A History of Harrow School

A HISTORY OF HARROW SCHOOL 1324–1991

Christopher Tyerman

OXFORD
UNIVERSITY PRESS

Great Clarendon Street, Oxford OX2 6DP
Oxford University Press is a department of the University of Oxford.
It furthers the University's objective of excellence in research, scholarship,
and education by publishing worldwide in

Oxford New York

Athens Auckland Bangkok Bogotá Buenos Aires Calcutta
Cape Town Chennai Dar es Salaam Delhi Florence Hong Kong Istanbul
Karachi Kuala Lumpur Madrid Melbourne Mexico City Mumbai
Nairobi Paris São Paulo Singapore Taipei Tokyo Toronto Warsaw
and associated companies in Berlin Ibadan

Oxford is a registered trade mark of Oxford University Press
in the UK and certain other countries

Published in the United States
by Oxford University Press Inc., New York

© The Keepers and Governors of Harrow School 2000

The moral rights of the author have been asserted
Database right Oxford University Press (maker)

First published 2000

All rights reserved. No part of this publication may be reproduced,
stored in a retrieval system, or transmitted, in any form or by any means,
without the prior permission in writing of Oxford University Press,
or as expressly permitted by law, or under terms agreed with the appropriate
reprographics rights organizations. Enquiries concerning reproduction
outside the scope of the above should be sent to the Rights Department,
Oxford University Press, at the address above

You must not circulate this book in any other binding or cover
and you must impose the same condition on any acquirer

British Library Cataloguing in Publication Data

Data available

Library of Congress Cataloging in Publication Data
Tyerman, Christopher.
A history of Harrow School, 1324–1991 / Christopher Tyerman.
p. cm.
Includes bibliographical references and index.
1. Harrow School—History. I. Title.
LF795.H32 T94 2000 373.421'86—dc21 00–035695

ISBN 0–19–822796–5

1 3 5 7 9 10 8 6 4 2

Typeset in Adobe Garamond
by Jayvee, Trivandrum, India
Printed in Great Britain
on acid-free paper by
T. J. International Ltd.,
Padstow, Cornwall

In Memoriam
D.T. and M.C.T.

Preface

This book has been an unconscionable time in the making. For their patience and forbearance as well as the invitation to write it and unsurpassed generosity in opening the archives in their possession for my use, I am delighted to thank the Keepers and Governors of Harrow School. Although there have been moments over the years when I felt less charitably towards those who first proposed me as Harrow's new historian, I am pleased to record my gratitude to Sir Lawrence Verney, Dr Jeremy Catto, and James Morwood for providing me with the opportunity. I am acutely aware of Lawrence Verney's vision of a well-organized archive and an unsentimental scholarly history: I hope his trust has received adequate recompense. My debts to those, including many old boys and former masters, who have supplied me with help, information, discussion, and advice are manifold and great. In particular I should like to acknowledge the assistance of Dr Toby Barnard, Ian Beer, Nicholas Bomford, Roger Ellis, Rita Gibbs, the late Herbert Harris, Dr Margaret Harris, Dr Michael Hart, Alasdair Hawkyard, Michael Hoban, John Hopkins, Janet Howarth, Professor John Honey, Peter Hunter, Jeremy Lemmon, James Morwood, the late Ian Scott-Kilvert, Dr Paul Slack, Andrew Stebbings, Dr Christopher Stray, and Ralph Thompson. Jeremy Catto and John Hopkins read the complete typescript; Jeremy Catto's encouragement and criticism over many years made this book immeasurably better and much more fun to write. The errors that remain are mine. My family have sensibly regarded the project with entertained but detached tolerance, a stance which recommends itself to anyone exposed to the febrile emotions stirred by public schools. I would not have written this book had I not been educated where I was. To the memory of those who introduced me to the school in the first place, and who may have been mightily amused at this outcome, the book is dedicated.

C.J.T.
Oxford
9 July 1999

Contents

List of Plates — xii
List of Maps — xiii
Acknowledgements — xiii
Abbreviations — xiv
Headmasters of Harrow School — xv

Introduction — 1

Part I The Foundation, 1324–1615 — 5

1. Origins — 7

2. Creation — 18
    John Lyon
    The Charter of 1572
    The Statutes and Rules of 1591

3. Birth — 36

Part II From Grammar School to Public School, 1615–1746 — 43

4. The Origins of a National Institution — 45
    The Early Masters
    The Mastership of William Hide

5. The Restoration School, 1661–1691 — 60
    William Horne, Eton, and King's

6. Heirs and Graces, 1691–1746 — 72
    The Chandos Connection
    Thomas Bryan
    James Cox

Part III The *Ancien Régime*, 1746–1844 — 95

7. The Classical School, 1746–1785 — 97

8. Eton Rules — 113
   Thomas Thackeray
   Robert Sumner
   The Election of 1771
   Benjamin Heath

9. A Glittering Scene: Joseph Drury and Byron's Harrow, 1785–1805 — 140
   Joseph Drury
   Byron's Harrow

10. Decadence and Change, 1805–1844 — 167
    I. Harrow's Nadir?
    II. Holding the Line, 1805–1829
        The Election of 1805
        The Chancery Suit of 1810
        George Butler
        The Failure of Discipline
    III. Towards the Brink, 1829–1844
        Charles Longley
        Christopher Wordsworth

Part IV Plenitude, 1844–1914 — 243

11. Charles John Vaughan, 1845–1859 — 245
    Change
    Staff
    Locals: The 'English Form'
    Boys
    Nemesis of a Head Master

12. Reform — 284

13. The Cult of Harrow: Montagu Butler, Sentiment, and Success, 1860–1885 — 303
    'A Harrow Hero'
    The Head and his School
    The Rise of the Federal School
    The Beginning of Modern Studies
    Reformed Harrow?
    Athleticism
    Songs

14. Imperial Harrow: The Origins of a Modern School,
    1885–1914   355
    Welldon
    Wood
    New Issues
    New Learning
    The Public School Profession
    The Battle for the Houses
    Rich and Poor
    A Conformist School?

Part V Staying On, 1914–1991   403

15. Challenges Old and New: Politics, Governors, and
    Money in the Twentieth Century   405
    Politics
    Governors
    Finance

16. Changing Identities, 1914–1991   440
    War
    Religion, Race, and Creed
    Playing the Game
    Sex, Obedience, and Violence
    Status

17. Clouded Eminence: Teachers and Taught, 1914–1991   488
    'Harrow' and Harrovians
    'Rich and Slack', 1918–1934
    Vellacott and the New House System, 1934–1939
    Crisis Survived, 1939–1953
    R. L. James and 'a Confident Conservatism', 1953–1971
    Modernization: Perception and Reality, 1971–1991

Conclusion   565

Select Bibliography   567
Index   575

Plates

(between pages 300 and 301)

1. View of Harrow Hill from the south-east *c*.1803
2. Modern aerial view of Harrow Hill from the east
3. The original schoolhouse, built 1608–15, from the south, *c*.1811–19
4. View from Church Hill looking south from the school gates towards the old Head Master's house, mid-1830s
5. View from outside the Head Master's house looking north, *c*.1900
6. The same view *c*.1960
7. The school steps outside the Old Schools in the 1850s
8. The Old Schools today from the south
9. Thomas Thackeray
10. Robert Sumner
11. From Robert Peel's copy of Tacitus' *Agricola* and *Germania*
12. C. J. Vaughan
13. H. Montagu Butler
14. 'Old Slybacon'; J. W. Cunningham
15. E. E. Bowen
16. J. E. C. Welldon
17. Lionel Ford
18. P. C. Vellacott
19. R. W. Moore
20. A. P. Boissier with W. S. Churchill
21. Dr R. L. James with H. M. Queen Elizabeth II
22. N. R. Bomford, B. M. S. Hoban, and I. D. S. Beer

Maps

1. Seventeenth-century Harrow — xvi
2. Eighteenth-century Harrow — xvii
3. Nineteenth-century Harrow — xviii
4. Twentieth-century Harrow — xix
5. Approach to the Old Schools, 1920 — xx

Acknowledgements

Plates 1, 3, 4, 7, 9, 10, 11, 12, 13, 14, 15, 16, 17, 18, 19, 20, and 21 are reproduced by courtesy of the Keepers and Governors of Harrow School; Plate 2 by courtesy of Halcyon Postcards of Bushey; Plate 5 by courtesy of John Murray Publishers; Plate 6 by courtesy of F. A. V. Fry & Co., London; Plate 8 photo by Lichfield; and Plate 22 by courtesy of W. Ralph Thompson Esq.

Abbreviations

DNB *Dictionary of National Biography*
GBM Governing Body Minutes (from 1871)
GM Governors' Minutes (to 1874)
HA Harrow Archives
HSR Harrow School MS Records
OH Old Harrovian
TUC Trades Union Congress
VCH *Victoria County History*

Head Masters of Harrow School

William Launce 1615–21
Robert Whittle 1621–8
William Hide 1628–61
Thomas Jonson 1661–8
Thomas Martin 1668–9
William Horne 1669–85
William Bolton 1685–91
Thomas Bryan 1691–1730
James Cox 1730–46
Thomas Thackeray 1746–60
Robert Sumner 1760–71
Benjamin Heath 1771–85
Joseph Drury 1785–1805
George Butler 1805–29
Charles Longley 1829–36
Christopher Wordsworth 1836–44
Charles Vaughan 1845–59
Montagu Butler 1860–85
James Welldon 1885–98
Joseph Wood 1898–1910
Lionel Ford 1910–25
Cyril Norwood 1926–34
Paul Vellacott 1934–9
A. P. Boissier 1940–2
Ralph Moore 1942–53
R. L. James 1953–71
Michael Hoban 1971–81
Ian Beer 1981–91
Nicholas Bomford 1991–9
Barnaby Lenon 1999–

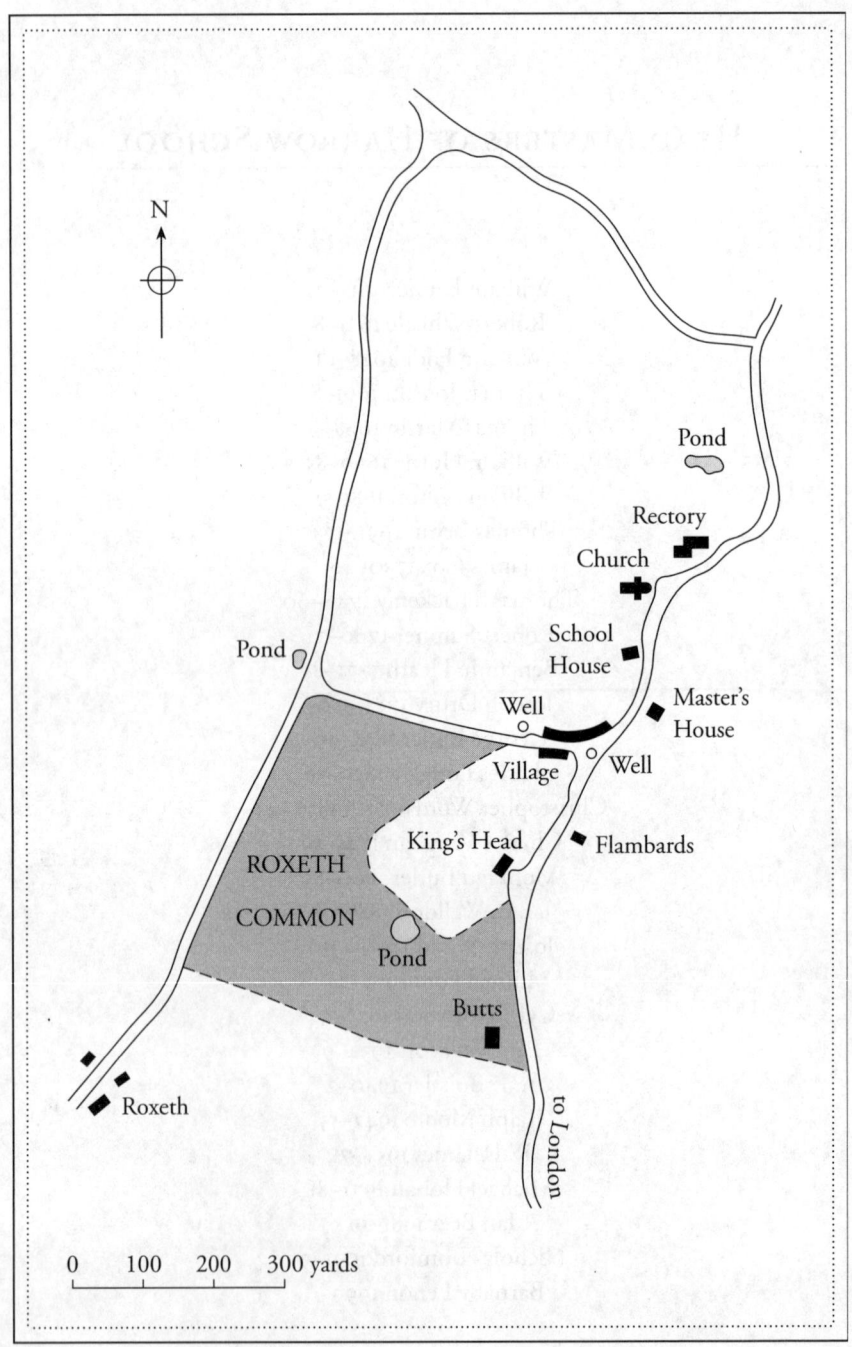

Map 1. Seventeenth-century Harrow

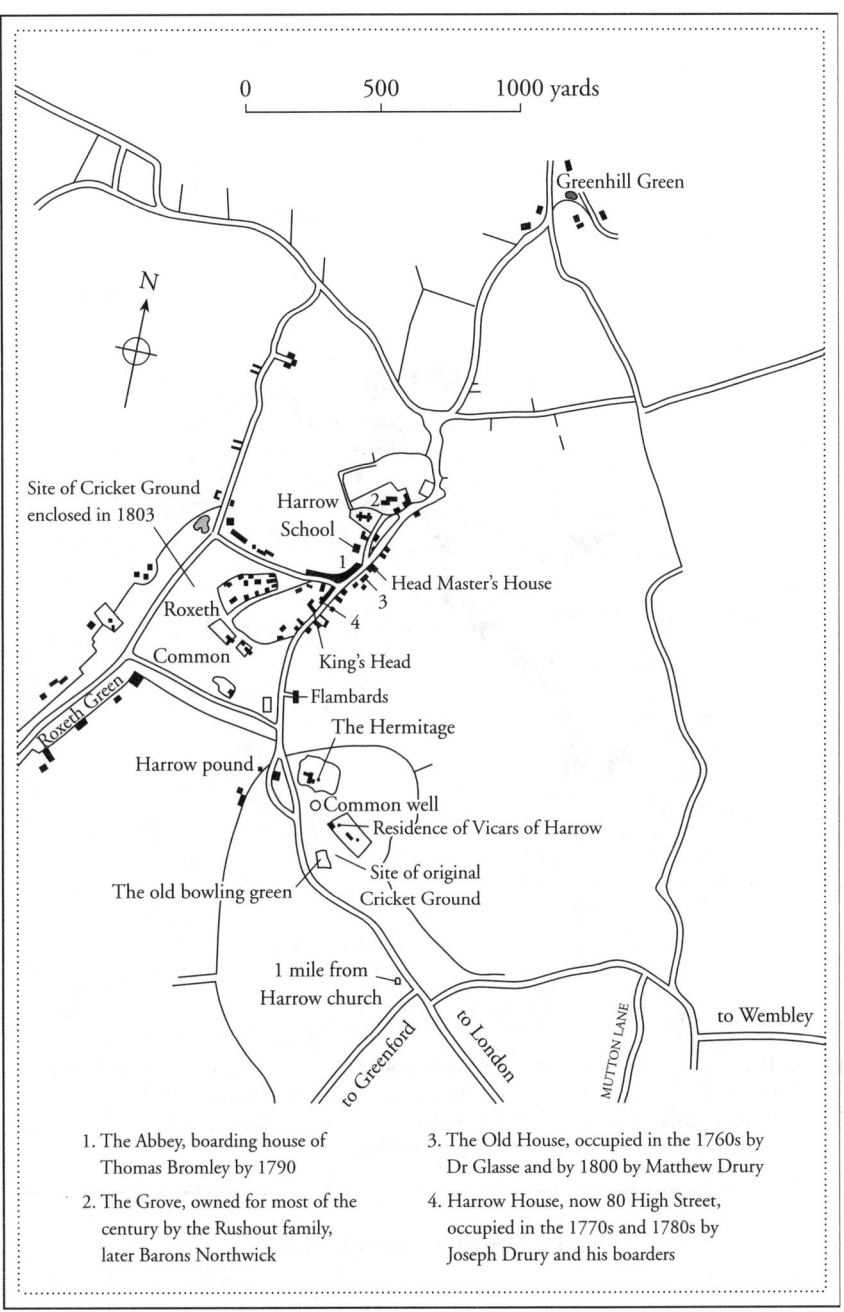

Map 2. Eighteenth-century Harrow

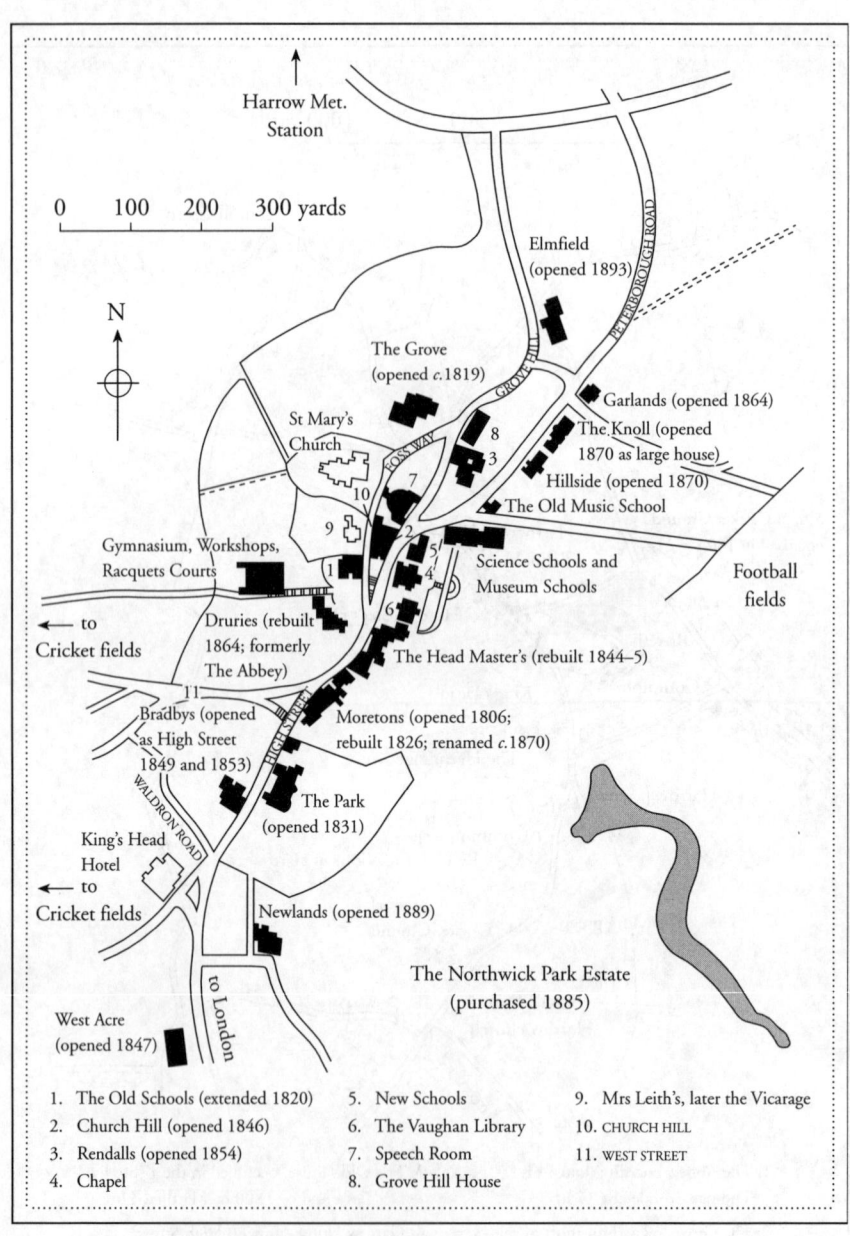

3. Nineteenth-century Harrow

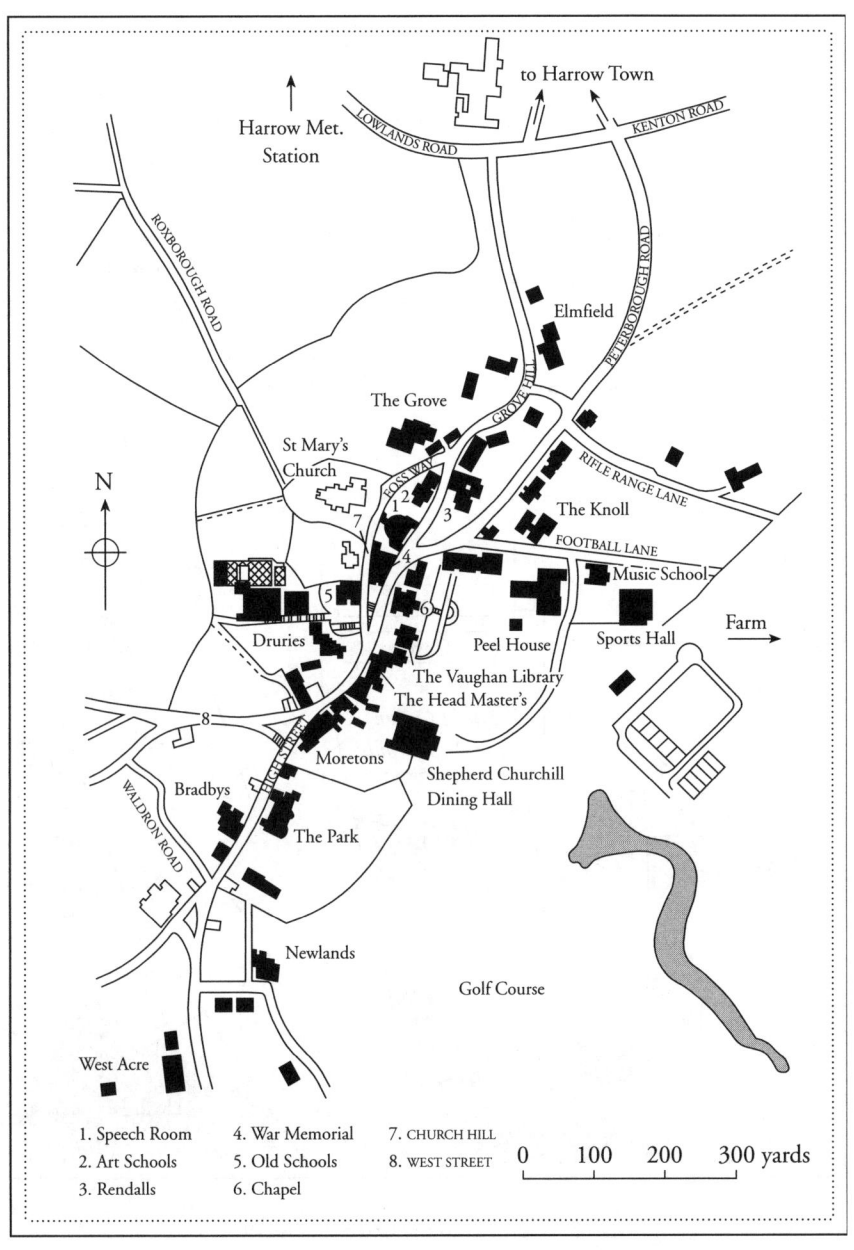

4. Twentieth-century Harrow

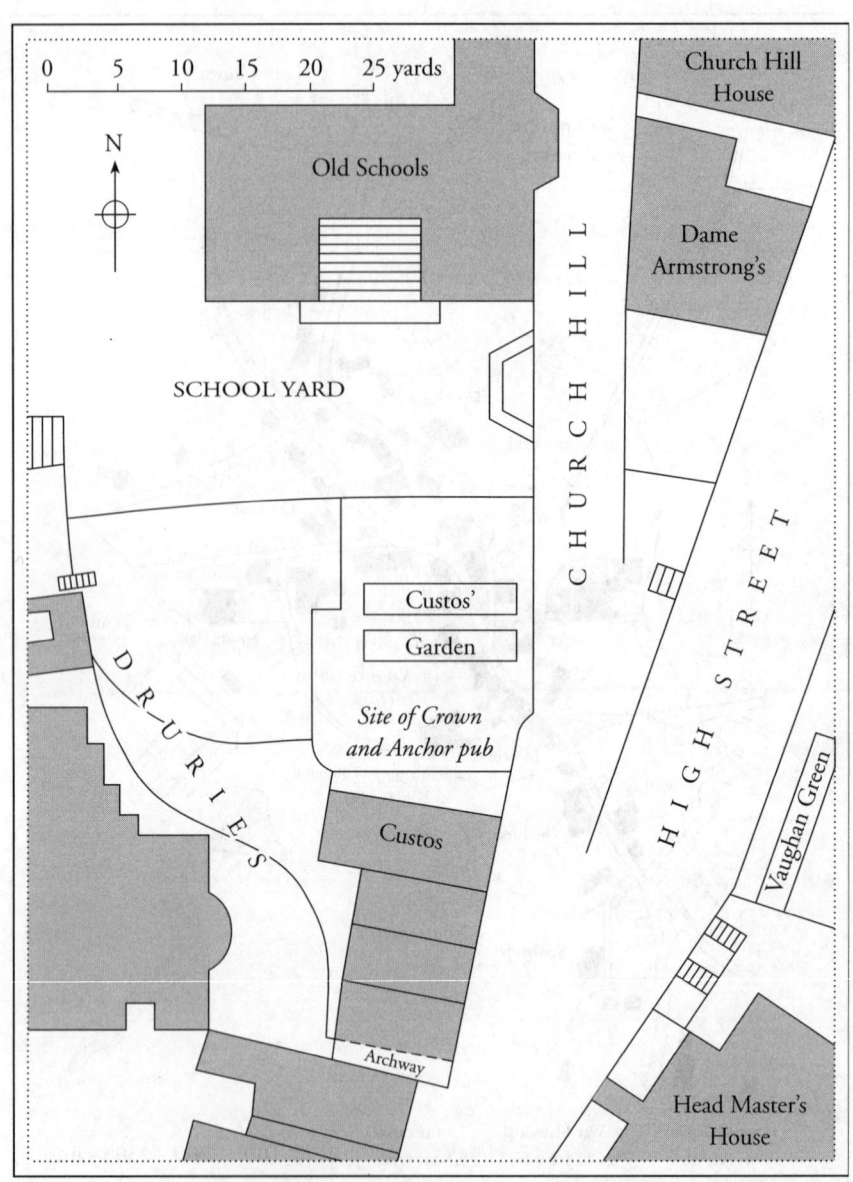

Map 5. Approach to the Old Schools, 1920

INTRODUCTION

'Once more let us see the revival of first-class men at Oxford—Wranglers, Medalists and Prizemen at Cambridge—and our school-bills (I mean 'Bills of the School') will grow away like Jonah's pumpkin'.

George Butler to Christopher Wordsworth, 6 March 1838.[1]

Harrow became the second most famous school in the English-speaking world, its name synonymous with class, social division, and privileged education. A very English phenomenon, it still arouses feelings of pride and unease, jealousy and hilarity, sentimentality and contempt, love and fury. Harrow remains common shorthand for a certain sort of exclusivity attracting the tawdriest excesses of snobbery and its inverted relative. The prominence of public schools in English political and social history may not be admired or even admirable but it is inescapable. In that context alone Harrow's contribution makes it worthy of study. While representing a characteristic example of the genre, Harrow's own story conforms to no obvious type. The conundrum that has moved its apologists for two centuries remains of interest. Harrow was one of scores of local grammar schools founded by pious and wealthy men in the sixteenth and early seventeenth centuries. Its advantages, while greater than some choose to recognize, were nevertheless modest compared with royal Eton, prosperous Winchester, or metropolitan Westminster. Yet from the eighteenth century it was established at the heart of the Establishment, as one well-entertained visitor put it in 1822: 'If hospitality and a generous Englishman-like feeling prevails anywhere, it prevails at HARROW.'[2]

When George Butler wrote to his successor but one in 1838, he hit on the guiding principle of Harrow's survival and eminence. Lacking available capital or a large endowment, Harrow always depended on numbers to secure its success. As Butler was indicating, the need for pupils demanded the constant reforging of a

---

[1] Harrow School Archives, Head Masters' Correspondence/Wordsworth/6 Mar. 1838, G. Butler to C. Wordsworth. The reference is to Jonah 4: 6.

[2] T. F. Dibdin, 'A Day at Harrow', *Reminiscences of a Literary Life*, 2 vols. (London, 1836), ii. 705.

good reputation. On occasion it may have been a school for aristocrats; it was never an aristocratic school. Most evidence survives from the years of Harrow's plenitude, yet it may be thought most interest lies in the ascent of Harrow from local parish school to nursery of a self-conscious elite in the seventeenth and eighteenth centuries when it adopted both style and teachers from Eton; from unreformed playground of boorish social and academic snobbery to a serious forcing house for Christian gentlemen and Imperial rulers in the nineteenth century; and, in the twentieth, from the seat of muscular self-confident ambition to a luxury school for the aspiring wealthy.

Harrow School is not short of histories. There exist over a dozen stretching back almost 200 years to R. Ackermann's *History of Harrow School* in 1816 and N. Carlisle's *Concise Description of the Endowed Grammar Schools in England and Wales* two years later. In addition, the school's past has been raked over by biographers and memorialists for as long. Oddly, the earliest histories are among the most dispassionate, content merely to recite information. Given the nature of the subject, much written is primarily of antiquarian interest. Otherwise, the tendency is towards polemic and teleology. Books on public schools are rarely neutral. As institutions they stir strong emotions of devotion and antagonism. Both extremes betray a sentimentalized view of the past, summoned to soothe or justify personal or contemporary prejudice or belief. What follows assumes no determinist inevitability of the school's success; nor does it seek to judge the social justice or morality of such schools. It merely attempts to investigate how the school developed and why and to locate its history within shifting social, political, and educational circumstances that gave rise to such institutions, later sustained them, and more than once threatened their extinction.

The excuse for a new history of Harrow is twofold. Since the early 1980s the school's archives have been collected together. It is now possible, as it was not before, to obtain a glimpse into the darker as well as the more familiar recesses of the past and to construct a rounded picture. The core of the school's holdings are the Governors' Minutes, complete from 1615, and their Account Books. Otherwise, the archives are uneven. Evidence from boarding houses has only recently begun to be centrally deposited with any regularity. Much of the collection comprises random donations, such as the valuable correspondence of the second Baron Northwick, a governor from 1801 to 1859. Beyond the school archives the sources are plentiful but scattered. The normal serendipity of historical research is immensely extended, many of the most interesting or important pieces of evidence being stumbled upon without expectation. Given that the history of any school is, in part, the collected biographies of thousands of individuals, this is inevitable. All views of school are partial. The published and unpublished autobiographical material presents its own hazards. School is special not necessarily because of the school itself but because of the age at which it is encountered. Adolescent memories constitute some of the most lastingly vivid. The experience of being a

Introduction

Harrovian at any time in its history was both distinctive and uniform; the historian has to remember both in order to avoid undue generalizing typology or excessive local special pleading. He has to tread a path between sociology and sentimentality.

It is also half a century since the publication of E. D. Laborde's *Harrow School: Yesterday and Today*. New evidence and different perspectives invite a fresh examination. The serious study of Harrow's past began with Percy Thornton's pioneering *Harrow School and its Surroundings* of 1885, which coincided with the cataloguing of the Lyon Trusts' muniments by E. J. L. Scott of the British Museum. Although silvered by a strongly emotional tone of loyalty and devotion, Thornton's work made use of the archives, some of which have since vanished. He established the true status of the founder, John Lyon, and discovered the existence of a pre-Lyonian school at Harrow. Sentiment and snobbery clouded his interpretations, yet his work remains the indispensable starting point for modern investigation. Further researches at the turn of the century into local parish records by W. Done Bushell and into the manorial rolls by W. O. Hewlett clarified issues of the parochial context and the relations of the school and the locality. E. W. Howson and G. Townsend Warner edited a valuable collection of historical studies and essays, *Harrow School*, in 1898. Some of the contributions were themselves as much evidence as interpretation, such as C. S. Roundell on the Harrow of the 1840s or J. E. C. Welldon on Chapel, an appropriate merging of primary and secondary sources typical of the school's endless dialogue with its own past. Histories of the school have a habit of becoming part of the school's history; Thornton displaying a confident, literary mid-Victorian vision; Howson and Townsend Warner a more diffuse, nuanced, critical, and, in the modern sense, academic approach. The twentieth century has witnessed a shoal of shorter surveys, some panegyric, such as Archibald Fox's *Harrow* of 1911, others more soberly affectionate, such as J. Fischer Williams in 1901 and P. H. M. Bryant in 1936. None extended the range of archival evidence, all largely feeding off earlier work. Their tone tends to be evocative and anecdotal rather than scholarly.

The most important contributions to the proper study of Harrow's history since 1898 have come from the succession of editors of the *Harrow Register*, collectively providing an invaluable biographical compendium. In the absence of any complete lists of entrants before the Head Mastership of Joseph Drury (1785–1805), W. T. J. Gun's volume covering the early centuries, 1571–1800, published in 1934, stands as a major advance in understanding of the nature of the early school and its relationship with contemporary society. To this can now be added the additional researches on eighteenth- and nineteenth-century Harrovians by J. S. Golland. Only by examining the origins and future careers of pupils can the rhetoric and reality of claims made for and by the school be tested.

The secondary literature on public schools is vast, much of it turgid, some of it sensational, most of it unscholarly. There are exceptions. No student of public schools can fail to have benefited from the researches of E. C. Mack, T. W. Bamford,

Introduction

B. Simon, J. Gathorne-Hardy, and J. R. de S. Honey. School histories tend to piety; general studies veer towards the opposite. What all openly or tacitly demonstrate is a continued fascination with one of Britain's most idiosyncratic yet successful social inventions, exported abroad even when vilified at home. It is hoped that this new study of one of the most prominent of these institutions will contribute to an explanation of this interest.

Part I

The Foundation, 1324–1615

I

Origins

By his own admission, John Lyon did not found Harrow School. The Charter he obtained from Queen Elizabeth I dated 19 February 1572 explicitly stated that he was re-endowing ('de novo erigere') an existing school. Of a school at Harrow before 1572 there is clear evidence; Lyon himself made provision to support its functions during his life. Neither did Lyon supervise the creation of his new foundation, the so-called Free Grammar School of John Lyon in the town of Harrow-on-the-Hill. This was the work of the Keepers and Governors of Lyon's bequests after the death of Lyon's widow in 1608, sixteen years after her husband. Lyon's foundation only reached physical reality after painful brushes with architects, builders, local hostility, and the court of Chancery in September 1615 when the new schoolhouse opened its door to the first pupils, nearly a quarter of a century after Lyon's death on 3 October 1592.[1]

It is probably true to say that almost all the favoured myths surrounding both founder and foundation are either misleading or downright wrong. Lyon was rich; his school precariously but well-endowed; his statutes in all respects wholly unoriginal; his intentions predictable. The provision for the admission of fee-paying boarders was not unusual in similar contemporary foundations, almost certainly envisaged as a means of increasing, at no cost to the Lyon trusts, the income of the Head Master, thereby attracting a better class of pedagogue. There was no sense of founding a national institution. Indeed, what evidence does survive suggests no special educational ambitions at all. Lyon's concerns as a founder were pious, charitable, and local, a product, a friend of his attested in 1579, of childlessness

---

[1] All histories of the school have accounts of the foundation. P. M. Thornton, *Harrow School and its Surroundings* (London, 1885), pp. 26–90, although sentimental, is both pioneering and evocative; W. O. Hewlett's chapters (1 and 4) in E. W. Howson and G. T. Townsend Warner (eds.), *Harrow School* (London, 1898) are detailed and authoritative; E. D. Laborde, *Harrow School: Yesterday and Today* (London, 1948), pp. 20–32, although unoriginal, is clear-headed and concise. The 1572 charter and 1591 statutes are edited and translated ibid., 216–40, the original text of the statutes in G. T. Townsend Warner, *Harrow in Prose and Verse* (London, 1913), pp. 50–73.

and local pressure not vision. 'I know his meaning is to bestow his lands for the re-erection of a school in the parish of Harrow, as he has no children. Some prefer him to this charge, to spare themselves'.[2]

Harrow School before 1615

These words of Sir Gilbert Gerrard, Attorney-General (1559) and later Master of the Rolls (1581), in many ways Lyon's *eminence grise*, confirm the context of the foundation; the continuance or resurrection of an older school on a new and financially more stable basis, protected by trusts rather than the inevitably more capricious charity of well-disposed and well-heeled parishioners. However, the exact nature of this pre-Lyonian school and its relationship both with the school Lyon subsidized during his and his widow's lives and with the subsequent Free Grammar School of 1615 are not entirely clear.

The plainest evidence for the existence of a school before 1572 comes from two contrasting sources: the records of entrants to Gonville and Caius College, Cambridge and a letter written in 1626 by an octogenarian resident of Bridgewater, Somerset, George Roper. The Caius Registers identify seven names of former pupils at school at Harrow, beginning with Richard Gerrard, who entered Caius in 1567 after, it is recorded, four years at Harrow. (He later migrated to Trinity before returning to Caius as a Fellow.)[3] That a school existed a decade earlier is shown by the Roper letter. In it, the aged writer recalled the death, seventy or so years earlier, of his father who had been Henry VIII's keeper 'of Enfield Chase, Hide Park and Marilibone' but who had left his family 'all unprovided for'.

I remember Queen Mary came into our house within a little of my father's death and ffound my Mother weeping and took her by the hand and lifted her up-for she neeeled-and bad her bee of good cheer for her children should be well provided for. Afterward my brother Richard and I being the two eldest were sent to Harrow to school and were there till we were almost men. Sir Ralph Sadler took order for all things for us there by Queen Mary's appointment as long as she lived.[4]

On the face of it, this school at Harrow must have had some reputation and standing. The Ropers were effectively royal wards. Of the other known pre-Lyonian Harrovians, the three sons of the local landowner, William Gerrard of Flambards, Richard became not only a fellow of Caius, but a chaplain to the Queen

---

[2] *Calendar of State Papers, Domestic. Addenda 1566–79*, p. 563: Sir Gilbert Gerrard to Mr Johns, clerk of the Signet, 12 Aug. 1579. (NB, the spelling varies between Gerrard and Gerard.)

[3] For an analysis of the Caius evidence see W. T. J. Gun, *The Harrow School Register, 1571–1800* (London, 1934), pp. viii–ix and under the individual entries listed there.

[4] Thornton, *Harrow School*, 383–4.

and a wealthy pluralist; Felix received a full education, which included Eton, Caius, and Gray's Inn as well as Harrow; and Philip rose to be a bencher of Gray's Inn. Their nephew, Thomas, followed his uncles to Gray's Inn. William Greenhill, who spent seven years at the Harrow school (1565–72), proceeded to Caius via Trinity before taking Holy Orders, securing the living of Brixworth, Northants in 1589. He also provided a direct link with Lyon's foundation, serving as a governor 1586–1613, the sole old boy known to have acted as such until William Fenn in 1683, almost a century later. As he had been admitted as a Sizar at Trinity, which meant he had to perform some menial serving functions to earn his keep at college, this Greenhill may have come from a branch of the extensive local family that had fallen, perhaps temporarily, on hard times. Greenhill's contemporary, John Stringe (1568–75), was also ordained, rising to be Rector of Elstree (1590–1612), where he apparently kept a school. Edmund Smythe (at Harrow 1575–8), after a similar university and clerical career, was academically even more distinguished, serving as Under (1588–92), then Head Master of Merchant Taylors' School (1592–9). From the Statutes of Merchant Taylors' (1561), it can be inferred that Smythe, a scholar of Caius and a MA, was learned in Latin and possibly also Greek.[5]

It is, therefore, clear that the school at Harrow was no mere Dames' school, to equip children of the locally ambitious but unprosperous with the literacy and numeracy to become apprentices. Still less did it resemble the educational service provided by Elizabeth Snell at Watford who it was said in 1579 'teacheth scholars to read and herself cannot read'.[6] The Harrow school had connections with London and the court, the patronage of parishioners of substance, and contacts with Cambridge University, almost certainly through Dr John Caius (d. 1573), refounder of the college to which he gave his name, who lived at Ruislip. Caius' college was that chosen by Lyon in 1591 at which to place the two exhibitioners to Cambridge he had determined to provide for in the 1572 Charter.[7] This association was most probably the consequence of a traditional and local connection, as Caius and his college were notorious for continued affection for Roman Catholicism in diametric contrast to the firmly Protestant nature of Lyon's foundation. The affinity was, therefore, not doctrinal but, as with so many Oxford and Cambridge colleges of the period, historical, regional, and personal.

The nature and location of the pre-Lyonian school are obscure. Perhaps it resembled the school that was, in 1599, being run by Thomas Hayward down the road at Ealing, a boarding school of eighteen boys, aged between six and seventeen, including sons of gentlemen and merchants as well as yeomen.[8] Yet it could have

---

[5] For the Merchant Taylors' statutes see N. Carlisle, *A Concise Description of the Endowed Grammar Schools in England and Wales* (London, 1818), ii. 49–69; for the biographical details see Gun, *Harrow School Register*, 10, 11, 26, 27.

[6] J. Guy, *Tudor England* (Oxford, 1988), p. 420.   [7] Laborde, *Harrow School*, 216–17, 230.

[8] J. Youings, *Sixteenth Century England* (London, 1984), p. 375.

been even more domestic. Sometime after the death of Joan Lyon in 1608 and his own death in 1611, the governors elected as 'schoolmaster at the free schole' Anthony Rate, described as being the 'schoolmaster at Flambards', the seat of William Gerrard on the southern crown of the Hill.[9] Rate does not appear to have been a graduate, at least of an English university, and four of the nine Harrovians recorded in the half century after *c*.1555 were Gerrard's sons and grandson. The school could have been simply the Gerrard's private schoolroom.

Superficially, the Roper story may lend some credence to this, as Sir Ralph Sadler certainly acted as a colleague of Gilbert Gerrard, William's brother, in Elizabeth's reign and may have known the family earlier. However, William Gerrard only came into possession of Flambards in 1566, finally purchasing it in 1573.[10] In 1576 a judgment of the Harrow Rectory Manorial court ordered Elizabeth Elkyn, widow, to remove from her house her maid, Elizabeth, and Matthew Spencer, 'schoolmaster'.[11] If Spencer were the local pedagogue (and as such the first recorded Harrow schoolmaster), his activities, the maid Elizabeth apart, have no stated association with Flambards. Moreover, by 1596, it appears that some sort of school was being or had been conducted in a building called the Church House, in the northeast corner of the churchyard, as Philip Gerrard, a former pupil at the Harrow school, was required to register his receipt of a lease on certain Lyon lands 'at the nowe Schoole or Churche house of the parish of Harrowe'.[12]

Other references to the late sixteenth-century pre-Lyonian school also suggest a parochial rather than domestic basis. In his letter of 1579 Gilbert Gerrard's remark that 'some prefer him[Lyon] to this charge, to spare themselves' may imply a parochially, not privately, funded school.[13] Even if the Attorney-General had only his brother's interests at heart, his words suggest a form of parish responsibility which was being gratefully handed over to a wealthy but childless local worthy. Lyon himself in his 1591 Statutes refers to the yearly payment of thirty marks 'which I . . . have used to give and to pay for the teaching of thirty poor children'.[14] As one of the first things the governors did at the opening of the Free School in 1615 was to increase the number of free scholars to forty, thirty may be taken as the scale both of Lyon's interim foundation and of the core of his intended Free School.[15] Whether that reflected earlier practice can only be guessed at. In 1593, the

---

[9] Howson and Townsend Warner, *Harrow School*, 54 Gun, *Harrow School Register*, 152.

[10] *VCH, Middlesex*, iv. 209.

[11] The Manorial Court roll is transcribed by W. O. Hewlett in Howson and Townsend Warner, *Harrow School*, 7 and in W. W. Druett, *Harrow through the Ages* (Uxbridge, 1935), p. 114.

[12] Harrow School MS Records (hereafter HSR), no. 170, in calendar prepared by E. J. L. Scott, *Records of the Grammar School Founded by John Lyon at Harrow-on-the-Hill AD 1572* (Harrow, 1886); Thornton, *Harrow School*, 388–412 provides a different calendar which does not tally with Scott or the numbers written, presumably by Scott, on the manuscripts themselves.

[13] *Calendar of State Papers Domestic. Addenda 1566–79*, p. 563.

[14] Laborde, *Harrow School*, 232.

[15] HSR II, fol. 5, Governors' Minutes, probably of 7 Aug. 1615.

topographer John Norden simply observed in his *Speculum Britanniae* that 'there is a schoole in Harrow, as yet not a free schoole, but intended to be'.[16]

There is, however, no concrete evidence that the school at Harrow had a continuous existence between the pre-1572 institution, the interim Lyon one, and the subsequent Free School. In detail of administration, and possibly curriculum, the Free School was explicitly different from its predecessors. Even after 1608, the appointment of the non-graduate Rate contradicted Lyon's statutes for the Free School. His apparent successor, one 'Mr Bradley', may have been an MA but was only paid £4 a year, rather than the forty marks (£26 13s. 4d.) provided for the Master of the Free School. Indeed, Bradley continued to be paid, possibly arrears, and be described as 'schoolmaster' into 1616. William Launce, on the other hand, the first active Master of the Free School, an MA of Trinity, Cambridge, was appointed in April 1615 on a seemingly entirely different footing, his terms exactly according to Lyon's rules.[17]

Some have tried to associate the pre-Lyonian school with some familiar literary references, thereby demonstrating its contemporary fame or status. Sentimentalists have long tried to lend Harrow schooling the magic glitter of Shakespearian connections. It is often asserted that Dr Caius of Ruislip appears in *The Merry Wives of Windsor*. However, this attribution may be spurious. The historical Caius was a Norfolk classicist as well as royal physician; Shakespeare's, although a doctor with court connections, is a comic Frenchman. If there lies wrapped in this characterization a subtle joke, it is hard to see how it could still resonate twenty-five years after Caius' death, when the play was written. At most, when lampooning a court physician, the writer may have come across the odd-sounding name of possibly the most famous of the Queen's doctors. To make him French suggests no very close intentional connection with any actual person of that name.[18]

Some have fondly imagined that Maria's description of Malvolio in *Twelfth Night* (III. ii) as 'like a pedant that keeps a school i' the church' concealed a reference to the school at Harrow. More—although perhaps only a little bit—serious has been the identification with Harrow of a school mentioned in *Love's Labours Lost* (v. i) when Don Armado asks the pedagogue Holofernes: 'Do you educate youth at the Charge House on the top of the mountain?' and Holofernes replies 'Or *mons*, the hill'. It is conveniently assumed that 'charge' is a corruption of 'church'.[19] While it is true that the sixteenth-century Latin for Harrow, as in the 1572 charter, was 'Harrowe super montem', it is hard to see that such a specific allusion can either be established or, perhaps, would have been employed when

---

[16] John Norden, *Speculum Britanniae* (London, 1593; repr. 1723), p. 23.

[17] Laborde, *Harrow School*, 228–9; Gun, *Harrow School Register*, 152; HSR V (Governors' Accounts), fos. 12, 17 for payments to Bradley in 1614 and 1616 and fos. 17–18 for payments to Launce; HSR I, fo. 20ʳ (Governors' Order Book, 29 Apr. 1615) for Launce's appointment.

[18] See the *DNB* entry for Caius by J. B. Mullinger; cf. Thornton, *Harrow School*, 50, 64, and 423.

[19] Ibid., frontispiece, pp. xii, 64, and 385; Laborde, *Harrow School*, 26 n. 2.

Shakespeare wrote the play in the 1590s. Possibly more concrete is the reference in Ben Jonson's *Bartholomew Fair* of 1614, the central character of which is the gullible young Bartholomew Cokes of Harrow-on-the-Hill, whose misfortunes on his day out in London supplies such unifying plot as exists in the play. At one point, a London cutpurse comments on the luckless Cokes 'I cannot persuade myself but he goes to grammar-school yet; and plays the truant today'.[20] If, and it is a big one, this can be taken as a description of the school at Harrow in its last pre-Free School days, then its nature as a grammar school, one in which Latin and possibly even Greek grammar was taught, would be established. It may equally be that Jonson gave Harrow as Cokes' home as being a known town, with an easily recognizable name and perhaps a reputation for commerce and supplying the capital with goods, which could have suggested to his metropolitan audience more money than sophistication or sense, with resonances similar to Luton for a London audience today. It may be noted, however, that Jonson, an Old Westminster himself, chose to call Cokes' servant Humphrey Wasp; there had been residents of Harrow called Wasp or Waps since the fourteenth century.[21]

Nevertheless, Lyon's interim arrangements, possibly from 1572, certainly in place by 1591, were evidently more academically elaborate than the most basic. Whether, if he indeed taught at Harrow, Matthew Spencer's pupils in the 1570s were supported by Lyon's largesse or not, the school he ran, like many others in Tudor England, could well have offered basic Latin as well as literacy in English. Whether there was more to it than that, either before or during Lyon's intervention, is probably unknowable. The Roper story is not inherently unlikely. In 1561 the Lord Keeper of the Great Seal, Nicholas Bacon, was urging a scheme on the Secretary of State, William Cecil, to provide adequate schooling for royal wards, albeit those of greater means than the Ropers.[22] The mystery of the Ropers' sojourn at Harrow in the 1550s lies not so much with the putative curriculum—to George Roper's overt regret his family seemed to have been destined to sink in the social race after their father's death—than in the choice of guardian. Sir Ralph Sadler, a former Secretary of State, diplomat, and Privy Councillor, lived at Standon in Hertfordshire during Mary's reign, in political retirement if not exile. An associate successively of Thomas Cromwell and Protector Somerset, Sadler had been in favour of the Protestant politics and religious changes under Edward VI and was only to be restored to court favour, office, and patronage under Elizabeth.[23] Queen Mary's generosity may have been less than magnificent except in the rosy reminiscence of an octogenarian. In any case, it is strange that the queen should have appointed somebody in such disfavour to supervise her support for her wards.

[20] *Bartholomew Fair*, IV. ii. 38–40; cf. I. i. 3–4.
[21] W. Done Bushell, *Harrow Octocentenary Tracts*, x (Cambridge, 1900), p. 31.
[22] R. Tittler, *Nicholas Bacon. The Making of a Tudor Statesman* (London, 1976), pp. 59–60.
[23] See Sadler's *DNB* entry by T. F. Henderson.

The question remains of the origins of whatever school existed in the parish of Harrow in the 1550s. One clue may be its association with the Church House in the churchyard, as the romantics would have it, Shakespeare's 'Charge House' on the Hill. The objective evidence for a school there dates only from 1596.[24] The Church House existed by 1475 and is mentioned again in 1538; on each occasion, as in 1596, it is the place at which legal conveyancing was conducted. The magisterial view of W. O. Hewlett, who did so much to clarify the early history of the parish of Harrow and its school, proclaimed 'nor can there be any reasonable doubt that the School of the time of Queen Mary was held in the same building'.[25] If so, it appears to have doubled as the local land registry, perhaps even court house. Lyon's own Statutes of 1591 envisaged his new schoolhouse being where rents were paid each half-year.[26] The 1596 phrase 'nowe Schoole or Churche house of the parish of Harrow' could imply recent occupation by the beneficiaries of Lyon's interim charity. That this was to be temporary is suggested by a lease granted by Lyon in 1572 that indicated his intention to house the schoolmaster of his Free School on a site to the south of the church and vicarage (where in fact the schoolhouse was later built), although, apart from his intentions as to the nature and capacity of a new schoolhouse outlined in 1591, neither he, his widow, nor the governors began to implement this scheme until after 1608.[27] On the other hand, it remains entirely possible that the Church House had been used by the Harrow school long before 1596.

It has been inferred from Court Rolls of the Harrow Rectory Manor, based on the Rectory which stood on the site now occupied by The Grove, that there was a school at Harrow as early as 1384. This evidence is essentially negative, that a bond-tenant of the manor was punished for sending his son to a school outside the manor and without his lord's (i.e. the Rector's) permission. This could imply the existence of a manor or parish school run by the church to which the offender, John Intowne, could have sent his son, William, presumably for a fee. William went outside Harrow in pursuit, the judgment stated, of learning in the Liberal Arts, a syllabus incorporating but going beyond grammar which may not have been available locally.[28]

If there existed a pre-Reformation school, the history of the sixteenth-century school and the role of John Lyon could become clearer, if only by inescapable analogy with dozens of similar institutions that nearly or actually collapsed in consequence of the ecclesiastical disendowments between 1536 and 1547. However, if such a school did exist before 1536, whether housed at Church House or elsewhere,

---

[24] HSR 170.
[25] Howson and Townsend Warner, *Harrow School*, 10. Hewlett's transcriptions of the local rolls are currently in the school's keeping.
[26] Laborde, *Harrow School*, 231.   [27] HSR 132, lease of 14 Mar. 1572.
[28] Howson and Townsend Warner, *Harrow School*, 6 for Hewlett's transcriptions of the court roll.

perhaps in the mid-fifteenth-century parvise, erected above the South porch by Rector John Byrkhede, builder of the spire, no unequivocal record of it survives.[29]

Many parishes had schools based on chantries of which Harrow had two:one, the chantry of the Blessed Virgin Mary, was housed in the parish church, possibly in the south transept. Hewlett, however, at his most final, declared of the chantry 'it is certain no school was attached to it'.[30] His claim is worth investigating, if only to see whether the school John Lyon re-endowed had its origins in the early fourteenth century. The chantry of the Blessed Virgin Mary was established at Harrow by the then Rector, William de Bosco, in 1324.[31] Given the frequency of medieval chantry schools being reformed, refounded, or re-endowed as grammar schools after the abolition of chantries in 1547, it is tempting to assume that Harrow was no exception. However, none of the Harrow records specifies that its chantry chaplain had duties as a schoolmaster. Hewlett regarded the absence of any such mention in the report of January 1548 by the royal Commissioners appointed to execute the abolition of the Chantries as conclusive.[32] More enigmatic is the reference to a chaplain at Harrow, possibly the chantry priest, being fined in 1521 as a common dice player, although whether this would preclude a pedagogic function must be a matter of conjecture and taste.[33] Some modern historians have adopted a similarly literal interpretation of the chantry evidence in general, including in their lists of chantry schools only those that had explicit educational functions attached to them.[34] Such a minimalist approach appears at odds with episcopal injunctions to all chantry priests to run schools.[35] For the chantry chaplains, teaching was both a method of supplementing income and of meeting the pastoral needs of local children. It has been argued that 'most of the chantry schools were casual and uninstitutionalized'.[36] This made them especially vulnerable, perhaps, after the abolition of the chantries in 1547.

The Harrow chantry of St Mary was certainly adequately endowed to provide sufficient income for a schoolmaster. The Chantry lands, according to the 1548 valuation, brought in £9 16s. 5d. a year, of which £9 6s. 0d. went to the chaplain.[37] It has been calculated that the median income of cantarist schoolmasters in Essex

[29] Done Bushell, *Octocentenary Tracts*, xi (Cambridge, 1903), p. 7.

[30] Hewlett, 'History of the Manors of Harrow', in Howson and Townsend Warner, *Harrow School*, 6.

[31] On the Chantry of the Blessed Virgin Mary, Done Bushell, *Octocentenary Tracts*, ix (Cambridge, 1897), p. 25; x. 29–32; xiii (Cambridge, 1909), 34–5, 43–6; *VCH, Middlesex*, iv. 253–4.

[32] Printed by Done Bushell, *Octocentenary Tracts*, ix. 25.

[33] From Hewlett's transcriptions of the court roll, Howson and Townsend Warner, *Harrow School*, 7; his gambling companions were seemingly servants of the founder's father.

[34] e.g. A. G. Dickens, *The English Reformation* (new edn., London, 1989), p. 235.

[35] W. H. Frere and W. M. Kennedy, *Visitation Articles and Injunctions* (London, 1910), ii. 17 (Worcester 1537), 56 (Salisbury 1538), 63 (Exeter 1538), 85 (London 1542); cf. the council held at St Paul's in 1529, C. Wilkins, *Concilia Magnae Britanniae et Hiberniae*, iii (London, 1737), pp. 722–3.

[36] A. Kreider, *English Chantries: The Road to Dissolution* (Cambridge, Mass., 1979), p. 60.

[37] *Octocentenary Tracts*, ix. 25.

at the time of abolition was £8 8s. 10d., something on the high side compared with equivalent figures for Wiltshire (£7 14s. 6d.), Warwickshire (£6), or Yorkshire (£5).[38] Indeed, the great ecclesiastical census of 1535, the *Valor Ecclesiasticus*, indicated that a third of all clerical incumbents claimed annual incomes of less than £5, although there was some understandable underestimation in places: in 1535, the Harrow chantry recorded annual income of only £6, which, even allowing for galloping inflation, looks distinctly meagre when compared with the assessment of 1548.[39] Another possible indication that the chaplain of the St Mary's chantry did more than sing daily masses for the soul of its benefactor is that, by the early sixteenth century at least, presentation to the chantry was in the hands of the parishioners, suggesting a wider parish role. The parishioners who took the lead included members of the extended Page family, from which two of the five original governors designated by Lyon in 1572 came, and, in 1534, one John Lyon, almost certainly the founder's father who died in the same year.[40]

The difficulty with linking any putative chantry school with the Harrow school of the 1550s and 1560s and so with the institution John Lyon rebuilt is compounded by the fate of the chantry lands. It has been said that re-endowment of ex-chantry schools after 1547 'was normally achieved through the efforts of local citizens who repurchased property from the court of Augmentations' (the court which dealt with the profits from the confiscated chantries).[41] Alternatively, but rarely, the crown, on petition of courtiers or influential locals, made grants from central funds roughly equivalent to those of the despoiled chantries. At Harrow, however, the government had sold the chantry lands in August 1548 for £747 6s. 8d. to William Gyes of the Strand. As with the two Harrow manors, formerly held by the archbishop of Canterbury and, indirectly, the Rector of Harrow which were appropriated by the crown from Cranmer in 1544 and 1545 and sold off by 1547, the Harrow chantry was seen as so much lucrative property. Just as the Manors went to non-residents, the North family and Christ Church, Oxford, so the chantry lands were alienated away from local ownership.[42] So neither had the crown the lands nor had locals the chance to buy them back in order to maintain or re-endow any school which may have existed. The only direct material link between the Chantry of the Blessed Virgin Mary and Lyon's provisions may lie in the appointment of Richard Edlyn as one of the 1572 governors, almost certainly a close relative of the John and Robert Edlyn of Pinner who had held chantry land at Hatch End in the 1540s.[43]

---

[38] Kreider, *English Chantries*, 62, Table 2. 2.
[39] Youings, *Sixteenth Century England*, 186; cf. pp. 120 and 192; *VCH, Middlesex*, iv. 253–4.
[40] *Octocentenary Tracts*, x; 'The Harrow Chantries', 32 n. 2.
[41] Guy, *Tudor England*, 205.
[42] The complicated fate of the Harrow church lands is explored in Done Bushell, *Octocentenary Tracts*, xiii, esp. the documents at, pp. 11–31 and 44–6; *Calendar of Patent Rolls 1547–8*, pp. 299–300 (6 Aug. 1548).
[43] Laborde, *Harrow School*, 218–19; *Octocentenary Tracts*, xiii. 44 and 46.

The Foundation

The balance of probability is that Harrow had a reasonably well-endowed chantry under the auspices of which children of the parish received an education beyond the rudimentary, possibly in the Church House. This school, like many others, was maintained, 'at no little cost, labour and charge', as was recorded in 1570 of the parishioners of Southwark in similar circumstances, by prominent local inhabitants.[44] Among these, William Gerrard of Flambards became the most conspicuous, if only because he had so many sons of school age. It is likely, therefore, that the medieval school continued on an *ad hoc* basis until John Lyon stepped in first to support then re-endow it.

The associations with London, the court, and Cambridge may have owed all to immediate contemporary acquaintances, but the pre-Reformation Harrow school, if it existed, would have been well-placed to acquire a reputation. Not only was the lord of the manor of Harrow the archbishop of Canterbury, but the Rectorship, although a sinecure generally held in plurality, attracted some distinguished and well-connected incumbents, some of whom actually resided in the Rectory, or Rectory Grove or, as now, The Grove. William de Bosco himself had been chancellor of Oxford University. John Byrkhede in the fifteenth century had been closely involved in the foundation of All Souls College, Oxford. Thomas Wilkinson (1479–1511) doubled as President of Queens' College, Cambridge (1484–1505), forcing a number of his university colleagues to seek him at Harrow, including, in 1493/4 Thomas Pate *bibliotiste*. In the sixteenth century, the prominent ecclesiastical politician, theologian, and administrator Cuthbert Tunstall (1511–22) cultivated pears in the Rectory garden (the so-called Hanging Gardens where the present Art School stands) before ascending to the sees of London, then Durham. His successor William Bolton (1522–32) was also prior of St Bartholomew's, London. William Warham (1532–7) was the nephew of Archbishop Warham. Even more prominent was Robert Layton (1537–44), Thomas Cromwell's chief agent in despoiling monasteries and the state terrorization of the religious orders in the late 1530s. He none the less found time to offer Cromwell lavish hospitality at the Harrow Rectory as well as sending his master some pears from Tunstall's orchard. His successor, Richard Coxe (1544–6), provides an even stronger link to the new age. In 1546 he effectively engineered the end of the Harrow Rectory (parochial clerical functions having anyway long since devolved completely on the Vicar) by, after the surrender of the Rectory Manor to the Crown (1545), securing its grant, with the all important tithes, to Christ Church, Oxford (1546) of which he just happened to be dean at the time. The last of the Rectors of Harrow, Coxe's subsequent career as prominent reformist divine, leading Marian exile, and Elizabethan bishop of Ely mirrored the fate of advanced Protestantism, the progress of which provided not the least important setting for John Lyon's charity. Although having only a fleeting association, Coxe remembered the poor of Harrow in his will

---

[44] Carlisle, *Grammar Schools*, ii. 578–81 (St Olave's).

(1581).[45] These Rectors provided, long before the scions of the nobility and gentry arrived, a wider dimension to local affairs not dissimilar to that which later allowed Lyon to obtain a royal charter.

The severance of the connection with Canterbury and the demise of the Rectory sinecure in the 1540s was probably less serious than the loss of church funding. Even after both manors had been obtained by Sir Edward North (1547), the potentially crucial tithes formerly belonging to the Rectory remained with Christ Church. The school continued but the 'charge', as Gilbert Gerrard put it, was clearly of sufficient weight as to make the encouragement of a new endowent a matter of interest if not urgency. In one way, however, although the political and fiscal aspects of the Reformation had in all probablity precipitated this problem, the theological developments eased its solution. No longer able to display piety by bestowing charity on chantries, gilds, shrines, etc., the religiously serious-minded found schools a more than acceptable substitute, not so much meritorious good works as channels to fructify the vineyard of the Lord by the raising up of new generations of the godly. Such was Lyon's implicit purpose. Yet to persuade him to it required a misfortune. From his memorial brass in the parish church, it appears that Lyon may once have had a child. By 1579, and probably for many years before, however, he was childless. It was this that helped persuade Lyon—or helped him be persuaded—to imitate the example of another childless school benefactor, Sir John Port at Repton (1556–7), and commit his fortune not to family but posterity.[46]

---

[45] For the details of these Rectors see *Octocentenary Tracts*, ix, 'The Vicarage'; x and xi, 'The Harrow Rectors' *passim*; xiii, esp. pp. 19–21.

[46] Thornton, *Harrow School*, 61, 419–20 for the brass, mutilated in 1847; for Port and Repton see Carlisle, *Grammar Schools*, i. 230–6.

2

CREATION

JOHN LYON

Of the personality of John Lyon we know almost nothing. Sentimentalists have endowed him with all the virtues, from visionary prophecy to the ruddy, healthy independence of the archetypal English squire of the sort so often praised at Harrow but so rarely seen there. All that remains are the records of his business transactions; his land deals; his prominent standing in the local community; and his establishment of the charitable trusts and corporation which were to sustain and administer his Free Grammar School and the roads from Edgware and Harrow to London. There is his brass in the church. His signature survives in the archives, from which it is evident that he retained a certain manual vigour until January 1591 when he signed every page of his statutes.[1] He must have been seventy-six years old as, from a Rectory Manor Court ruling of 1534, it appears that he was twenty at the time of his father's death that year.[2] According to a lease of 1572, we know he used to ride on horseback to Harrow village (then confined to the Hill itself) from his farm at Preston, stabling his mount on the site chosen for his future school.[3] His farmhouse at Preston dated in part from the fourteenth century. It became, certainly in the nineteenth century, a place of pilgrimage, visited by Harrovians in fiction as well as fact.[4] The governors sold the Preston lands, including the founder's farmhouse, in the 1930s, taking advantage of the demands of suburban housing, what Messrs Comden and Wakeling, the builders of Lindsay Park in the 1930s on

---

[1] HSR I, fos. 3ʳ–8ᵛ, 'Orders, Statutes and Rules'; Lyon's signature appears at the foot of each page.
[2] HSR 63, extract from roll of Court Baron held at Harrow, 14 Apr. 1534.
[3] HSR 132, lease of 14 Mar. 1572.
[4] Thornton, 'John Lyon', Howson and Townsend Warner, *Harrow School Register*, 24; H. A. Vachell, *The Hill* (London, 1906), p. 150.

part of Lyon's estate, called 'artistically developing'. The house itself was demolished by the local council in 1960.[5]

Of Lyon's thoughts, character, and motives, as opposed to his possessions, we are largely ignorant. In 1611, faced with charges of misappropriation of trust funds away from the upkeep of the roads, the governors insisted that building the school was their priority 'for that they well knew the same to be a worke of charity, which the said John Lyon above all Charitable uses most and principally affected'.[6] Of Lyon's prime concern for the inhabitants of Harrow, the governors were insistent. One of them, John Page of Wembley, was the last surviving from 1572, so their statements may possess authority, and are supported by the provisions of the Statutes of 1591. Some have tried to extrapolate Lyon's personality from the Charter and the Statutes.[7] Unfortunately these, in almost all details, are derivative or identical to other contemporary schemes.

Of Lyon's religion, his foundation may stand witness to Protestant conformity. Born an orthodox Catholic, Lyon was a young man at the time of the Henrician break with Rome in the 1530s. He appears to have followed the religious changes of the next thirty years with equanimity. He maintained good relations with his notoriously recusant neighbours, the Bellamys of Uxendon, but his circle included the Protestant Gerrards and, in his statutes, he prescribed Calvin's Catechism to be read to the pupils each Sunday. In 1591 he provided for the preaching of thirty 'good, learned, and godly sermons' in the parish church, sponsoring preachers being a characteristic of enthusiastic reformers, as well as urging the Master to lecture the scholars on Scripture. In the words of his Statutes, signed by him: 'I have only sought the advancement and setting forth of the glory of God and the good example, benefit, and furtherance of good Christian people.'[8] It may, however, not have escaped his notice nor have been accidental that the date of his Charter, 19 February 1572, was Ash Wednesday, in Lyon's youth and early manhood, at least, a day of penance.

The only flash of individuality, even a sense of humour, is in a quittance by Thomas Bellamy of Uxendon of a debt repaid him by John Lyon in 1569 at the foot of which Bellamy has written, as pretend witnesses, 'Jack Straw' and 'Wat Tyler', two famed leaders of the Peasants' Revolt of 1381. Lyon kept the document, but

---

[5] Druett, *Harrow through the Ages*, 149 and, for Messrs Comden and Wakeling's advertisement, 'Harroviana', ibid., pp. v–vi; for the farm's fate see *VCH, Middlesex*, iv. 251; cf. GBM 1930–8, *passim*.

[6] British Library, Add. MS 29,254, fo. 42^r, fos. 39^v–43^r transcribe British Library MS Harleian 2211, fos. 23^r–32^r, the record of the 1611 Chancery case and judgment written in the seventeenth century.

[7] Most notably Percy Thornton. For Page see Laborde, *Harrow School*, 218–19; Gun, *Harrow School Register*, 160. Oddly, Gun (p. 159) suggests that John Page was dead by 1608, which is contradicted by the Governors' Accounts, HSR V: John Page was still acting as one of the surveyors in 1616 (fo. 16).

[8] Laborde, *Harrow School*, 229–30, 233, 239; for Lyon and the Bellamys see W. Done Bushell, *The Bellamies of Uxendon* (London, n.d., bound with *Octocentenary Tracts*, ix–xiii), p. 98.

whether he appreciated the joke, whatever it was, let alone was a party to it, cannot be known.⁹ As in the quittance Bellamy admitted having lost the original bond, the subscriptions may have been a heavy reference to the destruction of records during the Peasants' Revolt. Apart from evidence of Elizabethan knowledge of the medieval past, the document cannot be taken as signifying anything concrete. John Lyon must remain forever two-dimensional, like his brass in the parish church: a public face; the image of a Tudor benefactor.

For his school, it was Lyon's property not his personality that mattered. Lyon was one of the richest farmers in a prosperous farming area. The valley of the Brent was highly regarded for the excellence of its corn.¹⁰ The rapid population growth in sixteenth-century England, as well as fuelling inflation, increasing poverty, and exacerbating certain social tensions, provided great opportunities for those who possessed agriculturally productive land. Markets were buoyant, even in years of plenty, and prices high. Inflation, as the governors discovered after 1608, presented a problem.¹¹ Although in his lifetime Lyon appeared content to issue leases to tenants of forty or even seventy and eighty years, in his statutes he insisted that the governors issued leases no longer than twenty-one years.¹²

Inheriting substantial property in 1534, by 1562 Lyon easily headed the parish rental list. In 1567 he was appointed collector of the Parliamentary subsidy and in 1580 appeared in Manorial records as 'prepositus et bedellus' (i.e. manorial reeve and bailiff). In 1590 his estate was valued as bringing in £179 6s. 8d., perhaps representing a capital value of £8,000. By purchase and lease Lyon had extended his holdings not only in Middlesex, but in Hertfordshire, Bedfordshire, Marylebone, and Paddington.¹³ The nature of Lyon's land transactions underwent a radical change after his decision to endow a school. It is impossible, from the surviving deeds, to be sure exactly when Lyon decided to put his money into property for the school, as opposed to his other business interests. A flurry of acquisitions between May 1570 and May 1575 show Lyon eager to build up his holdings in and around Harrow itself, including a substantial holding in Alperton bought for £140, a process which straddled the granting of the Charter in February 1572.¹⁴ Lyon, in association with his wife, had earlier acquired Harrow property, in 1564 and 1565, but his interests at this time seemed to be still directed to his business, in 1565

---

⁹ HSR 123, quittance of 3 July 1569 from Thomas Bellamy. Done Bushell assumes it is from Thomas's father, William. Thornton (*Harrow School*, 42) avoids the issue by simply referring to 'Belamy'.

¹⁰ Norden, *Speculum Britanniae*, 11.   ¹¹ British Library Add. MS 29,254, fo. 42ᵛ.

¹² e.g. HSR 115, 117, 120; Laborde, *Harrow School*, 235.

¹³ Thornton, 'John Lyon', in Howson and Townsend Warner, *Harrow School*, 21–3; *VCH, Middlesex*, iv. 172, 251, 269; v. 65, 289; British Library MS Harleian 2211, fo. 33ʳ; HSR 63, 88, 91, 101, 103, 104, 105, 113–20, 124, 126, 127, 129, 132, 133, 134, 136, 142–51, 156, 158–67, 169; for the valuation cf. Lawrence Sheriff's Will, July 1567, which envisaged an income of 45s. from land costing £100; Carlisle, *Grammar Schools*, ii. 662 *et seq.*, for the foundation of Rugby School.

¹⁴ HSR 126–9, 132–4, 136, 142–51; 134 for the Alperton purchase, Oct. 1572.

receiving permission to enclose common land at Preston.[15] Perhaps more significant was the purchase, for the substantial sum of £563 6s. 8d., of properties in Bedfordshire, in 'Maldon' (i.e. Maulden), Ampthill, Flitton, and Clephill. This may suggest a switch in investments.[16] By 1568, too, Lyon, again with his wife, had bought four tenements in Chipping Barnet.[17]

Of potentially greater significance was Lyon's purchase, some time between May 1560 and April 1569, for a sum under £500, of lands in North and South Mimms, Hertfordshire from Sir Gilbert Gerrard. Lyon's connection with the Gerrards was, as has been suggested, crucial in the endowing of the school.[18] Gilbert's brother William Gerrard, from whom Lyon bought property in the early 1570s, moved to Harrow in 1566.[19] It appears unlikely that Lyon had considered a school before then, but it is possible that the idea formed soon after.

The granting of the Charter in 1572 itself influenced Lyon's estate. Within a month of its sealing, a Lyon lease was referring to the building of new lodgings for a schoolmaster.[20] In 1575 the Harrow, Alperton, and Preston lands had been assigned to the Keepers and Governors of the Free School, appointed by the Charter, John and Joan Lyon only retaining a life interest.[21] Two of the most significant purchases after 1572 were of property in Marylebone for the express purpose of using the income on the upkeep of the Harrow and Edgware roads. In June 1579 Gilbert and William Gerrard bought lands in Kilburn from Alan Hoord for £340. A month later they sold these lands to John and Joan Lyon and the governors. After the deaths of the Lyons, the governors were to employ the yearly rents on the high road from Edgware to London, any surplus to be devoted to the Harrow road.[22] Gilbert and William Gerrard were both governors. The Charter had explicitly mentioned Lyon's determination 'to repair and mend at his own very great expense certain highways between Edgware and London as well as other places'. However, it omits any estimate of the actual annual value of the assets to be administered by the governors, presumably on the assumption that there would be additions to the trust and provision would be made for the roads. The Kilburn purchase can thus be regarded as part of a *quid pro quo*, managed by the ubiquitous Gerrards. In December 1582 Lyon spent a further £321 10s. on buying more land in Marylebone from William Sherington on almost identical terms to the Kilburn deal, except that the road to receive priority was the Harrow road through Harlesden and Paddington.[23]

---

[15] HSR 104; cf. nos. 101, 103.   [16] HSR 113–15.
[17] HSR 117.   [18] HSR 91, 120, 124.
[19] HSR 129; Lyon's association with William Gerrard is evident in the latter witnessing part of the Bedfordshire land deal of 1565, i.e. a year before Gerrard moved to Flambards: HSR 114.
[20] HSR 132.   [21] HSR 148, 149, 150.
[22] HSR 152, 153, 154–5, 156; this last, the sale deed of 6 July 1579, specifying the use to which the income was to be put (cf. Laborde, *Harrow School*, 231), in fulfilment of the promise made in the Charter (ibid., 216–17).
[23] HSR 165, purchase completed 19 Dec. 1582. Cf. Laborde, *Harrow School*, 321.

The desire to bequeathe money for the maintenance of local roads was not a novel idea. In 1552 William Sheafield's will provided both for a school at Leeds and for the upkeep of local highways. Around Harrow the roads were notoriously bad in winter, when the muddy clay 'waxeth both dyrtie and deepe'. Lyon's road trust was the fifth such to be directed at Harrow's roads since 1507. Elsewhere in the district, William Mulberry's charity had maintained the road from Bushy to London since early in the century.[24] Lyon's road provision may suggest one of the bases of his fortune; a market-gardener on a grand scale for the capital. However, the arrangements for the Harrow and Edgware roads were to cause trouble for the governors. Apart from the general problem that the income from some of the most profitable lands were assigned away from the school, in the governors' consistent view the prime charge on Lyon's bequests, the road trusts repeatedly involved them in heated litigation in Chancery or before charity commissioners during the fifty years after 1608.[25]

John Lyon was a man of substance who had increased his wealth to make himself, below the gentry, the richest citizen in a prosperous area, with significant landed interests in three counties. One of his cousins was Lord Mayor of London in 1554.[26] Yet he remained an essentially local man. Despite his contacts with courtiers and politicians, he received no royal preferment or office outside his parish, nor did he aspire to a social status above the misleading 'yeoman'. His whole career suggests the difficulty of establishing meaningful social categories in this period, as well as demonstrating the material upward mobility of an age of commercial opportunity as well as economic strain.

Yet Lyon needed help. Politically, the patronage of Gilbert Gerrard not only secured the Charter, valuable for legal and tax purposes as much as prestige, but assisted Lyon financially. In 1575, at Gerrard's special request, Lyon was excused the Manorial entry fine on the re-granting of his Preston lands as a life-interest from the governors.[27] In 1579, if Gerrard is to be believed, the Kilburn deal had stretched Lyon's liquidity beyond the limit. The Attorney-General, writing to the Clerk of the Signet to secure Lyon's release from a loan of £50, claimed that Lyon 'has not so much ready money, nor is likely to make so much presently of his goods', adding that he had to borrow (from whom, one wonders; Gerrard, perhaps?) to cover the purchase.[28] Given that, three years later, Lyon could contemplate spending over £300 for more land in Maylebone, Gerrard's claim may be hard to credit.[29] Perhaps he was simply rearranging Lyon's obligations.

[24] Carlisle, *Grammar Schools*, ii. 841–56; Norden, *Speculum Britanniae*, 11–12; *VCH, Middlesex*, iv. 170, 172; British Library Add. MS 29,254, fo. 41ʳ (cited by the complainants against the governors).
[25] e.g. the Chancery case of 1611, the challenge of 1651 and Leonard Sockdale's suit of 1655.
[26] Sir John Lyon of Perivale, a member of the Grocers' Company, Thornton, *Harrow School*, 53–7 and Appendix D. [27] HSR 150.
[28] *Calendar of State Papers, Domestic. Addenda 1566–79*, p. 563. [29] HSR 165.

In this letter, addressed from Sudbury, in which he explained Lyon's charitable intentions, Gerrard calls him 'my neighbour'. Although his primary seat was in Staffordshire, Gerrard had extensive property in the parish of Harrow at Greenford, Alperton, and Wembley as well as Sudbury, which qualified him as a governor as well as one of those from whom Lyon was removing a potential financial burden.[30] However, once the financial provisions for the Free School were established and formally conveyed to the new corporation, direct interest by the extremely busy Attorney-General and, from 1581, Master of the Rolls, dwindled. It seems likely that Lyon retained full and direct control of his estates during his life. A sign of how ineffective or superfluous the governors were during the Founder's lifetime came in 1586, when it was discovered that nobody had bothered to fill three outstanding vacancies in the Governing Body caused by the deaths of the incumbents, the bishop of London having to intervene to honour the requirements of the Charter.[31] Lyon seems not to have been unduly concerned by this legal hiatus.

THE CHARTER OF 1572

The most signal service Gilbert Gerrard performed was to ease Lyon's receipt of a Royal Charter.[32] In itself, the acquisition of royal Letters Patent for a school was not unusual. In a Parliamentary Statute of 1559 the government invited applications like Lyon's.[33] Control of education was a high priority of a regime intent on introducing lasting religious changes, the importance of schools, schoolmasters, and curriculum being explicitly recognized by the 1559 Parliament. In 1562 the court of High Commission was empowered to draft school and college statutes: indeed, Gilbert Gerrard himself was involved in doing this for Merton College, Oxford in 1567.[34] Among the fifty or so schools whose patrons availed themselves of the facility of Letters Patent under the 1559 legislation were schools of existing repute, such as Shrewsbury (1571), but most were local grammar schools, often of modest scale, such as Rothwell near Kettering (1581), with an endowment of £3 4s. 11d. Not all local benefactors, however, secured such royal imprimatur. Oundle (1566), Rugby (1567), and Oakham and Uppingham (1584) depended on the wills of their founders alone. A number of Letters Patent were granted in response to petitions from one or more local inhabitants (e.g. Wakefield, 1591, with very similar terms to Harrow's; Richmond, Yorkshire, 1568; or Woodstock, 1585). Frequently, the

---

[30] See above, n. 27; for the extent of Gerrard's estates at his death see his Will of 1593: *Index of Wills Proved in the Prerogative Court of Canterbury, 1584–1604*, ed. S. A. Smith and E. A. Fry, British Record Society (London, 1901), p. 170. In general see Gerrard's *DNB* entry by J. M. Rigg.
[31] HSR 168.   [32] The original is numbered HSR 130.
[33] 1 Elizabeth c.22, *Statutes of the Realm*, iv (1547–85), p. 397.
[34] J. Simon, *Education and Society in Tudor England* (Cambridge, 1966), pp. 291, 304, 307; *DNB*, vii. 1098.

element of re-foundation or re-endowment was even more explicit than at Harrow (e.g. Shrewsbury or Newcastle, 1600).³⁵

However, in many, perhaps most, cases, what distinguished those grammar schools that had and those that had not obtained Letters Patent was connections at court. Courtiers acted on their own behalf, as with Archbishop Grindal (St Bee's, 1583), Lord Keeper Sir Nicholas Bacon (St Alban's, statutes 1570; Redgrave, 1561); Sir Thomas Smith, Secretary of State (Penrith, 1564); Lord Treasurer Burghley (Alford, 1576); the earl of Huntingdon (Leicester, 1564); Sir Walter Mildmay, chancellor of the Exchequer (Godmanchester; Middleton, 1572); or the Lord Chief Justice Cholmley (Highgate).³⁶

Alternatively, they acted on behalf of others, as with Sandwich (1563), when Archbishop Parker and Sir William Cecil (later Lord Burghley) did so in support of Roger Manwood, although their protégé, as well as being a Kentish barrister, was also an exchequer official who later, as a Justice of the Queen's Bench, heard a case involving John Lyon.³⁷ In 1573 the Queen's favourite, the earl of Leicester, requested a charter on behalf of the inhabitants of Barnet, where the role of the influential was more than passing: one governor was Henry Knollys, Leicester's brother-in-law and cousin of the Queen; another was Robert Johnson, founder of Uppingham and Oundle, who had been encouraged to help Barnet by Nicholas Bacon. It may be significant that on either side of the Barnet schoolhouse was land owned by John Lyon.³⁸ The backing of courtiers, in the shape of Gerrard, for Lyon's schemes was, therefore, usual, although it was unusual for the patron not to be mentioned in the Letters Patent. Likewise, his grammar school shared its foundation charter with many others but was arguably more securely established than some comparable local schools, such as Rugby.³⁹

It appears that there existed a fairly coherent group of well-connected school patrons at Elizabeth's court in the generation after 1559 that often corresponded with the most vigorously protestant: Bacon, Leicester, Huntingdon, Mildmay. Central to this circle was Alexander Nowell, dean of St Paul's, from 1562 a key figure on the High Commission in drafting school statutes and curricula (e.g. at

---

³⁵ For a general survey see Simon, *Education and Society*, 304–32; for individual schools see Carlisle, *Grammar Schools*, ii. 214–19 (Oundle), 223 (Rothwell), 253–7 (Newcastle), 316 (Woodstock), 323–40 (Oakham and Uppingham), 374–95 (Shrewsbury), 875–82 (Richmond); M. H. Peacock, *History of the Free Grammar School of Queen Elizabeth at Wakefield* (Wakefield, 1892), pp. 10–15.

³⁶ Simon, *Education and Society*, 309–10, 315; Tittler, *Nicholas Bacon*, 59–62; *VCH, Middlesex*, i. 302–4; P. Collinson, *Archbishop Grindal, 1519–83* (London, 1979), pp. 33–4; Carlisle, *Grammar Schools*, i. 152–68 (St Bee's), 191–2 (Penrith), 555–6 (Godmanchester), 508–27 (St Alban's), 705–8 (Middleton), 770–4 (Leicester), 778–87 (Alford), ii. 162–3 (Highgate), 531 (Redgrave).

³⁷ Carlisle, *Grammar Schools*, ii. 594–615; HSR 136 (Michaelmas Term 1572).

³⁸ C. L. Tripp, *A History of Queen Elizabeth's Grammar School, Barnet* (Cambridge, 1935), esp. pp. 5–6, 220–3. Lyon's holdings at Barnet are the concern of HSR 117, leased by Lyon, 20 Oct. 1568.

³⁹ Rugby lacked a royal charter, depending instead on Sherrif's will. Carlisle, *Grammar Schools*, ii. 662–86.

Brentwood, Colchester, Tunbridge, Burnley, Middleton, and Bangor) and author of a widely circulated Protestant Catechism, recommended in Lyon's own statutes and elsewhere (e.g. Oundle and Bristol).[40] To this group Gerrard was closely associated, politically and personally. He acted as overseer of the will of Dean Nowell's brother. Joint treasurer of Gray's Inn with Nicholas Bacon in 1555, in 1579 he paid for a eulogy delivered at his friend's funeral. Like his colleagues, Gerrard lent his patronage to education, not only at Harrow but also at Hoddeson (1560).[41]

His and their purpose was clear. As Nicholas Bacon put it to William Cecil in 1561, 'I may remember diverse gentlemen that gave gladly great wages to their horsekeepers and huntsmen than to such as taught their children whereby they had very ready horses and perfect dogs, so they had very untoward children'.[42] Education was seen not only as a general beneficent force in society; it furthered orthodox religion and social control. Thus governments were intimately concerned, to the extent of even prescribing school textbooks, such as Lily's Latin grammar in 1542 or Ocland's Latin verse in 1582.[43] After 1559 the beliefs of schoolmasters were regarded as of supreme importance. The powerful cabal of Protestant divines, lawyers, and politicians, many of radical, Calvinist persuasion, was eager to plant serious reformed religion in England, a religion of Book and Pulpit. Learning and faith were two sides of the same coin. John Lyon was the instrument of this purpose at Harrow.

This context helps explain many features of Lyon's Charter and Statutes which, with only a very few exceptions, were directly comparable with numerous other contemporary foundations. The royal Letters Patent followed an almost invariable formula, providing for the establishment of a grammar school with a master and usher; the upkeep of the road from Edgware to London; the appointment of named governors, incorporated with a common seal and perpetual succession; the devising of statutes and ordinances by the founder or the governors and the supervision of those rules by the governors after the founder's death; the replacement of deceased governors; and the details of the administration of the endowment by the governors. The visitor was to be the bishop of London, although this was, perhaps oddly, contradicted by Lyon in his statutes of 1591, when the archbishop of Canterbury was substituted.[44] In common with practically all such Letters Patent, there was a clause which allowed the governors to receive endowments not subject to the restrictions of the Statute of Mortmain up to a specified sum, in Harrow's case £100 a year.

---

[40] Simon, *Education and Society*, 307, 309–10, 326, 329, 332; R. Churton, *Life of Alexander Nowell* (Oxford, 1809); Laborde, *Harrow School*, 239; Carlisle, *Grammar Schools*, i. 408–10 (Brentwood), 424–7 (Colchester), 626–32 (Tunbridge), 641–3 (Burnley), 705–8 (Middleton), ii. 214–19 (Oundle), 404–11 (Bristol), 923–4 (Bangor).

[41] Churton, *Nowell*, 143; Tittler, *Bacon*, 48, 191; *Calendar of Patent Rolls, Elizabeth I*, i. 297; Simon, *Education and Society*, 309.

[42] Tittler, *Bacon*, 60.   [43] Guy, *Tudor England*, 17–18; Simon, *Education and Society*, 324.

[44] Cf. Laborde, *Harrow School*, 220–3, 237.

The Foundation

In structure and often wording, these provisions follow the model established under Edward VI and standardized under Elizabeth I's legislation of 1559. Many contemporary charters are very similar, in essence and detail, such as those of Sandwich (1563), Highgate (1565), and Barnet (1573), where, as with Harrow, no fee was charged for the Letters Patent.[45] There were distinguishing features. Chief amongst these lay in the nature of the application of the endowment to charitable purposes beyond the school, mainly the roads. A number of schools were similarly associated with equivalent wider local charity. The name of the Harrow school was also distinctive. While elsewhere, in gratitude for funds or merely the charter, as at establishments very like Harrow, such as Barnet (1573) or Wakefield (1591), schools had taken the Queen's name as their title, John Lyon was permitted to give his own name to his school: the Free Grammar School of John Lyon.[46]

This may have been in recognition of the lavish scale of his endowment. One of the most enduring myths about Harrow School has been that it was poorly endowed. Whatever the management of the trust lands since Lyon, his own arrangements were, in the context of the time, substantial. Although not comparing with the huge funds placed at the disposal of schools by the crown at Christ's Hospital (1553), the Skinner's Company at Tunbridge (1552), or the Merchant Taylor's (1561), the allowance of £100 to be held in Mortmain, which relieved it of certain taxes up to that amount of income, easily outshines almost all other Elizabethan foundations, most of which were permitted an endowment limit of £40 a year or less, some considerably less. The level of this endowment limit was obviously crucial. In June 1572 the chancellor of the Exchequer, Sir Walter Mildmay, a veteran school patron, expressed the hope to William Cecil that the Queen would license a limit of £100 or at least 100 marks for Dean Nowell's school at Middleton 'for the increase of the stipends of the schoolmaster and usher'. The Queen was unmoved: Middleton's Charter of August that year set the limit at £20.[47]

Lyon already possessed substantial assets to which he added, as we have seen. But Mildmay's anxiety was well founded. Many Elizabethan schools went under, required further investment or charged fees. Lyon's exceptionally high tax relief indicated that his school had a better start than most. As John Norden commented a year after Lyon's death on his provisions: 'it is a good precedent, but I fear too good to be often followed'.[48] Despite the initially crippling capital costs incurred by the building of the schoolhouse, the annual current account of the Lyon Trusts was in surplus or balance for eighty of the first hundred years after Joan Lyon's death in 1608.[49] Ironically, in view of the increasing concentration on fee-paying boarders over this period, laden with profit for the schoolmasters, Lyon's bequest

---

[45] Carlisle, *Grammar Schools*, i. 594–615, ii. 162–3; Tripp, *Queen Elizabeth's*, 220–3.
[46] Explicit in the charter: see Laborde, *Harrow School*, 216–17.
[47] Carlisle, *Grammar Schools*, i. 705–8; cf. ibid., 626–32 (Tunbridge), ii. 20–37 (Christ's Hospital), 49–69 (Merchant Taylors'). [48] Norden, *Speculum Britanniae*, 23.
[49] HSR V, Governors' Accounts 1608–1709 *passim*.

not only fulfilled his non-school charitable purposes but allowed his Free School to live up to its name. A Free Grammar School was so called not, as some have suggested, because of its independence from the church, but because it was organized by an autonomous corporation possessed of 'perpetual succession' and, in the words of the will of Peter Blundell in 1599 which founded the school at Tiverton, it was 'not a school of exaction'.[50]

The scholars at Harrow were to be local and, apart from the necessaries of learning, such as writing materials, their education was entirely free of charge, a stipulation that underscored the essential parochial charitable intention, witnessed also by Lyon's instructions for sixty of the poorest householders to receive 6s. 8d. a year from the governors. These provisions are contained in Lyon's 'Orders, Statutes and Rules', dated 18 January 1591, with which the establishment of the Free Grammar School came a significant step closer.[51]

THE STATUTES AND RULES OF 1591

The Statutes were clearly made in recognition that the founder was nearing his end, although still vigorous. They have often been misleadingly called Lyon's Will. Although this latter document has been lost, the Statutes are not it. The confusion was of early making. When taken to court for misuse of the Trust funds in 1651, the governors' search for the 'Will' at the various possible probate courts was unavailing. For over two centuries thereafter, the governors, their agents, and historians of the school, including Percy Thornton in 1885, tried to locate it. In fact, the original of the Statutes lay in the school muniment chest all the time.[52] Still in the School Archives, each page is signed by the founder himself, a procedure identical to that pursued by the earl of Huntingdon with the Statutes he drew up for his school at Leicester (1574).[53] This conformity of practice is typical of Lyon's statutes as a whole. Whatever else, the founder's statutes were entirely unoriginal. While not surprising, given the circumstances of foundation and founder, this poses a problem for the historian. Previously, most students of Harrow School's past have ascribed the success of the school to the intentions and provisions of the founder. That intrepretation is clearly inadequate, if not misleading. It is largely to extrinsic not intrinsic forces that Harrow's ascent must be ascribed. In many ways it could be argued that, like grocer Lawrence Sheriff's school at Rugby, it rose by accident not design.

[50] Carlisle, *Grammar Schools*, i. 339–59.
[51] Laborde, *Harrow School*, 230, 232–3, 237, 240.
[52] HSR 209. For the 'Will' legend see, Thornton, *Harrow School*, 58, 427. Even Scott fell into this error when he wrote of Lord Ellesmere's 1611 judgment upholding Lyon's 'Will', when the manuscript itself only mentions Lyon's 'true intent and meaning' (*Records*, 62, no. 178).
[53] Governors' Order Book, HSR I, fos. 3ʳ–8ᵛ; Simon, *Education and Society*, 315.

The Foundation

Lyon's design was conventional, similar, in places identical, to many contemporary school statutes across England from the Lake District to Kent. Both administration and curriculum were standard, except, perhaps, for the expense of the provisions: on salaries and sundries, such as fuel, local charity outside the school, and fees for the running of the estates, the preaching of sermons, the ringing of bells, and the annual governors' dinner, the statutes imposed an outlay of over £130 a year, more or less the entire annual income from school trust land, which easily outstripped the resources of most other Free Grammar Schools.[54]

The Statutes implemented the principles and arrangements in the Charter. Details of how the Keepers and Governors were to conduct the business of managing the trusts and estates in their charge were carefully outlined, including the appointment of two surveyors to act as executive officers and a rent-collector; the manner and method of rendering accounts; the use of the school chest for storing records and surplus cash; the number of governors' meetings; their yearly feast; and their qualification, election, powers, and duties. That they had no free hand in management was explicit (and in the light of subsequent events wise). The Statutes were to come into force after the deaths of Lyon and his wife. Within six months, they were to appoint a Schoolmaster and Usher, an MA and BA respectively, who were to be unmarried. The teachers' salaries were to be forty marks a year (£26 13s. 4d.) for the Master and twenty marks (£13 6s. 8d.) for the Usher, each receiving five marks for fuel. Such salaries were much higher than the average, which was about £10, as at Merchant Taylor's; the Master at Eton received £16 and at Westminster £12.[55] Every year thirty sermons were to be preached in the parish church, the preachers, expected to be the Schoolmaster or the Vicar, receiving a fee of 6s. 8d. a time, the same amount as offered to the parish sexton for ringing the bell on these occasions over a whole year. The patronage of sermons was a characteristic of enthusiastic reformer laymen. Charity was common to all the prosperous pious. Twenty pounds were assigned to provide for sixty of the poorest parishioners in Harrow, excluding those in Pinner unless there was money to spare. Another twenty pounds was to be spent supporting two Exhibitioners at Gonville and Caius College, Cambridge and two at an unspecified Oxford college, each to last for a maximum of eight years: priority was to be given to the poorest pupils of the Free Grammar School and, in that category, Founder's Kin. The reservation of the income from the Hoord and Sherington lands in Marylebone for the Edgware and Harrow roads was repeated; and £4 a year added to maintain roads near Preston. The general terms and conditions of trust tenancies were fixed, as were even the minutiae of record keeping, such as entering the names of elected Masters and Ushers into a 'little pay book' and of newly elected governors into a special ledger.

---

[54] Laborde, *Harrow School*, 226–40. Cf. the 1590 estimate of income in British Library MS Harleian 2211, fo. 33ʳ and the annual sums received by the governors after 1608 (HSR V, fos. 1–23).

[55] Tripp, *Queen Elizabeth's*, 6. Cf. Simon, *Education and Society*, 371.

Creation

The archbishop of Canterbury was designated the arbiter of any unresolved disputes among the governors.

Special provision was made for the three years after the death of the surviving Lyon partner, a time clearly envisaged as most crucial for the successful implementation of the founder's schemes which would then be most vulnerable. During these three years, Lyon's subsidy for the education of thirty poor children was to be continued at a cost of twenty marks a year or until the new schoolhouse was completed. All over England, founders and patrons of schools, especially if local, apparently took immense pride in the building of the premises for their new grammar schools, emotions perhaps not unlike their ancestors' pleasure in new parish churches.[56] Lyon was no exception. He envisaged a building that would house accommodation of the Master and Usher and a schoolroom for the pupils. It was to be equipped with a chimney and cellars for fuel and was to be designed on a substantial scale. Over the three years specified, the governors were to set aside £300 to construct it.

In the event, the schoolhouse was to cost more than double that amount and take over twice the length of time to build than the Statutes allowed.[57] The governors' financial efforts to fulfil Lyon's instructions required borrowing money and facing a serious challenge in Chancery to the propriety of their management. Yet, in general, the Statutes were well founded, meticulous, and sensible. Even the cost and pain of erecting the schoolhouse was contained, such was the long-term value of the lands with which Lyon had endowed his trusts. A measure of the effectiveness of Lyon's provisions is their efficient longevity. Without direct royal court, City livery company, or university college patronage, Lyon's Free Grammar School prospered within the founder's careful and administratively modest, if financially comfortable framework.

That the institution grew during the subsequent century and a half from a school of and for one parish into a national institution has been ascribed to the 'Rules to be observed for the Ordering of the School' which Lyon appended to his Statutes in 1591, which together Percy Thornton called 'John Lyon's glimpse into the future'[58] The Rules detailed the authority and duties of the Schoolmaster, the nature of the curriculum, and the daily, routine management of the school and its pupils. Yet, like the statutes, they were unexceptional. The teachers were assigned a probabtionary period of six months. They were not to be absent for more than one day without good reason or ensuring adequate cover. The Master was to insist his pupils were clean, tidy, orderly, and polite. In common with many other

---

[56] Simon, *Education and Society*, 315.
[57] HSR V, Governors' Accounts, fos. 1–17; HSR I, Governors' Order Book, fos. 28ᵛ–30ʳ.
[58] Thornton, *Harrow School*, 26 *et seq.*; Laborde, *Harrow School*, 237–40. Cf. 'the wonder-dream of John Lyon which has materialised under the name of Harrow School' (Druett, *Harrow through the Ages*), 119.

schools of the time, corporal punishment was to be moderate.[59] The ritualized violence, sadism, and common assault with which schoolteaching was indelibly associated in the minds of old pupils and observers was a phenomenon not granted the approval of society until perhaps the later eighteenth, nineteenth, and twentieth centuries. It existed widely in the sixteenth and seventeenth centuries but everywhere ran counter to the expressed intentions of founders, governors, and parents. At Harrow, the only 'correction' permitted the teachers was 'a rod moderately, except it be a very thin ferule upon the hand for a light negligence'. If they exceeded this, they were, after warning, liable to be sacked. It may be instructive to note that institutionalized and accepted barbarity of man to pupil and pupil to fellow in the cause of learning and good order coincided with the transformation of the school into a finishing academy for the wealthy and social elite, a state far from the founder's Rules, and probably his intentions.

The Rules were a sort of prospectus, setting out the times, nature, and content of academic lessons and religious instruction as well as the obligations of pupils and parents. Lessons were to run from 6.00 a.m. until 11.00 a.m. and 1.00 p.m. to 6.00 p.m., although there was flexibility at the beginning and end of the day according to the distance the scholars had to come and the season of the year. These hours were entirely normal in such schools, if anything marginally longer at the end of the day, which in all circumstances was prefaced and concluded with prayers. School was on every day of the week, including Sundays, when the Master was instructed to teach from Calvin's or Dean Nowell's *Catechism*, where he would have found one of the fundamental principles of Lyon's establishment: 'For this age of childhood ought no less, yea also much more, to be trained with good lessons to godliness, than with good arts to humanity.'[60]

Holidays were restricted to one week to coincide with the great Christian festivals. Pupils were expected also to attend the parish church and to listen to the service and the reading and exposition of Scripture with 'reverence'. In school, they also learnt the Lord's Prayer, the Thirty-Nine Articles, the Ten Commandments, the Catechism, and the 'principal points of Christian religion', first in English (presumably for comprehension) then in Latin (presumably for education). Lyon's priority is clear. Education was fundamental in the creation of a godly society. As expressed in his charge to the governors in the Statutes, 'I have only sought the advancement and setting forth of the glory of God and the good example, benefit, and futherance of good Christian people.'[61]

---

[59] K. V. Thomas, *Rule and Misrule in the Schools of Early Modern England* (Reading, 1976), p. 10 and n. 39 and, in general on school violence, 9–12. For a racier but thought-provoking survey see J. Gathorne-Hardy, *The Public School Phenomenon* (London, 1977), ch. 3, esp. pp. 37–40.

[60] Alexander Nowell, *A Catechisme or First Instruction and Learning of Christian Religion*, tr. T. Norton (London, 1570), sig. B1, quoted in S. Schoenbaum, *William Shakespeare: A Compact Documentary Life* (Oxford, 1977), p. 62.

[61] Laborde, *Harrow School*, 233.

Profane recreation, or 'play', was given short shrift. Whereas in some schools acting (e.g. Sandwich or Westminster), music (e.g. Bedford), even chess (e.g. Camberwell and St Mary, Overey, south of the Thames) were encouraged, Harrovians were only allowed 'to drive a top, to toss a handball, to run, to shoot, and none other'.[62] Wrestling and 'leaping', found elsewhere, were not mentioned. The injunction to allow shooting has aroused much subsequent interest, most of it confused with the invention of an archery competition for a silver arrow in 1684 or sentimentalized in school songs as part of what could be called the 'Merrie England' version of Harrow's foundation. In fact, Harrow was by no means alone in having provision for archery in its rules, those at Dedham (1574) and St Alban's (1570) being almost identically phrased in specifying the equipment required.[63] The motives behind encouraging archery were much the same as those behind the whole educational project: a serious-minded attempt to inculcate stern, correct civic virtues as well as religous orthodoxy. In 1559 the Harrow Manorial Court ordered all boys over the age of twelve to possess bows and arrows.[64] Yet the academic earnestness of the Harrow Rules left little time for what were seen as essentially peripheral activities. What would now be called sport had almost no place in the original scheme of things. Like flogging, sport came into prominence as Harrow became increasingly a boarding school for the rich.

The priority of the Free Grammar School was academic education of a thorough, if narrow, sort. Some Elizabethan schools encouraged the study of French, Italian, even English, but the distinguishing feature of sixteenth-century grammar schools, in contrast to other charity or 'Dame' schools, was the concentration on classical languages, as a training for the mind and personality and a preparation for a public life.[65] Thus at Harrow, as in all other such grammar schools, the diet was, almost exclusively, petrifyingly classical, so much so that after the First Form all pupils had formally to speak Latin in school and when playing, presumably on the premises, although a certain amount of class work was inevitably conducted in English, notably translating from the Latin or Greek. As one object of this form of intensive education was to prepare pupils for the literate professions, this insistence on easy acquaintance with, in particular, Latin was prudent and probably not too onerous, given both the ease with which young children pick up spoken languages and their introduction to Latin at the same time as to written English. The central aim, however, seems to have been to repress the flightiness of youth and inculcate stern intellectual and hence personal discipline.[66]

The Rules provided for six forms, beginning with a reception class, 'the Petties',

[62] Thomas, *Rule and Misrule*, 17; Simon, *Education and Society*, 364–7; Carlisle, *Grammar Schools*, i. 606–7 (Sandwich's Christmas Latin play), ii. 559–62 (Camberwell), 582–9 (St Mary, Overey).
[63] Carlisle, *Grammar Schools*, i. 428–9 (Dedham), 508–27 (St Alban's).
[64] Druett, *Harrow through the Ages*, 113.
[65] Thomas, *Rule and Misrule*, 5–8; K. Wrightson, *English Society, 1580–1680* (London, 1982), 185, 191. [66] Thomas, *Rule and Misrule*, 1–15.

who were still learning English grammar and probably reading. In the First Form, pupils were introduced to Latin, using William Lily's grammar textbook, and taught to write. They practised their technical skill on classical anthologies of pithy sayings and Cicero's letters. Writing Latin sentences and translation into English was introduced in the Second Form where the literary models included pseudo-Cato's *Distichia* (begun in the First Form) and Aesop's *Fables* which, rather unexpectedly, Martin Luther ranked next only to the Bible as educationally useful. From Erasmus' *Dialogues* (or *Colloquia* 1512) pupils were provided with examples of conversational Latin and further edifying apophthegms could be derived from Antonio Mancinelli's *Carmina de quatuor virtutibus* (1502). In the Third Form prose composition was studied as were Terence's *Comedies*, Ovid's *De Tristibus*, and more letters of Cicero. Fluency in prose composition was completed in the Fourth Form through Erasmus' text on style, *De Duplici copia verborum ac rerum commentarii duo* (1511), or his collected letters, as well as reading Cicero (*De Amicitia, De Senectute*, or *De Finibus*); Virgil (*Bucolics* and *Georgics*); and the poems of Horace. With Vergil and Horace came instruction in verse composition. Now that a certain mastery of Latin was assumed, Greek grammar was begun, paving the way for the final year. The Fifth Form Latin syllabus included Virgil's *Aeneid*, Caesar's *Commentaries*, Cicero's *De Natura Deorum*, and Livy's *History of Rome*, while in Greek pupils read Demosthenes, Isocrates, Hesiod, Heliodorus (a Late Antique writer, printed in 1534 and translated into English—useful as a crib for the teacher if not his pupils—in 1587) or Dionysius of Parnassus. The Fifth Form were expected either to learn their texts by heart or to translate them into English. They also had exercises in writing essays in Latin. In addition the top three forms had to learn three Latin words at home each evening, a habit which in theory would have ensured a vocabulary of upward of three thousand words. These three forms also each had two hours a week (an hour a day was set aside for the purpose by the Master) during which they asked each other technical questions of grammar, syntax, vocabulary, and meaning. This training, at least, went beyond rote-learning, perhaps encouraging facility in public speaking. Certainly by the 1650s, Harrovians were orating in Latin and Greek freely and in public.[67]

This academic curriculum was as elitist as it was earnest. The locals Lyon intended to better had, or their parents had, ambitions beyond the menial, their eyes set upon the universities and professions, particularly the church. Education was a motor for upward social mobility, just as wealth was the fuel. In some grammar schools, pupils were openly warned to avoid 'apprentices and idle boys'.[68] The first Lyonian Harrovians may have been locals, they may not have been rich, but

---

[67] Bodleian Library MS Rawlinson D 1138, fos. 25ʳ–38ᵛ, speeches delivered by Harrovians between 1654 and 1656.

[68] Thomas, *Rule and Misrule*, 5–6; Wrightson, *English Society*, 190–1; Simon, *Education and Society*, 366–7.

they had to supply their own stationery and their own copies of the set texts, although the governors did later provide some basic reference books, such as Dictionaries, a Lexicon, standard editions of basic texts of Ovid, Vergil, and Demosthenes, as well as an English Bible (by then the new King James version).[69] The education that Lyon's generosity provided was deliberately segregating. After all, only a few families could afford not only the expense of the educational materials but, perhaps more crucially, the absence of their children's labour. It says much for the prosperity and social ambitions in the neighbourhood as much as the conservative tenacity of classical languages that such a curriculum retained its appeal among locals so sturdily for at least a century (the number of forty free scholars, agreed by the governors in 1615, still being attained in 1718).[70]

If they were not paupers, neither were the earliest Free Grammar school pupils necessarily infants. Although very sketchy, the evidence of seventeenth-century Harrovians is that they left aged about sixteen to eighteen, and therefore may have arrived as late as ten or twelve, although if they stayed for nine years, as did William Fenn (1637–46), some entrants were probably younger.[71] This relative maturity of entrants would explain the appointment from 1660 of so-called 'School Dames' to teach basic literacy to the younger parishioners before they were eligible to come to the Free School. The extreme youth of some later seventeenth-, but especially eighteenth-century, Harrovians, was once again in part a consequence of rich parents sending their children away to board as soon as possible.

In these provisions there was nothing out of the ordinary. Most grammar schools were conceived for modest numbers of local pupils. All studied Latin but not a few, from Westminster to Wakefield, added Greek. The textbooks reflected a common heritage of Renaissance New Learning; the religious instruction the more novel reformed religion. Nowell's *Catechism*, was ubiquitous; Calvin's was the first book bought for Philip Sydney at Shrewsbury in 1564.[72] In outline, many contemporary Statutes and Rules compare precisely with Lyon's schemes. At Archbishop Grindal's foundation of St Bee's (1583), there was provision made for a Governors' annual feast.[73] The school hours at Kirkby Stephen, in remote Westmorland, were identical to those at Harrow, as were many of the set texts: pseudo-Cato, Aesop, Cicero, Virgil, Terence.[74] The Charter (1591) and Statutes (1607) of the Free Grammar of Queen Elizabeth at Wakefield stand out in their similarity to Harrow's. There, a new school revived a previous one. The impetus for foundation was

---

[69] HSR II, Governors' Minutes (probably August 1615), fo. 3; provision by the pupils of their own stationery was specified in the statutory injunctions delivered to parents by the Master Laborde, *Harrow School*, 240. [70] Thornton, *Harrow School*, 112.
[71] Gun, *Harrow School Register*, 1–30. For Fenn, later a Governor of the School, see ibid., 9.
[72] Simon, *Education and Society*, 326.
[73] Carlisle, *Grammar Schools*, i. 152–68, at a cost of 6s. 8d. The Harrow governors did them themselves rather better (or inflation had taken its toll) spending 13s. 4d. on their dinner in 1617/18, rising to £1 6s. 8d. in 1620. [74] Carlisle, *Grammar Schools*, ii. 714–20.

The Foundation

explicitly local. The arrangements for governing the school and its funds are strikingly alike, even to the matter of the school chest and the term of tenants' leases. The school hours, religious instruction, and, in detail, the set-texts, even the Master's stipend, all mirror Harrow.[75] But more or less exact comparisons can be found across the kingdom. Even when the Harrow governors extended the Lyon benefaction in 1615 to include forty free scholars they were, consciously or not, aping Westminster (1560) and, less grandly and more locally, Highgate (1571).[76] Such correspondences leave the impression of a coherent national educational project of a sort not seen again until the nineteenth century.[77]

That Lyon was unoriginal needs little further emphasis. The monitorial system, which demanded two official informers each week and one secret Master's nark, was in essence copied from Westminster. Even the 'Articles' to be recited by the Master to all prospective parents, including the arrangements for attendance, expulsion, and for provision of ink, paper, pens, books, candles, bows, arrows (three), bowstrings, and bracers were copied verbatim from Bacon's St Alban's Rules of 1570.[78] Perhaps the most famous clause in the 1591 Rules, that allowing the Master to admit fee-paying 'foreigners', while certainly securing the later prosperity of school and, especially, Head Masters, and while expressly envisaging that some rich pupils could receive instruction at the Free Grammar School, merely reiterates a custom common elsewhere, for example at Tonbridge, Oundle, Wakefield, Sandwich, Reading, Tiverton, etc. This was no mark of a visionary founder, beloved of insular romantics, panegyrists, and tour-guides, but of a practical, conventional one.

In fact, there are perhaps only three unusual elements in Lyon's Rules. One is the absence of any mention of disease which features frequently in instructions for other schools. Perhaps it was recognized that Harrow, being rural, not urban, on an open site, had no need for the express barring of the sick enjoined elswhere. Perhaps this supports the idea that Lyon, while not being original, was at least intelligently selective in what he borrowed and copied and thus Percy Thornton's 'pious opinion' that Lyon, 'having more leisure' than men like Nicholas Bacon 'was the chief author of the said regulations'.[79] The evidence permits no verdict on this. The second oddity is more revealing, but, as before, of Lyon's generosity and wealth, not his nature. He envisaged that absolutely no entry charge would be made on those free scholars who enjoyed his benefaction. This was fairly exceptional, although, given the scale of Lyon's bequests, hardly significant. The most unusual clause in the Rules comes immediately after the injunction on the Master to keep the school

---

[75] Peacock, *Free Grammar School*, 3–15, 54–75.
[76] Carlisle, *Grammar Schools*, ii. 98–115 (Westminster), 162–3 (Highgate).
[77] cf. Wrightson, *English Society*, 186: 'something of a revolution in the provision of educational facilities'.
[78] Carlisle, *Grammar Schools*, i. 508–9, 517–18; Laborde, *Harrow School*, 240. Cf. Thornton, *Harrow School*, 78.   [79] Thornton, *Harrow School*, 64 note.

clean: 'He shall not receive any girls into the same school.'[80] Although some schools did admit both sexes, most grammar schools did not, girls' classical education being the preserve of courts and great houses. Yet, most compilers of statutes and rules felt no need to state the usual ban. Why was this thought necessary at Harrow? Perhaps Lyon was a stickler for accuracy, or something of an academic misogynist. Or perhaps the pre-Lyonian school had been open to the youth of the parish regardless of gender.

[80] Laborde, *Harrow School*, 239.

3

BIRTH

Joan Lyon died on 27 August 1608.[1] During his life, her husband had been careful to associate her in the ownership and transactions of his estate, in which she held a life interest.[2] After his death, she was regularly cited as acting with the Keepers and Governors in a similar fashion, using a version of her husband's seal.[3] She does not, however, appear to have taken much active part in the management of the estates. In September 1600 she used a cross to sign a power of attorney, suggesting she lacked the writing skill as well as business acumen of her spouse.[4] Immediately on her death, the governors entered into full possession and control of the Lyon trusts and endowments. Their behaviour over the next few years would determine more surely than any written instruction whether or not John Lyon's benefaction would survive.

Implementing founders' wishes could be risky. At Barnet in 1594 the Master was arrested because of the debts incurred in procuring floorboards for the new schoolhouse.[5] At Harrow, the discharge of their obligations led the governors into court in 1611 as defendants in a Chancery suit brought against them for misuse of funds and neglect of the terms of the trusts they managed. At issue was the alleged diversion to the building of the schoolhouse of income reserved to the upkeep of the Harrow and Edgware roads. The case and the judgment of Lord Chancellor Ellesmere revealed the problems faced by as well as the diligence of the governors while at the same time determining the parameters within which they could administer the proceeds from Lyon's bequest.[6]

---

[1] British Library Add. MS 29,254, fo. 42ʳ; W. O. Hewlett, 'Harrow School Buildings', Howson and Townsend Warner, *Harrow School*, 29.

[2] HSR 101, 115, 117, 120, 127, 129, 132, 134, 136, 143–9, 151, 156, 162, 163, 165, 169.

[3] HSR 172, 173, 175, 176.

[4] HSR 174, 29 Sept. 1600. The earlier association of wife with husband may suggest that Joan was considerably younger than John, her long widowhood predicted.

[5] Tripp, *Queen Elizabeth's*, 6.

[6] British Library, MS Harleian 2211, fos. 23ʳ–32ʳ; references below will be to the legible early nineteenth-century transcription, Add. MS 29,254, fos. 39ᵛ–43ʳ.

From the evidence and arguments presented in Chancery and the governors' own records, it is possible to piece together with some precision the construction of the schoolhouse and the opening of the Free Grammar School itself. That the schoolhouse took seven years to complete was not a comment on the governors' will but on the scale of the project to which they committed themselves. As they ruefully confessed to the court of Chancery in 1611, 'they had fallen into the common error of builders and had bestowed much more money thereabouts than at the first was meant or intended'.[7] It was a lesson not always remembered by their successors during the next four centuries. They also pleaded the wrecking uncertainties of inflation, arguing that 'difference of time did breed difference of charge', another cry with sharp twentieth-century echoes.[8]

At the heart of the governors' policy was—as it remained for generations—meticulous observance of what they perceived to be the founder's intentions as expressed in the Charter, Statutes, and Rules. But on Joan Lyon's death they were faced with a dilemma. The Statutes allowed the governors to spend up to £300 from the income of the first three years after her death on the schoolhouse. Yet it was by no means clear that any part of this considerable sum of money could be raised from yearly profits from the Marylebone estates set aside 'for ever' (said the Statutes) for the maintenance of the Harrow and Edgware roads, but only from the rest of the Lyon property. Yet the building of the schoolhouse, as the governors convincingly insisted in 1611, was the prime charge laid upon them in fulfilment of Lyon's bequest: no schoolhouse, no school, no charity, no point: 'they well knew the same to be a worke of charity, which the said John Lyon above all the said charitable uses most and principally affected'.[9]

Their plight was further complicated by the loss to the estate of land, including 116 acres in Kingsbury, valued at £50 a year, which Lyon had held in copyhold, because of the refusal of the lords of the manors to permit alienation to Lyon's charity: these properties went to Lyon's next of kin after 1608, not into the possession of the governors as Lyon had wished and intended.[10] This unexpected shortfall exacerbated the main burden on the governors, which was the cost of the building which far exceeded the provision allowed for in the Statutes. This, in turn, persuaded the governors to delay or ignore payments on the roads. This decision inevitably aroused the suspicion of those who stood to gain from the maintenance of the roads that not only had the governors not spent anything on them but that they had no immediate intention of doing so even after the three-year term had elapsed until the schoolhouse was finished, an impression apparently fostered by the governors' own possibly injudicious public statements to that effect.[11]

The Statutes had made clear that the schoolhouse was to be a substantial building. While keeping exactly to the founder's directions as to the number and nature

---

[7] British Library, Add. MS 29,254, fo. 42^r.   [8] Ibid., fo. 42^v.   [9] Ibid., fo. 42^r.
[10] Ibid.; *VCH, Middlesex*, v. 65.   [11] British Library, Add. MS 29,254, fos. 40^v–41^r.

The Foundation

of rooms, cellars, chimney, etc., the governors 'had made the same building of such strength as was fitting for such a worke so high situated'.[12] That meant brick, which alone had cost over £125 by the autumn of 1612.[13] This sum was, however, dwarfed by the bill run up by the main contractor, Thomas Page of Roxeth, whose costs and fees had, by the end of September 1610, come to £393 10s., swallowing up all but £22 of the trust's income in its first two years' operation. Much of this tiny remainder also went on costs associated with the school, such as scaffolding, timber, and £2 to 'Mr Sly the Surveyor', who had provided various plans for the new building.[14] Indeed, the governors had only avoided a deficit by accepting interest-free loans from their own number, such as the £50 lent by John Page of Wembley as early as August 1609.

The governors' accounts testify to their claim to have begun the construction of a 'faire' schoolhouse 'shortly after' the death of Joan Lyon as well as the heavy cost. It is also apparent that in trying to meet the expense of the schoolhouse, in the first four years they were able to generate an annual income around 50 per cent higher than that which appeared afterwards to have been the usual yearly return. Between 1608 and 1616 the governors' expenditure, largely directed to the schoolhouse, came to £1,140. Even so, despite protestations that they needed all the profits for five or six years after the three-year term to cover their costs, they had not bankrupted themselves, the spending, when averaged over those eight years, actually comparing quite favourably with subsequent annual costs once the school was running.[15] In fact, skilful and vigorous management of the estates kept the accounts in balance or surplus until the late 1620s and 1630s, when small deficits became regular.

From the accounts, although kept chaotically and copied inaccurately into different ledgers, it appears that the governors none the less had reason to be nervous.[16] As early as January 1610, the governors were in something like a panic faced with the 'charge of this building [which] did far exceed their purpose and expectation', realizing that 'once begunne it was of necessity to proceed in the same without intermission so far as fitting up of the roofe and the tyling thereof for the preservation of the whole'.[17] Although by 1611 the bulk of Thomas Page's expenses had already been met, there was still much to be done. Flooring, tiling, glazing, plastering, and furnishing continued into 1614–15, with finishing touches on interior decoration, pannelling, seats, and the school exterior and gate extending into

---

[12] British Library, Add. MS 29,254, fo. 42^r.

[13] For all the figures here and following on building costs and revenue see HSR V (Governors' Accounts) fos. 1–19 and HSR I (Governors' Order Book), fos. 28^v–29^r, Thomas Page's accounts 'concerning the building of the Free School'; the required borrowing is itemized ibid., fo. 30^r.

[14] HSR V, fo. 3. One of Sly's plans survives as HSR XI, now framed, reproduced by Thornton, *Harrow School*, 48–9 and the frontispiece to Scott, *Records of the Grammar School*.

[15] British Library, Add. MS 29,254, fo. 41^r.

[16] Cf. HSR I, fos. 28^v–29^r with HSR V fos. 1–3.   [17] HSR I, fo. 30^r.

1616. Indeed, it was only after September 1610 that payment was made for the demolition of the chimneys of the house which had previously stood on the site of the schoolhouse, probably between the new building and the street. (There is no reason to follow Thornton in imagining this 'old house' to have been a previous abode of the school.)[18] The area remained a considerable building site for years, a special sawpit being constructed some time after the autumn of 1614 to cater for the extensive carpentry yet to be completed.[19] Four years earlier, when the governors were taken to court, the prospects may well have seemed both unending and bleak, for them, their tenants, and those hoping to see repairs to the Harrow and Edgware roads.

The charge brought against the governors by the Attorney-General, Sir Henry Hubbard, 'at the relation of Charles Smith and other informants' (i.e. interested locals) in February 1611 was that a sum of £36 intended for the roads had been spent on the schoolhouse.[20] Further, it was argued that after the three-year term specified in Lyon's Statutes, the governors should be compelled to spend the income from the road trust estate on the roads as directed. The issue appeared urgent as the three-year term was to expire in August 1611 and the governors had made it known that, 'if not otherwise ordered' they would persist in spending all the trust profits on the schoolhouse for many years thereafter. The Charter, Statutes, and relevant indentures were studied by the court. In their defence, the governors pleaded Lyon's clear charitable intent to provide a schoolhouse; the loss of the £50 copyhold land; and the unexpected cost of building. They claimed not to have taken any fees, to which they were entitled, to have avoided 'superfluously unnecessary charge' by following Lyon's instructions exactly as to the dimensions of the schoolhouse, that some of them had spend 'great summes of money of their own Estates', that they had had to spend money going to law to reclaim rent and repair arrears (and, they might have added, preparing their defence in Chancery),[21] and that, in any case, they were empowered by the Statutes to use their discretion and resolve any statutory ambiguities. They calculated that even an additional three years' exclusive application of profits would 'hardly suffice to perfect the said building answerable to the intention of the Founder'. They even suggested that the Edgware Road did not need repair. At the centre of their defence was the argument that to divert money from the schoolhouse to the roads would run counter to Lyon's wishes and 'should break the trust reposed in them'. In a judgment of Solomon, the Lord Chancellor declined to uphold the complaint against the governors' previous conduct but insisted that after August 1611 the income from the properties so designated (i.e. the Hoord and Sherington lands in Marylebone) should be used

---

[18] HSR V, fo. 9; Thornton, *Harrow School*, 80.   [19] HSR V, fo. 14.
[20] The identity of Smith is revealed in HSR 158, the copy of the indenture concerning Lyon's purchase from the Gerrards of the Hoord lands used during the Chancery case, for which see above, n. 6.
[21] HSR V, fo. 7 for 15s. 6d. paid to the governors' solicitor.

exclusively on the roads and that, as provided for under the Statutes but not yet effected, two overseers be appointed to be responsible for the repairs to the roads. The first of many attempts by the governors and others to break the road trust to benefit the school had been frustrated. It would be another 386 years, and only after a privately sponsored Statutory Instrument (in 1991), before money from Lyon's Marylebone estates was again permitted to be applied, even indirectly, to the benefit of the school and its pupils.[22]

The judgment of 1611 left the governors free from legal interference to complete the establishment of the Free School. By September 1610 the basic fabric of the schoolhouse was nearing completion. The architectural design was that of Mr Sly, 'Old Sly', the surveyor. A drawing of his plan for a building similar both to Lyon's requirements and the actual schoolhouse as built still survives.[23] When compared to other similar schoolhouses, for example that at Barnet, the Harrow scheme appears lavish, including cellars for timber and coal on the ground floor; the large schoolroom on the first floor; on the second, two furnished rooms at either end for the Master and Usher to live in and in the middle one, slightly grander, for the governors to meet in (which they quickly equipped with curtains, leather-upholstered chairs, and a 'turkey carpet'); and on the floor above quite extensive attics.[24] Thomas Page was not the only local to benefit from the project. Felix Gerrard, a governor's son and brother, supplied bricks. The vicar, Humphrey Wildblood supplied large quantities of boarding. Lucrative employment was extended to neighbourhood painters, glaziers, bricklayers, tilers, carpenters, joiners, as well as labourers to carry the building materials and engage in unskilled work, such as the seven men who spent two days levelling the yard around the schoolhouse. One 'Goodman' Nicholas Elkyn was paid over £30 between September 1614 and September 1617 for a variety of handiwork: plastering, joinery, building the wall between the school and the vicarage garden, supplying coal for the cellar, and finishing the school gate on to the street.[25] For the next three and a half centuries the school helped sustain local Harrow tradesmen and artisans until, ironically, in the later twentieth century, driving them and the village of Harrow off the Hill altogether.

By 1615 the schoolhouse was nearing completion and ready to receive the first pupils of the Free Grammar School. Mr Bradley, who appears to have been the schoolmaster of the school for thirty poor pupils subsidized by Lyon, was paid off.[26] On 29 April 1615 the first Master of the Free Grammar School of John Lyon

---

[22] In the current John Lyon Trust, which since 1991 has been providing grants for charitable purposes and to projects in the boroughs through which the Harrow Road passes and which, in 1997, funded a scholar at Harrow School.

[23] See above, n. 14.

[24] For Barnet see W. H. Gelder, *Historic Barnet*, Barnet Historical Society (Barnet, n.d.), p. 41; Hewlett, 'Harrow School Buildings', in Howson and Townsend Warner, *Harrow School*, 30–1.

[25] For the foregoing details see HSR V, fos. 3–19.   [26] HSR V, fos. 12, 17.

was elected. William Launce, MA of Trinity College, Cambridge, a Suffolk man, was 27; the post at Harrow merely the start of a clerical career that embraced two London livings and, between 1625 and 1645, that of Harrow itself, a lucrative position in the gift of Lord North, one of the governors of the Free School who had appointed him to the Mastership in 1615.[27] Launce stayed as Master at Harrow from 1615 to 1621. On 25 September 1615 he was joined by his younger brother, Thomas Launce, BA, who was elected Usher, thus beginning the tradition of Harrow School as a family concern, a feature that persisted strongly into the nineteenth century.[28] Even after the entrepreneurial days of schoolteaching were ended by Victorian reform, dynastic links between teachers at Harrow remained a feature of the place.

The appointment of Launce as the first Master under the terms of Lyon's Statutes marks the beginning of the continuous history of the Lyon foundation. He was paid the first half-yearly instalment of his wages on 1 May 1615.[29] His arrival also signals the separation of functions between governors and Master. From 1615 there are two histories of Lyon's foundation, one that of the Lyon trusts, in the keeping of the governors, the other of Harrow School. Yet the two are closely related, not least because the governors' records, which contain much information obliquely or directly bearing on the nature and running of the school are more or less complete, while those of the school as an academic institution, of the masters who taught there and of the pupils who attended are fragmentary, occasional, partial, or absent. They are related, too, because, to an extent often ignored or unseen, the policy, decisions, even personalities of governors periodically exerted a profound influence on the direction of the school, not least in their appointment of and relations with successive Head Masters and their authority over the trusts. Indeed, the power of the governors to influence school life and policy immeasurably increased after the Public School Act of 1868 reordered the constitution of the foundation, stripping the Head Masters, and by extension the Assistant Masters, of their financial independence. Between 1615 and 1874, however, the original Lyon Statutes allowed the Master, armed with his 'foreigners' clause', to make as much money as he liked, in whatever manner he chose so long as it did not contravene the Statutes or the governors' interpretation of them. Thus Montagu Butler in 1868 was paid the same salary as William Launce in 1615, £26 6s. 8d.; yet Butler actually earned from his post as Head Master in the region of £12,000, none of it accountable to the governors.[30]

With the first Master appointed, the remaining elements of the Lyon bequest were brought to fruition. On 7 August 1615 the governors agreed to appoint Launce and

---

[27] HSR I (Governors' Order Book), fo. 20ʳ; for biographical details see Gun, *Harrow School Register*, 152. [28] HSR I fo. 20ʳ.
[29] HSR V, fo. 17.   [30] See below Chs. 12 and 13.

The Foundation

the Vicar, Humphrey Wildblood, as the preachers of the endowed sermons of which there were to be two on the first Sunday of every month, morning and evening, with additional sermons on 5 November, Ash Wednesday, Good Friday, and Coronation Day, a mixture of piety and loyalty that has clung to the school ever since.[31] Although nowhere stated, the remaining two sermons of the thirty specified in Lyon's Statutes were presumably preached at Christmas and Easter. It was typical of the essentially respectable nature of the foundation that, although these sermons bear all the marks of puritan lectureships often frowned upon by episcopal authorities, the preachers were licensed clergy who, as Vicar and Schoolmaster, were sustaining rather than challenging the local establishment and hierarchy. Wildblood and Launce were to receive ten pounds a year each for their services, which began in September.

By then, there was a school to attend these sermons. On the same day as the arrangements for the preaching were agreed, 7 August 1615, the maximum number of free scholars was fixed at forty and the first one, Macharie Wildblood, son of the Vicar, cosily admitted.[32] The mystery surrounding this entry in the Governors' Minutes, that it appears to be crossed out, may be explained by a probable subsequent decision that the Master would keep records of entries, the governors only recording the Lyon Exhibitioners to the universities. Such, at least, would explain the absence of any other names of entrants in gubernatorial records, as well as suggesting the undoubted later practice of Masters recording new boys' names.

That Macharie Wildblood was soon not alone is suggested by the provision in the following weeks and months of a small library by the governors and their payment for seats; for fuel for the teachers 'and their scholars'; and, most evocative of all perhaps, of three shillings 'to a poor woman for making clean the Schoole when the Scholars came first'.[33] The Free Grammar School of John Lyon, 101 years after its founder's birth, and twenty-three since his death, now existed.

[31] HSR II (Governors' Minutes), fo. 5. [32] Ibid.
[33] HSR II, fo. 3; HSR V, fos. 17–18.

Part II

From Grammar School to Public School, 1615–1746

4

THE ORIGINS OF A NATIONAL INSTITUTION

The first decades of the new Free Grammar School have traditionally been dismissed as Harrow's 'Dark Ages', the history of its Head Masters 'scrappy and uninteresting'. It has been argued that only with the arrival of William Horne from Eton in 1669 can there be discerned 'light in the darkness'. It has been customary to attribute Harrow's ascent towards its later prominence to Thomas Bryan (1691–1730) or even Thomas Thackeray (1746–60), described by one of his most noted nineteenth-century successors as the 'second founder of Harrow School'.[1]

Yet already in 1690 the then Head Master, William Bolton, described Harrow in print as a 'Public School'.[2] Two decades earlier, and possibly as early as the 1650s, the Head Master admitted boarders in his house. By the 1680s there existed a network of other landlords and landladies who offered accommodation to paying 'foreigners', for whom regular tuition and entry fees had been established. The numbers of fee-payers rose to about eighty in the 1680s. Of the identifiable Harrovians of the seventeenth century, over a third, possibly over 40 per cent, were foreigners, the earliest recorded being Hammond Claxton in 1630.[3] Although Horne seems to have brought with him from Eton not only teaching methods but some aristocratic connections, notably Francis and Charles Seymour, respectively the fifth and sixth dukes of Somerset, there must have been a strong fee-paying tradition to attract him to leave the under-mastership at Eton.[4] Even before his arrival,

---

[1] Thornton, *Harrow School*, ch. 4, pp. 65 *et seq.*, ch. 5, pp. 91 *et seq.*, p. 126 (the Head Master was H. M. Butler); B. P. Lascelles, 'Early Headmasters', in Howson and Townsend Warner, *Harrow School*, 54.

[2] W. Bolton, *A Poem upon a Laurel Leaf* (published by W. Crooke 'at the Green Dragon' without Temple Bar, 1690), frontispiece: 'A viris admodum Colendis Publicae Scholae, vulgo dictae Harrow super Montem Gubernatoribus'.

[3] Gun, 6. Claxton was probably a relative, although not the son of Edward Claxton, governor 1638–54. His father lived in Suffolk. Gun, *Harrow School Register*, 12 argues for William Greenhill, at Harrow *c.*1646, as the first recorded foreigner.   [4] Gun, 24.

money had been lavished on refurbishing the schoolroom with panelling and the construction of a gallery in the parish church to accommodate the schoolboys.[5]

The tone of the school became less parochial. Public corporate traditions were invented, such as, in imitation of other schools (e.g. St Paul's, Tonbridge), the annual Oration delivered by a pupil at the governors' audit meeting and the archery competition, both of which appear to have begun in the 1670s, the latter being endowed with a silver arrow as a prize in the following decade.[6] Rarely, and after the 1660s never, in this period, did the Head Masters preach any of the Lyon sermons. Harrow's development was reflected in the contrast between the laboured classical humour of surviving Latin speeches declaimed in the 1650s with the knowingly arch English heroic couplets composed by boys for their production of Nathaniel Lee's *Sophonisba*, given public performance at Harrow in 1698. The *dramatis personae* of this occasion illustrates clearly what the school had become. Mixing locals, sons both of the prosperous and the artisan, and foreigners, the cast ranged from the child of a Harrow ironmonger to one of a wealthy Hertfordshire landowner and London businessman, and included a Yorkshireman, later the first Harrovian known to have received a commission in the army. Near contemporaries of these actors were the first Harrovians—all 'foreigners'—to be elected as Members of Parliament.[7]

This apparent bifurcated nature of the later seventeenth-century school was unusual in one neither collegiate nor urban. Although other grammar schools had statutory provision for fee-payers and foreigners, Harrow's exploitation of such pupils was on an altogether more considerable scale. So, far from being solely or even mainly a local school, within a generation of opening its doors, Lyon's foundation instituted separate provisions for teaching locals to read (by 1651) and by establishing funds to bind parish boys as apprentices (from 1648) funded a route to advancement distinct from the grammar school, there being no clear evidence that all those taught to read went on to the school or that any of the apprentices had been previously educated there.[8] This policy of segregation within the educational charity may have begun accidentally. However, it certainly became a conscious policy of the governors during the mastership of the first great Head Master of Harrow School, William Hide (1628–61). It is with the governors, too, that responsibility for Harrow's wider distinctiveness probably rests.

After the so-called 'educational revolution' in late Tudor England, the seventeenth century created a hierarchy of education, at the bottom end of which

---

[5] HSR V, Governors' Accounts, fos. 130, 150, 152.

[6] Ibid., fos. 198 (1674/5); 225 (1678/9).

[7] Bodleian MS Rawlinson D 1138, fos. 25^r–38^v; Nathaniel Lee, *Sophonisba or Hannibal's Overthrow: A Tragedy* (London, 1697), copy in the Harrow School Archives; MS leaves bound into the beginning and at p. iv. Cf. cross-references between the list of actors (p. iv) and Gun.

[8] HSR V, Governors' Accounts, fo. 101; J. S. Golland, *The Harrow Apprentices* (London Borough of Harrow, 1981), p. 1; HSR IX (Governors' Apprentices' Book), fo. 1; HSR III, Governors' Minutes, fo. 2; Laborde, *Harrow School*, 32; below, n. 45.

literacy became a touchstone of social status as much as economic mobility. The growth of 'Dames' schools', reflected in Harrow's own provisions, prompted one observer in 1701 to comment that 'there are now not many but can write and read unless it have been their own or their parents' fault'.[9] This was almost certainly over-optimistic. Literacy remained patchy, but widespread, especially in parishes such as Harrow, populous, prosperous, with close links to the metropolis, opportunities for economic self-advancement and local access to basic educational instruction. If education at the base of society emphasized social stratification, so, increasingly, it did higher up. Education, particularly the grammar school curriculum of the classics that Lyon had so carefully prescribed for his school, created a cultural cohesion amongst those who experienced it. While in the late sixteenth century such cohesion may have been anticipated as encouraging a godly professional class, by the late seventeenth century the exclusivity and increasing vocational irrelevance of the classical training began to lend it a social cachet. Although this process reached its fullest flowering a century later, to Harrow's inestimable benefit, its progess was noted by John Locke, whose *Thoughts Concerning Education* (1693) admitted the benefits of a boarding school as making pupils 'bolder and better able to bustle and shift among boys of [their] own age', the 'emulation of school fellows' putting 'life and industry into young lads'. Locke recognized that parents sending their sons away to school 'have a strange value for words when, preferring the languages of the ancient Greeks and Romans' to English, they 'think it worth while to hazard [their] sons' innocence and virtue for a little Greek and Latin'.[10]

While recognizing the demand for the socially as well as educationally exclusive classical curriculum, Locke's complaint was with the standard of pedagogy. His ideal was for a Master 'to look after the manners of his scholars and ... care of forming their minds to virtue, and their carriage to good breeding, as of forming their tongues to the learned languages.' The problem in the later seventeenth century was that a decline in the popularity of the universities produced a shortage of quality schoolteachers, a difficulty possibly exacerbated in some schools by the political and personal disturbances of 1640–62 and the financial pressure placed on the supporting trusts by uniquely high levels of taxation in the 1640s and 1650s, and again in the 1670s and 1690s, all of which were reflected in the Harrow estate accounts.[11]

---

[9] Quoted by J. W. Adamson, 'Education', in A. Ward and A. Waller (eds.), *Cambridge History of Literature*, ix (Cambridge, 1912), p. 405; in general see K. Wrightson, *English Society, 1580–1680* (London, 1982), pp. 185–91.

[10] Quoted and discussed by J. B. Mullinger, 'English Grammar Schools', Ward and Waller, *Cambridge History of English Literature*, vii (Cambridge, 1911), p. 341.

[11] C. G. A. Clay, *Economic Expansion and Social Change in England, 1500–1700*, i (Cambridge, 1984), p. 186 and n. 6; HSR V, Governors' Accounts, *passim*.

Here, Harrow's experience was decisive in establishing a base from which to become a national instead of just a local school. Its governors, although, with the exception of Dudley, third baron North, not of the highest social rung, were prosperous and well-connected, including baronets, knights, MPs, wealthy merchants, and London Aldermen. Most notable was Sir Gilbert Gerrard, a governor for over sixty years (1609–70), owner of Flambards, baronet, and great-nephew of the founder's patron, who had purchased a baronetcy from James I, was a prominent supporter of Parliament in the 1640s, and continued to direct the Lyon trusts' affairs until a few months before his death. The governors' decisions on the direction of the school proved crucial. Although, on the face of it, severely constrained by Lyon's financial settlement, repeatedly challenged but confirmed (e.g. in 1651 and 1655), the governors possessed almost total discretion as regards interpretation of the statutes other than the provisions concerning the road money. Thus, to attract good Masters, they were able to permit them to live off the school premises (1650) and to marry (1669).[12] To keep Ushers, from the 1660s they repeatedly enhanced statutory payments to meet the new demands of the large numbers of 'foreigners'. The encouragement of 'foreigners' was central to Harrow's prospects in another associated way. Because fee-payers could—and did—earn the Master hundreds of pounds a year on top of his stipend, the governors could hope to appoint men of some distinction. The only statutory qualification for the Master was (and is) that he be an MA. Yet, at a time when the supply of well-qualified schoolmasters was in decline, the Harrow governors appointed proven professional teachers: Horne from Eton (1669), Bolton from Charterhouse (1685), Bryan from King's College School, Cambridge (1691), Cox from Harrow (1730: he had been the Usher), and Thackeray (1746: formerly of Eton). This looks like a consistent gubernatorial policy, unusual in other, local grammar schools, even where, as at Harrow, there was an exercised statutory link with Oxford and Cambridge through scholars or exhibitioners paid by the foundation.

Apart from the social contacts of the governors and the financial inducements and the flexible and attractive conditions of service for the teachers, the success of the school depended, to some degree at least, on those general qualities indicated by Locke. Harrow became a great school because, in the lights of its kind and its time, it had already become a good school. Thus it was able to ride the tide that was flowing in favour of socially as well as professionally elite classical education and the consequent growing popularity of fee-paying boarding. The cause of this success, one both academic and commercial, is to be found in the years before, not after, the Restoration.

---

[12] HSR III, Governors' Minutes, fo. 2; HSR I, Governors' Order Book, fos. 9ʳ–9ᵛ.

The Early Masters

The position of a seventeeth-century schoolmaster was usually lowly, far removed from the hierophants of the nineteenth century. Those who aspired to teach the classics did so, alleged Archdeacon Thomas Plume c.1675, 'out of necessity and only as a step to other preferment'.[13] This certainly fitted the first teachers at Harrow. William Launce, a native of Halesworth in Suffolk and an MA of Trinity College, Cambridge, was twenty-seven on his election in April 1615. He stayed for six years, assisted by his brother Thomas, appointed Usher in September 1615, before becoming rector of St Michael le Quesne, London. Launce probably owed his appointment to the patronage of Dudley, Lord North, a governor since 1613 and lord of the manor of Harrow. In 1625 Launce returned to Harrow as vicar, by which time Launce was described as North's domestic chaplain. It is possible that it was as such that he had received the Harrow mastership in the first place. Pluralism was not unknown to Lyonian Harrow's first Head Master, who combined his London rectorship with the Harrow living after 1625.[14] That North, whose lasting claim to fame was his discovery of the beneficial waters of Tunbridge Wells, was primarily responsible for Launce's preferment rather than the Gerrard cousins, Thomas and Gilbert, is suggested not only by Launce's employment but by his supposed churchmanship. Vicar of Harrow for twenty years, he was apparently excluded in 1645 'by reason of the contagious breath of the sectaries' at a time when the royalist influence on the Hill had collapsed with the flight to Oxford of, among others, Richard Page of Uxenden, the namesake and son of another governor, leaving Gilbert Gerrard of Flambards, a prominent parliamentarian, the dominant political figure in the locality.[15] North, although no religious partisan and by 1645 a moderate parliamentarian himself, lived far removed from Harrow, too far to protect his former protégé.

This image of Launce as a victimized champion of the Anglican Church may be less than the whole story, as he became rector of St Edmund the King, Lombard Street in 1648 and remained there until 1666. None the less, it is clear that the Mastership of Harrow was merely a stepping stone. He leaves almost no trace in the school records. The main achievement during his time was the building of an elaborate brick and timber 'house of office', later known officially as the 'boghouse', in 1619–20 at a cost of £10 12s. 10d., just under 8 per cent of that year's receipts.[16]

---

[13] Mullinger, 'Grammar Schools', 342; Plume was also a Fellow of Christ's College, Cambridge.
[14] For Launce's biography see Gun, *Harrow School Register*, 152; HSR I, Governors' Order Book, fo. 20ʳ; HSR V, Governors' Account Book, fos. 17, 36; Done Bushell, *Octocentenary Tracts*, ix, 20 and n. 1; for North see his *DNB* entry.
[15] Druett, *Harrow through the Ages*, 137, 139; Done Bushell, *Octocentenary Tracts*, ix, 20, n. 1.
[16] HSR V, Governors' Accounts, fo. 32; HSR VII, fo. 18 for 'boghouse' (Account 1714/15).

Thomas Launce lasted as Usher until 1636, supplementing his meagre income by assisting in the school sermons and, in all likelihood, acting as a sort of unofficial curate. After his departure, however, in 1637/8, Thomas was paid by the governors the not inconsiderable lump sum of £45, 20 per cent of that year's expenditure and the equivalent of over three years' Usher's wages.[17] The money was not arrears, as he had received his salary in full and on time. Possibly the money represented payment for effects he left behind in the narrow Usher's lodging above the schoolroom for the use of his successor. This was William Ponder, BA whose obscurity was so profound that he has entirely escaped the notice of all the school's previous historians, even though he held the post of Usher from May 1636 to September 1638.[18]

The Launce—and hence North—connection was further sustained by the appointment as Master in May 1621 of Robert Whittle, another East Anglian and Cambridge MA. Only twenty-three and ordained in the year of his appointment, Whittle combined his post at Harrow with acting as William Launce's curate at St Michael le Quesne. In 1627, some months before his effective resignation from Harrow, he became vicar of East Malling, Kent, where he remained for half a century, dying aged eighty-one in 1679.[19] For him, at least, the position of Harrow School was less than dominant. He evidently owed his preferment, modest though it may seem, to his wits, first as a sizar (i.e. poor scholar) at Magdalene, Cambridge then as a scholar of Emmanuel. Harrow was as good a first post as any, with the contacts with the governors possibly better than some. What is clear is that the position was not seen as one for the established scholar nor still for the loyal local teacher. Like many other similar establishments, the mastership, and hence direction of the schooling at Harrow was an adjunct to the wider patronage of individual governors and a vehicle for rapid promotion for the incumbents.

What is less clear is what these teachers actually did. Whittle supplemented the governors' initial provision of a library with books worth £1 10s. 4d. in 1623/4, the first evidence of academic attention by a Master.[20] Both Master and Usher still lived on site. The curriculum they followed and the discipline they administered may, or may not, have followed the Founder's instructions. More suggestive is that at least three of Whittle's pupils proceeded to Cambridge. Josias Barnard, son of James Barnard, a 'husbandman' of Harrow, after perhaps four years at the school went as a sizar to Caius in 1625, dying there in November 1628.[21] John Westbee, who went to Caius after two years at Harrow in 1627, may have been a foreigner,

---

[17] HSR I, Governors' Order Book, fos. 20ʳ, 21ʳ; HSR V, Governors' Accounts, fo. 74; Gun, *Harrow School Register*, 156; Done Bushell, *Octocentenary Tracts*, ix, 20, n. 1.

[18] HSR I, Governors' Order Book, fo. 21ʳ; HSR V, Governors' Accounts, fos. 74, 78; MS Act Book of the Court of Arches, A. 83 and A. 95, cited in a letter from H. E. Hyde to B. P. Lascelles, the school librarian, 19 May 1904, preserved in the School Archives.

[19] Gun, *Harrow School Register*, 152.   [20] HSR V, Governors' Accounts, fo. 43.

[21] Gun, *Harrow School Register*, 2.

having been born in London. His family seems to have been able to afford to support his education at Cambridge, possibly at Harrow too.[22] George Ashwell presents an altogether more substantial figure. Son of Robert Ashwell of Roxeth, he received the first Founder's Exhibition to Oxford in September 1627, aged fifteen. An undergraduate at Wadham, he became a fellow in 1636, serving as librarian and, twice, sub-warden. He earned his keep as a private tutor and chaplain, as well as holding the rectorship of Hanwell, Oxfordshire, from 1649, but secured his reputation as a noted and prolific High Church polemicist in a career stretching to the 1690s. Unless his translation in 1686 of an Arabic fantasy, *The History of Hai Elon Yochdan, an Indian Prince, or a Self-Taught Philosopher* conceals some hidden autobiographical reference or joke, it may be fair to assume that Ashwell received his basic linguistic grounding at the feet of Whittle in the schoolroom at Harrow, the first ripe fruit of Lyon's benefaction, even if his ideas would have been little to the Founder's taste.[23]

THE MASTERSHIP OF WILLIAM HIDE

Whatever the achievements of pupils or teachers in its first years, the establishment of Harrow School on firm and lasting foundations was the work of William Hide, Master from April 1628 until April 1661.[24] Whatever the character of the school in 1628, by 1661 the school was regularly attracting significant numbers of 'foreigners'; additional staff, in the form of a Writing Master, had been engaged; a system of teaching local children to read had been instituted; the library had been considerably extended; the Master was occupying a separate house away from the school; school hours were more strictly observed; links with Oxford and Cambridge had been strengthened by regular elections of Harrovians to the Founder's Exhibitions; and old boys were taking their places in the wider world as clergymen and lawyers.

Yet of Hide himself almost nothing is known. There are two William Hides who were Cambridge MAs of the right age, one of Jesus College (MA 1620, ordained 1625 aged twenty-five), the other St John's (MA 1627, ordained 1624).[25] It is not clear even whether Hide of Harrow was ordained or not. Twice he was described by the governors as being a 'Gentleman', on the lease for his house in 1651 and in the Accounts for 1655.[26] He certainly did not preach any of the Lyon sermons, that task devolving to the Vicar.[27] Thornton speculated that he may have been a distant

---

[22] Ibid., 29.
[23] HSR III, Governors' Minutes, fo. 4. For biographical details see Ashwell's *DNB* entry.
[24] HSR I, Governors' Order Book, fo. 20ʳ; HSR III, fos. 11, 14; HSR V, Governors' Accounts, fos. 51, 128.
[25] Gun, *Harrow School Register*, 153.   [26] HSR 211; HSR V, fo. 111.
[27] HSR V, Governors' Accounts, fo. 51. Cf. fo. 45, where Whittle is paid for sharing the preaching with the vicar and curate, 1624/6.

relative of the Founder; more likely he was a client of a governor.[28] His status as Master was recognized by his appointment as local Headborough (an officer or constable chosen at the Quarter Sessions) in 1652.[29] Of his personality, something may be deduced from his stubborn refusal to vacate the house he leased from the governors until evicted in March or April 1686, when he must have been over eighty years old.[30] Of his views, it may be significant that one of the many books he purchased for the school (in 1657) was by Calvin; that he retained his post throughout the Civil War and Interregnum, secure in the support of the parliamentarian Gilbert Gerrard; and that he was, it seems, asked to resign almost immediately after the Restoration in 1660.[31]

Some previous historians of the school have tried to gloss away Harrow's involvement with the anti-royalist party during the Civil War. Yet the two most prominent governors, North and Gilbert Gerrard, supported parliament. Gerrard, apparently disaffected for some time before 1640, was a prominent recruiter of forces against the king in 1642–3. Occupying the most prominent social position on the Hill, it is inconceivable that he did not acquiesce in the removal of Launce as Vicar in 1645. Furthermore, Launce's supplanter, Thomas Pakeman, was said to have been high in Gerrard's esteem. He certainly was appointed to deliver the Lyon sermons and may even have lodged some foreigners. His son attended the school. Pakeman was ejected under the 1662 Act of Uniformity.[32] Elsewhere, the governors paid taxes 'to the parliament' from the start of the Civil War in 1642–3.[33] The school itself under Hide seems to have retained its original Calvinist atmosphere; an inventory of school books in 1667 revealed the presence in the library of twelve volumes of Calvin.[34]

In these circumstances, it is in every way unlikely that Charles I, on his way from Oxford to St Alban's, passed through Harrow on the afternoon of 27 April 1646, still less that he lingered to water his horses, admire the view, and ponder his next move. The idea that the king, with only a few companions, would have taken the risk of literally riding past the door of one of his most tenacious foes (at Flambards) and then paused in the shadow of a church whose incumbent was a placeman of his opponents condemns the monarch as a bigger fool than even his worst enemies could have imagined. Of all the places between the Thames Valley and Hertfordshire, even in parliamentarian Middlesex, Harrow was one of the most conspicuous in its support for the king's adversaries, as Charles would have known as with him in Oxford were two prominent local royalists who had fled the county,

---

[28] Thornton, *Harrow School*, 86.   [29] Bodleian MS Rawlinson D 1138.
[30] HSR III, Governors' Minutes, fo. 53. Cf. fo. 55.
[31] British Library, Add. MS 29,254, fo. 34'; HSR III, Governors' Minutes, fo. 11.
[32] Done Bushell, *Octocentenary Tracts*, ix, 20–1 and n. 2; HSR III, Governors Minutes, fo. 17 (16 Apr. 1663); Gun (*Harrow School Register*, 20) makes a muddle of this; Druett, *Harrow through the Ages*, 137–8.
[33] HSR V, Governors' Accounts, fo. 86.   [34] Thornton, *Harrow School*, 87–8.

Francis Rewse of Headstone and Richard Page of Uxendon. The evidence for Charles's passage across the Hill comes from the testimony of one of his chaplains who had travelled with him, but his various statements under hostile examination are contradictory, possibly designed to shield those who had aided the king's progress. It may even have been a deliberate bluff to suggest that Charles had visited the very threshold of the home of a leading parliamentarian, an image that could have caused some embarrassment to his enemies. If Charles came anywhere near Harrow in 27 April 1646, which is by no means certain nor, from his itinerary, necessary; he probably skirted the foot of the Hill in some haste. The Charles I story and the commemorative plaque erected in 1925 probably owe more to certain Harrovians' envy and frustration at the royal connections of Eton than to recoverable historical fact.[35]

Away from the sentimental romanticism of snobbish royalists, it is evident that Harrow prospered as the Stuarts declined. Although rents failed to cover expenses throughout the 1630s and early 1640s, forcing the governors to borrow money to balance their current account, from 1647 substantial surpluses were regularly recorded.[36] In 1651 the governors saw off an attempt by local residents to extract more money from the Lyon trusts for the upkeep of the roads. They successfully asserted that the Commissioners established by the 1601 Act to prevent the misuse of charitable trusts, to whom the locals had appealed, had no jurisdiction over Harrow as the act exempted Free Schools run by governors.[37] A similar attack was launched in a parliamentary petition in 1655 by Leonard Stockdale of Kingsbury who complained that profits were misused or not used; that the governors were not making the most out of the estate; and that some governors were breaking the statutes as they were non-resident.[38] This assault in turn foundered on a repetition of the 1611 Chancery judgment. Another scrutiny of the governors' management may have been the cause of a review of all the estate leases in 1659.[39] In fact, although Stockdale's accusation of under-realization of assets was probably fair, and, indeed, recognized by the governors themselves, his complaint about misuse of funds was unjust. Ever since 1611 the governors had been scrupulous, if not always efficient, in applying all the profits from the two Marylebone estates to the roads, a sum which in 1655/6 came to a modest £40.[40] Only later in the century did the accounts benefit more obviously from the expansion of London and the consequent rise in property values and rents in the suburbs around Paddington.

That Hide was an energetic Master cannot be doubted. Apart from his teaching duties, he oversaw repairs to the fabric of the school; he supplied and maintained

---

[35] Ibid., 84–5 and n.; Druett, *Harrow through the Ages*, 136–40.
[36] For loans see HSR V, Governors' Accounts, fos. 58, 63, 78; for surplus/deficit see HSR V *passim*.
[37] HSR 209. Cf., for 1601 Act, *Statutes of the Realm*, 43 Eliz. I *c*.4, clause 39.
[38] British Library MS Harleian 2211, fo. 4ʳ–5ʳ; Add. MS 29,254, fos. 43ᵛ–44ʳ.
[39] HSR X, fos. 3ʳ–4ᵛ.   [40] HSR V, Governors' Accounts, fo. 113.

new clocks; he witnessed various documents for the governors.[41] However, his most distinctive contribution was in the academic and administrative management of the school. During his term of office, he spent at least £15 on books, probably reference works, including a repacement or duplicate of one of the dictionaries originally provided by the governors. Such purchases imply a thriving, growing school.[42] In 1650 he instituted two innovations in the educational system at Harrow. First he secured an annual stipend of £6 13s. 4d. for the teaching 'the free scholars' to write, a task devolved on a 'writing master', although after 1665 the job was done by the Usher.[43] It is clear that this service was provided for pupils already at school on the foundation. In the same year, however, Hide organized the teaching of poor children to read English in Harrow and the surrounding villages of Preston, Roxeth, Sudbury, Kenton, Wembley, and Weald. This was regularized by the governors as Hide was leaving in 1660. The 'Dames', so-called, usually women but occasionally men, were appointed by the governors, who also were to nominate their pupils.[44] There is later evidence that beneficiaries of this education were destined for the Grammar School. The general thrust of the system, which persisted, with only a short break 1709–18 after the governors had almost bankrupted the estate, was to segregate the Grammar School from the poorest local children whose ambitions did not stretch to a classical education yet, but who in Hide's and the governors' judgement, deserved part of Lyon's charity.[45] Thus the exclusivity of the grammar school education was preserved without undermining the charitable imperatives of the Lyon trust.

That the education Hide provided was increasingly exclusive can be variously illustrated. In the Governors' Accounts for 1632/3 mention is made for the first time to 'Free Scholars', as opposed simply to 'scholars' as before. The description was repeated with reference to a writing master in 1651/2.[46] There must be at least a presumption that this formula indicates the customary presence of fee-paying scholars. Of the thirteen identifiable Harrovians taught by Hide, possibly as many as five were foreigners; at least two became barristers; others received ecclesiastical

[41] HSR V, Governors' Accounts, fos. 52, 86, 101, 109, 116, 119; HSR 202, 204, 217.

[42] Ibid., fos. 63, 72, 89, 111, 116.

[43] Ibid., fos. 103, 105, 107, 109, 111, 114, 119, 122, 141 (after 1658 there may have been problems in finding a teacher as recorded payments ceased until the Usher was paid in 1665); HSR III, Governors' Minutes, fo. 22. The Governors seem to have paid the stationery expenses of the poor children learning to write (HSR V, loc. cit.).

[44] HSR V, Governors' Accounts, fos. 103, 105, 107, 109, 111, 114, 116, 119, 122, 125, 128 (where the names of the teachers are listed for the first time), 130, etc.; HSR III, Governors' Minutes, fo. 11; for men as teachers see HSR III. fo. 25 (Nathaniel Newman); HSR V, fos. 128 ('Mr Brisco'), 145, 152, 168, 204, 210, 290 (Nathaniel Newman, who (fo. 210) also taught writing), 309 (John Canon).

[45] HSR III, Governors' Minutes, fo. 97, 17 June 1709, where the Dames' duties were described as being 'to instruct poor children in reading so as to fit them for the free school'. Cf. fo. 112, 7 Nov. 1718 for the restoration of the system.

[46] HSR V, Governors' Accounts, fos. 60, 105.

livings in Buckinghamshire, Sussex, Lincolnshire, and Cornwall; and one, William Fenn (at Harrow 1637–46), went on to become the first OH governor.[47]

By the time Hide resigned, the importance of the fee-payers could not be underestimated. In 1662 the Usher was allowed to receive two-thirds 'of the profit' on those 'foreigners' he taught, namely in the First and Second Forms (out of five), that is: the Lower School. In 1665 the Usher was allocated ten shillings per 'foreigner' whether or not he was in the Lower School.[48] It is probably in this context that Hide's leasing of a house should be seen. In June 1650 the governors agreed to lease to Hide a tenement for an annual rent of £8. The lease was signed in August 1651, Hide paying £20 for it. This house, on the site of the present Head Master's, was Hide's home for the next thirty-five years.[49] Apart from comfort, the cause of the Master's migration from the accommodation provided in the schoolhouse may well have been to house boarders. Certainly by 1671, the then Master required somewhere to house 'his boarders'; it is likely the habit began with Hide.[50]

It is also worth noticing that Hide was able to afford both the entry fine and the rent, even though he was on an official stipend of only £26 13s. 4d. He may have been a gentleman of means: he was certainly able to keep up his payment of rent until his eviction in 1686. Alternatively, and more likely, he made money out of his pupils. By the 1680s tuition fees and board and lodging at the Head Master's house cost £22 a year.[51] The arrangements for paying the Usher in 1662 and 1665 suggest substantial profits available. The precise figures are unobtainable. However, it appears that boarding cost £14 in the 1680s, with schooling an extra sum of anything up to eight pounds. Certainly, from tuition alone, Hide could expect to make several pounds a year per foreigner, with more from those who may have boarded with him. The scale of fees may have been steep. In the 1650s the writing master's salary of £13 6s. 8d., the same as the Usher's, if calculated on a basis of the full forty free scholars, works out at 6s. 8d., half a mark, a head, a sum that foreigners presumably had to find themselves if they required or were provided with the service.[52] One of the most central reasons why Harrow flourished was that successive Head Masters, with the encouragement of the governors, treated the school as a business from which they obtained substantial profits. It was as a commercial enterprise that Harrow became a national institution, a 'public school'.

One oddity in this was the role of Gilbert Bamford. Unlike his successors, he did not take on the relatively lucrative job of writing master, even though his

---

[47] Gun, *Harrow School Register*, 6, 8, 9 (Fenn), 11, 12, 14, 17, 20, 23, 28.
[48] HSR III, Governors' Minutes, fos. 16, 21.
[49] HSR III, Governors' Minutes, fos. 2, 53; HSR 211.
[50] HSR III, Governors' Minutes, fo. 33.
[51] Details of fees in a letter from Mrs Anne Nicholas to her relative Edmund Verney of Claydon, July 1682: Townsend Warner, *Harrow in Prose and Verse, Harrow School*, 74; Laborde, 35 n. 1.
[52] HSR V, Governors' Accounts, fos. 107, 109, 111, 116, 119. When the Usher took over the task in 1665 the stipend was halved: HSR II, Governors' Minutes, fo. 22; HSR V, fo. 141.

university career as a Founder's Exhibitioner and sizar suggests no great private means: his father, Robert, was a local Harrow carpenter. Possibly a former pupil of Whittle and Hide, Bamford, a Cambridge MA, was appointed Usher in 1638 and, apart from drawing his salary and witnessing a lease in 1646, remained a shadowy presence until in October 1661 the governors lost patience with him: 'having been formerly admonished for neglecting his charge and having not hitherto amended, it is ordered that Mr Banfield [the spelling of the name being as elusively malleable as its owner] leave his said charge by the 20 March ensuing.' As this was the first meeting of the governors with Hide's successor, Thomas Jonson, it is likely that the Usher was victim of his colleague and protector's absence and of the new regime. Yet he was unmoved as, on 17 December 1661, he was summarily dismissed with immediate effect 'from this day . . . in regard his non-attendance'. Whether neglect of duty, incompatibility with the new Master, lack of sympathy with the changed circumstances of the Restoration, or sheer laziness lay behind Bamford's departure, his career speaks of the earliest days of Harrow: obscure and parochial.[53]

However, Hide, at least, seems to have been eager to foster scholarship as then understood. There survive hitherto unremarked transcripts of Latin speeches and declamations delivered by boys at the school in the 1650s. Of those that are dated, one set were delivered on 2 November 1654, another group just before the Christmas holiday in 1656. Although presented on festive occasions, together these speeches provide unique direct evidence of the classical curriculum and the use to which it was put.[54] Although probably deriving from the grammatical question and answer sessions prescribed in the Statutes, such declamations, alongside disputations, were a feature of seventeenth-century grammar schools, whether ordered by statutes or not.[55] There was a number of compendia and guides available, such as John Stockwood's *Disputiuncularum Grammaticalium libellus*, which ran to four editions between 1598 and 1634, providing pupils with an almost unimaginably dull list of possible questions for discourse or dispute, as did the Lincoln schoolmaster John Clarke's *Quaestiones aliquot declamatoriae* in his *Phraseologiae puerilis Anglo-latinae in usum tyrocini scholastici* (London, 1638).[56] Originally designed as an aid to learning and using grammar, there was often an element of display and occasion. At Tonbridge each year one afternoon in May was set aside for such public disputations. Orators were paid at St Paul's in the 1640s and

[53] HSR V, Governors' Accounts, fos. 35, 58, 72, 78, 111 (where Bamford is described as a 'gentleman'), 130; HSR I, Governors' Order Book, fo. 21ʳ; HSR III, Governors' Minutes, fo. 5 (where he is called 'Cranfield') fos. 6 and 16 ('Bamfield'), fol. 14 ('Banfield'), and fo. 15 ('Bamford'); Gun, *Harrow School Register*, 156; HSR 204. In 1662 Bamford was paid £10 as a gratuity, possibly compensation for his summary dismissal: HSR III, fo. 16.

[54] Bodleian MS Rawlinson D 1138, fos. 25ʳ–38ᵛ.

[55] Laborde, *Harrow School*, 238 for the statutory provision for the twice weekly oral grammar questioning for the top three forms; F. Watson, *The English Grammar Schools to 1660* (Cambridge, 1908), pp. 91–7, 465–7.

[56] Discussed by Watson, *Grammar Schools*, 96–7, 465–7.

Birmingham in the 1650s, where, as at Harrow, there were Christmas orations. At Harrow too, so the orator in 1656 asserted, payment was customary.[57]

These speeches, then, fit into the standard curriculum and pedagogic practices of the period. However, they should probably not be seen as the direct precursor of the annual audit oration first noted in 1674, known much later as the Contio Latina, except in so far as both display a tradition of Latin oratory at the school. The 1650s speeches are deliberately showy, often humorous, spiced with irony as well as erudition. The audience is described as hosts ('Benignissimi hospites'), possibly comprising the governors or the Master or, as at Tonbridge, members of the local community come to entertain the scholars of their local school. The chief orator was called the 'Janitor', apparently a post already traditional. This was probably the senior monitor who, from the 1660s and possibly from the beginning, sat at a special desk on the north side of the schoolroom door, literally the door-keeper. He was probably joined by a number of his peers.

In 1654, the speeches formed a disputation on the rival claims to precedence of doctors, orators, and philosophers. The Janitor's introduction is in light vein, but studded with classical allusions appropriate both to an exercise in Latin rhetoric and a speech delivered on a windswept Hill, thus there are explicit references to Aeolus, god of the winds, and Virgilian echoes ('magno cum murmure montis...'). The disputations themselves were more formal and unsurprisingly littered with famous classical models, including Ariadne, Hercules, Apollo, and Plato. The whole tone as well as content has a dessicated seriousness allied to a striving for wit and brilliance of form characteristic of much of the contemporary study of the classics where the intellectual satisfaction lay less in the arguments (here fairly banal: doctors struggle for health and life, orators existed amongst barbarians before philosophers, etc.) than in the words deployed on their behalf.[58]

The Christmas speeches of 1656 are more revealing and certainly more elaborately festive.[59] Some of the speeches praised company, wine, and Bacchus as well as the Muses, and were laced with quotations, for example from Horace. Others were more overtly academic. There was one on 'Metonymia', with allusions to Ovid and Virgil. The Janitor, who made a point of referring to the women in his audience, expanded on the themes of work and play, the 'bellum grammaticale', Harrow being likened to a small abode of the Muses, 'musarum domicilium'. More severely academic were a pair of speeches arguing the superior merits of Greek over Latin and vice versa. While one speaker pointed out that Latin's triumph was apparent in contemporary usage, the other cited the prolific but hardly popularly known Elizabethan Greek scholar and Regius Professor at Cambridge, Bartholomew Dodington (1536–85), in calling Greek the queen of oratory.[60] This

[57] Ibid., 93, 465; Bodleian MS Rawlinson D 1138, fo. 36ʳ.
[58] Bodleian MS Rawlinson D 1138, fos. 25ʳ–29ᵛ.
[59] Ibid., fos. 29ᵛ–38ᵛ.   [60] Ibid., fo. 31ʳ. For Dodington see *DNB* entry.

contest was implicitly continued in a supposed Dialogue between Quintilian, the first-century AD Latin teacher of rhetoric and a second century Greek successor, Hermogenes, which provided an excuse for literary pyrotechnics, including quotations from Homer in Greek.[61] In complete contrast were two bizarre speeches which conclude the transcripts: 'Quod tabaccum est planta nociva' and 'Declamatio quod tabaccum non est planta nociva', the former asserting that tobacco caused illness, the latter, producing Americans and, oddly, Arabs as witnesses, that it caused no harm.[62] If nothing else, such discourses on tobacco show how rapidly the smoking habit had caught hold of European tastes.

The chance survival of these speeches sheds light on the education provided by Hide and his colleagues. The Latin of the orations is classical, fluent, and rather dull. The allusions are sometimes subtly introduced, but as often dragged in pretentiously. Of the boys' command of the grammar and some rather arcane vocabulary, so fashionable in schools of the period, there is no doubt. The authors cited reflect the curriculum as laid down: Cicero, Ovid, Horace, Virgil, Homer. The senior boys evidently were competent in Greek. The knowledge of Dodington is impressive, but possibly the result of the edition of Demosthenes in use at Harrow being that which contained some prefatory Greek poems by the professor.[63] In general, beyond the demonstration of competence, there is a sense of vibrancy and enjoyment in these speeches, however formal, where the boys have concocted their own themes and felt free or were allowed to indulge in irreverence, if of a somewhat stilted kind. These speeches and the occasions at which they were delivered speak of a successful and confident school.

Hide clearly was good at his job. The changes of 1650 created a model that lasted unchanged in essentials for the next century. Yet it seems the governors felt the need to remove him. At their meeting on 5 October 1660 it was recorded that Hide 'hath declared himself willing to give over the imployment and that the Governors might proceed to the choice of another Schoolmaster . . . it is ordered that the said Mr Hide shall leave the school upon the first day of November next ensuing'.[64] This rather bleak sundering of an association of more than thirty years is unusual in form and content. Other Masters, according to the Governors' Minutes, either resigned, died, or were openly sacked. Hide seems to have been asked if he would step down and then given just a month's notice. In the event he stayed on until the following March or April before his successor was installed and remained an increasingly inconvenient tenant for another thirty-five years.[65] The motives of the

[61] Bodleian MS Rawlinson D 1138, fos. 32^v–35^r. For a Greek Homer quotation see fo. 32^v.

[62] Ibid., fos. 36^v–38^v.

[63] On which see the literary appendix to Dodington's *DNB* entry. For Demosthenes as a Harrow set text see Laborde, *Harrow School*, 29, 238 and HSR II, Governors' Minutes, fo. 3, for the copy bought by the governors in 1615. [64] HSR III, Governors' Minutes, fo. 11.

[65] Hide was paid half a year's salary on 25 Mar. 1661: HSR V, Governors' Accounts, fo. 128. He was still witnessing governors' leases on 20 Sept. 1661, in this case alongside his successor, Jonson: HSR 217. Evidently, as far as the governors were concerned, he was not in personal disgrace.

governors, chaired at the crucial meeting by Hide's patron Gilbert Gerrard, must remain obscure. However, the calibre of Hide's replacement, Thomas Jonson, not a Harrovian but one of the Founder's Exhibitioners at Cambridge, was hardly exceptional and does not suggest that he had been lined up for the succession in advance, especially as he was not appointed for some months after Hide's agreement to withdraw.[66] It may be that Hide was more identified with the Interregnum than can now be discovered and that he was viewed with disapproval by the new ecclesiastical masters, led by the freshly appointed bishop of London, Gilbert Sheldon. Alternatively, in order to retain the flow of 'foreigners' and the prestige of the school, the governors felt a change was essential. Although the commercial aspects of the school did not directly benefit the governors or the trust, it is not hard to imagine that the governors would prefer to preside over a thriving and significant establishment rather than an obscure and declining non-conformist seminary. The return of Charles II and the Anglican church may have made Hide suddenly seem old-fashioned. The sacrifice of Hide may also have balanced the continuing presence of the parliamentarian and probably presbyterian Gerrard and helped ward off too intrusive an interest by the Restoration regime which, as all its predecessors, took a keen interest in schooling. The governors could have been displaying the sort of political flexibility that was to stand the school in good stead for another two centuries before it became victim to its own class-sensitive success. On the other hand, Hide may have been removed because he was ageing.

At the same meeting as Hide's deposition was announced, as a sort of *quid pro quo* perhaps, his scheme of Dames' Schools was regularized under gubernatorial control and instructions.[67] If nothing else, he bequeathed that firm legacy to the parish. To the school he left the foundations of future development. What his socially more elevated and entrepreneurially more assured successors achieved during the following eighty years rested on his achievement.

---

[66] HSR III, Governors' Minutes, fo. 7 for Jonson's Exhibition to Cambridge, 29 Aug. 1652; fo. 14 for his election as Master, 10 Oct. 1661; Gun, 153.

[67] HSR III, Governors' Minutes, fo. 11.

5

THE RESTORATION SCHOOL, 1661–1691

Within thirty years of Hide's resignation, Harrow School had become a recognized competitor for the education of the gentry, a 'public school'.[1] A barometer of this progress was the extended argument between the Usher and the Head Master over the division of fees paid by 'foreigners'. In October 1662 the teaching of the first two forms of the five were assigned to the Usher, then a dim figure called 'Mr Blithe'. Pupils were only to be promoted to the higher forms and the supervision of the Master with gubernatorial consent. This division was financial as much as academic, it being agreed that the Usher was to have 'two parts of the profit and the Master one third part' for all 'foreigners' in these lower forms. Presumably the Master received all the fees from the 'foreigners' in the higher forms.[2] This arrangement proved transitory. In 1665 Blithe's successor, Thomas Robinson, BA, from All Souls College, Oxford, was awarded ten shillings a year for each 'foreigner' regardless of their place in the school, as well as £6 13s. 4d. ('twenty nobles') to teach the free scholars to write.[3] Although these provisions were made with the apparent endorsement of the Master, in June 1666 Robinson was complaining to the governors that the Master, Thomas Jonson, had refused to pay him the ten shillings per 'foreigner'. Jonson was ordered to explain himself at a special governors' meeting set for July 1666, for which, however, no record survives.[4] Matters were evidently settled amicably, as Robinson stayed as Usher until retiring in 1700. In the absence of further contention, it is likely that Jonson and his successors complied with the governors' order of 1665.

Whatever the resolution, it is unmistakable that 'foreigners' had become the central element in the school. In 1682 there were apparently about eighty of them,

---

[1] W. Bolton, *A Poem upon a Laurel Leaf* (London, 1690), title-page.
[2] HSR III, Governors' Minutes, fo. 16; HSR V, fo. 130 for Blithe the Usher.
[3] Ibid., fo. 21.   [4] Ibid., fo. 23; fo. 73 for Robinson's resignation in July 1700.

against the forty local free scholars.⁵ In 1690 the governors had to remind the Master and Usher of their obligation to teach 'for the founder's stipends' the full complement of free scholars even if it meant enrolling children not just of the poor but of 'the richer sort' from Harrow and Pinner.⁶ This anxiety about the numbers of local children ran concurrent with concern over the regulation of the entry of 'foreigners' into the eighteenth century.

There were other signs of the transformation of the school. It is improbable that Jonson moved back into the Head Master's old quarters above the schoolroom; certainly his successor, William Horne, lived in separate accommodation which he shared with fee-paying boarders.⁷ The schoolroom itself seems to have been re-panelled between 1661 and 1662. In 1663 the garret at the top of the schoolhouse was converted into two waterproof, boarded rooms. In 1669 the governors, flush with funds after a record surplus, spent £40 on new wainscoting for their meeting room.⁸ That numbers in the school were high and secure was confirmed by the building in 1667/8 of a gallery for the boys on the north side of the parish church, described over 150 years later as 'stifling and cavernous'. It was finally removed in 1887. At the same time, the special 'Master's pew' in church was renovated.⁹ By the 1670s the governors were employing a permanent custodian—one Adkins—to oversee the schoolhouse and perform a variety of menial functions, from ringing bells to cleaning the lavatories.¹⁰ In 1680 land was bought adjoining the school yard (or, in the pompous phrase of one of the deeds, 'next to the Atrium of the Free School') 'for the schollers' recreation'; the yard was then levelled in 1682.¹¹

By then, two lasting institutions had been established which helped define the corporate identity of the school. On 20 October 1674 John Dennis, a 'foreigner', delivered a Latin 'Oration' at the governors' annual audit meeting, a tradition that has continued, with some gaps and at least one foray into English, until the present. Unlike in later generations when the speech became the prerogative of the Head of School, the early Orators were probably those best able to deliver such an address. Dennis, for instance, proceeded to a Founder's Exhibition at Caius College Cambridge and a career as a minor poet, playwright, and literary critic. The institution of the Oration represents the deliberate addition of an annual ritual,

---

⁵ Anne Nicholas to Edmund Verney, 8 July 1682: Townsend Warner, *Harrow in Prose and Verse*, 74. ⁶ HSR III, Governors' Minutes, fo. 60.
⁷ Ibid., fo. 33.   ⁸ HSR V, fos. 130, 132, 136, 160; HSR III, Governors' Minutes, fo. 19.
⁹ HSR V, fos. 150, 152; Act Book of the Court of Arches, B. 13 b, quoted in letter from H. E. Hyde to B. P. Lascelles, 19 May 1904 for the faculty to build the gallery; Druett, *Harrow through the Ages*, 196; Laborde, *Harrow School*, 91 and n. 1 for the later comment.
¹⁰ HSR V, fo. 255 and *passim*. As so many occupations of the period, this may have been a family concern; in 1681 Goodwife Atkins was described as 'the keeper of the scoole': HSR III, fo. 47, while Sam Atkins was keeper in 1671 and the cleaner in 1685: HSR III, fo. 34; HSR V, fo. 255.
¹¹ HSR 250–2 for the deeds of the purchase; HSR V, fo. 230 for the price, £16, and fo. 231 for the new wall the expansion necessitated; fo. 242 for money spent 'for stuff and workmanship for levelling the schoolyard'.

symptom of a growing corporate self-consciousness and social posturing. This ritualistic element was emphasized in 1675, when the Orator, one Woodcock, was given the customary reward of ten shillings 'to buy him a pair of gloves'. The ceremonial presentation of gloves features in numerous arcane social ceremonies, such as the greeting of Assize judges on progress, and was associated with school orations elsewhere in the seventeenth century (e.g. St Paul's in the 1640s).[12]

One of the Founder's least significant provisions had been for archery. It was probably also one of the least effective until, in October 1678, the governors decided to reinstitute the practice, ordering that new butts be provided for the execution of the Founder's wishes at a site nearer and more convenient to the school than the old, now decayed site. The purpose was hardly utilitarian but wholly aristocratic, archery fitting well in the growing contemporary fashion for classical arcadian revival. The activity may have been popular, but the clearest evidence that survives suggests it was an elaborate but occasional game, a ritual display with overtones in terms of show more of the Eton Montem than any regular archery practice or contest. Within a few years of the restoration of the butts, a retired diplomat living in Harrow, Sir Gilbert Talbot, presented a Silver Arrow 'to be shot for by twelve young Gentlemen' annually. This competition became the social highlight of the school year, and was held without interruption from 1697 until abolished by Head Master Heath in 1772. It may be significant that none of those known to have shot for the Silver Arrow delivered the Oration and only one, the 1741 winner, received a Founder's Exhibition, suggesting that the skills involved in archery were not those of the schoolroom.[13]

The invention of public rituals and deliberately arcane customs suggests the social composition of the Restoration school. Non-academic social attainments were probably taken for granted, although how they were encouraged or catered for at Harrow in the seventeenth century is hidden. John Dennis, the son of a rich London saddler, was sent down from Caius for sword-fighting.[14] Domestic arrangements were expected to be comfortable for foreigners. In 1682 board and lodging cost one of them £14 a year (a sum thought by one observer in 1696 equivalent to the total annual income of a labourer or common soldier), his parents having to provide additionally '2 pair of sheets, 12 napkins, 6 towels; 2 puter plates & a poringer & a spone'.[15] Restoration Harrow was a school for barristers, doctors,

---

[12] HSR V, fos. 198, 204; HSR III, fo. 41; Gun, *Harrow School Register*, pp. xi–xii; Watson, *English Grammar Schools*, 465. The English experiment was in the 1920s, when the governors seemed keen to abolish the relic altogether. They failed.

[13] For the Statute see Laborde, *Harrow School*, 239, 240; HSR III, fo. 43; HSR V, fo. 225; Gun, *Harrow School Register*, pp. xi–xii and *passim* for participants; Laborde, *op. cit.*, 130.

[14] Gun, *Harrow School Register*, 7. In general see *DNB* entry for Dennis.

[15] John Nicholas, then eight years old and in his first or second year at school, son of Anne and George Nicholas: Townsend Warner, *Harrow in Prose and Verse*, 74–5; Gun, *Harrow School Register*, 19. For the comparative scale of incomes, devised by Gregory King in 1696 see G. N. Clark, *The Later Stuarts* (Oxford, 1965), p. 26.

academics, vicars, as well as landowners. Two became MPs, Joseph Girdler (Orator 1691, MP for Tamworth 1702–15) and Jermyn Wych (at Harrow 1684–8, MP for Fowey, 1713–15); both were Tories.[16] 'Foreigners' came from all parts of the kingdom, from Cornwall to Yorkshire, from Norfolk to Wales. The nonconformist tinge remained to temper the classics, as in the case of the philologist and antiquarian William Baxter, nephew of the puritan divine Richard Baxter, who arrived at Harrow from the Welsh Marches *c.*1668 knowing, so he later rather unconvincingly claimed, no English, only Welsh.[17] It may be possible to discern already the apartheid that existed later between the local free scholars and the 'foreigners': the most prominent ex-free scholar of the period, John Newman (Harrow *c.*1668), whose father Nathaniel taught English and reading to the poor children of the parish, had to be satisfied with the Headmastership of Colfe's Grammar School, Lewisham.[18] At one end of the social scale was John Maddox, son of a Harrow carpenter, a Founder's Exhibitioner at Caius in 1666 aged 16, who received regular additional subventions from the governors to complete his BA and MA degrees. Ordained, he became an Essex curate. However, by 1690 he appears to have lost both post and mind, the governors granting him forty shillings to buy clothes, he 'being now crazie in his intellectuals and very poor and helpless'.[19] At the other end were, *c.*1675, the Seymour brothers, Francis and Charles, respectively fifth and sixth dukes of Somerset.[20] Their attendance at Harrow owed everything to the person as well as personality of the Head Master, William Horne.

The identification of school and Master in early modern England was usually total. Only in the grandest or most ancient of foundations could the two exist in some degree of separation, their fates separable, but even there the reputation of Master was crucial for success and influence. In the seventeenth century Busby was Westminster and Westminster Busby in shared dominance of the educational world. It is no small sign of Harrow's growing status that it could not only survive a messy interregnum and a hasty dismissal of a Master in 1668–9, but could then attract a most distinguished and well-connected schoolmaster to the succession. The relationship was two-way—a good Master would only come to a school that had potential for personal profit or fame. If schools mirrored contemporary models of society, an aristocratic school demanded strong hierarchic leadership. It is entirely in keeping with the Caroline developments at Harrow that in 1672 a new Master's chair was installed in the schoolroom that resembled nothing so much as a throne, architecturally and pedagogically the centre of attention and authority.[21]

---

[16] Gun, *Harrow School Register*, 1–30, esp. pp. 10 and 30.
[17] Thornton, *Harrow School*, 92; Baxter's entry in the *DNB*; Gun, 2.
[18] For Nathaniel see HSR III, Governors' Minutes, fo. 25; HSR V, fos. 145, 152, 168, 204, 210, 290; for John see HSR III, fos. 30, 35; Gun, 19.
[19] HSR III, Governors' Minutes, fos. 23, 25–6, 29, 31, 33, 34, 35, 37, 60; Gun, 17.
[20] Gun, *Harrow School Register*, 24; *Complete Peerage*, xii. i (London, 1953), pp. 76–9.
[21] HSR V, fo. 183. It is still there.

Thomas Jonson, Master from 1661 to 1668, superficially appears of the old school. A former sizar at Trinity College, Cambridge and a beneficiary of a Founder's Exhibition from Harrow in 1652, he resumed his share of preaching the Lyon sermons, the last Master to do so.[22] In October 1668 he suddenly abandoned his post at a few days' notice, declaring to the governors 'his intentions of speedy removal on the Monday following to Lincoln'.[23] His motives remain wholly obscure, as does his future career. Traditionally, sudden departures tended to be caused by debt, as with Head Master Cox in 1746 or Under Master Mark Drury in 1826. Whatever Jonson's reasons, the governors were taken completely by surprise, the Vicar, Joseph Wilcocks, stepping into the breach.[24]

However, it is significant that, on Jonson's departure, there was no question of the Usher, Robinson, taking over *pro tem*. For one thing he was not statutorily qualified, holding only a BA degree. For another, his dealings with the governors and Jonson had established the inferiority of the Usher and the dominance of the Master, academically, administratively, and financially. This was an important confirmation of the authority of the Master, firmly relegating the Usher, despite his position under the statutes, to a subordinate role, allowing the Master almost unchallenged control of the lucrative income from 'foreigners', a perquisite vital in attracting popular and effective rulers. Jonson's years had also seen the physical expansion and refurbishing of the school building; the construction of the gallery in the parish church; the clear delineation of the duties of the Usher as regards the lower forms and the teaching of writing; and, above all, the open acknowledgement of the importance of 'foreigners' in the uneasy negotiations with the Usher in 1665–6.

The flight of Jonson led to the election, on 25 November 1668, of Thomas Martin, MA from Christ Church, Oxford.[25] It is unknown whether Martin, who was over 30 at the time of his appointment, had any previous schoolteaching experience. In any event, he was a disaster. On 14 June 1669, citing the provision in the Statutes allowing them to remove as Master within six months of his taking up his post if they did not believe him to be 'honest, godly, learned, discreet, diligent [and] sober', the governors sacked him. They claimed their decision had been based on their 'owne observation and convincing proof' and, in spite of Martin's denial of the evidence against him, they 'all thought and judged him a man not qualified according to the . . . statute.'[26] There is no unambiguous clue as to the nature of Martin's misdemeanours. Whatever they were, he received preferment as vicar of Stanwell, Middlesex in 1671. Possibly he was mentally unstable; he was reputed to have died insane in 1674. Of all things, an erratic, unsettling, or absent

---

[22] HSR III, Governors' Minutes, fos. 7, 14; HSR V, fos. 132, 135; Gun, 153. He need not have been a Harrovian to be elected to a Founder's Exhibition.

[23] HSR I, Governors' Order Book, fo. 21ᵛ.

[24] HSR V, fo. 159 for payment to Wilcocks 'for teaching the scholars in the absence of the Master'.

[25] HSR I, Governors' Order Book, fo. 22ʳ. [26] Ibid.

Master would have severely undermined Harrow's growing reputation. Ironically, the rising status of the school was recognized in Martin himself receiving, almost certainly *ex officio*, a BD. Such academic honours become more or less automatic for newly appointed Head Masters in the eighteenth and nineteenth centuries, although then they usually collected DDs.[27]

The sacking of Martin suggests another central feature of Restoration Harrow. Although not directly involved financially in the commercial success of the school, their personal stake being the small stipends allowed under the Statutes from the Lyon trusts, the governors displayed consistent interest and support in Harrow's transformation. It is clear from the growing bills for their annual dinners, the regular redecorating and re-equipping of the governors' room, as well as their own social standing, that the governors had aspirations for the school. They were happy to expend increased sums on the Dames' system, local charities, and subsidizing the Vicar and his curate; but they were also evidently willing to raise their investment in the school property, in books, and furniture. They supported the increasing numbers of foreigners, while being anxious lest the local community was excluded. Above all, in their decision to dismiss Martin and in their search, choice and handling of his successor, they showed they cared for the wider interests of the school. There was a clear risk in disposing of Martin. There was no Master for six weeks of schooling, Wilcocks again taking over. The new Master was only appointed three months after Martin's departure.[28] However, the risks of keeping Martin were clearly regarded as worse. It was a symbolic coincidence that the final meeting attended by Sir Gilbert Gerrard, the minutes of which may even have been written in his own hand, was that of June 1669 when Martin was sacked.[29] Gerrard, who died in January 1670, had been a governor since August 1609. Even though he may have missed the meeting in September 1669 which appointed Martin's successor, given that the successful candidate was the son of a prominent puritan schoolmaster of the 1650s, Gerrard may well have had a hand in the election. If so, he assisted at one of the most significant policy decisions ever made by the governors.

WILLIAM HORNE, ETON, AND KING'S

The new Master was William Horne, the Under Master of Eton College and a fellow of King's College, Cambridge. His appointment began over a century of domination of Harrow by Eton and King's. Between 1669 and 1785 only two Head Masters, Bolton (1685–91) and Cox (1730–46) were not from the two royal

---

[27] Gun, *Harrow School Register*, 153, where the BD is mistranscribed as a DD; B. P. Lascelles, 'Early Headmasters', in Howson and Townsend Warner, *Harrow School*, 56 gets it right.

[28] HSR V, fo. 168.   [29] HSR I, Governors' Order Book, fo. 22ʳ.

foundations, and Bolton, an Oxford man, was incorporated an MA at King's while Head Master, which suggests the interest of that college in Harrow was not entirely fortuitous or one-sided. In 1691 the provost of King's, Charles Roderick, in writing a testimonial on behalf of another Eton and King's man, Thomas Bryan, explicitly mentioned the success of Horne 'a master of Eton education'.[30] In 1691, 1746, 1760, and, controversially, 1771 the governors chose men with experience of Eton and King's as masters and fellows. In general they also sought as Masters men with teaching experience, not just good academic and social contacts, although these were undeniably useful. The inference was plain. The governors of Harrow were eager to imitate the Eton system, a point widely acknowledged in the eighteenth century. In that sense Harrow's later public competition with Eton began in colonization. The governors also desired a measure of professionalism not always sought by trustees of contemporary grammar schools.

Horne was the Under Master at Eton as well as a fellow of King's. His father, Thomas Horne, had been Head Master of Eton (1648–54) during the Interregnum.[31] His tenure of the Master's chair established Harrow in the forefront of fashionable boarding schools, in its way a competitor with the older collegiate schools despite the modesty of the buildings and formal provison of teachers. Eton in 1678 contained seventy-eight collegers and 124 oppidans. In 1682 Harrow educated forty free scholars and eighty 'foreigners'. Given the differences in scale of site and endowment, these figures alone tell of Horne's success. He attracted sons of professional families and country gentlemen. In the 1670s he even managed to seduce Francis, Lord Seymour, the future duke of Somerset, from Eton, with his younger brother Charles.[32]

Academically, Horne acquired a reputation as, in the word of his memorial in the parish church, a *preceptor strenuous*. During his time, he not only redesigned the schoolroom but spent at least £21 16s. on books for the school, possibly an indication of his efforts to introduce fresh, Etonian elements into the curriculum, although in essence the two programmes of study were already very similar.[33] The most striking element of his rule was that, by the 1680s, the 'foreigners', now an entrenched majority of pupils, were boarded out around the town very much in the Eton fashion. While the Usher still seemed to live in the schoolhouse and, indeed, had overall responsibility for its day-to-day upkeep, the Master lived elsewhere, with his boarders whom he charged £22 a year for lodging and schooling.[34]

---

[30] Thornton, *Harrow School*, 98–9.
[31] Sir H. C. Maxwell Lyte, *A History of Eton College* (4th edn., Eton, 1911), p. 241; Gun, *Harrow School Register*, 153; HSR I, Governors' Order Book, fo. 22^r.
[32] Thornton, *Harrow School*, 94; Townsend Warner, *Harrow in Prose and Verse*, 74; above, n. 20.
[33] HSR V, fos. 168, 204, 210, 230, 242, 244; Maxwell Lyte, *Eton*, 145.
[34] For Robinson's supervising of trivial repairs, not the Master, another sign of clear differentiation in status see HSR V, fos. 160, 168, 176, 182, 187, 193, 204, 210, 218, 224, etc.; Townsend Warner, *Harrow in Prose and Verse*, 74; Maxwell Lyte, *Eton*, 155.

Accommodation was a sore point. Wherever Jonson had resided, on his departure the governors looked for a suitable house for the Master. On his arrival, Horne had to rent a house, in 1670 being paid an extra £5 towards 'the better accommodating of his personal habitation'. This proved, according to the governors, 'not sufficient to accommodate him in his house of habitation but for want thereof he and his boarders have suffered and are still in danger of suffering cold and other inconveniences this ensuing winter.' Horne therefore was granted an additional £10 'towards the providing him with a house'. The governors' resolution to this effect on 24 July 1671 was the first time that boarders were mentioned in their records. In October 1672, as the lack of a suitable house persisted, Horne was allowed a regular £10 a year.[35] It was only after Horne's death in 1685 that the governors hit on a solution by giving the aged former Master William Hide notice to quit the tenement he had occupied since 1651.[36] Once the house was vacated in March 1686 it was discovered to be in need of extensive repairs, which prevented Bolton taking up residence for a year. The cost was estimated at £90; in fact between 1686 and 1693 the repairs and improvements to the house and its outhouses required at least £213 18s. 2d.[37]

The matter of the Head Master's house was of more than domestic importance. It was—and is—a matter of status. It was also, for Horne and his successors, a question of business. To make money, the Master needed 'foreigners'. To attract the sons of the gentry, as well as to maximize his income, he needed to be able to guarantee their care under his direct charge. As one parent noted in 1682, other landlords could die, leaving no male presence in the boarding house, or were, as at Eton, women anyway.[38] The establishment of the Master in a house of his own, from 1686 on the site occupied by all subsequent Head Masters until 1982, with one brief exception during the Second World War, placed him socially as well as physically in the centre of the community.

The other institutional change demanded by Horne equally emphasized the elevated status of the Master. In October 1669, the governors rescinded the statutory ban on marriage imposed on the Master and Usher by the Founder on the grounds of it proving 'by long experience . . . very inconvenient to the well-ordering of the school'. This suggests some previous difficulty in securing the best candidates for the Mastership or fears of scandal resulting from enforced bachelorhood, the new decree emphazing that a married Master must still avoid 'notorious' living and be sober and discreet, perhaps a backhanded reference to Mr Martin.[39] This order was repeated in 1699, 1704, and in 1722 extended to the Usher.[40] As well as being a sign of the times,

---

[35] HSR I, Governors' Order Book, fos. 33, 35; HSR V, fos. 159, 187, 192, 198, etc.
[36] HSR I, Governors' Order Book, fos. 53, 55; Hide was still apparently alive and paying arrears of rent after Michaelmas 1686: fo. 257.
[37] HSR V, fos. 255, 258, 262, 269, 274, 277, 278, 281, 285.   [38] See above n. 34.
[39] HSR I, Governors' Order Book, fos. 9^{r-v}.
[40] Ibid., fos. 9^v, 10^r; HSR III, Governors' Minutes, fo. 80 (for 1704 confirmation).

the new marriage clause placed the Master of Harrow on a par with heads of Oxford and Cambridge colleges, as well as rival schools such as Eton. Giving the Master the chance of a family made the post not only possibly more congenial, but created a potential dynastic interest as well as providing a greater incentive to make money. Head Masters soon became patriarchal figures, their network of local and national contacts enhanced by their progeny. It also allowed for the tradition of Harrow as a family business to emerge in the following century, when Masters were succeeded by sons-in-law, and employed sons, brothers, and nephews to the staff. In addition, it probably helped reassure nervous parents, at least of those boarding with the Master, that their sons were not being cast upon a world exclusively male.

Harrow School (first described as such by the governors in 1703) was a business and, for the Master, a lucrative one.[41] On the figures supplied by Anne Nicholas in a letter of 1682, there were eighty 'foreigners'. Each would pay an entrance fee, possibly of a few guineas, to the Master. Horne charged his boarders £22 a year, including school fees, although writing was possibly extra. Even a mere ten boarders would have set the Master up handsomely. In addition, Horne would have received all the schooling fees for the foreigners not in his house. From these, if the governors' order of 1665 was followed, the Usher received ten shillings per head, suggesting that the annual fee may have been about £2.[42] Whatever Usher Robinson received in addition to his £20 a year, and in 1682 it seems he may have received another £40, he had built up enough capital to buy two tenements in Harrow in 1697 for £46 2s.[43] However the calculations are achieved, Horne, through schooling and boarding fees, was making many hundreds of pounds a year, the income of a gentlemen of comfortable means.

Beside his personal fortune, Horne secured that of his school not just through personal contacts but, as has been described, through the creation of arcane elitist corporate rituals, archery and the Oration, and the physical emphasis on the authority of the Master on his throne/pulpit dominating the schoolroom. What Hide had begun, Horne enshrined: the distinctiveness of the school and the dominance of the Master. Both were essential to the appeal to the wealthy gentlemen upon whom late seventeenth-century Harrow's fortunes depended. As ever in its history, Horne's Harrow had to be sensitive to its commercial market to maintain its position and survive. It could not rely on the healthy reputation and convenient geographic location of the Hill alone. The trick was to combine social acceptability with academic respectability. Horne was evidently proficient at both.

---

[41] HSR III, Governors' Minutes, fo. 80 (13 Feb. 1703).

[42] A century later it was four guineas. For the Nicholas letter see Townsend Warner, *Harrow in Prose and Verse*, 74; the ratio of Usher to Master's income is related to the shares agreed in 1665 and the stated division of three-fourths to one-fourth made by the governors in 1721: HSR III, Governors' Minutes, fo. 114.

[43] HSR 309 (July 1697); in June 1700, Robinson undertook to rent two cottages at 20s. a year: HSR 317.

Horne fell ill in the autumn of 1685, delegating his duties once more to Wilcocks, the Vicar, a reminder of how different in establishment Harrow was from its collegiate competitors. This distinctive Harrow dichotomy of parochial and public continued to mark the school's character until the mid-nineteenth century. On this occasion, in the face of Horne's 'sickness and other weakness', the governors acted rapidly and decisively. Fearful of any hiatus in the management of the school, on 8 September they effectively sacked Horne on his deathbed, declaring that, unless he resigned by 5 October, they would declare the Mastership vacant anyway.[44] This may also have been because they already had a successor in mind, as they proceeded to an appointment on 12 October.[45] In the event Horne died before his ejection came into effect. The whole episode eerily parallels the circumstances surrounding the death and replacement of Dr Moore in 1953.[46] That the governors in 1685 acted with such dispatch was itself a sort of compliment to Horne's achievement.

The new Master, so promptly appointed, was William Bolton, an Oxford man who had been Second Master at Charterhouse, his credentials further proof of the school's new standing the governors were careful to preserve.[47] Bolton's election may also have marked a deliberate political shift. Of Horne's politics we have no record, but he came from puritan stock. Of Bolton's allegiances there is no doubt. The year before coming to Harrow, he had published two sermons extolling the monarch and non-resistance, a tactful move for an ambitious schoolmaster during the Tory reaction and personal rule of Charles II. The prevailing political wind blew strongly. In April 1686 the governors fixed the dates for the six non-monthly Lyon sermons.[48] They were to be delivered (by the vicar or curate) on Ash Wednesday, Good Friday, Christmas Day, and on three secular anniversaries: 5 November (the Gunpowder Plot of 1605), 30 January (the execution of Charles I, king and, to some, martyr), and 29 May (Restoration Day 1660). The last three are royalist and Anglican, an identity of devotion that the new Roman Catholic king James II attempted to divide at his peril. It was significant that, while after 1714 an annual Lyon sermon was preached on the current monarch's accession day, it was the late Charles II's accession, not that of his brother that was to be commemorated in 1686.[49] This was less a slight on James than an elevation of the Restoration of the Monarchy to providential status beside the salvation of James I and the 'martyrdom' of his son. It is wholly in keeping with the prevailing mood that two of Bolton's pupils, Girdler and Wych, were both future Tory MPs whose parliamentary careers were ended by the Hanoverian succession. The tone of Bolton's and his pupils' politics serve as a reminder that the eighteenth-century Whig ascendancy was far from inevitable.

[44] HSR III, Governors' Minutes, fo. 51.   [45] HSR I, Governors' Order Book, fo. 23^v.
[46] See below, pp. 532–3.
[47] HSR I, Governors' Order Book, fo. 23^v; in general, Gun, *Harrow School Register*, 153; Lascelles, 'Early Headmasters', 58.   [48] HSR III, Governors' Minutes, fo. 54.
[49] In fact initially the accession sermon was dropped after 1714: HSR III, Governors' Minutes, fo. 109, 23 Oct. 1716.

Bolton, as has been described, was the first Head Master to enjoy a separate house paid for by the governors (the rent was a peppercorn).⁵⁰ Clearly, for much of his time, his house, garden, and outbuildings were a building site. It was probably only in 1687 that he moved in. Given the expenditure on its refurbishment, Bolton's establishment was conducted on some scale. The lavish extent of the rebuilding, including barns and a cottage, suggests room for plenty of boys, Bolton seemingly being unmarried. If he maintained the numbers of his predecessor's reign, Bolton was wealthy. In his time the schoolhouse garret was further strengthened, probably for additional accommodation for teaching.⁵¹ However, that raises the question of whether Bolton or his predecessors employed assistants other than the Usher. If there was more than one classroom, this was likely. A generation later, Head Masters did.⁵² It is not impossible for Bolton's time.

The governors were clearly anxious lest the numbers of free scholars dropped or the Master and Usher ignored the local interest. In 1690 they pointedly confirmed their policy that forty free scholars was a 'competent' number to be taught for the founder's stated stipends.⁵³ The assumption must be either that the masters were asking for more money to teach the free scholars or that they were admitting fewer of them. Alternatively, there was a decline in local children wishing to go to the school, the governors declaring that, for want of poor children, sons of richer parishioners should be admitted. This foreshadows the long, unavailing struggle by the parish to wrest Lyon's school to their needs, which may have included reading and writing but not the classics. A classical education was of decreasing use for a poor child because it was becoming the preserve of the social elite: impractical, distinctive, and therefore exclusive and aristocratic. The governors' decree of 1690 on free scholars was tacit admission that the school envisaged by the Founder had changed out of recognition, the aristocratic, monied public school subsuming the charitable local grammar school. One of the oddities of the school's history, however, was that the myths of the former fed off the carcass of the latter until divorce was achieved in 1874. Bolton, two centuries earlier, had no doubts as to the direction he was taking. He was in business as Head Master of a public school.

Bolton was also adept at attracting patronage, as he combined the Mastership of Harrow with the living of Dunsby, Lincolnshire. More intriguingly, in 1690 he incorporated his Oxford BA at King's College, Cambridge, proceeding also to a Cambridge MA, a sign perhaps both of Bolton's connections and the college's sustained interest in Harrow.⁵⁴ Bolton's style of operation may be indicated by the Latin poem he published with an English translation in 1690. This was a sychophantic

---

⁵⁰ At least this was the case from 1703: HSR III, Governors' Minutes, fo. 80; Hide had paid £8 a year for the same property, 1651–86.   ⁵¹ HSR V, fo. 255.

⁵² HSR III, Governors' Minutes, fo. 115, 3 Apr. 1721: the Master was allowed to employ an assistant.   ⁵³ HSR III, Governors' Minutes, fo. 60.

⁵⁴ Lascelles, 'Early Headmasters', 58; Gun, 153. For King's details see letter from Joseph Romilly to C. E. Long, 28 Dec. 1855.

conceit describing how his rheumatism had been cured by the application of laurel leaves advised by his doctor 'and the repeated commands of the Honourable the Lady Gerrard', wife of Sir Charles, the third baronet, owner of Flambards, and governor of the school. She was the sister of the two Seymours, respectively fifth and sixth dukes of Somerset, who had been Harrovians in the 1670s. The dedication, to the six current governors of the school, headed by Sir Charles Gerrard, was delivered 'with great humility' by Bolton who called himself the school's 'Archididascalus', a pompous Renaissance Latin word for Head Master. He also called Harrow a 'Public School'. The verse itself is pretentiously mock-heroic, the translation suggesting no great confidence in the classical attainments of the audience. That it was printed by a publisher whose other authors included Thomas Hobbes points to elevated social aspiration or achievement.[55] Indeed, the *Poem upon a Laurel Leaf* captures some of the essence of Restoration Harrow. The dedicatee was aristocratic; the style and medium of the poem formal, classical, but fashionable; the author confident in the elevated place of both his institution and himself, yet displaying the obsequiousness to patrons so evident and so necessary to the school's success. All that was lacking was foresight: a year later Bolton was dead and, on 5 June 1691, so the Parish Register recorded, 'buried in sheepswool'.[56]

[55] W. Bolton, *A Poem upon a Laurel Leaf* (London, 1690), title-page, pp. 2–3, 5, 8.
[56] Letter from Revd J. W. Cunningham to C. E. Long, 17 Jan. 1856, quoting the Parish Registers, 5 June 1691.

6

HEIRS AND GRACES, 1691–1746

The election of Thomas Bryan in June 1691 confirmed Harrow's association with Eton and King's which lasted another hundred years. A scholar of Eton, fellow of King's, and Master of the King's College School, Bryan set the tone for the next century, in his own way as influential a Head as Hide, Thackeray, or Vaughan. On the deliberate policy of the governors to develop Harrow on Etonian lines much of the character of the eighteenth-century school depended. It was not so much a question of taking 'Eton's refuse', as one disgruntled Harrovian put it during the riots of 1771, as a matter of shrewd judgement of product and market.[1] The oppidan system at Eton provided an effective non-collegiate model of how to lodge an elastic number of fee-payers at little or no cost to the Foundation yet at considerable potential private gain to the teachers or landladies (Dames) who housed them whilst at the same time retaining for the Head Master full control over education, discipline, and academic fees. By the end of Bryan's reign even elements of Eton vernacular had migrated. In 1712 the Harrow phrase of 'free' or 'poor scholars' became the Etonian 'town boys' in the accounts. In 1733 the lowly Usher had been transformed into the grander sounding 'Under Master'.[2]

This is not to say that Harrow instantly sprung into being a nursery for the sons of peers. It did not. Then neither did Eton where the first school list in 1678 of seventy-eight collegers and 124 oppidans included only five baronets and only one son of a peer.[3] The attraction of public schools for the titled aristocracy grew slowly and fitfully in the early eighteenth century with many voices raised against the system and in favour of private tuition. Of those who held peerages carrying the right to a seat in the House of Lords in the eighteenth century born before 1710, just over 22 per cent were educated at Eton, Winchester, Westminster, Harrow, and St Paul's. Of those born after 1710, just over 65 per cent went to the same schools;

---

[1] Thomas Grimston to his father, 4 Oct. 1771, *Report on the Manuscripts of Lady de Cane, Historical Manuscripts Commission* (London, 1906), p. 230; on the Eton system see Maxwell-Lyte, *Eton*, esp. p. 155.   [2] HSR V, fo. 9; HSR III, fo. 128.

[3] Thornton, *Harrow School*, 94, quoting Maxwell-Lyte, *Eton*.

at Eton alone, the figures for the two periods were sixty-five out of 494 compared with 145 out of 460.⁴ Here Harrow had an advantage over competitors such as Westminster in being relatively cheap, by mid-century perhaps two-thirds of the all-in annual costs (c.£200 against c.£300).⁵ Yet by offering a similar syllabus, system of education, and extra-curricular activities under a Master from a grander institution, Harrow could guarantee a matching service. This was of particular importance as in the eighteenth century there was considerable mobility of pupils between certain public schools. Contacts and conformity were thus at a premium. From 1668 to 1805, every Head Master came to Harrow with previous experience of at least one of the schools within this loop of Eton, Westminster, Charterhouse, and Harrow. So, too, did most of the other teaching staff: Ushers Le Hunte (1700–5), William Cox (1747), and William Prior (1747–c.1765) being Etonians while John Hooker (1705–21) was a Harrovian pupil of Bryan. Of the grand schools, after 1688 Eton, by site, scale, and history, became by far the most prominent, being not merely royal and aristocratic but crucially, in the age of Walpole and the elder Pitt—both Etonians—fashionable. The governors of Harrow chose their model well. Although it took time, their policy bore noble fruit. Of those eighteenth-century peers born after 1740, seventeen were Harrovians compared to only seven Wykhamists. On the wider comparison of numbers, by 1800, Harrow had established itself as the second public school in the kingdom after Eton.⁶

No less significant of the consolidation of Harrow's position under Bryan was its ability to withstand two severe crises, one financial the other academic, which might have sunk the reputation if not the very existence of a school less secure of its place. In 1709 the Lyon estate teetered on the edge of ruin as the governors were forced to take out a mortgage equivalent to about two-thirds of normal annual income in order to cover the costs of rebuilding the farm at Preston which, at £581, was almost double the annual income from land rents. The debt was only cleared in 1714. The consequent economies directly affected the wider educational provision of the charity. Payment to the Usher to teach poor scholars to write was cancelled and the Dame system of teaching 'poor children in reading so as to fit them for the free school' was suspended. The former was restored in 1716, the latter only in 1718.⁷

In 1746 the Head Master since 1730, James Cox, absconded in the face of mounting debts after some years of drunken negligence which had, some said with

---

⁴ J. Cannon, *Aristocratic Century* (Cambridge, 1984), pp. 34–44 for these statistics and in general.
⁵ *Shardloes Papers of the Seventeenth and Eighteenth Centuries*, ed. G. Eland (London, 1947), pp. 76–7, 79.
⁶ Cannon, *Aristocratic Century*, 40; J. Lawson and H. Silver, *A Social History of Education in England* (London, 1973), pp. 116–17, 200; R. O'Day, *Education and Society, 1500–1800* (London, 1982), pp. 200, 204, 206.
⁷ HSR I, fo. 26ʳ; HSR III, fos. 93, 94, 96–7, 102, 105, 109, 112; HSR V, fos. 350, 351, 355–7; HSR VII, fos. 3, 15–16, 18; HSR 345 is a copy of the mortgage to Newman, 30 May 1709, with quittance for repayments, 1710–14 on the dorse.

perhaps only a little exaggeration, reduced numbers to forty, less than a third of the size of Bryan's school.[8] Such antics often presaged closure or reduction from a grammar to a primary school. That this was not Harrow's fate was clear evidence of its new position as a public school with the tenacity to survive as an institution despite temporary reverses of the sort that afflict such schools in all periods. While across England in the eighteenth century, schools with similar foundations were sinking into parochial obscurity and closure, their assets in places supporting mere sinecures, Harrow demonstrated that it had acquired resources of support that ensured its survival, in particular governors with wide experience, vision, and a network of social contacts that was already based on a tradition of schooling that stretched back three-quarters of a century. The governors as individuals were wealthy enough to guarantee the 1709 loan and resilient enough to replace Cox in 1746 with an experienced, well-connected, and highly regarded professional Master.[9] It says much for early eighteenth-century Harrow School, its acquired status and perceived potential, that Thomas Thackeray accepted the job.

The Chandos Connection

The governing body of Harrow was, characteristic of such corporations, dominated by nepotism. It was also marked by local interest and wealth. That Lyon's school was designed for the parish is certain. However, from the beginning the governors were often men with wider contacts and concerns, the Gerrards, Norths, and Rushouts combining county prominence with involvement at court and in government. Given the nature of local agricultural and commercial prosperity's dependence on London, even those strictly local families, notably the extended Page family, had metropolitan concerns. The election as governor in 1713 of James Brydges, successively earl of Carnarvon and duke of Chandos, Paymaster General of the Forces during the War of Spanish Succession, has traditionally been seen as placing the conduct of the trust's affairs and the contacts of the school on an altogether more efficient and exalted plane. This is to underestimate the social and financial standing of earlier governing bodies and to exaggerate the material influence of Chandos himself.

In one respect, Chandos's election was entirely consistent with tradition. He was elected a governor in 1713 in place of Warwick Lake, his first wife's uncle. In a period when office was often regarded as property, governors were frequently succeeded or joined by blood relatives, usually their sons. In 1713 Lake's son was too young (having to wait until 1745 to be elected in place of Chandos's son) and Chandos had just bought a local property, Canons in Stanmore, from another of his wife's uncles, Lancelot Lake. The Lake connection with Harrow was also dynastic,

---

[8] HSR III, fos. 140–2.   [9] Cf. Lawson and Silver, *Social History of Education*, 200.

Warwick Lake having married the heiress to Flambards and becoming a governor in 1701 in succession to his father-in-law, Sir Charles Gerrard. Of the thirty governors elected between 1660 and 1750, in addition to Chandos, thirteen were certainly sons of governors, one was a son-in-law, another five were members of the extended Page families of Uxendon and Wembley, three more were Old Harrovians, and one was the vicar. Most possessed, or acquired, property in the parish or nearby.[10]

However closely knit, the governors were not without means or experience. The Gerrards of Flambards were regularly MPs; the Waldos had made their money as London merchants with the consequent rewards of City office; others included barristers as well as landowners; the Grahams, father (1727–34) and son (1738–61) were successful society medical doctors; the Bucknalls became millionaires. They were men of substance, for many of whom, like Sir Thomas Franklyn (governor 1707–28) or Sir John Rushout (1715–75), becoming a trustee of the most significant local charity simply recognized their social position as prominent local landowners and employers.[11] Although when it mattered, as during the Preston Farm crisis after 1707, they were conscientious enough, there were times when meetings were adjourned because inquorate, as at the Audit meeting in April 1728.[12] The annual fee they paid themselves was small (one mark: 13s. 4d.), none the less, the style to which they treated themselves when conducting their business at Harrow suggests no undue disregard of status or scrimping. Throughout the seventeenth century new furniture was regularly acquired for the Governors' Room, which was repainted 'with a light colour' in 1705.[13] A measure of the conviviality of the Governing Body, as well as its collective expectations, may be found in the annual Audit Dinner. From a cost of one mark in the early seventeenth century, the expense gradually rose to £1 10s. 2d. in 1650, £4 5s. 0d. in 1675, £5 14s. 0d. in 1702.[14] In 1710 the governors invested in a set of a dozen oyster knives, by which time the dinners were held at the Anchor Inn, just by the school gate.[15] In the 1720s and 1730s, dinners included chicken, beef, ham, oysters, sturgeon, and asparagus, as well as wine.[16] In 1731 the cost was £10 9s. 7d., although usually the bill came to between £7 and £8.[17] The menu for six governors on 25 March 1735 included

---

[10] HSR I, fo. 26ᵛ for Chandos' election in 1713; for other gubernatorial elections see HSR I, fos. 18ʳ–32ʳ; Gun, *Harrow School Register*, 161–2; on Chandos and the Lakes see J. Johnson, *Princely Chandos: John Brydges, 1674–1744* (London, 1984), pp. 28, 62; Gun, op. cit., 159–60; *DNB* entry for Sir Thomas Lake (1567–1630).

[11] Gun, *Harrow School Register, passim*; for some comments on the gubernatorial families of Rushout, Waldo, and Bucknall see Thornton, *Harrow School*, 354–7.

[12] HSR III, fo. 122, 16 Apr. 1727; the meeting reconvened on 27 Apr. (fo. 123).

[13] HSR III, fo. 83 and *passim*; HSR V; and HSR VII *passim*.

[14] HSR V, fo. 29 (account for 1616–18), fos. 103 (1650), 204 (1675), 335 (1702).

[15] HSR VII, fo. 7: this account includes payment to a servant of Monk, the proprietor of the Anchor, for whom see fos. 37, 44, etc..

[16] HSR VII, fos. 31, 44, 47, 50, 53, 58, 62, 66, 70, 74, 78–9, 84–5.   [17] Ibid., fo. 70.

three lobsters, eight chickens, four ducks, and twelve pigeons as well as ham, beef, and lamb: with wine and service the bill came to £7 18s. 3d.[18] The governors were discriminating; in 1737, the ham and fowls came from London as did a barrel of oysters.[19]

As they perpetuated their families' interests in the charity, so the governors exploited the modest patronage at their disposal as trustees. In 1692 and 1695 Peter Waldo, brother of one current governor, Edmund, and son of another, Daniel, recently deceased, received money from the trust towards the costs of taking his Oxford BA and MA. He in turn became a governor in 1707, replacing his brother. In 1734 he nominated his own son for one of the Lyon Exhibitions at Oxford.[20] This was part of a convenient gubernatorial initiative to ensure that the Exhibitions were filled begun in 1724 when it was agreed that each governor in turn should have the nomination of new Exhibitioners. In 1734 the other Oxford Exhibition was filled by the duke of Chandos with his cousin's son, Henry Rodney. By 1737, however, this new system was summarily abandoned because of 'inconveniences'. Whether these arose from the lack or inability of candidates, the casualness or competition of patrons, or the disquiet of university colleges that had become used to suggesting names themselves is unclear. At the meeting which repealed the nominating privilege, Chandos had applied to appoint a successor to Henry Rodney, who had died. This may have been seen as not strictly within the rules of the scheme and, rather than disoblige the great duke, abolition was preferred.[21]

This incident, his election by dynastic and local connection, even the shared dinners, display Chandos as entirely complaisant with his colleagues and the traditions of the trust. Thornton hailed Chandos as 'the *deus ex machina*, whereby the business matters of John Lyon's foundation were placed upon the best possible basis'.[22] To his business acumen some have added his political contacts with the Hanoverian court in explaining how he furthered Harrow's fortunes. It is argued that after 1714 Dr Snape of Eton's well-aired High Church opinions deterred loyal Hanoverians from sending their children to his school, preferring Harrow, safe under the patronage of Chandos, whose gorgeous palace of Canons attracted the new elite of Georgian England. There is little to be said for this. The only Harrovians for whom Chandos is known to have been responsible were Henry Rodney and, if he actually went to Harrow at all, his brother George, the future admiral.[23]

---

[18] HSR VII, fo. 90.   [19] Ibid., fo. 100.
[20] HSR III, fos. 65, 67, 129; HSR I, fo. 26ʳ; Gun, *Harrow School Register*, 28 and 161.
[21] HSR III, fos. 119, 124, 129, 130, 132 (fos. 124 and 132 mention the Master of Caius as a nominator of candidates); for the Chandos–Rodney connection see Johnson, *Princely Chandos*, 165; Gun, *Harrow School Register*, 22.
[22] Thornton, *Harrow School*, 108 et seq. for the orthodox view of Chandos and Harrow. Cf. Howson and Townsend Warner, *Harrow School*, 157; Laborde, *Harrow School*, 36–7.
[23] Johnson, *Princely Chandos*, 165; Gun, *Harrow School Register*, pp. xiii–xiv.

The other governors displayed no signs of incipient Jacobitism which Chandos could have balanced. It was at a meeting that Chandos did not attend in October 1716 that the dates of the Lyon sermons were altered, that for Restoration Day being dropped, although, enigmatically, so was that for Accession Day.[24] (Both were restored later in the century.) Harrow's rise in popularity may owe more to Bryan and fashion than to temporary political complexion. In any case, Snape ceased to be Eton's Head Master in 1718, replaced by the aptly named latitudinarian Bland.

Chandos's transformation in the conduct of the trust's business may also have been exaggerated. His influence failed to ensure a regular quorum at the annual Audit. The complex financial deals surrounding the mortgage of £260 from Henry Newman in 1709 and the necessary retrenchment to provide an adequate series of surpluses to clear the debt had been achieved by 1714, before Chandos took an active part in the trust's affairs.[25] His personal involvement in the charity's business was fitful. Elected in June 1713, of the forty governors' meetings until that which received his resignation in April 1740, he attended just fifteen, nine of them between 1730 and 1738, when his national commitments had long ceased. During his twenty-seven years as a governor, he was Treasurer, that is, one of the two annual executive governors, four times, 1715/16, 1722/3, 1728, and 1734. On the first and last occasions, he presented his accounts in person: in 1728, he was absent and in 1723 represented by his agent, George Watkins, through whom he conducted much of his gubernatorial business and who, in March 1727, actually signed the accounts on Chandos's behalf.[26]

However, while the basic structure and policy of the trust remained unchanged, Chandos does seem to have been involved in some innovations of accounting and the beginnings of a broader investment policy. In each of his years as Treasurer, the surpluses were unusually high.[27] After his first year (1716/17) the governors began investing in Government Bonds, the start of a long and fluctuating relationship with the Stock Market.[28] After his second term of duty (1722/3), the accounts were rearranged to itemize income and expenditure under categories, a system pioneered, however, the year before.[29] Equally, the shift to beginning the accounting year at Lady Day instead of Michaelmas occurred in 1721, during a gap of almost six years in Chandos's attendance.[30] It was also in 1721 that the governors instituted a full survey of their possessions which allowed them, in 1724, to subsidize the construction of the Harrow Poor House.[31] Chandos may have been responsible for a

---

[24] HSR III, fo. 109.   [25] See above, n. 7.
[26] HSR III, fos. 103–33, esp. fo. 117; HSR VII, fos. 37, 55.
[27] £145 (1715/16), £103 (1722/3), £193 (1728), £141 (1734).
[28] HSR III, fo. 110; HSR VII, fo. 22.   [29] HSR VII, fo. 34 *et seq.*
[30] Ibid., fos. 31–2. Cf. shift in Audit date: HSR III, fos. 113, 114.
[31] HSR III, fos. 114, 116 (for survey of salaries and other standing charges), 119, 120; HSR VII, fo. 43 bis.; HSR XII, the bound copy of the survey plans for each of the Trust's estates, dated 1723.

most fortuitous intervention at the meeting of 1 April 1724 when it was agreed to remove the £157 10s. ½d. from the Chest kept in the Governors' Room on security grounds; almost exactly a year later burglars broke into the Chest but found only the silver matrix of the corporation's seal.[32] Overall, the annual receipts at the end of Chandos's tenure averaged around £500 compared with c.£400 at the start. As rent income remained fairly static over the period, the increase must be in part the result of better management of surpluses, for which Chandos's financial experience may take the credit. However, of greater significance than the easy financial skills of the duke was the manner in which the Master conducted the school and attracted pupils.

Thomas Bryan

In all schools in all periods self-image and public reputation reflect sharply the aspirations and, sometimes, the reality of the institution. On that measure, Bryan's Harrow thought of itself as a grand place. Both the Master's house and the schoolhouse were embellished beyond the strictly functional, the latter receiving 'beautifying' decoration in 1696/7 and a gilded weathervane, in the shape of a lion, in 1703/4.[33] Bryan's local status was recognized in the authority granted him to build his own pew in the parish church in 1706.[34] The tenancy of the Master's house was placed on a stable (and for Bryan and his successors distinctly advantageous) footing in 1703.[35]

Within the school, the Master's power was reaffirmed in 1699. The year before, he and the long-serving Usher had been in dispute. Now the governors made it clear that the Usher was not autonomous in the Lower School; that the Master had the ordering of the 'method of teaching' throughout the forms; and that the Master alone could admit foreigners.[36] These were important matters, given that the teaching of the Lower School was in the hands of the Usher. As the numbers grew, the proportion of foreigners in the Lower School increased until in 1721 the Usher Hooker taught sixty-six to Bryan's thirty-eight.[37] Without the 1699 assertion

---

[32] HSR III, fo. 119. See Howson and Townsend Warner, *Harrow School*, 5 for a transcription of the account of the burglary and the offered reward advertised in the *Whitehall Evening Post* of 6 Apr. 1725. For the costs of this and the repairs to the chest see HSR VII, fo. 47.

[33] HSR V, fos. 305, 337, 339 and the governors' accounts in general for these years. For the extension of Bryan's garden in 1698 see HSR III, fo. 68.

[34] Druett, *Harrow*, 165–6. He had refurbished his earlier pew—at the governors' expense—in 1698/9: HSR III, fo. 314.

[35] HSR III, fo. 80, when the governors also referred, for the first time, to 'Harrow School'. The lease is HSR 325, 1 Nov. 1703. The 1736 Map of the Harrow Road depicts the Master's House as a mansion: HSR XIII.

[36] HSR III, fos. 70, 71.   [37] Thornton, *Harrow School*, 117.

of the Master's authority, the institution could have split damagingly. Then, as now, a strong head was, in itself, a draw.

The financial settlement of 1721 calmed for a century the slightly anomalous relations between Master and Usher by allocating to the Master all foreigners' entrance money and three-quarters of the tuition fees regardless of their position in the school. The 1665–6 arrangement which gave the Usher ten shillings per foreigner was formally rescinded. Instead, as well as now receiving a quarter of all foreigners' tuition fees, ten pounds was added to the Usher's annual stipend on top of the £6 13s. 4d. already awarded him for teaching the Free Scholars writing. Although between 1660 and 1720 they had tended to become disgruntled at what they saw as the imbalance of reward, after 1721, despite Hooker's departure, presumably in dudgeon, Ushers appeared more content, possibly because of the greater opportunities to make money from the boys out of boarding or extracurricular teaching.[38]

In 1728 new arrangements for holidays recognized the transformed nature of the school. Hitherto, the school times for 'breaking up' had been a month at Christmas, and a fortnight at Easter and again at Whitsun. Bryan persuaded the governors to alter these to a month at Christmas and another month at Whitsun, effectively the whole of June, because of the inconvenience of the proximity of the two Spring holidays.[39] The inconvenience, it may be imagined, was suffered more by the pupils and their guardians than the Master, the new holiday arrangements fitting more easily the circumstances of the affluent foreigners.

Bryan was evidently a powerful figure, but one sensitive to the needs of his wealthy pupils as theirs and his so closely coincided. Aged about thirty on appointment, in thirty-nine years he gave Harrow stability and a clear reputation, what today is called profile, for being a public school in which parents could have confidence, secure in what their sons could experience. Bryan also began a Harrow dynasty. Married twice while at Harrow, two sons, Thomas and Samuel, were both at the school, at least one an Orator (Thomas later contriving to win £10,000 in a state lottery). One daughter married the Usher from 1722, James Cox, who succeeded his father-in-law as Master in 1730. Their sons, Bryan's grandsons, also went to Harrow one of them being given a Founder's Exhibition in 1741. Their daughter, Margaret, on marrying the local apothecary in 1763, became the stepmother of Samuel Parr, Harrow prodigy, master and competitor for the Headship in 1771.[40]

---

[38] HSR III, fo. 114. Cf. fos. 21 (1665), 23 (1666), and 70 (1698) for the previous transactions over the Usher's stipend.

[39] HSR I, Governors' Order Book, fo. 10ᵛ. Cf. HSR III, fo. 123 for consequent revival of the Oration at the Audit meeting, since 1721 held after Lady Day.

[40] HSR I, fo. 9ᵛ (1699) and HSR III, fo. 80 (1704) for Bryan's marriages; HSR III, fo. 113 for Samuel as Orator in 1719. Gun, *Harrow School*, 5 adds that Thomas was also Orator in 1715 but HSR III, fo. 107 mentions Nathaniel Ward instead. For Thomas also see Thornton, *Harrow School*, 114–15 n., for his grandsons, who both won the Silver Arrow, see Gun, *Harrow School Register*, and HSR III, fo. 134, for Margaret Parr see *DNB* entry for Samuel Parr.

Such dynastic links were repeated more than once, for example with the Heath-Drury clan from the 1770s until well into the following century, and the Butlers in the nineteenth century. In the Bryan case they illustrate both the continued parochialism of the school's management but also its profitability.

Financial success was the key to the status of Bryan and his school, the product of his academic and social repute. Precise figures are not available. It was decided in 1721 that the Master was to receive all the foreigners' Entrance money and three-quarters of all their tuition fees. On top of that, the Master took all boarding fees from boys in his house. If fees in the 1720s were the same as in the 1760s (four guineas a year) and given that there seem to have been around 100 foreigners at the time, this alone would have brought in over £300 a year. Basic boarding fees were between fifteen and twenty pounds a head.[41] The numbers in Bryan's house are equally obscure, but twenty boys could have brought in at least another £300 a year; thirty boys, £450, but possibly significantly more. Given that it was common for two or even three boys to share a bed, Bryan could have accommodated a considerable proportion of all foreigners.[42] Certainly, the numbers in the school swelled the Master's income in proportion to the educational problems of overcrowding, leading to his successfully petitioning the governors in 1721 to allow him to appoint an assistant master (without 'the power of the rod') at his own expense to cope with the 'great increase of the school'.[43] Within a few years, in addition to the Usher, paid directly by the governors, the Master, Bryan or his successor Cox, was employing two if not three additional members of staff, a Mr Weston, a Mr Evans and, by the late 1740s, a writing master, Henry Reeves. Weston it seems also boarded some boys and, as did Evans, took some for extra tuition in subjects not on the statutory syllabus.[44] This may have made the charge on the Master's purse less, as fees for tuition outside the formal curriculum went direct to the teacher, as did boarding fees to the landlord.

Thus the entrepreneurial structure of pre-reform Harrow was established. The Master possessed the greatest commercial opportunities, but it was essential to the scheme that his colleagues could make money beyond the stipends he (or in the Usher's case the governors) paid them through providing lodging for boarders and tuition out of school hours. One possible reason for Hooker's resignation as Usher in 1721 was that he was not only heavily engaged in the formal supervision and teaching of the younger boy but, as he still resided in the schoolhouse, he had no chance to make money from boarders. Only after 1722 were Ushers permitted to

---

[41] *Shardloes Papers*, 76. Cf. the remarkably comparable sums in 1682 from the Nicholas correspondence: Laborde, *Harrow School*, 35.

[42] J. Gathorne-Hardy, *The Public School Phenomenon* (London, 1977), p. 45.

[43] HSR III, fo. 115.

[44] For Weston and Evans, T. Barrett-Lennard, *An Account of the Families of Lennard and Barrett* (London, 1908), p. 579; for Reeves see Gun, *Harrow School Register*, 157 and refs. in the Governors' Minutes to the Writing Master, esp. Reeves, HSR III, fos. 144ᵛ, 146–7, and 181–2.

marry.⁴⁵ By contrast, Weston, Evans, and Hooker's successors who lived away from the schoolhouse could accommodate boarders, and could, as Weston and Evans did in the early 1730s, teach non-classical subjects, in this instance mathematics. This meant that Bryan and Cox could attract the extra staff numbers and the aristocratic curriculum demanded at modest personal cost. Whatever his exact annual income, Bryan made a comfortable living out of Harrow, perhaps increasingly so over time, in 1700 relinquishing the living of Prescot, Lancashire which he had held since 1692 and in 1714–15 extending his holdings on the Hill by leasing another tenement in the town.⁴⁶

The true test of Bryan's Mastership, as with any, lay in the pupils he attracted. Although direct evidence from his time is scarce, the outline of the education he provided can be reconstructed. He taught the standard classical curriculum, but with extras—handwriting, mathematics, probably some modern languages, drawing, dancing, and fencing. Although established by statute, the emphasis within the formal curriculum altered in the eighteenth century, as it did at Eton and Westminster. Horace replaced Ovid as the most read and influential Latin poet, fitting as he did the idealized self-image of the eighteenth-century aristocrat: rural, rational, rich, leisured, critical, but unpretentious, the pattern of the educated country gentleman. Almost certainly the emphasis, as at Eton, was heavily on poetry, mainly Latin but with Greek a continuing element. It may have been Bryan who added some Eton elements into the curriculum, such as Phaedrus. The core of the teaching method was repetition followed by imitation, language and some general moral or political content comprising what then passed for literary scrutiny or criticism.⁴⁷ This system too allowed for additional opportunities for profit. By 1700 the school week was hardly overloaded, there being whole days ('playdays') without formal lessons.⁴⁸ These in any case, given the nature of the pedagoguery and the ratio of pupils to teachers, consisted almost solely of oral construing and translating. Except in the Upper School, there was probably very little actual teaching in the modern sense. This tended to occur outside the formroom, even for the classics and entirely for other subjects, such as mathematics. For extra tuition, masters charged.

---

⁴⁵ HSR VII, fo. 21 for 1715/16 payment for redecorating Hooker's room in the schoolhouse, HSR I, fo. 10ᵛ for the governors' order that Usher be permitted to marry (29 Jan. 1722), which the new incumbent Cox promptly took advantage of by marrying Bryan's daughter. A comparison of Bryan's signature as witness in 1722 with that to the 1699 order allowing him to marry shows a far shakier hand.

⁴⁶ Gun, *Harrow School Register*, 153; HSR III, fos. 105, 107. Bryan paid £4 for the lease and offered it back to the sitting tenant a year later for £12 15s. HSR XII, 1723 Survey, Map I shows Bryan's extensive holding as Master from the governors and also his possession freehold of property opposite.

⁴⁷ In general see R. M. Ogilvie, *Latin and Greek: A History of the Influence of the Classics on English life from 1600 to 1918* (London, 1964), pp. 34–73, esp. 39–40. For the curriculum, including Phaedrus (which later was the name given to a form in the Lower School) at Harrow in 1755, see *Shardloes Papers*, 76. For maths and the system of charging for tuition outside the formal curriculum see Barrett-Lennard, *An Account*, 579.

⁴⁸ HSR III, fo. 73, in the instructions to the new Usher, Le Hunte (28 July 1700).

The point of a public school in the eighteenth century was not the academic information and skill imparted; these were better obtained fom private tutors, some of whom later in the century actually accompanied their charges to Harrow.[49] What a public school was supposed to deliver was conviviality, a toughening of social acumen, an early introduction to the rough world of a self-conscious elite, competitive within itself but collectively secure in its distinctive experience, traditions, and classical education against *hoi polloi* or, even worse, the commercial middle classes. Aristocratic tone not vocational skill was the essential ingredient.

Bryan's Harrovians sought a cheaper version of Eton. As has been noted, few were noblemen, but many were or aspired to be gentlemen.[50] As before, they became lawyers, dons, clergymen, and minor literary figures. Philip Bennet wrote a farce, *The Beau's Adventures* (1732). Sir Henry Blount, Bt. (Orator 1717) was an antiquary. Yet, some trod a wider stage, establishing in their careers as much as their education the standing of their school. It mattered less what they learnt at Harrow but more from what backgrounds they came and to what callings they went. John Cholmley (*c.*1698) was the first Harrovian known to have held a commission in the army, pioneer of the most enduring Harrow employment tradition. At least three others also received commissions from Bryan's benches, as well as possibly one admiral, Rodney (*c.*1730). The first Harrovian to hold a university chair was Robert Jenner (Orator 1729), Regius Professor of Civil Law at Oxford (1754–67). John Turner from Stanmore (Silver Arrow winner 1707) rose in commercial circles to the chairmanship of the East India Company, a baronetcy (1733), and a fortune of over £100,000—an early example of a Harrow sportsman making good in business. At Bryan's and his Ushers' feet sat six future Members of Parliament, including Joseph Girdler (Orator 1691), the first Harrovian MP, for Tamworth, in 1702. With them were George Forbes (*c.*1725), the future fourth earl of Granard; Matthew Moreton (Silver Arrow winner 1709), second Baron Ducie, described later as 'that best good man with the worst natured face'; Lord Rodney, the admiral; and probably John St John (Silver Arrow winner 1712), second Viscount St John, half-brother to the controversial Tory politician, Henry St John, Lord Bolingbroke. Besides these aristocratic luminaries were a few exotics, such as Edward Coke (Orator 1706), whose mother was Greek and who had been born at Constantinople, possibly illegitimate. Appropriately, one Harrovian in Bryan's school, although almost certainly not actually taught by him, was William Cooke, who spent three years at Harrow (1718–21) between the ages of seven and ten before proceeding to Eton and King's and a career as Head Master of Eton (1743–5) and Provost of King's (1772–80). Harrow's relationship with Eton could hardly have been more neatly caught. It also

---

[49] As was admitted by Thomas Barrett's wife in 1778 when removing his son from Harrow after three years of Latin and Greek there in preference for a private tutor, 'as at publick Schools very little is to be learned': Barrett-Lennard, *An Account*, 614. Cf. Cannon, *Aristocratic Century*, 36–40.

[50] For what follows see Gun, *Harrow School Register*, 1–30.

illustrates another feature of Bryan's school; the extreme youth of the pupils. Few stayed beyond sixteen; many came when little more than infants. School was school. There was no distinction between primary or secondary education, still less between a public school and a preparatory school, such distinctions being the result of competitive academic tests and examinations, beginning at universities from the later eighteenth century. Bryan's Harrow provided the services of both.

As suggested, the social education offered by Harrow was at least as important as the academic. One of the totemic rituals that gained in importance in direct proportion to its artificiality was the annual archery competition for the Silver Arrow. At least from 1704, the normally cautious and parsimonious governors regularly paid for the butts to be put in good order.[51] The names of winners and sometimes competitors were recorded. In 1723 the victory of Cross, son of a London brewer and nephew of Sir Thomas Cross, MP for Westminster, was mentioned in the *British Journal*.[52] The competition had become a society event. Corporate traditions and rituals are important signifiers. The governors' change of their audit meeting from Michaelmas to the week before Easter to suit the new accounting term of Lady Day in 1721 effectively ended the custom of an annual oration, as the new date coincided with the school's Easter break. In April 1728, with the Easter holiday abolished, the custom was revived, the oration to be spoken, as before, 'by one of the upper schollars'.[53] Such corporate gatherings were a formal acknowledgement of the identity of the institution, from boys to trustees. No less significant, perhaps, was the growing custom for boys to carve their names on the panels of the schoolroom, a sign of individual association with the institution and contributing visibly to a sense of tradition and continuity. The earliest name apparently dates from the 1660s; the earliest one identifiable is I. or T. Basil, 1701.[54] By mid-century, the habit was well-established. In this Harrow again imitated its older and grander collegiate competitors.

There survives one vivid, if unexpected, sidelight on the life of Bryan's Harrow. Sometime in 1697/8, possibly at the end of the Christmas term 1697, fifteen 'scholars at Harrow' performed Nathaniel Lee's verse melodrama *Sophonisba or Hannibal's Overthrow*, with a prologue and epilogue specially composed by two of the boys.[55] The Prologue was written by a pupil called Baggs, who also acted the

---

[51] HSR V, fo. 341, HSR VII, fos. 3, 6, 25 (when, in 1717/18, new butts were built), 44, 62 (a major refurbishment in 1729), etc.
[52] Gun, *Harrow School Register*, p. xii.   [53] HSR III, fo. 123.
[54] Gun, *Harrow School Register*, pp. xii–xiii, Laborde, *Harrow School*, 80–4.
[55] Nathaniel Lee, *Sophonisba or Hannibal's Overthrow: A Tragedy. Acted at the Theatre Royal by their Majesties' Servants* (London, 1697). The copy in the archives contains some notes by C. du Pontet, Vaughan Librarian, 1914–29. The additional manuscript Prologue and Epilgogue are on separate sheets bound into this copy at the beginning, with a manuscript dramatis personae in the same hand bound in at p. iv. For the biographical information on the players see Gun, *Harrow School Register*.

title role and was possibly Orator in 1701, and spoken by Charles Bressey, the 1697 Orator who played Massinissa, one of the male leads in the play. The other star, Capel Billingsby (Orator in 1696), who played Hannibal, delivered the Epilogue composed by the otherwise unknown Reuse. The nature of their heroic couplets, at once arch, formal, and knowingly coy, suggests that rather more than the strictly delineated statutory curriculum was enjoyed by Bryan's Harrovians. Baggs's Prologue went as follows:

> As when a yielding Maid does first essay,
> To act a woman's part in Love's Grand play,
> The more unskill'd, the better does her part,
> Excess of nature supplies want of art,
> So tho' our Virgin Action here to day
> May want th'address, and art shou'd grace a play
> We hope you'l pardon what you can't commend,
> Not to displeasure you is our utmost end,
> We treat you at our Modesties expence,
> Desire to please shou'd never give offence,
> For you we expose ourselves upon the stage,
> T'is a bold thing you'l say in a reforming age,
> But now I think on't better I've been told,
> He that wou'd make his fortune must be bold,
> Of merit take a drachm, of sense one grain,
> A pound of powder, with a Gauntie Mein,
> And much assurance mixt; a single dose
> Will do the bus'ness; let what will oppose
> You need not fear; secure to gain the prize,
> Tis a Probatum Recipe to rise;
> If what my Doctor says be true—why then
> We ought to practise now against more men,
> But t'is with the same fear that we begin,
> As he that first attempts to learn to swim,
> He tries in's depth, then farther does proceed
> And fear of sinking, makes him sink indeed.
> To shun his fate to'th Ladies we resort,
> By your fair hands held up we can want no support.

These verses suggest that play-acting, at least for these boys, was a novelty. They also indicate an easy poetic facility on the part of the author, Baggs, who was almost certainly only about eleven or twelve years old, playing, as he did, the female lead and not reaching the top of the school until 1701. The youth of the cast in general was emphasized in Reuse's Epilogue:

> To act Mens parts, so young, may seem a Crime
> We ask your pardon for it, and in time
> We hope to be like them, to learn and know

> The affairs of State and War, like Scipio.
> And when our country wants our aid, we all
> Will do the office of an Hannibal;
> (But since our wars are ceast) let us approve
> Great Massinissa's noble passion, Love!
> And Sophonisba's flame, twas kind in her
> To take the draught her husband did prepare
> And just in him to free her from the doom
> And punishment of proud and haughty Rome:
> Rosalinda's Charms overcame our Hannibal;
> Her courage and her love commanded all.
> She pitied prince Massina, but too late;
> Love not return'd, is certain cause of fate;
> Thus we, tho' Young, but yet to Love inclin'd,
> Shall be unhappy too unless you're kind:
> Ladies believe us then and think us true,
> And each shall a Massina be for you:
> Use us but tenderly in your commands,
> Forty to one, we mend upon your hands.
> If our Endeavours please, we have our end,
> Pardon our youth, and as we grow wel mend,
> Give us one clap, to shew you are our Friend.

Whether or not the *double entendres* were deliberate or effective, the self-regarding nature of this piece speaks of a self-confidence and social ease appropriate to Bryan's increasingly affluent establishment the more remarkable as the performers were all so youthful, Capel Billingsby who delivered this speech and played Hannibal, being at most fifteen. Of the rest of the cast whose ages can be discovered, they ranged from the oldest, like Billingsby, of about fourteen or fifteen, down to eight or nine. Yet their sense of position is marked, with the references to aspirations in 'State and War', military service, and, perhaps, to the Treaty of Ryswick (10 September 1697) in the phrase 'But since our wars are ceast'. It was appropriate, perhaps, that the *jeune premier* part of Massinissa was taken by the eleven-year-old John Cholmley from Yorkshire, who later served as an officer under Marlborough in the Low Countries, rising to become a colonel in the Sixteenth Foot Regiment (1717). The future careers of the rest of the cast confirm both the widening social and professional embrace of the school and the continuing local basis for recruitment. Although only two, possibly four, of the cast were 'foreigners', those from within the parish spanned the hierarchy from the well-to-do Capel and Arthur Billingsby or Drope Haly, all of Stanmore, who proceeded to university and Inns of Court, to John Hooker, son of a Harrow ironmonger who worked his way through Cambridge with financial help from the governors and who, after graduating as eighteenth Wrangler in 1705, returned to Harrow as Usher (1705–21) and took Holy Orders. By contrast, William Bucknall, of nearby Oxhey in Hertfordshire, and one

Buckley represented London commercial wealth, Bucknall becoming a governor of the school (1715–42). Of the cast of fourteen, nine can be indentified and of them at least six, and probably all, went on to university.

One figure likely to have watched this tyro production of *Sophonisba* was the Usher, Thomas Robinson, already in his fourth decade in post, assistant to five Head Masters and witness to the establishment of Harrow as a public school. Robinson was a member of All Souls College, Oxford, although it had taken him the unusually long time of ten years from admission to his BA, probably a sign of relative poverty, especially as he never progessed to MA.[56] He may have been a local poor scholar, possibly even an old boy; the name Robinson appears on the Hill, one Goody Robinson being the Dame for Harrow itself in the 1660s.[57] His ability to pay for his BA in March 1665 may have been consequent on his appointment as Usher, which came into effect in May 1665 and was formally confirmed in June that year.[58] He may have been an answer to urgent prayers. After the departure of the elusive Bamford, a Mr Blithe appears in the accounts as Usher for the remainder of 1662, but vanishes thereafter.[59] Whether out of piety or necessity, Robinson proved a devoted servant of the school. Living, perforce modestly, in the Usher's chamber in the schoolhouse, Robinson soon took on responsibility for overseeing all repairs and decoration to the building, a sensible arrangement given the removal of the Master to grander accommodation elsewhere, at least under Horne from 1669.[60] In addition, from at least the 1670s Robinson became the unofficial clerk to the governors, keeping the account book, witnessing leases, and holding deeds during a lawsuit over the application of the Road Trust income. He may even have been responsible for the more businesslike audit records from 1672.[61]

From his post of Usher, Robinson evidently made a comfortable, although not lavish income. As has been seen, he probably successfully enforced the 1665 agreement with the governors that he would receive ten shillings for each foreigner against a reluctant Jonson.[62] By the 1670s this could have been worth about £40 a year to him. From the start, he also earned £6 13s. 4d. for teaching the 'pettyes' or junior free scholars, to write.[63] Indeed, given the age of many Harrovians and the situation after he retired, it is likely that he was in charge of the larger portion of the school, the First and Second Forms that constituted the Lower School. From the foreigners therein he may also have derived fees for teaching to write. Certainly,

[56] Gun, *Harrow School Register*, 156. [57] HSR V, fos. 135, 138, etc.
[58] HSR III, fo. 21. [59] HSR V, fo. 130.
[60] Ibid., fos. 160, 168, 176, 182, 187, 204, 211, 218, 224, 242, 269, 282, 293.
[61] Ibid., fo. 225 (paid for entering accounts 1679), HSR 277, 289, 290, 304, 315, 322, HSR III, fo. 64, for the 1692 Road Trust case deeds in Robinson's custody. Robinson's increased involvement in gubernatorial and bursarial business seems to coincide with the arrival of Horne, testimony perhaps to that Head Master's sense of elevated status. [62] Ibid., fos. 21, 23.
[63] Ibid., fo. 22, HSR V, fo. 198 (1674/5) for the word 'pettyes'.

by the 1690s Robinson was able to invest in property by leasing three tenements from the governors at £3 a year and by purchasing two tenements for £46 2s. in 1697.⁶⁴

Yet Robinson represented the old order that Bryan wished to transcend, one rooted in the locality, as modest in ambition as in origin. The Head Master's victory in 1699 over the Usher symbolized the change.⁶⁵ There was to be no equality between the two; the Master's complete authority over the whole school was reaffirmed, perhaps a necessary injunction in the face of Robinson's entrenched position in charge of the Lower School. If Bryan had wished to ease his ageing Usher out, he may have achieved his purpose, as Robinson resigned a year later, perhaps when confronted with fresh financial terms consequent on the 1699 decision.⁶⁶ It may be no coincidence that from 1700 Bryan felt able to do without a second income from a parish, his troublesome independent senior Usher's removal allowing him to increase his share of the profits from the foreigners.⁶⁷ That Robinson opposed Bryan's insistence on sovereignty is clear from the appeal to the governors in 1698 that produced the statement of policy the following year. None the less, the governors, one of whom—Edmund Waldo—was an old pupil of his, bore Robinson no ill will: he continued to witness leases after retirement, no doubt a reflection on his expertise in their affairs amassed over a generation. He remained a tenant of the Trust until his death in 1714 almost half a century since the governors had paid £2 10s. 6d. for 'bringing the Usher from Oxford'.⁶⁸

The departure of Robinson—the first of Harrow's legion of Mr Chips—in 1700 marked an end to an interim stage in the consolidation of the school's status, one symbolically confirmed the following year by the death of the governor William Fenn, a barrister and local man who had been a boy at school under Head Master Hide in the 1640s.⁶⁹ Now Bryan could enhance his and his school's status by the appointment of Ushers more conducive to his project, John Le Hunte from Eton and King's, via a teaching post in Wisbech (1700–5), his (and Robinson's) old pupil John Hooker (1705–21), and, after falling out with Hooker over his financial cut, James Cox, the curate from Pinner, a graduate of Merton College, Oxford and, no doubt using his family connections, a rising figure on the London clerical scene.⁷⁰ All these were—as their predecessors had not been—MAs, men of breeding or academic distinction well able to cope with, as the governors put it in 1721, 'the great number of foreigners' now in the school.⁷¹ Bryan's final choice, however, to whom in a sense he bequeathed his school as well as his daughter, proved a less than trustworthy guardian of his legacy.

---

⁶⁴ HSR 308, 309, 317, HSR V, 315.
⁶⁵ Ibid., fo. 71.   ⁶⁶ Ibid., fo. 73.   ⁶⁷ Gun, *Harrow School Register*, 153.
⁶⁸ HSR 322, HSR V, fo. 141 (1665/6 account), HSR VII, fo. 14 (1713/14 account: his rent does not appear in the accounts for 1714/15).
⁶⁹ HSR I, fo. 25ʳ; Gun, *Harrow School Register*, 9.
⁷⁰ Gun, *Harrow School Register*, 156.   ⁷¹ HSR III, fo. 114.

JAMES COX

Head Master Cox is the black sheep of Harrow's past. Here is no flawed, tragic figure like Vaughan or frustrated failure like Wordsworth. He lurks in the shadows, the man who 'nearly ruined the school', about whom 'there is little good to be said', whose 'irregular habits' and 'evil ways' 'destroyed' 'much of Bryan's good work'. In the providential view of Harrow School, implicit in the works of Thornton, Lascelles, and Laborde, the school's manifest destiny and progress to its allotted 'place on the roll of fame' was obscured and interrupted by 'this most untoward event'.[72]

The factual basis for such ululation is less overwhelming, depending largely on the circumstances of Cox's dismissal in 1746. Yet Cox had ruled for sixteen years without the governors obviously objecting to his behaviour. Two governors at least, William Bucknall and Peter Waldo, had the confidence to entrust sons to Cox's care in the 1730s, although it must be said both were themselves Old Harrovians, among the earliest of what became and remains the cornerstone of the school's survival, 'Harrow families'.[73] The Head Master himself came from a respectable clerical family and, after Merton College, Oxford, took his MA to Pinner as Curate in 1716, being in effect curate to the Vicar of Harrow—Humphrey Henchman, another Merton man.[74] Appointed Usher in January 1722 Cox soon became the Head Master's son-in-law, the first Usher to be allowed to marry. He also held a 'lectureship' in London, which, on election in 1730 to replace Bryan, he promised to relinquish so as to 'apply himself strictly and solely to the instructing the Boys and care of the school'.[75] His own academic status and that of the school were recognized by his receipt of an Oxford DD in 1731. It is clear from the Minutes of the election meeting that Cox's succession had already been arranged and had received the express approval of four of the governors involved: Chandos, Rushout, Graham, and Bucknall although a fifth, OH Francis Herne, may have dissented.[76] Until the 1740s, at least, the governors' main concern was with the declining numbers of Free Scholars. In 1737 they asked Cox to produce an annual list and in 1739 agreed to increase the value of the Oxford and Cambridge exhibitions for Free Scholars.[77] That their numbers were declining (1738: 13, 1739: 14, 1740: 11) and were, even so, perhaps inflated by the children of affluent locals, such as Cox

---

[72] Thornton, *Harrow School*, 115–16; Howson and Townsend Warner, *Harrow School* (in chapter by Lascelles on the early Heads), 59; Laborde, *Harrow School*, 37.

[73] Gun, *Harrow School Register* 5, 28.

[74] Ibid., 153; Done Bushell, *Octocentenary Tracts*, ix. 21 and n. 2 for Henchman.

[75] HSR III, fos. 115, 126, HSR I, fo. 10^r (marriage waiver), 10^v (election as Head).

[76] The Minute Book entry of the election is witnessed by Chandos, Graham, and Rushout, with Bucknall sending his approval by letter to Rushout, later confirmed by hand in the Minute Book a year later (HSR III, fo. 126). The Order Book, however, lists Herne as having attended the election but not as having signed his approval. He does not appear in the Minute Book record.

[77] HSR III, fos. 130, 132.

himself or Bucknall, could be read as a sign of Harrow's success in providing for foreigners and the growing gulf between what the elitist curriculum the school offered and the accomplishments and education desired by the parishioners.[78] Under Cox the Ushers continued to be MAs, instead of the statutorily required BAs. That his third Usher, William Saunders (1743–7), was a former pupil may suggest a cosiness in which the habits of the Head Master could deteriorate without challenge. Saunders had been a foreigner but had relied on a Founder's Exhibition to gain his MA from Wadham College, Oxford.[79] However, his appointment by the governors may have owed more to his being a connection of the Vicar (himself a former Usher), Francis Saunders. It was surely another sign of the increasingly elevated self-image of the school that William Charles and William Saunders were appointed not just as Ushers but as Under Masters, confirming the borrowing from Eton.[80]

There survives from Cox's Head Mastership the first direct glimpse into life at Harrow from a boy's perspective which, among other things, exposes how little of the actual experience of school life and even the school's structure has been left in the official records. Thomas Barrett, later Barrett-Lennard and seventeenth Lord Dacre (1755), was at Harrow in Cox's early years. Born in 1717, by March 1732 he was describing himself in a letter from Harrow to his aunt and guardian as 'an old Border' (*sic*), one whose seniority, he felt, should have protected him from slights given by masters. This letter complains of the treatment Barrett had received from one Mr Weston who certainly taught Barrett mathematics and was probably his housemaster. Weston had refused to take Barrett on a field trip to teach 'the Gentlemen . . . to measure the ground' because he suspected him of wishing 'only . . . to be idle'. In revenge at this insulting and, so he insisted, false insinuation, Barrett asked his aunt to relieve him of being taught maths by Weston, urging her, revealingly, not to be 'mov'd by Weston's fawning and funning, who cares no more for you nor I than what money he can make off us'. On an earlier occasion, Weston had apparently entertained Barrett's aunt poorly, serving 'old heartychocks' and putting her up 'with frowsy Bet Rowsan to be devour'd by Buggs'. If his aunt complied with his request, Barrett assured her, he would not lose by it as he had already, unknown to Weston, begun taking maths lessons from a Mr Evans. He also, as earnest of his sincerity, promised to 'take double pains in Latin and everything else'.[81]

Thomas Barrett's self-pity, self-absorption, aristocratic contempt for masters, and elaborately acute sensitivity to his own hierarchical status is echoed in countless such letters over the next two and a half centuries, a form of writing that occasionally even approached a literary genre of its own when practised by such as Lord Byron seventy years later. Aside from adolescent petulance, Barrett indicates a school where subjects beyond the classical curriculum flourished, taught by

---

[78] Ibid., fos. 131, 132, 134.
[79] Gun, *Harrow School Register*, 28, 156.
[80] HSR III, fos. 80, 136.
[81] Barrett-Lennard, *An Account*, 579.

assistant masters evidently closely concerned with the financial aspects of their profession but yet who were socially acceptable as hosts to the aristocratic parents and guardians of their pupils. This suggests that the permission granted Bryan in 1721 to appoint a formal assistant was only part of the story.[82] What is more, Barrett takes this world and his situation in it for granted. Harrow was an established public school.

Confirmation of the insights provided by Barrett's experiences is suggested by the quality of his contemporaries. Cox's Harrovians were as well connected as Bryan's. This may, of course, represent an accident of evidence. For instance, more names of winners and participants in the Silver Arrow competition survive from 1731 than for previous years. This, however, may itself reflect the greater social status of the competition itself, attracting more public (i.e. London Society) notice. By 1746 a constable was employed to supervise 'Arrowday', as it was called.[83] Within the school, competitors vied with each other, as at the Eton Montem, in dressing up, the 1739 winner, fifteen-year-old John Jacob, being praised for having the 'genteelest' costume.[84]

In its archaic ostentation, the Silver Arrow contests well suited the aspirations of the entrants. Under Cox, Harrovians came from Ireland, Scotland, Wales, and all parts of England from Lancashire to Cornwall.[85] Robert Orme (c.1740), later prominent in the East India Company's administration of Madras and instrumental in appointing Robert Clive to command the Company's army, as well as writing the history of English involvement in 'Hindustan', was born at Travancore in India. Cox's lists are littered with sons of county gentlemen and London merchants, who returned to their shires or counting houses, often via the universities, or joined the legal, clerical, or military professions, although in the small Cox sample there appear to be fewer clergy than previously, a sign of changing social status and greater affluence. From the peerage, apart from Barrett, heir to the Dacre title, there was, c.1740, the son of the first Viscount Barrington. Daines Barrington became a lawyer, FRS, and FRSA and, in later life, encouraged Gilbert White to write his *Natural History of Selbourne*. In 1742 James Bruce, the African traveller and self-publicist, arrived with his step-uncle William Graham and his cousin William Hamilton, for forty years an MP (1754–96) for a series of Pocket and Rotten Boroughs, including the notorious Old Sarum, prominent in governing Ireland and notorious as 'Single Speech Hamilton', after his one memorable political intervention, his maiden speech in 1755. One early pupil, Brown, was the son of a commander of an East Indiaman. Another, the Silver Arrow winner in 1740, Bernard Hale, later a general (1793), was the son of a Baron of the Exchequer. Mervyn Archdall (c.1740) became a prominent Irish antiquarian. Thomas

---

[82] HSR III, fo. 115.   [83] HSR VII, fo. 136.

[84] Gun, *Harrow School Register*, 15 based on MS letters of Molly Downes (1738) and John Jacob himself: Harrow Archives, Materials Relating to Boys, Box I (unlisted).

[85] For biographical details see Gun and the relevant entries in the *DNB*.

Winslow from Gloucestershire retains the distinction of being the only winner of the Silver Arrow (in 1741) to receive a Founder's Exhibition, at University College, Oxford, a witness to the breadth, if not depth, of the education provided by Dr Cox. Family and professional links among parents and old boys continued to support local ties in providing scholars for Cox's school. Indeed, by the 1740s it is hard to describe Harrow as a local school at all, still less one that catered for the poor of the parish, with whom Cox's closest contact was through his *ex officio* position as Usher and Master, and as a Trustee of the Poor House.[86]

Despite these appearances of prosperity and social climbing, by the mid-1740s something had gone wrong with the school and, it appears, it was Cox. Although impossible to substantiate, it has been claimed repeatedly that numbers at the school fell by 1746 to forty.[87] This may be an exaggeration. None the less, if accepted, this decline from Bryan's peak of around 140 represents a loss of about 70 per cent. This compares with the two subsequent mid-century collapses in numbers, to fewer than seventy in 1844 and fewer than 300 during the Second World War—falls respectively of about 75 per cent and about 50 per cent from immediately previous highs. It is likely the governors were concerned about numbers as early as 1739. In 1737 their anxiety over Free Scholars may have been prompted by a traditional desire, tempered by many legal challenges, to follow the Founder's statutes. However, the additional sums added to the Founder's Exhibitions in 1739, while fitting the reforms to their granting made in 1737, in extending the increased funds to all Harrovians, including foreigners, may speak of diminished numbers proceeding to university and a decline in the school in general.[88]

Cox's running of the school does not appear on the surface to have differed in essence from his predecessor's. He secured a Founder's Exhibition at Balliol for his son James in 1741, this being very much in the nepotist tradition of the governors between 1724 and 1737.[89] That Cox is not mentioned in the Governors' Minutes, nor appears as witness to any of their leases after 1741, may or may not be significant. After 1740, however, he no longer reported the numbers of Free Scholars. Perhaps gubernatorial vigilance slackened. Not only did Chandos retire in 1740, to be succeeded by his dissolute son (who was reputed to have purchased his mistress, later second wife, from her husband 'with a halter round her neck' but more certainly lost most of his inheritance), but, of the six governors of 1730, only one, Rushout, remained in 1746.[90] There was also an unusually rapid turnover of

---

[86] e.g. HSR 402, for the lease of 1726, with, alongside the Head Master Bryan and Vicar Henchman, Cox, a Trustee, as Usher.

[87] Thornton is the source, referring in turn rather vaguely to 'the records of Archdeacon Thackeray's family' (p. 121 n.).

[88] HSR III, fo. 132.   [89] Ibid., fo. 134.

[90] Ibid., fo. 133 for the exchange of letters on Chandos' retirement (the duke's is printed by Thornton, *Harrow School*, 117). For the second duke see *Complete Peerage*, iii. 131–2 and n. f; Gun, *Harrow School Register*, 161–2.

Ushers, three in a decade and a half: Francis and William Saunders and William Charles (1732–43). That William Saunders was less than ideal may be suggested by his early departure only a year after Cox in 1747. Although this may have represented little more than a positive new policy by Head Master Thackeray, it may cast retrospective light on another potential weakness of Cox's rule. Neither he nor his Ushers had any Eton connections. It is unlikely to have been coincidence that Harrow's numbers rose sharply under Thackeray, from Eton, and his Ushers, William Cox (Eton and King's) and William Prior (Eton and Pembroke, Oxford).[91]

That Cox failed to strike a suitably imposing figure is perhaps witnessed by the widely circulated tradition that depicts him lounging in an armchair in the School Yard, sustained by a pint pot of beer, regularly replenished by a servant from the Anchor pub next door, smoking a long clay pipe of the sort then coming into fashion.[92] However, the only piece of hard evidence is contained in the governors' resolution of 26 April 1746:

Whereas the Rev. Dr. James Cox Master of the Free Grammar School has for a great while last past lived a disorderly, drunken, idle life and neglected the care of the school by which means it is very much decreased, and did, on or about Easter week (Easter was 30 March) abscond upon account of his great Extravagance and running in debt more than he was able to pay, therefore for these his misdoings we are of the opinion that he shall be displaced from being Schoolmaster and Declare the place to be void.[93]

If school numbers had suddenly fallen, Cox could easily have found himself financially embarrassed. He would not be the last notorious debtor on the staff; nor the last to flee creditors. He had leased and bought land in and around Harrow Town in his palmy days, but his lack of private means may have explained his need to combine the Ushership with a London 'lectureship' before 1730.[94] Cox's career shows how risky being Head Master could be if times were bad. To a modern eye, familiar with the much publicized symptoms of stress, Cox's retreat into sloth and alcohol suggests depression. Again, he would not be the last Head to suffer in this way and as a consequence to weaken public perception of the school. Yet he seems to have recovered, spending the last years of his life until his death in 1759 at Harrow, where he was buried. His drinking and his debts had not wholly incapacitated him even in 1746. He clearly fought his ejection, costing the governors fees of £15 6s. to get him out. Despite not paying his peppercorn rent, he was able to negotiate with the governors a payment of £50 'by Appraisement', presumably for whatever improvements he had made to the Head Master's House.[95]

Cox vacated the Head Master's chair under a cloud that cast a shadow over the future of the school. That the storm passed so quickly causing so little lasting

[91] HSR III, fo. 143 (Saunders' resignation), Gun, *Harrow School Register*, 156.
[92] Thornton, *Harrow School*, 116; Druett, *Harrow*, 86.
[93] HSR III, fos. 140–1. Cf. ibid., fo. 142.   [94] Ibid., fo. 127.
[95] HSR VII, fos. 134, 135, 136, 137.

damage suggests that the crisis had been brief and personal rather than systemic or of long gestation. Harrow did not go the way of Wellingborough or Coventry, local sixteenth-century Grammar Schools that were fast becoming sinecures for their Heads.[96] It did not revert to being a wholly local and domestic school, as did others. Harrow remained a school to which the prosperous and influential governors could attract a schoolmaster of eminence and experience in the hope that he could, in turn, secure pupils of substance and quality. This was not the work of providence, but of hard-headed governors and entrepreneurial Head Masters. Paradoxically, the Cox fiasco threw into sharp relief just how firm were the foundations of the Public School established by Horne, Bolton, and Bryan. By 1729 old boys were meeting for the 'Anniversary Feast of the Gentlemen Educated at HARROW SCHOOL', ticket-only affairs held regularly in taverns around the Temple and Strand in London, demonstrations of a lingering corporate identity that marked as clearly as anything the arrival of the school as an established institution—not least for the former pupils themselves.[97]

[96] Carlisle, *Grammar Schools*, ii. 226–31, 646–53.
[97] Harrow Archives MS 11D/N1/E (in box marked 'Press Cuttings'), from *The Daily Post-Boy*, Thursday, 8 Jan. 1729 (*sic*: *recte* 1730). Cf. *The Daily Advertiser*, 22 Feb. 1749, for that year's 'Harrow School Feast'.

Part III

The *Ancien Régime*, 1746–1844

7

THE CLASSICAL SCHOOL, 1746–1785

The arrival of Thomas Thackeray as Head Master in the Summer of 1746 marks an epoch in the history of Harrow School. Within a generation, the school acquired characteristics of a national institution, patronized by the aristocratic and wealthy from all corners of the British Empire, old and new, with a reputation for scholarship second to none and, no less significant, a self-conscious *esprit de corps* amongst pupils, staff, and old boys that, in glamorizing the past, secured the future. Thackeray and his two successors created a network of influential individuals and families disposed to regard Harrow as important to their own success and esteem thus lending the school a public reputation surpassing Westminster's and competing with Eton's as a seminary for the ruling classes in society, the state, and the professions. The extravagant actor-manager Tate Wilkinson, forty years later, remembered the standing of his old school when he arrived in November 1752 as 'second in this kingdom'.[1]

Harrow was established as fashionable. More than that, it began to display signs of permanent prominence through the invention and accretion of nostalgia. It is no coincidence that it is from Thackeray's and Sumner's years that the first detailed and lasting stories of schoolboy heroics and school heroes come. Whatever earlier Harrovians had achieved in later life, their schooldays left little personal record. By contrast, from the 1740s the place of Harrow in the lives of the famous old boys is evident and emphasized in what has appeared to many as Harrow's Golden Age. The *genius loci* was loudly proclaimed, encouraging one famous old boy, Sheridan (1762–8), to return to live there and another, William Jones (1753–63), to dream of doing so.[2] Not only did mid-eighteenth-century Harrow leave more records of school experience than all previous periods of its history

---

[1] T. Wilkinson, *Memoirs*, 4 vols. (York, 1790), i. 39.
[2] Sheridan rented The Grove from 1781. For Jones's supposed desire to retire to the Hill see Thornton, *Harrow School*, 154 and reference in n. 1, and R. Ackermann, *History of the Free School at Harrow* (London, 1816), p. 36.

combined, it also witnessed the birth of that most lasting and adhesive tradition, the cult of the school, with votaries indulging in smug self-importance and self-satisfaction as pupils and sentimental reminiscence as old boys. Regular reunion dinners continued to be held and alumni started to send their own sons and grandsons to their *alma mater* in large numbers.[3] In 1771 William Bennet (*c*.1757–63) wrote of the 'Genius of the school' waiting for a new Head Master.[4] In 1773 William Jones was able to joke to his former pupil, Lord Althorp (1769–75), about another Harrovian, Lord Folkestone (before 1764–*c*. 1766) speaking in the House of Commons 'for the honour of Harrow School'. Jones himself had composed a youthful Greek Oration in memory of John Lyon.[5] As for Lord Folkestone, Jacob Bouverie, he was the first of a dynasty of Harrovians that persisted in the late twentieth century, one of over forty families that can claim representatives as Harrovians in both the eighteenth and twentieth centuries.

These developments were less a consequence of radical changes to the system of schooling or direction of policy within Harrow than of altered external political, social, and cultural circumstances. It is clear from the long and loud debates amongst the higher reaches of society about the best manner of rearing children, led by such influential pundits as John Locke, that children were increasingly regarded as more than unformed adults, empty, even disposable, vessels into which knowledge and from which original sin were to be beaten with equal and indiscriminate savagery. Expressions of parental affection and sentiment became increasingly prominent, although the contrast with the supposed indifference of earlier generations to their offspring can be exaggerated. Coupled with the growing habit, already identified, of aristocrats sending children—almost exclusively sons—away to school, this trend towards more openly sentimental, individual concern led to closer attention to the schooling on offer which, in turn, provided those institutions with new potential for growth—or decline.

Interest in public schooling was also sustained by the shifting of boundaries between social classes consequent on the relative political stability and economic prosperity of mid-eighteenth-century Britain. Wealth unlocked doors. None the less, acceptance in the more elevated circles found beyond depended upon adoption of elite, aristocratic customs as money encroached on land and blood. Public

---

[3] Gun, *Harrow School Register*, p. xiii and *passim* for details of old alumni. The correspondence of Parr and Jones is littered with references to Harrow dinners from the 1760s. James Bruce, the explorer, after his return to England in 1773 cherished an ambition to be one of the stewards at the annual Harrow dinners. He was finally proposed, only to be denied by death, in 1794: Ackermann, *History*, 32–3. Cf. above p. 93 for the annual dinners, 1730–49.

[4] J. Johnstone, *The Works of Samuel Parr LLD*, 8 vols. (London, 1828), i. 53.

[5] G. Cannon (ed.), *The Letters of Sir William Jones*, 2 vols. (Oxford, 1970), i. 120, no. 68 (16 Feb. 1773). Cf. ibid., 82, no. 45 (2 Mar. 1771) for reference to the 'Harrow Feast'; John Shore, first Baron Teignmouth, *Memoirs of the Life, Writings and Correspondence of Sir William Jones* (London, 1804), p. 35, Teignmouth, himself an OH, describing Lyon in a sentimental tone familiar to successive generations of alumni as 'an honest yeoman'; the truth of the adjective was and remains unknowable.

schools became engines of social mobility because they guarded exclusive education. This self-conscious distinctiveness matched the increasingly fashionable operation of the social and professional elites themselves around overt symbols and rituals of identity and fraternity, from dining and drinking clubs to Freemasonry, status expressed by membership of defined, exclusive groups from 'The Club' of Dr Johnson's circle (1764) to Old Etonian and Old Harrovian dinners.

The social was inseparable from the academic. A classical education was a touchstone of class not intellect or learning and as such it appealed to the new capitalists and plutocrats of City and trading Empire. Social layers may have been porous, but the culture within each could be sharply distinctive.[6] In this process the universities were closely allied to public schools. While economic opportunity widened exponentially, educational scope contracted. Numbers of undergraduates admitted at Oxford declined by 40 per cent between the 1660s and 1750s, while the percentage of aristocratic or gentry students rose from 70 per cent c.1710 to over 80 per cent in 1760 and almost 100 per cent by 1800.[7] Even the prospect of becoming a sizar, i.e. act as a servant to pay for college fees, which had been the path for so many local Harrovians in the previous century, was anathema to the ambitious son of the Harrow apothecary, Samuel Parr (1752–61).[8] Governors and Head Masters of Harrow had been assiduous in cultivating the universities since the previous century, not least by the system of Lyon exhibitions, and so were well placed to identify themselves with this increasingly aristocratic process of education.

By 1759 the governors were referring to pupils as 'young gentlemen', instead of, as had been invariable practice, scholars.[9] As such, these aspirant rulers required the trappings of their class besides the smattering of classical allusion afforded by the public school curriculum. Thus at Harrow and elsewhere, French, maths, dancing, drawing (although not apparently before 1769), and fencing became standard additions to the formal school work and the classics themselves were, in the hands of Dr Sumner, explicitly related to future public life, notably in political philosophy and oratory.[10]

By becoming nurseries for the actual or aspiring aristocracy, the mercantile plutocrats and the successful professionals of law and medicine, public schools established a pre-eminence in education unchallenged until internal contradictions and external calumny forced reform in the middle of the nineteenth century. This

---

[6] Cf. J. Lawson and H. Silver, *A Social History of Education in England* (London, 1973), pp. 116–17.

[7] R. O'Day, *Education and Society, 1500–1800* (London, 1982), pp. 196–7, 204.

[8] Johnstone, *Parr*, i. 20, 30, 32; W. Field, *Memoirs of the Life, Writings and Opinions of the Rev. Samuel Parr LLD*, 2 vols. (London, 1828), i. 32. [9] HSR III, fo. 153ᵛ.

[10] See the accounts for Philip Francis in 1779: Gun, *Harrow School Register*, p. xix; Teignmouth, *Jones*, 19 (for French and maths under Thackeray); for the lack of drawing in 1769 see M. E. Ingram, *Leaves from a Family Tree* (Hull, 1951), pp. 85–6; for the presence of a drawing master. J. A. Greese, in 1773, see letter of Lord Althorp, 4 Apr. 1773, cited by J. S. Golland, Interim List of Amendments to Gun's Register, Harrow School MS, fo. 4; for Sumner's use of classics see Field, *Parr*, i. 55; T. Maurice, *Memoirs of the Author of Indian Antiquities*, i (London, 1819), p. 62.

culmination of developments beginning as far back as the 1660s had one significant local effect on Harrow, the effective exclusion of 'free boys' of the Parish. The emotions of William Peachey, a Free Scholar who was in the Phaedrus Class of the Lower School in 1770 and 1771, can only be imagined, surrounded as he was in his own form by a son of a former chancellor of the Exchequer, William Townsend, and others who went on to become MPs and colonial rulers.[11] Peachey stayed in Harrow to ply his trade as a shoemaker and part-time school porter. Quite why he needed Latin may well have remained a mystery to him.

More typical, perhaps, was the experience of the egregious Samuel Parr whose combination of precocity, loquacity, vanity, and longevity single-handedly provided much of the anecdotal substance of the mythology surrounding Harrow of the 1750s to 1770s. Sometimes called 'the Great Home Boarder' (i.e. day boy), Parr was at school from the age of five to fourteen, went to Emmanuel College, Cambridge in 1765, escaping an abortive apprenticeship in the family business. He returned to Harrow as an assistant master without a degree aged 20 in 1767 after being financially embarrassed at Cambridge following the death of his father, the Harrow apothecary, in 1766. On the surface this was a story of a poor scholar, a Jude the Obscure with good connections. In fact he was more typical of contemporary Harrow than merely his ability to befriend prominent boarders. His stepmother, whose avarice largely contributed to his inability to finance a complete school or university education, was the daughter and granddaughter to two Harrow Head Masters, Cox and Bryan. One of Parr's father's brothers had been a scholar at Eton and a fellow of King's. Parr's first Head Master, Thackeray, had suggested that Samuel might follow a familiar Harrovian path to Eton and, 'if the boy deserves', to King's. Parr himself resisted the social stigma of applying to Emmanuel as a sizar.[12] Neither a yokel nor a bumpkin, nor yet a Peachey, Parr was a freeholder (presumably inheriting his father's house after 1766), eligible to vote, a right he enthusiastically if injudiciously exercised on behalf of John Wilkes in the riotous Middlesex by-election in December 1768.[13] Such a 'poor boy' could hold his own with the gentry, even if he had no use for the dancing or fencing, well capable of brawling with Lord Mount Stuart, heir to the future Prime Minister Lord Bute, to protect a cat.[14]

In general, however, direct local educational interest in the school was squeezed out more or less in direct proportion to the increase in local economic interest, as the 'young gentlemen' brought employment and profit to labourers, tradesmen, and shopkeepers. This did little to placate a vociferous and growing section of the

---

[11] G. Butler, *A Selection of the Lists of Harrow School MDCCLXX–MDCCCXXVI* (Peterborough, 1849), pp. 14, 23. Daniel Peachey, his father perhaps, was also the school porter and witnessed leases c.1770, and so was obviously literate: HSR 512, 514, 515, etc. Thornton, *Harrow School*, 366 confuses the two.   [12] Johnstone, *Parr*, i. 11–37; Field, *Parr*, i. 4–16.

[13] Johnstone, *Parr*, viii. 234–5 for David Roderick's vivid account of Parr's vote in 1768.

[14] Ibid., i. 18.

parish community, the more prosperous part, who objected to the way the income from the Lyon Trusts was expended, with regard to both the roads and the school. It was a battle fought with tenacity from the suit brought against the governors by the new Edgware Road turnpike commissioners in the 1750s to the reforms of 1868–76, with its climax the fierce legal battle that was concluded by the judgment of the Master of the Rolls in 1810.[15] As the conflict applied to the school, it did no more than reflect the deliberate decision of the governors reaffirmed at every election to the Head Mastership. By insisting on the social contacts as well as classical attainments of the men they elected, the governors consciously excluded the interests of the 'poor scholars'. Their socially exclusive interpretation of the statutes—unsurprisingly preferred by the Master of the Rolls in 1810—allowed them to effect such a transformation with legality if not entirely with impunity.

There was one novel potential problem with creating a school for aristocrats and plutocrats. If the object of the exercise was to attract the children of the ruling classes and the purpose of the education to toughen them to face the competitive, cut-throat adult world, there were severe implications for discipline. In general, masters only exerted discipline within school or when a breach of the peace outside came to their attention, as for example when Dr Sumner flogged William Bird for trespassing on the field next to the school playing ground.[16] Only the Head and Usher had formal authority to beat.[17] Masters neither were nor did they see themselves as policemen or spies. The boys were left more or less to their own devices, hardly surprisingly as most of the grander pupils lived with their tutors in accommodation of their own hiring, sometimes on a lavish scale. Lord Althorp arrived at Harrow in 1769 'with a suite and attendance of such state as even at that time to be considered an intrusion upon the informity of school life'. He lived initially with his tutor, William Jones, one of the cleverest men of his generation and, until 1773 when he moved into the Head Master's house to board, rented a substantial property within a minute's walk of the school at 30 guineas a year.[18] His poor health and anxious parents may explain some of the princely aloofness. Elsewhere, a group of princelings, including the sons of the earls of Dartmouth and Radnor, lodged with the entrepreneurial Revd Dr Stephen Glasse in the Old House in the centre of Harrow, claiming immunity from normal school discipline, such as the regular call-overs in school. The bitterness of the battle fought over Sumner's ultimately successful attempts to bring Glasse's boarders under his authority and jurisdiction in 1768 testified to the independence of spirit of aristocratic Harrovians and their

---

[15] HSR 480–1 (1751–2), HSR III, fos. 150–1 (8 Apr. 1755); British Library Add. MS 29,254, fos. 44ᵛ–49ᵛ for the Chancery suit of 1810–11.

[16] Golland, Interim Amendments, 2. For Sumner's flogging in general see Maurice, *Memoirs*, i. 62.

[17] But Samuel Greg(g) complained that Parr, who was only one of the Head Master's assistants, had beaten him, Gun, *Harrow School Register*, 79.

[18] Ibid., 32; Cannon, *Letters of Jones*, i. 28–9, no. 16; Golland, Interim Amendments, 2.

parents.[19] Flogging for poor school exercises was one thing, no doubt to be applauded, but further limitations on a gentleman's life by a schoolmaster was far less congenial.

Such a semi-detached view towards discipline and authority was coupled with the extremely strong sense (and reality) of the boys' autonomous commonwealth, an aristocratic oligarchy within which complete freedom was considered a birthright but which stood implacably opposed to any challenge to their liberty (or licence) from below or above. Social snobbery was leavened by half-baked lessons in Greek and Roman history and political philosophy mixed, by Thackeray and Sumner at least, with vigorously promoted Whiggery, to produce potentially combustible material if the senior boys, as a group, felt slighted, ignored, or their perceived rights threatened. The result was that characteristic eighteenth-century public school phenomenon, the school rebellion. Most of the major schools experienced revolts in this period, most fought under the flag of preserving or defending rights and interests, a very Whiggish, unradical position: Winchester 1770, 1774, 1778, 1793; Eton 1768.[20] It may be taken as a sign of how far Harrow had exploited the aristocratic market for public school education that there were serious disturbances in 1771 and 1777. On both occasions the oligarchic pride of the boys was very much in evidence. In 1771 the petition to the governors objecting to their election of Heath as Head Master proclaimed loftily: 'as we (most of us) are in some degree independent of the foundation, whatever may be your opinions, we presume our inclinations ought to have some weight in determining your choice.'[21] The aggressive refusal of the governors to countenance this posturing led to serious unrest and considerable damage to property. In 1777 the issue was less dramatic, the timing of call-overs or bills, a regular source of tension under both Sumner and Heath. Again a petition was dispatched, this time to the Head Master, the key to the school stolen, and the Hill picketed. In the end, the boys consented to submit on condition that there were no expulsions. Indeed nobody was punished at all, signal witness to the power of the boys and the quality of their culture, indicative of which was the reaction of Dudley Ryder, the future Lord Harrowby, who had not stood out with his peers: 'I fear I have lost my character by having been so ready to submit.'[22] Pride and shame not obedience or guilt were the hallmarks of an aristocratic school, one weaned and fed on classics.

Whiggish insistence on the assumed liberties of the privileged was no less to the fore during wrangling between Heath and senior boys that ended the Silver Arrow

---

[19] For Glasse and his boarders see Thornton, *Harrow School*, 148–50; Johnstone, *Parr*, i. 57–8; Teignmouth, *Jones*, 26–7; Laborde, *Harrow School*, 39, 42.

[20] See e.g. E. C. Mack, *Public Schools and British Opinion, 1780–1860* (London, 1938), pp. 79–82.

[21] For Thomas Grimston's transcription of the petition in a letter to Sir Digby Legard, 15 Oct. 1771 see *Historical Manuscripts Commission. Report on the MSS of Lady du Cane* (London, 1905), pp. 275–6. For slightly different wording see Johnstone, *Parr*, i. 59–61.

[22] Harrow MS HM/D/2, Dudley Ryder to his father, Lord Harrowby, 1777.

The Classical School

competition in 1772. Whereas the Head Master saw the problem as one affecting his authority, at least one of the aspirant competitors, outraged at new rules insisting on their presence at school in the weeks before the contest, regarded himself as 'standing up for the Rights and Liberties of the Archers of Harrow . . . for our old customs and not patiently putting up with every encroachment'.[23]

The rebellions and the pupil culture that bred them provide backhanded compliments to the success of the school in the forty years after the flight of Dr Cox. Of this success there can be no doubt if measured either in the timeless currency of numbers or in the subtler assay of scholarship. Although numbers under Thackeray peaked at 130 and, by 1760 had, so Samuel Parr claimed, fallen back to eighty, he had established a nucleus of contacts and repute that formed the foundation of the startling increase that followed.[24] In Sumner's last year (1770–1) there were over 230 Harrovians and 242 in 1776, before a decline to 150 in 1785.[25] Two hundred was not reached again until 1799, the beginning of another surge in entries in the final plenitude of Dr Drury which reached its zenith in 1803 with 351. As impressive as sheer size was the nature of the entry. Already under Thackeray, the contours of the expansion were plain. Customers were British and Imperial, not just the aristocracy and landed gentry, but bankers and traders, the professional elite that was poised to rule India, North America, and the West Indies. With his scrupulously Whig credentials, in the years immediately after the '45 Thackeray was free to attract Scottish entrants in significant numbers; Gordons, Murrays, Frasers, as well as Lords Strathnaver and Mount Stuart. For his pains he was awarded a DD by Aberdeen University. Of even greater potential was the Irish connection Thackeray established—not only the sons of the earl of Massereene and the grandson of the earl of Granard (whose son had been at Harrow under Bryan), but gentry such as Robert Waller from County Tipperary or Richard Lytton and John Parnell from Queen's County. The further reaches of empire were represented under Thackeray too—John Law, son of a governor of Bombay, and John Lost from Jamaica.

In this geographic Embrace, Harrow, like its competitors, reflected the creation of the first British Empire and the consolidation of the political and hence social unity of the ruling classes of the British Isles. Harrow thus became both a national and an international school. Between 1760 and 1785 almost forty Harrovians can be identified as coming from the West Indies, the sons of planters, merchants, clergymen, and lawyers. There were a number of sons of those working and serving in or trading with India, making the careers of William Jones or John Shore in the subcontinent appear just part of the growing British diaspora of the eighteenth

---

[23] Ingram, *Leaves from a Family Tree*, 96–8 (pp. 97–8 for the quotation from Thomas Grimston's letter to his father). For the involvement of Philip Yorke, later third Earl of Hardwicke, see J. S. Golland, *Eighteenth Century Harrow* (typescript, priv. circulated, 1986), pp. 2–3, based on British Library Add. MSS 35377 and 35384.   [24] Thornton, *Harrow School*, 139; Johnstone *Parr*, i. 64.
[25] Butler, *Harrow Lists*, *passim*. For the details of Harrovians, unless otherwise stated, see Gun, *Harrow School Register*, *passim*.

century. The colonies of North America were represented by sons of governors of Massachusetts and New York, among others. There were some with even more exotic backgrounds: William Wrangham, son of a member of the council for St Helena; John Wilkes, nephew of the politician (whose illegitimate son was also at Harrow *c.*1769)[26] and son of the consul in Aleppo; Charles Imhoff, the German stepson of Warren Hastings; William Gomm, born in St Petersburg, son of an English merchant and diplomat domiciled there; and Francis Sapte, son of the foreign financial adviser to Frederick the Great.

Within the British Isles, the Scottish connection remained strongly aristocratic, including the son of the attainted Jacobite James Drummond, master of Strathallan, the future marquess of Abercorn and the earls of Erroll and Elgin (of Marbles fame). The relative paucity of Welshmen reflects the principality's poverty and lack of a social structure to mirror or match that of England. Very different was the Irish dimension. High Society in Dublin may have appeared both provincial and colonial, lacking both the independence of Edinburgh or the obscurity of, say, York, but it was prosperous, especially so in the boom of the mid-eighteenth century, possessed of a university of its own, and in close touch with mainland political and cultural interests and developments. The father of the most famous Irish Harrovian exemplifies this semi-detached relationship. Thomas Sheridan had a well-connected if maladroit clerical Irish schoolmaster as a father, but Jonathan Swift, disgruntled exiled Dean of St Patrick's, Dublin as a godfather. Thomas was educated at Westminster then Trinity College Dublin. In many respects he was equally at home on both sides of the Irish Sea. The choice of Harrow for his son Richard was also typical of how schools attracted pupils, being the result of a social encounter with Dr Sumner shortly before his appointment to Harrow in 1760 at which the elder Sheridan had been impressed by the schoolmaster's interest in rhetoric and oratory. Although ruined in 1754, Thomas Sheridan moved—if uneasily—in the highest literary circles and received a royal pension: hardly the 'poor player' of his son's snobbish tormentors at Harrow.[27]

The Sheridan experience indicates a particular feature of the Irish intake at Harrow in the mid-eighteenth century. Unlike the Scots, the Irish came from a wide section of affluent society. Forty Harrovians with parents living in Ireland have been identified entering the school between 1760 and 1785. Most came from the landed aristocracy and gentry and proceeded to English institutions—university, the law, or the army—before resuming their places in Irish society or staying in England, witnesses for an effective union among the elites of the Protestant Ascendancy long before any Act of Parliament. Thus Richard Martin of Galway, a noted

---

[26] For Wilkes's son, called undemonstratively John Smith, see Gun, *Harrow School Register*, 26. It is interesting that both of the main candidates in the 1768 Middlesex by-election had sons at Harrow.

[27] J. H. W. Morwood, *The Life and Works of Richard Brinsley Sheridan* (Edinburgh, 1985), pp. 2–8 for a concise account.

duellist and Irish MP both before and after 1801, was a co-founder of that most English of organizations, the RSPCA.[28] However, there were a sprinkling of those, like Sheridan, whose fathers may have been gentlemen who also worked for a living in the professions, but for whom, unlike the playwright–politician but more like his father, Harrow was only a stage in careers based in Ireland: Richard Chester, son of a Dublin attorney; Francis Hutcheson and the four Quin brothers, sons of Dublin physicians. All of these, as well as some others, proceeded from Harrow to Trinity, Dublin. That the use of Harrow—and indeed Eton, Westminster, etc.—as a finishing school or forcing house for the Irish upper classes was not entirely without risk was demonstrated by James Crosbie of County Kerry who was wrecked off the coast of Wales returning from the Christmas holidays, thereafter always spending the winter break in England.[29]

Most Harrovians came from England. Here, too, the balance reveals the sensitivity to social trends which lay—and lies—at the heart of a successful school. The nobility, as has been mentioned, begin to dominate the tone of the place, if not actual numbers: in the first surviving school list, of 1769/70, out of 236, less than 10 per cent were peers, heirs to peerages, or their siblings.[30] No less superior in their attitude to the rest of mankind were the country gentry, of whom a significant number went to Harrow. However, the mix was greater, with a marked presence of the children of directors of trading firms, such as the East India or Hudson Bay Companies, City merchants, and bankers. The important feature of the system was that by the end of their time at Harrow all boys were, as far as possible, ostensibly indistinguishable. The shared experience of dragooned academic and extracurricular uniformity of attitude deliberately smoothed away individual cultural idiosyncracies, even though activities outside the formroom remained highly personal.

The popularity of Harrow had a major and lasting effect on the structure of the school in the rapid extension of facilities for boarding and the increase in teaching staff. Apart from the very grand boys who set up their own establishments, supervised only by their private tutors and family retainers, it is likely that most, and certain that some of the masters, took in a few boarders each: the Writing Master Henry Reeves did so in the 1750s and 1760s; Joseph Drury did in the 1770s (including the future Prime Minister, Spencer Perceval).[31] In the 1760s Dr Glasse sought to cash in on the need for accommodation of an elevated nature. Much of the requirement was fulfilled, however, by a system of Dames' houses which had existed in some form for generations (and not, as most historians of the school have asserted, only from the end of Sumner's rule).[32] For the first time, some of them can

---

[28] Gun, *Harrow School Register*, 17.   [29] Ibid., 59.   [30] Butler, *Harrow Lists*, 8–16.
[31] Wilkinson, *Memoirs*, i. 43; Eland, *Shardloes Papers*, 76; D. Gray, *Spencer Perceval* (Manchester, 1963), p. 4; C. Drury, *Memoir of Rev. Joseph Drury DD, Annual Biography and Obituary* (1834), i. 9.
[32] Thornton, *Harrow School*, 151; Howson and Townsend Warner, *Harrow School*, 36; Laborde, *Harrow School*, 32, 174.

be named: in the 1750s Mrs King's and Mrs Hawkins'; in the 1760s and 1770s Mrs Crampton's; and Mrs Arnold's in the 1770s and 1780s.[33] Some of these establishments may have been quite extensive—Mrs Hawkins' house in 1757 boasting a schoolroom of its own and sufficient residents to resist an attack by boys from Thackeray's house to steal fireworks.[34] The Head Master continued to take in boarders, probably in some numbers: Sumner reluctantly had to direct Lord Grimston's son to Mrs Crampton's as he was full in 1769.[35] It was probably both for a greater measure of control as well as profit that Benjamin Heath built a large extension to the Head Master's house in 1772–4 which allowed him to accommodate between eighty and ninety boys. It cost him £1,000, only £200 of which would the governors, whose property it remained, reimburse.[36] Heath must have thought it a good investment; he certainly did everything he could to encourage boys such as Lords Althorp and Herbert to move from their separate private lodgings into his house.[37]

The circumstances of the boys were reflected in how they spent their times away from adult instruction. Some came to Harrow as scarcely more than infants, William Jones being only 7 in 1753; some, like James Powell, George Forbes, or Thomas Grimston, arrived after private boarding preparatory schools; some such as Thomas Grimston, delaying entrance until aged 16.[38] Conversely, many continued to use Harrow as a preparatory school for Eton, Westminster, or Charterhouse. Inevitably boys' pastimes suited their maturity and taste. What impresses is the diversity of activities in an age before the tyrannous ubiquity of games. There is something almost prelapsarian in the image of young Lord Althorp constructing an arbour in a corner of the playing field below the school yard in 1769.[39] In fact, it mirrored his tutor's own schooldays; in his first two years at Harrow, William Jones had divided his time between work 'and a little garden, the cultivation and embellishment of which occupied all his leisure hours'.[40] In 1780 Thomas Champneys rented a small garden which he fenced at his own cost.[41] It is recorded that Joseph

---

[33] Eland, *Shardloes Papers*, 76 (where it is clear that the overseer of the house called 'Hawkins' was a Mrs not, as usually assumed, a Mr Hawkins); Johnstone, *Parr*, i. 21, 25 n. 1; G. Cannon, *The Life and Mind of Oriental Jones* (Cambridge, 1990), p. 5; *Report on the MSS of Lady du Cane*, 228, 232; Ingram, *Leaves from a Family Tree*, 85–7; Accounts of T. S. Champneys, 1780–2, Harrow MS Materials Relating to Boys, Box V. (At least Mrs Crampton and Arnold were literate: letters from them of 1771 and 1783 respectively surviving.)

[34] Johnstone, *Parr*, i. 21.   [35] *Report on the MSS of Lady du Cane*, p. 228.

[36] HSR III, fos. 162, 166; letter of Lord Althorp, 29 Jan. 1775, cited Golland, Interim Amendments, 2.

[37] Cannon, *Letters of William Jones*, i. 139, no. 81; Golland, Interim Amendments, 3.

[38] Eland, *Shardloes Papers*, 75–6; Wilkinson, *Memoirs*, i. 7; Ingram, *Leaves from a Family Tree*, 79–81.   [39] Cannon, *Letters of William Jones*, i. 28.

[40] Teignmouth, *Jones*, 15; Jones also learnt chess, studied botany, and collected fossils: ibid., 22, 28.

[41] Champneys Accounts, Invoice for garden rent of 6s. 3d. for the quarter to Easter 1781. Cf. other expenditure on the garden in Mrs Arnold's bills for 1781 and 1782: Harrow MS, Material Relating to Boys, Box V.

The Classical School

Banks' interest in botany only began after his translation to Eton in 1756; but it could have been excited at Harrow.[42]

Drama was a feature of school life, with regular classical plays performed each Christmas until the early 1750s. Boys informally acted scenes or whole plays, classical, contemporary, and Shakespearean, in the 1750s and 1760s.[43] With Sumner's introduction of monthly speeches/declamations, outlets for both oratory and some acting were frequent; Jones and his pupil Althorp both in their time performed Mark Antony's funeral speech from *Julius Caesar*.[44] An elaborate, imaginative, semi-dramatic classical fantasy game, invented and organized by Parr, Jones, and William Bennet, involved many other boys in a sort of formalized brawl with classical overtones in the late 1750s.[45] Casual, individual, and general fighting was commonplace, that of Thackeray boys against Hawkins boys being immortalized in verse by Bennet in 1757.[46] The habit of writing poetry, picked up directly from school exercises, covered the Greek compositions of Jones to the English doggerel of Matthew Montagu's rhyming couplets on the scandal and dismissal of the Dancing Master Tassoni in 1779. It was fashion not aptitude that largely prevented romantic or sentimental verse which so characterized school poets after 1800. But an unashamed poetic tradition, complete with 'Harrow's Muse', existed before Byron began to extemporize on themes of Horace.[47]

Other less cerebral activities included the most popular of all early Harrow pursuits, stone-throwing, mainly, judging from the money paid by the governors to glaziers down the years, at the schoolhouse windows. This was habitually the initial recourse of rioters.[48] Much free time, of which there was no shortage, was occupied in eating and drinking, sometimes being taken to the King's Head for a 'fowl' by a visiting adult, more often supplementing diet and dispelling daily tedium with purchases from the local grocer and confectioner.[49] Daniell Griffiths enjoyed quantities of jam, cake, bread, ham, sugar, coffee, fruits (fresh and dried), sweets, ices, biscuits, tarts, custard, stews, pies, cordials, tea, and beer during his brief sojourn in 1785.[50] Harmless minor creative endeavours could fall foul of authority. John Sheldon was flogged by Sumner for floating a boat he had made, probably on

---

[42] Gun, *Harrow School Register*, 1.
[43] Wilkinson, *Memoirs*, i. 46–52; Teignmouth, *Jones*, 17, 20; Gun, *Harrow School Register*, 88 (for John Howe as Midas and Col. Teignwell); Johnstone, *Parr*, i. 18.
[44] Teignmouth, *Jones*, 25; Cannon, *Letters of William Jones*, i. 140–1, no. 82.
[45] Teignmouth, *Jones*, 20; Johnstone, *Parr*, i. 13; Field, *Parr*, i. 21.
[46] Bennet's poem was called *Pugna Maxima*, the only extant extracts of which appear in Johnstone, *Parr*, i. 21.
[47] Harrow MS HM/D/1a, b for Montagu's poem and its mention of 'Harrow's Muse'; for Jones as schoolboy poet, in Latin, Greek, and English see Teignmouth, *Jones*, 29–30; *The Works of William Jones* (London, 1799), ii. 627–56, iv. 477–95.
[48] e.g. 1771, HSR VII fos. 233, 235, 241 for window repairs 1770–2.
[49] Cannon, *Letters of William Jones*, i. 145, no. 85, Jones's invitation to Lord Althorp, 8 Mar. 1774.
[50] Harrow MS HM/D/25 fos. 1–7.

The Ancien Régime

the town pond or one of the wells. Such early check to his technical prowess did not prevent Sheldon from becoming a prominent surgeon with a special interest in embalming or from being possibly the first Englishman to take to the air, in a balloon from Chelsea in 1784.[51]

Other more formal, or at least more respectable, schoolboy occupations included sport. Writing to his pupil's mother in 1769, Jones sounded an almost nineteenth-century note: 'I strive to encourage him to play at cricket and fives and good exercises for I cannot bear to see a boy idling about with no object and spending hour after hour in making ducks and drakes in a pond or sauntering under tree.' His charge had already begun 'playing at cricket on the bowling green'.[52] This, according to a map of the Northwick estate in 1759, was at the southern end of the Hill, before the descent towards Sudbury, a spot idealized in a painting of the Mason brothers playing cricket in 1771/2.[53] It was only after the Enclosure Act of 1803 that the school obtained its own cricket pitch at the western foot of the Hill. Jones in 1769 speaks of cricket as a natural activity. Certainly his future biographer, John Shore, claimed to have acquired his own taste and developed his skill at the game when at Harrow as a boy in the mid-1760s.[54] Parr, a boy in the 1750s and a master in the 1760s, took cricket with him to Stanmore in 1771.[55] It may be that, as with so many things at this period, cricket was another import from Eton, where the game was certainly being played by 1736, and was innovated at Harrow by Thackeray or, more likely, Sumner. Given the often vulgar associations of the game at the time (high-class gamblers or rural hobbledehoys), only the earliest of stirrings of generally accepted rules and the school's lack of institutional structure to organize regular teams or contests, cricket under Sumner could still be just a recreation.[56]

If the settled increase in numbers of boys, especially after 1760, created a new school culture, the accumulation of staff was no less important. Since 1721 the Head Master had been allowed to appoint, at his own expense, an assistant to help him with the Upper School: Sumner had two; Heath four. In 1748 a Writing Master was appointed, Henry Reeves, ostensibly to relieve the Usher. In 1753 the power to appoint an assistant was extended to the Usher (now called Under Master).[57] There

---

[51] Gun, *Harrow School Register*, 24.   [52] Cannon, *Letters of William Jones*, i. 28–9, no. 16.

[53] Laborde, *Harrow School*, 41, 55 and n. 165. For a reproduction of the Mason picture see A. W. Ball, *Paintings, Prints and Drawings of Harrow on the Hill, 1562–1899* (London Borough of Harrow, 1978), p. 132.

[54] Second Baron Teignmouth, *Memoir of the Life and Correspondence of John, Lord Teignmouth*, 2 vols. (London, 1843), ii. 10.   [55] Thornton, *Harrow School*, 186.

[56] Ibid., 186 and n. 3. It might be noted that one of Thackeray's patrons, Frederick, prince of Wales, was also an enthusiastic promoter of cricket. For an intelligent, lively, and unsentimental account of eighteenth-century cricket see R. Bowen, *Cricket: A History of its Growth and Development throughout the World* (London, 1970), esp. pp. 27–67.

[57] HSR III, fos. 115, 144^r, 148–9; Butler, *Harrow Lists*, 7, 27, 35, etc.; F. de H. Larpent, *Reeves of Harrow School, 1745–1819* (London, 1911), p. 1.

was clearly a swarm of unofficial and semi-official academic hangers-on, from Evans and Weston in the 1730s to the private tutors of the 1760s and Dr Glasse.[58] By 1773, however, some of these had been regularized, thus beginning the division between Assistant and Extra Masters that continued until 1962. These latter included the Masters in writing, dancing, drawing, and French. Fencing, although more or less universal by the 1780s, remained on entirely private terms.[59] Although formally only the Head and Under Masters could beat, the presence of this larger adult academic body lent corporate solidity to the school as well as diversity and substance to the education provided.[60] It also created a close camaraderie—or mutual material self-interest—amongst the teachers themselves, reflected during the 1760s by collective jaunts to London and the tense discussions and initially united action following the sudden death of Sumner, an event which in earlier times could have emptied the school in hours.[61] The increase in staff also allowed for more effective teaching. This took place more or less exclusively outside the formal lessons, through tutors. These could be masters, even the Head Master, or privately engaged teachers, who usually doubled as companions/chaperones, such as Jones or the Yorke's Mr Weston or Lord Herbert's Mr Hetley.[62] From the 1760s, with the staff to make it possible, there seems to have been a concerted move towards masters as tutors, adding considerably to the cohesion of the school, consistency of learning, and accountability of instruction as well as reducing the precariously loose, centrifugal dynamics of the previous decades. The attraction for masters was obvious and perennial: money. When offering Samuel Parr the job of one of his assistants in 1766, Sumner explained that the departing master had been able to double the basic salary of £50 by tutoring, going on to assure his former pupil, 'I shall do everything in my power to make your situation both respectable and profitable'.[63] As with those with whom the boys lodged, the amounts payable to tutors could vary according, one parent was reliably informed, not to a standard fee but 'to the Parents' circumstances and Desires'. The informant continued, knowingly: 'to put your son upon a footing with the best in the School, a little money on these occasions is I always think well bestowed.'[64] Thus although a tutor, who was also a master, Head, or Assistant, could be engaged for as little as three guineas, Mrs Francis was quoted twelve guineas for a tutor for her son in 1779.[65]

[58] Apart from and more or less contemporary with Althorp's Jones were the Yorke's Mr Weston (any connection with Barrett's Weston in the 1730s?): Golland, *Eighteenth Century Harrow*, 1, and Lord Herbert's 'old Hetley': Johnstone, *Parr*, vii. 73 (so-called in a letter from William Bennett to Parr c.1769/70).

[59] See Butler, *Harrow Lists, passim* and e.g. Gun, *Harrow School Register*, p. xix; Golland, Interim Amendments, 4.

[60] But see Gun, *Harrow School Register*, 79 for Parr beating.

[61] Maurice, *Memoirs*, i. 149–51; Johnstone, *Parr*, i. 58, viii. 231–2; Field, *Parr*, i. 63 n. 2.

[62] Above, n. 58.   [63] Johnstone, *Parr*, i. 35 n. 2, letter Sumner to Parr, 10 Nov. 1766.

[64] Ingram, *Leaves from a Family Tree*, 86, letter to Thomas Grimston senior, 1769.

[65] *Report on the MSS of Lady du Cane*, 228; Gun, *Harrow School Register*, p. xix.

The Ancien Régime

Harrow successfully tapped into the growing lucrative market for public school education from 1750. However, this was neither inevitable nor necessarily easy. When the forceful Samuel Butler became Head Master of Shrewsbury in 1798 he inherited just eighteen boys.[66] That Harrow was able to take advantage of the new demands of the wealthy, well-born, and well-connected depended on its site, its cost, its tone, and its scholarship. A leisurely afternoon's ride away from London, especially convenient for the new suburbs of the West End around Hanover and Grosvenor Squares, but also within easy reach of the roads to Oxford, Bath, the Midlands (via Watling Street), and the North, Harrow Hill had a reputation for healthy air. This legend not only attracted asthmatics such as Lord Althorp, but was promoted by the boys themselves, William Jones in 1762 commenting to his sister how 'our bleak air' has worked wonders with Elisha Biscoe's complexion, 'now ruddy, which before was sallow and pale'.[67] It was claimed that between 1753 and 1763 only one Harrovian schoolboy died.[68] Given the foul water produced by the springs circling the crest of the Hill which ran through the graveyard, this was remarkable. Even Harrow was not immune. Boys contracted normal childish illness, such as whooping cough and measles. Boys did die, at least one succumbing during a serious outbreak of diphtheria in July 1771 when Sumner pursued the traditional Harrow policy of sending boys home—there to live or die—as soon as there were signs of an epidemic.[69]

The costs of schooling were judged on value as well as amount. On both scales Harrow emerged as being highly competitive. Fees varied according to house. Reeves charged £14 a year basic board in 1755, but £16 in 1759; Sumner and Heath £25 in 1769 and 1779; Mrs Crampton and Mrs Arnold £21 in 1769 and 1781/2 respectively.[70] There were, however, a myriad of hidden and not so hidden extras. Mrs Crampton charged Thomas Grimston an extra nine guineas for a private room in 1771, while Thomas Champneys paid only two at Mrs Arnold's a decade later.[71] A single bed cost extra everywhere, sharing being the norm.[72] Formal tuition, payable to the Head Master, remained throughout this period at four guineas, but the initial entrance fee leapt from five guineas under Sumner to nine under Heath.[73] As already noticed, private tutors, when masters, charged variable amounts: from Thomas Grimston three guineas in 1769; four guineas from Champneys in 1780/1;

---

[66] Mack, *Public Schools and British Opinion, 1780–1860*, 229.
[67] Teignmouth, *Jones*, 25; Cannon, *Letters of William Jones*, i, no. 1.
[68] Thornton, 152; Carlisle, *Grammar Schools*, ii. 161.
[69] *Report on the MSS of Lady du Cane*, 228–9; Golland, *Eighteenth Century Harrow*, 1 for Philip Yorke's flight.
[70] Eland, *Shardloes Papers*, 76; *Report on the MSS of Lady du Cane*, 25; Gun, *Harrow School Register*, p. xix; Ingram, *Leaves from a Family Tree*, 87; Mrs Arnold's bills 1781/2, Champneys' Accounts, Harrow MS, Materials Relating to Boys, Box V.
[71] Ingram, *Leaves from a Family Tree*, 95; Champneys 'Accounts', *loc. cit.*.
[72] Gun, p. xix (the Head Master's); Champneys Accounts, loc. cit. (Mrs Arnold's).
[73] *Report on the MSS of Lady du Cane*, 228; Gun, *Harrow School Register*, p. xix.

but twelve guineas from Philip Francis in 1779. *Mutatis mutandis*, similar variations applied to writing, drawing, dancing, fencing, French, and maths. The necessities and luxuries of life were also imponderable, but significant. In Champneys' bills for 1781/2, academic costs came to £38 18s. 9d.; living expenses to £35 13s. 3d., excluding any supplementary food. This, according to Daniell Griffiths' 1785 account with his supplier of food and drink of all sorts, John Bernard, could add another £20 a year to the total cost of a Harrow education.[74] Between 1755 and 1763, seven and a half years, James Powell's schooling came to £206 17s. 8d., which compared well with contemporary figures from Westminster, which could be double.[75] But Powell's tastes may have been ascetic or his accounts partial. For a Grimston, a Champneys, a Francis, let alone a Bouverie, Legge, or Spencer, the price must have been considerably higher, perhaps nearer £100 a year. Even so, this probably made it cheaper than Eton, although Heath seems to have based his fee structure very closely on that of his former school.[76]

Cost can operate in two ways. Cheapness can be seen as nasty and demeaning, while excessive expense convinces some that the product has style. Such cannot be said of the tone of a school. While discipline was not the mantra it became in the nineteenth century, and religion was largely ignored, the conduct of the school could make or break its reputation. Here Harrow was fortunate, Sumner reversing the rather chaotic atmosphere of the last years of Thackeray and Heath dealing with insubordination with public displays of firmness. Harrow also benefited from the lapses of others. One of the main reasons the earl of Huntingdon gave for advising the earl of Moira to send his sons to Harrow in the late 1760s was that they 'would have the advantage of a great school without running the risk of debauching their morals which was to be apprehended at Eton or Westminster'. Lord Hertford had recommended the school to Huntingdon, being well satisfied with the teaching and the boarding of his own three younger sons in a small house of only five boys. Huntingdon paid a visit and was 'so pleased with it' that he proposed to send Moira's 'dear little boys thither next week'.[77] Word of mouth, solid reputation, putting on a good show to prospective clients were all as much part of selling Harrow in the 1760s as in the 1990s.

There was a final element that secured Harrow's place, its scholarship which, by chance and good teaching, produced a remarkable generation of learned Harrovians; Parr 'the Whig Dr Johnson'; Jones, the inventor of comparative philology;

---

[74] See nn. 70–3. For Griffiths' spending see HM/D/25.

[75] Eland, *Shardloes Papers*, 76–7, 79.

[76] Gun, *Harrow School Register*, p. xix n. 1 for an Eton account of 1769 in which the entrance fee is nine guineas.

[77] Harrow MS, Materials Relating to Boys, Box I, Access no. 1984/55, transcript of a letter from the earl of Huntingdon to the earl of Moira, 23 June 176[ ]. Cf. Philip Francis to his wife, 16 Sept. 1776, 'I approve of . . . Harrow for my son. I hear a great account of the Master. I protest against Westminster or Eton': Gun, *Harrow School Register*, pp. xix–xx.

The Ancien Régime

William Bennet, expert on Roman roads and chief tutor at Emmanuel Cambridge for many years; Nathaniel Halhed, another pioneering Orientalist; or, of a slightly later vintage, under Heath, Richard Malkyn, first professor of History at the university of London. With scholarship, as with the atmosphere of the school, the fate of the institution was in the hands of the teachers and, overwhelmingly, in those of its Head Masters.

8

ETON RULES

The Harrow governors' policy of appointing Etonian Head Masters reached its consummation and faced its severest challenge between 1746 and 1785. The social and commercial success already described was inseparable from an academic reputation which was only securely established by its association with Eton. According to Canon Pyle of Salisbury writing in 1753, Dr Thackeray was 'a man bred at Eton and a great scholar in the Eton way, and a good one every way'. It was said at the time that, on election, Thackeray was directed by the governors to educate the scholars 'in every respect in the same manner as is observed in Eton school'.[1]

Such approval and preference reflected the achievement of Eton in satisfying its clients' complex social, political, and cultural desires as well as the decadence of the seventeenth-century powerhouse of Westminster. The remarkable wide acceptance of Eton's superiority was due in part to its unique nature. Although Winchester was comparable in being part of a dual-collegiate society that offered its scholars security of education at school and university followed by good prospects of church livings and aristocratic patronage, it lacked the crucial dimension of the aristocratic Oppidans, as well as being hidebound by incestuous parochialism and Founders' Kin. In common with all other eighteenth-century public schools, Winchester also lacked Eton's numbers, a significant factor when the families in the ruling class were numbered in dozens or scores rather than hundreds. Eton's networks were more extensive, embracing both the *haute monde* of the nobility and landed gentry and a self-perpetuating clerisy of gentlemen professionals whose academic and literary as well as social skills were honed by scholarships at Eton and King's and rewarded by preferment to college livings and lucrative or influential posts in schools, universities, and church. Externally, the Etonian system proclaimed the traditional elitism of the classics, tempered by the social training of aristocratic skills required in rulers of people and estates. Internally, the academic prominence

---

[1] J. T. Pryme and A. Bayne, *Memorials of the Thackeray Family* (priv. pub., 1879), p. 17; Thornton, *Harrow School*, 121–2.

was sustained by a close-knit circle of patronage and promotion that ensured that availability of amenable academic talent.

To this system Harrow became first an appendage, then an ally or partner, rarely if ever a rival. Indeed, the relationship of Eton and Harrow has never been that of contestants, except on the cricket field. They have been united in the same process of sustaining the dominance of the propertied classes in society and the state, collaborators in a system regarded for generations by its beneficiaries as an essential support for the betterment as well as survival of the established order of power and government. Thus Harrovians went to Eton and vice versa. Equally, the managers of the schools became closely linked by experience and dynastic ties. The younger Sir John Rushout, lord of the Manor of Harrow and a dominant governor from 1761 to 1800, went to Eton from Harrow in the 1750s. The world was a small one. In 1776 Elias Thackeray, eldest son of the Head Master, was presented with the Eton living of Walkerne, Hertfordshire to which he was succeeded in 1781 by another Etonian, Benjamin Heath, then still Head Master of Harrow.[2] The extended Heath family—Benjamin, Head Master of Harrow and fellow of Eton; brother George, Head Master of Eton; brother-in-law Joseph Drury, Head Master of Harrow—came to dominate both institutions for almost two generations. It was out of such shared links, rather than competition, that encounters such as the 1805 cricket match were spawned.

THOMAS THACKERAY

If the motive of the Harrow governors in seeking a Head from Eton in 1746 was grandiose, Thomas Thackeray's reasons for taking the job were apparently domestic: 'he took the school at Harrow to educate his own and other people's children.'[3] Although established comfortably at Eton, with an income from two Essex livings alone of £681 a year, by 1746 he already had fourteen children (two more were born at Harrow). His descendants were in no doubt that he accepted the Head Mastership 'on account of his very large family'.[4] As Head, he increased numbers (and thus profits), secured Lyon exhibitions for at least two of his sons, and continued to acquire lucrative and influential church preferment. In 1748 he became a chaplain to Frederick, prince of Wales, whose early death as much as George II's longevity blighted Thackeray's prospects. His latitudinarian Whig principles, which had served as a reason for his resignation as an assistant master at Eton, were rewarded by Bishop Hoadly of Winchester in 1753 with appointment to the archdeaconry of Surrey, a largely honorific post, with duties 'he might perform... yearly at the time of his leisure in the Easter holidays' but which brought in £130 a

---

[2] Pryme and Bayne, *Thackeray Family*, 36; Gun, *Harrow School Register*, 154.
[3] Canon Pile in 1753: Pryme and Bayne, *Thackeray Family*, 17.   [4] Ibid., 13, 15.

year 'with dependencies that may bring in a deal of money'. Thackeray died in September 1760, a month after retiring from Harrow, a wealthy man, leaving each of his fourteen surviving children £300. His widow, who died in 1797, left an estate worth £10,000, as well as a house at Eton.[5]

As far as the Harrow governors were concerned, Thackeray was quite a catch. Fifty-three on election, he possessed both contacts and repute in the circles they wished to cultivate. In 1743 he had narrowly missed election as Provost of King's. Socially, his regime appealed to the nobility, especially of Scotland (e.g. the duke of Gordon; the earl of Bute; the earl of Moray) and Ireland (e.g. the earl of Barrymore; the earl of Granard) as well as landed gentry and affluent professionals. Thackeray's connections with Frederick, prince of Wales were extended by his educating at Harrow in the later 1750s the sons of Lord Bute, the 'dearest friend', mentor, and future first minister of the new heir to the throne, Frederick's son, George. Some even argued that Thackeray resigned from Harrow in 1760 in expectation of the accession of George III (and Bute) and consequent high preferment.[6] If so, he miscalculated, the 77-year-old George II outlasting the 67-year-old pedagogue by exactly two months. However, through patronage such as Bute's, Thackeray's Harrow became an accepted adjunct to High Society, the interlaced world of politics and letters. At school, Bute's sons' tutor was Adam Ferguson, an active figure in the egregious Edinburgh intelligentsia and friend of David Hume.[7]

As befitted a coach of the aristocracy, Thackeray recognized the importance of corporate traditions, such as the Silver Arrow, the emblem of which he even incorporated into his coat of arms.[8] He increased payment to the annual Orator from 10s. to 10s. 6d.[9] Under him, the Eton system of boarding houses, with distinct identities, catering for different requirements, became more evident, as in the 1757 fight between the Head Master's house and Hawkins'.[10] Tate Wilkinson commented on his good fortune to board with the stage-struck Reeves family: 'had I been placed in a morose boarding-house . . . I must have led the life of a sulky Negro slave.'[11] The wider management of the school was placed in an order appropriate to its pretentions. The appointment of a Writing Master, Henry Reeves, in 1748/9, and the subsequent acquisition by the governors of the furniture of his classroom, alieviated a menial burden from the Usher, now usually known as the Under Master whose elevated status was further recognized in 1753 by the governors' permission to hire an assistant, subject to the Head's approval.[12] Thus, while his subservience to the Head Master was underlined, the Under Master's role was enhanced, a

---

[5] HSR III, fos. 148–9 (John Thackeray's exhibition, 24 Apr. 1753), 152–3 (Frederick's, 26 June 1758); Pryme and Bayne, *Thackeray Family*, 13–20.

[6] J. Steven Watson, *The Reign of George III* (Oxford, 1960), p. 1; Pryme and Bayne, *Thackeray Family*, 18.   [7] J. Y. T. Greig, *David Hume* (London, 1934), p. 248.

[8] Thornton, *Harrow School*, 130.   [9] HSR VII, fo. 173, Governors' Accounts for 1755.

[10] Johnstone, *Parr*, i. 21.   [11] Wilkinson, *Memoirs*, i. 51.

[12] HSR III, fos. 144^r, 144^v, 146–7, 148–9; HSR VII, fos. 143, 149, 153.

reflection of corporate values and expectations as much as increased numbers of pupils. In fact, at no time did Thackeray achieve the size of Bryan's Harrow at its greatest. The governors' request in 1759 for annual lists of pupils may have reflected anxiety about falling rolls, as such demands had done under Cox.[13]

However, distinction lay in quality as much as quantity. Thus it may have been for aesthetic reasons of convenience rather than necessity that prompted the addition of a lower playing field below the school yard, rented from the Trust's tenant after 1749. As nettles had to be cleared from the original yard in 1748, it does not seem that the demand on space was exactly acute.[14] Equally, the alteration and increase to the annual holidays, beginning in 1759, coincided with social rather than academic taste. Instead of a month at Christmas and another in June, as settled by Bryan in 1728, Thackeray, while keeping the winter holiday the same, restored an Easter break of a fortnight and moved the summer one to August.[15] Like Eton, Harrow now had three terms a year, an arrangement that has proved the most durable of the archdeacon's legacies to the school. However, to secure Harrow's place in the new market for public school education, administrative changes and social respectability had to be allied to excellence of scholarship which, in turn, depended on the masters.

Thomas Thackeray was suave, likeable, and literate, with a penchant for modern languages. To contemporaries and pupils he appeared amiable and avuncular. While Parr later described him as a 'strict disciplinarian', Wilkinson remembered him as reluctant to beat, 'as benign and humane a man as ever was placed at the head of such an unruly community as a public school'. As a teacher, his most noted quirk was his steadfast refusal to praise good work which he thought led pupils to vanity and idleness. Thus his approval of Parr's compositions had to be gleaned from his facial expressions and his appreciation of William Jones could only be voiced in private, to the effect that 'he was a boy of so active a mind that if he were left naked and friendless on Salisbury Plain he would nevertheless find the road to fame and riches'.[16] This aloof academic stance may have concealed detached indifference. It is perhaps significant of Thackeray's scale of values that while he was an involved and enthusiastic supporter of Harrow theatricals, and abetted Wilkinson's early steps as a prima donna, as soon as disquiet was voiced by 'public conversation in the circle of Harrow critics', he concurred in abolishing official drama completely, fearing the school could gain a reputation 'for breeding up actors in lieu of scholars'.[17] Even his friendliness to boys may have had an element of

---

[13] HSR III, fo. 153^{r-v}.
[14] Ibid., fos. 144^r, 145, 146–7, HSR VII, 145, 151, 155. Cf. ibid., fos. 162, 166, 167 for new tenant.
[15] HSR III, fo. 153^r.
[16] Thornton, *Harrow School*, 141; Field, *Parr*, i. 15–16, 19; Teignmouth, *Jones*, 20–1; Wilkinson, *Memoirs*, i. 43.
[17] Wilkinson, *Memoirs*, i. 51–2 and, generally, pp. 46–52.

calculation in removing himself from the disagreeable tasks of imposing discipline. To the undoubted benefit of his own reputation, Thackeray left the sadism demanded by the system to his deputies.

Of the assistant masters under Thackeray, very little survives. It may be assumed that the Head and Under Master took advantage of their power to appoint deputies. Sumner's assistant, Holmes, who resigned in 1766, may have been inherited from Thackeray.[18] Whoever served under Thackeray was likely to belong to that substantial class of university-educated clergy who had missed college fellowships and, more importantly, livings and were either marking time waiting for a church post or seeking alternative sources of respectable income. Until the 1780s assistant masterships at Harrow almost invariably led nowhere grander than a modest rural rectory. Strikingly, the 1771 secession apart, Harrow masters did not colonize other schools, a sign of the school's modest, if genuine eminence. For those extra masters hired to impart practical skills, Harrow could either, as in the case of fencing masters, be a recognition of repute gained in London society or, increasingly, a means of considerable family improvement. The children of Henry Reeves, Writing Master 1748–68, not only took advantage of cheap public school education, one succeeded his father as Writing Master for fifty years (1768–1819) and struck up a close and ultimately lucrative relationship with one of the governors, the wealthy Richard Page of Wembley; another rose in the East India Company to make a fortune in the subcontinent, retiring to East Sheen and ending his days as a JP for Surrey, a far cry from his mother who on her husband's early death, to support her family (they had thirteen children), had set up as a wine and spirit merchant in Fleet Street.[19] Of greater consequence, within and beyond the school, however, was the Usher or Under Master who had direction of the Lower School.

A year after Thackeray became Head, Cox's Old Harrovian Under Master William Saunders was replaced by William Cox, scholar of Eton, scholar and fellow of King's. To supplement his income, Cox combined his mastership with the curacy of Pinner. His appointment confirmed the direction of Thackeray's and the governors' intentions. Unfortunately, Cox almost immediately went mad, by March 1749 his absence from his post leading to his dismissal.[20] His place was taken in June 1749 by the more robust, although perhaps no more sane, William Prior.[21] Another Etonian, Prior held sway over the Lower School with a rod. Unimaginative, a slave to rules, insensitive to individuals, he was said to enjoy beating 'putting in force his love of torture' with 'exulting features'. Corporal punishment was administered by birch, aimed at the backside, and drew blood. A regular, not to say intrinsic feature of the public school, the moderation prescribed in the statutes was

---

[18] Johnstone, *Parr*, i. 35 n. 2.   [19] Larpent, *Reeves of Harrow School*, 1–3.
[20] HSR III, 143ᵛ, 144ᵛ; Gun, *Harrow School Register*, 156.
[21] HSR I, fo. 11ᵛ; HSR III, fol. 145; Gun, *Harrow School Register*, 156 misreads the Minutes, dating Prior's appointment to 1747.

honoured in the breach by such as Prior. Even the rule restricting the use of the rod to Head and Under Master seems to have been flouted, although beating with canes by monitors was only introduced by the evasive and squeamish Dr Drury fifty years later. Official monitorial powers of discipline remained restricted to identifying and reporting minor formroom infringements such as talking. Prior, however, was free to indulge his pleasure, 'in truth', Wilkinson recalled, 'a despicable, severe and disgreeable tyrant'. It may be no coincidence that he lasted only six months under the less *laissez-faire* Sumner, resigning with effect from Christmas 1760.[22]

Prior's brutality was not simply or even primarily a matter of controlling the behaviour of small boys. When it was, it is hard to see the direct logic: thus Tate Wilkinson, like many Harrovians since, was flogged for running away, although in his case eccentrically on the insistence of another boy's guardian.[23] Most beating, however, was strictly academic and administered as much for intellectual limitations as for laziness or moral turpitude. In 1756 William Jones, who had just returned from missing a year's school because of a broken thigh bone received in a fight for pears, was placed in the form he would have attained if he had not been away. During his year's convalescance Jones had read widely in English, but had not looked at any Latin and, consequently, was hopelessly out of his depth in class. No allowance for this was made by Prior who systematically flogged Jones as well as devising other humiliating punishments, all for insufficiencies beyond the pupil's control. Whether or not this treatment acted as a spur to Jones' success in rapidly making up for lost time and proceeding to progress far beyond the Lower School syllabus, it certainly scarred his personality and seared his attitude to the exercise of power. According to his biographer and Harrow contemporary, John Shore, Prior's behaviour 'made an impression on his mind which he ever remembered with abhorrence' leaving him with a lasting 'sense of injustice' which destroyed Jones' 'respect due to authority'. To this instance of pig-headed, conventional schoolmasterly cruelty was ascribed Jones' later extreme political radicalism and his sympathy with the oppressed, whether by society, culture, the law, or colonial condescension. Yet, again in Shore's opinion, as much as in Prior's abuse the fault lay in the inflexibility of rules in the public school system which 'must often preclude that attention to the tempers and capacities of individuals by which their attainments might be essentially promoted'.[24]

Such constraints may well have lain at the heart of Thackeray's studied indifference to his pupils' achievements: engagement with them as individuals could undermine the whole project which was based on a methodical, unvarying grind towards academic uniformity of exposure to the prescribed classics as models of

---

[22] Wilkinson, *Memoirs*, i. 43–4; HSR III, fo. 154ʳ. For the innovation of monitorial beating see Thornton, *Harrow School*, 207.

[23] Wilkinson, *Memoirs*, i. 39–43.   [24] Teignmouth, *Jones*, 15–17; Cannon, *Oriental Jones*, 5.

grammar and style. Not until Sumner and Parr did teachers regularly comment on literary quality or intellectual content. The structure of Thackeray's curriculum can be traced as it developed for one pupil, James Powell, through his purchase of textbooks.[25] The general pattern conformed to that current at Eton at least since the 1720s and at Winchester, the emphasis, except for prose anthologies and grammatical exercises, being almost exclusively poetical, with Greek introduced in the Upper School. Powell began, in 1755, with Phaedrus (a definite import from Eton), a book of Latin sentences, and a couple of grammars. To this some Ovid was added in 1756, more in 1757 along with Terence, a prose anthology, and a gradus (i.e. a dictionary to help composition of Latin verse). The use of these textbooks and the exercises of rote learning with written but mainly oral repetition that sprang from them were under the supervision of Prior, who must, therefore, have possessed at least a basic competence in Latin. Early in 1758 Powell obtained a Greek grammar, suggesting promotion to the Upper School and Thackeray's direct control. In 1759 Aesop's *Fables*, Ovid's *Metamorphoses*, Caesar's *Commentaries*, and a Greek New Testament appear among Powell's purchases. The following year saw substantial investment in classical heavyweights: two volumes of Homer, Martial, Horace, Virgil, Cicero's *Orationes*, as well as Cornelius Nepos and Lucian. The increasing importance of Greek was reflected in the purchases of 1761 and 1762, which included *Poetae Graeci*, two volumes of Sophocles, and Theocritus. Powell left Harrow at Easter 1763. Judging from contemporary and later evidence, his academic experience was standard, except that many left before attaining the Upper School and Greek, the retention of which marked Harrow as an elite establishment.

If Powell's academic career was unexceptional, its contours were shared by those of greater intellectual brilliance. For all his precocity, William Jones excelled mostly in degree, within the confines of the syllabus. In the Lower School he composed Latin verse in the style of Ovid, although verse composition, as opposed to translation, was not a requirement, but he only began Greek in the Upper School. The system, however, in which all boys slogged through the set texts repeatedly, not only allowed the young to rise according to merit not age—Parr reaching the top of the school in January 1761 aged 14—but also placed the gifted in a place of academic superiority above their station. Thus Jones's mastery of Terence in the Upper School was recognized by boys in the two forms above his whose exercises he wrote for two years. In 1760 it was Jones, not the Head Master's assistant (perhaps Holmes), who prepared a detailed account of the Upper School syllabus for Sumner.[26]

None the less, the narrowness and monotony of the curriculum and pedagogic method allowed the clever and industrious to extend their studies far beyond the

---

[25] For what follows see Eland, *Shardloes Papers*, 76.
[26] Teignmouth, *Jones*, 17, 18, 19, 21; Field, *Parr*, i. 19; Johnstone, *Parr*, i. 12.

confines of schoolwork, which thus formed merely a starting point. On the one hand Parr, Bennett, and Jones could explore an imaginary Greek political world of their own creation in the fields about the Hill. On the other, they could study, alone or more usually with private tutors, not only maths and French, but ancient history, classical natural history, metaphysics, and philosophy as well as literature not examined in the formroom. There was time for modern English writing, from Swift, Addison, and Johnson to pseudo-Ossian, as well as Shakespeare.[27] By allowing the talented to excel and pass beyond the normal curriculum, the Harrow system encouraged scholarship and created scholars, some, such as Parr or Bennett, in classical studies, but others, such as Jones, in non-classical disciplines.

However, this formed only a part, although an integral and important one, of a determinedly elite education which catered for as many clients as possible. Thus the curriculum supplied the dull with a patina of classical attainment and ersatz culture while promoting advanced individual study in arts subjects more or less without restriction. Unsurprisingly, for a prodigy such as Jones, university came as something of an intellectual anticlimax.[28] Yet his less committed or receptive peers also gained something considered of social if not strictly academic value. Even though Thackeray in his later years may not have been successful in maintaining numbers, he had lent Harrow 'a degree of celebrity' which, whether justified in fact, image, or tradition, it never subsequently lost.[29] He achieved this by using his suavity of manner, social contacts, and academic experience to harness the local advantages of the school to positive recruitment from influential aristocrats and plutocrats and the most rigorous enforcement of a conventional educational programme that allowed alumni of all sorts and orders to benefit according to their expectations and abilities, from commerce to the Commons and from fox-hunting to philology.

ROBERT SUMNER

Robert Sumner has claims to be one of the greatest of Harrow Head Masters. Under him, numbers reached previously unimagined proportions, allegedly as many as 280 at one time, certainly, from the mid-1760s, settling at well over 200.[30] Exploiting the cachet imported by Thackeray, he increasingly attracted the sons of the nobility as well as plutocracy by the excellence of his academic reputation, the strength of his personality, and a reputation for firm discipline and order. Under Sumner Harrow became a forcing house rather than a nursery for academic

---

[27] Teignmouth, *Jones*, 15–21, 27–30; Johnstone, *Parr*, i. 13, 18; Field, *Parr*, i. 18–24.
[28] Teignmouth, *Jones*, 31.   [29] The phrase is Field's: *Parr*, i. 13–14.
[30] Harrow MS, Materials Relating to Boys, Box I, Access no. 1984-55; Johnstone, *Parr*, i. 64; Butler, *Harrow Lists*, 7–25; J. S. Golland, *Catalogue of MS Bill Lists and Books 1770–1847*, Harrow MS, 1986, fo. 1.

prodigies and social lions. By the time of his sudden and early death in 1771, he had become in the eyes of some 'the best schoolmaster in England'.[31]

Much of his fame, it has to be admitted, rests on the roseate eulogies of his pupils who variously described him as one of the 'great ornaments of our literature'; 'another Demosthenes'. Not notably pious or religious, he was admired by those he taught for his learning, sense, and humanity. Richard Sheridan reportedly mourned him 'as a father'.[32] Sumner possessed a powerful, not entirely easy character; resilient, as when contesting threats to his authority from governors and parents; capable of exerting a strong and lasting ascendancy on those close to him, especially his staff. Samuel Parr modelled himself on Sumner not just as a teacher but even in his personal habits, such as smoking and solitary drinking.[33] Sumner's obsessive love of the work of Henry Fielding (another Etonian) influenced three of his assistants, Parr, Charles Roderick, and Richard Wadeson, to visit Fielding's old haunt of the Pillars of Hercules in Piccadilly in homage to the novelist's shade.[34] While both Parr and Roderick had been Sumner's pupils before they became his colleagues, Joseph Drury, the future Head Master, had not. Yet he could almost be said to have been created by Sumner, from his florid, emotional declamatory style of speech and love of providing modern examples in his classical teaching to his sense of humour, taste, and smooth social manner. All were ascribed by Drury's son to 'this early association' with Sumner.[35]

Sumner was Eton through and through. Born into an Etonian family in 1729, his uncle John being Head Master there, he was a scholar of Eton and King's, where he also gained a fellowship. He taught at his Alma Master from 1751 and married, on election to Harrow, the sister of an Eton and King's man. Even before coming to Harrow, he impressed potential parents with his distinctive style and learning. His one published work, *Concio ad Clerum* was noted for its Latinity.[36] He encouraged his best pupils, the monitors and those in the upper reaches of the Fifth Form, to read widely for themselves, establishing a library in the Old Schools for classics and philology, to which the monitors (i.e. the handful—four in 1770, six in 1771—of the most academically accomplished and hence senior boys) alone had keys, which thus became—and remain—symbols of their office.[37] Sumner's teaching had a deliberate slant towards preparing his pupils for lives in politics and the professions, particularly through the study of Greek and Roman history and the introduction of monthly declamations, on the Eton model of Head Master Bland in the 1720s.[38]

---

[31] *Report on the MSS of Lady du Cane*, 229, William Whately to John Grimston, 24 Sept. 1771.
[32] Field, *Parr*, i. 16–18, where there is also a translation of Jones's eulogy in his *Poeseos Asiaticae Commentariorum*; Johnstone, *Parr*, i. 51–2; Morwood, *Sheridan*, 10.
[33] David Roderick's testimony, Johnstone, *Parr*, i. 74–5.
[34] Johnstone, *Parr*, i. 54 n. 1, 63 n. 2; Maurice, *Memoirs*, i. 150–1.
[35] Drury, *Memoir*, 8.   [36] See Gun, *Harrow School Register*, 154 and Sumner's entry in *DNB*.
[37] Carlisle, *Grammar Schools*, ii. 153.   [38] Maurice, *Memoirs*, i. 61–2; Maxwell Lyte, *Eton*, 282.

Sumner fostered the social dimension of the school by hiring a Dancing Master and arranging for boys to have fencing lessons with one of the leading fashionable London instructors, Angelo.[39] Arrow Day flourished, especially when moved from the first Thursday in August to the equivalent day in July in 1761, a consequence of the changes to holidays made two years' earlier.[40] There was a marked gentility to the tone of the school. What had been called the bog or boghouse became known as the 'necessary'.[41] Although boys could dress very shabbily, there was strong peer pressure on them to have new clothes for Arrow Day. Hierarchical status was expected to be similarly recognized, in 1766 the 15-year-old Sheridan asking his guardian for a new suit 'as I have lately got into the 5 form, which is the head form of the school, I am under a necessity of appearing like the other 5 form boys'.[42] Parr attributed his ability to keep order in the Upper School among boys only a very few years younger (Parr was not yet 20 when he began to teach) to 'treating them with the respect due to young gentlemen'.[43] Although a stickler for discipline and the majesty of his own authority, Sumner had no time and his Harrow and Harrovians no place for the lurid sadism of Prior.

As a teacher, Sumner was rigorous, imaginative, and an intellectual snob. Those who fell short of his demanding standards faced neglect. His stars, however, were lavishly encouraged. He declared that William Jones knew more Greek than he did and had a better grasp of idiom. Unlike similar pedagogic hyperbole and lionizing, Sumner's was used to effect: he encouraged such pupils to read widely beyond the formal syllabus, including ancient history, logic, philosophy, and modern translations of the classics, such as Pope's Homer. He promoted verse composition in Latin and Greek and regularly set English essays on classical themes, a practice Parr exported to Stanmore. Those such as Jones who had exceeded the limits of the ordinary classical curriculum were introduced to other languages, including Hebrew and Arabic. Sumner possessed a particular interest in oratory and rhetoric, fostered by the monthly declamations, study of both Geeek drama and Cicero, and public performances of Shakespearean speeches. Although the three annual Speech Days were instituted by Benjamin Heath after 1772, the continuing Harrow tradition of declaiming extracts from classical and modern literature was begun by Sumner.[44]

---

[39] Ingram, *Leaves from a Family Tree*, 86; Butler, *Harrow Lists*, 7 (Tassoni is mistakenly called Drawing Master); Maurice, *Memoirs*, i. 92 (for two of Angelo's Harrow pupils Walter Pollard and William Jones).

[40] HSR III, fo. 154 bis^r; Butler, *Harrow Speech Bills, 1780–1829*, 10–11.

[41] HSR vii, fo. 225.

[42] Sheridan to Richard Chamberlain, 24 June 1766, Harrow uncatalogued MS, in C. Price (ed.), *Letters of Richard Brinsley Sheridan* (Oxford, 1966), i. 2.   [43] Field, *Parr*, i. 51.

[44] On Sumner as a teacher see ibid., i. 16–18, 57 n. 2; Johnstone, *Parr*, i. 20, 34, 51–2; Drury, *Memoir*, 8; Maurice, *Memoirs*, i. 61–2, 147–52; Teignmouth, *Jones*, 21–31; Teignmouth, *John, Lord Teignmouth*, i. 8–10; Cannon, *Letters of Jones*, i. 74, no. 40, letter of 1 Nov. 1770 declaring that Althorp with Sumner 'will learn more than with me, or any man in Europe' (cf. no. 42, p. 77 for reading).

The range of literature Sumner presented to his pupils was exhaustive and exhausting. John Shore remembered only the leading and obvious authors: Virgil, Horace, Cicero, Homer, and Sophocles. Yet, in the Summer Term of 1771 alone, Philip Yorke read Homer, Lucian's *Timon*, some Sallust, Pindar's *Odes*, some Sophocles, Virgil, at least six other Greek poets, including Sappho, the Greek New Testament (read with Sumner in his study on Saturday mornings as a model of language rather than faith), as well as a catechism and some geography and history. This was in addition to form work, which comprised construing, for example, Horace, and verse composition.[45] Sumner's speciality seems to have been Greek, but this may simply reflect the Upper School syllabus. Jones, for example, was equally proficient in composing Latin and Greek verse and pastiches. None the less, Parr, who increasingly shared Upper School teaching, went on to establish an outstanding reputation as an innovative teacher of Greek, prose and verse composition, history and philosophy as well as poets and dramatists.[46] Breadth was as important as depth. Almost as soon as he entered the Upper School, Lord Althorp was reading Hooke's *Roman History*.[47] Like his mentor Sumner, Parr was no mere grammarian, his method of citing modern English poets to parallel or illustrate the sentiments of the classical authors clearly echoing the technique of his master.

A flavour of the intellectual life Sumner stimulated can be obtained from surviving school exercises, including English essays written by his pupils. While Jones's schoolboy verses are exceptional, other survivals reveal a high degree of academic facility and intellectual seriousness at least amongst those with whom the Olympian Sumner could be bothered, such as John Sayer, head of the school in 1770, later lecturer in Greek at Cambridge, whose schoolboy English verse translations from Latin suggest an easy acquaintance with both genres.[48] The political tone of social awareness in some of the English essays or 'themes' is striking. Thomas Grimston rather pompously lamented the idleness of those 'whom Fortune has blessed with the means of life without any labours of their own'.[49] Philip Yorke, later third earl of Hardwicke, insisted on the efficacy of education in shaking off the tyranny of unreasoned 'influence of custom and bondage of vice'; 'that man is truly wise who, enlarged from the power of custom, is swayed only by the arguments which offer themselves to his unprejudiced judgement'. He was to become a staunch supporter of Catholic Emancipation.[50] John Hamilton, the future first marquess of Abercorn, argued, primly, that 'perfection is not to be attained but by earnest study', ability depending upon experience and 'judicious

---

[45] Teignmouth, *John, Lord Teignmouth*, i. 9; Golland, *Eighteenth Century Harrow*, fo. 5.
[46] M. L. Clarke, *Classical Education in Britain, 1500–1900* (Cambridge, 1959), 50; id., *Greek Studies in England* (Cambridge, 1945), pp. 17–20. Cf. Ingram, *Leaves from a Family Tree*, 87, 89, where Thomas Grimston admits to the advantage of buying second-hand textbooks 'being well-seasoned', i.e. with useful annotations by previous owners.
[47] Cannon, *Letters of Jones*, i. 77, no. 42.   [48] Harrow MS HM/D/7.
[49] Harrow MS HM/D/5.   [50] Harrow MS HM/D/9.

learning'. Innate advantages of mind or body are worthless 'if unenforced by Art'. For such solid Enlightenment principles, Hamilton sought confirmation in the career of William of Orange, 'the Great', who, despite physical infirmity and the power of Louis XIV, 'from little more than a private citizen of Holland' saved his own country 'from foreign slavery', was chosen king of England 'by the voluntary and unanimous offers of the whole people', thus 'becoming one of the greatest potentates of Europe'.[51] These impeccable Whiggish sentiments, when allied to strenuous *noblesse oblige* and an elevation of reason over tradition, marked these Harrovians, if not as radicals, then as critical observers of the status quo whether Whig or Tory.

Sumner promoted such sentiments. Under him, it was observed, the story of the sixth-century BC Athenian tyrannicides, the lovers Aristogiton and Harmodius, known as the Liberators, 'echoed from every tongue'. This devotion at least one pupil, William Jones, sustained into later life, incorporating the story into one of his literary works, although the origins of his hatred of tyrants was as much emotional—a reaction to men like Prior—as rational. At Sumner's Harrow, it was noted, 'the democratic spirit somewhat prevailed', in part because pupils were 'so well read under the tuition of their learned . . . master in Greek history', notably the stand against the Persians and Athens' resistance to Philip of Macedon.[52] Sumner certainly had little reverence for traditional views or people ex officio. It may be no coincidence that two of his pupils with whom he shared most adult converse, Parr and Jones, were both advanced radicals in their views. But Sumner was also a shrewd scholastic entrepreneur. He disapproved when in 1768 Parr, then his chief assistant, openly supported Wilkes in the Middlesex by-election. It was not that Sumner opposed Wilkes (as Jones did) but there were two sons of the government candidate, Sir William Beauchamp Proctor, in the school and he would have found it 'more agreeable' if Parr 'had not voted at all'.[53] Sumner needed the continuing patronage of the Establishment figures who were Wilkes's targets. Whatever abstract principles he inculcated into his clever boys, for the sake of the school and his income he could not afford to fall into the trap of political partisanship (thus, as has been noticed, he also admitted Wilkes's son to the school).[54] It has been suggested that the chances of preferment for Sumner's pupils, indeed for Sumner himself, were clouded by this 'democratic spirit', Parr and Jones being cited as examples.[55] Yet neither was typical, nor an easy protégé. Sumner, who retained the

---

[51] Harrow MS HM/D/10.

[52] Maurice, *Memoirs*, i. 61–2; Jones's poem, *Ode in Imitation of Callistratus*, 1782, is discussed by Cannon, *Oriental Jones*, 165–6 and 114–70 for Jones's politics in general.

[53] Johnstone, *Parr*, viii. 234–5 (a continuing support to 1770, to the disgust of one of his old school friends, Richard Archdale: ibid., vii. 225, 12 July 1770); Jones voiced his 'vehementer improbem illum Wilkensium', i.e. 'violent disapproving of that villain Wilkes' in Apr. 1768, *Letters of Jones*, i. 7 (tr. p. 10).

[54] Gun, *Harrow School Register*, 26.   [55] Thornton, *Harrow School*, 159–60.

support of a significant section of the highest nobility, died young, which deprived him of possible advancement (the new Prime Minister at the time, Lord North, being an Old Etonian) and his pupils of a lasting patron. None the less, Sumner was identified in the minds of some, including some governors, with an independence of mind and attitude that they found disconcerting, abrasive, and awkward.

However, such independence, or bloody-mindedness depending on your view, was crucial in Sumner's defeat of a concerted attempt to transform Harrow from a public school to a finishing academy for princelings, with profits dissipated among freelance local academic businessmen. By the early 1760s, the Revd Samuel Glasse, MA of Christ Church, Oxford and rector of Hanwell, Middlesex, had settled at what was later called the Old House, just down the street from the Head Master's house. Although the habit of boys living with their private tutors and of small groups of boys being boarded with recognized Dames, masters, or other landlords had been long established, Glasse posed a direct threat to the automomy and integrity of the school. Attracting the sons of the nobility, such as the earls of Radnor and Dartmouth, Glasse not only acted as their tutor, but took it upon himself to exempt them from attendance at normal school 'bills' (i.e. call-overs of the school lists) which occured several times each day.[56] Such bills were not only a means of keeping track of pupils during their free time, but also were seen by Sumner (and his successors) as symbols of the Head Master's authority. Glasse seemed to be exploiting the huge growth in numbers to create for himself an autonomous yet parasitic business which reduced the Head Master's power to that of a Holy Roman Emperor or a *roi fainéant*. As Harrow grew in size and prestige, the problem became acute, reaching a crisis early in 1768.[57] The problem for Sumner was twofold. Appropriate accommodation for the unprecedented influx of boarders and finding tutors for those not already so provided presented genuine difficulties. No less inconvenient were Glasse's powerful connections and allies among parents and governors.

The governors during the 1760s were an introverted lot.[58] Old Sir John Rushout, Lord of the Manor, who lived at what is now The Grove, had been a governor since 1715; his son, also John (Juliet to Wilkinson's Romeo in 1752), was elected in 1761 and became increasingly influential in his father's dotage.[59] Francis Herne, of Flambards, a governor since 1728, and John Bucknall of nearby Oxhey, elected in 1742, were both old boys. Francis Saunders, the vicar, a governor since 1747, had briefly combined his living with the Under Mastership of the school from 1730 to 1732. Their number was completed by Sir Charles Palmer, Bart., of Dorney Court,

---

[56] Johnstone, *Parr*, i. 57–8; Thornton, *Harrow School*, 133, 148–50; Laborde, *Harrow School*, 39, 42 for general accounts.

[57] *Historical Manuscripts Commission: Fifteenth Report*. Appendix Pt. 1, *Manuscripts of the Earl of Dartmouth*, iii (London, 1896), p. 187 (letter of 19 Mar. 1768); HSR III, fo. 156 for Governors' resolution, May 1768.

[58] Details from Gun, *Harrow School Register*.   [59] Wilkinson, *Memoirs*, i. 50.

Buckinghamshire and Pinner. They indulged in the customary nepotism, self-interest, and neglect, the audit meeting of 1766 being inquorate, and hardly covered themselves in glory in their manner of handling the difficult Head Master's election in 1771.[60] Although in the end upholding Sumner's authority over Glasse, they behaved in a mealy-mouthed fashion. By 1771, indeed, they seem to have withdrawn their support from Sumner, who vigorously opposed their abuse of their rights to grant school holidays.[61] This counted against Sumner's protégé Parr in the 1771 election, as, according to Parr himself, did his Sumner-like independence of spirit and radical politics.[62] Clearly, tensions between Head Master and some governors were acute. Sumner actively encouraged Parr and Jones to regard Saunders as a figure of fun and contempt, perhaps with reason. Another of Sumner's star pupils, William Bennett, fellow of Emmnauel, Cambridge, thought Saunders both stupid and malicious.[63] Over a year before the 1771 election, Bennett regarded the governors as hostile to the current regime and Parr in particular, to whom he wrote of the 'meanness of these men . . . their injustice'. Later he consoled Parr that failure to be elected to the Harrow headship at least meant he avoided 'obligations to the avarice of a Palmer or the malignity of an Herne'.[64] He could have added the tactlessness, bad-temper, and rudeness of a Bucknall.

Yet Glasse was thick with these men, appearing at times almost as a proxy Head Master or proxy governor. He attended the inquorate meeting in June 1766 when the trust's balance, by order of Herne and with the agreement of Bucknall, Palmer, and Saunders, was paid over into his keeping and when he witnessed a lease of trust land to Saunders. Over the next year, Glasse took charge of executing some of the trust's charitable payments, customarily the task of the annual treasurer or the vicar.[65] Beyond his house, he cut a significant figure within the school. In 1763/4 his advice even prevailed over Sumner's in persuading William Jones towards Oxford not Cambridge, while a few years later, he was instrumental in introducing Jones, now Lord Althorp's tutor at Harrow, to a form of religious understanding, if not orthodox belief.[66] This, however, was after the resolution of the serious constitutional row with Sumner. Yet religion may have played its part in the conflict. What little evidence there is suggests that Sumner was of a rationalist, secular bent, impatient with archaic obscurantism or religious mystery. John Shore, whose whole time at Harrow was spent under Sumner in the Fifth Form, remembered receiving

---

[60] HSR III, fos. 155ᵛ, 154*bis*ʳ for a Herne receiving a Lyon exhibition (3 Apr. 1762), fo. 154*bis*ᵛ for increased payment to the Vicar and assistant for annual sermons: the Vicar as governor attended the meeting on 23 Apr. 1762. This meeting, by being inquorate, was unable to grant Samuel Parr the vacant Lyon Exhibition.

[61] Field, *Parr*, i. 62; Maurice, *Memoirs*, i. 150: both were quoting another of Sumner's Harrovians, Lytton.   [62] Johnstone, *Parr*, i. 63–4.

[63] Ibid., vii. 74, viii. 233–4.   [64] Ibid., vii. 74 (letter, 1769/70), 78 (letter, 24 Oct. 1771).

[65] HSR III, fo. 155ᵛ, HSR 503, HSR VII, fo. 221: 'To Jane Aldy by Mr Glasse 5/-'.

[66] Teignmouth, *Jones*, 26–7, 64.

no religious instruction at all, beyond the literary study of the Greek Testament. Sumner predicted Parr would become a bishop, but for his learning rather than his piety. Parr's sudden ordination at Christmas 1769 was typically careerist.[67] To rise in the academic world, holy orders were essential; belief was not. However, the classical humanism of Sumner may have gone too far, not least with Saunders. Glasse's social Christianity, possibly tinged with commitment (as well as becoming a royal chaplain in 1772, he was a canon of Wells and then St Paul's), may have appeared more congenial, less threatening, as, perhaps, did Glasse himself.

The danger of the situation was clear. Harrow was changing, but to whose benefit, the Head Master or private contractors? It may be that the governors saw it rather differently, as a way of getting rid of Sumner. However, the duke of Radnor, a fervent supporter of Glasse with whom his sons boarded, agreed that at issue was not 'a matter of no consequence' between the two protagonists but 'a question of justice between the parents and master'. His argument was that parents should be allowed to have their sons exempted from the Head Master's control when out of school. He even claimed, perhaps to some governors' private embarrassment, that he had received assurances that this would be and remain the case, a guarantee which, if it ever existed, smacks of the laxer days of Thackeray.[68]

The result of the contest would have profound results, even if the governors appeared unaware of the precariousness of the position. Radnor threatened that, if Glasse lost, he would destroy the school. However, if Sumner lost, the teaching staff could have been relegated to hired lackies serving a galaxy of well-connected independent tutor-housemasters. The balance of influence would have resided with parents. Almost inevitably, given the developments in the fashion for such schools, Harrow would soon have ceased to have been a match for Eton, Westminster, and Winchester, the odd automonous commonwealth of the public school having been fatally diluted. On the other hand, more immediately, if Sumner misjudged his stand, other schools were eager to take advantage. In March 1768, before the formal resolution of the crisis, the countess of Dartmouth received a letter from the Lower Master at Eton, Dr Dampier, who had heard that she and the earl were 'under some distress about their sons, owing to the quarrel that had lately happened between Dr Sumner and Mr Glasse at Harrow' and begged 'to recommend Eton'.[69]

The Dartmouths were unimpressed. They adandoned Glasse and placed their sons in Sumner's house.[70] The governors were in a bind. If Sumner was forced to submit, he would presumably resign. His departure would more certainly than his retention risk the ruin of the school given his contacts, commercial and academic success, and the many satisfied customers. Yet the governors' personal sympathies

[67] Teignmouth, *John, Lord Teignmouth*, i. 9; Johnstone, *Parr*, i. 20, 37–8.
[68] Radnor's letter, now lost, is quoted in Thornton, *Harrow School*, 149–50.
[69] *MSS of the Earl of Dartmouth*, 187.   [70] Johnstone, *Parr*, i. 58 and cf. ibid., 56.

as far as they went were for Glasse and against Sumner. However, despite individual shortcomings, the governors of the mid-eighteenth century almost unfailingly, if occasionally accidentally, acted in the better corporate interest. At their meeting in May 1768, they resolved the dispute, after 'serious consideration', mentioning neither names nor details, by ordering 'that all the young gentlemen who shall be admitted into the Free Grammar School shall conform to the rules thereof'.[71] This verdict, though pusillanimous and evasive, was decisive. The Head Master's authority was confirmed.

However, this did nothing to solve the problems of overcrowding, accommodation, or tutors, which were in fact exacerbated by Glasse's withdrawal. Before his death, Sumner only had time to tackle some of these. It was left to his successor urgently to build a large extension to the Head Master's house, although Sumner tried to offer lodgings to as many boys as possible and had begun domestic improvements. It seems he extended the number of Dames' houses and allowed them to take more boys. More masters also meant greater scope for supervised boarding. Control was maintained by the Head Master's absolute power to admit boys, license boarding houses, and supervise discipline throughout the town, although within some houses life must have been a shambles. Increasingly, even before the Glasse incident, the Head and assistant masters offered themselves as private tutors: Sumner, Holmes, Parr, Roderick, and Drury all did so.[72] Such private tuition was essential to the academic effectiveness of the formal curriculum in preparing for the formroom construing, translation, and composition exercises, as well as providing opportunities for additional subjects such as French and maths. In 1770 William Jones was angrily appalled at the prospect of his former charge Althorp attending school for three months without a tutor, a problem quickly resolved by Sumner providing the private tuition himself.[73] The use of masters as tutors was to form the basis of the academic organization of the school for the next century and a half, only finally disappearing under Lionel Ford (Head Master 1910–25), even though private tutors not members of the staff continued to attend the great, such as the duke of Dorset in Byron's time, into the nineteenth century. In Sumner's often *ad hoc* responses to the changing nature of the school lay the foundations of its future success and his own stature as Head Master.

Central to his policy were his staff. The Under Master, Richard Wadeson, appointed in December 1760, may already have been an assistant, as he had witnessed a lease for the governors the previous May. If so, his place as assistant may have been filled by the Mr Holmes whose departure in December 1766 opened the way for the return of Samuel Parr early in 1767 as the Head's principal assistant. Within a couple of years Parr had been joined in teaching the Upper School by

[71] HSR III, fo. 156.
[72] Cannon, *Letters of Jones*, i. 74; Johnstone, *Parr*, i. 35 n. 2; Maurice, *Memoirs*, i. 82.
[73] Cannon, *Letters of Jones*, i. 69 (no. 37), 74 (no. 40).

Charles Roderick, and Joseph Drury had been engaged by Sumner to assist Wadeson in the Lower School.[74] This assigning of masters to forms rather than to subjects across the whole age and ability range was central to the structure of teaching for more than a century and, in attenuated form, survived until the 1970s. Of the four, Parr was the only outstanding scholar. Wadeson was unambitious and apparently second-rate, staying at Harrow until 1789, but Roderick pursued a long and moderately successful teaching career while the urbane Drury slid almost without effort into the Head Master's chair vacated by his brother-in-law Heath in 1785.[75] A feature of this group was similarity of background and social status. Parr's father was an apothecary; Wadeson's a husbandman; both were entered as sizars at Cambridge. Parr, Drury, and possibly Wadeson could not afford to complete their degrees without taking up teaching. All of them, including Roderick, were dependent on their master's salaries and tutorial income, a useful incentive to loyalty and industry. In that sense they were all self-made men, in contrast to their socially more elevated employer. They were also very young: on appointment Wadeson had been 24, Roderick 23, Parr rising 20, and Drury only 18, almost a sort of pupil–teacher. As a group, Wadeson was nearly the same age as Sumner (he was born in 1734, Sumner in 1729), while Roderick (b. 1745) and Parr (b. 1747) were of an age, with Drury (b. 1751) slightly younger, although Parr soon affected to look much older. Age and circumstances may explain their easy conviviality. One holiday, Wadeson, Parr, and Roderick spent an evening and stayed the night at the Pillars of Hercules in Piccadilly.[76] In March 1771, Roderick and Drury together spent three nights on the town, taking in plays and a performance of Handel's *Messiah*.[77] On Sumner's death the surviving masters attempted to act in concert over the succession and held the school together during the interregnum.[78] The younger three, at least, although their paths diverged after 1771, remained friends for the rest of their long lives.[79]

Sumner treated these young masters, and Jones when he returned as Althorp's tutor in 1769, as students as much as colleagues. He ostentatiously kept a book of his favoured pupils' best exercises on view. He would discuss Parr's current reading with him and regularly entertain him and Jones to dinner. Jones, it seems, chaffed at this tutelage; Parr lapped it up. For him, Sumner was 'the instructor of my

---

[74] HSR III, fo. 154ʳ, HSR 497; Johnstone, *Parr*, i. 35 n. 2, 36–7, 42; Drury, *Memoir*, 6–7; Butler, *Harrow Lists*, 7.

[75] For the careers of these masters, apart from the not wholly reliable Gun, *Harrow School Register*, 157 and refs. see Johnstone, *Parr*, i. *passim* and esp. pp. 51–2, 58, vii. 77, 226 (re Wadeson's doctorate); Field, *Parr*, i. 67–9 (Roderick); Maurice, *Memoirs*, i. 82; Drury, *Memoir, passim*.

[76] For Roderick's version see Johnstone, *Parr*, viii. 234. Cf. Maurice, *Memoirs*, i. 150–1; Field, *Parr*, i. 63 n. 2.   [77] Johnstone, *Parr*, viii. 231–2: Roderick to Parr, 23 Mar. 1771.

[78] Ibid., i. 58 (the account is Roderick's).

[79] Drury and Roderick both received rings in Parr's will. Parr died (1825) aged 78 years; Roderick (1830) aged 85 years; and Drury (1834) just short of 83 years.

boyhood and the guide of my youth'.[80] Sumner's influence over Drury was no less profound and lasting. If this regime had been perpetuated, the orgy of mutual admiration and self-congratulation could easily have curdled. While it lasted, it left a vivid impression on all who experienced or witnessed it, masters, boys, and parents.

In an institution now as large as Sumner's Harrow, there was something if not unhealthy then precarious in this reliance on the personality of one man. Robert Sumner, as his surviving portrait shows, was no ascetic. He chain-smoked, probably drank freely with or without company, and by 1771 never went up to school before eleven in the morning. He happily left Parr to cope with the Fifth and Fourth Forms in his absence.[81] An inspirational teacher of the able, he matched a keen railing sense of humour with a sharp critical judgement. In his prime cheerful, witty, and learned, he exerted an almost mesmeric hold over pupils and listeners with what Parr described as his 'fine voice, fine ear, fine taste'.[82] An objective assessment would also mark him as domineering, confident in an ability he declined to undervalue. He was intolerant of the stupid, dull, or idle, spending little time to modify first impressions. It was Parr, when standing in for him, who brought Sheridan's virtues to the Head's attention; Sumner had not noticed them.[83] Sumner's virtues were intellectual, secular, and humanist; so, possibly, were his vices.

Towards the end, although there were no signs of it in his correspondence or the outward management of the school, there were hints of a decline or a shadow falling across his life. Jones, who had kept in close touch with his old master even before returning to the Hill in 1769, had a row over Althorp's tutorial arrangements in 1770. A year later, on Sumner's death, Jones admitted to his friend William Bennett, 'my confidence in him had been considerably decreased for the three last years and I began to take less pleasure in his company than ever'.[84] Jones had remained close to Samuel Glasse even after the 1768 passage of arms and had, to a degree, turned towards religion.[85] Sumner may have appeared increasingly cynical or flippant. Or, as is the common disillusioning lot of pupils who outstrip their mentors, the genius of the teacher that had shone so brightly for the boy, in adult light may have seemed faded, perhaps a little flashy or superficial. Jones also disapproved of Wilkes, for whom Sumner's closest accolyte Parr was so strong. There was more; Jones continued starkly to Bennett: 'as to himself, he had too many misfortunes to

---

[80] Teignmouth, *Jones*, 63; Cannon, *Letters of Jones*, i. 81 (no. 45), 103 (no. 56); Johnstone, *Parr*, i. 42, 54–5, 74–5, viii. 233–4; Field, *Parr*, i. 54, 57 n. 2.

[81] Laborde, *Harrow School*, 134 (for portrait); Johnstone, *Parr*, i. 75; Golland, *Eighteenth Century Harrow*, fo. 5; Field, *Parr*, i. 52–3. Thomas Grimston's description of the school day for the Fourth Form in 1769/70, with lessons ending at variable times ('sometimes sooner, sometimes later') might confirm a certain relaxation—or the variable enthusiasm of the master, probably Parr: Ingram, *Leaves from a Family Tree*, 87.   [82] Thornton, *Harrow School*, 161–2.

[83] Teignmouth, *John, Lord Teignmouth*, i. 8–9; Field, *Parr*, i. 51–3.

[84] Cannon, *Letters of Jones*, i. 69, 74, 77 n. 3.   [85] Teignmouth, *Jones*, 64.

make life any longer desirable'. Strong, if pious, stuff. However, even Bennett, a staunch devotee, lamented to Parr on hearing of Sumner's death: 'Ah! my friend, was he not too careless in his conduct? Were his talents always applied to the glory of his Maker?'[86]

It is now impossible to discover what lay behind these remarks: drink? money? sex? family misery? Certainly, Bennett's remark suggests an unhealthy lifestyle which could well have been the cause of the sudden stroke Sumner suffered on 12 September. He lingered speechless for a few hours, surrounded by the school doctor and the faithful Parr, Drury, and Roderick, before he died.[87] He was 42. Thornton likened Sumner to 'a splendid meteor'.[88] Meteors bring brief, sudden, bright illumination causing both wonder and damage. They also destroy themselves.

THE ELECTION OF 1771

The ultimate test of the governors' Eton policy now arrived. Sumner's death presented them with a choice: whether to continue Sumner's system with or without his particular, at times eccentric, slant, whether to affirm independent local distinctiveness, or to reassure prospective clients by a confirmation of Harrow's openness to the grandest public school tradition. As the Glasse incident and its aftermath had shown, Sumner's work was incomplete, still largely dependent on his own personality and a close group of loyal, uncritical, subservient colleagues lacking significant social connections of their own. Whatever decision reached by the governors would inevitably have lasting repercussions.[89]

The small group gathered around Sumner's corpse immediately settled that if, as expected, Wadeson was not interested, the succession should be Parr's. His friends had been scheming for his succession for some time and Parr himself declared that Sumner had always seen him as his heir. In the days after Sumner's death, he took over the running of the Upper School, Sumner's tutors, and oversaw his boarders. His lack of the qualifying MA was rapidly amended. With the support of a number of Heads of Houses, by the end of September he received his Cambridge MA *per literas regias* from the Chancellor of the University, ironically the duke of Grafton, one of Wilkes's prime targets.[90] Trying to create irresistible momentum

---

[86] Cannon, *Letters of Jones*, i. 103; Johnstone, *Parr*, i. 53.

[87] Johnstone, *Parr*, i. 58 (Roderick's account); *Report on the MSS of Lady du Cane*, 229, William Whately to John Grimston, 12 Sept. 1771. [88] Thornton, *Harrow School*, 145.

[89] The following narrative is largely based on the memoirs and letters of some of those involved or present to be found in: *Report on the MSS of Lady du Cane*, 229–37 (the Grimston correspondence); *MSS of the Earl of Dartmouth*, 194–6; Johnstone, *Parr*, i. 53–65, 82, vii. 78 (Parr, Roderick, Bennett, and Lytton, with some letters of Heath); Field, *Parr*, i. 58–62 (Parr, Lytton); Golland, *Eighteenth Century Harrow*, fos. 1–2 (the Yorke perspective).

[90] Field, *Parr*, i. 61–2; Johnstone, *Parr*, i. 56 (letter from the Master of Caius to Parr, 19 Sept. 1771), 58. For plans for Parr to succeed see Bennett's letter on 1769/70, ibid., i. 74.

to his candidature, Parr submitted his application to the governors the day after Sumner's death, emphasizing his local birth, attendance at the school as a boy, and experience as a master, rather pointedly excusing himself attendance on the governors because of his duties at the school during this 'perplexity of our affairs'. He also immediately sought the patronage of influential parents, such as Lord Dartmouth.[91]

However, other interests were soon engaged. Two further candidates emerged by the end of September: Sumner's cousin, Humphrey, and Benjamin Heath, both masters at Eton and strongly backed by that school and its network of aristocratic contacts. There was fevered lobbying of governors and parents by all sides, the ferocity of the contest a tribute to the strides Harrow had made under Sumner. His succession was seen as both valuable and important. The governors kept their counsel, which, as four of them lived on the Hill, cannot have been easy, their reticence possibly the cause of Parr accusing them of 'meaness, injustice and perfidy'.[92] He was only informed of his fate the night before the election.

On 3 October, the governors elected, the often factually economical minutes insisting 'unanimously', Heath, a decision clearly reached before the meeting as they had already intimated their intention to the successful candidate who arrived shortly after the completion of the election.[93] This had been held in the Governors' Room in the schoolhouse which now became the focus of events as the governors entertained Heath to dinner, Parr not being invited. Heath's arrival sparked a riot. Parr, visibly upset, went up to confront the governors, none of whom dared look him in the eye. It was left to Heath himself to tell Parr that he had been rejected solely because of his age, 24. Meanwhile, outside, the crowd of boys turned nasty, one complaining: 'is it fit that we should always take up with the refuse of Eton?'.[94] Immediately a petition, written by three senior members of Fifth Form, Thomas Powell, Walter Pollard, and John Crooke, and signed by the twenty-six most senior boys, was presented to the governors by a deputation.[95] A splendid example of adolescent self-importance and outrage, it none the less perceptively exposed the central issue and acutely struck at the heart of the governors' policy, even if impotent to alter the fait accompli. Vigorously voicing support for Parr and his credentials, academic and local, it attacked the Eton policy of the governors 'as there appears so many objections to anyone from that place' (Sumner was excepted as transcending this disadvantage by his unique talent). Harrow, the boys declared, 'ought not to be considered as an appendix to Eton', concluding darkly, 'we hope

---

[91] Johnstone, *Parr*, i. 55–7.
[92] Ibid., 61–2, a rather embarrassing letter from Parr to Heath, 6 Oct., to which Heath, reasonably as Parr's secession seriously threatened his own prospects, declined to reply.
[93] HSR III, fo. 160. [94] Thomas Grimston, *Report on the MSS of Lady du Cane*, 230.
[95] For the text see ibid., 275–6; Johnstone, *Parr*, i. 59–61. Roderick later claimed the petition had been signed by all the boys. Philip Yorke more credibly says only the top twenty-six: Golland, *Eighteenth Century Harrow*, fo. 2.

your determination, private attachment or personal affection will not bias your choice to the prejudice of the school'.

The reaction of the governors, who almost certainly thought, wrongly, that Parr and Roderick lay behind this demonstration, was implacable and, in one case, inflammatory. The millionaire Old Harrovian Bucknall angrily called the boys' delegation 'no better than a parcel of blackguards'.[96] For his pains his carriage was promptly wrecked, its wheels removed and the remains pushed down Sudbury Hill. Other governors' property was threatened. The windows of the Rushout residence, The Grove, were smashed as were all the windows of the schoolhouse. Herne's house, old Flambards, escaped more lightly through the intercession of Parr and Roderick who both spent much of the evening quelling the riot. Next morning, Heath slipped back to Eton and two governors, Bucknall and Palmer, went home 'in a hack post-chaise, with the blinds up and 'Parr for ever' written in chalk on the outside'.[97]

However, the rebellion achieved nothing. Heath took over as Head on 14 October and, with the support of the majority of parents, soon imposed his authority. Some, perhaps as many as forty or fifty, left or seceded with Parr. The school tottered but survived. Given Parr's subsequent record as a schoolmaster, the governors were probably vindicated. Although popular, immensely learned, and an original teacher, Parr was vain, solipsistic, and irritable, a self-pitying self-publicist with a pride and affected eccentricity that ensured he never held the confidence of parents or possessed the solid determination to stick at an uncongenial task long enough for lasting success. In fact, despite his apparent surprise and shock on the day of the election, Parr had foreseen the outcome as he had already made provision for setting up a separate school by renting a large house at Stanmore.[98] On hearing of his defeat at Harrow, he immediately resigned and offered Roderick and Drury posts at his new school. The governors, alarmed at the prospect being left with a Head and no members of staff, asked the two assistants to stay: Roderick declined while Drury, after some hesitation, decided to stay. It appears, therefore, that although the riot was spontaneous, there had been a tacit compact struck by the three assistants to stand together in an attempt to force Parr on the governors which only broke down in the face of their unanimous rejection of him.

In devising a contingency plan in case of failure Parr was displaying realism. It was widely accepted that, with the possible exception of the younger Rushout, the governors were hostile to his interests.[99] His close association with Sumner and clear determination to continue in his master's independent footsteps would have

---

[96] Reported by William Whately to John Grimston, 8 Oct., *Report on MSS of Lady du Cane*, pp. 233–4.

[97] *Report on the MSS of Lady du Cane*, 231 (Thomas to John Grimston, 4 Oct.).

[98] He had acquired the house by 4 Oct. and published his terms as early as 7 Oct.: *Report on the MSS of Lady du Cane*, 231, 232. Cf. Roderick's rather enigmatic memory: Johnstone, *Parr*, i. 58. Parr had borrowed £2,000 from Sumner's brother for the venture: see *DNB* entry.

[99] Johnstone, *Parr*, i. 74.

counted against him. The governors stated that age was the sole reason for his rejection. Parr and his friends believed that his support for Sumner in the row over gubernatorial interference in granting holidays and, probably, the Glasse affair, as well as his public support for Wilkes weighed more heavily.[100] Parr would have seemed a looser cannon even than Sumner. Parr, after all, was the son of a Harrow apothecary too poor to finish his degree at Cambridge, while Heath came from a wealthy, well-established academic and well-connected Devon family. It may also not have escaped Parr's attention that John Rushout, the future first Baron Northwick and the governor who chaired the election meeting in place of his octogenarian father, old Sir John, had been at school with Benjamin Heath—at Eton.[101]

The 1771 election was a pivotal moment in Harrow's history. The governors' decision to remain openly associated with the highest national social and academic circles of the academic world, to resist local cabals and parochialism, and to regard the school in a wider context than simple consideration of who could manage the school as it was, confirmed a policy that had brought Harrow its prominence. It also set a distinctive precedent. To date only one Old Harrovian has become Head Master—Montagu Butler. Apart from the disastrous Cox, Joseph Drury, and the temporary wartime expedient of Boissier, no Head Master has been appointed from inside the school. The reasons, as in 1771, were both institutional and social. Heath was elected in part because of snobbery; in part because of contacts; in part because of petty personal animosities towards his main rival; but also in part because the governors' disengaged perspective on the school allowed them to ignore the passions of the moment and the place in preference for a longer vision of the interests of the charity. To the outside world, Parr was 'irregular and unfit.'[102] Parr was a risk; Heath was safe: and the opinion of the world mattered.

BENJAMIN HEATH

Benjamin Heath was eminently qualified as a Head Master by intellect, temperament, and background. His father and namesake was a wealthy town clerk of Exeter who had established a very distinguished reputation as a Greek scholar and critic. Heath himself had been a scholar of Eton and King's and an assistant master at Eton from 1763, where his brother was to become Head in 1796.[103] One of his

---

[100] Johnstone, *Parr*, i. 63–4; Field, *Parr*, i. 62; Maurice, *Memoirs*, i. 150.

[101] After leaving Harrow.

[102] Dean Kaye of Lincoln's opinion, quoted by Thornton, *Harrow School*, 184 n. Parr closed Stanmore in 1776, moving to Colchester then (1779) Norwich. He stopped being a schoolmaster altogether in 1785, retiring to the living of Hatton, there taking some private pupils.

[103] For Heath and his family see W. R. Drake, *Heathiana* (priv. pub., 1881). On the reputation of the elder Heath see R. M. Ogilvie, *Latin and Greek: A History of the Influence of the Classics on English Life from 1600 to 1918* (London, 1964), pp. 71–2 and his entry in *DNB*.

Eton pupils, in reprimanding his younger brother for leading the Harrow revolt, talked of Heath as 'a steady friend and a faithful adviser . . . exceedingly affable in his manners and profoundly learned, without any mixture of pedantry'.[104] A bibliophile, Heath's library outgrew his house at Harrow by 1781, ultimately being sold for £9,000 in 1810. His academic reputation preceded him, even Parr conceding he was 'a very great scholar and a very good man', a sentiment soon echoed by so stern a judge as William Jones.[105]

His social manner was important. On his first evening when the school reassembled after his election Heath visited each boy in their houses 'to ask . . . if they meant to meet him as friends'.[106] He soon won them over, and through them their parents, not least by continuing the familiar methods of Sumner. From an initial group of about sixty, numbers rose to ninety by the end of October and by March to 155. In June 1772 Heath asked the governors for money to extend boys' accommodation in his house. Within three years numbers had revived to more than 200, over eighty in the Head Master's alone.[107] By 1776 one prospective client complained that, although hearing 'a great account of the Master', Heath's 'school and houses are too much crowded'.[108] Parr's secession to Stanmore, potentially lethal to Harrow and to Heath's personal profit, had been withstood.

To charm was added severity and a determined will. The condition attached to boys returning to Harrow was that Heath had the parents' authority 'to enforce a proper submission to those regulations . . . necessary for the establishment of discipline'.[109] Heath, nicknamed 'Black Ben', was an enthusiastic flogger, even though some pupils doubted the effectiveness of his ministrations. One parent commented a few years later on Heath seeming 'a well behaved man and reckoned very severe in his school', adding: 'this I think an advantage'.[110] He moved swiftly to repair the damage of the departure of Parr and Roderick. By the time school reopened on 14 October 1771 he had hired two new assistants, one of whom, the 22-year-old Thomas Bromley, had just come down from Cambridge as Eighth Wrangler and with the Chancellor's Medal. He took over Roderick's private pupils and probably his teaching.[111] Bromley was to stay at Harrow for thirty-seven years,

---

[104] Maurice, *Memoirs*, i. 82–3: John Pollard to his brother Walter.

[105] *Report on the MSS of Lady du Cane*, 231 (in Parr's speech trying to quell the riot of 3 Oct. 1771); Cannon, *Letters of Jones*, i. 130, no. 75 (23 July 1773). Cf. i. 104, no. 57 (26 Nov. 1771) and i. 139, no. 81 (1 Jan. 1774).

[106] *Report on the MSS of Lady du Cane*, 235–6: letter of Thomas Grimston, 15 Oct.

[107] Ibid., 235–7; Golland, *Eighteenth Century Harrow*, fo. 2; HSR III, fo. 162; Butler, *Harrow Lists*, 28–34; Golland, Interim Amendments, 2.

[108] Philip Francis on 16 Sept. 1776: Gun, *Harrow School Register*, pp. xix–xx.

[109] Copies of the circular dated respectively 5 and 6 Oct. are printed by Johnstone, *Parr*, i. 62–3 and *Report on the MSS of Lady du Cane*, p. 232.

[110] Quoted by Gun, *Harrow School Register*, 154. Cf. Harrow MS HM/D/1a; Townsend Warner, *Harrow in Prose and Verse*, 167.

[111] *Report on the MSS of Lady du Cane*, 231, 235; Gun, *Harrow School Register*, 157.

amassing a modest fortune in the process as housemaster. Like Wadeson, Bromley had been a sizar at St John's, Cambridge, as probably had another of Heath's appointments, Richard Glover, a master by 1774 who stayed for more than two decades. Joining them were, briefly, a Mr Bradley of Corpus Christi College, Oxford and a Mr Cooke who, like Glover, remained for twenty years.[112] Heath's prompt recruitment reassured parents both as regards the formal school work and, perhaps more importantly, the provision of private tuition.

A punctilious scholar and efficient manager, Heath none the less appears moderately accident-prone. Within nine months of taking office he was faced with a confrontation with senior boys over Archery Day.[113] Sumner had been a great supporter of this festival and preparations began as normal, the governors as usual spending money on preparing the butts.[114] However, Heath not only refused to allow the traditional exemption from school work for the month prior to the contest to the twelve boys who had put themselves forward, he had also insisted on their presence at six o'clock bill from which archers had customarily been excused. After the boys appealed to the eagerly interfering governor, Herne, Heath, probably disingenuously, pleaded ignorance of custom. This drew a fine reposte in the circumstances of Parr's recent departure, to the effect that Heath might have consulted his senior masters beforehand. The quarrel led to the withdrawal of half the archers and Heath's cancellation of the contest, as it turned out for good. In place of the high jinks of fine clothes, archaic sporting ritual, fashionable audiences, excitable parades, and a lavish party, Heath substituted three Speech Days which served part of the same social function of attracting parents and the well-connected down to the school while maintaining sober academic discipline. (The tradition has been sustained, although the number of Speech Days was reduced to two in 1829 and one in 1844. When Hawtrey abolished Montem at Eton in 1847 he diverted attention by arranging a cricket match; a sign of the times.)[115]

It is likely that Heath deliberately provoked, or at least consciously risked, a row. He carefully chose his ground, that of school discipline and the Head's authority, the same position occupied by Sumner in 1768. In the process, he could assert his independence from the past, his current power, not least in regard to a difficult governor, and abolish a potentially disruptive social extravagance. It says much for his ability to ride out storms unabashed and unresentful, that he got away with little

---

[112] Gun, *Harrow School Register*, 157; Butler, *Harrow Lists*, 27, 35 (Bradley seems to have stepped in briefly for Cooke 1774/5, although see Golland, Interim Amendments, 4), 45, 53.

[113] For the 1772 confrontation see Ingram, *Leaves from a Family Tree*, 97–8; Golland, *Eighteenth Century Harrow*, fos. 2–3.

[114] HSR VII, fo. 241: 14s. 6d. was spent, more than the usual 10s. 6d., but less than the £1 1s. of 1771 (fo. 236).

[115] Butler, *Harrow Speech Bills*, Introduction, (p. 8); for the abolition of Montem see J. Gathorne-Hardy, *The Public School Phenomenon* (London, 1977), p. 146. Ironically, Heath had been captain of Montem in 1759.

more than some adolescent sulking. Victory was of more than passing significance. For Heath and Harrow to gain a reputation for discipline cast it in a favourable light when compared to the licence and excess of competitors such as Westminster and Eton itself. Supervision of boys out of school, through the mechanism of regular and, for the boys, inconvenient call-overs, was as important for Heath as it had been for his predecessor. One of the grievances in 1772 had been the new bills at nine and six on holidays. Heath's willingness to outface opposition on this issue was confirmed in 1777 when his institution of two additional bills on Sunday, at nine and five, led to an organized rebellion which lasted three days. A monitorial petition was followed by theft of the school keys, the boycott of Sunday bill, and picketing of the London road. In the end, by threatening expulsion of the ringleader, Chaloner Chute, and heavy retribution for the rest of the rebels, Heath engineered a settlement through compromise. No boy suffered, but the bills remained.[116] The importance of the issue is shown by Heath's willingness to face such insurrection.

Academically, Heath pursued the existing Harrow/Eton model. Looking at the books studied, the hours worked, and the exercises set, little altered, even if the atmosphere was less intense than under Sumner. From Philip Yorke's reading, the change of regime in 1771 is imperceptible, except that Heath rather ostentatiously introduced the Upper School to books on Christianity, although doing little to provide any time for formal religious instruction. He seemed happier taking boys through Herodotus. School hours, on full days, remained leisurely: two hours from Prayers at 7 a.m. to 9 a.m.; Breakfast; Second School 11 a.m. to Prayers at 12 noon; Third School 3 p.m. to 4 p.m., followed by Preparation until Fourth School from 5 p.m. to Evening Prayers at 6 p.m.[117] Whole holidays were plentiful, including at least one a week. Something of the sceptical tone of Sumner's day hung on. In an essay on Virtue, John Richardson suggested that 'religion . . . is very apt to draw us on to unaccountable lengths, being deluded by foolish and superstitious ideas', citing as illustration the devoted enthusiasm of adherents to what he saw as the Roman Catholic conspiracy of a hundred years earlier to capture England.[118] Heath maintained the focus on public life through the cultivation of oratory in the annual Speeches and monthly declamations and the encouragement of pupils such as Althorp in their English essays to consider the best use of rhetorical devices, in his case Satire.[119] Heath himself looked over essays with some care, as witnessed by his manuscript corrections to an essay about the importance of emulation in human nature by Theophilus Salwey.[120] One innovation was the

---

[116] See the vivid account by Dudley Ryder, later Lord Harrowby, one of the participants in Harrow MS HM/D/2.

[117] Golland, *Eighteenth Century Harrow*, fos. 5–6. See Thornton, *Harrow School*, 183–4 for school hours *c*.1780. Cf. Ingram, *Leaves from a Family Tree*, 87 for the hours under Sumner and Thomas Gisborne's recollection of Heath's religious instruction (Carlisle, *Grammar Schools*, ii. 148).

[118] Harrow MS HM/D/8.   [119] Harrow MS HM/D/14.   [120] Harrow MS HM/D/13.

creation, when numbers or talent suggested, of a Sixth Form, which first appeared in 1775, although without permanent existence possibly until Dr Drury. Heath also seems to have been the first Head to apply the title of Shell to a form, in this case one waiting for promotion between the Fourth and the Fifth Forms in 1780. Monitors remained at the same number as Sumner had left, six.[121] In keeping with his policy of close academic direction and eagerness for giving book prizes, from 1778 the annual Orator was no longer paid money but received a volume of a classical author, usually Pine's Virgil.[122]

After the heated world of Sumner and the rebellions of the 1770s, Harrow under Heath appears calm. Even scandal barely disturbed the placid surface of a school at ease with success and itself. In 1769 Sumner had appointed a Dancing Master, Antony Tassoni of Hanover Square who built a Dancing School for the boys in 1770. In 1779 he gave way to the equally improbably named Dominic Velloni, who leased from him the Dancing School, a conveniently large room by then the scene of the annual Speeches. Velloni's lease allowed for Tassoni to visit the Hill twice a year to inspect the premises.[123] This injunction may not have been a legal formality, rather an agreed restriction on Tassoni's presence on the Hill. From a poem written on 14 October 1779 by Matthew Montagu to Dudley Ryder, later earl of Harrowby, it appears that Tassoni had made himself *persona non grata*.

> Tassoni is gone for a great misdemeanour
> (Indeed I ne'er heard of a thing that was meaner)
> For the which I could wish that we'd kicked him a mile hence.
> Was papaw (i.e. pawpaw) with the boys and then bribed them to silence:
> No crime he committed but such indecencies.
> As no Man would have done in his right senses.[124]

Tassoni had abused boys and tried to buy their silence. As is not uncommon in such circumstances, his wife tried to plead for him ('Came down here at night dress'd to move our compassion | Quite in negligée, in the pink of fashion'). Equally typical was the immediate but surreptitious removal of Tassoni by Heath. The pantomine elements in the story should not disguise its exposure of some pitfalls of a thriving boarding school and its witness to the clear moral line habitually drawn by otherwise easygoing boys. Once again, however, Heath handled the situation well, which is to say he got away without publicity.

Heath's rule consolidated the position of the Head Master's office. Heath himself, his power confirmed by the rows over bill, entrenched his position, financially as well as magisterially, by building a large extension to the Head Master's house between 1772 and 1774. From a school of about 200, Heath could expect to receive

---

[121] Butler, *Harrow Lists*, 8, 17, 27, 35, 45, 46–7.
[122] HSR VII, fo. 265 and cf. fos. 245, 268, 271, etc. For Heath giving book prizes see Golland, *Eighteenth Century Harrow*, fo. 3.
[123] Ingram, *Leaves from a Family Tree*, 86; HSR 513, 524.   [124] Harrow MS HM/D/1.

towards £1,000 a year from schooling, tuition, and entrance fees. A house of eighty to ninety boys would have brought in over £2,000. Not that Heath necessarily needed the money. He was able to pay £800 from his own pocket to the extension of his house and, from 1781, he also held the living of Walkerne.[125] This comfortable cushion of wealth may have been one of his attractions for the governors in 1771, aware of possible hard times ahead. It may also have lessened Heath's anxiety at the steady decline in numbers from 242 in 1776 to 150 when he retired in 1785.

Heath's position was also secured by a unique family arrangement. In 1777 his two senior assistants, Drury and Bromley, married his sisters, Louisa and Rose. Heath himself was unmarried, living with his mother (who lived until 1808, her ninetieth year).[126] The tradition of Harrow as a family business, begun by Bryan and Cox, was powerfully revived, creating a dynastic succession as Head and assistant masters which lasted unbroken until 1863, by which time the even more tenacious and extended Butler kindred had surplanted it. The cosiness of the dispositions at Harrow under Heath was well caught by a visitor to Speeches in the early 1780s, Dean Kaye of Lincoln:

Harrow: The school an old high Hous, about 180 boys, a Head Master and 4 junior masters, Dr Heath, Dr Drewry (*sic*) and Mr Bromley who married his sisters. His mother. At the Speeches Mrs Bromley got up at three to provide custards etc. which would not keep, clouted cream. She has the conduct of the whole. Mr Drury is most likely to succeed to the school. On Dr Sumner's death He wish'd Mr Parr to succeed.[127]

Dr Kaye's prophecy, coupled with his recall of the events of 1771, point to one of Heath's most obvious achievements. There was no disruption when he informed the governors of his election as a fellow of Eton and his retirement from Harrow at Easter 1785. The succession was seamless. In his resignation letter of December 1784 Heath had not only pressed Drury's claims, stressing his character as a gentleman, but suggested that 'it might be of some service if I could add, when I inform the friends of my young men of my intended resignation, that I had reason to hope for his success'.[128] Although the governors took no official notice of Heath's letter until May 1785, there was no contest.[129] Heath's brother-in-law entered into his kingdom. For Heath, the first Head Master to leave for a better job since 1628, there were the lush, corrupt pickings of an Eton fellowship. Yet he discovered that his time at Harrow was not free of penalty. In 1809 George III, on the verge of final insanity, vetoed Heath as a candidate for the Provostship of Eton on the grounds 'He will never do, for he ran away from Eton'.[130]

---

[125] HSR III, fos. 162, 165, HSR VII, fos. 245, 265. For his scale of fees see Gun, *Harrow School Register*, p. xix; for numbers see Butler, *Harrow Lists, passim*; Golland, *Catalogue of Bill Books*, 1–2; id., Interim Amendments, fo. 2; Thornton, *Harrow School*, 187.

[126] In general see *Heathiana, passim*; Drury, *Memoir*, 9.

[127] Thornton, *Harrow School*, 184 n., quoting British Library Add. MS 18,556, fo. 22.

[128] Harrow MS, uncatalogued HM Correspondence, 28 Dec. 1784, from Eton.

[129] HSR III, fo. 185. [130] Maxwell Lyte, *Eton*, 372.

9

A GLITTERING SCENE: JOSEPH DRURY AND BYRON'S HARROW, 1785–1805

Harrow school at the end of the eighteenth century presents a deceptive image. As with English society itself, behind the successful pursuit and maintenance of traditional outward forms and structures, supporting fundamentals were beginning to change, the start of a shift in the ground which ultimately swept away much that had seemed so stable and so effective. Just as the aristocratic hierarchy in politics, based on land and commerce, resisted French revolution and imperialism only to be challenged and changed by reform consequent on new economic and social imperatives of burgeoning industrialization, so the patrician culture and classical curriculum of the eighteenth-century public school that Harrow had come to embody and which had seemed to shine so brightly when nurturing the likes of Palmerston, Peel, and Byron, was soon to appear obsolete and corrupt. The Head Mastership of Joseph Drury appeared a Golden Age but its glamour and self-satisfaction concealed a transience and an inertia that were soon exposed. At the height of its prestige, when it challenged to be the first, certainly the most aristocratic school in the realm, Harrow was at once ossified and beginning to be confronted by material forces that were to alter its character for ever. While the Harrow of the 1850s is still recognizable, that of 1800 is alien. Most contemporaries, not least Harrovian governors, masters, parents, and boys, were unaware of the imminence of change. Defiance and victory over the French if anything reinforced a sense of complacency in old systems and values. However, Drury's Harrow, so memorably evoked by Byron's sharp, sensuous sentimentality, now appears less a reaffirmation of lasting certainties than a fleeting, gorgeous *fin de siècle*.

The Governors' Minutes and Accounts reveal both hidebound traditionalism and new currents of economic development. With one eye firmly—and as it proved wisely—on the strict legal interpretation of the Charter and Statutes, the governors continued to display unbending parochialism. Despite the aristocratic patronage of governors such as the lords Clarendon, Northwick, and Grimston, all with local estates, the governors' concerns remained dominated by the problems of running what then was hardly a huge estate, there having been only tiny accretions of property to the original trust lands bequeathed by John Lyon two centuries earlier. In 1801 estate income was £777 1s. 11d.[1] The 1801–2 accounts in many ways conformed exactly with their predecessors since 1615. Apart from the salaries to Head and Under Masters, payments to the vicar for sermons, to local tradesmen for repairs to the school's fabric and fittings (reflecting as ever the boys' habitual entertainment of glass breaking) and for firewood, money was disbursed on local charity, Dames' salaries, and apprenticeships. Ten pounds went to the Sunday school at Pinner; twenty to the poor of the parish of Harrow. By an equally traditional contrast, £19 19s. 9d. went on the governors' annual feast, although now, at least, they also stumped up for a meal for the tenants.[2] Peachey was paid £8 for ringing the school bell and, a special payment, two guineas for cleaning out the latrines, which had been extensively rebuilt in 1791.[3] Harrow was, after all, considered the healthy school. The Orator received his Virgil, costing £1 7s. This was hardly the stuff of high finance. Sudden capital expense could shake the Accounts. In 1799 the schoolhouse was deemed to be 'in a dangerous state'. The school builder was instructed to make all required repairs provided 'nothing shall be done but what is absolutely necessary'. As it was, his bill was for over £268, a significant percentage of annual income but still just under twice the estimated cost of a two-up, two-down brick town house.[4] Occasionally the governors were forced into considering extreme measures. In 1805 the governors only narrowly avoided having to take out a mortgage. It was with some relief that, the mortgage threat removed, Lord Clarendon noted that 'nothing now, of course, need be said of it in our Order Book'.[5] Nor was it.

However, in common with the general trend in land management, the previous decades had witnessed some modifications in administration of both property and income. From 1772 a land agent–legal adviser was employed, a precursor of the later clerk to the governors. The bankers Denne and Co. replaced the wooden chest and treasurer's pocket as the depository for annual surpluses in 1787, a move consistent with the increasing importance to the trust of investments, notably government bonds. Rents rose. In 1801 the governors for the first time employed professional accountants and surveyors, Kent, Claridge and Pearce, a reflection of growing complexity in the trust's business.[6] As turnpikes were established along the

[1] Harrow School MS, Governors' Accounts, 1801–2; additions had been on the scale of the 1680 purchase of land for extending the school yard: HSR V, fo. 230.
[2] The tenants' entertainment cost only £3 9s., Governors' Accounts, 1801–2; an annual tenants' breakfast had been instituted in 1790: HSR VII, fo. 316.
[3] HSR III, fo. 198, HSR VII, fo. 325, etc.; Governors' Accounts, 1801–2.
[4] HSR III, fos. 215–16, HSR VII, fo. 355.
[5] Harrow School MS, Governors' Records, Correspondence of 2nd Baron Northwick, 12 Aug. 1805. Cf. HM/Bg/file.　　[6] HSR III, fos. 161–2, 193–5, 199–200, 224; HSR VII, fol. 296.

The Ancien Régime

Edgware and Harrow roads, the governors were involved in lengthy negotiations about contributions to their upkeep and the control of rents from properties affected.[7] The enclosure movement reached trust lands in Bedfordshire in 1797 increasing the value of tenants' lands thus allowing the governors to raise rents.[8] In the same year it was decided a watch be kept on the line of the proposed Grand Junction Canal, for which in 1803 some of the Marylebone land had to be sold.[9] This was merely a foretaste of the complete transformation in the fortunes of the road trust with the early nineteenth-century suburban spread, partly encouraged by the new canal, into Paddington, Kilburn, Maida Vale, and St John's Wood. By 1840 the Marylebone estates were regularly producing annual balances two or three times that of the school trust. Increasingly, the emphasis of the governors' routine activities was concentrated on coping with these changes. School business took up less of their time as the frequency of meetings increased, now often held away from the Hill, at the Essex Arms in Watford to suit Lord Clarendon or at Lord Grimston's house in Grosvenor Square, a pattern of detachment becoming more prominent as the decades passed and not altered until the last quarter of the twentieth century. Even on the Hill, given the dilapidated state of the schoolhouse and the overcrowding caused by the numbers in the school, except for the formal annual Audit, meetings around 1800 took place in an upper room at the King's Head.[10]

These changes did not leave the school wholly unmarked. The advent of income tax in 1798 persuaded the governors that they would have to extend their traditional habit of paying some tenants' land tax to this new levy on masters' salaries.[11] Most notably, the governors lent their support to the Harrow Enclosure Act of 1803 which provided for the enclosing of Roxeth Common.[12] This benefited not only some trust tenants (for whose new fences the governors agreed to pay) but the school, as part of the Common was taken into the governors' direct control and used as a cricket field, the present Sixth Form Ground. For once the interests of the school and the governors' concern to increase the value of the trusts' endowment coincided. However, the order of priorities was clear. Roxeth Common was enclosed because it offered local landowners, including the governors, the prospect of greater profits from their tenants at the cost of depriving inhabitants of common rights such as grazing. It was not enclosed to foster Harrow school cricket.

This active congruence of interest by its rarity underlines the independence of governors' concerns with those of running the school. The school trust could net less than £1,000 a year, but the school itself generated vastly greater sums. In 1797 Dr Drury's annual fees, including a single bed (5 guineas extra), servants, mending, etc., but excluding entrance fees (which totalled 10 guineas) or private tuition

---

[7] Laborde, *Harrow School*, 45. For turnpike business see e.g. HSR III, fos. 219, 220–1, 222, 223, 225, 232, 235–7, etc.   [8] HSR III, fos. 207–8.
[9] Ibid., 245–6; Governors' Accounts, 1801–2 for payment to J. Duckett for surveying land taken for the canal.   [10] HSR III, fos. 216, 217, 218, 220.
[11] Laborde, *Harrow School*, 44; Governors' Accounts, 1804.   [12] HSR III, fos. 229, 239–40.

(4 guineas), were just under £42, but this made no allowance for extras which, as in the previous decade, could well have doubled the eventual bill.[13] At Bromley's house, at about the same time, a total cost of at least £100 was suggested after enquiries by a prospective parent, about half of which was likely to have gone on boarding, i.e. to the housemaster.[14] On a modest estimate of an average of £50 on tuition and boarding and ignoring the money paid to local tradesmen or on extra activities such as fencing or dancing run by semi-independent entrepreneurs, a school of about 140 pupils, as in 1797, would have generated £7,000 a year. In 1801–4, with numbers fluctuating around and above 300, income would have been upwards of £15,000.[15] Thus, superficially penurious as a corporation, Harrow school under Dr Drury was big business, generating huge profits, the chief and direct beneficiaries of which were the masters, in particular the Head. Charles Roderick observed that by staying at Harrow after 1771 and becoming Head Master, his former colleague Drury had 'accumulated a huge fortune'.[16] He was not alone. According to the alert Admiral, the earl of St Vincent: 'Mr Bromley is said to receive some thousands per annum for his boarders and Pupils, he has of course accumulated great Wealth, but so fond of his occupation he cannot quit it'.[17]

The admiral was not exaggerating wildly. In 1804 there were forty-three boys at Bromley's house the Abbey, one he had been running by then for at least fifteen years. In that year, if most of his boys were also his private pupils and he charged more than the Head Master for board and lodging, as did all assistant masters as they lacked the Head's economies of scale, at a conservative estimate Bromley could have grossed well over £2,000. In the same year, when the school roll stood at around 300, with seventy-five boys in the Head Master's house, with fees the same as in 1797, and including entrance fees, and the private tuition he strongly recommended, on his own calculations Drury earned, net of salaries, £7,217. A year earlier, in 1803, with 320–50 in the school (including seventy new boys that year paying entrance fees) and eighty-five in his house, Drury earned £6,319. In twenty years as Head, he made over £80,000 from the school. Even his brother Mark, receiving £31 1s. 8d. as Under Master, could have earned from his house of about thirty boys (on the site of the present Old House and Bookshop: Peel boarded with him) in 1803 and 1804 as much as £1,500 each year. In addition, he received a quarter of the schooling and entrance fees.[18] No wonder Mark Drury

[13] Harrow School MS HM/D/26.

[14] Undated letter Lord St Vincent to his brother W. Jervis, c.1800, transcript in Harrow MS, Material Relating to Boys at the School, Box I (loose).

[15] For numbers here and below see Butler, *Harrow Lists, passim*; Harrow School MS Bill Lists 1785–1805; Golland, *Catalogue of Bill Books*, 1–5; Dr Drury's surviving Entrance Book; M. G. Dauglish and P. K. Stephenson, *Harrow School Register, 1800–1911* (London, 1911).

[16] Johnstone, *Parr*, i. 82.

[17] Harrow School MS, Materials Relating to Boys, Box I, St Vincent letter, as above, n. 14.

[18] For house figures, see MS Bill Lists; Drury's Entance Book (MS 1871–2) contains his annual income on a loose folio: the average is over £4,000 p.a.; the lowest is over £2,500 p.a. (1792–4).

was eager to succeed his brother. These figures compare with the average income of a peer of £8,000; a baronet would be doing well on about £4,000; substantial merchants might have earned only about £2,500; and a comfortable shopkeeper about £100 a year.[19] Drury's official salary from the governors remained £30, but his earnings at the height of his school's popularity made him unequivocally wealthy. It is striking how vigorously his son, Charles, attempted to rebut Roderick's charge that Joseph Drury had 'accumulated a large fortune'. It was clearly a sensitive point: the son protested too much.[20]

These potential and actual riches depended, of course, upon the numbers of boys in the school. Under Drury, Harrow reached a size greater than ever before, not again reached until Dr Vaughan fifty years later. Yet this was not a gradual expansion but a sudden spasm of popularity. Inheriting a school of 150 in 1785, Drury presided over gentle decline, numbers reaching as low as 120 in 1793–5. In 1793 the Dancing Master Richard Blake secured from the governors a halving of his rent for the Dancing School 'in consequence of the reduced number of scholars'.[21] Thereafter the rise was initially modest: over 130 in 1796, 141 in 1797. Then growth accelerated. There were 180 boys listed in 1798; over 200 the following year when Henry Temple, later the second Viscount Palmerston and Prime Minister, remarked on the rapid influx of boys: 'the school now consists of 188 boys . . . about seventy more than . . . when I first came [in 1795] and it is most likely will be increased by ten or fifteen more after the holidays.'[22] It was. During 1800 and 1801 numbers surged upwards, from 222 until finally topping 300. Throughout the next two years, 1802 and 1803, numbers ranged at historic heights, between 313 and a peak of 351. Although then falling away below 300, George Butler inherited a school of over 250 in 1805. Even though this startling crescendo was brief and except for his last four years Drury was merely restoring the proportions of the school he first knew under Dr Sumner, his success in attracting pupils established for his successors a new benchmark and, less expected, a legend. It also, most significantly for the school's future, created the largest ever pool of Old Harrovians, from whom could be gained pupils or, as for the rebuilding of the schoolhouse in 1819, donations.

The explosion in size reflected and promoted the school's reputation. It also lent Harrow the crowded and hectic atmosphere alternately loathed and loved by Byron, the contrast between the frenzied schoolboy rivalries, arguments, fights, games, and friendships with the tranquillity of the churchyard and views of the surrounding countryside providing piquancy to some of the poet's early school

---

[19] These were calculations by Patrick Colquhon in 1803 in his *Treatise on Indigence* and *Treatise on the Population and Resources of the British Empire*; R. Porter, *English Society in the Eighteenth Century* (London, 1982), p. 81.

[20] Drury, *Memoir*, 16.   [21] HSR III, fos. 202–3.

[22] B. Connell, *Portrait of a Whig Peer* (London, 1957), pp. 421–2: Palmerston to his mother, June 1799.

verse.²³ The Harrow Byron created went beyond predictable Harrow arcadian nostalgia as displayed in Savillon's 1780s *Elegies* or George Holford's *Invocation to Harrow Muses* (published in 1801 but composed 1794).²⁴ In particular, Byron, anxious of his own pedigree, identified with the aristocratic element in the school, such as his friends the duke of Dorset, Earl Delawarr, and the earl of Clare.²⁵ To many subsequent writers it was the combination of talent—Drury taught five of the seven Harrovian Prime Ministers—and breeding that was so attractive about Harrow around 1800.

The school had grown into a serious rival to Eton not just on the backs of men doing well out of the French wars but from the patronage of the highest reaches of the peerage. As Percy Thornton excitedly put it, Drury 'ruled over the most patrician assemblage of which record remains'.²⁶ He cited the school list of 1803 where among the 345 names were one actual and three prospective dukes, a future marquess, two current and five future earls and viscounts, four lords, twenty-one honourables, and four baronets. There were forty-one peers, sons, heirs, or brothers of peers, just under 12 per cent of the total. Cynics might argue that, courtesy of the younger Pitt's orgy of peerage creations (there were 94 new creations 1780–99, 113 new grants in all) there were more peers about, 267 in 1800, seventy-eight more than twenty years earlier.²⁷ However, it seems that sons of only three Pittite creations—Calthorpe, Lilford, and Bradford—found their way to Harrow.

The reasons for this dual phenomenon of sudden popularity and aristocratic connection are not easily unravelled. Although Harrow prided itself on being the healthy school, there were deaths from scarlet fever in 1795 and measles in 1803.²⁸ The trend of the rich and titled to educate their sons for public life at public schools was accelerating, a sign of increased social mobility among the plutocracy and, perhaps, a collective reaction to the sense of embattlement caused by the French wars. By the 1790s public schools portrayed themselves as peculiarly English and peculiarly elitist. More specifically, growing realization that the war was not to be short and of the need for toughened military and political leaders may have made public schools more attractive. Locally, the decline in repute of Westminster—Dr Drury's old school—almost certainly acted as a direct benefit for Harrow which could appeal to a similar London-based market. In general, however, overall numbers attending public schools rose, so poaching was not a central cause of Harrow's

---

²³ See esp. the poems e.g. *Hours of Idleness*, in Byron, *Poetical Works*, i, ed. J. J. McGann (Oxford, 1980), pp. 39, 66–9, 75–6, 94–8, 116–21, 123, 132, 138–9, 157–72 (*Childish Recollections*), 172–3.

²⁴ *Savillon's Elegies* (London, 1795), pp. 1–3 (*Adieu to Harrow*), 73 (*Sonnet on a Distant View of Harrow School*); Invocation to Harrow Muses: To Defend the Use of the Heathen Mythology, in G. Holford, *The Cave of Neptune* (London, 1801), pp. 3–7.

²⁵ Byron, *Poetical Works*, i, nos. 47, 59, 66, 71.

²⁶ Thornton, *Harrow School*, 205. Cf. ibid., 196 and n. 2.

²⁷ Cannon, *Aristocratic Century*, esp. pp. 21–2.

²⁸ Connell, *Whig Peer*, 320 (cf. p. 424 for a serious case of mumps in 1800); *Register, 1800–1911*, 21: S. Jenyns died of measles, 27 Oct. 1803; Butler, *Harrow Lists*, 62. For mumps see HM/D/22.

The Ancien Régime

increase, although accommodation was. From the mid-1790s, new masters provided fresh opportunities to house boys ostensibly in comfort, as did Benjamin Evans, Byron's future housemaster, who bought a house in Hog Lane (now Crown Street) after his arrival in 1792.[29]

Family loyalty also played a part. Drury's Harrow contained many sons and grandsons of Harrovians. They, like their Head Master, were a direct link to the 1760s when Harrow had well over 200 pupils who, thirty years later, had children of their own to place. This should not be exaggerated. In October 1800, out of over 230, just under forty had previous family links with Harrow, not counting the sons of masters and Benjamin Heath's nephew, who became one of Byron's fags.[30] None the less, by 1800 pupils of Sumner, Heath, and Drury himself had reached positions of power and authority and not only had sons of their own to be educated but, by word of mouth and by example, could influence others in the close world of the English upper classes.

One traditional reason advanced for Harrow's popularity can be discounted. The argument that Harrow was a Whig school attracting those who disapproved of Pitt the Younger's policies at home and abroad or disliked George III's patronage of Eton holds little water. As before, Harrow complemented as much as opposed Eton, Drury himself sending his two eldest sons there as teenagers.[31] Harrow's flirtation with radicalism ended with the defection of Parr. Where even the extreme Whig Sumner advocated political neutrality, Drury was decidedly conventional, as was his school. Among the special additional holidays still observed by the school were the anniversaries of the King's birthday, the Queen's birthday, the Coronation, the Accession, the Martyrdom of Charles I, and the Restoration of Charles II, hardly evidence of a hotbed of Whiggish liberty.[32] If Byron affected romantic radicalism and if one of his friends, Thomas Wildman, was the son of a friend of Wilkes and a nephew of the controversial Horne Took, also seated on the benches with them were the Tory Peel and the sons of the rigidly reactionary Spencer Perceval. Indeed, it could be argued that Harrow's very catholicity was a draw.

The aristocratic influx may also be more apparent than real as well as holding a clue to one reason for Harrow's rapid advance. As much as Harrow attracted aristocrats, aristocrats attracted Harrovians. While the percentage of boys from the families of peers in 1803 was 12 per cent, in 1796, in a much smaller school (139 as against 345), it was actually higher, over 15 per cent.[33] Even in decline, Drury kept a refined establishment which gained adherents—such as the parvenu first

---

[29] On Evans see Gun, *Harrow School Register*, 157; Thornton, *Harrow School*, 270, 272. It is claimed that Evans served for fifty years, but that would place him at Harrow in 1783, aged 18 years and before matriculating at Cambridge: he came in 1792: HM/D/45.

[30] Thornton, *Harrow School*, 204 n. 2, 273; Drake, *Heathiana*, 24; *Register, 1800–1911*, II and 1–14 for the Bill List: 10 Oct. 1800.   [31] Gun, *Harrow School Register*, 65.

[32] Harrow School MS HM/Bg/file; Thornton, *Harrow School*, 228.

[33] Butler, *Harrow Lists*, 53–72. On aristocrats under Drury see Drury, *Memoir*, 13–14.

Sir Robert Peel or the sceptical Irish first Viscount Palmerston—by virtue of its existing tone. The place in the affections of the English aristocracy first gained by Sumner was carefully tended by his successors thus preventing the school from drifting into a social obscurity to match its shrinking size in the 1780s and 1790s. Sumner's and Heath's modifications to the Eton system by offering assistant masters as both tutors and housemasters reassured parents. Of those with sons at the Abbey the Palmerstons found Mrs Bromley intelligent and capable while the Spencers thought her husband 'a gentleman having very moderate pretensions to scholarship and no recommendations beyond a good nature and a long residence as tutor in the family of the earl of Pembroke'.[34] Bromley certainly helped the young Lord Althorp cope with the death of his younger brother with intelligence, sensitivity, and tact. As much as to underlying trends, Harrow's eruption in size can be credited to Drury and his colleagues: the announcement of the Head Master's retirement late in 1804 knocked fifty off the roll.[35]

Joseph Drury

Joseph Drury was Head Master of Harrow for twenty years, 1785 to 1805.[36] When he retired, he had been teaching at the school for thirty-six years. The circumstances of his original appointment, his inability to complete his Cambridge BA owing to lack of money, may have fired in Drury, coming as he did from a respectable background, a certain material ambition. In 1771, only 20, he clearly saw where his interest and opportunity lay, to be a grateful Heath's right hand rather than number three to the mercurial and difficult Parr. Heath, a wealthy man, was unmarried. By becoming his brother-in-law in 1777 as well as his coadjutor, Drury soon occupied the position as heir to Heath's business, outstripping his competitor Thomas Bromley who married the other sister. It is likely that Heath and Drury became friends as well as business associates: they were to be buried beside each other. Drury learnt early the vital principle of eighteenth-century success: connections. It was said he had not progessed from Westminster to Christ Church because of the lack of them. As a schoolmaster, he sought to remedy the omission for reasons certainly professionally prudent but also, perhaps, more deeply psychological. At once basking in the approval of the great, he declared he was more proud to be 'the exclusive architect' of his own fortunes than in any pedigree.[37] Yet he married into a wealthy and well-connected family. For all

---

[34] Connell, *Whig Peer*, 323; D. Le Marchant, *Memoir of John Charles, Viscount Althorp, 3rd Earl Spencer* (London, 1876), pp. 32, 37–8 (for Bromley's letter to 2nd Earl, 23 Jan. 1791, a masterpiece of rare sensible and sensitive housemastering).

[35] Harrow School MS Bill Lists; Golland, *Catalogue of Bill Books*, 4–5.

[36] On Drury see Drury, *Memoir*, passim.

[37] Ibid., 3. Cf. ibid., 6 for Westminster and university.

The Ancien Régime

the encomiums showered upon him, some apparently sincere, Drury remains an elusive personality. A man whose career was founded upon amiability and social charm, he none the less harboured an almost pathological refusal ever to have his portrait drawn, carved, or painted and, from a young age, was obsessive in destroying correspondence. He seemed determined to leave few traces apart from his energetic patronage of Edmund Kean at the Drury Lane Theatre late in life.[38] After he retired from Harrow, he only once returned, to a hero's welcome in 1807.[39] (By contrast, Parr kept on returning to Speech Days until shortly before his death in 1825, an increasingly odd relic from a past age in a funny wig.)[40] For most of his almost thirty years of retirement on his Devonshire estate, Drury gave the distinct impression that, in his grandson's words, he 'had had enough of boys' society'.[41] Drury has extravagantly been called 'the most exceptional schoolmaster that history records',[42] yet it is clear that, his pile made, he more or less immediately abandoned his vocation almost as if he could not leave it fast enough. He never looked back. That it took him twenty years to amass adequate funds should not disguise that they were one of his objects throughout. His ambition was not for status: he received only trifling ecclesiastical preferment. It was for the security that is brought by money and land.

From Sumner, Drury learnt his rather overblown pedagogic technique, characterized by his son as 'a tendency to the *Asiaticum dicendi genus*'.[43] Under Heath, he learnt his trade as an educator of the aristocracy, more accomplished socially than academically. His degree (a BD) was finally achieved in 1784 by occasional residence in Cambridge during the holidays; the DD arriving with the rations, as it were, after his appointment as Head Master, in 1789. It appears that Drury was technically unqualified to be elected Head, as he lacked the MA specified in the statutes, another indication, perhaps, of a certain cosy decadence that was never far from the elbows of the school's managers. Even before succeeding to the Head Master's chair, Drury began to cultivate the great, the good, and the potentially useful, including Old Harrovians such as Sheridan and his former pupils the earl of Harrowby and Dr Stephen Demainbray, chaplain and astronomer to the king. Staying during the holidays with the banker Henry Drummond, another pupil, at Uxbridge, Drury encountered political luminaries such as Lord North, then Prime Minister and Henry Dundas, later Lord Melville, Pitt's closest henchman.

[38] Drury, *Memoir*, 24.
[39] B. H. Drury, 'The Drury Family', in Howson and Townsend Warner, *Harrow School*, 64–5. See Butler's letter inviting Lord Northwick to dine with Drury, July 1807, Harrow School MS, HM Correspondence Butler G File, unnumbered.
[40] Thornton, *Harrow School*, 182–3 and n., quoting the eye-witness of Richard Chevenix Trench, later archbishop of Dublin.
[41] Charles Merivale, *Autobiography and Letters*, ed. J. A. Merivale (Oxford, 1898), p. 21.
[42] P. H. M. Bryant, *Harrow* (London, 1936), p. 32.
[43] i.e. 'florid, emotional, declamatory style of rhetoric': *The Oxford Classical Dictionary*, ed. M. Cary, *et al.* (Oxford, 1949), p. 767.

Elsewhere, he struck up friendships with the likes of Admiral Meadows, the future Earl Manners; Thomas Powys, later Lord Lilford; the king's doctor, Sir George Baker; Repton, the fashionable landscaper of rich men's estates; as well as a host of other members of high society and literary or musical hangers-on.[44] Almost by definition Drury or any schoolmaster in his position and time were attendants at the courts of the wealthy and influential. It helped that Drury revelled in such society, spending his vacations, his son purred, 'in a manner still more congenial to his disposition, among friends whom his many engaging qualities had first attracted and afterwards united to him by bonds of closest attachment'.[45] Many sent their sons to Harrow as well. Even before 1785, Drury, at his house, now 80 High Street, took in as boarders distinguished sons of prominent fathers, including the future Marquesses of Westminster and Hastings and Harrow's first Prime Minister, Spencer Perceval, son of Lord Egmont.

As Head Master, Drury continued Heath's precedent of running the school as a family business. His brother-in-law Bromley ran the largest boarding house after Drury's own. Their wives, the Heath sisters, were powerful forces. Rose Bromley effectively ran her husband's house while Lousia Drury, according to one of her grandsons, was 'the soul of the old establishment at Harrow', probably not the first and certainly not the last dominant Head Master's wife. Although both artistic, the Druries must have cut an incongruous pair, he reserved and deferential, all suave friendliness and studied charm, a model of conventional social grace; she, highly strung, a prolific writer of forgettable verse with a sharp tongue and keen wit, 'highly lauded and perhaps a little feared', an impression no doubt considerably enhanced by the forbidding green shade she wore over a blind eye.[46] Besides his wife, Drury surrounded himself with relatives. Soon after becoming Head, he appointed his younger brother, the portly and popular Mark Drury, to the staff, later securing his promotion to the Under Mastership on Wadeson's retirement in 1789. In 1801 Henry Drury, Joseph's eldest son, became an assistant master. When, announcing his own retirement in 1804, Joseph Drury advised the governors to appoint Mark to succeed him, Harrow displayed a remarkable dynastic spectacle. The Head and Under Masters were brothers; the senior master was the Head's brother-in-law; the Head's eldest son was a master, tutor, and housemaster; and the Head of School was Charles Drury, the Head Master's third son.[47] Allied to the obvious financial gains was the consideration of status. Joseph Drury tried to ensure his family were established as gentlemen. His two eldest sons were sent after Harrow to Eton as scholars, in turn becoming scholars and fellows of King's; both were later strong candidates for Headships, Henry at Harrow (1829), Benjamin at

---

[44] Drury, *Memoir*, 10–14, 22 (for Repton).   [45] Ibid., 11.
[46] Merivale, *Autobiography*, 21–2; Drury, *Memoir*, 26 for Joseph's singing and piano playing. For Mrs Drury's role in running the house and supervising the younger boys, see Harrow School MS HM/D/31.
[47] Harrow School MS HM/D/40; MS Bill Lists 1804; Gun, *Harrow School Register*, 65.

Eton (1809). The presence as a fellow of Eton of their uncle, Benjamin Heath, cannot have harmed their prospects. This Heath–Drury, Eton–Harrow network was also significant of the sense of common identity, mutual elitism, and shared superiority between the top public schools which has never quite vanished.

Joseph Drury's place in the traditional history or mythology of Harrow has been rivalled only, perhaps, by Vaughan. He not only took the school to unprecedented numbers and social distinction, possibly more remarkably he appears to have been almost universally liked and admired. Lacking the intellectual clout of a Sumner or Heath, he relied on impressing his pupils with his personality. The Victorians saw in this the pioneering first step towards what became the keystone of Arnoldian educational reform, 'school government by personal and moral influence'.[48] This is to misunderstand the context of Drury's regime. Unlike Arnold and his followers, Drury did not base his authority on the pulpit, only very rarely preaching. Although in general terms invoking religion or morality to counter disorder, misconduct, or vice, Drury's preferred weapon was ridicule, embarrassing culprits rather than putting them in fear for their immortal souls. As befitted a system so steeped in the recitation of the classics, shame not guilt lay at the heart of Drury's system of rebuke. He also preferred to discuss disciplinary problems privately, allowing boys to express intimate feelings away from the glare of peers' disdain.[49]

In Byron's often heightened memory, Drury was 'the best and worthiest friend I ever possessed'. From his correspondence, it is clear Drury treated pupils with immense patience and consideration. He regularly used to visit boys in their rooms and ask them to join him on walks. Writing in 1804 Byron commented: 'there is so much of the Gentleman (Drury would have been pleased with that), so much mildness, and nothing of pedantry in his character that I cannot help liking him.'[50] Palmerston, who left in 1800, later declared that to be reprimanded by Drury was a positive pleasure.[51] Drury's secret was that he took pains to know each boy as an individual and to pretend to them and to their parents that each had a unique place in his attention. He also perfected the art, useful to all pedagogues, of the soothing report. In 1777 he had let Sir William Lee down gently in a letter about a Latin prose by young William Lee which was so bad it was, by agreement of master and pupil, thrown in the fire, even though Sir William had praised it. Drury used this to illustrate why promotion of young William to the Fourth Form 'would be doing him an essential injury', concluding in delphic vein, 'there is not

---

[48] Thornton, *Harrow School*, 194. [49] Drury, *Memoir*, 17–21.
[50] Ibid., 19; Byron, *Letters and Journals*, ed. L. A. Marchand (London, 1973–82), i. 50; Thornton, *Harrow School*, 197. An excellent example of his style is the letter to 'The Captain of the School and Monitors', 29 Nov. 1808, where he carefully explains to the then rebellious Sixth Form the duties of the Head Master and the boys' obligations to him: Harrow School MS HM Correspondence Butler G. File, unnumbered.
[51] K. Bourne, *Palmerston: The Early Years, 1784–1841* (London, 1982), p. 6.

the least harm to be found about him, at the same time I must say he is not always so attentive'.[52] A similar gambit was used about Byron's close friend Cecil Tattersall in 1804, when Drury wrote: '[He] is a very amiable boy and possesses sufficient talent to distinguish himself but I think he wants energy and ambition and confines himself rather to what is necessary than attempts to go beyond it'.[53]

One crucial reason for Drury's success with the Upper School was that he declined to beat senior boys and was reluctant even to set them lines. He prided himself on his verbal reprimands. These were effective, it seems, only because his 'Jobations', as Byron called them (the derivation is from Job), were made to fit the criminal as much as the crime.[54] One consequence of this highly unusual reluctance to flog was that Drury allowed monitors to beat, with canes rather than birches. As they could beat more or less at will and given that physical violence was a normal solution to everyday problems among the boys, Drury's self-denying ordinance, which extended in practice beyond the senior forms, was remarkable, at once insouciant and self-interested. It could be argued that Drury's desire above all things to be liked led to the construction of a system of devolved discipline over which he could preside in avuncular and detached manner, more of a Thackeray than a Heath. The key lay in Drury's relations with the members of the highest forms. Byron said that Drury was 'respected and feared' by the older boys who, in awe of the Head Master's acute yet generous appraisal of character, disciplined the rest of the school harshly more or less on his behalf. It is notable that even his indulgent son and biographer, Charles Drury, did not recommend this system for universal application.[55] If, however, the direct discipline meted out by senior boys caused trouble, Drury was quick to write reassuring letters to parents or guardians whose goodwill he tended so assiduously. On one occasion in 1798 he was stung by a mother's accusation that her sons had been bullied into a time-honoured professional defence: 'As to any serious act of cruelty . . . I must suspend my belief, till the charge is substantiated by better authority.'[56]

This incident revealed the dark side of Drury's Harrow. It was plausibly alleged that two new boys, the Webb brothers in the Head Master's, had been assaulted, the elder, aged 12, kicked in the stomach and thrown to the gound by a senior boy, Lancelot Holland, an injury exacerbated by a subsequent punch during a fight; the younger, aged 10, hit about the head with a toasting fork, probably by his fag master. Drury's spirited defence, while casting doubt on the charges themselves, exposes a Harrow far from arcadian or edenic. The elder Webb he described as a pathological recluse with possible suicidal tendencies who avoided all company

---

[52] Harrow School MS HM/D/16, 17.
[53] Harrow School MS HM/D/no number, 22 Apr. 1804, Drury to Revd W. D. Tattersall.
[54] Byron, *Letters and Journals*, i. 53.
[55] Ibid., i. 54 and 53–5, 56, 58; Drury, *Memoir*, 17–20; Thornton, *Harrow School*, 206–8. Cf. Byron, *Poetical Works*, i, *Childish Recollections*, i. 92, re as a monitor being flogged by Butler: 'And he who wields, must, sometimes, feel the rod'. [56] Harrow School MS HM/D/34.

but absented himself in local alehouses. Drury admitted that other boys may have teased and bullied him because of his eccentric behaviour ('laughed at' and 'plagued' were Drury's words) but he thought Webb should be 'endebted to them for their exertions'. The cause of compulsory sociability, it appears, was allowed to commandeer force and inflict casualties. The younger Webb was cleverer and popular, but, Drury complacently opined, 'boys of different ages do . . . sometimes take improper liberties and exercise crude authority over those younger than themselves'.[57] Drury's sympathies with his pupils did not extend to challenging the status quo. One of the few not susceptible—at least in retrospect—to Drury's charm was, perhaps inevitably, the austere and awkward Robert Peel, who wrote later in life: 'I would not send my boys [to Harrow] . . . unless it is better conducted now than it was when I misspent my time there.'[58]

Palmerston, in the late 1790s, bore witness to the prevalence of fighting (at which he excelled), swearing, and drinking ('fashionable at present', i.e. 1798).[59] There were no bounds physically and few socially. Privacy was impossible. Fagging was endemic and, although often benign in the sense of being merely a process of service, could degenerate into intrusive harassment, as Drury more or less conceded in the Webb case. For those below the Fourth Form, fagging was compulsory; in 1796 this meant that 50 out of 139 were fags; in 1803, 93 out of 345, respectively just over and just under a third of the school. In large houses the tasks were liable to be both more onerous and more hazardous. Casual, possibly unremarked brutality was likely in a school containing such a wide age range. Byron was unusually old in going to the school at 13. Many arrived before they were 10. In 1801 the oldest boy in the school was rising 18; the youngest $6\frac{1}{2}$. Bullying was widespread, Byron earning himself a particularly bad reputation. Like the adult world it affected to mirror, beneath the glamorous, studious, or vibrant display Harrow was a place of violence and scarcely suppressed licence.[60]

The structure of the school did little to discourage this. Indeed as the numbers grew, overcrowding made conditions worse, a state positively encouraged by the venality of the masters. Drury, so far from being modest in his material ambition, tried to maximize his profits whatever the price paid by the pupils he supposedly cherished. His wife having already retired to the west country, her nerves apparently shot to pieces, in his later years, Drury abandoned living in the Head Master's altogether, renting a cottage nearby instead (possibly with one of the Harrow

---

[57] Harrow School MS HM/D/33–5, letters to and from Drury Apr.–May 1798.
[58] N. Gash, *Mr Secretary Peel* (London, 1961), 46.
[59] E. Ashley, *The Life and Correspondence of Henry John Temple, Viscount Palmerston*, 2 vols. (London, 1879), i. 4–5, 6–7, ii. 453. Cf. Harrow School MS HM/D/21.
[60] In addition to works already cited, see L. A. Marchand, *Byron. A Biography*, 3 vols. (London, 1957), i. 65–100 ('The Harrow Years'); C. J. Tyerman, 'Byron's Harrow', *Journal of the Byron Society*, 17 (1989); Merivale, *Autobiography*, 22 n. 1; Ashley, *Palmerston*, i. 7; Butler, *Harrow Lists*, 52–72; MS Bill Lists, 1801; Byron, *Poetical Works*, i. 369.

Dames, Ann Batt), while he crammed as many boys as possible into the house which he allowed to degenerate into a slum. After he retired, the governors were so shocked at what they found that they wrote into his successor's terms of employment that 'in future the Master of the School be bound to keep the Master's house in repair'.[61] Such avoidance of repairs to fabric and fittings was not unique to Drury. A broken window in young Althorp's room at Bromley's house was left unmended during the winter holidays of 1790–1 thereby soaking the wallpaper.[62] The furnishings and decorations were provided and paid for by the boys. They also supplemented their rations, by choice or necessity, contributed to servants' wages, and provided for themselves basic items for washing and mending as well as paper, pens, ink, tea, and sugar, not to mention linen and clothes. A single bed was usually extra; nightshirts were rarely worn.[63] From their riches, housemasters were expected to pay for food and servants; Drury also had to pay the Assistant Masters their salaries: it is difficult to determine on which he lavished least.

Almost all the masters were involved in this commercial enterprise by taking in a few boarders. In 1803, apart from the Head Master, Mark Drury, and Bromley, Henry Reeves, Writing Master and first official school Librarian, had seventeen; Evans had twenty-one in 1804, in which year Henry Drury had twelve. The other two assistants, Bland and Roberts, and Webb the Dancing Master received a handful each. With a full school such perks were easy to dispense, saving the Head from worrying over much about his assistants' basic salaries of 60 guineas.[64] Large numbers also boarded at Dames' houses, principally Mrs Leith's, on the site of the modern vicarage, and Mrs Armstrong's where the War Memorial steps are now. Here life was even less ordered than in master's houses and the food notoriously bad. They attracted clients because they charged less.[65] Yet boarding houses were sufficiently lucrative to persuade the school doctor to open his doors to a few boys. Transfers between houses was easy and common. Byron had the opportunity to compare the regimes in three houses. Initially placed in 1801 with his tutor, Henry Drury (not then established at what became known as Druries, then the Abbey and still occupied by Bromley), he transferred in February 1803 to Evans's house in Hog Lane for a couple of terms. Finally, on his return to school after his long vacation in January 1804, he stayed with Dr Drury, thus finding himself in Dr Butler's house for the new Head Master's first term, Byron's last, in the summer of 1805.[66]

---

[61] HSR III, fos. 255–6, 259; Drury had rented the cottage, garden, coachhouse, and field since 1793: Ann Batt took over the cottage and garden after Drury left, 11 Apr. 1805; for Mrs Drury see Merivale, *Autobiography*, 21–2; Drury, *Memoir*, 23.   [62] Le Marchant, *Spencer*, 37–8.
[63] Cf. the Palmerstons' experience: Connell, *Whig Peer*, 322, 323, 323–4; Harrow School MS HM/D/26 for single-bed supplement.
[64] MS Bill Lists, 1803, 1804; Carlisle, *Grammar Schools*, ii. 149 *et seq.* for salaries, terms, and conditions. Cf. the £50 offered to Parr by Sumner in 1766.
[65] Howson and Townsend Warner, *Harrow School*, 36–7.   [66] Marchand, *Byron*, loc. cit.

The Ancien Régime

The teaching staff assembled by Drury were a very mixed bunch, but, in sharp contrast to Sumner's time, they were academically distinguished, very different from the callow ingénu that Drury himself had been in 1769. All were in Holy Orders. Henry Drury and Robert Bland were distinguished academics in their own right. Mark Drury had gone from Harrow to Trinity College, Cambridge where he completed his degree. Henry Drury was a fellow of King's. Edmund Outram, a master 1791–5 had, like Bromley, attended Manchester Grammar School and St John's College, Cambridge, where he was a fellow, having been Second Wrangler in 1788. Benjamin Evans, who probably succeeded Outram, had been at Eton, and then Pembroke, Cambridge, winning the Chancellor's Medal in 1789. William Roberts, a master from 1801, was a fellow of Queens', Cambridge. Robert Bland, appointed in 1802 as the Under Master's assistant (by whom he was paid), was an Old Harrovian, a pupil of both the older Drurys, who had proceeded to Pembroke, Cambridge before returning to Harrow on graduation.[67] It is a mark of Harrow's academic reputation sustained by Heath that Drury could attract a number of Cambridge fellows, the lure being as much financial as intellectual. While their teaching skills were less certain, although in his early days Mark Drury had been a conscientious teacher of the very young boys, their academic attainment was a sign of things to come.[68]

By contrast, among the so-called Extra Masters, the Writing Master Henry 'Quilley' Reeves was a man of no academic standing, having succeeded his father in 1768 aged 17. The Dancing Master after 1793, James Webb, survived long enough to take advantage of a boom in his business after 1800. The French master was a middle-aged Swiss, Jacques Butticaz, who was succeeded in 1805 by a M. Briod.[69] Such Extra Masters were still paid directly by their pupils, but the establishment of a more or less formal post of French master is another sign that the school curriculum outside the classical formwork was increasingly directed from the centre and not left to individual arrangements with a host of private tutors, as had been the case in the 1760s.

What it was like being taught by these men is difficult to know. Some evidently could behave with sociability towards their pupils, Byron being friendly with Henry Drury after early tantrums (Byron's, not Drury's) and Robert Bland. As a breed, Byron reasonably found schoolmasters fit for ridicule as prudish, as in *Don Juan*, or snobbish, as in the poem to the duke of Dorset, written just after Byron left school in the summer of 1805:

---

[67] Gun, *Harrow School Register*, 65, 157.
[68] Le Marchant, *Spencer*, 36–8; Harrow School MS HM/D/32 for Mark Drury's tutorial advice, 1798.
[69] HSR III, fo. 205 for Webb taking over Blake's position 1793/4 and fo. 256 for Reeves becoming Librarian, 1805; Gun, *Harrow School Register*, 157–8; Butler, *Harrow Lists*, 73; MS Bill Lists.

> Tho' passive tutors, fearful to dispraise
> The titled child whose future breath may raise,
> View ducal errors with indulgent eyes
> And wink at faults they tremble to chastise.[70]

Masters were judged by most boys as social figures, models of behaviour and tone rather than as intellectuals. Learning, after all, occurred largely outside the form-room. The Spencers felt socially at ease with Bromley. Byron praised Drury as a gentleman but was furious at what he regarded as ill-bred behaviour by Henry and, later, Mark Drury whom he described as 'this upstart son of a Button maker'.[71] Indeed, Byron is guilty of precisely the snobbery at which he poked fun in his poem to the duke of Dorset when he composed his almost exactly contemporaneous lampoon on Dr Butler, or 'Pomposus' as Byron gleefully nicknamed him;

> Not formed to grace the Pulpit, but the Shop;
> The *Counter*, not the *Desk*, should be his place.[72]

Elsewhere Byron calls Butler a Barbarian possessed of no social virtue. This feeling that gentlemen should be educated by gentlemen was not new.[73] The respectful and dutiful Dr Drury himself never missed the chance to get pupils to convey to their parents his humble service. He paid especial court, for example, to Byron's guardian, Lord Carlisle, perhaps hoping for an invitation to Castle Howard.[74]

The discounting of the academic for the social was understandable, even inevitable. Eighteenth-century public schools evolved their distinctive *esprit de corps* in a process that created and sustained the very English combination of aristocratic egalitarianism and elitism, free, within the peer-group, from the rigidity of caste that ossified the aristocracies of some continental nations. As Byron expressed it in *Don Juan*, public schools taught pupils:

> . . . all as such can be said
> To be the most remote from common use.[75]

The ability to quote the classics at will was a sign of breeding, the attribute of a gentleman, however loutish in other respects.[76] Cocooned in this superiority, the internal structure of the school admitted no class distinctions of wealth or blood, except for a recognition of titles in the bill lists. It was this egalitarianism that persuaded the American ambassador Rufus King to send his two sons to Harrow in

---

[70] Byron, *Poetical Works*, i. 67, no. 47, ll. 13–16. Cf. *Don Juan*, ibid., v. 21–2, Canto i, stanzas 39–44. [71] Id., *Letters and Journals*, i. 49–50.

[72] Id., *Poetical Works*, i. 172–3, no. 93a, ll. 2–3.

[73] e.g. Daniel Defoe, in the *Compleat English Gentleman*, cited Cannon, *Aristocratic Century*, 38–9.

[74] T. Moore, *Life of Lord Byron* (London, 1851), 19–20.

[75] Canto I, stanza 40, *Poetical Works*, v. 21.

[76] Connell, *Whig Peer*, 434, the first Viscount Palmerston's estimate of the value of a classical education, c.1800: 'nothing contributes more to set off and ornament natural talents' giving 'a young man a reputation even beyond its real value.'

1803.⁷⁷ Some awesomely well-bred Harrovians, such as the duke of Dorset, still lived separately with their private tutors. But even they came under monitorial discipline from which, until the upper forms were reached, 'very properly', Byron noted, 'no rank is exempt', although there survives an anecdote of doubtful authenticity which has Byron himself unsuccessfully attempting to get his protégé, Lord Delawarr, excused a monitorial beating on the grounds 'he is a fellow peer'.⁷⁸

Drury's Harrovians display a variety already familiar. They were wealthy, their schooling, including extras, costing between £100 and £200 a year. The sons of the peerage, gentry, professional classes, and a few new self-made men, such as Peel's father, they later followed predictable careers in the law, church, politics, or on their ancestral estates. There were some oddities. One of Rufus King's sons went on to be President of Columbia University, the other to be Governor of New York, unique Old Harrovian achievements. Others had more dramatic fates, none more than Edward Drummond who, as Peel's private secretary, was assassinated in mistake for his employer in 1843. Of the more prosaic, many passed through the universities, then, for most Harrovians, little more than finishing schools in social graces and fast living. Such comfortable progressions into adult power and influence would have been the near universal lot of Drury's Harrovians but for the French wars. Many Harrovians around 1800 expected to join the colours on leaving school and there was much discussion in upper forms of commissions. A number of Byron's closest friends went into the army, some, such as John Wingfield and Edward Long, Alonzo and Cleon in *Hours of Idleness*, were to die in it. There were many Harrovians at Waterloo. Byron's generation was the generation of *Vanity Fair*. Ever since, the army has provided the single most popular career for Old Harrovians. It may be that such an environment and the experience of such early losses of close friends made the infirm Byron more determined to seek a military role in Greece in the 1820s.⁷⁹

Drury's Harrow was and, through his correspondence and verse, remains Byron's Harrow. The poet's voice conjures up inescapable images of youth and pastoral beauty, his poems weaving an aura of enchantment about what must have been a distinctly pragmatic, earthy community. Although following a tradition that extended back at least half a century, Byron became Harrow's poet, he set a style and created a world far more seductive and appealing than the laboured, hearty, dictatorial corporate verse of the Victorian eulogists. Such was Byron's posthumous reputation that by the end of the nineteenth century he had become enshrined as part of the myth of Harrow that his poetry helped create, 'by far her

---

⁷⁷ Carlisle, *Grammar Schools*, ii. 149.
⁷⁸ MS Bill Lists, 1804; Byron, *Poetical Works*, i. 369; Moore, *Byron*, 23; Thornton, *Harrow School*, 435 for the tutors of Dorset, Herbert, and Plymouth.
⁷⁹ Gash, *Mr Secretary Peel*, 43; Byron, *Poetical Works*, i, no. 93, *Childish Recollections*, ll. 243–64, 325–40; *Register, 1800–1911*, passim.

greatest son'.[80] Unlike more recent claimants for that dubious honour, such as Winston Churchill, Byron left a uniquely varied corpus of evidence about his time at school, his own poems, letters, exercises, and textbooks as well as the reminiscences of others which acknowledge if not his genius then his skill at self-publicity. Although much of it plainly distorted or wrong, Byron's evidence can open a window into the Harrow of his often remarkable contemporaries. It allows a glimpse into what the education provided at Harrow felt like and how it may have influenced at least one exceptional pupil on levels wider and deeper than the sort of philological training received by the likes of Samuel Parr or William Jones. Through Byron, it is possible to understand something of the experience of Harrow at the end of its golden age.[81]

BYRON'S HARROW

'There goes Birron, straggling up the Hill, like a ship in storm without rudder or compass.'[82] So the schoolboy was described by fellow poet, the scary Louisa Drury, herself a victim of his not entirely friendly pranks. Her remarks point to the most obvious superficial characteristics of Byron at Harrow, his name and his lameness. That his surname was pronounced 'Birron' at school is confirmed by at least three other, independent sources, all Harrovian contemporaries, including his formmate Robert Peel who went on calling the poet Birron until his death in 1850.[83] Byron's aggressive compensation for his disability, a club foot, is attested by a number of his friends and his own obsessive accounts of his physical prowess in games and in fighting. One of his room-mates remembered him as a terrible bully. Yet Byron's carefully crafted romantic image of himself ill-matched the boy, recalled by another contemporary, 'with an iron-cramp on one of his feet, with loose corduroy trousers plentifully relieved by ink, and with finger nails bitten to the quick'. Schoolboys are habitually cruel and there is one anecdote of Byron waking up to find his bad leg in a tub of water.[84] At Speeches in July 1804 he preferred to

---

[80] J. G. Cotton Minchin, *Old Harrow Days* (London, 1898), p. 298.

[81] For what follows see Tyerman, 'Byron's Harrow'; *Poetical Works*, i, *Hours of Idleness* and *Childish Recollections* and the poems, pp. 132, 138–9, 172–3, 201–3, 210, nos. 76, 80, 93a, 93b, 109, and pp. 369, 370, 383; v, *Don Juan*, pp. 21–2; Byron, *Letters and Journals*, i. 41–3, 48, 49–64, 68–73, 110–12, 118–19, 144–5, 176–7, iii. 210, viii. 23–5, ix. 12, 14, 16, 42–4; R. E. Prothero, *Letters and Journals of Lord Byron*, i. 12–13, 27–8, 42, 70, 178–9, vi. 304; *Medwin's Conversations of Lord Byron*, ed. E. J. Lovell (Princeton, NJ, 1966), 61–4; Moore, *Byron, passim* to p. 48; Marchand, *Byron*, 65–100; C. S. Parker, *Sir Robert Peel*, i (London, 1899), pp. 12–16.

[82] Thornton, *Harrow School*, 239, quoting Merivale.

[83] Gash, *Mr Secretary Peel*, 43; J. A. Froude, *Thomas Carlyle: A History of His Life in London*, 2 vols. (London, 1884), ii. 45; Sir Algernon West, *Recollections* (London, 1899), i. 2; Minchin, *Old Harrow Days*, 192.

[84] Howson and Townsend Warner, *Harrow School*, 188; Marchand, *Byron*, i. 66 n. i, 67.

take the sedate role of Latinus in performing an extract from the *Aeneid* (Peel played Turnus) to avoid having to stand. The almost invariable image Byron presents of himself in his poems about Harrow is of a carefree youth roaming the Middlesex countryside with his friends. Real life was less idyllic. To reach the bathing place, almost two miles away, he used to have to hire a pony because, he wrote, 'it is too far to walk'.[85]

Byron spent little more than four years at Harrow, between April 1801 and July 1805, missing one term, being absent between July 1803 and January 1804. When at school he shone at making trouble, public speaking, and passionate friendships. Academically, although soon placed in the Fourth Form, alongside the outstanding Peel, and ending a monitor and third in the school, he achieved little, admitting to being an indifferent classic, which given his high position may say much for the qualities of his peers. He left school with a dislike of Virgil and Horace and a feeble grasp of Greek vocabulary. Of natural sciences, like most of his contemporaries, he was almost wholly ignorant. A few years later, he confessed that mathematics gave him a headache. However, he did pride himself on what he called 'my general information', mainly historical and literary. Despite rising to be a monitor and much praised (not least by himself) as a public declaimer, it is hard to say that Byron's school career was, as a school career, successful. Even his monitorial status and triumphs at the two Speech Days in 1805 were almost denied him as Drury had tried to get rid of him six months earlier.[86]

Byron found it easy to fritter away his time, to the exasperation of his teachers. His first tutor and housemaster, Henry Drury, talked of his 'inattention to business' and disruptive behaviour; more than one master called Byron a 'blackguard'; and Drury's correspondence is littered with unflattering and somewhat weary references to 'negligence', 'childish practices', idleness, indifference, animal spirits, and want of judgement. Byron's schooldays only acquired the familiar patina of charm, excitement, and success long after they were over. It is instructive to compare the highly critical things Drury wrote about Byron when he was in the school with the statement he gave Byron's biographer, Thomas Moore, for publication after the poet's death, in which the bright, rebellious, lazy, self-centred boy of 1801–5 is transmuted by memory and later fame into a shy 'mountain colt' led by 'a silken string'.[87] Such myths obscure much of Byron's life, many propagated by the poet himself. However, the real importance of Harrow to Byron—and vice versa—was that as a schoolboy he began to write poetry, the start of the career of the first professional poet of the modern age. Thus of more importance than his brawls and pranks; his attempts to prove himself as an athlete and cricketer; his rebelliousness and quickwitted skill at doing the minimum of preparation for

---

[85] Byron, *Letters and Journals*, i. 50.
[86] Prothero, *Letters and Journals*, i, Drury to Hanson, 29 Dec. 1804. Cf. Byron, *Letters and Journals*, 59; Moore, *Byron*, 19–20, 46–7 for a startlingly long list of books read at school.
[87] See above, nn. 81, 86.

form-work; or even his famed friendships with glittering young aristocrats, was the present he received, not from a peer or a peer's son, but from the son of a banker, Henry Boldero who, in 1803, gave his friend, then 15, a copy of the poetical works of Alexander Pope.[88]

Byron's indulgence of his muse reflected both the leisure available to Drury's Harrovians and the enormous variety of recreations in such a large congregation of boys of so diverse ages. To fighting, swimming, dancing, and fencing must be added cricket, football, tennis, raquets, boxing (often a form of organized bullying as a spectator sport), and skating in winter. Younger boys sailed boats on the Duck-puddle (the school bathing place); older boys made catapaults and all threw stones. The young Lord Althorp, not yet in his teens, collected grubs and silkworms, reared squirrels and greenfinches, and was taught by an older boy how to use a skipping rope. Sometimes conjurors performed for the boys, to the delight of the young Palmerston. Older boys indulged in more adult pursuits. Illicit horse-races were arranged. Palmerston owned a quarter share in a ferret for rat-catching and once asked his mother for a burning-glass, for what pupose he did not say. Many boys used to fish. Peel arranged for a local cottager to keep his guns for him so that he and his friend Robert Anstruther could spend their afternoons illicitly beating the surrounding hedges and woods for small game to shoot. In such a crowded and relaxed school, with unbridled physicality and naked boys sharing beds, it is extremely unlikely that there was no homosexuality, but the evidence is meagre and often ambiguous. However, Byron cannot have been alone in being emotionally attracted to boys, if physically fastidious. Equally, opportunities for relations with the opposite sex, especially servants, were much greater, in term and during the holidays, than in later more rigid and morally tense times. As Palmerston noticed, swearing was rife, as was alcohol. One memory of Byron is of his singing rowdy choruses at one of the Hill's outlets for liquor, Mother Barnard's. In short, Harrow prepared its pupils in almost every respect for their adult futures.[89]

Byron, an enthusiastic swimmer like many lame people, prided himself on his skill at cricket, even to the extent of exaggerating his meagre contribution to the first Eton–Harrow match in August 1805. The then captain of the school said that if he had had his way, Byron would never have played at all. In fact the match had little to do with a sporting contest, being arranged by the boys themselves largely as an opportunity for subsequent drunken socializing in London, carousings that ended in both teams causing noisy scenes in the Haymarket Theatre.[90] As it was,

---

[88] Marchand, *Byron*, i. 85 n. to l. 11.

[89] Townsend Warner, *Harrow in Prose and Verse*, 90–1; Le Marchant, *Spencer*, 30–44, 54–5, 58–60; Ashley, *Palmerston*, i. 4–9; Gash, *Mr Secretary Peel*, 40–8; Bourne, *Palmerston*, 6–11; Connell, *Whig Peer*, 320–5, 419–34; Marchand, *Byron*, 65–100, esp. p. 90 and note for Byron and homosexuality; Moore, *Byron*, 19–31, 33; Byron, *Letters and Journals*, i. 41–73; Parker, *Peel*, i. 14–15 and above, n. 81.

[90] *Letters and Journals*, i. 70–2 (Byron's own account of the drunken proceedings), vii. 229, ix. 12; Marchand, *Byron*, 97–8; Prothero, *Letters and Journals*, i. 70; Thornton, *Harrow School*, 238–9.

Byron's disability required him to employ a runner (presumably he did not field much either). This was a habitual occurrence. In a poem written many years later, Henry Page, a Harrow wheelwright, recalled Byron and how, as a boy, 'Oft at the famous game of cricket | I've served his lordship at the wicket.'[91]

Relations between Town and Gown were not always so harmonious. The school generated considerable wealth for the local community: the cobbler, barber, draper, baker, tailor, confectioners, butcher, and blacksmith. Leading beneficiaries included Mr Bliss, publican at the Crown and Anchor (locally known as the Abode of Bliss) who found himself unexpectedly having to entertain George III on an impromptu visit to the Hill in 1804, and Mother Barnard, 'this old girl', as Byron called her, who nevertheless was sufficiently businesslike to insist on the early payment of his bill. Against this, Harrovians caused resentment by their snobbery and bad manners, thefts, assaults, and widespread poaching, even by otherwise upright boys such as Peel. The local farmers were especially hostile. Tension turned to violence in 1803 with the enclosure of Roxeth Common, part of which was to be used as the school's cricket pitch. This had earlier been sited at the top of Sudbury Hill at the southern end of the Hill. The enclosure of the new field provoked a pitched battle between boys and locals over which the masters had no control (or perhaps even interest). Byron vividly recalled narrowly escaping being bludgeoned with a musket butt wielded, in his less than egalitarian phrase, by a 'grovelling savage'. This was a symptom of a more lasting conflict. Shortly after Byron left, some local parishioners, including employees and tenants of the Lyon trust, met to begin a legal challenge to the governors, accusing them of departing from the founder's statutes and charitable intentions.[92]

Such freedom to roam, play, or write depended on the modest demands of the formal curriculum. The school day was the same as under Heath: five hours in school broken up into four periods; only three hours on Thursday and Saturday; some scripture study on Sundays; a day off lessons, although not exercises, every Tuesday. Drury may well have continued Sumner's tradition of missing First School, which was taken by his assistants.[93] Because of numbers and delapidation, a major refurbishment of the schoolhouse was conducted between 1799 and 1803, including the rebuilding of the Cockloft or attic, completed in 1802–3. Every space possible was used, forms having to share whatever room was available. These forms stretched from the Sixth down to the Third Form, below which the introductory divisions retained the names of the texts or exercises studied: Phaedrus, Terence, Ovid, Grammar. Form size varied greatly, the smallest in 1803, Ovid, being of seven, the largest, the Shell, between the Fifth and the Fourth Forms, of forty-eight.

[91] 'Henry Page's Opinion of Lord Byron', photocopy, unlisted, in Harrow School Archives.
[92] On the general relations between school and parish see T. May 'Relations between Harrow School and the Parishioners of Harrow', unpub. MA thesis (1974), *passim*; on Byron and the locals see *Poetical Works*, i, *Childish Recollections*, ll. 273–82.
[93] Thornton, *Harrow School*, 434–5.

Placing depended not on age but on mastery of the classical languages gauged by oral recitation of exercises.[94]

Drury was not entirely impervious to educational theory, but not keen enough to consult Samuel Butler of Shrewsbury about 'modern' techniques of classical instruction.[95] However, he was no innovator. The formal system of learning was the Etonian one of Heath and Sumner. Drury balanced Latin and Greek, concentrating on grammar and philology. In Greek the great fifth-century tragedies received almost as much prominence as Homer. In Latin, apart from the customary obeisance to Virgil, there was a typically eighteenth-century preference for the convivial, speculative, and satirical Horace who, despite Byron's later disdain, clearly exerted a profound influence on his poetic style and tone. Drury recognized the limited use of such expertise to most of his senior pupils and so, as had Sumner, he illustrated the sentiments of, for example, Greek tragedians with modern English verse. He was keen on Latin prose but most of all employed the English essay, another Sumner legacy, and encouraged writing of free English verse translations of classical poets.[96] When he set Lord Bessborough the traditional punishment of twenty nonsense verses, the culprit produced twenty-eight.[97] The unrelenting monotony of construe and composition, recitation, exercises, and themes was variously received. Some, like Peel, found they could almost think in Latin and Greek while others, such as Audley Macdonald, 'a dunce who could only play upon the flute', failed to cope with any of it, even though in the Sixth Form.[98]

The limitations of this system are obvious. If a boy was good at this academic drudgery, school presented no challenge; if not, the challenge was avoided by getting help from a tutor or another, more scholarly boy. Under Drury, promotion up the school for the inept was largely by seniority and group solidarity. One reason Palmerston's father adduced for removing his son from Harrow once he had become a monitor was the limitations of subjects and people: 'boys remaining in the upper class of a public school . . . can only pursue the common routine of classical instruction and . . . must associate principally with companions from whom they can derive no improvement.'[99] Even within the narrowness of the curriculum, excellence was rare. Only after years of admitting Harrovians to Christ Church was the dean, Cyril Jackson, an old school fellow of Drury, able to say 'Harrow has sent us up at least one good scholar, in Mr Peel'.[100] To the early nineteenth-century Harrovian, literature, ancient or modern, was, at best, a source of *bons mots*. As Byron admitted, reading Burton's *Anatomy of Melancholy* was 'most useful to a man who wishes to acquire the reputation of being well read, with the least trouble'.[101]

---

[94] Butler, *Harrow Lists*; MS Bill Lists.
[95] Mack, *Public Schools and British Opinion, 1780–1860*, 228, 233 n. 3 confuses Joseph with his son Henry. [96] Drury, *Memoir*, 16–18.
[97] Le Marchant, *Spencer*, 39–40. [98] Byron, *Letters and Journals*, ix. 43.
[99] Connell, *Whig Peer*, 426. [100] Gash, *Mr Secretary Peel*, 52.
[101] Marchand, *Byron*, i. 85.

Drury's encouragement of versifying was not wholly pointless, stimulating in some precision of thought and expression as well as a degree of literary appreciation. Under the date 1 December 1804 Byron wrote: 'My first Harrow verses (that is English as exercises), a translation of a chorus from the Prometheus of Aeschylus, were received by Dr. Drury but coolly':

> Great Jove! to whose Almighty throne
> Both Gods and mortals homage pay,
> Ne'er may my soul thy power disown
> Thy dread behests ne'er disobey.[102]

Later, Byron caricatured such exercises. In 1810, from Constantinople, he sent Henry Drury a doggerel version of the Nurse's Dole in the *Medea* of Euripedes:

> Oh how I wish that an embargo
> Had kept in port the good ship Argo!
> Who, still unlaunch'd from Grecian docks,
> Had never pass'd the Azure rocks;
> But now I fear her trip will be a
> Damn'd business for my Miss Medea.[103]

Drury's passion for poetry, ancient and modern, clearly rubbed off, on Byron and others. In their valedictory letter in March 1805 expressing gratitude for his services, the governors felt the infection in the air: 'We could have wished upon this spot (inter hac Musarum sedes) to have caught the Spirit of Composition and to have been able to grace the merits which we are anxious to acknowledge.'[104]

Outside the formroom, boys pursued other intellectual or academic interests. Byron read widely, if superficially, in history and literature. Palmerston taught himself Spanish; Althorp studied some Ancient History and geography between attending to his menagerie.[105] One subject conspicuous by absence was religious instruction—or even religion itself. Sunday worship in the parish church was an occasion for discomfort, gossip, and boredom. Even though he fancied himself as an orator, Drury preached as rarely as possible, at most twice or thrice a year.[106] The omission of religious education in a school staffed exclusively by clergymen would be striking if it had not been so traditional. Here, again, Drury emulated his mentor Sumner as he did in another distinctive aspect of his teaching which offered his pupils an outlet uncommon in other schools.

On the testimony of his son, Drury liked the sound of his own voice and enjoyed training others. He was a veteran, perhaps inveterate, theatregoer since the 1760s; it was to be the passion of his retirement. One favourite exercise he set was the English essay which, if good enough, was then rehearsed by the author for declaiming aloud to the rest of the school, presumably at the monthly or terminal declamations

---

[102] *Poetical Works*, i. 370.   [103] *Poetical Works*, i. 284, no. 144.   [104] HSR III, fos. 253–4.
[105] Le Marchant, *Spencer*, 36–7; Ashley, *Palmerston*, i. 6–7.   [106] Drury, *Memoir*, 21.

instituted by Sumner. It was this exercise, rather than, as usually assumed, one of the Speech Days, that provided Byron with his first taste of oratory. On this occasion, Drury was surprised that Byron, unknowingly, departed from the prepared text only to recover himself before the end without interrupting the flow of speech. Such recitations may have served as auditions for the public Speech Days in the summer.[107]

Here, it has often been said, was Harrow's training ground for the political orators of the future, the Prime Ministers Perceval, Goderich, Peel, Aberdeen, and Palmerston and the architect and pilot of the Great Reform Act, Althorp. No evidence survives for Perceval, but each of the rest performed at least once: Althorp and Goderich in 1798; Palmerston and Aberdeen in 1800; Peel in 1804. The pieces they performed were standard fare for Speeches: extracts from Virgil, Tacitus, or Sallust, or modern poetry, such as Gray's *Bard*, spoken by Palmerston in 1800. (Aberdeen was Dido the same year). Other Speeches from Drury's time included Greek tragedy, Horace, Cicero, Ovid, and Livy but also, most revealing of the Head Master's tastes: Shakespeare, Milton, Dryden, Addison, Hume, as well as Gray and a number of other contemporary poets. It must be acknowledged, however, that the standard of speaking could be very low and that none of Drury's Prime Ministers as an adult was particularly noted for the elegance and power of his oratory.[108] Perceval and Goderich were businesslike and mundane; Peel formal, clear, reluctant to indulge in rhetoric; Aberdeen sparse, elliptical, and austere; Palmerston heated in language, at times bombastic, with the occasional memorable phrase, but delivered in a rather shambling manner; Althorp down to earth. None of them ranked beside the Pitts, Fox, Brougham, Gladstone, or Disraeli in virtuosity of harnessing thought and argument to words. However, what the Harrovians (and notice that the elder Pitt, Fox, and Gladstone were from Eton where declamations had been staged since the 1720s) possessed, except for Goderich, was parliamentary courage and a manner that enabled them to dominate an assembly. Presence rather than rhetorical genius may have been Drury's legacy to them.

Byron, who performed in Speeches in 1804 and twice in 1805, dallied with politics, making a few speeches in the House of Lords, one at least amusing.[109] But he lacked the necessary gravitas or concentration to be a successful politician. None the less, when older he liked to see himself as a radical, a rebel with innumerable causes, a pose he traced back to his schooldays. Drury's Harrow, like the English aristocracy, became increasingly reactionary as the French wars progressed, although the old Whig tradition was strongly maintained by Althorp and others. At school, Byron's one overt political gesture was fighting to protect the bust of

---

[107] Ibid., 16–17, 20–1.
[108] For Palmerston senior's low opinion of the orators in 1795 see Connell, *Whig Peer*, 324–5; in general see Howson and Townsend Warner, *Harrow School*, 164, 171; *Harrow School Speech Bills*.
[109] Marchand, *Byron*, i. 83–4, 96, 170, 344–6.

The Ancien Régime

Napoleon he kept in his room when the French war started again in 1803. This may have been rooted as much in a desire to be different than in political conviction, especially as he later remarked of the French emperor 'I don't want him here'.[110] It is difficult to see in the self-obsessed boy who courted the gilded scions of the nobility the man who would pose as Liberty's warrior. Indeed, although he would have hated to think it, Byron's mother's fondness for the French Revolution was probably more of an influence than Harrow. However, Byron described himself as rebellious and leader of a serious revolt, against the new Head Master, George Butler, in the summer of 1805. If true, it would suggest Drury left the school out of control.

There are many anecdotes about Byron at Harrow. Some are palpably false, such as the tale that he protected Peel from bullying by monitors. This never happened, the bullying of Peel occurring before Byron's arrival.[111] The most dramatic story concerns the election of Drury's successor, George Butler, instead of Mark Drury in 1805. The election was long and contentious. The boys took an active part in the debate on the side of Mark Drury, an unsurprising gesture of schoolboy insularity and conservatism. Originally, the pro-Drury party was led by Thomas Wildman who surrendered the leadership to Byron in order, legend has it, to secure his charismatic adherence. When, in late March 1805, it was announced that the archbishop of Canterbury had broken the governors' deadlock by appointing Butler, there were ugly incidents. Byron was supposed to have torn the grating from the Head Master's windows; refused to dine with Butler at the end of the summer term; and, most sensationally, to have been involved in an attempt to blow up the new Head Master in the schoolhouse, an attempt only aborted by Byron urging the preservation of the names carved in the panelling.[112]

Such is the legend. What truth lies in it? As in 1771, the boys were strong for the defeated internal candidate, although, even allowing for the intervening Easter holiday, the supposed time-lag in resisting the new incumbent is in suspicious contrast to the events thirty-four years earlier. Certainly Byron lampooned Butler mercilessly in verse, both at the time and in *Hours of Idleness* (1806). There was a serious breach between the two that was healed, as much on Butler's wishes as Byron's, only in 1808.[113] Yet there is no mention of gunpowder in Byron's correspondence. In his poem 'Childish Recollections' he observes, talking of Harrovians and the Fourth Form Room:

> And, here one night abroad they dared the room
> While bold Pomposus [*i.e. Butler*] staid at home[114]

---

[110] Byron, *Letters and Journals*, iii. 210.   [111] Parker, *Peel*, i. 13.
[112] Thornton, *Harrow School*, 218; Moore, *Byron*, 29; Harrow MS HM/D/40, 42, 43; Byron, *Letters and Journals*, i. 62–3; HSR III, fos. 252–4; Marchand, *Byron*, i. 94.
[113] Byron, *Letters and Journals*, i. 110–12, 144–5, 147, 153–4, 155, 166, 176–9, 206, 208, 239.
[114] *Poetical Works*, i, *Childish Recollections*, ll. 179–80. Cf. ibid., ll. 151–65.

hardly a description of a revolt, more a prank to test the new Head's nerve. In 1808 Byron openly expressed his resentment at Butler, but without any sense that he had behaved in a way other than a normally turbulent schoolboy. When, in November 1808, there *was* a serious rebellion, led, Byron claimed, by two of his former fags and clearly aimed at ousting the rather prim Dr Butler, Byron commented that his ex-fags 'had now obtained the honour to which their master [*i.e. himself*] aspired in vain'.[115] It may be noted that the 1808 revolt was against Butler's attempts to curb the monitorial excesses established by Dr Drury.[116] Commenting on the 1805 gunpowder plot legend, Drury's grandson, Charles Merivale, declared that when he was at Harrow (1817–24), the story of the boy who saved the panelling from explosion was told (almost equally implausibly) about Judge Richardson, who had been at school in the 1780s. Regarding the refusal to dine with the Head Master, Butler himself categorically denied the story. As for Byron being a leader of a rebellion, some contemporaries denied he was *ever* a leader.[117]

There is a further piece of evidence, the letters of Thomas Wildman, first leader of the anti-Butler party. On 17 May, ten days after the beginning of Butler's first term, Wildman wrote to his mother: 'Butler is extremely civil . . . very strict . . . while he behaves to *us* more as young men at university, there is not the smallest idea of a row, for though we all regret that Mr Drury did not succeed, yet in other respects we could not . . . wish it in better hands.' Some days later, Wildman wrote again: 'I like Butler more and more and I have a good deal to do with him lately, and have been to him very frequently both alone and with Lord Byron . . . and he has always behaved in the most handsome manner.' Throughout that summer term Byron seems to have remained in harmony with Butler who appears to have appreciated Byron's Speech Day performances. From the available evidence it must be concluded that the rebellion of 1805 is a myth: it never happened.[118]

The cause of the ill-feeling between Butler and Byron, the latter regarding himself as libelled and slandered by a malicious Head Master, lay not in the poet's heroic deeds of defiance but in his verse. Some end-of-term leaving pranks in his house and in the schoolhouse (a night raid perhaps) may have occurred: not for the first or last time. But what sparked Butler's fury, resentment, and later insinuations that Byron had been expelled—which were untrue—and was an unsuitable person for Harrovians to consort with—which had more weight—was Byron's wit and pen. A series of poems evidently circulated within and around the school almost certainly after the last Speech Day in July 1805, but before the end of term. Byron later unconvincingly claimed the offending verses were dictated by him when ill.[119] Whatever the circumstances, they represent possibly the most extreme, damning,

---

[115] Byron, *Letters and Journals*, i. 176–7.   [116] Thornton, *Harrow School*, 219–20.
[117] Ibid., 238–9; *Medwin's Conversations*, 64.
[118] Harrow School MS 1984/13/i–iii (copies: originals were in possession of Mrs H. S. Escott).
[119] Byron, *Letters and Journals*, i. 144–5, 153–4. Cf. ibid., 110–12.

rude, and effective public attack by a boy on a master ever. They must also rank among the most stylish. One of the poems, *On a Change of Masters at a Great Public School*, is dated 'Harrow, July 1805'; the other marginally more offensive, *Pomposus*, is of the same vintage.[120] Their satire and venom would not only have stung Butler's pride, but, if widely circulated, could have threatened his livelihood, dependent as it was on his reputation and the goodwill of the great. His anxiety showed in his persuading his predecessor to admonish his former pupils for their hostilty to the new Head.[121] In the circumstances of his controversial election, Butler had every right to be sensitive.

Byron's poems on Butler may serve as a fitting testimony both to the atmosphere of Drury's school—free, boisterous, snobbish, occasionally dangerous, sometimes intense, loudly self-conscious, confident of its prominence—and to the poet's own development, his talent still raw but lit by skill, energy, imagination, and excitement, leaving Harrow a rudderless ship no longer:

> Of narrow brain, yet of a narrower soul
> Pomposus holds you, in his harsh controul;
> Pomposus, by no social virtue sway'd,
> With florid jargon, and with vain parade,
> With noisy nonsense, and new fangled rules,
> Such as were ne'er before enforced in schools;
> Mistaking pedantry, for learning's laws,
> He governs, sanctioned by self-applause.
> With him, the same dire fate, attending Rome,
> Ill-fated IDA [*Byron's name for Harrow*]! soon must stamp your doom;
> Like her o'erthrown, forever lost to fame,
> No trace of science left you, but the name.[122]

In a backhanded way, *On a Change* and *Pomposus* are tributes to Byron's former master.[123] The secret of Joseph Drury's success with parents and boys was his facility at making friends, a rare gift when extended over so many years to so many pupils. A figure at once popular but reserved, recalled with affection, academically conservative and intellectually timid, a quiet man with a passion for the stage, Drury through hard work not personal brilliance completed what Sumner had begun, bringing Harrow to an apogee of fame and glamour. In gratitude, the boys subscribed to a leaving present worth 330 guineas.[124] Drury would have liked that too.

---

[120] Byron, *Poetical Works*, i. 132, no. 76, 172–3, no. 93a. Cf. *Childish Recollections*, ll. 89–92, 99–120 and i. 173 no. 93b.
[121] Drury, *Memoir*, 21 (cf. Drury's similar behaviour in 1808).
[122] *Poetical Works*, i. 132, no. 76.   [123] Whom Byron called Probus in his Harrow verses.
[124] Byron, *Letters and Journals*, i. 62–3.

10

Decadence and Change, 1805–1844

I. Harrow's Nadir?

Early nineteenth-century Harrow witnessed the school's descent from the second most popular and, for its meagre endowment, easily the most successful public school in England to one facing closure. In 1805 George Butler inherited over 250 pupils and an established reputation. In December 1844 Christopher Wordsworth left just sixty-nine on the roll, with probably fewer in residence, the governors, in June of that year, having acknowledged 'the probable Dissolution of the School'.[1] Arthur Haygarth, the future compiler of the seminal *Cricket Scores and Biographies* and a boy in the school from 1839 to 1843, recalled forty years later that during his time 'the grass grew in the streets of Harrow'.[2]

The reasons for this apparent collapse are not as obvious as a bare recital of the elements of decline might suggest. Failure, although cumulative, was not permanent nor irreversible. Fallings rolls were not unique to Harrow; in this period Rugby, Winchester, Shrewsbury, and Westminster all suffered sharp reversals of fortunes. There were external challenges common to all public schools, notably prolonged agricultural depression, the great financial crash of the autumn of 1825, and the economic crises of 1837 and 1842, 'no gloomier year in the whole nineteenth century'.[3] However, the consequences of industrialization had some direct benefits. Like Rugby, but in contrast to Shrewsbury, the arrival of the railway in 1837 offered prospects of future growth.

More insidious than the vagaries of the new industrial cycles or the malaise in agriculture following the end of the French wars were the vociferous attacks on the

---

[1] Harrow School Archives, HM/W/Free Scholars Dispute File (hereafter HM/W/FSD), letter Henry Young to Wordsworth, on or just after 6 June 1844.

[2] Thornton, *Harrow School*, 283 n. 2.

[3] A. Briggs, *The Age of Improvement* (London, 1959), 295.

public school system of education from two distinct quarters.[4] Liberal and radical reformers criticized the intellectual and academic conservatism of the classical curriculum, as well as the uncontrolled barbarism of schoolboy life and the negligence of the teachers. Beginning with Sydney Smith's famous onslaught in the *Edinburgh Review* of 1810, there was a sustained campaign in the Whig and reformist press against public schools in general as well as individual schools for being both damaging and useless to their inmates. Despite energetic defence in Tory organs such as the *Quarterly Review*, there was a danger that public schools if not reformed from within or by Parliament, would simply be ignored by the wealthy *arrivistes* of the newly enriched and soon to be enfranchised bourgeoisie, especially as utilitarian concepts were being translated into curriculum reform in private and technical schools. Harrow fell victim to its own success and national prominence, its perceived shortcomings being paraded in public beside those of its collegiate companions to the disquiet of its supporters.[5] Although escaping the scrutiny of Henry Brougham's parliamentary committee of 1816 to 1818 and the resulting establishment of the Charities Commission in 1818, Harrow's deep conservatism was questioned even by loyal old boys, such as the Prime Ministers Goderich and Peel.[6] Internally, criticisms of academic and disciplinary procedures were voiced by successive Under Masters, William Mills and Henry Drury, and by Benjamin Kennedy, the most intellectually prominent assistant master of his time and future Head Master of Shrewsbury.[7]

However, Harrow's particular characteristics lent it a degree of immunity from calls to modernize. If the purpose of critics was to force Harrow to be more sensitive and attractive to the needs of the new upper middle classes, they had chosen the wrong target. At no time in this period did the school try to attract middle-class pupils. When in the 1790s a pupil of Heath recalled with nostalgia 'the spot . . . where the sons of Nobility and Traffic went hand in hand', his memory or his social awareness played him false.[8] Heath and Drury's Harrow had been exclusive seminaries for gentlemen. This was no less true under Butler, Longley, and Wordsworth. Land and title remained the boys' predominant backgrounds and, no less importantly, the dominant tone, even when commercial parvenus, like Peel, were recruited. It has even been argued that 'more exclusively than either Eton or Winchester, Harrow devoted itself to educating sons of the gentry and titled

---

[4] Mack, *Public Schools and British Opinion, 1780–1860*, esp. chs. 3 and 4; B. Simon, *The Two Nations and the Educational Structure* (London, 1974), 98–100, 342.

[5] e.g. *The Quarterly Journal of Education*, 9 (1835), 75–83 and refs. to vol. 5 (1833).

[6] Harrow Archives, *Letters to Dr Longley and MSS in his own Writing, 1829–36*, Peel to Longley, 7 Dec. 1829, Goderich to Longley, 28 Dec. 1829.

[7] HM/1829/H. Drury to Lord Northwick, 5 Jan. 1829; HM/1829/W. Mills to Governors, 10 Jan. 1829; S. Butler (ed.), *The Life and Letters of Dr. Samuel Butler*, 2 vols. (London, 1896), ii. 134.

[8] *Savillon's Elegies or Poems written by A Gentleman A.B. late of the University of Cambridge* (London, 1795), p. xi.

nobility'.⁹ The typical product was what has been described as the 'gentlemen professional' in the traditional occupations of the army, the church, the law, public service, or politics. Between 1825 and 1850, at most half of 1 per cent of Harrow fathers and between 4 and 6 per cent of their sons were or became businessmen. This, at least, was one public school that did little to ease the path of a new commercial establishment. Harrow did not breed entrepreneurs or educate their children. Rather its function was to reinforce the aristocratic values to preserve the traditional character of the English ruling class in a world of disturbing change. John Keble had it right when, perhaps only half jokingly, he congratulated W. W. Phelps on his appointment to Harrow in 1826, hoping that his friend would remember him 'when you become a bishop in consequence of your judicious operations upon the head or heels or whatever it may be on any little Duke or Prime Minister'.¹⁰

The other front of attack was moral and religious. Here utilitarians, liberals, radicals, and the pious united in their criticisms. As religion began to play a greater part in public discourse, especially, but not exclusively, among the evangelical and evangelically influenced upper and middle classes, the absence of it at public schools caused outrage and contempt amongst their opponents, pain and anxiety to their natural supporters. The one feature that almost all early nineteenth-century memoirs of Harrow comment upon is the absence of religious instruction and atmosphere. Some of these reminiscences were sharpened by the cultural gulf between the intellectual world of their youth, *c.*1810–30, and that of their adulthood created by the brief triumph of 'godliness and good learning'.¹¹ Although this strenuous Christianity is often associated in the context of public schools with the march of evangelicalism across the consciousness of the English establishment, it applied in no less measure to High Churchmen and devotees of the Oxford Movement. Isaac Williams, a prominent Tractarian, at Harrow 1817–21, later lamented that there was 'no-one in that little opening world to guide me or speak of Christianity'.¹² He only found religion at Oxford, from, in particular, the preferment-hungry John Keble. Williams encapsulated the retrospective distortion that coloured many accounts of their casual schooldays by subsequently prim early-Victorians. His first encounter with Byron, whose tenacious influence ('noxious taint' as one moral reformer put it) at Harrow and elsewhere was regarded as a

---

⁹ E. A. Allen, 'Public School Elites in Early-Victorian England', *Journal of British Studies*, 21 (1982), 90 and *passim* for what follows. Cf. T. W. Bamford, *The Rise of Public Schools* (London, 1967), esp. pp. 210–19; id., 'Public Schools and Social Class, 1801–50', *British Journal of Sociology*, 12 (1961), 224–35.

¹⁰ C. Hole, *The Life of Archdeacon W. W. Phelps*, 2 vols. (London, 1871–3), i. 445.

¹¹ D. Newsome, *Godliness and Good Learning* (London, 1961), 1–91; Mack, *Public Schools and British Opinion, 1780–1860*, 213–19, 236–333, 341–6; J. R. de S. Honey, *Tom Brown's Universe* (London, 1977), esp. pp. 1–46.

¹² G. Prevost, *The Autobiography of Isaac Williams BD* (London, 1892), 10 and, generally, pp. 4–24.

severe block to moral improvement, was through a copy of poems given by the author himself in the school library:[13]

> Into these poems I ventured to look, feeling at the time that I ought not to do so, but was most agreeably surprised by finding so very little harm in them; indeed nothing but what *I thought* one might read with safety, and from this was but a slight step to great admiration. The subtle poison of these books did me incalculable injury for many years; the more so as the infidelity was so veiled in beautiful verse and refined sentiment.[14]

This autobiographical dislocation of sympathy and perspective probably stimulated reminiscence. To those solid Victorians or passionate divines who had been at Harrow before the 1840s, their schooldays must have seemed not just another country but a different planet. Although the realities of life in public schools such as Eton and Harrow changed far less than reactionaries and reformers alike pretended, the perception of change, so vital an element in the psychology of the educated elites of the mid-nineteenth century, may itself have provided the motive to publish memoirs. Added to the fashion for prolix biographies of the 'life and letters' variety, a habit at once prurient and reverent, these unreformed years were exposed to particularly intense scrutiny. Later Victorians, let alone twentieth-century Harrovians, did not rush into print with memories of their schooldays with anything like the enthusiasm of their predecessors. Possibly the gap between private experience and public image became increasingly difficult to bridge. Growing habits of secrecy and discretion, of orthodoxy, reaction, and fear, the closure of the ranks of the elite against the threatening excluded but articulate masses acted as further deterrents. For whatever reason, Harrow in the first half of the nineteenth century is uniquely well-served by memorialists, many, like Williams, anxiously bemused by their young, impious, and irreverent selves.

That Harrow under Butler and Longley lacked a religious dimension is, however, undoubted, confirmed by contemporary diaries no less than the attacks of external critics. Even the formal motions of faith were degraded: in 1823 Francis Trench, a future vicar of Islip, Oxfordshire, turned his mind to confirmation only a fortnight before the ceremony.[15] The following year, a future bishop of St Andrew's received no preparation for his confirmation beyond his tutor, the improvident William Drury, inquiring if he knew his catechism. Holy Communion was unknown, either at confirmation services or any other time.[16] This absence and casualness, with religion ignored or despised, was a greater problem at Harrow than elsewhere as, until 1839, all worship was in the parish church, a setting uncongenial even to the religiously enthusiastic Dr Wordsworth.

---

[13] Newsome, *Godliness*, 16; Mack, *Public Schools and British Opinion, 1780–1860*, 76, 198, 268, 300, 341; E. S. Purcell, *The Life of Cardinal Manning*, 2 vols. (London, 1896), i. 20.
[14] Prevost, *Williams*, 6–7.
[15] F. Trench, *A Few Notes from Past Life, 1818–1832* (Oxford, 1862), p. 36.
[16] Charles Wordsworth, *Annals of My Early Life* (London, 1891), p. 21.

The Christian attack on public schools was, however, aimed at transformation or redemption rather than root and branch reform. While critics of the curriculum demanded radical change in the institutions, their statutes, and their social function, the Christian reformers had a subtler, clearly conservative purpose to employ these schools in God's work of reviving religion in society. Most of them, from Low Church Thomas Arnold of Rugby to High Church Christopher Wordsworth, wished to protect and enhance public schools and their academic values from the march of materialism and rationalism.[17] Though partly inspired by disenchantment and the demands of the newly religiously enthusiastic middle classes, these Christian reformers only posed a threat to public schools where those schools resisted their influence.

Harrow did not resist, its decline not simply being due to a lack of godliness. George Butler was said to prepare boys in his house thoroughly, if hastily, for confirmation.[18] There were serious and powerful evangelical housemasters from the 1820s. Less conclusively, Charles Longley was the first public school Head Master to become archbishop of Canterbury. Ironically, Harrow's steepest decline occurred under the Christian reformer Wordsworth who fell foul not of irreligion but, typically for early Victorian Anglicanism, of the envy and distaste of his evangelical brethren in Christ, led by the malign and meddlesome vicar, J. W. Cunningham. Harrow did not neatly fit the standard generalizations of early nineteenth-century public school decadence and unpopularity. While the bastion of the old guard, Henry Drury, asserted as late as 1836 the ideal Head Master should be 'a Gentleman, Scholar and Public School man' who 'could do verses', George Butler in 1830 instead identified the necessary qualities as those of 'a gentleman, a Christian and a man of learning'. Harrow was open to change.[19] In his first address to the school in 1836 Wordsworth proclaimed 'it will be my earnest endeavour to make you all, first, Christians; secondly, gentlemen; and, thirdly, scholars'.[20] This reordering of Butler's priorities was no mere semantic or rhetorical shift, but a sea-change in attitude and approach to education. Wordsworth's ideas were identical to those of Arnold and his pupil, C. J. Vaughan, who was to use precisely the same formula in his application for Wordsworth's job in 1844.[21] Vaughan had heard the words as a monitor at Arnold's feet. But Harrow was not Rugby and Wordsworth was not Arnold.

If the reasons for Harrow's decay do not conform to a general stereotype, being as much local as general, the facts are none the less compelling. Joseph Drury's legacy

---

[17] Newsome, *Godliness*, 1–91; C. Stray, *Classics Transformed* (Oxford, 1998), p. 100 for Christopher Wordsworth's explicitly reactionary defence of classics as a barrier against 'vernacular radicalism and materialism'.

[18] Trench, *Notes*, 36.   [19] Butler, *Samuel Butler*, ii. 139; Hole, *Phelps*, ii. 66.

[20] H. J. Torre, *Recollections of School Days at Harrow* (Manchester, 1890), p. 126; C. S. Roundell (né Currer), 'Dr Christopher Wordsworth', Howson and Townsend Warner, *Harrow School*, 99.

[21] Newsome, *Godliness*, 34; A. P. Stanley, *The Life of Thomas Arnold*, 2 vols (London, 1858), i. 100; Harrow Archives, *Printed Testimonials for C. J. Vaughan, 4 December 1844*, pp. 3–4.

was golden but poisonous. With the aristocrats, he bequeathed riot, indiscipline, idleness, and vice, in the early nineteenth-century sense of drinking, gambling, etc., and an educational system that bored all but the most talented or the most moronic. Unsurprisingly, his successors, lacking his charm and deft footwork, encountered problems. Of the three Head Masters in this period, two were asked to resign and the third, on his own admission, only took the job to further his chances of a bishopric, the pursuit of which occupied much of his time and possibly more of his thoughts. If Wordsworth's failure was most palpable, Butler had to be reprimanded by the governors for the chaos in the school in 1826.[22] He left only 110 to 120 boys in the Spring of 1829.[23] Longley was incapable of keeping order, a point forcibly brought home to him on 21 September 1832 when a Sixth Former, G. F. Wilbraham, went to school drunk and threw up in front of the Head Master. On another occasion, Longley himself had to run after a couple of boys illicitly engaged in pistol shooting in the fields near the bathing place. Impressively, he caught them, although, when confiscating the gun, he betrayed acute nervousness lest it were loaded.[24] More humiliating still was the implied rebuke by the leaving scholarship examiners in 1833 at the poor standard of candidates.[25]

Many of the signs of decay were familiar from other schools. The curriculum was sclerotic, designed to favour the few and ignore the many, indifferent to education, open to mechanical cribbing. Discipline in school and by masters was brutal. Amongst boys it was either barbaric or non-existent. Drinking, gambling, smoking, fighting, and bullying, as well as a whole range of illicit outdoor pursuits and sadistic initiation rituals, were standard. When Wordsworth tried to tackle these problems, he was accused of publicizing them to the school's detriment, a paradox familiar to less turbulent regimes than his.[26] Yet many boys remembered their schooldays with intense almost elegiac affection despite—or because of—it all.

At Harrow, a particular set of accidents added to the impression of disintegration. In consequence of the abolition of Dames' houses; their replacement by more luxurious accommodation provided by masters desperate to make money; the near extinction of the resident private tutor; and the decline in fee-paying pupils, from being a relatively cheap school, Harrow became one of the most expensive. In hard times this was a problem, one exacerbated by the opening of new, less costly rivals in the early 1840s, such as Cheltenham and Marlborough.[27] Harrow under Butler gained a reputation for being a lazy school, as it awarded itself seemingly endless

---

[22] HSR III, fo. 346, 9 Feb. 1826.
[23] MSS Bill Books. See J. Golland's *Catalogue*, fos. 9–10; Hole, *Phelps*, ii. 34.
[24] MSS Diary of G. J. Pouchée, xerox copy, Harrow Archives Accession no. 1984–7, fos. 18 and 41–2.   [25] Governors' Minutes (hereafter GM), 20 June 1833.
[26] HM/W/FSD, Wordsworth to Governors, 16 Mar. 1844; HM/W/Charles Perry to Wordsworth, 18 Apr. 1842; Roundell, 'Wordsworth', 89.
[27] In general see Thornton, *Harrow School*, 248–84; Howson and Townsend Warner, *Harrow School*, 66–107. Cf. the cursory treatment in Laborde, *Harrow School*, 50; and below, p. 227.

extra days, sometimes weeks of holiday. There were well-publicized scandals which were festooned across the national press. Less public, but more damaging, were the internal tensions between Heads and masters over changing the curriculum, the distribution of fees, school charges, and the allocation of boarding houses. Harrow was also unlucky: the Grove was burnt down in 1833 and, catastrophically, the Head Master's house and its boarding side in 1838. A lengthy lawsuit, 1808–10, between the governors and local parishioners drew attention to glaring anomalies in the school's constitution and function. Two senior housemasters absconded in 1826 to avoid creditors.[28] Most damaging of all was the feud between the governors and successive Heads, culminating in the volcanic row over the admission of Free Scholars from 1842 to 1844 which, while largely a result of declining numbers and shortsighted reforms in the boarding system, in turn caused a further and near-terminal haemorrhage in numbers.[29]

One prosaic but telling indication of the steely nerves required by Harrow parents, let alone the Harrow boy, at the end of Wordsworth's rule, is the experience of Charles Currer. He entered the eccentric but definitely aristocratic and successful Dame's house, Mrs Leith's (on the site of the present vicarage) in January 1841. At the end of the year, on the closure of Leith's, he transferred to the Grove, under T. H. Steel. After another year Steel departed, to be replaced at the Grove by Richard Shilleto, the eminent Greek scholar who, finding himself facing ruin, left in a fury within months, closing his house. Showing great faith (Currer's father had been at Harrow under Joseph Drury), Currer then removed to the Park in 1844: three houses and four housemasters in just over three years, seemingly an almost frenzied rush to oblivion.[30]

Yet Currer's career is suggestive of a rather different picture. He stayed at Harrow to be Dr Vaughan's Head of School and, half a century later, wrote a reasoned apologia for Dr Wordsworth in which he recognized that he had been a reformer who, in some respects, had laid the ground for Vaughan's success. Despite Harrow's vicious reputation, one owing not a little to the slanders of Cunningham, Vaughan claimed to have expected Harrow to be a desert 'and I found a garden'.[31] Currer's Harrow under Wordsworth was not as different from what followed as many—then and now—have claimed. Under Wordsworth, before the advent of Vaughan, Currer received a first-class classical education (rapid promotion to the Sixth was more or less inevitable given the non-existent competition), was taught some higher mathematics, played serious cricket, and became a monitor at a ceremony in chapel, sure foundations for following his father in becoming a loyal old boy.

It has become fashionable (and publishable) to emphasize the unlicensed and licensed mayhem of the unreformed public schools of the early nineteenth

[28] Mark and William Drury. [29] Below, pp. 235–9.
[30] Roundell, 'Wordsworth', 92; *Harrow Register, 1800–1911*, 174.
[31] Roundell, 'Wordsworth', 90.

The Ancien Régime

century.³² The experience of Harrow insists on a subtler interpretation. On the one hand, reform of the Arnold–Vaughan type had less effect than once argued. The boyish habits of drinking, swearing, fighting, and bullying continued. Drummond Smith's account of the Head Master's in the 1820s, or George Pouchée's diary of Druries in the 1830s reveal a no more disreputable or decadent world than Augustus Hare's Grove of the late 1840s or John Addington Symonds' Rendalls of the 1850s. Indeed, neither of the earlier two far from innocent witnesses mentions sex, which to Symonds appeared all pervasive as well as all important. Neither did reform make any discernible difference in what Harrovians went on to do: 'the moral revolution of the 1840s and 1850s had no real effect on the boys of that generation if their ultimate choice of career is any guide.'³³

If the closing years of Harrow's *ancien régime* did not give way to a brave new world, neither were they devoid of change. Between 1805 and 1844 the whole structure of the school changed, with boarding becoming increasingly concentrated on a few large houses run by masters to the near-extinction of all others. Signs of house identity, rather than identity with the master whose house it was, begin to appear. Distinctive colours were worn at sport, at least by the 1830s.³⁴ In 1839, for the first time, when W. W. Phelps left the Park he passed on a house and its boarders intact to his successor, a development of vast future significance, in some senses the real beginning of modern Harrow.³⁵ Organized games, football and cricket, had begun under Butler and became compulsory, much earlier than in other public schools. The first cricket professional was engaged in the 1820s and regular matches with other schools began.³⁶ Butler's sporting enthusiasm was further reflected in the creation of the new Duckpuddle in 1809, a dangerous, swampy place, the water the consistency of soup, that claimed at least one boy's life, in 1826.³⁷ Longley tried to introduce French and Wordsworth succeeded in intruding maths into the formal curriculum. Form masters were instituted in 1840; prizes and leaving scholarships in the 1820s; regular, later termly examinations from 1829. The tutor system was regularized, as was fagging and the role of the monitors. In a rare concern for academic values, in 1831 the governors insisted that Longley restore the library to its proper use by vacating it as a form room.³⁸ The average age of entry rose from 11 to 13–14 in this period, although there were still some entrants, such as Anthony Trollope, as young as 8 and a division could have as many as six years dividing the oldest and youngest.³⁹ After Butler, flogging by the Head Master was reduced and

³² e.g. J. Chandos, *Boys Together* (London, 1984). ³³ Bamford, *Rise of Public Schools*, 215.
³⁴ Pouchée's Diary, fo. 21 (2 Oct. 1832). ³⁵ Hole, *Phelps*, ii. 139.
³⁶ Charles Wordsworth, *Annals*, 10.
³⁷ HSR III, fo. 276; Minchin, *Old Harrow Days*, 164; C. Stretton, *Memoirs of a Chequered Life*, 3 vols. (London, 1862), i. 7; Roundell, 'Wordsworth', 95; Thornton, *Harrow School*, 253; *Harrow Register, 1800–1911*, 116.
³⁸ GM 23 June and 10 Aug. 1831. For the other details see below, pp. 206–41.
³⁹ *Harrow Register, 1800–1911, passim*; HM/W/Boarding House (hereafter HM/W/BH), G. Butler to Wordsworth, 6 Mar. 1838 (ii).

came close to abolition, although that by other masters and monitors remained unaltered in savagery. The policy of employing, as assistants, fellows of Oxbridge colleges was expanded until there occurred the ludicrous spectacle of Benjamin Kennedy, of Latin Primer fame, one of the most distinguished philological classicists of the nineteenth century, later, after being Head Master of Shrewsbury, Regius Professor of Greek at Cambridge, spending his time at Harrow, 1830–6, teaching the Fourth Form. Not surprisingly, they hissed him.[40]

Old habits were dying: between 1817 and 1829 Mr Webb the Dancing Master received no pupils. Although he survived in service until 1840, after, he reminded the governors when appealing for a pension, a stint of forty-seven years, it must be doubted whether he was fully employed for much of his last quarter century.[41] Extravagant diversity of dress, such as rainbow coloured ties, was reined in; uniform began to be introduced as Wordsworth prohibited any neckties other than black or white at Bill.[42] New buildings were rising. In the boldest decision hitherto made, the governors agreed to a new schoolhouse, erected 1819–20, provided the old one remained within it and that they only paid for those alterations that effected the original 1615 structure. In 1839, after a dogged campaign of trench warfare with the egregious Cunningham, Wordsworth was able to have a chapel consecrated (Rugby had had one since 1813). For all its ugliness—according to Currer 'a plain, hideous, red-brick building, something between a conventicle and a racket court'—and bizarrely sloping floor following the contour of the Hill eastwards, it provided the essential forum for the moral revolution sought by Wordsworth and ostensibly realized by Vaughan.[43]

Less tangibly, but no less significant, the cult of the school itself was developed. In 1813, at the annual old boys' meeting, Sam Parr presided over the funding of a memorial to John Lyon in the parish church.[44] Wordsworth instituted Founders' Day in October 1842, to mark the two hundreth and fiftieth anniversary of Lyon's death. Nobody worked harder to cultivate the bonds that a sense of the past can bind those of the present to an institution than George Butler. It has been suggested that the first school use of the term 'Old ———ian' was applied to Old Rugbeians in 1840. Yet, in March 1838, Butler, signing himself *Harroviensis*, had already coined the phrase 'Old Harrovian', an example followed a year later by the governors themselves.[45] Here lies a paradox perhaps typical of these years. Butler, in his retirement as during his Head Mastership, was an obsessive supporter of Harrow,

---

[40] Pouchée's Diary, fo. 25.   [41] Butler, *Samuel Butler*, i. 361; GM, 25 June 1840.

[42] A. Fox, *Public School Life: Harrow* (London, 1911), p. 22; Wordsworth's MS Head Master's Book in HM/Vaughan, Jan. 1845.   [43] Roundell, 'Wordsworth', 95.

[44] An account of the meeting on 8 May 1813, HM/Bg/Book of Subscriptions to Lyon Memorial Fund; OHs going back to the 1750s, the Head and assistant masters and boys at the school raised a total of £136 19s.

[45] G. M. Young, *Victorian England: Portrait of an Age* (Oxford, 1936), p. 96; HM/W/BH, Butler to Wordsworth, 6 Mar. 1838 (ii).

as fundraiser and antiquarian, to an extent that Joseph Drury, who shared Butler's mercenary interest but not his indiscretion about it, would have found bewildering. Yet Butler had effectively been sacked in 1829 for his conspicuous inability to maintain numbers or discipline, his failure only concealed from future generations by his own endeavours—not least as a significant landlord on the Hill to whom masters, including the Head, owed rent—and the piety of his powerful and plausible son, Montagu. George Butler exposes the contradictions of the time. Harrow was seen as a great school. Sumner, Heath, and Drury's work in this, as in much else less fortunate, endured. Even in its darkest days its supporters never relinquished the concept of its national importance. It was at once able to be a comfortable sink of unquestioning habit and an uneasy forcing house of innovation. Its contacts and traditional eminence, expressed by the concerns of its old boys, as well as its unique characteristics ensured a presumption of survival.

II. Holding the Line, 1805–1829

The Election of 1805

The succession to Joseph Drury was another pivotal moment, as significant as that to Sumner in 1771. The governors' resolve was again tried in a contest that embodied the competing influences within a successful and self-confident institution: to perpetuate an existing, proven system or to respond to wider pressures and interests. The issues were reflected in the candidates. Joseph Drury announced to the governors his intention to resign at Easter 1805 in a letter of 25 November 1804 in which he strongly pressed the claims of his brother Mark to the succession.[46] Within five days two internal candidates presented themselves, Mark Drury, then Under Master, and Benjamin Evans, an assistant master.[47] Both were in their forties. The younger Drury was an old boy, popular, affable, and lazy, a sought-after tutor and housemaster, most noted for his massive bulk which made it necessary for him to have a specially huge chair constructed to fit his size. Evans, an Etonian, Eighth Wrangler and Chancellor's Medallist at Cambridge had run a successful house since his arrival in 1792, later being described as 'a blunt specimen of a generation of pedagogues even then (1818) passing away'.[48] In their applications, both stressed their services to the school, of twenty-two and thirteen years respectively, with Drury emphasizing his Harrow education and Evans his Eton connections. The governors being in no hurry to make an election, an increasingly bitter feud developed between the two masters, culminating in Joseph Drury writing an intemperate letter on 11 March 1805 in support of his brother and accusing Evans

---

[46] HM/D/40.   [47] HM/D/42, 43, 45, 47.
[48] J. A. Merivale (ed.), *Autobiography and Letters of Charles Merivale* (Oxford, 1898), p. 37.

of underhand campaigning.[49] Unsurprisingly in such circumstances, the boys took sides, most of them on behalf of the Under Master, their typically conservative instincts regarding his accession as confirming their own sense of self-esteem. As in 1785, Harrow should be kept in the family, very much the departing Head's desire.

What the Drurys seemed not to know was that there was a late entrant onto the field, for whom some governors, including Lord Northwick, had been waiting. George Butler, fellow of Sidney Sussex College, Cambridge and former Senior Wrangler, applied on 5 March: on 7 March the governors set the election meeting for 18 March.[50] Butler had first been suggested to Northwick on 10 February by an Old Harrovian, Lord John Fitzroy, youngest son of the duke of Grafton, then at Trinity, Cambridge. Fitzroy made it clear that Butler was Cambridge University's candidate, adding 'the university have expressed on various occasions their concern for the future success of the school, but a still greater concern on hearing that Mr Drury and Mr Evans were the only candidates'.[51] Among Butler's testimonials were ones from almost every Head of House in Cambridge. Another Butler supporter emphasized his experience of Europe, his literary polish, and that he was 'the perfect gentleman', ideally suited to educating what he called 'the flower of Britain's youth'.[52] Some of Drury's adherents began to switch to Butler whose academic credentials and prowess were repeatedly cited, second only, even equal some hyperbolists claimed, to the famous professor of Greek, Richard Porson himself (who, needless to say, was also a Butler referee).[53] Even Sam Parr lent his voice in Butler's praise.[54] It was a carefully and effectively orchestrated campaign. Lord Northwick, to whose support Butler himself later paid tribute, recalled that it was to the Cambridge testimonials that 'we are solely endebted for the present Head Master'.[55]

This interest in Harrow taken by one of the universities, rather than, as previously, another school, marked a new stage in how Heads were appointed and in Harrow's status. The parochial cosiness of 1785 or even, for all its disturbances, 1771, were a world away. Harrow had become, in a sense, public property, the destiny of its Mastership a matter of more than local or narrow interest. It was, literally, a national school: in 1800 at least twenty-five English counties were represented among the boys.[56] The interest of Cambridge, with its recently established examinations for first degrees, also reflected the stirrings of a new, rigorous, self-conscious elevation of academic facility in addition to social connection as the touchstone of university achievement and hence future influence and success, a move which was to transform secondary and higher education over the next seventy years. Schools such as Harrow, in imitation of the older collegiate ones,

[49] HM/D/44, 54. For the boys' campaign see above, pp. 164–6.   [50] HM/D/48, 52.
[51] HM/D/46.   [52] HM/D/55. Cf. nos. 49–51, 53.   [53] HM/D/60.
[54] Minchin, *Old Harrow Days*, 85; E. Graham, *The Harrow Life of H. M. Butler* (London, 1920), p. 11.   [55] HM/1829/Lord Northwick to S. Evans, 28 Jan. 1829.
[56] *Harrow Register, 1800–1911*, 1–14; the corresponding figure for 1830 is 24: Bamford, 'Public Schools and Social Class', 227.

were now regarded as essential wells from which the universities drew their talent and social allure.

At the Harrow election meeting, the choice was plain: a continuance of the existing regime and atmosphere, essentially complacent, introverted, a profitable business concern and benefit society of the extended Drury–Heath family (with Butler's intervention Evans was not a serious candidate); or a fresh start, based on the traditional curriculum and the social values of the gentleman, but infused with the best modern scholarship, with an eye for the needs and opportunities of the wider world. The governors met on 18 March and voted by ballot, a tactical error as the result was a tie, three each to Butler and Drury. It is likely that the three peers, Northwick, Clarendon (who had arranged the date of the election), and Grimston voted for Butler, with the three locals, Williams the vicar, Moody, and Page supporting the parochial status quo. They had no alternative but to submit the decision to the Visitor, the archbishop of Canterbury.[57] To increase their embarrassment, the governors immediately publicized their plight by communicating the result to Joseph Drury, whose reply was of a man in shock, alarmed at the expected propect of his brother's succession being dashed.[58] For it was pretty obvious whom the Visitor would choose. Charles Manners-Sutton had not risen to the chair of St Augustine, which he had ascended only a month earlier, by ignoring patrons with the heavier clout. Butler got the job.[59]

It proved a crucial election, exerting a strong influence on its immediate successors. All subsequent vacancies in the Head Mastership were advertised, at least around Oxford and Cambridge. Never again, regardless of their final choice, were the governors to be stuck with such unimpressive candidates as they were in 1804–5 through inaction on their part. Since 1805, no internal candidate—barring the exceptional circumstances of 1940—has gained election: after 1829, few have stood. If not always an attractive post, the Head Mastership of Harrow has been seen as important within the public school world, not a perquisite of a private cabal or local faction. It had been a close thing. The ultimate election of Butler not Drury signalled and secured Harrow's place in both the social and educational worlds. Butler was to found a Harrow dynasty even more pervasive and tenacious than Drury's, but one always sensitive to the outside reputation of the school.

The Chancery Suit of 1810

Unfortunately for the governors what was good for the school was not obviously so good for the parishioners of Harrow. The development of some Elizabethan and Jacobean grammar schools into public schools had occurred almost imperceptibly, without statutory changes. What had begun as local charities were now the preserves of 'the sons of the nobility and gentry of this kingdom'. From the end of the

[57] HSR III, fos. 252–4.   [58] HSR III, fos. 253–4; HM/D/57.
[59] For the appeal to the archbishop see HM/D/58, 59; for his decision see HSR III, fo. 255.

eighteenth century until the 1860s, across England the new reality of these schools was challenged by local inhabitants who reckoned their rights under the original founders' statutes had been ignored. Epic battles were fought at Rugby and Shrewsbury. The bases for the attacks varied according to the statutes, but in essence they shared common themes: upwardly mobile local traders, farmers, and businessmen resented the social and educational privileges enjoyed by 'foreigners' to the exclusion of their own children for whom they imagined the schools had been established. The logic of their appeals was to alter the character of these public schools entirely under the guise of a return to statutory legality. These cases were just one aspect of a general scrutiny of the administration of trusts and charities that led to the establishment of the charity commissioners in 1818. As a despised Free Scholar, Anthony Trollope (1823–4, 1831–4) had ample personal opportunity to understand the emotions aroused by such diversions of local charities which, together with his experiences of Winchester, informed his portrayal of the case of Hirams' Hospital in *The Warden*.

At Harrow the attack began in 1806 with a parish meeting to discuss the operation of Lyon's statutes.[60] Oddly, neither the parishioners nor the governors at any time until long after all issues between them had been settled in the 1870s actually had access to the originals of Lyon's Statutes, Rules, and Orders, relying on various copies made for the 1611 case and subsequent litigation. Lyon's autographed Statutes lay undetected in the school chest until rediscovered by E. J. L. Scott in the 1880s. Previous litigation against the governors had mainly concerned the administration of funds and, increasingly, the operation of the Road Trusts. These remained a source of confusion and irritation, not least because the relative income of the school and road trusts altered rapidly. Building on the Paddington estate began in earnest from 1808.[61] By 1827 the surplus on the road trusts was still only £571, compared to an unusually high balance from the school estate of £1,400. By 1836 these balances had been reversed, £1,550 to £545; in 1844 £1,440 to £345.[62] Any attempts to reallocate the Road Trust to support the school foundered on the shoals of Elizabethan legal skill and the lack of a united Harrovian will in Parliament to tamper with the Founder's intentions. It provoked the only sour note at the Tercentenary (*sic*) celebrations in 1871, introduced appropriately by the rebarbative Robert Middlemist.[63]

However, the parishioners in 1806 had a less complex but bigger target: the school itself. They believed that they were being cheated of their rights to free education for their children and that the Founder's intentions and his Statutes were being flagrantly abused by governors, staff, and pupils. Their grievances were legal,

---

[60] May, *Relations between Harrow School and Parishioners*, esp. p. 17; Thornton, *Harrow School*, 223–6; Howson and Townsend Warner, *Harrow School*, 67.
[61] HSR III, fos. 266, 268–9.   [62] HSR III, fos. 357; GM 27 June 1836, 20 June 1844.
[63] *The Commemoration of the Tercentenary of Harrow School* (Harrow-on-the-Hill, 1871), pp. 44–5.

educational, social, and venal. In their depositions for the case in Chancery, made in 1808–9, a succession of locals aired their complaints.[64] Some were painful, if legally trivial. John Withers recalled being beaten up as a Free Scholar by the other boys in the 1790s, representations to Drury merely making matters worse. At that time there were only two foundationers. William Winckley had experienced harassment as a 'Charity boy' in the 1770s and, as an adult, had had his house attacked and his wife molested by Harrovians. It was attested that poaching, violence, and vandalism were endemic. Numerous local tradesmen complained that their premises and employees were frequently abused. Some attributed the problem to the excessive pocket money enjoyed by 'foreigners' who 'are thereby enabled to commit and are nearly daily committing or engaging in Scenes of Dissipation'. Yet even if locals did wish to attend, the expenses of books and clothing and, most serious of all, the exclusively classical curriculum deterred them from taking advantage of Lyon's charity. There was, of course, an implied complication. One of the strongest complainants was assistant to the school doctor; another, John Bliss, ran the Crown and Anchor pub. Financially, Harrow traders did well out of the school they disapproved of so greatly.

When it came to court in August 1810, the charges levelled against the governors had been arranged into eight counts arguing breach of the statutes: five governors were non-resident; they had not been duly appointed; £2,000 of trust money had been spent enlarging and glorifying the Head Master's 'to the prejudice of the poor inhabitants'; the Head Master did not live, as specified in the statutes, in the schoolhouse; few local children attended the school because of the dominance of foreigners who maltreated any Free Scholars; the expense of the school made it impossible for locals to be 'on the same footing . . . especially as they are too apt to imbibe the extravagant and expensive ideas as well as pernicious habits of the young men of fortune'; a land agent had been appointed 'at a large salary'; foreigners were admitted without gubernatorial agreement. The plaintiffs, through the Attorney General, demanded the removal and replacement of the governors and for a new scheme 'for the better regulation of the school and the admission of the children of the Inhabitants . . . and generally for the Establishment of the Charity'.[65]

The defence insisted that the governors were fit persons to serve, all living within two hours of the school, available for local consultation and rejected 'imputations of mismanagement'. Regarding the Head Master's house, the defendants noted that it was only 80 yards from the school and that the governors had subsidized the repairs after Drury's departure only on the existing house, not Butler's extension, to the tune of £1,200 not £2,000, none of which was 'to the prejudice or exclusion'

---

[64] May, *Relations between Harrow School and Parishioners*, passim. For the evidence prepared see the boxes of MS files in the Harrow School Archives: Chancery Case 1808–10; HSR III, fos. 264–5, 267, 272–3, 277, 282–3.

[65] A transcript of the case and judgment are in British Library Add. MS 29,254, fos. 44ᵛ–49ᵛ.

of the locals. No local children had been refused entry. They then tackled the essential issue of principle. Lyon had founded a classical school 'for teaching Grammatically the learned languages and not for the instruction of the children of the Town in general learning'. Classical learning 'is in the opinion of those best capable of judging not well adapted ... for persons of low condition, but better suited to those of a higher class, intended for the learned professions'. This, the governors' lawyers argued, was what deterred locals, rather than any supposed expense which, beyond textbooks, did not arise unless the Free Scholar had private lessons. This was, of course, disingenuous, as the system of learning, such as it was, depended on boys having private tutors. The defendants also sought to minimize the seriousness of ill-treatment by foreigners, claiming that all boys in such a large school were liable to such difficulties. Institutionalized bullying was denied, although it was admitted that tensions arose when 'boys of different fortunes and situations in life' were brought together. The whole school benefited from the fees paid by the foreigners which attracted 'Masters of much greater learning and better qualified for the Office than ... otherwise'. The policy of admitting foreigners was, it was asserted, generally approved by the governors.

The two sides were arguing at cross-purposes, both claiming strict adherence to the letter of the statutes while actually promoting contrasting interpretations of the spirit. The nervousness of the governors, who privately must have recognized that Lyon's local grammar school was a far cry from Butler's public school, was evident. Much of their case was bluster and nit-picking, alternating with a direct appeal to the snobbery and class interest of the judge. The suit had occupied their attention since 1807; in 1809 they had not immediately replaced Lord Grimston because of anxiety about their rights.[66] However, while the Attorney-General scored some palpable hits, as with the residence of the governors, he could not pretend that the statutes, meagre as they were, had been explicitly contravened just by *ad hominem* discrimination. Unfortunately for his case, Lyon had specified a classical curriculum and had allowed for the admission of an unspecified number of foreigners. The parishioners had a strong moral argument, although one vigorously denounced by the sychophantic Sam Parr, perhaps the first professional old boy in the school's history.[67] The governors, on the other hand, because of long experience of legal challenge, had always been careful to act within the letter of the statutes. Thus they supported local educational charities, such as the Sunday school at Pinner and, later, the Harrow National School, but consistently refused to subsidize clergy or churches at Pinner or Harrow Weald.[68]

The Master of the Rolls, Sir William Grant, was a Scot with a taste for madeira who had impressed William Pitt, whose placeman he became. He cannot have

---

[66] HSR III, fos. 272–3.
[67] HM/Bg/Butler to Lord Northwick, 14 July 1807, quoting a letter from Parr.
[68] HSR III and GM, *passim*.

been unaware of Harrow's reputation and character, not least as the then Prime Minister and leader of his party, Spencer Perceval, was an old boy. Grant's judgement formally settled the status of the school until the Public School Act of 1868 but, in essence, for good. Harrow was to stay a public school if needs be at odds with local people and opinion, whatever the cost in terms of legal sophistry. Grant enshrined the fiction of the inspired vision of John Lyon 'who did not mean to erect a mere parochial school'. Like so many apologists since, Grant failed to understand the context of Harrow's foreigner clause, let alone the charitable intent of the founder. While trying his best to be faithful to the statutes as composed, Grant was inevitably as prone to anachronistic convenience and modernist misinterpretation as either of the parties pleading before him.

Grant divided the case into three. He dismissed the plaintiffs' demand for the removal of the governors on a technicality: they could only be displaced by petition to the Great Seal. On the question of the management of the trust revenues, which the plaintiffs claimed were not fully realized, he rejected charges of general wrong doing by the governors, although he did suggest that there was a possible conflict of interest for one governor, Williams, the vicar, as a lessee of lands of which he was also a trustee. Nevertheless, Grant conceded to the plaintiffs that the current administration of the trust funds required overhaul and proposed that a new scheme for the application of the charity's revenues be drawn up taking account both of the Founder's directions and changed circumstances.

However, 'the most material object of the suit' was the accusation that the Founder's money 'is employed rather in providing for the more commodious education of the Rich than in supplying a gratuitous education to the poor' and that local children were deterred from attending the school because of ill-treatment by foreigners and the dangers of acquiring expensive habits. The solution of banning foreigners was dismissed as counter to Lyon's express intention and the wider interests of the school and parish. Grant found no compelling evidence 'of the alleged conspiracy against parish boys' and, given the immutable classical curriculum, the numbers of locals taking advantage of the school even if foreigners were banned or restricted would be minimal. The one change he countenanced was the possibility of an allowance paid by the trust to the Head Master for each foundationer (as operated at Rugby). Grant even turned the plaintiffs' argument on its head by noting that it was perfectly proper for the school to continue whether there were any locals in it or not, the test of propriety in the use of revenues being their expenditure on the school rather than specifically on Free Scholars. In this context, Grant approved of the subsidy to Butler for the rebuilding of the Head Master's house, noting that although the governors were contributing £2,000, Butler himself had spent £5,000. The judgment concluded with Grant citing the recent precedent of the Rugby case heard by the Lord Chancellor which had been resolved in favour of the governors not the parishioners, thus preserving 'a great Public School'. Any alterations to the curriculum or discipline in the school in future could, as in the past, be determined by the governors and Head Master, with ultimate appeal to the Visitor.

However well founded in law, there was something artificial about Grant's judgment as he simultaneously allowed himself to be swayed by the current nature of the school while hiding behind the statutes when convenient to his general intention of preserving the status quo. His refusal to believe in the well-attested discrimination against parish boys revealed his true attitude to the whole business. The effect of his judgment was, perhaps as intended, negligible. In the Spring of 1811, to test the attitude of the school, the parishioners formed a committee which sent twenty-nine boys to be admitted as Free Scholars. Butler examined them and took just four, those, he claimed, who could read.[69] By 1816, out of 295 pupils, three were Free Scholars.[70] As the painful and humiliating experiences of Trollope a decade later revealed, parish boys continued to be treated with contempt and abuse by boys, and even masters, including Butler.[71] This was, of course, merely a symptom of a much wider and more deep rooted snobbery. Even Charles Merivale (1817–24), grandson of Joseph Drury and nephew of Henry, thought he had been scarred for life by 'the sense of social inferiority which was impressed upon me at Harrow'.[72] Despite the silence on the subject in Grant's judgment, the behaviour of foreigners persisted in thuggery, vandalism, loutishness, and larceny in dealings with local inhabitants in general or, indeed, anybody else to whom they took a dislike. Crucially, the one positive proposal made by the Master of the Rolls, that a new scheme for allocating revenues be devised, was completely ignored. The only subsequent signs of anxiety or appreciation of how close they had come to disaster appeared in the extreme caution shown by the governors over any possible breach of the statutes. Thus Butler formally asked permission to marry in 1818, presumably so that the precedents could be declared; in 1821–3, the governors were careful to insist that they contributed only to the repairs to the old schoolhouse fabric and not to the new rooms added in 1820; and in 1823 the invitation to Lord Aberdeen (of, among other places, Bentley Priory, Stanmore) to become a governor contained the somewhat unwelcoming rider that, in accordance with Lyon's will, he should resign if he moved out of the parish.[73]

By legitimizing the de facto constitution of Harrow, Grant's judgment spared the school the trench-warfare between the charity and its supposed local beneficiaries experienced by Shrewsbury where it lasted until 1866.[74] It also confirmed an inertia inherent in the administration of both school and trust which slowed or

---

[69] Thornton, *Harrow School*, 226–7; Johnstone, *Parr*, vii. 431, Butler telling Parr, a former Foundationer himself, of the outcome (letter misdated to March by Johnstone).

[70] Butler, *Harrow Lists*, 107–19; HSR III, fo. 301.

[71] The relevant extracts from Trollope's autobiography are in Townsend Warner, *Harrow in Prose and Verse*, 130–8.   [72] Merivale, *Autobiography*, 43.

[73] HSR III, fos. 306–7, 319, 320, 321, 329–30, 333.

[74] Mack, *Public Schools and British Opinion, 1780–1860*, 355.

prevented adaptation and change. In allowing the governors to escape without any commitments not to their taste, the Master of the Rolls paved the way for the statutes to be used by them as a shield to resist reform and a club to beat reformers, not least when these proved to be their own Head Masters. The 1810 judgment itself was employed to help crush Dr Wordsworth's attempts to place both the admission and the funding of Free Scholars on a rational basis in the 1840s. Ironically, by upholding a specious literal interpretation of the statutes, Grant made possible the wholly venal subversion of the Founder's intentions by wealthy newcomers to the parish in the 1830s and 1840s, attracted by the lure of a free education at an expensive, elite public school. As elsewhere, this late triumph of the *ancien régime* merely served to hasten its decay, highlight its contradictions, and plant seeds that nearly choked the life out of it.

George Butler

The 1810 judgment secured Harrow's status as an aristocratic school and the mixed constitution of adult tyranny and juvenile republic that went with it. George Butler exercised the one and suffered the other for almost a quarter of a century, the longest tenure since Bryan.

Butler was the son of a private schoolmaster from Chelsea. A small, wiry man of immense intellectual and physical energy, he was something of a polymath, interested in science and expert in modern languages as well as proficient in classics and, when young, distinguished in mathematics. He swam, rode, and skated with vigour as well as claiming, with characteristic lack of modesty, to be an expert fencer.[75] His academic and social contacts were impeccable. He was a natural member of the Athenaeum Club after its foundation in 1824.[76] Potential boarders were directed to his house because of 'the advantages in point of learning and connections'.[77] Although cruel, Byron's early judgements were not so very far from their mark. Although much cleverer than the poet could recognize, Butler was fond of 'florid jargon', was often conspicuously pleased with himself, flogged with enthusiasm, liked to brag about his continental visits, and took pains to create an image of learning and authority which at times appeared not to match the reality.[78] Butler wanted to impress academically and socially, occasionally perhaps straining too hard, lacking the effortless ingratiating quality of his predecessor. Careful to cultivate the great, assiduous in his dealings with local governors, even to the extent of marrying the daughter of one, John Gray of Wembley, he nurtured the style and manner of a gentlemen.

[75] For Butler see Graham, *H. M. Butler*, 7–17; Merivale, *Autobiography*, esp. pp. 36–7; Minchin, *Old Harrow Days*, 84–90, 225–40; Fox, *Harrow*, 14; Charles Wordsworth, *Annals*, 22–3; Howson and Townsend Warner, *Harrow School*, 66–80; Thornton, *Harrow School*, 215–64; *DNB*.
[76] HM/Longley (hereafter HM/L), Longley to the secretary of the Athenaeum on Butler's behalf.
[77] Harrow Archives, Harrow Masters, File T. S. Hughes, 13 Oct. 1809.
[78] Byron, *Poetical Works*, i. 132, no. 76, 157–72, no. 93, 172–3, no. 93a.

This was made easier by his considerable personal fortune. On arrival, Butler spent £12,000 on repairing the slum that the Head Master's house had become, adding dormitories and studies for boarders (which he described as his 'Barracks') and considerable extensions to the private side. The governors had provided just £1,200.[79] He added a large stable-block to house his horses and carriage. Throughout his time, Butler steadily bought land on the Hill, both adjacent to his house and beyond, especially on the northwestern slopes where his estate is still commemorated in the road names of Gayton (after the Northamptonshire rectory to which he was preferred by his college in 1814) and Peterborough (of which cathedral he was dean from 1842). More than one of his assistants were also his tenants, as were his two immediate successors. When his eldest son was in the school under Longley and Wordsworth, he used to deduct the rent they owed him from the half-yearly school bills.[80]

From the school, despite the collapse in numbers in his last decade, he earned enough to make him regret leaving. His view of the Head Master's income was that it should be sufficient 'so that he may retire in good time to enjoy his well-earned affluence'.[81] From schooling fees (ten guineas a head) he was guaranteed an income of at most something over £3,000 and at worst well over £1,000. Each new boy paid four guineas on top of this. Set against these, the Head paid sixty guineas to each assistant (four or five at any one time) and a quarter of the schooling fees to the Under Master. Butler also took private pupils at between ten and twenty guineas each. The big profits came, as ever, from his boarders who were, by 1819, being charged £67 a year. It was as a business speculation that he had enlarged his house to accommodate as many as 120 boys. Given that the Head could expect a profit of as much as 66.66 per cent on his income from boarders, this could have meant that Butler cleared over £40 a head.[82] The division of the boys' accommodation between the dormitories and studies tempted overcrowding, in 1814 Butler being criticized by a favourite pupil for 'taking more boys into his house than he has studies for', some little boys in the Head Master's being forced to eat their breakfast and supper in the house yard or even the street.[83] By such commercial realism, Butler's

---

[79] R. Ackermann, *History of the Free School at Harrow*, 18–19; HM/Bg/ Butler to Sir John Richardson, 15 Dec. 1828; HM/W/BH, Butler to Wordsworth, 6 Mar. 1838 (i and ii); HSR III, fos. 255–6, 261–2; British Library Add. MS 29,254, fos. 44ᵛ, 45ᵛ, 49ʳ; for a drawing of Butler's extensions at the back in 1815 see, W. C. Trevelyan's Diary, *The Harrovian*, 11, 26 Feb. 1898, between pp. 6 and 7.

[80] See correspondence in files HM/W/BH, 19 Feb. 1838 and undated, Colenso to Wordsworth, 1838; HM/W/Butler to Wordsworth, 22 June 1837; Cockerell to Butler, 27 June and 20 Aug. 1838; Butler to Wordsworth, 26 Dec. 1838; HM/W/24, etc..   [81] HM/W/4.

[82] For estimated percentage profit see 'Colenso's plan' 1838 in HM/W/BH file; Butler's 1819 fees HM/Bg file, unlisted MS circular to parents and 1829 memo on school history: Carlisle, *Grammar Schools*, ii. 149.

[83] This according to Henry Fox Talbot: A. Hawkyard, *William Henry Fox Talbot* (Harrow, 1989), p. 21 quoting from Talbot's letters now at Lacock. Cf. H. J. P. Arnold, *William Henry Fox Talbot* (London, 1977), pp. 32–6.

The Ancien Régime

income in good years matched all but the most spectacular years of Dr Drury and, over the period of his Head Mastership, he must have recouped his initial investment many times over.

However, it was typical of the man that Butler was always worried about money almost to the point of obsession. In 1828 he mused wistfully that the money he spent on the Head Master's 'would by this time have amounted to a large sum'.[84] During negotiations over providing a piece of land for the new chapel in 1837, he commented to Dr Wordsworth on the 'very high price' he had paid for his Hill properties.[85] Yet his investment proved sounder than he could have imagined. In 1838, a year after the opening of the London to Birmingham railway and the station at Harrow Weald, he was assured by the architect of the chapel, C. K. Cockerell, 'it is quite certain that the railroad has at least doubled the value of your ground' and was encouraged to indulge in some speculative property development as a consequence.[86] None the less, even when appointed dean of Peterborough in 1842, he was concerned lest he would lose out financially. Yet, at his death, aged 79, in 1853, he left his widow in comfort—she took a house near Hyde Park—and his many children far from destitute.[87]

For the school, however, Butler's close interest in money was fortunate as well as fortuitous. Not only could he be generous—as when endowing three prizes in 1820—but he was ideally suited to initiate and lead the appeal in 1818–20 that paid for the new east wing of the Old Schools for which he acted as treasurer and secretary. He was also by far the greatest individual contributor, subscribing £500 towards the ultimate total of more than £7,600: the next largest sum was £100.[88] This appeal was of the utmost significance, the first of what became a regular feature of Harrow whose nineteenth-century transformation was almost entirely the result of private donations or appeals on the model of 1818–20. Butler himself was instrumental in attracting benefactions for prizes, starting a habit that continues to proliferate. Until the reform of the financial arrangements of the school in the 1870s, all capital expenses on new buildings depended upon successful public appeals as the governors had neither the funds nor the legal authority to subsidize any building other than the old schoolhouse, now the west wing of the Old Schools. The first to follow the 1818–20 model was the subscription for the new chapel in 1839 (c.£4,000). Thereafter, such appeals were regular. Between 1820 and 1870, for buildings and other, non-academic facilities, just under £59,000 were raised. Butler had set the pattern for the future.[89]

As a pedagogue, Butler's record was more chequered. If not the monster of pomposity of Byron's poems, he was fussy, nit-picking, and pedantic, displaying the

[84] HM/Bg/Butler to Sir John Richardson, 15 Dec. 1828.
[85] HM/W/Butler to Wordsworth, 22 June 1837.
[86] HM/W/Cockerell to Butler, 27 June and 20 Aug. 1838.   [87] Graham, *Butler*, 17, 53.
[88] A list of donors is printed in *Tercentenary of Harrow School*, 79–90.
[89] Howson and Townsend Warner, *Harrow School*, 135–52.

rigidity and smugness of the excellent second-rate. His teaching was methodical and uninspiring, George Batten (1817–24) noting in 1823: 'when one is thinking of poetry, he is thinking of whether you have put your right stops, marks of exclamation etc.' Charles Merivale (1817–24) was even more damning, recalling Butler as excellent in maths 'but in classics he was nowhere, nor can I remember getting any insight into classical lore from his immediate teaching, nor, which was much worse, being directed into any course of learning, or in any way kindled to interest or enthusiasm in its pursuit.' Or, as Byron had put it, he dealt out precepts 'as if dealing lace'.[90]

None the less, although the gifted may, like Merivale, have thought the work 'very easy', Butler's system could produce scholars and scholarly habits. Isaac Williams (1817–21) believed he thought in Latin while at Harrow. Charles Wordsworth may have been showing off to his brother (and future Head Master of Harrow) Christopher at Winchester when he described his work in the week ending on Saturday, 17 February 1824. This, he claimed, had included composing 120 lines of Latin hexameters, fifty lines of Latin prose, and nineteen verses of Lyrics, as well as construing and learning thirty lines of Juvenal a day. That very evening he had learnt 120 lines. Extra work included six or seven chapters of Thucydides, Herodotus, or a Greek play, as well as some Livy and Tacitus. The bolder tackled Aristophanes. Even allowing for hyperbole, the implied volume of study is impressive. However, there was also much leisure for private reading, as both Williams and Francis Trench (1818–24), among the scholars, testify.[91]

They were not typical. For the idle, bored, or less intelligent school work was dudgery to be endured not enjoyed. Butler himself worked hard, taking the Sixth Form and Monitors (a class of up to thirty-five or even, in full years, forty) for all periods every day; hearing the lessons of every other form at least once a month; and setting and examining the tests which, every alternate term, determined the form order and promotion. However, the circumstances of teaching as well as the syllabus were against fruitful formal instruction for the majority who were anyway mainly at school to socialize. It says much for the formality of teaching in school that, until the new rooms were finished in 1820, three forms: the Sixth, Lower Fourth, and Third, all worked—or more accurately sat—in what is now the Fourth Form Room; upstairs the Fifth Form met in the Governors' Room (now part of OS2); the Upper Fourth in the southern chamber (part of OS4); the large Shell in the Cock Loft or attic on the second floor.[92] The size of forms precluded sensitive instruction or efficient learning. In the last year of the old schoolhouse, 1819, Butler's own form comprised forty-three boys; the Fifth Form, fifty-two; the

---

[90] Harrow School Archives, Letters of G. M. Batten, typescript, no. 7, 23 Feb. 1823; Merivale, *Autobiography*, 36; Byron, *Poetical Works*, 172–3: 'Portrait of Pomposus', l. 3.

[91] Merivale, *Autobiography*, 34; Prevost, *Williams*, 4–5; Charles Wordsworth, *Annals*, 18–19; Trench, *Notes*, 2, 23–5.

[92] Thornton, *Harrow School*, 240–2 for Merivale's account.

combined Shells, under Henry Drury, seventy-two; the Upper Fourth, twenty-one; the rest of the Fourth, thirty-four; the Third Form, just twelve. The provision of more rooms was not matched by additional masters until 1826, when the full classical teaching complement, including Head and Under Masters, was eight—for 211 boys. Until then the ratio had been considerably worse.[93]

Even the pupil room system failed to provide much education. On the one hand, the exercises being prepared were mechanical for all but the most earnest or gifted, one such, Charles Merivale, remembering Henry Drury's pupil room as providing stimulus, intensified interest, and closer understanding. On the other, there was no even distribution of pupils. In 1820, in a school of about 250, Henry Drury was tutor to ninety of them, as well as form master to sixty or seventy and housemaster to a further forty.[94] At twenty guineas each, pupils were eagerly sought, new masters, such as Batten or Phelps, labouring hard in slowly gaining a reputation and, hence, enhanced income. Here, too, social acumen or religious inclination played as great a part as academic or pedagogic skill. Thus S. E. Batten, a clever evangelical with a taste for the nobility, was no scholar but was keen to attract private pupils. So he set about becoming proficient as a tutor of Latin verse, the main staple for the ordinary boy, by learning chunks of Ovid by heart.[95] Even Henry Drury, when young regarded as the most inspiring tutor in the school, lost heart and energy as the years rolled on in unremitting sameness. He became lazy and disillusioned, although still popular as a tutor. The fault was only partly his. As his nephew shrewdly observed, 'his was the sore mischance of having been put too early into an easy position beneath his abilities'.[96] The common image of the early nineteenth-century public school master is of a sadist, idler, toady, mercenary, or incompetent. However, there were also some who were probably as bored by the whole system as their pupils, but, unlike their charges, they had a living to make.

Butler recognized the need to lend greater purpose to the academic process. Taking his lead from his Cambridge contemporary, but not relation, Samuel Butler of Shrewsbury, the Harrow Butler began to emphasize examinations as a means of ensuring that classics were learnt. He was not alone: even Eton followed Shrewsbury, introducing the Newcastle Prize in the 1820s.[97] At Harrow, Butler offered prizes for Latin and Greek verse in 1820, regularized by the governors in 1821.[98] These were altogether grander and more elevated than the traditional book prizes handed out for excellence in form-work, as candidates had to compose in the required form on set subjects, the successful entries then being declaimed on a Speech Day. Charles Wordsworth, an incorrigible hearty and fanatical cricketer as well as the future author of a definitive Greek grammar, explained one reason for their success: work was a 'counter-stimulus' to games 'in the prizes given almost too

[93] Butler, *Harrow Lists*, 107–18, 135–44. [94] Merivale, *Autobiography*, 37–8.
[95] Thornton, *Harrow School*, 242. [96] Merivale, *Autobiography*, 38–9.
[97] Mack, *Public Schools and British Opinion, 1780–1860*, 232. [98] HSR III, fo. 323.

freely'.[99] Prizes satisfied adolescent competitiveness bringing glory almost on a par with that won on the games field. Isaac Williams later admitted that 'my ambition ... was excited in getting prizes and boyish admiration'.[100] The public recognition of these prizes was carefully nurtured by the staff, tutors vying to ensure their pupils' success to a degree that casts some doubt on the unaided originality of some winning entries. None the less, when Francis Trench and Robert Sheppard, both in Mrs Leith's, won two of the three prizes in 1823, their Dame 'expressed her satisfaction that we could do something in this way, besides beating the school at cricket'.[101] Thus individual ambition and corporate pride were harnassed together in a manner most familiar to later generations of Harrovians.

Butler extended the range of prizes by securing the endowment of a medal for Latin prose from Robert Peel, even though the protracted negotiations, lasting well over a year (1825–7), saw Butler at his most pernickity and obsequious. Peel wanted 'to promote the sound learning by exciting the honourable emulation [*i.e. in the sense of rivalry or competition*] of the Scholars'.[102] This was exactly the intention of the governors when, in 1824, they began to investigate the conversion of the more or less moribund, uncompetitive Lyon exhibitions into objects 'of desire or competition to the Upper boys of the school'. These leaving scholarships, two a year worth £50 per annum for four years held at either Oxford or Cambridge, apart from financial value, were to be academically respectable, special papers being set each spring by external examiners from the universities. The first competition was held in 1828. The following year John Sayer, who had been Sumner's head of school in 1770, lavishly endowed a similar scholarship for Harrovians proceeding to Gonville and Caius College, Cambridge, a restriction he insisted on despite objections from both Butler and Henry Drury.[103] These scholarships soon became the blue riband for Harrow scholars and, for the first time, introduced an element of external scrutiny of the school's curriculum and standards in a foretaste of the strenuous academic meritocracy that dominated Victorian education.

Even this introduction of serious academic competition failed to shift the prevailing sloth. The formal working day was if anything less full than it had been in Sumner's or even Drury's time. On a full teaching day, First School lasted just under an hour, finishing at 8 or 8.30 a.m.; Second School from after the daily Masters' meeting at 11 a.m. theoretically until noon, but could be as little as half an hour; Third School from 2 p.m. until 2.30; Fourth School from 4.30 to 5.30. As

[99] Charles Wordsworth, *Annals*, 9, 15.   [100] Prevost, *Williams*, 4.
[101] Trench, *Notes*, 35–6.
[102] Peel to Governors, 4 Oct. 1825, *MSS Correspondence Respecting the Foundation of the Peel Medal and the Sayer Scholarship*, bound 1828; HSR III, fo. 360; Howson and Townsend Warner, *Harrow School*, 139–40.
[103] HSR III, fos. 338, 342, 362, 366, 374, 381; Howson and Townsend Warner, *Harrow School*, 140; *MSS Correspondence of Peel Medal and Sayer Scholarship*, passim; M. C. Buck, 'John Sayer', *The Harrovian*, 94 (1981), 131–2.

The Ancien Régime

before, Thursday and Saturdays were half holidays, cutting lessons to one and a half or two hours; Tuesdays were whole holidays. Even the Sunday Greek New Testament lesson was stopped after Vicar Cunningham's election as governor in 1818 on the grounds that any violation of the sabbath rest offended his evangelical sensibilities, an early example of his interference. Frederick Shore's full school day in 1814 lasted just two and a half hours, with at most two hours in pupil room. In 1826, as a new master, assistant to the Under Master, W. W. Phelps spent three hours in school (with no Third School) and two hours with his solitary private pupil.[104] This compares with the four hours, three days a week spent playing cricket by the Sixth Form Game in 1827.[105] It is hardly surprising that Wordsworth was able to double the amount of time spent on academic work when he arrived in 1836.[106]

As if school hours were not sufficiently relaxed, Harrow had a penchant for granting itself additional whole holidays and exemption from 'exercises', i.e. homework or preparation. In 1806 there were fourteen additional holidays, a mixture of religious and secular festivals, some with some without 'exercises'. If these did not fall on a Tuesday or a Sunday, the school routine was disrupted. The victories in the French wars provided another frequent excuse in Butler's first decade, as did visiting grandees and the Head Master's own wedding in 1818, when the only issue was whether the boys would get a week or a fortnight off. On more than one occasion, the monitors requested holidays directly from the governors, which irritated Butler more because of the potential undermining of his authority than any interruption to academic endeavour.[107] Although generally profligate, occasionally the governors were cautious, refusing a holiday in 1819 on the birth of Princess Victoria and only agreeing to a week to mark the coronation of George IV if 'other Public Schools adopt that means'.[108] Given the increased public scrutiny of such schools and, since 1810, acute local interest, Harrow's conduct was feckless and risked scandal. One fifteen-day period in June and July 1813 included seven whole holidays and two half-holidays, that Summer term containing as many as eighteen whole holidays, let alone innumerable individual exeats for particular boys.[109] Although Francis and Richard Trench's mother approved of the 'numerous holidays' as providing time for willing boys to perfect their work, in the light of the hardly overcrowded school timetable, such specious special pleading convinced few.[110] In July 1818 the following poem on 'a growing evil at Harrow' was left, helpfully, at Cunningham's house:

---

[104] F. J. Shore to his sister, 13 Oct. 1814, *The Harrovian*, 30 (1917–18), 86–7; Thornton, *Harrow School*, 242; Hole, *Phelps*, ii. 7–8.
[105] Drummond Smith to Fanny Smith, 30 Apr. 1827, Catto MS Drummond Smith Letter Book, pp. 125–6.   [106] GM, 26 Feb. 1838.
[107] HM/Bg/1806 memo on holidays; HM/Bg/Butler to Lord Northwick, 29 Nov. 1806; 16 July 1808, 10 June 1814, 17 July 1815, 17 Mar., 24 Mar. 1818, 20 Dec. 1822.
[108] HSR III, fos. 296, 300, 316, 323.
[109] Diary of W. C. Trevelyan, printed in Townsend Warner, *Harrow in Prose and Verse*, 107–12.
[110] Trench, *Notes*, 2.

> Sing Muse! of Harrow Hill and Harrow boys!
> Their Num'rous Holidays! their Bats! and Toys!
> But Learning—*that* dull theme Oh never name
> Let Play and frolic lead the way to Fame.
> Ye Sages say who live through Space and Time
> Can Holidays at Harrow be a crime?
> Will idle Masters—idle pupils make?
> Or loit'ring Boy become a Fool or Rake?
> > Methinks I hear their Sighs,
> > Lamenting from the Skies
> That Time once lost can never be regained.
> The Truth resounds, but what can Mortals say?
> The Doctor's married and is fond of play—[111]

Yet nothing was done. Holidays of one or more days continued to be freely, almost casually given. In 1826, Drummond Smith, commenting to his sister that his birthday, 13 April, was an extra holiday, admitted 'I really do not know what for'. After Butler left Longley immediately requested that all one-day holidays be allocated to Tuesdays and reduced the number of Speech Days.[112]

Outside the formal curriculum, the extensive free time encouraged without discrimination wide reading, the indulgence of hobbies, intellectual or otherwise, and mischief. Butler himself tried to promote an interest in science through lectures and conversation. He allowed Henry Talbot (better known as Fox Talbot, pioneer of photography) to conduct chemical experiments in the Head Master's—until one exploded—and turned over part of his large new greenhouse to his pupil's botanical specimens.[113] Butler always insisted that Talbot was his cleverest pupil. But private encouragement had its limits. Neither Butler nor the governors was prepared to alter the curriculum, even though the 1810 judgment had implicitly allowed them to. Deviation from the classics was seen as tantamount to conceding the liberal criticisms. As with many cornered conservatives, Butler made changes to the form but not the substance. Outside the school or pupil room, regular lectures were organized on general subjects and in 1819 Butler, after some hesitation, allowed a display of an orrery to the school, something that Keate of Eton persisted in refusing, possibly because the owner charged 7s. 6d. a head for showing it.[114]

Although singularly lacking his predecessor's charm and skill with the young, Butler shared his passion for public speaking or, more accurately, declamation. His new schoolhouse was conceived around the new Speech Room as much as the need for more classrooms. The care he lavished on preparing the speakers, who

---

[111] HM/Bg/'Left at Cunningham's July 22 1818'.

[112] Drummond Smith Letter Book, 75–6; HM/W/Head Master's Memorandum Book from 1815, fo. 71.

[113] Hawkyard, *Talbot*, 11–31; Arnold, *Talbot*, 32–6; Howson and Townsend Warner, *Harrow School*, 68.

[114] Letters of G. M. Batten, no. 2.

performed to the whole school in rehearsals before the three public Speech Days, struck Charles Wordsworth, himself to become a schoolmaster, as excessive, taking up 'perhaps more of the time of the head master than he could well spare'. Like much committed schoolteaching, Butler's enthusiasm was born of frustrated skill and vanity. Again according to Wordsworth, 'although somewhat too slight and short in figure for the great parts of Tragedy, he would have made a first rate actor, and of this he was not perhaps altogether unconscious'.[115] This emphasis on the tradition of artifical, histrionic declamation began to appear old-fashioned or inappropriate. As soon as Butler retired, the number of Speech Days was reduced to two and, in 1844, to one.[116]

Butler's other passion was physical exercise. Apart from creating a new bathing place, he was happy for the leisure hours of the boys to be occupied with cricket and racquets in the Summer and football as well as skating in the winter, although the new schoolhouse of 1820 reduced the scope for racquets to one wall—the western—where before there had been three.[117] Both cricket and football were played on what is now the Sixth Form ground, although by the end of Butler's period unofficial games of football were arranged on the fields to the east of the Hill on the way to the new Ducker. By then, games had become effectively compulsory, organized entirely by the boys themselves but licensed by the Head Master who occasionally, as in 1805 and 1818, and from 1821 annually gave permission for teams to play Eton and, from 1825, Winchester at Lord's, the first of such contests that were to become such a marked feature of public schools' calendars and, indeed, characters.[118]

Harrow was precocious in developing a sports obsession a generation or more before other schools. By the 1820s, games had come to dominate boys' leisure, although had not yet driven out what Charles Stretton described as 'more dubious' pastimes.[119] Devotion to cricket pre-dated football which only became a habitual feature of half-holiday afternoons, between 2 and 4, in the early 1820s.[120] The Sixth Form ground was levelled in 1827, largely at the boys' cost.[121] Earlier, Charles Wordsworth became a school hero because of his extraordinary sporting prowess. As he himself put it, he may have been second in school academically (to Arthur Martineau) but out of it was 'facile princeps'. Wordsworth was a sporting prodigy, a member of the cricket eleven for five years (1820–5), one of three 'club-keepers' elected annually, and virtual captain 1823–5. Later, at Oxford, he played in the first Oxford versus Cambridge cricket match (1827) *and* rowed in the first varsity boat race (1829). He had been sent to Harrow as a weakling and the school doctor, Dr Bowen, widely regarded as an ingratiating quack, had predicted he would not

---

[115] Charles Wordsworth, *Annals*, 22–3.   [116] Laborde, *Harrow School*, 87.
[117] A complaint made by Francis Trench in 1821: Trench, *Notes*, 17–18.
[118] Charles Wordsworth, *Annals*, 10–11. All accounts of Harrow lavish space and chapters to sport, especially cricket.   [119] Stretton, *Memoirs*, i. 5.
[120] Charles Wordsworth, *Annals*, 19.   [121] HSR III, fo. 361.

see 20: he died aged 86. So keen was his generation to perfect its skills that they hired, at their own expense, a professional coach, John Anderdon, an Old Harrovian and Henry Manning's brother-in-law. Manning was in the eleven in 1825 alongside Richard Trench and Wordsworth, a unique trinity of a future cardinal, an archbishop, and a bishop.[122]

Sport did not exist in isolation from the temper of the school as a whole. Rivalries between houses previously conducted by contests of snowballing or stonethrowing began to be channelled into house matches, as that between Leith's and the school in 1823, although not, as later, to the exclusion of older forms of competition.[123] The annual election of the cricket club-keepers witnessed a more or less legalized brawl as each boy filed up in front of the whole school in the Fourth Form Room to declare his vote only to be promptly set on by the supporters of the other candidates. This was known as 'the Squash' and scarred the memory of more than one frightened little boy, even if it toughened him for the adult exercise of the franchise.[124] Football developed in hierarchical fashion, the junior boys simply running after ('following up') the seniors. Fagging was incorporated as an essential part both of racquets, where junior boys acted as ballboys, sometimes perched precariously on the roof the Old Schools, and of cricket, where they supplied outfielders and long-stops. As elsewhere, the frontier between play, discipline, and abuse was sometimes blurred. Commitment grew in intensity, Drummond Smith opting out of the Sixth Form game because of the time devoted to it, at least twelve hours a week. In his poem on school life, written in October 1826, Smith acknowledged the now established importance of sport:

> The morning comes with it the bell
> And shortly, Upper Shell
> Goes up. The reverend Mr Mills
> The duties of the morn fulfils.
> Then three more schools come and so on
> Until our work at least is done.
> Now this sort of life is all much the same.
> We should die of ennui, if t'were not for the game.
> Either football or rackets, the last I like best
> (As in that you are likely to get hurt much the least.)[125]

For a blood such as Charles Wordsworth, more thoughtful and perceptive than most of his kind, games presented subtler incentives: 'I took intense pleasure in games of all kinds, doubtless chiefly for their own sakes, but in some measure too

---

[122] Charles Wordsworth, *Annals*, 6–19; Thornton, *Harrow School*, 246; Minchin, *Old Harrow Days*, 228–9. [123] Trench, *Notes*, 36.
[124] Howson and Townsend Warner, *Harrow School*, 34, 97; Thornton, *Harrow School*, 369–70; Minchin, *Old Harrow Days*, 237–8.
[125] Drummond Smith Letter Book, 93, 125.

for the sake of the distinction which success in them among boys—and, as the world ever goes, among men and women too—never fails to bring with it.'[126]

The Failure of Discipline

Butler possessed a forceful personality, unafraid of confrontation, although equally incapable of forestalling trouble, either in his house or in the school in general. His self-confidence, which easily slid into self-righteousness, concealed a battle for self-control. This may explain his rigidity as Head Master, refusing even to allow a colleague's harmless experiment of rearranging his pupils' seating according to their weekly form position, an effort to make the academic grind more engaging.[127] Butler was very sensitive to his own position. As with many small men, he needed to dominate. Every teaching day, he would hold a masters' meeting at his house before Second School (11 a.m.), after which he would lead a procession of his assistants up to the Old Schools, his eagerness and determined bearing contrasting with the rather more shambling and possibly reluctant gait of his colleagues.[128] A tense individual, Butler's nervous energy customarily found an outlet in hard, physical exercise. Occasionally, however, he lost control. In 1822, in a rage, he punished fifty-three boys for missing a call over by denying them their remove to a higher division.[129] In 1812 Butler set Lord Brudenell 160 lines from Virgil to learn for returning late from a holiday, refusing to listen to the boy's excuses: within an hour and a half the future leader of the Charge of the Light Brigade had left Harrow for good; but not before Butler had called him a liar. One of Brudenell's contemporaries noted at the time: 'Dr Butler forgot the character of a gentleman and could not, master his passion, but . . . seems to have a sort of pleasure in punishing—as we have lately had (I am sorry to say) too many examples.'[130] From start to finish, Butler beat enthusiastically, occasionally, it seemed to his victims, with prejudice. Charles Stretton, a typical Harrovian wastrel and layabout, sensed Butler disliked him personally, perhaps not without cause, claiming that the Head Master, when about to beat him, always chose a long, fresh birch rod, 'one that was not divested of its buds by prior use'. Stretton recalled that when he was double flogged in 1827 it gave 'an immense amount of satisfaction to the reverend gentleman who so ably did his duty'.[131] Butler's treatment of the 8- or 9-year-old Anthony Trollope, even if exaggerated in the self-pitying author's memory, was brutal. The Head Master shouted insults at him in the street for being dishevelled and dirty, although he knew of Trollope's straitened circumstances. The victim laconically recalled: 'He must have known me had he seen me as he was wont to see

---

[126] Charles Wordsworth, *Annals*, 9.   [127] Merivale, *Autobiography*, 37.
[128] Thornton, *Harrow School*, 239, quoting Charles Merivale.
[129] Letters of G. M. Batten, no. 4. Cf. Maxwell Lyte, *Eton*, 398, where the story is misdated to Longley's regime.
[130] Hawkyard, *Talbot*, 23.   [131] Stretton, *Memoirs*, i. 16, 18.

me, for he was in the habit of flogging me constantly. Perhaps he did not recognise me by my face.'[132]

In mitigation, it could be argued that Butler's excesses were not in the Keate mould of compulsive whipping; his sadism was tempered by being directed mostly at criminals not idlers or idiots. However, it cannot have been a coincidence that in 1829, at the end of this reign of violence, if not terror, the conservative Henry Drury argued for an end to the barbarism, hoping that if he succeeded Butler flogging could be phased out.[133] He would have been amazed at how long it would be before that was achieved—over a century and a half.

Many observers, of course, regarded a flogged school a good school. They ignored the evidence of their eyes. Butler's Harrow confirmed that excessive punishments act as much as incentives as deterrents. As a system of control, it was centrally flawed in failing to provide any constructive mechanism for improvement of manners or attitude. For twenty-four years Butler beat: for twenty-four years Harrovians misbehaved. Each succeeding generation was unaffected by the lashing of their predecessors. Flogging did not, could not, was not even intended to improve the moral tone or organization of the school, especially as it was meted out so frequently. It was not the least influential of the mid-century reforms to flog more occasionally but more pointedly, to make, as it were, each stroke count, morally as well as physically, a badge of shame but also an ordeal allowing for subsequent redemption. It was with the beatings of Arnold and Vaughan that the usually disingenuous or, if sincere, perverted concept of 'this will hurt me more than it hurts you' became a commonplace.[134] For Butler beating was meant to hurt physically. It did. But its influence on school discipline stopped as soon as the boy staggered, still half-naked, out of the Fourth Form Room (for some reason, victims were not supposed to readjust their clothing in front of the Head Master).[135] It says as much for the paucity of intellect as well as sympathy that Butler and his profession failed to see or understand the contradictions before their eyes. Even ignoring its damaging wider social and psychological effects, while possibly useful as a goad to the academically idle, flogging as a means of disciplinary control simply did not work.

Throughout Butler's rule there are accounts of fighting, excessive drinking, illicit smoking, thieving, and bullying. Sidney Herbert, later the saintly Peelite minister, was such a ferocious bully at Mrs Leith's that he was nailed into his own room by mutinous fags.[136] Stonethrowing and snowballing were so common as to

[132] Trollope, *Autobiography*, published in Townsend Warner, *Harrow in Prose and Verse*, 131–2.
[133] *Memoir of Rev. F. Hodgson*, ii (London, 1878), p. 192.
[134] Cf. Arnold's advice to Longley that flogging 'should be administered in earnest': Harrow Archives, *MS Correspondence of Drs Longley, Wordsworth, etc.* (1884), fos. 27–31. For Vaughan's innovative vigour and rigour see F. M. Norman, alias 'Martello Tower', *At School and at Sea* (London, 1899), 11, 32.   [135] Stretton, *Memoirs*, i. 18.
[136] Minchin, *Old Harrow Days*, 88; the identification is mine.

The Ancien Régime

be almost recognized school sports. Target practice with pistols, riding tandems, and carriages as well as a variety of nocturnal escapades teetered on the cusp of high spirits and crime. Attacks on locals continued with unabated ferocity; local Baptists were attacked; in 1826 the blacksmith's was wrecked.[137] One encounter in 1824 drew both Butler and Henry Drury into a brawl on the High Street, with some shoving and name-calling.[138] In 1827 Batten was beaten up by a pupil returning in the early hours from a drinking club the boys had founded. This was the 'Red Nightcap' club, named after the insignia of membership, a red cap 'emblazoned with a pot of porter standing on two crossed pipes, all in gold lace, with the exception of the froth, which was admirably imitated in silver'. The culprit was flogged but not expelled.[139] On another occasion, Butler similarly spared a boy he found helpless with drink.[140] Expulsion was a dangerous resort for a Head Master presiding over a declining school. Nevertheless, some boys took matters into their own hands by running away. In the nature of the evidence, and perhaps the more relaxed times, there is little evidence of sexual abuse, although it may be significant that, on learning of Henry Talbot's acute but inarticulate distress after his first week at Harrow, Butler, while rather too firmly telling him that 'he never wished to know the cause of animosity between boys', allowed him to change beds.[141]

It is hard to see Butler at any point attempting to control and only occasionally to police the boys. His house appears to have been in a constant uproar, with Butler powerless to stop vandalism. In 1827 his efforts to restrict illegal access and egress at night by putting bars on the windows were thwarted when a boy took an axe to them.[142] In a sense, Butler made himself powerless by acquiescing in unsupervised monitorial authority and the fagging system. As a 10-year-old, Charles Merivale fagged for the head of his house, brushing his clothes, looking after his shoes (cleaned by servants), making his breakfast, as well as answering the general demands of the Fifth and Sixth Formers: 'from one or more of these "masters" I suffered many things, but generally they afforded me a sort of sublime protection, coupled sometimes with bitter taunts.'[143] His reactions could stand for the experience of Harrow fags at any time during more than two centuries: time-consuming drudgery and helpless vulnerability to the caprice and cruelty—and kindness—of older boys with the compensation of protection of fag by fag-master against anybody else who wished to usurp the privilege to exploit. In 1827 Butler did outlaw night-fagging in his house. However, despite Percy Thornton's confident claims, probably derived from Butler's doting son Monty, that the rituals of blanket-tossing and 'rolling-in' (where the whole house pelted a new Fifth Former with hard rolls with the successful aim of hurting him) were abolished, such painful

---

[137] Druett, *Harrow*, 217; Thornton, *Harrow School*, 251 n.
[138] Drummond Smith Letter Book, 43–4. [139] Stretton, *Memoirs*, i. 8–19.
[140] Trench, *Notes*, 39–41. [141] Hawkyard, *Talbot*, 11–13.
[142] Drummond Smith Letter Book, 131–2. [143] Merivale, *Autobiography*, 31–2.

initiation rites survived and flourished.[144] Given this catalogue of brutality and mayhem, it is all the more remarkable that Charles Wordsworth was sent to Harrow in 1820 because of its reputation as having 'a milder and more indulgent system' than the 'rougher discipline of Winchester'.[145]

Butler's attempts to impose his authority on the near-autonomous, self-regulating subculture of the boys exposed the strengths and the weaknesses of both sides. Early in November 1808 Butler discovered that, instead of reporting boys causing trouble, the monitors had begun to cane them themselves in the Fourth Form Room, in imitation of floggings by the Head Master. One victim was so severely beaten about the arms and body that he had to be confined to bed. Butler instantly confiscated the monitors' canes and declared that they had no right to inflict corporal punishment: they immediately resigned en bloc. However, the five in Mark Drury's house soon recanted and apologized to Butler, the other five reluctantly following suit, upon which all were reinstated. However, as in earlier disputes, the general body of the boys disapproved of such capitulation, seeing it, as ever, as a surrender of privileges. At the afternoon bills on Thursday, 3 November, Butler was hissed and his desk decorated with a banner proclaiming 'Liberty and Rebellion'. By evening there was a full-scale riot in the street. One of the ringleaders, John Kemmis in the Fifth Form, was apprehended stealing the school key from Peachey's house. For this he was summarily expelled. Over the next four days, while the boys paraded through the streets with shouts of 'Liberty!', 'Rebellion!', and 'No Butler!', and blocked the London road with chains to prevent communication with their parents, Butler and his colleagues continued to process daily to the deserted school where they sat in empty formrooms. Butler persisted in calling Bill, even though there was nobody to answer. Adamant in his refusal to back down, Butler, despite being pelted with stones, hissed, and booed wherever he went, tried to restore order on the streets and raided a few boys' rooms in search of hidden caches of gunpowder. Seeing his obduracy, the revolt gradually subsided. When order was restored only seven boys were expelled, and two of them subsequently pardoned, the rest of the school escaping further penalty. As under Heath, the issue of principle was the Head Master's authority. Beyond that, Butler did not choose to disturb the boys' regime. Private monitorial beatings in houses continued, more or less licensed.

It might have been expected that Byron would have congratulated his old school mates on their boldness. Less predictable, but more significant, were the reactions of some former and current masters, as well as the press, in which Butler was blamed for the whole outbreak as he had broken into boys' studies. Sam Parr, while publicly supportive of Butler, was delighted that he had been so lenient on offenders. Joseph Drury wrote a long and characteristically emollient and elegant letter to

---

[144] Drummond Smith Letter Book, 125–6; Thornton, *Harrow School*, 220–2; Letters of G. M. Batten, no. 11. [145] Charles Wordsworth, *Annals*, 6.

The Ancien Régime

his 'dear young friends' the monitors in which he admonished them but, having exhorted them to respect Butler's authority and discipline, invited them to visit him in Devon. Throughout he was at pains to understand the boys' grievances, even though he regarded them as illegitimate. More worrying for Butler was Henry Drury's reaction. The day after the rebellion ended he wrote to John Kemmis's father a very warm letter, expressing his sadness at the boy's expulsion. While condoning Butler's behaviour, Drury none the less emphasized Kemmis's good behaviour, wishing to be remembered kindly to him; 'I do not feel less his friend now'. As well as asking Mr Kemmis to settle John's claret bill separately, Drury offered his advice on Oxford colleges and tutors, clearly viewing the whole incident of the rebellion and expulsion as unfortunate but nothing to interrupt polite and gentlemanly relations. It may be that Drury felt—as indeed he was—compromised by the stay he had enjoyed with the Kemmis family in Ireland: he would not be the last housemaster to undermine his independence and probity by accepting the hospitality of parents.

Together, these rather equivocal reactions indicate how institutionally difficult the imposition of discipline was. The rights of the boys were taken seriously, Parr's main objection to the rebellion being that the privilege of beating was not, as claimed by the monitors, immemorial custom but a new invention. There were limits on Butler's freedom of action. If he offended parents by excessive harshness, boys would be withdrawn; if too lenient, the school would collapse into a sink of unregulated chaos and violence. Thus the independence of the boys' world had to be respected, whether Butler liked it or not. At least his firm handling of the crisis attracted one admirer: King George III. This evidently cheered Butler enormously. It may have been unfortuate for his chances of preferment that the old king soon lapsed into permanent insanity.[146]

Disturbances twelve years later were much tamer. Stirred by the widespread publicity of the feud between the new king, George IV, and his estranged wife Caroline, whose cause had been taken up by some Whig opponents of the government, the boys began to demonstrate in her favour. They paraded along the High Street wearing white cockades and some illuminated their studies as a show of support. Butler acted quickly. Summoning the whole school to his new Speech Room, he harangued them on the evils of 'party spirit' in a school as leading to factions and enmities. Not much attention was paid, one boy commenting at the time that his remarks on the divisive effects of political partisanship were 'quite mistaken'.[147] These demonstrations, as the Queen Caroline affair itself, proved a nine-day wonder. However, the boys had once more displayed an independent corporate will.

---

[146] For these details of the 1808 rebellion see Thornton, *Harrow School*, 219–20; Graham, *Butler*, 12–14; HM/Bg/Joseph Drury to Captain of School, 29 Nov. 1808 (via Mrs Leith); HM/Bg/Dr Parr to Dr Butler 10 and 17 Dec. 1808; Harrow Archives Kemmis Correspondence, letters from Dr Butler, 21 Nov. 1808, and H. Drury, 8 Nov. 1808.

[147] Trench, *Notes*, 14–15; Byron, *Letters and Journals*, i. 176–7.

Closely in touch by family connection and avid scrutiny of the press with the political world of London, Harrovians were highly politicized. Their eccentric devotion to radical slogans and fashions formed a means of expressing a self-consciously distinct identity as a group in tension, if not outright opposition to authority, the sort of sentimental upper-class radicalism popularized by the poet Shelley. The 1820 demonstration simply reaffirmed this solidarity in open display and implied rejection of authority.

A scandal in October 1826 further emphasized how powerless the school authorities were in the face of events. Three boys in Mills' house were expelled for 'acts of gross indecency'. These were part of a pattern of criminality, the boys apparently having organized a crime ring, selling items they had stolen, forcing younger boys to steal for them, and presiding over a regime of terror that enforced silence. When the intervention of a parent led to their exposure, the reaction of the monitors was swift and brutal. Each culprit was given a total of sixty lashes delivered on the hands and back, some by a twisted toasting fork, others by the handle of a post-boy's whip. They were then reported to Mills and Butler and were expelled immediately. The extent of the boys' outrage and the measures they took before involving any master speak volumes for the crude power of self-regulation and the brutal but clear boyish moral code as well as for the impotence of adult authority in policing the school. Despite the brave words of 1808, Butler was not only unable to prevent monitorial beating but, in this instance, condoned it. Rumours reached the press forcing Butler to issue a formal public statement to allay suspicions that the culprits had either been victims of unnecessary violence or, on the contrary, had been harboured from punishment for a time.[148] The publicity was extremely damaging when school numbers were collapsing. During the winter of 1826–7, Drummond Smith from the Head Master's repeatedly referred to the decline in his letters, in January commenting 'a great many have left out of this house and there is not one new one come'.[149]

The 1826 scandal added to a catalogue of misfortunes that lent an appearance of disintegration to the school. 1826 was a truly horrific year. Numbers slid below 200. In April, a recent new boy, Charles Lemon, drowned in the congealed waters of Butler's new Ducker amid suspicions of negligence and a concealment of the truth.[150] More damaging was the sudden disgrace and departure of two senior masters. Late one night in early February that year Mark Drury and his son William fled the Hill to avoid their creditors, William alone allegedly owing between twenty and thirty thousand pounds. They found refuge on the continent.[151]

---

[148] HM/Bg/Butler's letter to the press, 31 Jan. 1827; Drummond Smith Letter Book, 97–9.

[149] Drummond Smith Letter Book, 102.

[150] Stretton, *Memoirs*, i. 7: 'Will it be believed that we could not save him?' The boy's father removed the body immediately, preferring to pay a fine rather than face an inquest.

[151] HSR III, fo. 345; Drummond Smith Letter Book, 71–2, 73–4; HM/Bg/Butler to Lord Northwick, 14 Nov. 1826.

Although Mark's nephew Henry avoided bankruptcy, he too was revealed as living beyond his means and by the end of the year was forced to sell his remarkable library: his nephew thought he never really recovered from this blow. Mark and William were victims of the 1825 crash; Henry of a bibliomania that netted him a fabulous collection of medieval manuscripts and incunabula, some of them acquired in the aftermath of the French wars from sales of such famed libraries as that of the Visconti in Milan, including Petrarch's own copy of Suetonius. When finally sold in 1827, Drury's books fetched just under £9,000, a gross undervaluation. Henry's method of coping with such humiliation was to take to his bed for long periods, which exacerbated the school's troubles as he ran by far the largest pupil room as well as a house and form. With Butler himself also suffering from a series of minor debilitating aliments, possibly psychosomatic, the academic direction of the school was rudderless.[152]

The Drurys were also sufferers from the decline in numbers from which, as housemasters and tutors, they lost income. This was no less true for the other masters and lay behind a nasty spat between Butler and Benjamin Evans, appointed Under Master in place of Mark Drury in February 1826. Evans complained to the governors that Butler insisted he shared calling over the whole school, something that Joseph and Mark Drury uniquely had done as Head and Under Master but which had ceased in 1805. He also desired clarification as to whether the Third Form was part of the Under School, and so his responsibility. Evans' main object was less to avoid work—even with the Third Form, the Under School in 1826 comprised just twenty-one boys—than to increase his pay, as he suggested that if he had to share calling over, he should receive half of the schooling fees, instead of the traditional quarter. He also wanted to prevent Butler depriving him of a quarter of the entrance fees. Unsurprisingly in the light of previous disputes stretching back to the late seventeenth century, the governors found against him on all counts. Yet they failed to clarify the Under Master's anomalous position which continued to cause tension and resentment until its final abolition in 1868.[153]

The flight of the Drurys allowed Butler to refashion the teaching staff by the appointment of an additional assistant to the Upper School, a sign of misplaced optimism, the experiment of five instead of four Upper School assistants lasting only two years, such was the continued collapse in numbers and financial liquidity.[154] 1826 also marked the end of an era longer even than Drury dominance. In March, Henry Reeves died at the age of 75. He had succeeded his father as Writing Master in 1768, being additionally appointed the school's first official librarian in 1805. In 1814 he persuaded the governors to pay him £6 13s. 4d. (i.e. the 'twenty

---

[152] HM/Bg/Butler to Northwick, 14 Nov. 1826; Merivale, *Autobiography*, 39; Drummond Smith Letter Book, 94–5, 101, 109–11, 113–15; *Catalogue of the Library of Rev. Henry Drury*, Harrow Archives, H. Drury file, 262 for total. Petrarch's Suetonius is now in the library of Exeter College, Oxford.
[153] Harrow Archive, Harrow Masters Evans File, 27 Feb. 1826; HSR III, fos. 348–50.
[154] HSR III, fo. 350; Butler, *Harrow Lists*, 135; *Harrow Register, 1800–1911*, 902.

nobles' of 1665) as of right out of trust funds for teaching Free Scholars. The last living professional link with Sumner's Harrow was severed. Astonishingly, his successor, Jacob Marillier, maths master since 1819, held the post until he retired in 1869, by then custodian of the brand new Vaughan Library.[155] Such personal continuities imply a tenacious conservatism easily overshadowed by the more transitory careers of Head Masters. Of George Butler's appointments in 1826, the Old Harrovian William Oxenham (né Oxnam), who took over William Drury's house (now Moretons), survived in post until his death in 1863, four Head Masters—including Butler's son Monty—later, after a career that grew in eccentricity and incompetence, inspiring amused or exasperated affection, increasingly a symbol that some changes were as much apparent as real.[156]

Butler was not insensitive to changing influences on education. To those masters he inherited, notably the Drurys and Evans, he added not only traditional figures such as William Drury, William Mills, and Oxenham, but also two bright evangelicals, Batten and Phelps, who pioneered a new style of housemastering by their purchases, respectively, of the Grove (c.1820) and the Park (1831), lavish establishments that secured an aristocratic atmosphere and select company very much in tune with fashionable sentiment. The moral tone of these establishments appeared, at least to external view, more elevated and the discipline more secure than the traditional houses of Henry Drury, Evans, Mills, Oxenham, or even the Head Master himself, creating a model which was to become the ostensible norm a generation later.[157]

By contrast to these ambitious evangelicals, for all his energy, Butler decreasingly gave the impression he was in control of his charges. His house was anarchic; the school no less so. Again, 1826 proved a personal milestone in the destruction of his Head Mastership. At the same meeting of the governors on 9 February that received Mark Drury's letter resigning as Under Master 'immediately', they issued a startling rebuke to the Head:

> The Governors having reason to believe that sufficient care and attention have not been given to secure the confinement of the scholars in their respective houses after the hours of locking up thereby exposing the inhabitants of the Parish to interruption and discomfort, the Governors have judged it right to call upon the Head Master . . . to adopt such measures as will prevent the recurrence of this evil.[158]

Such an admonition, formally written into their minutes, was unprecedented, a measure perhaps of the governors' exasperation and, possibly, of Cunningham's meddling. In his reply of 19 February, Butler blustered. He regretted that the

---

[155] Larpent, *Reeves of Harrow School*, 2; HSR III, fos. 256, 292, 295–6, 350; *Harrow Register, 1800–1911*, 902; Harrow Archives, Harrow Masters, Miscellaneous File, 1826 for references for the Writing Mastership. [156] See below, pp. 257–66.
[157] Thornton, *Harrow School*, 241–2, 257–8; Hole, *Phelps*, ii. 59–60, 89–95, 135–9.
[158] HSR III, fo. 346.

governors felt the need to complain, but he insisted that 'no pains have been wanting on his part to prevent the evil thus complained of', although he tried to lay the blame for recent disturbances on town boys.[159]

Unfortunately for him, at least one of the governors was soon to have direct evidence of the effectiveness of Butler's disciplinary regime. In July 1826 George Rushout, nephew of Lord Northwick, was removed from the school after being seriously injured as a result of being ducked in water repeatedly for half an hour by two bullies—Robert Adair and the Hon. James Ramsay. Only his uncle Northwick's intervention, so George's father claimed, saved the boy's life, as the subsequent medical attention had been so careless as to aggravate his condition through excessive use of leeches that had left unhealed wounds. This incident occured only a few weeks after the suspicious drowning of young Lemon. Butler, although significantly not denying the substantive charge of bullying, reacted with a typical display of denial, insisting that young Rushout's continuing illness was due not to the water he had been forced to swallow or medical negligence but to constipation caused by eating too many cherries. Rushout was not convinced: young George did not return, his father lamenting 'the poor fellow may live (if he does live) to rue the day that first brought him acquainted with Harrow School'.[160] In fact thirty-three years later, young George Rushout, now third Baron Northwick, succeeded his uncle as a governor of Harrow School, which he remained until his death in 1887. He may, however, have voted against George Butler's son Monty in the close Head Mastership election of 1859. The fate of the bullies stands as testimony to Butler's attitude to the affair. Robert Adair stayed at Harrow to become a monitor in 1828, ultimately being elevated to the peerage as Baron Waveney after a modest career as politician, military expert, and prominent freemason. James Ramsay, as marquis of Dalhousie, left Harrow over a year after the Rushout episode, later serving as Governor General of India and becoming a member of Harrow's nineteenth-century pantheon of heroic statesmen, commemorated to this day by a portrait in Speech Room.[161]

The events of 1826 ensured that Butler's days as Head Master were numbered. His stress-related illnesses were more frequent and his attention increasingly centred on fundraising. Numbers sank seemingly inexorably, by the end of 1826 to fewer than 200; a year later to fewer than 150. Yet Butler seemed unmoved. In November 1826, he wrote 'I am happy to say that the school is going on in all respects to my satisfaction'.[162] Two years later, with the roll below 130 and still falling, he had entered a fantasy world, claiming 'our late increased and increasing admissions show us to have "weathered the storm" and to be more "proceeding in

---

[159] HM/Bg/Butler to Governors, 19 Feb. 1826.
[160] HM/Bg/George Rushout to Butler, 23 July 1826 and 29 July 1826, this annotated with detailed rebuttals by Butler; Butler to Lord Northwick, 19 Aug. 1826.
[161] *Harrow Register, 1800–1911*, 107, 117 for the boys' school careers.
[162] HM/Bg/Butler to Lord Northwick, 14 Nov. 1826.

a prosperous course"'.[163] In 1827 forty-four new boys entered the school; in 1828 just twenty-six.[164] The governors had had enough. After a quarter of a century, Butler had become a liability, protected only by his governor father-in-law, Gray, who died in November 1828. Informally, Butler was then persuaded that, in the interests of the school, he might consider resignation. He took the hint. With a characteristic love of show and ceremonial, he arranged to announce his depature to a special conclave of governors on 9 December 1828. Alone, this gesture did not halt the slide; numbers continued to fall until Butler had finally gone at Easter 1829.[165]

Butler spent much of his vigorous twenty-four-year retirement preserving and inventing the history of the school for posterity. In his time as Head Master he oversaw the beginnings of a new house system, competitive examinations, the cult of games, and even the first school newspaper.[166] He created a new dynasty, continued by his brother-in-law, as Oxenham became by marrying Mrs Butler's sister, and his descendants as boys, Head and assistant masters, and governors of the school. One of his grandsons only retired as a governor of Harrow in 1962.[167] In retrospect, there is an almost proprietorial air to the new school motto George Butler coined: *Stet Fortuna Domus*.

III. TOWARDS THE BRINK, 1829–1844

The choice of George Butler's successor in 1829 completed the work of 1805.[168] The governors set the election for 16 March. As late as 27 February there were just five candidates. The externals were Dr J. W. Niblock, proprietor of a failing London private school, and C. W. Stocker, Principal of Elizabeth College, Guernsey and a future professor of Moral Philosophy at Oxford. There were three internal candidates. The evangelical S. E. Batten, a defeated rival of Dr Arnold for the Rugby Headship in 1827, had harboured ambitions for the Harrow post since at least 1823, his credentials resting on his success as housemaster of the Grove and the support of Cunningham and his party, his testimonials including a highly aristocratic element of seven earls, four barons, and a couple of marquesses.[169] William Mills, a stickler for discipline who took the Fourth Form, was dismissed by one old boy as

---

[163] HM/Bg/Butler to Sir John Richardson, 15 Dec. 1828.
[164] *Harrow Register, 1800–1911*, 118–23.
[165] HM/Bg/Butler to Lord Northwick, 8 Dec. 1828; HSR III, fo. 373; that Butler was persuaded to resign was revealed in 1844: HM/W/FSD, Henry Young to Wordsworth on or after 6 June 1844; Golland, *Catalogue of Bill Books*, fos. 9–10.
[166] The first, shortlived, *The Harrovian* in 1828.   [167] Prof. J. R. M. Butler.
[168] The main documents are collected in HM/1829 file and *MS Correspondence of Drs Longley, Wordsworth*, fos. 1–3, 5–9, 11–17, 19–31.
[169] He made his interest clear as early as 27 Nov. 1823, Letters of G. M. Batten, no. 12. For Rugby see Hole, *Phelps*, ii. 32.

'an honest man and seemed to do his best'.[170] He was also ambitious. With his application, Mills presented a fashionably radical manifesto addressing the faults of Butler's regime, including proposals for more local scholars, an end to bullying, secure lock-up, more emphasis on academic work, and a tighter control over the curriculum.

The favourite was Henry Drury who presented himself as the candidate best able 'to raise Harrow to the highest pitch of eminence' by virtue of his Harrovian connections and his proven popularity as housemaster and tutor. He proposed to abandon flogging below the Fifth Form, possibly reduce fagging, and 'to adopt what the world calls for and will have from all of us hereafter', namely 'the Private Reading of subjects connected with modern literature'.[171] Drury mustered over sixty testimonials, including ones from the duke of Sussex, a younger son of George III; Lord Chancellor Lyndhurst; the old Harrovians Palmerston, Goderich, and Peel; Samuel Butler of Shrewsbury; seven bishops, and six Heads of Oxbridge colleges. He had the support of his Alma Mater Eton and, ironically in the light of his views on beating, its head, the notorious flogger Dr Keate. Drury's canvassing, Butler observed unflatteringly, was 'overwhelming'.[172]

Yet the governors were unhappy. Cunningham bemoaned the quality of the field, although admitting a preference for Batten. He was careful to cast damaging aspersions against the name of Drury, associating Henry by innuendo with the financial ruin of his uncle and cousin. Drury vigorously tried to rebut this.[173] Cunningham had been conducting an increasingly bitter feud with him for years, even before Drury presided over the funeral of Byron's illegitimate daughter Allegra at the parish church in 1822 against the vicar's wishes. Drury made no secret of his mutual contempt, yawning in church whenever given a chance which, in view of the long evangelical orations on offer, came not infrequently.[174] If his malice was unique, Cunningham's opposition was not. The austere Aberdeen was anxious 'to make a stand' against Drury and even one of Drury's own referees admitted that his recommendation was made solely because friends had asked him.[175] The governors' efforts to widen the field by writing to the Vice-Chancellors of Oxford and Cambridge, despite rumours, appeared by late February to have failed. Yet, at the last moment— indeed after it, as the election meeting was postponed for five days—Charles Longley, Student of Christ Church, was nominated and elected unanimously on 21 March, the only Oxford Head Master in the 150 years between Cox and Wood.[176]

[170] Merivale, *Autobiography*, 37.
[171] HM/1829/H. Drury to Lord Northwick, 13 Dec. 1828 and 5 Jan. 1829; *MS Correspondence of Drs Longley, Wordsworth*, fos. 24–6.
[172] HM/Bg/Butler to Lord Northwick, 9 Jan. 1829.
[173] HM/1829/Cunningham to Lord Northwick, 22 Dec. 1828, 29 Feb. 1829; H. Drury to Northwick, 5 Jan. 1829. [174] See below, pp. 231–3.
[175] *MS Correspondence of Drs Longley, Wordsworth*, fos. 11–13; the lukewarm referee was Lord Beauchamp: HM/1829/Beauchamp to Northwick, 29 Dec. 1828.
[176] HSR III, fos. 376–8.

Longley's election was the consequence of a Christ Church conspiracy. Shortly after Christmas, Lord Aberdeen received an account of Longley, then Senior Censor of Christ Church, from one of his Harrovian undergraduates, James Lord Grimston, son of Lord Verulam, also of Harrow and Christ Church. Verulam was 'very anxious that Drury should not succeed'. Under his guidance, the Christ Church don was quietly talked up as a possible candidate. Grimston's brother, Edward, began mentioning Longley's name around the school. Longley was interested, but he was in an awkward position because Drury was married to his brother-in-law's niece. Throughout his eminent career, Longley took pains to be liked. This did not put him above ambition. Keen to avoid any accusation of hypocrisy or double-dealing, as late as 15 March Longley stipulated that, to keep his conscience clear and reputation clean, he would not be a candidate unless and until the governors had ruled out Drury. Appearances were all. Behind this apparent rectitude, a fierce campaign was now waged, with Longley's tacit approval. Aberdeen engineered a postponement of the election to allow Longley's friends to gather testimonials. Grimston secured the Students of Christ Church. Aberdeen, then Foreign Secretary, prevailed upon the Home Secretary, Harrovian and Christ Church man, Robert Peel to persuade the dean of Christ Church and the bishop of Oxford to write. Leaving nothing to chance, Verulam squared the archbishop of Canterbury, William Howley, 'in case his casting vote was required'; Howley had been a canon of Christ Church. Aberdeen himself may have already encountered Longley, as he was in the process of placing his ward, Abercorn, at Christ Church, where he matriculated in July 1829. Although not a university man himself, the senior governor, Lord Northwick's father, brother, and nephew (who also matriculated in 1829) all went to the House.[177]

The election, at the delayed meeting on 21 March, came after a week of frenzied lobbying. The unanimous approval of Longley was due, so Drury bitterly remarked later, to the 'abstract idea of a "young lean stranger"' which 'was from the first sure to weigh over any claims, testimonials or private friendship'. Drury thought he had been badly treated, insulted at such a public declaration of his 'incompetency'.[178] He did not know the half of it. Although three governors assured him that if Longley had declined, he would have been the unanimous choice, Cunningham, purring with pleasure, made it clear to Longley himself that 'many circumstances ... rendered it next to impossible for the governors to elect any of the existing candidates'.[179] So, as he desired, Longley, the declared non-candidate, was able to accept election as if by invitation.

This election confirmed the sort of candidate the governors now sought; dons, former dons, existing head masters, from outside the school, of academic

---

[177] The evidence for the conspiracy is in *MS Correspondence of Drs Longley, Wordsworth*, fos. 1–3, 5–9, 11–17, 19–26. [178] Ibid., fos. 24–6. Cf. Butler, *Butler*, i. 354–5.

[179] *MS Correspondence of Drs Longley, Wordsworth*, fo. 21.

prominence if not excellence, possessed of good prospects, fashionable views, and appropriate religious seriousness. A dash of myopia or self-delusion may have helped in this instance. Writing to his future wife, Longley insisted he had 'done everything to prevent myself from being nominated', conveniently forgetting his own laying down, on 15 March 1829, the precise circumstance in which he could be so considered. He claimed that in the setting aside of the other candidates and the offer to him 'the hand of Providence seemed so distinctly visible in the affair'.[180] It is hard to believe he had not noticed the rather more obvious and active hands of his own friends and college.

Charles Longley

The one characteristic that most observers noted in Charles Longley was his good nature and good manners, qualities to which Trollope ascribed his later ecclesiastical success.[181] A referee described him in 1829 as 'conspicuously preeminent as a religious and gentlemanly man'.[182] Half a century later a former pupil remembered him as 'a perfectly well-bred and courteous gentleman, who knew how to treat his boys as gentlemen'.[183] Not given to confrontation or harsh words, to most of his pupils he appeared polite, pompous, aloof, and ineffectual. As a bachelor at Oxford he had been nicknamed 'Rose'. At Harrow, he was known as 'Jacob' after his pet parrot.[184] Some thought him a good teacher whose scholarship was elegant rather than exact, cultured but not rigorous. His academic attainments were recognized as 'respectable' but lacking the 'profound erudition', i.e. philological pedantry, of his Cambridge predecessor and successors.[185] He published no scholarly works, the nearest being an edition of maps for use in the school. His churchmanship was Low in the old-fashioned sense of being fiercely anti-papist rather than evangelical. One of the few occasions he set intellectual blood racing was his introduction of H. H. Milman's *History of the Jews* into the school which, because of its secular and historical rather than scriptural and religious approach, was seen by evangelicals as 'infidel', provoking loud protests from Batten and Phelps.[186] Longley was not a very committed schoolteacher or schoolmaster. He enjoyed the prominence afforded by the Head Mastership, its social and political contacts, then potentially much wider than those of an Oxford College. Certain aspects of Harrow life he enjoyed, affecting the habits of a country gentleman. He kept cows.[187] His true

---

[180] *MS Correspondence of Drs Longley, Wordsworth*, fo. 19.
[181] Trollope, *Autobiography*, in Townsend Warner, *Harrow in Prose and Verse*, 136.
[182] *MS Correspondence of Drs Longley, Wordsworth*, fos. 13–17.
[183] H. L. Jenner, 'Dr Longley', Howson and Townsend Warner, *Harrow School*, 82.
[184] Thornton, *Harrow School*, 275–6. Cf. ibid., 267; Minchin, *Old Harrow Days*, 94–5.
[185] Jenner, 'Dr Longley', 81–2. Cf. A. J. B. Beresford-Hope's remarks quoted in J. E. Overton and E. Wordsworth, *Christopher Wordsworth, Bishop of Lincoln* (London, 1890), p. 83 and Hugh Pearson's: Fox, *Harrow*, 111.   [186] Hole, *Phelps*, ii. 55.
[187] GM, 9 Feb. 1832 (request for timber for his 'cow house').

motive in seeking and accepting the post was, as he wrote in 1836, that the Headship 'essentially contributed' to his subsequent preferment.[188]

In the mean time, Longley was content to earn as much as he could. While the governors had restricted his commercial scope in 1829 by prohibiting the Head Master from taking private pupils, causing 'a very serious diminution' in his income, Longley asserted that the best candidates for the post would be deterred unless their income was sufficient to allow a Head 'to retire before his strength is exhausted', the line consistently adopted by George Butler.[189] This was disingenuous. Numbers under Longley did not merit such gloom. From the depths of under 120 in April 1829, within two years 200 had been reached and, in 1833, 250, gradually declining below 200 again in 1836. Longley was reputed to have saved £30,000 from his seven years at Harrow.[190] This may not have been an exaggeration. From his own accounts for 1834 and 1835, from schooling and entrance fees to school and house he received over £2,800 and £2,550 respectively, out of which he paid not more than £400 in masters' salaries. There were between fifty and sixty boys in Longley's house at the time, bringing in another £4,000 or so a year, of which around £2,400 may have been profit. In good years, therefore, Longley's receipts were c.£6,500 and even in his worst years £5,000, with a profit margin of anything from 60 to 70 per cent.[191]

Longley realized that his income depended on his making a success of his job academically as well as socially. Immediately on appointment he charmed Drury into cooperation. He consulted Thomas Arnold about flogging, receiving a typically self-confident statement of policy wrapped in the language of principle: 'I never did nor do I believe that it can be relinquished altogether, but I think it may well be reserved for offences either great in themselves or rendered great by frequent repetition and then it should be administered in earnest.'[192] Longley was never quite able to live up to this, his decisions to beat being rather erratic, ranging from savagery when confronted with a Harrovian throwing stones at a boy not in the school to benign acceptance of some of the worst excesses of insubordination, breaking of bounds, criminality, and drunkenness.[193] Henry Torre, who spent five years under Longley flouting a wide range of rules, was never beaten.[194] Like his predecessor, Longley found it easier to think the best of his pupils and to construe their behaviour in the most favourable manner possible. In 1831 he went so far as to defend his boys in the press against charges of beating up two slightly drunk

---

[188] GM, 14 Mar. 1836.
[189] HM/Longley Correspondence (hereafter HM/L)/Longley Memorandum, 10 Mar. 1830.
[190] Honey, *Tom Brown's Universe*, 298. For school numbers see Golland, *Catalogue*, 10–15.
[191] HM/L/Accounts 1834, 1835; terms 1830; W. H. Gregory's bill 1831; for the calculation of percentage profit see HM/W/'Colenso's Plan', undated, 1838.
[192] *MS Correspondence of Drs Longley, Wordsworth*, fos. 24–31; Butler, *Butler*, i. 353.
[193] Minchin, *Old Harrow Days*, 194–5; Pouchée's Diary, *passim*.
[194] Torre, *Recollections*, 5 and *passim*.

visitors. While conceding that boys had pushed their chaise into a pond, bombarded them with eggs, and hurled abuse if not blows, Longley insisted that the victims were not gentlemen but 'sporting characters . . . elevated by drink' who enjoyed 'equally with the young people (about thirty in number) the affray'.[195] Small wonder that Harrovians from his time were reputed to have been 'among the most loyal and devoted sons of the school'.[196]

Academically, too, Longley was eager to learn. He authorized Drury to consult Samuel Butler on textbooks and examinations and, together with Drury, visited Shrewsbury to observe Butler in action. At the end of 1829 examinations for the Sixth Form on the Shrewsbury model were introduced.[197] Already Longley was considering curriculum alterations. These proved modest. Extra holidays were to be confined to Tuesdays and Speech Days, with their attendant rehearsal days, cut to two.[198] Despite the approach to Samuel Butler, the old Eton grammar and Drury's own Harrow textbooks were retained for classics. With most masters, teaching continued to be 'in dry, formal manner' without 'genuine appreciation of classical literature'. Some remembered the common standard as 'most defective', the whole system 'bad'. The exception was Benjamin Kennedy, Butler of Shrewsbury's star pupil and eventual successor, who arrived at Harrow in 1830, having acted as external scholarship examiner that year. His presence inspired the few clever boys who were his pupils (his form teaching was of the most basic with the Fourth Form who used to hiss him) and put other masters on their mettle, a necessary model of academic excellence as Henry Drury sank into sloth and decline.[199] Elsewhere, there was some tinkering. The Sixth Form were given half a lesson and one lecture a week on modern European history within the timetable. But no English history or English literature were introduced, and ancient history consisted solely of facts and dates with no attention given to social life, arts, politics, or religion.[200]

One issue Longley could not avoid. The introduction of French and maths into the school timetable was a central demand of reformers. Even the conservative Robert Peel argued that if Longley combined classics with maths and 'an efficient system' of modern languages or just French he would 'remove almost every objection which used to apply to the course of study pursued at a Public School'.[201] Eton and Harrow were reactionary even by public school standards. Compared with

---

[195] HM/L/note on 'Outrage at Harrow' to be placed in the *Morning Chronicle*, 8 Apr. 1831.
[196] Jenner, 'Dr Longley', 82.
[197] Butler, *Butler*, i. 354–5, 361, 363; Harrow Archives, *Letters to Dr Longley and MSS in his own Writing, 1829–36*, Peel to Longley, 7 Dec. 1829; Goderich to Longley, 28 Dec. 1829.
[198] HM/W/Head Master's Memorandum Book, fos. 67, 71.
[199] Lady Gregory (ed.), *Sir William Gregory: An Autobiography* (London, 1894), 31–8; Hole, *Phelps*, ii. 74, 81. For Kennedy being hissed see Pouchée's Diary, fo. 25.
[200] Gregory, *Autobiography*, loc. cit.; Longley's Timetable, Thornton, *Harrow School*, 436–7.
[201] *MS Correspondence of Drs Longley, Wordsworth*, Peel to Longley, 7 Dec. 1829.

Arnold's curriculum at Rugby, Longley's, except for the tiny provision for history exclusively classical, appeared exceptionally old-fashioned and narrow. Where Harrow under Longley had a weekly total of sixteen periods of up to an hour, never more, often less, all classical except for the half lesson on European history, Rugby's week comprised twenty periods of between one and two hours, two for mathematics, two for modern languages, and the remaining sixteen for classics, scripture, and history, both English and European, medieval and modern as well as ancient.[202] Although Longley's chosen model, Shrewsbury, maintained an exclusively classical curriculum, Samuel Butler's style of teaching and system of examination meant that, for the intellectually able, there was genuine academic challenge and inquiry largely absent from Harrow.[203]

Change would entail disturbing the habits of the masters and the attitudes of the boys. The status of the extra masters who taught maths and French, since 1819 the Marillier brothers Jacob and Jacques, was palpably inferior to the classical assistants. Christopher Talbot, for over fifty years MP for Glamorgan (1830–85), remembered that in Dr Butler's time the French master 'lived the life of a dog' and that whenever the writing and arithmetic masters appeared 'they were received with hallooing and hooting'. Peel saw additional difficulty. While the French master 'is often a Quiz [i.e. an eccentric] little calculated to maintain his influence over his pupils', lazy boys would dislike the extra work of compulsory French, while the ambitious clever ones would resent the time spent away from the classics on which prizes and scholarships were awarded.[204] There were other practical obstacles. The addition of French or maths would be regarded as a potential threat to the financial monopoly of the classicists' pupil rooms or represent an additional cost to parents, as, without pupil rooms, the masters teaching those subjects would have to be paid out of school funds (i.e. fees) to make it worth their while.

In the event, Longley moved with characteristic circumspection. Not until 1834–5 did he formulate a scheme for French, with the option of Italian, 'as an integral part of the school business', which he announced in a printed circular of 31 March 1835. To pay for this, an extra guinea was to be added to the general schooling fee. Longley's caution was justified. His scheme failed utterly and was abandoned before his departure the following year. The precise reasons for this are obscure, Longley merely recording that teaching French in school was 'inexpedient'. One problem may have lain with the French master, Jacques Marillier, who seemingly preferred, because more profitable and less effort, exclusively teaching private pupils. If he was as bad a teacher as his brother, this may also have contributed to the collapse of the scheme. Serious teaching of modern languages had

---

[202] For Arnold's curriculum see Newsome, *Godliness*, 64–6. Cf. Thornton, *Harrow School*, 436–7; Hole, *Phelps*, ii. 7–8.

[203] Mack, *Public Schools and British Opinion, 1780–1860*, 232; Butler, *Butler*, i. 5.

[204] Thornton, *Harrow School*, 269; *MS Correspondence of Drs Longley, Wordsworth*, Peel to Longley, 7 Dec. 1829.

to wait until the establishment of the Modern Side in 1869, their continuing absence from the timetable being noted with disapproval by the Clarendon Commissioners five years earlier.[205]

Longley was more decisive and effective with maths. He did nothing. When presented with a modest proposal from Jacob Marillier to include some actual mathematics in the leaving scholarship papers in addition to the two set books of Euclid and his offer to pay for a three guinea prize for the best maths papers each year, Longley rejected both completely. Even Henry Drury was dismayed by this, commenting shrewdly 'for the sake of Cambridge we must some day or other enlarge our sphere of Mathematics'.[206] There was the rub. While Cambridge rather oddly insisted that mathematics was studied as well as classics for the Tripos, Oxford disdained such dilution for Schools. Some Oxford dons thought boys were wasting their time by studying maths when they should have been concentrating on Latin and Greek.[207] Longley was clearly of their number. It was for his successor, the acme of the Cambridge system, to introduce mathematics into the curriculum. However, at no stage was the utilitarian view that maths was practical and useful conceded. All the Harrow arguments revolved around its role in the education of a gentleman and a scholar.

Outside the formroom, Longley was more of a reformer. On election, he was instructed by the governors to investigate the 'custom of charging Fines to the boys for Breakfasts'.[208] This referred to the practice whereby boys provided lavish breakfasts for themselves after First School by buying food and drink from the local shops on credit. The usual name for this was 'Finds', as the meals were 'found' by the boys themselves not their housemasters or Dames. It was a habit that reached back to the previous century. Large, expansive breakfasts after First School were important social events, but they were funded by debt, the bills run up being paid at the end of term by parents not boys. This extended to other provisions which were consumed voraciously by eternally hungry boys. Local shopkeepers were only too eager to extend credit, confident that parents would settle the accounts. Early capitalist nineteenth-century England, as so many of its novels show, was obsessed with the moral as well as material dangers of debt. Easy credit and consequent improvidence provided the temptation that allowed the delights of materialism to be judged and condemned with reassuringly traditional moralizing. Charles Stretton attributed his lifelong habit of debt to his Harrow schooldays: 'the system of "Find" bills . . . was the nucleus of ruin to many young men . . . the first germ of thirst for attaining that which was desired, without feeling the pressure of present payment.'[209]

---

[205] HM/L/Circular, 31 Mar. 1835; HM/W/Memorandum, 18 Feb. 1842; Jenner, 'Dr Longley', 84; Minchin, *Old Harrow Days*, 22–5; *Report of Clarendon Commission* (1864), i. 216, iv. 230.
[206] HM/L/unlisted, undated MS on maths prizes.
[207] Roundell, 'Wordsworth', 98.   [208] HSR III, fos. 381–2.
[209] Stretton, *Memoirs*, i. 3. Cf. the debts of the eldest son of George Butler: Graham, *Butler*, 28.

In January 1830 Longley abolished Finds in the interests of reducing costs to parents and restricting the danger of their sons incurring 'heedless debts'. Parents were urged to refuse to pay any tradesmans's bill unauthorized by the Head Master. At the same time, parents were requested to desist from sending game to their sons, as this also incurred unsupervised costs (e.g. dressing, etc.).[210] In February 1834 Longley announced that he had secured the written agreement of all the Harrow tradesmen bar one (Parsons) never again to extend any credit to boys, although he had to repeat his request about game.[211] Costs were an important cause of this anti-debt campaign. Harrow was becoming an expensive school. In 1831 the half-yearly bill for a boy at the Head Master's, the cheapest house, excluding any extra food, sweets, clothes, or other luxuries, came to nearly £90, £35 of which was linked to schooling. At the Grove, board and lodging alone came to £150 a year.[212] In 1835, in a further bid to cut 'all unnecessary expense', Longley asked parents to supply boys' clothing from home rather than ordering suits from Harrow tailors (who could be expected to overcharge) and to send their sons to school already furnished with the money needed to pay the various compulsory subscriptions, such as for cricket (15s.) and the lending library that had been established (2s. 6d.).[213]

Longley expressed concern with 'the great moral injury resulting from the temptation to run into debt to which boys at Public Schools are too frequently exposed.'[214] Unlike his predecessor, who saw evil and vice as products of individual miscreants, he recognized the potential for corruption in the unregulated system itself. Yet he lacked the personality or support from his colleagues to attempt more than external tinkering. He would lecture the boys with memorable ponderousness on iniquities such as the night time game of hide and seek known as Jack o'Lantern.[215] He would deal with breaches of discipline if he stumbled across them. But he did nothing to stop his favourite pupil, William Gregory, spending all his free time poaching in the company of a local ne'er do well, Billy Warner or Henry Torre and his friends spending a whole night at the Pinner Fair. Boys could climb in and out of his house at will. Rolling-in and blanket-tossing continued unchecked. Across the road in Drury's house, then called the Abbey, drinking, smoking, and fighting were unrestrained. Throughout the school, boys indulged their sporting habits, including post-chaise racing, shooting, fishing, keeping dogs, and beagling. Informal games, such as hare-and-hounds, a radical form of steeplechase, and football on the eastern fields occupied any other spare time.[216]

---

[210] HM/L/Circular, Jan. 1830; Memorandum, 10 Mar. 1830.
[211] HM/L/Circular, Feb. 1834, and attached printed form.
[212] HM/L/W. H. Gregory's bill, Dec. 1831; Hole, *Phelps*, ii. 59 n. 2.
[213] HM/L/Circular, 31 Mar. 1835; for subs. see Gregory's Dec. 1831 bill.
[214] HM/L/Circular, Feb. 1834.   [215] Jenner, 'Dr Longley', 86.
[216] Gregory, *Autobiography*, 34, 35; Torre, *Recollections*, 4–47; Minchin, *Old Harrow Days*, 93–5; Jenner, 'Dr Longley', 81–6; Pouchée's Diary, *passim*.

The impression that many boys spent much of their time simply loafing about is amply confirmed by the diary of George Pouchée of Druries between May and November 1832. When not lounging about the street throwing stones, picking fights with locals and visitors, escaping or suffering regular punishment for idleness, he fished in Park Lake, boxed with friends, watched brutal but unexciting contests on the Milling Ground below the Old Schools, set off fireworks inside Druries, threw water at maidservants, shot pistols, and played billiards, football, and cricket. One afternoon, he occupied time by watching girls on the treadmill at the workhouse. He learnt to smoke in late June, reaching three cigars a day in just over a fortnight. There were lavish illicit suppers and extended drinking sessions in Druries, fuelled by whisky punch, wine, port, sherry, or gin, leaving Pouchée drunk or complaining of hangovers. The only unjaundiced enthusiasm shown by Pouchée was for sport.[217]

One of the few areas of control and discipline were games which, to Benjamin Kennedy's disgust, were 'so zealously pursued and with such organisation of the whole school that it is vain to expect anything like extensive reading and sound scholarship'.[218] Cricket remained dominant. Apart from school games there were house matches. For the Sixth Form games, the professional in the 1830s was another old boy, Henry Anderson, an enthusiastic cricketing Scotsman who, after giving up the City for sport, lived for some time in a gypsy encampment. For a couple of summers, a professional from Lord's also attended for a fortnight, one year bringing a bowling machine or catapult. In 1832 a pavilion was built. As with all the cricket, this was paid for by boys' subscriptions, not school funds. The independence of the game was more or less total, run as a club by elected officers (the 'club-keepers').[219] There was no official supervision.

Cricket became a central mechanism in binding old boys to the school, as numbers of them came weekly to play against the eleven in the Sixth Form. After matches the old boys would usually entertain the eleven and others to extremely bibulous dinners. Around the sides of the feasts lurked fags waiting to pounce on any discarded but not empty bottles. The evenings would regularly conclude with drunken parades along the High Street, with Harrovians young and old singing loudly and swearing eternal comradeship.[220] Thus the immensely powerful socializing force of cricket which so characterized later nineteenth- and much of twentieth-century Harrow was forged. Cricket provided a conduit for the uniquely strong influence exerted over the school by its old alumni. It came to represent the values, health, even nature of the school itself. Yet, until early Victorian godliness was superseded by the cult of manliness and hearties, some of them Old

---

[217] Pouchée's Diary, fo. 21 and *passim*.   [218] Butler, *Butler*, ii. 134.

[219] Jenner, 'Dr Longley', 85; Torre, *Recollections*, 109–27; *Harrow Register, 1800–1911*, 66. It may be noted that the two greatest stalwarts of Harrow cricket in the Victorian age, Robert Grimston (1828–34) and Frederic Ponsonby (1830–3), both played in the Sixth Form Game in Longley's time.

[220] Torre, *Recollections*, 109–10.

Harrovians, began to be appointed to the staff from the 1850s, including the former member of the cricket eleven Montagu Butler as Head, there was no active involvement by the masters. Although Christopher Wordsworth, like his Harrovian brother Charles, may have been a keen and successful cricketer, as Longley's successor he encouraged masters to attend cricket matches as a necessary disciplinary precaution not for love or veneration of the game.[221] This rampart between the academic and the athletic remained until the arrival of masters such as F. W. Farrar (in 1855) who would have left Longley mightily puzzled by his famous evocation of 'the great cricket-field of life'.[222]

What distinguished Harrow in the 1830s was the degree of compulsion in playing games, either as fags for cricket and racquets or, for those in the Fourth Form and below, as players in football. A clever boy, such as William Gregory, placed in the Shell between the Fourth and the Fifth, not only avoided fagging but football as well, allowing him plenty of time to indulge in his passion for poaching. For those in more junior forms, football was compulsory not by school rule but the much more effective boys' *lex non scripta*, enforced with remarkable efficiency by the Sixth Form, again with no involvement by masters.[223] Whole-school games were huge melées with scores of boys of all ages and sizes which could degenerate into brawls. The young, the small, and the weak were particularly vulnerable. Following cricket's lead in the 1820s, football was also played between houses. In 1832, in one match the Longleyites and Kennedyites (i.e. the Head Master's and the Grove) took on the rest of the school; on another the Head Master's teamed up with Mrs Leith's. Players were beginning to wear distinctive clothing. In one of the earliest detailed accounts of a game of Harrow football, that played on 2 October 1832, George Pouchée described boys wearing striped 'nightcaps' (probably ancestors of the fez) and blue or red and white striped shirts.[224] The contours of later house colours, house spirit, and house competition were already visible. What secured the place of games, long before the sententious philosophizing of such archpriests of athleticism as E. E. Bowen, was their popularity. Following the official two-hour football match at 2 p.m., boys would, after the 4 p.m. bill, eagerly join unofficial games on the eastern fields for the rest of the afternoon. The later cult of sport was an imposition to regulate existing tradition, a measure of discipline rather than innovation, a process exactly parallel with the wider academic and social changes associated with Vaughan and Butler. Bizarrely, the only limitation to the general enthusiasm for football in the 1830s was the weather. As in cricket, rain stopped play.[225]

If the boys were able to construct order out of chaos, Longley had less success with his own staff. The oldest, Evans, Under Master since 1826, survived as a relic

---

[221] HM/Vaughan (hereafter HM/V)/Wordsworth's Head Master's Book, 21.
[222] F. W. Farrar, *In the Days of Thy Youth* (London, 1889), 373.
[223] Pouchée's Diary, fo. 21-2; Jenner, 'Dr Longley', 85.
[224] Pouchée's Diary, fos. 21-2, 30.   [225] Ibid., fos. 23, 28.

of a lost age to die in June 1833 aged 68, still in office after more than forty years' service. One pupil from his last years fondly recalled his encouragement of English, then wholly ignored by more progressive masters: 'Read a number of the *Spectator* of a morning at breakfast and begin to get up some modern history of Europe. Don't forget your Shakespeare.'[226] Evans' deficiencies as a classical teacher of the Fifth Form, his by virtue of seniority, could have been rectified by a younger Henry Drury, but after 1829, 'Old Harry' was a broken man. Massive, like his uncle, jealous of his distinguished past, he rarely allowed boys to forget he had been Byron's tutor. Having ruined himself by profligate bibliomania, he maintained a large house and a larger pupil room (claiming at one time to have tutored 112 boys at the same time) but to decreasing effect and with diminishing control. Inheriting the Under Mastership and the Fifth Form from Evans, like his father he became fonder of declamatory monologues than actually listening to boys' construing. A lover of fires, rushing to see the Grove and the Head Master's burn down or to watch from the churchyard the distant conflagration that destroyed the old Palace of Westminster in 1834, Drury became increasingly eccentric, bad-tempered, and indolent. He frequently missed First School, scouts being placed around Druries to relay his movements or lack of them. He received boys in his favourite flowery dressing gowns, ate fruit in lessons, and borrowed cigars from boys in his house when he had run out. By the 1830s the visits with boys to London to view the sights, including Cato Street, scene of the plot to assassinate the entire Cabinet in 1820, were just a memory. Although claiming harmony with Longley, his resentment at losing the Headship in 1829 left him an awkward colleague, untamed and untameable.[227] Without his library, his intellect festered, not the form or pupil-room teaching nor his continuing reputation among similarly old-school classics such as Samuel Butler providing much compensation.[228] Familiar with the *ancien régime* at its roughest, he maintained more or less open warfare with Cunningham and the evangelical party which the vicar's part in the election of Longley did nothing to pacify. Rife since the late 1810s, the so-called Cunninghamite–Druryite feud split the adults and boys on the Hill in a manner not repeated until the Venables–Boissier conflict in the 1930s.[229] Already isolated since the removal of his uncle and cousin in 1826, Drury found himself further diminished by the ambitious, reforming evangelicals Batten and Phelps as a housemaster and by Kennedy as a scholar. Yet he retained the affection of boys as a character. His tragedy was that his financial position and large family (he had eleven children) prevented retirement,

---

[226] Thornton, *Harrow School*, 270.
[227] HM/1829/H. Drury to Lord Northwick, 13 Dec. 1828; Minchin, *Old Harrow Days*, 196, 227–8; Jenner, 'Dr Longley', 82–3; Torre, *Recollections*, 40; Pouchée's Diary, esp. fo. 11 (cadging cigars); Merivale, *Autobiography*, 37–40; Thornton, *Harrow School*, 270–1; B. H. Drury, 'The Drury Family' in Howson and Townsend Warner, *Harrow School*, 65.
[228] Butler, *Butler*, i. 354–5, 361, ii. 129, 139–40.
[229] Minchin, *Old Harrow Days*, 227–8. See below, pp. 519–20.

forcing him to cling to his income as Under Master and housemaster long after he was physically and psychologically fit enough. Under Longley, still only just past fifty but prematurely aged, Henry Drury's presence spoke of disappointed hopes and a different age.

Drury's frustration was the common lot. William Oxenham's notorious foul temper and worse tongue covered what most observers recognized as an amiable nature and good scholarship. Little shocked him, his anger providing a safety valve for boredom not anxiety, being almost entirely self-generated as he was famously immune from boys' baiting. Teaching the Shell was little incentive to humanity, mainly comprising hearing boys stumble through familiar, indeed unchanging passages of prepared Horace, Virgil, and Homer, leavened with some verse composition and grammar tests. To earn a respectable income meant coping with one of the larger houses (now Moretons), with anything between fifteen and thirty-five boys, a task for which he was entirely unsuited, even though he had completely rebuilt the premises in 1828. Neither in form nor house could he muster the interest, energy, or strategems to impose order. That this persisted for over thirty years says much for his stamina and the tolerance of a system that still regarded a master's teaching post, like his house, as his property rather than a salaried job.[230]

Similar frustration marked the Harrow career of William Mills, who had the misfortune to teach Pouchée in the Upper Shell in 1832, for which labour his pupil drew a cartoon of him in characteristic pose beating a boy on the palm of the hand, complete with unavoidable tag: 'palmam qui merit ferat'.[231] However, Mills was more ambitious than Oxenham and his house less lucrative. His ideas for reform and tighter discipline having cut no ice with the governors in 1829, he sought promotion elsewhere, leaving to be Head Master of Exeter Grammar School in 1834.[232]

Without either a large boarding house or pupil-room, Harrow masters under Longley struggled to maintain their status and make an adequate living, especially as one of the incentives of becoming a schoolmaster for a college fellow was that it allowed him to marry. Another was that however modest initial rewards as a Harrow master, they were probably greater than the c.£200 earned by most dons at the time. The competition for boarders' and pupils' fees was therefore intense. Success had no necessary connection with effective formroom teaching. The outstanding master when Longley arrived was Samuel Batten. He had bought the Grove for £5,125 in 1819/20 and, through his close contacts with the prominent evangelical Clapham Sect (his wife was one of the daughters of John Venn, rector of Clapham), quickly built up his house and pupil room. In 1826 his forty-two boarders paid £150

---

[230] Hole, *Phelps*, ii. 8; Jenner, 'Dr Longley', 83; Torre, *Recollections*, 37; Minchin, *Old Harrow Days*, 10–16; Pouchée's Diary, fo. 19; Norman, *At School and at Sea*, 9; Howson and Townsend Warner, *Harrow School*, 44; Graham, *Butler*, 31. [231] Pouchée's Diary, fo. 7.

[232] See above, pp. 203–4 for Mills' application for the Headship of 1829. For a failed bid for Bury St Edmund's (which went to his colleague John Edwards) in 1828 see Hole, *Phelps*, ii. 33; Pouchée's Diary, fo. 19; Thornton, *Harrow School*, 270; *Harrow Register*, 902.

each giving a gross income of £6,450. Four years later, with just over thirty boys, Batten was supposed to be earning from them around £5,000, half of which was profit. As Charles Merivale noted, Batten's Grove 'constituted a new era in . . . school economies'.[233] The price was high, the comfort and facilities commensurately luxurious. The Grove was the first of the new, grander, more pretentious houses that formed the basis of Harrow's prosperity after 1850, whose housemasters aped the style (and occasionally substance) of their wealthy clients. The 1830s spartan chaos of Druries, the Head Master's, Mrs Leith's, or Oxenham's looked increasingly antediluvian by contrast.

Yet Batten's arrangements owed nothing to the governors and little to the Head Master, whose only role was to have appointed Batten in the first place and to admit his boarders to the school, as far as he was concerned the more the better. Masters came to Harrow with their own fortunes to make. W. W. Phelps only began to break even three years after arriving in 1826 and, despite gross receipts of £880 in 1830, remained considerably in debt, prompting sympathy from George Butler and his own search for a more profitable position elsewhere.[234] This did not prevent him from joining the feeding frenzy on the sudden death of his friend and fellow evangelical Batten in 1830. Any change in staff, especially the removal of a successful housemaster, offered financial opportunities to the other masters. Before the 1829 Head Mastership election, for which the two most popular housemasters were candidates, it was suggested to Phelps by Mrs Batten that 'it must be of advantage and increase my numbers should Drury succeed, but much more if her husband does'.[235] Within eight days of Batten's unexpected death on 3 May 1830, Phelps had bid for the lease of the Grove only to find that B. H. Kennedy, then a fellow of St John's, Cambridge, had already been accepted by the Batten family as tenant for £360 a year, exclusive of rates, taxes, and repairs. Longley had moved with lightning speed to attract the austere scholarly Kennedy, whose first contact with the school had been as a scholarship examiner that March. The result of Kennedy's arrival was that Phelps gained only eight of Batten's boarders, instead of the full thirty or so.[236]

Undaunted, in 1831 Phelps, still alert to entrepreneurial opportunities, pulled off a major coup when he bought the whole of the Park estate, the second Baron Northwick's former residence, for £6,000, including the great house. The property had come on the market because of the current owner's bankruptcy. If Phelps had not submitted a bid, the house was to have been demolished. The agents, eager for a quick sale, arranged easy terms for a mortgage in addition to a loan to Phelps from a friend. Such was the success of the venture that the loans were paid off within six

---

[233] Merivale quoted by Thornton, *Harrow School*, 241–2. Cf. Merivale, *Autobiography*, 37; Letters of G. M. Batten, no. 16; Hole, *Phelps*, ii. 59 n. 2, 59–60.
[234] Hole, *Phelps*, ii. 17, 34, 58–9, 63, and n. 1, 61–73.   [235] Hole, *Phelps*, ii. 34, 47.
[236] Ibid., ii. 74–5; Butler, *Butler*, i. 374.

years, by which time the Park was the largest house in the school as well as one of the most aristocratic. Phelps himself proudly recorded that when he left Harrow in 1839, seven of the thirteen titled pupils then at Harrow were in his house, as well as two sons of Sir Robert Peel.[237]

Phelps's financial gamble paid off handsomely. As his biographer commented, it required 'as much nerve for a boarding tutor . . . to fit himself out as it does to establish an hotel'.[238] Phelps also demonstrated that Batten's success could be repeated and sustained, even in the more straitened times of the 1830s. He did more. When Batten died, it was assumed that some parents would transfer their sons to another master and tutor, not necessarily the new tenant of the Grove. This continued to be the assumption when his successor Kennedy left in 1836. However, when Phelps left the Park in 1839, he had created a permanent boys' house which his successor, J. W. Colenso, 'had nothing to do but keep up there what he found'.[239] This was the beginning of the identification of boys with a house rather than a housemaster, the foundation of a system that came to dominate Harrow life as separate houses developed their own characteristics and traditions that lent them powerful autonomous status, independent of both school and incoming housemasters. By the end of the nineteenth century, Harrow had become almost a federal school— admissions, sport, social life, and finance revolving around established houses proudly distinct in nature and history, the housemasters operating as an oligarchy of over-mighty barons who regularly forced Head Masters to Runnymede.[240]

Batten and Phelps operated their houses as private businessness to the exclusion of the Head Master. Except for major disciplinary problems, the Head had no involvement, unless as a rival for boarders. This was wholly traditional, the independent financial incentive providing the basis for recruiting ambitious and able staff. Given the lavish scale of these new houses, however, their informal relationship with the school presented commensurately greater risks. As with the Battens at the Grove, Phelps retained ownership of his house after he ceased to be a master, renting it to his successors. In theory, he was free to lease it to anyone, with or without a school connection. Each transfer of tenancy, therefore, was fraught with potential hazard for the general management of the school, particularly in the 1830s and 1840s when numbers were falling and the profitability of boarding houses less conspicious than previously.[241]

Commercial competitiveness seeped into academic rivalry. Phelps not only resented Kennedy the Grove but also his academic reputation. Kennedy, when young a protégé of Samuel Parr, had, after all, won the Cambridge University Porson Prize for Greek iambics while still at school. When, in Kennedy's first year,

---

[237] Hole, *Phelps*, ii. 89–91, 93, 94, 120, 138–9.   [238] Ibid., ii. 88.

[239] HM/L/Kennedy's Circular to Parents, 9 Mar. 1836; Hole, *Phelps*, ii. 139.

[240] To some OH disapproval: Roundell, 'Wordsworth', 90, comparing the school in the 1890s to his time in the 1840s: 'Harrow has become a conglomeration of houses instead of being Harrow'.

[241] Phelps complained of this in 1841: Hole, *Phelps*, ii. 150.

The Ancien Régime

one of Phelps' pupils won a leaving scholarship, the tutor gloated: 'I cannot but look on it as a peculiarly kind Interposition of Providence in my favour, so soon after the appointment of a new master the éclat of whose name is so calculated to obscure men of inferior calibre.'[242] Such animosities are the stuff of institutional life. The independence of the masters was unchallenged by Longley, ever sensitive to his popularity, despite their palpable inadequacies. Drury was increasingly remote from reality even when physically present. Mills's efforts to impose order and inculcate academic seriousness were regarded by his pupils as faintly sinister and definitely eccentric. Oxenham should never have gone into schoolmastering. 'Lisping' Phelps was admired for his coolness, but reacted badly to any rigorous academic demands made of him. Although inspiring to clever private pupils, 'Baity Benji' Kennedy displayed a notoriously short fuse in form and house, a man almost wholly out of sympathy with the intellectually casual if not slovenly Harrow of the 1830s. Given both his lowly standing in the school and the near catastrophic destruction of the Grove by fire in January 1833, his perpetual state of fury may have had some justification. George Gepp, who came in 1832, made no impact except, as a new master, attracting the usual insults ('Last tho' not least in his own opinion | Comes Jepp [*sic*], a nasty, surly, cocky minion').[243] The extra masters, the Marillier brothers, knew little and cared less. Without the political advantage his successors enjoyed of a host of junior masters dependent on the Head Master's patronage for promotion to the fleshpots of large boarding houses, Longley was powerless to impose order or efficiency on his assistants.

Longley's priorities became clear. Despite good intentions, he was not cut out to be a schoolmaster. Too aloof, too affable, too easily teased, his ambitions lay elsewhere. He cultivated Peel assiduously. By the autumn of 1835, it was widely accepted that his expectations were to be satisfied with a bishopric. He possessed the great advantage in the eyes of the Whig Prime Minister, Lord Melbourne, that he was neither an evangelical nor a sympathizer with the new Tractarian movement. That he was a Tory and opposed Melbourne's Irish policy mattered less than that he was not an ecclesiastical partisan. Longley's translation was, however, a typically muddled affair. On 28 February 1836 Melbourne offered either Hereford or Chichester. On 3 March this had become Bristol or the brand new see of Ripon, with the promise of the reversion of Durham. Characteristic of Melbourne's style of administration, the second offer was sent to Ireland by mistake.[244] Longley accepted Ripon and had to wait twenty years before ascending to Durham, but Harrow, as he recognized in his letter of resignation to the governors, had 'essentially contributed' to his elevation.[245] However, his later eminence scarcely

[242] Hole, *Phelps*, ii. 81.
[243] This and the nicknames from J. W. Fergusson's poem on the masters in 1833: Pouchée's Diary, fos. 19–20. On Kennedy's temper see Jenner, 'Dr Longley', 83.
[244] *Historical Manuscripts Commission: National Register of Archives, Letters and Papers of C. T. Longley (Lambeth) Catalogue*, pp. 3–4, fos. 65–7, 68–9, 86–8.   [245] GM, 14 Mar. 1836.

218

concealed even from admirers and apologists that he had been, in the words of one of Phelps' correspondents, 'a failure', the least effective Head Master of Harrow between Cox and Wood, a period of 150 years.[246]

Christopher Wordsworth

Whatever else, Christopher Wordsworth was not ineffective, even if, as a jaundiced Richard Shilleto acidly remarked, he seemed content for Harrow to bear witness to 'the blessing of unity' by reducing it to one boy.[247] His unsuitability for the post was active where Longley's had been passive. His election none the less marked another step by the governors towards fashionable reform. They had seen that the existing system under Longley had failed to galvanize the school and were prepared to accept that being a gentleman, although important, was not enough. They now sought a man of high scholarship and serious religion. In the event they found themselves one of serious scholarship and high religion.

An initial approach, conducted at the instigation of Cunningham by Lords Aberdeen and Northwick, was made as early as December 1835 to Benjamin Kennedy to see if he would stand. He turned them down, preferring to compete for the Headship of his old school Shrewsbury instead. Kennedy was scathing about Harrow. He could probably earn more money there but he would 'take no school where fagging is a legalised system ... learning cannot flourish in it', Harrovians tending to be 'well-mannered ... gentlemanly ... but as a body ... reckless ... idle and careless of self-improvement'.[248]

Kennedy's withdrawal, and subsequent success at Shrewsbury, left the field open. Thomas Arnold suggested the Old Harrovian Charles Wordsworth, but he preferred to remain as Second Master of Winchester on £1,400 a year.[249] Once again, the governors advertised in the universities. There were ten declared candidates. Between them they produced such a torrent of testimonials that it is hard to see how the governors absorbed all of them in the four weeks they allowed themselves before the scheduled election on 31 March. James Garbett, fellow of Brasenose, a future professor of Poetry at Oxford, was a fancied runner with thirty-five sponsors, including John Keble and the implied blessing of Arnold. He was mentioned as a good disciplinarian. Christ Church produced two strong candidates, Canon Robert Hussey, later Regius Professor of Ecclesiastical History and Charles Dodgson, a friend of Longley's (who later appointed him to a canonry at Ripon), backed by forty-one testimonials, who argued he was the candidate of continuity who would maintain Harrow 'in the highest rank among the great

---

[246] Hole, *Phelps*, ii. 132.
[247] J. E. C. Welldon, *Recollections and Reflections* (London, 1915), p. 107.
[248] Butler, *Butler*, ii. 120, 122–3, 134, 140.
[249] *Letters and Papers of C. T. Longley (Lambeth) Catalogue*, p. 5, fo. 105, Arnold to Longley, 7 Mar. 1836.

The Ancien Régime

Christian institutions of the country'.[250] That must have raised some eyebrows on the Hill. Thomas Peile, Old Salopian and fellow of Trinity, Cambridge represented the new breed of acute, religiously minded scholars, his supporters emphasizing his academic accomplishments and 'sound religious principles': he was later to become Head Master of Repton. By contrast Thomas Mitchell, a tutor at Oxford, was supported by a very few, very grand aristocrats, such as the sixteenth earl of Suffolk, whose sons he had taught.

A very late applicant was Christopher Wordsworth, whose name first appears on 25 March. A fellow of Trinity, Cambridge and recently elected Public Orator, at only 28, the son of the Master of Trinity and nephew of the most famous living English poet, he already possessed the aura of a rising star. His name had been brought to Lord Northwick's attention by an old schoolfriend, now a fellow of Trinity, who insisted that no other Cambridge man had 'obtained equal honours and prizes.'[251] More pertinently, he had examined the Harrow leaving scholarships for the previous three years (1834–6), well placed when his brother Charles decided not to run. He was actually on the Hill the day Longley's resignation was announced.[252] His fellow examiner, William Jacobson, vice-principal of Magdalen Hall, Oxford, also applied.

According to Lord Northwick, before they met on 31 March, at Lord Aberdeen's London house, 'no one of the Governors until the hour of our meeting was at all aware who would be the successful candidate'.[253] They proceeded to whittle down the list, first to six, still including Mitchell, then to three: Wordsworth, Dodgson, and probably either Garbett or Peile. Although it is impossible to reconstruct their motives, the governors may not have been immune to traditional instincts. In the shortlisting process, Dodgson may have been preferred to his fellow Christ Church competitor Hussey because one referee, comparing the two, mentioned the former's 'superior manner in society'.[254] A factor weighing against Peile, a candidate with an outstanding academic record from Shrewsbury and Trinity, an experienced schoolmaster and teacher, backed by Samuel Butler, may have been, as one referee honestly but fatally pointed out, that he was 'by birth a Cumberland man, and his father is agent to Lord Lonsdale for his coalmines at Whitehaven', the earl being an Old Harrovian.[255] None the less, Northwick insisted that any on the long shortlist would have been satisfactory. In the end the governors chose *jeunesse*

---

[250] HM/1836/Dodgson to Lord Northwick, 24 Mar. 1836. In general the HM/1836 file includes almost all the relevant documents and correspondence on this election.

[251] HM/1836/H. R. Reynolds to Lord Northwick, 25 Mar. 1836.

[252] GM, 19 Feb. 1834, 12 Mar. 1835; HM/L/27 Jan. 1836, Wordsworth to Longley and Wordsworth to Jacobson; Longley's Circular to Parents, 8 Mar., the day fixed for the Leaving Scholarships.

[253] HM/1836/drafts of letters from Lord Northwick to the earl of Suffolk and his sister Anne, 1 Apr. 1836, in which the details of the election are given. Cf. HM/L/Aberdeen to Longley, 17 Mar. 1836 seeking his views on who should succeed him.

[254] HM/1836/Frederick Calvert to Lord Northwick, 20 Mar. 1836.

[255] HM/1844/Printed Testimonials for Revd T. W. Peile, which include those of 1836.

d'orée, Christopher Wordsworth, whose own examiner's report was considered at the very meeting he was elected Head Master.[256] It says much for contemporaries' self-restraint or the narrowness of the classical curriculum that nobody in retrospect felt moved to quote Tacitus's apt comment on the Emperor Galba *omnium consensu capax imperii nisi imperasset*. Modern observers, by contrast, are left wondering what if Charles Dodgson had come first not third and had brought to Harrow his four-year-old son, the future Lewis Carroll.

The 1836 election, in candidature and result, showed how far Harrow was now entrenched in the academic religious establishment that ran early Victorian upper-class education. Head Masters and, increasingly at posh, profitable schools like Harrow, the assistant masters were drawn from a small coterie or mafia of well-connected, financially comfortable, socially respectable dons, clergymen, and schoolmasters equally at home in college, vicarage, or schoolroom. In the way of such tight-knit, often interrelated circles, destinies were shaped early, preferment achieved young. These heroic hierophants existed in a world elevated from their colleagues. At Harrow, none of Wordsworth's assistants matched his prominence even though all were older. Much the same had been true of Arnold at Rugby and was to be true of Tait and Temple at Rugby, Cotton at Marlborough, Lee at St Edward's, Birmingham, Benson at Wellington, and Vaughan at Harrow. These were men of intense earnestness and moral seriousness, men of Christian action who were almost from youth identified by their peers—and often by themselves— as possessed with a mission to reform English society from the top. Mostly, but not exclusively, towards the evangelical wing of the church, as Head Masters their doctrine was, as Arnold and Wordsworth alike proclaimed, the fostering of 'first, religious and moral principles; secondly, gentlemanly conduct; thirdly intellectual ability'.[257] Their task, as they perceived it, was the protection and promotion of Christian civilization in the face of attacks by materialism and reason. Religion and education were inseparable. In this they were zealots who felt justice was theirs regardless, in Wordsworth's case heedless, of public opinion.

Although a High Churchman, Wordsworth was a typical product of this generation which has been misleadingly dubbed Arnoldian. As late as 1835, Samuel Butler confided to Benjamin Kennedy, 'I don't know what you mean by Arnold's reform of Rugby . . . I have never heard of such an act.'[258] Butler was not interested in anything except classical learning, a tradition Kennedy maintained at Shrewsbury for another thirty years in the teeth of moral, educational, or social reformers. Wordsworth was no less independent and would have resented any suggestion that he followed Arnold's creed, though he did seek his advice on the establishment of

---

[256] GM, 31 Mar. 1836.
[257] Thus Arnold: Stanley, *Arnold*, i. 100. For Wordsworth see Torre, *Recollections*, 126; Roundell, 'Wordsworth', 99. In general see Newsome, *Godliness*, 1–91; Honey, *Tom Brown's Universe*, 1–46.
[258] Butler, *Butler*, ii. 122–3.

a chapel and the advisability of having a separate chaplain. His aims and attitude were none the less characteristic of his generation. Writing to his father in 1842, Wordsworth, arguing for the merits of greater Visitorial authority, declared 'the Church... must find her way into the *Grammar* schools where the *upper classes* are educated; and this she will never do if she does not do it *now*.'[259] According to his redoubtable daughter, Wordsworth came to Harrow 'with very high and noble aims, with a longing to unite religion and scholarship in education, as he felt that he had the power beyond most men of his time to do.'[260]

Unfortunately, Wordsworth overrated the power of reason and underestimated the limitations of his personality. Brilliant, austere, with the blinkered self-assurance of the over-bright, he was as tactless as he was energetic. Although not without charm and social skill, he was impatient, lacked circumspection, was no respecter of persons, and suffered fools not at all. He possessed a sharp, donnish wit and a caustic shrewdness that frightened and irritated.[261] Despite his own athletic prowess, he cut no ice with the majority of boys for whom 'success at games counted for more than success in the school work.[262] Even his Sixth Form were more likely to be moved by respect than affection. An eager moral reformer, he never seemed able to bridge the empathetic gulf that separated his religious idealism from the many—boys, parents, and even masters—for whom, as one of his younger pupils was to put it, 'a great public school is not so much a place where book learning is to be acquired, as a sphere for the formation and development of the habits, character and physique of an English gentleman'.[263]

In common with many of his like-minded contemporaries, there was about Wordsworth something of the self-righteous, something of the prig. He dressed in silk doctoral robes, complete with velvet cap.[264] He pontificated to his colleagues about what and how they should teach even though almost all of them had experience where he had none and one of whom had been teaching at Harrow before he had been born. Once his chapel had been built, he concocted a special ceremony at which he solemnly invested the monitors with their keys intoning 'Sis tu Monitor Scholae Harroviensis', blithely unaware of any bathos.[265] Unafraid of public opprobrium, he tended to broadcast expulsions instead of hushing them up thereby giving the school an inevitable bad name, courting, as one Trinity colleague put it in 1842, 'the notoriety which is necessarily given to any moral offence by the exercise of a strict and wholesome discipline.'[266] Before removing the improbably named bully Vicesimus Knox Vade, head of Leith's and a future

---

[259] HM/W/Wordsworth to his father, 25 Oct. 1842.
[260] Overton and Wordsworth, *Wordsworth*, 364.
[261] Overton and Wordsworth, *Wordsworth*, 83–5, 93; Norman, *At School and at Sea*, 3; Roundell, 'Wordsworth', esp. pp. 89–90, 99, 102–5; Minchin, *Old Harrow Days*, 96–8; Torre, *Recollections*, 126–7. [262] Roundell, 'Wordsworth', 91; Welldon, *Recollections*, 109.
[263] Norman, *At School and at Sea*, 17. [264] Ibid., 11; Roundell, 'Wordsworth', 104.
[265] Roundell, 'Wordsworth', 102. [266] HM/W/Charles Perry to Wordsworth, 18 Apr. 1842.

parson, he allowed him to be publicly 'licked' by the other boys.[267] When the head of the Park in 1837 was expelled for beating up his fag, the boy's father threatened Wordsworth: 'I court publicity; I court investigation'. Wordsworth, as usual, stuck to his guns. However, in 1844 he did advise his successor that it was much better to let parents remove their children than to expel them.[268]

Much of this artlessness came from naivity and an extraordinary inability to understand boys as well as their parents. When he caught a couple of Harrovians in a pub, he set them each the task of putting Psalm 119 (easily the longest) into Greek iambics, subsequently not noticing that both the finished products were the work of just one of the culprits, Percy Smythe, later Viscount Strangford, a talented linguist. In chapel, his sermons flew well over the heads of his audience as he 'breathed the atmosphere of the Council of Nicaea'. He never hid his disdain for the mundane business of schoolmastering or his dislike of flogging, which he conducted sometimes during lessons in the Fourth Form Room with perfunctory haste using birches that were too big and bushy to inflict any damage or act as a deterrent.[269]

At times it appeared that Wordsworth was conducting an elevated discourse with himself while far below 'moderate anarchy' prevailed.[270] He may have been the first Head Master to try to define the duties and privileges of monitors. He banned all fagging after 8 p.m. and persuaded the boys to regulate cricket fagging in 1838.[271] Such administrative reforms had little impact. Boys continued to throw stones and snowballs at will. In July 1836 a post-boy was killed in the traditional end-of-term carriage race from the Hill to Marble Arch. There was a pitched battle with the navvies building the railway in 1837. One morning the masters found themselves locked out of the Old Schools because boys had filled up the lock. Billy Warner, the drunken oyster-seller with a horse and cart useful for illicit trips off the Hill, 'purveyor of illegitimate and objectionable amusements', was still allowed more or less free access to boys in search of fun.[272] In 1837 Henry Holland, future Secretary of State for the Colonies and Baron Knutsford dressed up as a girl to entertain a man lured down from London, the object apparently being the humiliation of the unsuspecting swain rather than sex.[273] As soon as the railway to London was

---

[267] Roundell, 'Wordsworth', 100 (the identification is mine).
[268] HM/W/25 for the correspondence connected with the expulsion of Thomas Smith; HM/V/Wordsworth's Head Master's Book, fo. 17ᵛ.
[269] Welldon, *Recollections*, 109; Roundell, 'Wordsworth', 105; Norman, *At School and at Sea*, 11.
[270] Roundell, 'Wordsworth', 99.
[271] Torre, *Recollections*, 121–2 reproduces the new cricket fagging rules.
[272] Ibid., 7 and n. 1, 24–6; Druett, *Harrow*, 218; Roundell, 'Wordsworth', 99–102; Norman, *At School and at Sea*, 6–7.
[273] For a poetic account of the incident see 'The Adventures of Tom Spicer', *The Harrovian*, 11 (1898), 13–15 (the identification of the central character is mine); Torre, *Recollections*, 31. Cf. Roundell, 'Wordsworth', 100 who suggests the prank was habitual, naming another similar occasion, with C. F. Surtees as the lure; Harrow Archives, B. A. Acland to his sister, 12 Nov. 1837 for another account of the same or similar incident.

opened in 1837, Harrovians regularly took advantage of the half-hour ride to London to spend afternoons at Lord's—and no doubt elsewhere.[274] With the decline in numbers, the continuing mayhem was, of course, limited in local effect. None the less, in Vaughan's early months many remaining 'Wordsworthites' continued to run amok and one governor suggested to the new Head that he sack all those he had found on the roll.[275]

If the boys were out of sympathy with Wordsworth, so were some of his colleagues when confronted with change. Wordsworth reformed both the curriculum and the method of instruction. In 1837 maths was introduced as 'part of the regular course of education', with a specialist mathematician to teach it.[276] He continued the tradition of attracting scholarships and prizes. In 1838–9 Richard Gregory, the Old Harrovian great-uncle to one of Longley's brightest pupils, William Gregory, endowed a leaving scholarship and a medal for Latin composition in memory of his first wife Isabella, with whom he had conducted a lengthy premarital affair, during which she dressed as a man, calling herself Jack the Sailor. Whether Wordsworth or the governors were aware of this is unclear.[277]

The syllabus was overhauled to the extent that Wordsworth claimed in 1838 that he had doubled Upper School work.[278] The Fifth Form was to prepare four exercises a week instead of one. The general aim, Wordsworth explained to Lord Aberdeen, was 'the establishment ... of uniformity of system in the whole business of the school'.[279] He wished to control every detail of the syllabus, down to prescribing the parts of speech to be learnt and the balance between Latin and Greek, verse and prose, composition or construe. All internal examinations, now to be termly instead of every other term as under Longley, were to be supervised by the Head. Detailed rules were specified for the award of good work prizes and 'copies' (given in the Sixth Form for any translation with fewer than three mistakes). New textbooks were introduced, such as Charles Wordsworth's new Greek grammar; old ones, such as the venerable Eton grammar and anthologies of minor classical authors, including that complied by Henry Drury, were removed. Pupils were distributed more evenly to tutors and in 1840 form sizes were reduced and consigned to individual masters, instead of the previous system of huge divisions taken by one master, assisted by another. The Head expected to receive weekly reports on all

---

[274] Roundell, 'Wordsworth', 101; Hole, *Phelps*, ii. 125 for earliest impact of the railway on visits to and from London in the Summer of 1837.

[275] Minchin, *Old Harrow Days*, 95–6; Roundell, 'Wordsworth', 103: the governor was Cunningham.

[276] HM/W/15, 16, 17; GM, 8 May 1837; HM/W/22; Printed Circular, 10 June 1837.

[277] Gregory, *Autobiography*, 6–7, 9; Howson and Townsend Warner, *Harrow School*, 142.

[278] GM, 26 Feb. 1838.

[279] HM/W/Aberdeen to Wordsworth, 28 July 1840. Cf. for the details, HM/W/Head Master's Memorandum, 5 Feb. 1840; Wordsworth to H. Drury, 24 Feb. 1840 (with Drury's MS comments in margin); Wordsworth to Aberdeen, 2 Nov. 1840; HM/W/BH undated H. Drury to Wordsworth; and, in general, HM/V/Wordsworth's Head Master's Book; Overton and Wordsworth, *Wordsworth*, 83–4.

boys from their masters. An attempt was made to reduce absenteeism among masters and institute cover for emergencies. Masters' meetings were held once a week, on Wednesday evenings, with an additional one on the penultimate Tuesday of term to consider examinations. This *dirigisme* extended even to boys' mealtimes, rules for absence, the saying of Grace, and house prayers.

The spasm of regulation caused inevitable dissent, although there was at least one master who felt, by 1840, that Wordsworth had not gone far enough.[280] Unsurprisingly, there was a running battle with Drury over the efficient and uniform teaching of the Fifth and Sixth Forms. Not only had Wordsworth outlawed Drury's own anthology and criticized his lax and old-fashioned teaching, he also insisted that no tutor should correct Sixth Formers' work—thus doing the Under Master out of money—and proposed that Drury's form-work (in the Fifth) be done by the dissident master, Steel, who otherwise would leave. Drury, wracked with gout and scarcely able to function, simply ignored appeals to set more work or follow a prescribed and agreed syllabus, which had induced the exasperated reforming Steel to threaten resignation. Disagreement bred disloyalty. Visiting his old school after the Lord's cricket match one year, when asked by Etonians how many Harrovians there were, Drury replied: 'I do not know exactly; but I think there are eleven.'[281] An increasingly bad-tempered row continued until the obstinate but increasingly pathetic Under Master's death in 1841. Wordsworth's forensic pursuit of the old man in a series of prissy memorandums makes depressing reading less because of Drury's palpable incompetence but for his Head's cold, unfeeling rectitude. In the end, almost too late, Wordsworth's essential humanity found a solution in appointing, to Drury's delight, his son Ben to the staff as both a help and a palliative.[282]

Phelps was openly hostile to Wordsworth, on religious and academic grounds, resenting changes to the pupil system and the insistence on masters following the curriculum as devised by the Head. He may also not have relished changing teaching habits that included allowing boys to use dictionaries in exams. Having been refused any clerical duties in the new chapel, in the Summer of 1839 he resigned.[283] His opposition could have been expected, as could that of Jacques Marillier, who in 1837 opted out of teaching French throughout the school in favour of taking a few private pupils and left in 1839.[284] Crueller was the behaviour of J. W. Colenso. He had been brought to Harrow by Wordsworth in 1837 to teach maths and had taken over the Head Master's boarding house the following year. Negotiations during this transfer and subsequently after fire had destroyed the house occupied

---

[280] HM/W/Wordsworth to Aberdeen, 2 Nov. 1840 referring to threatened resignation of 19 Oct. by Steel. For Wordsworth's tactless handling of this see Overton and Wordsworth, *Wordsworth*, 83–4. For Drury's grief and rage see his letter to Lord Northwick, 29 Oct. 1840, printed in *The Harrovian*, 18 Feb. 1952, p. 62. [281] Welldon, *Recollections*, 107.

[282] HM/W/Wordsworth to Aberdeen, 2 Nov. 1840. Cf. Longley to Wordsworth, 9 Mar. 1841 and above, n. 279. [283] Hole, *Phelps*, ii. 133–4.

[284] HM/W/Memorandum, 18 Feb. 1842 re teaching of maths and French.

The Ancien Régime

much of Wordsworth's time and goodwill working in Colenso's interests. That did not stop the new recruit seizing the opportunity of Phelps' departure in 1839 to switch his ambitions to the Park, leaving Wordsworth in the lurch. Once safely ensconced, Colenso had no compunction in admitting to his house late in 1839 two Etonians who had been just been expelled for fireraising on Guy Fawkes Night, an act hardly conducive to enhancing Harrow's reputation.[285]

Of the rest of the staff: Gepp left in 1837, T. H. Steel, who Wordsworth had brought with him from Trinity to take over the Grove, gave up in 1843. His successor, Richard Shilleto, once a favoured Cambridge pupil of Kennedy, lasted only one bad-tempered year. Increasingly, the fall in numbers made Wordsworth an isolated figure. Colenso departed, almost bankrupt in 1842; his mathematics replacement, J. P. Birkett, followed in 1844.[286] By then, with the boys' side of the Head Master's still a gutted ruin, there were only three boarding houses: Moretons under Oxenham, with whom, rather surprisingly, Wordworth got on well, Druries under Harry's son Ben, and the Park, under Wordsworth's friend George Harris, a Salopian fellow of Trinity who had been brought to the Hill in 1837. At least Wordsworth had the no mean accolade of the approval of the indestructable Custos, Sam Hoare.[287]

A vicious circle of bad publicity, bad economic circumstances, the legacy of bad management, bad luck, and bad judgement led to a catastrophic decline in numbers that merely accentuated the problems. Harrow was not alone in suffering wild fluctuation in numbers and serious decline. Westminster went from 300 in 1821 to 67 in 1841, still only reaching 96 twenty years later. Winchester and Shrewsbury both sank towards the 100 mark in mid-century. When Arnold inherited Rugby in 1827, he found just over 120 boys. At Harrow, numbers remained steady at above or around 150 until 1839 when entries, which had briefly risen, slumped to 31 in 1840, 33 in 1841, 26 in 1842, 21 in 1843. Given the average stay of four years, to reach the optimum level of 200 suggested by George Butler, 50 new boys a year were required, a number only achieved under Wordsworth in 1837 and 1838 (56 and 55 respectively). At Easter 1843 there was only one new boy. Even some of its most faithful supporters were deserting the school: both Peel and Butler sent sons elsewhere. The whole of 1844 brought thirteen new entrants, admissions being so unusual and Wordsworth so distracted that the name of one of only four new boys at Easter 1844, H. E. Hutton, was not even transcribed in the Head Master's Entance Book: the boy had to write in his own name later.[288]

---

[285] HM/W/15–17, 20; HM/W/Printed Circular, 10 June 1837; Memorandum, 18 Feb. 1842; HM/W/BH *passim*; Hole, *Phelps*, ii. 134; GM, 24 and 29 May 1839; Maxwell Lyte, *Eton*, 483: the boys were A. H. Farmer and W. Spottiswode.

[286] *Harrow Register, 1800–1911*, 902; Honey, *Tom Brown's Universe*, 298–9; for Colenso's debts of £5,000 see P. Hinchcliff, *John William Colenso* (London, 1964), p. 31.

[287] Overton and Wordsworth, *Wordsworth*, 104; Thornton, *Harrow School*, 368.

[288] Harrow Archives, Wordsworth's Entrance Book in Admissions Register, 1829–92, sub. Apr. 1844 and *passim*, 1836–44; *Harrow Register, 1800–1911*, 159–181 (a total of only 287 boys); for

With total numbers plunging below 100, senior boys may have complained of a lack of fags, but for masters the situation was more serious.[289] Because of its small available endowment (c.£1,000 p.a. compared to Eton's £20,000), almost the entire income of the Head Master and all that of his assistants, whose basic salaries came out of the Head's pocket, derived directly from schooling, boarding, and tuition fees: no boys, no money; no money, no teachers; no teachers, no school. By 1844 Harrow provided insufficient boarding or tuition income to support its masters; even the Head reckoned he was making a loss.[290] In such circumstances it was impracticable to expect wide let alone unconditional support from those whose livelihood appeared to be vanishing, some of whom had incurred considerable debts in setting themselves up at Harrow.

Wordsworth was an inept Head Master. He was also a very unlucky one. The hostility and awkwardness with the masters was not entirely of his making. Asked to introduce a new system of management and financing by the governors in 1836, his efforts to oblige were dogged by mishap, from the continuing economic recession after 1837 to the resistance of the masters to lower boarding and tuition rates. The governors had become anxious that Harrow was pricing itself out of the market. After taking the advice of Longley, Wordsworth, and Drury, in 1836 they reduced the fees.[291] Private tuition went from twenty to ten guineas; payments to extra masters were fixed at an annual standing charge of 3 guineas a year. More controversially, boarding fees were set at 65 guineas for the Head Master's and Dames' houses; ninety guineas for those run by assistant masters. In Longley's time, the Head Master had charged 70 guineas and assistant masters anything between a £100 and £150. After representations from the Masters, the governors relented to the extent of allowing private tuition fees of 15 guineas and payments for extra subjects of four guineas. In the light of Harrow's past, these controls were draconian, especially as there was an attempt to limit the number in each assistant master's house to thirty-five, presumably in an attempt to maintain as many flourishing houses as possible. Traditionalists such as Phelps were angry and scornful: from the Summer of 1836 until he left three years later, numbers in The Park never dipped below thirty-five.[292] Yet the governors were fully justified in seeking economies not only because of the general economic conditions but because of new, cheaper, self-proclaimed public schools such as Cheltenham (1841) and Marlborough (1843) to which, with King's and University College schools in London, Liverpool College, and Bristol Grammar School, Wordsworth attributed part of Harrow's decline.[293]

---

fluctuating numbers, esp. see Roundell, 'Wordsworth', 87 n. 2, 98; *Report of the Public Schools Commission*, i. 6; Thornton, *Harrow School*, 251 and 280–1 and Graham, *Butler*, 28 for Peel and Butler; for Butler's optimum, HM/W/Butler to Wordsworth, 6 Mar. 1838 (i).

[289] Thornton, *Harrow School*, 283.
[290] HM/W/FSD/Wordsworth to Aberdeen, 17 Aug. 1843.
[291] GM, 6 June, 27 June, 5 July, 11 July, 1 Aug. 1836; HM/W/6, 7, 9; HM/W/Circular, 10 June 1837.
[292] Hole, *Phelps*, ii. 94, 139.   [293] HM/W/FSD/Wordsworth to Governors, 16 Mar. 1844.

The other gubernatorial initiative was more directly damaging. In 1829 they had removed the Head Master's right to take private pupils which had existed since Sumner's time. Early in 1836 they conceived the idea that the Head Master should no longer be burdened with the supervision of boarders, a change 'likely to advance the interests and secure the character of the school'.[294] When they got wind of the scheme, both Henry Drury and George Butler immediately noticed the central flaw in the proposition: 'whence will there be sufficient emoluments to the Master?'[295] The governors, however, seemed to wish to elevate the dignity of Head Master of Harrow onto a similar footing to the Heads of Eton or Winchester without much thought as to financial realities. At more comparable schools, Rugby and Shrewsbury, the Heads accepted boarders. Arnold saw it as important to his moral influence and authority. Samuel Butler took a rather more prosaic view. He and his wife ran *three* boarding houses, containing in all 150 boys, allowing him 'to put by full £4,000 a year'. Even Longley, given his own experiences unsurprisingly an enthusiastic supporter of the scheme, wondered how the governors proposed to 'indemnify the Head Master for the loss of so profitable a source of income'.[296] Wordsworth's response was a carefully balanced memorandum setting out arguments for and against which recommended the compromise of appointing an assistant to run the house under the Head's overall supervision. In July 1836 the governors dropped the idea because of the difficulties of implementation.[297]

However, Wordsworth greatly disliked the chores of housemastering and in February 1838 revived the scheme, this time successfully. The key to his proposals was the arrival the year before of J. W. Colenso who, being a mathematician, had not been allowed to take boarders or private pupils. By suggesting that he take over the Head Master's boarders, George Butler's 'barracks', Wordsworth was not invading anyone else's vested interests, nor was he reducing the number of boarding houses. Colenso, who would now assume equal status with the other assistant masters, was to build a house for himself, at his own cost, on the High Street to the north of the boys' rooms which would then be detached from the Head Master's house to the south. Although, as was pointed out by George Butler, the Head would still have the noise of the boys next door, he would, in Wordsworth's words, be more able to concentrate on 'the moral and intellectual superintendance of the school', especially necessary in view of the great increase in Upper School business.

Financially, Wordsworth reckoned that he was earning 1,206 guineas in 1837–8 from schooling alone, to which, under his scheme, would be added Colenso's income as a maths master minus his new salary as an assistant master, making an additional sum of 260 guineas, total 1,466 guineas or just over £1,500. This

---

[294] GM, 21 Apr. 1836. Cf. HM/L/Aberdeen to Longley, 17 Mar. 1836.
[295] Butler, *Butler*, ii. 139–40 (Drury to S. Butler, 14 Mar. 1836); HM/W/4 (G. Butler to Wordsworth, 27 May 1836).
[296] HM/W/Arnold to Wordsworth, 18 Sept. 1839; Butler, *Butler*, ii. 125, 127; HM/W/Longley to Wordsworth, 31 Mar. 1838.   [297] HM/W/5; GM, 5 July 1836.

compared with just over £2,000 Wordsworth declared he currently earned. Colenso calculated that his income, which as the maths master was around 320 guineas, would, on the numbers in the Head Master's in 1838 (28) and a few private maths pupils from the Upper School whom he would now be permitted to take, be in the region of £1,100 gross a year. Bizarrely, these arrangements meant not only that Colenso but the Head as well would actually be earning less than Phelps, Drury, or Oxenham, whose *net* incomes were between £1,750 and £2,500. The governors saw the problem of the Head Master's loss of earnings and, in accepting the proposal, raised his income from schooling fees by five guineas per head and one guinea extra on entrances, ironically, in view of their recent attempts to lower general costs to parents. It was calculated that an annual entry of fifty, would, in the fourth year of the scheme, produce an income for the Head of just over £2,600. Compared to the riches enjoyed by his predecessors—and some current housemasters—this was small beer, but Wordsworth highmindedly accepted the severe financial consequences for the good of the school, despite a vigorous critique of these terms by George Butler. Wordsworth was so committed to the plan that he lent Colenso £1,600 towards the building costs of his house.[298]

In the event, the scheme nearly wrecked the school, almost ruining both Colenso and Wordsworth. The calculations of the Head Master's income rested on estimates of entrants that were hopelessly optimistic. By 1844, with the fall in numbers, Wordsworth would have been fortunate to receive much more than £1,000, this lack of income proving a crucial issue during the rancid altercation with the governors over Free Scholars. Whether Colenso could have made a success of his side of the deal was never put to the test. On the night of 22 October a fire broke out in one of the boys' studies in the 'barracks', apparently as the result of the ever-ingenious Colenso's new heating system. The gimcrack lathe and plaster rooms of Butler's annexe burnt fiercely. Within a few hours the boys' side and Wordsworth's house were completely destroyed, although Colenso's own house, finished that Summer, escaped unscathed. No boys were killed, although all their clothes and other possessions were lost. Wordsworth's wine cellar, furniture, plate, and most of his books were saved, but his clothes and linen were consumed. Thieves had a fine time, one almost making off with a manuscript Greek New Testament Wordsworth had brought back from Mt. Athos. Colenso had luckily insured his property only two days earlier. In contrast, the Head Master's private house, home to every Head since William Bolton in 1686 and to William Hide before that, had been massively underinsured by the governors.[299]

---

[298] The central documents for this and for what follows are in HM/W/BH, esp. Memorandum, 19 Feb. 1838; 'Colenso's Plan', undated 1838; and undated financial calculations by Wordsworth; HM/W/4; HM/W/G. Butler to Wordsworth, 6 Mar. 1838 (i & ii); GM, 26 Feb., 13 Mar., 2 Apr., 21 June 1838; Harrow Archives, Harrow Masters, Colenso File, Wordsworth's agreement with Colenso, 29 Apr. 1838.

[299] Overton and Wordsworth, *Wordsworth*, 94–5; Howson and Townsend Warner, *Harrow School*, 39–41; Welldon, *Recollections*, 106; GM, 7 Feb., 27 June 1839.

The impact of the destruction of the Head Master's was immediate and insidious. Colenso's boys were housed elswhere. Drury grudgingly took in some; but, pyrophile that he was, the conflagration had afforded him great excitement: 'It was a magnificent sight in Mr Colenso's long passage to see hall, playroom, study and every window in the yard sending out volumes of flames.'[300] The governors were wholly unable to meet the cost of rebuilding the boys' side which was left ruinous until 1845, although a new Head Master's house was ready on the original site by the autumn of 1843, at a cost of over £4,600, £2,000 of which came from a mortgage.[301] Meanwhile, Wordsworth lived in a cottage on the Park estate, symbolically severed from the centre of the school. Colenso, after negotiating a lease from the governors on the charred ruins on 24 May 1839 promptly abandoned the idea a few days later preferring to move into the Park on Phelps's departure in July.[302] The fire had effectively reduced Harrow's resources to three large houses and a declining Dames' house (Mrs Leith was ageing) and exposed the fragility of the governors' financial arrangements. It all seemed a metaphor for Wordsworth's Harrow; heat that destroyed instead of purifying.

The whole episode had lasting effects. The idea of the Head Master being a housemaster was revived by Wordsworth in 1844 and the practice was resumed by Vaughan, acting on Arnoldian precepts.[303] The issue was not raised again for half a century. Finding himself overwhelmed, Welldon appointed an assistant housemaster and around 1900 it was planned and confidently predicted that the Head Master would be settled in his own separate establishment without boarders, probably at the Grove. This never happened. Only in 1980 was the Head Master withdrawn from technical management of a house, a move confirmed by the erection of a new residence for the Head Master in 1982 away from boys and the heart of the school.[304] One less tangible result of the 1838 fire was that the question of the financial management not only of the school but also the Lyon trusts was seriously reviewed for the first time since 1810. Once again the sage of all things Harrovian, George Butler, pointed the way, writing to Wordsworth in 1843 of the need for a new financial settlement of trust income 'by a change in their appropriation for the *Highways* to the *Hill*'.[305]

Neither fire nor declining prosperity seemed to daunt Wordsworth's pursuit of 'sound learning and religious education'. More undermining by far was the presence at Harrow and on the governing body of the vicar, J. W. Cunningham, who seems to have taken upon himself a struggle to forge a school in his own image, a mixture of aristocratic favour and religious sententiousness. Apparently loved by his parishioners and dogged by domestic tragedy, Cunningham had the best of

---

[300] Howson and Townsend Warner, *Harrow School*, 40–1.
[301] GM, 7 Feb., 11, 27 June 1839, 5 Feb., 13 Apr. 1840, 7 Aug. 1843.
[302] GM, 1 Mar., 24 Apr., 24, 29 May, 4 July 1839.   [303] GM, 22 Feb. 1844.
[304] Welldon, *Recollections*, 116; see below, pp. 392–3, 552–3.
[305] HM/W/FSD/G. Butler to Wordsworth, 18 Aug. 1843.

evangelical connections, at one time being curate to John Venn (S. E Batten's father-in-law) at Clapham. He was provided with the living at Harrow in 1811 by his father-in-law who had bought the presentation, remaining vicar for fifty years, dying in post in 1861. As Harrow was one of the two richest livings in England, its vicars felt no need to leave: between 1702 and 1922 there were just six. It was also customary for the vicar to be a governor of the school as both Cunningham's predecessors had been. Clearly viewed with some trepidation, the new vicar had to wait until 1818 before he too was elected a governor. Any anxieties about his awkward religious zeal were fully justified as, for the next forty-three years, he spied on five successive Head Masters, interfering and plotting at will.[306]

A crashing bore and self-righteous bully, Cunningham sought to impose his religious opinions on the school. In a mood of righteous sabbatarianism, he managed to ban the Greek New Testament lessons on Sundays under Butler. He directed his friends in various Church missionary and Bible societies to pester successive Heads. Butler and Wordsworth resisted their approaches but, as Butler commented, 'Dr Longley, I believe, was more liberal, or more under *Cunningham influence*'. As with many high-minded men, he could be abjectly petty. In 1835 he tried to get the school to pay for their pews and, as part of his vendetta against those of whom he disapproved, harassed masters over the space they occupied. He liked to dominate. Few were allowed to usurp his pulpit, where a hidden high chair was placed to give the impression that, in spite of the extreme length of his sermons—three-quarters of an hour was standard—he was able to stand throughout, sustained by his fervour and mission. A social toady of extravagant proportions, he became petulant when boys with aristocratic evangelical connections, such as S. J. Gambier in the 1820s, refused to become 'one of his'.[307] Mr Slope in Trollope's *Barchester Towers* is said to have been modelled on him.

Cunningham certainly aroused as much dislike as he did reverence. Sam Parr despised him.[308] The public feud with Drury was long and bitter. Once Cunningham stopped in mid-sermon to insult Drury's nieces whom he suspected were laughing at him; thereafter every time Drury passed the vicar in the street he would shout 'brawler'.[309] Samuel Butler's opinion could have hardly been blunter. Writing to Benjamin Kennedy in 1835 after Cunningham had floated the idea of Kennedy taking the Head Mastership of Harrow, Butler's invective flowed freely:

You are in the hands of a man who professes to wish you well, and who may be your friend, but he is a known meddler and *intriguant*, and he is a man who I believe would flatter and

---

[306] His first wife died as did four daughters in one cholera outbreak. In general see *DNB* entry; Druett, *Harrow*, 194, 198–201; Hole, *Phelps*, ii. 2 on the fears at his arrival; HSR III, fos. 304–5.

[307] Thornton, *Harrow School*, 242; HM/W/G. Butler to Wordsworth, 22 June 1837; Druett, *Harrow*, 168–9; GM, 12 Mar., 15 May 1835; HM/W/Cunningham to Wordsworth, 7 May 1838, 20 Jan. 1843; Norman, *At School and at Sea*, 37; Minchin, *Old Harrow Days*, 225–8, 236.

[308] On the evidence of Samuel Butler of Shrewsbury see Butler, *Butler*, ii. 122–3.

[309] Druett, *Harrow*, 199–200; Minchin, *Old Harrow Days*, 227–8.

betray any one to serve his own views. They are plain to me. His apparent object is specious and laudable. His real one ... is to make it a school for his own evangelical clique ... I dread him for my friends and I despise him for myself.

Anthony Trollope, who knew Cunningham well, called him 'a most cringing hypocrite and a most confounded liar'.[310] Cunningham's correspondence amply confirms such verdicts. Behind a habitually silken almost oleaginous tone, he was implacable in his own rectitude and pursuit of opponents. Wordsworth's brother-in-law warned him of Cunningham's hypocrisy in 1843: 'I am sure Mr Cunningham (notwithstanding all his friendly professions) wishes personally to get rid of you and must be the object of all mistrust.'[311] Not for the last time, a nickname devised by the boys hit its target: they called him 'Old Slybacon'.[312]

Cunningham's particular disapproval and probable dislike of Wordsworth, inspired by the Head Master's churchmanship and lack of deference, prompted a concerted campaign of interference, antagonism, and treachery justified by whining specious legalism. Wordsworth was overtly High Church. Although Cunningham admired Newman's preaching (perhaps characteristically noticing style not substance), he and allies such as Phelps were increasingly alarmed after Keble's Assize Sermon of 1833 on National Apostasy at the drift of the Tractarians; Wordsworth's own interest in the early church made him sympathetic to such views.[313] In 1837, to the vicar's alarm, Wordsworth invited Keble to act as a leaving scholarship examiner.[314] Cunningham soon put it about that Wordsworth was leading the boys to Rome, which was unfair. Wordsworth was a High Churchman, a philologist, theologian, and historian of the early church, but strongly anti-papist. Ironically, he even managed to elicit from Henry Manning, long before his smooth translation to Rome, a letter in which the future cardinal condemned 'a Romanizing friend'.[315] However, his views on authority within the church were hardly to the vicar's taste, for example when Wordsworth implied that the Visitor, i.e. the archbishop of Canterbury, had precedence over the governors on matters of religious observance at the school.[316] Equally, Wordsworth failed to conceal his contempt for Cunningham. Although not as crude as Drury, who ostentatiously

---

[310] Butler, *Butler*, ii. 122–3 where Butler also accused Cunningham of deliberately trying to destroy the Society for the Promotion of Christian Knowledge 'to the great advantage of the Bible Society'; V. Glendinning, *Trollope* (London, 1992), p. 33.

[311] HM/W/FSD/G. Frere to Wordsworth, 23 June 1843.

[312] Norman, *At School and at Sea*, 37.

[313] For Cunningham's admiration of Newman's preaching at St Clement's, Oxford see Hole, *Phelps*, ii. 130, letter to J. Hunter, 16 June 1832.

[314] HM/W/12, 26 Nov. 1836; Hole, *Phelps*, ii. 130; Roundell, 'Wordsworth', 89–90 and 90 n. 1. Cf. Overton and Wordsworth, *Wordsworth*, 84.

[315] HM/W/Correspondence on restoration of school galleries in the parish church, Henry Manning to Wordsworth, 23 Sept. 1842.

[316] HM/W/Wordsworth to his father, 25 Oct. 1842; Cunningham to Wordsworth and vice versa, three letters, all 20 Jan. 1843.

yawned and groaned during sermons, the Head Master showed exactly what he thought of the inaudible monologues by whiling away the time reading his Bible—in German.[317]

From the beginning, Cunningham sought to make mischief. In October 1836 he received complaints from boys who, thinking they were to be unfairly punished, had sought his protection. The vicar claimed the right to hear appeals as 'the resident governor', insisting, with unconscious irony, his conduct 'was becoming my character as a Governor and a Gentleman' and in no way merited Wordsworth's stinging rebuke. At the same time he tried to countermand Wordsworth's ban on a home boarder going riding. Yet, in 1842, he had the gall to suggest that Wordsworth's regime of discipline and punishment was not severe enough.[318] Cunningham consistently supplied boys, parents, private tutors, and potential clients with his own often critical or misleading views on school management without any consultation with Wordsworth. The *casus belli* of this guerrilla campaign was the building of a school chapel, which was anathema to the vicar, jealous of his control over the school's religious practices and suspicious of the Head Master's. Having lost that battle, Cunningham did all he could to destroy Wordsworth, his chosen weapon being the question of the Free Scholars. In the process, the two of them almost destroyed the school.

The significance of the new chapel was summed up half a century later by one of Wordsworth's monitors, Alexander Beresford-Hope: 'with this work the old order ceased and Harrow School took its place in the general revival of Church interests'.[319] For Wordsworth, as for Arnold, a school chapel was central to his educational purpose as a place where boys could receive 'such religious instruction as is most appropriate both to their present position as members of a large school and also to their future destination as persons likely to exercise considerable influence over society at large'.[320] Services in the parish church inevitably lacked 'this particular instruction', as well as any suitable seating. In Chapel, the Head Master could inculcate religious virtue appropriate to the age and interests of his pupils and demonstrate how faith was bound up in their everyday lives. As Arnold wrote to Wordsworth when he learned of the Harrow project, a school is 'a distinct congregation' and 'the Head Master is the natural preacher to boys placed under his care . . . what he says will have . . . much more weight with them than what they hear from any one else'.[321] Wordsworth emphatically agreed. An educational institution without a chapel, a friend once delighted him by saying, was 'an angel without wings'.[322]

---

[317] Roundell, 'Wordsworth', 95.
[318] HM/W/10; HM/W/Cunningham to Wordsworth, 11 Oct. 1842.
[319] Overton and Wordsworth, *Wordsworth*, 84. There was also the more prosaic reason that the growing numbers of parishioners made the presence of the school increasingly inconvenient.
[320] HM/W/Printed Circular 'For Private Circulation Only', 11 Dec. 1837.
[321] HM/W/Arnold to Wordsworth, 31 May 1837.
[322] Overton and Wordsworth, *Wordsworth*, 217.

The Ancien Régime

The governors took some persuasion. Wordsworth had begun to raise money for his plan as soon as he took up the Head Mastership in April 1836, the enthusiasm of his correspondents being measured by their contributions: Longley gave £300; Cunningham £5, later increased to £10.[323] However, it took a year from his initial proposal to the governors in May 1836 before they agreed in principle. In June 1836 and again in February 1837, under the influence of Cunningham, they had procrastinated, Wordsworth's letter of November 1836 not even being considered until three months later when a response was postponed indefinitely.[324] Cunningham himself employed Fabian tactics. He first tried binding Wordsworth to the parish church by offering him a share in administering Holy Communion, as he insultingly put it, 'to remind the Master of the necessity of religion as well as learning . . . and to unite the school with the parish, as all members of one great family'. Next, to avoid the expense of a new building, he suggested the archbishop of Canterbury be asked to license the Speech Room for occasional divine worship. He argued strongly, against Arnold's advice and central belief, that the Head Master should not act as chaplain.[325] Wordsworth was unmoved, showing skill in marshalling strong political support, including Archbishop Howley of Canterbury, Bishop Blomfield of London, Sir Robert Peel, Bishop Longley, and George Butler.[326] At the special meeting in May 1837 to consider the plan, Cunningham, having made his views plain, left the room while the rest of the governors reached their decision. They agreed to the scheme on condition that control of the chapel would rest with them and on Wordsworth producing satisfactory details of funding and management.[327]

Cunningham did not give in. He refused to help raise the money and persisted in sniping at the project, as late as the laying of the foundation stone 'with due masonic precision' by Lord Aberdeen on 4 July 1838, commenting 'I cannot contemplate the event without a measure of anxiety for the future'.[328] He resurrected the matter of charging the school and masters for the use of the pews in the parish church, complained about the boys' behaviour in church, and attempted to block any innovations in Chapel services.[329] Wordsworth, however, displayed unexpected flexibility. Although insisting on acting as chaplain, an arrangement that

---

[323] HM/L/Wordsworth to Longley, 4 May 1836; HM/W/Chapel Account, total £2,704, includes both Longley's and Cunningham's donations; HM/W/4; HM/W/Cunningham to Wordsworth, 30 Apr. 1836, no date 1837.

[324] GM, 27 June 1836, 1 Feb. 1837; HM/W/12 Memorandum, 26 Nov. 1836; Laborde, *Harrow School*, 92.

[325] HM/W/Cunningham to Wordsworth, 30 Apr. 1836 and undated 1836.

[326] HM/W/18; HM/W/Wordsworth to Peel, 27 Nov. 1838.

[327] GM, 22 May 1837; HM/W/Cunningham to Wordsworth, 22 or 23 May 1837; HM/W/ 18, 20, 24 for the subsequent planning.

[328] HM/W/Cunningham to Wordsworth, 2 May 1838; Howson and Townsend Warner, *Harrow School*, 141. Cf. ibid., 103–4.

[329] HM/W/Cunningham to Wordsworth, 7 May 1838; 11 Oct. 1842, 20 Jan. 1843 (2 letters).

persisted for sixty years, he agreed the link with the parish should remain. The school would continue to attend St Mary's for Matins on Sunday, but assemble in chapel for Evensong. In fact, this was a smoke screen. Wordsworth showed little intention of allowing the governors—lay or clerical—to influence his conduct of the chapel, pre-empting their interference by obtaining the archbishop's sanction for Chapel celebration of certain Saints' Days, the institution of a Founder's Day ceremony, a termly Sacrament Sunday, communion for all confirmed boys, and catechism at the regular Sunday afternoon services. All these were vigorously, but unavailingly, opposed by the vicar.[330]

The chapel itself, designed by C. R. Cockerell, the architect of the 1820 Old Schools, was, by all accounts, hideous and inconvenient. Built on land given by George Butler, it cost £3,847 12s. 9d., all raised by subscription, and was finally consecrated on 24 September 1839.[331] For all its physical limitations, it provided Wordsworth with his chosen setting to pursue his educational ideals. Opposition was not restricted to governors or parents. Boys, out of innate conservatism and philistinism as much as religious conviction, were suspicious of the change, bored by the Head Master's verbose intensity, and hostile to his innovations. When he thought he had persuaded the Fourth Form to join his wife in singing a hymn, they and the rest of the school sat staring silently while the unfortunate lady performed an impromptu solo. Even getting boys to respond audibly during prayers took five years and was made easier by there being by then so few of them. None the less, despite all the doubts and disadvantages, 'the spirit of the thing was there' and no Head Master for another 150 years would hesitate in naming Chapel as the centre of the school.[332]

Dissent within the staff; idiosyncratic imposition of discipline; indifference to hostile press and public opinion; religious controversy; deliberate provocation of the influential evangelical party; disapproval by Oxford University of the introduction of maths into the formal curriculum; the loss of the largest and cheapest boarding house; national economic difficulties; competition from new public schools; the greater accessibility of existing rural schools because of the railways: to this catalogue of problems both self-inflicted and unavoidable was added the most dangerous of all, a bitter, open, protracted dispute between the Head Master and the governing body over the admission of Free Scholars.

The problem of the Free Scholars had changed since 1810. Then it had been a question of there being too few; by the late 1830s it had become one of the prospect of there being too many. Before the problem had been parishioners being of a social and economic standing below that which desired a classical education; now wealthy incomers were enthusiastically claiming the privileges once designed for

---

[330] HM/W/Wordsworth to his father, 25 Oct. 1842.
[331] Laborde, *Harrow School*, 92; HM/W/24; HM/W/Cockerell to G. Butler 27 June 1838 with appended groundplan: printed Laborde, *Harrow School*, 94.
[332] Roundell, 'Wordsworth', 99; Overton and Wordsworth, *Wordsworth*, 84, 108.

the poor. Unlike at Rugby, no formal financial provision was made by the governors to pay for the tuition of Free Scholars; they received a high-class education without charge. Thus there were two issues that came to be in dispute. Should Lyon's benefaction be enjoyed by those who could easily afford to pay the fees instead of being reserved for the needy and should the governors actually support Lyon's benefaction with money as well as goodwill? With the decline in the number of foreigners, both issues increased in significance, particularly for a Head Master with moral scruples whose income, after losing his boarders in 1838, was wholly dependent on schooling fees. Unlike in 1810 or under Dr Vaughan, when disputes revolved around the nature of the education required by most parishioners, the core of contention in the 1830s and 1840s was fees and the consequent eligibility for exemption. Bound up with the central points in dispute were the authority of the Head Master in relation to the governors and the nature of the school.

As in 1810 the governors took their stand on a literal interpretation of the statutes combined with an insistence on the immutablity of subsequent wholly unLyonian changes. It was this awkward, not to say contradictory stance that persuaded so many Hergaphiles, including Percy Thornton, to pretend that Lyon not only would have approved of an academy of the rich and privileged but actually envisaged it. Counsel's opinion delivered in favour of the governors in May 1843 by Thomas Pemberton Leigh went so far as to suggest, on no evidence whatever, that the influx of such wealthy foreigners was a benefit to the parish 'which the founder may be held to have had in his contemplation'. He was merely following the lead given by the case presented to him by the governors in which they admitted to a desire to 'encourage' the admission of the sons of the local 'respectable and wealthy' in order to maintain the school's 'present celebrity'.[333] In their world view, the rights and interests of the poor or the intentions of the Elizabethan benefactor scarcely merited notice.

At the height of the crisis, in August 1843, Cunningham made his and the governors' attitude plain in a letter to Lord Northwick:

It is especially ... from your Lordship and from myself that the guardianship of the rights of the Inhabitants of the Parish is to be expected. To them the decision that the class of persons to whom Dr Wordsworth objects should not be admitted would be little short of *ruin*—and such would be the case with regard to *property* in general.[334]

The High Tory Wordsworth may appear an unlikely revolutionary, but his attack on the exploitation of the Lyon benefaction by the rich under the banner of upholding the rights of the poor may have touched a domestic as well as political nerve. One of Cunningham's own sons had been a Home Boarder under Butler and another was due to go the Harrow in 1845.

[333] HM/W/FSD Counsel's Opinion for the Governors, 4 May 1843 and Case, a copy of which was sent to Wordsworth, 5 June 1843, cf. GM, 3 June 1843.
[334] HM/W/FSD/Cunningham to Lord Northwick, 4 Aug. 1843.

According to George Butler, he, his predecessor, and Henry Drury had all taught Foundationers for nothing both in school and in their pupil-rooms regardless of their ability to pay. They had thought it their duty and, in any case, many were the sons of masters.[335] With the growth of suburban development on the Hill from the early nineteenth century, free schooling became a lure. In 1830 one lease on the Hill was offered at a higher rent to those bringing children to be educated at Harrow explicitly because of the expected fee exemption. Advertisements for houses to let mentioned the prospect of free public school education. The arrival of the railway in 1837 accelerated this trend. In 1838 Cockerell proposed to George Butler a speculative housing development scheme for the land next to the new chapel 'suited to persons desiring residence during the education of their sons at Harrow ... as I am assured such houses are in great demand at Harrow and the rail road will greatly increase it'.[336] By the Summer of 1839, in a school of 160, there were twenty-six Home Boarders, double the number at the beginning of the decade. In Wordsworth's last five years, 1839–44, the proportion of Home Boarders admitted rose from 10 per cent to 30 per cent.[337]

Longley, in March 1830, complained to the governors about the unrestricted admission of the sons of these carpetbaggers. He wanted 'all those who take houses in Harrow obviously for the sole purpose of sending their sons to the school' to pay fees. Free education of the sons of these incomers neither followed the intentions of the Founder nor benefited the school. Large numbers of Home Boarders, he argued, presented discipline problems. In any case, fees would not deter them. He proposed a test of eligibility. All freeholders and copyholders would be entitled to a claim to free education, subject to the traditional procedures of acceptance by Head Master and governors, but only those who rented their properties if they had been 'naturalized as it were by a residence of five years'. The governors avoided the central issue by allowing Longley a discretionary payment per Foundationer. This was not continued for his successor who only learnt of the arrangement in 1843, long after battle had been joined.[338]

The first shots were fired in January 1837, when, in response to his enquiry, Cunningham informed Wordsworth of the tradition that the resident governor, previously Lord Northwick now himself, examined potential Free Scholars 'when called upon'. Wordsworth was presumably concerned when he heard that, in addition to his own examination, three candidates had seen Cunningham as well, especially as the vicar had also been spreading the idea that private tuition was unnecessary and

---

[335] HM/W/FSD/G. Butler to Wordsworth, 18 Aug. 1843.
[336] HM/L/Memorandum to Governors, 10 Mar. 1830, part 3; HM/W/Cockerell to Butler, 20 Aug. 1838.
[337] *Harrow Register, 1800–1911*, 125, *et seq.*, 170–81; Hole, *Phelps*, ii. 139; HSR III, fo. 393 (22 June 1830).
[338] HM/L/Memorandum, 10 Mar. 1830; HSR III, fo. 390; HM/W/FSD/Wordsworth to H. Young (Governors' Clerk), 17 June 1843.

not compulsory at Harrow, when de facto it palpably was. The vicar assured Wordsworth that the object of the gubernatorial scrutiny was to weed out 'improper persons'.[339] There the matter rested. The trickle of Free Scholars continued unremarked.

In the autumn of 1841 Thomas Sanctuary, a former High Sheriff of Sussex, moved to Harrow to claim a free place for his son. His application provoked Wordsworth to demand a judgement from the governors as his understanding of the statutes led him to consider Sanctuary 'not a fit object of the Founder's charity'. In line with his predecessors, Wordsworth was concerned with his authority, arguing that no Free Scholar could be admitted by the governors without the Head's prior approval. Citing the contrast with Rugby (he had extracted the relevant information from Arnold specially), Wordsworth argued that as Harrow masters were not paid for teaching Foundationers, if more came the Head Master would likely be ruined and certainly earn less than his assistants who, unlike him, could charge for private pupils and take in boarders. Although Sanctuary backed away from a fight by withdrawing his claim (albeit temporarily), the governors ruled in February 1842 that all parishioners possessed the rights laid down by the statutes.[340] This did not satisfy Wordsworth. He remained convinced that their interpretation did violence to Lyon's intention to reserve his charity for the poor of the parish and, more importantly, constituted an attack on his livelihood.

Open warfare erupted early in 1843 when Wordsworth rejected the claims of two parents (B. Williams of Byron House, Harrow and H. C. Vernon, primarily of Hilton Park, Stafford) to free education for their sons.[341] The financial implications were tiny, a matter of 15 guineas a year each, those of the principle considerable. Wordsworth refused to accept the governors restatement of their interpretation of the statutes and a new procedure for the admission of Free Scholars. Both sides consulted lawyers. After the governors received counsel's opinion in May favourable to their case, Wordsworth clarified his position in two unrepentant, unequivocal memorials.[342] He refused to admit a Free Scholar who was not 'poor . . . upon a fair and liberal interpretation of the word', believing he was 'following the design of the Founder'. If, however, this were ignored, there must be a limit to the numbers admitted and remuneration from the trust for their schooling. While the trust income had risen twelve times since the foundation of the school, the original stipend of £30 designed to cover the teaching of the Free Scholars had stayed the same.

A blizzard of letters between Wordsworth and the governors in June 1843 failed to break the deadlock, even after the Williams and Vernon boys were formally elected

---

[339] HM/W/13.

[340] HM/W/Wordsworth to Lord Northwick, 22, 28 Sept. 1841; GM, 21 Feb. 1842.

[341] The bulky and exhaustive correspondence, memoranda, and legal opinions from 1 May 1843 to 6 June 1844 are collected in HM/W/FSD.

[342] HM/W/FSD/Wordsworth's Memorials, 13 May and 17 June 1843.

to Free Scholarships and the Head instructed to admit them as such.[343] Wordsworth's legal adviser, his brother-in-law George Frere, although suggesting resignation would be preferable to a long fight and ultimate surrender, persuaded Wordsworth to shift his ground from the high moral argument about Lyon's intentions and the rights of the poor—which legal opinion had consistently rejected—to one of finance.[344] It must have surprised Mr Williams to be told by Wordsworth on 27 June 'I should be very happy to see the benefits of Free Instruction extended as widely as possible to the inhabitants of Harrow', provided he were remunerated appropriately.[345]

Only after the Attorney-General ruled that admission as Foundationers was the right of all inhabitants, the Head Master's consent advisory, and his persistent refusal could constitute grounds for dismissal under the Statutes did Wordsworth surrender, on 17 August agreeing to the admission as Foundationers of Williams and Vernon.[346] By now the governors were not in magnanimous mood. Breaking their own stated procedures they tested Wordsworth's resolve and loyalty by electing nine new Free Scholars between September 1843 and June 1844, ignoring his protests about his consequent financial loss. With the school trust's balance varying between £165 in 1842, almost £500 in 1843, and £345 in 1844, they declined to act on the Head Master's stipend, instead scoring cheap points by declaring disingenuously that it was not obligatory for a Free Scholar to employ a private tutor, one of Cunningham's pet causes.[347]

On 22 February, the governors moved in for the kill. The school's crisis had provoked 'strong and repeated appeals . . . by some of its oldest and warmest friends'. Turning the Head Master's persistent attempts to extract an increased stipend against him, they expressed regret at the reduced numbers that were the cause of his decline in income 'and wished to express their anxiety to receive from him any explanation of its cause'. More ominously they added that they believed 'some material change in [the school's] system would be requisite to create any considerable return of its former prosperity'.[348] Ignoring the implied threat, Wordsworth's reply took the form of an apologia. He insisted the decline in numbers was not due to a lack of industry in masters or boys, still less to the system of education, religious, moral, and literary. Recent changes, Wordsworth declared, had actually improved the school 'as a seminary of sound learning and religious education'. That fewer than eighty boys were benefiting seemed not to have dented the Head

---

[343] In the file there are twenty-seven documents from 22 May to 2 July; alone, the day after the Governors' meeting of 21 June elicited an exchange of four.

[344] HM/W/FSD/G. Frere to Wordsworth, esp. 23 June, 12, and 16 July 1843.

[345] HM/W/FSD/Wordsworth to B. Williams, 27 June 1843.

[346] HM/W/FSD/Attorney-General's Opinion, 5 Aug. 1843; R. Palmer (Wordsworth's lawyer), 15 Aug. 1843; Wordsworth to G. Butler, 16 Aug and Butler's reply, 18 Aug. 1843; Wordsworth's surrender to Young and Aberdeen (separate letters), 17 Aug. 1843; GM, 8 Aug. 1843. Cf. GM, 9, 14, 27 Mar., 21, 27 June 1843.

[347] HM/W/FSD/Correspondence from 18 Sept. 1843; GM, 30 June 1842; 22 June 1843; 22 Feb., 6, 20 June 1844. [348] GM, 22 Feb. 1844.

Master's equanimity. The true causes of the school's difficulties were the general economic malaise that had afflicted other, richer establishments, but had hit Harrow harder because of its limited endowment, poor financial management, and an inability to attract donations. More particular causes included competition from newer, cheaper public schools, the loss of the largest, cheapest boarding house with the consequent dependence on three expensive ones (Shilleto had shut the Grove), the imposition of strict discipline which 'does not always gain goodwill and support at the time when it is applied', and, finally, the dispute between the Head Master and the governors which had undermined confidence in the school.[349]

Wordsworth's critique was remarkably fair. Yet, apart from the rebuilding of the boys' side of the Head Master's, he offered no suggestions as to how to reverse the disintegration of the school and his description of its health was fantasy. His unrepentant attitude was both obtuse and provocative, the result of shattered nerves. He was living in a cocoon of anger and self-righteousness. In a peculiarly graphic image, George Frere had warned him of the dangers of confrontation: 'the beginning of Strife is as when one letteth out water—therefore leave off Contention before it be meddled with.'[350] Wordsworth had ignored the advice and was swept away.

The governors were left with no alternative. After a meeting on 6 June they asked Wordsworth to resign in language that bore no prospect of misinterpretation:

so strong a feeling has taken possession of the public mind as to leave them no hope of the Restoration of the School, either by the cooperation of those attached to it, or from any other source without a complete change in the administration. It is under this conviction, and not from any disrespect to yourself, or forgetfulness of your many high attainments, that they feel themselves called upon by a sense of Duty, to suggest to you the propriety of your tendering the Resignation of your Office of Head Master... They beg you to believe that they have not made this suggestion without much pain to themselves, but the obligation to make it appears to them imperative when no other means present themselves of averting the probable Dissolution of the School.[351]

Unequivocal though this was, Wordsworth refused to comply immediately. Not only had his health suffered, his finances were wrecked. Unlike his predecessors, Wordsworth had 'derived no emolument from my office... beyond the mere maintenance of myself and family'.[352] In February 1843 he had failed in his efforts to become Regius Professor of Divinity in Cambridge, his desire to leave Harrow for a university chair being acidly hurled in his face by the governors.[353] It was clear

---

[349] HM/W/FSD/Wordsworth to Governors, 16 Mar. 1844.
[350] HM/W/FSD/G. Frere to Wordsworth, 23 June 1843.
[351] HM/W/FSD/Young to Wordsworth, after GM, 6 June 1844.
[352] HM/W/FSD/Wordsworth to Aberdeen, 17 Aug. 1843.
[353] Overton and Wordsworth, *Wordsworth*, 101; his health was suffering even then. Cf. V. Strudwick, *Christopher Wordsworth, bishop of Lincoln, 1869–85* (Lincoln, 1987), p. 4; in the letter proposing resignation Young referred to Wordsworth's professorial applications as evidence of Wordsworth's agreement on 'the expediency of some such measure'.

he would only leave if suitable alternative empoyment was found. As was to happen eighty years later, a loyal Old Harrovian Prime Minister came to the rescue. Peel had offered Wordsworth's father, now retired from the Mastership of Trinity, a canonry at Westminster. The elder Wordsworth and Archbishop Howley, Harrow's Visitor, persuaded Peel instead to install Christopher Wordsworth. On appointment to Westminster, the Head Master resigned on 21 October 1844. As his successor but two, J. E. C. Welldon, explained, 'fortunately Sir Robert Peel loved Harrow more than he hated Wordsworth—so he gave him with a sore heart a Canonry at Westminster and saved Harrow from extinction'.[354]

Wordsworth had been a disaster for Harrow. He had contributed much to his own failure, notably his eagerness to divest himself of boarders, his insensitivity to public opinion and private interest, and his obsessive obstinacy over Free Scholars. Others also played full parts, not least the governors whose financial management and administrative decisions were as culpable as the Head Master's. Cunningham's vendetta might have been handled more skilfully by a flexible or experienced Head, but Wordsworth, still only 37 when he resigned, was as full of his own moral certainty as the vicar yet lacked his adversary's malign deviousness. Intriguingly, all they had in common was that, at different times, they both frequented Dr Jephson's sanitorium for nervous illnesses in Leamington.[355] Economic, fashionable, and religious circumstances increased the risks involved in Wordsworth's reforms. Yet the introduction of maths and the building of the chapel were lasting achievements. Wordsworth's successes showed that change was possible; his failures that it was essential.

[354] Overton and Wordsworth, *Wordsworth*, 107–8; HM/W/FSD/Wordsworth to Governors, 21 Oct. 1844; GM, 5 Nov. 1844; Strudwick, *Wordsworth*, 5; the parallel is with Baldwin's dispatch of Lionel Ford to the deanery of York in 1925.

[355] Cunningham in 1830; Wordsworth after leaving Harrow at the end of 1844; Hole, *Phelps*, ii. 79; Overton and Wordsworth, *Wordsworth*, 105.

Part IV

Plenitude, 1844–1914

11

CHARLES JOHN VAUGHAN, 1845–1859

On 22 January 1845 the Easter Term began at Harrow under a new Head Master, a 28-year-old clerygman and former Cambridge don with no previous experience of being a schoolmaster. The school he inherited was close to extinction; the few remaining boys so riotous and vicious that the new Head was advised to sack the lot of them and begin again.[1] Fifteen years later, the same Head retired to national regret and applause having re-established Harrow, now boasting its longest roll ever, with sure foundations at the forefront of the esteem of the Victorian Establishment, an eminence on which the school basked for the next three generations.

The scale of the achievement of Charles Vaughan has never been doubted. For his favourite pupil and successor, Montagu Butler, he was 'almost the refounder of Harrow'. Another pupil, Charles Dalrymple, scanning the half century after Vaughan's arrival, called him 'the restorer of Harrow . . . he recreated the school'. James Welldon, his successor but one, wrote in 1915 that 'the Harrow of today is, in its essential features and characteristics, still his Harrow'. In 1945 yet another occupant of his chair, Ralph Moore, concluded: 'This was the greatest Head Master Harrow has had'.[2]

The gratitude and sentimentality might well have amused Vaughan who once confided to Welldon that 'the worship of Harrow among certain Harrovians had perhaps been a little overstrained', a remark that neatly captures one of his qualities that so disturbed his contemporary admirers.[3] Vaughan's lack of exaggeration or overt enthusiasm, his sense of the ridiculous, cool, some thought cold, reserve of manner, and barely contained irony and sarcasm made him an awkward mid-Victorian hero. He was also well aware of what he owed to Wordsworth, especially the chapel; and he soon found himself fighting—with more success—many of his predecessor's battles, over Free Scholars, the governors' commitment to the poorer

---

[1] By the vicar: Roundell, 'Wordsworth', 102–3.
[2] Graham, *Butler*, 30; Dalrymple, 'Dr. Vaughan', Howson and Townsend Warner, *Harrow School*, 113; Welldon, *Recollections*, 110; R. W. Moore, *Charles John Vaughan Centenary Address* (Harrow, 1945), p. 1. [3] Welldon, *Recollections*, 85.

locals, and the vicar. In the essentials of administration and the curriculum, Vaughan was hardly an innovator. His subsequent reputation was heavily influenced by the need of almost all nineteenth-century public schools to have heroic Head Masters. Vaughan's crisis of numbers was not unique. In 1841 Westminster contained just sixty-seven boys; Repton in 1854, when S. A. Pears arrived from Harrow, contained fifty, itself a considerable advance on the single pupil of some years earlier; at Uppingham in 1853 Thring found twenty-eight.[4] Vaughan inherited a system of financing the masters through large and small boarding houses that potentially allowed for rapid growth and big, quick profits. None the less, it is hard to diminish the substance of Vaughan's achievement. When he left, in December 1859, instead of sixty-nine there were 438 Harrovians: no subsequent Head managed such a relative improvement. With the numbers came new facilities: boarding houses; formrooms; a rebuilt chapel; extended playing fields; a new, confident *esprit de corp*; an enhanced public reputation, with grand public figures now eager to associate themselves with the school by accepting invitations to visit; and a newly extensive network of grateful old boys and parents.

If perceptions of the extent of Vaughan's public achievements at Harrow can now be more realistic and less roseate, the view of his general conduct and personality was radically changed by the publication in 1964 of references to and in 1984 of the complete *Memoirs* of John Addington Symonds (1840–93), Victorian writer, pioneering art historian, self-confessed homosexual, and Old Harrovian (Rendalls 1854–8). Written after 1889, these paint a startlingly vivid picture of Harrovian lowlife in the 1850s and, sensationally, tell the story of how Vaughan himself was blackmailed into resigning as Head Master of Harrow in 1859 because of his sexual advances to one of his monitors.[5]

Charles Vaughan was born in 1816, the son of the vicar of St Martin's, Leicester. His family was prominent in what Noel Annan described as the 'Intellectual Aristocracy' characteristic of the nineteenth century: prosperous, clever, well-educated, inter-married, mutually helpful and successful in church, school, and university. A first cousin was H. H. Vaughan, Regius Professor of History at Oxford, whose son, W. W. Vaughan, became Head Master in turn of Giggleswick, Wellington, and Rugby (and who married one of J. A. Symonds' daughters). T. H. Green, the Oxford philosopher, was one of Vaughan's nephews (and he married Symonds' sister). A younger brother, Edwin Vaughan, was brought onto the Harrow staff in 1849.[6]

[4] J. Gathorne-Hardy, *The Public School Phenomenon* (London, 1977), pp. 94–5; Thornton, *Harrow School*, 251; *Clarendon Commission Report*, i. 6.

[5] P. Grosskurth, *John Addington Symonds* (London, 1964), esp. pp. 30–41; id. (ed.), *The Memoirs of John Addington Symonds* (London, 1984), esp. pp. 84–121.

[6] *DNB* entry by C. E. Vaughan; N. Annan, 'The Intellectual Aristocracy', in *Studies in Social History: A Tribute to G. M. Trevelyan*, ed. J. H. Plumb (London, 1955), pp. 280–1.

In 1829, the year of his father's death, Vaughan was sent to Rugby, a move which shaped his life by introducing him to the forceful Thomas Arnold. Nicknamed 'Monstrous Cute', apparently an allusion to his cleverness, Vaughan soon became one of Arnold's favourite pupils, an acolyte through whom Christian morality was dispersed through the school.[7] Vaughan represented to the highest degree Arnold's ideal of intellectual facility harnessed to intense, evangelical moral earnestness. Even beyond the grave, Arnold's patronage, which was reciprocated with adoration, proved crucial in Vaughan's career.

From Rugby, Vaughan went, like his predecessor and successor at Harrow, to Trinity College, Cambridge where he graduated in 1838 as Chancellor's Medallist and Senior Classic, a distinction won by four successive Head Masters: Wordsworth, Vaughan, Butler, and Welldon. Elected a fellow of Trinity in 1839, Vaughan began to read for the Bar but, in 1841, changed course to be ordained, accepting the family living in Leicester. In 1842, on Arnold's early death, he stood as a candidate for the Head Mastership of Rugby. He was unsuccessful by the narrowest of margins, the post going to A. C. Tait, a future archbishop of Canterbury.[8] In 1844, when Wordsworth resigned, Vaughan, after visiting the Hill and sensing an opportunity to effect work of which his mentor would have been proud, applied for the Headship although advised by Dean Turton of Peterborough not to throw himself away on the place.[9]

The election of Vaughan was dominated by ecclesiastical and educational politics. There were thirteen candidates, including T. W. Peile, the rather indifferent Head Master of Repton (defeated in the 1836 election); C. T. Penrose, another Rugby and Trinity man, also a candidate at his old school in 1842 and from 1845 an ineffectual Head Master of Sherborne (his one innovation in five years there being Rugby football); A. Phillips, principal of Cheltenham College; the mathematician and historian N. Pocock, fellow of Queen's, Oxford; and J. Chapman, a prominent evangelical master at Eton and future bishop of Calcutta. They possessed very similar qualifications. All could have subscribed to Chapman's declaration: 'Education I believe to be the great hope, as well as the great work of our day.'[10]

However, Vaughan garnered powerful backing. Lord Aberdeen favoured him after being told by a governor of Rugby that Vaughan had missed election at Rugby solely because of the perceived awkwardness of there being three members of staff who had taught him. Cunningham's vote was eagerly solicited by all candidates. Initially leaning towards the stoutly evangelical Chapman, he was bombarded by private letters in support of Vaughan from his referees. In the end Cunningham acted as a whip for Vaughan, gathering in the vote of Lord Northwick by arguing

---

[7] Chandos, *Boys Together*, 304.

[8] HM/1844/Cunningham to Lord Northwick, 9 Dec. 1844.

[9] Thornton, *Harrow School*, 287.

[10] HM/1844/Chapman to Lord Northwick, Dec. 1844. For the testimonials and other correspondence on the election see HM/1844, *passim*.

that Vaughan 'would raise the school to a state of high distinction as to character and scholarship'.[11]

Although Vaughan elicited the public support of a wide range of impressive referees, including Bishop Davys of Peterborough, Dean Peacock of Ely, and his cousin Professor Vaughan, more potent was his acknowledged position as Arnold's torchbearer, confirmed by testimonials from Arnold's widow; his biographer, Vaughan's close school friend and future brother-in-law, A. P. Stanley; G. E. L. Cotton, a Rugby housemaster, future Master of Marlborough, the 'Young Master' in Thomas Hughes's *Tom Brown's Schooldays*; and even from Arnold himself from beyond the grave in a letter offering Vaughan a post at Rugby in 1840. All stressed Vaughan's intimacy with Arnold and understanding of his ideas. They presented Vaughan as the candidate of the reforming establishment as a whole, although in fact he represented only the Arnoldian tendency within that establishment. W. C. Lake, another of Vaughan's intimates at Rugby and a fellow of Balliol, spoke for many of this party: 'I know of scarcely any one to whom those who themselves are interested in the work of Education would be so thankful to see Harrow entrusted as to Mr Vaughan' who would make his pupils 'good as well as learned men', the touchstone of Arnoldian correctness. Vaughan was a scholar, in the lights of the time, described revealingly by another supporter, W. H. Thompson of Trinity, as possessing 'literary taste of unsurpassed purity and elegance'. However, it was not learning as such that mattered. Vaughan himself set out his manifesto unequivocally in his letter of application. He promised to devote himself 'earnestly to the furtherance of the great work of Christian Education', continuing, 'I cannot forget that however arduous the task set before me, I should always have one firm ground of encouragement and hope (the possession of which, I am well aware, must be my principal recommendation . . .) in my affectionate and lively recollections of the example and instructions of Dr. Arnold.'[12]

This explicit association with Arnold was not some introverted donnish ploy. Non-Arnoldians, like Wordsworth, were as earnest in their efforts in the cause of godliness and good learning. Yet the Harrow election occured at the early peak of Arnold mania which was to sweep across public schools in the following decades. A few months before the Harrow election, Stanley's biography of Arnold appeared. In it, Arnold, in real life a somewhat narrow-minded, arrogant, bad-tempered bully, who suffered many failures of administration and popularity at Rugby where he spent much time plotting an escape to a university chair (which he obtained in plurality in 1841) and whose only real virtue was that he took schoolteaching, moral training, and his pupils seriously, was transformed into a modern hero, a champion of Christian progress against the insidious vices of idleness, ungodliness, and democracy. This was the man who could save the schools—and religion—of the

---

[11] HM/1844/Cunningham to Lord Northwick, 9 Dec. 1844; Thornton, *Harrow School*, 287.
[12] HM/1844/C. J. Vaughan Printed Testimonials, 4 Dec. 1844.

aristocracy from the taunts and outrage of the middle class. Arnold and his disciples stood for reform; they also openly and unapologetically promoted a continuance of social elitism expressed most fundamentally in the classical curriculum which they defended as stoutly, if more ingeniously, as the most diehard reactionary. Governors were offered a coherent system of education justifiable academically and morally in a way that 'unreformed' schools could not be, through the written authority of the *Life* of Arnold and the articles, sermons, speeches, and pamphlets of his followers. Stanley's biography was immediately popular, not least with the few remaining Sixth Formers at Harrow.[13] Few readers could have missed the great man's approval of his star pupil, Charles Vaughan. Whether or not they too had been swept up in the Arnold worship, the governors of Harrow unanimously elected Vaughan Head Master on 18 December.[14]

CHANGE

Vaughan's Head Mastership is incomprehensible without Arnold and his principles. These, as understood and operated by Vaughan, comprised an assertion of the Head Master's independent and absolute authority over routine, discipline, and academic syllabus; a curriculum which was essentially traditional and classical, a formation of habits of learning and a patina of erudition rather than an acquisition of useful knowledge; an emphasis on the school as a community, specifically a Christian community, within which assistant masters played a pastoral as well as academic role; and a policy of delegation of power over the discipline of boys to senior pupils, the monitors, under the control of the Head Master. All authority derived from the Head whose position in the school was further defined by his acting as chaplain. The pulpit was the centre of the Head Master's influence; Vaughan reckoned to preach every Sunday of term at Evensong. There was fostered the cult of godliness, not as an abstraction but as a series of practical responses to school life. Central to this was prayer (Vaughan urging his pupils to pray to God on their knees every night before bed); submission to the word of God as expressed in Scripture (and interpreted by the Head Master); and the encouragement of the strength of character needed to follow Christian precepts despite the ridicule of friends and temptations of adolescence.[15]

Neither Arnold nor Vaughan confused godliness with athletic manliness. Their concerns were moral and spiritual. Muscular Christianity was an invention of the next generation. Arnold rather disapproved of hearties and Vaughan regularly teased and mocked the school for their sporting, particularly cricketing obsessions, although he was pleased when his house did well at games and it did his reputation

---

[13] Roundell, 'Wordsworth', 106–7.   [14] GM, 18 Dec. 1844.
[15] For Arnold and Arnoldism see Newsome, *Godliness*, 1–91; Honey, *Tom Brown's Universe*, 1–46.

no harm when there was a run of victories over Eton in the 1850s. His prorities were unequivocal: 'the soul stands first, far first . . . next to it comes the mind . . . third and last comes the body . . . essentially inferior . . . in proportion as man himself is superior to the beasts that perish.'[16] At Harrow, games, both compulsory and casual, had been pervasive and popular for at least two generations before Vaughan arrived, but the cult of games as a disciplinary and moral force came with Montagu Butler and E. E. Bowen after 1860. In Vaughan's day, 'exercise' meant 'prep.'; sport he usually called 'excitement'.[17]

When Vaughan took up the Head Mastership, Harrow had nowhere else to go but up or out. The drama and chaos of Wordsworth's last years had left demoralization as well as desolation. Discipline and academic study were, beyond the Sixth Form, minimal, the school excelling only at cricket, although the victories over Eton in 1843 and 1844 may say something about a continuing, if attenuated, corporate spirit. The motley crew of assistant masters were all facing financial ruin. Physically, the school was a wreck. Twenty years later, G. F. Harris described the form rooms as 'infamous . . . not fit for any gentlemen's sons to be in'.[18] The sanitation was appalling. There were five waterless privies, which were soon recognized as a health hazard. No boys' house had bathrooms or even bathtubs. There was no sanitorium.[19] The boys' side of the Head Master's still lay in ruins; the Grove was untenanted, the few boarders being scattered in Moretons, Druries, the Park, and a few private houses. Surrounding a depressed school was a depressed village, the school being a major landowner, employer, and customer. The few boys left failed to pay their debts, a fact exploited by a local shark, Joseph Page.[20] Resentment on the part of the wealthier tradesmen and farmers at what they saw as the continuing abuse of the Lyon charity simmered only barely below the surface. Even the well-to-do gentry found their victory over Wordsworth empty. In such a remnant of a school, what was the free education worth?

Yet the gloom was neither total nor unique. The early forties were nationally a period of economic depression, agricultural slump, and financial instability. Small numbers were mirrored elsewhere. Compared to Winchester, Westminster, and Shrewsbury, the targets Harrow had set for itself, of 200 to 250, were expansive. Throughout the first half of the nineteenth century, of the leading public schools, only Rugby compared to Harrow in numerical pretensions, Eton, of course, being a universe of its own. Wordsworth had established at least a blueprint for renewal: Chapel; regulated fagging; codified punishments; ordered house and school religious observances; the definition of monitorial power; regular Masters'

---

[16] C. J. Vaughan, *Harrow Sermons* (London, 1853), pp. 267, 269; id., *Memorials of Harrow Sundays* (London, 1863), pp. 80, 193.

[17] Vaughan, *Memorials*, 191, 193, 361.   [18] *Clarendon Commission Report*, iv. 202.

[19] Ibid. and pp. 154–230 for the detailed evidence of school conditions. For sanitation problems see GM, 25 Nov. 1847, 10 Mar., 14 June 1853, 3 Feb. 1854.

[20] Graham, *Butler*, 28.

meetings; a credible examination system; magisterial supervision of cricket matches at which alcohol was banned; a wider curriculum to include serious mathematics; the continuance of the system of profit through boarding fees for all masters; even the institution of Founder's Day which recognized and encouraged the cult of the Old Boy which was to prove so vital in funding Harrow's physical expansion over the next century and a half. Less tangibly, Harrow possessed one essential ingredient for survival. Despite its rapid decline, it was still regarded as a great school. It attracted thirteen candidates, some of genuine ability and distinction, to become its head in 1844, their referees falling over themselves to stress the need 'to restore its ancient reputation'.[21] This fame and position cannot have been unaffected by its distinguished old boys. In 1845, the Prime Minister, Peel, was an Old Harrovian. Between August 1827 and October 1865 there were only three brief periods of a few months (January–June 1828, December 1851–December 1852, and February 1858–June 1859) when an Old Harrovian was not either Prime Minister or Foreign Secretary: Goderich, Aberdeen, Palmerston, Peel, the legacy of Joseph Drury.

More generally, the position of Harrow in the consciousness of the Establishment remained secure however low its current reputation. Although still heavily linked to the capacity and perception of the Head Master, unlike in 1746, the last similar crisis, the school's fame now possessed independent life. It is a striking feature of English public schools that, despite all social and economic vicissitudes, those identified as pre-eminent at any given time retained their unofficial status over centuries. The collegiate schools of Eton and Winchester were and are protected by property. Yet, elsewhere, once secured, prominence, whenever gained, almost guaranteed survival: Westminster, Charterhouse, Harrow, Shrewsbury, and Rugby. These, with St Paul's and Merchant Taylor's, were those investigated by the Clarendon Commission in 1861–4. They were considered an elite then: they remain members of a rather wider public school elite today. It is far harder to identify schools that, having once attained popular recognition as major public schools in the eighteenth century or later, and however precarious their fortunes on occasion, have subsequently closed.

Vaughan was also lucky, as many of his supposedly successful predecessors and successors have been. His policy of what he later called 'appropriate and salubrious' progress suited the fashion of the times.[22] Vaughan was a liberal by political and personal inclination, although he was careful to disguise the fact. He was probably one of the most politically radical Head Masters in Harrow's history, closer to Hide and Sumner than most of the rest. When all Harrovians and most masters, including Montagu Butler, had rejected Gladstone in the 1880s, Vaughan quietly approved of Home Rule. Forty years earlier, when to be a Tory master at Harrow

---

[21] Dean Peacock of Ely, HM/1844/Vaughan Printed Testimonials, 7, 27 Nov. 1844.
[22] *Harrow Tercentenary*, 27.

was apparently worthy of note (there were only three under Vaughan; later there was none but), there was wide acceptance on all sides of the social and economic efficacy of progress.[23] Peel's budgets in the 1840s, the repeal of the Corn Laws in 1846, and Gladstone's budgets after 1853 marked the triumph of Free Trade and inaugurated a quarter of a century boom which propelled Britian, for the last time, to a supreme position in world commerce. Liberal–Whig administrations ruled for thirty out of the forty years 1846–86. Economic reform and technological innovation increased the profits of investors and entrepreneuers; both Isambard Kingdom Brunel and George Hudson 'the Railway King' sent sons to Vaughan's Harrow.[24] Aristocratic shareholders did too. The material confidence displayed at the Great Exhibition of 1851 translated into initiatives by central and local authorities to improve standards of living. As a result of the Board of Health's complaints, water closets were introduced to the school's sanitation in 1853–4.[25] Vaughan's liberal instincts ran entirely with the grain of informed opinion.

Equally, however, his moral and religious instincts, his Arnoldian rather than political side, were conservative in ways that, paradoxically, also gained favour. With the mid-century material improvement came anxiety, among the educated classes, for the moral health of the nation, a fear lest their increasing prosperity was corrupting. The greater the material advantages of early and mid-Victorian England, the louder the calls for spiritual renewal. This fitted precisely the thrust of Vaughan's pastoral approach which warned of the snares of the physical and material world and urged concentration on the eternal, spiritual, and divine. Even in Harrow's small world, better resources presented their own dangers. As Vaughan put it in 1857, 'the multiplication of outward help and facilities for learning has a direct tendency to counteract true knowledge'.[26] Thus, in both his material improvements and his moral message, Vaughan was fashionable.

Vaughan came to Harrow realizing that 'the new Head Mastership must be marked by some important alterations, both in the discipline and in the general economy' of the school.[27] No compulsive or methodical administrator, lacking the obsessive attention to minutiae of his predecessor and successor, through presence and personality he exuded calm determination and clear priorities. Sensitive to the traditions of the school, Vaughan's tact and vigour soon attracted praise. Cunningham, writing on 29 January 1845, thrilled 'there are already more new boys than we had for a year . . . [Vaughan] has conciliated both masters and boys . . . I feel no doubt that the Governors have been directed to the right person', although this did not stop the vicar's espionage or febrile defence of his vested interests.[28] Satisfaction

---

[23] G. G. Coulton, *Fourscore Years: An Autobiography* (Cambridge, 1943), pp. 142–3; Minchin, *Old Harrow Days*, 276.
[24] *Harrow Register, 1800–1911*, 176, 182, 206, 246, 281.   [25] GM, 10 Mar. 1853.
[26] Vaughan, *Memorials*, 61.
[27] HM/1844/Vaughan Printed Testimonials, 4 Dec. 1844, 4.
[28] HA Governors' Records, Cunningham to Lord Northwick, 29 Jan. 1845.

was confirmed by *The Times* (3 March): 'Harrow is now under the direction of one who is able and willing to carry out the Arnold system of education.'

As all his predecessors had experienced, confidence was the key. This Vaughan inspired from the start. When his first term began, there were already seventy-eight boys. In his first recruits there were significant names: Boldero, son of an MP from a family that had been Harrovians since Byron's day; Hudson a son of the Railway King; Kindersley, son of a leading judge; and two other MPs' sons, including Spencer Perceval, grandson of the Prime Minister.[29] Vaughan's presence restored faith in the school even before he had achieved much. As often, reputation lay in the eye of the beholder. Vaughan recaptured Harrow's traditional clientele. George Butler's eldest son, a Harrovian under Longley, persuaded him to send his youngest, Montagu, to Harrow rather than Rugby as planned.[30] In sociological terms, Vaughan's title of restorer is appropriate. No new classes were attracted. The known parental status of entrants to Vaughan's Harrow in the late 1840s matched almost exactly that of entrants to George Butler's Harrow: at least one third from the landed gentry and another fifth from titled families. The only perceptible change, given the unevenness of the evidence possibly more apparent than real, was an increase in the numbers of clergyman's sons. Harrow once more became in fact as in image a national school; by 1850, Harrovians came from twenty-six counties, compared to only thirteen in 1840.[31] The ultimate seal of approval came in 1848 with a visit from Queen Victoria.[32]

The restoration of confidence produced a steady increase in numbers. The size of the school doubled in 1845 and doubled again in 1846, creating urgent problems of formroom space. The 300 mark was reached in 1847; 400 in 1852, a historic high, Drury's peak of 350 having been overtaken in 1849. When Vaughan left, the roll was just fifty down from its peak a few months earlier of 488, almost twice the optimum size envisaged by George Butler twenty years before.[33] Such expansion demanded redrawing the scale of the school and modification of its internal structures. Like Joseph Drury before him, Vaughan's skill was to achieve this without apparently altering the nature of either pupils or curriculum. While Vaughan was certainly cashing in on contemporary prosperity, he was also responding to the twin pressures of the growing popularity of public school education among the propertied classes and the increased competition from new or reformed schools offering a similar system, often, as with Cotton at Marlborough, under Arnoldian Heads, but at a lower cost. In that context, Vaughan had little choice but to maintain social

---

[29] *Harrow Register, 1800–1911*, 182–3.

[30] Thornton, *Harrow School*, 287. His regular reports on boys reassured parents: *Clarendon Commission Report*, i. 220.

[31] Bamford, *Rise of Public Schools*, 210, 212, 215; Allen, 'Public School Elites', esp. pp. 108–17; Bamford, 'Public Schools and Social Class', esp. p. 227.

[32] Thornton, *Harrow School*, 293.

[33] *Clarendon Commission Report*, ii. 275; *Harrow Register, 1800–1911*, 182–324.

as well as academic elitism; he had to persuade parents that Harrow was not just a good or suitable school, but that it was a grand one. In the modern jargon, going down market was not a practical option. It was not until the last twenty years of the nineteenth century, with the collapse of agricultural prices and the growth of monopolistic trading companies that in order to maintain its relative exclusivity Harrow became the haunt of plutocrats.

Vaughan's popularity was crucial as numbers underpinned improvements to buildings, sports facilities, housing, and academic staff. Harrow was still governed by the old financial system. The governors' funds were doubly circumscribed by the modest income from the School Trust estate (worth about a £1,000 a year) and the strict legal limits set upon its use. The balance (i.e. a combination of current and past surpluses) on the School Trust, varied from a maximum of £543 in 1848 to a meagre £148 in 1851 and £127 in 1856; the average annual balance during Vaughan's time being *c*.£340. After the disastrous year of 1851, the governors took out a mortgage of £2,000 which took a decade to repay.[34] Except for basic repairs to the fabric of the original part of the Old Schools and the renovation of the school's sanitary arrangements, any material improvements had to be paid from boarding and tuition fees which the governors did not control. A school of 100 produced an annual turnover of perhaps £15,000; one of 400, perhaps £60,000. Of that, perhaps just under a quarter represented tuition fees available to the Head Master for the school, the rest going as the individual housemasters (including the Head) wished.[35] Thus the number of boys determined the extent to which they could be accommodated in reasonable surroundings. New buildings had to be financed by the masters or donations from parents and old boys, which depended on their confidence in the Head Master and his management. Thus, for all his advantageous circumstances, Vaughan must take his share of the credit for the revival he led.

The physical transformation of the school was impressive and permanent. Vaughan's immediate priority was to rebuild the Head Master's boarding house.[36] For financial and pedagogic reasons, he insisted that the mistake of 1838 was reversed: boarders would place the Head and the school on sounder footing as regards income and entrants and as a good Arnoldian he felt his influence could be spread more directly and effectively through running a house. Even before the Head Master's was rebuilt, Vaughan took in boarders from the start of his Head Mastership. The new boys' side was paid for by subscription; the governors refused even to pay for the boys' stoves and grates. A committee had been established in 1843, after Wordsworth's volte-face in trying to persuade the governors to rebuild

---

[34] GM, 22 June 1848, 3 July 1851, 23 Feb. 1852, 19 June 1856.
[35] For a general financial assessment, based on 1861–2 figures but also referring explicitly to Vaughan's time see *Clarendon Commission Report*, i. 209–10, 224, 226, ii. 269–75, 283–6, iv. 156–7.
[36] HA Governors' Records, Vaughan to Governors, 31 Mar. 1845; Lord Aberdeen to Governors, 7 Apr.; GM, 11 Apr., 3 July 1845.

had failed. By April 1845 £1,500 had been raised, with another £2,000 promised. Leading figures on this committee were the two professional old boys, Frederick Ponsonby and Robert Grimston; a parent, T. W. Beaumont, MP for Northumberland, donated £1,000, the new house costing £4,000.[37] No less important, the Grove was reopened by one of Vaughan's new recruits, the Cambridge classicist J. N. Simpkinson, and four new large houses were opened or built by assistant masters, with the Head's encouragement: Church Hill in 1846 by R. Middlemist; West Acre in 1847 by G. T. Warner; Rendalls in 1854 by F. Rendall; and the two houses that later became Bradbys by H. Keary in 1849 and E. H. Bradby in 1853 respectively. In addition a number of small houses were established to allow masters to increase their income and status. The most striking of these was the reopened (1846) Vicarage, the former Mrs Leith's, which from 1855 to 1866 was put under Mrs Wood, in Vaughan's eyes a deserving widow, with H. E. Hutton as resident tutor. Mrs Wood's daughter, nicknamed 'Sunshine', who cut quite a dash on the Hill, is better known as Annie Besant, the energetic theosophist, socialist, and radical reformer.[38]

These new houses reflected and stimulated the school's growth, as new housemasters sought customers, with some success: the Grove was full by February 1848.[39] Yet the school's teaching accommodation was small or decayed or both. When the available space in the Old Schools was exhausted, the New Schools were built in 1855 paid for by subscriptions from the Head and Assistants Masters and parents. Dearer to Vaughan, the peculiar, ugly little chapel of 1839 was totally rebuilt between 1854 and 1857 to designs by the fashionable George Gilbert Scott, the Head Master himself paying for the chancel, at a cost of £3,000. Also out of his own pocket, Vaughan spent £1,000 improving Ducker between 1845 and 1851. In 1849 the first six acres of the Philathletic ground were bought and in 1850 the first racquets courts built.[40] By the late 1850s schemes existed for a new Speech Room, a gymnasium, and a library, all of which were realized under Vaughan's successor.[41] The building programme under Vaughan set the architectural and aesthetic tone of the school that persisted until the hotel–superstore style of the last quarter of the twentieth century. Scott's Chapel is French Gothic; the New Schools and Rendalls are grand Jacobeathan with late Gothic touches around arches and windows. The oddity of the chapel was, and remains, its flint finish, entirely inappropriate for the local geology or the brick, stone, wood, and plaster of the rest of the buildings on the Hill.

---

[37] HA Governors' Records, Hon. F. Ponsonby to Governors, 5 Apr. 1845; Cunningham to Lord Northwick, 5 Mar. 1845; Howson and Townsend Warner, *Harrow School*, 41; Laborde, *Harrow School*, 180.   [38] *Harrow Register, 1800–1911*, 912–16; Druett, *Harrow*, 202–3.

[39] HA Governors' Records Lord Saye and Sele to Lord Northwick, 3 Feb. 1848.

[40] *Clarendon Commission Report*, iv. 157, Laborde, *Harrow School*, 52, 95–9, 121, 201; Howson and Townsend Warner, *Harrow School*, 142–3.

[41] GM, 14 June 1853; 6 Mar., 15 June 1854.

Vaughan's impact on the school's organization was equally lasting. He gave official sanction to the establishment by the boys of the Philathletic Club to run school sport in 1852–3; the Musical Society in 1857; and the Rifle Corps in 1859, when the scare of a French invasion inspired the creation of volunteer groups across the country. The origins of a formal Debating Society and the Essay Club can be traced to the 1850s, the latter being Vaughan's especial charge at which he presided over papers presented by the stars of his Sixth Form, past and present.[42] Although wedded to the traditional classical curriculum even for the academically inept, Vaughan recognized the needs of those wishing to pass into the armed forces. Throughout the nineteenth century the armed forces provided the most popular single profession for Harrovians: 18.6 per cent of entrants in 1830 and 1845, rising, because of the Crimean War and Indian Mutiny to over 30 per cent of entrants in 1850 and 1855 before settling back at around 20 per cent in the 1870s and 1880s. The Memorial Aisle in Chapel consecrated in 1858 to those fallen in the Crimea recognized the importance of these military links and provided a tangible focus for corporate pride. To cater for the demand, Vaughan instituted the Army Class in 1851 which, by 1857, contained forty-five pupils who received additional instruction in maths and 'Military Science'.[43] With that exception, Vaughan made little alteration to the nature of the curriculum, beyond encouraging the endowment of more prizes in a wider range of subjects (he himself gave a prize for English). The only new departure was the introduction of further compulsory modern languages, with French for all and German for those good at French in 1855. In an effort to grade and teach the swollen numbers of boys more carefully, in January 1859 a new form or block, the Remove, was inserted between the Shell and Fifth.[44]

In 1854, after a well-publicized scandal involving the abuse of their power, Vaughan, to show confidence in this most essential Arnoldian institution, increased the number of monitors from ten to fifteen.[45] The importance of monitors to the system cannot be exaggerated; when the former Rugby master G. E. L. Cotton went to Marlborough in 1852, a boy commented: 'the Sixth Form are to govern the school.'[46] Although the formal position of monitors was traditional, and despite Wordsworth's reforms, Vaughan injected a new element of responsibility and duty into what previously had been largely an office of privilege. He allowed them almost complete power provided it was always understood that their

---

[42] According to the Essay Club minutes, kept by Vaughan himself, H. M. Butler was a regular visitor after he left. See, in general, HM/Wordsworth's Head Master's Book: Vaughan Additions, fos. 61ᵛ–65ʳ; HA Debating Society Minute Book 1852–71; HA Captain of School Book, 1851–72 *passim*; Laborde, *Harrow School*, 54, 191; Graham, *Butler*, 174; *Clarendon Commission Report*, i. 222–3; Dalrymple, 'Vaughan', 123; Sir H. Trueman Wood, 'Harrow in the Fifties', *Cornhill Magazine* (Apr. 1921), p. 411.   [43] GM, 19 Feb. 1957; Bamford, *Rise of Public Schools*, 210.

[44] HM/Wordsworth's Head Master's Book: Vaughan Additions, fo. 62ᵛ; Captain of School Book, 1851–72, fo. 19; *Clarendon Commission Report*, i. 216; Howson and Townsend Warner, *Harrow School*, 142–3.   [45] HA Captain of School Book, 1851–72, fo. 46.

[46] Honey, *Tom Brown's Universe*, 104.

authority derived directly from his. So he would allow one Head of School to deliver a brutal public thrashing in the Fourth Form Room in front of the whole school to two boys caught torturing a cat while insisting that another, Henry Yates Thompson, apologize to the whole Sixth Form for attacking two fellow monitors out of pique at being beaten by them in a scholarship exam.[47] Vaughan retained the rigid system of academic seniority that selected monitors, who continued to be the boys best at classics tests and the longest in the Sixth Form. The introverted, unathletic, precious J. A. Symonds was Head of Rendalls at 16, and remained so for almost two years, having to beat bullies considerably larger than himself. The fastidious and tender-conscienced W. D. Legh expressed scruples at beating boys for impertinence and insubordination, although he was happy to thrash bullies 'without temper'.[48] More aggressive or uncontrolled natures could find expression just as easily; some thought monitorial canings far more painful than Head Master's beatings.

It was over the system of monitorial beating that Vaughan nearly came unstuck. The Platt–Stewart incident in 1853 was a test case for Arnoldian orthodoxy as well as a cause célèbre, the Head Master's vindication at the tribunal of public opinion being of wide significance. As Arnold's disciple, Vaughan had strong views about beating: he approved of it. Monitors beat with canes—'whopping'—across the clothed backs or shoulder-bades of their victims, usually in private in the school library (now Old Schools 1), only rarely in public. Alone in the Fourth Form Room, with only Custos as a witness, the Head used a birch—'swishing'—on the exposed backsides of culprits. Whereas Wordsworth's birches were reputedly feeble, being old, big, and bushy, Vaughan insisted on a new birch for each 'swishing' (leaving his used ones to the furious Under Master Oxenham), ordering each one 'to be reduced in bulk so as to sting more'. These he kept locked in a cupboard (also to his deputy's rage). When, on one occasion, its lock was blocked up as a prank, Vaughan threw a tantrum, threatening to punish the whole school (by then, February 1847, over 250) unless the perpetrators confessed. Following Arnold, Vaughan did not beat often or recklessly, but when he did he meant it to hurt. He would deliver six, eight, or ten cuts and draw blood, leaving birch buds imbedded in the wounds causing scars that could last for a fortnight.[49] This final sanction was used so rarely precisely because the monitors were allowed the power of the cane. It remained an unpleasant anomaly until the 1970s that most masters were not allowed to beat, while boys were permitted, often instructed by adults, to beat other boys. Vaughan saw this as essential to effective education. As late as 1873 he persuaded his colleagues on the Governing Body of Winchester to issue a

---

[47] S. Daryl ['An Old Harrovian'], *Harrow Recollections* (London, 1867), pp. 31–3; Symonds, *Memoirs*, 87–9. Cf. *Clarendon Commission Report*, i. 221.

[48] Symonds, *Memoirs*, 87; 'C.L.H.', *Memorials of a Harrow Schoolboy* (London, 1873), p. 20.

[49] Norman, *At School and at Sea*, II, 30–2; A. J. Hare, *The Story of My Life*, i (London, 1896), p. 219; Minchin, *Old Harrow Days*, 14.

statement after a beating scandal defending 'the practice of allowing prefects ... to inflict bodily punishments on their juniors', against the opinions of counsel: the earl of Derby and Sir Stafford Northcote resigned in disgust.[50] Vaughan would certainly have remembered the similar case he had faced twenty years earlier at Harrow.

In November 1853 a Fifth Former, the Hon. Randolph Stewart, son of the earl of Galloway, was thrashed by a senior monitor, H. E. Platt, son of a judge, for insolently disputing an umpiring decision at football. Before the caning, Stewart appealed to Vaughan who, following his almost invariable custom, having ascertained that the incident had occurred, ordered Stewart to submit to the beating or leave the school.[51] In the school library, Platt administered thirty-one blows to Stewart across the shoulders with, it was alleged, a cane of one inch diameter, 'as hard as he could'. Stewart staggered off to the school doctor, the sleek entrepreneur Hewlett, who immediately reported to Vaughan. Platt was summoned and demoted on the spot (but not expelled).

Unwisely Platt, who later became a clergyman, instantly wrote to Stewart to explain his action, which he admitted was severe, 'but not in any way excessive', adding sententiously, 'I never looked upon the matter as an affront to me, but to a monitor'. Stewart was not appeased. Both fathers wrote to Vaughan protesting, Lord Galloway calling for reform, Baron Platt asking for reconsideration 'for the sake of his family, for the sake of Harrow and, with sincere respect', he added nastily, 'for the sake of yourself'. With this threat both sides rushed into print, Platt printing his exchange with the Head Master without permission, to Vaughan's annoyance ('and with misprints too').[52] The press and public had a field day. In the vollies of correspondence the issue soon became that of the monitorial system itself. The attack was on two fronts. On the left were those who agreed with *The Times* of 13 April 1854 that 'the monitorial system, as illustrated in the case before us, is entirely indefensible'. On the right, the voices of reaction clamoured against the new 'Rugbean' system which reduced monitors to spies, 'tools of the Head Master'.

Vaughan's response saw him at his most effective; politically astute, calm, clear, dispassionate, and firm. He arranged for a public exchange of letters with the then Home Secretary, Lord Palmerston, well-known not only for being an Old Harovian but also for unreconstructed views on public schools. Vaughan acknowledged that ill-considered popular opinion was against his system and that abuse was

---

[50] J. Vincent (ed.), *A Selection from the Diaries of Edward Henry Stanley, 15th earl of Derby, 1869–1878*, Camden Fifth Series, iv (London, 1994), pp. 124–5 and n. 6.

[51] The correspondence and full details are in HA Pamphlets and Printed Forms of Nineteenth Century, letters from Galloway and Platt, 1853–4; 'A Few Words on the Monitorial System at Harrow'; 'A Reply to "One who was once a Monitor"'; Vaughan to Palmerston: Thornton, *Harrow School*, 448–51. Cf. Chandos, *Boys Together*, 239–44.

[52] HA MS E. Latham Letters, Vaughan to Latham, 9 Dec. 1853.

possible, but he rejected the liberal clamour against corporal punishment by quoting Arnold's charge that such opponents, in elevating the individual above the community, were 'neither reasonable nor Christian but essentially barbarian'. (He could have added that they were also hypocritical, as most parents thrashed their own children without compunction.) Vaughan insisted that the monitorial system was 'capable of great good' and, more important, 'impossible to replace'. Tellingly he surveyed the alternative: 'a body of ushers, masters of a lower order whose business it shall be to follow boys into their hours of recreation and rest and avowedly as spies . . . reporting to their superiors.' Such magisterial espionage would, he asserted, ruin 'the great glory of an English Public School—its free development of character, its social expansiveness, in short its liberty'. Clearly, modern methods and organization of discipline would have appalled him. Vaughan rejected the idea that the senior boys were his spies: to be effective and gain respect monitors needed freedom and independence. Yet, the key Arnoldian point was that they and the other boys were aware that monitorial power derived from the Head Master. Manners were for monitors; morals for him. Thus was discipline differentiated and rendered acceptable to boys and masters alike.

Vaughan's justification, for all its self-referential logic, worked. Reactionaries were reassured that monitors were not spies; reformers convinced they acted under the Head's control. Lord Galloway was even moved to praise Vaughan. Platt left. In the privacy of the Hill, however, Vaughan increased the number of monitors to fifteen; forbade any monitor to beat in his own cause; and redoubled his efforts to keep them orderly, his severity on Yates Thompson being an illustration. In general, his measured persuasiveness won the day perhaps because he did not disguise the realities of school life while insisting that his authority was sufficient. Vaughan's assertion of clear-sighted autocracy aimed at the corporate good, unbending to public opinion, grounded in principle and confident in its rectitude and efficacy, went down well with old boys, existing and potential parents. The Platt–Stewart affair was not Vaughan's Waterloo but his Marengo.

Staff

That the case attracted so much notoriety in a sense was a measure of Vaughan's success. As the school grew in size and repute, this rested increasingly on his staff as much as on him. Perhaps the greatest transformation he achieved was in the numbers, calibre, and material prospects of his assistants.

The motley crew he inherited may never have entirely warmed to him or his methods. Oxenham, increasingly foul-mouthed, violent yet indolent, regularly swore in public at Vaughan's very name, habitually calling him a 'damned fool', a dislike possibly feigned, possibly caused by the restriction on his power of the rod. Vaughan tolerated Oxenham's incompetence, late arrivals in Chapel, non-appearance at bill which, by 1859, was all the old man had to do, having hived off his teaching. Vaughan, in his feline way, saw that Oxenham was pure gold with the reactionaries and, he must certainly have noticed, with the Butlers, whose in-law he was.[53] The existence of George Butler (who only died in 1853) as a major local landowner and school benefactor and of his family as pupils and later trustees for his estate was not the least test of Vaughan's famed tact.

Harris, at the Park, was a Trinity man only four years senior to Vaughan, but a product of Samuel Butler's Shrewsbury, very far from Arnold's Rugby. Known as 'the Governor', prim, sanctimonious, pompous, and reactionary, a clever but rigid classicist, Harris preferred neatness to understanding in his pupils' work, was easily gulled by genuinely clever boys, such as C. S. Calverley (né Blayds), and, it was said, 'to a budding scholar [he] was about as genial as a black frost'. Harris was an uncomfortable colleague for Vaughan, his main interest, as he revealed perhaps inadvertently to the Clarendon Commissioners in 1862, being his house and its operating profits.[54] There, at least, he was to have much to thank Vaughan.

Given the rather desperate circumstances of his appointment in 1841 and the grandeur of his name, not least in the eyes of his grandfather's ageing but influential pupils, Ben Drury, a learned bachelor who retained close links with his Cambridge college to which he finally returned in 1863, led a rather separated existence running his house, the Abbey. He was popular and friendly, a loyal and faithful Old Harrovian who continued to attend Speech Day until the late 1890s, he was unmarked by any notions that the Gospel according to Arnold meant anything.[55] In very stark contrast with his predecessor, Vaughan did nothing to upset living Harrow traditions. These included the maths master Jacob Marillier, only just past the meridian of his fifty years of service, and the ex-patriot French drudges, A. J. and P. M. G. Ruault, *père et fils*.

Vaughan realized that rather than disturb the old guard, Masters' meetings and Chapel excepted, if he could attract large numbers of pupils, as house masters or extra masters who gained per capita, they would be financially happy. Academically, the pupil room system would allow new minds and higher standards despite their continued presence, although even there Vaughan could not and never attempted to disturb the hold of the housemasters, Harris, Drury, and Oxenham. He merely provided clever boys with additional tuition, free of charge, given by himself, later (1852) assisted by B. F. Westcott. Unlike Wordsworth, Vaughan could cope with diversity. In the 1850s there were few worse housemasters than Oxenham

---

[53] Minchin, *Old Harrow Days*, 13–15; Graham, *Butler*, 31; Norman, *At School and at Sea*, 9; Trueman Wood, 'Harrow in the Fifties', 398; *Clarendon Commission Report*, iv. 154; Hare, *Story of my Life*, i. 236–7.

[54] Minchin, *Old Harrow Days*, 18–20; W. J. Sendall, *The Literary Remains of C. S. Calverley* (London, 1885), pp. 21–2; *Clarendon Commission Report*, iv. 192–203.

[55] Trueman Wood, 'Harrow in the Fifties', 399; Howson and Townsend Warner, *Harrow School*, 65; *Clarendon Commission Report*, ii. 285.

or tutors than Harris; there were few more effective (judged by university results) combinations of school tutors than Vaughan and Westcott.

The distinction of Vaughan's school lay in the masters he recruited. Never before or since was such a galaxy of talent assembled so rapidly. From six in 1845, by 1859 there were twenty-one assistant masters, marking a definitive move away from the traditional confines of a small coterie of educational shepherds drilling huge classes in grinding repetition: in 1803, with almost 350 boys in the school, there had been, including the Head Master, only seven teachers.[56] Although careful not to disturb the hierarchy of seniority in allocating form-masterships (thus Westcott acted only as the Head's assistant in the Sixth Form), Vaughan believed in appointing tutors of talent and distinct specialisms. Following Wordsworth, he was especially keen to place mathematics on a proper academic footing.[57]

In fifteen years Vaughan appointed twenty-two masters, some outstanding beyond the narrow confines of the Hill. S. A. Pears (1847–54) became Head Master of Repton. B. F. Westcott (1852–70) was successively Regius Professor of Divinity at Cambridge, canon of Westminster, and bishop of Durham. While at Harrow, F. W. Farrar (1855–70) wrote the numbingly sentimental and cloying but massively popular *Eric or Little by Little* (1858) which is largely about death by masturbation, an early, vivid, agitated example of the Victorian sex-panic or, as one critic observed, 'the kind of book which Dr. Arnold might have written had he taken to drink'.[58] Farrar, whose photo-album, begun in 1859, shows his own keen appreciation of male adolescent beauty, became a pundit on educational reform, Master of Marlborough, archdeacon of Westminster, and dean of Canterbury. With another of Vaughan's appointees, the mathematician R. B. Hayward (1859–93), he was elected a Fellow of the Royal Society and actively promoted the Natural Sciences as a serious activity. One of Vaughan's last appointments, E. E. Bowen (1859–1901) became possibly the most famous assistant master in the country, a pamphleteer on educational reform; archpriest of the adoration of games as a serious activity for adults and boys alike; and the author of many of the most famous Harrow School Songs—although after Vaughan, who was tone deaf.[59]

Some of Vaughan's appointments were of eccentrics. T. H. Steel, lured back in 1849 after fleeing Wordsworth's devastation six years before (he was to stay until his death in 1881, aged seventy-five, forty-five years after arriving with the new Head Master in 1836) always carried with him a blue umbrella, rain or shine.[60]

[56] Butler, *Harrow Lists*, 58–72.
[57] For basic biographical information on the masters see *Harrow Register, 1800–1911*, 902–4.
[58] Gathorne-Hardy, *Public School Phenomenon*, 87 and cf. 84–8. Farrar's photograph album is in the Harrow School Archives. I am grateful to the late Revd H. L. Harris for drawing my attention to it.
[59] W. E. Bowen, *Edward Bowen: A Memoir* (London, 1902); J. A. Mangan, 'Philathletic Extraordinary: A Portrait of the Victorian Moralist Edward Bowen', *Journal of Sport History*, 9 (1982), 23–40; Graham, *Butler*, 174.
[60] Minchin, *Old Harrow Days*, 40; this was especially remarkable as boys never carried umbrellas at the time.

C. F. Holmes (1853–87), known as 'Skipper', was a cruel, vindictive disciplinarian who preferred spending three nights a week in London, at the theatre or playing billiards at his club, to supervising his Small House in the High Street.[61] The French historian and writer Gustave Masson (1855–88) was a widower, hired when working as a tutor to a local Harrow family. Forced by custom and prescript to teach Harrovians to pronounce French with an English accent, he spent much time writing flirtatious poems to his colleagues' wives, Catherine Vaughan included, usually in French. His relationship with Mrs Vaughan was close, a poem of June 1859 intimate, their correspondence teasing and affectionate: she wept at his farewell note in December 1859.[62] By complete contrast and most bizarre was the maths master, Robert Middlemist (1845–76), House Master of Church Hill, to all appearances the driest of dry sticks, a misanthropic confirmed bachelor with an intmidating manner. In school he showed blatant favouritism to boys in his house or 'sons of people who sent game or could be of use to him' but mercilessly persecuted others, such as Randall Davidson, the future archbishop of Canterbury. In Holy Orders, through which he derived further income from the living of Little Linfold, Oxfordshire, he was a woeful preacher, his only good sermon later being discovered to have been lifted wholesale from J. H. Newman. Naturally he excited hostile comments from his former pupils. 'Cynical and acrid'; 'naturally unpopular ... the most charitable critic could not say that he was suited for a schoolmaster'; 'a bully, a tyrant'; 'he was a terrible man' are just some, representative comments on 'Old Middy'.[63]

Yet on his death in January 1877, to the astonishment of everybody from Montagu Butler downwards, it was revealed that he had a wife and children living on the south coast whom he visited at weekends and during the holidays, which explained his otherwise unaccountable fury if asked how he spent his free time. Unknown to any on the Hill, he had married one of his servants and such were the social conventions of the day and such were the profits of a Harrow housemastership (which he calculated in 1862 as £1,330 net a year), that Middlemist adopted this stategem of duplicity which he sustained for decades.[64] He was materially aided by the invention of the railway, his pathetic story providing an unexpected example of how the transport revolution affected social behaviour. Middlemist would have felt his decision grimly justified by the events surrounding his funeral

---

[61] Minchin, *Old Harrow Days*, 21–2; Trueman Wood, 'Harrow in the Fifties', 401; J. Rawcliffe, (ed.), HA MS *Harrow Verses, 1873–4* (1927), p. 18 n. 3. (MS copies of poems—many are also in HA, Materials Relating to Boys, Box III).

[62] Trueman Wood, 'Harrow in the Fifties', 403; Collings MSS, *Poésies intimes*, esp. nos. IV, V, VII, XI (to Mrs Vaughan), XV, XX, XXXVII, XLI, etc.; ibid. for Mrs Vaughan's farewell letter and later correspondence from Doncaster. I am grateful to the late Rex Collings Esq. who allowed me to read and transcribe these documents.

[63] Trueman Wood, 'Harrow in the Fifties', 402–3; Minchin, *Old Harrow Days*, 25–30; Rawcliffe, *Harrow Verses*, 15 and n. 2 and p. 16. Cf. MS poem on Middlemist by R. H. Doulton, c.1870, Materials Relating to Boys, Box III.   [64] *Clarendon Commission Report*, ii. 285.

at Harrow. His widow insisted on attending with their four children. Butler, snobbery struggling with hypocrisy, anger, and disgust, anxious to avoid gossip, placed a man at the railway station to turn back all old members of Middlemist's house from going to the service.[65] A life of deceit and concealment had soured Middlemist, although his actions could be seen as a noble compromise in not abandoning his lover while resisting the crushing opprobrium of snobbish social mores. He paid a high price. Even the saintly and more than slightly crazy John Smith (1854–82), on hearing of Middlemist's wife and family, could only manage to remark: 'Thank God that there was somebody to love him.'[66]

The group of masters Vaughan gathered were almost all of high academic achievement. Among the Wordsworth survivors, Drury had been Ninth Classic and remained a fellow of Caius, Cambridge while Harris had been Third Classic and a fellow of Trinity. Of Vaughan's twenty-two appointees, fourteen had first-class degrees, nine college fellowships. Rendall and Westcott had been, like Vaughan, Senior Classics at Cambridge, Steel Second Classic, Bowen and Farrar Fourth Classics, and H. W. Watson Second Wrangler. They came from a close web of school and university contacts that made the old Harrow Etonian mafia appear random. There were four Rugbeians (Edwin Vaughan, E. H. Bradby, W. J. Bull, A. G. Watson); four from King Edward's Birmingham, ruled by J. P. Lee, who, as a close colleague and admirer of Arnold's at Rugby, had taught Vaughan (H. Keary, F. Rendall, B. F. Westcott, J. Smith). No fewer than eleven had, like Vaughan, studied at Trinity, Cambridge (Simpkinson, Warner, Keary, Rendall, T. H. Steel, Westcott, Bull, Smith, Farrar, H. W. Watson, Bowen), four had also been fellows: small wonder that by the mid-1850s some 15 per cent of undergraduates at Cambridge's largest college were Harrovians.[67] Fourteen of Vaughan's masters were in Holy Orders, although it is significant of the dramatic secularization of public school teachers in the second half of the nineteenth century that all Vaughan's first twelve appointments (to 1853) were of clergymen but only two (out of ten) thereafter. Too independent yet too similar to cooperate easily or admire their Head overmuch, his assitants instinctively and by training shared his educational purpose if not his method.

For all their glittering prizes, Vaughan's staff were not necessarily good teachers. Middlemist, Holmes, Oxenham were unsympathetic and bad. Masson and Westcott were scholars but no schoolmasters. German lessons with Ruault were to be dreaded. Bradby was a bore. Smith exerted his influence through his peculiar not quite sane personality; his deliberately ingenuous and innocent style, although adored by his Fourth Form, was no good with older, wiser, cleverer boys for whom

---

[65] Rawcliffe, *Harrow Verses*, 15 n. 2, where he provides eye-witness testimony. On the Middlemist episode see Minchin, *Old Harrow Days*, 27–9; G. W. E. Russell, *Fifteen Chapters of Autobiography* (London, n.d.), pp. 50–4.   [66] Minchin, *Old Harrow Days*, 28.
[67] Graham, *Butler*, p. xxxvii, in G. O. Trevelyan's introduction.

his childish Christian simplicity grated. The young Bowen could not keep order; the old Marillier remained ineffective. However, Drury and Steel were sound and respected; Hutton popular if not particularly learned; Edwin Vaughan was considered a good house master as was Simpkinson. Farrar's main contribution was the encouragement of science outside school hours, hardly surprising as he, a fellow of Trinity, Cambridge, and A. G. 'Vanity' Watson, a fellow of All Souls College, Oxford, each with outstanding classical qualifications, were confined in their formal duties to teaching the Shells.[68]

For all the splendid array, as in previous generations, the key to Harrow's academic reputation was the Sixth Form where Vaughan presided, assisted by Westcott who marked the language work (astonishing drudgery for one of the leading theologians of his generation). There clever boys could arrive at an early age and stay for years gilding their linguistic erudition and facility by constant exercises and occasional prizes and scholarship competitions. From the start, Vaughan produced excellent scholarship candidates who went on to shine at university, such as the Wordsworthians C. S. Currer, H. N. Oxenham, and J. K. Rennie. From the intake of his first two years, 1845 and 1846, Vaughan's pupils included five future Oxbridge fellows, including T. C. Baring, the re-founder of Hertford College, Oxford and two Senior Classics (F. W. Hawkins and H. M. Butler) and one Second Classic (C. S. Calverley, né Blayds) at Cambridge.[69] Such was his reputation that his name at Trinity became a sort of triumphal totem. What went on in other forms scarcely seemed to matter, although for those masters with equal academic prowess, Vaughan's monopoly of influence and credit may have been galling.

Away from the classics and the pursuit of prizes and pots by Vaughan's many Sixth Form highfliers, modern languages was taught by Masson and the Ruaults and maths, especially important to Cambridge candidates, by Middlemist and later H. W. Watson and Hayward in the Upper School and, in the Lower, by Marillier. Otherwise, there was some non-Ancient History out of school; entirely voluntary natural science under Farrar; Scripture on Sundays. Geography was, apparently 'a farce'.[70] Below the Sixth Form, especially in the Lower School, the standard of classical instruction and learning was as low as it was in maths and modern languages. The classical curriculum remained narrowly linguistic; the weight of verse composition crushing; the belief in its educational benefits near universal. It was only in the 1860s that Farrar and Bowen called for reform,

---

[68] For impressions of the teaching see Minchin, *Old Harrow Days*, 13–67; Daryl, *Recollections*, 17, 119; Trueman Wood, 'Harrow in the Fifties', 396–405; Norman, *At School and at Sea*, 9–15; Hare, *Story of My Life*, 242; Rawcliffe, *Harrow Verses, passim*. From the other side see A. Westcott, *The Life and Letters of Brooke Foss Westcott*, 2 vols. (London, 1903), pp. 173–5, 189–98, 229–30, 240, 247, 260, etc.

[69] *Harrow Register, 1800–1911, passim*.

[70] *Clarendon Commission Report*, iv. 230; Trueman Wood, 'Harrow in the Fifties', 401, 403–5 for science. In general, the impression of narrowness and low achievement is confirmed by the *Clarendon Commission Report*, i. 15–26, 213–20, 222–3, iv. 154–230.

although in retrospect some regretted the narrowness of the system. C. S. Currer, one of Vaughan's early scholars, a first-class classic at Oxford and a fellow of Merton, became disillusioned that the time 'that might have been given . . . to the cultivation of the faculties of an ordinarily educated man was wasted upon the inanities of Latin verse composition'. The writer Augustus Hare, in a lowly form in 1846–7, remembered even more harshly: 'I never learnt anything useful at Harrow and had little chance of learning anything. Hours and hours were wasted daily on useless Latin verses with sickening monotony. A boy's school education at this time, except in the highest forms, was hopelessly inane.'[71] Vaughan was an absolute conservative and, by successfully imposing his views on his star pupil Monty Butler, ensured that change in the curriculum came but glacially at Harrow, a conservatism that was rarely challenged by the masters.

One emotion towards Vaughan his assistants may all have shared, if reluctantly, was gratitude. As striking as their academic credentials was their wealth, in which they took their lead from him. On a conservative estimate, by the late 1850s Vaughan was earning from tuition and entrance fees, capitation, and boarding charges, between £10,000 and £12,000 gross a year, the equivalent of a modern millionaire. Out of this he paid the salaries of his assistants which he unilaterally increased from £60 to £150;[72] he had to provide the necessities of the new boarding house (to which he added an extra floor at his own expense); his generosity towards the school was massive. None the less, he may still have made profits of over £5,000 a year. Married (in 1850 to his best friend A. P. Stanley's vivacious sister), but without children, he lived at the Head Master's in some style, his household including a governess, housekeeper, lady's maid, cook, maidservant, six housemaids, a butler, a coachman, and a footman. His early eagerness to have the boys' side rebuilt, and later to pay for its extension, is understandable in terms of financial investment. It was no coincidence that of the seventy-three boys he admitted to Harrow in 1845, thirty were assigned to his house.[73]

What applied to the Head applied to his assistants. By increasing their salaries and offering almost all the chance to take boarders, Vaughan attracted his talented staff, the boarding fees being described by Westcott as 'a means for making it possible for a junior Assistant Master to live at Harrow . . . it is in fact payment for his School services', without which he could not have remained.[74] The stipends of college fellows varied from £200 to £300 a year. Even after dons were allowed to marry, the lure of an income three to ten or more times greater proved effective. To Vaughan's success his staff owed their fortunes. Whatever his personal feelings,

---

[71] Roundell, 'Wordsworth', 98; Hare, *Story of my Life*, i. 242.
[72] *Clarendon Commission Report*, i. 210.
[73] Much of the financial details can be extrapolated from the fees and numbers. See the Clarendon Commission evidence, esp. ii. 269–75, MSS circulars outlining fees, and termly Bill Books. For his household see the Harrow Rating Survey, 1851–2 and Shaw, *Relations between Town and Gown*, ch. 4.
[74] *Clarendon Commission Report*, iv. 209.

Oxenham declared in 1862 that until Vaughan came to the school, over twenty years 'my whole profits were nil'. How differently he fared after 1845. By the mid-1850s Oxenham's income was well over £5,000 a year and he felt secure enough to give up formroom teaching altogether, paying £300 to John Smith to do it for him.[75] George Harris lived at the Park with a substantial household, earning over £6,000, with £2,000 annual profit. He claimed to run up a butcher's bill of £600 a year because he fed his boys so well: for Sunday lunch he would serve a whole sirloin and most of the ribs of the carcass, weighing 80 pounds. Even more extraordinary was that Harris insisted on carving all the meat personally.[76] Drury and Middlemist, charging around £100 per boarder, made annual profits in excess of £1,000 from their Large Houses. Westcott, in a Small House, could charge around £150 per boy; as few as seven in residence producing £1,000 a year gross to go with £750 from salary and pupils. Frederick Rendall, known as 'Monkey', estimated an annual net profit on the boarding house he built of £1,044 'the maximum result of a successful speculation', Rendall being able to delegate all his private tuition work and much of his house pastoral duties, John Smith again being the proxy.[77] Even the old maths master Jacob Marillier cashed in. His accounts for 1845 record an income of £950, of which over £500 came from private sources, with a surplus of over £100. By 1859 he was earning £2,300, over £1,700 from the school (i.e. the boys) and was able to invest that year alone over £1,000 in such things as Life Insurance, Railway Stock, and Consols.[78] With no capital gains tax and income tax varying in this period between 6 per cent and 2 per cent such men were the Great Moguls of British education.

Yet they did not warm to their chief. There was little *esprit de corps* despite, perhaps because of, his weekly masters' meetings. Westcott noticed in 1852; 'we are so far independent that one master knows little of another'.[79] Oxenham apart, some masters clearly disliked Vaughan, perhaps because of his aloofness, his steely blandness or simply the awful feelings of obligation they all must have felt towards the provider of their riches. He was thought to lack sincerity and he made no secret that he regarded boys more honest than masters. In the numerous memories of him, there are few scenes of him with other masters, almost always the stories detail his relations with and impact on boys. After he left it was said he made enemies and, his old pupil Butler excepted, the masters never talked about him.[80] Perhaps they then knew what before they may have sensed that Vaughan's quiet, rigid

---

[75] *Clarendon Commission Report*, ii. 283, 285, iv. 154; HA Oxenham Collection, House Lists, which reveal that he deliberately misled the Clarendon Commissioners about the number of boys usually in his house and therefore the size of his income (ii. 285).

[76] Ibid., ii. 285, iv. 201.   [77] Ibid., ii. 284–6, iv. 209–11.

[78] Ibid., ii. 285, iv. 211; HA MS Masters' Papers, J. F. Marillier: Cash Book, sub ann. 1845–59. For a general discussion of public school masters' wealth see Honey, *Tom Brown's Universe*, 296–307.

[79] HA MS Masters' Papers, B. F. Westcott/Westcott to A. C. Benson, 8 Mar. 1852(?).

[80] Minchin, *Old Harrow Days*, 99–100; Graham, *Butler*, 29.

facade sheltered hypocrisy of proportions startling even for the most enthusiastic reader of contemporary novels. Middlemist was not alone in leading a double life.

Locals: The 'English Form'

Another source of possible unease was Vaughan's and his wife's social work. Except for Harris, Middlemist, and Holmes, the masters tended politically towards the mid-century liberal consensus. Yet their philanthropy did not imply social reform. The Vaughans, however, were more than do-gooders in the tradition of *noblesse oblige*. Mrs Vaughan set up an industrial home for girls; Dr Vaughan became the first chairman of the Harrow Local Board. They held parties for locals of all classes at the Head Master's and began annual lectures in Speech Room open to people from the town.[81] Vaughan was no socialist, but neither was he a patrician philanthropist like Lord Shaftesbury. He accepted, indeed insisted upon the separation of classes, but saw no reason why each should not enjoy available advantages of their own, especially if theirs by moral if not legal right. His pupils deserved as well as earned their places in the sun. So did the farmers and tradesmen of Harrow deserve their rights under the statutes of John Lyon.

The problem remained threefold: the preponderance of foreigners; the exploitation of the charity by rich incomers; the exclusion of the non-gentry, commercial community from any practical benefit from the Lyon Trust. To justify the first, Vaughan addressed the other two. As the suburbanization of Harrow continued, the problem of wealthy Free Scholars remained, although their proportion no longer constituted a major financial drain on the school's resources. The exploitation of Foundationer rights was blatant. *The Times*, 17 September 1855:

> Harrow School—To be let, furnished, a good roomy house known as the Old Vicarage, situate near Harrow Church. This is a good opportunity for a family who may wish to avail themselves of the advantages of the school for their sons whose admission into it can be obtained at once and even free if desired to.

In 1853 Vaughan, bravely in view of Wordsworth's experience, revived Longley's idea of imposing a residence qualification: he suggested two years. After initially hiding behind their judgments of 1843 and 1844, the governors conceded the expediency of such a plan and referred the question to the Charity Commissioners prior to an approach to Chancery. With their approval obtained, the governors were prepared to proceed in 1854 when Vaughan suddenly got cold feet. He reported that a prominent local businessman, R. Chapman, had expressed his strong objections to the governors' application to Chancery leading Vaughan to state he had 'no wish to evade any liability in the shape of gratuitous education which either Law or Equity

---

[81] See e.g. Laborde, *Harrow School*, 52; Bamford, *Rise of Public Schools*, 202.

might impose upon him'. Exasperated, the governors wondered whether Vaughan, who had instigated the process in the first place, had changed his mind or would prefer a limit of twelve months.[82] The application to Chancery was not cancelled but the entry requirements for Free Scholars went unchanged until the 1868 Public Schools Act. Vaughan's retreat can be explained by his prudence. Chapman was the school's regular builder, local, efficient, and cheap, at that very moment constructing new privies and shortly to be engaged in the larger projects of the chapel and the New Schools. Vaughan knew when not to pick a fight. Instead, following Wordsworth, he restricted the availability of free education for the gentry by banning riding to school and maintaining compulsory attendance at the 2 p.m. bill, for which day-boys, including Foundationers, had to have returned from their lunch, which they took at home. Vaughan's measures caused anger among those living at the further-flung corners of the large parish, which extended from Pinner to Wembley and Harrow Weald to Sudbury, as he effectively restricted access to the school to those living on or around the Hill, a move that helped concentrate suburban development.[83]

Chapman had represented the interests of the farmers and tradesmen. In 1849, the governors had rejected a petition to use Trust funds to establish a 'commercial school', i.e. one designed to cater for the needs of those not wishing for the classical curriculum of the public school but for more than the very basic skills provided by the local National School (which the governors did support in lieu of paying Dames in Harrow Town itself).[84] The issue did not go away, not least because of the increasing prosperity of the public school. Above the abiding problem of Lyon's intention in establishing his charity, the mismatch of the wealth of the school and the relative poverty of the school trust aroused local suspicion because it was thought either that the governors must be concealing their assets or that trust money was being diverted towards the interests of foreigners. Between 1851 and 1854 the campaign to force the school to contribute to founding a school for the middle classes was led by John Morris, a Scottish self-made philanthropist living in Sudbury, who conducted a vigorous correspondence in the national press and with the Visitor, governors, and Head Master. The destruction of his fences by Harrovians in 1851 lent a sharp edge to his vituperation.[85] Such vociferous protest provoked much inevitable, visceral snobbery from the defenders of the status quo.

[82] GM, 28 May, 14 June, 4 Oct. 1853, 6 Apr., 15 June 1854.
[83] Simon, *The Two Nations and the Educational Structure*, 314. Cf. Wordsworth's Head Master's Book, Jan. 1845 and his row over Home Boarders riding, above, p. 233.
[84] GM, 21 June 1849. In general see Shaw, *Relations between Town and Gown*, ch. 5.
[85] For Morris's campaign, apart from Shaw, ch. 5; see HA *Notes to Pamphlets Printed for John Morris in 1854 Regarding Harrow School*. It is worth noting that the Clerk to the Governors bought up all outstanding copies of Morris's pamphlets on his death in 1867: HA MS, Letter Book of Henry Young, fo. 400, 24 Dec. 1867.

However, Vaughan sought his own solution. In July 1851 he proposed to the governors 'an extension of the benefits of the foundation to the farmers and tradesmen of Harrow' by the establishment of an 'English school ... of commercial character' as a separate, inferior form of the public school. The governors' liability would be to pay the master of the school and act as patrons. After obtaining counsel's opinion, the governors rejected the scheme in February 1852.[86] Undaunted, ignoring the governors, in May 1853, at his own cost, Vaughan opened the so-called 'English Form' in a converted shed. He paid the teachers' salaries and a charge of £5 a year levied for all non-classical tuition, which included English grammar and composition, history, geography, maths, music, etc. By 1859 Vaughan had satisfied himself that his commercial school, which took boys up to about fourteen years old, 'had answered its purpose having quite extinguished all complaints on the part of the Parishioners which formerly used to break out'. However, the rules of the new form, Vaughan admitted, 'were so arranged as to prevent these boys from interfering with the higher school'. Furthermore, parents had to agree to the school and pupils being 'entirely separate in all respects from those at the public school'.[87] This implied waiving rights to free education under the Lyon statutes, as Vaughan hoped the governors would admit boys to the English Form as if on to the foundation.

In the event, the governors did no such thing. Hardly surprisingly, some locals regarded the whole enterprise as a sham and a bribe 'to preserve the Upper School from the contamination of the classes who were looked down upon as tradespeople'.[88] As it stood, despite Vaughan's complacent optimism, the English Form provided no permanent solution. If part of Lyon's foundation (which the governors denied until 1859), why was it cut off from the public school? If not, it failed to answer the demands for the Lyon trust to provide suitable education for locals. Either way, it looked like a device to cheat parishioners of their rights on Harrow School and, in its renovated stable some distance from the main school buildings, was stigmatized as inferior. Vaughan's motives may have been philanthropic, but his rules and stated aims were clearly more in the interests of his own school than in appeasing the grievances of the parish, even if his own governors were too hidebound to recognize this. The conflict over the Foundation rumbled on until bursting out with renewed energy during the protracted debates surrounding the 1868 Public Schools Act. Nevertheless, Vaughan's initiative, however patronizing it appeared, showed regard for the interests of local farmers and tradesmen. Although a compromise, and lacking gubernatorial support, Vaughan's English Form was the first constructive attempt to resolve the educational, as opposed to legal issues involved

---

[86] GM, 10 July 1851, 23 Feb. 1852.
[87] GM, 1 Dec. 1859. For Rules see *Morris Pamphlets*, where a prospectus, dated 13 May 1853, is included.
[88] Chapman's view: see Shaw, *Relations between Town and Gown*, 60. Cf. Graham, *Butler*, 197.

in the dispute over the Lyon charity that had dogged the Hill for half a century. Compared with other Head Masters in similar situations, notably at Rugby and Shrewsbury, Vaughan's solution was sympathetic and enlightened. It was also practical. For all its faults, shortcomings, and anomalies, the English Form provided the precursor and blueprint that led, eventually, to the creation, by the reluctant Harrow governors, of 'The Under School of John Lyon' in 1876.

Boys

The pupils whose exclusivity Vaughan was so eager to protect were, a recent comparison with Merchant Taylor's school has concluded, underachievers, even at Oxford and Cambridge where about a third of leavers went.[89] Harrovians proceeded to unexceptional careers. Vaughan's restoration hardly altered the pattern. While the army maintained its primacy, the church, for all Vaughan's attempts to recruit, attracted a gradually decreasing percentage, falling from 12 per cent of 1845 entrants to 9 per cent of those admitted a decade later, a steady decline that persisted until in the 1880s only 2 per cent to 3 per cent took the cloth. The law was moderately popular, with between 10 per cent and 20 per cent. Few went into industry or manufacture, unless to a family firm, often brewing or distilling. The City was relatively unpopular, claiming 4 per cent of leavers in 1852–3 and only 2 per cent—i.e. one person—in Vaughan's last term. Most Old Harrovians were and regarded themselves as gentlemen. According to one of them, Montagu Butler, they were 'from the landed aristocracy', although he conceded with a delicate whiff of disdain that 'great numbers also are the sons of persons who have more recently become wealthy', as in all periods since the eighteenth century, wealth-inheritors rather than wealth creators.[90]

When at school, most had little interest in form work. Sport remained the most time-consuming extra-curricular activity. Football was still compulsory for all below the Fifth Form. Although Vaughan never went to watch it, cricket occupied fifteen to twenty hours a week in the Summer.[91] As with football, it was run entirely by boys, each having to pay the annual subscription to cover costs, which it sometime failed to do. Adult involvement came from the ubiquitous Ponsonby and Grimston. Until the arrival of Bowen in 1859, the only master to play cricket—or any games—with the boys was the Old Harrovian H. E. Hutton, one of Vaughan's first pupils who had played at Lord's in 1846 and 1847.[92] It was more Vaughan's

---

[89] Allen, 'Public School Elites', 90, 95–9, 107–16.
[90] *Clarendon Commission Report*, iv. 183. For statistics see *Harrow Register, 1800–1911, passim*; Bamford, *Rise of Public Schools*, esp. p. 210.
[91] Dalrymple, 'Vaughan', 113; *Clarendon Commission Report*, i. 222–3, iv. 193, 220–1, 230.
[92] Trueman Wood, 'Harrow in the Fifties', 402.

good fortune than design that the 1850s witnessed an unprecedented run of success against Eton. The paradox of a Head who 'hated athletics' succeeding in winning the respect of hearty pupils and parents after a great athlete, Wordsworth, had failed so abjectly was one recalled with characteristic glee by their successor Welldon.[93] Although acknowledging sport's potential for instilling community spirit, Vaughan warned against its tendency to encourage 'selfishness, self-importance, self-indulgence and self-will'.[94] He was not alone. Robert Lang, five years in the cricket eleven, two in the football, captain of cricket 1858–9, a Cambridge cricket blue and all-round sportsman, confessed to the Clarendon Commission that he thought games had received disproportionate time and prestige. However, Matthew Ridley, a Parkite (1856) future Home Secretary, in his evidence to the Commissioners, placed the sports-mad into a perspective which would have encouraged Vaughan: 'Boys distinguished in games have influence, but . . . I should never have dreamt of any such class of boys exercising a paramount influence when I was at Harrow'.[95] By then, however, the dam was breaking, the flood of athleticism imminent. Vaughan would have been intrigued, amused possibly, but hardly delighted at the thought that perhaps his most influential pupil was C. W. Alcock (Druries 1855–9), one of the inventors of Association Football.

Evidence of the social life of Vaughan's Harrovians is inevitably patchy and partial. Symonds portrays the school in general and Rendalls in particular in the 1850s as places of vulgarity, violence, and vice, shameless in bullying, aggressive in sodomy. His description of the sexual abuse of N. C. Cookson—'a red-faced strumpet, with flabby cheeks and sensual mouth, the *notissima fossa* of our house'—and his subsequent sufferings at the hands of former lovers makes grim reading. Yet, although prurient, Symonds presents such scenes as almost prosaic, the normal exchange between sexually active adolescents denied alternative release. There was little apparent rape. Whether psychologically damaged or not, Cookson became a coalowner and a noted grower of fine orchids. Attractive and willing younger boys were given female nicknames—the son of the Master of Pembroke College, Cambridge was known as Bum Bathsheba; an Irish Home Boarder Leila. The practice was not unique to Harrow. According to Symonds, only once—when a note from a Grovite inviting 'Leila' to his bed between Third and Fourth Schools (4–5 p.m.) was intercepted—did the authorities take action or even notice. Vaughan's solo confrontation of the whole school was clearly impressive; it even received a veiled mention in Dalrymple's published eulogy on Vaughan in 1898.[96] Yet the culprits only received a beating and some lines respectively. Symonds suggested that the masters did not know the nature or scale of active homosexuality in the school. It may be subtler than that. Vice for early nineteenth-century

---

[93] Welldon, *Recollections*, 109–10.   [94] Vaughan, *Sermons*, 269.
[95] *Clarendon Commission Report*, i. 221, 222–3, iv. 230.
[96] Symonds, *Memoirs*, esp. pp. 94–7, Dalrymple, 'Vaughan', 110.

schoolmasters meant drinking, gambling, lewd conversation, even idleness. Homosexuality as an indentifiable condition—or even word—was not recognized until the end of the century. Sodomy and masturbation were regarded as similar coarse habits, the existence of which bore no relation to the sentimental idealism of friendship or the extreme, passionate language of innocent affection that saturates Victorian correspondence. It was attitudes to sex not altered sexual behaviour that led to the increasingly shrill sex-panic in schools from the 1850s onwards, although it has been argued that the cult of athleticism contributed to encouraging precisely what it was aimed to combat.[97]

Symonds was obsessed with sex with men and boys. Other contemporaries were less fussed. Hare acknowledged that he had heard of the sexual immorality at Harrow in his time, but had not come across it partly, he thought, because he was not interested in it. He was far more worried by rampant bullying and the flogging of fags. Yet he also recorded his delight at performing in elaborate drag shows in the Grove and frying chips with an almost modern enthusiasm. His outrage was not at sex but at the sort of unrestrained violence that allowed Parkite Sixth Formers on the football fields to flog reluctant little boys with thorn sticks until 'blood poured down their jerseys', this six years before Platt's tantrum.[98] Harrow had a justified reputation for bullying. Matthew Ridley revealingly commented that a Parkite who had left because he had been bullied 'was a great deal too good natured.'[99] Frightening initiation rituals flourished and Vaughan made a habit of visiting each new boy on his first evening to prevent the house yahoos doing their worst. Bullying was one of the most serious crimes in Vaughan's view, meriting certain birching and probable expulsion. One head of the Park was expelled for excessively thrashing his fag for breaking his tea set.[100]

Hare's view of school life is of boisterousness not sin, brutality rather than sustained viciousness. Others were more anxious. One warned future Harrovians: 'set your face and ears against lewd and obscene jokes and jests, and shun, like the touch of a leper, any approach to acts of immorality . . . you will see all things going on about you that will shame.'[101] This is a vision of a world part-Symonds, part *Eric*. Yet for many serious-minded boys, as for the school moralists such as Farrar, the chief problem was masturbation not sodomy. In his diary entry on 23 March 1851 W. D. Legh admits that staying in bed in the morning 'still continues to be a great source of temptation and sin to me, but which I must continue to struggle

---

[97] See Mack, *Public Schools and British Opinion, 1780–1860*, 213–19; Honey, *Tom Brown's Universe*, 185–96; Gathorne-Hardy, *Public School Phenomenon*, 79–93, 144–80.

[98] Hare, *Story of My Life*, i. 217, 228, 241–4, 245.   [99] *Clarendon Commission Report*, iv. 222.

[100] K. E. Digby, 'Dr. C. J. Vaughan', *The Harrovian*, 20 Nov. 1897, p. 102; HA Head Master's House Prize Book, 1851–93; J. E. Mylne, 'Autobiography' (Feb. 1860), esp. fo. 23^{r-v}; *Clarendon Commission Report*, i. 221, ii. 281, iv. 200–1, 229.

[101] Daryl, *Recollections*, 68. But see also his more relaxed view of schoolboy life: ibid., 59–67.

against with vigilance and prayer'.[102] This is hardly the stuff of iniquity. For those, such as Hare who was not interested in immorality or for scholars such as C. S. Blayds, who was too busy composing Latin verses and finding quiet corners in which to smoke, school was not a vale of tears or sump of unbridled sensuality and lust. None the less, the fagging system was inevitably open to abuse.[103] Peter Withington (Head Master's 1849), writing at school in 1851, accused older boys of 'flagrant partiality towards any of the fags to whom on account of good looks or any other cause they may have taken a fancy'.[104] The Head of School, Monty Butler, commented on H. C. Stanley being 'dear to the big fellows' (he was withdrawn after only a year) and warned his successor: 'For God's sake, I say it solemnly, *do not let* FitzGerald (C.L., 1848) corrupt the new fellows.' It was almost certainly the habit of taking up with younger boys to which Butler referred when he wrote to a school friend in January 1852 celebrating the attack on what he called the 'petting system'.[105] Yet the calm, unsensational realism of Withington's comments on fagging in 1851 or J. E. Mylne's (Head Master's 1858) 'Autobiography of a Harrow Boy' of February 1860 must be placed in the balance against Symonds' morbidly overheated recollections.

Vaughan did not conceal the unflattering aspects of school life. His sermons confronted the crimes and temptations he wished his charges to guard against: drinking, gambling, lying, swearing, idleness, bullying, and sex.[106] Many Head Masters hid or ignored the potential for sin within their schools: Vaughan repeatedly chose to highlight it, as he did other less morally corrosive misdemeanours, such as stone-throwing, the hallmark of unreformed Harrow, and smoking. One source of corruption which particularly exercised Vaughan was light and comic literature, which, of course, he never read. His reaction to the discovery of actual pornography was, unsurprisingly, extreme.[107] However, to dwell on the sordid and prurient alone is to mislead. Of course the system was the source of its evils and the gap between the public rhetoric and the private lives yawning and unbridged. Yet, on its own terms, monitorial control maintained order within boarding houses, most problems deriving from mischief, boredom, and high spirits not malice or vice. At a school where the Under Master taking call-over was invariably a cue for riot, boys may well have been able to protect the weak better than some masters.[108] Vaughan managed, with a struggle, to abolish the worst excesses of the previous era, such as the 'Squash' ritual, the 5 November revels, access to pubs, hare and

---

[102] 'C.L.H.', *Memorials*, 22–3.
[103] Sendall, *Claverley*, 12–29; Minchin, *Old Harrow Days*, 259.
[104] HA MS Head Master's House Prize Book, 1851–93; P. Withington, *Schoollife at Harrow*, fo. 10ʳ. In general, see ibid., fos. 9ʳ–10ᵛ.
[105] Latham Letters, Butler to Latham, 5 Nov. 1851, 13 Jan. 1852.
[106] Vaughan, *Sermons*, 5, 16, 17, 78, 178–9, 181, 249, 281, 306, 317, 341, 342, 406, 439; id., *Memorials*, 93, 144–52 (an astonishingly critical catalogue of school sin), 191, 304, 310, 333, 347, 441.
[107] Id., *Sermons*, 449, 532; id., *Memorials*, 195.
[108] Trueman Wood, 'Harrow in the Fifties', 398.

hounds, massed snowball fights with the locals, and the malign influence of Billy Warner.[109] Vaughan was a realist. He understood boys and, to a degree unusual in his contemporaries, both tolerated and trusted them. Many of his pupils enjoyed their schooldays, learnt something, and retained fond memories. To that extent, Vaughan's Harrow did not distort adolescence more than other boarding schools, and probably less than some. For this, the Head must take some credit. Harrow was marginally less Hobbesian for his efforts. Masters did not need to treat all boys as vermin fit only as victims of their inner frustrations, outward posturings, or sadism. Thus, Vaughan instituted a special mischief charge in his boarding house 'applicable, for instance, to the case of a boy taking a poker, as is not infrequently done, and sending it through a partition wall'. It is 'not infrequently' that most strikingly captures the atmosphere of mutual recognition.[110]

In fifteen years Vaughan established Harrow on a pinnacle of renown and respectability. Speech Days saw the great and the good flock down to the Hill. In the highly competitive world of Victorian public schools, Vaughan ensured Harrow's eminence. In part this was due to the accident of history; in part to deliberate policy. Vaughan's conservative reluctance to confront vested interests or traditions produced two fundamental legacies that left Harrow bracketed with Eton rather than its natural peers, Rugby or Shrewsbury. The continuance and expansion of the system of autonomous Large Houses, pioneered under his immediate predecessors, coupled with the pervasive use of Small Houses, allowed Harrow masters to earn more than almost any other public school masters, Eton included. The Master of Marlborough earned less than a Harrow housemaster.[111] This allowed for the boys' living accommodation to be less cramped than elsewhere, as well as lending a distinct house-based tone to school life. There were no vast dormitories, not even in Vaughan's rebuilt Head Masters', unlike its predecessor. Equally, Vaughan did not follow the trend adopted almost universally elsewhere of centralizing by physically integrating forms and living quarters in combined school buildings, usually constructed in close proximity, such as around a quadrangle. The motive for centralization, as at Marlborough after the 1851 rebellion, was disciplinary, to reflect the authority of the Head and the unity of community under him. Harrow developed differently, on more Etonian lines, although lacking the collegiate focus.[112] From a commonwealth of boys in 1800, by 1900 Harrow had become a federation of houses, a source of particular strengths and weaknesses very different, then and now, from other public schools in atmosphere as well as physical aspect. That Harrow resisted current orthodoxy was due in considerable measure to the confidence as well as conservatism of Charles Vaughan.

[109] So Norman, *At School and at Sea*, 4–5; Thornton, *Harrow School*, 290, *et seq*. But, for a rather different set of impressions, cf. Hare, *Story of My Life*, i. 219–21, 223; Daryl, *Recollections*, 63–7; and Lang's evidence on accepted drinking and gambling: *Clarendon Commission Report*, iv. 229.
[110] *Clarendon Commission Report*, iv. 165.   [111] Honey, *Tom Brown's Universe*, 301.
[112] Cf. Gathorne-Hardy, *Public School Phenomenon*, ch. 5, esp. pp. 105–8.

Nemesis of a Head Master

In this heroic age of the reformed, refounded, or created public schools, the personalities of Head Masters proved vital. Here, Vaughan presents a problem. He left instructions on his death that all his papers be destroyed and that no biography be attempted. In life, too, he was the most hidden and elusive of men. Richmond's portrait, although concealing Vaughan's large nose and short chin, captures a quality commented upon by others: the face is a mask, the figure an icon. All witnesses testify to his quietness, his soft voice, his deliberate tread, his studied courtesy, a 'blandness behind which evidently lay a large reserve of determination and action',[113] above all his self-possession. Monty Butler remarked on Vaughan's battle to control his sarcastic wit and his lively, often irreverent conversation.[114] There was the suspicion of insincerity in his manner, knowing all but feigning innocence, all things to all who mattered. Yet of one thing there can be certainty. Although disliked by some, C. L. FitzGerald dismissing him as 'the little man', his chosen pupils adored him.[115] With them he relaxed; he could allow himself to be witty, provocative, challenging, inspirational, confiding. His reward was their devotion and friendship, a rapport of a sort he never achieved with colleagues. Writing in his first term at Cambridge in 1851, Monty Butler recorded that 'nearly all the Harrow men's rooms have Vaughan's picture in them'.[116]

Vaughan exerted influence in three ways: teaching, conversation, and preaching. His teaching was the least remarkable. Even the devoted Butler admitted that, despite excellent literary taste, he possessed a 'disproportionately narrow range of general reading'. Kenelm Digby (The Grove 1849–55) thought him 'not a man of wide reading or knowledge'. His pupils were given no Ancient History or Philosophy (i.e. Plato) in form, although the specially favoured read more widely in private sessions, including the *Phaedo*. His Scriptural teaching was confined to literal paraphrasing. Another witness described Vaughan as 'a teacher of pure and undiluted grammar ... no purely literary discussions were encouraged'. Vaughan's enthusiasm was for composing Greek verse and in 'verbal criticisms' of Greek dramatists, especially Sophocles and Aristophanes. One Harrow quip was that Vaughan's two strong points were tact and Greek iambics.[117]

Vaughan compensated for his small mind with expansive care for his pupils. It was in his long talks with the Upper Sixth or with the older boys in his house, sometime far into the night, that Vaughan had most effect. His 'wonderful sympathy' is

---

[113] Norman, *At School and at Sea*, 4.   [114] Graham, *Butler*, 30; Dalrymple, 'Vaughan', 108.
[115] Latham Letters, C. L. FitzGerald to Latham, probably *c.*Easter 1852.
[116] Latham Letters, Butler to Latham, 5 Nov. 1851. Cf. Butler's memories: Sendall, *Calverley*, 12–29 and G. O. Trevelyan's: Graham, *Butler*, esp. pp. xix–xx.
[117] Digby, 'Vaughan', 100; Dalrymple, 'Vaughan', 109; Graham, *Butler*, 30; Minchin, *Old Harrow Days*, 13, 105–6.

hard to reconstruct. According to G. O. Trevelyan, 'he gave us an unbounded freedom of remark and reply, to an extent which sometimes bordered on presumption, but never on impertinence. He seemed to like us better for our faults which, after due reflection, made us the more heartily and sincerely ashamed of them'.[118]

In one sermon Vaughan argued, 'He who feels his own sinfulness . . . can warn a sinner of a danger common to them both . . . for that he himself also is compassed with infirmity'. Although such intimacy and freedom courted exploitation, disappointment, even disaster, and clearly satisfied his own emotional needs, Vaughan's sympathy appears to have been genuine. He got on well with these boys. Whatever his private discourse, in public he repeatedly emphasized that 'it is only as a sinner that any of us can approach God'.[119] Vaughan may have been a dissembler, but on occasion he could be refreshingly unsanctimonious.

Of his sarcastic vein, little evidence survives. He liked to pour scorn on politicians. Once he insisted that 'he found boys always fair, masters sometimes, the parents never; and as for widows, he confessed he had sometimes been tempted to reconsider his objections to sutee.' His method of signalling to boys when to go at the end of a party was to advance on the shyest, hand outstretched, murmuring 'Must you go? Can't you stay?' Vaughan used to reduce, and be reduced by, his Sixth Form to raucous laughter.[120] He also came across as interested in their welfare. The benefit he derived is apparent. In 1851 he wrote to George Butler about his son Monty who had just left school: 'he has been for the last year I may truly say *everything* to me at Harrow.' To Monty himself, Catherine Vaughan, married only the year before, wrote 'to him (i.e. Vaughan) who has taught you for so long, it is no trifling sorrow to part with you in one sense for ever'.[121] Mrs Vaughan knew her husband.

Vaughan's sermons were once thought one of the glories of mainstream midnineteenth-century Anglicanism. Today they appear intellectually shallow in their literalness of Scriptural interpretation. Every paragraph proclaims Vaughan as no theologian. However, the pulpit was his favoured platform. By careful manipulation of the governors and by even more skilful outmanœuvring of the jealous and meddling Cunningham, by 1857, when his new chapel was opened, Vaughan had extracted the school from any formal attendance at the Parish Church. Judging from recorded responses, his weekly sermons to the whole school were effective: inspirational to some; moving to others; memorable to most. The reasons are not hard to find. His language was precise; his arguments possessed internal logic and structure; his subjects almost always relevant to the preoccupations of his congregation; his tone pleading and personal. Again and again, Vaughan drew the great Christian truths of sin and redemption in images and examples from school life.

---

[118] Graham, *Butler*, p. xx. Cf. Dalrymple, 'Vaughan', 112.
[119] Vaughan, *Sermons*, 71, 181.
[120] Graham, *Butler*, 29; Moore, *Vaughan*, 6; Sendall, *Calverley*, 20.
[121] Graham, *Butler*, 41.

He was uncompromising in his insistence on man's and boys' sinfulness; the risk of eternal damnation; and the difficulties of leading a Christian life especially at school, which he repeatedly warned was a place of temptation where bad habits condemned the unwary to Hell. At a simple level, Vaughan's sermons were appeals to the boys to pray regularly and to behave properly by avoiding idleness, swearing, bullying, deceit, and unclean thoughts or acts. There was a strained urgency in them at odds with his suave, relaxed conversational manner, but which was the more impressive for being directed to them rather than merely at them. Vaughan kept faith with his mentor. In the sermon, as nowhere else, lay the essentials of Arnold and Vaughan: authority, community, instruction, spiritual direction, moral responsibility, and religion. To these, Vaughan added his own obsessions: the possibility of repentance and forgiveness.

In 1859 there was no obvious reason why Vaughan should not have continued at Harrow until an important see became vacant. It was a myth that he had always said fifteen years was enough: he only said it after his resignation, which came with unpredicted, shocking suddenness; even Cunningham was surprised. In correspondence with the clerk to the governors, as late as 24 August there was no hint of retirement. Yet on 16 September he sent a rather abrupt note announcing his intention to resign at Christmas.[122] He was only 43, a royal chaplain, at the height of his powers and reputation, still planning for Harrow's future. He had sat on the 1856 Royal Commission into the University of Cambridge and was talked of, to the horror of the fellows, as a possible Master of Trinity.[123] His serene progress had been punctuated by school scandals of a routine nature, most of which can only be traced in allusive private correspondence and oblique references in sermons. There were comments that discipline was wearing thin.[124] Yet other sources suggest no slackening of his grip. One ploy was to summon a whole house (as in one stone-throwing incident) or even the whole school to the Speech Room in the Old Schools where he would confront them with the offence and challenge the culprits to confess. When he exposed the projected homosexual liaison between 'Leila' and his admirer and criticized the school in general for their habit of bestowing female nicknames on each other (a bit unfairly as Vaughan's brother-in-law, A. P. Stanley had been called 'Nancy' at Rugby), alone, he held over 400 boys in complete stillness.[125] Vaughan had courage as well as presence.

Neither could save him from blackmail. Symonds' account of the fall of Dr Vaughan is so extraordinary that, since its revelation by Phyllis Grosskurth in 1964 it has been attacked not just by loyal Old Harrovians and has formed the basis

---

[122] Young Letter Book, fos. 49, 51–2, 52–3. Cf. the printed circular dated 16 Sept.
[123] Dalrymple, 'Vaughan', 111; Graham, *Butler*, 82; Coulton, *Fourscore Years*, 142.
[124] Graham, *Butler*, 29. There are also hints throughout his sermons 1857–9: Vaughan, *Memorials passim*.
[125] Symonds, *Memoirs*, 96; Dalrymple, 'Vaughan', 110. Cf. Hare, *Story of My Life*, i. 218–19.

of a novel.[126] In January 1858 Symonds was informed by a fellow member of the Upper Sixth, Alfred Pretor, that the Head Master had begun a love affair with him, in proof of which Pretor showed the disbelieving Symonds some passionate letters from Vaughan. Symonds, at the time a repressed homosexual, was incensed by prurient indignation and jealousy. Even though Pretor and Vaughan continued their affair, largely conducted in the Head Master's study overlooking the High Street, Symonds did not speak out, taking solace, as did so many nineteenth-century classicists of his persuasion, in Plato. Symonds and Pretor left Harrow in July 1858. It was not until a year later, at the beginning of his first Summer vacation from Oxford in 1859 that he divulged the secret to John Conington, the professor of Latin. In corroboration, Symonds produced one of Vaughan's letters to Pretor. Conington immediately insisted Symonds inform his father. Symonds senior, a Clifton doctor of grand connections and powerful personality, immediately wrote to Vaughan revealing that he possessed proof of his affair with Pretor. Unless Vaughan resigned immediately and promised to seek no further advancement in the church, he would be exposed. Vaughan, apparently as calm as ever, travelled to Clifton to inspect the evidence, accepted it, and, with the advice of his brother-in-law Stanley and Canon Hugh Pearson, an Old Harrovian friend, agreed terms. A few days later Catherine Vaughan followed to beg for mercy. She knew of what she called her husband's 'weakness', but argued that it had not interfered with his running of the school. Dr Symonds was implacable. Vaughan resigned.

Vaughan soon learnt that this alone was insufficient to appease his persecutors. On leaving Harrow, Vaughan was offered the see of Rochester by the Prime Minister, Palmerston. Vaughan accepted, his decision being sufficiently definite for him to have offered the chancellorship of the diocese to a friend and for Farrar to have given his Form a free lesson in celebration.[127] Within hours the acceptance was withdrawn (and Farrar's lesson reinstated) after the arrival of a telegram from Dr Symonds. When later in 1860 he was proposed for Worcester, Vaughan turned it down immediately, as he did subsequent offers of even grander sees, to the baffled fury of his friends and the disbelief of his enemies. Instead, he became vicar of Doncaster and, in 1869, Master of the Temple in London. Only after Dr Symonds' death did Vaughan accept higher preferment, becoming dean of Llandaff in 1879. Ironically, and no doubt to the anger of the Symonds family, Vaughan made a virtue of his predicament. He became a symbol of humility. In a sense he was forced to live up to his own precept. In an uncannily prophetic sermon in May 1859, he urged the virtues of renunciation, hoping some would be 'contented ... to stand aside ... to live under reproach and even to die under misconstruction, if a sense of the national interests both made a certain course their obvious duty and

---

[126] The account is in Symonds, *Memoirs*, 97–100, 110–16.
[127] Thornton, *Harrow School*, 300 n. 1; Coulton, *Fourscore Years*, 142; Grosskurth, *Symonds*, 37 conflates the two offers of 1860 and misdates them.

debarred them from an immediate explanation of reasons and motives'.[128] For the next forty years Vaughan had to practise what he had preached. Yet such was his personality, resilience, and position the restoration of Harrow had won him in the eyes of the ecclesiastical establishment, that he carved out a unique role for himself. Between 1861 and his death in 1897, privately and for no fee he tutored 461 young ordinands for the priesthood, including the future archbishop, the Old Harrovian Randall Davidson. These pupils were known as Vaughan's 'doves' and their devotion to their teacher was as firm and ardent as any of his Sixth Form at Harrow. They even built a church in his memory in Kensal Rise. Of Vaughan, Archbishop Benson remarked, apparently without irony, 'no living man has laid the Church of England under greater obligations'.[129] However, it was hardly the career that had beckoned before the fateful Summer of 1859.

Is Symonds's story true? For any verdict on Vaughan, this is crucial. Circumstantial evidence supports Symonds. Dalrymple, one of those school friends of Pretor and Symonds supposedly in the know, confirms the 'Leila' scene in Speech Room and, in a strikingly guarded, unengaged, enigmatic, and reserved published encomium in 1898, casts doubt on Vaughan's insistence that his resignation merely followed Arnoldian precept, claiming it 'took most people by surprise'. Dalrymple, who supposedly strongly condemned Symonds for breach of confidence, even refers, rather gratuitously, to Vaughan as 'a great letter-writer'.[130] There is no doubt Vaughan's resignation came out of the blue, nor that Catherine Vaughan was genuinely distressed in December 1859, as if the move was scarcely of their making.[131] For some years after 1859 there was much high-class clerical gossip about Vaughan's reasons, the *nolo episcopari* stance from a man of known ambition fuelling incredulity and speculation. It may be significant or coincidental that one of Vaughan's first visitors at Doncaster was William Johnson Cory, the Eton master who became a sort of high priest of intellectual pederasty.[132]

Against this, Symonds' memoirs were composed thirty years after the event. He had a fertile imagination, especially when describing his homosexual awakening. Some of the other Harrow passages are littered with small errors of detail, while, in possibly suspicious contrast, the setting of Vaughan's and Pretor's affair is graphically described. Symonds implies that Vaughan was in the habit of sitting next to pupils on his sofa stroking their thighs while going over their Greek verses. More seriously, the memoirs as a whole constitute an extended propagandist essay on the nature of homosexual orientation and Symonds' heroic passage to enlightenment.

---

[128] Vaughan, *Memorials*, 362.
[129] Dalrymple, 'Vaughan', 113; Coulton, *Fourscore Years*, 141; Moore, *Vaughan*, 7 and 8–12 for a sermon preached in memory of Vaughan by one of his 'doves': R. L. White, 21 Jan 1945.
[130] Dalrymple, 'Vaughan', 110, 113.
[131] See her letter to Gustave Masson in the Collings MSS.
[132] Recalled by G. O. Trevelyan, Graham, *Butler*, p. xix. For gossip see Grosskurth, *Symonds*, 37–40; Symonds, *Memoirs*, 113–15.

If Symonds' story is true, then there are few finer examples of the closed society of the Victorian establishment at work than the covering up of the scandal not just from public gaze but from those inside the charmed circle. Unless we posit astounding levels of communal irony and self-control, the encomiums for Vaughan that showered on him must have been genuine. For a reprobate old gossip such as Welldon, who would have had more than one reason to be interested in Vaughan's destruction, to have written as he did if he had known stretches creduilty: 'few headmasters, indeed perhaps few clergymen have been so generally trusted as Dr Vaughan.'[133] If Welldon did not know it is testimony either to a standard of discretion that Symonds himself denies Pretor, who supposedly was free with the story, or to the fact that the whole thing is untrue. Certainly, the scandal if it existed never spread beyond a very close circle. One of Vaughan's doves, an unlikely one as it transpired, the historian G. G. Coulton also knew Pretor, who was a fellow of St Catherine's College, Cambridge. In the same autobiography in which Vaughan has an honoured place, Coulton described Pretor as 'a favourite pupil of Vaughan at Harrow [who] drew his dividend [at St Catherine's] practically as a sleeping partner . . . a man of refined taste who condescended at rare intervals to show his attractive face and select dress at High Table'.[134] For neither Welldon nor Coulton to have known is impressive.

No letters of Vaughan to Pretor survive: Symonds apparently ordered all relevant papers he possessed to be destroyed at his death in 1893. None the less, some of Vaughan's correspondence does survive which may help assess if not the truth then the plausibility of Symonds' account. Edward Latham was in the Head Master's 1845–52, a monitor and head of house in his final year, 1851–2. Twenty-two letters to him from Dr Vaughan survive in the Harrow School Archives. To provide some control when reacting to the linguistic fashion for extremes of expression and the nuances and connotations of words and phrases, the Latham letters can be compared with those from Vaughan to two other contemporaries, Monty Butler and H. M. Jackson. In all three collections, Vaughan's tone is affectionate, often playful; his and their use of 'love', 'beloved', 'long for', etc. are free of sexual overtones.[135] Even so, some of the Latham letters are arresting.

On a scrap of sealed paper, Vaughan writes to his head of house: 'Dearest Latham, Will you accept this little remembrance? from your ever affectionate CV'; or: 'Dearest Latham, Will you accept this little, very little trifle in aid of your travelling expenses—from your ever attached and affectionate friend C Vaughan. PS Your visit will live in my recollection for a long time.'[136] Once Latham has left, inevitably for Trinity, Cambridge, a strain of nostalgic longing enters Vaughan's

---

[133] Welldon, *Recollections*, 110.   [134] Coulton, *Fourscore Years*, 117–18.
[135] HM/Vaughan, *passim*; I must thank Sarah Tyerman for her immaculate transcriptions, surely the oddest convalescence therapy.
[136] Latham Letters, both undated, except the first which just has 'Sunday night'.

letters, coupled with a persistent and unexpected sense of insecurity. On 17 February 1853, Vaughan wrote:

I do not know whether you care for letters: I rather doubt it—at least for letters such as I could should care for . . . I long to see you . . . I often wonder whether you have forgotten or changed towards me. But I do not know why I should suppose it—except that it seems improbable that anyone should remember me when I have been two or three months out of their sight.

At the top of this letter, Vaughan wrote 'Burn this'.[137] While invigilating an examination in Speech Room on 20 July 1853, Vaughan penned these thoughts: 'the more I think of all your kind thought and care about me . . . and then in what you said and did for me here, the more sure do I feel that you will not change nor forget me . . . dear, dear Latham.'[138]

In November 1853 Vaughan suggested Latham might prefer to visit when they will be 'entirely alone'. On 16 January 1854, Vaughan wrote: 'I always feel towards you so very much more than I can write—and I fear it makes my letters very absurd. But you are indulgent and kind—I do not fear you.'[139]

Whatever should be made of the Latham correspondence, it reveals that Vaughan was no stranger to emotional letters. Those to Pretor were, perhaps, not so unusual. The Latham letters also display a vulnerability not wholly disguised by jocularity. Vaughan, in common with many of the best public school masters of the last two centuries, involved himself emotionally with his pupils. In consequence he reaped harvests sweet and bitter.

Despite the difficulties surrounding believing such a remarkable cover-up, the evidence of Symonds' story is, on balance, credible. This does not require out of hand condemnation. In the light of the vulnerability exposed in the Latham letters, Vaughan appears if anything more remarkable, not least in coping with his fall. This seems to have been the verdict of Monty Butler who perhaps knew Vaughan as well as anybody was allowed. Preaching in Llandaff Cathedral on 24 October 1897, a few days after Vaughan's death, on the text 'He served his generation', Butler goes almost as far as he could in lifting the veil on Vaughan's secret and his character. For Butler, it is uncharacteristically acute and poignant: he must have known.

Nature had meant him for an ambitious man . . . But along with this current of a natural ambition there was another, a supernatural current of quite exceptional devoutness, a dread of himself, a profound prostration before God in Christ, an overwhelming sense of the danger of personal sin, and of being led by the tempter to a pinnacle and a pitfall. It is I believe in the recognition of these two sweeping currents of temperament and of the

---

[137] Ibid., Vaughan to Latham, 17 Feb. 1853.
[138] Ibid., Vaughan to Latham, Wed., 12 noon, 20 July 1853.
[139] Ibid., Vaughan to Latham, 16 Jan. 1854.

pathetic struggle carried on between them, that we shall best see the beauty of his life, the secret of his influence, the key, it may be, to some unexplained decisions at some critical moments.[140]

Butler's words, Vaughan's 'dread of himself', are borne out in the most astonishing setting, his sermons to the school. Again and again, they appear as dialogues with himself as much as with his pupils, almost a personal commentary. One recurrent theme was deceit: 'One man, by a plausible manner eludes for many years the discovery of his wickedness; perhaps he dies with it still hidden'; or: 'we enable ourselves to do wrong, to gratify our sinful desires to the very uttermost, and yet all the time to do our appointed work, as though we had been upright', almost the very words of Catherine Vaughan at the feet of Dr Symonds.[141]

Vaughan can with justice be accused of grossest hypocrisy, as in a famous passage when he condemned any older boy who leads astray a younger one as 'a murderer, in the worst of ways; a murderer of the soul made in God's image'.[142] Yet he was almost playful in challenging perhaps himself. On 6 November 1859, his fate sealed, he calmly preached a sermon on letters.[143] More serious was his acute sensitivity to sinfulness, in himself as well as others: 'we must not look in this world for freedom from temptation . . . even victory, the victory of years, does not exterminate the foe.'[144] In May 1858, when apparently involved with Pretor, he described physical desire as always with us, the 'enemy in the very camp'.[145] The following September, he digressed on remorse, repentence without God: 'if repentence is loneliness, remorse is desolation.'[146] Yet he believed—he had to—that sinners could help save souls. There may have lain his anguished justification. His mission, as he put it in the peroration of the last sermon as Harrow's Head Master, was to 'make this place all that a Christian school may be—diligent, faithful, pure, religious—the nurse of Christian men, the trying place of souls for heaven!'[147]

Judged on this programme, Vaughan, the stupendous hypocrite, could claim he had at least tried to honour his calling. He was no great prophet or academic. He may not compare with Butler of Shrewsbury, Cotton of Marlborough, Thring of Uppingham, or Benson of Wellington or the other pioneering paladins of nineteenth-century public schools. As a disciple he never outshone his mentor Arnold. Yet his task, compared with theirs, was more delicate, more important. His rule was never out of the limelight. If he had failed at Harrow, his principles could have gone down with him. The position of the Arnoldians was by no means impregnable in the 1840s as it was a decade later. His pivotal role not just for Harrow but for an educational movement, may help explain the concealment of the scandal: it

---

[140] H. M. Butler, '*He Served his Generation': A Sermon Preached in Llandaff Cathedral on 24 October 1897* (n.p., 1897), p. 12.   [141] Vaughan, *Sermons*, 326, 462–3.
[142] Id., *Memorials*, 148. Apparently during his affair with Pretor.
[143] Ibid., no. XXXVI, p. 459.   [144] Id., *Sermons*, 342.   [145] Id., *Memorials*, 192.
[146] Ibid., 208.   [147] Ibid., 528.

was vital to secure the survival of a system, a creed almost, in which so many believed and from which, it must be said, so many derived so much material profit.

At Harrow Vaughan's success was stunning and his legacy, not least in the shape of Montagu Butler, endured. Vaughan created a rationally ordered community that worked, a garden out of a wilderness. If a serpent lurked in that garden, that hardly diminished the public achievement nor, even, the inspiration given many of his pupils, however shifting the sands on which it was built. Vaughan felt the contradictions keenly. On his deathbed he persistently asked 'Is there forgiveness?'[148] From there in 1897 he addressed the Triennial Dinner of old Harrovians with typical remorse and self-deprecation: 'The Harrow of 1845–1859 would not know me now—an old man, full of regrets and sorrows for many things, but most of all for this—that he is laden with a gratitude which he does not deserve, and with love which he can now repay only by idly loving back.'[149]

Charles Vaughan was a remarkable man and a remarkable Head Master, one of the few who managed convincingly to share in the personal and spiritual anxieties of his pupils. Unlike many who attempt this, he was never smug or self-important. He may have lectured his pupils; he did not patronize them; rather he agonized with them, even if they only dimly realized it. He helped them. Some thought him a humbug; others a saint. He was neither. Rather he was a flawed hero, whose humanity, at once attractive and repulsive, was forged on the anvil of his private combat with sin. In words he put in the mouth of an imaginary—perhaps not so very imaginary—confessor:

I was once as you are now. I lived as you are living. I sinned as you sin. I have suffered for it. Behold me now. Hear my tale of sorrow—how my sin found me out—how it pursued me all my life long—how it brought me to a condition which you cannot envy—how it has aggravated all my difficulties and poisoned all my joys. Hear and fear.[150]

---

[148] Moore, *Vaughan*, 8.   [149] Graham, *Butler*, 395.   [150] Vaughan, *Sermons*, 524.

12

REFORM

Of all the nineteenth-century Royal Commissions of inquiry and subsequent reforms of established English institutions such as the army, civil service, and universities, the oddest by far concerned public schools, 1861–4. Initiated by liberal reformers in response to a growing critical clamour, reform of the grandest public schools in the event was conducted by moderate sympathizers who desired to strengthen rather than transform. The subsequent legislation was largely a House of Lords Bill, finally piloted through parliament by a Conservative administration. While ostensibly reforming corrupt and inept corporations, the changes both intended and effected confirmation of some of the very practices that had originally aroused criticism, notably the classical curriculum, social elitism, snobbery, and headmagisterial despotism. Public school reform was proudly conservative, at best placing the existing educational systems at such schools on an unchallengeable legal basis; at worst, an elaborate and costly manœuvre by the ruling elite to restrict access to their ranks. Put crudely, public school reform succeeded triumphantly in what some saw as its essential purpose: to save Eton.[1]

The wider implications of the Clarendon Commission (1861–4) and the resulting Public School Act (1868) were more startling. As part of the general scrutiny of education which included the Endowed Schools Act (1869) and Forster's Education Act (1870), public school reform established a national educational system explicitly based on class. Unlike Brougham's Charity Commissioners in 1818, there was no mechanism for public accountability in the 1868 reforms, last ditch attempts to ensure a measure of external scrutiny through statutory school inspections being successfully resisted. Head Masters' power remained as unshaken as their classical education; their curriculum and discipline were held up as models

---

[1] In general on reform see C. Shrosbree, *Public Schools and Private Education: The Clarendon Commission, 1861–64 and the Public Schools Act* (Manchester, 1988), *passim*, esp. pp. 92, 188–9 for Eton as a separate target; Mack, *Public Schools and British Opinion since 1860* (New York, 1941), pp. 3–49, 91–100.

for emulation; traditional charitable purposes were either separated or dissolved, it being an article of faith that classes could not mix educationally, that each required distinctive intellectual training while, as has recently been remarked, 'the classics fulfilled the same sociological function in Victorian England as calligraphy in ancient China—a device to regulate and limit entry into a governing elite'.[2] The commercial principle underpinning the transmutation from grammar to public schools, that of paying fees for education despite or in addition to existing endowments for the purpose, was accepted without demur. Public schools were not just confirmed as resorts of 'Englishmen of the higher class', they were praised as setting the moral tone for the educational of lower orders. According to the Clarendon Commission:

> It is not easy to estimate the degree in which the English people are indebted to these schools for the qualities on which they pique themselves most—for their capacity to govern others and control themselves, their aptitude for combining freedom with order, their public spirit, their vigour and manliness of character, their strong but not slavish respect for public opinion, their love of healthy sports and exercise. These schools have been the chief nurseries of our statesmen ... and they have had perhaps the largest share in moulding the character of an English gentleman.[3]

Hardly surprising sentiments from a panel of Etonians, Wykehamists, Westminsters, and Rugbeians, yet they were of immense future significance. The acceptance by parliament of the status of public schools as beyond reproach or control in their academic, social, and moral aspects and the confirmation not just of their independence but of their superiority enshrined a hierarchy of schooling that persists. No serious, lasting partnership between public and private educational provision has subsequently been possible in England, the parliament of 1868 effectively condemning succeeding governments to concern themselves with educating the openly branded lower classes and ensuring the continuance of public schools as the accepted training ground of the ruling class. While other Victorian reforms increased access to institutions on merit, the 1868 Act closed access to public schools, now officially acknowledged as deserving 'to rank among English institutions', to all but a few, privileged by birth, wealth, and nothing else. As the *Harrow Gazette* fulminated in June 1867, 'it is a rich man's Bill'.[4]

The process of public school reform fell into three distinct phases: the examination of nine leading public schools by the Royal Commission chaired by the earl of Clarendon between 1861 and 1864; the parliamentary battle between 1865 and 1868 to devise and pass a Public Schools Act to deal with seven of the investigated schools; and the creation of new governing bodies and their framing of fresh

---

[2] Shrosbree, *Public Schools*, 59.
[3] *Report of the Royal Commission on Public Schools* (*The Clarendon Commission*) (London, 1864), i. 10, 56.   [4] Ibid., i. 56; *Harrow Gazette*, no. 154, 1 June 1867, p. 1.

statutes and regulations in accordance with the Act between 1868 and 1874. While the Commission had investigated all aspects of the management of the schools' finances, structure, entry, discipline, and curriculum, the 1868 Act only tackled administrative and financial matters, the new governing bodies, statutes, and rules being vetted by Special Commissioners whose brief ended once the provisions of the Act had been fulfilled. At Harrow, the alterations were spread over more than fifteen years from the arrival of the questionnaires from the Public School Commissioners in October 1861 until the opening of the Lower School of John Lyon in 1876 and the final implementation of the financial and administrative changes a year later.

Throughout, the governors and masters, especially the Head Master, Montagu Butler, were determined that there should be as little upheaval as possible and less external interference in the way the public school was run. None the less, although insistent that Harrow already fostered general intellectual and moral qualities that prepared boys 'to become profitable members of the Church and Commonwealth', after 1864 Butler shrewdly introduced significant changes to the academic system of the school in the spirit of the Commission's inquiry and report before legislation was enacted.[5] In part this was to demonstrate one of his and his colleagues' central arguments, that parliamentary reform was unnecessary as the Head Master held exisiting powers to implement alterations.[6] The Harrow parishioners, on the other hand, were by turns fearful and outraged that their rights were being trampled beneath the march to secure the exclusivity of the public school. However, the force of their arguments was dissipated through the clear division of interest between the rich gentry eager to maintain their privilege of free education and the tradesmen and farmers who still desired all Lyon's money to go where he had wished, to educate the poorer of the parish.

The Public Schools Commission was hardly the vehicle for radical change, the Etonian Gladstone, then chancellor of the Exchequer and a prime mover in its establishment, insisting that its purpose was to examine, not attack.[7] The aim was to improve the schools rather than coerce or destroy them. At all stages of the process from 1861 until the new statutes and regulations were approved in 1874, schools had been closely and sympathetically consulted, even if at times witnesses were harried, excesses revealed, and inadequacies exposed. The reaction of schools mixed aggression, smugness, myopia, and subterfuge. A number of Harrow masters, including Butler, simply lied about their income.[8] Yet the Commission's

---

[5] Graham, *Butler*, 198 and, in general, pp. 195–211.
[6] Expressed in a printed open letter from the Head and Assistant Masters, 31 Mar. 1865.
[7] Mack, *Public Schools and British Opinion, 1780–1860*, 27–8.
[8] Both Oxenham's and Marillier's statements: *Clarendon Commission Report*, ii. 285 as to profits and numbers paying them can be demonstrated to have been misleading by a comparison with their personal financial records. Bradby admitted that his statement was of the calculated profit he used for Income Tax purposes (ibid., ii. 284). Butler, ibid., i. 209 and ii. 272–3, declared a vague gross figure

composition was hardly threatening. Lord Lyttleton and Sir Stafford Northcote, the Tory frontbencher, were Etonians; the earl of Devon, a Westminster; Edward Twistleton, a Wykhamist; Halford Vaughan, a Rugbeian; William Thompson, a don. Their effectiveness was doubted even by their chairman, who described Northcote as pedantic, Devon as weak, Twistleton as quirky, Thompson as idle, and Vaughan as mad. Lyttleton, of whom the chairman approved, was no more flattering: Northcote was consumed by political ambition; Devon devoid of humour; Twistleton erratic; Thompson indolent; and Vaughan intolerable.[9] The most radical of them all was perhaps the chairman himself. Lord Clarendon had not attended a public school, although his eldest son was in West Acre (1858–63). With extensive experience of Europe, his perspective on English education was not conventional. For example, he believed that 'a parent was likely to be better acquainted with the disposition of his own son than the headmaster', a heretical view that cut at the heart of Arnoldian magisterial omniscient tyranny with its insistence on the insulated autonomy of the public school's world but one that Clarendon pursued through his keen interest in his own son's progress.[10] A former and future Whig Foreign Secretary, Clarendon probably owed his chairmanship to the desire of Palmerston and Russell to get him out of the way. He proved himself a sharp interrogator, his forensically deadly exposure of the gigantic, time-honoured, illegal profit-taking by the fellows of Eton on the first day of hearing evidence there in 1862 being matched by his ruffling of the smooth Montagu Butler in 1865 before the House of Lords Select Committee.[11] Butler had argued against the appointment of men of science as governors, as proposed in the Public Schools Bill then being considered, claiming they might interfere with the academic running of the school. Clarendon commented with measured sarcasm that Butler only preferred the status quo because it allowed him to be an absolute dictator. This exchange is the more remarkable as Clarendon had, since January 1861, been a governor of Harrow, throughout and after the period of the inquiry a regular attender at governors' meetings at which the implications of his Commission's findings were discussed.[12]

The Commission concerned itself with three areas of scrutiny and two general targets. The scandal of the management of Eton by its fellows as well as the high and often lurid profile of the school in general made it a case in itself. The other eight schools could almost be seen as a smokescreen for the main object. However, by including these, the Commission was implying a distinction between them and other public schools which was in fact arbitrary. The original proponents of a

of c.£10,000 when, on his own figures, he should have admitted to over £12,700. He was usually a most punctillious administrator.

[9] Shrosbree, *Public Schools*, 94; Mack, *Public Schools and British Opinion since 1860*, 28 nn. 46, 47.
[10] Shrosbree, *Public Schools*, 124. Cf. pp. 61, 77, and 125.
[11] Gathorne-Hardy, *Public School Phenomenon*, 97; Mack, *Public Schools and British Opinion, 1780–1860*, 46 n. 85. [12] GM, 18 Jan. 1861, *et seq*.

Royal Commission had argued for the inclusion of all Endowed Schools, some of whom resented the elite status given to the Clarendon schools, while two of those covered by the Public School Commission—St Paul's and Merchant Taylor's—thought their inclusion as mainly day schools inappropriate in predominantly boarding company: they were omitted from the final legislation. The Commission itself recognized the artificiality of their brief by collecting evidence from Marlborough, Cheltenham, and Wellington, new foundations claiming to provide a distinctively public school education, as well as the metropolitan day schools of the City of London and King's College. Some witnesses provided further comparisons with schools such as King Edward's, Birmingham, Christ's Hospital, and Repton. Thus the third, unofficial, more general remit was to investigate a whole type of education. Yet for all the targets remained the same: the financial management of the endowments by governors and the educational administration of the schools by the Head Master and his colleagues.[13] Despite the cosy establishment links, no school investigated emerged unscathed.

Harrow fared better than some for the mundane reason that the Trust assets were so meagre.[14] Unlike at Eton or Winchester, there was little scope for serious fraud or corruption, the modest sums the governors paid themselves scarcely meriting a mention. More serious was the application of the trusts to local education. Here, Harrow had the advantage of the 1810 judgment to support the legality, if not the morality, of current arrangements. The Head Master's unfettered financial control over all tuition fees was a matter of greater concern, the Commissioners politely indicating their disbelief of Butler's statement of his income by suggesting that his 'real emoluments are unascertained, and indeed unascertainable'.[15] There was much interest in the direct relation of boarders to Assistant Masters' profits and what they got for their money. More damaging to the school was the published oral and written evidence supplied by the Head, masters, and old boys. From it Harrow appeared as an expensive school run by wealthy entrepreneurial masters who did no actual teaching, even as tutors. Despite the introduction of maths and modern languages over the previous quarter of a century, the staple academic diet was classics of a non-scholarly kind, yet the academic standards of leavers, even those going to university, was 'low'.[16] Even the Head Master admitted 'there is really but a small literary interest among the boys', confessing in his covering letter to the Harrow evidence that when a Harrovian left 'his actual acquirements are probably extremely scanty'.[17] Sport, especially cricket in the Summer, occupied almost as much time each week as formal lessons, which took up perhaps twenty-two hours a week, up to eighteen of which were for classics. Such was the status of other

---

[13] Honey, *Tom Brown's Universe*, esp. p. 242; Shrosbree, *Public Schools*, esp. pp. 92–3.
[14] For the Harrow evidence see *Clarendon Commission Report*, i. 6–49, 209–28; ii. 269–86, 494–7; iv. 154–230. [15] Ibid., i. 226.
[16] Ibid., i. 26. [17] Ibid., iv. 183; Graham, *Butler*, 198.

subjects that masters openly disagreed over when either maths or modern languages had been introduced. In any case one witness claimed that at Harrow he had forgotten what French he knew when he came.[18] Other subjects were cursorily dealt with in the curriculum, natural science not at all, being entirely voluntary. Divinity meant weekly tests on bits of the Bible prepared out of school. Most classrooms were poorly ventilated slums. Boys' houses lacked bathrooms, there was no school sanitorium, and not all houses had sick rooms. The monitorial power of boys to cane was not just defended but lauded, for Butler 'the only true way to govern boys is to train them to govern themselves'.[19] Yet the theme of bullying and the example of the Platt–Stewart incident coursed through the evidence. The Commissioners were prepared to give Arnoldian principles the benefit of the doubt, but they allowed discrepancies between the evidence on pupils' manners and morals from masters and old boys to stand. The best that could be said was that there were no gaffes or startling revelations. The obsessive traditionalism of Butler and many of his staff who appeared as witnesses, Westcott perhaps excepted, occasionally grated, as when the Commisioners dismissed all arguments in favour of the boys' uniform of 'an evening dress coat': 'we see no sufficient reason for obliging them to wear at school a coat which they are sure never to wear at home'.[20] Intriguingly, this most trivial of absurdities still survives when the more significant deficiencies identified by the Clarendon Commission have long gone.

The final report of the Clarendon Commission published in 1864 recommended changes to the structure of the trust, the management of the school, and the details of the curriculum while carefully preserving the essential social character of the institution. It proposed a new governing body of twelve for whom there was to be no residence qualification but a new religious test of membership of the Church of England instead. These governors were to have the power to regulate the studies, discipline, and management of the school. Local Foundationers' rights were to be abolished both to free education at the public school and to election as Lyon scholars at the universities. Instead, Lyon Trust money should be spent on the establishment of a Lower School and the erection of a building for the English Form, for which the governors should take responsibility. Numbers in the public school should not exceed 500. There should be introduced a superannuation rule for admission, promotion, and leaving. The curriculum should be modestly reformed. Classics, maths, and divinity should be taught throughout the school; modern languages and natural science, music, and drawing to every boy up to the Fifth Form; a history prize should be instituted; in classics, there should less verse and prose composition and more translation; at the Head Master's discretion 'some specialising was to be allowed'. A 'school council' of masters should meet the Head regularly to effect school business. The fate of the Lower Mastership was to be

---

[18] *Clarendon Commission Report*, iv. 230.   [19] Ibid., ii. 281.   [20] Ibid., i. 224.

decided by the new governors, who were also to tackle the inadequate provision of sanitation, formroom ventilation, and space to play cricket.[21]

For any except extreme reactionaries, these were hardly radical suggestions. While destroying Lyon's statutes and rules, they accepted the existing public school on most of its own terms. Games, monitors, and fagging were untouched; the curriculum only slightly amended. Although advising a shift of authority from Head Master to Governing Body, the Commission left the system intact. Abolishing parishioners' rights was seen as protecting the ethos of the public school. It also cut the Gordian knot that had shackled Harrow so damagingly over recent decades. The most progressive aspects of the Commission's conclusions were the abolition of the old, legally binding statutes that had caused Harrow such trouble and the proposals for the improvements in the academic training and physical environment of the boys. This was not the barbarism and Jacobinism feared by defenders of the system such as Charles Vaughan.[22]

None the less, the Report of the Clarendon Commission aroused fury from more or less all sides. Liberals were dismayed at its timorous conservatism and refusal to contemplate utilitarian reforms or public accountability. Such voices were not heard at Harrow, where the loud debates were conducted by a wide spectrum of conservatives and diehards. The governors were anxious for their powers; the Head Master for his autonomy; the Assistant Masters for their independence; the local gentry for their free education; and the tradesmen and farmers for their rights to the charitable trust. While the Clarendon Report itself was merely advisory, the ferocity of reaction was focused by the introduction of a Public School Bill in the House of Lords in 1865 and its subsequent tortuous passage through parliament. Amid the political and legislative chaos of 1865–8, the measure, delayed, amended, and thrice reintroduced only began its passage through the House of Commons in the autumn of 1867, finally receiving Royal Assent in July 1868.[23] This glacial progress served to maintain and amplify the popular debate at a high pitch.

Butler's initial response to the Report had been constructive. Before any legislation had been prepared, he urged the governors in September 1864: 'the present opportunity is manifestly one which it is for our interest to embrace'. With immediate effect, he proposed to introduce entrance examinations for all and a superannuation rule. He argued that Harrow should also introduce Entrance Scholarships to compete not just with the collegiate schools of Eton, Winchester, and Westminster but with more direct rivals such as Rugby (which had such scholarships from 1862) and Wellington (in 1864) as well as serving to go some way to mitigate

---

[21] *Clarendon Commission Report*, i. 227–8; summary in Graham, *Butler*, 199–200.
[22] Quoting Arnold during the Platt–Stewart affair: see above pp. 257–9.
[23] 31, 32 Victoria c.CXVIII; Shrosbree, *Public Schools*, esp. pp. 111, 128, 177, 182, 185–206; Mack, *Public Schools and British Opinion since 1860*, 42–3, 91.

the disadvantage of high fees as compared with Marlborough, Cheltenham, Haileybury, and Clifton. Butler was concerned lest Harrow be seen as and become a preserve solely of the very rich, already 'the professional element among us . . . is decidedly lower than I could wish'. Butler agreed with the need to introduce natural science onto the curriculum, but not drawing or music which, characteristically, he thought would best be covered by encouraging vocal music through house singings—'the *esprit de corps* of Houses being very powerful'. He had, after all, appointed John Farmer to do precisely that in 1864. Equally, as an enthusiast he was keen to find ways of purchasing the large cricket field, the Philathletic ground.

Most of the rest of Butler's advice revolved around finance, masters' incomes, gubernatorial control of fee-income, and the arrangements for the English Form after the abolition of Foundationers' rights, his suggestions forming the basis for the statutes and regulations adopted a decade later. In applauding the proposed destruction of Lyon's statutes he invoked the shade of the Founder himself who, Butler sentimentally and conveniently imagined, would certainly not wish to reverse the history of Harrow 'to reduce it from a great national institution to a humble village school'. Butler's solution, like that of the Commission, was to separate the public school from any provision of local education on which, none the less, Trust money should be spent. Only towards the Report's recommendation of three governors with attainments in literature or science did Butler express outright hostility, fearing intrusion into his control of the curriculum: 'for the studies of the School you cannot make the Head Master too exclusively responsible'.[24]

Once the Public School Bill was introduced in March 1865, battle lines were clearer. The Bill was less radical even than the Clarendon Report, confining itself to the creation of new governing bodies, their powers, and the drafting of fresh statutes (when reintroduced in 1866, the provision for Special Commissioners to oversee these procedures was added). No specific reforms to the details of curriculum were mentioned. None the less, the Head and Assistant Masters combined to attack the measure as 'seriously injurious to the welfare of the school', objecting to the intended new governing body's control over discipline, management, and the curriculum. They argued that any desired improvements could be introduced by the Head Master under his existing authority.[25] They had a point, at least on the academic side. As well as entrance exams and superannuation, the 1860s saw a shift in the structure of the curriculum. In 1867 Farrar, as editor of *Essays on a Liberal Education*, concluded 'our present system of exclusively classical education as a whole and carried out as we do carry it out, is a deplorable failure'. Another contributor, his colleague Bowen, argued for the inclusion of science and a radical

---

[24] HA Public Schools Commission and Act File (hereafter PSCA); H. M. Butler, *A Letter to the Governors of Harrow School on the Principal Recommendations of the Public Schools Commissioners* (priv. pub., 1864); see GM, 23 June 1864 for Butler's agreement to produce the document.

[25] PSCA, Open Letter by Head and Assistant Masters, 31 Mar. 1865; F. Rendall, *The Foundation of John Lyon: Remarks on the Present Distribution of its Funds* (Harrow, 1865).

change in classics: 'teaching by means of grammar is repulsive and infructuous.' He even went so far as to challenge Monty Butler's pet obsession: 'verses ought to be (almost) abolished.'[26] Although having very little general impact, the *Essays* struck certain domestic chords. Butler was moved to establish a Modern Side under Bowen in 1869 and at least one other master, Bowen's close friend the energetic polymath R. Bosworth-Smith, replaced verses with geography and history in the same decade. However, he was regarded as highly unconventional by his stuffier colleagues.[27] In the end the clause giving the new governing body control over academic studies stood but with the addition that any regulations concerning the curriculum should be constructed with the advice of the Head Master.[28]

Apart from innate conservatism and a common fear of changing academic routines that however dull were at least familiar, the Harrow masters' real anxiety may have been financial. Independence from governors' control could be seen as a code for freedom from scrutiny or interference in profit-taking. They need not have worried. In 1864 Butler, although accepting the capping of his income by means of a salary (a theoretical c.£4,000 a year) and the number of boys in each house, vigorously supported the masters' right to keep all boarding fees in addition to their salaries. In the event, none of the Public Schools Bills, Act, statutes, or regulations seriously diminished the earning capacity of the masters, who could after 1874 still expect to earn anything up to £4,000–5,000 a year if in a large house and £1,000–2,000 in a small one. Only the Head, whose post-1874 annual salary from the school hovered around £3,000 instead of the profit of £4,000 plus he had enjoyed previously (his house profits remaining much the same, c.£2,000) may have suffered a marginal decrease in income.[29] After reform as before, most of the money generated by the school went into the pockets of the masters, if in a reduced ratio (still more than 2:1), although additional charges to the governors for the creation of a School Fund increased the cost to boys. Given the moderate nature of the legislation, the masters' main campaign was reserved for the details of the new statutes and regulations. Here, helped by Butler's insouciant diplomacy (and perhaps the convenient death of the awkward Lord Clarendon in 1870), they secured most of their interests. It was only in the long term, over the following century, that the governors' new powers were used to restrict the autonomy of housemasters and to support Head Masters, such as Welldon and Ford, in reforming masters' working habits.

By contrast, for the parishioners, the battle for the Bill was crucial. They suffered from a number of disadvantages. Split along lines of class and self-interest, they

---

[26] Mack, *Public Schools and British Opinion since 1860*, 61–4; C. Stray, *Classics Transformed* (Oxford, 1998), 86 n. 9, 94–5.

[27] Lady Grogan, *Reginald Bosworth Smith: A Memoir* (London, 1909), pp. 113, 119–23.

[28] For the Harrow pressure see Graham, *Butler*, 203–4.

[29] See HA Head Master's Book, 1874–92, fo. 87, Harrow School Regulations, 21 Feb. 1874 for the financial details.

were opposed by the very Foundation to which they claimed access. The school approved of the abolition of the Foundationers' rights as they stood, preferring, as Butler explained at a meeting in March 1865, the Trust money to pay for a Lower School with only a very limited number of Foundation awards for locals from there or elsewhere to the public school, with the great majority of Home Boarders paying fees.[30] Essentially, Butler proposed choice between a very cheap subsidized Lower or commercial school and paying modest fees at the public school. Thus, he argued, rights to the public school would not be replaced or substituted by the creation of a Lower School. His desire was, like Vaughan's before him, to separate the classes. Although accused by the vicar of 'a fatal gift of eloquence', Butler made no attempt to disguise the real losers under both his scheme and the bill, the local gentry. He neatly exposed the most fundamental weakness of the parishioners' case but pointing to the opposing interests among them: farmers and tradesmen; gentry with permanent residence; in-coming gentry with temporary residence in order to enjoy Foundationer rights; builders and speculators. He was very firm in his belief that priority should be given the farmers and tradesmen: the very poor had a National School; the gentry could well afford the day-fees at Harrow; the profits of property speculators were of no concern to the Lyon Trust. He even declared his support for a two-year residence limit on any trying to claim even the modest surviving benefits on the Foundation he proposed. In many ways, Butler's address of 20 March 1865 was Wordsworth's revenge.

Appropriately, the resistance was led by the vicar. Francis Hayward Joyce harboured some personal grievances against the governors. His assumption that he would *ex officio* succeed to his predecessor's governorship was contradicted by the election of the earl of Verulam instead, a decision casting an intriguing light on his colleagues' perceptions of Cunningham's use of his position. When Joyce continued to hand out apprenticeships, he had to be reminded that it was a governors' prerogative: he could only recommend. In 1864 the £25 paid annually to the vicar in Cunningham's time was reduced to £10.[31] Whatever his private emotions, to the end Joyce remained vigorous in objecting both to the legislation and then the proposed new statutes. In retrospect, it might have been more sensible to have elected him a governor like his three predecessors. Yet his separation from the school reflected the final transformation of Harrow into an autonomous national school that happened to be on the Hill, a status accelerated by the removal from the Parish Church in 1857 and recognized by Clarendon and the Public Schools Act.

Joyce's most difficult task was to keep a coalition of parishioners intact. While a Vestry meeting rejected the abolition of Foundationer's rights root and branch in March 1865, divisions were soon apparent.[32] One local gentleman, in an open

---

[30] PSCA, H. M. Butler, *An Address Delivered Before the Inhabitants of Harrow-on-the-Hill on Monday the 20th March 1865*, 1–35; for a sychophantic account see Graham, *Butler*, 201–2.

[31] HA Young's Letter Book, *passim*; GM, 5 Feb. 1862; 23 June 1864.

[32] PSCA, Butler, *Address on 20 March 1865*, pp. iii–vi.

letter to the vicar, rejected any change to the existing arrangements, arguing that the gentry should not surrender their rights to benefit the tradesmen and farmers, as Butler had suggested: they should be content with a separate Lower School, leaving the existing Foundationer arrangements in the public school, with the Home Boarder element secured at a fixed proportion (a seventh, roughly what it was in practice).[33] At the same time, Joyce had to contend with the interests of those, such as his Vestry clerk, W. Winckley, a local bookseller and house agent whose two sons attended the English Form on behalf of whom he had had to sign the waiver of any rights to the public school which, as he pointed out, effectively was 'saying that though they are upon the foundation, they are not upon the foundation'.[34]

Throughout, Joyce attempted to maintain unity. The first open letter to the governors in February 1865 was signed by representatives of the gentry and tradesmen.[35] By 1872, when the gentry rights were hardly an issue after the 1868 Act, the vicar none the less made it clear to the governors that the proposals he presented them, while drafted by a meeting of farmers, tradesmen, and 'Middle Class residents', nevertheless had the backing of the gentry's 'Defence Committee'.[36] The problems disunity presented Joyce were the undermining of the credibility of parochial complaints in general, the lack of common cause, and the ease with which one group could be picked off or played against the other, a manœuvre which the governors were happy to leave to the adroit operations of Montagu Butler.

The most effective means of keeping a united front was blanket opposition to any infringement of the existing Lyon statutes. Even this could prove awkward. The Public Schools Bill 'confiscates the just rights of present inhabitants of Harrow', thundered the *Harrow Gazette* of April 1867: 'an illiberal measure... it denies the opportunity of Public School Education to the sons of poor men.' A Petition to the governors signed by 110 parishioners urging them 'to keep inviolate the rights conferred' by John Lyon was appended. However, the majority of the signatures were of wealthy not poor parishioners, from Agnes, countess of Buchan to the school doctor, Hewlett and one of Guardians of the poor and tenant of Preston Farm, Thomas Sneezum.[37]

Butler exploited this schism to the full. In February 1868, after another bravura three-hour performance of sophistry and verbal legerdemain at a public meeting, this time to tradesmen and farmers, he secured sixty signatures to a memorandum he then forwarded to Members of Parliament. This supported Butler's 1865 scheme for the Lyon Trust both to continue local places at the public school and to create a 'Modern School' more appropriate to the needs of the majority. To Lord Enfield, the Liberal MP for Middlesex, Butler had disingenuously stressed the spontaneity

---

[33] PSCA, Printed Letter, J. W. Cunningham to F. H. Joyce, 31 Mar. 1865.
[34] Shrosbree, *Public Schools*, 208 n. 49; GM, 5 July 1860 for the Winckleys in the English Form.
[35] PSCA, Printed Letter, F. H. Joyce, J. W. Cunningham, Richard Chapman, 15 Feb. 1865.
[36] HA Minutes of the Governing Body of Harrow School Established 1871 (hereafter GBM), 20 Feb. 1872.   [37] *Harrow Gazette*, 1 Apr. 1867, pp. 1–4.

of support for this plan. More questionably, he also sent a second memorandum of his own that he had not shown the petitioners in which he set out seven reasons for supporting the contentious Clause 14 of the Bill which provided for the end of the Harrow Foundation, implying slyly that the petitioners had in some way approved of this support.[38] Unluckily for Butler, Enfield, now confused as to who wanted him to table what amendments, alerted Joyce. The Harrow 'Defence Committee', who represented the gentry of the parish, had already refused to sign Butler's petition;[39] now they angrily denounced Butler's sleight of hand, insisting that fifty out of the sixty who had signed his first memorandum had been unaware of the second and hostile to it. Butler, the governors' willing public stalking horse, had been caught out. Joyce led a deputation from the 'Defence Committee' to Enfield bearing a petition of their own signed by 442 locals which supported two amendments to the bill then in committee: the first, Enfield's own, secured the rights of locals to entry to Harrow as fee-payers as well as Foundationers; the second altering Clause 14 from establishing 'a separate school either in connexion or not in connexion with the existing school' to establishing 'a lower school in connexion with the exisiting school'.[40] Inevitably, the weight of influence was against the parish. The Public Schools Act as passed legislated for the end of the traditional statutory rights of local parishioners to free education at Harrow School.

The Act itself did not create any replacement. There was a period in limbo when the 1868 law prevented certain traditional actions, such as the appointment of a Lower Master, while leaving the rights of the Foundationers intact until fresh statutes were framed by the new governing body.[41] Nowhere was the nature of the Act as a measure designed to prevent radical change more apparent than in its delegation of detailed reform to these new bodies which were to be constituted by the existing governors with the approval of the Special Commissioners. In fact only Eton and Winchester complied, all the other schools having new governing bodies imposed upon them.[42]

At Harrow the negotiations between the governors and the Special Commission over the constitution of the new governing body lasted for two years from the Spring of 1869.[43] The main problems arose over the power to nominate the new governors. Initially, the existing governors wished to choose all of them, five of themselves and four new members. When the Commission made it clear that four of the new body had to be nominees from outside bodies, the governors suggested

---

[38] See transcripts in PSCA, the Harrow Defence Committee's Printed Circular Letter, 10 Mar. 1868. Cf. Graham, *Butler*, 204–6, who typically glosses over the problems.

[39] PSCA, MS of Resolutions of the Harrow Defence Committee, 24 Feb. 1868.

[40] *Harrow Gazette*, no. 164, 1 Apr. 1868, pp. 1–6 and above, n. 38.

[41] Young Letter Book, fos. 426–36; GM, 6 Jan. 1869.

[42] Mack, *Public Schools and British Opinion, 1780–1860*, 43.

[43] Apart from GBM, *passim*, the Young Letter Book fos. 445–510 provide the best detailed evidence.

the universities of Cambridge, London, the Royal Society, and the Lord Chancellor, rather pointedly omitting Oxford.[44] The Commission was unimpressed. Until the last minute, the governors wanted the perpetual nomination of five places on the new body: in the end they settled for two, with the additional power to nominate three more in the first instance.[45] This was seen as important as one of the eccentricities of the 1868 Act was that in some cases, Harrow being one, the new governing bodies would have control of the schools while the existing governors were to continue to manage the old trusts. This led to the bizarre spectacle between November 1871 and January 1874 of two separate bodies, the Keepers and Governors of the Free Grammar School of John Lyon, managing the Lyon trusts, and the Governing Body of Harrow School, charged with establishing and operating the new statutes and regulations, each with a different composition, meeting places, and minute books. The inevitable confusion was only resolved by the Public School Shrewsbury and Harrow Act of 1873 which dissolved the old governing body, which met for the last time on 14 January 1874 to approve its own demise, and incorporated the new one with the title and seal of the old.[46]

The new governing body that met for the first time comprised ten members. The duke of Abercorn, the earls of Verulam and Spencer, Lord Northwick, and W. H. Stone, MP elected themselves. The Head and Assistant Masters elected C. S. Roundell (né Currer), Old Harrovian, former Head of School and captain of cricket, a Liberal, a fellow of Merton, and a member of the Royal Commission on the Universities in 1871. The Vice-Chancellor of Cambridge nominated B. F. Westcott, who until appointment as Regius Professor of Divinity in 1870 had taught at Harrow for eighteen years as the Head Master's classical language dogsbody. The university of Oxford governor was Montague Bernard, professor of International Law and a fellow of All Souls who had been secretary to the Clarendon Commission, whose chairman had first suggested him as a governor in 1869.[47] The Lord Chancellor's appointee was the pedantic vice-chancellor, Sir John Wickens. The Royal Society chose Professor John Tyndall, superintendent of the Royal Institution, a noted physicist who had taken close interest in science education in schools in the late 1860s.[48] Not likely to be revolutionary, the externally nominated governors displayed two sides of the same coin, that of Harrow's national prominence which required, on the one side, public scrutiny, however discreet and indirect and, on the other, the recognition of its importance by public bodies.

It took two years before draft statutes were agreed and another nine months before they received the approval of the Special Commissioners and the Privy Council. One rather unexpected reason for this was the frequency with which the

[44] Young Letter Book, fos. 459–60, 13 May 1869.
[45] Ibid., fos. 496–510; GM, 29 June 1871.
[46] GM, 14 Jan. 1874; the Act is 36, 37 Victoria c. XLI; Minute Books, GM and GBM.
[47] Young Letter Book, fos. 445–6, 8 Apr. 1869. Full list: GBM, 22 Nov. 1871.
[48] On Tyndall see Mack, *Public Schools and British Opinion since 1860*, 61, 66.

new governing body was inquorate: in 1874 four out of ten meetings, including the Audit meeting and that which officially received the newly approved statutes.[49] Only a few governors, Westcott but especially Roundell and Stone, took much active interest, most of the work on Home Boarders, the Lower School, and all the school regulations being done by Butler, who revelled in such complexities.

Reaction to the framing of the statutes and regulations was predictable. On a practical level, the rights of foundationers and the numbers of Home Boarders soared, as local gentry hurried to exploit the privileges before they were extinguished. In July 1869 there were fifty-six; two years later there were eighty-eight—sixty-two of them on the Foundation, forcing the governors to impose a limit of seventy Foundationers in July 1871.[50] If he ever heard of it in his episcopal palace in Lincoln, Christopher Wordsworth may have allowed himself a wry smile.

The Assistant Masters voiced concerns over their insecurity of tenure and lack of any right of appeal to the governors against dismissal, which Butler, in true Arnoldian spirit, opposed as an infringement of his untrammelled authority: the compromise reached allowed no right of appeal but insisted that the Head explain his reasons to the governors who would be prepared to hear a statement from the dismissed master.[51] Security of tenure represented a serious problem. Butler himself offered James Robertson a post at Harrow after his summary dismissal from Rugby in 1871 and in 1875 openly sympathized with Oscar Browning when he was sacked from Eton.[52] However, just as the masters resented gubernatorial interference in the school so Butler resisted any attempt to allow them direct access to the governors or the formal right to challenge his decisions. Elsewhere, there was greater agreement. Led by Bowen, Rendall, and E. M. Young, a future Head Master of Sherborne, the masters displayed anxiety lest the Lower School drain resources from the public school, beginning a tradition of aloof disdain for the sister institution that lasted for over a century. They were also jealous of their prerogatives to take boarders, which they wanted explicitly recognized. In general, the masters were supportive of the main principles of the new statutes which were regarded as defending rather than undermining their position.[53]

There was less unanimity over the proposed Conscience Clause allowing non-Church of England pupils to be admitted both as boarders and day boys. Some wanted housemasters to have the right to remove boys who opted out of religious instruction (such as it was) and Chapel services; others wished for a blanket exemption clause provided substitute religious instruction and observances were

[49] GBM, 27 Jan., 11 Feb., 25 June, 21 July.
[50] GM, 11 July 1871; GBM, 25 July, 26 Nov. 1872; parishioners' complaint, PSCA, *Memorial to the Governing Body of Harrow School*, 12 Dec. 1872.
[51] PSCA, Comments to the Public Schools Commissioners on the Governors' Proposed Regulations from a Meeting of Assistant Masters, 31 Oct. 1873, signed by Bowen and Young; Observations on the Proposed Statutes, 4 Nov. 1873, by Rendall and Bowen; Graham, *Butler*, 209–11.
[52] Graham, *Butler*, 209–10, 215–16, 243–4. [53] See above, n. 51.

compulsory. This too was a live issue. In 1869, in the teeth of an angry and rather disreputable complaint from the vicar, Butler admitted the Roman Catholic duke of Genoa to the school as a Home Boarder (he lived with Matthew Arnold in Byron House) but exempted him from Chapel attendance. (He was rewarded with the Order of a Commendatore of the Corona d'Italia for his pains.)[54] Less publicly, discussions were held in 1872 and 1874 on the possibility of Jewish boys attending the school as Home Boarders or in a boarding house of their own, a scheme that was realized in 1881.[55]

Religion also caught the attention of the parish. After objecting to the admission of the duke of Genoa, Joyce remained alert to any dilution of the Anglican nature of the school. Until the very last stages of negotiations, the parish Vestry, presumably spurred on by the vicar, loudly opposed the statute that declared that 'any graduate of an university within the British empire shall be eligible for the office' of Head Master. Thus a Head need not be a cleric or an Anglican or even a Christian. Given the importance of the chapel as 'the main source of pesonal influence . . . were the post to be filled by a non-conformist, a Roman Catholic, a Jew or still worse by a atheist, the consequences would . . . be calamitous'.[56] Lyon's statutes had assumed that all graduates would be members of the Established Church and so did not specify a religious test. The new public schools almost all insisted on the Head being a member of the Church of England to such an extent that some ambitious young schoolmasters even in the later twentieth century still became confirmed Anglicans to enhance their career prospects. Harrow, for reasons of tradition not broadmindedness, was and remains different, at least constitutionally. In practice, the habit of clerical Heads continued until 1925, and there has been only one obviously anti-clerical Head Master since Reform.[57] The desire for religious tests in public schools, which emerged over the qualifications for governors as well, stood in marked contrast to general social legislation. It revealed the anxieties and the insecure self-image of promoters of public schools which were regarded as bastions of faith against the hordes of irreligious barbarians (and democrats). It was less a matter of belief but of identity. The clerk to the governors, C. W. Young, summed this up in 1870 answering an inquiry from the Special Commissioners about religious tests for governors: 'There is not to my knowledge in the Constitution of the Governors anything to require them to be members of the church of England. They have I believe invariably been so in practice but this has arisen, I conceive, rather from the social position of the Governors selected than from any other cause'.[58]

[54] GM, 6 Jan. 1869; Young Letter Book, fos. 435–6, 6 Jan. 1869; Graham, *Butler*, 188–90.
[55] GM, 27 June 1872; GBM, 14 Jan. 1874; *Harrow Register, 1800–1911*, 916.
[56] PSCA, MS Draft of Observations to the Special Commissioners under the Public School Act 1868, Jan.–Feb. 1874. Cf. *Objections of the Vestry*, 14 Jan. 1874. [57] A. P. Boissier.
[58] Young Letter Book, fo. 486, 17 Mar. 1870. The issue was raised in parliament when a late-night Commons resolution struck out the proposed religious test for governors, to the fury and disingenuous outrage of the duke of Abercorn in the Lords: see e.g. Mack, *Public Schools and British Opinion since 1860*, 99 n. 19 and refs. to Hansard and cf. the rather different account of Graham, *Butler*,

The central objections of the parishioners still revolved around the arrangements for the Foundation and the disposal of Trust income.[59] Just as the masters were suspicious of school money, i.e. from fees, being diverted to the Lower School, so the locals persisted in their belief that Trust income was either liable to be syphoned off to subsidize non-Foundationers or that locals were being denied free access to their rights, for example by having to sit examinations not merely for entry but for the newly constituted 'Foundation Exhibitions' to be funded each year by half the Trust income. Ironically, at the start of the process in 1868 the balance on the Harrow School Trust fund was £742; in 1873 and 1874 it was three times that: £2,117 and £2,498 respectively, even before any of the economies proposed as part of the new financial structure.[60] This sudden rise in income permitted the governors some confidence that their plans for establishing a Lower School could work and thus they could more easily dismiss parishioners' fears that somehow the whole operation was designed to cheat them of their rights. Although accommodating in receiving objections until the last moments, the governors were hardly deflected from their central purpose which was to take financial control of the public school and settle the Foundationer problem by establishing a Lower School to fulfil Lyon's charitable purpose as regards the education of the parishioners. Following Butler's advice, they were not even willing to allow any members of the Lower School Committee of Management to be elected by the parish Vestry.[61] The governors retained control. Their basic premiss, that the public school should remain inviolately aristocratic, was not negotiable.

As late as June 1874, the final agreement to the new statutes was delayed by a legal challenge from a local barrister, Lewis Gaches, and by a last, abortive attempt by the Special Commissioners to impose some control over the curriculum by the addition of a clause imposing regular school inspections to check on the studies conducted at the school.[62] Finally, the new statutes were approved on 7 July 1874. All parishioners resident on the day the Public School Act became law (31 July 1868)—but only they—retained their rights of free education. The Trust income was to be divided: after paying for various salaries, the Head Master's private house and a Lyon Scholarship (a single award consolidating the old Lyon leaving exhibitions), one-half of the balance was to go to the Lower School, the other to pay for Foundation Entrance exhibitions. The Lower School was to be a day school for local boys 'intended for Commercial and other similar occupations' with fees from

206–7. In 1871 the Privy Council rejected the religious test for governors who simply ignored this, assuming a religious ban until reminded of the true position by a surprised Privy Council clerk in 1974: GBM, 30 May 1974.

[59] PSCA, Objections of Harrow Parish Vestry to Statutes Proposed by the Governing Body of Harrow School, 23 Oct. 1873 (cf. *Harrow Gazette*, 1 Dec. 1873).

[60] GM, 25 June 1868, 26 June 1873; GBM, 25 June 1874.

[61] Graham, *Butler*, 209 for Butler's patronizing anti-democratic opinion.

[62] GBM, 10 June 1874.

£5 to £12 and a curriculum compromising Latin, English, modern languages, writing, maths, natural science, history, and geography. The Foundation Entrance Exhibitions were to be open to sons of parishioners who had been resident for at least two years, reviving Vaughan's suggestion of twenty years earlier. The Head Master of Harrow was to be paid from fee-income not Trust property. The Lower Mastership was abolished (the last incumbent, Harris, had resigned late in 1868) and the details of the Head's power of appointment and dismissal of assistant masters established. The old statutes were formally repealed.[63]

The details of the new arrangements for Harrow School were laid out in the Regulations.[64] Here were specified the details of superannuation rules which, by insisting on a minimum level of academic progress in theory altered the nature of the school profoundly, although probably encouraging the promotion of favoured dullards whose tutors, formmasters, or housemasters did not wish to see leave. Nothing in the new rule affected the system as described to the Clarendon Commission whereby of the numbers promoted from each form two-thirds were those who did best on the termly examination with the other third comprising boys who had been in that form for three terms.[65] The universal Entrance Examination introduced in 1863/4 was formalized, as was the limit set on Home Boarders (80). The total numbers in the school were fixed, initially at 576. Fees, boarding payments for each house, and other charges were laid out, as were the salaries for the Head and Assistant Masters. All income from fees and school charges were to go into a School Fund administered by the Head Master from which, apart from the teachers' salaries and other expenses, £2 10s. per pupil was to go to the governors to establish a 'Surplus Fund', initially to cover the remaining boys on the Old Foundation if the Trust income proved inadequate, thereafter to support the Lower School up to £250 a year; to subsidize Open Entrance Scholarships, the subjects for which were specified; and in consultation with the Head Master, to pay for anything else required by the public school. From 1877 the Head Master was to submit the accounts of the School Fund annually to the governors. General guidelines of study were set out including maths throughout the school; science and modern languages for at least nine terms for each boy, and, for those who excelled at these, throughout a school career. Further specialization was left to the Head who was also allowed to phase in science teaching pending the appointment of requisite staff. Otherwise, the Head had full control over the studies of the school, the organization of Chapel and Divine Worship, and the employment of teaching and other staff. A Conscience Clause allowed Home Boarders by right and boarders by permission of the governors to be exempt from attendance in Chapel, school prayers, and religious instruction, no boy to be disadvantaged in exams or prizes as

---

[63] PSCA, Harrow School Statutes, published 18 Dec. 1873, pp. 2–8; Graham, *Butler*, 208.
[64] Harrow School Regulations, 21 Feb. 1874, Head Master's Book, 1874–92, fo. 87.
[65] *Clarendon Commission Report*, i. 212.

1. View of Harrow Hill from the south-east *c.*1803 by George Barret the Younger

2. Modern aerial view of Harrow Hill from the east

3. The original schoolhouse, built 1608–15, from the south, *c.*1811–19

4. View from Church Hill looking south from the school gates towards the old Head Master's house, mid-1830s

5. View from outside the Head Master's house looking north, *c.*1900; Church Hill is on the left; Chapel on the right

6. The same view *c.*1960, showing the clearance of the central area in the front of the Old Schools on the left and the War Memorial in the centre

7. The school steps outside the Old Schools in the 1850s

8. The Old Schools today from the south; the original schoolhouse survives behind the left hand (western) wing

9. Thomas Thackeray, Head Master 1746–60

10. Robert Sumner, Head Master 1760–71

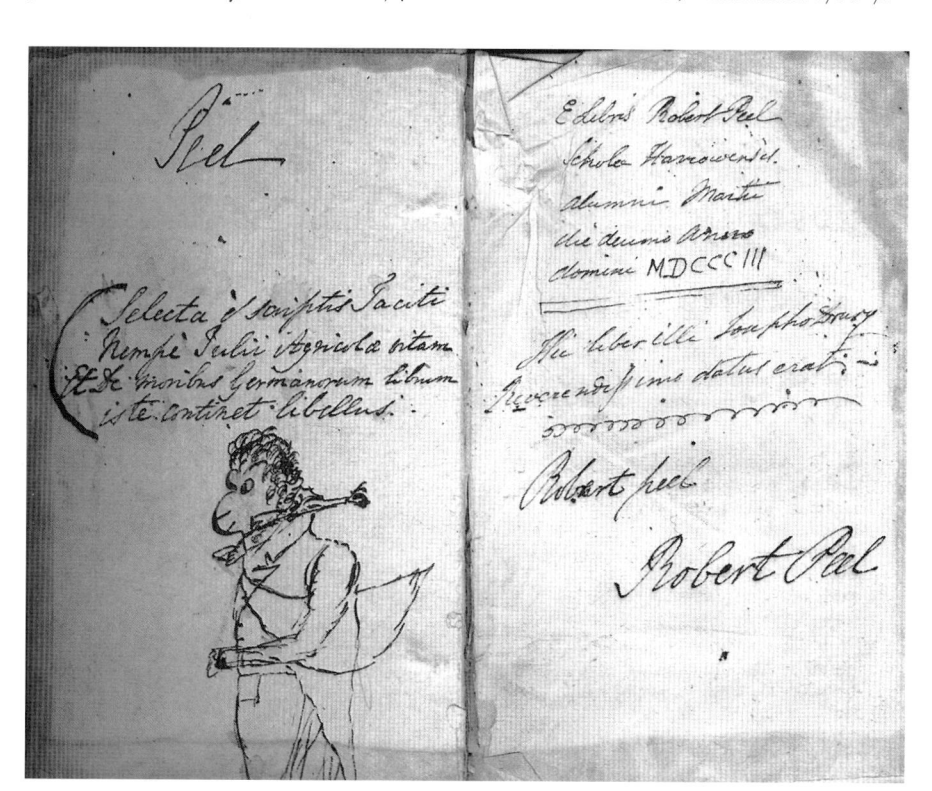

11. From Robert Peel's copy of Tacitcus', *Agricola* and *Germania*, acquired by him in 1801, with an inscription on the right hand page, dated 1803, by Joseph Drury, Head Master 1785–1805; the cartoon is by Peel

12. C. J. Vaughan, Head Master 1845–59

13. H. Montagu Butler, Head Master 1860–85

14. 'Old Slybacon'; J. W. Cunningham, Vicar of Harrow 1811–61; governor 1818–61

15. E. E. Bowen, Assistant Master 1859–1901

16. J. E. C. Welldon, Head Master 1885–98, in 1898

17. Lionel Ford, Head Master 1910–25, in 1919

18. P. C. Vellacott, Head Master 1934–9

19. R. W. Moore, Head Master 1942–53, in 1951

20. A. P. Boissier, Head Master 1940–2, with W. S. Churchill on the way to Songs, November 1940. One eyewitness later described Churchill on this occasion as 'red-faced' and 'emotional'

21. Dr R. L. James, Head Master 1953–71 with H.M. Queen Elizabeth II during her visit in February 1971 to mark the school's Quatercentenary; in the background, with spectacles, is Lord McCorquodale, Chairman of the Governors

22. Modernizing Harrow; three Head Masters in front of the memorial to the fallen of the Second World War; from left to right, N. R. Bomford (1991–9); B. M. S. Hoban (1971–81); and I. D. S. Beer (1981–91)

a result. Appended schedules presented the details of the Entrance and Scholarship exams; the limits to the numbers in each house; the school, tuition, optional, and boarding fees; the length of holidays; the subjects on the curriculum; and the details of the masters' salary structure. Gentlemanly agreement had been replaced by bureaucratic accountability; an aristocratic finishing school by an academy of tested achievements, however modest; the unfettered discretion of a despotic Head Master by the constitutional supervision of a new governing body. A fortnight after the new arrangements were sealed, the governing body signalled a definitive end to the old order by ceasing payments for apprenticeships and announcing the withdrawal of charitable donations to local National and Sunday schools; after the current recipients died, there were to be no more ex gratia gifts to local widows.[66]

Yet, in many ways little had changed. Reform had always been intended to protect rather than tear up, conservative not radical. As Vaughan congratulated his successor: 'You have guided the vessel through what might have been a shipwreck of a change to a Governing Body'.[67] Butler enjoyed considerable assistance in the circumstances and contents of the 1868 Act itself; the divisions among the opponents of reform, especially within the parish; the influence and inclinations of the Governors and Special Commissioners; and the absence of damaging scandal at the wrong moment. Butler's own early flexibility and support for the main thrust of the legislation were crucial. He saw how he could preserve what he thought important while adapting to suit the temper of moderate change. Butler was a fine propagandist. Continuity was a passion of his. It is no coincidence that precisely the years of Reform, 1864–74, saw the creation of the tradition of Harrow School Songs that, with the Tercentenary celebrations of 1871, consecrated a vision of Harrow's past, present, and future that deliberately excluded suggestion that the school after 1874 was, in any essential way, new. Butler concealed change, brutal choices, and casualties behind rhetoric and song, shrewdly appealing to concocted sentiment and feeling not intellect. On 7 July 1876 the 'Gentry and other parishioners', as the invitation rather characteristically put it, met the governors for a lunch in celebration of the completion of the building of the Lower School of John Lyon at which the assembled company was entertained by the singing of Bowen and Farmer's song *Queen Elizabeth Sat One Day* about Lyon's building of the original school. The austere academic Westcott was reduced to tears of laughter. What the locals made of it is not recorded.[68] The awkward present could be wished away in

---

[66] GBM, 21 July 1874.   [67] Graham, *Butler*, 211.
[68] Ibid., but cf. a piece of anti-Reform doggerel preserved by the Vestry's lawyer: J. T. Prior, PSCA Undated Poem:

You free born Harrowonians	wich was left for ever free
Where is your boasted bravery	Now this great school is uptaken
Can you rightly sit and see	By this cursed lawless law
Your rights and your libertys	…
taken away from you	

good-humoured verse and music that, more carefully than it may have appeared, invented a very particular past for the purpose.

The great achievement of reform was the ending of the parishioners' rights by accepting that Lyon's statutes were inappropriate for a great public school. As such, 1874 marks an epoch in the school's history. Yet, reform recognized an existing condition, it did not create a new one. It was more a process of legitimization than renewal. It also provided for the first time a regular, clear view of the school's financial situation. One direct result of the new regulations was the appointment in 1881 of a bursar to assist the Head in managing the School Fund, A. C. Tosswill, a mathematician and housemaster of the small house of Garlands. He was paid an extra £100 a year, suitably five pounds less than the organist Farmer.[69] The new arrangement allowed a degree of transparency. What was revealed was perhaps unexpected; it was certainly significant. Each year from 1873 to 1876, on a turnover of c.£14,500 to c.£15,500, the School Fund saw a deficit. When numbers picked up, very modest surpluses were recorded. In 1884, on receipts of just over £18,000, the surplus was just £800, around 4.5 per cent. Other years in the 1880s saw the surplus vary from as much as 7 per cent to under 3 per cent.[70] Thus, from its inception, the School Fund revealed a systemic problem in the school's finances. Fees never comfortably covered expenses. With the Road Fund unavailable, the Harrow Trust Fund largely committed elsewhere, the school for all its grandeur and expansion could not afford any significant capital expenditure (all such forays being paid for by subscription or gifts) and was vulnerable to its fluctuating market, the economy, and occasionally poor financial management. Before reform, only the funds controlled by the governors were under the scrutiny of the Charity Commissioners and law. Now all the public assets were. Where before many of the financial difficulties could be laid at the door of Elizabethan lawyers, after 1874, behind the wealthy facade and wealthier masters, was a highly precarious financial structure, prone to debt, that had to support the whole school. Ironically, the reform of 1868–74 that was meant to set the school free merely added a new and lasting element to the conundrum of the poor rich school.

Now you free born Harrowonians
Rowse from the lethargy
and exert your manly skill
Down with those tyrants
Stick up for your liberty
Let your sons their places fill

[69] For the accounts of the School Fund 1873–84 see Head Master's Book, 1874–92, fo. 39; for Tosswill, sub anno 1881; GBM, 24 June 1880, 1 Feb., 3 Mar. 1881.

[70] See above, n. 69. This insolvency occupied much of the governors' attention in the years immediately after 1874.

13

THE CULT OF HARROW: MONTAGU BUTLER, SENTIMENT, AND SUCCESS, 1860–1885

In twenty-five years, Montagu Butler admitted more than 4,000 boys to Harrow.[1] Such numbers secured the school's status as a national institution. Their social prominence was assumed. When advising his successor on teaching the Upper Fourth in 1879, John Smith suggested that during the first month of term each new boy should be asked to explain his family motto to the form; he never doubted they possessed one.[2] Such extensive ties of association within the ruling elite provided the basis for Harrow's fame. Even appointments to Assistant Masterships were deemed of sufficient public interest to warrant gazetting in *The Times*.[3] When deliberately fostered by Butler, 'the public school esprit de corps', created a 'strong passion new in man's history'.[4] Sentiment thrived on success. Privileged by birth and wealth, Butler's Harrovians achieved much on their own account in those spheres most cherished by Victorian public schools: public service, sport, the professions, the church, and academic life. Butler presided over one of the great powerhouses of the late nineteenth-century British Establishment during a Head Mastership that defined Harrow's reputation, character, and standing.

The statistics impress.[5] At Oxford, Butler Harrovians won 41 scholarships (9 at Balliol), 19 exhibitions, 71 Firsts (34 in Finals), 11 University Scholarships, 19 prizes, and 18 Fellowships. At Cambridge there were 58 scholarships (38 of them at Trinity), 12 exhibitions, 58 Firsts in the Triposes, 9 university scholarships, 25 prizes,

---

[1] The total was 4,099: *Harrow Register, 1800–1911*, 325–637.
[2] E. D. Rendall and G. H. Rendall, *Recollections and Impressions of the Rev. John Smith MA* (London, 1913), p. 47.
[3] W. Done Bushell, *et al.*, *William Done Bushell of Harrow* (Cambridge, 1919), p. 3.
[4] Honey, *Tom Brown's Universe*, 147.
[5] What follows is based on Graham, *Butler*, 299–300.

and 15 Fellowships. (Unlike Eton or Winchester, the only closed college award for Harrovians was the Sayer at Caius until 1874, when T. C. Baring endowed 3 at Hertford College, Oxford.) By 1920, 5 of Butler's pupils had become heads of Oxbridge colleges, 9 professors, and 1 Public Orator. Another 5 had become public school Head Masters. Thirty-three Harrovians won cricket blues, 8 for rowing. Of those ordained (less than 5 per cent), 2 became deans, 9 bishops, and 1, Randall Davidson, archbishop of Canterbury. In the armed forces, by the end of the First World War Butler's Harrow had produced 1 admiral, 64 generals, and 4 VCs. In April 1884, for a brief period, there were 64 Old Harrovian MPs, including some Butler pupils, split with unexpected evenness: 32 Liberal; 32 Conservative, an equality soon unimaginable as Home Rule began to destroy public school political Liberalism.[6] Of more than 100 Butler Harrow MPs, at least 30 rose to the Privy Council. One, Stanley Baldwin (1881–5), became Prime Minster: Butler had once had to beat him for sending pornography ('Harrow filth') to Eton, a slur that blighted his last terms at school and set him on his course to Downing Street.[7] Four Viceroys, 9 colonial governors, and 12 ambassadors as well as 5 British High Court judges were taught under Butler. So was one of Harrow's 2 Nobel Laureates for Literature, John Galsworthy (Winston Churchill being the other): the future novelist and dramatist was a notorious hearty at school (1881–6, monitor 1884) but later turned against the system, accusing public schools of being socially divisive 'caste factories'.[8] Beyond these notables were scores of civil servants, barristers, JPs, Lords Lieutenant, High Sheriffs, junior officers, and men distinguished by action or status in their communities across the British world. There is some truth in the comment of Butler's pupil, colleague, and biographer, Edward Graham, that 'it would be hard to convict the generation of Harrovians trained under Dr Butler of inefficiency or stagnation'.[9] To all appearances, Butler's Harrow was a huge success. Its intellectual certainty, emotional tone, and physical influence pervaded later generations through the single-minded policies of perhaps its greatest success, the Head Master himself.

'A HARROW HERO'[10]

Like many successful schoolmasters, Montagu Butler never really grew up. To the end of his long life, in many essentials he remained an eager, earnest, energetic sixth former addicted to verse composition and school. As Master of Trinity (1886–1918)

[6] Thornton, *Harrow School*, 374; Graham, *Butler*, 231 for the Baring scholarships.
[7] K. Middlemas and J. Barnes, *Baldwin: A Biography* (London, 1969), pp. 15–17.
[8] Mack, *Public Schools and British Opinion since 1860*, 284; H. V. Marrot, *The Life and Letters of John Galsworthy* (London, 1935), pp. 703–5.   [9] Graham, *Butler*, 300.
[10] The phrase was Lionel Ford's in Jan. 1918: G. H. Hallam, *et al.*, *Rev. H. M. Butler DD* (memorial vol., Harrow, 1918), p. 17.

his eccentricities could degenerate into ripe absurdity;[11] as Head Master of Harrow (1860–85) a puppyish naive enthusiasm for interests shared by the young rendered him a powerful force. Prolix, pompous, tireless, affectionate, emotional, devoted, his personality lacked the artifice of his verses. A supporter wrote of him in 1860 that, unlike Vaughan, 'no one will ever fancy him insincere'.[12] His religion was the simple, generally evangelical, undogmatic, almost undenominational, broad-church piety of his youth. His politics remained the Peelite liberal conservatism of his teens. Neither a theologian nor philosopher, his conversation concerned not ideas but people, usually Harrovians or Trinity men. Not 'speculatively minded nor critically minded',[13] very clever in the old, narrow Cambridge philology style, blessed with a prodigious memory, he never strayed from the pattern of character formed as a precocious, somewhat priggish, and universally spoilt youth at Harrow and Trinity. This allowed him to share the life of his pupils; he enjoyed it, from talking classics to cricket. Prone to hero-worship, 'he paid an almost superstitious homage to Authority'. Unlike Vaughan, who made people uneasy, Butler was open and uncomplicated, by no means threateningly intellectual: 'he never arrived at his conclusions by any process of serious reasoning . . . he held strongly and conscientiously a certain number of conventions'.[14] His considerable, unforced personal charm was matched by a spectacular ability to provide epitaphs and memorial speeches at will: even his son described it as an 'extreme facility and felicity'.[15] Suitably sonorous sentiments poured from him almost uncontrollably. In an age that gloried in commemoration, his skills were in great demand. Meticulous and gentlemanly in manner, his childlike sense of enjoyment and guileless human sympathy were often obscured by a ponderous formality that led G. C. Warr, who helped teach the Sixth Form for a term, to comment that although 'his conversation is faultless . . . you have a faint impression as of a reporter present'.[16] It is difficult to know whether the torrent of facile commentary, verse, anecdotes, admonition, and advice protected something more sensitive or merely an ossified juvenile sentimentality. Narrow in learning, keen on games and physical exercise, unmusical, uninterested in science, obsessed by rules, traditions, family, and institutions,

---

[11] e.g. the wonderful story told by Edmund Gosse and recorded by A. C. Benson: D. Newsome, *On the Edge of Paradise* (London, 1980), pp. 89–90.

[12] Henry Sidgwick to Roden Noel, 18 Feb. 1860: Graham, *Butler*, 130. In general, apart from Graham's biography which contains sharp criticisms as well as correspondence, memoirs, and hagiography see Hallam, *Rev. H. M. Butler*; Mack, *Public Schools and British Opinion since 1860*, esp. pp. 95–100; and memories of pupils: Minchin, *Old Harrow Days*, 116–29; G. W. E. Russell, *Fifteen Chapters of Autobiography* (London, n.d.), pp. 36–9; H. A. Vachell, *Fellow Travellers* (London, 1923), pp. 21–3; C. M. Leaf, *Walter Leaf, 1852–1927: Some Chapters of Autobiography* (London, 1932), pp. 45–8.

[13] Hastings Rashdall's judgement: Graham, *Butler*, 334.

[14] Both remarks come from G. W. E. Russell's surprisingly acerbic tribute in Hallam, *Rev. H. M. Butler*, 12.   [15] Graham, *Butler*, 377.

[16] Ibid., 158.

Montagu Butler's personality shaped a whole public school mentality, a sort of refined philistinism that found nothing strange in reducing all adult life to the image of school:

> whether it be in matters of cricket, or in matters connected with the Church, or in matters connected with politics, or in matters connected with our professional engagements, there is hardly any motto which I would more confidently commend for the guidance of the dear friends who are sitting round me... than 'Play the Game'. Remember the School and 'Play the Game'.[17]

Sixty-two years before he spoke those words, in his speech to the governors as Head of School in 1851, the 18-year-old Butler urged his audience: 'Let us strive earnestly that the name and fame of Harrow may never be marred by carelessness or fault of ours.'[18] Throughout his life Butler was consumed by a mystical devotion to the school that he projected onto its past, present, and future. He gave early notice that his schoolboy enthusiasm was more than adolescent practice for adult endeavours in a letter to his successor as Head of the Head Master's house, Edward Latham, in September 1851: 'when I get to think about Harrow matters and above all Harrow discipline, I feel a kind of professional enthusiasm come over me quite indescribable.'[19]

The youngest son of George Butler, born when his father was almost 60, Montagu's academic career was meteoric. From the Eagle House, Hammersmith preparatory school, whose Head Master, Edward Wickham, in addition to Butler, produced five other public school Heads, including Warre of Eton and Ridding of Winchester, Montagu arrived at Harrow in 1846. He won all the prizes, played cricket at Lord's (with a runner, as he always did in deference to his supposed poor health), won a scholarship to Trinity, became Head of House and School and was comfortably installed as Vaughan's favourite pupil. His glittering success continued at Cambridge, where he was President of the Union, Senior Classic in 1854, and a fellow of Trinity in 1855. He did not neglect Harrow, often visiting socially, to play cricket or attend Vaughan's Essay Club. In 1859 he examined for the Harrow Leaving Scholarships. It was as if he were keeping the seat warm for his own return.[20]

The roots of his lasting affection for the school are unclear. For all the verbosity of his mountainous correspondence, memorandums, sermons, and speeches, there is apparently no diary, no intimate document of self-analysis, exposure, or recognition. His sense of Harrow's importance and its history was fostered by his aged father, memorials of whom the son repeatedly donated to the school and to whom he paid pointed tribute in his Governors' Speech of 1851.[21] Perhaps Montagu felt some need to expiate what may have appeared, in the memories of his uncle

---

[17] Graham, *Butler*, 398. [18] Quoted Hallam, *Rev. H. M. Butler*, 20.
[19] HA Latham Letters, Butler to Latham, Sept. 1851.
[20] See esp. Graham, *Butler*, 18–86. [21] Graham, *Butler*, 37.

Oxenham and other Hill old stagers, his father's failure, although neither parent nor child was given to regard himself as unsuccessful. Perhaps he was bewitched by sentimental, gilded memories of an idealized Harrow spun by hours of parental reminiscence. Perhaps he never felt so happy, fulfilled, or confident as when at the head of the school. One trait that remained with Butler all his life was a reluctance to embrace serious change; his natural stance was to look backwards. It is sobering to realize that between the ages of 13 and 52, thirty-nine years, Montagu Butler spent thirty of them living in one part or another of the Head Master's House at Harrow. Even afterwards, he was scarcely absent. All his many sons from his two marriages were Harrovians, the first in 1880; the last in 1907; one daughter married a Harrow master; his eldest son, Edward, who in Butler's last term, as captain of the Eleven, melodramatically hit the winning four against Eton with only a few minutes of the match left, became one in 1891. In 1901 Butler himself was elected, and remained to his death, the Master's governor.[22] Thirty years after retiring as Head Master Butler's body was returned to the Hill for burial in January 1918 next to his first wife and his mother. The bond had been forged early. On hearing of his election as Head Master in 1859, Butler's brother-in-law, the explorer and eugenicist Francis Galton, congratulated him: 'They say *les mariages se font en ciel*, and I am almost ready to believe that you and the school were created for one another.'[23]

Whatever drove it, Butler's devotion was not the passive pleasure of memory. As Head Master he deliberately strove to spread his sense of loyalty and sentimental attachment to the school for positive ends. His twin purpose in planning the elaborate Tercentenary celebrations in 1871 was to 'extend the range of patriotic devotion' of old boys and then to use that new affection to raise money to re-equip the school.[24] In both he succeeded triumphantly. Decorated by speeches from his predecessors, Wordsworth (which showed how little actual history most knew) and Vaughan (which showed how little of anything was known), sanctified by the presence of Byron's fag, Baron Heath, and serenaded by songs carefully pointed to encourage nostalgic generosity, the festivities provided a memorable focus for supporting the Lyon Memorial Fund, which ultimately raised £38,000 to pay for a new Speech Room and Science Schools. Butler himself led the way with almost profligate gifts throughout his rule.[25]

His proselytizing went beyond a fund-raising gimmick. There was something overtly spiritual in his conception of the school. It stood for the Christian life 'with every grateful retrospect and every chivalrous aspiration' transmitting 'from term to term, from year to year, from master to master, from boy to boy, from friend to friend of the richest of all blessings which, with all reverence, we call the Spirit of

---

[22] HA HM/We/Minutes of Master's Meetings, 1893–1910, 10 June, 24 June 1901.
[23] Graham, *Butler*, 130.   [24] Ibid., 219.
[25] *Harrow Tercentenary*, 24–8, 30, and *passim*; Howson and Townsend Warner, *Harrow School*, 145–6. For Butler's munificence see Graham, *Butler*, 318–19.

God'.²⁶ Through this combination of nostalgia for youth and the intensity of adolescent friendships with Christian purpose, what could be described as a marriage of the Byronic to the Arnoldian, Butler, as others were doing perhaps less convincingly for their public schools (Eton, Winchester, and Westminster excepted: they had genuine pasts upon which to reflect), was forging for Harrow a new quasi-religious, quasi-secular cult of the school. This differed markedly in intensity and range of emotional and personal engagement from previously existing manifestations of filial piety to the Alma Mater from Parr and Sheridan to Byron and Palmerston, who regarded their old school affectionately as merely scenes of their youth. Montagu Butler's new devotion was not just about old friends but about an almost platonic ideal of Harrow, more than just a place or a school, an ennobling symbol far removed from Vaughan's testing ground of sin. Butler's views may have owed not a little to his father, a pioneer professional old boy and exploiter of school nostalgia to raise money. Yet, they went further, were more embracing, more defining of the adult. Butler was eager to collect and commemorate hagiographic stories linking schooldays to later virtue, a theme picked up by the songs of Bowen, Howson, and others.

The most famous example of this squirrelling of uplifting legends fell into Butler's lap by chance. On a walk with the philanthropist Lord Shaftesbury in 1876, outside the Old Schools the aged earl told Butler the now famous story of how on that spot as a boy over sixty years earlier he had seen a pauper's funeral conducted by a couple of drunks: 'that sight was . . . one of the influences which led me to choose my life's career'. Before that walk, nobody seemed to know of the story. Thereafter, Butler publicized it, as in a memorial sermon on the earl in 1885. It made its first entrance into Harrow Song mythology in 1891 and in 1897 a tablet was erected on the wall nearest the spot to record the event.²⁷ (Interestingly, John Smith, the unstable, saintly formmaster of the Fourth, recalled an almost identical scene from his childhood which formed 'the turning point of my life', although in his case the drunken bearers tipped the corpse, a child, onto the road.²⁸ By 1885, when the Shaftesbury story was aired, Smith had long gone into a mental asylum.) Such tales possessed an inspirational rather than historical purpose, one aimed at Old Harrovians but more directly at boys in the school.

On Speech Day 1883, when presenting his eldest son with a prize, Butler cited the boy's dead grandfather and recently dead mother in support of a very public admonition: 'you must never forget that you are the servant of the school'.²⁹ Young Edward went on to be a monitor, captain of cricket, and a master, as if he had much

---

[26] Mack, *Public Schools and British Opinion since 1860*, 100.
[27] Graham, *Butler*, 247; Laborde, *Harrow School*, 71 and n. 1; Howson's song: *Stet Fortuna Domus*, verse 4, ll. 7, *Harrow School Songs* (new edn., Henley, 1993), p. 93.
[28] Rendall, *Recollections of John Smith*, 18–19.
[29] Minchin, *Old Harrow Days*, 119.

alternative: he retired aged only 53 (he lived to be 81) the year after his father died.[30] The point of Butler's new cult of Harrow, one so gently mocked by his beloved Vaughan to his chosen successor Welldon, was that it should be personal and lifelong, as he put it at the Tercentenary lunch, a 'unity of life, which binds together the various generations of a great Public School' a 'consciousness of brotherhood'.[31] This open freemasonry was sustained by beliefs that cut across formal religion and by rituals and liturgies (jargon; Songs; house and school singings; Founder's day; reunion dinners; Tobacco Parliaments; etc.) familiar only to the initiates: by 1900 most public schools had much the same, if less gawdy and elaborate. The emotional and practical consequences of such forged bonds cannot be overestimated. Benefactions from Old Harrovians in the nineteenth century totalled above £150,000; between 1885 and 1898 £90,000 was raised to increase the Harrow estate, which was further extended beyond the Watford Road in 1905 when 254 acres were purchased for over £80,000. More crucially, in 1885 The Park with its forty-seven-acre grounds were saved for the school by a specially formed Harrow Park Trust at a cost of £16,000.[32] Without such old boy largesse Harrow could not have survived as a front-rank school, a fact redoubled in emphasis throughout the twentieth century.

The emotional ties which underpinned this generosity reached a public climax when Baldwin, on forming his first government in 1923, included six Old Harrovians so that it would, he joked to the Harrow Association, be 'a Government of which Harrow should not be ashamed'.[33] (It lasted eight months.) What is most remarkable about Baldwin's later public devotion is that he hated his last months at Harrow, sullen at his humiliation over the pornography scandal and resentful at the arbitrary power of the Head Master (also his housemaster) who seems to have cut him consistently. He left a year early and sent his own sons to Eton. Yet, the embodiment of a self-created world of misty, rural English nostalgia, sentimental, emollient patriotism, and conservative values, Baldwin had to be seen as a loyal Old Boy and this may even have influenced his political decisions. In 1923, in high office for just two years, the most unlikely Prime Minister between Perceval and Major, he needed all the friends he could get. Harrow provided one network worth exploiting.

Without the commitment and longevity of Montagu Butler himself, the cult and myth of Harrow that so characterized the school's self-image for a century after his resignation may have proved less focused, less pervasive, or less tenacious. Although not accidental, owing its fruition to Butler's deliberate nurturing of it in

---

[30] *Harrow Register, 1800–1911*, 571; J. W. Moir and L. J. Verney (eds.), *Harrow School Register, 1885–1949* (London, 1951), p. 678.

[31] Welldon, *Recollections*, 85; *Harrow Tercentenary*, 30.

[32] Howson and Townsend Warner, *Harrow School*, 144–6, 152–6; Laborde, *Harrow School*, 198; Head Master's Book, 1874–92, fo. 83.

[33] Mack, *Public Schools and British Opinion since 1860*, 385.

the fertile soil of mid-Victorian culture, its origins lay not in some rational scheme to compensate for the lack of school endowment, although that came into it. Butler's vision that found expression in this newly invigorated cult of the school sprang from his own very personal feelings for Harrow established over years. When he finally resigned in 1885 he felt he had 'signed away youth and romance and sacred memories that are life itself': 'I came back to the dear study and sobbed like a baby'.[34]

The Head and his School

Ironically, Butler was very nearly not Head Master. Although regarded by many as Vaughan's natural heir, the suddenness of the vacancy and Butler's extreme youth, 26, cast the outcome of the 1859 election into the hazard. Vaughan had urged the governors to proceed with dispatch, but their holiday arrangements meant that the process took two months, with some administrative slips on the way, one candidate's testimonials being misdirected to 'Mr Grosvenor, Harrow School'.[35] The system of election was modified. As well as soundings from the Oxbridge Vice-Chancellors, advertisements were placed in the university newspapers, *The Times*, and *Daily News*.[36] Although ten candidates applied, the choice came down to two: Butler and the refined High Churchman, Alfred Barry, son of the architect, Head Master of Leeds Grammar School, later Master of Cheltenham, and Primate of Australia. Apart from their ages (Barry was 33), churchmanship, and teaching experience, there was little to choose between them. Both were committed Christians in holy orders; both first-class academics and fellows of Trinity. Fortuitously, Butler, using his entitlement as a fellow of Trinity, had been hurriedly ordained a deacon only in September 1859 because, although still a layman, he had accepted the living of Great St Mary's in Cambridge: after election to Harrow, he was hastily advanced to priestly orders in December.[37]

Butler's testimonials displayed the backing of the Cambridge academic and ecclesiastical establishment (but so did Barry's), with a sprinking of the great, including Lord Macaulay. There was support from three distinguished younger Old Harrovians: F. Vaughan Hawkins, C. S. Currer, and W. H. Stone, all later to become governors in Butler's time. Butler based his candidature on his associations with Harrow and Vaughan coupled with a determined conservatism to preserve 'those wise and generous principles on which the education of its scholars, physical, intellectual and spiritual has so long been based' in order that the school

---

[34] Butler to Hastings Rashdall, 20 Feb. 1885, Graham, *Butler*, 285.
[35] Young Letter Book, fos. 57^{r-v}, 68, and in general, fos. 51–92.
[36] GM memorandum placed between minutes for 7 July and 16 Nov. 1859.
[37] Graham, *Butler*, 84–6.

should 'continue to justify its great name as a place of training for manly Christian gentlemen'.[38]

No candidate was interviewed, that modern ritual appearing only in 1885. All depended on personal knowledge and private lobbying. Vaughan worked hard behind the scenes on his pupil's behalf, but the contest was fierce, the outcome uncertain. At a preliminary meeting, the spectre of 1805 arose when the six governors voted 3:3, with Aberdeen and Abercorn for Butler, but Cunningham and, perhaps, Northwick for Barry. Cunningham's initial opposition to Butler is strange. As a schoolboy, the young Montagu had treated the vicarage as a 'second home' and Barry's High Churchmanship was anathema.[39] Perhaps Cunningham had learnt of the Vaughan debacle. Barry was married. Butler, a close friend and pupil of Vaughan, was not. Perhaps Butler appeared too much the internal candidate or just too inexperienced. Whatever the reason, in contrast to 1805, after the deadlock no formal vote was taken, the governors adjourning until the next day, 16 November. Cunningham, back home, was visited by F. W. Farrar who later claimed to have persuaded the vicar to change his vote by citing the near unanimous support for Butler amongst the teaching staff.[40] Next day, Butler was elected, the Governors' Minutes pregnantly declare, 'by the greater part' of the governors, in its frankness clear evidence of bloody conflict to the last. Typically, the turncoat Cunningham was first to communicate the result and his joy to the Butler family.[41]

As Head Master for a quarter of a century, Montagu Butler stamped his personality on the working of the school. He was immensely conscientious, hard-working, sometimes so tired that he fell asleep in form, famously incapable of delegation.[42] When absent convalescing from a serious illness in the Spring of 1882, he still could not let go, Bowen commenting that Harrow during this time was run by 'Government of a Deputy tempered by post-cards from Brighton'.[43] His correspondence shows all the signs of rapid composition allied with serious verbal diarrhoea. Intensely self-regarding, his habitual method of communicating by writing with others outside his immediate family, however near-at-hand or often encountered the recipient or trivial the matter, was as laborious as it was unremitting.

In fact, Butler was not a very accomplished administrator. Masters meetings were an agony for his colleagues. Governors were bombarded by paperwork congesting their business. Good at managing the human dimension of running the

---

[38] Ibid., 122–3 and for the election in general, pp. 119–32; Young Letter Book, fo. 69.
[39] Graham, *Butler*, 32.
[40] Ibid., 127. The story was told by Farrar to Revd W. E. H. Sotheby who told Graham.
[41] GM, 16 Nov. 1859; Graham, *Butler*, 127–8.
[42] F. E. Marshall in Hallam, *Rev. H. M. Butler*, 7 and in general, pp. 6–12 on his working habits; Graham, *Butler*, 187, 305 and, generally, pp. 301–32. Welldon embellishes Butler's sleepiness with typical amusement in *Forty Years On* (London, 1935), pp. 125–6.
[43] Graham, *Butler*, 251.

school, Butler was found out when it came to taking responsibility, after 1874, for the finances. Perhaps his vagueness over his income in 1862 had been as much a matter of incompetence as concealment. Although he had been used to some part-time accounting help, he simply could not get the School Fund accounts right. In 1877 he forgot to provide the annual accounts at all; in 1879 he was accused by the governors of mismanaging the Fund; and by 1880 the accounts had slid into chaos. So busy, he repeatedly forgot to brief himself for governors' meetings or provide information as requested: it took him three and a half years to supply a report on science teaching first demanded in 1877.[44] His plight was recognized in 1880 by the appointment of a Head Master's secretary, the first of a redoubtable line, W. Moss, who stayed to serve four Heads over four decades, and of a Bursar, first A. C. Tosswill in 1881, then, from 1882, M. G. Glazebrook, later High Master of Manchester Grammar School and Head Master of Clifton.[45] After 1875 Butler was even assisted in the complicated process of adding up the weighted marks for examinations and prizes by W. D. Bushell's 'Harrow Mark Reducer', a special slide rule designed (and publicly marketed, the first branded Harrow product) for the purpose.[46]

Despite his incessant, voluminous correspondence within the school and beyond, Butler never reduced himself to a manager. His conception of a Head was fully Arnoldian. He insisted on his full share of teaching, both of the Sixth and on a regular rotation occasional periods with all classical divisions. The chapel remained at the centre of his school work, not least because it provided the only direct, regular contact he had with the majority of the 500 and more boys under him for whom he was otherwise a distant disciplinarian. He preached at almost every Sunday Evensong during his Headship and, despite a weakness for orotundity, over the years became a highly effective practitioner, not least in his own eyes. Even after his much loved first wife died in 1883, he allowed himself only two days off. By the mid-1870s he became one of the most sought after Establishment preachers, earning the usual accolade of an Honorary Chaplaincy to the Queen in 1875 followed by appointment as Chaplain in Ordinary in 1877.[47]

Like his sermons, the tone of his regime was industry and faith. Idleness was anathema to him. Writing to Farrar in 1862, he realistically complained: 'the listlessness of the Harrow boys will, I fear, continue to be our thorn in the flesh as long as we continue to labour here'.[48] Not an original thinker or innovator, his achievements in moving slowly but steadily towards a wider curriculum were considerable, placing Harrow in all cases on a par with competitors and in some instances ahead of them. His personal obsession with classics and verse did not make him dogmatic. In 1878, with other distinguished public schoolmasters, he signed a

[44] GBM, 15 Mar., 6 July 1877, 28 Feb. 1879, 13 Jan., 30 Apr., 16 Nov. 1880, 1 Feb. 1881.
[45] GBM, 8 Mar. 1881, 25 Apr. 1882; Graham, *Butler*, 184–5.
[46] See HA Masters' Papers, W. Done Bushell file for information and advertisement.
[47] Graham, *Butler*, 238–9, 257, 355–62; Minchin, *Old Harrow Days*, 120; Russell, *Autobiography*, 37–8.   [48] R. Farrar, *The Life of Frederick William Farrar* (London, 1904), pp. 123–4.

petition to the university of Cambridge calling for an end to the Greek entry requirement, to no avail: the country parsons would not tolerate it. Butler showed flexibility of mind and action. His motives for retaining Greek, which he confessed was far too difficult for most boys, were as much pragmatic as ideological: if he abolished it, all the brilliant boys would go elsewhere.[49]

Change was possible. The 1860s witnessed Entrance examinations for all; the institution of Entrance scholarships in 1865 and the controversial superannuation rule in 1868. The Modern Side established in parallel to the traditional classical system in 1869 was only the second in the country (Cheltenham was the first, although Rugby had also begun to teach science). Music, in the form of unison singing in Chapel and Harrow songs, was introduced as an integral part of the school experience, although not as a form subject. The Rifle Corps was revived in 1863, reorganized and provided with an armoury beneath the Old Schools.[50] New buildings were erected to cater for the expansion of studies, including the Library, Science, and Music Schools. A school Sanatorium was established.[51] His very last years as Head Master were taken up with discussions on the overhaul of the timetable to respond more realisticly to individual academic needs, although these changes, which aroused fierce emotions, were left to his successor.[52] Of possibly even greater long-term significance was the introduction in 1875 of the annual examination of the Sixth Form by the Oxford and Cambridge Examination Board for the Certificate of Proficiency, a device to ease boys' passage into the newly (but only very slightly) competitive universities.[53] Although in mild form, this instituted external examinations not by hand-picked individuals, as in the case of the Leaving Scholarships, but by outside academic bodies not just, as already happened, the army, navy, or Indian Service. Such intrusion was vociferously opposed by some, such as Bowen, on the grounds of academic independence, the incapacity of university examiners, and the inability of such narrow examination to judge the true quality of a school, arguments familiar a century and a quarter later.[54] None the less, external examinations became a dominant theme of the next century, from Common Entrance, to School Certificate, to O, A, and GCSE Levels, all of which undermined and ultimately destroyed the school's academic independence that Butler and his contemporaries so cherished and fought so vigorously to defend. Butler's object, as demonstrated in his handling of the Clarendon Commission and the Public Schools Act, was to preserve the nature and status of the school which inevitably implied, as Vaughan helpfully pointed out to the assembled old boys at the Tercentenary celebrations, not just faith and zeal but progress.[55]

[49] Head Master's Book, 1874–92, fo. 63; Minchin, *Old Harrow Days*, 129.
[50] GM, 19 June 1862; Graham, *Butler*, 170–1 and *passim*; Laborde, *Harrow School*, 58–9.
[51] Laborde, *Harrow School*, 207; Graham, *Butler*, 166; GM and GBM, *passim*.
[52] GBM, 23 Mar. 1882, 2 Mar. 1883, 20 Mar., 25 June 1885.
[53] Head Master's Book, 1874–92, fo. 10; GBM, 17 Nov. 1875.
[54] Stray, *Classics Transformed*, 198 n. 92; Bowen, 141–4.   [55] *Harrow Tercentenary*, 27.

Curriculum reform frightened Butler much less than change to the internal system of independence of schoolboy life under monitorial rule. This he supported without contradiction, partly because he imposed an overriding discipline of some strictness and severity which his pupils and his successor thought extravagant.[56] Twenty years after leaving, Butler himself displayed lachrymose regret at his harshness.[57] As Head Master, he was very alert to sin, playing a prominent role in establishing the Church of England Purity Society in 1883.[58] Some of his colleagues were also less than vigilant. Holmes was regularly absent from Druries in the evenings; as Harris' health deteriorated The Park descended into a pit of bullying; while Steel apparently never went into the boys' side at The Grove: he believed in letting them alone, unlike his successor Bowen, known for obvious reasons as 'the Sleuth'. Butler had a series of disciplinary problems in his first years and W. D. Bushell remembered Harrow even in the early 1870s as 'a little hell'. Yet Butler was hardly aided by 'his tendency to treat the tiniest breach of a school-rule as if it was an offence against the moral law'.[59]

Rather than alter the self-government of the young, in 1869 Butler, bowing to the inevitable, opened the Upper Sixth and the monitorial body to boys with attributes other than academic ability, in Graham's words 'such as character and influence', i.e. bloods. In 1876 the restriction in the number of monitors was lifted. The result of these changes, thrilled E. D. Laborde seventy years later, was that Harrow gained 'the reputation for turning out leaders of men'.[60] Butler was probably more interested in policemen of the young, but he would not have been too unhappy with Laborde's eulogy. In a fashion curiously typical of his time (Thring of Uppigham being the prototype) Butler combined a condescending belief in the moral and intellectual superiority of the classics with an enthusiasm for the ordinary, vigorous, monoglot pupil on whom most formwork was wasted, those described by Farrar in 1867 as 'completely ignorant of—altogether content with—their own astonishing and consummate ignorance'.[61] In his Tercentenary sermon Butler summed up his vision of the school by listing 'those influences which exercise so potent a spell over all ages and every variety of taste and pursuit': intellectual thoroughness; 'the wonderful charm of pure, disinterested friendship'; the 'first growth of public spirit'; the 'battleground for inward moral struggles'; the first call to Christ. Above all, 'never can any one of us be more truly and typically and traditionally Harrovian . . . as never to forget that he is also a gentleman.'[62]

---

[56] Graham, *Butler*, 314–15; Russell, *Autobiography*, 12; Welldon, *Recollections*, 86–7.
[57] P. Lubbock (ed.), *The Diary of Arthur Christopher Benson* (London, 1926), p. 107.
[58] Honey, *Tom Brown's Universe*, 180.
[59] Russell in Hallam, *Rev. H. M. Butler*, 12; Russell, *Autobiography*, 47–8; Bushell, *Done Bushell*, 11; HA, W. Rawcliffe, *Harrow Verses* (1927), pp. 18, 20; Leaf, *Autobiography*, 51–2; Vachell, *Fellow Travellers*, 26; Graham, *Butler*, 157.
[60] Laborde, *Harrow School*, 59; Graham, *Butler*, 301.   [61] Farrar, *Farrar*, 101.
[62] *Harrow Tercentenary*, 16–19.

The Rise of the Federal School

A direct corollary of Butler's conservatism was his passive acceptance of the trend begun under Wordsworth, confirmed under Vaughan, and reinforced by the new Statutes and Regulations that houses, large and small, not only provided the wealth of the masters but formed the basis and the structure of the boys' social life and identity. Butler presided over the full flowering of the house system. He accepted the status quo as immutable: 'the *esprit de corps* of Houses being very powerful'.[63] Even though the problems in securing The Park for the school at the end of his Headship and the row over the housemasters' constitutional rights over the question of sanitary inspections signalled that the separation of house and school was fraught with dangerously divisive consequences, these were problems for his successors to try to resolve, a matter that occupied them for the better part of a century.

Thus, although a tight disciplinarian, outside his house and his form, Butler did not control the school in the way that a Sumner had or even a Vaughan had. There were too many boys, too many autonomous houses, too many masters for that. The only boarding house owned by the school was one part of the Head Master's, the rest were owned or leased privately by the masters. The very geography of the school, so different from most other public schools in being spread along almost two-thirds of a mile through the town, militated against the Arnoldian ideal of control. Paradoxically, this most imperious seeming of Head Masters (who maintained a pious correspondence with Arnold's daughter until the First World War)[64] had far less effect on most of his boys than did the individual housemasters and tutors. Although his personality pervaded every aspect of school life, the school had become too Balkanized for any Head Master to sum up its parts in himself. Butler's unique empathy with his school concealed this development, but none after him, however hard he tried, could seriously be considered as more than a figurehead.

Some observers remarked on Butler's ability to unite his staff in a common purpose even when riven with antagonisms over details, Butler's Harrow presenting to the world a school with a set of clear values, articulated by a Head of secure authority.[65] The reality, of course, was rather different. By the time he left, all but eight of the twenty-six masters were his appointments. While he inherited such warhorses as Oxenham and Ben Drury, he bequeathed men who continued to teach at Harrow until after the First World War. His colleagues straddled a complete century, from Marillier (1819–69) to Graham (1882–1919). Yet Butler was far from

---

[63] Butler, *Letter to the Governors*, Sept. 1864 and above, p. 291.
[64] Graham, *Butler*, 422, an annual task he 'inherited' from Dean Stanley in 1881.
[65] Hallam, *Rev. H. M. Butler*, 4.

being an autocrat. Ever sensitive of his youth and even more youthful looks, he tended to defer rather than confront. His 'blow ups' were always in writing, never face to face, and even then, he admitted, usually futile.[66] One of his faults was a reluctance to dismiss or ease out elderly masters who had long ceased to be effective, a result of sentiment, conservatism, and a reluctance to challenge vested interests. Almost as soon as he went, the system of seniority whereby promotion to forms and to houses was decided on rigid seniority, was abolished and a superannuation rule for masters, discussed by the governors as early as 1875, was introduced.[67]

His handling of his colleagues typified his methods in general: suave and affectionate in private; anxiously ponderous in public. Despite his best efforts, he was rarely able to persuade all of them to attend the weekly masters' meetings, favourites such as Westcott and Smith being especially remiss, the latter never going. One reason may have been timing; from nine o'clock at night until midnight. Another may have been Butler's habit of introducing business by reading lengthy memorandums which dealt indiscriminately with issues great and small with equal detail, seriousness, and laboured concern.[68] In business as in life, Butler lacked a sense of proportion. These memorandums, and those hundreds he sent to the governors, pointed to industry and vulnerability. Like some of his conversation, Butler was rarely *ex tempore*, the occasional unscripted sermon, forced on him, for example, by a broken writing arm, attracting notice.[69] Part of this inhibition was probably the natural result of his early difficulties as Head. Nine of his colleagues had been masters when he had been a boy. Although impressively self-assured in public, he looked even younger than 26, a difficulty he attempted to counter by always wearing Geneva bands with the more usual cap and gown and by growing a large and distinctive beard when ill in 1867.[70] He adopted a very formal attitude on the Hill. He always allowed enough time to climb from the Head Master's to his formroom in the Old Schools to avoid ever being caught out of breath. To boys such as H. A. Vachell, later the author of *The Hill*, the most glutinously sentimental of all novels about the school, Butler appeared a remote figure when riding slowly across the Hill, silently and solemnly acknowledging their presence by a tip of his hat, an 'Olympian'.[71]

For a Head whose intellectual powers were admired, political presence unchallenged, and achievements for the school unquestioned, Butler's handling of his masters consistently lacked ease. He conspicuously failed to quell their squabbles and enmities, his managerial methods at times appeared quaint or ludicrous.

---

[66] Graham, *Butler*, 144. [67] Ibid., 146–7; Hallam, *Rev. H. M. Butler*, 5.

[68] HM/Bm/Wescott Correspondence, Butler to Westcott, 28 May 1861. Cf. Butler to Westcott, 22 Dec. 1868; Rendall, *Recollections of John Smith*, 24; Graham, *Butler*, 144–5, 187; comments of colleagues Hallam and Marshall, *Rev. H. M. Butler*, 5, 6. [69] Russell, *Autobiography*, 38.

[70] Russell in Hallam, *Rev. H. M. Butler*, 11; Graham, *Butler*, 139, 192 and n. 2.

[71] Vachell, *Fellow Travellers*, 21; Graham, *Butler*, 187.

To pacify one colleague who had lost a bruising argument, Butler penned the following:

> Thus with a tear in either eye
> For fear I've raised the Furies,
> 'For auld lang syne' I forward my
> Eirenicon to Druries.[72]

What the bruiser C. F. Holmes made of this entirely typical offering from his Head is unrecorded. Butler's conservative rigidity lost him at least two masters against his will. Butler insisted that all Harrow housemasters should possess First Class degrees (which astonishingly they did). His refusal to shift caused the resignation of the popular and effective Lancelot Sanderson after five years in 1869: he went to found Elstree Preparatory School which became one of Harrow's most loyal 'feeders'.[73] Ironically, that very year Butler began to dilute the intellectual qualifications for the Sixth Form and monitors. Robert Quick, an Old Harrovian and a believer, like Butler, in the efficacy of the Arnoldian system and narrow classicism, left in 1874 exasperated at the sheer incompetence of the system and the technical ignorance of his colleagues which led, he argued, to 'overworked masters and under-taught or ill-taught boys'. He deplored the rule of athleticism amongst the boys that bred bullying and the crushing of individualism, a world 'in which the schoolmaster has as much share as the coastguard officer in the world of the smuggler'. Quick was popular and, although he regarded Butler, an old school contemporary, as a self-obsessed solipsist, was seen by the Head as an asset. Yet, despite acknowledging him a 'hero with children' and a genial colleague, Butler refused to accelerate Quick even to a pupil room, let alone a house. The offer to make Quirk a sort of house tutor at the Head Master's with a variety of menial tasks failed to keep him on the Hill.[74] Perhaps this was inevitable, but the seniority system and the refusal of the old to die, retire, or relinquish positions for which they were conspicuously unsuited meant that much of the formal teaching under Butler was poor and the masters frustrated. Farrar, with a national reputation as a classicist and educational innovator, never taught a form above the Upper Remove. Unsurprisingly, he grew impatient with his dull and backward charges and, despite gaining a large house, The Park in 1869, was eager to leave.[75]

Butler was aware of the problem but unable to fight against what, everywhere else, he praised: tradition. In December 1868 G. F. Harris retired through ill health. Butler offered his form, the Lower Sixth, to E. M. Young, a former fellow of Trinity in his late twenties who had joined the staff in 1863, instead of F. Rendall, the formmaster of the Upper Fifth, a veteran of twenty years and an appallingly

---

[72] Bryant, *Harrow*, 88.   [73] Graham, *Butler*, 141–2.

[74] Mack, *Public Schools and British Opinion since 1860*, 167–8; Graham, *Butler*, 213–14.

[75] Farrar, *Farrar*, 92. Cf. the comments of A. D. Godley, 1869–74, scholar of Balliol and fellow of Magdalen, *Rev. H. M. Butler*, 9.

dull, inept teacher. There was a mutiny at the Masters' meeting, led by Farrar whose fustration at being stuck with the Upper Remove erupted at the prospect of promotion being blocked by the elevation of the upstart Young. Farrar accused Butler to his face of 'almost every kind of injustice and caprice' and threatened to 'take public steps to gain redress'. T. H. Steel, now well into his sixties, stirred the pot by pronouncing for all to hear that he hated the very sight of Butler's handwriting. Butler tried to rally support from the masters not at the meeting, confessing to the absentee Westcott, 'I am in great trouble... grieved and humiliated'. He failed. Young, whose political skills were sufficient to secure him the Headship of Sherborne in 1877 although not enough to keep or save himself from largely unfair public obloquy and dismissal in 1892, saw how the wind sat and tactfully refused the offer of the Lower Sixth. The diehards had won, leaving Butler to lament 'I cannot hope that my error in judgement will be very soon forgotten'. However, three years later, with Farrar gone to the Mastership of Marlborough, Westcott to his Cambridge chair and others, such as Bowen, engaged on the new Modern Side, Butler was able to establish the principle that the succession to the Lower Sixth, but only to that form, should rest with the Head's discretion not on seniority.[76]

Such public defeats were comparatively rare, although tactical withdrawals were common. In 1863, against his advice, the masters insisted on one of the most unpopular and spectacularly silly rules to be introduced even at Harrow. Trouser pockets were banned, ostensibly to prevent boys slouching, but more probably because of the new sensitivity to adolescent sexual habits. Ridicule was heaped on the school. Butler perceived that the boys would resent the imposition, if only as an interference with their independence in a period when uniform was only beginning to be prescriptive (a trend in which Butler played a prominent part). After a few months, Butler argued for the ban to be lifted (or, as he characteristically phrased it, 'I acknowledged frankly my disposition to recede'), but was overruled, despite petulantly announcing that he would refuse to enforce the rule.[77]

Such essentially trivial rows revealed how loose the Head's control could be. If his silken persuasion failed, he had little else with which to discipline his colleagues. It is sometimes forgotten that the authority of the great public school

---

[76] HM/Bm/Westcott Correspondence nos. 10, 11, Butler to Westcott, 22, 23 Dec. 1868; Minchin, *Old Harrow Days*, 44–6; Graham, *Butler*, 146–7; on Young see Honey, *Tom Brown's Universe*, 334–5.

[77] Graham, *Butler*, 182–4. Cf. *Ode to a Certain Friend* by J. G. Lawson (1870–4):

By thy large and ugly nut,
By thy beard of formal cut,
By thy robes of sable black
By thy lordly noble hack,
Tell, oh! tell what evils hide
In the pockets by my side

HA, Rawcliffe, *Harrow Verses*, 24 and cf. p. 19 re Bowen, 'Wondering where they wear their pockets'.

paladins was contingent on the support of staff as well as parents, governors, and old boys. For every Thring or Butler there was a Hayman of Rugby or Young of Sherborne, both removed as Heads, in 1874 and 1892 respectively, after concerted campaigns by their colleagues.[78] At Harrow this was an especial problem with so many of them, as well as having independent relations with influential parents as housemasters, were distinguished in their own right. G. H. Hallam calculated that as Harrow masters in the years just after he came, 1870–2, there were five Senior Classics (he was one), six future Head Masters, two Fellows of the Royal Society, one future bishop, two deans, and two Oxbridge professors, not to mention the old guard, such as Steel, who was once a colleague of Henry Drury, or Middlemist, a housemaster since 1845.[79] Men such as Rendall, Holmes, Farrar, or Bowen were not likely to submit easily to anything they disliked. Even the apparently other-worldy Smith bombarded the Head with written criticisms.[80]

One of the bitterest conflicts occured over the new Speech Room. Built between 1874 and 1877, both the exterior and interior designs by the fashionable C. F. Burges met with fierce opposition. Internally, the narrow dais was thought too small to accommodate the large orchestras and choirs (i.e. most of the school singing in unison) required by the Director of Music, John Farmer. Music was regarded with suspicion by many, such as Rendall, who saw 'the essential principle of Farmer's teaching' (i.e. mass community singing rather than elite ensemble or, even worse, solo performances) contradicted by the plan. However, as Butler pointed out, a wider platform would require huge further expense and distort the overall design. So the peculiar feature of Harrow Songs, with the audience sitting on a stage being sung at by the school sitting in the auditorium, was instigated. In November 1872 Rendall, a member of a sub-Committee of the Building Committee, resigned in protest accusing Butler of 'a distinct breach of faith' and warning of the design's 'practical inconvenience and moral mischief attendant on the exclusion of the school for the glorification of a select few'. Burges' exterior fared no better, one observer likening the whole edifice to 'a cross between a swimming bath and a tennis court'. Most dismissed it as an eyesore. On 8 July 1873, when Butler presented the plans to his colleagues, only four out of twenty-six supported the Burges design. Yet Butler pushed it through despite warnings of 'a very grave sense of the evil that was smouldering' and 'a wide-spread dissatisfaction which was disturbing our peace and engendering distrust where all should be harmony'. Butler's problem was that Burges was the pet architect of the forceful chairman of the Building Committee, A. J. Beresford-Hope, MP, trustee of the British Museum and the National Portrait Gallery, patron of church-building, and leading light in organizing the Lyon Memorial Fund. The Speech Room debacle provided an interesting test of the relative strengths of masters and old boys: the outcome was

---

[78] See on this aspect Honey, *Tom Brown's Universe*, 325–35.
[79] Hallam, *Rev. H. M. Butler*, 3.   [80] Graham, *Butler*, 139.

not in doubt. Butler meekly accepted *force majeur*.[81] Ironically, Burges's Speech Room, with rather truncated towers completed only in 1919 and 1925, has probably survived as a greater aesthetic success than Gilbert Scott's then much admired Chapel. Although Butler was able to secure Burges's design despite his colleagues' hostility, so far from being a demonstration of strength, the incident revealed the weakness of the Head Master in the face of external pressure and the masters' freedom to attack him. Behind the facade of harmony, much was discord which Butler was powerless to resolve.

The system increasingly weighted the balance against the Head. In 1862, two years before he joined the staff for thirty-seven years, Reginald Bosworth-Smith, a pupil of Cotton at Marlborough and a fellow of Trinity, Oxford, examining the Leaving Scholarship, noted: 'the school gives me the impression after Marlborough of being too much split up into small divisions by the number of houses'.[82] This did not prevent him from accepting Butler's invitation in 1869 to build himself a large boys' house (the Knoll) where, in the words of one colleague, 'he was able to establish his own traditions and stamp his character upon the life of his boys'. Butler's only subsequent role was to provide the Knoll with its first head of house, Robert Yerburgh, whom he recommended in typically effusive manner: '*Ecce*, he is a remarkably good-looking, active, manly fellow, just the one to be head of your new house.'[83] However, Bosworth-Smith had identified a central feature of late Victorian Harrow. While the boys might be over-disciplined, the masters enjoyed institutional liberty that bordered on licence.

Butler's correspondence reveals the wearying battles he waged to get his way. Even junior masters felt free to sign petitions opposing his actions.[84] On cherished issues, his power could still be limited. At one masters' meeting he threatened to resign unless they agreed common methods and content in religious instruction. They refused. Butler did not resign.[85] In an age of indifference, religious conformity had been easy to obtain; in one of enthusiasm, it proved impossible. He had greater success in 1878 when another resignation threat prevented the governors accepting Bowen's offer to endow a Modern Side Scholarship that deliberately omitted a Divinity examination, but it was Bowen's horror at the prospect of losing Butler, rather than the merits of the case, his subservience or gubernatorial fiat, that persuaded him to withdraw his proffered endowment.[86]

Religion remained a thorny issue. As Harrow's reputation grew, parents of all religious persuasions were eager for their sons to enjoy its advantages. Butler

---

[81] Graham, *Butler*, 224–7; Laborde, *Harrow School*, 135–7 for the later building history; copies of Burges' rather fine drawings and elevations are in the school archives.

[82] Grogan, *Bosworth-Smith*, 63.   [83] Ibid., 67, 74, 105–6.

[84] Graham, *Butler*, 145. Butler's reply to H. G. Hart, a junior master who had joined in public opposition by masters to Butler; Hart later became Head Master of Sedburgh.

[85] Graham, *Butler*, 144–5.

[86] GM, 26 June 1873; GBM, 27 June, 29 Nov. 1878; 20 Jan. 1879; Graham, *Butler*, 179–80.

admitted the first overtly practising Roman Catholic in 1869. With more applying for admission, Butler tried to establish certain principles in 1875. Butler believed that Catholics offended against the traditions of the school far more seriously than nonconformists. As Vaughan had insisted in 1871, Harrow was a Reformation school. It remained a predominantly evangelical one. Suspicion of Romish influence continued to be surprisingly keen and tenacious. In 1897, a suggestion for a Roman Catholic house came to nothing.[87] Only in the last quarter of the twentieth century did Roman Catholics in any numbers apply to Harrow, become housemasters, or even governors. The Conscience clause of the 1874 Regulations, strongly promoted by Butler, aroused considerable hostility among the masters, the majority insisting that housemasters had the right to refuse or expel any boy who opted out of Chapel and Anglican religious instruction. The application of this clause provided another sign of housemasters' independence. Bowen, first at Grove Hill (1864–81) and then The Grove (1881–1901) was a notorious freethinker, Chapel being important mainly for its expression of community, in which it in any case fell far short of games. Nevertheless, although enthusiastic for the Conscience clause, he opposed the admission of Jews on the grounds they might miss some Saturday school, thus breaking the grip of the total shared experience that he regarded as fundamental.[88] None the less, he admitted N. C. Rothschild to the Grove in 1891. Bosworth-Smith admitted to the Knoll (1870–1901) boys from India, Persia, Egypt, and Zanzibar, giving it, in the revealing phrase of one colleague, a cosmopolitan 'tincture'. Others were less coy 'over this admittance of coloured races'; in 1896 Welldon insisted on being consulted before any 'foreign boys' were entered.[89]

As early as 1872 the governors raised the question of the possibility of a Jewish house, an idea strongly backed by C. S. Roundell (né Currer).[90] This apparently presented Harrow opinion with less anxiety although more practical difficulty than Roman Catholics. Among the boys (and more discreetly among the masters) there was much unthinking, traditional upper-class, overt anti-Semitism, but both the Head Master and the governors accepted that a school for the rich could not ignore a possibly lucrative market. It was accepted there was a demand. Both Cheltenham and Clifton were to establish Jewish houses. Jewish boys such as J. F. Waley, F. A. Davis, and H. M. Beddington were admitted in 1877 and 1878, boarding individually with masters such as the Drawing Master, Edward de la Motte. In 1880 the governors agreed to establish a separate Jewish house which was opened a year later

---

[87] Graham, *Butler*, 188–9; GBM, 16 Mar. 1875 and, for Welldon's anti-Catholic views, 2 Feb. 1886; *Harrow Tercentenary*, 27–8; Minutes of Masters' Meetings, 1893–1910, 29 Nov. 1897.

[88] Bowen, *Bowen*, 134–5, 201, 217; above, pp. 297–8.

[89] Grogan, *Bosworth-Smith*, 107–8; Minutes of Masters' Meetings, 1893–1910, 26 Apr. 1896.

[90] GM, 27 June 1872. Cf. GBM, 14 Jan. 1874. For what follows see GBM, 27 May 1875; 30 May 1876; 4 May, 28 June, 6 Aug. 1877; 28 Jan. 1879; 20 July, 16 Nov. 1880; Minchin, *Old Harrow Days*, 70–1; *Harrow Register, 1800–1911, passim*; HA Jewish House file.

by Dr Joseph Chotzner from Belfast (whose name the bewildered clerk to the governors initially rendered as Schottsner).[91] This was situated first at the top of Waldron Road, accommodating eight to nine boys, one wag nicknaming it 'Junipers'. After some trouble with the drains of a new house he had moved to in 1886, Chotzner returned to Belfast in 1892, the Jewish house being taken over by Charles Sankey who had recently come to Harrow from the Headship of Bury St Edmunds School. Under Sankey, a gentile, Jewish religious instruction, a cause of some concern before 1881, was conducted by a visiting rabbi from Cambridge. Increasingly, the Jewish community pressed for Jews to be admitted to exisiting houses, under Christian housemasters, provided they were allowed time for Divine Worship on Saturday mornings.[92] This pressure to integrate came largely from parents. With numbers of 'conforming', i.e. non-observant Jews in other houses rising, it appeared to some of the masters that the need for a separate Jewish house was receding. After a decision made in 1898, it closed in 1903.[93] The federal nature of the school which had made it possible in the first place, also precipitated its demise as individual housemasters had the freedom to decide whom to admit and, within the Regulations, under what terms, an attempt to impose a common form of entry being rejected by the masters in 1898.[94] In Butler's time there was no obvious religious quota, except that a small house, of up to nine, imposed a de facto limit on the number of observant Jews. However, the decision to close the Jews' house in 1898 went further towards an open quota. It was decided that, after closure, observant Jews could be received into boarding houses but only two per house, with any housemasters free to refuse to take any, thereby ensuring the total remained effectively no higher than when the house existed. Along with many other public schools, thereafter Harrow operated religious and ethnic quotas, with the tastes and prejudices of housemasters as much as school policy providing the determinant factor.

In many ways, Butler and his colleagues were establishing a new relationship, reflecting the new power of the housemasters and the new conditions imposed by the Statutes and Regulations of 1874. Bowen, one of the chief belligerents, even composed a song about a House hero (*Tom* 1893). Battles were often triangular. The Head wished to preserve his authority, which meant at times supporting the masters against the governors, as over the curriculum; at others the governors against the masters, as with sanitary regulations; and occasionally his own independence, such as over the right of appeal for dismissed masters or the place of Divinity. Masters were fearful of the Head's despotic right to hire and fire but

[91] GBM, 16 Nov. 1880. Cf. 30 Nov. 1886 for recognition as a Small House.
[92] *Jewish Chronicle*, 5 May 1882, 11 Oct. 1895 See HA Jewish House file; GBM, 5 Feb. 1889.
[93] GBM, 6 Nov. 1888, 5 Nov. 1889, 25 June 1891, 4 Feb. 1902, Minutes of Masters' Meetings, 1893–1910, 29 Jan., 12 Feb., 19 Feb. 1894, 30 Sept. 1895, 17 Feb. 1896, 16 May, 6 June 1898, 17 Nov. 1902. Cf. 29 Nov. 1897 for attitude to Catholics.
[94] Minutes of Masters' Meetings, 1893–1910, 2 May 1898.

resented any interference from the governors, presumably because they knew they had some leaverage over the Head which they wholly lacked with the governing body. The masters were undoubtedly more powerful as a group than previously. The Entrance Scholarship system, for example, depended on contributions from each housemaster, which caused resentment but lent them authority, not least in ensuring that each house had its own scholars rather than them being concentrated under the Head or a Master of Scholars as elsewhere.[95] The 1874 Regulations, that specified their boarding fees, enshrined their coequal importance with the Head, whose finances were, if anything, more closely controlled than theirs. As all masters who stayed long enough received a small or large house regardless of their suitability, even those juniors not yet on the ladder of preferment were eager to support housemasters' rights confident that their turn would come. As a group, they also benefited from the late nineteenth-century obsession with institutional identity. The boys' boarding house readily lent itself to the emotions of belonging, especially as, by the 1870s, all boarders were in their housemaster's pupil room (unless, as in the case of Bushell in Rendalls, he was not a classicist). Shared domestic experience was a strong bond. School rituals were aped by distinct house songs, jargon, colours, and rules.[96] Increasingly, boys from different houses did not mix socially outside school teams until they were quite senior. There was general acceptance of this oddly fissiparous world. Butler's successor, Welldon, believed that a good house was more important than a good school.[97]

This presented no great difficulty provided housemasters were loyal. The new Statutes and Regulations tested that loyalty. In their submissions to the governors throughout the reform process, the masters had feared erosion of their independence. Although anxious about tenure, they were particularly concerned with interference from the new governing body. As it seemed that only one new governor, Professor Tyndall, appeared interested in actually scrutinizing academic studies and then only science which affected two masters at most, fears over control of the curriculum proved unfounded, joint committees over the timetable, for instance, essentially leaving the decisions with the Head.[98] In 1874, immediately the new Statutes and Regulations were in force, the housemasters tested their position by requesting an increase in their boarding fees. Greed was matched by laziness, as they failed to provide the governors with supporting information for nine months.[99] None the less they secured their rise of 6 per cent on basic boarding fees, making the cost for boy in a large house £90 a year, small houses remaining unchanged at £135. Given the fixed maximum numbers in each house, this meant

---

[95] Head Masters' Book, 1874–92, fo. 95 for arguments about scholarships' scheme in 1880; Minutes of Masters' Meetings, 1893–1910, 8 Mar., 7, 14 June, 1 Nov. 1897. Cf. Statutes and Regulations of 1874; in general, Bowen, *Bowen*, 134; Laborde, *Harrow School*, 59.
[96] e.g. Druries has one by Howson and Thatcher. [97] Welldon, *Recollections*, 99.
[98] GBM, 15 Mar. 1877, 16 Nov. 1880, 1 Feb., 15 Feb. 1881, etc.
[99] GBM, 10 June, 23 Nov. 1874, 16 Mar. 1875.

that a master in a full large house, on top of his salary, anything between £150 and £300, and his pupil-room fees, c.£600, would receive around £3,500 a year. Those in small houses often took more pupils, but from their boarders could expect between £1,200 and £1,350. At the same time, to meet the expenses of new subjects and facilities, a problem the traditionalist Percy Thornton warned darkly could endanger the school in any future slump, school charges were raised by 16 per cent, making the total annual academic fee just under £50.[100] Basic fees, therefore, could vary from c.£140 to c.£185; with uniform and casual expenses thrown in, Harrow was a very expensive place, almost twice as costly as Marlborough or Haileybury.[101] The masters were the main beneficiaries. Small wonder that of the forty-five academic masters appointed to permanent posts by Vaughan and Butler between 1845 and 1885, twenty (almost 45 per cent) stayed at Harrow for more than thirty years (Bowen for forty-two, six others for thirty-five or more), with another six for twenty four or more years.[102] In all senses, at Harrow seniority was serious.

Although the masters were financially appeased, a constitutional row developed over health and safety. In 1875 the governors decided on sanitary inspections of all school houses conducted on their authority, although they did not organize one until 1879, with another in 1880.[103] What was revealed shocked them. As Butler confessed, most occupiers were 'ignorant of hygiene', as a result 'many of our Boarding Houses during the last fifty years have been faulty from a sanitary point of view', the recent inspection showing 'that nearly all required important improvements'.[104] The governors moved quickly to establish new regulations giving themselves power to order regular inspections by their appointed inspector and the right to close unsatisfactory Boarding Houses.[105] For housemasters this presented two distinct challenges. Although all except the Head (a tenant of the governors) occupied their houses as freeholders or tenants of non-school landlords, under this scheme they would be financially liable for any changes ordered by the governors, as they would be obliged to carry out the Sanitary Inspector's recommendations or face the governors' refusal to allow them to continue to take boarders. This also raised a serious constitutional issue of intrusion by the governors. In January 1880 the masters' voiced their opposition to the scheme through C. F. Holmes.[106] The issue of principle was expressed forcefully by the legalistic Bowen. He and J. Stogdon, who lived in the two sides of Grove Hill (later Grove Hill House and the Foss), had been criticized over dangerous lobbies and landings in their premises. Bowen rejected the governors' letter on the subject, arguing that he

---

[100] GBM, 27 May, 11 June 1875; Head Master's Book, 1874–92, fo. 43; HA Copies of Statutes and Regulations with post-1875 amendments in HM/Bm/file.
[101] Honey, *Tom Brown's Universe*, 296–302.   [102] *Harrow Register, 1800–1911*, 903–6.
[103] GBM, 27 May 1875, 30 May 1876, 6 July 1877, 26 June 1879.
[104] Head Master's Book 1874–92, fol. 43, Butler 'Strictly Confidential' Circular, Feb. 1881.
[105] Head Master's Book, 1874–92, fo. 43, Lord Verulam to Butler, 30 Nov. 1880.
[106] GBM, 13 Jan. 1880.

was responsible only to the Head Master. Immediately, the governors determined that in future all communications with Assistant Masters should be conducted through the Head.[107] The substantive issue of governors' intrusive authority remained. They pressed ahead with further inspections, formulating and imposing their sanitary orders and amending the School Regulations to recognize their supervisory power. Butler quietly sided with the governors because he did not want to take the responsibility of imposing expensive changes to sanitation on reluctant colleagues. His interference in the running of their houses would only cause trouble. Too close to the housemasters, he much preferred the impartial and impersonal control of the governors. Refusing to be cowed, the masters continued to protest. In a memorandum of February 1885, presented by a delegation led by Holmes, the masters argued that the new regulations broke the statutory relationship of the Head with both governors and assistants who, hitherto, had no direct formal relationship with the governing body.[108] Sanitation inspections were regarded as the thin end of the wedge. Armed with this precedent, the governors might begin to determine masters' duties, even salaries. Although in the long run entirely accurate in their prophecy, without the Head's support the masters made no headway, the governors' imposing their regulations following favourable counsel's opinion in April 1885.[109] However, it said much for the self-image of the housemasters that, in spite of Butler's opposition, they felt able to pursue their claims to the point of forcing the governors to go to law.

THE BEGINNING OF MODERN STUDIES

Butler's period witnessed the age of the dominant assistant master in more than housemasterly autonomy, financial acquisitiveness, or administrative bloody-mindedness. Through the intellectual energy of the few, the educational opportunities and range of academic interests vastly expanded. Narrow in his own cerebral pursuits, Montagu Butler presided benignly, if at times supinely, over the diverse activities of his staff and, in creating a Modern Side in 1869, almost in spite of himself signalled the beginning of the end of the monopoly of classics, the single most significant revolution in the academic history of the school.

The openness of some Harrow masters after 1860 to broader notions of education, both academic and non-academic, owed much to their intellectual calibre but no less to the changing culture in the universities. The pious clergymen of Vaughan's day were replaced by the vigorous freethinkers of Bowen's. By the 1870s

---

[107] GBM, 13 May, 20 July 1880.
[108] Head Master's Book, 1874–92, fo. 65, Memorandum of Protest, 7 Feb., signed by C. F. Holmes. Cf. GBM, 1 Feb., 8 Mar., 10 May 1881, 28 Feb., 21 Nov. 1882, 18 Nov. 1884, 3 Feb. 1885.
[109] GBM, 20 Mar., 13 Apr., 1 May 1885. Cf. Graham, *Butler*, 238 for a distinctly mealy-mouthed account of the affair.

intellectual fashions at Oxford and Cambridge were religiously sceptical, fed on the Scriptural criticism of Jowett, the aestheticism of Pater, the agnostic philosophy of Mill or Spencer, the theories of Darwin and the empricism of Sidgwick.[110] Bowen approved of boys in his house not being confirmed.[111] Such men were not in holy orders: only nine out of Butler's twenty-seven appointments were ordained; in 1885 only five out of twenty-five masters were clergymen (at 20 per cent marginally less than the average in twenty-three leading schools) and none of the seven most senior.[112] They wore their classics lightly, their range of cultural references and interests determinedly eclectic. In their company, Butler, although a contemporary, appeared, as in so much else, old fashioned by 30.

Much of the change in intellectual atmosphere began outside the formroom, in houses or pupil-rooms or in more or less licensed extra voluntary lessons, such as Farrar's botany classes in the 1860s, made possible by a combination of bright, inquisitive pupils; bored, undertaxed, yet sympathetic masters; and masses of free time.[113] The influence of such changes should not be exaggerated or pre-dated. By 1885 the ice floe of classical repetition and rote-learning had scarcely begun to crack, as it was to under Welldon. Within the formroom, of course, most of teaching remained narrow, mundane, inept, neglecting, in Farrar's words, 'all the powers of some minds and some of the powers of all minds', unsatisfactory for the few, 'utter and irremediable waste' for the many.[114] The Modern Side grew only erratically and slowly, from 27 in 1869, to 55 in 1876, and 80 in September 1881; in a school of between 500 and 550, these were modest pickings.[115] Many masters were as bad as ever. Some, such as the septuagenarian Steel, were the same as ever, although his old fashioned neglect did not prevent him introducing boys to the poetry of Wordsworth (whom he had entertained on the Hill when the poet's nephew was Head Master). Others displayed the usual symptoms of an educational system curiously but stubbornly impervious to what pupils actually learnt or enjoyed, such as W. J. Bull, (1853–88, housemaster of West Acre 1864–80), 'a square man arduously trying to fit himself into the round hole in which a mischievous providence had placed him'; or the bullying clubman C. F. Holmes; or W. D. Bushell (1866–99, Rendalls 1881–98), a mathematician not good at teaching maths, better at astronomy, happier, as a cleric, commanding the Rifle Corps; all of them in their own ways distant and out of sympathy with the boys.[116]

---

[110] Newsome, *Godliness and Good Learning*, esp. pp. 227–34 for a brief account of these changes, which can be augmented by Mack and in Honey, *Tom Brown's Universe*.

[111] M. Moorman, *George Macaulay Trevelyan* (London, 1980), 22.

[112] Gathorne-Hardy, *Public School Phenomenon*, 190–1. Compared to seven leading HMC day and boarding schools, Harrow's lack of clerical masters was even more marked, the average of these being 40% in 1880 and almost 29% in 1889: Honey, *Tom Brown's Universe*, 308.

[113] Farrar, *Farrar*, 84, 138–9.   [114] Ibid., 100–1.

[115] Bowen, *Bowen*, 103–15; Laborde, *Harrow School*, 59.

[116] Russell, *Autobiography*, 41, 49; Minchin, *Old Harrow Days*, 7; Bushell, *Done Bushell*, 11–15, 19, 30; HA MS Diary of E. C. Richardson, 26 Jan. 1889, *et seq.* for Bushell's Astronomy.

They were victims of the system in which education was strangled by convention. Even Butler, whose Upper Sixth usually came to admire, trust, even adore him, employed fear as a teaching tool: 'in form he inspired terror even in those who most admired and loved him'.[117] He preferred to humiliate rather than help boys in difficulties over oral translation. In form he deliberately perfected techniques to frighten: his Monday Greek Testament tests left few without lifelong scars.[118] Yet, away from the awesome task of imparting the glories of what many regarded even then as a very narrow range of the classics, Butler could be genial, charming, inspirational. His lecture on Napoleon's Italian Campaign of 1796 entered legend. If only to extend their range of allusions when translating the classics, he encouraged his pupils to read widely in standard gentleman's English literature: Shakespeare, Scott, Macaulay, but also introduced one to Disraeli's *Sybil*. Fond of political oratory, he informally taught some English parliamentary history from the Stuarts onwards, no doubt in the Macaulay line, partisan and prone to hero-worship.[119] This was not usual. One Harrovian in his house left school in 1868 not knowing that Peel had repealed the Corn Laws.[120] In Butler's eyes, this would not necessarily have condemned the system, merely the boy's lack of curiosity. Butler wished to train the mind not impart knowledge, hence the obsession with linguistic accuracy, the martinet pedantry only barely concealed beneath bluff joviality. The ability to learn rather than learning itself was the ideal, leaving Butler to confess with equanimity to the Clarendon Committee in 1862: 'With many of the most useful mental accomplishments [the Harrovian] is imperfectly equipped. To many of the highest branches of knowledge he is practically an entire stranger.'[121]

The key to understanding Butler's wholly traditional purpose lay in his desire that boys left Harrow believing that the 'moral welfare' of the institutions to which they did or would belong—school, family, college, club, regiment, nation—could only be maintained by leaders 'distinguished by vigilance, courage, love of justice, sympathy, and courtesy'. Hence the Butlerian, indeed public school, equation of morality and social habits, of religion and status. Thus, as he once thundered to a chastened school, lying was 'not only un-Christian but ungentlemanlike'.[122]

This was the context in which the oddest of Butler's colleagues was not only tolerated but revered. John Smith actually delighted in his own academic inability, once insisting on Butler privately translating for him impromptu, such was his wonder at the Head's facility (the result of whose internal battle between flattery and exasperation was never in doubt). Smith represented an older tradition of religious emulation, a licensed holy man, battling with depression, fear of alcoholism (he

---

[117] Leaf, *Autobiography*, 45.
[118] Ibid., 45–7; Graham, *Butler*, 301–16; Hallam, *Rev. H. M. Butler*, 9–11.
[119] Graham, *Butler*, esp. p. 301, *et seq.*; Russell, *Autobiography*, 36–9; Minchin, *Old Harrow Days*, 122; Leaf, *Autobiography*, 47; Godley, *Rev. H. M. Butler*, 9–11.
[120] Minchin, *Old Harrow Days*, 114–15.   [121] Graham, *Butler*, 198.
[122] Russell, *Autobiography*, 37.

was a pained teetotaller), and madness, occasionally violent but devoted, sincere, unaffectedly naive, and adored by the unintellectual masses who passed through—or stayed—in his Upper Fourth. He taught manners more than anything else coupled with a childlike version of Christianity as in:

BOY: Have you ever been to Switzerland, Sir?
SMITH: No, laddie. It is the first place I hope to go when I am dead.[123]

Smith made it his business to speak to every new boy individually about the dangers of public school life, sex in particular. In these notorious, strange, and for many bewildering or embarrassing encounters he would confess to all sorts of sins, whether in thought, deed, or imagination none could fathom. He took care to conduct these talks in a public place, if possible with witnesses 'perhaps . . . to avoid the evil flavour which secrecy behind closed doors may give to the most well-intentioned conversation'.[124] Smith's concern was not that homosexual activity was a growing menace, although the *Journal of Education* in November 1881 warned that it 'has been of late increasing among the upper classes in England'.[125] No aristocrat himself, he was none the less in a long line of moralists who saw education for the ruling class as fundamentally non-academic; as Butler trained the mind so Smith wanted to train the soul. Neither had much time for learning for its own sake. In the eighteenth century, elite knowledge defined a gentleman; in the nineteenth, it had become the other way round.

Smith's mawkish religiosity was a world away from the younger reformers' belief that education should impart information appropriate to the individual and his times. Moral training was not to be found in the nature of the academic curriculum so much as in religion, social behaviour, and games. Manliness and citizenship replaced godliness and refinement.[126] This allowed for an exponential expansion in subjects both worthy and necessary to be studied. It also, most crucially, began to break down barriers between the apparently clever and the supposedly stupid. The traditional classical curriculum concentrated on those adept at exams, prizes, and scholarships to the effective exclusion of everybody else for whom school was a socializing rather than an educative experience. The most famous victim of this in late nineteenth-century Harrow was Winston Churchill (1888–92), acknowledged by his teachers to be bright but, no good at classics, diverted into the Army Class as even the Modern Side required Latin. The reformers' argued that a wider curriculum would reach more boys, be more inclusive not exclusive. It was a slow process. Catering for the academically less gifted positively rather than, as before, passively

---

[123] Rendall, *Recollections of John Smith*, 25 and *passim*.
[124] Ibid., 10; Minchin, *Old Harrow Days*, 33; Vachell, *Fellow Travellers*, 28; Graham, *Butler*, 137–9.
[125] Mack, *Public Schools and British Opinion since 1860*, 126–7.
[126] See e.g. Bosworth-Smith's ideal of 'a citizenship of manhood': Grogan, *Bosworth-Smith*, 130.

marked a new path for Harrow, which, although beginning in the 1860s, took a century before it reached its logical end.[127]

The need for a fresh approach cannot be doubted. John Galsworthy (1881–6), in the Upper Sixth for Butler's last year, remembered the reverse side of the Head's disdain for useful learning:

not encouraged to think, imagine, or see anything we learned in relation to life at large ... we were crammed not taught ... debarred from any real interest in philosophy, history, art, literature and music or any advancing notions in social life or politics.[128]

Yet reformers had to tread carefully. Seniority and tradition were against them. Hearing of proposed changes to the curriculum, one quite youthful old boy wrote to Butler from Bermuda, 'I trust they are not going away too much with the classics and trying to become over-practical'; to prevent this he proposed endowing a prize on the 1662 Prayer Book.[129]

In many ways the reformers were themselves deeply imbued with reverence for public schools and the ideal of aristocracy. All were pure classicists by training. Farrar, Bowen, and Colbeck were fellows of Trinity, Cambridge; Bosworth-Smith of Trinity, Oxford. Farrar, the most scathing of all in fulminating against the old ways, was ordained, subsequently proceeding to enjoy a very traditional career as Head Master, canon, and dean. Although a leading figure (with Bowen) in the Bishop Colenso Defence Fund, he reassured in his novels and sermons, despite their overheated obsession with, as Butler tactfully put it, 'two haunting visions, the one of boyish innocence, the other of boyish wickedness'.[130] Bosworth-Smith, regarded by some as 'a red-hot Radical', although a layman and strongly influenced by the Christian socialist F. D. Maurice, campaigned vigorously against the disestablishment of the Church of England.[131] Bowen presented the most striking of contrasts. A pioneer in broadening the curriculum, a champion of the concept of divisions rather than forms to give every boy 'his proper place' in each subject, contemptuous of traditional teaching methods and artificial barriers between master and pupil, he was none the less a savage beater, notoriously given to spying on boys, a public school sentimentalist, and co-creator of Harrow's cloying pseudo-history. An aggressive, not to say bullying, elitist who had little time for those who lacked his own compulsive energy, he kept a mechanical duck on his desk which he would set to wag its head at those boys he considered fools.[132] No less than Butler, Vaughan, or Arnold, Bowen believed that teaching (and learning and therefore life) was a matter of what he chose to call character—i.e. adherence to certain

---

[127] On the coming of Modern Sides in general see Mack, *Public Schools and British Opinion since 1860*, 50–100. Cf. Stray, *Classics Transformed*, 47–100.
[128] Marrot, *Galsworthy*, 42–3.   [129] HM/Bm/J. S. Curling to Butler, 1 June 1869.
[130] Farrar, *Farrar*, 140. Cf. Ibid., 116–17 for Colenso fund.
[131] Grogan, *Bosworth-Smith*, esp. pp. 49, 53, 63–101, 105–41.
[132] Vachell, *Fellow Travellers*, 26–7; Bowen, *Bowen, passim*, esp. 111–14, 195–6, 206–7, 253.

prescribed patterns of respectable upper-class social behaviour—by boys and masters alike. No less than John Smith, Bowen believed education to be essentially moral not didactic, an attitude he summed up before the Bryce Commission on Secondary Education in 1894: 'A bad man teaching history well is a far worse thing than a good man teaching history badly'.[133]

The central contrasts between the reformers and their colleagues was their outside interests and their overt sympathy for and direct encouragement of their pupils. Farrar despised the school's introspection: 'You can't think how society stagnates here. Conversation is unknown. Harrow forms the sole topic of Harrow.'[134] He broke out of this snug carapace, his philology and polemics, in favour of science and the reform of classical teaching adding to his public stature as a novelist. Bowen, a prolific author of articles and pamphlets, became the most sought-after pundit on secondary education in the country, as well as taking a leading role in organizing groups such as the United Ushers, an association–dining club for public school assistant masters. Bosworth-Smith maintained a lively social life with some of the leading intellectuals of the day, becoming a noted historian, biographer, and author of the hugely successful *Mohammed and Mohammedanism*, his total ignorance of Arabic and lack of any personal experience of the Muslim world not seeming to deter him or his readers. There can have been few public school masters who could claim, with 'Bos', to have been 'prayed for in the mosques along the west coast of Africa'.[135] In contrast to Bowen, who tended to be reclusive and entirely wrapped up in his school work, 'Bos' reckoned his outside interests improved his teaching.

These masters got to know their pupils as people. Farrar and Bowen regularly invited individual Harrovians on holidays to the continent. In the winter of 1867–8, Bowen and E. M. Young travelled to Italy with the 15-year-old Walter Leaf whom they taught to smoke cigars. After a similar jaunt, Farrar commented to a friend, 'the Harrow boy who came with us I had always liked, but now I love him tenfold, having been cheered by his ruddy face in perils and pleasures'.[136] In Bowen's case, this intimacy could slip into sentimentality and, by the end of his long career, dependence: the shock of the death of one favourite, Ernest Reade, during the Boer War left him murmuring inconsolably: 'I want my boy.'[137] In general, however, excessive emotion was held in check, although it was said that Farrar 'was inclined to spoil the boys who responded to his appeals and to rate them higher than they deserved'.[138] The nature of these appeals was summed up by Thring of Uppingham. Farrar, he declared was 'not a mere knowledge-box with the lid open, but a true guide and teacher, able and willing to help, inspirit, and lead the way'.[139]

[133] Bowen, *Bowen*, 238.   [134] Farrar, *Farrar*, 128.
[135] Grogan, *Bosworth-Smith*, 141. Cf. ibid., 89, 112, 134.
[136] Leaf, *Autobiography*, 43–4, 64; Farrar, *Farrar*, 131.   [137] Bowen, *Bowen*, 247.
[138] Russell, *Autobiography*, 40. Cf. his remarks in Graham, *Butler*, 136–7.
[139] Farrar, *Farrar*, 84.

Bowen's vision was even clearer, if more intense and psychologically exposed: 'If you talk with them, you may be a comrade without pretending to be a child: when they work with you, they will be your companions, wayward, frivolous, stupid, peevish, intractable perhaps, but companions, fellow-travellers, playmates.'[140]

Aesthetically, the mentor of the reformers was Ruskin. Their chosen vehicles were English literature, history, geography, and science, all part of the syllabus of the Modern Side created in 1869. Boys unable to learn Latin verse were set Milton instead by Farrar, who taught his Remove division Coleridge, urged his pupils to read poetry for themselves, and introduced geography. Bosworth-Smith replaced Latin verses with geography and history, as well as Milton. Both Farrar and Bowen fiercely opposed the adoption of Kennedy's Latin Primer in 1867 as standardizing and prescriptive, although Farrar himself produced a Greek syntax card. Bowen did all he could, through literature and history, to hold the boys' interest. Farrar and Bosworth-Smith gave lessons in botany, an ideal subject for their pedagogic purpose, as boys could be individually involved by being asked to be aware of their surroundings and collect their own specimens. Although 'Bos' was a keen gardener, Farrar's expertise was painfully bought and never great, but he passionately believed in the importance of science, founding a Natural History Society and attracting lecturers such as Tyndall, Ruskin, and Huxley. After all, he had been proposed as an FRS by Charles Darwin (who confessed to have learnt nothing from Samuel Butler at Shrewsbury who used to sneer publicly at his pupil's chemistry experiments).[141]

The introduction of science was more than an academically desirable necessity. It was symbolic of modernity, of change. Rugby had already introduced it. Pressed by Farrar, in the autumn of 1866, Butler agreed to its introduction at Harrow for very characteristic reasons:

we need to spread broad-cast over England among the gentry some knowledge of the elements of Natural Science . . . we want ordinary English gentlemen to have some decent notion of the direction in which the investigations of the great Masters of each Science are tending . . . we want to get rid of the nonsense . . . which regards Natural Science as naturally Godless, or at least 'uncanny'.[142]

The plan was to teach some science to all boys in lower forms for up to two years and then to allow a few specialists to continue. In the Spring of 1867 the first science master was appointed, George Griffith, a friend of Butler's brother-in-law. Not until 1874 was he provided with a state-of-the-art laboratory which was equipped only in 1876 after an appeal though a 'Scientific Apparatus Fund'.[143] Griffith none

---

[140] Bowen, *Bowen*, 247.

[141] Farrar, *Farrar*, 82–5, 88, 96–107, 116–17, 136, 139; Grogan, *Bosworth-Smith*, 113–15, 119–30; Stray, *Classics Transformed*, 192–3; Bowen, *Bowen*, 99–101, 187, 208–10.

[142] Graham, *Butler*, 172. For introduction of science in general, see ibid., 171–4.

[143] Head Master's Book, 1874–92, fo. 53. Cf. HM/Bm/Butler to Griffith, 4 May 1871; Laborde, *Harrow School*, 148. Some windows were specially designed for the easy emission of gases.

the less provided a basic grounding at least in physics (e.g. refraction of light) and botany. By 1880 boys were taking notes from Griffith on optics, magnetism, galvanism, induction, telegraphy, and biology, including the classification of species.[144] However modest, science attempted modernity, unlike the mathematicians who still used Euclid as a textbook in the 1870s and as late as 1900, refused to allow boys to consult logarithm tables which were viewed on a par with classical cribs. A second science master was appointed in 1876, Sydney Lupton, described by Galsworthy as 'a complete noodle', hardly surprising as Butler had sought a 'high-minded and able man' of 'general capacity' willing to bone up on the subject rather than 'a professed chemist' of 'actual attainment'.[145] Thereafter, with the appointment of the six foot ten inch 'Oxford Giant', B. P. Lascelles in 1885, C. E. Ashford (1893), and Archer Vassal (1896), science became an established, if for many peripheral and optional part of the standard curriculum. Although as late as the 1960s it was possible for a Harrovian to pass through the school without taking any science, during the first half of the twentieth century Harrow was in the forefront of national innovations in teaching science in schools. Yet, while supportive, Butler had no scientific knowledge or interest, never once visiting the Science Schools after their opening, and none of his successors for almost a century possessed a science degree.[146]

The advent of science in 1867 was regarded by Butler and Farrar as the precursor to the major reform, that of the Modern Side. Hitherto, apart from the freelance activities of the reformers, non-classical subjects had only been studied for prizes. In the wake of Farrar's *Essays on a Liberal Education* in 1867 and relentless pressure from him and Bowen, Butler finally agreed to establish a Modern Side in 1869. The subjects to be taught were to exclude Greek but comprise maths, modern languages, history, Latin, science, and English taught in a self-contained group of forms mirroring but separate from the classical side under the autonomous management of its own head. As Farrar was applying for Headships elsewhere, Butler appointed Bowen to run it. To avoid the Modern Side becoming a sump for the idle, stupid, or poor classicists, initially entry was only after the first year at school; until 1890 there was no Modern Fourth, the Shell being the lowest; entrants had to be of proven diligence and, from 1874, when new boys were allowed directly, they had to sit a special Modern Side entrance exam.[147] Although regarded as radical by most, and providing a model copied throughout the public school world, Harrow's Modern Side found parallels with the curriculum changes of Ridding at Winchester and Temple at Rugby.[148] For Bowen it did not go far enough. He believed the best system would be an integrated, unified syllabus, with Greek as a late option,

---

[144] See the MSS note books of G. P. Bidder, 1878–81, HA.
[145] Marrot, *Galsworthy*, 663; HM/Bm/Westcott Correspondence no. 21, Butler to Westcott, 23 Aug. 1875.   [146] Graham, *Butler*, 173.
[147] Bowen, *Bowen*, 101–17; Graham, *Butler*, 178–80.
[148] Mack, *Public Schools and British Opinion since 1860*, 92–4.

and subject divisions throughout, a fundamental change in the academic approach and structure of the school that had to wait another century from the opening of the Modern Side.[149]

Until the 1890s, when Welldon's reforms altered its relationship to the curriculum as a whole, the Modern Side moderately prospered. By 1881, with over seventy boys, and four masters the experiment could be judged a success, even if Bowen himself had had to learn German from scratch to undertake the modern languages teaching.[150] The formmasters were the classicists Bowen himself; Colbeck; H. O. D. Davidson, another Trinity man, but with the added kudos of winning the Inter-University Weight Putting three years in a row; and W. G. Guillemard. Higher maths was taught by Bushell and Hayward; natural science by Griffith and Lupton. Bowen believed the boys liked their work 'to a greater degree . . . than under the Classical regime' because they felt they were 'being helped to learn instead of . . . being put through the mill'.[151] Between 1876 and 1880 there was a Modern Side scholarship; thereafter the maths scholarships were open to both Sides. Modern Side boys did well in 'Modern' subject prizes, such as history, English or modern languages, as well as winning mathematics awards at the universities. Bowen, unsurprisingly, became highly proprietorial, refusing to admit the need for a separate status given to the Army Class in 1888 and resigning as Master of the Modern Side when the rules for admission were modified (he thought eased) in 1893. There remained suspicion among the old guard over this interloper and Butler's conservatism killed Bowen's leaving scholarship scheme, yet the Modern Side persisted until the distinctions were abolished in 1917 as part of Lionel Ford's attempts to widen choice in the syllabus for all.[152] By the end of the nineteenth century, if the elite of brilliant literary philologists in the Butler mould were no more, there was a greater diversity of academic achievement, potentially involving a wider section of the school.

Outside the teaching in form, the presence of the Modern Side influenced the academic tone of the school by establishing the status of science, English, history, and geography. One effect of this is evident in the examinations for various prizes in 'modern' subjects not confined to Modern Side candidates. In 1881 the English Essay Prize was a criticism of Tocqueville's *Ancien Régime*. A contemporary Bourchier History prize consisted of a general paper on the leading events in Europe since Charlemagne and a Special Subject paper on the Norman Conquest, broadly defined to cover 1066 to 1135, with Stubbs' *Select Charters* as a set text, the study of which a decade later convinced the young G. M. Trevelyan of his destiny as a historian.[153] Three plays a year were set for the Shakespeare prizes: *King Lear*,

---

[149] Bowen, *Bowen*, 111–14.   [150] Ibid., 101 and the 1881 memorandum, 103–15.
[151] Bowen, *Bowen*, 109.
[152] Ibid., 114–16; or curriculum change in general, Laborde, *Harrow School*, 58–64.
[153] Head Master's Book, 1874–92, fos. 77, 78; Moorman, *Trevelyan*, 23.

Richard II, and *Much Ado About Nothing* in 1884; *As You Like It*, *Coriolanus*, and *Romeo and Juliet* in 1885.[154] Although the palmiest days of the Modern Side possibly had to await the arrival of the historian G. Townsend Warner in 1891, the general leavening of the academic life of the school of which it was both a symptom and a cause is unmistakable, yet more testimony to the influence of the most remarkable Harrow master of his, or possibly any, period, without whom change would not have occured as rapidly or effectively, Edward Bowen.

Twice passed over for the Headship, mistrusted by pious, conservative, and lazy colleagues, austere to the point of asceticism, arrogant, opinionated, given to Gladstonian circumlocution, utterly consumed by working with and for his pupils, in form, house, and on the games field, of national stature, Bowen was the dominant figure at Harrow for thirty years, an eminent Victorian who refused to conform to anything other than his own idiosyncratic 'love of institutions and idealisation of custom which in him was not pedantry but poetry',[155] a faith at the heart of which lay his devotion to educating boys by entering their world and becoming their companion. Although respectful of his seniors, even reading the lesson at Vaughan's funeral, Bowen's concept of manliness and athleticism was Arnoldianism's nemesis, for good and ill.

Reformed Harrow?

However significant the changes to the curriculum, the pattern of life for most boys and many masters varied rather less. The great watershed of the agricultural depression from the 1870s had been barely felt at Harrow. Although one snobbish critic in 1869 criticized the school for its atmosphere of *nouveau riche* dandyism, the decisive transformation into a plutocrats' school came a generation later.[156] Butler's Harrovians continued to proceed to the same professions, or lack of them, as their predecessors.[157] The issue of the Empire, which came to dominate the public school world and the careers of its old boys, had yet to be resolved. Beaconsfieldism had, thanks largely to domestic economic problems it is true, been defeated in the 1880 election. News of Gordon's death at Khartoum reached London just as Gladstone was offering Butler the deanery of Gloucester (the crisis not deterring the indefatigable Head Master from pestering the Prime Minister with one of his most tortuously solipsistic letters about the offer).[158] The defining debate over Home Rule raged a year after Butler left Harrow. As yet, the Empire

---

[154] Head Master's Book, 1874–92, fo. 79. Cf. the classical and modern side diets, HA Materials Relating to Boys, Box 1, H. A. Cohen to A. L. Cohen, 17 July 1885 describing classical side Lower Sixth Trials with HA G. P. Bidder's Essay Book, Oct. 1880–June 1881.

[155] The phrase is G. M. Trevelyan's: Bowen, *Bowen*, 206–7.

[156] Quoted in Mack, *Public Schools and British Opinion since 1860*, 121.

[157] Bamford, *Public Schools*, 210, 212.   [158] Graham, *Butler*, 278–9.

was still as J. S. Mill had dismissed it, little more than a 'vast system of outdoor relief for the upper classes' rather than the emotional core of the public schools' religio-patriotic mission in the 1890s.[159] Even so, both Butler and the governors noticed changing demands and were anxious lest excessive fees determined the character of the institution. One of Butler's less intellectual pupils from the 1860s later praised Welldon for keeping 'our good ship Harrow off the rocks of plutocracy'.[160] He was wrong, but his attitude is significant. Another Butler Harrovian, H. A. Vachell, enshrined this snobbery in his best-selling *The Hill* (1905), in which virtue lay with the sons of public servants, great landed aristocrats, rural gentry, and country parsons. Sin, vice, torpor, and bad manners were the characteristics of the lounging sons of successful trade or the middle classes. Yet, while Butler could with impunity indulge in quietly amused snobbish disdain for the antics of the newly wealthy, his successors had to be more careful.[161]

The consecration of the boarding house as the centre of Harrow life provoked the invention of myriad instant traditions, a host of new shibboleths, and a lexicon of jargon. Harrow, it seems, was the birthplace of the later ubiquitous form of slang called by lexicographers the 'Oxford-*er*', perfecting its climactic form: 'wagger-pagger-bagger' for waste paper basket.[162] In place of classics, public school slang marked boys' entry into an aristocracy to which they may not have born. Socially, emphasis was increasingly on the group not the individual. Within what has been called the 'total society' of school, self-obsessed, hostile, ignorant, and fearful of outsiders or those who declined to conform, were the smaller circles of the houses that controlled behaviour in equal proportion to providing members with security and identity. As school dress became uniform, so these groups adopted distinctive clothing for games. As monitors ceased to be the cleverest boys, so they assumed symbols of office, such as the crest on their hatbands. The tension between the individual and the group, inevitable in schools, was decisively resolved in favour of the latter. Boys were increasingly expected to see themselves not so much in a personal, moral relationship with peers and God but as active participants in a collective enterprise—team, house, form, school—through which and only through which, standards and values were expressed. This extended to academic groups; on one occasion Farrar's Remove A played Bowen's Remove B at football. While pretending care for the individual, Bowen organized his teaching and house to produce what he called 'exalted conventionalism', a code of conduct and set of rules within which the individual could go his own way but only within the prescribed parameters.[163] Conventions

---

[159] F. C. A. Dietz, *A Political and Social History of England* (New York, 1927), p. 551.
[160] Minchin, *Old Harrow Days*, 262.
[161] Ibid., 65–6 for one such anecdote.
[162] Honey, *Tom Brown's Universe*, 235; Howson and Townsend Warner, *Harrow School*, 276–83.
[163] Farrar, *Farrar*, 89; Bowen, *Bowen*, 242. In general see Mack, *Public Schools and British Opinion since 1860*, Pt. II; Gathorne-Hardy, *Public School Phenomenon*, esp. pp. 105–14, 204–10; Honey, *Tom Brown's Universe*.

could present nasty dilemmas. Both H. A. Vachell and Walter Leaf were short-sighted. Because wearing spectacles would have made them objects of derision and worse, they were unable to shine in the one area that would have ensured popularity, games. In desperation, Leaf wore a monocle, which, oddly, was considered acceptable.[164] Conforming to a consensual type became increasingly compulsory, the main mechanism for its imposition being athletic. The increasing dominance, formal and informal, of bloods was an inevitable consequence of this apparatus, which essentially was one of control.

Certain assumptions combined from earlier years to support this structure, notably fagging that, as so much else in public school life, was increasingly idealized as a form of character training, instead of a convenient, exploitative way for older boys to live comfortably and run their houses easily. More generally, Harrow in the 1880s as in the 1850s or 1820s was disciplined by an embracing culture of mundane written punishments punctuated by extreme ritualized but none the less personal violence. Leslie Stephen, among other things an old Etonian, wrote in 1873 of flogging as 'a sacred initiatory rite', the flogged forming a 'sort of strange chivalry'.[165] This was typical of the fraudulence of much Victorian reform. Instead of change, old habits were confirmed through rhetorical transformation into noble, improving traditions. The culture of beating was too ingrained in institutions and masters to be abandoned, despite publicized incidents such as the 'tunding' scandal at Winchester in 1872 and the Charterhouse whipping affair of 1874. Saintly John Smith promised to harry an idle boy: 'I'll set him lines; I'll punish him; I'll send him up, and have him flogged *for I love the lad*.'[166] Butler later regretted his harshness, but at the time showed no qualms. He made no connection with the violence of the flogging block and that in the school in general. He may have deplored the public semi-licensed fights in the milling ground below the school yard, that persisted until the 1870s, to the extent of proposing, with familiar absurdity, to rename the site the Quoits Ground.[167] Not only were his colleagues less concerned, many of them joining the crowds of boys to witness these bloody combats, but Butler's refusal to curb monitorial beating or deny housemasters a more or less free hand ensured that his legacy was as violent as his inheritance.

Beating cannot be dismissed as a peripheral or small part of school life. Although the sadistic and erotic connotations may not have been perceived or understood, the psychological impact on floggers and flogged of *le vice anglais* is unmistakable. Given the exhaustive catalogue of petty crimes inviting such penalty, including leaning out of windows or walking in the middle of the road, the vast majority of boys at some time were caned in the house. Perhaps growing uneasiness is apparent

---

[164] Leaf, *Autobiography*, 40; Vachell, *Fellow Travellers*, ch. 2.
[165] *Cornhill Magazine*, Mar. 1873, p. 284. Cf. Honey, *Tom Brown's Universe*, 196–203.
[166] Mack, *Public Schools and British Opinion since 1860*, 93; Rendall, *Recollections of John Smith*, 14.
[167] Welldon, *Recollections*, 143–5; Russell, *Autobiography*, 76 for 1868 fight; HA Rawcliffe, *Harrow Verses*, 10, 11a, for fights in 1872 and 1875.

in George Townsend Warner's coy account of the ultimate fate of an idle boy: 'A bad card, however, will take him to the Fourth Form Room, and what happens then is not to be described; it is sufficient to say that small pieces of birch twig may sometimes be gathered from the floor.'[168] It is remarkable that this oldest, most common feature of schoolboy life is absent from the Harrow School Songs of Bowen and company (there is a single reference in one of the earliest and another in a song written by a recent old boy)[169] while almost every other aspect of school life is loving or teasingly portrayed.

Yet the stereotype of the sadomasochistic master and the brave or terrified victim, while accurate enough, misses an important truth. Boys liked beating boys. To beat could be as character-forming as being beaten. In a remarkable passage of autobiography, Walter Leaf, Homeric scholar and financier, recalled the first caning he administered as head of The Park in the summer of 1869:

> I thought that a weakling like myself could not inflict any caning at which the victim would not smile . . . in fear and trembling I set to work on a big bully. I could hardly believe my ears when after only three or four strokes I found that he was actually whimpering and begging me to stop. That moment I regard as perhaps the greatest crisis of my life. I had found myself and my self-reliance. I finished his full ten strokes, of course . . .[170]

There are strong parallels here with Symonds' account of caning brutes in Rendalls fifteen years before. Like Symonds, Leaf went on to experience emotional and sexual problems, in his case a prolonged, uneasy celibacy until marriage in early middle age.

If in discipline Harrow preserved its traditions, Butler's school expanded its horizons as befitted a great national institution of what was agreed to be the greatest nation on earth. This not only meant that pupils were gathered from foreign lands and different faiths. Harrow became part of the fashionable world. This found expression most glaringly at the Lord's cricket match against Eton. More domestically, the new music master, John Farmer, could intice Clara Schumann and the violinist Joachim to give recitals. Butler invited the great and the good to Speeches, from Lord John Russell to Robert Browning (who did not come). There were visits from Gladstone, the queen of Holland, and the emperor of Brazil, as well as the prince and princess of Wales. Informal intellectual life flourished with German readings, Shakespeare recitations, lectures by Ruskin, Huxley, Tyndall, and, intriguingly, Professor Conington of Oxford. At breakfasts with the Head Master boys were introduced to some of the grandest literary or political figures of the time.[171] Butler established a Masters' Essay Club, which began in 1872 with Henry Nettleship's paper on 'The Religion of the Romans in the time of Cicero',

---

[168] Howson and Townsend Warner, *Harrow School*, 277; Gathorne-Hardy, *Public School Phenomenon*, 115–16. [169] *Lyon of Preston*, 1869, v. 4, l. 3; *Jerry*, 1885, v. 1, l. 7 by Spencer Gore.
[170] Leaf, *Autobiography*, 54.
[171] Graham, *Butler*, 171 and *passim*; Grogan, *Bosworth-Smith*, 73.

just a year before he left for the Chair of Latin Literature in Oxford. In this setting Bosworth-Smith first aired his views on Islam.[172] Neither scene would have been imaginable twenty years earlier.

However, Butler's Headship was pivotal in the school's history in two other, contrasting but intimately related dimensions which together formed twin pillars of the cult of the school: games and Songs.

Athleticism

Vaughan's memorial was a library; Butler's was the purchase of the football fields.[173] Harrow had been the first great school to countenance compulsory games. Their social and cultural prominence was matched by the time lavished upon them. Institutionally, games provided an ideal solution to the problem of what to do with boys between lessons and sleep; they occupied time, energy, and emotion, a form of acculturation to the hierarchies of school and house. With the attendant bullying and brutality came a perceived benefit in terms of health, fitness being regarded by the authorities, somewhat bizarrely, as an antidote to vice. Boys were less precious in their enthusiasm and more single-minded in their hero-worship of sporting Gods. While academic scholars pursued activities beyond the reach or understanding of the mass, sport was the common experience. Sporting success, therefore, guaranteed populist devotion and social power. More surprising to anyone of Arnold's or Vaughan's generation was that adults, schoolmasters, began to pay as much lip-service to this devotion as their pupils. One of Butler's pupils from the 1860s observed without undue hyperbole that masters worshipped at the shrine of the cricket eleven. Butler could publicly deplore 'Athlete-worship', yet he once grovelled to a sulky Captain of the Eleven to beg him to play at Lord's.[174] The 'Moloch of Athletics' claimed the grandest victims.[175]

Between 1840 and 1870, the ideal of Arnoldian manliness, the virtue of one who fought for truth, right, and religion, was being transformed into the complementary cults of muscular Christianity and games. As Norman Vance has described it, 'manliness was moving from the chapel to the changing room'.[176] Key prophets were Thomas Hughes, whose *Tom Brown's Schooldays* recast Arnold's Rugby from the perspective of a non-scholarly hearty; Charles Kingsley, the best-selling writer

---

[172] HM/Bm/Westcott Correspondence, no. 18, Butler to Westcott, 21 Apr. 1872; Graham, *Butler*, 217–18.   [173] Laborde, *Harrow School*, 198.
[174] Minchin, *Old Harrow Days*, 146; Graham, *Butler*, 315.
[175] The phrase is G. W. E. Russell's: *Autobiography*, 75; on athleticism in general see Newsome, *Godliness and Good Learning*, 195–239; Honey, *Tom Brown's Universe*, esp. pp. 104–17; N. Vance, 'The Ideal of Manliness', in B. Simon and I. Bradley (eds.), *The Victorian Public School* (London, 1975), pp. 119–29; Gathorne-Hardy, *Public School Phenomenon*, 144–80.
[176] Vance, 'Ideal of Manliness', 123.

and publicist for whom 'Christian practice seems not seldom to mean little more than being clean and physically well-developed' and Edward Bowen.[177] Writing in 1884, Bowen pronounced the ultimate benediction on this new cult, one which would have shocked many of his predecessors and baffled more: 'There lives more soul in honest play, believe me, than in half the hymn-books'.[178]

The physical and the religious were inseparable. Hard exercise was a craze amongst the educated classes. The late nineteenth century was the golden, heroic age of Alpine walking and climbing: D. R. Hadow (1860) was killed returning from the first successful ascent of the Matterhorn in 1865. Success in sport could confer instant fame on an institution: Cotton at Marlborough and Thring at Uppingham both exploited this. The universities were, if anything, more obsessed; the reputation of the new Keble College, Oxford was secured by its athletic successes under Warden Talbot. To justify this pandering to the non-intellectual, this surrender, some argued, to the lowest common denominator, physical activity had to be elevated into a moral virtue. The apparently damaging and divisive aspects of aggressive competition and concentration on success required refashioning into qualities that were valuable and of intrinsic moral worth. 'The best boys', insisted Bowen, 'are, on the whole, the players of games'. This led easily to a sort of physical fascism, verging on the pantheistic in its praise of games: 'when you have a lot of human beings, in highest social union and perfect organic action... I think you are not far from getting a glimpse of one side of the highest good.'[179]

Their creed was practical, often mundanely so, as in their obsession with physical cleanliness. It embraced, as Arnold's did not, all manner of boys, the stupid as well as the bright. It was a demotic faith, its adherents often blinded to the realities of their pursuits. Most boys were less than convinced but went along with the moral rhetoric because it suited them. They knew that favouritism as much as skill determined selection for Lord's, but if their enjoyment was afforded quasi-religious status, they did not complain.[180] Their conventional adoration of bloods was now consecrated by their masters: a fateful alliance.

Bowen did not believe that masters should run games. He did believe they should play them: he was still playing Harrow football with his boys a few weeks before his death in 1901 aged 65. He despised gym—'the mere Greek iambics of physical training'—and other solitary or individual sports.[181] Games were far more important than exercise. Said the former fellow of Trinity College, Cambridge, prominent educationalist and pioneer of modern studies: 'in our whole system there is nothing which, in my opinion, approaches [games] in value.' Games bred dignity, courtesy, cooperation, 'a permanent corrective' to 'laziness, foppery,

---

[177] Newsome, *Godliness and Good Learning*, 199. Cf. Mack, *Public Schools and British Opinion since 1860*, 103–208.
[178] In a paper delivered to the United Ushers in 1884, later published in the *Journal of Education*: Bowen, *Bowen*, 224. [179] Ibid.
[180] Minchin, *Old Harrow Days*, 174–5. [181] Bowen, *Bowen*, 225.

man-of-the-worldness'. The root of Bowen's philosophy was a startling reversal of what had been common before him: 'I have often been told that the mind is superior to the body; I do not think this has ever been proved.' To support this he argued that people were more influenced by bodies than minds. Whereas he admitted to having dull-witted friends, he denied he had any ugly ones.[182] In Bowen, who retained an undogmatic belief in Christian principles if not God, such priorities only hinted at what appears throughout his life to have been a latent homoeroticism. For Hellenists such as Symonds or W. J. Cory, beautiful bodies, preferably with beautiful minds, translated athleticism into aestheticism.

Although Bowen was an extremist and a zealot, his friend Bosworth-Smith still supporting 'intellectual energy' as the paramount school requirement, his general principles accorded with contemporary values.[183] The great public issues of the late nineteenth century were not of the mind but of power. Bowen and his followers made one crucial error. They corrupted their pupils by encouraging, almost insisting on, the analogy of adult with school life. As David Newsome has concluded: 'the worst feature of the earlier [i.e. Arnoldian] ideal was the tendency to make boys into men too soon; the worst feature of the other . . . was that . . . it fell into the opposite error of failing to make boys into men at all.'[184] It did no service to pupils to pretend that adult choices were no more taxing than setting a field in cricket or following up in football. Few more fatuous and potentially damaging analogies have been drawn than Farrar's description of 'the great cricket-field of life'.[185] Boarding schools inevitably had a tendency to retard certain social development: the cult of games accentuated this.

It was not Bowen's fault that his cults of physical manliness and muscular Christianity were recruited by less intelligent schoolmasters to serve the cause of philistine anti-intellectual conformity, and by society at large to foster the ideals of sentimental patriotism and militarism that equated the battlefield with the gamesfield and sent officers and men to their deaths on the Somme kicking footballs. Yet his attitudes were directly responsible for a loud, proud pandering to athletic achievement which lay at the heart of the crushing conformism that was the sign of athleticism's triumph. This was a sad paradox for one so wedded to the individual.

Athleticism spawned another distortion: the cult of youth. If fitness was next to godliness, not only were the weak or infirm ipso facto condemned, so was the decrepitude of age. A central feature of old boy devotion was nostalgia for the evanescence of youth. Harrow Songs drip with it. The world of *The Boy's Own Paper*, founded in 1879 as a by-product of what could be called the Tom Brown Schooldays enthusiasm, was immensely influential—it was Baldwin's favourite

---

[182] All from the 1884 paper on games, ibid., 222–5.
[183] Grogan, *Bosworth-Smith*, 127.   [184] Newsome, *Godliness and Good Learning*, 238.
[185] F. W. Farrar, *In the Days of Youth* (London, 1889), p. 373.

reading—and intensely juvenile.[186] The world of youth was depicted as possessed of its own fulfilment. Adult life and, almost by definition, the burden of rule, wealth, and power, somehow detracted from the noblest ideals. The world of youth was uncomplicated by responsibility, compromise, or women, the main crises, if novelists were believed, being bullies, cads, and manly romantic attachments to other boys. The glorification of youth in the setting of the public school was a potent force.

In Vachell's *The Hill*, subtitled 'A Romance of Friendship', Charles Desmond, the Prime Minister, watches his son, Harry Desmond, play at Lord's. He is taking time away from a major international crisis, but, as two Eton boys put together a large stand, 'the Minister is frowning; things may look black in South Africa, but they're looking blacker in St John's Wood.' Around him, Old Harrovians meet, their divergent adult achievements forgotten: 'they stroll off together, mighty prelate and humble country parson, once again happy Harrow boys.' Near the end of the match, Harry, nicknamed 'Caesar' Desmond takes a spectacular, crucial catch 'in his lean brown hands':

How does Desmond feel? It is futile to ask him, because he could not tell you if he tried. But we can answer the question. If the country that he wishes to serve crowns him with all the honours bestowed upon a favoured son, never, *never* will Caesar Desmond know again a moment of such exquisite, unadulterated joy as this.[187]

A few months later, young Desmond is killed in action in South Africa. In a memorial sermon in Chapel, the Head Master annunciates the terrible concluding logic to the cult of youth:

To die young, clean, ardent; to die swiftly, in perfect health; to die saving others from death, or worse—disgrace—to die scaling heights; to die and to carry with you into the fuller ampler life beyond, untainted hopes and aspirations unembittered memories, all the freshness and gladness of May—is not that cause for joy rather than sorrow? . . . I would sooner see any of you struck down in the flower of his youth than living on to lose, long before death comes, all that makes life worth living. Better death, a thousand times, than gradual decay of mind and spirit; better death than faithlessness, indifference, and uncleanness.[188]

The Hill went into nine editions in its first year of publication, 1905, and twenty-one by 1913. In 1905 one hundred and forty boys entered Harrow: thirty one of them (22 per cent) were killed between 1914 and 1918 in the First World War, rather less than the average cull of Harrovians of those years.[189] One of them was Richard Vachell, the author's son.

---

[186] Mack, *Public Schools and British Opinion since 1860*, 148.
[187] H. A. Vachell, *The Hill* (9th edn., London, 1906), pp. 257, 261, 269, 270.
[188] Ibid., 313–14.
[189] *Harrow Register, 1885–1949*, 255–66 (the average of all OHs in the war was 27%); Gathorne-Hardy, *Public School Phenomenon*, 211.

Plenitude

Harrow was less overwhelmed by games mania than some other schools. Academic elitism remained important. The string of university scholarships continued. High calibre academic masters continued to be appointed. Although a few, such as that of the Old Harrovian Cambridge cricket Blues M. C. Kemp in 1888 or E. M. Butler in 1891, were men whose lives were dominated by sport, Harrow offered sufficient material prospects to attract men with Blues and Firsts, such as another Old Harrovian, C. G. Pope, in 1899. However, athletic obsession among masters was inescapable as the universities were saturated with it. The effect of games on the intellectual tone of the school was apparent even to apologists. Torn between pandering to current fashion and maintaining that academic standards were as high as ever, E. W. Howson, Butler's son-in-law, nervously admitted in 1898 that 'the finer flowers of scholarship have faded before the boisterous breath of athleticism'.[190]

Butler and his successor were keenly aware of the dangers but were helpless to divert them. They were forced, by circumstance, prudence, and predilection, to acquiesce. Welldon seemed unequivocal: 'It is the clear duty of every master in a Public School to set his face against the worship of athletic games.' Yet, a great footballer himself, he also believed the corrosive propaganda that games provided 'lessons in some of the qualities which have given the British race its supremacy in administrative work among strange races in far-off regions'.[191] Butler enjoyed watching and talking cricket. He admired Bowen's influence in the school: 'More probably than any other master who has ever lived at Harrow, he gave his heart to their games as well as their work,' in Bowen's 'deliberate judgement' of cricket and football being 'second to nothing in fostering a healthy, manly, unselfish, corporate life'. Butler argued, almost certainly correctly, that the effect on boys of Bowen's wide intellectual contributions to the school, in form and through his lectures and Shakespeare readings were enhanced by his being 'their tried and tested companion on the cricket ground and the football field'.[192] Publicly Butler disapproved of boys feeling 'a kind of idolatry' for Lord's which, in the 1870s, he thought had 'assumed too ambitious proportions'.[193] Yet he had once begged a boy to play and in 1885, on the morning of the second day, wrote to his son, the Harrow captain, suggesting tactics.[194] He and the governors recognized the importance of Lord's, spending much time and effort trying to find the ideal dates for the annual contest in 1877.[195] The moral dimension of cricket was also not lost on Butler: 'a Cricket Ground is no mean school of character,' teaching 'valuable lessons in manliness and self-government'.[196]

The growing prominence of games under Butler is unmistakable. The Philathletic ground was bought for the school; so too, after Butler's departure, were the

[190] Howson and Townsend Warner, *Harrow School*, 264.   [191] Welldon, *Recollections*, 96–8.
[192] Bowen, *Bowen*, 187.   [193] Graham, *Butler*, 236–7.
[194] Vachell, *Fellow Travellers*, 22.
[195] GBM, 13 July, 6 Aug., 13 Dec. 1877; Graham, *Butler*, 235–8.
[196] Graham, *Butler*, 263.

football fields, the largest extensions of school property since the Enclosure of 1803. Apart from a gym, new racquets courts were built and the football fields drained. This was not a sudden process: Robert Grimston and Frederick Ponsonby had been supervising and encouraging cricket since the 1840s. It was a sure one. In 1884 Percy Thornton could write with some justice that 'the life of Harrow was mirrored forth in her cricket'. Football only occupied a lesser status because it could not be played against any other school, although in the 1850s Harrow Football was played on Parker's Piece in Cambridge by Old Harrovians and other undergraduates.[197]

The advantages games brought were enhanced discipline within and fame without. As a much later Head Master of Harrow remarked, in many ways it was easier to control boys on the playing fields than in the classroom. Brawn is far easier to appease and satisfy than brain. Games were the perfect reflection as well as occupation for the masculine world of the boarding school, even if it encouraged as much as it exhausted mutual male admiration. It was by chance only that there were no Cory or Browning incidents at Harrow as at Eton. In the brutalized world of the boys' house, extroverts thrived, sharing their qualities of strength, bravado, openness, and self-confidence with the successful gamesplayer. The social and emotional bonds of the team reinforced the tyranny of the group over the individual and subsumed the increasingly claustrophobic cult of romantic friendship. Masters, too, could perpetuate their schooldays for decades by playing alongside their pupils, such contact mitigating the licentiousness of pupil culture. If masters had themselves been sporting gods in their youth, so much the better.

Butler's objections to games amounted only to his fear lest it supplanted religion. He did little to ensure it did not. When G. C. Cottrell was killed in June 1871, hit on the head by a cricket ball when umpiring the Sixth Form game, he was buried with the school cap he was to have worn at Lord's.[198] For J. G. C. Minchin, in the Head Master's from 1864 to 1868, 'ours was an aristocracy of the finest cricketers and the "footer" players', such as the legendary Walker brothers. Warming to his theme Minchin explained the aesthetic of the passion:

No thinking man will blame us for idolising the athlete. The cricketer in his flannels was our hero, not the student immersed in his books. Can there be any question as to which is the more picturesque figures? Was there ever a race more intellectual than the ancient Greeks, and did not they worship the human form divine.[199]

J. A. Symonds and other Hellenists would have agreed with him, no doubt to his discomfort. Such sentiments turned Butler's educational conservatism on itself. Not fully appreciating how his own enthusiasms for games had been transformed

---

[197] Thornton, *Harrow School*, 372; Graham, *Butler*, p. xxxviii.
[198] This detail remembered by Welldon: *Recollections*, 97–8.
[199] Minchin, *Old Harrow Days*, 150; like Thornton, Howson, and Townsend Warner, Minchin devotes a separate chapter to cricket. Cf. an identical attitude reflected by A. Lunn (1902–7) in *The Harrovians* (London, 1913), p. 44.

Plenitude

into a new exclusive and intolerant devotion, he was helpless to prevent its growth. This failure, one of Butler's two most potent legacies, rang down the following hundred years, when athleticism more completely than any other single quality defined the nature of school life.

Songs

The other surviving Butler legacy were the school songs. These were not designed for ephemeral entertainment alone. Butler was quite clear on this: 'the songs proved from the first, and never lost their spell, of quite extraordinary value in promoting good fellowship among the boys and in forging links of love and loyalty between the passing generations of Harrow men.'[200] Edward Graham, a Harrovian of the 1870s and master for thirty-seven years from 1882, recorded their value 'as interpreters of school-life and as a bond of brotherhood'. Harrow songs had both a function and a message. They seduced old boys: 'when we hear them sung by Harrow boys we are young again'; 'the old school songs have kept alive my love for the school.'[201] They also carried a didactic purpose not far removed from that of the cults of games and youth. For the diminutive Leo Amery (1887–92), fellow of All Souls, Cabinet Minister, and ardent imperialist, the songs were 'an all round education in themselves, the embodiment of a manly conception of personal life, of public duty and public policy', i.e. conservative, patriotic, and hierarchic.[202] Forty-five years after he left Vachell, in Desmond vein, acknowledged that the songs were not neutral amusements:

> Harrow Songs, verbally and musically, made for something greater than entertainment. They are instinct with public school spirit, a clarion call to strenuous endeavour, an injunction to work and play with faith and courage, to fight against odds, to follow up wherever the Light may lead, and to sacrifice self, if need be, to the common end. No finer sermons have ever been preached, and none that lingers longer in the memory.[203]

Bowen would have been delighted in his old pupil, although what Vachell made of Welldon's opinion that the songs were truer to Harrow than his books is not recorded.[204] The Songs preached and preached extraordinarily successfully because seeming not to. Songs learnt in youth stay in the mind for life. Almost subliminally, the music and words mould the singer's emotions and shape his perceptions. This was no accident, but part of a deliberate policy to create a lasting, fixed identity of school and schooldays. Winston Churchill felt their power: 'they shine through the

---

[200] Bowen, *Bowen*, 189.
[201] Graham, *Butler*, 177; Minchin, *Old Harrow Days*, 74; R. Meinertzhagen, *Diary of a Black Sheep* (London, 1964), p. 183 (he had been at Harrow in the 1890s).
[202] Honey, *Tom Brown's Universe*, 139.   [203] Vachell, *Fellow Travellers*, 30.
[204] Welldon, *Recollections*, 131. Cf. ibid., 126–30.

memories of men . . . They cheer and enlighten us. They breed a bond of unity between those who have lived here and I think they are, on the whole, the most precious of all Harrovians.'[205]

Of their effectiveness and wide impact, there can be no doubt. They have been sung regularly within Harrow, at house-singings and School concerts, every term since the 1860s, now forming the most distinctive of the school's communal rituals reaffirming corporate identity. They have been sung in praise of baseball; by Antarctic explorers; by schools across the Empire (in one instance to the disgust of the Old Etonian George Orwell); even by South London GPDST girls schools after the First World War. (John Farmer had been musical adviser and inspector to the GPDST for twenty-five years.)[206] In the early 1920s an Old Harrovian Home Secretary quelled a prison riot by telling the governor to order the band to play *Forty Years On*: the rioting prisoners immediately stood to attention before returning quietly to their cells. At least, that is what the Old Harrovian Prime Minster was told.[207] In his Silver Jubilee address to both Houses of Parliament in May 1935, King George V quoted two lines from *When Raleigh Rose*. His speech writer for that occasion, the historian G. M. Trevelyan, regularly sang Harrow Songs at home with his family.[208] Harrow Songs have been and are still regularly played at Harrovians' weddings and, especially, funerals. The Songs represent the grip of the old school at its tightest.

Yet they belong almost exclusively to one narrow period of the school's history, from 1864 to 1897 when upwards of fifty were composed.[209] There are fewer than ten twentieth-century Harrow Songs. Their vision is restricted and specific, the product of a particular set of circumstances. Harrow in the 1860s and 1870s was not alone in articulating in song and verse new post-Arnoldian values as instruments to foster nostalgia.[210] The Eton Boating Song dates from 1863, its hold so tenacious that Lord Rosebery, at Eton at the time of its composition, had it played to him on his deathbed in 1929. Appropriately, Cory, the high priest of muscular Hellenism, wrote the verses. Across the public school world, poems and songs quarried history, sites, and habits to evoke innocence, romantic attachment, and reaction against change. In this enterprise, none compared to Harrow.

The original inspiration for these usually smug, often triumphalist commentaries on public school values and life came from an unusual source. John Farmer

---

[205] *The Harrovian* (1955–6), 39. In general see Howson and Townsend Warner, *Harrow School*, 205–16.

[206] See introduction to 1993 edn. of *Harrow School Songs*, p. vii. For Farmer see his *DNB* entry.

[207] *The Times*, Diary, 2 May 1986 refers to this incident/anecdote.

[208] Moorman, *Trevelyan*, 223–4.

[209] See the fuller pre-1885 range in J. Farmer (ed.), *Harrow Songs and Glees* (London, 1885). All songs quoted hereafter can be studied in 1993 edn. *Harrow School Songs* and cf. E. D. Laborde's MS 'Notes to Songs' in HA, referred to in GBM 7 Nov. 1959.

[210] Mack, *Public Schools and British Opinion since 1860*, 143–6; Newsome, *Godliness and Good Learning*, 225; Honey, *Tom Brown's Universe*, 138–41.

was the son of a Nottingham lace manufacturer. Most of his musical training and experience had been in Germany and Switzerland, where he had been close to Wagner, to whom he became a sort of amanuensis, assisting him in a staging of *Tannhäuser* at Coburg. A self-made man of enormous confidence, energy, directness, uncompromising enthusiasm, and sarcastic wit, he never lost his Midlands accent which, because his only other dialect was the broad Swiss of his Zurich-born wife, was regarded by some boys as a form of broken English. In 1862, when playing daily at the International Festival in London as a salesman to advertise a make of piano, he was noticed by some Harrovians who engaged him to run the Musical Society, then five years old. Coming to live at Sudbury, Farmer, despite sticking out as a social and personal oddity among 'the eminently prim, donnish, scholastic staff', was encouraged by the civilized Westcott to organize singing parties, first at Grove Hill then, after January 1864, Moretons. These proved so popular that the habit soon spread to other houses. One of the earliest supporters was Harris of the Park: the last to admit Farmer and his mixture of German *Lieder* and familiar British patriotic songs were Middlemist in Church Hill and Steel in The Grove, where Farmer was once greeted with a hail of boots. By 1864 all houses held regular singing parties, sometimes as often as once a week, and in March that year a chorus of thirty-six boys drawn from the Head Master's and Moretons performed at a concert in front of the whole school. Butler correctly remarked: 'this represents a great revolution in Harrow ideas.'[211]

Initially, Farmer held no official post at Harrow, the Musical Society, like the cricket club being technically and financially independent. In 1864 Butler, seeking a new Chapel organist, offered the post, combined with a mathematical mastership, to a Cambridge friend, the Revd Charles Gray, who refused. Already, at a casual meeting on Sudbury Hill, Farmer had harangued Butler on the virtues of music as a force to civilize, inspire, and unite boys in a school. Butler, who was wholly unmusical but saw he needed an organist quickly, now offered Farmer the job, probably impressed more by his social rather than educational arguments. It proved to be one of his most significant appointments.

Although a vigorous and sympathetic teacher of musical boys and the designer of a serious music syllabus, Farmer believed that music should be taught to and experienced by everybody. This almost inevitably implied singing as the main vehicle, an educational tradition that held sway throughout the British educational system for another century. Although an early devotee of Bach and a champion of Brahms as well as Wagner, Farmer sought the most effective common denominator in his general school work. This meant mass unison singing. In Chapel he abolished the choir; all hymns and psalms were sung in unison. 'Mass production'

---

[211] Graham, *Butler*, 174–8; Howson and Townsend Warner, *Harrow School*, 203–10; Farmer's *DNB* entry; Leaf, *Autobiography*, 50, 55–6; Russell, *Autobiography*, 73–4; Minchin, *Old Harrow Days*, 68–71.

was how one early initiate described Farmer's methods.[212] In house singing every boy had to participate even if he could only speak or shout along to the music. In choosing who sang in the School XII, a sort of elite corps used for special solos or choruses, Farmer would opt for the glamorous hearty over the excellent singer because he wanted music to be accepted by an essentially philistine body of boys and masters.[213] By 1874 it was accepted that his method required the involvement of hundreds of boys performing at concerts, one of the causes of the row over Burges' new Speech Room. Farmer's skill was to render music, seen by many as the preserve of the interested or gifted elite, as an inclusive experience, as much a team or corporate activity as games.[214] It was in this spirit that, taking his model from German schools and universities, he introduced to the repertoire songs specially composed for Harrow.

The earliest compositions sat awkwardly between the unreformed classical curriculum and Farmer's new populism. The very first of Farmer's school songs was Westcott's *Io Triumphe* of 1864, in Latin, cheerfully praising the school. Three more Latin songs from Westcott in 1864–5 to existing German tunes and E. H. Bradby's *Herga* of 1865, with Farmer's music, set the tone of what was to follow with their local piety and adoration. Yet these refined verses from classical scholars were too precious for Farmer's demotic purpose. This was only fully realized by his collaboration with Bowen which began in 1867 with *Willow the King*, a whimsical song about cricket, dedicated to Ponsonby and Grimston. From that moment, the vision contained in Harrow Songs was shaped in over thirty songs by Bowen's own preoccupations and philosophy: the centrality of games, the rewards of effort, the experience of the schoolboy, the embrace of Harrow present and past, the cult of youth.[215] Games dominate, from *Willow the King* to *If Time is Up*, written in 1889 but performed in 1895, with its almost resigned call to accept whatever fate has in store: 'Heigh ho, follow the game, and shew the way to more.' His verse was playful in a rather arch manner, the underlying didacticism and sentimentality never completely strangling his humour. Bowen's skill was that his words appealed to boys because they were deliberately boyish. He also understood the power of words and music. In one of his and Farmer's finest compositions, *Songs*, written as a tribute to their collaboration on Farmer's departure for Balliol in 1885, Bowen recognizes the potency of their creations:

> Down in the chamber
> Hearts hold deep
> Cradled in amber—
> So songs sleep!
> ...
>
> When droops the boldest

---

[212] Leaf, *Autobiography*, 56.
[213] Minchin, *Old Harrow Days*, 69–70.
[214] See above, pp. 319–20.
[215] Bowen, *Bowen*, 117–20, 157–62, 181–3, 185–6, 219–21, 226–8.

> When hope flies free
> When hearts are coldest,
> Dead songs rise;
> Young voices sound still,
> Bright thoughts thrive,
> Friends press around still—
> So songs live!

Bowen's praise for manliness was both personal and deliberate. His Harrow was one full of ordinary, possibly not very academic, probably rather lazy boys (e.g. *St Joles* 1885) who liked games, disliked hard work, and wanted to enjoy themselves, each boy a 'child of hope, and courage and endeavour' (*Good Night* 1880). His songs had a message for them:

> Is the music random?
> Honour keep it true;
> Fellowship and clandom
> Start the notes anew.

The songs were designed to create a uniform image of the school that existed only in the imagination and thus could be permanent, heedless of objective reality. There were two reasons why his first song (of many) about Harrow Football, *Forty Years On* (1872), became the school anthem. Farmer's music is for once portentous, neither playful nor lyrical, redolent of German hymns, stately, rousing. He apparently wrote the music within minutes of being presented with the text, the author himself suggesting the tune for the loudly sporty chorus ('Follow up! Follow up! Follow up! Till the field ring again and again with the tramp of the twenty-two men. Follow up! Follow up!').[216] Bowen's words, written while on holiday in Switzerland, capture more explicitly than in any other song the twin bonds of shared experience and nostalgia in order to unite Harrovians past and present. As memory itself, the song looks forward and back simultaneously on school and youth in ways mystical, magical, and, self-referentially, musical.

> Forty years on, when afar and asunder
> Parted are those who are singing today
> When you look back, and forgetfully wonder
> What you were like in your work and your play.
> Then, it may be, there will often come o'er you
> Glimpses of notes like the catch of a song—
> Visions of boyhood shall float then before you,
> Echoes of dreamland shall bear them along.

Apart from the solitary word 'work' in the fourth line, in the full four verses there is not a single reference to academic pursuits. The 'great days in the distance

---

[216] Bowen, *Bowen*, 157–8.

enchanted' (v. 3) were 'days of fresh air, in the rain and the sun'. Age means physical decline: 'What will it help you that once you were young?' (v. 4). Yet all life can be—should be—played as a game, so the song ends with a prayer to the deity of athleticism:

> God give us bases[*i.e. goals in Harrow football*] to guard or beleaguer,
> Games to play out, whether earnest or fun;
> Fights for the fearless, and goals for the eager,
> Twenty, and thirty, and forty years on!

This appeal to God was deemed controversial, the approval, presumably aesthetic rather than theological, of Matthew Arnold being sought before its final inclusion.

When tired of sporting triumphalism, Bowen turned to patriotism and history, insidiously but effectively combining the domestic with the national. These themes were far from accidental. The year after the Public School Act came the jovial nonsense *Lyon of Preston, yeoman John* in 1869. Sung at the Tercentenary, its point was both institutional and political, the boys, as one observer commented, 'seemed almost personally familiar with the founder thanks to the soul-inspiring songs of Mr Bowen.'[217] As then almost nothing was known of Lyon, he could easily be hijacked for the purposes of identity and continuity, his approval for the public school (rather than the locals) being both insinuated and assumed. *Queen Elizabeth sat one day* of 1875 is even more bizarre. Sung at the completion of the Lower School in 1876, it embodies an entrenched philistinism that probably even Bowen did not espouse:

> SPENSER carries you well along
> And the SWAN OF AVON is rich in song—
> Still, we have sometimes found them long.

This is the song that began the unfortunate association of Harrow with 'Merrie England' and 'good Queen Bess' (namely: references to 'the bold sea rover'). In it Lyon asks for a charter for a school at which the curriculum is to be sternly traditional ('verse and prose'), the climax is an extraordinary evocation of the dominance of sport combined with a scarcely veiled attack on any critics of the school (i.e. most of those who heard it at the Lower School opening in 1876):

> And this is my charter, firm and free,
> This is my royal, great decree—
> *Hits to the rail shall count for three,*
> *And six when fairly over:*
> And if any one comes to make a fuss,
> Send the radical off to us
> And I will tell him I choose it thus...

[217] Thornton, *Harrow School*, 306.

Singers and audiences may not have taken or have been intended to take the words too seriously; Gladstone apparently enjoyed singing it.[218] However, the association with Elizabethan England was serious, emphasized by both Drs Wordsworth and Vaughan in their Tercentenary speeches as well as by Butler's Tercentenary sermon. The link provided Harrow with a share of a glorious past, one to stand comparison with the more genuinely illustrious histories of their rivals (alluded to with customary tact by Wordsworth in his 1871 speech), a history of which to be proud, even if of recent manufacture. Evoking Drake, Raleigh, Shakespeare, and Philip Sidney, Bowen's words and Framer's lilting tune made the point directly in *When Raleigh Rose* of 1878:

> For we began when he began,
> Our times are one;
> His glory thus shall circle us
> Till time be done.

This fame by association was partly made possible by ignorance of the school's history, an ignorance that had been exploited to the school's advantage in 1810 and again during the reform disputes. Bowen's early songs fill this gap. Ironically, between 1883 and 1885 Edward Scott of the British Museum and Percy Thornton, an Old Harrovian author, had investigated the muniment chest for the first time. This produced the first catalogue of school and estate documents and the first even remotely scholarly history, Thornton's *Harrow School and its Surroundings* (1885).[219] Undaunted, the myth-makers merely incorporated the new information. *Grandpapa's Grandpapa* (1884) focused on the different manners of the early eighteenth century; *St Joles* (1885) acknowledged that the schoolhouse had been built under James I not Elizabeth. In one of the two most musically lyrical of the Farmer–Bowen songs, *Byron Lay* (1884; the other being *Good Night* of 1880 about boyish hard work and fair play), the coincidence of Byron and Peel in Joseph Drury's Harrow is used to ram home some central articles of faith for the school cult. Both idling poet and scholarly statesman have their place; so do sportsmen, Bowen slipping in the lines ' "Even a goose's brain has uses" | Cricketing comrades argued thus'. Byron was the most celebrated Old Harrovian of and in the nineteenth century; Peel the most revered politician, although Palmerston was the most loved. However, Bowen's point was not antiquarian but propagandist and, in the school context, populist, expressed in one of the most quoted yet syntactically opaque lines, which is supposed to mean the opposite of what at first sight it appears to suggest: 'None so narrow the range of Harrow'. The resonance of Bowen's anti-intellectualism rings down the decades.

The almost liturgical use of songs in the worship of school and youth was made possible by Bowen's mercurial versifying skill and the quality of Farmer's music, his tunes being uncannily appropriate to the mood of the verse and as memorable as

---

[218] Bowen, *Bowen*, 190.   [219] GBM, 12 June, 20 Nov. 1883, 5 Feb., 21 May 1884.

anything by Sullivan. Before Farmer left, other masters, J. Robertson, later Head Master of Haileybury, E. W. Howson, and an old boy, Spencer Gore, supplied him with texts. Howson in particular developed a style of his own that he continued to exploit with Farmer's successor, Eaton Faning. Howson's eight songs were more overtly sentimental, less whimsical, less mystical, his focus sharp on specific aspects of schoolboy life: the new boy (*Five Hundred Faces* 1883); fagging (*Boy!* 1883); football (*Three Yards* 1885; *Play up!* 1887); swimming (*Ducker* 1887); bill (*Here Sir!* 1888); the Rifle Corps (*Left! Right!* 1897). While Bowen's later efforts lacked the passion and subtlety of his Farmer songs, Howson's verse reflected the established myth. Where Bowen invented, Howson gilded. Sport is as ever dominant: 'They tell us the world is a scrimmage, | And life is a difficult run' (*Three Yards*), but Bowen's irony was missing. Howson was more emphatic, cruder. Harrow and Harrovians are 'like an ancient river flowing . . . to the wider life to be . . . where duty's voice is ringing clear' (*Here Sir!*). Howson's triumphalism marked the success of the cult of the school and reflected its recruitment into a wider imperialism of the 1890s. In the nakedly arrogant and self-satisfied *Stet Fortuna Domus* of 1891, dedicated to an Old Harrovian Lord Mayor of London, Howson's 'patriotic chorus' lauds the 'magic thrall that unites us all | The name and fame of Harrow', earnestly hoping that Harrovians 'long continue | From Harrow School to rise and rule':

> And as the roll of Honour's Scroll
> Page after page is written,
> May Harrow give the names that live
> In Great and Greater Britain.

The song is still sung today.

The language and music of the songs indelibly marked the self-image of Harrow. Howson's demand for nostalgia in one of Farmer's happier settings, *Five Hundred Faces*, was quoted by an Old Harrovian in a letter to Butler just two years after its first performance in 1883:

> Yet the time may come, though you scarce know why
> When your eyes will fill
> At the thought of the Hill,
> And the wild regret of the last goodbye![220]

The phrase 'forty years on' entered the national language. Songs remained a potent weapon in the service of the school. In the autumn of 1896 the War Office requested the Head Master's Conference encourage recruitment into their Rifle Corps as 'a matter of national importance'.[221] Within months Howson and Faning composed a recruiting song, *Left! Right!*:

---

[220] Graham, *Butler*, 294; G. W. E. Russell to Butler, 21 July 1885.
[221] HM/We/Lord Wolseley to the Head Masters' Conference, Oct. 1896. Cf. anxieties that the Corps was undermanned and therefore financially unsound, Minutes of Masters' Meetings, 1893–1910, 1 Feb. 1897.

> So listen all, both great and small, and may there be some more
> To rally round to the bugle sound, and join the Rifle Corps!

Following the traumatic Boer War, the first great test of the cult of school, athleticism, and youth, George Townsend Warner and the new Director of Music, Percy Buck (shortly to take Warner's 19-year-old daughter as his mistress), produced *You?*, that tackles the grief and loss in an attempt to be reconciled with them. Apart from *Avete* to greet Edward VII in 1905, Buck, an expert on Tudor music, only composed one other song in his twenty-six years at Harrow. In 1910, at the height of the battle to pass the People's Budget and reform the House of Lords, when public schools were once more being attacked for unjustified elitism, an old India hand, C. J. Maltby wrote *The Silver Arrow* (a reference both to the archery contest abolished for rowdyism in 1772 and to the school crest) which tried to imply that Harrovians were the patriotic heirs of patriotic 'yeomen and burghers'. The almost Elgarian tune graces an unworthy piece of doggerel:

> ... Arise our youth,
> Rise in your strength, and show
> By word and by deed ye are worthy seed
> Of your Sires who drew the bow.

The chances of many ancestors of the plutocratic assembly that first sang this being so descended or being pleased to be reminded of it was an irony lost on Imperial Harrow.

The power of songs to rebut the present or reconcile it with a mythic past was not lost on Cyril Norwood, Head Master 1926–34. Post-First World War Harrow was vulnerable to a prying, prurient press; to creeping suburbia; and to internal divisions occasioned by educational changes. Norwood revived the Bowenesque tactic of dealing with each through new songs. *The Twentieth Centur-ee* (1931/2) reassures that the present is not worse than the past, merely different, with a warning not to give copy to 'The Daily This and Daily That | Grow hot about the Harrow Hat' and to 'bring no shame upon the name | And build no less a Harrow'. *John Lyon's Road* (1932) argues that the immutable 'secret' of education remains constant despite modernity, 'arterial roads where'er one roams, | And quite a lot of aerodromes'. The annual calendar is evoked in *East is East* (1933) as a sign of permanence. Yet Norwood fancied himself as a reformer. His most controversial innovation was the introduction of Rugby Football as the main school game from the Autumn Term in 1927. Diehards were appalled (as they were later when Association Football was seen to threaten rugby). A noisy campaign was launched against the change, reaching the national press. A unique referendum of the whole school was conducted, which Norwood won, a novel exercise in rule by plebiscite.[222] Feelings remained raw. So in 1933, to signal the acceptance of the new regime and

---

[222] Laborde, *Harrow School*, 200 and below, pp. 471–2.

secure its abiding place in Harrow life, Norwood wrote a song, *The Song of the Forwards*, dedicated to the unbeaten Fifteen of the autumn of 1932. No less than the most pointed of Bowen's compositions, Norwood employed the medium for a precise purpose, to create a new acceptable part of the school myth by enshrining it in unison singing. The myth and the cult remained essentially unchanged, with rugby joining the cricket and football of Bowen's day:

> There's plenty of bumps, and there's plenty of bruises:
> They'll teach you much more than a game.
> On, On, On, On, take strength and good temper and courage and speed—
> On, On, On, On, they're not a bad oufit for life and its need.

Edward Bowen might have phrased it more subtley, but he would have approved the sentiment which Norwood expressed more romantically and emotionally, with music by his collaborator R. S. Thatcher to match, in his last song, *Leavers* of 1934:

> And each and all own Harrow's call,
> True children of her story
> ...
>
> And far or nigh, beneath the sky,
> Wait fields both broad and narrow,
> In larger loyalties to try
> The lessons learnt at Harrow.

The cult of Harrow was Monty Butler's most fateful gift to the school he loved so obsessively.

Butler left Harrow reluctantly in 1885. After declining some grander posts, he was persuaded, after a very heavy, concerted campaign, to accept the surprisingly modest deanery of Gloucester, both in prestige and, importantly for Butler, income a far less exalted post. His performance in the later years had become increasingly uneven, his concentration frayed by illness and the death of his first wife in 1883. It is hard to avoid the impression that Butler was pushed out, the governors fearing an endless Headship. Gloucester was presented to him by friends as preparation for a grander role in the church, a bishopric at least. This never materialized, although in 1886 he did decline the archbishopric of Melbourne, the colonies being a common dumping ground for former Head Masters (e.g. Barry to Sydney; Cotton and Welldon to Calcutta). His career was saved by Lord Salisbury's offer of the Mastership of Trinity, Cambridge in 1886, a shrewd move to conciliate Liberal Unionists in the aftermath of the first Home Rule Bill.[223] Unlike with Vaughan, there were no cries for further advancement. Butler was a victim of his early precocity; having adopted so completely the opinions and habits of his elders, by middle age he seemed already out of date.

---

[223] Graham, *Butler*, 230–300, 384–5.

His impact on Harrow was indelible, if only in what one pupil called 'terrible combinations of red and black brick'.[224] In Butler's time the Hill was transformed by the Vaughan Library, the new Druries (1864), Speech Room, the Science Schools, the Gym, the 'New Side' of the Head Master's. The Museum Schools, designed by Basil Champneys, was begun in his last months. Butler had brought Vaughan's method to fruition. He presided over constitutional reform and, with science and the Modern Side, began processes of academic curriculum development that set the school on a long road of modernization. All this was effected without too must cost in terms of public support. He left the house system alone. Butler himself stood as a guarantee of the adherence to tradition. Athleticism and the cult of the school were enshrined in song. He was not a popular Head Master with boys, becoming so only when they grew up to become Old Harrovians. A curiously distant figure, while Vaughan's final act as Head Master was to shake the hand of each boy individually, Butler's was to pass, weeping and alone, from Chapel to his house through a line of cheering boys, a monumental figure, a Harrow icon.[225]

---

[224] Russell, *Autobiography*, 59.
[225] Interestingly, almost all accounts mention his unpopularity; for his last day see the eye-witness Graham, *Butler*, 295.

14

IMPERIAL HARROW: THE ORIGINS OF A MODERN SCHOOL, 1885–1914

On the 15 June 1912 King George V and Queen Mary attended Speech Day at Harrow, receiving a loyal address from the boys, hearing Songs, and taking tea with the Head Master and a fair proportion of the British Establishment. *The Times* oozed reverence for this 'gracious recognition by the crown of those services, both past and present, which have been rendered by . . . Harrow'. Their Majesties were introduced to Harrow's current celebrity, the racquets professional Charles Williams, who had survived the sinking of the Titanic a few months earlier. This was pre-war England at its palmiest, most confident, most powerful with Harrow at its centre, 'a national possession'. The only blot on the day's proceedings appeared at lunch before the royal party arrived when the Head Master, with customary gaucherie, revealed that his predecessor had preferred to play golf that day rather than pay homage to Crown and school.[1]

Beneath the bunting, all was rather less secure. Numbers had been declining for a decade and were about to slip below 500 for the first time in over a generation. For forty years, the governors had been waging an unsuccessful campaign to balance the books. A year before, the Board of Education had criticized certain fundamental features of the Harrow academic system. The new Head, Lionel Ford, had just embarked on radical reform of the curriculum—the second in twenty-five years—which controversially threatened to revolutionize masters' methods of teaching and earning. The school had undergone two critical external inspections in the previous six years. Perceived threats were crowding in, from the taxation policies of the Liberal government to creeping suburbia that was reaching the very foot of the Hill. Public attacks were increasingly vocal. The Labour MP J. Ramsay

---

[1] *The Harrovian*, 29 June 1912, pp. 62–7.

Macdonald in 1907, and delegates to the Trades Union Congress in 1910 and 1911 demanded government investigation of the disposal of Harrow's funds.[2] In January 1912 the senior science master at Harrow, Archer Vassall, published a stinging attack on the system of education, concluding that 'the average boy at a public school either gets an education unsuited to his powers or falls by the wayside and gets no true education at all', leaving those serving in the empire 'sound in character' but lacking 'plasticity, resourcefulness and any ability to adapt himself quickly to his new environment'.[3] Only a few days before the King graced Speech Day, the prominent Old Harrovian novelist and playwright, John Galsworthy published a damning condemnation of the ethics of his old school, 'Public Schools as Caste Factories', accusing the system of fostering the social divisiveness responsible for the growing industrial unrest of the period.[4]

Harrow as much as any public school had been in the forefront of shaping and sustaining the ideology and practice of imperialism. Harrovians served as proconsuls, soldiers, and administrators and reaped the profits as speculators, bankers, and merchants. A Harrovian was killed on the Jameson Raid into the Transvaal in January 1896;[5] Harrow provided more infantry officers in the Boer War than any other school except Eton.[6] Its chapel was a shrine to the imperial dead. In his valedictory sermon in 1898 Head Master Welldon identified the two great principles for which Harrow and Harrovians should stand: the church of England and the British Empire, it being 'the prerogative of this age to weld those two together'. He told boys of the 'divinely ordained mission of their country and their race', attempting to excite in them 'a lively interest in the British Empire . . . and the solemnity of the duties imposed upon it'. Welldon's Harrow celebrated Empire Day; one of his colleagues, G. H. Hallam, produced an annual *Empire Calendar*.[7]

Yet Welldon's imperialism, in common with many others of his generation, was not a crude militaristic or exploitative creed, even if militarism and exploitation were inescapable consequences of it. Welldon was sufficiently Arnoldian to cling to civilizing and missionizing ideals; the realities of violence, oppression, power, and wealth he chose to ignore. His was an empire of 'Blues ruling Blacks', based on 'truth, liberty, equality and religion'. As Bishop of Calcutta (1898–1902) he put

---

[2] GBM, 30 Apr. 1907; *TUC 1910* (London, 1911), p. 174; *TUC Ninth Quarterly Report*, June 1911, p. 30.
[3] Quoted from the *Times Educational Supplement*, Jan. 1912 by Stray, *Classics Transformed*, 260.
[4] Mack, *Public Schools and British Opinion since 1860*, 284 and n. 47; Marrot, *Galsworthy*, 703–5.
[5] G. B. L. Lambe, 1882–5, *Harrow Register, 1800–1911*, 602.
[6] G. Best, 'Militarism', in Bradley and Simon, *Victorian Public School*, 133.
[7] HA Welldon file, unlisted newspaper report; Gathorne-Hardy, *Public School Phenomenon*, 194–5; R. Wilkinson, *The Prefects: British Leadership and the Public School Tradition* (London, 1964), p. 101; Welldon, *Forty Years On*, 116; G. H. Hallam, 'Empire Calendar with Notes for the Year', *The Harrovian*, 24 Feb. 1912, pp. 8–9.

precept into practice by preaching in Bengali and inviting some, probably rather bewildered, local non-Christians to attend a Masonic festival. Welldon's confessional hatred was reserved for Roman Catholics and his racism for Jews and Chinese. His empire, by contrast, was naively eirenic, similar in purpose to Hallam's *Calendar*, 'to promote mutual understanding, help and intercourse between all citizens'.[8] In 1890 he proposed a scheme for a Muslim boarding house at Harrow under a Muslim housemaster.[9]

Harrow's experience in the generation before the First World War belies a crude image of aggressive imperial triumphalism tempered by mawkish sentimentality, although there was much of both. The new traditions and cults devised by Butler and Bowen were, for all their superficial bravado, essentially introspective and introverted. Harrow's outward image was older, more established than, for example, Rugby's. The heroes of *Tom Brown's Schooldays* of 1859 contrast oddly with Charles Dickens' Harrovian, the dowdy, declined Matthew Pocket of *Great Expectations* (1860; Dickens knew his quarry: Pocket had proceeded from Harrow to Trinity, Cambridge). Unlike new schools, such as Clifton, Cheltenham, or Marlborough, still less like the army school of Wellington, Harrow's older traditions of rule and military service, its academic staff of a calibre higher than at most other non-collegiate schools, and its boys still drawn to a larger extent than elsewhere from established gentry and professional social groups, tempered the rush to follow the populist fashion. Until the Boer War, the Rifle Corps remained an eccentric and minority activity, genuinely voluntary until 1914. Harrow's military links went back to the Napoleonic Wars; its imperial associations to the early eighteenth century. The dominant support for the new imperialism was matched by the clear hostility to militarism expressed by Bowen, Bosworth-Smith, and Welldon. The Harrow Mission in Nottingdale, West London, founded by Butler in 1883, was as significant an expression of Harrovian *noblesse oblige* as any protestations of imperial longings.[10] Direct entry into the Indian or other colonial service was remarkably low, at most between 2 per cent and 4 per cent in the quarter century after 1885, although the surprising number of engineers produced around 1900 often found employment overseas. There were almost certainly more Harrovian farmers and businessmen than District Commissioners or lawyers in the late Victorian and Edwardian Empire. The heavy intake of Harrovians into the regular armed forces not only declined in this period (25 per cent of total entrants in 1890; 16 per cent of 1900 entrants; 15 per cent of 1905 entrants), but often indicated a comparatively short stay under the colours, as in the case of Winston Churchill (1895–9).

---

[8] Welldon, *Forty Years On*, esp. pp. 89–90, 110–11, 119–20; id., *Recollections*, esp. p. 98; Wilkinson, *The Prefects*, 101–2; Gathorne-Hardy, *Public School Phenomenon*, 194–5; *The Harrovian*, 24 Feb. 1912, pp. 8–9.

[9] GBM, 26 June 1890. Cf. ibid., 5 Nov. 1889.

[10] M. Burnett, *History of the Harrow Mission and Club in Notting Dale* (London, 1983), esp. pp. 1–15.

Harrow's engagement with Empire, in contrast to the majority of Victorian public schools, tended to be of rulers not servants.[11]

Harrow espoused empire but was not defined by it. The rhetoric was adopted, careers were adapted, but Harrow imperialism bore a local stamp. The numerous dead came from a tradition of enlistment that had nothing to do with empire as such. The impact on masters, until the Boer war, was more likley to be in the shape of numerous sons of African or Indian potentates striving to associate themselves with this nursery of upper-class Englishness, from relations of the Khedive of Egypt, the sultan of Zanzibar, the king of Siam, or Indian maharajahs to the clever, ambitious, conformist son of the very rich Indian lawyer Motilal Nehru.[12] In 1910 a strenuously loyal Old Harrovian Archibald Fox was moved to comment on 'the comparative frequency of foreign appellations in the *Harrow Register* among which not a few are Eastern'.[13] Bosworth-Smith 'thought imperially' and recruited for the Knoll accordingly, to the disapproval of one of his successors, C. H. P. Mayo who pointedly quoted Kipling: 'East is East and West is West', the fraternal Imperialism of Welldon or Bosworth-Smith, however aristocratic scraping awkwardly against Harrow's traditional ingrained racism.[14] For the governors throughout this period the empire took far less precedence than drains.[15]

None the less, the political tone of Harrow altered significantly and permanently. Inevitably, Harrow supported the propertied interest. This had worn various colours. Welldon confidently proclaimed Harrow historically a Whig school.[16] Class as opposed to party interest allowed the management of the school to be shared between Tories like Abercorn and Whigs indiscriminately, the governors retaining a distinctly Liberal hue. The fifth Earl Spencer, a Liberal Cabinet Minister, was a governor from 1870 to 1908 and chairman from 1888. C. S. Roundell, the first Master's governor, remained a committed Liberal reformer throughout thirty years (1871–1901) as the most energetic member of the board. While in 1829 it would have been inconceivable for them to elect a Head Master with unsound views on the Anglican Ascendancy, in the 1840s the governors sponsored reform and appointed a closet liberal, Vaughan.[17] The fundamentally conservative Montagu Butler saw himself as politically progressive as did many of the scholarly intelligentsia of his youth. For the school in the mid-nineteenth century, the political issues were of progress towards improving the standard of education in order to maintain

---

[11] Figures from *Harrow Register, 1800–1911* and *Harrow Register, 1885–1949, passim*; on militarism see Best, 'Militarism', *Victorian Public School, passim*. Cf. Gathorne-Hardy, *Public School Phenomenon*, 194–200.

[12] Welldon, *Forty Years On*, 111; *Harrow Register, 1800–1911, passim*.

[13] A. Fox, *Public School Life: Harrow* (London, 1911), p. 97.

[14] C. H. P. Mayo, *Reminiscences of a Harrow Master* (London, 1928), pp. 46–7, 86. He believed in aparthied as regards boarding houses: ibid., 152–3; Grogan, *Bosworth-Smith*, 107–8.

[15] GBM, 1881–94, *passim*.   [16] Welldon, *Recollections*, 99.

[17] For the political context of the 1829 election see HM/1829/Cunningham to Lord Northwick, 27 Feb. 1829.

aristocratic ascendancy over the newly enriched and enfranchised middle classes, an ambition well-served by the Arnoldian Christian scheme of education pursued by Vaughan and Butler. Although highly political in purpose and effect, this project was not partisan, as the conservative reforms of the 1860s and 1870s revealed.

However, as society began to change in ways impossible to contain within traditional aristocratic attitudes or classical curriculum, the slide to reactionary politics began, Gladstone providing the catalyst for the change. In the 1860s, only three masters were Tories and were regarded as oddities.[18] In the 1880 General Election, Bowen stood as the Liberal candidate against Arthur Balfour at Hertford (losing creditably by 400 to 564 votes). He was considered in connection with a seat in Leeds (1883), briefly adopted for Oxford (1884), and on the shortlist for Harrow (1885). The governors began to be alarmed, a sign of Old Harrovian feeling, discussing the question of masters standing for parliament at an unminuted closed session in November 1884.[19] However, this was not an expression of partisanship, as one governor was himself standing in the Liberal interest and another could expect office in any Liberal Cabinet. In 1884 Harrovian MPs were equally divided between the parties. By December 1910 not only were there fewer of them (34 instead of 64) but of those Harrovians elected, only nine were Liberals, one of them a renegade Tory, Winston Churchill.[20]

The sea-change occurred with Home Rule in 1886, although this may have served as a useful pretext for many to abandon a party no longer wedded to the supremacy of the aristocracy. As early as 1881 Butler voiced concern lest Gladstone's pacific and lukewarm imperialism would threaten British rule in India and Ireland. In the election of December 1885 Butler for the first time voted against the Liberals in Harrow (and their candidate the future imperial proconsul Alfred Milner).[21] Welldon argued that 'Mr Gladstone's first Home Rule Bill was indirectly a damaging blow aimed at Harrow [*seen by Welldon as a non-Tory school*], as it set almost the whole aristocracy on one side in politics'.[22] This meant, in parochial terms, that Harrovian parents now saw no reason not to send their sons to Eton. Having encouraged middle-class, nonconformist radicalism (which ostensibly caused Butler's defection in 1885), Gladstone now threatened the integrity of the burgeoning empire. This lost him not only natural conservatives but also instinctive radicals such as Bowen. Thereafter, Harrow nailed its colours to the Tory and imperial mast.

This united all elements in the school as the boys had long been solidly Tory, certainly since the death of Palmerston in 1865. During the 1868 election, according to one account only five Harrovians—Lord Grey, Walter Leaf, W. A. Meek, M. G. Dauglish, and G. W. E. Russell—displayed the Liberal colours, although they were probably joined by F. H. Villiers, son of Lord Clarendon. Most of these were influenced more by family tradition than personal conviction. Masters notorious

---

[18] Minchin, *Old Harrow Days*, 22, 276. [19] Bowen, *Bowen*, 175–9; GBM, 18 Nov. 1884.
[20] Thornton, *Harrow School*, 374; *The Harrovian*, 8 Apr. 1911, p. 19.
[21] Graham, *Butler*, 362–5. [22] Welldon, *Recollections*, 103–4.

for Liberal politics, such as E. M. Young, the future Head Master of Sherborne, were ragged mercilessly for their opinions. By the 1890s all had changed. From the Head Master downwards, including 'red hot radical' Bosworth-Smith, there was political unity and uniformity around the Unionist cause.[23] G. M. Trevelyan, a cradle Liberal, found himself almost alone in opposing the Conservatives in the 1892 election. Uniformity bred indifference, assumed agreement spawned ignorance, Trevelyan fulminating 'in a school of 600 boys I have found just two people capable of talking sensibly about politics... I might just as well talk Greek politics to the rest.'[24] Occasionally boys could be engaged by the national political debate, as during the constitutional crisis of 1909–11. It is significant of the shift in Harrovians' social origins as much as for the future direction of Conservative politics that, at a meeting of the school Debating Society in the autumn of 1910, a motion in favour of Tariff Reform was carried by 73 votes to 11.[25]

The identification of Harrovian masters and governors with political conservatism and, increasingly, the Conservative party became complete from the early twentieth century with the rise of socialism and corporatism, the collapse of liberalism and the creation of a state secondary system after 1902. This was mirrored by a withdrawal of Harrow, along with the other public schools, from the mainstream of educational debate and change. Although leading officials at the new Board of Education, such as the highly influential Wykehamist Permanent Secretary Robert Morant, saw public schools as models, after 1902 the focus of state attention was not on them, their relationship becoming increasingly detached. While grammar schools often aped the style and manners of public schools, by the 1920s, the familiar state/independent division had become an entrenched feature of the United Kingdom educational system. No longer could governments tacitly accept that public schools were, in the sense they had been regarded in the 1860s and 1870s, national institutions. Instead, however envied and emulated, public schools almost by definition became synonymous with class elitism and, often unfairly, educational conservatism.

Within Harrow, the conformity of political view now matched the conformism of manners which was such a feature even of such a diverse and decentralized school. Bowen and Bosworth-Smith followed the dreary path to reaction trodden by so many radicals, their insistence on reform of the 1860s curdling to blinkered refusal to accept it in the 1890s. Suggestions to abolish the university Greek requirement now came from Oxford not the public schools. Welldon, with the majority support of his staff, emasculated the Modern Side by admitting to it the less able. He encouraged science but insisted it was no substitute for arts, especially classics.[26] The emphasis appeared to be on the necessary rather than the sufficient. The acceptance

[23] Russell, *Autobiography*, 72; Minchin, *Old Harrow Days*, 272–3, 276; Bowen, *Bowen*, 179.
[24] Moorman, *Trevelyan*, 22–3.   [25] Fox, *Harrow*, 70.
[26] Mack, *Public Schools and British Opinion since 1860*, 213; Bowen, *Bowen*, 115–16.

of rule by bloods was enshrined in new regulations for the appointment of monitors in 1894 when half their number were to be reserved to heads of houses and 'athletic boys of high character'.[27] The cult of Harrow as a brotherhood of devotion and service was now pervasive. In a way that would have astonished Vaughan and his pupils, Harrovians were expected to love and worship their school, set, in C. H. P. Mayo's words, on its 'Mons Sacer'.[28] In 1910 George Townsend Warner, the most brilliant teacher of his time, Harrow boy (1880–3) and master (1891–1916), declared his passionate emotion to Lionel Ford after the new Head Master's first Founder's Day: 'Ah! now you can understand what Harrow is, and what a joy beyond words it is to be allowed to serve her', a significant feminine association in a world of men.[29] This pattern of thought, loyal, uncritical, engrossed, defensive, conservative, transferred from the local to the national. As Welldon insisted: 'An English Head Master, as he looks to the future of his pupils, will not forget that they are destined to be the citizens of the greatest empire under heaven; he will teach them patriotism, not by his words only but by his example.'[30]

The surrender of the ideal of service to the City of God to service to the City of Man was just one more symptom of how the anxieties of economic and social change had replaced theological religion with political religion. Of the Harrovians who entered the school in 1890, seven (4 per cent) took Holy Orders; a decade later, just one; from the 1905 intake none. On Speech Day 1912 George V heard Harrow Songs and inspected the Corps; he did not visit Chapel. His host, Lionel Ford, was the last ordained Head Master of Harrow.

WELLDON

James Edward Cowell Welldon personified this transition. A lifelong advocate of the cultural supremacy and world mission of the English, he believed that 'the true good ... of the education in English Public Schools is not scholarship so much as citizenship'. At the same time, he thought 'a Head Master who cannot give his boys Holy Communion is like a Head Master who cannot teach his Sixth Form' and insisted that all his colleagues regularly attend Chapel on pain of dismissal. Yet, whatever its spiritual effect, Welldon's Chapel was where the school 'learns that it has a corporate life; there ... the lessons of brotherhood can be enforced', a markedly secularized version of the Vaughan–Butler tradition.[31]

---

[27] Minutes of Masters' Meetings, 1893–1910, 5 Mar. 1894.
[28] Mayo, *Reminiscences*, 173.   [29] *The Harrovian*, 18 Nov. 1916, p. 93.
[30] Wilkinson, *The Prefects*, 101.
[31] Welldon, *Forty Years On*, 119, 158; Wilkinson, *The Prefects*, 55. Cf. Welldon, 'Harrow School Chapel', in Howson and Townsend Warner, *Harrow School*, esp. pp. 128–31; HM/We/18 Jan. 1893, Welldon to the Masters re. Chapel attendance and cf. Minutes of Masters' Meetings, 16 Apr. 1894: Welldon's strictures seem to have had only limited success.

Yet Welldon owed his position to his clerical status. As one candidate he defeated for the Harrow Headship acidly remarked, 'he owes his own rapid promotion entirely to taking Orders and speaking about church problems'.[32] A star product of Eton and King's, a Senior Classic like his three Harrow predecessors, Welldon had taken deacon's orders in 1883 when he went from his King's fellowship to the Headship of Dulwich aged only 29. He stood unsuccessfully against the experienced, games-mad Warre at Eton in 1884 and was ordained a priest in 1885, the year of his election to Harrow. He belonged to that typically Victorian cult of the clerical Elect, those chosen almost it seems from birth by God and man to succeed, a sort of establishment Calvinism whose Chosen belonged to a tight knit social group reinforced by school and university, knowing and being known by the right people. Welldon, unlike many such, had used his fellowship to publish some academic work, on Aristotle. There, Butler spotted him for his successor.[33]

Welldon was also in some ways one of the last of the line. The late nineteenth century saw the parting of the ways between dons and schoolmasters as universities were secularized, allowed married fellows, and provided adequate stipends. Between 1875 and 1925, two largely separate professions emerged creating a clear distinction between secondary and higher education, in management, teaching, and learning. Schoolteaching was no longer the preserve of clergymen. At Harrow, Welldon was one of only seven ordained masters out of thirty-nine, the practice of appointing laymen having been established since the 1850s. By 1893 sometimes as many as half the masters would skip Chapel.[34] His successor at Dulwich, A. H. Gilkes, was a layman, as were his three rivals on the Harrow shortlist in 1885.[35] The self-professed great public schools clung to the tradition of clerical Heads for another forty years, often in the face of reason. While convenient if governors wished to ease out a Head to a deanery or colonial bishopric, the clerical tradition narrowed the field of candidates while not conspicuously enhancing the religious tone, which remained conventionally Anglican whether masters wore dog collars or not. Although the operation of an establishment Elect continued for another three-quarters of a century, tempered only modestly by conspicuous merit, increasingly it was a secular one, drawn from within the public school world. While Welldon was the first Head Master of Harrow since Bryan to have been a Head elsewhere, his precedent has been followed by all bar two (the very different Vellacott and Boissier) of his eleven successors to date.

In another way Welldon represented this new Elect that relied on less overt group identity than the Trinity, Cambridge or Arnoldian mafias. As were many undergraduates of the 1870s, Welldon was a freemason, which may be linked to his

---

[32] T. E. Page to W. H. D. Rouse, 18 June 1893, quoted by C. Stray, *The Living Word: W. H. D. Rouse and the Crisis of Classics in Edwardian England* (Bristol, 1992), p. 16.

[33] On Welldon, apart from his own *Recollections* (1915) and *Forty Years On* (1935), see J. W. S. Tomlin's article for the *DNB*.   [34] HM/We/18 Jan. 1893, Welldon to Masters.

[35] GBM, 13 Apr. 1885; Stray, *Classics Transformed*, 189; Honey, *Tom Brown's Universe*, 308–14.

rabid hostility to Roman Catholics ('a nation within a nation . . . against national unity').³⁶ He remained prominent in the Craft, openly demonstrating his allegiance while in India and, in 1924, acting as chaplain when the Old Harrovian Lodge (no. 4653) was consecrated.³⁷ There had already been some grand Harrovian freemasons, such as the first duke of Abercorn, a governor from 1834 to 1885. Other governors who were freemasons included Lord Ridley (governor 1885–1904); Lord George Hamilton (governor 1900–24, chairman 1908–24); the second marquess of Zetland (governor 1925–42); and Walter Monckton (governor 1930–47).³⁸ There have been many others. Leading Harrow families apart from Hamilton and Dundas embraced the Craft, such as the Pleydell-Bouverie earls of Radnor, Yorke earls of Hardwicke, and Powys Lords Lilford. Between 1885 and 1971 Head Masters tended to be freemasons, as did many governors and often powerful groups of masters and housemasters. C. Norwood and R. L. James made little secret of their freemasonry; in 1937 Vellacott gave the school an additional half-holiday at the request of the Grand Master of the Masonic Order.³⁹ Among the upper classes in the late nineteenth and early twentieth centuries there was less concealment of membership than later. Membership was not seen as conflicting with mainstream broad Anglicanism. Two of the first thirteen annual Masters of the OH Lodge were clergyman, one, F. C. N. Hicks, was bishop of Gibraltar, later bishop of Lincoln, as well as a governor of the school, 1927–42.⁴⁰ The new chapel at Charterhouse, built as a memorial to the dead of the First World War, is festooned with masonic symbols. Christianity and the cult of the school were easily embraced in the Craft. In 1929 two Harrovians from the 1890s, C. T. Clay and C. H. C. Pirie-Gordon, gave the Harrovian Lodge ceremonial cups mounted on plinths of oak from Old Speech Room and olive wood from Jerusalem. In 1934 Norwood presented the Lodge with 'rough and smooth ashlars cut from a stone taken from the School Chapel at Harrow'.⁴¹ For clever and ambitious middle-class men, freemasonry was fashionable, as it continued to be among public schoolmasters who, almost by definition, relished institutional male cameraderie. As well as a sign of clubbability, that most precious quality in the eyes of so many English institutions, freemasonry operated almost as an adjunct to their professional identity. Unlike other associations (e.g. United Ushers), it offered contact with the great and influential beyond but often linked to their own immediate sphere. Its

---

³⁶ Welldon, *Forty Years On*, 172–3.

³⁷ Ibid., 291; Herbert Greene, 'Miscellaneous Papers', Bodleian MS G. A. Middl. 65, record of the dinner at The Savoy, 8 Dec. 1924. Greene was an OH (1870–5), a barrister, and a fellow of Magdalen College, Oxford, 1880–1910 as well as a freemason.

³⁸ *Harrow School Register, 1845–1937*, ii (1899–1937), ed. J. H. Stogdon (London, 1937), p. 351: 'Prominent Old Harrovian Freemasons'; Greene, 'Miscellaneous Papers', list of membership of OH Lodge, 1935–6 circulated by H. Pirie-Gordon.

³⁹ *The Harrovian*, 22 June 1937, 'Here and There'.   ⁴⁰ *Harrow Register, 1845–1937*, ii. 351.

⁴¹ Greene, 'Miscellaneous Papers', List of gifts to OH Lodge.

prevalence at Harrow was a symptom of this fashion, one network of community, another team, among many.

If Welldon neatly combined past prejudice and contemporary change, so did his election. The governors advertised more widely; references were limited to six per candidate; and the shortlisted four were interviewed before a decision was reached, a Harrow first. Of course, some of this procedure was merely formal, the candidates emerging through contacts rather than open competition in accordance with Harrow tradition. Welldon was the favourite, appearing at the top of all lists drawn up by the clerk of the governors. Yet although favoured by Butler and clerical status, he faced stiff competition.[42] Some at Harrow advanced the cause of Bowen. Although undoubtedly the dominant figure in the school, his political and religious views told against him. At a special Masters' Meeting called at the invitation of the governors, he received only eight votes, the rest going to Welldon, no doubt in deference to Butler. None the less, not all were happy with the idea of Welldon, there being a move to propose John Percival, founding Head Master of Clifton (1862–79), subsequently President of Trinity College, Oxford, Head Master of Rugby, and bishop of Hereford, one of the heroes of the public schools' Golden Age.[43] Nothing came of this, although the prospect of Percival at Harrow is intriguing, not least in the light of how he exhausted Rugby with his reforming energies between 1887 and 1895. In the event, the governors interviewed three candidates as well as Welldon: P. A. Aitken of Glasgow University; H. C. Goodhart of Trinity, Cambridge, later classics professor at Edinburgh; and T. E. Page, renowned classics master at Charterhouse and co-founder of the Loeb Classical Library, a man well-qualified for important Headships but repeatedly thwarted by his lack of Holy Orders. Given their inherent conservatism and the overt pressure from Butler and the majority of the masters, the outcome was scarcely in doubt, but it was reached only after serious discussion. The Minutes of the meeting on 1 May 1885 suggest Welldon was not elected by acclamation.[44]

Welldon was huge, ugly, and physically imposing. Known to boys as 'the Porker', he exuded self-confidence which bordered on arrogance.[45] He rarely sought or heeded advice.[46] With his irreverent, often mischievous but sharp wit and general contempt for the manners and ethics of schoolmasters as a class, he was more popular with boys than his staff. He possessed to an extraordinary degree the gift of remembering for years his pupils' names, faces, and careers, even if they had not been in his form. One of his central tenets was to trust boys, especially when it

---

[42] GBM, 21 Feb., 5 Mar., 13 Apr., 1 May 1885; Graham, *Butler*, 288.
[43] Bowen, *Bowen*, 191–2.   [44] GBM, 1 May 1885.
[45] 'Harrow in the Eighties', *The Harrovian*, 7 Dec. 1961; in general, as well as the works cited above see *The Harrovian*, 17 Dec. 1898, pp. 105–7.
[46] According to one of his assistants at Harrow, R. C. Gilson to J. W. Headlam, 29 Mar. 1891; I am endebted to Christopher Stray for a transcript of this letter.

was a matter of believing their word against that of a master.[47] Few Heads have so successfully penetrated and exposed the inherent weaknesses, bluster, vanity, pettiness, and mendacity involved in the teaching profession. He attributed 'troubles which occur in Public School life . . . largely, if not mainly . . . to the failure of masters in discipline'.[48] He did not follow the Arnoldian belief in the natural viciousness of youth. Although a keen supporter of games, an accomplished footballer himself, he deplored 'muscle worship'.[49] On the other hand, his realism led him to accept that hero-worship was part of school life, just as he recognized that Chapel services would be more appreciated by boys the fewer there were of them: he reduced Sunday services from three to two, and sermons from two to one. He regarded Harrow as over-disciplined, at least in contrast to Eton; 'I tried to relax a little the discipline of the school'.[50] His Punishment Book records that between 1888 and 1898 he conducted 917 floggings (never fewer than five strokes of the birch; often more) at a steady rate of a hundred a year.[51] If this constituted relaxation, the mayhem under Butler must have been savage indeed.

Welldon's method of administration was autocratic. One colleague described Welldon's 'immense power, vigour and unquestioned authority . . . ill-fitted to brook opposition', unkindly adding 'he called to mind the picture of a Roman dictator or Cardinal Wolsey'.[52] Initially, Welldon faced a problem not unlike that presented to Butler in 1860. Of the twenty-eight masters he inherited in 1885, sixteen had been there for fifteen years or more, including eight with more than twenty-five years' service. Twenty of his colleagues were older than him.[53] To survive he chose to dominate. Although he was careful to consult his colleagues when formulating his radical curriculum reforms in 1886, he made it clear that, while he would only proceed with their general assent, he would not compromise the central thrust of his policy. In the teeth of opposition from some senior masters he introduced new, more valuable scholarships in 1897 and, while disapproving of it for boys, imposed a superannuation rule for masters, coupled with a pension scheme. In making appointments, he apparently never 'asked or took advice'. At the very end of his Headship, he refused to be bullied by Bowen into diluting his new provision that the ultimate power of allocating scholars to houses rested with the Head Master.[54] Unlike the devoted and ponderous Butler, the more mercurial and

---

[47] Welldon, *Forty Years On*, 139–40.   [48] Ibid., 107, 133.
[49] The phrase is Arnold Lunn's: *The Harrovians* (London, 1913), 61.
[50] Welldon, *Recollections*, 87.
[51] HA Head Masters' Punishment Book from 1888 to 1965, entries Sept. 1888–Dec. 1898.
[52] I. Quigley, *The Heirs of Tom Brown* (Oxford, 1982), p. 37.
[53] For details see *Harrow Register, 1885–1949*, 674–8.
[54] HA HM/We/Report of the Head Master on Studies, 30 Oct. 1886; HM/We/26 May 1897, Welldon to Masters; Minutes of Masters' Meetings, 1893–1910, 8 Mar. 1897 (vote against scholarship proposal 14:5), 7 and 14 June, 1 Nov. 1897; GBM, 7 Nov. 1893, 2 Feb., 11 May, 12 and 22 July, 2 Nov. 1897, 1 Nov. 1898; for refusing to take advice see above, n. 46; Head Master's Book, 1874–92, fo. 81.

contemptuous Welldon thought Masters' Meetings generally a waste of time 'apt to degenerate into duels between individual masters', usually involving the increasingly locquacious and difficult Bowen who never stopped talking and sometimes the ageing Bosworth-Smith who insisted on reading out his views *in extenso*.[55] Impatient of such unnecessary indulgence of egos, in 1892 Welldon reduced the number of meetings to one a fortnight, instead of once a week, changing the time to 4.30 p.m. on Tuesday afternoons rather than 9 p.m. on Wednesdays.[56] He rarely displayed much trust in his colleagues. He would patrol the High Street just before First School at 7.30 a.m. to catch any masters who were late; in 1889 he insisted on knowing exactly how many lessons each master actually, rather than notionally, taught; and he voiced a clear suspicion of those who used textbooks they had written themselves.[57] What probably grated even more was his vein of heavy sarcasm. When threatening colleagues with dismissal for non-attendance at Chapel, he did not accuse them of irreligion but implied their idleness by insisting that any habitual absentee be required to produce a medical certificate stating that 'it is impossible for him to attend without danger to his health'.[58] Occasionally he was baulked, as over attempts to establish a uniform system of admission to houses or his suggestion in 1895 that the annual Head Boy's speech to the governors, the Contio, be abolished.[59] Although admired by some younger colleagues and recalled with increasing affection during the disastrous rule of his successor, the immediate result of his behaviour was predictable. Regarded by many, with justice, as an unscrupulous careerist, within five years of his appointment, it was alleged, only a little unfairly, that if the masters had been given another vote, Bowen would have won unanimously.[60]

The boys, whose interests Welldon prided himself on protecting and understanding, were less hostile. Seventy years later, one Rendallian of the 1890s paid him a tribute that would have delighted him: 'he was respected and loved by the boys... Welldon knew us, trusted us, and believed in us.'[61] Although occasionally uneasy with the highly intelligent and opinionated, such as G. M. Trevelyan, he was capable as few Heads were of discussing the weaknesses of the school intelligently, openly, and sympathetically.[62] This rather detached pose attracted pupils as much as it irritated masters. Welldon's lack of intensity in his job, his detachment from obsessive, all-consuming engagement with Harrow must have appalled those used to Butler and their own devotion. Even the governors were slightly put out

---

[55] Welldon, *Recollections*, 88; Mayo, *Reminiscences*, 23; Bowen, *Bowen*, 231–2; Grogan, *Bosworth-Smith*, 118. [56] Head Master's Book, 1874–92, fo. 61, 26 Feb. 1892.

[57] *The Harrovian*, 17 Dec. 1898, 105–7; Bryant, *Harrow*, 90; Head Master's Book, 1874–92, fo. 69; HM/We/21 Sept. 1896, Welldon to Bushell.

[58] HM/We/18 Jan. 1893, Welldon to Masters.

[59] Minutes of Masters' Meetings, 1893–1910, 2 May 1898, 6 May 1895.

[60] Bowen, *Bowen*, 192.   [61] Meinertzhagen, *Diary*, 181–2.

[62] Moorman, *Trevelyan*, 34.

when he failed to turn up for the first day of the Spring Term 1890.[63] Boys were less censorious. E. F. Twiss (West Acre 1890–4) was amused at the idea that Welldon's main anxiety during an outbreak of scarlet fever in March 1893 was whether it would interfere with his holiday plans to visit Jerusalem.[64]

For the boys, it seems that his greatest ability was communication, a quality which he lacked so spectacularly in his dealings with adults, as his later career demonstrated. Ironically, Welldon saw himself as a great prince of the Church and pillar of the State, even being quite pleased with the see of Calcutta when offered it at the age of only forty-four, whereas he was actually most effective as a schoolmaster. His imperial patriotism left its mark. Recalled one 1890s Harrovian, 'whilst I was at Harrow I awakened to the glorious magnificence of the British Empire'.[65] Welldon even delivered interesting sermons. While condemned by some adult judges as simple, monotonous, unoriginal, and platitudinous, his style appealed to the young. Twiss confided to his diary that Welldon had preached a 'very good' sermon on Holy Communion in March 1893. By his final year E. C. Richardson (Moretons 1885–9), later called 'the father of British skiing', had become a connoisseur of Harrow preachers. During the Easter Term 1889, while dismissing the efforts of J. A. Cruikshank, Bushell ('fearfully humhuggy') and E. C. H. Owen ('drivelling'), he noted a 'good sermon by Welldon' on the child Samuel and an 'extraordinary sermon from Welldon about courtesy'.[66] It must have helped that the Head Master did not assume, as had his two predecessors, that he was fighting a losing battle against his audience's sin.

This did not mean he was unaware of it. Cheating, idleness, bullying, gambling, swearing, passing counterfeit money, keeping and distributing pornography were the stock in trade of those sent up the Welldon for punishment. One boy was flogged for setting fire to his bedclothes; another, with traditional insensitivity, put on daily reports for 'constant failure'; a third kept back at the end of term for what Cruikshank regarded as 'unnecessary questions'.[67] Winston Churchill was flogged (seven strokes) for missing detention (an encounter milked as a story in later years) and held back at the end of one term for impertinence to his far from able maths master, J. W. Welsford.[68] Sexual misdemeanours were distinguished between 'indecency' and 'immorality', a distinction possibly semantic, possibly criminal. One consequence of his clerical status and his prurient enthusiasm for confession before confirmation was that boys admitted to him crimes of homosexual seduction. Occasional sex scandals were dealt with in the usual way: in 1890 four were

---

[63] GBM, 4 Feb. 1890.   [64] HA MS E. F. Twiss, 'Diary for 1893', 21 Mar.
[65] Meinertzhagen, *Diary*, 210.
[66] Twiss, 'Diary', 18 Mar. HA MS E. C. Richardson, 'Diary 1889–i', 27 Jan., 3 Feb., 24 Feb., 31 Mar. For a less flattering opinion on Welldon's preaching by his bishop at Durham, Hensley Henson see Honey, *Tom Brown's Universe*, 314 n.
[67] Punishment Book, 1888–1965, 8 Oct. 1888, 7 Mar. 1889, 25 July 1893, and *passim*.
[68] Ibid., 20 Oct. 1890, 21 Mar. 1892.

expelled from the Knoll; in 1891 four more were expelled from Newlands, although one had been 'terrorized into sin', this ring also involving three Rendallians who had just left.[69] This was the small change of a boys' boarding school, heterosexual activity (if any) seemingly being conducted more discreetly. Welldon took a relaxed view of adolescent sex. Poking fun at one cherished belief of the games fanatics, he recalled that when he saw boys coming up the Hill after football: 'I knew they had enjoyed such exercise as would keep their animal spirits tolerably quiet for twenty-four or forty-eight hours.'[70]

In all that he did and wrote, Welldon appeared as a man apart, an observer even of his own actions and professional and social circles. This made him a refreshingly incisive and malicious raconteur, capable of mocking himself as well as others. His solitariness and cynicism he shared with Vaughan, with whom he got on well. Yet, while appearing to his school as a man of confident authority, there was another side.

It is dangerous, often false and usually unprofitable to ascribe to a novelist the emotions revealed in his fiction. None the less, Welldon's *Gerald Eversley's Friendship* published in 1895 with the wholly misleading subtitle *A Study in Real Life* cannot entirely be dismissed on those grounds, not least because neither he nor his biographer nor any previous historians of Harrow ever mention it. They were probably too embarrassed. It is a truly dreadful book, an empty, dull sentimental love story about an unprepossessing middle-class scholar and a glamorous aristocratic blood. It is a tale of boy meets boy, nearly loses boy, wins boy but can only have boy by getting engaged to boy's sister ('to be linked to her was to be linked to him perpetually') who then dies, imposing on boy a life of good works and celibacy.[71] There are some startling passages. Praising Harry Vennicker, the 'lithe' object of Gerald Eversley's affections, a 'splendid animal, healthy, vigorous, proud' whose 'bright complexion and soft blue eyes were passports to favour', Welldon comments: 'No being, perchance, is so distinct, none so beautiful or attractive, as a noble English boy.'[72] This, from a Head Master of a public school, writing under his own name and title, in the year of Oscar Wilde's trials is remarkable.

Welldon did not enjoy the naivety of Farrar thirty years before. Maybe he did not seek it. There is much in *Gerald Eversley* that was repeated in Welldon's two volumes of memoirs (of 1915 and 1935). The Head Master trusts a boy's word above the suspicions of a housemaster (who bears more than a passing resemblance to Bowen in age, crustiness, snobbishness, devotion, heartiness, and radicalism). As in all his books, Welldon cannot resist attacking marriage. The only female character of any substance is, unsurprisingly, the ethereally beautiful mother of the love-object Vennicker, although it is her son's physique that continues to inspire the author's

---

[69] Punishment Book 1888–1965, July (no day entered) 1890, 17 Nov. 1891, 26 Jan. 1898; Welldon, *Forty Years On*, 157.
[70] Welldon, *Forty Years On*, 116.
[71] Id., *Gerald Eversley's Friendship: A Study in Real Life* (London, 1895), 288 for quotation. For a brief discussion see Quigley, *Heirs of Tom Brown*, 134–6.   [72] Welldon, *Gerald Eversley*, 3, 33.

greatest admiration: 'a tall, manly, splendid creature,' 'strong and beautiful'.[73] His doomed sister is much less vivid. There are some strange interludes, as when the housemaster is described as an expert in the sleeping positions of his boys.[74] Much of the time, the tone is that of the conventional public school novel, although the standard elevation of an exaggerated, overheated ideal of friendship is paralleled by Welldon's own views published years later. On one level it is possible that Welldon was being ironic. Thus, to describe a vital house match 'it would need a pen of a Thucydides'.[75] As with Vachell's Desmond at Lord's a decade later, when Vennicker scores the winning goal he is told 'you will never be a greater person in life . . . than you are today'.[76] Unlike Vachell, Welldon did not believe this. Yet it is hard to credit his writing a 354-page novel merely as an exercise in irony, not least because, amid the banalities, he insists on saying serious things about public schools.

However the fiction is read, the novel contains extraordinary, scarcely veiled attacks on Welldon's own school and its system. He talks of schoolboy morality as 'the morality of a savage tribe'; he attacks the Procrustean insistence at 'St Anselm's' (i.e., unmistakably, Harrow) on conformity; public school, he admits, 'has its victims', is 'the home of the commonplace'. 'There . . . mediocrity sits upon her throne . . . the spirit which conforms to custom is lauded to the skies . . . the spirit which is independent and original is apt to be crushed'. His remark that masters 'take their tone from the boys . . . they admire the boys whom the boys admire' must have gone down well.[77] In places, the references are specific to Harrow, showing the Head Master's House of the 1890s as little changed from forty years before. Junior boys were still forced to box each other for the amusement of the Fifth Form. Initiation rituals were still tinged with hostility and violence. Welldon's description of 'fag-spotting' outdoes that of Peter Withington in 1851: 'the nearest parallel to it may be said to have been the sale of slave girls in the market at Constantinople', 'cleanliness was a recommendation in a fag as well as attractiveness of appearance or alacrity'.[78]

Gerald Eversley could be taken as a failed attempt to cash in on a lucrative market. Parts of it can also be read as a deliberate indictment of some characteristics of schooling that Welldon found distasteful but was too realistic or lazy to confront directly. It is notable that he found the time to write it at all. However, there remain elements of the work that strike more personal notes. Welldon in later life displayed a very low estimate of human nature in general. Himself unmarried, he harped on the subject of the over-grieving widower who inevitably marries again, his example being quite clearly Montagu Butler.[79] He was a settled misogynist, even though he supported women's suffrage and, in the 1930s, the ordination of women. Very alert to hypocrisy and the absurdities of the human condition, he was

---

[73] Ibid., 169, 232.   [74] Ibid., 20.   [75] Ibid., 163.   [76] Ibid., 166.
[77] Ibid., 73–4, 75–6, 77, 78.   [78] Ibid., 88, 89, 123.
[79] Id., *Forty Years On*, 24. Cf. the sentiment expressed over thirty-five years earlier, Newsome, *On the Edge of Paradise*, 56.

prudish about sex, 'a rather unhealthy aspect' of life.[80] None the less, he retained an intensely romantic view of friendship, writing in 1935 of 'that abiding benediction of human life, especially among the unmarried, a benediction even more highly esteemed ... in the pagan than in the Christian world ... one of the safeguards which render life's journey not only less painful but happier and easier than it could otherwise be'.[81] Here lay the reason for the subtitle to his novel, for this was Welldon's 'real life'.

In 1933 he resigned from the deanery of Durham, his last post in a career of gentle decline from the heights of Harrow thirty-five years before. His biographer for the *Dictionary of National Biography*, J. W. S. Tomlin, Welldon's Head of School in 1889, explained his retirement followed 'shortly after the death of a faithful servant who had been with him in close companionship for nearly fifty years'.[82] Although Tomlin did not say so, the servant's name was Edward Perkins. Together, Welldon and Perkins, also described by his employer as 'my faithful servant', travelled the globe, the latter on one occasion in Uganda even upstaging his master at a ceremonial reception.[83] Their relationship provided a frame for Welldon's awkward personality, his isolation and enjoyment of the role of outsider. It may also explain his lack of the highest preferment he could have expected. As they traipsed across the Empire year after year, they may have cut odd figures, although such loyal bonds of male affection, of master and servant, or mentor and associate, is a cliché of late nineteenth- and early twentieth-century fiction if not society. Their trips began in bizarre and hilarious circumstances. In 1887 Welldon planned to travel to the United States of America with his old Eton friends, Stuart Donaldson, the future Master of Magdalene College, Cambridge and George Curzon, MP, future Viceroy of India, Foreign Secretary, and notorious stickler for abstruse aristocratic etiquette. Perkins went too: 'It happened that my chief footman at Harrow was very anxious to travel abroad. I liked him and wished to give him as much pleasure as was possible; and so I told him I would take him with me.' The sequel found the ill-assorted quartet stranded at a crowded hotel somewhere in the Midwest whose proprietor suggested accommodating them in two beds, proposing that Curzon sleep with the footman. The budding pro-consul's outrage must have been wondrous; at least it secured them each a single bed.[84]

WOOD

The choice of Welldon's successor was unhappy. Governors tended to choose worst when least adventurous. When Welldon announced his intention of accepting the bishopric of Calcutta in the summer of 1898, the governors had time to survey the

---

[80] Welldon, *Forty Years On*, 187, 209, 212–13, 233.   [81] Ibid., 50.
[82] *DNB Supplement, 1931–40*, ed. L. G. Wickham Legg (London, n.d.) s.v. 'Welldon'.
[83] Welldon, *Forty Years On*, 72–3.   [84] Ibid., 68–9.

field. A shortlist of four was drawn up, including the Eton master Lionel Ford, then 33, ordained, a friend of Welldon, and clearly a coming man, two years later to be appointed to the Headship of his old school, Repton.[85] Yet none of these was elected, the governors, before any interview, deciding to offer the post to Joseph Wood, then Head Master of Tonbridge.[86] Although a successful Head Master of the old-fashioned classical teacher tradition first at Leamington (1870–90), then Tonbridge, Wood was an unusual choice. All previous Heads since Thackeray had been in their thirties or twenties on appointment; Wood was 56, twelve years older than the man he was succeeding (and only nine years younger than Monty Butler). Perhaps the governors felt the responsibility resulting from the school's undoubted status. Welldon had been told by an Old Harrovian Cabinet minister in 1885 that 'the headmastership of Harrow was an office second only to the Premiership in the demands which it necessarily made upon its occupant'.[87] Experience may have seemed at a premium. The governors may have feared a young Head Master would fall victim to the substantial number of powerful senior masters. Bowen, Bosworth-Smith, Bushell, Stogdon, Tosswill, Hallam, Marshall, Gilliat, and Colbeck had each served between twenty-eight and forty years, most retaining considerable energy if only to disrupt. In the event, the plan backfired as Wood was faced with a rapid turnover of staff and consequent loss of stability as these figures retired or died. Still more unfortunate was the sight of a Head Master trying to implement the new policy of enforced retirement for masters at 60 when he himself, appointed at 56, went on to 68. The issue arose almost immediately when Bushell pleaded desperately to be kept on after his due retirement date in the Summer of 1899, even without salary. (He hardly needed the money, as he had already managed to buy Caldy Island when housemaster of Rendalls.) Wood curtly refused: 'I deem it best, and less invidious to enforce impartially and in all cases the retirement of masters at the age of sixty'.[88] This was wholly disingenuous, as he had just asked Bushell's exact contemporary Bosworth-Smith to stay on for two more years and Bowen, who was even older, enjoyed his own special dispensation as a past and future benefactor of the school. Bushell's consolation was to be made honorary (i.e. unpaid) school chaplain which he remained until the year before his death in 1917.[89]

While creating as many problems as it solved, the appointment of Wood suggests an unexpected timidity and lack of confidence. Perhaps the governors agreed with Welldon's self-regarding opinion of 1898 that 'it would take a very strong man to damage Eton and Winchester . . . but a weak man might ruin Harrow', even though in the event that is exactly what they got.[90] Wood's election also revealed a streak of gubernatorial amateurishness in appointing Heads that recurred. Only

---

[85] Newsome, *On the Edge of Paradise*, 55; GBM, 11 Oct., 1 Nov. 1898; C. Alington, *Lionel Ford* (London, 1934), pp. 46–7.   [86] GBM, 1 and 2 Nov. 1898.
[87] Welldon, *Recollections*, 85.   [88] HA HM/Wood/Head Master's Letter Book, fos. 2, 4, 5.
[89] Bushell, *Bushell*, 8–9; Grogan, *Bosworth-Smith*, 100–1.
[90] Newsome, *On the Edge of Paradise*, 55.

after Wood was in office did it emerge that he had not been informed of the full financial terms of his appointment. The governors had omitted to tell Wood that out of his salary of £500 plus £6 capitation on four hundred boys and the profits from his boarders, he was required to pay the governors £800 rent for his boarding house and a fixed charge for each boarder above the agreed quota. As the Governors' Minutes laconically recorded, Wood 'had thus formed an incorrect idea of the amount of the income of the Head Master when he accepted the post'.[91] The governors were hoist with their own ineptitude. Given they could hardly force Wood to take less than he had been led to believe was on offer and retain his services, they were forced to raise the school fees more than twice the intended increase in order to compensate themselves for the loss of income from the Head Master's rent, this at a time when Harrow was already notoriously expensive and numbers were beginning to sag.[92] Such casual attention to salary was not unique; seven decades later, at the culmination of a lengthy selection process, another candidate had to inquire of the Chairman of the governors whether the post being offered him carried any remuneration.

Wood's main virtues were elegant old-fashioned scholarship, good looks, good manners, a large private income, and Holy Orders. He was almost a complete failure.[93] Bad Head Masters usually come in two guises, of commission and omission. Wood was a good example of the latter, his ineffectiveness only countered by an awesome acerbity of epistolary style. His incapacity was soon apparent. On 6 December 1900 the governors passed a resolution stating that the Head Master 'from failure of health or from some other cause, does not take that part in the teaching of the higher forms, in the general administration of the school, and in the superintendance of his own Boarding House which his office requires'. When Wood protested, two months later the governors coldly 'decided to inform the Head Master that they adhere to their resolution'.[94] In 1904 they had another go after considering 'certain allegations affecting the position of the school and the Head Master'.[95] As early as June 1899 Wood had decreed that he only wished the most serious offences to be brought to his attention: the number of floggings declined to an average of forty-four a year, less than half Welldon's rate, even though some of the offences may appear less than heinous: in 1906 one boy was birched for displaying 'a photograph of himself smoking'.[96] Certainly, in retrospect, Wood was accused of a failure of discipline, an inability or disinclination to

---

[91] GBM, 7 Feb. 1899. Cf. ibid., 6 Feb. 1900.
[92] GBM, 9 May 1899. The capitation to the governors had to be raised by £2 15s., which meant the tuition fees charged to the parents had to rise by £5 from £33 9s. to £38 9s.
[93] Laborde draws a veil over Wood's period. Bryant, *Harrow*, 93–5 is more forthcoming, basing much of his account on Mayo, *Reminiscences*, 90–108 which is the fullest published consideration.
[94] GBM, 6 Dec. 1900, 26 Feb. 1901. Cf. GBM, 6 Nov. 1900.   [95] GBM, 16 June 1904.
[96] Minutes of Masters' Meetings, 1893–1910, 13 June 1899; Punishment Book, 19 June 1906 and *passim*.

impose order. The philistine and intimidating rule of the bloods was challenged more effectively by one of his Heads of School, J. R. M. Butler, than by Wood himself.[97] Although at times he could be extremely brusque in requiring parents to remove their sons, he was reluctant to expel boys. In 1899, when Lady Forwood refused to remove her son Eric for 'bullying and maltreating a younger boy', Wood capitulated.[98] There was a want of energy to support his literary bluntness. A younger, more ambitious man might have been more eager to impress, to stamp his mark on the school's regime. Wood was the first Head Master of Harrow for whom the post was a retirement job. He relied heavily on his assistant housemasters at the Head Master's and, probably even more than governors and masters, was disappointed that it proved financially impossible to sever the Head's links with a boarding house altogether. He was no doubt relieved to have Bushell as chaplain, another significant departure from the Victorian tradition. Wood displayed all the symptoms of a man enjoying a possibly unexpected late boost to his standing, if not income, at the end of a worthy but otherwise less than outstanding schoolmaster's career.

None the less, Wood attempted with some success to maintain a high standard of classical scholarship for a chosen elite by creating the so-called Twelve, a small group within the Sixth Form that worked directly under him.[99] In terms of academic success at Oxbridge, this worked well and deflected attention from more general shortcomings in the curriculum and the boys' attainments identified in the annual Oxford and Cambridge Certificate Examiners' reports. However, in general Wood was inimical to educational change, even modest modernization such as that imposed after the 1906 inspection of the school by the university of London: the abandoning of Euclid, the creation of practical maths 'Laboratories' and the ending of the formal Pupil Room lessons in Ovid's *Fasti*.[100] Away from his chosen few pupils, Wood provided no lead. There were fewer Masters' Meetings with less business. Wood opted out of choosing staff. Departments, especially maths and science, were left to their own devices. In 1903 he delegated plenipotentiary authority to George Townsend Warner as 'Head Master of the Modern Side', including control over the timetable and appointments.[101] Other Head Masters openly disdained the mundane aspects of their jobs, not least Edward Lyttleton of Eton (1905–16), but whereas Lyttleton consistently displayed a certain style, at once hearty and elevated, Wood appeared merely to abdicate. It was difficult to know what he was for. At his leaving there were no trumpets sounded or scenes of lingering applause. On the last morning of the Summer Term in July 1910, shortly after

---

[97] This is the clear indication of Lunn, *The Harrovians*, 274–80: Butler is called 'Dale'. Cf. ibid., 254 *et seq.* for Wood. [98] Wood Letter Book, fos. 16, 22.
[99] Larborde, *Harrow School*, 63; *Harrow Register, 1885–1949*, *passim*.
[100] GBM, 6 Feb., 12 June 1906; Mayo, *Reminiscences*, 99–100, 130–2; Laborde, *Harrow School*, 155.
[101] Wood Letter Book, fos. 95–6, 97, 99–100.

Plenitude

the boys had left, he quietly drove off the Hill in his motor car, pausing only to wish goodbye to an aged local resident.[102] The surprise was that he had stayed so long.

Of the Head Masterships begun and completed between 1898 and 1999, Wood's lasted the third longest, of those not cut short by higher preferment or death only bettered by James. He was the oldest on appointment of all Harrow Head Masters, barring the exceptional case of Boissier in 1940, and the oldest on relinquishing the post since Thackeray in 1760. There were perhaps two salient reasons for his retention. At the height of its fame, although not fortune, Harrow could not afford a messy, enforced, or acrimonious resignation of its Head. Wood was a genial enough figure when presiding over the visit of Edward VII in 1905 (his fourth visit after 1864, 1871, and 1894). Harrow's public image was secure. The Rifle Corps won shooting competitions at Bisley.[103] The Cricket XI won as often as it lost at Lord's. Field Marshal Lord Roberts himself laid the foundation stone of the Boer War memorial transepts in the chapel in 1902 in commemoration of the fifty-five Harrovians who had died, about 10 per cent of those who had fought.[104] Just as Wood's weakness showed how the school no longer relied on its Head alone, his remaining in office suggested that even Imperial Harrow could not afford signs of discord.

More than that, the governors had reason to be thankful to Wood for helping in the increasingly urgent quest to save the surroundings of the school from suburban developers. The visit of Edward VII in 1905 was arranged to mark the purchase of 254 acres of the Northwick estate beyond what is now the Watford Road. Despite the fuss over his salary in 1899, in 1903 Wood promised to forgo part of it in order to secure a regular surplus on the precarious School Fund account. From 1906 he underwrote from his salary the annual interest payment of £1,650 that the governors were paying on the loan required to buy the Northwick land.[105] Even allowing for the Head Master's likely income of around £4,000 net, this was an order of generosity to compare with any of the past. The school had reason to be in Wood's debt. In this very traditional way, the power of the Head Master's purse helped secure his position.

Wood's image of the scholarly, slightly other-worldly philanthropist may have been carefully and deliberately designed. His correspondence reveals another side: abrupt, clear, direct to, and beyond rudeness. He did not mince words: in dampening one master's hopes of preferment in 1899 he told the man: 'I . . . must at once and frankly say that I cannot hold out to you any hope whatever of my sanctioning your taking one of the existing Large Houses'.[106] Four years later the same master,

---

[102] Mayo, *Reminiscences*, 108.

[103] For this, and, in general, a sympathetic view of Wood's Harrow see Fox, *Harrow*, 61 and chs. 3 and 4.   [104] Laborde, *Harrow School*, 100–1.

[105] GBM, May 1903, 8 Dec. 1904, 21 Feb. 1905, 6 Feb., 8 May 1906. Cf. ibid., 2 Nov. 1909 when Wood's impending retirement was seen as casting the whole operation of the land purchase scheme in jeopardy. For Edward VII's visit see Laborde, *Harrow School*, 198–200.

[106] Wood Letter Book, fo. 18.

Welsford, who taught maths to the Army Class, was demoted from its second to third division: 'I have constant complaints made to me of [your] teaching. . . . The evidence seems to me to be overwhelming that the boys under you do not make the progress which they ought to make.'[107] E. M. Butler received a similarly unadorned rebuke at his total failure to teach his Third Fourth—'the Greek nursery'—any Greek.[108] During his two years' probation, Wood dismissed P. A. Micklem, an Old Harrovian in Holy Orders: 'I hardly think your best line of work lies in a schoolmaster's profession.'[109] More remarkable was the identical tone he adopted when sacking the mathematician W. N. Roseveare in 1905: 'You are not suited for school work. Your discipline and methods of teaching are alike unsatisfactory.'[110] Roseveare, Sixth Wrangler and a fellow of St John's College, Cambridge, had been teaching at Harrow since 1889. Wood's style embraced a pleasing vein of tactlessness. When informing Lord Aberdeen that his son Dudley would have to leave at Easter 1902 because of the superannuation rule, he added that the boy was also lazy and disorganized.[111] When appointing George Townsend Warner to the Headship of the Modern Side, he noted that the post required 'tact and temper' but continued: 'if you have a fault it is that you do not suffer fools gladly.'[112] It was just such maladroit honesty that lay behind his owning up to preferring a round of golf to the royal Speech Day in 1912.

Wood cuts an improbable figure as Head Master of Harrow. Apparently a relic from the past, yet he knew how to enjoy himself with modern amenities, even if his staff suffered. On 22 January 1908 he wrote to his groom and coachman: 'Dear Peek, I have finally decided to give up horses altogether. I therefore must give you notice that I shall not require your services after a month from today, and that you will have to vacate the cottage on Feb. 22nd. I shall be happy to help you in any way I can to secure another place.'[113] Wood was going into motor cars. Almost without noticing, he, and his school, were entering a new age.

New Issues

Wood's successor Lionel Ford appeared to be cast in an entirely different mould. Well-connected (his mother was one of the ubiquitous Lyttletons), an experienced Head Master with a reputation for discipline, athleticism, and devout Christian faith, a defeated candidate at Harrow in 1898, successful, constructive Head Master of Repton since 1901, apparently energetic, certainly self-confident, Ford had been an obvious choice to succeed Wood. His election proceeded without much difficulty in April/May 1910, the only oddity being the clerk to the governors' passion for obfuscation which led to the actual appointment being omitted from

---

[107] Ibid., fo. 84. [108] Ibid., 15 May 1900. [109] Ibid., fos. 85–6.
[110] Ibid., fo. 118. [111] Ibid., fo. 61. [112] Ibid., fos. 99–100. [113] Ibid., fo. 148.

the Governors' Minutes altogether.[114] Although protesting that he had been reluctant to accept the Harrow offer, only acceding to pressure from the 'dear people' at Repton, he had in fact lobbied for the job, its prominence, and income.[115] In Holy Orders, Ford was 45, conforming to the new pattern of appointments to the Headships of the most prominent public schools. His arrival, according to Archer Vassall, was welcomed by the staff who, in general terms, recognized that the drift under Wood could not continue.[116]

In his speech to his luncheon guests on Speech Day 1912, who included both Butler and Welldon, Ford deliberately argued the case for change. In his first few years he persuaded his colleagues and observers that he was a radical, intent on tearing down and rebuilding the academic, religious, even sporting life of the school. In fact much of what was put in place by Ford followed logically from the changes instituted by Welldon and fresh administrative, financial, and educational circumstances whose origins could be traced back thirty years. For all its heavy patina of nostalgic continuity, compared to 1885 Harrow in 1910 was already a very different place confronting a very different world.

On the surface, the backgrounds of Harrovians 1885–1910 remained constant. Yet although the largest numbers, some 40 per cent to 45 per cent, came from England and Wales outside London and its adjacent counties, among these there was a marked shift towards the south-east, a sign of the commercial pull of London and the spread of commuter railways. Boys with London addresses ranged from just under 20 per cent to nearer 30 per cent in some years (e.g. 28 per cent in 1905). Compared to mid-nineteenth-century Harrow, there was a significant and growing shift towards money rather than land as the basis of Harrovian wealth and an increasingly Home Counties quality. Even the merchants from Merseyside, who had provided a significant number of entrants in the 1880s and early 1890s, more or less disappear by 1910. An obvious change in the nature of Harrow was revealed in the career destinations of leavers. Of those whose future occupations can be discovered, of the 1890 entrants 37 per cent went into the armed services, 17 per cent the law and 23 per cent business, trade, and banking; of the 1900 intake, 25 per cent went to the armed forces, 14 per cent the law and 30 per cent business, trade, and banking; of the 1905 entry the figures, distorted by the 22 per cent killed in the First World War, were respectively 32 per cent, 3 per cent, and 36 per cent.[117] Harrow was ceasing to be an aristocratic school and becoming a cradle of plutocracy.

This was reflected in the fees which, at between £150 and £200, were among the highest of public schools, nearly double some competitors. In 1899 and 1910 the

[114] On Ford, Laborde, *Harrow School*, 63–4; Bryant, *Harrow*, 95–8; Mayo, *Reminiscences*, 168–72, et seq.; Alington, *Ford*, esp. pp. 81–113.
[115] Newsome, *On the Edge of Paradise*, 270. [116] Alington, *Ford*, 93.
[117] Statistics derived from *Harrow Register, 1800–1911* and *Harrow Register, 1885–1949*. Cf. T. W. Bamford, 'Public Schools and Social Class, 1801–50', *British Journal of Sociology*, 12 (1961), 225–33; id., *Rise of Public Schools*, 210, 212, 218–19.

tuition element of the fees was raised, by 15 per cent on each occasion.[118] Boarding was pricey and all additional but often compulsory activities, including music, games, specialist science, workshop were paid for separately. On top of that came uniform and inevitable expenses on clothing and laundry, let alone food to supplement often spartan rations and pocket money. In all senses, Harrow was very expensive. Although affecting to despise materialism, the values of the school became solidly upper middle class.

The context of the school altered conclusively. Physically, Harrow was brought closer to London by the extension of the Metropolitan Line to Harrow-on-the-Hill in 1880 (thereafter providing special trains for the end of term and Speech Day) and the arrival nearby of the Great Central Line (1899) and District Railway (1903). One general consequence was the rapid growth in local population. In 1841 the population of the old parish of Harrow (i.e. stretching from Harrow Weald to Wembley) was 4,627; in 1911 the new, smaller Urban District of Harrow-on-the-Hill contained over 17,000 people.[119] Unfortunately for the governors and the school's income, the new development that swamped the old hamlets of Greenhill and Roxeth did not occur on school property, although a glance at the road names of modern Harrow testifies to the school's prominence. It was even alleged that for generations the school's Head Masters were the only people in the parish who could be licensed as pawnbrokers. On the Hill, urbanization galloped ahead, with new roads (Byron Hill, Middle Road, Peterborough Road) and new housing, artisan on the western slopes, plush middle class down London Road, Sudbury Hill, and South Hill. Even the Hill of the mid-1890s seemed a lost Eden in the eyes of one master thirty years later.[120]

External influences on the school became more bureaucratic. From the 1880s elected local authorities impinged on school affairs, particularly through early planning and health regulations, although the Middlesex and London County Councils and the various borough, rural, and urban district councils were more concerned with the operation and management of the Road Trust and estate.[121] The Charity Commissioners had frequently intervened to regulate the financial management of the school trusts, particularly as the governors began to try to sell trust land in an increasingly desperate attempt to fund the lavish scale to which the school now unavoidably aspired. Yet they presented no public threat, as the negotiations over reform indicated. For many years the Commission was run by the son of a former Harrow Head Master, Longley. However, from 1899 Harrow's affairs came under the scrutiny of the newly constituted Board of Education under a political head. Although lacking the supervisory role over public schools that the Bryce Commission of 1895 had recommended, this new department not only had

---

[118] GBM, 9 May, 8 June 1899 to £38 9s., 24 Oct., 1 Nov. 1910 to £45. Boarding fees varied from £90 to £135 depending on the size of house.   [119] Laborde, *Harrow School*, 18–19.
[120] Mayo, *Reminiscences*, 1–3.   [121] GBM, *passim*, e.g. 18 Feb. 1890, 7 May 1895.

to approve financial dealings of the Trust but had powers to organize school inspections and, after the 1902 Education Act, direct authority to regulate county and borough secondary schools. Harrow's immediate contact with the Board was through submission of annual accounts (which allowed the President of the Board, Walter Runciman, in March 1911 to assure a deputation of the parliamentary Committee of the TUC that Harrow's endowment income was only £1,700 a year) and the inspection of the school it conducted at Ford's request in 1911.[122]

That same year Harrovians sat the consolidated Schools Certificate examinations for the first time, an extension of the existing annual Oxford and Cambridge university certificate examinations.[123] From 1917 Schools Certificates, offered by eight examination boards, were supervised by a national Secondary Schools Examination Council, Harrow sticking to the Oxford and Cambridge Board. Loss of independence was thus combined with a requirement to prepare boys for nationally recognized and validated tests not of the school's devising. By 1938 about 170 Harrovians a year, a third of the school, were sitting School Certificate and Higher School Certificate exams.[124] To a lesser extent, similar constraints were voluntarily embraced by accepting the Common Entrance Examination in 1904. Both developments paralleled a widening of the formal curriculum and an inevitable diminution of the local particularism of the Harrow curriculum, a trend which led by the end of the century to the acceptance of a National Curriculum. Whereas in the mid-nineteenth century, teachers such as Farrar or Bowen could fashion their own educational reforms and Welldon could construct his own syllabus as well as timetable, a century later the desire of parents to see their sons acquire the same qualifications as their fellow citizens, only better, left most innovations in the curriculum to national examination boards and governments. As much as anything, the move towards standard examinations and curriculum marked the end of the golden age of public schools as empires unto themselves. The consequence of these apparently merely administrative changes was in the long term to create the bifurcation, some would say paradox, of the modern public school, at once lauding independence while increasingly reliant for its reputation on its relative position within a national system of examinations and in comparison with state-funded secondary education. Unlike Eton, which resisted government inspection until 1938,[125] or Winchester and Westminster that retained their own Entrance Examinations for at least some applicants, Harrow was always willing to accept, or insufficiently self-confident to reject, enforced uniformity and comparability. While

---

[122] GBM, 9 May, 15 June, 7 Nov. 1911, 30 Apr. 1912; Laborde, *Harrow School*, 63; Mayo, *Reminiscences*, 207; *TUC Ninth Quarterly Report*, June 1911, p. 30 (I am grateful to Dr Janet Howarth for this reference). [123] Alington, *Ford*, 101.
[124] HM/Vellacott/31 Jan. 1938, Bursar's Memorandum on Fees: the fee for taking Certificate exams. was £2 5s. The total thus spent on it a year was c.£350.
[125] Mack, *Public Schools and British Opinion since 1860*, 430.

retaining the trappings of eccentric grandeur and ersatz tradition, the education offered became increasingly less distinctive. Harrow's usually flexible, sympathetic, or realistic reaction to this process provides yet another indication that its nature was more akin to those of Shrewsbury and Rugby than to the great collegiate schools.

New Learning

The first task presented to Welldon was the construction of a new academic syllabus. His instructions from the governors had been to investigate specialization, postponement of starting Greek and Latin verse, and the arrangements for maths and science.[126] The issues were not merely academic, as Welldon saw. Given the salary structure, pupil room system, and limited resources available to the governors, 'educational questions, as touching vested interests, are apt to merge themselves in finance'. 'To ask for Extra masters is impossible when the school fund is already taxed to the utmost. To diminish the incomes of the present Masters is to create a sense of insecurity and perhaps of injustice'.[127] The reforms intended to equip Harrovians with a broader academic education. Some have argued that this was forced on the school by the requirements of the examinations for the Home and Indian Civil Services and the Armed Forces.[128] This cannot be entirely true as relatively few Harrovians tried for the former and the latter, despite Welldon's overhaul of the Army Class, still required boys to attend specialist crammers. Welldon's motives appear less crudely utilitarian. He argued that Greek 'cannot properly be taught to all boys', its retention being largely due to the requirements of the universities, although Latin 'will always be a necessary subject'. Science, as an alternative major component of the curriculum, was not suited 'to the needs of the many' but 'the general ignorance of scientific facts is a blot upon liberal education'.[129] His promotion of Art, long before it became fashionable elsewhere, the appointment of W. E. Hine as Art master in 1892, and the building of an Art School in 1896, suggest Welldon was moved by principle and personal taste.

The political battle was carefully waged. Welldon warned the governors his proposals would take a year. He consulted widely amongst other Heads, Wilson of Clifton proving especially helpful. Within the school, he canvassed views, paying especial tribute to the veteran Watson, the leading mathematician, Bushell, and the ambitious young Balliol classicist and Bursar, M. G. Glazebrook, soon to be High Master of Manchester Grammar School (1888) and Head Master of Clifton (1891). By contrast, Bowen and Bosworth-Smith were obstructive. After a series of 'very full and frank' meetings the masters approved the new draft timetable

---

[126] HM/We/Report of the Head Master on Studies, 30 Oct. 1886, p. 1.   [127] Ibid., 2.
[128] e.g. Laborde, *Harrow School*, 60.   [129] HM/We/Report on Studies, 7–8, 9, 10.

by a 'large majority'. Welldon's final report was presented to the governors in November 1886 and approved in February 1887 for implementation from 1888.[130]

Welldon's reforms marked a decisive break with the traditional, exclusive, classical curriculum of Greek and Latin verse and rigid form-based teaching for all subjects. For the first time entry was restricted to boys no older than 14 (Welldon himself preferring admission at 13), the 1880s average being nearer $14\frac{1}{2}$, although in one famous later case at least a blind eye was shown to infringement of the rule: in 1905 Jawaharlal Nehru joined the school aged 15.[131] The school was divided into three blocks of forms A (VIth and Vth), B (Remove and Shells), and C (IVth and Army Class). The distinction was retained between the Classical and Modern Sides, one centred on Classical the other modern languages. Some science and modern languages as well as maths were now taught on the Classical Side where English history was added as a form subject. The Modern Side was to contain no more than a third of the school, but access to it was extended to the Shells. In 1893 Bowen, in a fury at his ideas being ignored, resigned as Head of the Modern Side at what he saw as Welldon's mendacity. Bowen had always insisted that entry to the Modern Side should not be a refuge for failed classicists. Welldon dispensed with this but pretended otherwise. Although reactionary in some matters, Bowen would also have noticed that Welldon's changes failed to live up to their own logic, which indicated an integrated curriculum with divisions according to ability throughout, a scheme Bowen himself advocated.[132] As it was, on both Classical and Modern Sides, there was only a modest extension of divisionalization, in French and science in the A Block. None the less, even this was a significant development on which Ford's later reforms built.

Elsewhere, sacred cows were being slaughtered. Greek was no longer an entry requirement, Harrovians now being able to begin it from scratch. There was a move towards a common broad curriculum with Latin, French, English, divinity, maths, and science, in various combinations, treated as core subjects for all boys in the first years. While botany and chemistry (which in practice subsumed elements of physics) formed the initial basis for science, by his retirement Welldon had added biology.[133] The introduction of compulsory science, modern languages, and English history on the Classical Side in B Block breached the defences of the purists. For the first time English literature was taught as a subject in its own right, defended by one of Welldon's protégés, the classicist E. C. E. Owen in 1906 as of parallel importance to classics.[134] Through two more Welldon appointments, Townsend Warner and Somervell, Harrow soon led the field in the systematic

---

[130] HM/WE/Report on Studies, *passim*; GBM, 30 Nov. 1886, 1 Feb. 1887; Head Master's Book, 1893–1910, fos. 21, 133.

[131] Head Master's Book, 1893–1910, fos. 1, 21; HM/We/Report on Studies, 18; Jawaharlal Nehru, *An Autobiography* (Oxford, 1989), p. 17.   [132] Bowen, *Bowen*, 111–16.

[133] GBM, 9 and 27 June 1898; *The Harrovian*, 17 Dec. 1898, p. 106.

[134] Mack, *Public Schools and British Opinion since 1860*, 239.

teaching of English language. Unlike his predecessors, Welldon showed himself flexible, alert to different needs: in 1893 he allowed G. M. Trevelyan to substitute a history essay for Greek verse for Saturday evening prep.[135] More generally, he introduced specialization in the A Block for a few hours a week, in classics, maths, history, geography, science, and modern languages. This presented the additional benefit of allowing junior masters with low forms to teach in the Upper School, lending the work, Welldon hoped, 'greater intellectual attractiveness to University men'.[136] Welldon abolished the seniority rule for appointing formmasters. Drawing and singing were added as options in the IVth forms and gymnastics was introduced for the Shells. The Army Classes were reorganized, probably as a result of parental pressure to reduce the need to spend money on crammers (although they still did). Boys destined for the Army remained technically with their ordinary forms but received additional lessons in subjects of particular relevance for the Army entrance exams, such as arithmetic, algebra, geometrical drawing, geography, and French.[137] Initially run by Colbeck and Welsford, from 1890 the Army Class was placed under L. M. Moriarty, who had come to Harrow the year before from the chair of French Literature at King's College, London (a move testifying to the relative financial rather than academic inducements of the two institutions). The Army Class added greatly to the diversity of academic activity but at the same time condemned its members to lowly status, as their extra Army Class work made it almost impossible for them to shine in their notional forms. Thus Winston Churchill, who joined the Army Class in 1889, never rose beyond the Lower School before he left in 1892 even though he won prizes.

The increase in subjects and options inevitably altered the structure and nature of school life. There were more school periods and the amount of time allocated to the increasingly fatuous pupil room reduced. More radically, lessons became occasions where boys were actually taught. To assist this, First School was reduced by a quarter of an hour. Masters were required to teach. Some were excellent, such as Townsend Warner in history and English; Somervell in English language; Gilson in classics; Vassall in science. A richer academic atmosphere than previously is suggested by E. C. Richardson's diary for the first term of 1889, when he was in Bowen's Modern Upper Fifth. He had French with A. J. Duhamel, a new, talented teacher from France who, with his colleague B. J. Minssen, were described as 'pioneers in a revolution' of teaching colloquial French; German with W. G. Guillemard; Roman history with E. H. Kempson, future Principal of King William's College, Isle of Man; as well as Latin, history, and English with Bowen. Bushell taught him astronomy, an interest he pursued by visiting a local observatory; Lascelles provided private lessons in chemistry, including practicals: when he failed to turn up

---

[135] Moorman, *Trevelyan*, 23. [136] HM/We/Report on Studies, 17.
[137] For one pupil's experience of the Army Class see R. S. Churchill, *Winston S. Churchill*, i (London, 1966), pp. 126, *et seq.* Cf. Head Master's Book, 1893–1910, fo. 2; GBM, 30 Nov. 1886.

Richardson whiled away the time glass-blowing.[138] This was another world compared with that of twenty years earlier.

Of course, sport retained its grip on time and emotions, Welldon being a keen supporter, believing success at games 'one of the great passports to the success of the school'.[139] Here, Welldon was very fortunate. Two of perhaps the greatest, certainly the best known international sportsmen Harrow ever produced were F. S. Jackson (1884–9) and A. C. MacLaren (1886–90), both long-standing members of the cricket eleven, captain in their final years, university blues, Test cricketers, and captains of England. In 1905 Jackson, later a soldier, Indian pro-consul, influential Conservative, and governor of the school, was possibly the most successful captain of all time: he won the toss on every occasion, headed both bowling and batting averages, and won the rubber against Australia. Yet Welldon's Harrow, while not changing boys' cultural attitudes that dictated that work was to be avoided or despised, placed a new emphasis on matters academic and intellectual that affected boys at all levels of the school.

That is not to say Welldon's changes transformed the scholastic standards of the school. In 1890 Welldon admitted that, in contrast to the equipment, science teaching was unsatisfactory. Griffith was past it and Lascelles increasingly bored, preferring his work as Vaughan's Librarian.[140] After Griffith's retirement in 1893 matters were improved with the appointment of C. E. Ashford in 1894, later Head Master of the Royal Naval Colleges of Osborne (1903–5) and Dartmouth (1905–19), and, in 1896 F. E. Allhusen and A. Vassall, the latter being paid by the Head Master until 1899. However, in 1895 the Oxford and Cambridge Certificate examiners reported on the poor performances in Scripture, Roman and English history, and natural science. Such criticisms were repeated in 1897, the governors asking Welldon to explain 'the apparent low level of work and ineffectiveness of much of the teaching which it discloses'.[141] As with all schools and with Harrow in all periods, educational reform risked foundering on the incompetence or intransigence of masters. Bosworth-Smith, on whom Welldon had pinned some hopes for specialist history teaching, simply took no notice of the changes. Some called him 'a chartered libertine'; the Head Master might have thought a broken reed a more apt image.[142] Bowen's flouncing out of managing the Modern Side concealed a decline in power: boys began to notice that the questions he asked in history were all coming from the textbook. Hayward, an FRS in 1876, appeared senile, smugly inept in the formroom. Bushell, while admired by junior maths masters, cut an increasingly decrepit and distant figure. Welldon had recognized the problem in his 1886 curriculum proposals when he commented on the inadequacies of Ruault

---

[138] E. C. Richardson, 'Diary', *passim*; Mayo, *Reminiscences*, 109–18 for French, but cf. the rather different impression left on Nehru: *Autobiography*, 18.
[139] E. D. W. Chaplin, *The Book of Harrow* (London, n.d.), p. 51. Cf. Welldon, *Recollections*, 97–8.
[140] GBM, 29 Apr. 1890; Mayo, *Reminiscences*, 32–3.   [141] GBM, 5 Nov. 1895, 2 Nov. 1897.
[142] HM/We/Report on Studies, 13; Grogan, *Bosworth-Smith*, 117–18.

and Masson in French, Griffith in science, and Hayward in maths. His solution was the retirement and pension schemes and effective recruitment.[143]

If a Head Master is as good as the staff he appoints, Welldon must rate highly. The historians Townsend Warner and Somervell, who had turned to academic work and teaching late in life after a decade in business;[144] the classicists N. K. Stephen (1888–1925) and R. C. Gilson (1890–1900, thereafter Head Master of King Edward's Birmingham); and the scientist Vassall were of exceptional calibre. G. M. Trevelyan (1889–93) thought his teachers excellent, especially grateful to Gilson and Egerton Hine the Art master as well as Townsend Warner and Somervell: 'I was better taught in history than any other schoolboy then in England . . . the adaptation to school teaching of modern methods of studying history owes much to Harrow experiment at that period.'[145] Some of the less outstanding appointments were nevertheless above average. E. C. E. Owen (1886–1918) was a conscientious and popular classicist. F. C. Searle (1887–1904), a saintly mathematician who acted as Welldon's housemaster in the Head Master's, impressed many, although his ostentatious piety was not for everyone. His death after less than a year as housemaster of Moretons in 1904 was greeted with terse but unalloyed, undisguised pleasure by his Head of House.[146] Duhamel and Minssen reinvigorated the teaching of French, as well as importing their own claret by the barrel.[147] Moriarty was shrewdly effective with the Army Class. Even when confronted with appalling teaching conditions, some of the young masters worked hard to teach and enthuse their pupils. C. H. P. Mayo (1893–1919) taught in the turret of Speech Room, approached only by a ladder and trap door, dark, airless, cramped, with desks actually pointing away from the teacher. None the less, he seems to have made a genuine effort to impart some mathematical basics into the likes of Churchill.[148]

However, the problem of low academic standards remained. The Oxford and Cambridge examiners were again damning in 1900.[149] Trevelyan's and Churchill's very different contemporary experiences suggested that for the industrious scholar, academic standards could be exceptionally high while the culture of sport, idleness, and philistinism could stunt the intellectual ambitions of the less obviously talented. Although for ever grateful to Robert Somervell for his then idiosyncratic teaching of the structure of the English language (on which Townsend Warner later wrote a popular textbook), Churchill underachieved academically, although finding considerable compensation in becoming public schools' fencing

---

[143] See the Twiss and Richardson Diaries, *passim* (Richardson, 'Diary', 25 Jan. 1889 for Bowen's history questions); Meinertzhagen, *Diary*, 178–80, 184–7; HM/We/Report of Studies, 18; Mayo. *Reminiscences*, 12–13.   [144] R. Somervell, *Chapters of Autobiography* (London, 1935), pp. 1–85.

[145] Moorman, *Trevelyan*, 23–4; Somervell, *Autobiography*, 104.

[146] As recorded in the Moretons Head of House's Book, 1904.

[147] Mayo, *Reminiscences*, 117 for the claret.

[148] For a drawing of this room see Mayo, *Reminiscences*, 7 and cf. ibid., 5–9, 45–6.

[149] GBM, 6 Nov. 1900.

champion.¹⁵⁰ The difficulty for educational reformists lay not just in the lumpen indifference of pupils but in the priorities of some of the staff.

Change once initiated can prove unstoppable. Welldon's reforms only began a process of amending and integrating the whole curriculum. The old order was swept away piecemeal. Although Wood's creation of the elite Classical Twelve was irrelevant for the majority, the Inspection of 1906 caused the abolition of Euclid in maths and Ovid's *Fasti*. It also coincided with the new mathematics laboratory in the Copse under the management of A. W. Siddons (1899–1936; 1943–6) viewed with abiding distaste by the traditionalists such as Mayo.¹⁵¹ The Inspection of 1911 paved the way for the completion of Welldon's work by Ford and the burial of the remains of the traditional educational system. In 1913 the pupil-room, the central feature of the *ancien régime*, was finally abolished, its former significance lingering tenaciously only in name: forty years later one room in the Knoll was still known as 'Pupe'.¹⁵² At the same time Ford introduced more lessons, clearing the mornings for academic work. Forms were to be of equal size, twenty-five, in the Middle and Lower Schools. Learning Greek could be deferred until the second year. Divisions were extended to modern languages, now including Spanish as well as French and German, and science throughout the school. In place of a monolithic uniformity, Ford established a Babel of options in the Sixth Form, including economics for the first time. In 1917 Bowen's dream of an integrated timetable was achieved by the abolition of the distinction between the Classical and Modern Sides. The logical conclusion to Ford's changes, and to an extent to those begun by Welldon, was the establishment between 1920 and 1925 of specialist Upper School forms in classics, history, maths, modern languages, and science, the subsidiary optional subjects being taught in divisions. The transformation of the Victorian syllabus was total and complete.

Ford's innovations were not uncontested. He was criticized for failing to protect classics, especially Greek, although the abandoning by Oxford and Cambridge of the universal Greek entry requirement after the First World War played its part in its apparent decline. Mayo claimed that in 1918 only six boys were doing Greek. The plethora of options aroused much complaint, Ford being accused of being 'too ready to follow new and fashionable gods'.¹⁵³ Harrow fancied itself as a bastion of tradition: Ford seemed to be pandering to modernity. In fact, his structural changes, the abolition of the pupil-room, the integration of the curriculum, and

---

¹⁵⁰ Churchill, *Churchill*, i. 110–85 where Winston's *My Early Life* is exposed as an inaccurate romanticized version of events; Townsend Warner's *On the Writing of English* was published in 1914.

¹⁵¹ Laborde, *Harrow School*, 155; Mayo, *Reminiscences*, 130–4.

¹⁵² GBM, 9 May, 15 June, 7 Nov. 1911, 30 Mar. 1912. See, in general, Alington, *Ford*, 84, 93, 101–3; Laborde, *Harrow School*, 63–4; Bryant, *Harrow*, 95–6; Mayo, *Reminiscences*, 168, 207–8; I am grateful to J. P. Lemmon (The Knoll 1949–54) for local information.

¹⁵³ Mayo, *Reminiscences*, 208; Alington, *Ford*, 84. On the wider decline of classics see Stray, *The Living Word*, 28–34; id., *Classics Transformed*, 270 and *passim*.

the creation of specialist Sixth Forms put Harrow only very slightly ahead of some competitors and behind others. As one observer shrewdly put it at the start of Ford's reforms: 'We're moving with the times. In fact, we're trying to forestall the times.'[154]

Ford was no eccentric or radical. He was no Sanderson of Oundle. His new timetable and curriculum became the standard conventional model for all public and grammar schools, at Harrow lasting in essence unchanged for much of the rest of the century. His problem was that his changes were superficial as regards the intellectual life of the school and opposed by many of his staff. The collapse of classics was temporary but suggested to some a lack of effort or attention. By 1930, not least because of the arrival in 1925 of one of the most effective public school classics masters of the century, E. V. C. Plumptre, classics revived. Ford was evidently a difficult man to work for and became the butt of inevitable anxieties among the masters when faced with a rapidly changing world. Much of the hostility to Ford's new timetables had more to do with devastating war and unsettling peace than the nuances of lesson times or choice of optional subjects. None the less, Ford's draconian changes were pursued by him with an apparent lack of human sympathy, as if men and boys were made for the timetable not vice versa. Although wholly ignorant of it, E. M. Venables, an indifferent Arts man, was required to teach maths in the Upper School. In 1924 a relatively new master, R. M. Baldwin (1922–57), a Balliol historian, wrote to Ford to complain about his timetable for the following academic year that comprised mainly teaching French and Latin. If this were to continue, Baldwin remarked icily, 'I cannot help feeling that the privilege of serving you . . . will have been somewhat dearly bought'. He concluded in even chillier vein: 'We feel the Timetable tends to become a piece of machinery to which the human element . . . is liable at any moment to be sacrificed.'[155] Such, perhaps, was the inescapable price for an educational revolution that stradled the public school world and transformed the experience of being and teaching at Harrow.

The Public School Profession

The wider curriculum and more systematic examination structure was parallelled by a growth in the perception of schoolteaching as a profession. Public schoolmasters in general, and Bowen in particular when giving evidence to the Bryce Commission on Secondary Education in 1894–5, rejected the idea of teacher training, external control, and national examinations.[156] Few, if any at schools such as

---

[154] Lunn, *The Harrovians*, 309: the speaker in 1912/13 was, ironically, 'Mr Ingolsby', i.e. Mayo.
[155] HA Head Masters' Files on Masters, 1903–71, R. M. Baldwin to Lionel Ford, 2 July 1924; E. M. Venables, *Bases Attempted* (typescript, priv. circulated, n.d.), p. 16.
[156] Bowen, *Bowen*, 235–8. See, in general, Honey, *Tom Brown's Universe*, 296–342.

Harrow, joined the Assistant Masters' Association, founded in the 1890s (incorporated 1901), let alone a trade union. Rather, teaching was a matter of character not technique, its organization—like its profits—personal. Professional *esprit de corps* was fostered by personal contacts and informal groups, such as the United Ushers, founded by Bowen and Browning of Eton in the 1870s or the bizarrely religious annual meetings of 'Dons and Beaks'. Freemasonry played a part in identifying group interest and professional solidarity. Above all, individuals contributed to a new respect that Assistant Masters enjoyed by 1900 in comparison to the reputation of seedy, sadistic, or merely sad ushers of half a century earlier. In particular, the image of teaching was transformed by those, like William Johnson Cory at Eton or Farrar and Bowen at Harrow, who deliberately transcended the merely instructional. Pastoral schoolmasters did indeed have to rely on character not just brain and cane, with all the attendant risks. If successful, they also demanded devotion from pupils and respect of parents and old boys. Bowen freely described teaching at a public school as a profession with a confidence and justice inconceivable and unintelligible to a Harry or even Ben Drury, let alone his one-time colleague William Oxenham.[157]

This informal creation of a respected and self-conscious profession depended on personal influence and contacts away from clubs however informal. The symbiosis between Assistant as well as Head Masters at Harrow and Eton was vital to the self-respect of the former earlier in the century. The explosion of the number of public schools instead of creating separate systems encouraged colonization and exchange. Harrow governors regularly sought information from similar schools and the government legislation in the 1860s emphasized a communal identity. Most influential were individual connections as in the Arnoldian network. In the following generation, Imperial Harrow played a prominent role. Counting Sam Parr, up to 1869 only seven Harrow Assistant Masters had proceeded to Headships elsewhere, six between 1834 and 1869, including Pears to Repton in 1854 and Bradby to Haileybury in 1867. From 1870 to 1912 twelve left for public school Headships (while only eight during the same period arrived at Harrow with teaching experience elsewhere).[158] This alone bound Harrow within the public school community at least as firmly as membership of the Head Masters' Conference. This had been founded in 1869 in response to the perceived threat to the non-Clarendon public or 'Endowed' schools contained in the Endowed Schools Act of that year but was quickly taken over by the great schools, providing a conduit for information and concerted lobbying. At any one time there would be groups of

---

[157] Bowen, *Bowen*, 235: 'I have often thought that the craving for influence, especially for spiritual influence, is one of the chief "temptations", "snares" of our profession.'

[158] To Marlborough; Sherborne; Radley; Haileybury; Sedbergh; King's Canterbury; Manchester Grammar; King William's, Isle of Man; King Edward's, Birmingham; Glenalmond; RN College, Osborne; Newcastle Grammar; the eight came from Marlborough (two), Westminster, Rugby, Haileybury (two), Dulwich, Clifton.

HMC Heads who had previously worked as colleagues at schools such as Eton and Harrow. In 1870 Haileybury, Marlborough, and Radley were led by former assistants of Butler of Harrow. In 1891 the Heads of Sherborne, Sedbergh, King's Canterbury, and Clifton were all former Harrow masters.[159] Not the least feature of Imperial Harrow was as a training ground for Headmasters, remarkably as assistant masters' incomes on the Hill were so high and their social cachet elevated. The Harrow influence did not necessarily take the form of Harrovianization of other schools, although Young introduced songs to Sherborne.[160] The significance of such transfers lay in the demonstration of a communal bond and shared experiences that began when the future Heads were at their own public or even prep schools and continued at university and beyond. Just under half of all the masters appointed at Harrow 1801–99 had been educated at one of the Clarendon schools (only 14 per cent at Harrow itself) with a further 14 per cent from other public schools. Thus, in contrast to Eton where for much of the century the number of OE masters was nearer 75 per cent,[161] Harrow embodied and refreshed the wider public school community. By offering large incomes and aristocratic pupils, posts on the Hill were highly desirable. Through recruitment and exchange Harrow assumed a leading position among HMC schools which has never entirely been eroded.

The construction of this network enhanced public schools' exclusivity. Only 16 per cent of nineteenth-century Harrow masters had been educated at grammar schools. The appointment of Wood was not the least remarkable for his being an old boy of Manchester Grammar School, apart from George Butler, educated at his father's school in Chelsea, the first non-Clarendon school educated Head Master of Harrow since Cox in 1746, whose schooling is unknown. Wood's five immediate predecessors had attended Westminster, Winchester, Rugby, Harrow, and Eton. The circulation of men with similar backgrounds and assumptions reinforced the tendency to complacent self-regard for the exclusive superiority of the public school which could be very narrowly defined. It is alleged that sometime in the 1870s, in reply to a request from nonconformist Mill Hill for a games match, itself a potent mechanism of communal identity, Harrow sent a postcard: 'Eton we know, and Rugby we know, but who are ye?'.[162]

None the less, for all their hauteur most Harrow masters were forced to fight some professional battles identical to those waged by their despised colleagues in state-aided secondary schools over tenure, superannuation, and pensions. The new direct relationship with the governors since 1874 scarcely helped their cause, the governors' attitude to the relative importance of masters being exposed unexpectedly in 1894 when they refused permission for relatives to erect a memorial

---

[159] Ibid.   [160] Honey, *Tom Brown's Universe*, 139.
[161] Bamford, *Rise of Public Schools*, 121.
[162] Honey, *Tom Brown's Universe*, 285. See, in general, for the public school community, ibid., 238–95.

tablet in Chapel for W. J. Bull, a master from 1853 to 1888, while at the same time allowing one for an Old Harrovian fallen for the Empire.[163] The governors were prepared to afford masters neither independent status regarding the Head nor access to gubernatorial largesse. The governors suspected there were too many masters costing too much (in fact they cost *c.*60 per cent of the expenditure from the school fund, a figure that remained impressively constant over the next century).[164] Despite their personal wealth, Harrow masters did not possess legal tenure, although in practice almost nobody was sacked. During the interminable wrangling over sanitary inspections that rumbled acrimoniously into the mid-1890s, the threat of withdrawal of permission to accommodate boys could be held over the heads of housemasters with little redress except obfuscation, obstinacy, and obstruction. The new Statutes and Regulations of 1874 had deliberately excluded any protection against summary dismissal. However, Welldon and the governors recognized that unless conditions of service were agreed Harrow could easily become a stumbling gerontocracy. Superannuation for masters had first been discussed in the 1870s. In 1887 Welldon introduced a retirement age of 60 and a pension scheme by way of compensation, the financial arrangements, management, and scales of contributions by masters and governors finally agreed in 1889.[165] There were difficult confrontations with Hayward, Hutton, and Watson, all of them over 60, with over a century of service between them, who sought in vain for additional pensions beyond these arrangements. The refusal, by a majority vote, to make Hutton any ex gratia payment in 1890 marked a sour end to a career at Harrow as boy (1844–7) and master (1855–90), but not a unique one as the Harrow Masters' Pension Fund regularly failed to provide adequately over the century of its existence.[166] Inevitably the most difficulty was caused by Bowen. One source of funding for the scheme had come from the payments of £150 a year extra to the four senior masters being transferred into the pension fund to secure them a pension. Bowen, one of the four since 1888, because he decided to remain outside the scheme, insisted on receiving the additional £150, even though financially he did not need it. He kept up his usual mixture of guerrilla tactics and sharp practice for two years until in 1891 he won his money but not his point of principle.[167]

Bowen, however, was both *sui generis* and the last in a tradition of almost provocative independence. His sudden death on a bicycling tour of France on Easter Monday 1901 marked a period in the school's history, coinciding as it did with the retirements of Bosworth-Smith, Gilliat, and Tosswill, two years after the departure of Bushell from teaching and two years before the death of Colbeck and

[163] GBM, 17 Apr. 1894; Bull finally received one in 1903: GBM, 3 Nov. 1903.
[164] GBM, 25 Apr., 29 June, 7 Nov. 1893, 6 Nov. 1894, 5 Nov. 1907, 3 Nov. 1908, etc.
[165] GBM, 27 May 1875, 1 Feb., 23 June, 1 and 29 Nov. 1887, 7 Feb., 28 June, 6 Nov., 11 Dec. 1888, 5 and 26 Feb., 14 May, 5 Nov. 1889. For the Pension Fund accounts see Head Master's Book, 1874–92, fo. 81.   [166] GBM, 15 July 1890. Cf. GBM, 18 Feb., 29 Apr., 26 June 1890.
[167] GBM, 5 Nov. 1889, 4 Feb., 1 and 29 Apr., 26 June 1890, 3 Feb., 21 Apr., 3 Nov. 1891.

departure of Stogdon: with Bowen these had served a total of 240 years. Already, the erosion of masters', especially housemasters' autonomy had begun. The phyrric victory of the governors in 1894 over sanitary inspections was the last conflict of the old order.[168] Despite a titanic and often acrimonious struggle, the housemasters, led by Bowen and Marshall, failed to prevent the introduction of a new Entance Scholarship scheme in 1897–8 or reduce the Head Master's discretion over placing scholars.[169] The fissiparous nature of the Harrow staff began to be reduced. In 1894 there were proposals for a masters' Common Room which would have signalled a radical departure from masters' traditional detachment, again in contrast to the new campus Victorian public schools. (It was characteristic of the order of priorities that, although nothing came of this idea for masters, the monitors were provided with a common room by Welldon in 1895.)[170] In 1904 it was proposed to use the residential side of the Copse for accommodating bachelor masters as the availability and cost of property on the Hill was beginning to become prohibitive for new, young teachers, although it was only after 1918 that the policy of housing staff where possible in school accommodation was systematically instituted.[171] Greater control over the terms of appointment began to be exercised. Under Wood masters were appointed on probation, usually of two years, without guaranteed seniority, promise of pupil room, or of house.[172] As the curriculum expanded and became more diverse and flexible, the old rigidity of allocating forms by seniority crumbled, but in the process master's inadequacies became more palpable, their positions more vulnerable.

The Battle for the Houses

The status and condition of the boarding houses became urgent. The protracted dispute over sanitation between 1881 and 1894 touched on crucial issues of housemasters' autonomy; the houses' adequacy and safety; and their ownership. Improved medical provision, hygiene standards, and the introduction of electric lighting (to Newlands 1889, other houses and school buildings 1896–98) could not be left to piecemeal arrangements. The sanatorium, opened in 1867, was extended in the early 1890s and a new one proposed in 1903, although nothing came of this for another quarter century.[173] There was a concerted but contentious attempt by Welldon to impose a single school doctor on housemasters, a policy Wood

---

[168] For the protracted sanitation row see GBM, *passim*, esp. 28 July 1892, 6 Mar. 1894; Head Master's Book 1874–92, fo. 91.

[169] GBM, 7 Nov. 1893, 25 June 1896, 2 Feb., 11 May, 12 and 22 July, 2 Nov. 1897, 1 Nov. 1898; Minutes of Masters' Meetings, 1893–1910, 8 Mar., 7 and 14 June, 1 Nov. 1897; HM/We 26 May 1897, Welldon to Masters. [170] GBM, 6 Feb., 17 Apr., 28 June, 6 Nov. 1894, 5 Feb. 1895.

[171] GBM, 9 June 1904. [172] Wood Letter Book, fos. 3, 12, 13, 38, 85–6, etc.

[173] GBM from 5 Nov. 1889 to 3 Mar. 1896, 3 Nov. 1903; Laborde, *Harrow School*, 207–8.

endeavoured to maintain against vigorous opposition.[174] Welldon was unhappy with the accommodation provided at most houses. Perhaps bearing his Eton childhood in mind, he strongly advocated the creation of more single bedroom/studies in each house. Bowen had remodelled the Grove to allow almost all boys to have singles in the 1880s, but Welldon, who hoped to build up to fifty singles for the Head Master's, more or less made it a condition of appointment that new housemasters follow suit, as did even well-established housemasters such as Stogdon at West Acre in 1895.[175] Increased numbers and inertia limited the extent of the reform (to about twenty rooms) and at a time of financial weakness this policy threatened to stretch resources beyond breaking. None the less, Welldon's determination was decisive in confirming what remained one of Harrow's most distinctive features, its lack of dormitories.

The school was bursting with boarders. The 600 mark was reached in 1890 and bettered for all but the last months of Welldon's rule, reaching a peak of 636 in the Summer of 1896.[176] To pursue a consistent policy across the school required extensive renovations to existing buildings, therefore money, and the consent and cooperation of the owners of the houses, not necessarily the housemasters who were often tenants. The case of the boarding house in High Street highlighted the problem. In 1890 'Vanity' Watson was about to retire after twenty-two years as housemaster there. He was a tenant of the Dr E. H. Bradby who had bought the two parts of the house in 1853 and 1863 before leaving for the Headship of Haileybury in 1867. Already in 1888 Bradby toyed with selling the house and two years later had insisted on being reimbursed for the money spent on new drains in consequence of the enforced governors' sanitary inspection. In July 1890 he was informed that in its present state the house would be closed to boarders after Watson retired the following year, a circumstance which would have certainly reduced the property's rental value. However, if Bradby were willing to renovate the house and install an adequate number of single rooms, the governors would cover half the cost and retain the house for boarders. Bradby refused to cooperate so the governors decided to close the house and accepted the offer of H. O. D. Davidson to build another Large House elsewhere. After temporarily occupying the High Street site, Davidson opened his new house at Elmfield in 1893, leaving the High Street house as a Small House.[177] Thus the future of the school lay in the hands of absent landlords and the entrepreneurial ambitions of assistant masters.

This increasingly inconvenient situation suggested one obvious but immediately unattainable solution: the school should itself buy the boarding houses. The

[174] Wood Letter Book, *passim*.
[175] GBM, 15 July 1890, 27 June, 3 Nov. 1895; *The Harrovian*, 17 Dec. 1898, p. 106; Laborde, *Harrow School*, 60.
[176] See printed Bill Books and the regular return of numbers to the governors: GBM, *passim*.
[177] GBM, 6 Nov. 1888, 15 July, 4 and 25 Nov. 1890, 3 Feb., 25 June 1891; Laborde, *Harrow School*, 188. For the fire that delayed occupation of Elmfield see Mayo, *Reminiscences*, 4.

problem was that it did not possess the funds to do so: when offered Garlands by R. B. Hayward (then housemaster of the Park) in 1887 for £4,000, the governors were forced to decline, as they were, more seriously, the offer from the Batten family to sell them the Grove in 1896. The £2,000 mortgage for the purchase of the south wing of the Head Master's from Butler in 1885 alone took almost thirty years to pay off.[178]

None the less, through the agency of the Harrow Park Trust, a beginning was made. The Trust had been established in 1885 to buy the Park for £16,000. It was funded by offering fixed-return shares (at 4 per cent) to investors, mainly Old Harrovians, to create capital to effect purchases, the repayments to investors depending on the profits of managing the estates, namely the rent from the Park. To provide more income as well as to cater for the increasing school numbers and the demand for greater comfort, in 1889 Newlands was opened on Trust property under F. E. Marshall.[179] Although the Chairman of the Trust was Spencer Gore, who also served as the governor's land agent 1893–1902 (first winner of the Wimbledon Lawn Tennis Championship in 1877, author of the song *Jerry* in 1885, and a declared bankrupt in 1907),[180] the key figure was Charles Colbeck, from 1890 housemaster of Moretons, secretary of the Trust. When Bradby's house and Druries were thought to be for sale in 1888, Colbeck proposed the governors sold land away from the Hill and take out mortgages to buy them.[181] Although it proved impossible at the time, this provided the model for funding later purchases of property on the Hill. In 1893 the Park Trust itself bought Druries from the Holmes family (G. F. Holmes, who died in 1887, had bought it from Ben Drury in 1863), as well as a number of surrounding houses between it and Church Hill to create more open access. By 1898 the Trust's capital had grown to £30,000. The governors underwrote the Trust's purchase for £2,000 from Montagu Butler of Dame Armstrong's, opposite the school gates, in 1900. By 1914 The Trust had bought the Knoll and Elmfield.[182] It was a unique demonstration of practical old boys' support for their Alma Mater. Although conspicuously loyal, these Old Harrovians owned a stake in the school unlike those who contributed to appeals to buy land outright, although a Harrow Football Field Trust administered the Butler Memorial purchase. The connection with the school was reinforced on Colbeck's death in 1903 by the appointment of the school's Bursar, Robert Somervell, as the Trust's secretary.[183] Thirty-five years later one of the Trust's former solicitors argued for the

---

[178] GBM, 4 July 1887, 2 Feb. 1897, referring to the Batten offer of 26 Dec. 1896. For the Butler purchase see GBM, 1 Feb. 1910, 3 Nov. 1913, 11 June 1914 (finally paid off).
[179] C. Colbeck, 'The School Estate at Harrow', in Howson and Townsend Warner, *Harrow School*, 152–3; Head Master's Book, 1874–92, fo. 83; Laborde, 188.
[180] GBM, 5 Dec. 1893, 12 June 1902, 5 Feb., 5 Nov. 1907; *Harrow Register, 1800–1911*, 366.
[181] GBM, 6 Nov. 1888.
[182] GBM, 5 Dec. 1893; Colbeck, 'School Estate', 153; GBM, 6 Dec. 1900.
[183] Somervell, *Autobiography*, 97.

significance of this symbiotic relationship: 'Harrow owes the position which it holds today in the front rank of English Public Schools entirely to the close cooperation between school and Old Harrovian in all matters vital to the life of the school'.[184]

The original scheme had allowed for the governors at any time to buy Trust property on reasonable terms; however, in 1917 the governors themselves succeeded to the management of the Trust properties and liabilities.[185] Thereafter, supported by selling land off the Hill, mortgages, and, until the mid-thirties, rent from housemasters, the governors pursued a policy of buying the remaining boarding houses: for example, Moretons in 1919 for £7,000; West Acre from the Stogdons in 1925 for £10,000. The last house to be bought was, ironically, Bradbys in 1930. With all the housemasters now tenants of the governors, control was easier. In 1930 housemasters' terms of office were for the first time limited—to fifteen years. In 1936 a scheme was introduced under which they surrendered their financial independence in return for fixed salaries and set capitation grants, the last of the old private hoteliers leaving Elmfield in 1948.[186] As in the two previous centuries, the exigencies of the balance of finance and cohesion determined some of the most fundamental elements in the structure of the school.

RICH AND POOR

The context of this transformation in financial and political control was a severe and unresolved financial crisis. Ironically, the chief windfall assisting centralization was the bequest to the school of the Grove and other property and investments, amounting in capital value to tens of thousands of pounds, by Bowen, the archdefender of federal independence. Bowen had bought the Grove estate from the Battens in 1900 for £14,000. In his lifetime he was lavish in endowing the school, including an extension of the cricket fields and £1,000 to help buy part of the Northwick land. In 1888 he endowed the Fifth Form Scholarship (its first winner being Leo Amery). In 1893 he settled his whole estate on the school, which had the secondary consequence of rendering him impossible to sack or even discipline, a luxury Bowen enjoyed with all his renowned energy.[187] On his death in 1901 the school received one of the most valuable gifts in its history, not merely financially but in regard to the whole setting of the school. Although Bowen and the school's original intention had been to close the Grove as a boarding house and convert it into a residence for the Head Master, needs of economy forced a change of plan,

---

[184] HA Papers of H. J. L. Gorse, Memorandum of L. M. Hewlett 'On the Future of Harrow School', Feb. 1939. [185] GBM, 28 June 1917, 12 Feb. 1918.
[186] Laborde, *Harrow School*, 176–7, 182, 186, and below, pp. 515–18.
[187] Bowen, *Bowen*, 245–6; GBM, 21 Feb. 1888, 14 May 1889, 7 Nov. 1899, 14 June 1900, 26 Mar. 1901.

the Head remaining a housemaster until 1980 despite generations of opinion that it was a poor combination.[188] Without Bowen's generosity it is extremely unlikely that even the Park Trust could have competed for the Grove estate (which by 1901 included the Copse, built by Bowen for his retirement) on the open market. The governors certainly could not have afforded it.

In acute form, Imperial Harrow demonstrated the most persistent Harrow paradox: an expensive school, full to the brim, oversubscribed, both popular and famous, of international renown yet unable to balance its books. This was not for want of tenacity or ingenuity. Until 1897 W. H. Stone, then Walter Leaf, a chairman of the Westminster Bank and, from 1908, Frederick Huth Jackson, a director of the Bank of England, oversaw the school finances until a separate finance committee of the governors was established in 1910, the precursor to the later powerful General Purposes Committee.[189] The structural problems were manifold. As early as 1887 Stone revealed that income from the Lyon estate (i.e. the lands left for the school not the roads) had, over the previous five years, failed to cover charges against it, a result of the sustained agricultural depression that hit even good farming land such as Preston where Sneezum regularly applied for a reduction of his rent.[190] Estate deficits continued into the 1890s. Income from the now immensely lucrative Road Trust lands remained inaccessible, hopes of finding loopholes in the restrictions on the use of the income being dashed. From 1 January 1894 all Road Trust moneys were secured in a separate bank account to prevent them being 'drawn upon for school purposes' and the Charity Commissioners began an investigation into the Trust's operation.[191] New local authorities also began to take an unsympathetic interest, such as Hendon District Council and Middlesex County Council.[192] Not even the counsel's opinion of H. H. Asquith in 1897–8 aided the governors' cause.[193] Profits from the richest part of the estates for which they were legally responsible were not available to them, the perpetuation of the governors themselves in street names across the Road Trust estate in Paddington and Maida Vale (e.g. Hamilton Terrace) providing ironic commentary on their predicament.

The school fund, established after 1877, exposed stark systemic difficulties. Annual Head Master's budgets even at their most optimistic never envisaged a surplus of more than a few hundred pounds in a turnover of above £21,000, too low to meet the obligations placed on the fund by the 1874 regulations. Shortfalls were

---

[188] Bowen, *Bowen*, 245–6; GBM, 1 Nov. 1898, 18 Apr. 1910; Minutes of Masters' Meetings, 1893–1910, 26 Sept 1898, 10 Oct. 1898 (when they voted 19 to 5 against the Head having a boarding house).

[189] GBM, 18 Apr. 1910 and, in same book, minutes of Finance Committee meetings, 28 July, 12 and 24 Oct., 7 Dec. 1910.

[190] GBM, 3 May 1887; Sneezum died in 1890, GBM, 29 Apr. 1890. For his rent reductions see e.g. GBM, 23 June 1887. [191] GBM, 5 Dec. 1893, 6 Feb. 1894.

[192] GBM, 6 Mar. 1894, 7 May 1895, 4 Feb., 11 Aug., 3 Nov. 1896.

[193] GBM, 2 Nov. 1897, 9 June 1898.

Plenitude

often made up from the Head Master's annual rent, which made the fiasco over Wood's salary in 1899 so damaging. Deficits on the school fund were common. That in 1893 was due, Welldon explained, to loss of fee income because of a flu epidemic and an increase in masters' salaries, not least the ex gratia £150 a year to Bowen backdated to 1889.[194] Here at least the governors could act by instructing the Head Master to reduce staff costs in 1893–4 which, with the help of the retirements of Hayward and Griffith, he achieved. None the less, it was inescapable that, even when the school was full, fees did not satisfactorily cover expenditure.

The problem was exacerbated by the need to maintain Harrow's prestige by improving educational and domestic facilities. The single-room policy was expensive; even where houses were not owned by them, the governors usually offered to contribute to renovation costs. Demands on the school's income came from the drainage of the football fields in 1893; further acquisitions of playing fields (e.g. in 1895) and the Grove fields (1897–1902); the mortgage to secure the large 1905 Northwick Park purchase (only feasible with Wood's donation); re-equipping the Science Schools; added teaching costs consequent on the expansion of the curriculum; the building of the Museum Schools (1885–6), the fever cottage at the sanatorium in the early 1890s, the Music Schools (1890–1), and the Art Schools (1896); equipping the Copse for mathematics in 1904; improving arrangements for rifle shooting (in 1904); and the creation of a parade ground (1910–11).[195] Some of the capital for these projects, such as the Butler Memorial fund's for the Gymnasium and Workshop or H. Yates Thompson's gift of the Art Schools, came from other sources, but not the recurrent, often hidden, cost of running and staffing new buildings. The governors were trapped. They could not afford to run a great school but equally they could not afford not to.

While annual balances varied, the general health of the school's finances deteriorated. A cash-in-hand balance at the bank of £3,000 in 1890 became a deficit of £700 in 1894. Overdraft arrangements had to be agreed regularly, as in 1897 and 1911.[196] Only the trusts for prizes and scholarships flourished. The indefatigable bursar from 1888 to 1919, Robert Somervell, gradually consolidated all school financial business in his own hands. While lending administrative efficiency and a measure of accounting clarity to the school's affairs, alone he could do nothing about income and expenditure. Raising fees did little to ameliorate the problem.[197] Short- and long-term loans became customary from the early 1890s, often of £1,500 to £2,000 a time, simply to meet current commitments.[198] The governors were not helped by the sudden collapse of their bank, Hopkinsons, in 1898, which left them at the same time without a Head Master or a banker, as well as losing their

---

[194] GBM, 7 Feb. 1893.
[195] Apart from GBM, *passim*; Laborde, *Harrow School*, 206–7; Fox, *Harrow*, 60.
[196] GBM, 4 Feb. 1890, 6 Nov. 1894, 2 Feb. 1897, 15 June 1911.
[197] Somervell, *Autobiography*, 92–8.   [198] GBM, 6 Feb. 1894, etc.

money on account. It took until 1911 for the last dividend from the receiver to be paid, producing a final return of 13s. 6d. in the pound.[199] Given that there was at least one influential and well-informed banker on the board, the governors may appear to have been less than vigilant. However, with or without sound bankers, more drastic measures were required.

The failure of the new system of financial arrangements to support the school that Harrow had become prompted a fateful necessity. In 1883, for the first time in three hundred years, the governors, using the freedom lent them after the 1868 Act and 1874 Statutes, decided to sell parts of the Lyon estate: Alperton and a piece of Preston Farm. The Preston buyer withdrew and it took another seven years for the Alperton sale to be agreed with a purchaser and approved by the Charity Commissioners, the sale price of £1,700 being considerably less than originally expected.[200] In 1891 the sale of part of Preston Farm was again mooted.[201] In 1897, to pay off the overdraft at the bank, the governors sold their property in central Barnet and some cottages at Maulden in Bedfordshire.[202] The rest of Maulden Farm went in 1904 for £3,750, £2,000 of which was earmarked for the renovations of the Grove (which Bowen had left as an austere slum) and the changes to the Copse.[203] Beside selling off land, at one of the least propitious times for agriculture, the governors were repeatedly forced to sell stock, culminating in the sale of £16,703 of Consols in 1899.[204] After a radical review of finances in 1910, a more long-term strategy was finally adopted with the creation of an Endowment Fund in 1913, although this did little to save the school from near financial ruin twenty-five years later.[205] It is hard to see what else the governors could have done before the First World War. They exploited the wealth and goodwill of Old Harrovians to the full. They attempted to preach economy to Head Masters. There was a limit to how far they could increase costs (not above Eton, perhaps). Yet they felt obliged to maintain Harrow in the style to which it and its clients had grown accustomed. This imposed hand-to-mouth short-term expediency, the radical, historic nature of which should not be passed over lightly. The investments they sold had been built up over the previous 175 years. The land had belonged to John Lyon.

A Conformist School?

In 1913 Arnold Lunn, an old Knollite (1902–7) and inventor of the skiing slaalom, published his novel *The Harrovians*, based on a diary he had kept at school. It immediately caused widespread outrage and indignation, Lunn being forced to

---

[199] GBM, 11 Oct. 1898, 7 Nov. 1899, final dividend: 22 Nov. 1911.
[200] GBM, 27 Apr. 1883, 4 Nov. 1890.   [201] GBM, 21 Apr. 1891.
[202] GBM, 4 Feb., 3 Mar., 11 Aug. (when the Charity Commissioners tried to stop it) 1896, 2 Feb., 24 June 1897.   [203] GBM, 1 Nov. 1904.
[204] GBM, 7 Feb. 1893, 8 June 1899.   [205] GBM, 4 Feb., 3 Nov. 1913, 2 Feb. 1914.

resign from his five London clubs.[206] His crime was to have written a book about Harrow without sentimentality. It was not that Lunn hated Harrow, any more than Alec Waugh's even more notorious *Loom of Youth* of 1917 showed a hatred of Sherborne. What rankled was its prosaic 'documentary' style and content. Nothing much happens in Lunn's novel. There are no grand passions for other boys or even the school. It is the antithesis of Vachell's cloying emotings (at which fun is poked in a delicious description of Lord's). In his preface Lunn commented that 'life for the average Harrovian is monotonously uneventful and happy'.[207] Lunn, son of the founder of Lunnpoly the travel agents, sought to portray life at Harrow as it was rather than as it should have been. Yet he refused to preach or indulge in polemic. Recalling the uproar the book caused, forty years later Lunn put his finger on the source of the outcry: 'The trouble was, of course, that I had kept a careful record of the cynicism of Harrow youth rather than the sentiment of Old Harrovians.'[208] For that, he, like others since, was not forgiven.

Lunn's account of Wood's Harrow is distinguishable from that presented by other memorialists of the Imperial age only in its quiet sustained irony. He presents a world that outwardly conformed: ' "Conform or be kicked" is the command written over the portals of every school . . . they teach the lesson that the brilliant individualist is often a nuisance in the game of life.' Yet he recorded the triumph of one intellectual Head of School—clearly J. R. M. Butler—in defeating the bloods in matters of precedence and privilege which comprised the boys' ruling obsession. He is honest about boys' habits and interests: sporting, anti-intellectual ('Harrow caters not for the exceptional but for the average boy'), trivial. He recounts with minimal emotion the waves of bullying (a feature confirmed by L. P. Hartley, West Acre 1910–15), the tedium and violence of compulsory mass house football, relationships between boys of different ages, 'the aristocracy of muscle', 'muscle-worship', adolescent interest in sex, anti-Semitism, philistinism, and snobbery.[209] His picture is three dimensional. Bullying 'is infectious', bullies often charismatic figures who develop 'into the best type of virile manhood', oddly a point that formed the basis of the dreary, limp saga of endeavour, friendship, and redemption, *Follow Up! The Story of a Commonplace Harrovian* (1908) by Archibald Fox (Newlands 1892–7).[210] There are no heroes, no villains, just boys—some strong, some loutish, some feeble, some dull. Lunn's irony can be comic, as in his descriptions of the absurdities of Chapel and 'the litany of Nationalism' or the religious nature of Lord's, 'not the creed of the Lord who delighteth not in any man's legs' or the

---

[206] Gathorne-Hardy, *Public School Phenomenon*, 309.
[207] Lunn, *The Harrovians*, pp. v–vi, 113–14 for the Lord's scene.
[208] Quoted from A. Lunn, *Memory to Memory* (London, 1956) by Quigley, *Heirs of Tom Brown*, 155.
[209] Lunn, *The Harrovians*, 43, 44, 45, 61, 77, 139, 143, 150, 196, 274–8, 280, etc.; L. P. Hartley, 'The Conformer', G. Greene (ed.), in *The Old School* (Oxford, 1984), pp. 65–82; the first edition had appeared in 1934. [210] Lunn, *The Harrovians*, 57, 59, 61.

worshipped Olympians themselves 'clothed in white samite, mystic wonderful'.[211] He is realistic, not hysterical about the incidence of sodomy 'where five hundred young men are gathered together'. He is shrewd and often affectionate about his teachers, especially praising 'Mr Gerant', i.e. George Townsend Warner. He refuses to pass over social tensions, as when boys attacked a group of unemployed who were marching through Harrow.[212] The local working class had been making their feelings about the *jeunesse d'orée* clear for years by systematically dumping rubbish on the path down to the cricket fields.[213] For all his apparent detachment, Lunn was as much trapped in the 'total society' of school as the most ardent sentimentalist. However, he committed the ultimate solecism by placing Harrow in the context of leaving and growing up.

Lunn's novel suggests a paradox. There is no doubting the collective corporate conformism of Imperial Harrow; the reaction to *The Harrovians* alone indicates as much. Galsworthy remembered 'all sorts of unwritten rules of supression' in the mid-1880s which remained in force thirty years later. E. C. Richardson talked of 'these beastly petty little rules that spoil one's enjoyment here'. Trevelyan insisted the whole period witnessed 'the leisure and initiative of the individual boy . . . increasingly sacrificed to meet the needs of the athletic timetable, with the organized mass opinion of the boys and often of the masters to enforce obedience to the stereotype ideal of games and "good form"'.[214] Yet L. P. Hartley, although he entitled his memoir 'The Conformer', remembered 'we were a collection of oddities such as would have rejoiced the heart of Herbert Spencer or any individualist philosopher', a view confirmed by Lunn and diarists from the 1880s and 1890s.[215]

Conformity operated at a number of levels; on not all were individualism and eccentricity crushed. Bowen preached the absolute importance of the individual boy, to the extent of encouraging Grovites to leave early rather than stay on merely for the sake of the house or school. Yet he was also obsessed by Harrow as an ideal as much as a place or institution.[216] The majority of Harrovians were untouched by good or extending teaching, still less transformed by timetable reform. As even the devoted Fox admitted, it was fashionable to slack and cheat at work, as, in real life, Churchill's steady academic decline testifed.[217] H. M. Butler's refined philistinism soon lost its refinement. The hardworking boy was already a 'groize' before the First World War.[218] Yet the same boy who could call his classics 'great rot' and express bewilderment at his housemaster visiting the sublime church at

---

[211] Ibid., 109, 138–9. The Tennyson reference adds insult to injury as the late poet laureate's moments of lush emotionalism were treasured by cultists such as Bowen and his followers. Cf. Richardson, 'Diary', 2 and 7 Apr. 1889 for Bowen reading from *Idylls of the King*.

[212] Lunn, *The Harrovians*, 143, 222, 243–6. [213] GBM, 20 June 1889.

[214] Marrot, *Galsworthy*, 43; Richardson, 'Diary', 16 Feb. 1889; Trevelyan, *British History in the Nineteenth Century* (London, 1922), p. 172. [215] Hartley, 'Conformer', 68.

[216] Bowen, *Bowen*, 206–8. [217] A. Fox, *Follow Up!* (London, 1908), 54–5.

[218] Hartley, 'Conformer', 74.

Patrington, could also enjoy and shrewdly criticize the content and performance of concerts of classical music.[219] More generally, although the charge of public school anti-intellectualism levelled by experienced schoolmasters such as A. C. Benson in *The Schoolmaster* (1902) was both just and widely corroborated, much of the burden of the attack was on the stultifying classical curriculum still prevalent at places such as Benson's Eton.[220] Harrow, by contrast, had moved decisively towards a broader education. There, hidebound traditional philistinism was as much of the spirit as of the mind.

There was a culture of uniformity at Harrow but it was self-conscious. L. P. Hartley, writing in 1934, almost had to apologize for not following the expected line of diatribe against the damage inflicted by the system. That conformity was and remains such an issue among boys might suggest a less than unthinking acceptance. In this Harrow may have differed from many other public schools where conformity was much more a necessity for survival in schools where boys congregated in quadrangles and dormitories. Harrow had neither. However, it did have the tyranny of the house, as well as hierarchies, privileges, and orders of precedence as fine tuned and as viciously protected as at any court of the *Ancien Régime*.[221] These helped lend shape to the otherwise flat world of the schoolboy. Boys ran their own affairs and the lowest common denominator tended to suffice in matters of opinion and social behaviour, especially as so much of the time was given over to escaping boredom. Here games played a practical if mundane role, occupying time, interest, energy, violence, and competitiveness. Archibald Fox could talk in 1911 of games providing 'invaluable lessons in self-control, self-subordination, pluck, endurance and fair play', none of which was usually apparent to most when actually forced to play them.[222] The cult of games was the creation of old boys and masters. In its virulent form, so was the insistence on conformity. The chief conformists at Harrow were the teachers not the taught.

The artificial transmutation of schoolboy enthusiasms, prejudice, deference, fear of loneliness, and bullying into an insistent code of uniform behaviour was experienced by Jawaharlal Nehru (Head Master's 1905–7). On arrival he determined to conform at work and play but found 'how dull most of the English boys were as they could talk about nothing but their games'. A shrewd observer, he noticed that while Paramjit Singh was a misfit, the son of the Gaekwar of Baroda was 'popular because of his cricket'. Nehru, known as 'Joe', took the hint, joining the Corps, the chess club, and taking up shooting. He later remembered Songs with affection. His desire to follow the crowd had unsavoury, but not uncommon, consequences: 'there was always a background of anti-semitic feeling. They were

---

[219] Twiss, 'Diary', 20 Jan., 23, 24 Feb., 4 Mar. 1893.
[220] Mack, *Public Schools and British Opinion since 1860*, 220, *et seq.*; Stray, *Living Word*, 34.
[221] Lunn, *The Harrovians*: e.g. p. 310 for importance of the house implicit throughout, as it is in Hartley, 'Conformer'.
[222] Fox, *Harrow*, 58. Cf. Hartley, 'Conformer', 68 and Lunn, *The Harrovians*, *passim*.

"damned Jews", and soon, almost unconsciously, I began to think that it was the proper thing to have this feeling'.²²³ Such sensitive acculturation was not untypical of the smooth future Prime Minister of India; nor was it untypical of his peers: the ethics of the mass, 'Conform or be Kicked'. Although he was later to romanticize his time at Harrow, Nehru's comments, written thirty years afterwards, on his emotions on leaving school penetrate to the heart of the process of conformity and help explain the paradox of the conforming individual: 'I wonder how far I was really sorry at leaving Harrow. Was it not partly a feeling that I ought to be unhappy because Harrow tradition and song demanded it? I was susceptible to these traditions for I had deliberately not resisted them so as to be in harmony with the place.'²²⁴

The most devastating effect of conformity was emotional. L. P. Hartley, who visited the theme of stunted emotions in his novels, summed up the effect: 'The necessity of disguising what one felt, of keeping the stiff upper lip when cursed by a Sixth Former or wounded by a friend or hit by a cricket ball, sometimes found its logical outcome: after many repetitions one felt nothing at all.'²²⁵

This is more or less what Archer Vassall was suggesting from an academic perspective in 1911. It echoed the memories of John Galsworthy of Harrow in the 1880s. Harrovians were inflexible, timorous, conservative, deferential, 'half-developed' in Lunn's phrase.²²⁶ However, this was not unique to Harrow but a tendency of all boarding schools. To protect themselves, acceptance of whatever it took to ensure survival at school was of paramount importance to boys. Public schools at the turn of the century have been seen as imposing the restrictions of an obsessively introspective 'total society' on their members.²²⁷ In many cases this was not only inevitable but essential, not just for the institution's purposes of indoctrination and control, but for the comfort of the pupils. For many Harrovians were, in some senses, homeless, their parents abroad or, in a variety of senses, even when living in London, distant. Despite appeals for Foundationers' rights that persisted for decades after 1874 and fears of an unprofitable glut of day boys, the number of Home Boarders steadily declined to a mere handful by the First World War.²²⁸ Harrow's status as a boarding school was secure. Therefore, the vast majority of Harrovians inevitably spent far more time at school than at any other home. The world of school was more completely the world of their youth than any other. To obey the household gods was not simply prudential it was natural and, importantly, reassuring. Thus it was considered 'bad form' to discuss home lives or

---

²²³ Nehru, *Autobiography*, 17, 18; M. J. Akbar, *Nehru: The Making of India* (London, 1989), pp. 47–54; J. M. Brown, *Nehru* (London, 1999), p. 26.
²²⁴ Nehru, *Autobiography*, 19.   ²²⁵ Hartley, 'Conformer', 77–8.
²²⁶ Lunn, *The Harrovians*, 61.
²²⁷ Gathorne-Hardy, *Public School Phenomenon*, esp. pp. 204–10.
²²⁸ GBM, from 13 Apr. 1885 at intervals until 3 Feb. 1903; for Home Boarders: 3 Dec. 1895, 25 June 1896; Minutes of Masters' Meetings, 1893–1910, 4 Nov. 1895.

families, encounters at school or at Lord's with one's own parents let alone those of others occasioning embarrassment and confusion.[229]

However, behind the public facade of unquestioned duty and manly heartiness, Imperial Harrow could be a rather raffish place, more of 'Demon' Scaife than Harry Desmond, let alone John Verney. The cultists of sport rarely dwelt on the pitched-battles that occurred at the end of Lord's each year.[230] Still less did they stifle the private mockery at their devotions. Nobody stopped or seemed to mind E. C. Richardson's daily walk and smoke in 1889. Bullying was unconfined. Richard Meinertzhagen (1891–5) used to poach and once rode up to London on a butcher's cart and back before 9 a.m. bill. The habits of the rich upper and middle classes, in particular drinking and smoking, were not shed at the foot of the Hill. At least until 1908, beer was drunk after football by Knollites quite officially. Sporting demi-gods may have been worshipped, but according to L. P. Hartley starquality was earned rather differently: 'by being beautiful, by being wicked, by being a wit, by being a butt, by being good-natured, by being foul-mouthed (a field, however, in which pre-eminence was hard to win), by being daring, by being always in trouble.'[231]

What was true for boys was true for some of the masters. The conventional Old Harrovian hearty M. C. 'Bishop' Kemp cultivated the eccentricity of keeping his spaniel, Bus, in form to bite offending pupils on command. There was something of the Oxenham about him. When faced with a new proposal of the Head's he once banged the table exclaiming 'my God, Head Master, I hate the whole scheme'. His response to a new prayer in Chapel would be to whisper loudly to his neighbour 'Pass along to Mr Du Pontet to kick the Head Master'.[232] John Stogdon enticed the young Leo Amery to join West Acre rather than the Head Master's after entertaining him to a discussion of Indian politics over a dish of olives. Percy Buck was criticized by Wood for allowing senior boys to smoke freely in his house. Griffith was so delighted by the possibilities of electricity that he even tried using it to treat scarlet fever victims in Druries.[233] According to Richard Meinertzhagen, Bushell, his housemaster, was obsessed with vice, bewildered new boys being confronted with a harangue of revealing absurdity, even for 1891: 'Cast out the sins of the flesh for they are the Devil himself. When I was a small boy another larger boy said unto me "Be unto me as a woman" and I cast him down stairs and that was my salvation. I ask you all to do unto such a boy as I did unto him.' At the time, Meinertzhagen had no idea what Bushell was talking about.[234]

---

[229] Marrot, *Galsworthy*, 43.   [230] e.g. in 1900: Quigley, *Heir of Tom Brown*, 137.
[231] Richardson, 'Diary', *passim*; Meinertzhagen, *Diary*, 177, 207; Mayo, *Reminiscences*, 142–3, 155–8, 223; Hartley, 'Conformer', 77.
[232] Meinertzhagen, *Diary*, 180; Bryant, *Harrow*, 154–6.
[233] *The Harrovian*, 20 Dec. 1919, 10–11; Wood Letter Book, fo. 136 (Buck also missed lessons frequently); Twiss, 'Diary', 17 Mar. 1893.   [234] Meinertzhagen, *Diary*, 178–9.

The contrast between the idealized world of Bowen's and Howson's songs or Fox's panegyric enthusiasm, as in his *Harrow* (1911), and the diverse, eccentric, often irreverent reality is unsurprising. Some Harrovians did embrace the school's self-image with enthusiasm. The poem *On Leaving Harrow* by J. W. Jenkins, Head of School 1897–8, was typical of both emotion and literary skill, sincere but ill-formed, 'Farewell, beloved Hill', etc.[235] However, many boys were indifferent, taking what came as part of the order of things, only later gilding the memories and realizing the social cachet their school bestowed on them.

Nowhere is the gulf between what is customarily believed and retrospectively presented as public school values and the actual habits of Harrovians more keenly observed than in the story of the Rifle Corps. Imperial Harrow, like Imperial Britain, was militaristic in a sentimental, theoretical, rather than a grimly practical, Prussian manner. For much of the period before the Boer War, the Harrow Rifle Corps was a shambles. The 1919 dictum of M. G. Glazebrook, a captain in the Harrow Rifle Corps in the 1880s, that 'every sound public school boy wears khaki' was wishful thinking before 1914.[236] Founded in 1859 as the 18th Middlesex Rifle Volunteer Corps, it was revived in the 1860s by Butler, who foisted on it a rather elaborate, fussy uniform.[237] Run by boys, there were few recruits, most of them interested more in shooting than soldiering. In 1882 the Corps was taken over by Bushell, beginning a sequence of clerical Commanding Officers over the following twenty-five years: E. H. Kempson (later bishop of Warrington); during the Boer War, the exquisitely pious F. C. Searle, who was apparently incapable of issuing orders and was distinctly squeamish at being asked one Field Day to 'beat the Hell' out of the opposition; and Edgar Stogdon, future head of the Harrow Mission and vicar of Harrow. Predictably, the Corps was called the Church Militant.[238] Under Bushell, numbers rose from around thirty to about 200 although by 1888 this had declined to 'scarcely over 100, the majority of whom are inefficient', disliking drill and regarding membership simply as a good way of being allowed off the Hill for shooting matches.[239] Until the Boer War (1899–1902), organization was relaxed. Drill was weekly on Wednesday evenings 7.30–9 (singing practice being another option at that time) in a local drill hall, the venue depressing, the standard low, despite which keen boys, such as Churchill, greatly enjoyed the regular Field Days. The Corps Bandmaster was noted mainly as a beer drinker.[240] Despite the War Office appeal of 1896–7, the Corps remained voluntary; only briefly, during the

---

[235] Fox, *Harrow*, 90.
[236] Bushell, *Bushell*, 16. For militarism see Best, 'Militarism', *passim* and cf. Gathorne-Hardy, *Public School Phenomenon*, 196–200.
[237] Graham, *Butler*, 170–1; Laborde, *Harrow School*, 206.
[238] Bushell, *Bushell*, 15; Mayo, *Reminiscences*, 48–59.
[239] Bushell, *Bushell*, 15; Churchill, *Churchill*, i. 115–18.
[240] Meinertzhagen, *Diary*, 197–8.

Boer War, were attempts made to enlist all boys over 15.[241] More significantly, after 1900 the Corps became popular with the bloods as yet another arena in which to exercise their power and a compulsory subscription was levied on all boys (of 3s. 4d. a term).[242] After 1900 drill moved to mornings until Ford's timetable reforms of 1913. In 1908 the Rifle Corps was re-established as an Officer Training Corps without making much greater impact, drill being widely used in the late nineteenth century and again under Ford as a form of punishment not a preparation for war, a rather nasty form of physical jerks for delinquents.[243] More masters became involved as officers, attracted by the additional money. Provision for shooting was improved in 1904 when a fifty-yard range was built below Garlands to replace the old one below the School Yard. In 1910/11 a parade ground was constructed. However, numbers in the OTC still remained little more than half the school: 296 in 1909, with 114 going on Corps camp; just over 300 with 146 going to camp in 1910.[244] The uniforms remained faintly Gilbert and Sullivan; the training hardly meeting Lord Roberts' 1912 call—widely ignored—for National Service.[245] There was, in some houses, absolutely no pressure to join the OTC. Patriotism was not seen as necessarily imposing any personal military obligation.[246] Imperial Harrow was not Adolescence in Arms. The outbreak of war in 1914 changed all that. In 1898 J. W. Jenkins could write, of Harrow: 'Thou sendest me to fight | For home and school and right' as a metaphor of service.[247] The First World War brought savage reality to the call. In the words of Philip Bryant, who saw many of them go, the last generation of Imperial Harrow 'was practically immolated'.[248]

---

[241] HM/We/Oct. 1896, Lord Wolseley to HMC Head Masters; Minutes of Masters' Meetings, 1893–1910, 25 Mar. 1900.
[242] GBM, 12 June 1902, although this was because of the financial shortfall owing to lack of numbers not the reverse.
[243] HM/We/3 Feb. 1898; Head Master's Book, 1910–16, Lionel Ford Memorandum, 1 Mar. 1911.
[244] Laborde, *Harrow School*, 206–7; Fox, *Harrow*, 59–60.
[245] *The Harrovian*, 29 June 1912, pp. 74–5 for Roberts' open letter. Cf. Fox, *Harrow*, 59–60 for similar sentiments eighteen months earlier.
[246] e.g. West Acre, Hartley, 'Conformer', 68.   [247] Fox, *Harrow*, 90.
[248] Bryant, *Harrow*, 94.

Part V

Staying On, 1914–1991

Part V

Starting On 1914–1907

15

CHALLENGES OLD AND NEW: POLITICS, GOVERNORS, AND MONEY IN THE TWENTIETH CENTURY

The distinctive nature of Harrow must be preserved... to be seen to be producing from the School pupils who will become men of integrity to manage our own country and its institutions, and also pupils who are motivated by the power of the spirit to go out into the world to work to the service of others.[1]

These sentiments would not have disgraced Montagu Butler, echoing with clarity his apologia to the Clarendon Commissioners in 1862. In fact, they belong to a document on 'Long-Term Priorities' drawn up by Head Master I. D. S. Beer in 1989. Such continued confidence in Harrow's role in providing rulers in the late twentieth century would have astounded many observers of public schools since 1914 as much as the assumption of spiritual inspiration would have intrigued them. It is less a question of whether Beer was justified than of how such hopes could still be held after almost a century when the forces threatening public schools regularly appeared to be about to engulf them. While as vulnerable to national economic and political developments as any other public school, Harrow's precarious financial base made it more susceptible to financial malaise while its high social profile and proximity to the London Press exposed its shortcomings more cruelly to hostile gaze. Above all, the survival of a system which 'arbitrarily confers upon its members advantages and powers over the rest of society' and of schools which 'confer such advantages on an arbitrarily selected membership which already starts with an advantageous position in life' sat ill with much prevalent social thinking as Britain embraced electoral democracy after 1918 and welfare egalitarianism after 1945.[2]

---

[1] HA Policy Document on Long-Term Priorities, May 1989, p. 3.
[2] From the Report of the Royal Commission on Public Schools 1968, J. Stuart Maclure, *Educational Documents: England and Wales 1816 to the Present Day* (5th edn., London, 1986), p. 338.

Yet the anomaly of state versus private education enshrined in legislation and government policy from 1868 remained unaltered.

Survival did not leave the institutions untouched. As the Newsom Report of 1968, from which the above description of public schools comes, fairly observed, the schools themselves regretted being forced into an exclusive ghetto of selection by wealth, not least because of the consequent restricted calibre and nature of recruits and the glaring perpetuation of social inequality. Harrow long held to a fond ideal of the perfect schoolboy as one with, as a loyalist described it, a 'background of service' rather than a desire to purchase 'social prestige', possessing the *noblesse oblige* of the landed gentry rather than the material security of the idle rich.³ Nevertheless, if the public schools became caricatures of their opponents' criticisms, those critics' prophecies of dissolution or destruction proved wholly misplaced. In 1934 Graham Greene, introducing a collection of public school reminiscences by fellow writers, commented: 'like the family album, this book will, I hope, be superficially more funny than tragic, for so odd a system of education does not demand a pompous memorial . . . For there can be no doubt that the system which this book mainly represents is doomed.'⁴ He could not have been more wrong.

Politics

The truth . . . is to any normal person that inequalities start more or less in the mother's womb and certainly in the home and the worst public schools can be accused of doing is that they have a preponderance of the children of upper and middle class parents in their schools.⁵

So Dr R. L. James, Head Master of Harrow 1953–71, dismissed the hostility to public schools of the Labour government in 1966 and, in particular, of the ex-public school (Highgate) minister, Anthony Crosland. Reg Prentice, the junior minister responsible for schools and future convert to the Conservatives and Mrs Thatcher, James described as 'a man of quite monumental ignorance on the whole thing . . . quite fantastic!'⁶ He wrote during the deliberations of the Royal Commission on Public Schools of 1965–8, the first since the Clarendon Commission, the appointment of which sent a frisson of fear through the schools examined.

The normal position of proponents of public school education in the 1960s and 1970s appeared defensive and apprehensive. The Harrow governors expressed dark

---

³ Venables, *Bases Attempted*, 27–9. I am grateful to the late Revd H. L. Harris for lending me his copy of this revealing essay in sentimentality and self-justification.

⁴ G. Greene (ed.), *The Old School* (Oxford, 1984), p. vii.

⁵ HM/James/16 Feb. 1966, James to Dudley, marquess of Aberdeen.

⁶ HM/J/16 Feb. 1966.

concerns in the mid-1960s about the political 'climate' or 'atmosphere'.[7] There were rumours of Irish estates being offered for Harrow-in-exile. The Labour party manifesto of 1964 proposed the abolition of independent schools; that of 1974 the withdrawal of their charitable status. Ideological conflict revolved around opposing definitions of freedom. Supporters of the principle and practice of public schools argued they represented freedom of choice; opponents insisted such freedom was a cover for the retention by a monied elite of a stranglehold on the British establishment and institutions which denied the freedom of the majority to aspire to equal opportunities. The more detailed issues were traditional: public schools were socially divisive per se; the education they provided outmoded, even harmful to pupils; their existence distorted and weakened the state system. In the late 1960s the Head Masters' Conference retaliated by hiring a Public Relations firm and establishing a lobbying organization, known as the Independent Schools Information Service.[8] In the event the electoral successes of the Conservative party, in 1970 and 1979–92, proved a more effective defence. Yet such was the nervousness of public schools that, on his first Speech Day in 1982, Head Master Beer urged his audience to support the ISIS campaign against renewed Labour party proposals for their abolition and in 1983 counsel's opinion was sought on the implications of an end to charitable status, despite the overwhelming evidence against the likelihood of a Labour victory in that year's general election.[9] A decade later it was felt necessary for the Head Master to voice opposition to the Labour plan to abolish Assisted Places even though Harrow had not entered that scheme.

Whether public schools were justified in such continued anxiety must remain a matter of debate. The Labour government in the mid-1970s found the problem of separating the charitable status of public schools from that of other charities a near-impenetrable legal thicket, especially for an administration with barely a settled majority. In any case, in response to the Newsom Report in 1968, the Harrow governors had calculated that the school could survive the withdrawal of charitable status, partly because of its relatively small endowment and dependence on fee income.[10] The schools potentially worst off without tax-relief were those with proportionately massive endowments, from Eton to Monckton Combe. Furthermore, in the mid-1980s it was variously calculated that the cost of abolition could have been between £300 and 500 million on salaries alone (day and boarding, primary and secondary schools) with a further £2 billion on capital costs.[11] By the late 1990s, abolition was hardly a political issue. The question at the end of the century as often earlier was whether expensive boarding schools would wither of their own

[7] GBM, 16 Nov. 1963, 14 Nov. 1964.

[8] J. Wakeford, *The Cloistered Elite* (London, 1969), p. 24. Cf. generally M. Sanderson, *Educational Opportunity and Social Change in England* (London, 1987).

[9] HA Minutes of the General Purposes Committee of the Governing Body (hereafter GPC), 4 Nov. 1982; GBM, 12 Nov. 1983.   [10] GBM, 26 Sept. 1968.

[11] Sanderson, *Educational Opportunity*, 9.

accord or would again reinvent themselves to suit new demands and markets. Despite raucous debate, the history of public schools since 1914 has been as much of protean change and optimism, even arrogance, as of grim rearguard actions against a domineering populist foe.

The First World War may have eventually exposed the sentimental, ignorant cant of the Edwardian public school value-system. Immediately, however, in the eyes of their supporters, the costly victory confirmed the superiority of the English way of educating its leaders, not least in contrast to the German habits previously praised by educational reformers. When Stanley Baldwin opened the cavernous and gloomy Harrow War Memorial building in 1926, it was of rededication not reform that he spoke (in marked contrast to Churchill's mood in 1944).[12] In many ways, Harrow of the 1920s witnessed the apogee of militarism, compulsion, conformity, and the games cult which acted as a justification to those who had sent their pupils to die; a denial of the horror; a corporate tribute to, in the words of C. H. P. Mayo, those 'many bright, sunny, happy lives who played the game to the end'.[13]

For those who came after, this triumphalism could weigh heavily. To avoid the Corps, Cecil Beaton (1918–22) had to pretend to be a cripple by wearing surgical boots with metal leg splints, while the rebellious Giles Playfair (1924–7) was flogged for being bad at drill.[14] Cyril Norwood's *The English Tradition of Education* written in 1929, during his Head Mastership, contains a chapter headed 'The Danger from Individualism' as well as some unexpectedly florid absurdities from so superficially dour an educational theorist. Central to Norwood was his 'ideal of chivalry', which he defined as 'physical fitness and bodily prowess, beauty and the service of beauty, courage and self-sacrifice, honour and honesty'. This had

> inspired the knighthood of medieval days, the ideal of training for the service of the community... has been combined in the tradition of English education. It is based on religion; it relies largely upon games and open-air prowess, where these involve corporate effort... the ideal which the public schools are seeking... is the true ideal that... answers to our national needs.[15]

One of Norwood's Old Harrovians accurately described the book as 'ridiculous'. Professional critics such as Bertrand Russell or E. M. Forster could sneer, with some justice.[16] Yet the virtues Norwood eulogized or invented found many adherents. If nothing else, the war had revealed the bravery if not the intelligence of public school men. Even R. C. Sheriff's bitter war play *Journey's End* (also of 1929)

[12] Laborde, *Harrow School*, 155–7; *The Harrovian*, 6 Dec. 1944.
[13] Mayo, *Reminiscences*, 158.
[14] H. Vickers, *Cecil Beaton* (London, 1993), p. 20; G. Playfair, *My Father's Son* (London, 1937), pp. 107–8.
[15] C. Norwood, *The English Tradition of Education* (London, 1929), pp. 10, 19, 225.
[16] Gathorne-Hardy, *Public School Phenomenon*, 302; Wakeford, *Cloistered Elite*, 22–3; Mack, *Public Schools and British Opinion since 1860*, 441–2 and 323–452.

could be interpreted as 'the most effective propaganda for the British upper classes written in our time'.[17] There was a startling confidence in public school mores and men. Between 1920 and 1940, 68 per cent of Conservative MPs, who sat on the government benches for all but two and a half years during that time, were from public schools. R. H. Tawney calculated in 1931 that 75 per cent of holders of high office in church, state, and industry had been educated at 135 HMC schools, of these 63 per cent came from fourteen 'great' schools. In 1942 a WEA pamphlet suggested that of the 76 per cent public school office holders, 40 per cent had gone to Eton, Winchester, Rugby, Harrow, and Marlborough.[18] In 1927 Welldon, now a provincial dean, opined that the first Labour government in 1924 had suffered from having no Etonians in the Cabinet.[19] In that same year, the Prime Minster, Baldwin, and over a third of his Cabinet; the archbishop of Canterbury, Randall Davidson; and the new Regius Professor of Modern History at Cambridge, G. M. Trevelyan, were all Old Harrovians.

Yet the context of this public school hegemony had changed. Demands for social reform were increasingly associated with those for economic reform. The coal and General Strike of 1926 were popularly seen in class political terms. During the coal strike, a preacher at Harrow was almost booed in Chapel for suggesting the miners deserved more sympathy than the mine owners. Baldwin was formally congratulated by the school on his handling of the crisis.[20] More widely, the post-1918 world had lost its innocence. The heroes of boys' stories were no longer the noble characters of Rider Haggard or the two-dimensional imperial conquerors of G. A. Henty. Instead appeared the cynical brutality, almost pathological butchery of Sapper's Bulldog Drummond or the scarcely less bigoted and prejudiced if rather more pallid characters in the thrillers of the Old Harrovian Dornford Yates, heroes who struggled against dastardly subversion of the English upper-class universe. The World War appeared to some to have unleashed deadly threats to public school values. Speaking at the Harrow Luncheon Club in 1923 the Old Harrovian Sir Gerald du Maurier called for 'a sort of Klu Klux Klan of Public Schoolboys which when the Beacon flares on the Hill, would come down and restore England once more to law and order, and make her what she used to be and what she always should be, the pattern country in the world'.[21] In 1925 a governor of Harrow, Sir Hugh Anderson, FRS and Master of Caius, Cambridge, reported to his colleagues 'that he had received two complaints with reference to some masters showing socialist tendencies', being instructed 'to assure the two correspondents that the Governors discouraged any political propaganda as part of a Master's

---

[17] Mack, *Public Schools and British Opinion since 1860*, 415.
[18] B. Simon, *The Politics of Educational Reform, 1920–1940* (London, 1974), p. 272.
[19] Mack, *Public Schools and British Opinion since 1860*, 404.
[20] Playfair, *My Father's Son*, 84; HM/Norwood/19 May Baldwin to Norwood (in the PM's own hand).
[21] Mack, *Public Schools and British Opinion since 1860*, 393 (he mistakes the du Mauriers *père et fils*).

office'.²² Presumably opinions with which they agreed were not classified as propaganda. One master had displayed a Labour party poster in his window during the 1924 general election; thereafter he found keeping order in form very difficult. In the same term Anderson took his stand against the Reds, Giles Playfair was knifed by a fellow pupil in the Head Master's for writing a feeble socialist manifesto. Playfair's housemaster, C. W. M. Moorsom, who 'ran the house more or less as he would have a battalion', initially threatened the culprit with the direst penalties, which he waived once he heard the nature of the provocation.²³ However, neither Moorsom nor Anderson could return the world to 'what it should be'. Debates over public schools in the nineteenth century had concerned function; in the twentieth, until the 1990s, they increasingly revolved around the degree of independence and, ultimately, their existence.

Between the wars the political threat hardly disturbed the surface of Harrow's smugness; suburbia and scandal were far more troubling. No Labour government achieved a parliamentary majority; the public school generation educated during the heyday of the 1880s and 1890s ruled, Harrow alone providing four dominant political figures: Baldwin, Churchill, Leo Amery, and Sam Hoare (Amery and Baldwin being governors of the school; Hoare only briefly after the Second World War). Yet chronic financial problems and declining numbers not only posed threats in themselves but forced Harrow, along with other public schools, to confront the possibility of state aid. Ironically, from the perspective of the 1960s and 1970s, the approach for accommodation with the state came from the public schools.

In 1920 a Report of the Select Committee on National Education, a body heavy with public school men, called for public money for the public schools as it had begun to be directed at Oxford and Cambridge.²⁴ However, it took the prolonged economic and financial depression of the 1930s and the demographic effects of the First World War on the public school classes to place government intervention in the centre of public school thinking. Numbers began to slide alarmingly after the boom decade of the 1920s when public schools grew by anything from 10 per cent (Eton) to 50 per cent (Oundle). Over a comparable period (1918–31) Harrow grew by almost 28 per cent, from 515 boys to 669. These gains were wiped out over the next decade. By 1938 Cheltenham had lost almost 23 per cent of pupils, Clifton 14 per cent. At Harrow from a peak of 675 in May 1928, numbers held up above 650 until 1931 before declining steadily, at times steeply. Between May 1931 and May 1939 Harrow lost 22.5 per cent in size, from 665 to 516. Admissions between 1934/5 and 1938/9 alone collapsed by 37 per cent.²⁵ The effect was dramatic. Masters were

---

²² GBM, 12 Feb. 1925.   ²³ Playfair, *My Father's Son*, 75–8, 84.
²⁴ Simon, *Politics of Educational Reform*, 31.
²⁵ For Harrow figures see, *Harrow Register, 1885–1949, passim*; Bill Books; GBM, *passim* for the Head Masters' returns of numbers. Cf. Mack, *Public Schools and British Opinion since 1860*, 381, 394.

laid off and one house, West Acre, closed even before the outbreak of war in September 1939 depressed numbers still further, to their lowest since the late 1840s. Harrow was in a particularly difficult situation. Despite valuable bequests and a vigorous policy of selling land and stock to cover capital expense, the school became increasingly uneconomic. The governors had spent lavishly but prudently on buying land and housing on the Hill since the First World War, incurring long-term debt. The 1930s fall in fee income exposed the structural weaknesses in the school accounts familiar from before 1914. Temporary economies appeared inadequate. Even a scheme to sell up and remove the school to a country location in 1938/9 proved to be financially impossible as well as institutionally suicidal.[26] After Head Master P. C. Vellacott had explained the reasons for closing West Acre by the end of the year, its housemaster, F. A. Leaf, a devoted and quietly loyal Old Harrovian (1904–9) and master (1915–50), wrote, on 31 January 1939, 'it takes a little time to grasp the idea that the existence of Harrow is not assured'.[27]

Some thought help should come from the government. In October 1938 Norwood, now President of St John's College, Oxford, but still recognized (not least by himself) as a spokesman for public schools, wrote to the Permanent Secretary at the Board of Education: 'Headmasters are literally spending half their time in commercial travelling and touting on preparatory school doorsteps.'[28] While difficult to imagine the suave and aloof Vellacott dunning for trade, the point was well made. Harrow was partly a victim of its own complacency and previous success: Leaf's bewilderment at the hard financial realities was merely an extreme form of a general denial of fundamental danger that pervaded the school regardless of Vellacott's constant efforts to bring home the true situation. This was underlined by the stunned reaction of some Old Harrovians (including masters) in January 1939 when Walter Monckton deliberately leaked the information that the governors were preparing plans to move the school away from the Hill.[29]

In the winter of 1938/9 the HMC organized a private ballot of 86 schools on whether there should be a new Royal Commission. The governors of Harrow, worried at the open-ended nature of any such scrutiny, with another 50 schools voted against the idea, 35 voting for it. In private, however, in November 1939 and again in the winter of 1941/2, the Board of Education was approached for a financial grant to save the school from closure. Baldwin, who made the second approach, received sympathy but the less than reassuring, or even accurate advice that if more economies were entertained, the school would survive the war.[30]

In 1940 the irrepressible Norwood suggested a Royal Commission specifically to investigate the integration of the public schools into the state system. He envisaged

---

[26] See below, n. 121.   [27] HA Masters' Files, F. A. Leaf to P. C. Vellacott, 31 Jan. 1939.
[28] Simon, *Politics of Educational Reform*, 275, *et seq.*
[29] HA Gorse Papers, 25 Jan. 1939, Vellacott to Gorse.
[30] GBM, 15 Mar., 15 Nov. 1939, 17 Dec. 1941, 11 Feb. 1942; Simon, *Politics of Educational Reform*, 275.

a settlement similar to the state aid to the grammar schools after 1902 but without the administrative interference of central or local government. Public schools would accept 10 per cent of poor pupils with no strings attached, a neat, if modest, move in the direction of social responsibility without losing sight of the core need for financial assistance.[31] In March 1940 an internal Board of Education report proposed a Royal Commission to study the relationship of public schools to the maintained sector, adding the far from equitable or egalitarian idea of tax relief for school fees.[32] In April 1941 E. C. Mack, the pioneering historian of attitudes to public schools since the eighteenth century, no uncritical friend of traditional boarding schools, predicted that after the war 'the most likely solution . . . would be one in which the Public Schools would take state money and accept state interference in order to bring into their ranks the best elements of the working class'.[33] Finally, under concerted pressure from the public schools, in July 1942 R. A. Butler, as President of the Board of Education, established a departmental committee, chaired by the Scottish judge, Lord Fleming, 'to consider means whereby the association between the public schools [defined as members of the HMC and the newly formed Governing Bodies Association, including Harrow, set up to champion wholly independent schools] and the general educational system . . . could be developed and extended'. Unlike in 1861, the public schools had made the running under the banner of wishing to embrace some idea of equality. They were powerfully represented on the Fleming Committee by men such as Spencer Leeson, by then Head Master of Winchester.[34]

High-mindedness and self-interest coincided. Many public schools wanted a way to attract government money while retaining their independence and avoiding political opprobrium. The Harrow governors, in again rejecting the idea of a Royal Commission in June 1940, had feared lest a request for state money would appear 'as an attempt to benefit these schools at the public expense' and arouse 'strong political opposition'. A commitment to 'draw their boys from wider sources' provided schools with the means to avoid this.[35]

When the Fleming Committee reported in 1944 its proposals as they affected boarding public schools (known as Scheme B) were accepted in principle by both the HMC (conveniently chaired by Leeson) and the GBA. The plan was for the state, through means-tested Board of Education bursaries or Local Authority grants, to subsidize initially at least 25 per cent of public school entrants who were to be drawn from the maintained sector, with a view to increasing the proportion over time to make such schools 'equally accessible to all pupils'. There were no

---

[31] Mack, *Public Schools and British Opinion since 1860*, 455–7.
[32] Simon, *Politics of Educational Reform*, 275.
[33] Mack, *Public Schools and British Opinion since 1860*, 462.
[34] On the Fleming Committee, Report, and its fate see J. C. Dancy, *The Public Schools and the Future* (London, 1963), pp. 16–21; Sanderson, *Educational Opportunity*, 65–6.
[35] GBM, 11 June 1940; Dancy, *Public Schools*, 17.

provisions for any direct administrative interference by the state. Nevertheless, the thrust of the scheme was the integration of boarding schools into the state system. Given a guarded welcome by the public schools, including Harrow,[36] the Fleming proposals failed through government indifference. R. A. Butler was more concerned with his far-reaching Education Act of 1944 which, while admitting a role for boarding education, also referred to the need to restrain public expenditure. In 1946 his Labour successor Ellen Wilkinson, while encouraging individual Local Authorities' arrangements with boarding schools, suggested there should be a national scheme. Most Local Authorities were lukewarm and ministers, of both parties, refused to provide incentives or a lead. Only a few, mainly Conservative, Local Authorities opened negotiations with local boarding schools. Although the GBA revived the idea of state aid in 1958[37] there was no systematic integration of state and independent secondary education, the provision of boarding except for the disabled, disturbed, or criminal remaining in private hands. This dichotomy of approach was reinforced by the Newsom Commission Report of 1968 from which it could be inferred (and was by the Harrow governors) that the state regarded boarding 'need' primarily in terms of abnormal or defective backgrounds and 'maladjusted' children. If that was what was intended as a basis for admission of state pupils, the governors noted dryly, 'the Public Schools would have to change fundamentally'.[38]

The significance of the Fleming Report lay in its identification of a social conscience in public schools which persisted, at least in public, even after the financial imperatives that had first encouraged its discovery had disappeared. Middlesex was one of the few Local Educational Authorities that remained enthusiastic, Harrow the beneficiary. For a quarter of a century from 1947 Harrow admitted five Middlesex scholars a year selected from local grammar schools on interview and record, the proportion of fees paid by the council determined by parental means test.[39] Although this went some way towards the Fleming principle, it did little to leaven the plutocratic mass. The numbers were proportionately tiny (at most twenty-five at any one time). Some housemasters needed to be cajoled into accepting them.[40] If known, some Middlesex scholars suffered the condescension of snobbish adolescent peers. As Dr James remarked in the 1960s, the scheme required careful presentation to avoid suggestion of poaching clever boys from local grammar schools, such as the first-class Harrow County.[41] Even as a mild form of social engineering, the scheme had limits: in 1952 it was reported that all the Middlesex scheme entrants came from private schools.[42] This was not entirely surprising as the 1944 Education Act's introduction of the Eleven-Plus Examination had increased the

---

[36] GBM, 20 Sept. 1944.   [37] GBM, 15 Feb. 1958.   [38] GBM, 26 Sept. 1968.
[39] GBM, 6 Nov. 1946, 5 Feb., 8 Nov. 1947, 8 May 1948, etc. Cf. HM/J/18 Feb. 1966, James to marquess of Aberdeen.
[40] HA Minutes of Housemasters' Meetings 1949–67, 6 Feb. 1950.   [41] HM/J/18 Feb. 1966.
[42] Minutes of Housemasters' Meetings, 1949–67, 2 June 1952.

divergence of state and independent schools, where the usual transfer age to secondary level was 13. As early as September 1944 the idea was floated that any state bursaries under the Fleming scheme should cover sending a successful candidate to Preparatory School for two years at 11. A version of this proposal was revived in the report to the governors of their Long-Term Planning Committee in 1978, this time with the school not the state footing the bill.[43] In the event the plan proved too expensive, although a similar scheme was pursued by Eton. The demise of grammar schools in the 1970s effectively severed links between Harrow and LEA schools for a generation, the two sectors increasingly inhabiting different, highly politicized, and mutually antagonistic universes.

The commitment to educate the less wealthy persisted beyond the days of financial crisis. In 1944, launched by Winston Churchill at his annual winter visit to Songs, an appeal was begun to raise money to enable indigent sons of Old Harrovians killed or ruined by the war to enter Harrow, as after 1918, and to allow entry into the school of boys from poorer classes. Churchill voiced supreme confidence in the efficacy of a public school education but argued for a broader social intake.[44] In the main, the War Memorial Appeal, following the similar fund established in 1917, aided sons of Old Harrovians, there being no internal desire nor obvious external demand to widen the school's social embrace. This and numerous other funds established for similar purposes, were used primarily to protect the older class of Harrow entrant rather than encourage entry from new ones. As the relative incomes of clergymen, academics, and schoolteachers declined in relation to increasing school fees and those of business, banking, and industry, Harrow governors and Head Masters, keen to maintain a high proportion of old boys' sons, used these funds to shore up the social mix as it had existed in some notional pre-1939 or even -c.1914 school. However, on Churchill's death in 1965, a Churchill Memorial Appeal raised well over £20,000 to provide assistance for pupils who would not otherwise go to Harrow. Although the resulting endowment was relatively modest, for some years from 1967 it provided for one scholar a year from the borough of Harrow.[45] However, this failed to fill the gap left by the end of the Middlesex scheme in the 1970s. From the late 1980s various attempts were made to attract at least one local scholar a year despite the difficulties of matching the state and private curriculum. The most recent attempt to acknowledge the local geographical and social environment of Harrow was also the most historic. In 1996 £20,000 was allocated from the John Lyon Charity towards paying for Sixth Form scholarships from local state schools. Known as the John Lyon Scholarships, they were funded by income from the former Road Trust lands released for local charitable purposes by a Statutory Instrument in

---

[43] GBM, 20 Sept. 1944, 17 July 1978.
[44] *The Harrovian*, 6 Dec. 1944; GBM, 13 Feb. 1917; Laborde, *Harrow School*, 155–6.
[45] GBM, 7 June 1966, 11 Nov. 1967, 9 Nov. 1968, 21 Mar. 1970.

1991.[46] For the first time in four hundred years, the express intent of the Founder that no money from his Paddington estates be spent on the school was overcome.

The desire to challenge the entirely accurate perception of Harrow as a rich man's school remained. Much of the inspiration for local bursaries or scholarships was cosmetic and political. As experience showed, there was little local demand. In any case, the governors managed an increasingly successful local day school, John Lyon School. For Harrow, the social issue was viewed in national terms as the demand from less wealthy local families for boarding education evaporated. In 1989 the school committed itself 'to devise schemes whereby boys from poorer families in the British Isles may attend the School' and to increase the number of bursaries 'so that the school may accommodate a wide range of candidates'.[47] This was not to be met by public funds. The idea of a state Assisted Places Scheme had been proposed by the GBA in 1970. The idea was revived by the new Conservative government in 1979. Introduced in 1981, the scheme was rejected by the Harrow governors, although they joined it on behalf of John Lyon School. They argued that the Assisted Places grants helped parents with education, not boarding fees and were thus primarily aimed at day schools.[48] In part to compensate for this and to fulfil the objectives described in 1989, P. A. Beckwith allocated half of a £5 million donation to the school in 1992 to assisted places.[49] Because of bursaries for sons of Old Harrovians and other categories of indigent boys, music and art awards and the academic scholarships filled each year since the 1970s almost exclusively by candidates who were down for Harrow in any case, full fees have been paid by perhaps 80–85 per cent. In 1968 it was claimed that 100 out of 700 boys received financial assistance of one sort or another.[50] Whether such policies widened the social complexion of the school, still less its atmosphere or attitudes, must be doubted; the assumptions behind the curriculum matched those of a particular conservative social group, from the maintenance of classics to the dominance of sport.

The image of Harrow as a socially exclusive school for the very well off matched reality. One of the most striking features of the school's twentieth-century experience has been the extent to which, not least since 1945, this circumstance received only modest political challenge and much active encouragement.[51] The chief threat to the elite status of Harrow was not that it trained snobs but that it trained fewer leaders in a less distinctively superior manner. Competition from other public schools in standards of academic and extra-curriculum education and in the level of fees proved more challenging than state scrutiny. Successive government education policies have, whatever their intent, worked to the advantage of independent

---

[46] GBM, 30 Nov. 1996; *Statutory Instruments 1991 No. 1141 Charities: The Charities (John Lyon Road Trust) Order 1991*.
[47] Policy Document on Long-Term Priorities, May 1989, pp. ii, 2.
[48] GBM, 7 Nov. 1970, 10 Nov. 1979, 5 June 1980, 12 Mar. 1983.
[49] GBM, 30 May 1992.   [50] GBM, 26 Sept. 1968.
[51] For what follows see Sanderson, *Educational Opportunity*, 8–10, 67–9.

secondary education. Both the 1902 and the 1944 Education Acts, by increasing the state funded element in grammar schools, drove certain socially sensitive middle-class parents to the private sector. The introduction of the Eleven-Plus Examination after 1944 denied access to grammar schools for the less academic, regardless of class or income. Although this mainly benefited day schools, the move of the expanding wealthier middle classes towards the private sector provided an important constituency of goodwill even among those who could not personally afford boarding fees. This trend was accelerated by the wholesale comprehensivization of secondary education by both Labour and Conservative governments in the 1960s and 1970s; the abolition of Direct Grant schools in 1975; and the perception of a decline in state schools under the Conservative government in the 1980s. The Assisted Places scheme of 1981, which appealed directly to social as well as academic aspirations, appeared to confirm a view that state schools were in some ways regarded by the government as less good than public schools. Unsurprisingly, this caused resentment in the state sector for which the government was responsible. The re-banding of public schools as 'independent schools' from the 1970s suited the prevailing political mood. It also acknowledged that, despite a rise in the percentage of pupils educated privately in the mid-1980s, numbers at boarding schools were declining and that many independent schools (e.g. former direct grant grammar schools) had never conformed to the stereotype of the traditional public school.

The general benefits of sympathetic government policy were great, especially if the tax system befriended high-earners, as in the 1980s and 1990s when Harrow fees were rising at more than twice the rate of inflation (1983–93 fees up 127.5 per cent; inflation 51.7).[52] In 1951, just after the Conservative election victory, some Harrow governors suggested asking the Royal Commission on Taxation and Profits to consider tax relief for school fees.[53] The twentieth-century dominance of right-of-centre governments helped the survival and prosperity of all independent schools. Harrow's political associations proved especially useful. Conservative politicians were a familiar sight on the governing body in the first three-quarters of the century. In 1926 the governors proposed to lobby the Old Harrovian chancellor of the Exchequer, Winston Churchill, to relieve school profits of Income Tax leaving the Head Master to contact OH MPs, three of whom were governors anyway (L. S. Amery, E. C. Grenfell, and F. S. Jackson).[54] Without Churchill in 10 Downing Street, Harrow's chances of survival on the Hill in 1940–2 would have been sharply diminished: moving would have been fatal. Mrs Thatcher, a Harrow parent, used to visit the school as Prime Minster and in 1987 hosted a fund-raising reception at Downing Street which alone raised almost £360,000 towards the school Appeal.[55] Such cosiness was not inevitable; the local Conservative MP provoked Head

[52] GBM, 26 Feb. 1994.   [53] GBM, 10 Nov. 1951.
[54] GBM, 20 May 1926.   [55] GBM, 6 June 1987, 27 Feb. 1988.

Master Beer's withering scorn when he voiced support for local residents' anxieties over school building plans in the early 1990s.

Nor was it of any help when the economy failed. While political storms were weathered with remarkable ease, financial difficulty could threaten disaster. As was recognized of the 1930s but often forgotten in the 1970s, Harrow's success could be charted by scrutiny of the Stock Market. Vaughan and Butler were great Head Masters partly because of the favourable economic climate. Just as James in the 1950s and Beer in the 1980s were fortunate to coincide with propitious economic and political circumstances, so Head Master Hoban was unlucky with both in the 1970s. As was recalled in 1989, 'the greatest danger to the independent schools over the past twenty five years was in 1974 when the Financial Times index fell below 150'.[56]

Governors

Although Harrow's fortunes were inevitably associated with its Head Masters, on the governors lay responsibility for the school's strategic policy. After the new governing body and statutes of 1871–4, no major decision was the Head's alone. This relative standing found physical illustration in their waiting to be summoned into governors' meetings, in their study to be fetched by the Custos; sitting on a chair at the door; or pacing around outside.[57] For most observers, governors tended to be shadowy figures receiving attention only in times of crisis or when they appointed Head Masters, their personalities, backgrounds, and supposed predilections suddenly becoming the subject of much speculation. At other times, the school took little cognizance of its governors; there are relatively few portraits or busts of any of them in the school, those that there are, with a few exceptions, marking public not gubernatorial achievement.

For much of the century, the governors reciprocated this detachment, only meeting at Harrow once a year. Under the 1871 and 1874 Statutes, the only formal contact between masters and governors was through the Head Master, although the governor elected by the Head and Assistant Masters often acted as a conduit of information, primarily from the governors to the school: it was Leo Amery, as Masters' governor, who communicated the bad news of salary cuts in January 1940 and received the complaints against Boissier's dismissal of his arch enemy Venables in 1942.[58] Although active behind the scenes and often involved in surprising trivia

---

[56] Policy Document on Long-Term Priorities, 1.
[57] Respectively Dr James, Mr Hoban, and Mr Beer.
[58] GBM, 15 Nov., 6 Dec. 1939; Masters' Files, L. W. Henry, 19 Jan. 1940; HM/Boissier/8 Mar. 1942, H. J. L. Gorse to Boissier containing copy of letter Gorse, Henry, and Plumptre to Amery, 7 Mar. 1942; HM/Bos/11 Mar. 1942, Amery to Henry.

(e.g. the debate over the exact shade of blue for the school jacket or 'bluer' in 1978), as one retired senior housemaster commented in the 1940s, 'neither masters nor boys see much of the governing Body, whose activities are estimated rather than observed'.[59] The descent by a number of governors on the Hill following the night-club scandal of 1925, when some Harrovians were caught *in flagrante delicto*, caused a sensation. More usual was the experience of E. M. Venables, a master 1917–42, with Dr F. W. Pember, chairman of the governors 1924–42: 'In all my twenty-five years at Harrow I had thirty seconds with Dr Pember, who asked me when I was at Cambridge.' Venables was an Oxford man.[60]

Certain individual governors were more communicative than Dr Pember, for example his colleague and vice-chairman, the banker E. C. Grenfell, later Lord St Just (governor 1922–41). Naturally, for a body comprised overwhelmingly of old boys (of the 100 governors appointed 1900–86, only seventeen were not Old Harrovians: between 1900 and 1976, there were only five), personal social links with masters and parents were legion.[61] Head Master Boissier complained of one of his housemasters, the historian L. W. Henry, 'if things do not go his way he rushes off to some governor . . . and slangs the whole place'.[62] Most contacts were more convivial. There were always OHs not on the governing body of great influence, none more than Sir Francis Fladgate, a solicitor like his grandfather and namesake who had been clerk to the governors 1802–22. As chairman of the War Memorial Committee after 1918 Fladgate not only raised over £100,000 for the memorial building and bursaries for sons of Harrovians killed in the war but supervised the physical and aesthetic transformation of the centre of the school and the Hill in the 1920s.[63] Some Old Harrovian masters, such as E. M. Butler or M. C. Kemp, acquired privileged status: in retirement the former became chairman of the Harrow Association (founded in 1907), the latter a trustee of the Football Field Trust. During the acute financial crisis of 1938–40, the governors secretly consulted a number of important old boys about the possibility of leaving the Hill, such as T. G. Blackwell, of Crosse and Blackwell, a trustee of the Land Trust, Endowment Fund, and Apcar Bequest.[64] A regular attender at these conferences was H. J. L. Gorse, at that time simply an assistant master teaching science, but a Head of School (in 1921), prominent in the Lodge and treasurer of the Endowment Fund. He joined a select group dined by Walter Monckton and Blackwell in January 1939 to test initial reactions to the idea of moving the school. What he heard so upset Gorse that he immedi-

---

[59] GBM, 1 June 1978, 31 May 1979; Venables, *Bases Attempted*, 46.
[60] Venables, *Bases Attempted*, 46.
[61] For lists of governors see *Harrow Register, 1800–1911*, 898; *Harrow Register, 1885–1949*, 670–1; L. J. Verney (ed.), *Harrow Register, 1986* (London, 1987), pp. 795–7.
[62] HM/Bos/7 Aug. 1942, Boissier to R. W. Moore.
[63] Laborde, *Harrow School*, 155–7; GBM, 13 Feb., 10 June 1918, etc. Fladgate was also a prominent freemason: *Harrow Register, 1845–1937*, 351.   [64] GBM, 7 Dec. 1938.

ately wrote describing the evening to Head Master Vellacott who, it transpired, knew nothing about Monckton's scheming.[65]

Such informal links contrasted with the rigid constitutional procedures. For most of the century the governors' business was conducted in circumstances of secrecy and clubland intrigue, their *ex cathedra* judgments being handed down to the school through the Head Master. Governors repeatedly refused to receive formal delegations of masters or admit their specific advice, for example on names for Head Masters, as in 1925 over the succession to Ford.[66] Although meeting a group of disgruntled parents over Boissier's handling of the dismissals of Venables and his son-in-law John Bostock in 1942, the governors had no formal contact with the three masters who were leading the discontent: Henry, Gorse, and Plumptre.[67] Individual governors or *ad hoc* committees did frequently conduct sensitive or contentious negotiations, as over certain senior masters' pension entitlements in the 1970s and 1980s. Yet the principle contained in the statutes that so alarmed Bowen and his colleagues in the 1870s, that of refusing masters right of appeal against the Head, was vigorously defended, even in cases involving senior and powerful school figures. In 1929 C. G. Pope, exercised his statutory right to make a statement to the governors against his dismissal as housemaster of The Grove and from the staff. As a concession to his standing as an OH and Master-in-Charge of Cricket, he was allowed to present his argument in person but, as in similar circumstances fifty years later, the governors refused to countenance any questioning of the Head Master's decision, on the later occasion twice explicitly informing the dismissed housemaster that they supported the Head's action.[68] Although causing factional discontent, such unwavering public support was inevitable if the governors wished to retain Head Masters' services. This behaviour did not mean that the governors always approved of all that Heads did but it reinforced their official detachment. The relationship of the Head with the governors was crucial. At least two post-1914 Head Masters suffered from whispering campaigns that appeared to some to have been orchestrated by certain governors: the exasperation at Wood was mirrored by the harrying of Ford. It is a strange feature that most Head Masters in the first half of the century had less than warm relations with the governors. Not the least part of the image of success engendered by James and Beer was that they managed the governors well.

With added pressure on funds and the need to modernize the fabric, administration, and planning of the school from the 1970s, the Governing Body became less remote, meeting at least three times a year at Harrow and regularly entertaining masters and monitors. The governors' Long-Term Planning Committee of

[65] Ibid., 1 Feb., 7 Mar., 10 May 1939, 13 Mar. 1940; Gorse Papers, 5 Jan. 1939 (Monckton to Gorse), 25 Jan. 1939 (Vellacott to Gorse). [66] GBM, 5 Nov. 1925.
[67] GBM, 10 and 18 Mar. 1942; HM/Bos/11 Mar. 1942, Amery to Henry.
[68] GBM, 13 Nov. 1929, 10 Nov. 1979, 1 Mar. 1980.

1978 had a master as secretary[69] and subsequent strategic planning attempted to integrate the wishes and perspectives of masters as well as governors. The last quarter of the twentieth century saw a radical shift in the nature of the governors' role. Hitherto cautious, conservative, sceptical of innovation, often fearful of change, bound up with legal and financial niceties, from the mid-1970s the governors adopted a more positive approach to the immediate and longer-term plans for the school. This may in part have been forced upon them by the economic blizzards of that decade and the building of the Central Feeding block and the new boarding house, the New Knoll, followed by the progressive refurbishment of the old houses. Whether they liked it or not, the governors' actions were effecting the detail of the school's life in ways previously unimagined except in wartime. Increasingly, the Harrow governors, like their counterparts across the HMC, confronted the financial problems of the 1970s and 1980s by conceiving of the school as a business with assets that required greater commercial exploitation (e.g. holiday lets, hiring out public rooms, marketing the name, etc.). By the end of the century, this commercial arm of the school's activities initially embodied in a company called Lyon Services, contributed importantly to the school's bank balance, some years making the difference between profit and loss.[70]

In their own deliberations, the governors began to display enthusiasm for current administrative, managerial, and educational fashion, developments presided over by R. A. A. Holt (governor 1952–82) with sixteen years as Chairman of the GPC, ten as vice-Chairman, and eight as Chairman, and driven by figures with commercial not just financial backgrounds such as R. H. Boissier (elected 1976), N. A. S. Owen (1979), and the American businessman G. R. Simmonds (1975), as well as the future Cabinet Secretary F. E. R. Butler (1975) as member and Chairman of the GPC and later Chairman of the board himself. Significantly, of the twenty governors appointed or elected between 1976 and 1986, eleven were not Old Harrovians; two were women.[71] The provision of five-year terms, introduced in 1939, was exercised more effectively as the turnover of elected governors increased as well as numbers.

From traditional Olympian aloofness and occasional condescension, cooperation became the watchword, even when honoured in the breach. Although the gulf remained between the parochial interests of masters and the wider—but not always clearer—perspectives of governors, from the 1980s a résumé of decisions taken at governors' meetings was shown to masters.[72] Parents and old boys were

[69] M. A. Crofts, GBM, 17 July 1978.

[70] See GBM and GPC 1978 onwards; 13 June 1998 for Lyon Services' halving the running deficit.

[71] Lady Soames, daughter of Winston Churchill, in 1980; the duchess of Abercorn in 1986, keeping alive the Hamilton connection begun by John Hamilton, first marquess of Abercorn, at Harrow under Sumner and a governor, 1811–18.

[72] For moves towards engagement see GBM, 10 Nov. 1984 re role of Masters' governor; 4 June 1988 re 'the great improvement in communication with the Masters' Room [sic]'.

included in the public gubernatorial embrace. In 1976 the governors experimented by electing a 'parents' governor', as well as a local governor in 1978, followed twenty years later by moves to include representatives from the Harrow Association on the governing body.[73] In 1990 there appeared the suggestion that Harrow should have a resident governor on the Hill, the equivalent to Eton's Provost: when consulted the Head Master-elect, N. R. Bomford, with characteristic tact, did 'not feel able to express a view'.[74] The idea may have seemed an intimacy more intrusive than helpful. Yet, despite such actual or proposed changes, with the exception of the senior, well-connected, or inquisitive, unless being urged directly to assist in another round of economies, masters of the later twentieth century followed their predecessors in holding only the haziest notion of governors' strategy, policies, and priorities.

The business of governing Harrow became progressively more complicated as the twentieth century proceeded. For much of the time the governors had to deal with a variety of separate Trusts established to control various chunks of property or endowment.[75] Although they took direct control of the Park Trust in 1917, there remained the 1913 Endowment Fund; the Land Trust (which controlled the Northwick estate); the Philathletic (i.e. cricket) Field Trust; and the Football Field Trust. Until the pooling of scholarships and prizes, many bequests were managed separately as were the funds generated by the massive legacies of Shepard Churchill and Gregory Apcar. Investment, sale, and application of income and the management of credit had variously to be negotiated with the Public Trustee, the Board of Education, and the Charity Commissioners. Before direct control, the governors had to borrow from the various Trusts and funds established for the school's benefit and repay the loans. After the Second World War appeal money was held separate from the central funds of the school by the War Memorial Trust (as after the First), the Harrow Trust, and, from 1984, the Development Trust which, to avoid involvement in any possible future statutory attacks on the school's finances, controlled its own assets.[76] The Road Trust generated much work and no useable income until 1991 when it was replaced by the John Lyon Charity, which in turn added a new administrative load. So too did the administration, through a separate Management Committee, of John Lyon School for which the governors of Harrow retained a statutory responsibility. In addition to managing the school and the estate, for much of the century the governors operated a masters' pension scheme which, with its modern replacement, involved them in delicate, often acrimonious negotiations with the supposed beneficiaries. The 'New System' of running houses in 1936, fully adopted by 1948, placed the auditing and monitoring of house

[73] GBM, 27 May, 6 Nov. 1976 (J. Macdonald-Buchanan), 11 Nov. 1978 (A. de la P. Beresford).
[74] GBM, 1 Dec. 1990.
[75] The bulk of the evidence upon which the following is based is in GBM and GPC.
[76] GBM, 16 June 1984. For pooling of funds see ibid., 10 Nov. 1956, 5 June 1980.

accounts under the governors' direct scrutiny, a process of control that was completed by the centralization of house accounting in the 1980s, the role of the Bursar, and the numbers employed in the Bursary growing in proportion to the governors' direct authority.[77]

The policy of protecting the school by buying most available property on the Hill as well as the boarding houses before and after the First World War involved the governors in new responsibilities as purchasers and landlords, very different from their previous relations with their Middlesex farming tenants. To cope with the new demands, in 1918 the pre-war Finance Committee was replaced by a General Purposes Committee[78] which, from the late 1940s, assumed the central executive role as regards school property and accounts, making it the cockpit of decision, even if the full Governing Body retained the power to reject or amend GPC proposals. After the Second World War a separate Committee was established to oversee fee remissions, bursaries, and scholarships.[79] In 1955, following legislation and a vital court ruling that released two-thirds of trust income for unrestricted investment, an Investment Committee was created, including financial experts not on the Governing Body as well as the governors' brokers.[80] With the mushrooming of committees and subcommittees, permanent, semi-permanent (e.g. the Heraldry Committee, wound up in 1987),[81] and *ad hoc* (e.g. for various Appeals or the Quatercentenary celebrations) the number of governors was expanded from the original ten of 1871, to fifteen in 1939, twenty in 1974, and twenty-five in 1997.[82]

In 1939, as part of an attempt to enshrine Old Harrovian influence on gubernatorial decisions by way of a new financial advisory committee, the solicitor L. M. Hewlett argued that governors were 'not able to give the time and attention to detail which is essential if the finance of the school is to be carried on on sound lines'. This was not entirely fair, especially as a special financial standing committee had been formed in 1936 comprising Grenfell, Amery, Monckton, and the Head Master.[83] None the less, Hewlett had a point. Since 1871 governors were—and are—unpaid. At any one time, only a few governors were consistently active on school business and even then usually in conjunction with other occupations.

---

[77] See GBM, 27 Feb. 1988 for an increase in Bursary staff of four, in part to cope with new centralized accounting systems for which see GBM 19 Nov. 1988, 25 Feb. 1989. Somervell managed with one secretary, a method that persisted through Goodden and Ledward to the Second World War. By the 1990s the Bursary staff occupied a whole building. Another guide to the increase in business is the inexorable rise in salaries paid to Bursars who by the 1980s and 1990s were more highly paid and received more substantial benefits than any other employee except the Head Master.

[78] GBM, 10 and 27 June 1918.

[79] Partly as a consequence of the Harrow Trust taking over remissions: GBM, 6 Oct., 13 Nov. 1948.   [80] GBM, 7 May 1955.

[81] On L. J. Verney's retirement as governor see GBM, 21 Feb. 1987.

[82] GBM, 14 Apr. 1939, 30 May 1974, 29 Nov. 1997.

[83] Gorse Papers, L. M. Hewlett, 'Memorandum on the Future of Harrow School', Feb. 1939; GBM, 4 Nov. 1936.

Challenges

However, the only serious strategic error of which the governors can be accused was their reluctance until the 1970s to increase fees sufficiently to tackle the systemic as opposed to immediate weakness in the school's current account where income inadequately covered expenditure. Sole reliance on numbers solved only half the equation. The need to establish an impregnable endowment had been recognized before the First World War, leading to the creation of the Endowment Fund in 1913, but almost all subsequent attempts to reserve bequests or investment income or appeal money were vitiated either by short-term financial current account debts, as in the 1930s and 1940s, or by huge capital expenditure, on property in the 1920s and 1930s; repairs and modernization of the fabric from the 1960s to 1990s; or new buildings, such as Central Feeding and a new house in the 1970s, a Sports Hall and a CDT centre in the 1980s, and a theatre in the 1990s.

For most of the century the school account required an overdraft at the bank at times of astronomical proportions. By the end of the 1920s it had reached £40,000 (c.£1.2 million today); in February 1939 it stood at £95,000 (around £3 million today).[84] In 1951, with the Ministry of Education inspectors soothingly commenting that the school's 'indebtedness does not appear unduly large in relation to the capital assets and . . . the existence of the Harrow Trust' (which contained the money raised by the appeal at the end of the war), the bank overdraft was around £80,000, rising to over £88,000 in December 1953, with interest charged on £66,000 of it; this latter element was paid off only by 1970.[85] Despite regularly running surpluses of up to £500,000 in the late 1980s, which still represented less than the 10 per cent of turnover, the building programme led to an overdraft in 1988 of almost £1,170,000 as cash outflow ate away any profit.[86] Yet, in the 1980s and 1990s as in the 1920s and 1930s, dexterous juggling of funds and occasional windfalls allowed the governors to fulfil the same function as their predecessors before 1914 in satisfying the imperative of providing the luxury and quality of facilities and resources, human and material, demanded by an expensive school with a grand reputation.

If money lay at the heart of the governors' business it did not necessarily dominate their approach or mentality. Not all governors were businessmen; not all businessmen governors saw their role purely in financial terms. The tradition of annual inspection of the School's Charter, a characteristic invention of Monty Butler when Masters' governor (1901–18), only ceased when the document returned to the school archives in the 1980s.[87] The dominant figures over the century have

---

[84] GBM, 23 Feb., 11 May 1927, and *passim* until 20 May 1935 when it began to increase sharply; GBM, 1 Feb., 10 May 1939.
[85] *Report by His Majesty's Inspectors on Harrow School, Middlesex, May 1951* (Ministry of Education, London, 1951), p. 3; GBM, 11 Nov. 1950, 3 May 1952, 7 Feb., 11 June 1953, 8 Nov. 1969.
[86] GBM, 19 Nov. 1988. For closer details for these figures see relevant GPC reports.
[87] GBM, 6 June 1987.

varied considerably more than the school's financial predicament. There were no coherent patterns in appointment or election of governors. There has been a strong masonic element, from Lord George Hamilton onwards. Awareness of public sensitivity to this was reflected in the decision in 1979 not to commemorate the OH Lodge's gift of £1,500 to renew the chairs in the Old Harrovian Room (where the Lodge held meetings) by erecting a plaque or frame 'recording the source of the donation' because 'it would not be appropriate'.[88] In the early 1970s it was joked that the governors were becoming an Elmfield mafia: Holt; his predecessor as Chairman, Lord McCorquodale and A. McCorquodale, between them governors 1947–52, 1963–71, 1972–82; the Marquess of Zetland (1962–72); K. R. M. Carlisle (1966–76); Sir Donald Cameron (1967–77); Sir Peter Studd (1971–80); E. A. R. de Rothschild (1976); J. R. Findlay (1977–82); Sir Michael Thomas, who helped arrange the transfer of the school's investment portfolio from Lazard's to his own firm of Buckmaster and Moore in 1972.[89] In addition to the statutory external appointees of Oxford, Cambridge, the Royal Society, the Lord Chancellor, and the Masters, the Governing Body customarily included a clergyman (Archbishop Davidson 1905–29; Bishop Hicks of Lincoln 1927–42; Dean White-Thomson of Canterbury 1947–62 and 1965–70; Canon Gilliat of Sheffield 1970–5; Dean Mann of Windsor 1976–90; Bishop Jones of Sodor and Man, 1991). Soldiers were regularly elected, including General H. S. Horne (1924–9), Major-General Sir Allan Adair (1947–52), Field Marshal Earl Alexander of Tunis (1952–62), and Lt-General Sir John Akehurst (1982–97). Bankers and financiers have inevitably loomed large since Walter Leaf and Frederick Huth Jackson from before 1914 and E. C. Grenfell between the wars. Politicians traditionally constituted a significant element, this century including W. H. Long (1918–24); F. S. Jackson (1923–7; 1939–47); L. S. Amery (1925–55), S. Baldwin (1930–45), S. J. G. Hoare (1947–8), M. S. McCorquodale (1947–52, 1962–71), J. D. Profumo (1952–7), W. T. Monckton (although in his legal days 1930–47), and the legal politician D. B. Somervell (1944–60). It is striking that no active or retired national politician sat as a governor for the last quarter of the century, perhaps a sign of political tact and the increased expectations of commitment in both positions. Some politicians were anyway purely iconic if not decorative. Whereas Leo Amery was one of the most active and influential governors of the first half of the century, Baldwin, although elected in 1930, attended his first meeting only in 1938, his main contribution being to chair the tricky meetings with Old Harrovians over the financial crisis of 1939 and the school's possible move.[90] Sam Hoare's brief tenure was wholly ephemeral as he confessed he was unable to attend any meetings.[91] Next to money men from banks, industry, and the City, lawyers, barristers, and solicitors, have played as

---

[88] GBM, 3 Mar. 1979.   [89] GBM, 10 Nov. 1972.
[90] GBM, 14 June 1938. It could be argued that in the mean time he had had other things to do.
[91] GBM, 15 Sept. 1947.

large a role as any other group: Pember, Monckton, Somervell, Holt, L. J. Verney (1972–87), about whom his colleagues recorded: 'there was no Old Harrovian who was more dedicated to the school';[92] and M. B. Connell (1983).

Perhaps the most important lawyers have been the successive clerks, i.e. solicitors, to the governors, only eight since Francis Fladgate in 1802, each with their own style. As takers of minutes, where the nineteenth-century H. and G. W. Young were prolix, W. G. King was positively terse. M. Percival Hardy (1916–35) and G. F. Finch (a relation of Francis Fladgate, 1935–60) attempted to record much of the flavour of discussion, if any, while J. B. Gilbart-Smith (1960–83) was as circumspect and as brief as sense allowed, although he did introduce typed minutes in 1965.[93] A. J. F. Stebbings (1983) returned to fuller minutes that permitted the reader to understand the context for decisions without having to refer to those of the various reporting committees. The most signal clerk's triumph was the partial breaking of the Road Trust by Statutory Instrument in 1991 after a five-year process and repeated earlier failures (e.g. 1939, 1945, 1966, 1967, 1968, 1980), the key having been to suggest application of the trust income to local charities in the boroughs bordering the Harrow Road not directly to the school.[94]

Recruitment depended on the old boy network; from the 1970s, with increasing numbers, order was lent the procedure by one governor organizing nominations. The Harrow governing body did not operate in isolation, many governors being associated with its work before election, for example as members of the Investment Committee, successive Appeal committees, the Quartercentenary Committee, as informal financial consultants or as officers of the Harrow Association. Typical of this process was the committee established in May 1939 to investigate the financing of the school which comprised four governors and six Old Harrovians, of whom four (F. S. Jackson, then president of the Harrow Association, the earl of Radnor, M. S. McCorquodale, and G. C. Rivington) later became governors.[95] Three of these rose to be Chairman, Rivington, with his close links to the Harrow Association, which he also chaired, exerting a strong influence throughout his time as a governor (1939–69).

With few exceptions, the dominant governors were Old Harrovians. Yet there was no bias towards occupation, merely availability. Twentieth-century Chairmen have been political grandees (the Liberal Earl Spencer 1888–1908 and the Tories Lord George Hamilton 1908–24, Walter Long 1924, F. S. Jackson 1942–6, and M. S. McCorquodale 1964–71); lawyers (the academic Pember 1924–42, the political Somervell 1947–53, the solicitor Holt 1971–80, and the High Court Judge

---

[92] GBM, 21 Feb. 1987.
[93] GBM, 6 Feb. 1965. Committee minutes had been typed for years before, GPC since 1948, GBM, 7 Feb. 1948.
[94] GBM, 7 Mar. 1939, 2 May 1945, 12 Feb., 7 June 1966, 11 Nov. 1967, 30 May 1968, 8 Nov. 1980, 7 June 1986, 21 Feb., 21 Nov. 1987. See above, n. 46.
[95] GBM, 10 May 1939.

Connell 1997); a publisher (G. C. Rivington 1953–64); a cleric (M. A. Mann 1980–8); a civil servant (F. E. R. Butler 1988–91); and a soldier (J. B. Akehurst 1991–7, not an OH), a telling roll-call of the active British Establishment of twentieth-century public service, witness to Harrow's tenacity in holding its corner of the commanding heights. Notably, none of them has been a professional financier.[96]

Once elected a governor, a consequence of contacts, what counted most was personality and inclination. The externally appointed governors demonstrated this. Like his predecessor C. S. Roundell, but unlike many of his successors, Leo Amery was a powerful Masters' governor, not least because of his wide social and political contacts. He did not see himself simply as a spokesman or protector of one interest group. While most Royal Society governors have either observed proceedings with a faintly bewildered air or concentrated their energies on science teaching, Sir Hugh Anderson (1922–7) served as deputy chairman and made it his business to scrutinize the general finances of the school, which he embodied in a comprehensive financial report in 1923.[97] Between the wars business was controlled by governors appointed by the Lord Chancellor, Pember, who became Warden of All Souls, and by Oxford, A. W. Pickard-Cambridge, a classicist, fellow of Balliol and Vice-Chancellor of Sheffield. With Grenfell, they sat on most committees and were party to all the significant decisions. They also managed to curb if not entirely frustrate Monckton's capacity for svelte intrigue and backstairs influence. Pickard-Cambridge was almost a professional school governor, at one time or other sitting on the boards of Rugby, Stowe, Trent, and Mill Hill as well as Harrow, a useful source of comparative knowledge in the difficult days of the 1930s. The undoubted influence of two history dons, the Cambridge governor J. R. M. Butler (1925–62) and the Oxford governor C. H. Stuart (1958–81, Oxford governor from 1969), especially but not exclusively in matters academic including the election of Head Masters, depended more on their status as Harrovians, knowledge of OHs and staff, and mastery of political processes than to their official capacity.

One oddity of composition was of the Governing Body's own devising. In 1974, when planning for a change of statutes to increase membership from fifteen to twenty, the governors returned to the question of the statutory religious qualification which had been simmering for decades. It had last been discussed formally in 1948–9.[98] This time they petitioned the Privy Council to abolish the requirement, as they understood it, for governors to be members of the Church of England. The response of the Clerk of the Privy Council is worth quoting:

so much of the original Statutes of 16 May 1871 as had imposed upon any person as a qualification for appointment to the Governing Body membership of the Church of England had been expressly disapproved by Her Majesty in Council at that time. It was not known

---

[96] They often acted as deputy chairman, as, for example, did Grenfell.
[97] GBM, 9 Nov. 1923.   [98] GBM, 7 May 1949.

how it had come about that the copy of the Statute in the [governors'] Clerk's possession still retained the words requiring such qualification without reference to the disapproval by Her Majesty, but it was evident that no amendment was now required . . . since membership of the Church of England had never since 1871 been required as a qualification for appointment as a governor.[99]

What could have occurred in 1871 was that the then relatively new clerk, Waring Young, already submerged by the weight of drafts and redrafts of new statutes, either had simply not noticed the Privy Council's dissent or, much more likely, in collusion with the Chairman Lord Verulam and the senior governor, Lord Abercorn, had supressed it. The statutes had been tabled in parliament and Abercorn's attempt to insert a religious test in the House of Lords had been successfully challenged by the Liberal majority in a shambolic late night sitting in the Commons as well as by the Privy Council. Abercorn, a pillar of the Protestant Ascendancy in Ireland and a governor for over fifty years (1834–85), with fine aristocratic hauteur, may have chosen to interpret the affair in line with his religious prejudice. More remarkable is that nobody challenged what was, as Waring Young had admitted in 1870, not a defence of tradition but a new restriction, the old statutes making no mention of any religious test.[100] Reactionaries as well as revolutionaries can find inventing the past useful. The practical effect of Abercorn's and Young's deceit had been to exclude those, such as Anthony and Lionel de Rothschild in the 1930s, on whom the governors were happy to rely for financial advice.[101] It also caused William Chawner, Master of Emmanuel College, Cambridge to feel he had to resign when he left the Church of England in 1908. On that occasion, the clerk, Percival Hardy, agreed to ask the Privy Council if the statutory religious test remained in force; either he failed to do this or he concealed the response (Abercorn's son Lord George Hamilton had just been elected Chairman) or he had merely inquired whether there had been any amendments to the 1871 statute which, of course, there had not.[102] The resolution of this bizarre story was that after 1974 recruitment to the governing body was religiously neutral, with Catholics and Jews gaining election to join the Anglicans, agnostics, and atheists that had been allowed in before.

Inevitably, governors frequently disagreed with each other. Finance was the commonest sources of dispute, such as whether to move in 1939 or to pursue an even more expansionist policy in the 1980s.[103] Nominally unanimous, Head Master elections often proved less than easy: at least one governor since the Second World War later claimed he resigned in disgust at his colleagues' choice. Occasionally ideological or principled divisions surfaced. One governor insisted on the

---

[99] GBM, 30 May 1974.
[100] Young Letter Book, fo. 486, C. W. Young to Public Schools Commissioners, 17 Mar. 1870 and above, pp. 298–9.   [101] GBM, 10 May 1939.
[102] GBM, 2 Feb. 1909.   [103] GBM, 12 Mar. 1983.

clerk recording his dissent to the decision to allow daughters of Masters into the Sixth Form in 1977.[104] In 1918 Pember, Walter Leaf, and A. D. Godley, fellow of Magdalen and Oxford governor, protested strongly against the majority decision to accept the terms of the Evelyn de Rothschild Scholarships. These were intended to be awarded for qualities other than intellect or financial need, the non-academic qualities which, the protesters acidly observed, 'are sufficiently encouraged by the Public School system' without further financial inducement. The relatively high value of the scholarships, they argued, would actually 'depreciate those [academic] attainments a certain neglect of which is already imputed to the great Public Schools'.[105] This academic cry against the prevailing culture of the 'good chap' failed to sway the opinion of the rest of the governors, including the President of Queens' College, Cambridge, the Revd T. C. Fitzpatrick. Pember and his allies were correct in their diagnosis of school priorities but wrong in thinking that there was much they could do to alter it. Twentieth-century Harrow always prided itself in being a school for the 'all-rounder': the de Rothschild Scholarships merely acknowledged this.

Even when most distant, the governors were jealous of their power. Strategic decisions, such as the repeated confirmations from the 1970s that Harrow would remain a single-sex fully boarding school without girls or day boys, rested solely with them.[106] Yet they needed the tacit approval of the wider constituency of parents and old boys, to a significant extent the same people, as in many years between a quarter and a third of Harrovians at any one time were sons of OHs.[107] Between the wars, the governors were criticized for not adequately consulting the Old Harrovian community.[108] The only reason they involved so many old boys in the discussions of the 1939 crisis was they intended to appeal to them for at least £300,000. Similarly, in the post-1945 period of almost constant appeal for donations, planning for the future necessarily took account of the wishes of those educated during Harrow's past. 'What will OHs think?' was not a casual refrain but central to the long-term funding of the school, lending the formulation and public presentation of policy a Janus-like dimension. This was not new; the technique had been pioneered by Monty Butler in the 1860s and 1870s.

Equally traditionally, the governors felt free to interfere in the detailed running of the school, often willing ends without providing means. In 1945 they expressed

---

[104] GBM, 26 May 1977.

[105] GBM, 12 Feb., 14 May 1918. The scholarships were established in memory of E. A. de Rothschild (Newlands, 1899–1904) who had died of wounds in Egypt the previous November.

[106] GBM, 17 July 1978, 6 June 1987.

[107] Apart from the volumes of the *Harrow Register* see the termly breakdowns of OH sons as new boys in GBM from 10 Nov. 1962 onwards. Cf. on the phenomenon more generally, Wakeford, *Cloistered Elite*, 94; Sanderson, *Educational Opportunity*, 9, 69.

[108] By L. M. Hewlett, Gorse Papers, 17 Feb. 1939, Hewlett to Gorse, including his 'Memorandum on the future of Harrow School'.

great concern 'at the low standard of cricket' and wanted curriculum changes to provide even more time for it. In 1953–4 it was the relative dearth of Harrovians entering Sandhurst (27 between 1945 and 1952) that exercised them.[109] At other times, executive action was ordered as in 1924 when, under the new chairmanship of Walter Long, the governors resolved to abolish the Contio although deciding to experiment with it in English before finally consigning the 250-year-old tradition to oblivion. Naturally change caused uproar and, although it had been Long's idea, the already unpopular Ford was blamed: the Contio in Latin was restored the following year.[110] Ironically, Ford suffered from governors' conservatism as well as innovation. In 1924–5, led by Pember and Godley, the governors instructed Ford to encourage the study of Latin which they—and Ford's many critics—thought was being neglected.[111] No less significant of incipient reactionary tendencies was the governors' response to the nightclub scandal in the Summer of 1925, which had involved a number of school monitors. To improve discipline they suggested that Ford resumed frequent Masters' Meetings and revived the old pratice of promoting boys to be Head of the School and monitors 'by position in School Order', in short a revival of the practices of Montagu Butler, under whom a majority of the governors had been educated.[112] Once, instead of trying to change the present to match the past, the governors tried with some success to change the past to suit the present. In 1963 they declared brazenly: 'Notwithstanding the doubts which had been expressed in some quarters, it was decided that the year 1571 should continue to be accepted as the year of the School's Foundation'.[113]

Overt engagement with the internal operation of the school was usually the result of financial or managerial crisis. Controversial actions of Head Masters, such as the introduction of Rugby Football in 1927 or the dismissal of senior housemasters in 1929, 1942, or 1979, attracted formal gubernatorial backing.[114] In 1953 the governors were forced into the delicate position of having to relieve the dying Moore of the Head Mastership even though the knowledge that he was mortally ill had been kept from him.[115] Support for Head Masters was not always forthcoming. The governors seemed to have tried to rid themselves of Ford some years before his final depature.[116] The schism Boissier created in the school did not incline the governors to accept his offer to continue in post after the agreed term of two years in 1942, despite the difficulties in securing a replacement.[117] While often not up to date with educational changes, the governors tended to be highly sensitive to the school's reputation, especially within their own social circles. Hence the

---

[109] GBM, 7 Nov. 1945, 9 May 1953, 6 Feb. 1954.
[110] GBM, 9 May 1924; Alington, *Ford*, 109.
[111] GBM, 24 June, 16 Oct. 1924, 12 Feb. 1925.   [112] GBM, 7 May 1925.
[113] GBM, 16 Nov. 1963. The decision was taken in the context of relaunching the current Appeal.
[114] GBM, 19 Jan. 1927, 13 Nov. 1929, 10 and 18 Mar., 22 Apr. 1942, 10 Nov. 1979, 1 Mar. 1980.
[115] GBM, 7 Jan. 1953.   [116] GBM, 11 Nov. 1919, 10 Feb. 1920.
[117] GBM, 8 Apr. 1942; HM/Boissier/2 Dec. 1941, Pember to Boissier.

disapproval of socialist masters in 1925 and of numerous critical articles that appeared in the school newspaper over the years. While anxious not to be unpopular, once agreed, the governors pursued their policies often with almost gleeful disregard for other sensitivities. Although extracting the highest return on any property sale was incumbent upon them as trustees, they occasionally behaved like philistines. In 1954–5, they encouraged potential buyers of the Roxeth Farm, a listed building, to get planning permission to pull it down for development.[118] In 1959, when approached by the Wembley History Society, they refused to lift a finger to help save and preserve Lyon's farmhouse which they had sold twenty years earlier: it was demolished by the local council the following year.[119] When their own plans to demolish the mid-Victorian Hillside, Knoll, and Garlands as part of a major school and commercial redevelopment of Peterborough Road came partly unstuck in 1979, one governor railed at the 'Betjemanesque sentimentality' of those who had opposed the scheme.[120] Even greater lack of tact, some said taste, was on display during passages of planning and presenting the theatre and West Street development in 1987–92. Intolerance of external opposition is probably an occupational hazard of governing bodies. It has certainly been a robust tradition at Harrow at least since the rumpus of 1771. However, their main task, apart from electing Head Masters, was to manage the school's finances. Thus their perspective on school policy and expenditure as Trustees was always hemmed in by legal and financial constraints, often not appreciated by observers, a circumstance which more than anything caused them and their decisions to be misunderstood or resented.

Finance

The closest Harrow came to closing its doors since 1844 was during the financial crisis of 1938 to 1942.[121] Numbers declined from over 500 in 1938 to fewer than 300 in 1942; registrations for the future were down to a meagre seventy in the year 1941–2. An overdraft of £95,000 secured early in 1939 was covered by a massive sale of stock. Repayment of mortgages and loans were more or less suspended. In 1940 £15,000 was borrowed from one of the inter-war windfall bequest funds, the Clifford Smith, and another overdraft negotiated to meet the £40,000 Baldwin

---

[118] GBM, 13 Nov. 1954, 7 May 1955.
[119] GBM, 14 Feb. 1959. Cf. purchaser's promise to leave the farmhouse to Wembley District Council as a 'Memorial to John Lyon', GBM, 14 June 1938.
[120] GBM, 30 July 1979 (when secrecy was urged), 10 Nov. 1979; the governor was C. H. Stuart.
[121] The crisis of 1938–42 can be traced in GBM, 26 Oct., 7 Dec. 1938; 25 Jan., 1 and 7 Feb., 7 and 15 Mar., 10 May, 13 June, 25 Oct., 15 Nov., 6 Dec. 1939; 13 Mar. 1940, 19 Feb., 14 May, 12 Nov., 17 Dec. 1941, 11 Feb., 8 Apr., 6 May 1942; Gorse Papers, 5 Jan. 1939, 25 Jan. 1939, 16 Feb. 1939, 17 Feb. 1939, 3 Mar. 1939, 21 Mar. 1939, 12 Apr. 1939, 22 Dec. 1939; Memoranda by G. F. Finch, Jan., Mar. 1939, and by L. M. Hewlett, Feb. 1939; Architect's Report and Plan for new school, Feb. 1939.

told Old Harrovians in March 1940 was needed for the school to survive until 1943, provided numbers remained around 400: in January 1941, they were 332. West Acre had been closed at the end of 1939; Newlands and Rendalls followed in 1940 and 1941; Bradbys in 1942. Housemasters still in the old, hotelier system faced heavy losses. Staff were laid off in 1939 and 1942; salaries were drastically cut. In February 1941 it was bleakly predicted that, even with another loan to tide the school over until Christmas 1942, unless an income of £20,000 was found from somewhere, at that date 'all the existing assets of the school will have been exhausted'.[122] A year later the governors were gloomily discussing whether the school's endowment would be available to pay pensions 'in the event of dissolution'.[123]

The crisis was exacerbated by the outbreak of war, but had not been caused by it. Declining numbers since 1931 and insufficient fee-income had undermined the basic solvency of the school which was already encumbered with long-term debts from the policy of property purchases which continued until the eve of war. There was no longer much land to sell, Preston Farm itself having been sold between 1930 and 1938 for almost £190,000 mainly to pay off the overdraft and other loans.[124] The acquisitive John Lyon would hardly have been amused. The deficit on the school account for 1936–7 was £19,000; that for 1937–8 £27,000 on a turnover of about £100,000. Although assets in property and trusts were valued at around £500,000, mortgages and loans, by January 1939, were estimated at £116,000, not counting the then overdraft of over £80,000.[125]

Four possible solutions were aired, all but one dependent on a massive injection of endowment through an appeal to Old Harrovians for £300,000. The school could stay on the Hill by suspending repairs, dismissing masters, cutting salaries, closing houses, and raising fees. It could remain at Harrow but sell most of its property to build a new centralized school in compact blocks to encourage economies of scale. The school could sell up and move to a rural site. The governors pursued this to the extent of preparing architect's drawings and detailed plans as well as an appraisal of cost. After consultation with Old Harrovians at a series of meetings, rebuilding on site was regarded as financially 'ruinous'. Moving, which some argued would also encounter legal difficulties, especially as regards the application of funds, appeared even more expensive and, the governors commented, 'what was built would not be Harrow', a judgement amply confirmed by the groundplans prepared.[126] The decision to stay on the Hill, made on 7 February 1939, was accompanied by a declared policy to restrict numbers to 500 and implement drastic economies. Whether these would have worked is impossible to judge as the outbreak of war plunged the school into fresh crisis. A new round of cuts was agreed in October 1939 and again in December 1941. The final option, a temporary

---

[122] GBM, 19 Feb. 1941.   [123] GBM, 11 Feb. 1942.
[124] GBM, 13 Nov. 1929, 19 Feb., 14 May, 12 Nov. 1930, 16 June 1932, 15 Nov. 1933, 8 June, 27 Oct. 1937, 14 June 1938.
[125] Finch, 'Memorandum', Jan. 1939 for details.   [126] GBM, 7 Feb. 1939.

closure of the school, discussed in May 1941, exposed the governors' position even more starkly. Without fees, the school's annual income was a mere £15,500, about half of which came from the scholarship and prizes trusts. Yet the upkeep of the school property during any closure would be c.£27,000. The governors could not afford to keep the school open; nor could they afford to close it.[127]

This conundrum was resolved by the arrival of Malvern College in the summer of 1942 paying rent for the houses they occupied. The governors had sought this solution for some time. They had failed to entice Westminster School to the Hill during the winter of 1941–2.[128] After Baldwin's attempt to extract government money from the Board of Education had failed, Malvern provided Harrow's salvation. It was but a temporary reprieve. With the coming of peace and the departure of Malvern in 1946, Harrow's precarious finances were once more revealed.[129]

The cost of maintaining Harrow as a luxury school consistently imposed crippling weight on its finances. At the end of the century as in 1914 and 1945 the need persisted for an increased capital base. Because of the small size of endowment relative to demands and pretentions, the governors could never afford the desired large capital projects, including essential refurbishment, out of their own resources. There were two great periods of spending. Between the Bowen legacy of 1901 and 1939 £165,000 were spent on property, not counting the money spent by the First World War Memorial Trust on the War Memorial and the refashioning of the central area of the school.[130] Not only were all the boarding houses bought, but large swathes of housing on both sides of the High Street as far as West Acre, along Harrow Park and down West Street and Grove Hill. The motive was to protect the school from suburban sprawl and uncongenial development on the Hill, as well as providing the governors with the ability to house staff in some decency.[131] After a quarter of a century of consolidation and repair, from 1970 the school re-equipped itself with a range of public buildings as decisively as under Vaughan and Butler. Between 1975 and 1990 £13.7 million went on buildings and improvements, not including the cost of the school theatre or the completion of the house refurbishment scheme.[132] The physical and institutional nature of the school was fundamentally altered by the construction of the Physics and Maths Schools, the Churchill Schools (i.e. the CDT Centre), a Sports Hall including an indoor swimming pool (rendering the decaying Ducker redundant), a separate house for the Head Master, a new boarding house, a gallery in the Old Speech Room, and, most important of all, a central feeding block. Just as the Harrow of the 1880s looked alien to veterans of Dr Wordsworth, so the school Head Master Beer left in 1991 looked and was a very different place from that of Dr James.

[127] GBM, 14 May 1941.   [128] GBM, 17 Dec. 1941, 11 Feb. 1942.
[129] GBM, 10 May 1947: 'It was clear that the school could not continue indefinitely on its present financial basis.'   [130] GBM, 15 Mar. 1939.
[131] Gorse Papers, Finch, 'Memorandum', Jan. 1939.   [132] GBM, 1 Dec. 1990.

Inevitably, therefore, the history of Harrow's twentieth-century finances parallelled that of the nineteenth in being one of fund-raising, from the Endowment Fund of 1913, that raised £40,000 in its first year, to the Development Fund of 1984, that by 1990 held over £2m.[133] Before 1914 capital projects were met by direct appeal to old boys (e.g. the Tercentenary, Park, and Land Trusts). Between the wars, the chance of bequests, not least the morbid windfalls resulting from the casualties of the Great War, and the sale of local farmland for development allowed the governors to protect the school by buying property on the Hill without recourse to living Old Harrovians. The financial crisis of 1938–42 encouraged a return to pre-1914 practices. Between 1944 and 1974 the school launched four Appeals (in 1944–7, 1948, 1960–6, 1971–4) which together realized many hundreds of thousands of pounds. The post-war Harrow Trust alone contributed £173,000 to the school between 1947 and 1960; the various appeals of the early sixties raised over £330,000; that for the Quartercentenary, by 1974, £579,000.[134] The Appeal begun in 1978 was to be continuous, with a permanent secretariat, adapting to changing capital or endowment requirements, its first phase, before it 'totally lost momentum' in 1982, raising almost £750,000.[135] Without these external sources of income Harrow could not have survived, at least in the form it did. On either side of the First World War, the choice would have been between a smaller school swamped by suburbia, unable to attract staff or pupils because the environment would have become cramped, run down, and expensive, with fees high and salaries too low to match local property prices. After 1945, without the Appeals, the continuation of a fully boarding system would have been in jeopardy. As late as the 1970s the governors recognized that without continued injection of endowment, any decline in applications would impel them to consider the admission of girls or day boys, house closures, and a reduction in staff and subjects taught.[136]

The problem was that by far the largest element of the school's income were fees, at times between 85 per cent and over 95 per cent.[137] Harrow was a relatively expensive school before 1914; by the end of the century it was consistently one of the most expensive, if not *the* most expensive. In 1910 the basic combined tuition and boarding fee in a large house was £135 a year, rising to £150 in 1916, £162 in 1918, £192 in 1919, and £207 in 1920.[138] Even these figures were deceptive, as games, music, art, Corps, workshops, specialist science, etc. were all extra, adding between 15 per cent and 20 per cent to the bill. In 1938 Head Master Vellacott cautiously introduced a

---

[133] Alington, *Ford*, 104, GBM, 2 June 1990.
[134] GBM, 9 Feb., 1 Nov. 1944, 7 Feb. 1945, 1 May 1946, 8 May, 13 Nov. 1948, 4 Nov. 1950, 12 June, 9 Nov. 1957, 13 Feb., 6 Apr. 1960, 7 June 1966, 29 May 1969, 21 Mar. 1970, 27 May 1971, 9 Mar. 1974.
[135] GBM, 13 Nov. 1982.   [136] GBM, 17 July 1978.
[137] e.g. GBM, 14 May 1941: fee income c.£85,000; other c.£15,500, i.e. 15% of total. Cf. 15 Sept. 1947 investments (£6,000 a year) provided just under 4% of gross income; 10 Nov. 1979 investment income supplied about 6%.
[138] GBM, 24 Oct. 1910, 8 Feb. 1916, 12 Feb. 1918, 13 May 1919, 11 May 1920.

consolidated fee of £230 which was almost immediately increased to £250 to stave off bankruptcy. (Eton had had consolidated fees since 1919, in 1938 £245.)[139] After a wartime reduction, in 1945 Harrow fees were restored to £234 a year, thereafter rising steadily, passing £300 in 1949, £400 in 1956, £500 in 1961: at the beginning of the great inflation of the 1970s they stood at just over £1,000; in 1983, after another consolidation of compulsory extras, they were £5,000; in 1990, £10,000.[140]

Mistakenly, until the 1960s successive Heads and governors were content to shadow Eton.[141] The pressures of the 1970s and 1980s saw an end to that as Harrow fought to do more than keep pace with rising costs. Record numbers of boys (consistently above 700 from 1968 and 750 since 1985) presented an opportunity to settle the historic problem of a current account for a full school in which fee income could slide easily below annual expenditure. Put crudely, if the Harrow fees in the late 1990s had reflected the same real cost as those of the early 1930s they would have been, extras included, just over £8,000: they were in fact more than 50 per cent above that.[142] The driving up of fees was not some profligate attempt to fleece gullible parents, however it may have seemed to them at the time. In the mid- to late 1970s, the by then termly fee increases, sometimes of more than 10 per cent a time, were not only to offset inflation but to attempt to secure a surplus over gross turn-over of 5 per cent. By the late 1980s the annual surplus target was 10 per cent.[143] Even so, deficits were not unknown: after years of healthy surplus, inflation produced deficits of almost £80,000 in 1974–5 and £32,000 the following year. Despite energetic fee rises, in 1988 once again the estimated surplus appeared to be evaporating. Even high surpluses of over £500,000 in the 1980s fell short of the desired required 10 per cent: in 1990–1 the surplus of £555,000 represented only 7 per cent of income, the governors, as so often, calling for economies.[144]

One reason for nervousness was that capital expenditure, even when ultimately covered by sales of property, appeals, or windfalls, incurred borrowing. From the early 1920s the school's overdraft had grown gradually from £25,000 in 1922 to £50,000 in 1936; three years later it was £100,000, equivalent to 20 per cent of the

---

[139] HM/Vellacott/28 Mar. 1935, 31 Jan. 1938 (Bursar's Memorandum), Sept. 1938, Vellacott memorandum for governors, 10 Nov. 1938, 3 Dec. 1938, 16 Dec. 1938, 24 Jan. 1939, 16 Jan. 1939; HM/V/ G. A. Harrison's bill, Spring Term 1936 and 6 May letter from father to Vellacott; HM/V/Boys' Bills 1938-3; GBM, 26 Oct. 1938, 25 Jan. 1939.

[140] GBM, 6 Jan. 1943, 20 Feb. 1945, 5 Feb. 1949, 2 Jan. 1956, 15 June 1961, 9 Mar. 1974, 13 Nov. 1982, 12 Mar. 1983, 24 Feb. 1990. Harrow was consistently above the average of boarding public schools. Cf. Sanderson, *Educational Opportunity*, 69.

[141] HM/James/21 Nov. 1960, Robert Birley from Eton smugly comparing notes with James. On Birley's chart, the two schools matched each other exactly since 1939 and, while their percentage increases were less than other comparable schools, their totals were higher. Cf. the governors' attitude, GBM, 5 Feb. 1949.

[142] The accepted multiplier 1930 to late 1990s *c.*30. I am grateful to Dr R. Van Noorden for this calculation. For fees growing faster than inflation: GBM, 26 Feb. 1994.

[143] GBM, 17 July 1978, 21 Nov. 1987.

[144] GBM, 13 Mar. 1976, 5 Mar. 1977; 19 Nov. 1988; 30 Nov. 1991.

entire assets of the school, with most of the school property already mortgaged.[145] A similar pattern appeared after 1945, although by then numbers were going up not down, there was no great campaign to buy property, merely to restore much neglected exisiting buildings. The governors received a gloomy prognosis of the future in 1947 and in 1948 called for cuts of £10,000 a year, yet by 1953 the overdraft was creeping above its limit of £80,000 to nearer £90,000.[146] On neither occasion was the interest rate prohibitive. This was otherwise in the late 1980s with interest rates in double digits (the so-called 'Lawson boom'). In 1987–8, while the annual surplus was £425,124, the overdraft was £1,169,354 with a continuing annual deficit on capital expenditure. Thus, even with record numbers of boys, with fees rising faster than inflation, and a windfall of £500,000 from the sale of land at Greenford, in the middle of an unavoidable renovation programme for the boarding houses (building and repairs in 1989 costing c.£2 million a year) the apparently thriving school, increasingly dependent on the commercial income from Lyon Services and the continued health of the Development Fund, needed to be run with tight economy: new schemes, such as the theatre project, were envisaged as being only possible if self-financing.[147]

There were differences in the circumstances of financial management between the early fifties and the late eighties. Parochially, the most significant change was the management of investments. Until 1955 the governors were restricted to investing their trust money in gilt-edged stocks and Trustee securities. Under an Order sought by the governors from Mr Justice Danckwerts in February 1955 the governors were thenceforth allowed to invest up to two-thirds of the value of their Trust funds freely in stocks, shares, or property.[148] This and subsequent changes both to the Stock Market and the consolidation and organization of school Trust funds liberated the governors' investment opportunities. None the less, the nature of the problems facing governors in the late 1980s would have been recognizable to their predecessors, the difference being that the modern governors had taken deliberate steps to try to solve the underlying problems.

It is hard to imagine any time since 1914 when the governors' best efforts would not have been rendered futile without the extraordinary and consistent generosity of old boys. Encouraged by the creation of the Endowment Fund in 1913, Lionel Ford remarked complacently to Walter Monckton in 1919 on the 'endowments flowing

---

[145] GBM, 12 May 1922, 29 Feb. 1936, 1 Feb, 10 May 1939; Gorse Papers, Finch, 'Memorandum', Jan. 1939.

[146] GBM, 10 May, 15 Sept. 1947, 7 Feb., 8 May, 6 Oct., 13 Nov. 1948, 11 June 1953.

[147] GBM, 27 Feb., 19 Nov. 1988. Cf. open letter M. B. Connell of the GPC to Beer, May 1989, in 'Policy Document on Long-Term Priorities', p. ii.

[148] Copy of Order of 14 Feb. 1955 in Minute Book, June 1980–June 1987; GBM, 7 May 1955. Cf. ibid., 8 May 1954. The application came under the terms of new legislation freeing Trust assets for general investment.

in', much of the 'very large sums' coming from Old Harrovians killed in the war or donated by grieving relatives in their memory. Ford himself understood the need to attract funds to pay for the house purchasing policy, describing himself as a 'beggar': he was apparently very successful, raising over £400,000.[149] Many of his successors were more fastidious. With the arrival of the continuous appeal in the late 1970s, a permanent fundraiser spared Head Masters an overtly Fordian role, although they inevitably played an important part in creating public and private atmospheres conducive to giving.[150]

The impact of Old Harrovian donations cannot be underestimated. Before 1914 old boys had bought for the school the football fields, almost all the cricket fields, the Park, Druries, the Knoll, and Elmfield, and had built Newlands. Some complained that after 1918 the financial policies and buying plans had been undertaken without enough OH involvement. After 1945 the Harrow Trust, which controlled the money from the 1944 Appeal, funded repairs and fee remissions as well as *ad hoc* capital costs.[151] For most of the century all academic Entrance Scholarships, except for a handful which came to be known as Head Master's Scholarships, and all Leaving Scholarships were funded by gifts, some of great value, such as the Clifford Smith bequest in 1932 (initially providing an income of £2,200 a year) or the L. C. Wilson Scholarship fund (first endowed 1962, estimated in 1978 at between £300,000 and £400,000, producing an income of up to £30,000). The Clifford Smith fund was large enough to supply a loan of £15,000 to keep the school operating in 1940.[152] Cumulatively, the Scholarship and Prizes Fund produced a consistent profit which could be used in certain circumstances under firm rules to assist the central funding of the school. This dependence on chance donations created problems. Some failed to keep pace with inflation; others imposed restrictions on eligibility. From the 1970s there were moves to increase full fee scholarships from school funds, of the sort Welldon had pioneered in 1897–8. Such provision was dependent on increased endowment, but many donors and governors preferred non-academic bursaries to elite intellectual awards as a means of recreating or maintaining the diversity of entry. Without the past donations, the school could afford neither.

Over the last century the two most significant individual gifts between the Bowen legacy of 1901 and the Beckwith gift of 1992 were the Shepard Churchill bequest of 1916 and the Gregory Apcar Reversion of 1936 both of which exerted a profound effect on the school until the 1980s. The will of Augustus Shepard Churchill, a Harrovian 1860–3, left the school his property in stocks and land, both substantial. Of the former, in 1917 £50,000 of Consols were transferred to the

---

[149] Alington, *Ford*, 107 n. 1; Bryant, *Harrow*, 96–7; *The Harrovian*, 27 Feb. 1926, p. 2.
[150] GBM, 20 May 1977, *et seq.*
[151] GBM, 6 Feb., 1 May 1946, 6 Oct., 13 Nov. 1948, 4 Nov. 1950, 12 June, 9 Nov. 1957, 13 Feb. 1960.
[152] GBM, 16 Nov. 1932, 15 Feb. 1933, 10 May, 15 Nov., 6 Dec. 1939, 13 Mar. 1940, 7 Nov. 1953, 13 Feb. 1962, 17 July 1978.

Challenges

Endowment Scholarship and Prizes Fund, the remainder going into the Estates Account. Money in the Scholarship Fund could be used elsewhere, as in 1919 when £250 was transferred to the games fund. In general, Shepard Churchill money cascaded through the school's finances. With a loan of £17,200 from the Shepard Churchill Fund in 1920, the governors were able to buy Moretons and numbers 7, 12, 14, 16, 32, and 34 High Street.[153] The land was potentially even more lucrative, comprising as it did Shepherd's Market in west London, among other things a well-known red-light district. The Public Trustee repeatedly urged the governors to sell, but they sensibly resisted until the windfall could be used, which was not until the 1970s.[154] In the mean time, the only trouble the Shepherd's Market estate gave were its brothels which, between 1956 and 1970, regularly provoked evictions and proceedings against tenants.[155] Finally, as part of plans to develop the school in the early 1970s, between 1971 and 1973 Shepherd's Market was sold for £1,185,000 allowing the school to build a central feeding block, the dining rooms in which were called, in honour of the source of the funding, the Shepherd Churchill Hall and Room. (The spelling of Shepard changed over the century, perhaps because of confusion with the man, Shepard Churchill, and his property, Shepherd's Market.)[156]

The Apcar Reversion was even more spectacular in its day. Gregory Apcar was an Anglo-Indian merchant from Calcutta, one of a clan of Apcars in the school under H. M. Butler in the 1860s and 1870s. One, J. A. Apcar, had already left a substantial legacy to the school in 1921.[157] The Gregory Apcar bequest, accepted in February 1936, was described by the governors as 'an endowment which has never been equalled in all [Harrow's] history', exhibiting 'a shining example of love and care for Harrow and her needs and a splendid generosity the memory of which can never be extinguished in the hearts of Harrovians'.[158] If such pious optimism proved misplaced, the bequest itself was remarkable. Apcar left the school an estate valued in total at around £320,000, about £10 million in modern terms, which would have increased the value of the school's property and Trusts by almost two-thirds. The estate was divided in half between the school and Mrs Apcar who retained a life interest in property valued at £160,000 which would revert to the school on her death: she survived for another four and a half decades.[159] The rest was payable to the school immediately. The capital was only to be spent on buying

---

[153] GBM, 14 Nov. 1916, 13 Feb., 8 May 1917, 11 Nov. 1919, 10 Feb. 1922; Board/Ministry of Education Order, 22 June 1920. (Copy in 1980–7, Minute Book. At the same time the Endowment Fund was subsidizing the purchase of 94, 96, 98 High Street.)

[154] e.g. GBM, 12 May, 22 June 1922, 23 Feb. 1927. The governors' full control of the Trust only came in 1941, GBM, 14 May 1941.

[155] GBM, 10 Nov. 1956, 9 June 1964, 12 Feb. 1966, 11 Feb. 1967, 21 Mar. 1970.

[156] GBM, 27 May, 10 Nov. 1971, 10 Nov. 1973, 8 Nov. 1975. £400,000 was still available from the Fund to contribute to a Sports Hall in 1985: GBM, 16 Nov. 1985.

[157] GBM, 13 May 1921.   [158] GBM, 26 Feb. 1936.   [159] GBM, 23 Mar. 1980.

property; otherwise it must be invested or, if spent, replaced. Already by 1939 over £80,000 had reached the school, £10,000 of which had been invested to produce money for the Cricket Fund.[160] As a sign of the desperate financial condition of the school, in 1937 £20,000 of Apcar stocks were sold at a loss in order to reduce the overdraft, but which had to be replaced from school income over thirty years.[161] Apcar money continued to provide an important supplement to the school's income for two generations. In 1971 some Apcar property was sold for £51,000; in November 1981 sale of Apcar investments realized £585,759.[162]

Generosity on this scale was inevitably unusual, yet the instinct was widespread. Almost as impressive as huge individual gifts were the numbers of Old Harrovians prepared to give. Writing in 1939, one enthusiastic if critical OH, the Land Trust's solicitor L. M. Hewlett, argued that it was only the largesse of Old Harrovians that allowed Harrow to compete with the well-endowed Eton and Winchester as 'one of the leading Public Schools', 'the result of this has been to inspire in Old Harrovians a greater love for their school, or at any rate one more actively apparent, than in the case in other schools'.[163] For those actually running the school, such proprietorial interest possessed dangers and inconveniences as well as benefits. Between 1960 and 1966 over 2,000 Old Harrovians contributed to the various appeals, nearly half the total number of old boys. The 1970–4 Appeal attracted around 1,500 donors (not all OHs); that of 1978–82 about 1,000.[164] The obsessive, passionate, almost universal devotion displayed by pre-war Old Harrovians may have slackened but it was replaced by a greater determination to encourage gifts from parents. Non-Harrovian companies and public trusts, such as the Industrial Fund for the Advancement of Science, that gave £10,000 to improve the Science Schools in 1957, could also be targets.[165] Although especially fashionable in the late twentieth century, the importance of public relations has thus lain at the heart of Harrow's success since the eighteenth century. Since Montagu Butler and Reform, it has been as explicit as it has been crucial.

There was less direct correlation than might have been expected between contemporary perceptions of success or failure of the school and OH generosity. The 1900s, 1920s, 1930s, and 1970s, times of some difficulty for the school, were all periods of quite lavish giving. What mattered as much as current impressions were the feelings generated by the quality of donors' memories of his schooldays over which fundraisers had little control. Just as no Head Master could ignore Old Harrovians,

---

[160] For the details and early payments see GBM, 6 May, 9 June 1936, 26 Oct. 1938; Gorse Papers, Finch, 'Memorandum', Jan. 1939.   [161] GBM, 27 Oct. 1937.

[162] GBM, 6 Nov. 1971, 14 Nov. 1981. The final traunch realized over £720,000 1980–2, GPC 23 Mar. 1980, 18 Sept. 1980, 28 Jan. 1982.

[163] Gorse Papers, Hewlett 'Memorandum on the future of Harrow School', fo. 4.

[164] GBM, 13 Nov. 1965, 7 June 1966, 24 May 1973, 9 Mar. 1974, 27 Feb., 13 Nov. 1982.

[165] GBM, 13 June 1957. This fund provided c.£3 million for public school laboratories: Sanderson, *Educational Opportunity*, 68.

Challenges

so he could not diminish the past which, because of the school's financial imperatives, exerted something of a stranglehold on the present. 'No place is more saturated with tradition', a non-Harrovian master commented on Harrow in the years after 1918.[166] For all the rapidly changing curriculum, appearance, and structure of the school, the requirements of school finance demand obeisance to the past. This is of fundamental importance to the understanding of the nature of the shifting identy of Harrow since 1914, especially in the last third of the twentieth century. Change, for example central feeding in the late 1970s, had to be introduced in two specific ways, either with the trappings of tradition intact (e.g. houses retaining autonomy and identity at meals) or as a sign that the modern school was striving to maintain Harrow's position of excellence that it had inherited from the past (e.g. the CDT centre of the 1980s). It is in this context that the survival of obsolete or dignified, rather than efficient, elements of school life should be judged: hats, tails, Songs, Contio, Harrow Football, gowns, etc. They may attract certain new clients; they may, as an analysis in 1989 argued, be a clear strength of the school in competition with others; they may lend a cohesive identity to current members of the school society.[167] They certainly encourage continued loyalty of old boys. Every twentieth-century reforming Head Master encountered opposition to trivia as much as to substance: from compulsory Greek and the introduction of Rugby Football to the abolition of the Contio or the Harrow hat. Most traditional of all was the recognition by late twentieth-century fundraisers of the power of nostalgia and that the best context in which to use it to encourage the sympathetic sentiments that might lead to giving money was Songs. Monty Butler had worked that out by 1871.

[166] Venables, *Bases Attempted*, 27.   [167] Policy Document on Long-Term Priorities, pp. i, 2.

16

Changing Identities, 1914–1991

A Harrow master in the 1950s, reading Vachell's *The Hill*, was struck by its relevance half a century on.[1] Twenty years later, boys remained subject to rules of privilege, such as not rolling umbrellas or visiting other boarding houses, familiar to Galsworthy almost a century earlier. The buttoning of the 'bluer' jacket was as sensitive a point of etiquette in 1970 as in 1910.[2] Fagging persisted until the 1990s; the wailing call of 'Boy!' still heard a hundred years after being immortalized in song by Farmer and Howson. Beating ended only in the 1980s. Victorian and Edwardian slang persisted; 'tosh' (bath); 'eccer' (exercise/sport); 'groize' (hard worker) still greeted bemused new boys in the 1970s, even if many of the richer seams of local dialect had gone.[3] 'Beaks' wore gowns; Farmer's Songs were sung; cricket was played against Eton at Lord's in what many still viewed as the climactic ritual of personal and corporate achievement. Houses stayed autonomous fiefdoms, known by their housemaster's initials, each with their own nineteenth-century colours, individual subcultures, traditions, and shibboleths. The hierarchy of boys continued to manage their own social structures to the exclusion of masters. Head Masters continued to lionize their monitors. Boys still romanced about themselves and their friends, were still loyal to peers, resentful of change, and obsessed with games; still drank, smoked, bullied, swore, avoided work and punishment. Harrow still prided itself on producing leaders and, in Head Master Beer's phrase, wealth-creators of the future; still gloried in its breadth of intellectual entry; still fancied itself as the second best school in the country. Yet the school Vachell described, part-Edwardian ideal, part mid-Victorian memories, had changed radically even by the 1950s in curriculum, management of houses, and uniform. Boys sat public examinations; they no longer fagged at cricket; Harrow football was no longer a compulsory mass activity; there were baths in boys' houses. The experience of

[1] Gathorne-Hardy, *Public School Phenomenon*, 394.   [2] Fox, *Harrow*, 75.
[3] Howson and Townsend Warner, *Harrow*, 281–2; Hartley, 'The Conformer', 74. Unless separately noted, the evidence for Harrow from the 1960s comes from personal knowledge and private interviews with OHs.

being a Harrow boy or master in the 1950s or 1960s was only superficially the same as John Verney's or L. P. Hartley's.

The setting had been transformed, not just by encroaching suburbia. For the old guard, the ripping out of the centre of the school in the 1920s to create the War Memorial Building and open the vista from the High Street to the Old Schools, meant 'the reverence linked with age [had] gone'.[4] The 'architecture of hearty and confident gloom'[5] was jostled by 1970s functionalism (physics and maths schools) and supermarket vernacular (Central Feeding block) or by 'Marks and Spencer masonic' (the theatre) in the 1990s, only the indigenous Harrow alpine design of the new Head Master's house (1982) and its echoes in the late 1980s brutalism of the CDT centre preserving a local if peculiar style. Dutch elm disease left the eastern fields naked in the 1970s and the cows were expelled by golfers.

Nevertheless, the 1950s master hit on a truth. Harrow's culture was conservative and determinedly traditional. What linked late twentieth-century Harrovians with those who went to war in 1914 was a belief that they were linked. All schools possess a double time frame. Constant renewal of pupils is concealed by the sense in each of them that their time is the school's permanent state, an impression encouraged by teachers for whom change is hidden by routine and familiarity, the annual repetition of the school year, each different, each the same. Harrow fostered the conviction that, in Platonic fashion, the school had not altered its essentials, embodied in selective memory, the creation of myth and the school songs. The most fervid reformers, Ford or Beer, operated within the security of confident continuity, their outward alterations acceptable because regarded by many as both superficial and transient. The modern transformation of Harrow, delayed until Dr James's retirement in 1971, its foundations laid by Michael Hoban over the next decade to be developed and proclaimed by Ian Beer in the 1980s, followed similar patterns elsewhere. Yet often radical administrative alterations hardly constituted what John Rae, a Head Master at King's Taunton and Westminster and a Harrow master 1955–66, described as a revolution.[6] The school's conservatism engorged novelty with ease. The newness of necessary and unavoidable innovation was quickly forgotten. In an institution limed with the past, present habit acquired the standing of immutable practice, until the next change. Thus central feeding under Hoban and the one-term entry, five-year course under Beer, both fundamental to the nature of the school, left barely a scar in the memory. Perhaps the most successful twentieth-century Head Master, Dr James, an instinctive and confident conservative, survived the 1960s by pretending to ignore them while being quietly accommodating. His policy presented a paradigm of Harrow which even the noisiest of reformers was forced to respect because in it lay one of the secrets of survival

[4] Mayo, *Reminiscences*, 174.   [5] Vickers, *Beaton*, 20.
[6] J. Rae, *The Public School Revolution, 1964–79* (London, 1981). Cf. Gathorne-Hardy, *Public School Phenomenon*, 369–410.

and material success. Between 1914 and 1991, the school's habits, attitudes, structures, and manners underwent enormous shifts, yet all the time comfortably concealed behind a mask of tradition.

WAR

Two thousand nine hundred and seventeen Harrovians served in His Majesty's armed forces during the First World War. Six hundred and ninety were wounded and 644—22 per cent—were killed, not counting those who died later from their physical and psychological wounds.[7] The First World War remained Harrow's Great War, casting a shadow so profound that the memory of the 344 who fell between 1939 and 1945 found accommodation within the vastness of the shrine to their predecessors. The silent emptiness of the War Memorial Building is appropriate for the hollow anguish and grief caused by the losses sustained. The Great War transformed the physical structure of Harrow, implanting a dead heart in the school. It enshrined a corporate sense of worth. 1914–19 defined Harrow for more than a generation. The subsequent militarism in boys' timetables and the attitudes of masters, many of them war veterans, would have alarmed the Edwardians for whom the cult of war had been of rhetoric not bayonet practice. While promoting traditions of military training, conformity, and obedience, the legacy of the First World War was as much of duty and service as triumph. Appropriately, when the next World War broke out, Harrow was led by a Head Master, Paul Vellacott, DSO, who had been badly gassed in the trenches and made a prisoner of war.[8]

Some, not the participants, glorified the war as validating the aims and methods of public schools. C. H. P. Mayo excitedly recalled memories of 'a wonderful time of promise and of hope', 'years of wonderful opportunity, most wonderfully responded to' when he had been inspired by the example of youth 'who never faltered, their only expressed fear . . . lest it should be over before it was their time to go'. The inspirational cliché was somewhat diminished by his immediate comment that, as a housemaster, 'catering was very difficult'. However, even this inconvenience was linked to his central thesis of public school superiority as he confessed to illicitly providing extra rations for his boys 'who, if the war lasted, would be required to officer the new armies and whose physical strength must therefore be sustained even though older and more useless people suffered'.[9]

There was evidence to support Mayo's vision. In October 1915 two 17-year-old Moretonians, R. Peel and R. K. McFarlane, ran away from school in an unsuccessful

---

[7] Laborde, *Harrow School*, 155, 159–60 for a consideration of the casualty figures in both wars.
[8] P. Pattenden, 'Peterhouse Honours May 1913', *Peterhouse Annual Record* (Cambridge, 1995–6), pp. 75–6. I am grateful to J. H. W. Morwood, Esq. for this reference.
[9] Mayo, *Reminiscences*, 177–80.

attempt to enlist.[10] If the Head Master's punishment book is a guide, boys were better behaved, or more discreet, or masters less willing to punish. This may have had other causes. Mayo's ecstasy in his proxy relationship with war was eccentric. More common were the emotions recorded by E. M. Venables who joined the Harrow staff in 1917: strain, nerves 'suffering widespread and intense'.[11] Pride was tempered by the awful reality of the fighting. Week after week at Sunday Evensong, the Head Master read out the names of the dead. Month after month the pages of special supplements to the *Harrovian* recorded, often in gruesome detail, precisely how the dead had fallen, in prose stiff with stoicism yet laced with ghoulish prurience. Some of the statistics of the slaughter are almost unbearable. Of the forty-two boys who entered Harrow in Wood's last term, Summer 1910, sixteen were killed in the war, 38 per cent; the figure was just under 30 per cent for the whole of the academic year 1909–10, excluding those who died of illnesses contracted in the course of military service. To those who heard the lists of the dead, especially the adults, each was an individual tragedy. Three masters were killed. One of them, Charles Werner, scholar, athlete, former housemaster at the Head Master's and a devoted member of the Alpine Club, was last seen leading an attack on German trenches on the Aubers Ridge, near Fromelles, on 9 May 1915 carrying the ice axe he had specially requested be sent him at the Front.[12]

Despite these horrors, Harrow experienced the ordinariness of war. Gardens were converted into boys' allotments, run on characteristically commercial lines. Insurance against air-raids was taken out; to combat bombing, fire appliances were acquired. Fear of air attacks led to suggestions for the easing of restrictions on Home Boarders. The most lasting change was to the uniform with the adoption of the blue jacket, the 'bluer', instead of tails for normal school dress on all days bar Sunday. The Corps, now compulsory, drilled with dummy rifles, the real ones having been requisitioned.[13] Masters reacted in different ways. Some joined up. Others, such as Townsend Warner, assisted the war effort, in his case by writing articles on war management that earned him a posting to secret work with the Foreign Office, a strain that probably caused the ulcer that killed him in the autumn of 1916. Ford retreated into devising the Crypt Chapel in which, to the disquiet of some, he would pray for the dead; or he would spend his time fussing over the rights of non-Old Harrovian masters to admission to the Field House enclosure during cricket matches.[14] With the school beginning to recover its numbers from

[10] Head Master's Punishment Book, 1888–1965, 20 Oct. 1915.
[11] Venables, *Bases Attempted*, 14.
[12] A. Lunn, *Memory to Memory* (London, 1956), p. 45; *Harrow Register, 1885–1949*, 679 and, for the 1910 statistics, 310–21.
[13] Mayo, *Reminiscences*, 181, 188; GBM, 1 Nov. 1915, 8 Feb., 9 May 1916; HA Lionel Ford, Head Master's Book, 1910–16, 22 Feb. 1916; C. Harman, *Sylvia Townsend Warner* (London, 1989), p. 28; Hartley, 'The Conformer', 68.
[14] Harman, *Townsend Warner*, 28–33; Alington, 83, 85.

1916, mundane routines if anything intensified. Ford's new timetable was perfected in 1917. Absent masters were replaced, in one case by a woman; dead ones with new staff. With typical lack of finesse, Ford wrote to Fred Leaf in May 1916: 'I think we must assume that both Werner and Lagden are dead, and therefore I need not any longer delay to confirm your appointment here as a master.'[15]

The end of the Great War did not mark a return to Edwardian Harrow. Pride in Harrow's contribution, in the generals Smith-Dorrien, who had skilfully prevented the retreat from Mons in 1914 from turning into a rout, and Horne who had led the British back there in 1918; in the eight VCs and countless other service decorations; in the dead and wounded, was tempered by bitterness and loss. A boy with a German father was refused entry by the governors in February 1919.[16] The War Memorial was the largest school building erected during the century between 1877 and the mid-1970s. It did more than commemorate the dead. Housed in the building were separate common rooms for masters, monitors, and members of the Philathletic Club, then a self-electing oligarchy that ostensibly ran games; a large hall for meetings, later known as the Old Harrovian Room, where boys and parents could assemble; and a room dedicated to the memory of Second Lieutenant Alex Fitch, killed aged $19\frac{1}{2}$ at Jeancourt on 18 September 1918, a year after leaving Harrow.[17] Originally, the walls were lined with portraits and busts of old boys and Head Masters stretching back to the eighteenth century, the War Memorial acting as a shrine for Harrow as well as its war dead. Although deserted for most of the day, it provided a social and business centre for masters and senior boys that had not existed before and a place of congregation for the present school and past members: the OH Lodge regularly held its meetings there (Sir Francis Fladgate, its inspiration, being a prominent mason). The War Memorial altered the way the school functioned by creating a centre that was not, like Chapel or Speech Room, purely ceremonial. It suited the structural reforms and creeping centralization of Ford and his successors; appropriately but inevitably the command post of the ARP wardens during the Second World War was sited there. Yet the building was not solely functional; the new concentration of school activity exisited in the presence of the shrine to the dead and the eternal light shining above the portrait of young Alex Fitch.

The interpretation of Harrow embodied in the War Memorial was unmistakable. It stood for secular ideals of permanence, solidity, tradition, and duty. It showed Harrow taking itself seriously, solemnly, pompously, a fulfilment of the emotions created by the Butlers in the previous century. Wartime sacrifice proved that the cult of the school represented more than the nostalgia of Songs (there is

---

[15] Masters' Files, F. A. Leaf, 5 May 1916, Ford to Leaf. For women teachers at Harrow, 'D.P.H', 'A Woman's Invasion of a Famous Public School', ed. L. Huxley, *Cornhill Magazine* (Oct. 1932); Alington, *Ford*, 106.   [16] GBM, 11 Feb. 1919.

[17] Laborde, *Harrow School*, 155–72. For a sample of later disputes over the use of the Fitch Room see GBM 15 June, 11 Nov. 1961, 7 June, 12 Nov. 1962, 9 Nov. 1968.

none about either World War), sentiment, and reunions. Harrow could be proud of itself through its contribution to the national cause, an offering that required constant proclamation to inspire future generations. Although dedicated by Archbishop Davidson, the Harrow War Memorial was, like so many others across the kingdom, an expression of civic and corporate identity as well as loss. Its defining message and massive presence became so familiar that both were taken for granted. In the generations born after the World Wars and especially after the 1960s, the War Memorial may have appeared gloomy and ponderous, losing its power to give pause, empty of living emotions, no longer a recognized or accepted statement of Harrow's place in the world. Nevertheless, unnoticed or not, the War Memorial witnessed the extent to which the experience of war penetrated and shaped the school's self-image and aspirations.

The human responses to the Great War at Harrow in the 1920s matched those elsewhere, a mixture of triumphant but uneasy conservatism, material hedonism, and exasperated radicalism, with the ratio heavily in favour of the first two. The masters who returned from the war exerted a profound influence. Eleven appointed before 1918 served in the war, one, the exotically named Albert Marie Elie Begouën de Meaux, in the French army; two were clergymen. Of those arriving in the ten years afterwards, fourteen had been in the armed forces. An extra-master, E. G. Mercer, who taught music and drill, rose to be a temporary Brigadier-General, before returning to Harrow to command the Corps.[18] Some did not let people forget their wartime role. In common with many others who had joined up in 1914 (Clement Attlee was another), E. J. Housden (master 1920–52) continued to be known as 'Major' for the rest of his life (to the boys he was 'Tichy').[19] He had won the MC, later commanded the OTC (1933–44) and acted as secretary to the Imperial Cadet Association (1940–64). Others were more reticent, although often continuing as loyal Corps officers. Of the Harrow masters who went to war in 1914 and returned, the Revd D. B. Kittermaster had won the MC, J. H. Hollingsworth the DSC, and C. W. Carrington, his time with the Grenadier Guards leaving him 'rather detached', the DSO. Even without war service, E. W. Freeborn, 'Juggins' to the boys, commanding officer of the OTC 1914–19, was known as 'Major'.[20] There was a group of masters who had taught at one of the naval colleges, Osborne or Dartmouth: C. W. M. Moorsom (1908–34, described by both pupil and colleague as a 'militarist');[21] C. L. Bryant (1913–41); L. W. Henry (1919–44); and A. P. Boissier (1919–42). C. R. Browne (1919–48) had been educated at both. A. Wyatt-Smith, master and unsuccessful defender of the Army Class, a veteran of the Boer War, lent enthusiastic support to the new militarism.

---

[18] *Harrow Register, 1885–1949*, 679–85, 690 for masters' details.
[19] HA Materials Relating to Boys, Box 1, H. R. Bridgeman MS Diary, 29 Sept. 1939.
[20] Vickers, *Beaton*, 21.
[21] Playfair, *My Father's Son*, 73; Venables, *Bases Attempted*, 74.

The OTC became a central feature of school life. In 1921 the governors formally recognized it as a compulsory feature of the curriculum for all boys over 15. Parades were twice a week, on Wednesday afternoons and Friday mornings before lunch, with some additional exercises on Sundays. New facilities for shooting were constructed in 1925, the rifle range almost being sited next to Park Lake. The same year asphalt was laid on the the parade ground.[22] Masters were expected to join the Corps. Not the least ground for general suspicion of the refined, prickly High Church cleric Malcolm Venables when he came in 1917 was his refusal to join the Corps even though he had been Commanding Officer at his previous school, Felsted, an experience that had persuaded him that the Corps and the cloth did not mix.[23] This was not a Harrow view. The Corps had been commanded by clergymen for most of the quarter century before 1914; in 1932, a VC and MC, G. H. Woolley, was appointed as Venables' successor as chaplain. The belligerent Wyatt-Smith never bothered to conceal his disapproval of Venables.

Boys found it much harder to escape Corps. Even if they did not go to Cecil Beaton's extravagant lengths to avoid it, those less inclined or less fit for military enthusiasm found themselves persecuted. 'Slacking at Corps' in the 1920s was a ubiquitous charge levelled at so-called aesthetes, punishable by inevitable beating. The rebellious Giles Playfair not only suffered in this fashion but also failed a history exam because he had been forced to spend the previous afternoon polishing his corps belt. Militarism was pervasive in action as well as spirit. The rituals of preparation formed an integral part of school life, from usually failed attempts to tie puttees correctly to the endless cleaning of belts and boots. Some, such as Playfair's OH theatrical impresario father, protested when military routine interfered with academic work.[24] These were lone voices. More typical was the behaviour of Terence Rattigan (1925–30). While openly criticizing the excessive prominence of Corps training, he none the less insisted that his hapless fag, Michael Denison (1929–34), cleaned his Corps belt properly, a chore familiar to fags for another half century.[25]

On one level, Corps was regarded by the majority of Harrovians in the same way as any other compulsory school activity, a necessary evil to be reviled but accepted. Few probably shared Giles Playfair's sense of 'mental degredation' at the bullying he suffered because of his incompetence at drill. Corps bullying would not have seemed much different from all the other kinds.[26] The emphasis on the martial did not achieve greater enthusiasm for the armed forces as a career. Harrow had been a military school since the Napoleonic Wars; it did not become more so in the 1920s. In 1924, responding to Ford's proposal to close the Army Class as part of a final uni-

---

[22] GBM, 23 June 1921, 10 Nov. 1922, 21 June 1923, 8 Feb., 9 May 1924; Laborde, *Harrow School*, 202–3, 206–7.

[23] Venables, *Bases Attempted*, 14 and 22–3 for Wyatt-Smith's disapproval.

[24] Playfair, *My Father's Son*, 104–8.   [25] G. Wansell, *Terence Rattigan* (London, 1995), p. 41.

[26] Playfair, *My Father's Son*, 107.

fication of the curriculum, Wyatt-Smith protested that applicants to Harrow would decline as there were commonly between 100 and 120 prospective army recruits in the school.[27] The figures are less impressive when divided by years and by results. Of the 155 entrants in 1919, twenty-two joined the regular armed services (one the Australian army), 14 per cent, with another six volunteering for the Territorial Army. Excluding TA recruits, the figures for 1924 entrants were twenty-six out of 156, 16.6 per cent; for 1930, twenty-six out of 157 entrants, 16.5 per cent. These proportions exactly match those from the entries in 1900 (16 per cent) and 1905 (15 per cent). Proportionately fewer Harrovians went into the professional armed services in the 1920s than at any time during the last thirty years of the nineteenth century. Harrow's post-1918 military obsession was more for internal, institutional identity than for the education or future of the pupils. As so often, what has been portrayed as the character of the school in fact comprised the habits and mentalities of adults, the masters not the boys.

This was vividly demonstrated in the handling of the Corps 'mutinies'. With what Norwood condemned as 'the damage that has . . . been done by the rapid spread of free speculation', some intelligent boys developed ideological doubts about compulsory militarism.[28] At the beginning of Norwood's term, a monitor refused to attend parade claiming he was a conscientious objector.[29] More serious, because more public, were the complaints about excessive drill made to the new OTC commander, Colonel Harold Ozanne, early in 1928. Terence Rattigan, in his third year at The Park, passed the story to his then lover, Geoffrey Gilbey, racing correspondent of the *Daily Express*, adding that some boys had threatened not to parade. The ensuing publicity caused a tremendous row until Rattigan confessed he had been the source of the story, after which the outrage abated. Rattigan was probably not expelled because of his useful combination of academic ability and promise as a batsman.[30]

The objections to excessive Corps did not disappear. In the winter of 1929–30 the *Harrovian* carried a heated correspondence on this issue stimulated by a detailed attack on the practical and legal basis of compulsory Corps by a boy calling himself 'Sufferer' who made the neat debating point that His Majesty's Government was spending £100,000 on the League of Nations but £150,000 nationally on the OTC. The real target was the second parade on Friday lunchtimes as much as compulsion. 'Sufferer' followed this up early in 1930 with another letter advocating voluntary Corps; this time he was joined by a supportive letter from Rattigan who, having opened the batting at Lord's the previous July, must have regarded himself as invulnerable. Rattigan's signed letter may have been

---

[27] Masters' Files, A. Wyatt-Smith, 1 June 1924, Wyatt-Smith to Ford. See *Harrow Register, 1885–1949* for statistics.
[28] C. Norwood, *Religion and Education, The Teaching Church*, paper no. ix (London, 1932), pp. 7–8.
[29] Playfair, *My Father's Son*, 105.   [30] Wansell, *Rattigan*, 37–8.

a bluff and he was 'Sufferer'. This is suggested by the acid reposte of 'Eupy' to the first 'Sufferer' letter, accusing the author of uncertain gender, effeminism acting as an unsubtle code for homosexuality, Rattigan's uninhibited sexual activity being widely known. 'Sufferer' shared Rattigan's views and interest in history. The authorities bore down with ponderous fury through Ozanne's rebuttal of 'Sufferer's' claim that compulsion was illegal without an active Conscription Act in 1929, the Colonel citing numerous Militia Acts to prove his point.[31]

This failed to defuse the discontent. Rattigan, arguing that it was absurd for boys to be forced to drill on Sundays, as some houses insisted, while not being permitted to play games such as squash or fives, continued to write letters to the *Harrovian* as well as one to *The Times*. The latter was noticed by Stanley Baldwin. A bigger explosion, leading to widespread press coverage and questions in the House, was caused by a petition dated 28 May 1930, claiming to bear 400 signatures of Harrovian NCOs and cadets, addressed to John Bostock, an officer in the Corps and housemaster at the Head Master's. This declared opposition to more than one parade a week, claiming that no other similar schools had as many. 'Excessive parades' had transformed 'an institution necessary for discipline and training' into 'a military torture, a thing to be dreaded and avoided and now universally condemned'. The petitioners called for 'a reduction to one parade a week' to 'abolish this hatred and restore success, so essential to its success'. The protest's ringleaders were three Elmfieldians, C. D. Yarrow, P. G. Roberts, and I. M. Carlisle. Their stance was against the excesses of the military obsession, not for pacificism; Yarrow was wounded at Dunkirk and Roberts, a future Conservative MP, became a major in the Coldstream Guards. The authorities, faced with questions of Harrovians' patriotism and loyalty as well as implied criticism of the school's management, counter-attacked, although it took them a month to come up with a strategy. Ozanne denounced the petition as a fake, the official line wavering between accusing the petitoners of obtaining signatures by concealing the nature of the protest and asserting that the signatures themselves were forged. The petition still survives in a box in the school archives, folded in an unconsidered envelope addressed to Bostock. Some signatures look genuine and are accompanied by pertinent comments; the scripts of others are suspiciously similar. Only one, that of Roberts, appears on the sheet with the petition, the rest on attached slips of paper. Undoubtedly, there was an element of faking. Yet the ruse touched on a genuine grievance that divided otherwise well-disposed pupils from their teachers. Bostock did not dismiss it as a prank and the intensity of the reaction suggests acute official sensitivity. There was widespread unease among the ruling elites at how to perpetuate respect for the Great War and its perceived lessons of duty, control, and order. It must have been especially galling for Harrow veterans as well as militarists to read

---

[31] *The Harrovian* (1929), 167–8, 195–6 (1930), 55; Wansell, *Rattigan*, 41; M. Darlow and G. Hodson, *Terence Rattigan: The Man and his Work* (London, 1979), pp. 41–2.

headlines such as 'Die Harrowschuler protestieren gegen den Korporalstoct' in German newspapers.[32]

The public fuss was hardly mirrored at Harrow. All three organizers of the petition, like Rattigan before them, became monitors. Friday lunchtime parades continued for the rest of the decade.[33] The episode held potential for much embarrassment for Norwood as he had just published, in his *English Tradition of Education*, a prescription for an unoppressive, nonmilitarist OTC. Fortunately for him, few noticed that his own school singularly failed to conform to his proclaimed ideals.[34] The Harrow Corps continued as before; so did pupils' reactions to it. There was no change in the numbers joining the armed forces; no lack of patriotism after 1939; no lessening of independent thought. On 25 February 1939 the motion at the school debate that 'Conscription is the only means of preserving this country' was defeated by 40 votes to 14.[35] The 'mutinies' were expressions of frustration at what seemed an unthinking and exaggerated obeisance to habit and control as much as of hostility to overt militarism, reactions to what Giles Playfair noted in connection with the Corps, 'the fundamental trouble with Harrow— nothing was ever explained or tempered with reason'. It may not have surprised the protesters of the 1920s and 1930s that compulsory Corps only ended in 1973.[36]

With figures such as Colonel Ozanne at the helm, the school's leaden response was unsurprising. Lacking a university degree, he was one of a number of unfortunate Norwood appointments. Apart from the 'mutinies', the intensity of which probably reflected Ozanne's intransigence, a member of the school Shooting VIII, Robin Negus, died on Corps camp in 1932, possibly due to military medical negligence, although naturally the War Office inquiry exonerated all attending doctors and nurses.[37] Whatever his skill as a military commander, Ozanne cut a grasping figure at Harrow, combining his unpopular command of the OTC with the Estates Bursarship. By November 1932 the governors instructed Norwood to sack him, remaining deaf to all appeals.[38] It is likely that Ozanne's control over finances of part of the school as well as the Corps proved too much for him. Once made compulsory, the Corps had had two non-academic masters as commanders, Mercer and Ozanne. This may well have exacerbated the incipient autonomy of Corps funding, accounting, and auditing. Whatever the reasons for his dismissal, Ozanne was the last 'professional' CO of the Harrow OTC, his successors being assistant masters, under the usual control of the Head.

---

[32] HA CCF File (unsorted) for the petition, correspondence, and newpaper cuttings on the affair.
[33] Bridgeman Diary, 16 May 1939.
[34] Mack, *Public Schools and British Opinion since 1860*, 423 n. 47.
[35] Bridgeman Diary, 25 Feb. 1939.
[36] Playfair, *My Father's Son*, 106. In contrast see the uncritically positive account of Corps and Harrow life in *Young Colt's Diary*, 'ed.' C. Terrot (London, 1936); GBM, 17 Mar. 1973.
[37] GBM, 16 Nov. 1932, 15 Feb. 1933.
[38] GBM, 16 Nov. 1932. Cf. ibid., 15 Feb. 1933. Housden replaced him: GBM, 17 May 1933.

The Second World War exerted an entirely different influence. The war itself and modern war in general no longer came as such a traumatic shock; the Great War had accustomed a generation to the idea and some of the realities of industrialized warfare. There was no false optimism; if anything false pessimism was more apparent. War could no longer be seen as culturally cleansing, as some had believed before 1914. The tone of the Second World War was more demotic, more democratic, the propaganda reliant less on upper-class Anglican prejudices, more genuinely populist. Owing to inescapable circumstance, Churchill's rhetoric was not about Imperial glory or even playing the game. It appealed to basic instincts of national solidarity in the face of destruction. Not even the most blinkered public schoolmaster imagined that the war against Hitler was going to be won by public school pluck. There was none of the snobbish Mayo nonsense of Harrow boys being more useful than others. Victory would justify a whole nation not one set of class values.

Locally, there were other significant differences. Unlike in 1914–18, the school itself was in the front line. The war's onset was long expected; as early as February 1937, ARP planning had begun. Classes on air raid protection started in June 1938. Detailed plans for dispersing the school during the anticipated aerial bombardment were in place by September 1938 when gasmasks were issued.[39] Under the skilled and good-humoured management of the Senior ARP Wardens I. W. Bankes-Williams (1938–41) and H. L. Harris (1942–5), the school survived the bombs, occasionally only narrowly, with boys and masters providing the fire watch. During the Blitz in the autumn of 1940 all boys had to be accommodated in overnight shelters, with separate daytime shelters, the stoicism of the instructions to masters on how to behave if a raid occurred during lessons being a model of detached understatement. On the night of 2 October 1940 thirty-three fires in school buildings were ignited by incendiary bombs, the first of which fell directly in front of the Head Master, A. P. Boissier, as he entered the ARP control station in the War Memorial. The main damage was caused to the Speech Room roof. Bombing remained a serious threat almost to the end of the war. There was a near-disastrous raid on 22 February 1944, Ash Wednesday, and the bombing intensified the following autumn.[40] Once again, the ordinariness of the experience shines through contemporary records and accounts. However, it is little wonder that numbers in the school fell by almost a quarter between the Summer of 1940 and January 1941.[41] By staying on the Hill, Harrow was vulnerable, less to direct attack than to German pilots losing their way or dropping excess loads after flying across

---

[39] GBM, 24 Feb. 1937; HM/Vellacott/Accession no. 103, paper by I. W. Bankes-Williams; HM/V/Sept. 1938, Memorandum Vellacott to parents; GBM, 13 June, 18 July 1939.

[40] GBM, 23 Oct. 1940, 20 Sept., 1 Nov. 1944; HM/V; HM/V/ARP Arrangements from E. V. C. Plumptre's papers; *Sunday Times*, 17 Nov. 1940 for a description of 200 firebombs at Harrow. Cf. Laborde, *Harrow School*, 66, 144–5, 151, 180 for other raids.

[41] From 435 to 332.

London before turning back eastwards to their continental bases. Logistic problems increased with the arrival of Malvern in 1942, although, in terms of manpower for fire-watching and fire-extinguishing, it provided valuable assistance. As H. L. Harris wrote later 'Malvern College could not have done more for its own buildings than it did for Harrow'.[42]

The impact of casualties also differed from the Great War. They were less heavy, although two serving masters were killed, both airmen: G. T. Swann and R. de W. K. Winlaw. Casualties occured in campaigns of movement on land and sea and in the air, with clear gains and losses, not with a relentless, remorseless, grinding inevitability in an apparently endlessly static bloodbath. This did nothing to mitigate individual tragedies. Yet, although many were to lose their own lives before the war ended, there were far fewer boys to hear the roll of honour. There were fewer masters too. Including those who went to fight, thirty-four masters of Edwardian Harrow served through the 1914–18 trauma, some, like E. M. Butler, C. H. P. Mayo, and E. C. E. Owen, to retire early immediately afterwards. Only twenty-two served through the whole of the Second World War, seven of whom were away on war service.[43]

Whereas in 1918 many had looked to return to pre-war certainties, in 1945 it was recognized that the world, even on Harrow hill, had been altered irrecoverably. Winston Churchill spoke to the school in 1944 of change as an opportunity not a betrayal.[44] The Second World War had been waged against militarism. The peace promised radical new departures. With the loss of Empire over the next quarter of a century, in ideological if not employment terms Harrow's occupation had gone. The very core of Harrow's mission, so confidently proclaimed in the Victorian and Edwardian era, so stridently reaffirmed between the world wars, was eroded. Instead of a creed of Christian duty and *noblesse oblige*, Harrow, with other public schools, was increasingly forced to refashion its function in more utilitarian terms of providing a different or better education than elsewhere. The twilight of assumed greatness was deceptive, long, and lingering.

The military dimension of the school's identity survived. Most of the new intake of masters under R. W. Moore (Head 1942–53) had fought in the war and nearly all those appointed until the mid-1960s had done National Service. The Corps itself, renamed in 1940 the Junior Training Corps and, after the war, with the advent of naval and R.A.F. sections, the Combined Cadet Force, diversified.[45] With such a wealth of military experience there was no shortage of masters available to act as officers. Thus the Corps continued as an integral part of the Harrow scene, so much so that, although parades were reduced to one a week and the emphasis on bayonet practice and endless drill was dropped, its profile remained large. Externally, as the British armed forces shrank and, after the end of National Service,

---

[42] *The Malvernian*, Summer 1946, p. 14.
[44] *The Harrovian*, 6 Dec. 1944, p. 19.
[43] *Harrow Register, 1885–1949*, 679–88.
[45] Laborde, *Harrow School*, 206.

became more professional, so school Corps received if anything more attention as recruiting grounds for future officers. Internally, because of the experience and inclinations of the post-war and National Service generation of masters, serving in the Corps became an established route to social acceptance and professional advancement for a new master long after any of them possessed genuine military credentials.

This commitment to training for the armed forces failed to elicit much response from pupils in the thirty years after 1945. Of Harrovians entering the school in 1945, just 11 per cent (11 out of 98) stayed in the professional services, with two more active in the TA and RNR. From the new boys in 1951, when the governors were sufficiently alarmed at the prospect of another world war that they laid plans to evacuate to Malvern, the figure had declined to 9 per cent (12 out of 133), not counting the special case of King Hussein of Jordan. The governors, newly afforced by Field Marshal Alexander, were disturbed to learn that between 1945 and 1952 only twenty-seven Harrovians had passed into Sandhurst: they wanted more to enter the armed forces.[46] Yet this pattern remained into the 1970s. Ten out of 174 new boys in 1970 joined up, just under 6 per cent; from 1975, 12 out of 165, just over 7 per cent.

Yet from the late 1960s, when other schools were abandoning their CCFs, Harrow's commitment remained unshaken, with ever more resources being attracted from the Ministry of Defence. Despite Head Master Hoban's recognition in 1973 of the times in which he was living by offering alternative activities for Wednesday afternoons, thereby earning him the disapproval of some powerful colleagues, the Corps remained a dominant force, not least because the alternatives were inadequate.[47] Arguably, apparently voluntary Corps advanced its cause as a school activity. Other options, such as Community Service, could not accommodate the same numbers and, more importantly, attracted social opprobrium in many quarters of the school. In some, perhaps most houses in the 1970s and 1980s, pressure from peers and housemasters to join the Corps was irresistible. To opt for alternatives was thought by some to be unmanly, in local patois 'shag'. Given the predominance of sporting priorities in a school with a wide range of academic abilities this is less surprising than the adult pressure. Yet the Corps, as well as giving the boys something tiring to do on Wednesday afternoons, provided tangible standards and goals which could show the school in a good light. By the 1980s, with the language of nationalism fashionable once more and the Falklands War acting for some as an icon of national revival, there were obvious institutional benefits in running an active and successful Corps, not least with an important section of Harrow's traditional clientele. Masters derived enjoyment, fresh contacts with a range of boys different from those they taught, and a few perks. For both boys and masters it could be seen as games with guns. Although in the 1980s the rhetoric of militarism

[46] GBM, 9 May 1953, 6 Feb. 1954; *Harrow Register, 1986, passim* for the statistics.
[47] GBM, 17 Mar. 1973.

was distinctly muted, echoes of Edwardian Harrow were unmistakable, from the fervour of some recruits to the indifference, ennui, or mockery of others. If, viewed from a national or even HMC perspective, Harrow's nurturing of the military tradition appeared eccentric, it suited the school's traditions and self-image. Harrow remained a military school, in some ways more so than before 1914, precisely because its commitment to the Corps was less common.

Significant of this increase in status was the school CCFs reversion to using the title of Harrow Rifle Corps which it had carried between 1859 and 1908, a title redolent of self-confident traditionalism.[48] At the top of the Corps, this change was fully justified. In the 1980s the Corps was one of Harrow's clear successes. In December 1990 Head Master Beer revealed that over the previous eight years Harrow had won more than sixty service scholarships, more than any other school in the land.[49] Here, at least, Beer seemed to be saying, Harrow was best. For a century and a school scarred by war, this forms an intriguing epitaph. What most of Beer's predecessors would have made of it is unimaginable. Beer nevertheless recognized that an essential element in Harrow's identity since the Great War, one maintained against surrounding changes, had, as the century was ending, retained importance in the image the school presented the world and, powerfully, in the image it held of itself. Alex Fitch might have approved.

Religion, Race, and Creed

Religion, specifically the Church of England, lay at the heart of Harrow's identity in the first four centuries of Lyon's foundation. In spite of the concurrent secularism of games, academic competition, and war, Victorian ideals of godliness persisted in providing the rhetoric and structure for social and moral education. As Waring Young had appreciated in 1870, Anglicanism defined class as well as faith.[50] By the twentieth century, Harrow comfortably occupied its own niche in the facade of the British Establishment of which the national church was a chief adornment. Anglicanism may have been next to godliness; it was certainly next to patriotism. Religion at Harrow, as elsewhere, concerned cultural, ethnic, and racial identity as well as belief. Debates over the nature of Anglican churchmanship presented within the school mirrored the imposition of religious restrictions and tests on potential entrants, the equation of religion, class, and race only dissolving in the last quarter of the twentieth century, a century in which, at one time or another, Harrow discriminated against Roman Catholics, Jews, Muslims, Hindus, and Buddhists partly on the grounds of defending its 'English', not to say Anglican identity. As society and the constituency of wealthy parents eager to take advantage

---

[48] Laborde, *Harrow School*, 206. [49] HA HM/Beer/Head Master's Newsletter, Dec. 1990.
[50] Young Letter Book, fo. 486.

of Harrow's education became more cosmopolitan, so old shibboleths lost their meaning. None the less, every Head Master between 1914 and 1991 followed their predecessors back to Wordsworth in locating the centre of the school in Chapel, in deliberate or inadvertent exclusion of others.

Even though Harrow abandoned the habit of clerical Heads in 1926, sooner than Eton (1933), Winchester (1935), and Westminster (1937), many Head Masters between the First World and Gulf Wars were men of conspicuous Anglican piety. In religion, the attitude of the Head was crucial, as he was statutorily charged with the supervision of worship in the school, as Paul Vellacott testily had to remind his turbulent priests in the late 1930s.[51] Vellacott himself, after repeated difficulties with the warring clerics on the staff, wearily—and possibly ironically—confided to Malcolm Venables, one of the most troublesome of all, that 'no man ought to be Head Master of Harrow who is not in Holy Orders.'[52] Vellacott was a layman with little patience for the theological, liturgical, and ecclesiological squabbling that marked inter-war Harrow. A man of orthodox Anglican views, he believed in Chapel as an important aspect of the school's corporate life.[53] Much the same was true of Dr James twenty years later, who chose not to parade his personal faith and deplored public excesses of religious enthusiasm. In many ways, Vellacott and James reflected the prevalent attitudes of boys and parents. Religion, i.e. Anglicanism, was accepted as an integral part of private education. Whatever individual faith was inspired or acquired, public school religion was essentially conformist and conventional, the majority of boys, it was often accurately feared, accepting confirmation because it was expected of them, a social as much as religious ritual. As Welldon had discovered in the 1890s, beyond the religiously committed, possibly a minority even then, most masters shared uncommitted attitudes which could prove especially awkward with housemasters on whom, until the 1960s, fell much of the burden of preparing boys for confirmation. Formmasters, of whatever degree of religious interest or knowledge, continued to 'teach' Divinity until late in the century. Many masters rarely attended Chapel, a lament of chaplains in the 1930s as much as the 1890s or 1990s.[54] The opening to more non-Anglican pupils blurred even the traditional conventions. Yet, as with the Corps, loss of monopoly led to an increase in seriousness among the school's religious authorities—now no longer exclusively Anglican—rather than a disintegration into obscurantism or casual indifference. In the 1980s Harrow experienced an official religious revival to match its military one, except its base amongst boys was necessarily narrower.

Such shifts and doubts were not apparent in the public rhetoric. Lionel Ford, precisely in the manner of Wordsworth or Vaughan, once declared: 'My order in

[51] Masters' Files P. H. M. Bryant, 10 Feb. 1939, Vellacott to Bryant.
[52] Venables, *Bases Attempted*, 102.
[53] Masters' Files, H. McL. Havergal, notes by Vellacott in response to Havergal's memorandum of 26 May 1938. [54] Venables, *Bases Attempted*, 57, 187; above, p. 366.

the relative importance of the Education of schoolboys is, first, the Christian Faith, then character based on it, and then intellectual achievement.'[55] Cyril Norwood was equally unequivocal: 'spiritual values must go through all the schools of our country ... I do not know any sure foundation for it other than the foundation of the Christian religion' which, he made very clear, he found in a firmly Protestant Anglicanism.[56] Ralph Moore did more than voice his devout Christian principles, he taught Divinity in the VIth Form and published a series of devotional studies between 1941 and 1950.[57] Ian Beer, as befitted a former Head Master of a Woodard school, regarded the promotion of 'the spiritual life of the community' as essential to his educational objective. In language redolent of Victorian values, he wished pupils to be 'motivated by the power of the spirit' to serve others; they were to be 'presented with faith in action so that such a faith may be "caught" by the individual'. This programme demanded commitment from believing adults and 'a joyous approach to a living religion in the Spirit' in Chapel which, like Ford before him, Beer depicted as God's house. Norwood, who equated Anglo-Catholicism with irreligion, would have been appalled at such expressions but he would have been more sympathetic to Beer's argument that a threat to Harrow lay in 'parents no longer look[ing] for a Christian education'.[58]

This continuity of religious sentiment was not unique to Harrow, despite its marked traditionalism. Of the eighty-nine public schools identified by the Fleming Report in 1944, forty-one demanded that their Head be members of the Church of England. Harrow was not one of these, but shared with another twenty schools some formal tie to the Established Church, for example the school's visitor being the archbishop of Canterbury (or, depending on which foundation document is followed, the bishop of London) and the Head Master technically acting as the Ordinary with regard to Chapel worship. Only twelve of the Fleming Report's eighty-nine schools had no 'definite links with a particular denomination'.[59] The gulf between the intentions of Head Masters and chaplains and their achievements is common to all professedly Christian public schools, as are the general patterns of change in the role of Chapel, increasingly voluntary, and the office of chaplain which, after 1945, tended towards the pastoral. The schoolmaster in a dog collar was replaced by the chaplain as a school's parish priest. Academically, no less than in the inculcation of morality and ethics, the popular association of formal religion with educational order and discipline continued to be seen as working to the advantage of all traditional public schools.

---

[55] Alington, *Ford*, 102; Bryant, *Harrow*, 97.
[56] Norwood, *Religion and Education*, 7.
[57] *The Harrovian*, 28 Jan. 1953, pp. 47–52; among his devotional works were *Where God Begins* (1941), *Christ the Beginning* (1944), *The Moving of the Spirit* (1947), and *The Furtherance of the Gospel* (1950). [58] Policy Document on Priorities, 1989, pp. 2, 3, 4, 5.
[59] Dancy, *Public Schools*, 67 and, generally, pp. 67–73.

Harrow's particular religious identity was distinctive and frequently controversial. As Welldon diagnosed in 1915, nineteenth-century Harrow was an evangelical school, in a Broad Church sense.[60] The religion preached by Vaughan, Butler, and Welldon himself tended to provide 'a supernatural sanction for morality', behavioural not mystical.[61] The sermon rather than the sacrament sat at the heart of Harrovian worship. Not only was anti-Roman Catholicism rife and freely voiced, by Welldon, for example, even the mildest hints of a more Anglo-Catholic style of worship were greeted with suspicion and anger. The Oxford Movement found few supporters on the Hill before Lionel Ford; the experience of Christopher Wordsworth remained a living precedent. Until the autumn term of 1898, Sunday preachers wore academic dress: gown and hood, and only changed then because Welldon had been appointed a bishop and was very sensitive to status. When Wood, on arriving at Harrow, adopted the eastward position in celebrating Holy Communion he was accused of 'galloping to Rome'. Ford's Anglo-Catholicism went some way to breaking his Head Mastership.[62]

Trained as a priest at Cuddesdon, a nursery of High Churchmen, Ford shocked many of the traditionalists at Harrow by his clear emphasis on the sacraments and the beauty of 'holiness'. His protégé Venables described the battleground: 'Ford believed in the Catholic Church as the Body of Christ. Schoolmasters prefer to regard it as a congregation of moral beings. Ford believed in the priesthood. Schoolmasters prefer parsons. Ford wanted to beautify ... worship. Schoolmasters, as a whole, prefer vigour to beauty.'[63] Additional celebrations of Holy Communion on Sunday and during the week were introduced, including a Sung Eucharist on Sundays, which not only disturbed the evangelicals but attracted the fierce opposition of the anti-clerical, free-living, if not free-thinking Director of Music, Percy Buck. Ford appeared to undermine the influence of housemasters by seeing each confirmation candidate individually, although Welldon had done much the same. Ford's difficulties, inevitable because of his desire for change, were compounded by a perceived secretiveness in his failure to explain his innovations and an apparent predilection for favourites and divisive cliques. He said Matins daily after First School in the Crypt Chapel with a circle of sympathetic masters, a service boycotted by some of the ordained masters. In making appointments, Ford frequently considered the candidate's churchmanship. Venables commended himself at interview in 1916 as 'a real Cuddesdon man' while E. J. Housden's Baptist upbring in 1919 was a matter of concern whereas, during his interview in 1925, E. V. C. Plumptre revealed himself not only as an Anglican but 'sympathetically minded religiously'.[64] This did not mean that Ford deliberately packed the school with

---

[60] Welldon, *Recollections*, 104.   [61] The phrase is Dancy's, *Public Schools*, 70.
[62] Welldon, *Forty Years On*, 172–3, 180; Alington, *Ford*, 84–5, 100.
[63] Venables, *Bases Attempted*, 38 and, in general, pp. 32–44; Alington, *Ford*, 50, 89–113.
[64] Ford's interview notes in Masters' Files, E. M. Venables, 17 Sept. 1916; E. J. Housden, 12 Aug. 1919; E. V. C. Plumptre, 2 Apr. 1925.

Anglo-Catholics. One of his earlier appointments, the Revd D. B. Kittermaster, led the opposition to the changes in Chapel. In any case, the main difficulty lay with senior masters, such as E. Graham and C. G. Pope and later A. Wyatt-Smith who were not afraid to voice their hostility. As one of Ford's supporters later observed, his churchmanship 'was so pronounced in type as to make its acceptance . . . extremely difficult' as he attempted 'to remove religion from the circumference to the centre of school life'.[65] Yet this attempt to blacken Ford's opponents with the tar of 'moral apathy' was unfair on some of them. Not all were lazily conformist or prejudiced conservative bigots. Kittermaster had a genuine evangelical vocation. After retiring from Harrow he served as chaplain at a Borstal in Rochester. However, he could not share the concerns of the Anglo-Catholics who in consequence branded him as 'at heart . . . a lay slum worker', a comment typical of the High Churchmen's only too apparent social as well as spiritual snobbery.[66]

Almost as soon as Ford left, Norwood, an anti-Catholic of the old school, abolished almost all his sacramental innovations, apparently with the approval of Archbishop Davidson. Norwood's lay status required a chaplain to be appointed. Ironically, this turned out to be the Anglo-Catholic Venables. He managed to salvage the Wednesday Holy Communion, regarded by one housemaster's wife as 'one of Ven's Anglo-Catholic dodges'.[67]

Norwood represented the mainstream of old-fashioned public school Anglican protestantism. Venables's somewhat paranoic account of Harrow religion, 1925–40, confirms that nuances of attitudes to religion mattered, however arcane the issues may appear. Religion returned to its traditional place as the declared foundation of the essentially secular public school values embodied, according to Norwood, in 'games and open-air prowess' and 'corporate effort'.[68] Ford, for all his obsession with games, could not have written as Norwood did to the Cambridge blue E. T. Killick in 1929: 'I should like to have a man who is a good cricketer and in Holy Orders.'[69] All seemed directed at outward civic virtue rather than inner spiritual life. Chapel once more resounded to massed unison singing at compulsory Matins or Evensong, led by a choir with 'its traditional personnel of lordly athletes'.[70] When Henry Havergal, Director of Music 1937–45, tried to introduce a Harmony Choir in 1938, he received a blast of disapproval from Head Master Vellacott. When the Old Harrovian clergyman Philip Bryant resigned from the staff in 1939, complaining that his idea for voluntary Sunday services had been rejected by his clerical colleagues, Vellacott showed he was shrewder than Ford. Arguing that any changes in Chapel worship needed to be gradual, he

---

[65] Venables, *Bases Attempted*, 48.   [66] Ibid., 42.
[67] Ibid., 76–82; GBM, 14 Nov. 1926.
[68] Norwood, *English Tradition of Education*, 19.
[69] Masters' Files, 10 July 1929, Norwood to Killick.
[70] The phrase is Venables': *Bases Attempted*, 42.

commented 'Nor is, in such a society as this, a strong element of conservatism a bad thing'.[71]

The bitterness of the sacramental and ritualist row scarcely abated during the 1930s. It was said at the time that Old Harrovians 'had felt towards Ford's religious activities much as the Scots felt towards Laud and Charles I'.[72] Venables, as chaplain 1926–31, provided both lightning conductor and lightning for regular storms. Sensitive to criticism, self-serving, and, in his memoirs, dishonest, but also a sincere priest, perceptive schoolmaster, and sympathetic housemaster, Venables thought himself persecuted for his beliefs. He was right. In 1929, he was told a delegation of boys from Moretons had protested to Norwood against his possible appointment as their housemaster on the grounds of his churchmanship. He was not appointed. When chaplain, he identified nine of his colleagues as supporters, with six implacably hostile, the rest suspicious or indifferent.[73] There were frequent rows, even after Venables become housemaster of the Park in 1932 and Geoffrey Woolley succeeded to the chaplaincy. Vellacott's plan for Kittermaster to stay on after retirement in 1937 as chaplain, with the enthusiast Bryant as his deputy, came to nothing, the dominant clerical figures remaining at odds with communal practice.[74] In December 1938 Vellacott had to veto the clergy's attempt to get the octogenarian Bishop Winnington-Ingram of London, notorious as the demagogic imperialist Christian cheerleader for the Allied cause in the Great War, to wear his cope and mitre at Confirmation. Despite the Head Master's ban, Venables telephoned the bishop asking him to dress up none the less. Vellacott, whose temper frightened even experienced schoolmasters, was unamused.[75]

The departure of Woolley in 1939 and Venables in 1942 allowed Ralph Moore a free hand. Judged by the minimal numbers of boys entering the church and the number of masters in Holy Orders, from 1940 never more than three or four at any one time, battles over the liturgy may appear to have lacked relevance. However, Chapel was one of the few places where masters and their wives as well as the boys met together regularly and it remained a focus for ceremonies, visitors, and returning old boys. The tenor of worship was very visible. Post-1945 religious debates in public schools revolved around the teaching of scripture/Divinity, the effectiveness of religious instruction at Confirmation, and compulsory Chapel. Issues of liturgical practices and ecclesiology lost much of their capacity to inflame as the Church

---

[71] Masters' Files, H. McL. Havergal, memorandum of 26 May 1938 and Vellacott's notes; P. H. M. Bryant, correspondence with Vellacott, 9–10 Feb. 1939.

[72] Venables, *Bases Attempted*, 75.

[73] Masters' Files, E. M. Venables, 6 Feb. 1929, Venables to Norwood (and Norwood's vesuvial reply, 7 Feb. 1929); *Bases Attempted*, 76, 82.

[74] For the abortive Kittermaster scheme see Masters' Files, P. H. M. Bryant, 28 June 1942, A. G. Elliot-Smith, Head Master of Cheltenham to R. W. Moore; Elliot-Smith had taught at Harrow 1925–40. Cf. GBM, 24 Feb. 1937.

[75] Masters' Files, E. M. Venables, 13 Dec. 1938, correspondence between Vellacott and Venables.

of England itself slipped its moorings from fixed party positions, the Authorized Version of the Bible and the 1662 Prayer Book. Whereas modern theological ideas and scriptural criticism had been effectively denied the average Harrovian for most of the century, by the 1960s, chaplains, such as the liberal M. L. Hughes (chaplain 1961–73), and their assistants, felt free to air fresh, even challenging ideas. The increasing parochial concentration on Holy Communion began to effect school practices without attracting accusations of popish sacramentalism. Especially from the late 1960s, traditional Harrovian attitudes to worship ceased to impose high barriers to development. Yet Anglicanism remained an integral part of the school's portrayal of itself.

One of Moore's first acts in 1942 was to re-appoint Bryant as a chaplain.[76] Together they experimented with voluntary Chapel services as Bryant had proposed in 1939. Although this did not prove an unqualified success, Moore's willingness to inject a sense of personal choice and devotion into school religion set a pattern that was to be repeated after the early 1970s. Although devoutly orthodox, Moore combined faith with humanity, charity, and common sense. He was the first Head Master not to require a divorced master to resign and to welcome his second wife. His realistic approach to adolescent religion did not find favour with all, but he suffered none of the reactionary outrage of Ford, not least because he was not an Anglo-Catholic. Moore's clergy found it difficult to agree on a Divinity syllabus, yet they maintained close, amicable relations. Inevitably there were some reactionary voices.[77] In January 1946 the fussy, compulsive note-writer Cyril Browne, housemaster of Elmfield, objected to the idea of the school playing football against boys from the Nottingdale Harrow Mission club on the specious grounds that the game would break the Fourth Commandment.[78] He may have been more worried about social contamination than Divine wrath.

The lack of passion in Chapel politics was reinforced by James who, unlike Moore, was sceptical of the value of encouraging public religious enthusiasm. For most of James' long Head Mastership, 1953–71, there was daily compulsory Chapel for the whole school, except for Mondays, when the weekly notices given out in the Speech Room were prefaced by prayers. There was one service on Sundays, Evensong. The daily services tended to comprise opening and closing hymns (James was fond of community singing and religous music), a lesson, and prayers. There was little scope for individuals bearing witness to their own faith, as became fashionable from the late 1960s onwards. There was a minimum of ritual. Wholly sung Evensong was not common although by now a Harmony Choir was tolerated. Holy Communion tended to be weekly, early on Sunday mornings; Hughes's enthusiasm for a mid-morning Marbecke Eucharist not being shared by the Head

---

[76] Masters' Files, P. H. M. Bryant, esp. 20 June 1942, Moore to Elliot-Smith.
[77] Ibid., 25 June 1942, A. P. Boissier to R. W. Moore. For a retrospect on Moore's innovations see HM/James/1 June 1962, James to Bishop Stopford of London.
[78] Masters' Files, C. R. Browne, 24 Jan. 1946, Browne to Moore.

Master. Responding to concerns that 'only in schools and prisons does compulsory worship still go on', James explained to the bishop of London in 1962 that he was in favour of daily compulsory worship at Harrow because the Founder had willed it.[79] What appears breathtakingly disingenuous concealed a highly efficient and practical approach. Chapel services expressed a corporate solidarity. The religious element was rarely diluted by gimmickry; neither was there any aggressive insistence on active personal faith. The weekday services tended to be brief, hardly worth complaining about, yet provided a useful shared daily event in a still Balkanized school. Sunday preaching lacked the urgency of Vaughan or Butler or the absurdity of the desiccated J. W. Coke Norris (1903–30), the model for the central chartacter in Rattigan's *The Browning Version*, who reputedly always began his sermons with 'Thucydides tells us . . . '[80] Some sermons, for example those of the scientist cleric H. J. L. Gorse, were performing *tours de force*. Hughes and his assistant and successor were happy to startle congregations with the possibilities of finding the bones of Christ in Palestine or of reincarnation as a flower. James was not impressed; neither was he disturbed as he knew, from personal experience, that faith and religion were not synonyms and that, for most adolescents, their conversion experiences, if any, or commitment to God came as a result of private response not public ritual.

He may have been surprised at the turn of events in the twenty years after his retirement when both enthusiasm and High Church practices became firmly entrenched in Harrow's Anglicanism. In 1973, as part of wide-ranging reforms, Hoban ended compulsory Chapel for the whole school, although Chapel attendance remained obligatory on all who did not openly profess another denomination or faith.[81] On Sundays boys could choose from one of three services, including Holy Communion. During weekdays the school, now too large to be easily accommodated together in Chapel, was divided into the Upper and Lower schools, each with two 'non-liturgical' services a week. This abandonment of set form, pioneered in the late 1960s, opened the way to new diversity, immediacy, and directness, from appeals to faith to more secular presentations of moral or ethical issues. The escape from traditional liturgy coincided with the wider Church of England reforms that led to the Alternative Service Book of 1980 as well as with a clear shift in churchmanship. Hughes's successor as chaplain, his assistant B. A. Boucher, inclined towards Anglo-Catholic liturgy and theology, even though he presided over the demise of the 1662 Prayer Book. It was alleged that, to save storage space, large numbers of the now redundant copies were incinerated.

The High Church trend was intensified by the arrival of Ian Beer from Lancing in 1981. Not only were vestments and ritual more elaborate, the chaplains began to

---

[79] HM/J/31 May and 1 June for the very revealing correspondence between James and Bishop Stopford in which the Head Master discusses the history of his own faith as well as his attitude to corporate religion.

[80] Wansell, *Rattigan*, 32.   [81] GBM, 17 Mar. 1973.

be called, and expect to be called, 'Father' in an emphasis on their priestly function. One even sported a biretta. Yet this was no slide to Rome. Parallel to such Anglo-Catholic practices came a resurgence of a fundamentalist evangelicalism, among masters and boys.[82] Many of the old categories and party labels lost validity as the attempt was made to display 'faith in action' from all parts of the theological spectrum. Beer was positively Arnoldian in his belief in the centrality of religion in education, placing his programme for Personal and Social Education, begun in 1989, under the Religous Studies Department.[83] A new chaplaincy was established, including others than the Anglican chaplains such as lay readers and lay people. Dialogue with other denominations and faiths was opened. The variety of religious attitudes proclaimed would have disturbed the Broad Church evangelicals of Victorian and Edwardian Harrow; the Catholic practices would have appalled them. Yet, while deploring the means, they might have recognized and sympathized with the end, a renewed attempt to enshrine personal witness to a Living God within a corporate structure, a brave stand in the secular society on and off the Hill. The uncertain effect of such efforts would also have seemed familiar. To say that Harrow as an institution took religion seriously is not the same as asserting that Harrovians did so too.

Harrow had been founded as a Christian school but for most of its history the teaching of Christianity had been dire. Until abolished by Ford after the First World War, Sunday afternoon New Testament lessons provided the only formal Divinity instruction, the vestige of the Greek New Testament periods of Victorian Harrow. Housemasters, of whatever intellect, aptitude, or religious interest, were responsible for Confirmation preparation until the 1960s. A glimpse of what these sessions were like is revealed in a minute from a housemaster's meeting just after the death of Philip Bryant in June 1960. Lance Gorse, the ordained housemaster of The Grove, undertook to take candidates on doctrine, leaving the other housemasters to deal with the Ten Commandments and 'ethical teaching', although they were asked by Gorse 'not to make a particular connection between sex and Confirmation'.[84] This role for housemasters indicates strong tacit assumptions about their backgrounds and beliefs. With the ending of this function in the 1960s, the religious inclinations of housemasters became irrelevant in the context of the Anglican nature of the school. By the end of the century there was a Roman Catholic housemaster, an appointment inconceivable a quarter of a century earlier. With the advent of GCE O Level examinations in 1951, the problem of what to

---

[82] Manifested by the weekly evangelical prayer and discussion group known as 'Flambards' after the house in which it first congregated.

[83] Known as 'The Way of Life'. Beer's religious policies mirror closely Dancy's ideas of 1962: *Public Schools*, 67–73. Beer had taught at Marlborough and was Head of Lancing; Dancy had been Head of Lancing before becoming Master of Marlborough.

[84] Minutes of Housemasters' Meetings, 1949–67, 7 June 1960. For Sunday Divinity, see Venables, *Bases Attempted*, 16; Bryant, *Harrow*, 109.

teach in scripture/Divinity was reduced. None the less, away from the examination syllabus, formal religious instruction, or education remained minimal yet compulsory throughout the whole school, ranging from Bible stories to ethics, according to the taste of the master and the age of his class. Here too, the crowding of the curriculum and the advent of greater flexibility and choice revolutionized the provision of religious education. By the 1980s 'Religious Studies' had become an academic subject, taught by specialists, with an emphasis, for boys under 16, on comparative religion. Divinity was no longer compulsory for all.

This late twentieth-century bifurcation of approach to religion, of greater institutional intensity with increased diversity and choice, represented a radical departure from traditional Harrovian attitudes. Anglicanism was important to Harrow because it formed part of its settled world view. The anti-Catholicism was partly explained by this, as was the acceptance of freemasonry which was embedded in Harrow's clerical as well as lay fabric. It would not have seemed at all odd for the freemason classicist J. W. Moir (master 1922–48) to urge Moore in 1947 to appoint an openly freemason clergyman to the staff.[85] The decline in anti-Catholicism, although not paralleled by an equal decline in freemasonry, forms one of the sharpest transformations in Harrow's religious identity. In the later 1930s, there were less than a dozen Roman Catholics in the school (in 1938 less than 2 per cent).[86] By 1984, with seventy Roman Catholics (over 9 per cent) in the school, the governors appointed the first Catholic school chaplain, a monk from Ealing Abbey.[87] By the end of the century, with a number of Roman Catholic masters, including a housemaster, and over a hundred Catholic boys, a permanent residential Roman chaplain was appointed; Roman Catholic services were conducted in Chapel. Ironically, although in school terms historically revolutionary, the rise of Roman Catholicism fitted Harrow's identification with the conservative wealthy social classes within which Roman Catholicism had gained ground in the later twentieth century, not least through converts from the Church of England. Competitive and socially aware parental ambitions allied to the changes after the Second Vatican Council rendered Roman Catholicism less exclusive and the traditional Catholic schools, such as Downside, Ampleforth, or Douai, less popular. Eton's acceptance of Roman Catholics had pre-dated even Harrow's.

The effective collapse of institutional prejudice against Roman Catholics acknowledged the greater diversity of Harrow's market. The integration of non-Christians and foreigners had a longer, more troubled history. Since the 1870s Harrow presented a contradiction. While accepting individual boys from a wide variety of

---

[85] Masters' Files, J. W. Moir, 14 Dec. 1947, Moir to Moore.
[86] HM/V/31 Jan. 1938, Bursar's memorandum on fees to Vellacott; Catholics then paid an extra 27s. a term. [87] GBM, 10 Nov. 1984.

faiths, denominations, and countries, as an institution Harrow remained culturally monochrome, with racism and anti-Semitism endemic. Thus, Nehru submitted to the name 'Joe' and embraced the prevalent anti-Semitism in a school that educated the Rothschilds.[88] Only occasionally were the institutional assumptions Harrow governors, masters, and boys shared with the British propertied classes revealed in overt discrimination or persecution. That such prejudices existed, even if coded, was none the less evident. While Roman Catholics and dissenters attracted suspicion, white Christians increasingly aroused less anxiety: facilities for Christian Science instruction were provided (at parental cost) in the 1920s and 1950s.[89]

The experience of Jews at Harrow epitomized the school's religio-racial 'schizophrenia'. From the end of the nineteenth century Harrow attracted consistent numbers from the Jewish community. Yet many masters were less than relaxed about admitting them. Lionel Ford had to insist that each new housemaster guaranteed to admit some 'Jewish and foreign boys', a significant association. When offering the housemastership of Bradbys to E. W. Freeborn in 1918, Ford insisted 'you agree to take your share of the burden of providing for boys of alien extraction or religion, to the extent of one (or possibly two) boys at a time'. Freeborn, who equated Jews and foreigners together as 'undesirables', tried to wriggle out of the commitment.[90] In August 1942 Boissier, in handing over the Head Mastership to Moore, expressed his concern about the new housemaster of Druries: 'Between ourselves I am a little worried by the number of "aliens" that Snell is taking', a group later described as 'foreigners'.[91] The code is easy to penetrate by scrutiny of the *Harrow Register*. What Boissier meant were Jewish children of foreign extraction, at least one a German with an Anglicized name. In November 1945 the governors took up the theme, expressing their concern to Moore on 'the number of Jews in the school'.[92] There appeared for some time after the Second World War an institutional inability to cope normally with Jewish boys. In February 1952, when considering arrangements for the Choral Society's performance of Haydn's *Creation*, the housemasters collectively agreed: 'If any Jews want to attend the "Creation" they must get their parents to write to the Housemasters concerned'.[93] This religious unease echoed the most dramatic individual demonstration of anti-Semitism in twentieth-century Harrow.

On Tuesday, 30 May 1939 the Revd E. M. Venables wrote to a Jewish school monitor from Newlands:

I am writing to you in regard to your having read the lesson today in chapel. You know me, I am sure, to be your friend, and am genuinely interested in all that concerns you; and I am

---

[88] Nehru, *Autobiography*, 18; Brown, *Nehru*, 26.
[89] GBM, 16 Nov. 1927; Minutes of Housemasters' Meetings, 1949–67, 4 Feb. 1952.
[90] Masters' Files, E. W. Freeborn, 12 Dec. 1918, Ford to Freeborn, 17 Dec. 1918, Freeborn to Ford. Regular religious instruction was allowed on Sundays. When the Old Music Schools were used for this they were nicknamed 'Tin Tab' by the boys, Laborde, *Harrow School*, 151.
[91] HM/Boissier/7 Aug. 1942, Boissier to Moore.   [92] GBM, 7 Nov. 1945.
[93] Minutes of Housemasters' Meeting 1949–67, 4 Feb. 1952.

in no sense personally antipathetic towards the faith that you profess. But I protest, with all the conviction of my heart and mind that I possess, against your reading the lesson—let alone a New Testament one—in Chapel. In my view it should be as impossible for you to wish to do it as for anybody to allow it. It is absolutely and entirely indefensible, and it has wounded me (not that this itself matters) intensely. I cannot conceive anybody approving of such a thing, and I hope it will never happen again. But I write this to you concerning principle and it does not affect my personal regard for you at all.[94]

The self-righteous tone and self-exculpatory asides are typical Ven; his apparent inability to perceive the burden of his own message characteristic of his time and place. The correspondence survives in the school archives because the Head Master when Venables was retired in 1942 was Boissier, Ven's bitterest personal enemy, who decided to leave it on the file. Yet Boissier—who used his unexpected elevation to remove or destroy his own file—shared the general unease at Jews in the school. Although that very term Harrow had 'adopted' a refugee family from continental Europe, Venables' letter was crass, its crude insensitivity matched only by its offensiveness.

The boy's father was incandescent with outrage and distress, only barely prevented by an agile Head Master from going public.[95] Vellacott was scarcely less furious. Whatever his own opinions, a charge of anti-Semitism coming at a time when he was trying to charm Old Harrovians, including two de Rothschilds, into bailing the school out of financial ruin was more than unhelpful. He rounded on Venables, accusing him of lack of judgement and bullying: 'a boy [is] always at the mercy of a master.' He was tempted to 'have EMV out on this', relenting only after agreeing with the taciturn senior master, C. W. Carrington (who, at the age of 59, had just become a father) that, in the light of the current round of staff dismissals and resignations, the school's reputation could not stand 'the enforced resignation of a senior man'.[96] However, the secret was not well kept. A month later there arrived at Vellacott's house a plain postcard, franked 'Paddington W.2', addressed to 'Hitler the Head Master, Harrow School, Harrow-on-the-Hill'. On the back, where the postman and anybody else could read it, the message ran: 'E. M. Ven. the Jew Baiter. Goebels'. The date was 24 June 1939.[97]

What the victim made of Venables' behaviour would provide an interesting study: he later became a distinguished professor of psychiatry in the USA. For a master to let his guard slip was unusual. Routine, low-level 'Jew-baiting', usually by younger boys, persisted for years, certainly into the late 1960s, even in enlightened houses, much of it reflecting the narrow introspection of the world of the old monied

---

[94] Masters' Files, E. M. Venables, 30 May 1939.

[95] Ibid., 5 June 1939; Bridgeman Diary, 6 Feb. 1939 for adoption scheme.

[96] Masters' Files, E. M. Venables, Vellacott's notes. For Carrington's son see Bridgeman Diary, 9 Feb. 1939.

[97] Masters' Files, E. M. Venables. The postcard is attached to the correspondence on the affair.

upper and middle classes and the attitudes of small, reactionary rural boarding preparatory schools. Harrow itself, in common with most other leading boarding schools, was accused of operating a semi-formal Jewish quota, commonly estimated at 10 per cent into the 1970s.[98] Some houses were notable by their absence of Jews. However, like anti-Catholicism, anti-Semitism, at the institutional level, evaporated as the school came to terms with the post-war world in the 1970s. Helped by the arrival of comparative religious study in the formroom, attitudes shifted. While never reviving the 1880s experiment to attract Orthodox Jews, a century later the position of the visiting Jewish rabbi and the community he served was secure and uncontroversial. Other 'aliens' had come to take the place of Jews in Harrow's anxieties.

Certain masters, such as C. H. P. Mayo, had long disapproved of racial diversity at Harrow.[99] However, as an Imperial school, Harrow could not afford to deny admission to sons of wealthy or aristocratic subjects of the empire, as Welldon's scheme for a Muslim house testified.[100] Yet the ambivalence remained, pride in educating a cosmopolitan elite vying with the reluctance of housemasters such as Freeborn to accept foreigners. Such was their resistance that, by the end of 1926, all the Indian and Siamese Harrovians boarded privately with the maths master, R. T. Hughes, Norwood being forced to insist, not very effectively, that they be spread around among the established boarding houses.[101] As long as the majority of foreign Harrovians possessed impeccable pedigrees, such as the kings of Jordan and Iraq in the 1950s, prejudice could be contained. However, the double standard was never far from the surface. At Lord's in 1968, Harrow's Singhalese captain was greeted with shouts—not all Etonian—of 'Get back to the plantations', taunts that did not unduly upset Dr James.[102]

As British public schools increasingly began to tap a lucrative international market from the 1970s, the issue of race and identity assumed a more than anecdotal importance. In November 1977 the governors, noting the rise in the number of foreigners in the school, required the Head Master to specify foreign nationals in his termly reports.[103] In March 1978 there were fifty-two out of 730 (7.1 per cent), rising erratically to around 12 per cent in 1984–6 and 13.6 per cent in 1990.[104] In a careful, almost painfully worded, passage in July 1978 the governors' Long-Term Planning Committee proposed 'as a guideline only not in any sense as a rigid rule', a quota: 'not more than 10 per cent of the boys accepted by House Masters should be from backgrounds unfamiliar with the ethos of a British Public School'.[105] The relevance of this quota to the school's identity was further explained by Beer in November 1982 when he declared 'that he did not apply a quota system in regard

---

[98] Rae, *Revolution*, 147 and refs. there to the *Jewish Chronicle*.
[99] Mayo, *Reminiscences*, 152–3.   [100] GBM, 26 June 1890.   [101] GBM, 14 Nov. 1926.
[102] HM/J/13 July 1968, J. Riddell to Dr James; 22 July James to Riddell.
[103] GBM, 5 Nov. 1977.   [104] GBM, 4 Mar. 1978, 1984–6, *passim*, 1 Dec. 1990.
[105] GBM, 17 July 1978.

to the admission of non-U.K. nationals, but exercised discretion with a view to ensuring that the school retained its overriding character as an English school—a quality desired as much by the overseas nationals who sent their sons to it as by British parents'.[106] As the school sought closer links with Arab and Japanese sponsors, the issue was delicate. Yet the existence of the foreign quota was openly recognized, in at least one edition of Existing Customs, which the then Vaughan Librarian quietly removed from the shelves in case it fell into hostile hands. The 1989 'Long-Term Priorities' document stated the objective: 'to maintain the best single-sex boarding community possible educating pupils from all over the British Isles with representatives from as many foreign countries as possible within [a?the?] prescribed limit of foreign nationals.'[107]

Whatever private or institutional concerns, market forces drove the percentage of foreign nationals at Harrow beyond 14 per cent in 1991 and 1992 to more than 16 per cent in 1994.[108] As Beer had noticed, this addition to the school's constituency if anything encouraged conservatism and the maintenance of the school's traditional image, even though provision for Muslim or Hindu worship lagged far behind that offered Jews and Roman Catholics. This new inclusiveness was possibly assisted by the reality of the new secularism. It was perhaps symbolic that a huge dinner in London's Guildhall rather than, as a century before, a religious service formed the climax of the Quartercentenary Celebrations, held, like those for the Tercentenary, a year early, in 1971.[109] Nevertheless, almost in disregard of its increasingly heterogeneous ethnic, cosmopolitan, and religious complexion, Harrow remained a self-consciously old-fashioned English public school, still defined by traditional methods of teaching, Corps, Chapel, and games. Definition, per se, imposes limits.

Playing the Game

The Public Schools, if they taught nothing else, would more than justify their existence by their teaching of this one lesson—Play the game . . . It is one of the greatest human lessons of all religions . . . This small island race . . . would [not] ever have attained to its unique position in the world—or have been such a great civilising agency among backward races, if it had not learnt on its playing fields to carry on, though tired and exhausted, to act with fairness and not to be afraid to face responsibility.[110]

C. H. P. Mayo's reaffirmation of the classic doctrine of the games cult in 1928 found emotional almost mystical agreement from Cyril Norwood whose

---

[106] GBM, 13 Nov. 1982.
[107] Policy Document on Long-Term Priorities, 2, 'Opportunities', para. iii.
[108] GBM, 30 Nov. 1991, 28 Nov. 1992, 26 Nov. 1994.
[109] GBM, 20 Mar. 1971. A suggestion of a service in St Paul's had come to nothing.
[110] Mayo, *Reminiscences*, 196–7.

English Tradition of Education proclaimed the full Bowen-esque doctrine. Through athletic games the ideal of chivalry, of physical fitness, and bodily prowess 'answers to our national needs' as 'the training of the body develops the right type of character' through team spirit, fair play, and the willingness to suffer physical hurt. Gentlemanly games, such as rugger, transcended mere exercise for those 'morally and physically fit to play'. In schools they formed 'part of the discipline by which Satan is prevented from providing mischief', by which, of course, Norwood meant sex. Unlike his Victorian predecessors, Norwood derived the purest athletic doctrine from what he supposed was the chivalry of the Middle Ages rather than the Classical world because, he observed, 'the Greeks had no team-spirit'.[111]

Extravagant claims for team games strongly affected the nature of Harrow and its education for much of the twentieth century. Writing of the 1920s, Giles Playfair remarked without exaggeration 'compulsory games were considered equally, if not preferentially, with compulsory lessons'.[112] E. M. Venables lamented the tradition that games time was sacrosanct, any unexpected intrusions into the timetable, such as play or concert rehearsals or even sports practice, being accommodated from lessons or prep. periods.[113] This habit persisted. In 1950 housemasters agreed that certain boys could be excused the final quarter of an hour of the last lesson of the morning in order to practise in the cricket nets.[114] For much of the century the school timetable was suspended for a mass visit to the annual Varsity rugger match at Twickenham. Lord's was even more important, the central festival of the games cult. In 1955, when it was discovered that the dates for A Level Maths and Geography clashed with Lord's, the possibility of changing examination boards was agreed by housemasters.[115] In the 1980s and 1990s, First Eleven cricketers (as at Eton) received specially sought permission from public examiners to sit A Levels at special times to allow them to play at Lord's. Although himself an enthusiastic cricketer, Ford's reputation suffered considerable damage, especially among Old Harrovians, because during his Headship Harrow never won at Lord's which, one cool observer commented, each year 'loomed on the horizon in too baleful and tense a glow'.[116] The institutional priorities occasioned self-parody. Cyril Browne, housemaster of Elmfield, described by a friend as 'always the bachelor sportsman, the lover of open-air life', began his final report on the future Permanent Secretary Anthony Part in July 1934: 'Although he has not fulfilled his early promise at games, he did become twelfth man to the School Cricket XI. He also won a scholarship to Trinity College, Cambridge.'[117]

The games obsession was not quixotic. It provided important cohesion within the school. Inability to converse at length and in detail about school and other

---

[111] Norwood, *English Tradition of Education*, 10, 19, 69–70, 95–7, 101, 103, 104, 107.
[112] Playfair, *My Father's Son*, 104.   [113] Venables, *Bases Attempted*, 24.
[114] Minutes of Housemasters' Meetings, 1949–67, 28 Mar. 1950.   [115] Ibid., 7 Nov. 1955.
[116] Venables, *Bases Attempted*, 50–1; Alington, *Ford*, 87.
[117] A. Part, *The Making of a Mandarin* (London, 1990), p. 12.

sport placed boys at a considerable disadvantage. Until paper rationing during the Second World War, the *Harrovian* carried full reports of all house as well as school matches, including, for cricket, complete scorecards. Games inspired approval from parents as well as old boys. In the words of one inter-war housemaster, 'to many parents, a good bowling action wipes out any blots on their son's reports'.[118] The governors' concern at the poor standard of cricket in 1945 was based on more than sentiment or passion.[119] They believed the school's prestige was at stake, no doubt recalling how the unexpected victory over Eton at Lord's in 1939 concealed from many the true state of the school. Even though greater academic competitiveness and educational utilitarianism in the later twentieth century promoted the importance of form work, sport retained an institutional primacy in the attitudes of the school and in its structures. If sport's moral dimension was emphasized less overtly, it survived in the minds of many teachers as a general justification. As the range and nature of the games being played diversified from the 1960s, the rhetoric shifted to concentrate on the physical benefits of exercise, in Beer's words 'so that [Harrovians] may enter society as fit adults'.[120] None the less, assumptions equating sporting skill and success with positive social and personal qualities persisted not least in Head Masters' Speech Day addresses. Many masters continued to take for granted that lessons as important as those received in formrooms could be learnt on the gamesfield, even if they were more shy in articulating precisely what these were.

Sport attracted considerable financial investment, largely through old boy donations, from the bowling shed of the 1920s to the new racquets courts of the 1960s to the sports complex of the 1980s, facilities that continued to figure prominently in any assessment of the school's external standing with prospective clients.[121] In the age of Appeals, it was easier to elicit money for sport than for scholarship. The cult may have appeared to have degenerated into a hobby, but sporting success still mattered and, when attained, was loudly proclaimed. Athletic achievement was visible, easily quantified, involving all conditions of boys. Participation could be engrossing even for the majority of the less talented. In a school consistently committed to admitting a wide range of intellectual ability, only a few could win genuine academic success. The mass could play, enjoy, and understand sport. It occupied time, expended energy, and, frequent injuries apart, provided health advantages.

The chief problem was that while the elevation of games still suited the internal organization and self-image of the school, it was increasingly introspective. As the century drew to a close, employers and universities were less impressed by sporting achievements alone at a school level and the end of the leisured amateur meant that

---

[118] Venables, *Bases Attempted*, 24.   [119] GBM, 7 Nov. 1945.
[120] Policy Document on Long-Term Priorities, 1989, 4.
[121] Wansell, *Rattigan*, 32; GBM, 10 Nov. 1962, 11 June, 16 Nov. 1963, 7 June 1966, 11 June 1983, 16 June 1984, 9 Feb. 1985.

few leavers would ever play team-games again, certainly not with the intensity of their school days. From being a passport to rule, as Monty Butler, Bowen, Mayo, and Norwood imagined, team sport, in particular, became increasingly confined to relevance only within a school context, no longer an accepted, recognized, or actual preparation for adult life. Social change had emasculated the potency of the games cult. From being a scene of thousands, the annual Eton and Harrow match at Lord's increasingly found the ground echoing and deserted, only the substantial catering receipts encouraging the MCC to persist in acting as hosts. In 1980, Eton even proposed abandoning Lord's altogether: Harrow disagreed.[122] No longer were matches concluded by fights in front of the pavilion as they were regularly until the Second World War.[123] Even in 1954, at his first Lord's, Dr James had been 'absolutely horrified at what went on—shouts insults and certainly no punches pulled from the spectators'. By the late 1960s, not only had James 'long ago got used to this', the behaviour was better.[124] A quarter of a century later, incidents in the largely empty ground were tamer still, the improvement in manners charting a sure decline in importance.

Traditionally, one of the attractions of teaching at a public school for the athletically inclined was the chance to go on with sport. Playing games had been a sine qua non of gentlemen schoolmasters since the 1860s. Before the First World War, unlike less affuent schools, Harrow did not need to appoint masters solely for their sporting prowess. Intellect and games-worship were combined by men such as the talented fives player Townsend Warner or the cricketers Kemp and Pope, all OHs. Ford continued the tradition, although he was realistic enough, for example when appointing E. J. Housden, to recognize that Harrow needed some masters whose use and interests were primarily athletic.[125] Norwood was either less discriminating or more enthusiastic in taking men whose chief qualifications were Blues or national caps, his two internationals materially assisting the successful introduction of rugger.[126] Too many good sportsmen could produce rivalries and frustrations. One of Norwood's last appointments, the Cambridge cricket blue R. de W. K. Winlaw (1934–42), who turned down an invitation to tour the West Indies with the MCC in 1934–5, was very put out when Vellacott chose the Oxford blue, D. F. Walker (1935–9) as master in charge of cricket in 1936.[127]

[122] GBM, 8 Nov. 1980, 28 Feb., 4 June 1981. The compromise was agreement on Eton's insistence on a one-day match during term.
[123] Bryant, *Harrow*, 109–10; Masters' Files, J. W. Moir, unsorted letters, 1939; HM/J/13 and 22 July 1968 for Riddell correspondence.
[124] HM/J/22 July 1968, James to J. Riddell; James cited the memories of three OHs (P. Carlisle, R. A. A. Holt, and J. Gilbart-Smith) to support his contention that behaviour was better than before 1939.   [125] Masters' Files, E. J. Housden, Ford's interview notes, 12 Aug. 1919.
[126] I. M. B. Stuart (1927–31) had played for Ireland; W. H. Stevenson (1931–57) for Scotland.
[127] Masters' Files, R. de W. K. Winlaw, correspondence with Vellacott 1936: he claimed Norwood had promised him the post.

Norwood established a lasting tradition of schoolmasters whose real passions were more or less exclusively sporting rather than academic or intellectual. One ambitious private schoolmaster, from a long line of public school housemasters, on his own initiative applied to Norwood to teach 'IV Form subjects and games'. His university academic record was dismal (a Third and a Pass) but he had won a blue and, in the words of his referee, was 'always a gentleman and a sportsman'. Norwood took him and he stayed at Harrow for the rest of his working life.[128] When Moore was restocking the staff after the Second World War, seven of his first nine appointments in 1946 were Oxbridge blues, at least three of whom possessed no academic pretensions at all.[129] The tradition of advertising combined academic and sporting posts had been well established by the end of the 1930s, R. H. Dahl's appointment in 1938 being designated as being in 'Modern Languages with Rugger'.[130] Many less athleticly talented masters greatly enjoyed sport, some playing long after it was good for them or their team mates. The administrative Head of Classics under Vellacott and Moore, J. W. Moir, died playing fives in 1948 aged fifty.[131]

The Head Masters epitomized the tradition. Monty Butler and Welldon had both been games-players of note when young, but Lionel Ford continued to play fives and cricket to the threshold of old age; in 1922, aged 57, he scored forty-five for a fathers' team against Elmfield, including six sixes. He once summoned a probably rather alarmed new boy simply to tell him how better to defend his leg stump.[132] What Norwood lacked in personal sporting achievement he supplied in his devotion to the cult and his belief in the transcendant moral virtues of rugger. The election of 1934 broke with tradition as Paul Vellacott was the first non-classicist to be appointed Head Master; his First had been in History. None the less, perhaps of equal importance in persuading the governors of the suitability of choosing a Cambridge don, was his hockey blue. Moore, energetic in all he did, played fly-half for the Masters against the school rugger XV in his first term, possibly *faute de mieux* as he was the second youngest on the staff.[133] The conservative revival of the 1980s, witnessed in the Corps and in school religion, extended to sport as the governors appointed a former rugger international and Cambridge blue as Head Master in 1981.[134] Ian Beer placed sport behind only religion near the centre of his vision of education and, in his early years at Harrow, could be seen in a tracksuit himself.

Yet the sporting ethos of Harrow in the 1980s, while sharing features with that of earlier periods, was more pragmatic and diverse. The cultural claims for team games were more muted, both a cause and a consequence of an acceptance of sport

---

[128] Masters' Files, J. W. Greenstock, Greenstock to Norwood, 22 Feb. 1930; reference from E. L. Browne, 21 Feb. 1930.   [129] *Harrow Register, 1986*, 808–10.
[130] Masters' Files, R. H. Dahl, 8 Apr. 1938, E. A. Greswell to Vellacott.
[131] Masters' Files, J. W. Moir, 18 Feb. 1942.   [132] Alington, *Ford*, 88, 116.
[133] *The Harrovian*, 28 Jan. 1953, pp. 47–52.   [134] GBM, 1 May 1980.

as primarily a utilitarian activity, exercising the body not moulding the character. Although a few masters clung to it, the old hierarchy of value that differentiated games had largely dissolved, especially among pupils. In the mid-1950s cricket was effectively compulsory. Twenty-five years later, Harrovians could select from a list that included tennis, athletics, and golf as well as racquets, squash, fives, etc.[135] By the end of the 1980s, Association Football had been accepted as a significant school game, as it had been before Norwood's introduction of rugger in 1927, the conflict between the two codes exposing attitudes to the role of sport more sharply than any other example. Norwood thought soccer had been ruined by professionalism, thus 'for school purposes', of character building, 'pride of place will come to be given to Rugby Football'.[136] What he meant was that, after the turn of the century, soccer had become increasingly proletarian. Both cricket and rugger retained their amateur status, one into the 1960s, the other into the 1990s. They were games for gentlemen. To the uninitiated, the contempt for soccer may appear unintelligible but it was strong and lasting. At a meeting of housemasters with the Head Master on 30 January 1967 (the year after England won the World Cup) 'some discussion took place about the seeping and insidious threat of soccer.'[137] Norwood, but perhaps not many others, would have understood.

Ironically, the introduction to Harrow of what became the iconic and quintessential winter game aroused the same hostility as, in some quarters, did the revival of soccer half a century later. Before Norwood arrived in 1926, the school's prime winter game was Harrow Football which only Harrovians, Old Harrovians, and Harrow masters could understand let alone play. Suitable to local conditions, Harrow Football had been a mass participation sport within the school but, by definition, could not be played against any other school. Norwood, with experience as a boy or Head Master of three other public and two grammar schools, was keen for Harrow to compete against other HMC schools. Soccer, which Harrow had played against schools such as Westminster for over a generation, he despised and was willing to sacrifice. Unfortunately, his decision to make rugger the official school sport for the winter term from 1927 was seen as an attack on soccer only by the perceptive few.[138] Most regarded it as a direct threat to the primacy and near-monopoly of Harrow Football and, hence, an assault on a core element of Harrow's distinctive tradition, the moral qualities of which lay at the heart of so much of Bowen's cultic verse. Led by the obstinate and self-confident OH housemaster of The Grove, G. C. 'Cocky' Pope, the defenders of the Harrow Football status quo launched a furious campaign to oppose the proposed change. Norwood outmanœuvred them by conducting the process of persuasion very publicly. In the winter of 1926–7, he

---

[135] For a wider view see Rae, *Revolution*, 115.
[136] Norwood, *English Tradition of Education*, 103.
[137] Minutes of Housemasters' Meetings, 1949–67, Dr James's note, 1 Feb., on the meeting of 30 Jan. 1967. [138] See the correspondence in *The Harrovian*, 18 Dec. 1926, pp. 132–5.

involved the governors who received a protest from Pope and a number of conflicting letters from OHs as well as the Head's plan. They unanimously agreed to the principle of Norwood's scheme.[139] Norwood then held an unprecedented referendum within the school, although careful to reserve the right to ignore its result.[140] Opposing manifestos were produced; there was scarcely concealed campaigning. The masters and boys gave him overwhelming support; the Philathletic Club and Old Harrovians were equally clearly against. Both sides accused the other of dirty tricks and a vehement, venomous correspondence appeared in the *Harrovian*.[141] Unabashed, Norwood proceded to appoint an Irish rugger international, I. M. B. Stuart, to supervise rugger's implementation. On 7 October 1927 the first school match was played against St Edward's, Oxford.[142] Within six years, with the unreconciled Pope sacked, Harrow's rugby football XV went through a successful season and Norwood wrote a song about it. Without knowledge of the game, much of *The Song of the Forwards* is incomprehensible. None the less, its propagandist purpose and moral message are clear enough in the final verse. Playing rugger teaches 'much more than a game', its required strength, 'good temper', courage and speed providing 'not a bad outfit for life and its need'.[143]

Harrow Football did not die; it gradually withered. Still attracting keen *aficionados*, often non-OH masters, it remained compulsory for the Easter Term for more than half a century, continuing to be played on a house basis. However, in the face of other sporting activities, its continuance increasingly relied on its place in Harrow's past. By the 1990s 'School' matches, against motley collections of old boys, attracted almost no watchers, being played in eerie isolation on otherwise deserted football fields. By the end of the century Harrow Football had been reduced almost to the state of the Harrow hat and tails, part of Harrow's dignified not efficient constitution, its main function being to give returning old boys something to play against their houses on the afternoon of the annual Founder's Day.

A similar fate was meted out to the Philathletic Club the progress of which was highly revealing of the changed nature of the organization of sport in twentieth-century Harrow. In the nineteenth century the boys ran games. Bowen himself disapproved of excessive magisterial interference.[144] Consequently, the Phil., comprising the leading bloods, held considerable authority as well as status, recognized by their distinctive waistcoats and bow ties and their right to walk down the middle of the road, a privilege abandoned only in the face of the motor car. Norwood's victory over rugger and the Phil. represented both a political and practical

---

[139] GBM, 19 Jan. 1927.
[140] For a boy's view of this see Playfair, *My Father's Son*, 114. Cf. the adults Laborde, *Harrow School*, 200; Bryant, *Harrow*, 99; Venables, *Bases Attempted*, 120–1.
[141] Pope's letter of 9 Dec. is probably the angriest; he also prints his manifesto: *The Harrovian*, 18 Dec. 1926, pp. 132–3. Cf. I. M. B. Stuart's memories, HM/J/13 June 1967, Stuart to James.
[142] HM/J/13 June 1967 for Stuart's suggestion of a fortieth anniversary game.
[143] *Harrow Song Book*, 112–13.   [144] See above, pp. 339–40.

milestone as the new game was clearly under masters' control as coaches. Harrow Football had been 'taught' and organized by the boys themselves. Professionals were hired for some minor games, such as racquets, and especially for cricket, paid through boys' subscriptions (games remaining a notionally separate item on bills until the 1970s).[145] Nothing indicates the importance attached to cricket more clearly than the engagement in 1930 of the legendary Yorkshire all-rounder Wilfred Rhodes as the professional (Eton had recently acquired the services of the other great Kirkheaton left-arm bowler and right-hand batsman from cricket's Golden Age, George Hirst). Rhodes, an austere, dedicated northerner, came across to spoilt, gilded southern youths as taciturn, critical, and curmudgeonly. He was soon replaced by another famous England cricketer, the Middlesex professional 'Patsy' Hendren whose genial nature and acute social sense ensured his success.[146]

From Norwood's time, the control of masters over coaching and arrangements for all games increased. By the late 1940s some masters were engaged primarily for their supposed coaching skills and inevitably assumed control of organization, internally as well as the older function of supervising away matches. At the same time, the role of school monitors was progressively enhanced, particularly under Dr James, leaving the Phil. as increasingly honorific, with little practical to do except as a consultative body and a club of privilege. In 1966 the Head of School, a future Conservative MP, recognized the logic of events and proposed to the Head Master that the Phil. be abolished.[147] He argued that the Phil. in much of its activities and membership duplicated the monitors and no longer promoted 'manly sports'. Bloods received adequate rewards elsewhere; the administration of games could rest perfectly happily with the captain, master-in-charge, and Head; and 'for the amount of positive work it does the Philathletic Club is an unqualified waste of money for any parent who has a son in the Phil.' He went on to argue that the Phil. did 'positive harm' by instilling in boys 'a wrong sense of values', creating 'false friendships' and disrupting monitorial cohesion and authority. He concluded that 'the old Phil. died some time ago' and its successor 'has brought more trouble than it is worth to the school'. Dr James was unimpressed. He dismissed the Head of School's arguments as those of 'a young man in a hurry' whose real concern was with the Phil.'s unique privilege of wearing bow ties, one denied monitors. Although firm that 'there is no question of the Phil. being abolished', he consulted his two senior OH masters, both former members of the Phil., H. J. L. Gorse and G. R. McConnell, who warned of the effect of abolition on Old Harrovian opinion which the Head Master was equally keen not to infuriate.[148] While all three

---

[145] Laborde, *Harrow School*, 201. Cf. the Crosbys, father and son, as racquets professionals, GBM, 7 May 1949, etc., GBM, 27 May 1971, 9 Mar. 1974 and Bryant's description of masters' involvement in rugger, in contrast to Harrow Football: *Harrow*, 105.
[146] A. A. Thomson, *Hirst and Rhodes* (London, 1959); Venables, *Bases Attempted*, 204.
[147] HM/J/8 May 1966, Head of School, R. A. Nelson, to James.
[148] HM/J/11–12 May 1966, four letters to and from James, H. J. L. Gorse and G. R. McConnell.

masters recognized that the Phil. had almost no practical purpose, it remained in its impotent finery, a symbol of how the image of Harrovians' traditional independence concealed the late twentieth-century reality of adult control. Diehard old boys might complain that 'we are getting like a grammar school (or should we now say, going comprehensive)',[149] but, paradoxically, given the continued institutional importance of games, not least the public relations involved in inter-school competition, closer adult supervision was inevitable. As with much of traditional Harrow, the maintenance of old forms required new structures carefully camouflaged to avoid immediate detection. While, as one old Harrow hand put it in the 1960s, 'two years are usually about enough to establish tradition in boys' minds'— and often less in masters'—Old Harrovians, whose interest, especially in cricket, remained intense, took a little longer.[150]

Change was inexorable, in ideology, administration, and practice. Old Harrovians retained an almost proprietorial concern with cricket through the Field House Club. More than one post-war master-in-charge of cricket was deliberately undermined by coteries of old Flannels.[151] Yet cricket's strangehold over time and sentiment loosened until by the 1990s the game had become a minority passion, under Beer clearly less encouraged or pervasive than rugger. The break with the previous century and a half or more of school experience would be hard to exaggerate if it had not occured almost imperceptibly. Other stalwarts fell by the wayside. Boxing, regarded by Norwood as integral to the ideal of public school athletics, could not be sustained.[152] One OH from the 1950s, later an Amateur Boxing Association judge, claimed he owed 'the moulding and structure of my character' to the sport he regarded as a 'means of expression'.[153] This cut little ice when bouts, particularly among heavier boys, could develop into crude slogging matches. From the mid-1960s, boxing began to be run down to its ultimate abolition as a school sport.

New sports have replaced the old warhorses in the affections of boys and masters. Although the introduction of rowing failed in the 1960s, by the end of the century there was much greater diversity, with more emphasis on individual sports rather than team games. This reflected the general social rise of the cult of fitness which replaced games per se as a cultural ideal. A. C. Maclaren or F. S. Jackson, still probably the most successful OH sporting internationals, would have been dismayed at the idea, let alone practice, of 'pumping iron'. The building of a small golf course in the 1970s, part of the tidying of the eastern Hill fields consequent on the construction of a reservoir in Harrow Park, encouraged golfing. Squash and other small ball games became seen as important parts of general health regimes.

---

[149] HM/J/11 May 1966, G. R. McConnell to James.   [150] Ibid., McConnell to James.
[151] i.e. members of the First XI at Lord's.
[152] Norwood, *English Tradition of Education*, 107.
[153] HM/J/30 Oct. 1964, D. Savill to James; 2 Nov. James to Savill. Cf. HM/J/Transcript of telephone conversation with a *Daily Mail* journalist on the matter, 21 Jan. 1964.

Compulsion remained, sometimes, as with cross-country running, justified on the vaguely moral grounds of the benefit of obedience and pain. It was difficult for any late twentieth-century Harrovian to avoid rugger, cricket, and Harrow Football entirely. Most were content that this was so. The majority of Harrovians in 1990 as in 1930 or 1900 enjoyed sport. By the late twentieth century, those who did not, while experiencing social exclusion, were no longer as vigorously or sadistically persecuted as their unathletic predecessors.[154] None the less, Harrow's games reputation and lavish sporting facilities still proved a draw for many like-minded parents and preparatory schools. In response, and in line with society's new elevation of sport as an icon of civilization, there developed an increasing pseudo-professionalism about the way certain sports were approached. In the 1980s demotic 'rugger' became serious 'Rugby'. Sport and games persisted as central to Harrow's practice and identity. Stripped of overt association with unquestioned moral or psychological benefit, they reclaimed their eighteenth-century place as recreation not education.

Sex, Obedience, and Violence

One of the arguments for games used to be that they reduced schoolboys' libidinous habits and expended much of their aggression. Neither happened to be true.[155] If anything, the games cult reflected rather than confined the physical habits of adolescent boys in a male environment, the concept of sublimation being as wishful as Bowen's sillier flights of fancy. Sex and violence were intrinsic parts of school experience. The main contrast between them was that one was practised almost exclusively between the boys themselves; the other by both boys and masters. The traditional nexus of sodomy, fagging, bullying, and beating persisted far into the twentieth century. However, the boys' world existed only as the largest element in the school; the context and guardians were adult.

There are very few examples of masters engaging in active sexual relations with boys, although it was not unknown. There is much more evidence of heterosexual alliances between boys and local girls, not infrequently masters' daughters. Too often consideration of sex and public schools has been restricted to homosexual relations. It should also be remembered that boys were surrounded by adults and children of both sexes. Not all sexual relationships were physical. Twentieth-century Harrow was sexually charged in ways peculiar to such an institution. One example of the possibilities is suggestive. In 1913 Percy Buck, the devastatingly handsome married 42-year-old Director of Music and father of five, began an affair with his 19-year-old piano pupil, Sylvia Townsend Warner, daughter of George,

---

[154] Playfair, *My Father's Son*, 63.
[155] Wakeford, *Cloistered Elite*, 82; Gathorne-Hardy, *The Public School Phenomenon*, 144–80, 365–8.

then housemaster of Bradbys. Sylvia was besotted with her father; part of Buck's appeal was probably explicable in those terms. George Townsend Warner was an expert fives player. One of the pupils he coached was Ronald Eiloart (1901–6), a senior boy in Bradbys when Warner took over the house. Eiloart became an architect and spent holidays with the Warners. After the First World War he became Mrs Townsend Warner's second husband.[156] The community of the Hill and the parallel one of the school always provided essentials for sexual attraction: proximity and opportunity, supported by an intricate network of social acquaintances away from Harrow dependent on shared schooldays. It is a social cliché of Victorian and Edwardian public schools that old boys, like the hapless Gerald Eversley, married their schoolfriends' sisters. Harrow was no exception. Neither was it in the continued dynastic associations that bound masters' families to each other and to those of their pupils.

While boys gossiped about their own liaisons and friendships, Harrow's adults were no less engrossed in their own affairs. Marriages of masters were annexed to Harrow ritual. All new wives before the Second World War, and some since, were expected to wear their wedding dress when first entertained on the Hill, as if they were marrying the school, which, in many cases, it may have seemed to them they had. The first wife who worked professionally away from the school was probably Dr Alice Stewart, the expert on radiation, wife of L. D. Stewart (master 1934–48) shortly before the Second World War. She used to avoid the grim ritual of mutual visits to the grand ladies of Harrow by delivering her visiting card when she knew the wives would be out attending a rugger or football match.[157] Professional working wives remained a rarity for another thirty years. Such were the expectations of service that in 1959 there was a proposal that housemasters' wives receive a separate salary, an idea vetoed by the governors' General Purposes Committee; Head Masters' wives were luckier, being paid from 1981.[158] Until the 1950s the birth of a master's son (but not necessarily a daughter) automatically gained the school a half-holiday, as, until the Second World War, did the marriage of a master's daughter. These were the rituals of a tribe.

Not all masters behaved with expected dutiful decorum, although none attained the quality of Middlemist's deceit. In the 1930s one master left a daughter of a housemaster almost at the altar, certainly after the presents had been received.[159] Another housemaster was reported to have been found regularly by his boys with his mistress on his knee. More recently, wife swapping was not unknown. Harrow

---

[156] Harman, *Townsend Warner*, esp. pp. 16–17, 21–2.

[157] According to her own reminiscences in a BBC2 biographic profile in 1996. While at least one wife, Mrs P. H. F. White, taught in her husband's place during the Second World War, the second wife with a profession away from the school was Dr Margaret Harris, an academic chemist, wife of H. L. Harris from 1945.   [158] GBM, 11 June 1959; GPC 1981–91, *passim*.

[159] HM/V/1 Jan. 1935, letter to Vellacott; Masters' Files, E. M. Venables, 1 Jan. 1935, an irate Venables to Vellacott.

society in the first two-thirds of the century was little different from the rest of the class to which it belonged. Sexual concealment was as commonplace as repression. The school context added strains and, for some, temptations. There were occasional indiscretions by homosexual masters, sometimes leading to dismissal, sometimes not. Yet the school depended on homosexual masters for some of its most inspired and committed teaching, as much in the half century after 1945 as in the century before. It is incontestable that there existed greater potential harm in the heterosexual wielding the cane than the homosexual channelling his personality into education.

Many masters, in private at least, were fully aware of the sexual potential in Harrow society. Under Vellacott at least seventeen supposedly pornographic books were placed on a school Index. Housemasters in the 1930s considered the introduction of sex education, only to reject it as provocative and intrusive. Hysteria at the 'moral septicaemia' of adolescent homosexuality was matched by a shrewd understanding of it.[160] Until the 1970s most Harrow masters had themselves been to boarding schools. 'The school tart' was a phrase employed by masters as well as boys.[161] When discussing whether or not boys at Ducker should continue to bathe naked in the 1950s, opponents of this innovation asserted confidently that 'a young boy in swimming trunks was more erotically attractive to older boys than if he was in the nude'.[162] Head Master James was well aware that younger boys could present 'a danger to older boys'.[163] While some of the most serious scandals, in 1925 or 1979, concerned boys' heterosexual antics, homosexual liaisons continued to haunt the school's imagination and reputation. Yet simultaneous to expressing the most absolute disapproval of homosexual relationships, Harrow often turned a blind eye to bullying (a 'toughening' process some believed), encouraged beating of boys by boys and perpetuated a system of fagging and boy government that, in certain circumstances, could encourage or conceal sexual activity. It may be pure chance that the eradication of the acceptance of homosexuality as part of Harrow boarding life coincided with the demise of fagging. There again, it may not.

The classic doctrine of fagging was summed up, with typical bravado by C. H. P. Mayo in 1928: 'Those who hope to rule must first learn to obey . . . to learn to obey as a fag is part of the routine that is the essence of the English Public School system . . . the wonder of other countries. Who shall say it is not that which has so largely helped to make England the most successful colonising nation, and the just ruler of the backward races of the world?'[164] (It might be noted that the Empire was lost while at least Harrow's fagging was still operating at full blast.) Mayo was merely parroting the orthodoxy handed down from Vaughan and the Arnoldians who saw in regulated fagging the basis of the independence of public school boys

---

[160] Venables, *Bases Attempted*, 149–51, 155, 156–7, 162.
[161] Rae, *Revolution*, 127; Vickers, *Beaton*, 23.   [162] Rae, *Revolution*, 128.
[163] HM/J/22 Mar. 1957, James to Revd O. J. T. Roberts.   [164] Mayo, *Reminiscences*, 150–1.

to which was ascribed the chiefest glory of the system. E. M. Venables, writing in the 1940s, dismissed critics as those 'who know it only in theory' or 'who probably did not have enough of it'.[165] A common theme of fagging apologists, from Vaughan onwards, including both Mayo and Venables, was that it was worse before their time, the bitter experiences of old boys belonging to an antediluvian period long superseded by a beneficent present. Cumulatively, this is unlikely. For many, at some time or another, personal or general fagging imposed drudgery, inconvenience, intrusion, and fear. As such, it could be argued, it provided excellent training for public school life for the young boy. For the monitors and fagmasters it added to the enclosed hubris allowed them as temporary heads of the school world. Fagging may have encouraged obedience; it also fostered hectoring assumptions of ruling, which may or may not have proved useful in later life. If fag masters wished to exploit fags there was little to stop them, especially if their housemaster approved the system, as almost all did until the 1970s. One of the greatest changes in the daily experience of boys at Harrow in the quarter century after 1970 was the gradual elimination from most houses of officially condoned fagging. Alone, that made late twentieth-century Harrow, for all its continued institutional and individual adherence to tradition, a foreign country to those who had gone before.

More spectacular was the end of beating, part of a national phenomenon of startling, if stealthy, revolutionary effect. For thousands of years, beating children in order to instil learning or obedience formed a basic educational assumption. In little more than a generation, beating in the United Kingdom not only fell out of fashion, it became illegal. At Harrow, the Victorian tradition of beating by Heads, housemasters, and school monitors remained essentially untouched into the 1970s. The anomaly that some boys could wield the cane but most masters could not caused scarcely a disturbed murmur.[166] The regime was often characterized by its advocates as benign, even beneficial, although to whom was not always entirely clear. There were some housemasters' voices raised, even in the 1940s, against the 'spurious discipline' of excessive reliance on the cane to be found 'only in such places as pride themselves on the toughness that they mistake for virile efficiency'.[167] Such places existed into the 1970s. If complaints are a guide, abuse was usually the prerogative not of boys but of housemasters, some of whom held to a misty belief in the purgative and character-forming qualities of the ritual of the rod, one which they insisted had done them no harm.[168] How could they tell? Not all housemasters beat and less militant floggers argued that caning provided a

---

[165] Venables, *Bases Attempted*, 124.
[166] Rae, *Revolution*, 122–3. Cf. Norwood, *English Tradition of Education*, 71–3; Venables, *Bases Attempted*, 160, etc. [167] Venables, *Bases Attempted*, 160.
[168] See unsorted correspondence scattered through HM/J/file; boys beat comparatively rarely in the 1930s according to Bryant, *Harrow*, 103.

useful final sanction for serious misdemeanours for which the alternative—e.g. suspension or expulsion—would have been too draconian. In only a minority of houses was there a beating frenzy in the 1950s–1970s. Harrow was far from alone in cherishing the beating tradition. In 1966 Graham Kalton, in a survey of HMC schools, found that 145 out of 166 schools (87 per cent) allowed masters other than the Head or Deputy Head to beat, with 103 out of 166 permitting boys to inflict corporal punishment (62 per cent).[169]

The Head Masters' Punishment book suggests a sharp decline in floggings by the Head Master. Wood flogged 529 times 1899–1910, about fifty a year. Ford, known as a disciplinarian from his Repton days, managed only 264 over fifteen years, under twenty a year. He largely abandoned the full ceremonial of birching in the Fourth Form Room for the more intimate caning in his study. Norwood, despite a fondness for discipline, recorded only thirty-three occasions when he beat between 1926 and 1934.[170] Vellacott was more fastidious, drawing a veil over the darker side of school life. He wrote in the Punishment Book late in 1935:

'I decided at the end of my first year here to discontinue this tale

of degredation, ugliness and tears,
A record of disgraces best forgotten,
A sullen page in human chronicles
Fit to erase.

The picture the foregoing pages give of life in a school, as lived by a Head Master . . . fills me with a sense of shame.'[171]

His lead was followed by Boissier. So there is no evidence of how many they beat. The pious but slightly prim Moore disagreed. Under Vellacott's statement he commented: 'I consider the foregoing a sentimental view. This book is not intended as the presentation of a picture, but as a private Head Master's record maintained in the interests of justice and consistency. No corporal punishment should be administered without record kept; and memories are fallible.'[172] In his elegant and stylish hand, Moore recorded twenty-seven beatings in ten years. Entries under James became increasingly sparse before the Punishment Book was abandoned in 1965.

Housemasters could be less fastidious. Many ordered their Heads of House to administer the punishment. Increasingly, some boys were reluctant to carry out their housemasters' dirty work. The radical winds of the 1960s reached Harrow, if only as gentle zephyrs. One Head of House told his housemaster he refused to beat. When thus forced to resume the habit himself, this experienced housemaster noticed on one occasion the victim becoming sexually aroused during the

---

[169] Tables reprinted by Gathorne-Hardy, *Public School Phenomenon*, 453 from G. Kalton, *The Public Schools: A Factual Survey of Headmasters' Conference Schools in England and Wales* (London, 1966).
[170] HA Head Master's Punishment Book, 1888–1965, *passim*.
[171] Head Master's Punishment Book, fo. 238.   [172] Ibid., fo. 239.

caning.¹⁷³ He never beat again. It was surprising, perhaps, that he had not earlier made the connection. Not all his colleagues either experienced or registered such responses. Some were wedded to the procedure almost as an article of faith, certainly of policy. Yet within a decade of the retirement as housemasters of some of the worst floggers of the century, officially the cane was no more. When challenged in 1987 by the pressure group STOPP, the Head Master was instructed by the governors to declare that 'the cane had not been used at Harrow since 1982'.¹⁷⁴ It seems that the last boy to be beaten at Harrow received his punishment in 1987, the last of a very long, distinguished, and crowded line.

While fagging and corporal punishment were liable to the constraints of authority, sodomy was not. Like bullying and recurrent degrading, dangerous, or frightening initiation rituals, the level of homosexual activity was not constant. Rather it conformed to the familiar twentieth-century public school pattern of rapid shifts in fashion.¹⁷⁵ This phenomenon explains the discrepancies in old boy memories. Two boys in the same house, who have overlapped for a term or so, may not only have entirely different recollections but genuinely different experiences. The exception to this rule was the caesura that appeared when, from the 1970s, the school allowed greater access by parents and more flexible, frequent, and longer Exeats for boys. With these changes, the enclosed conditions within which, as one veteran of the 1920s recalled, 'we were all homosexual for a while at Harrow', no longer applied.¹⁷⁶ Conveniently, as ages of initial heterosexual activity fell, so Harrovians' opportunities increased. Instead, there emerged signs of a corporate homophobia, in an almost pathological, hypocritical mass rejection of the past.¹⁷⁷ Until then, boys' attitudes to homosexual activity appeared closely related to those of previous generations, a matter of appetites not morality, of temporary enjoyment not lifelong vice, carnal but natural. There is little evidence of rape, encounters being casual and consensual. Many of the most intense emotional involvements almost by definition never reached physical expression.

Active sexual experiences at school proved more psychologically ephemeral than bullying. Sometimes masquerading as discipline—in the house or on the gamesfield or parade ground—sometimes as initiation ceremonies, bullying was endemic in Harrow, partly because neither boys nor many masters understood how it operated or what forms it could take.¹⁷⁸ Harrow was fortunate in lacking

---

¹⁷³ Norwood was aware of the possibilities. In 1928 he expressly denied he had ever seen a boy derive pleasure from the pain of being beaten: *English Tradition of Education*, 73.
¹⁷⁴ GBM, 21 Feb. 1987.   ¹⁷⁵ Gathorne-Hardy, *Public School Phenomenon*, 162–3.
¹⁷⁶ Wansell, *Rattigan*, 27–8.
¹⁷⁷ But cf. the nasty homophobic story from a public school in the 1950s: Gathorne-Hardy, *Public School Phenomenon*, 163.
¹⁷⁸ When contrasted with boys' memories, the unanimity about the lack of serious bullying in reactionaries' (e.g. Fox, Mayo, Norwood, Venables) published work is revealing.

dormitories. More casual than institutional, bullying was tacitly condoned because often unseen. Despite the prestige afforded it by Vaughan and his followers, the habit of leaving boys to run their own affairs, one which persisted in some houses into the later twentieth century, was an invitation to abuse. It could be argued that the surprise was the lack of mayhem. Yet, certain aspects of bullying were almost lovingly tended, protected by the victims' greater loyalty to the boyish code of solidarity and the easy indoctrination of the closed society. The most bizarre example of this process was the resurrection of initiation rites in some houses from the 1970s, as if they were permanent Harrow traditions, instead of sporadic excesses of pampered but emotionally confused 17- and 18-year-olds. Putting little boys in packing-trunks and pretending to throw them out of high windows; mock executions; superficial but painful physical torture; and a nasty custom known as 'Death Yarder' could, and did, exert psychological as well as physical damage.[179] Harrow's ascent to a kinder, more tolerant environment was neither inexorable nor constant in the twentieth century.

Inevitably, there had always been homosexuality at Harrow. In the early 1920s as the mid-1850s or late 1960s, boys would traverse the Hill at night for sex.[180] There has probably been no twentieth-century decade when a boy has not been expelled or removed for sodomy.[181] The dozen years after 1918 witnessed heightened sexual activity, its features shared with other similar periods (although it must be remembered that the most notorious boys' sex scandal, the night club affair of 1925, was primarily heterosexual).[182] Cecil Beaton recalled how, in some houses in the early 1920s, sodomy was rampant. Given his only moderate indulgence, he felt aggrieved that because he wore make-up, dressed himself in fine fabrics, painted his Bradbys study mauve or green, and 'was frightfully pretty and luscious' people thought he 'must be a little tart'.[183] A few years later, Giles Playfair earned a bad reputation because he exposed a sex ring in the Head Master's leading to the main seducer's expulsion (he later became a schoolmaster).[184] Terence Rattigan's outrageous flirting and more appeared to be tolerated at the end of the decade.[185] Norwood's supposed new strict regime appeared to make little difference. Neat sociological comparisons between the state of society and the incidence of sodomy at Harrow do not appear to work. After 1945 neither rationing nor economic revival had any distinct impact. Nor did the decline of religion (any more than had

---

[179] All examples occurred in the late 1980s.
[180] Vickers, *Beaton*, 23, based in part on Beaton's own diary, is most graphic for the 1920s. Cf. Symonds in the 1850s.
[181] For the 1880s to 1960s see the Head Master's Punishment Book.
[182] Gathorne-Hardy, *Public School Phenomenon*, 302.
[183] Vickers, *Beaton*, 24 for extracts from Beaton's Diary, 27 Feb. 1924.
[184] Playfair, *My Father's Son*, 75, 78–80; Head Master's Punishment Book, 1888–1965, entry for 24 Mar. 1925. [185] Wansell, *Rattigan*, 27–8, 32, 43.

its nineteenth-century rise).[186] In one sense, the school recognized homosexuality for what many boys regarded it, a transitory indulgence. Most masters understood it even if they felt compelled to punish it. Despite the opprobrium of moralists, both inside and beyond the public school world, homosexual behaviour was recognized as only occasionally damaging to the boys involved, carnal rather than vicious, a case of *faute de mieux* not lifelong sexual orientation. As the events surrounding The Grove fire of 1974 revealed, it was publicity of sex not sex itself that caused damage to the institution.[187] The same incident suggested that Harrow low life, including casual sexual advances, had changed in essence but little over the centuries, one continuity with tradition the school authorities could have done without.

Status

In 1914 Harrow was the second most famous school in the world. Its old boys, as politicians, generals, clergymen, financiers, businessmen, colonists, farmers, and games-players, sustained a reputation on which it appeared the sun would never set. The world turned. The confidence in empire seeped away even before the proconsuls departed. In the half-century since 1945, the elite that sent its sons to Harrow was transformed, in power narrower as in origins more diverse. Between 1918 and 1955 almost 45 per cent of all Conservative Cabinet ministers (in office for all but nine of those years) had gone to Eton and Harrow, as had over a third of Tory MPs.[188] In 1997, for the first time since 1722, no Old Harrovian was returned to the House of Commons in a general election.[189] In the City, although Harrow had rarely produced entrepreneurs, Harrovians continued to flourish. Yet, while its name ensured publicity when things went wrong, Harrow no longer occupied a central place in the Establishment, even if, collectively, public school products still occupied a disproportionate, though decreasing area of the nation's commanding heights.

This decline resulted from external forces outside the school's control. The status of a school operates on two separate but associated levels. When Welldon commented in 1928 that he did 'not know that any other Public School has ever played a greater part in national life than Harrow is playing today', he was paying tribute to the boys of his own and his predecessor's Headships between thirty-five and fifty years before.[190] They had risen in competition with their generation. Harrovians

---

[186] The evidence from the Head Master's Punishment Book and Head Masters' correspondence supports this.

[187] See e.g. the coverage in the *Daily Mail*, 20 May 1975 (after the arsonist's trial), which was fairly representative. [188] Gathorne-Hardy, *Public School Phenomenon*, 451 and refs.

[189] An OH, Matthew Moreton, was returned in a by-election in 1723 (Gun, *Harrow School Register*, 18) leading to uninterrupted Harrovian presence until May 1997.

[190] Welldon, 'Introduction', Mayo, *Reminiscences*, pp. vi–vii.

from the later 1920s were a different breed, their times increasingly unrecognizable to any surviving Victorians. Yet they may have been sent to Harrow because of the lustre to the school's name provided by Baldwin and the rest. Therefore, the status of such a school related to its past fame. However, its current or future place continued to rely on its sensitivity to present changes. Harrow's twentieth-century survival as a prosperous and, in public school terms, a widely acknowledged 'great' school depended on its protean capacity to recognize change and to act upon it. This was not easy, for the transformation was enormous.

A senior Harrow housemaster in the 1920s could earn, gross, something in the region of £5,000; the net figure after paying for his boarders could be as much as £3,000 a year, perhaps the equivalent of £80–90,000 seventy years later.[191] After the introduction of the new system of financial tenure from 1936, when housemasters ceased to be hoteliers and accepted salaries for their house duties and allowances for their expenses, while financially more secure, their entrepreneurial earning potential was almost eliminated. Despite increasing salary allowances and a highly advantageous new salary scale in 1989, housemasters no longer cut the same affluent figures as their predecessors.[192] Unlike in earlier periods, a Harrow house was no longer more lucrative than most Headships elsewhere. A similar progress applied to Head Masters. In 1926 Cyril Norwood was paid £4,500, with an additional £500 entertainment allowance, a combined figure closer to £150,000 today.[193] In spending power, senior masters and Heads were paid less at the century's end than at its beginning. The mid-century financial collapse meant that in 1953 James began on £3,500, with £800 entertainment allowance; in 1971 Hoban received £5,000, with £1,000 for entertainment. Inflation pushed the Head's salary to £20,000 by the end of 1980; three times that a decade later.[194] Even with further annual increases, late twentieth-century Heads were not the moguls their earlier twentieth- let alone nineteenth-century predecessors had been. Assistant masters' salaries, at least taking the scale as a whole, followed a different career. The scale in 1918 varied from £400 at the bottom to £1,070 for a master with twenty-seven years' service, figures that remained more or less static for the following decade.[195] Thirty years later, after successive crises, it stood at £450 to £1,000. In 1968 with substantial rises to meet the inflation of the 1950s but before the massive paper increases of the 1970s onwards, the range stretched from £1,050 to £2,800.[196] However, by the 1990s, the scale compared favourably in real terms with that of the 1920s, if only slightly.[197] The reason was obvious. Unlike in earlier periods, the profits of the top jobs (i.e. housemasterships) paled in comparison and the proportion of masters likely to

[191] Figures based on numbers in houses, boarding fees, salaries, and expected profits.
[192] GBM, 25 Feb. 1989.   [193] GBM, 1 Dec. 1925.
[194] GBM, 5 Mar. 1953, 7 Nov. 1970, *et seq.*; GPC 18 Sept. 1980, *et seq.*
[195] Masters' Files, T. E. J. Bradshaw, Salary Scale 1918; GBM, 11 May 1927.
[196] GBM, 3 June 1948, 30 May 1968.
[197] The top of the scale reached over £32,000, broadly comparable with the 1930 maximum.

obtain such posts was considerably less as the number of houses remained the same but the size of the staff doubled between 1914 and 1991.[198]

The salary scales point to a definite shift in class identity among the masters, one which paradoxically strengthened devotion to Harrow and its traditions. Assumptions of public school inbreeding, affluent backrounds, even private means underpinned much recruitment until the 1970s. Ford commented on candidates' personal wealth in his interview notes.[199] C. G. Pope's butler at The Grove was recruited from his family estate. Until the introduction of service tenancies in 1948, masters in school accommodation paid rent as leaseholders.[200] As late as 1968 a bachelor OH master and former housemaster could afford to employ and accommodate, at his own expense, a housekeeper and her husband.[201] By then, such private affluence was no longer the rule; salaries, not least for those with families or who would not attain the riches of boarding houses, needed to be not only competitive but realistic to attract teachers without capital.

If education provides any insight into the sociological complexion of a group, twentieth-century Harrow displayed novel features. Although, in marked contrast with their nineteenth-century predecessors, none of the twentieth-century Head Masters except for Hoban (Charterhouse) had been educated at schools covered by the 1868 Act, they came from similar backgrounds, middle-class professional or modest gentry. Until the last quarter of the century, a large majority of assistant masters had been educated at British public schools: 73 per cent in 1920, when a number had been privately educated; 84 per cent in 1930; 78 per cent in 1950; and 79 per cent in 1970. The figure for 1985 was 58 per cent.[202] Fewer came from Clarendon schools or even the more prominent of the new nineteenth-century foundations. Either a new meritocracy or a wider search for possible candidates lay behind the significant shift under Hoban and Beer.[203] This change produced at least one intangible result. Harrow traditionally enjoyed a reputation for a factious, fractious, and highly self-critical staff.[204] The non-public school, and non-boarding origins of the staff produced a softening of conflict and dissent, a greater acceptance of the positive features of the school, and easier acceptance of corporate spirit.

---

[198] Depending on how it is calculated, i.e. whether all or some extra-masters are included, the 1914 figure was *c.*40, the 1991 figure *c.*80. The number of boys had risen by 55%, *c.*500 to *c.*775.

[199] Ford noted Venables' private means at interview in 1916. They allowed him to swap a tenured post at Felsted for an initially temporary one at Harrow: Masters' Files, E. M. Venables, 17 Sept. 1916.

[200] GBM, 8 May, 3 June 1948. For the origins of Pope's butler I rely on information from G. R. R. Treasure, Esq., his successor but four at The Grove.

[201] G. R. McConnell, GBM, 30 May 1968.

[202] Statistcs derived from *Harrow Register, passim*.

[203] But cf. with Policy Document on Long-Term Priorities 1989, 6–7 that assumes the need to recruit masters 'from schools such as these willing to come back and teach here'.

[204] See above, *passim* and cf. Bryant, *Harrow*, 99. *The Harrovian*, 6 June 1998, p. 198 records an external view of how 'detestable' Harrow masters were. Judging from Venables' memoirs and the evidence of other correspondence, that judgement may have possessed foundation.

Unity was probably important when externally the identity of the school no longer guaranteed privileged access to traditional ladders of promotion and success. One barometer for the loosening of Harrow's grip on elite institutions is provided by Oxford and Cambridge. Professor Honey calculated that in the mid-1850s, Harrovians comprised almost 20 per cent of all entrants to Balliol College, Oxford. In the same decade, Trinity, Cambridge was admitting up to thirty Harrovians a year, almost 14 per cent. In 1867, over 5 per cent of all Oxford undergraduates (71) were OHs, second only to Eton (121:8.9 per cent). Thirty years later, of those who matriculated at Oxford in 1897 2.9 per cent (26) were from Harrow, which then sent more boys to Cambridge.[205] As the universities expanded gently, the proportion of Harrovians decreased, but numbers remained high. Sixty-two of the 157 entrants to Harrow in 1920 went to Oxbridge, almost 40 per cent. From the 1930 new boys, 42 per cent (67) followed suit. The Second World War marked a turning point. Of Harrow's intake of 119 in 1950, only 33 proceeded to Oxbridge, still over 27 per cent.[206] In 1960, to the consternation of the Head and housemasters, it was announced that in the future Oxford would insist on candidates achieving two A Levels. With Cambridge likely to follow, they gloomily observed that 'only high grade A Levels will be of use'.[207] Dr James, although a scholar himself, shared the views of some of his less cerebral colleagues (at least three of the housemasters at the 1960 meeting had Thirds or worse). In 1968 he wrote to a former pupil: 'twenty years ago the universities were far broader in their outlook and much less dominated by competition and the emphasis on the academic to the excluson of other things . . . education at a university becomes far less of a training for life than it used to be in my day'.[208] That he meant Oxbridge was not in doubt. Three years earlier he congratulated another leaver on obtaining a place at Bristol rather dampeningly: 'it is a very good University from all accounts . . .'.[209] He seems to have ignored the fact that in 1960 'redbrick universities' (the housemasters' phrase) required three not two A Levels.

The philosophical gulf between newly academic, meritocratic, and competitive Oxbridge and the traditional all-round, in John Dancy's word 'total' education of the public schools was, to the benefit of the latter, obscured by removal of the Direct Grant which drove many good, academic day schools into the private sector. In 1976 Oxford admitted 55 per cent undergraduates from non-state schools; Cambridge 53 per cent; of these only 19 per cent and 18 per cent respectively were

---

[205] The Honey statistics were presented at a seminar at Nuffield College, Oxford on the history of the university in 1982; for Trinity see G. O. Trevelyan's introduction to Graham, *Butler*, p. xxxvii.
[206] Figures from *Harrow Register, 1885–1949*, 411–23; *Harrow Register, 1986*, 131–46, 361–72.
[207] Minutes of Housemasters' Meetings, 1949–67, 1 Nov. 1960.
[208] HM/J/4 Sept. 1968, James to Hugh Montgomery-Massingberd, who had decided not to take up a place at Selwyn College, Cambridge.
[209] HM/J/3 Feb. 1965, James to J. F. Appleton.

independent schools, the rest were Direct Grant.[210] Before that, Harrow's statistics looked buoyant, a credit to James and some of his housemasters' vigorous policies of recruiting an academic elite as well as admitting the non-academic. Of the 144 1960 entrants, thirty-five reached Oxbridge, just over 24 per cent, figures that remained fairly constant through the decade.[211] In December 1969, with sixteen awards out of thirty-five places, Harrow won more honours than Winchester, a feat repeated in December 1970, with seventeen awards (out of thirty-eight places), one of the best results from any school in the country that year.[212] From the mid-1970s, the numbers going to Oxbridge each year was usually somewhere in the twenties, bolstered by the ability of Harrovians until the mid-1980s to stay an extra year in order to apply twice. From the mid-1970s proportions of both entrants and leavers going to the old universities fell below 20 per cent and 15 per cent.

Diehards muttered at what they saw as a bias against public schools or Harrow. This was misleading on two fronts. Oxford and Cambridge had deliberately changed their admissions policies, first to attract the new academic elite in state secondary education caused by the 1944 Education Act; later to accommodate the comprehensivization of the 1960s and 1970s. Yet, stubbornly the proportion of independent undergraduates remained at or near 50 per cent far higher than strict proportionality either in application or secondary education. Just as the attitudes and aspirations of universities and public schools converged in the mid-nineteenth century, so, in their emphasis on academic criteria, universities (and increasingly not just Oxbridge) were challenging traditional public school assumptions. Oxford and Cambridge no longer acted as automatic finishing schools for Harrovians engaged in a ritualized passage from prep. school to adult grandeur.

On the other hand, Harrovians went in greater numbers to other universities in Britain and abroad or sought other vocational training. Instead of clinging to past certainties, while still regarding Oxbridge successes as academic blue ribands, the school increasingly adapted itself to a different market, decisively rejecting the Victorian academic model. As James' comments of 1968 suggested, much of that ideal had already become moribund. The greater corporate introspection resulting from political attack in the 1970s and material success in the 1980s produced an educational model that challenged Harrow's distinctive identity and traditional values. This was achieved less by their open destruction than by a re-articulation of older forms. Games became sport for all. Corps remained a mass activity by also assuming characteristics of uniformed games. The syllabus was extended so that all could achieve qualifications. Boys were no longer left to their own devices. Risks of neglect or initiative were avoided. Instead of the whole system—not least games—being based upon the belief that it tended to the inculcation of qualities of service,

---

[210] Gathorne-Hardy, *Public School Phenomenon*, 450.
[211] *Harrow Register, 1986*, 486–99.
[212] I am grateful to R. B. Venables, Esq. (master 1952–83) for supplying me with these statistics.

command, and rule, courses in leadership were established. In common with all other successful late twentieth-century public schools, Harrow ceased to be an ideal and became a product.

The plumes, gongs, and gowns so adored by Monty Butler and his heirs ceased to rain down on Harrovians; so did the blows of the cane and birch, the unquestioning assumptions of privilege and authority, the pleasure in the right to rule. However, Harrow's identity towards the end of the twentieth century, compared with the pretensions of the Imperial school, may have operated not only to the advantage of the institution, but to the benefit of the pupils as well. Beneath the patina of tradition, the school was more open to parents, more culturally diverse, more educationally comprehensive, and more attuned to its clients, leaving only outward forms, institutional arrogance, and introspective self-satisfaction as ties to its glorious past.

17

Clouded Eminence: Teachers and Taught, 1914–1991

'Harrow' and Harrovians

In a famous aside, Cyril Norwood commented: 'The business of a school is to work and to get on with its life without bothering about whys and wherefores, and abstract justice, and the democratic principle.'[1] In daily administration and instruction, Harrow cherished the spirit of Norwood's apophthegm throughout the twentieth century, Giles Playfair's 'fundamental trouble with Harrow . . . nothing was ever explained or tempered with reason'. Lionel Ford advised new masters, with characteristic elusiveness, 'the Harrow boy is a courtier—don't tell him too much'.[2] In an institution whose Head possessed dictatorial powers of decision, arbitration, appointment, dismissal, and patronage, deference was not restricted to pupils. Welldon had identified discipline as Harrow's main characteristic, by which he meant obedience, its imposition generally regarded by public school teachers as the basis of successful education.[3] It implied anything from maintaining order in form to unchallenging acceptance of social rules, restrictions, and traditions by masters as well as boys. Throughout the twentieth century the apparent price of the 'total' education of independent boarding schools was submission; its package insularity.

Unfortunately for such orderly theories, circumstances intruded. The image of a self-governing Parnassus was a myth before 1914 and over the following seventy-five years repeatedly exposed as a sham. Unquestioning obeisance to authority and the power of a received collective ethos, manifested in a network of arcane practices of compulsion and communal integration, may have supplied firm

---

[1] Norwood, *English Tradition of Education*, 75.
[2] Playfair, *My Father's Son*, 106; Venables, *Bases Attempted*, 36.
[3] Welldon, *Recollections*, 86–7.

cement for Harrow's variant form of what Erving Goffman defined in 1961 as a 'total society'.[4] However, while fully active and protective for its members, the 'total society' of Harrow was not immune from external pressures enforcing change, discussion, debate, even dissent. The Harrow paradox, which it shared with similar institutions, lay in its need for validation by the world outside, while always seeking to persuade its members that school provided its own justification. Harrow needed the support of parents, donors, and old boys; it had to respond to the demands of public examinations, universities, and employers. Legislation concerning health, hygiene, safety, ancient monuments, corporal punishment, employment, and education itself directly influenced the management and nature of the school.

By mid-century, the school was part of suburban London. John Betjeman thought this worked to Harrow's advantage: 'Being near London its masters can get away from each other'.[5] Alternatively, boys could get out and others in, including parents, undermining one of the central features of the 'total society' of the school. In response, the number and length of Exeats, when boys were allowed off the Hill for nights at a time, actually decreased in the first two-thirds of the century as compared with rural, Victorian Harrow. With improved communications, culminating in a motorway system of fortuitous but almost unsurpassed convenience for Harrow, the school's isolation, maintained as fiercely as possible until the 1970s, was eroded out of recognition. Thereafter, a growing tension arose between the requirements of local Harrovians (a clear majority with that locality now embracing the whole of London, the South-East, Home Counties, and southern Midlands) and the sons of parents from further-flung regions of England, Wales, Scotland, and Ireland, as well as from abroad. The very concept of a fully boarding school was challenged, the governors repeatedly having to reiterate this most fundamental aspect of Harrow since the eighteenth century.[6]

Inevitably, with external forces challenging social and academic inertia, while affording to ignore 'abstract justice', boys as well as masters bothered 'about whys and wherefores'. Norwood himself dabbled with 'the democratic spirit' when it suited him. To cope with such developments and to disguise the inadequacy of Norwood's dictum, while unconsciously confirming its narrow-mindedness, a distinctive official tone was perfected. With origins in the high-minded elitist complacency of Monty Butler, Harrow's tone held at its centre the ideals of service and leadership, based on a disdain for plutocratic materialism and a nostalgia for the supposed virtues of the English country gentleman: a love of honour, justice, truth, and vigorous independence. The snag lay in Harrovians themselves, from the late nineteenth century increasingly drawn from business not title or land.

---

[4] Gathorne-Hardy, *Public School Phenomenon*, 204–10. Cf. Dancy, *Public Schools*, 81–9.
[5] J. Betjeman, *Letters*, ed. C. Lycett-Green, ii (London, 1995), p. 177.
[6] e.g. GBM, 14 Oct. 1975, 17 July 1978, 6 June 1987; Long-Term Priorities Document, 1989.

Philip Bryant ingeniously confronted this difficulty in his 1936 history of the school, a paean of praise on 'the continuity [which] has never been broken . . . in which is to be found the spirit which has made, and still makes, "Harrow"'. Sympathetic to the OH 'new poor' making 'great sacrifices to have their sons educated as scholars and gentlemen at Harrow', Bryant none the less whimsically speculated on the Founder's possible approval of 'the "new rich", whom the worship of money leads to give accidentally to their children the very education that may save them from becoming its slaves'. Bryant, a future chaplain, ascribed the school's ability to transcend the bourgeois origins of its pupils (and staff) to a mystical force in Harrow, personified as female. 'Her god is still a god of the hills—hardy, independent, daring'.[7] This was the desired tone of the school. In 1989 the purpose of the school looked much the same dressed in more prosaic clothes; to produce 'men of integrity . . . to work to the service of others'.[8]

More realistically, Harrow reflected its constituents' habits and attitudes, as it had always done, often more 'Demon' Scaife than Harry Desmond. One of many truths about the school was recognized by Ian Beer: 'Some would see a blemish here, as in some comparable schools, in the complacent acceptance of, even glorification in some euphemistic way, of inequalities in society which appear to have become more pronounced in recent years'.[9] Such attitudes were not unique to Harrow; they infected a whole class. The popular stereotype of the twentieth-century Harrovian is as untrue of any individual as are all anecdotal generalizations. One version concerned a young lady in a room with an Etonian, a Wykehamist, and a Harrovian. The Etonian orders a chair for the lady; the Wykehamist fetches it; and the Harrovian sits on it. Interestingly, it is a joke told by Harrovians. Beneath it lurks the hint of 'bad manners', that Harrovians for all their wealth, position, sophistication, and social style are, and know they are, in Nancy Mitford's category, not quite 'U', or, in that splendid Victorian snobbism, 'hairy at the heel'.[10]

Harrovians present no objectively discernible social characterisitics beyond their class and a shared school experience. Again Betjeman, in praise of his favourite school, thought that 'for its size [Harrow] has produced more varied distinguished men'.[11] This cuts both ways. The variety Betjeman saw as typical posits lack of uniformity, the characteristic of being a Harrovian was to be untypical. Harrovians' future careers depended on their original circumstances not the school, in the late twentieth century as in the nineteenth. Except in legend, there may be no 'Harrow type', neither the swaggering parvenu nor the dutiful philanthropist, although Harrovians have been both. Nevertheless, there may exist a 'public school type', to which Harrovians, as a subset, have conformed. In the early 1960s John Dancy, then Master of Marlborough and considered a fashionable reformer, believed in such a type, comprising 'self-confidence, loyalty, capacity for

---

[7] Bryant, *Harrow*, 158, 159, 162. [8] Long-Term Priorities Document, 3.
[9] Ibid., Pt. II, 'Faults', iv. 3. [10] Vachell, *The Hill*, 266. [11] Betjeman, *Letters*, ii. 177.

leadership and the "quality of being a good mixer"'. These characteristics, he argued, were not the result of boarding school education but 'tendencies pre-existing in . . . the English middle class', by which he meant what today might be called the upper middle class rather than the 'Middle England' of modern psephologists.[12] Dancy's point, though crude, is apt. For all the rhetoric, propaganda, mystique, and sentiment, Harrow produced pupils distinctive by general class more than by school, a fact easily discernible at universities where public school products live in a wider social mix. Only within the tight world of grand boarding schools were subtle differences of language and associations noticeable. Obviously, for individuals, school memories were particular, yet even here inspirational masters often counted for more in the lives of remarkable pupils than the institution itself.

If the twentieth century furnished proof of the relatively superficial social and cultural influence exerted by Harrow on its pupils as opposed to their pre-existing backgrounds, more serious for idolators was the inexorable confluence between Harrow and other schools. By the 1980s, one hardened veteran of the public school world could describe Harrow as 'Radley-on-the-Hill'; another, less charitably, called it 'Millfield-sur-M25'.[13] To meet the competitive requirements of parents, the demands of public examinations, and finally a national curriculum, Harrow became more like other schools in teaching, games, extra-curricular fashions, and facilities, only its wide national catchment area and the privacy of single or shared rooms marking it, with Eton, as clearly different. Indeed, there appeared to be a competition in sameness. Whereas in the nineteenth century Harrow had been unusual in its Music, Science and Art Schools, a century later it chased its partners and competitors in central feeding blocks, CDT centres, sports halls, and theatres as hard as it had once in building a chapel. This was what parents expected. As HMC boarding schools became homogenized, distinctive local traditions loomed more important for external marketing and internal self-confidence. The ease with which Harrow slid into conformity reiterated its essential pragmatism as did its determination to aim for a particular clientele by remaining fully-boarding and single sex, another nod to its traditional pairing with Eton.[14]

The extreme loyalty and interference of Old Harrovians has formed one of the school's most particular traits. Yet, this undeniably intimate connection has been unevenly registered in the numbers of old boys who sent their sons to twentieth-century Harrow. As a proportion of the school, the numbers of sons of OHs have varied unexpectedly, as the following table indicates:[15]

---

[12] Dancy, *Public Schools*, 89–92.
[13] As in previous chapters, certain information from the post-war period and especially from the 1960s is derived from personal knowledge and interviews with eye-witnesses.
[14] See above, n. 6.
[15] Statistics derived from GBM *passim* and the relevant editions of the *Harrow Register*.

Date	(new boys)	percentage sons of OHs
1900	(165)	24.2
1910	(130)	19.2
1920	(158)	23.4
1930	(157)	26.1
1940	(74)	28.3
1950	(119)	37.8
1960	(144)	38.8
1965	(150)	44.6
1970	(174)	38.5
1975	(165)	32.7
1980	(191)	25.6
1985	(190)	16.8

Faced with this decline, Head Master Beer concentrated his considerable energy to reversing the trend, encouraging old boy visits to the school, delivering exhaustive presentations at reunion dinners across the world, and consulting retired former masters from the days of Moore and James. By the end of Beer's Headmastership (1991) it was claimed that the proportion had risen once more to nearer 25 per cent.

Harrow's attitude to its old boys was ambivalent. While desperately anxious to milk them of goodwill and money, the school authorities frequently bemoaned the restrictions such subservience imposed on reform or change. The governors often acted as the guarantors of OH influence, even to protecting the Harrow hat.[16] Their concern late in 1977 at the number of foreign nationals in the school may in part have been occasioned by the sudden collapse in numbers of OH sons, from 38 per cent of new boys in 1972, to $c.33$ per cent 1974–6, to under 25 per cent in 1977. The steeper decline under Beer 1981–5, possibly a delayed response to bad publicity in the 1970s and spectacular fee increases, led to careful consideration of relations with the Harrow Association in particular and old boys in general, with an increase in promotional material specifically aimed at them. From 1984 the Head Master no longer specified the numbers of sons of OHs entering the school.[17]

The nervousness at the falling proportion of sons of OHs lacked clear historical perspective. As the figures above reveal, the share of places taken by children of old boys in the late 1970s and 1980s conformed to the pre-Second World War pattern. The quarter-century after 1945 appears wholly exceptional. The peak was reached under James: in 1963 and 1964 42 per cent of new boys were OH sons; in 1965 44 per cent.[18] Consequently, many of those OHs advising Head Masters from the 1970s imagined that the post-war situation was normal, leading to exaggerated anxiety over what were in fact traditional levels of old boy support. There are no

---

[16] GBM, 28 Nov. 1992, 20 Feb. 1993.
[17] GBM, 5 Nov. 1977. Cf. 26 Feb. 1984 with 16 June 1984, *et seq.*
[18] GBM, 1963–5 record these statistics. Cf. *Harrow Register.*

simple explanations for the post-war phenomenon. In the later 1940s to 1960s, the real cost of fees compared to earnings may, for one of the few periods in the school's history, have favoured the parent. The effects of war, peace, and the comforting conservatism of Dr James may have created a sympathetic atmosphere. The social profile of the wealthy and influential remained stubbornly traditional. After 1945, for the first time, the majority of old boys were regularly approached to donate money to the school, possibly encouraging devotion and reminding old boys of their school and the value it placed on them. L. M. Hewlett may have been correct that dependence on old boy largesse inspired 'a greater love for their school'.[19] Handled with discretion, appeals may have generated loyalty as well as money, the relative decline 1975–85 having causes beyond the power of appeal brochures to counteract.

The proportion of old boys' sons in the school, even at the mid-1980s levels, was higher than at most HMC schools. There was more to this than good promotion. For much of the century, the school prospectus insisted that all completed application forms specified the names of 'Harrow references and connexions': the cloister of this elite was closely guarded.[20] Until the late 1970s, when a serious attempt was begun to institute a central register of applicants and to force underbooked housemasters to accept boys from it, entry to Harrow was exclusively through houses.[21] Dr James abandoned the central listing that had existed under Moore, preferring to keep surplus names on the Head Masters' House list.[22] Some houses traditionally attracted startlingly high numbers of old boys' children almost regardless of circumstances. In the early 1960s one house boasted 80 per cent OH sons.[23] In 1958 the governors only agreed to accelerate the programme to build more rooms in Elmfield because the pressure on its places was coming from Old Harrovians.[24] Dynastic loyalties often operated on a level below that of the school, as Boissier discovered when he closed Rendalls in 1941, a house which then had had only five housemasters since its opening in 1854.[25] The peculiar loyalty of old Elmfieldians to their house, while deliberately fostered by certain domestic rituals (a house song; the quasi-liturgical turning towards Speech Room during the singing of *Forty Years On* at house singings, etc.), owed much to the stability in the succession of housemasters, only three, including the founder H. O. D. Davidson, between 1893 and 1948. The third of these, the sporty Cyril Browne, a bachelor, approved of the idea of his successor being either unmarried or childless, presumably so that distractions would be minimal.[26]

[19] Gorse Papers, Hewlett Memorandum, Feb. 1939.
[20] HM/Vellacott/May 1939: School Prospectus; Rae, *Public School Revolution*, 144.
[21] GBM, 13 Mar. 1976, 10 Nov. 1979, 28 Feb. 1981.
[22] Minutes of Housemasters' Meetings, 1949–67, 29 Oct. 1962.
[23] Wakeford, *Cloistered Elite*, 94; Sanderson, *Educational Opportunity*, 69.
[24] GBM, 8 Nov. 1958. [25] See below, pp. 525–6.
[26] Masters' Files, C. R. Browne, Browne to R. W. Moore, 7 Mar. 1947.

The continued concern for retaining a uniquely high percentage of sons of old boys in the school, as well as being sound business, fitted an overriding theme of twentieth-century Harrow. Although the past was often conjured up to excuse or justify the present, it was rarely an actual past. Harrovians of the 1930s found it hard to credit that there were proportionately far more sons of OHs in the 1960s than in their day. Radical change and the late-century loss of much of the domestic distinctiveness remained concealed behind both myth and a genuine stability. A Harrovian in 1938 could have found himself taught by masters, appointed by Wood, who had begun as colleagues of men hired by Montagu Butler sixty years earlier. Thirty years later, in 1968, there remained masters appointed by Norwood and Vellacott. Archer Vassall had been given his first, temporary post to teach science at Harrow by Welldon in 1896; his pupil Lance Gorse, who overlapped with him for a year (1932–3), retired as a science master in 1968. The last Moore recruit to retire left in 1988: his father had also taught for over thirty years at Harrow, being appointed by Ford in 1915. The youngest James master has a retirement date thirty-eight years after his employer's departure.[27]

This human dimension, once tactfully described in an inspectors' report as 'over-stable', coincided with two long periods of academic stability, that of School Certificate until 1951 and of GCE which stretched unchallenged from 1951 to 1987. Thereafter, the introduction of a combined GCSE, incorporating O Level and CSE, and alterations to examinations to suit the National Curriculum produced near constant change in curriculum content and teaching methods. Yet the palmy days until 1987 concealed significant shifts of emphasis. Oxford and Cambridge became genuinely academically competitive from the early 1960s; from the mid-1980s they abolished their post-A Level scholarship and entrance examinations which led directly to the establishment of a one-term entry and a five-year course. Gone were the days when a scholar could sit all his O Levels by the end of his first year and spend up to four years in the Upper School. By then attitudes to public examinations had altered. As late as the mid-1960s, for clever boys A Levels were modest interruptions in the specialized academic process; for the less able they were not attempted at all. The standardization of Harrow owed much to the demand for universal qualifications which left academic independence, relaxation, and eccentricity less accepted and less sustainable.

One consequence of the new utilitarianism of the 1980s was a decline in public schools' academic prominence. Lavishly funded and selective, their examination results continued to shine in comparison with most state schools. However, they were no longer in the vanguard of national educational innovation and reform. With the mass markets of GCSE, examination boards devised syllabuses without much consideration of the independent sector. The national curriculum was

---

[27] For basic information see *Harrow Register, 1885–1949*, 674–89; *Harrow Register, 1986*, 800–22.

constructed by governments with interests in uniformity and accessibility.[28] Certain subjects at secondary level were confined almost exclusively to public school ghettos, such as medieval history or classics. In science independent schools, not least Harrow, had long pioneered new approaches and techniques. In 1981 twenty out of sixty-six members of committees of the Association of Science Education giving schools as their addresses were from public schools. Of the fifty-eight Trial schools in A Level Nuffield Physics, seventeen were independent: Harrow fully participated from 1974.[29] By the 1990s curriculum development, classics excepted, increasingly marginalized independent schools.

This reflected a gradual removal of schools such as Harrow from the limelight of serious national attention and importance. Every nineteenth-century Head Master of Harrow received an entry in the *Dictionary of National Biography* or its supplements; of their twentieth-century successors, only Norwood was included. In 1914 Harrow was a national and imperial school, at the height of prestige and acclaim, at the heart of power, influence, and the Establishment. Its status was recognized beyond the self-regarding public school universe; in the 1930s Southern Railways named a locomotive after the school.[30] By 1991 Harrow continued to be national and international only in the sense of its entrants not its importance. Royalty visited because of the school's past not its present. The stripping away of the reality and, more slowly, of the illusions of grandeur may have assisted the school to adapt to modernity. Harrow of the 1990s, for all the attempts to preserve the show of tradition, was a very different place from the school Lionel Ford had set out to reform three-quarters of a century earlier, even if not everyone noticed.

'Rich and Slack', 1918–1934[31]

Harrow between the wars provided a scene of startling contrasts. Numbers rose to unprecedented heights only to fall to depths not visited since the 1840s. Still widely respected and admired, its pupils justified in retaining confidence in their future social positions, the school suffered from an academic system in constant flux marked by 'indolence of habit'. It enjoyed an atmosphere of 'tolerant idleness' in which boys fully exploited what Graham Greene described as Harrow's combination of 'extraordinary barbarity in discipline with a really civilised attitude of trust' while masters easily spared time from mundane teaching and elaborate socializing to conduct vigorous personal feuds and lasting vendettas.[32] Presiding over them as Head Masters were successively a despised wreck attracting concerted

---

[28] One of its drafters was an OH and future governor, N. W. Stuart (The Park, 1956–60).
[29] G. Walford, *Life in Public Schools* (London, 1986), 191–2.
[30] Gathorne-Hardy, *Public School Phenomenon*, 351.
[31] The phrase is Betjeman's: *Letters*, ii. 177.
[32] Venables, *Bases Attempted*, 30; Mack, *Public Schools and British Opinion since 1860*, 447.

disloyalty; a confused and aloof autocrat disdained alike for his origins and appearance; a mildly eccentric don whose plans were submerged by economic catastrophe and ignored by internal bickering; and, appointed in the midst of near-fatal crisis, an ageing agoraphobe who hated appearing in public and never held masters' meetings. The wealth of parents, boys, and masters and the relaxed management which prompted Betjeman's admiring description of 'rich and slack' attracted as many brickbats as plaudits.

Lionel George Bridges Justice Ford lived up to the pompous sonority of his name. His public manner combined ponderous hesitancy with insouciant tactlessness. Awkward in private, his powerful mind exhausted itself in tortuous vacillation. Acutely aware of his impressive family connections, he rarely concealed his snobbery. Candidates for teaching posts were assessed on their social acceptability. In his interview notes on E. J. Housden, a public school and Cambridge mathematician and hearty, Ford commented '*Quite class enough?*'.[33] He chose to live in style, lavishly refurbishing and extending the private side of the Head Master's.[34] In his elevated opinion of the importance of class he was ably abetted by his equally snobbish wife. Such were the awesome tones in which they referred to their grand relatives (Ford's mother was a Lyttleton), which they did regularly, that on one occasion when the inevitable subject was introduced by Mrs Ford, C. W. M. Moorsom murmured 'Shall we kneel?'.[35]

Seeing himself as a doer, not much of a reader and a poor judge of character, Ford easily inspired hostility. Intolerant of colleagues' failure or weakness, by which he often meant their disagreement, his tactlessness was comprehensive. His offer in 1914 of a Small House to the pedestrian but polite scientist Bernard Middleditch was typical: 'Sleeman, Werner, Prior, Edwards and Cruttwell having definitely declined my offer of Hillside, I am now writing to offer its succession to you.'[36] To enemies such as Edward Graham this 'frankness' displayed 'a certain lack of sympathy'. Some of the assistant masters saw him as a dangerous radical: 'the reddest of Reds could not have been more sceptical of the established order.' Other conservatives, more acute or more suffering, remembered his reforming zeal producing a system 'whose complexity was at first sight more obvious than its effectiveness'.[37] As much as the excessive complication of detail and fussiness of administration, it was the manner in which Ford introduced his curriculum changes that grated. A first-class classicist himself, he appeared to wish to downgrade

---

[33] Masters' Files, E. J. Housden, Ford's interview notes, 12 Aug. 1919. For Ford at Harrow in general see Alington, *Ford*, 81–113; Venables, *Bases Attempted*, 52 for Ford's snobbery.

[34] GBM, 16 June, 28 July, 1 Nov. 1910, 7 Feb., 17 Feb., 9 May 1911. To Ford belongs the credit for the balcony outside the Head Master's study which some have found a convenient means of escaping awkward visitors. [35] Venables, *Bases Attempted*, 53.

[36] Masters' Files, B. Middleditch, 30 June 1914, Ford to Middleditch.

[37] Alington, *Ford*, 92; Mayo, *Reminiscences*, 168; *The Harrovian*, 27 Feb. 1926, p. 1.

classics in his quest for a better standard of education for the majority, 'the greatest advantage for the greatest number'.[38] This challenged the central anti-utilitarian assumption of traditional Harrow that academic excellence equated more or less exclusively with excellence in classics, a lasting prejudice that G. M. Trevelyan had fought in the 1890s but was endured sixty years later by another scholar who opted to specialize in history, his choice earning him a blow on the head from the Head of Classics' umbrella.[39] Thus, although Ford increased money for Entrance Scholarships, he was not forgiven for substituting maths and science for the school-funded classics prizes in 1918. In the end, the governors forced him to modify his arrangements which were further reversed by Norwood. Yet Ford seemed oblivious to criticism, deliberately inviting controversy and working 'in an atmosphere of suspicion'.[40]

For one thing he was rude to people who mattered. An obsessive cricketer himself, Ford offended the OH cricketing mafia, which included the irascible senior master M. C. Kemp.[41] He outraged the pious with his ritualism, Anglo-Catholic enthusiasm, and implicit criticism of previous religious observances and instruction. By challenging the tyranny of classics he forged a hostile alliance of traditionalists and intellectuals, a rare and dangerous combination. He showed conspicuous favouritism. E. M. Venables suffered from being so obviously Ford's creature, his patron appointing him to a Small House only five years after his arrival. Even Ford's supporters thought him unwise after 1918 to rely so heavily and openly on Archer Vassall, whom Ford had made housemaster of Elmfield in 1913. Vassall, a scientist, was suspected of influencing Ford's apparent preference for his subject, the role of *eminence grise* seeming to fit well a personality described by one long associate, meaning to be unflattering, as 'astute, persuasive, subtle and elusive'.[42] An eager controversialist and public critic of the dominance of classics, of private means and supported by a wife devoted to Harrow and Elmfield, Vassall was an effective intriguer, even managing to poach a master from under the usually vigilant stare of the future archbishop of Canterbury, Geoffrey Fisher, then Head Master of Repton. The sneering tone of some contemporary comments, such as Mayo's 'science is in pride of place today', may reflect a suspicion of Vassall's undue power.[43]

Such was the dislike of Ford that few gave him the credit for the rapid increase in numbers from just over 450 in 1916 to almost 650 by the time he left at the end

---

[38] *The Harrovian*, 27 Feb. 1926, p. 1; Alington, *Ford*, 84.   [39] Moorman, *Trevelyan*, 23.
[40] Alington, *Ford*, 83. Cf. ibid., 81: 'an atmosphere of controversy'; GBM, 28 June 1917, 12 Nov. 1918, 24 June, 16 Oct. 1924, 12 Feb. 1925, 14 Nov. 1926; *The Harrovian*, 20 Oct. 1934, 151.
[41] Alington, *Ford*, 111.
[42] Venables, *Bases Attempted*, 49–50, 55. Vassall's nephew was the notorious spy of the early 1960s. Ford's son Neville was in Vassall's house, Elmfield.
[43] Masters' Files, H. J. L. Gorse, 16 Feb. 1931, Gorse to A. Vassall, 17 Apr. 1931, G. Fisher to C. Norwood; Mayo, *Reminiscences*, 208; Alington, *Ford*, 93.

of 1925, one critic commenting 'this popularity was so universal as to be independent of either teacher or school'.[44] His critics seem to ignore his popularity with the boys and his ability to get on with them. They could not see that his affectations in dealing with adults concealed a genuine enjoyment of teaching and the company of pupils. The governors appeared equally unimpressed. Ill health, brought on by the emotional strains of the war, forced Ford to take the autumn term of 1919 away from Harrow, the school being run in his absence by Kemp, a hardened foe.[45] It is clear the governors hoped he would not return. One obstacle to this desired end was the inadequacy of Ford's pension provision. With the dual object of enhancing his pension and covering his departure with a dignified gloss, in November 1919 the governors wrote to the President of the Board of Education 'as to Headmasters in the future receiving considerations in elections for Church preferment'.[46] Despite receiving an unsatisfactory response, the governors persisted in wishfully assuming Ford's tenure of office was drawing to a close. In May 1920 they reassured Moorsom, housemaster at the Head Master's, that they would recommend his confirmation in post to a new Head and provide compensation if he were not retained.[47] In 1924, although devastated by the death of his son Richard at Eton, Ford had not sought time off and was therefore surprised, if grateful, to receive another offer from the governors of a sabbatical term. This time his place was taken by the clever, cool, witty, and incisive classicist N. K. Stephen (inevitably known as 'Inky'), Kemp having retired in 1921.[48] This second leave of absence seriously damaged his standing within the school and outside.

Fault was not restricted to Ford. His staff were increasingly disloyal, attacking him behind his back and to the boys. They and the governors freely blamed Ford for the experiment of the Contio in English in 1924, although many (and all the governors) must have known it had been Walter Long's idea.[49] Ford's own difficulties were not entirely of his making. The war took an enormous toll. No emotional or professional training could have equipped him to cope with certain events. In June 1914 he had expelled a monitor for 'immoral conduct with a small boy'; two years later he was reading out the older boy's name in Chapel as one of the fallen on the Somme.[50] When he had arrived from Repton in 1910 his mandate to reform was not accepted by his senior staff, settled in relaxed gentility under the 'urbane and dignified repose' of Dr Wood.[51] The long-term benefit and necessity of his changes remained hidden, only appreciated a generation later. The sincerity of his churchmanship not even his enemies denied, indeed it formed a central plank of their opposition.

[44] Mayo, *Reminiscences*, 171. [45] Alington, *Ford*, 109.
[46] GBM, 11 Nov. 1919, 10 Feb. 1920. [47] GBM, 11 May 1920.
[48] Alington, *Ford*, 111; Venables, *Bases Attempted*, 44.
[49] Alington, *Ford*, 109; GBM, 9 May 1920.
[50] Head Master's Punishment Book, 26 May 1914; *Harrow Register, 1885–1949*, 315.
[51] The phrase is Venables': *Bases Attempted*, 28.

None the less, Ford proved a disappointment. Not only did he lack the political acumen and thuggery of Welldon, he also displayed what a friend called 'a certain vein of indolence'.[52] As so often, an effective reformer at one school did not transfer his success to another. In the twentieth century Harrow was unfortunate in the growing habit of appointing men on their second or third headships. However competent, they rarely brought to Harrow the energy, sensitivity, and skill that had gained the attention of the governors in the first place, only Moore and James standing as clear exceptions. Partly this was a consequence of age. From Wood onwards, second- or third-time Heads tended to possess experience and confidence in their own abilities, but often lacked the energy to sustain new programmes, the interest to repeat past triumphs, or the flexibility to learn that Harrow required different treatment. They were also confronted by staff whose tenure had extended back to many predecessors and would stretch far beyond to numerous future incumbents. Twentieth-century Head Masters often gave the impression of short-term lease-holders among a curmudgeonly body of freeholders, interlopers to be humoured or denigrated at will. This was certainly Ford's destiny, his provocative policies and personality combining with growing exhaustion to leave him a beleaguered figure. This was more surprising because he had led the school unflinchingly through the worst corporate tragedy in its history. Few allowed him much praise for that.

Masters' Meetings presented a paradigm of Ford's problems. They were held in the Vaughan Library, the Head and senior masters sitting at one table, the rest spread around the large reading room. In Ford's early years few apart from the elderly OHs said or were encouraged to say anything, business being the jealously guarded privilege of Graham, Kemp, Townsend Warner, and E. M. Butler. This was facilitated by the conversation at the Head Master's table being conducted in tones largely inaudible to everyone else in the room. This segregation continued after 1918. Once, following a long whispered discussion at the top table, Ford turned for his opinion to the French master, holder of the Croix de Guerre and Chevalier of the Légion d'Honneur, A. M. E. Begouën de Meaux, who had been quietly reading a book at the other end of the library. Begouën de Meaux was startled; 'What, what is this? Oh, my opinion? So sorry, but I haven't heard a word! We can't hear anything this end of the room'.[53] Such factional apartheid militated against easy acquiescence to Ford's schemes. Many of the senior masters, like Graham, did not disguise their dislike of Ford's policies.[54] To deflect open confrontation, Ford adopted laborious, vacillating circumlocution: perhaps a consequence of what friend and foe agreed was the tortuous, over-scrupulous 'slow-workings of his mind'.[55] This merely exacerbated his difficulties as he could

---

[52] Alington, *Ford*, 71 (and Alington was a friend).
[53] Venables, *Bases Attempted*, 35.   [54] Ibid., 34.
[55] Alington, *Ford*, 96; Venables, *Bases Attempted*, 34, 48–9 and, generally, pp. 32–55.

appear deliberately devious and secretive. Half-way through one particularly agonizing vacuous statement, as tension and irritation mounted in the room, one exasperated master, probably Kemp, banged the table with his fist and shouted 'My God, Sir, cannot we have the truth?'. After a moment's dead silence, Ford, his face thunderous, slowly resumed his unintelligible statement.[56]

This inability to control his staff was not unusual in a Harrow Head Master of any period: Norwood had to resort to firing dissidents to get his way. Ford's failure was more unexpected given his impeccable social and public school credentials at Eton and Repton. Yet he was up against some powerfully independent personalities. Of the thirty-eight assistant masters he inherited in 1910, exactly half lasted through and beyond his fifteen years as Head.[57] Between 1918 and 1922 the old guard retired: Graham; Butler; Kemp; Mayo; the Christian fundamentalist Owen; the brilliant but increasingly blind Moriarty who had once out-talked A. J. Balfour at a dinner party; and the scholarly but inept housemaster of Newlands, Sir Arthur Hort. Together they had taught at Harrow for 218 years, an average of thirty-one years each. Remaining were the locquacious Vassall as the power-behind the throne; the bad-tempered, unacademic bully Wyatt-Smith; the dull, 'unruffled disciplinarian' with a prominent Adam's apple, Coke-Norris; the scholarly du Pontet for whom 'schoolmastering was, perhaps, too much of a trial';[58] the lame W. G. Young, who, because of a riding accident, always taught in his house, West Acre; the increasingly irrepressible 'Cocky' Pope, 'Bishop' Kemp's natural successor as resident guardian of the OH flame of tradition and cricket; the witty and versatile Bradshaw; and Stephen, 'whose swift insight and capacity for freezing courtesy and shafted irony was equal to any occasion'.[59] Ford himself had appointed powerful characters and men who early assumed status: the historian L. W. Henry; the mathematician A. P. Boissier; the sporty C. R. Browne; the confident R. M. Baldwin; the well-connected O. G. Bowlby; and the versatile T. F. Coade, the future Head Master of Bryanston, renowned for his promotion of drama as a director of plays and, according to one pupil, although 'the last of whom we boys were most frightened in [the] class room', a 'most delightful man'.[60] As he grew older, Ford was decreasingly able to control such men, especially housemasters. With impunity, Pope, at The Grove, encouraged his boys to refuse to follow the rest of the school in continuing to wear 'bluers' during the week, Grovites sporting their tails every day.[61]

[56] Venables, *Bases Attempted*, 49; Alington, *Ford*, 92, 96, 110.
[57] For career details see *Harrow Register, 1885–1949*, 676–84. For accounts of their personalities, apart from Masters' Files, see Venables, *Bases Attempted*, 15, 20–3, 42, 58, 73–4, 82–3.
[58] Venables, *Bases Attempted*, 20, 21, 24; Wansell, *Rattigan*, 32 for Coke-Norris's Adam's apple.
[59] Venables, *Bases Attempted*, 35.
[60] Private Correspondence, G. J. Poke to J. P. Lemmon, 2 Dec. 1994, p. 4. I am grateful to Jeremy Lemmon for permission to quote from this letter.
[61] Bryant, *Harrow*, 110 gives a misleadingly cosy view on this.

Increasingly Ford appeared out of touch. Despite his obsession with the timetable, which became so complicated that he resorted to the appointment of Coke-Norris as Harrow's first Organisation Master,[62] and his concern to raise academic standards throughout the school, those few new masters with experience elsewhere found that Harrow, compared with other public schools, failed to take academic work seriously. The proliferation of extra half and whole holidays (e.g. for Baldwin's OH ministers), intrusions into lessons and prep. periods by games and other extra-curricular activities became so extreme that an 'Interruption to Work' committee was established, chaired by the respected and distinguished veteran mathematician A. W. Siddons.[63] The governors intervened in 1924–5 to reimpose what they regarded as more appropriate arrangements for teaching classics throughout the school, even though this still left a surplus of classical masters with little to do.[64] The maths teaching could still deliver for alert boys such as Giles Playfair results in School Certificate Maths as dismal as two out of three hundred. Cecil Beaton spent much of his time cheating: as a teachers' favourite nobody seemed to mind.[65] There were patches of excellence. The eccentric Egerton Hine, whose misplaced nationalism or literal-mindedness caused him to object to the hanging of El Grecos in the National Gallery, still inspired artists. Siddons was class, as was the Head of History, Leonard Henry, when health permitted. Coke-Norris put off clever boys such as Terence Rattigan, to whom he taught Greek, but excelled at conscientiously coaching the IVth, i.e. bottom, Form. Stephen's refined old-fashioned classical scholarship was available to talented initiates, although he scorned lesser pupils with such encouraging remarks (deemed witty by his colleagues) as: 'if you go on improving at your present rate, you will soon be a half-wit'.[66] In general, though, formal academic life in Ford's Harrow remained flaccid. 'Juggins' Freeborn's report on Beaton for entrance to St John's College, Cambridge in 1922 admitted that while his English was good 'with ordinary school subjects such as Mathematics and Latin, he is very weak indeed, in fact bad . . . But he is a very nice boy and I feel sure you would not regret admitting him to the College'.[67]

Actually, neither Beaton nor many of his schoolmates was particularly 'nice'. Extravagance of behaviour and dress, institutionalized bullying, and casual sodomy were commonplace, only occasionally being brought to the notice of authorities. One reason for the apparent decadence of much of life in Harrow in the 1920s was overcrowding. Numbers rose by over 40 per cent in Ford's last decade, 1915–25. Houses became warrens, in many places delapidated, crumbling, insanitary, and unheated. Housemasters had little incentive to improve conditions

---

[62] Masters' File, L. W. Henry, 2 Apr. 1923, Ford to Henry.
[63] Venables, *Bases Attempted*, 23–30, esp. pp. 24–5; GBM, 23 June 1925.
[64] GBM 26 June, 16 Oct. 1924, 12 Feb. 1925; Masters' Files, J. W. Moir, May 1925, Moir to Ford.
[65] Playfair, *My Father's Son*, 125; Vickers, *Beaton*, 22.
[66] Vickers, *Beaton*, 21; Darlow and Hodson, *Rattigan*, 34–5; Venables, *Bases Attempted*, 21, 73.
[67] Vickers, *Beaton*, 26.

other than to comply with health regulations and the requirements of clients. The governors were directing their resources to buying property around the Hill and old boy donations were largely concentrated on the War Memorial Appeal. The surprise is not that Harrow was hit by scandal but that it was not so bludgeoned more often.[68]

The Easter Term of 1925 marked a low point in Harrow's reputation. Giles Playfair and his father had persuaded a disbelieving then reluctant Moorsom to break a homosexual circle in the Head Master's.[69] To the unconcealed surprise and disgust of many of his colleagues, Ford had returned from his second sabbatical. He cut an increasingly pathetic figure, weighed down by family tragedy and what must by then have dawned on him as the prospect of professional failure. His successor as Head Master of Repton, William Temple, was already a bishop. Yet he remained resilient and apparently immovable. He continued to get on well with pupils. His notorious conversational hubris remained undimmed. Ford liked to trump everyone else's experiences. On half overhearing one of his female guests confide to his wife that she had recently undergone a serious gynaecological operation with a complicated Greek name, he immediately declared to the astonished pair: 'Oh yes; when I had one of those . . .'. Such *bêtises* apart, while outwardly maintaining appearances, Ford's mood cannot have been cheerful and even his equanimity was severely tested by the scandal that struck in March 1925.

'Ferocious buggery' was not the only sexual outlet for senior Harrovians. London beckoned. One interested observer, John Betjeman, recalled that 'whenever the police raided the Hypocrites Club or the Coconut Club, the '43 or the Blue Lantern there would always be Harrovians there. They used to go down on the Metropolitan Line'.[70] One night in March a group of seven chose to travel by motor car instead. They were caught by the police 'in flagrante delicto'; the news reached the papers. Ford's reaction scarcely helped. Privately shattered at the prospect of the bad publicity, he appeared unfortunately insouciant in public, being quoted as commenting by way of defence: 'Only seven out that night!' Despite the presence at these clubs of public schoolboys from most of the fashionable schools within a thirty-mile radius of London, Harrow bore the full brunt of the ridicule and hostility, not least because the seven miscreants were led by the Head of School—a school hero and Triple Blood—and two monitors. They were instantly withdrawn by their parents. Of the other four, only one left immediately, later to serve as Churchill's personal pilot at the end of the Second World War; the remaining three stayed another term, one of them for obvious reasons. He played at Lord's (though Harrow still failed to win).[71]

---

[68] Playfair, *My Father's Son*, 69–80; Vickers, *Beaton*, 21–5.
[69] Playfair, *My Father's Son*, 79–80; Head Master's Punishment Book, 24 Mar. 1925.
[70] Quoted by Gathorne-Hardy, *Public School Phenomenon*, 302.
[71] Gathorne-Hardy, *Public School Phenomenon*, 302; Venables, *Bases Attempted*, 46; Head Master's Punishment Book, 26 Mar. 1926; *Harrow Register, 1971, passim*.

Thus to decadence was added a sense of disintegration. Governors rushed to the Hill like impotent vultures, their suggested remedies hardly taking cognizance of the twentieth century, their proposal that Ford should actually increase the number of Masters' Meetings being, in the circumstances, only one of a series of unconsciously comic touches.[72] With some masters in more or less open revolt, discipline was lax everywhere. The whispering campaign against Ford began to deafen. As with Wordsworth eighty years earlier, the question for the governors was how to remove him with the added caveat that any change required careful publicity. For the sake of the school, Ford could not be seen to have been sacked. In any case, he displayed no signs of wishing to leave. There was one obvious solution which depended on whether Baldwin would play the same role as Peel had in 1844. It seems he did. There exists a possibly apocryphal story of Baldwin, when approached by the governors about elevating Ford out of Harrow, declaring that, as Prime Minister, there was nothing he took more seriously and about which he resisted outside pressure more firmly than ecclesiastical preferment... *however*, he was a loyal Old Harrovian. The next day a special edition of the *London Gazette* announced Ford's appointment as dean of York. Although events may not have occurred in precisely that fashion, one of Baldwin's Cabinet, Leo Amery, a man not knowingly averse to intrigue, had recently been elected the Masters' Governor. The archbishop of Canterbury was an Old Harrovian. Certainly, the appointment to York was sudden. There is another story of how a surprised Ford was unexpectedly summoned from his dinner table to be informed of his preferment. Such was the speed of events that the governors received only two months' notice of the vacancy, although it took them less than a month to decide on Ford's successor who, it was said, was pressed to accept the post by two stalwart OHs, the Prime Minister and the archbishop.[73] Whatever else, the removal of Ford to the deanery of York, a position barely grand enough for one of his social sensitivity, saw the Establishment working at its sleekest.

Ford's reputation had been left indelibly tarnished. He had always presented observers with a series of contradictions. A classicist of the old school, a double First, a cricketer, former Head of his school, and President of the Cambridge Union, he came from a background of assumed destiny to rule. Yet he was accused of denigrating the classics and failing in sympathy with his assistants. A man of massive self-confidence, he was a poor, diffident public speaker, whose addresses to the boys were hesitant and whose sermons, delivered in a deep, booming nasal voice, obscurely intellectual.[74] Yet they were his greatest admirers, sharing his sporting interests and responding to his unaffected concern for their well-being. His problems were with adults, especially those consumed by self-interest, self-importance, and religious bigotry, those, as one of Ford's supporters put it, 'whose outlook was

---

[72] GBM, 7 May 1925.   [73] GBM, 5 Nov., 1 Dec. 1925; Venables, *Bases Attempted*, 69.
[74] Playfair, *My Father's Son*, 113; Alington, *Ford*, 92.

bounded by the Hill'.[75] It is hardly surprising that one of his greatest pleasures and a source of much solace was the supervision of the daily feeding of his many pigs he kept at the bottom of the garden of the Head Master's, which he had lovingly restored after his predecessor had allowed it to degenerate into a chicken run. One of his first acts as Head Master had been to construct new and luxurious sties for his pigs, the governors, perhaps taken aback at the request, declining to pay for them.[76]

Obsessed with the qualities of a gentlemen, Ford could be brusque, tactless, secretive, and devious in his professional dealings. An intellectual, he read little and cultivated the image of a hearty. His paradoxical nature was neatly captured by one Harrow wit who remarked that Ford 'was not half as good as most people thought, but much much cleverer.'[77] He presided over Harrow in its darkest days, his term of office the second longest of the century. His devotion to Harrow, for all its treatment of him, remained undimmed. His legacy was a timetable that, for all the excessive complexity that matched its framer's mind, allowed the curriculum to grow and adapt according to the educational needs of the pupils not just the convenience, habits, or prejudices of the teachers. Unlike his reforming and conservative predecessors, whose rule tended to be based on precept, Ford's primary interest was pragmatic, the education of his pupils. When demonstrated on a broad scale, this presented something of a novelty to Harrow. It was entirely in keeping with Ford's concerns and devotion that his parting gift to the school were nine films, silent movies, shown to the boys on 18 December 1925.[78] The boys reciprocated by presenting Mrs Ford with a fur coat. At the very end of his farewell speech to the school, Ford quoted his wife's letter of thanks: 'Every time I wear it I shall feel I am wrapped in the love of Harrow. Yours sincerely, May Ford'. Her husband broke down in tears before he could finish.[79]

The speed of Cyril Norwood's election indicated prior collusion, the advertisements placed in the press, as the statutes demanded, providing an even less substantial smokescreen than usual. The effect of Ford's last years and the measure of the governors' desperation were everywhere apparent. Norwood was the first layman of modern times to be elected Head Master of Harrow, an unusually bold step as it was taken before Eton or Winchester. The scars of the ritualism conflicts were vivid. Norwood's churchmanship, however 'sound', could not, by definition, assume such a prominent role in Harrow affairs. Norwood was also the first Head Master on whose tenure was imposed an age limit. It was agreed on his appointment that, then aged 50, he would retire at 60, with an option for renewal to 65.[80] This removed the tensions that had accompanied Ford's last years, nobody knowing when or if he would go. The model of the 1925 arrangements remained

---

[75] Venables, *Bases Attempted*, 46.   [76] Alington, *Ford*, 96, 118; GBM, 1 Nov. 1910.
[77] Alington, *Ford*, 117.   [78] *The Harrovian*, 27 Feb. 1926, p. 10.
[79] Playfair, *My Father's Son*, 113.   [80] GBM, 1, 8, 15 Dec. 1925.

standard for over seventy years. Norwood appeared eager to come. Offering the post on 1 December 1925, the governors assumed an interregnum, making arrangements for N. K. Stephen, who was about to retire, to act as interim Head Master. By 8 December Norwood had not only accepted election but announced his intention to start the following month; there would be no hiatus. For all concerned, not least the governors of Marlborough where Norwood had been Master since 1916, less than a month's notice was remarkable.

Norwood provided an almost complete contrast with his predecessor. The son of an obscure drunken clergyman and failed headmaster, Norwood was a self-made man whose life demonstrated the virtues of industry and temperance. He never spoke of his childhood, but to his youthful experiences he probably owed his often chilling reserve and social awkwardness as much as his ambition. His passion for effective management and authority may have acted on a hidden inner insistence to vindicate his father's weaknesses. A product of Merchant Taylor's, after Firsts in Mods and Greats at Oxford, he had begun his professional life as a civil servant before entering teaching at Leeds Grammar School. He retained the manner and habits of an austere, Olympian mandarin, an administrator rather than a teacher, a theorist not a formroom practitioner. Between 1906 and 1916 he was Head Master of Bristol Grammar School, establishing its lasting reputation before moving to the lusher pastures of Marlborough where he was probably happiest. Many believed he never took to Harrow; some said the feeling was mutual.[81]

As a young man Norwood had begun to air his views on public school education. In *The Higher Education of Boys in England*, co-authored with Anthony Hope in 1909, he voiced approval of public schools' 'training of boys outside the classroom in the manlier virtues and to a keen, if narrow patriotism'. Yet he was highly critical of their elitism and snobbery and their failure to encourage 'a wider citizenship and a higher duty, and the subordination of self to the community': 'Our young barbarians at play are a pleasing spectacle, but a boy of forty, with a horizon bounded by sport and by *The Spectator* is perhaps something of an anachronism.' Boys should be trained to hard work and individual thought. The solution, Norwood believed, lay in the then very radical notion of merging public schools into the state system, an idea to which he returned with vigour thirty years later.[82] By the mid-1920s, now an acknowledged educational pundit, his enthusiasm for public schools was less qualified. Although the themes of disciplined work, ennobling sport, team spirit, and corporate effort remained central to his philosophy, there came now an acceptance of the moral and hence social superiority of the public school system and thus the public school classes. The radical young Head Master had developed some reactionary tendencies. In his *English Tradition of Education*

---

[81] See Norwood's entry in *DNB* by G. C. Turner. See, in general, Venables, *Bases Attempted*, 69–175; Bryant, *Harrow*, 98–9; Playfair, *My Father's Son*, 113, et seq.
[82] Mack, *Public Schools and British Opinion since 1860*, 281–4.

of 1929 he enthusiastically embraced Bowen's vision of games; the efficacy of beating; hostility to external examinations, including Common Entrance and School Certificate; and a belief in the importance of aristocratic values. Edward Thring of Uppingham, hearty apostle of manliness, subordination to the community and educational populism for the ordinary boy, drew his strongest approval. He felt an increasing dislike of the promotion of the individual. Unless a shared communal experience, excellence was pernicious: 'of the ten thousand evils that now exist (1929) in Britain and America nothing is worse than the world-champions in sport and all that goes to produce them'.[83] One of the few photographs of Norwood smiling is one taken of him sitting surrounded by Harrovians about to play Harrow Football on Founder's Day, a festival of team spirit, although even then his attitude suggests tension.[84] Norwood was equally dismissive of those claiming insight, acuity, or knowledge: 'there is nothing of which I have so great a horror as the expert'.[85] A freemason, strongly anti-Catholic, Norwood advocated Head Masters being conspicuous believers, even if not in Holy Orders, and insisted on the centrality of religion in school life.[86]

In practice, Norwood found implementing his ideas less straightforward. He simplified Ford's options system, reducing the number of subjects and combinations; restored Latin for Upper School non-classicists; tightened the provision of prep. time; and introduced the idea of a year-long syllabus, with the assumption that form groups (not necessarily of the same age or entry date) moved up the school in annual blocks, instead of piecemeal, term by term. His theoretical hostility to the demands of School Certificate had not prevented him encouraging Marlburians to sit the exam or Harrovians working seriously for it. When he left in 1934, success in School Certificate provided one measure of his achievement. However, his attempt to create a specialist Sixth Form centre in the Copse stalled, with only the History Sixth moving there.[87]

In common with many theorists, Norwood indulged in fads. One of the most notable was a desire to assess and equate Harrow in relation to the outside world of education and adult work. His chosen instrument was his fellow freemason E. D. Laborde, head of geography, whom he created Harrow's first Careers' Master in 1932 as a statement of principle rather than an expression of anxiety about Harrovian unemployment.[88] Laborde's self-made career probably appealed to Norwood.

---

[83] Norwood, *English Tradition of Education*, 106. For Thring see ibid., 18, 116, 198.
[84] Reproduced by Gathorne-Hardy, *Public School Phenomenon*, opposite p. 193.
[85] Written to Nigel Playfair, Playfair, *My Father's Son*, 110.
[86] Norwood, *English Tradition of Education*, 29–30, 51–2, 54–5.
[87] On Norwood's curriculum changes see GBM, 14 Nov. 1926; Laborde, *Harrow School*, 64, 155; Venables, *Bases Attempted*, 168–70; *The Harrovian*, 20 Oct. 1934, p. 151; *DNB* entry. Cf. Norwood, *English Tradition of Education*, 141–2.
[88] Masters' File, E. D. Laborde, correspondence, 1921–1939, *passim*; GBM, 16 Nov. 1932; interestingly, Laborde's masonic associations, which are recorded in *Harrow Register, 1971*, 704, were omitted from the next edition, *Harrow Register, 1986*, 802.

Educated privately and at London University, he had not risen on the escalator of effortless privilege, the lack of a public school or Oxbridge education later costing him at least one headship. After a career in the Colonial Service as a Head Master in Fiji, Laborde came to Harrow to teach modern languages in 1919, shrewdly switching his interests to Ford's new specialist subjects geography (of which he became head in 1925) and the short-lived economics. An over-strict disciplinarian, eliciting a reprimand from Ford, Laborde reinvented himself as a considerable popular geographer and successfully completed a Ph.D. at London University, an almost unique pre-war example of a genuine higher academic degree among the Harrow staff.[89] On one famous occasion he displayed some humour. Teaching Terence Rattigan French in the Lower Remove, Laborde returned the stage-struck pupil's exercise, an unexpected melodrama, with the comment: 'French execrable . . . Theatre sense first class. Two out of Ten.'[90] Laborde's methodical if uncritical history, *Harrow School Yesterday and Today*, published in 1948, justly held the field for half a century, his approval of Ford, Norwood, and 'modernity' barely concealed beneath apparent objectivity. As Careers' Master, Laborde arranged for boys to be tested by the National Institute of Industrial Psychology. It says much for Norwood's personality that Harrovians submitted to this. One encounter revealed the cultural gulf between the gilded Olympians on the Hill and what is now called the world of work. One scholar received high marks on his IQ tests and was reported by the Institute as having 'a quick mind, organising ability and powers of initiative'. They recommended he might be suitable for the Home Civil Service, to which the boy inquired 'What does that do?' He later found out as a Permanent Secretary in no fewer than four government departments.[91]

Bolder was Laborde's publishing of the results of a school-wide intelligence test conducted by the National Institute of Industrial Psychology in 1934 in which Harrovians were compared with other public and state secondary schools. That the tests occurred was testament to Norwood's meritocratic determination; that detailed results and graphs were published in the *Harrovian* a sign of extraordinary (and unrepeated) confidence.[92] Compared in a group of four other public schools, Laborde calmly reported, 'it will be seen that in each age group [of five 13.6 to 18.6], except the 13.6–14.5 the Harrow curves are inferior to the norm'. In case readers failed to grasp his meaning, Laborde continued that while the 13.6–14.5 group showed 'a high proportion of intelligent boys', the 15.6–16.5 and 17.6 to 18.5 years revealed a 'comparative absence of Grade A boys', that of 16.6 to 17.5 containing 'a substratum of stupid boys'. On the face of it, Harrow was admitting less academic boys than elsewhere and was succeeding in reducing their intellectual abilities during their stay. The School Inspectors of 1931 did not seem bothered; they reported

---

[89] Masters' File, E. D. Laborde, Ford to Laborde, 2 Dec. 1921.
[90] Darlow and Hodson, *Terence Rattigan*, 34; Wansell, *Rattigan*, 29–30.
[91] Part, *Making of a Mandarin*, 19. [92] *The Harrovian*, 31 Mar. 1934, pp. 39–44.

that Harrow's education was 'satisfactory', their only specific recommendation concerning the need for new formrooms in the now very overcrowded and cramped school (with over 660 boys).[93] What may have worried Norwood was that the 1934 survey was taken at the end not the beginning of his term of office. It may not be a surprise that public disclosures of such information did not form part of Norwood's legacy.

Nevertheless, these results match certain features of Harrow's system confirmed by anecdotal evidence elsewhere across the century. The range of intellectual ability at entry was traditionally very wide, including many not very able, not to say, as Laborde did, stupid boys. One effect of the Harrow ethos was to increase the proportion of those not using their minds to much active purpose. The few scholars, while qualitatively as good as any in the land, did not quantitatively compare well with some other schools. The relative improvement from the fourth to fifth years was explicable in terms of the really slow boys leaving before those with the prospect of qualifications. Although only a blurred snapshot taken from what many argued was a misleading angle (where did the Institute test for manliness and character?), the 1934 IQ results provide a useful, if for some disquieting, insight into the very nature of the school.

Norwood's attempts to mould the school in his image encountered more severe obstacles even than the relative stupidity of the intake. He never accurately gauged the tone of the school nor the requirements for its teaching staff. Half his twenty-four appointments averaged only nine years' service each, at a school where the average length of tenure was over twice that. One veteran of Ford's time commented 'some strange people appeared and disappeared from time to time'.[94] A number of them left teaching altogether, for example to become School Inspectors. The successful introduction of rugger in 1927 exposed a far greater threat to Norwood's schemes, namely the outright hostility of certain senior masters.

Where Ford exuded late Victorian Establishment refinement, Norwood appeared as a philistine. Harrow snobbery condemned him as 'plebeian'. Many years later, one master fulminated that Norwood failed to 'clean Harrow up' not, as E. M. Venables argued, because it 'began too late' but 'because he wasn't really a gentleman'. 'His nickname here was "Boots"—not quite-quite. He never got Harrow in his grip. He retreated to write his ridiculous book, to sit on Whitehall committees and eventually to St. John's College, where he made an even worse mess'.[95] This was only partly accurate, Norwood's extended absences, to Canada in the early Summer of 1930 or as Chairman of the Secondary School's Examination Council after 1931, occurred after he had imposed the main features of his policy.[96]

---

[93] GBM, 18 Feb., 23 Oct. 1931, 17 Feb., 16 June 1932.
[94] Venables, *Bases Attempted*, 170; *Harrow Register, 1971*, pp. 706–9.
[95] Quoted by Gathorne-Hardy, *Public School Phenomenon*, 302. Cf. Playfair, *My Father's Son*, 113.
[96] GBM, 19 Feb., 18 Mar., 14 May 1930, 18 Feb. 1931.

Contempt for his humble origins and middle-class appearance and manner was fuelled by his own cold reserve and absence of affability, but had its origins in what many perceived as his threatening behaviour.[97]

Norwood courted publicity, being 'a little abundant in the newspapers' as one supporter tactfully observed, in 1931 even allowing Paramount Sound News to make a film of the school.[98] He used this weapon to deadly effect against his opponents during the rugger debate in 1926–7. Some never forgave him. His enemies tended to be senior housemasters who rightly diagnosed his determination to extract 'perfect loyalty' from his staff, whereas they had been happy to conduct themselves and air their opinions on school matters without let or hindrance during the lotus years under Ford whose headmastership some had helped destroy.[99] In 1928 the governors agreed that all future housemasters would be appointed for a fifteen-year term.[100] Norwood's proposal to provide them with fixed salaries instead of boarding profits was rejected, but news of it must have leaked out. These plans only affected future housemasters, but such undermining of jealously guarded rights and privileges marked Norwood as a dangerous man. This image was confirmed in May 1929 when Norwood, in the face of concerted opposition from housemasters, obtained governors' approval empowering him to insist that each house admit an Entrance Scholar at least once every four years.[101] This issue had been contested by Welldon and his housemasters in 1897–8, Bowen arguing against any infringement of his independence.[102] It raised the crucial principle of the limits of houses' autonomy and Head Masters' control. Even towards the end of his time, Norwood could be forced to modify declared decisions in the face of housemasters' opposition.[103] Although often seen later as a matter of personalities, Norwood's battles were fought over the fundamental constitution of the school, his victory paving the way for further reforms under his successor and, ultimately, after another half-century, to the emasculation of Harrow's federal system.

As in the 1890s, the fulcrum of opposition resided in The Grove. C. G. Pope was of the old school. A clever hearty in the Bowen mould, Pope assumed special privileges as an Old Harrovian. By the late 1920s he was the second senior housemaster after Vassall. Unlike Kemp, he chose not to put himself out to socialize or even converse with new masters who were not old boys. A studiedly old-fashioned 'rather forbidding' teacher of classics, very popular with the boys in his house, he made few concessions to his pupils outside. Form master of Lower Classical Fifth, on meeting his class for the first time at early School (i.e. 7.30 a.m.) in September 1929, he strode into the room of total strangers, picked up the sole prayer card and announced: 'We'll start with the General Confession. Speak up!' As one of the

---

[97] Cf. *The Harrovian*, 20 Oct. 1934, p. 151.
[98] Bryant, *Harrow*, 98; GBM, 20 May 1931. Cf. Venables, *Bases Attempted*, 167–8.
[99] Bryant, *Harrow*, 99. [100] GBM, 28 Feb., 9 May 1928.
[101] GBM, 8 May 1929. [102] GBM, 1 Nov. 1898.
[103] G. Poke to J. Lemmon, 2 Dec. 1994, p. 5 over a play, *Outward Bound*.

rather stunned form later recalled 'we had trouble in identifying the General Confession, let alone speaking up'. By then, however, Pope had other things on his mind than the feelings or the liturgical grounding of his Lower Fifth.[104]

Pope ran his house as an allod, independent from outside influence or control, but his powerbase extended beyond the school to the Old Harrovian community, especially cricketers and their citadel in the Field House Club. Pope was not only powerful but wilful and bloody-minded. His letters to the *Harrovian* in 1926-7 reveal a poor loser, his outrage wrestling for mastery with anger and self-pity. Accused of offensive opposition to Norwood's rugger proposals, he counter-attacked against what he saw as misuse of schooltime for 'Rugby propaganda'. He deplored the use of the plebiscite, protested vigorously to the governors and attempted to derail the plans by a series of guerrilla tactics.[105] Faced with final defeat, he remained unrepentant. He had been flouting Head Masters since the First World War by insisting his boys wore tails up to school. He refused to change his spots. Conservatism, even of the most diehard variety, was tolerable; flagrant disobedience was not.

Pope assumed he was invulnerable, especially as he was due to retire in 1932. Norwood decided to sack him. The Head Master had signalled his own ruthlessness and, vitally, the support he had from the governors not only during the rugger debate of 1926-7 but also early in 1929 when he managed to remove the learned but inept du Pontet from the staff after thirty-one years but six short of retirement.[106] The dismissal was sugared by the governors' agreement to pay du Pontet one year's salary and an immediate full pension. Another malcontent, Wyatt-Smith, housemaster of Moretons, departed in the Summer of 1929.[107] Norwood was picking off his enemies one by one. 'Cocky' Pope's turn came soon enough. It had long been Pope's habit not only to accompany the cricket XI on away matches but to entertain them lavishly during their return, often arriving on the Hill late, the boys well lit up. Norwood seized on this. It is said he instructed Pope that on no account must the practice continue, on pain of his dismissal. He knew his man. Pope ignored the command; Norwood fired him, giving him a term's notice to quit.[108]

As in 1926, Pope misjudged his power. He protested to the governors by letter, as did various sympathetic Old Harrovians and parents; he attended a governors' meeting on 13 November 1929 to plead his case; all to no avail. After listening to his statement, the governors concluded they must support their Head Master, telling Pope that 'they regretted that they could not see their way to making any representations to the Head Master in respect of the exercise of his authority in this matter'.[109] A month later Pope left The Grove, his successor, T. E. J. Bradshaw, at 43

[104] Part, *Making of a Mandarin*, 8-9; Venables, *Bases Attempted*, 15.
[105] GBM, 19 Feb. 1927; *The Harrovian*, 18 Dec. 1926, pp. 132-3, 26 Feb. 1927, p. 16; HM/James/13 June 1967, Ian Stuart to Dr James on 'the little tricks to wreck Norwood's innovations'.
[106] GBM, 20 Feb. 1929; Venables, *Bases Attempted*, 20 for du Pontet's aptitude.
[107] *Harrow Register, 1971*, p. 702.   [108] GBM, 13 Nov. 1929.   [109] Ibid.

becoming the first housemaster with fixed tenure, an irony unlikely to have been lost on anyone.[110]

Norwood's cull of the old-guard of Harrow masters, by no means all for the reasons that had cost Pope his job, was extensive. Apart from Pope, Wyatt-Smith, and du Pontet in 1929, Sleeman, Edwardes, Coke-Norris, and Hollingsworth all departed before retirement age, as, through ill health, did Vassall. Norwood was a good butcher, adding the Superintendent of the Gym, Captain Hibbert as well as Colonel Ozanne to his tally in 1932.[111] However, it is far from certain this produced added efficiency let alone 'perfect loyalty'. If anything, the 1930s were just as poisonously rancorous within the staff as the previous decade. His own appointments fed resentments. Venables never forgave Boissier for being preferred to him for the housemastership of Moretons in 1929; though Norwood soothed his feelings by the offer of The Park in 1932, the damage had been done.[112] Despite his own strong views, Norwood failed to resolve the tensions within the clergy and amongst the decreasing number of pious adult laity. Perhaps his greatest problem remained himself. Even his 'exituary' in the *Harrovian* talked of his 'forbidding reserve'.[113] Most noticed the evident signs of strain he displayed almost as soon as he arrived at Harrow.[114] Many boys regarded him as distant and tyrannical, even though he only flogged thirty-three times in his eight years.[115] In common with many of his colleagues, he displayed lack of understanding of boys for whom the school and its disciplinary system was inadequate. One Elmfieldian was sent up to him and warned for 'shiftiness'. John Amery, a lost soul later executed for treason in 1945, elder son of Leo, the Masters' governor and Cabinet Minister, was warned for shoplifting, 'moral breakdown, unsatisfactory work'; yet he had to endure a further two years of Harrow, although he moved out of the Head Master's.[116] Even in his early days, Norwood hardly appeared engaged in the individuals in his charge. A fortnight after conducting a long interview with Giles Playfair, then aged sixteen, Norwood failed to recognize him, calling him by the wrong name.[117] However, other pupils found him 'a delightful man'. He was especially approachable over any scheme that involved the central tenet of his educational philosophy, team effort; thus he approved of the making of a film by boys in 1931 and the creation of an Old Harrovian Dramatic Society a few years later.[118] Yet, towards the end of his time, few doubted his attention was elsewhere, interests that bore fruit when he was elected President of St John's College, Oxford, his old college, in 1934.

---

[110] Laborde, *Harrow School*, 177. [111] GBM, 16 Nov. 1932.
[112] Masters' Files, E. M. Venables, 6 and 7 Feb. 1929, Venables to Norwood.
[113] *The Harrovian*, 20 Oct. 1934, p. 151. Cf. Bryant, *Harrow*, 98.
[114] Venables, *Bases Attempted*, 70.
[115] Playfair, *My Father's Son*, 113; Head Master's Punishment Book, entries 1926–34.
[116] Head Master's Punishment Book, 4 July 1926, 1927–i: no date for 'shiftiness'.
[117] Playfair, *My Father's Son*, 114. But Playfair was somewhat irascibly vain.
[118] G. Poke to J. Lemmon, 2 Dec. 1994, pp. 2–3, 5.

Norwood had been appointed specifically to restore order to the school, its masters, boys, chapel, curriculum, and reputation. He achieved only partial success in any of them. Typical of self-confident and not unsuccessful self-publicists, Norwood was honoured less by those working closest to him than the outside world. Although he later insisted that Harrow had been a friendly place, he became a somewhat distant figure, never shaking off the domineering demeanour of the tense and shy. Privately affectionate and concerned, he was viewed by snobbish boys and masters as common, dictatorial, insensitive, a poor listener, and, in his views on education, faintly absurd, judgements that his admirers were forced to acknowledge if not support. As many other Head Masters of Harrow, Norwood found it a very difficult school to dominate. His victories were local and limited: a less cumbersome timetable, fewer ravaging dinosaurs on the staff, a reassertion of the constitutional unity of the school and authority of the Head Master and, perhaps above all, rugger.

Vellacott and the New House System, 1934–1939

If Norwood left a palpably battered and tired figure, the governors decided to replace him with comparative youth. When establishing the committee of Pember, Pickard-Cambridge, and Bishop Hicks to find a successor in February 1934, the governors 'decided that steps be taken to ascertain whether Mr Spencer Leeson, old Wykehamist and Head Master of Merchant Taylor's School would accept the Headmastership if it were offered him'.[119] Leeson, an Imperialist friend of Leo Amery, possessed the advantages of youth (he was 42), intellect, and faith (he was to be ordained in 1940, dying as bishop of Peterborough). Something of an administrator, a former civil servant, Leeson was an effective educational politician and theorist in the Norwood mode, although much more of an academic. He decided to save himself for Winchester, whither he went in 1935.

By 10 March the governors after 'considerable discussion' decided to ask P. C. Vellacott, fellow of Peterhouse, Cambridge to an interview the following week, after which he was offered the Head Mastership.[120] Thus Harrow copied Eton, who had appointed a Cambridge don, Claude Elliot, as Head in 1933. Paul Vellacott was 43, a historian of the Glorious Revolution, his distinguished war record matched by administrative achievements as Tutor (i.e. Senior Tutor) at Peterhouse, 'responsible for making the basis of the modern college what it is'.[121] Presumably J. R. M. Butler, a fellow Cambridge historian, near contemporary, and the university's Harrow governor would have known Vellacott. Even as an undergraduate before the Great War, Vellacott appeared a formidable presence. As a young don he

---

[119] GBM, 7 Feb. 1934.   [120] GBM, 10 and 17 Mar. 1934.
[121] Pattenden, *Peterhouse Annual Record* (1995–6), p. 76.

cultivated a deliberately donnish persona, calm, precise, unworldly. He would claim never to have travelled by bus or visited a cinema. So effective was he, in the phrase of his successor as history tutor and Master of Peterhouse Herbert Butterfield, at making 'a legend of himself' that undergraduates speculated that 'he went periodically to London to have his umbrella rolled'.[122] At Harrow he honed his style to tease the school, as when he once stood up in Speech Room to declare with heavy straight-faced assumed naivety: 'I am informed by the Captain of Rugby Football that there is to be a match between Oxford and Cambridge at Twickenham tomorrow.'[123] His assumed detachment from reality could have alarming consequences for the young. Vellacott used to interview junior boys in pairs. On one occasion, a couple of nervous boys presented themselves in his study, one an aristocrat with a consumptive cough; the other bearing a famous Harrow name. (After a pause) Vellacott, to coughing lordling: 'Why did you come to Harrow? Your family usually go to Eton.' Aristocrat: 'Well, er, the Hill, you see; it might be better for my, er, cough.' Vellacott (unabashed), turning to the other boy, 'You must be Peel. Why did *you* come to Harrow?'[124]

For all his affectation, as Head Master Vellacott was incisive, unruffled, and shrewd. *Persona grata* with the great and good, he lacked the snobbery or sychophancy of the courtier. In 1938 Winston Churchill arrived to judge the school's reading competition, then conducted postprandially in Speech Room before the whole school. Churchill had enjoyed Vellacott's hospitality and slept throughout the boys' readings. When roused at the end to deliver his adjudication, Churchill displayed his practised quickness of wit by brazenly awarding the prizes wholly inappropriately in the alphabetical order the boys' names appeared on the programme before rolling forth his overripe prose on subjects that interested him, unconnected with the competition.[125] Vellacott was unimpressed, remarking: '*That* man will never come to Harrow again.' It probably gave him wry amusement later to see how he could not have been more wrong.

A stylish public speaker, Vellacott's correspondence is littered with sharp character appraisals. The masters who cited him as a referee for headships elsewhere were presumably unaware of his honesty. When Oliver Bowlby, whose irreproachably grand public school connections had encouraged Ford to appoint him in 1923, applied for the Headship of Bradfield in 1939, Vellacott advised that his appointment would be 'unsafe', adding, for good measure, that as housemaster of Bradbys he failed to attract a 'good clientele' to his house.[126] He scuppered J. W. Moir's chances at St Paul's in 1938, even though he had suggested him in the first place.[127]

---

[122] Quoted ibid., 77–8.
[123] *The Harrovian*, 23 Jan. 1940, 'PCV' exituary for this and other details.
[124] I am grateful for this memory to G. F. Peel.
[125] Venables, *Bases Attempted*, 143. For other details I am grateful to the late H. L. Harris.
[126] Masters' Files, O. G. Bowlby, Correspondence between Vellacott and A. B. Ramsay, 26, 29 June, and 9 Aug. 1939.   [127] Masters' Files, J. W. Moir, 29 May 1938.

Vellacott was an unusual Head Master in seeing no absolute virtue in concealment, obfuscation, or deceit. It was common in the 1930s, and later, for wives to be taken into account when appointing to public schools, Vellacott himself receiving reassurance from R. H. Dahl's referee in 1938 that as the candidate was 'socially impeccable . . . I cannot imagine that his wife would not be so also'.[128] This extended Vellacott's range of testimonial observations. In 1936 Laborde and E. D. Gannon, a talkative modern linguist whom Vellacott quite liked, were being considered for the headship of a school in Scotland. To the chairman of governors, Vellacott commented on their spouses: 'both these ladies are good looking: Mrs Laborde the more striking so and perhaps I ought to say that she does lend some aid to her beauty.'[129] However, Vellacott was not simply misanthropic. He defended Gannon vigorously against sly accusations of being difficult: his crime was to be a great talker. When Philip Boas came to him in some agitation after breaking off his engagement to Venables's daughter, Vellacott told him not to worry, that if he had doubts he had done the right thing, and that his post was secure. (Ven. was unamused.)[130]

As Head Master, Vellacott neither minced words nor suffered fools. When Philip Bryant offered his resignation in 1939 when his plans for voluntary Chapel were rejected by his fellow clergymen, Vellacott accepted it by return—which from the tone of his letter Bryant probably had not expected—the Head adding that the basis of Bryant's grievance was false.[131] When John Bostock, having declined to join the new housemaster system, found he was making a loss on Rendalls and no longer able to pay his wife from the boarding profits, Vellacott merely pointed out that it was now impossible for him to enter the new scheme as numbers and hence central income was too low, and that he either had to stick it out or resign his housemastership.[132] Henry Havergal's proposal for a Harmony choir in 1938 presented Vellacott with the opportunity to deliver a crushing general condemnation of the Director of Music's organ-playing and musical style.[133] The handling of the increasingly difficult Venables, over Chapel and the 'Jew-baiter' incident, showed Vellacott at his best: unemotional, chillingly clear, realistic. Faced with such formidable forensic authority, Venables, for all his bluster, was brought to heel, Vellacott noting calmly after one interview that Ven. 'was disturbed and alarmed'.[134]

Although wedded to composing elegant memorandums and dispatching pithy notes, Vellacott did not use his love of paperwork as an excuse to avoid decisions.

---

[128] Masters' Files, R. H. Dahl, 8 Apr. 1938, E. A. Greswell to Vellacott.
[129] Masters' File, E. D. Laborde, 23 Oct. 1936, Vellacott to J. H. Bruce-Lockhart.
[130] Masters' Files, P. H. Boas, 1 Jan. 1935, Boas to Vellacott; E. M. Venables, 1 Jan. 1935, Venables to Vellacott.
[131] Masters' Files, P. H. M. Bryant, 9 Feb. 1939, Bryant to Vellacott; 10 Feb. 1939, Vellacott to Bryant.
[132] Masters' Files, J. Bostock, undated MS notes in Vellacott's hand.
[133] Masters' Files, H. McL. Havergal, 26 May 1938, Vellacott to Havergal (unsent but contents conveyed).
[134] Masters' Files, E. M. Venables, MS note in Vellacott's hand, Dec. 1938.

In the deepening financial crisis the Bursar since 1920, C. P. Goodden, OH, freemason, naval officer, and former Army accountant, proved incapable of implementing the economies prescribed by the governors, attracting 'special criticism'.[135] Despite Goodden's length of tenure and influential friends, Vellacott smoothly engineered his removal and replacement by the Domestic Bursar, P. A. Ledward, a change that proved vital in the crisis of 1938–42. When it became unmistakable that J. W. Moir was a feeble housemaster of Druries, with discipline lax to the point of absence, possibly the result of his love of the bottle, Vellacott replaced him without fuss in 1939, clearly hinting that unless Moir accepted the usual covering story of ill health and went quietly there would be full revelation of the true reasons for his dismissal.[136]

There was no hiding behind the mountain of paper Vellacott generated. Indeed, some regarded Vellacott as rather too sure of himself and his grasp of Harrow which they fondly assumed required half a lifetime fully to understand. He achieved this by close attention to detail, an inquiring not to say intrusive energy, an observant eye, and, to the surprise and possibly alarm of those used to the distracted Norwood or the opaque Ford, an excellent memory.[137] Norwood's management was described by one as work 'upon a large canvas, using big sweeping strokes, even if a few rough edges might be left'; by contrast Vellacott 'preferred the smooth finish of a Dutch interior'.[138] He established committees to report on many aspects of school life and was meticulous in assessing any proposals, slovenly thought, or prose being alike victims of his scrutiny. Unlike Norwood, Vellacott was both sociable and accessible; unlike Ford he established a rapport with his senior masters by openly consulting them without feeling obligated to them. In 1938, disturbed by growing evidence of incompetent teaching, he conducted an informal round table discussion of the problem, which had the effect of cleverly associating his colleagues in the unpleasant business of dismissals.[139]

Vellacott's most significant reform he introduced almost immediately. Even before taking office, he investigated ideas for the introduction of a new system of paying housemasters, reviving Norwood's proposal of 1928. The pioneer of transforming housemasters from private hoteliers into salaried housekeepers had been Charterhouse, whose example had been followed by Repton and Marlborough. Frank Fletcher, Head Master of Charterhouse, presciently warned Vellacott on 8 May 1934 that, although the system worked and was popular in his school, 'I suspect you will have to go very cautiously if you want to introduce this at Harrow. I foresee all sorts of objections and possible resentments'.[140] On 16 May 1934 Vellacott,

---

[135] Masters' Files, P. A. Ledward, 13 Oct. 1937, Ledward to Vellacott; GBM, 27 Oct. 1937.
[136] Masters' Files, J. W. Moir, correspondence between Moir and Vellacott, 3 Apr., 4 Aug., 24 Sept. 1938, and undated 1938/9.
[137] See the highly selective account by Venables, *Bases Attempted*, 179–83.
[138] Ibid., 180.   [139] Ibid., 188.
[140] HM/Vellacott/8 May 1934, F. Fletcher to Vellacott.

still not in post and only two months from election, presented his scheme to the governors. They waited until the autumn to appoint a subcommittee to investigate the idea, but agreement was reached in February 1935. The new scheme was to apply to all housemasters entering office after January 1935; existing houses were given the option of joining, which by May seven Large Houses and one Small House had done, leaving only The Park (Venables), Moretons (Boissier), Elmfield (Browne), Rendalls (Bostock), and Garlands (Laborde) outside.[141] Under the new system, in return for handing all income from boarding charges to the school, housemasters were to receive an additional salary of £600 a year, a fixed capitation sum for each boy in the house to cover his maintenance, food, housing, etc. (Allowance A) and an annual capital grant for structural improvements, repairs, and boys' facilities (Allowance B). Additionally, housemasters and their families were to receive their food, board, and lodging free under Allowance A. House staff would be hired and paid by the housemaster who would recoup his expenditure from the Bursar.

Opponents of Vellacott's proposals regarded them as a direct attack on the independence of houses as much as housemasters and thus on 'the genius of Harrow'.[142] Yet the plan was well timed. Profits were declining as numbers fell steadily from the peak of over 650 between 1926 and 1931 to below 600 by 1935, with the evidence of registrations suggesting further deterioration in the years ahead. Of those who stayed outside the new system, two, Bostock at Rendalls and Laborde at Garlands, soon regretted it as their income from decreasing numbers of boys failed adequately to cover their costs.[143] Of the rest of those *non placet*, Boissier had long overbooked Moretons, so could afford to live off accumulated fat, in money and boys; Venables' assiduous cultivation of prep. school headmasters kept the Park unusually well-stocked; while Elmfield reaffirmed its reputation as the Tibet of Harrow, an enclosed, separate world, proud in its strong, distinct, living tradition. Most houses had become uneconomic by 1939; without the new scheme, their housemasters would have faced personal ruin and the school a messy, unplanned series of house closures. As it was, four houses did close (West Acre, Newlands, Bradbys, and Rendalls) but at least their fate could be supervised with some degree of decorum to minimize the extent of the damage to the school.

Desirable in terms of efficiency and equality between houses, the new housemaster scheme contained a number of serious flaws. The system was not accompanied by strict auditing procedures at the level of the house. Not all Heads were as rigorous as Vellacott who used to scrutinize in detail each account privately with

---

[141] GBM, 16 May, 16 June, 7 Nov. 1934, 20 Feb., 15 May, 6 Nov. 1935; HM/V/printed and draft circulars, *passim*.

[142] Venables, *Bases Attempted*, 195 and, generally, pp. 194–6 and ch. 13, *passim*.

[143] Masters' Files, J. Bostock, Vellacott undated MS notes; 21 Oct. 1940, Bostock to A. P. Boissier; GBM, 19 Feb. 1941; Laborde's Small House, Garlands, closed at Christmas 1940.

the housemaster.¹⁴⁴ The potential for imaginative use of the house accounts, especially for family needs, became embedded in the system as an expected perk of the job, some post-war housemasters travelling many inconvenient miles during the Summer holidays to buy expensive cuts of meat on their house accounts at Harrow. There was little check on the destiny of the capital grant, Allowance B, which could as well be spent on housemasters' holidays or hobbies as on the house. Until centralized in the late 1980s, the appointment of domestic staff and the wages claimed were often taken on trust, not always merited.¹⁴⁵ Although overspending the Allowances was common after the war, occasionally abuse was so blatant that housemasters were surcharged or, as with West Acre and Bradbys in the early 1970s, their spending placed under supervision.¹⁴⁶ Venality did not necessarily entail profligacy. Bursar Ledward pointed out to the Head Master in October 1940 that Gannon of Druries was actually making a surplus on Allowance A which, he noted, given the small numbers of boys and consequent lack of economies of scale, 'looks like plain starvation'.¹⁴⁷

The other serious weakness of the system was that it created an anomaly, reducing housemasters' independence of financial manœuvre while leaving their monopoly over admissions, political authority, and social status intact. The school could suffer from continued Balkanization, although some regarded this diversity as a definite strength. In 1952, as Harrow was emerging from its wartime crisis, some housemasters were 'not keeping their houses as full as they might'.¹⁴⁸ In the 1970s and 1980s successive Heads began to erode this independence. In 1976 the length of tenure for housemasters was reduced from fifteen to twelve years, this accidentally creating a novel problem of greater numbers of younger ex-housemasters who stayed on the staff yearning for past wealth and influence.¹⁴⁹ In 1979 and 1981 the governors reiterated their insistence that housemasters were obliged to take boys from a central list if their own numbers fell short of the agreed quota.¹⁵⁰ By then, the advent of central feeding, as well as threatening house exclusivity and identity, removed much of the vestigial financial independence, houses no longer needing to employ their own cooks, etc. At the end of the 1980s separate house budgets were reduced still further by the centralization of all accounts and management of domestic staff. The anomaly bequeathed by Vellacott only then emerged in full clarity.

While the reform of 1935 had succeeded in changing the basis of a housemaster's position, in typical Harrow fashion, it had maintained traditional appearances and

---

¹⁴⁴ HM/Boissier/16 Oct. 1940, Ledward to Boissier.
¹⁴⁵ GBM, 19 Nov. 1988, 25 Feb. 1989.
¹⁴⁶ GBM, 6 Feb. 1954 (Newlands: surcharged), 12 Nov. 1955 (The Foss), 17 Nov. 1959 (Bradbys), 10 Nov. 1962 (West Acre, Rendalls), 12 Nov. 1966 (The Park, Bradbys, The Knoll), 17 Feb. 1968 (Newlands), 8 Nov. 1969 (West Acre: surcharged), 7 Nov. 1970 (West Acre surcharged and under supervision, Bradbys, Moretons), 10 Nov. 1972 (Bradbys, under supervision), etc.
¹⁴⁷ HM/Boss/16 Oct. 1940, Ledward to Boissier.   ¹⁴⁸ GBM, 3 May 1952.
¹⁴⁹ GBM, 23 May 1976.   ¹⁵⁰ GBM, 10 Nov. 1979, 28 Feb. 1981. Cf. 13 Mar. 1976.

some substance. A house remained the palm of Harrow life, appointments to which were ferociously sought and largely decided on seniority not suitability. Thus Harrow housemasters remained senior men, in contrast to most campus boarding schools where the post was a rung of the preferment ladder accessible to the young and ambitious, not just the settled and respectable. The unchanging seniority system not only inevitably produced as many dreadful housemasters as good ones, it also encouraged Harrow masters never to leave. It remained difficult for a Head Master to impose his will on recalcitrant housemasters who no longer needed his patronage, had direct privileged access to boys and parents, as well as to a pool of old boys, their own or their predecessors'. If, in addition, housemasters were sporty or Old Harrovians, or both, their status verged on the impregnable. Whatever the provocation or incompetence, it took a brave—some said foolish— Head to dismiss such figures, as difficult in the 1970s as in the 1920s. However, by the end of the 1980s although retaining control over entry, the financial power had gone and their houses were increasingly used in the holidays for commercial lets. In 1988 the housemasters complained to the governors of their 'feeling of loss of status'.[151] What they actually meant was loss of money, as they were immediately comforted by a new salary scale that raised incomes, compensated for any loss of perks and ensured that, however long the gap between leaving a house and retirement, ex-housemasters would receive enhanced pensions as if they had retired in post.[152] It was recognized that, despite increased assistance from deputies, housemasters held the most difficult pastoral posts in the school and still determined much of the nature of the school's intake as recruitment officers. Yet, ultimately because of Vellacott's reforms, they no longer enjoyed the baronial authority of a Bowen or a Vassall.

Vellacott possessed intelligence and style. He entertained generously. Candidates for posts would be interviewed at his London club in scenes reminiscent of Evelyn Waugh or Anthony Powell. One of his most lasting contributions to Harrow was aesthetic, the creation of the VIth Form Room underneath the Vaughan Library for the Classical Sixth for which he designed the chairs and the ingeniously conceived tables that could be used separately or fitted together in a set pattern to form a large smooth surface.[153] Vellacott himself taught history to the Sixth, but this nod in the direction of the classics did him no harm. More functional was the conversion of the Sheridan Stables into formrooms using money bequeathed by Herbert Leaf.[154] Vellacott was imaginative in initiating an exchange scheme with boys from the USA; and practical in helping to devise schemes with the local council to regulate motor car traffic on the Hill.[155] The problems of Ford's day and the habits of

---

[151] GBM, 19 Nov. 1988.   [152] GBM, 25 Feb. 1989.   [153] Venables, *Bases Attempted*, 189.
[154] As suggested by the School Inspectors in 1931: GBM, 16 June 1932, GBM, 26 Feb. 1936; Laborde, *Harrow School*, 172.   [155] GBM, 24 Feb. 1937.

Norwood he alike repudiated in an almost pathological dislike of publicity (he forbade masters to write to the press) and obsession with security. At one stage he imposed tickets for Chapel as well as securing the school bounds with fences and locked gates.[156]

His anxiety to retain Harrow inviolate may not have been unconnected with its internal divisions. Harrow in the 1930s presented an extraordinary spectacle. With its finances spinning towards bankruptcy, the school as a whole seemed largely oblivious. 'We masters knew very little' appeared to some senior figures sufficient explanation.[157] Many soon learned all too much as masters began to be dismissed in 1938–9. The internecine backbiting and feuding continued unabated, senior figures such as Carrington lacking the character or the interest to foster unity, even though the school faced closure.[158] Moir of Druries, a connoisseur of claret whom Vellacott consulted before his dinner parties, was accused by colleagues, within earshot behind his back, of being 'an irreclaimable drunkard': his nickname was 'Duck'; his hold over his house negligible.[159] Gorse, a principled depressive and housemaster at the Head Master's, staggered from one crisis to another before insisting on resigning his post.[160] F. W. T. James, housemaser of Newlands from 1937, was thin-skinned and querulous.[161] The central schism revolved around Boissier and Venables, an animosity fuelled by pique and pettiness masquerading as principle. Each encouraged their boys to despise those in the other house, at times Parkites and Moretonians deliberately refusing to walk on the same side of the road (which as they were almost next door presented difficulties). Venables regarded Boissier as a crook; Boissier thought Venables a charlatan. Venables never forgave Boissier, two years his junior in years served (the absolute Harrow rule of seniority), for stealing a march on him by succeeding to Moretons. Such were their forceful personalities that other masters were drawn into the tightening vortex of their conflict, Venables especially cultivating a circle of sympathetic, thoughtful supporters, such as Henry of The Grove. In his memoirs, Venables, who had to overcome the death of one of his daughters, appears as neurotic as well as a practised liar, as in his account of his relations with Vellacott over Chapel and his astonishing feat of omitting any mention of Boissier in the entire work. Even Boissier's outdoor production of *The Tempest* in 1938 is attributed to A. R. D. Watkins, who played Prospero.[162] Boissier, a more worldly figure, was little better, the boys in his house warming more to his wife, 'Mrs Boss', whose forceful appearance on

---

[156] Venables, *Bases Attempted*, 181–2.   [157] Ibid., 178, 189.

[158] Ibid., 22–3, 177 whose dismissal of Carrington may have been because of his lack of support over the 'Jew-Baiting' incident.

[159] Masters' Files, J. W. Moir, 13 May 1942, Moir to Boissier; various informal and formal obituaries (unsorted) Feb. 1948; letter of Edgar Stogdon, 29 Feb. 1948.

[160] Masters' Files, H. J. L. Gorse, 2 Aug. 1937, Gorse to Vellacott.

[161] HM/Boss/16 Oct. 1940; Masters' Files, F. W. T. James, *passim*.

[162] Venables, *Bases Attempted*, 140, 183. Cf. Chapel rows with Vellacott above, p. 458.

touchlines and boundaries in support of her husband's house became legendary. As with most such hothouse feuds, reason or justification became irrelevant; the hostility providing its own rationale and momentum. Given his dry sense of humour, Vellacott may not have thought it inappropriate that in 1939 Harrow suffered an infestation of rats.[163]

After his brief experience at Harrow, Vellacott probably could hardly wait to return to Cambridge when he was elected Master of Peterhouse in the Summer of 1939, although, true to form, he offered to stay until a successor could be found.[164] By then he had begun to implement the economies necessary to stave off ruin, his calmness and clarity in drafting options for the governors and in explaining difficult decisions to masters, revealing the quality of his personality as well as intellect.[165] Inevitably, the nature of his task aroused hostility among some colleagues, especially, perhaps, because of his unchanging, apparently detached, imperturbable manner. If the quality of appointments is one gauge of a Head Master's ability, Vellacott can hardly be judged, as he released more than he engaged. However, of the eight permanent members of staff appointed, only two failed, although one of his last, temporary appointments turned out to be a thief and a con-man.[166] Vellacott's period of office was the shortest since Thomas Martin was sacked after only six months in 1669. Yet in the new house system, the creation of the Sixth Form Room, the manner in which he administered decline, managed the most acute crisis since 1844, and coped with fractious, intemperate colleagues, he provided a model of how the problems of a school could be tackled successfully by the power of intellect and reason.

To many, however, the victory at Lord's in 1939 would have counted for more. Inter-war Harrow was rich and slack; that latterly it was also materially failing as an institution seemed hardly to have impinged on the masters and almost not at all on the boys. In a manner strongly reminiscent of the old boys of Longley's time, Old Harrovians of the 1930s, when the school was sinking faster than they knew, became some of the most devoted and loyal. Any picture of Harrow of these years is incomplete without recognition of the fulfilment many boys found: academic, athletic, social, musical, and dramatic. Cecil Beaton practised his photography; he and Giles Playfair enjoyed themselves in elaborate house theatricals.[167] There were school plays as well as the theatrical interludes (still called 'Speeches') on Speech Day. These latter gave stage-struck Harrovians a chance to indulge their passion: in 1927 Terence Rattigan, apparently no actor, appeared as Olivia in *Twelfth Night*

---

[163] GBM, 13 June 1939.   [164] GBM, 18 July 1939.
[165] GBM, 26 Oct. 1938 for Vellacott's crisis memorandum; Masters' Files, F. A. Leaf, 31 Jan. 1939; HM/Boss/Circular Apr. 1939; above, pp. 430–2.
[166] HM/Moore/re guardian of A. E. G. Grey; GBM, 11 Feb. 1950; Bridgeman Diaries, 2 Oct. 1939; *Harrow Register, 1885–1949*, p. 687.
[167] Vickers, *Beaton*, 21, 25; Playfair, *My Father's Son*, 100–3.

'hardly within the sphere of practical politics with boy actors but Rattigan made a charming looking and dignified countess'.[168] The homogenity of boy culture was on display six years later in the school Dramatic Society's production of John Drinkwater's *Abraham Lincoln*. The lead was taken by Dorian Williams, later a BBC commentator on equestrian events; other roles were played by Michael Denison, the future professional actor; John Profumo, appropriately for a future minister portraying one of Lincoln's Cabinet; and Charles Laborde, the Captain of the the Rugby XV, a fine mix of the aesthetes, the ambitious, and the athletic.[169] Elsewhere, there were concerts as well as cricket. Enjoyment was as possible as ennui or unhappiness. In the Summer Term of 1931, Norwood gave permission for a group of boys to make a Chaplin-Keatonesque film. Shooting culminated one morning before First School in a mass chase down the High Street by more or less the whole school, to the fury of one housemaster's daughter whose sleep was disturbed.[170] The absurdities and iniquities of adults rarely violated the general tenor of schoolboys' lives: they rather expected such things. Most published memoirs recall Harrow as a place of incident, usually unpleasant, or boredom (cold baths, dull teaching, narrow-minded boys, etc.). Perhaps an equally accurate image of Harrow between the wars can be exhumed from *Young Colt's Diary*, 'edited' by C. H. Terrot (Elmfield 1929–33). The hero 'John Colt' is a breezy philistine, greatly enamoured of the school, its games, the Corps, and the 'jolly chaps' he knows. 'Colt' 'is not spotty and his time is so well filled that he has none to waste upon those tiresome habits . . . "repressions" or "inhibitions". He is just a healthy young Englishman of seventeen, as good looking as his lovely sister Heather'.[171]

CRISIS SURVIVED, 1939–1953

In congratulating R. W. Moore on his appointment as Head Master of Harrow in June 1942, the Head Master of Cheltenham, former Harrow master A. G. Elliott-Smith, commented that 'Harrow has had terribly bad luck for some time now'.[172] This was an understatement. The deepening financial crisis of the late 1930s, the collapse in numbers, changing Head Masters, austerities of war and fratricidal strife among the staff had combined to bring Harrow near to destruction even without the aid of the Luftwaffe.

Vellacott announced his departure in July 1939; he would leave Harrow at Christmas. By the time the appointing committee met for the first time in mid-September the Second World War had begun and it had become apparent that the

---

[168] According to *The Harrovian*'s account of Speech Day 1927; C. Tyerman, 'Harrow Drama', *Inauguration of the Harrow School Theatre* (Harrow, Dec. 1994).
[169] *The Harrovian* review of the play, 22–4 Feb. 1933.   [170] See above, nn. 60 and 103.
[171] C. Terrot (ed.), *Young Colt's Diary* (London, 1936), p. 7.
[172] Masters' Files, P. H. M. Bryant, 19 June 1942, Elliott-Smith to R. W. Moore.

decision to stay on the Hill made in May 1939 and the economies agreed the previous January would fail to restore the school's finances or numbers.[173] Just thirty-four new boys arrived in September 1939, the lowest autumn intake since 1845; the roll of boys actually present, as opposed to registered, stood at 423 compared to 516 the term before. The figures on which the governors had based their calculation to stay at Harrow assumed numbers of over 450. In October further drastic cuts were fixed for 1940. Newlands was to follow West Acre into closure, with another house likely to follow; the chaplain, Woolley, was encouraged to retire; the salaries of housemasters under the new scheme were to be reduced by 12.5 per cent; other masters' by between 5 per cent and 10 per cent. Further dismissals were not ruled out.[174] In these circumstances it was hardly surprising that the governors encountered difficulties in finding a new Head. Not only had the war effort diverted possible candidates, the job itself could not provide guaranteed tenure as the governors recognized the renewed prospect of closure.

With time running out, the governors opted for a temporary solution. They elected the senior housemaster A. P. Boissier for a fixed period from 1 January 1940 until the end of the Summer Term 1942.[175] The terms of Boissier's appointment were later wrapped in distortion, many after the war claiming he had only been an acting Head. In fact he received all the powers his predecessors had enjoyed, his subsequent demotion in Harrow legend a consequence of surviving friends of Venables on the staff and the unfortunate events of his tenure. He was even denied the customary portrait until over twenty years after his death.[176] However, in late 1939, his appointment had much to commend it to hard-pressed governors. He was retiring in 1942 anyway. In two years, the effect of the war and Harrow's own financial propects would, they hoped, have become clearer. Boissier was a known quantity. His election saved money, effectively a third of his Head Master's salary. The other senior masters were either older, less experienced as administrators or, like Venables, unsound.

Boissier, a mathematician by training, had spent most of his Harrow career since arriving in 1919 in administrative posts. Housemaster at the Head Master's from 1925 and at Moretons from 1929, he had managed the school stores and tuck shop in the 1920s. He was well connected, having taught King George VI at the Royal Naval College, Osborne before the First World War. He and his wife had established a circle of loyalty around themselves and in Moretons. Since the early 1920s Boissier, a member of OUDS when up at Balliol, had, with colleagues such as Coade and Elliott-Smith, vigorously maintained Harrow's acting traditions, performing as well as directing numerous plays and operettas involving boys, masters,

---

[173] GBM, 10 May, 18 and 31 July 1939.
[174] GBM, 25 Oct. 1939; *Harrow Register, 1885–1949*, pp. 618–20; *Harrow Register, 1800–1911*, pp. 186–8.
[175] GBM, 15 Nov. 1939.   [176] GBM, 13 Mar. 1976.

and masters' families, broadening his contact with the school and raising his profile with a wide cross-section of the Harrow community.[177] The showman surfaced when he entertained Churchill to Songs, a tradition that began in the autumn of 1940 as a government publicity stunt but which soon acquired the status of a significant annual corporate ritual that continued, in reaffirmation of Harrow's special self-importance, long after the Prime Minister's loss of office and death.[178]

However, the governors were taking a serious risk. Boissier had revealed himself something of a buccaneer as a housemaster. In 1931 he was reprimanded for cramming sixty-three boys into his house when his quota was fifty-five.[179] It was rumoured by his enemies that he manipulated the rationing system so that, by using his boys' entitlement, his table was always well stocked. There was about Boissier more than a whiff of two of his 1920s acting roles, Bottom and Falstaff, but tempered by a reserve that touched neurosis.[180] In 1931 he had suffered a serious nervous breakdown which it was claimed had left him a severe agoraphobe with an 'invincible unwillingness to appear in public'.[181] As Head Master he felt unable to hold Masters' Meetings and conducted often delicate personal and professional business solely by letter. Highly sensitive to criticism but not the feelings of others, Boissier displayed an unfortunate streak of vindictiveness. This appeared damagingly in his selection of the three masters to be dismissed in 1942. To contemporary observers his choice did not look coincidental: his old enemy Venables, justified on the possibly specious grounds of his nearness to retirement; Venable's son-in-law, Bostock, still only in his mid-forties who, apart from his family allegiance, had clashed with Boissier over the closure of Rendalls; and F. W. T. James, the semi-invalid 'pig-headed' former housemaster of Newlands, also in his forties, who in 1941 had made the mistake of accusing Boissier of being dictatorial and lacking 'common humanity'.[182] When he was leaving the Head Mastership in August 1942, Boissier could not resist sending his successor gratuitously hostile portraits of two of Venables' strongest supporters, describing Leonard Henry of The Grove as 'underhand, spiteful and without influence in his house' and Lance Gorse as having 'altered completely' since taking Holy Orders, his judgement now being 'biased and ... unsound'.[183] Presumably unknown to Boissier, Moore had already seen Henry and Gorse together for a private meeting at the Connaught Hotel a fortnight before receiving his predecessor's diatribe.[184]

---

[177] *The Harrovian*, 14 Oct. 1953, pp. 7–8; 'Tempest in the Making', *Harrow 1938* (boys' magazine published at Harrow), pp. 16–17, including photograph; *Harrow Register*, etc.

[178] HA Churchill File, *passim*.   [179] GBM, 18 Feb. 1931.

[180] He had played Bottom in 1921 and Falstaff, in *The Merry Wives of Windsor*, in 1924.

[181] GBM, 18 Nov. 1931; *The Harrovian*, 14 Oct. 1953, pp. 7–8.

[182] See their relevant Masters' Files and below; for James, HM/Boss/16 Oct. 1940 for Ledward's comment; Masters' Files, F. W. T. James, 9 July 1941, James to Boissier; 11 July 1941, Boissier to James, making his resentment very clear.   [183] HM/Boss/7 Aug. 1942.

[184] Oddly the evidence is in Masters' File, P. H. M. Bryant, 21 June 1942, Leonard Henry to Moore.

To Boissier's sclerotic managerial style and his personal antipathies was added a clear perception of his own self-interest. A condition of his Headship was the closure of Moretons in 1940. Once in post, he persuaded the governors to change their mind. From the Summer of 1940, he continued as Head Master and as housemaster of Moretons, although the governors insisted he came under the new house system, Boissier receiving an additional £500 a year on relinquishing the boarding profits.[185] Instead of Moretons, Newlands closed in July 1940, depriving James of income, to be followed in December 1941 by Bostock's Rendalls and in the Summer of 1942 by Bradbys, although Bowlby, its housemaster, was more generously treated by being transferred to Moretons on Boissier's departure.[186] It appeared that Boissier was happy to sacrifice others to the crisis while safeguarding his own. Having successfully improved one part of his contract by remaining a housemaster, in late in 1941 he offered to stay on as Head Master after the following Summer on a term-by-term basis. This time the offer was politely but firmly declined as it had become clear that Boissier provided no hope for the future.[187] This was not to underestimate Boissier's work in grappling with the governors' suggestions for economies; his public calmness in the face of increasing difficulties and his cheerfulness when sharing the dangers of wartime Harrow. Nevertheless, abetted by some purblind colleagues, Boissier persisted in fighting the battles of the 1930s, his Head Mastership forming an appendage to his predecessors' in ways the governors had not envisaged. Even in extraordinary times, Boissier displayed all the disadvantages of the successful internal candidate. With German bombs nightly threatening the physical survival of the school and its inmates, with the financial prospects bleaker than for a century, with governors openly admitting the possibility of imminent closure, Boissier and some of his assistants could not shake off their past bickering, content to play out with almost ritualistic thoroughness the petty rivalries with which they had become so comfortably familiar.

The difficulties generated by Boissier and his masters paled beside the threat to the school's existence that persisted almost throughout his tenure. In January 1940 the governors had presented a projection of the funds required to maintain the school until 1943 based on a school of 400 pupils.[188] By early 1941 numbers were down to just over 300. Rendalls, whose capacity was over fifty, accommodated fewer than thirty; by the autumn of 1941 this had shrunk to just nineteen before the governors decided to close the house.[189] 1942 saw the school with fewer than 300 pupils for almost the whole year. It is hard not to sympathize with the governors' dismissive exasperation at a request put to them in March 1940 by the aged but

---

[185] GBM, 11 June 1940.
[186] HM/Boss/no date, draft circular re Bradbys and Bowlby; GBM, 11 Feb. 1942.
[187] HM/Boss/2 Dec. 1941, Pember to Boissier; GBM, 17 Dec. 1941, 11 Feb. 1942.
[188] GBM, 13 Mar. 1940; see above pp. 430–2.
[189] Masters' Files, J. Bostock, 21 Oct. 1940, Bostock to Boissier; GBM, 12 Nov. 1941; HM/Boss/13 Nov. 1941, Pember to Boissier.

indefatigable H. A. Vachell that he be allowed to use the school premises and pupils in a film he hoped to make of *The Hill*.[190] Even before the bombs fell and the flow of pupils almost dried, Harrow was facing collapse. Most of the younger staff were away at the war, although some of their replacements, such as Mrs P. H. F. White, who taught her husband's biology timetable, were more than adequate replacements, Betty White's expertise being recognized by her employment as the first full-time woman teacher at Harrow in extension of the Great War precedent, one not followed again until the 1990s.[191] More immediate danger was presented by air-raids and the consequences of staying on the Hill. It was said that Boissier, reputedly the only Head Master in the country personally acquainted with both Prime Minister and monarch, played an important role in preventing Harrow's evacuation.[192] He certainly eased the arrival of Malvern at the end of his Headship, the move that, through the rent payable on the houses occupied and facilities used, saved the school. Ironically, Harrow's near dissolution had provided this opportunity for survival, its emptiness allowing the space for Malvern to live, work, worship, and play.

By then, the search for a permanent new Head Master was almost complete. The last months of Boissier's term present a bizarre picture of bitter feuding and division among a small but vociferous group of masters. The closure of Rendalls, Boissier's style of leadership, and the required dismissals of masters formed a noisy coda to the simmering divisions of the previous decade. In November 1941 Bostock, who, despite finally being admitted to the new housemasters' scheme earlier in the year, had found he could neither make Rendalls pay nor match others in attracting pupils, was given a month's notice that his house was to close.[193] Boissier's letter, unusually beginning with the recipient's forename, 'Dear John', was drafted on 19 November, but only sent on 24 November. The failure of Boissier to arrange an interview and the tone of the letter ensured trouble. The whole affair proceeded through hostile letters passing between Moretons and Rendalls, sometimes at the rate of two or three a day. Crucial notes from both sides were mislaid. Bostock's requests to redraft the circular to be sent to parents and to appeal to the chairman of the GPC, Pickard-Cambridge, were refused. Leonard Henry acted as Bostock's mediator, but at no time did the protagonists meet nor even speak on the telephone. No sharper contrast could be found between the acrimonious mismanagement of the Rendalls closure and the cooperative manner in which Vellacott and F. A. Leaf had closed West Acre two years earlier. Bostock was less emollient than

---

[190] GBM, 13 Mar. 1940.
[191] Masters' [*sic*] File, Mrs Betty White, *passim* for correspondence with Boissier over terms.
[192] In press cuttings in 1942 and his obituary in *The Harrovian*, 14 Oct. 1953.
[193] GBM, 19 Feb., 12 Nov. 1941. For the details of the closure of Rendalls and the correspondence between Bostock, Boissier, Pember, and Pickard-Cambridge: HM/Boss/13 Nov., 17 Nov., 19 Nov., 21 Nov., 24 Nov., 27 Nov. (two), 29 Nov. (two), 30 Nov., 1 Dec. (three), 4 Dec. 1941.

Leaf. An Old Harrovian and mathematician, service in the Great War had left him without any sort of university degree, adding to a sense of insecurity. It was likely no other school would employ him.

Despite there being only nineteen boys in Rendalls, Boissier met strong resistance from the parents. The governors' hopes that the boys be transferred to Druries were largely frustrated. Of the nineteen, five left, seven went to Bostock's father-in-law at The Park, three to Henry at The Grove, and two each to the Head Master's and Druries.[194] The circular sent to parents expressed the belief that membership of the school was more important than belonging to a particular house. One old Rendallian parent was unimpressed: 'I heartily disagree with your views that a change of house is a matter of secondary importance, it may be to you and the Governors, but the unfortunate victim finds himself a social outcast and naturally the new House Master is not particularly pleased at being landed with someone not of his own choosing.'[195] There spoke the authentic voice of federal Harrow. The upset was emotional as much as practical. For Bostock it was more serious. He was allowed to stay in the private side of Rendalls until Easter 1942, but was given no guarantee of housing thereafter. More threatening was the decision, taken on 17 December in the midst of the Rendalls row, that up to five masters were to be dropped by September 1942.[196]

If the closure of Rendalls had been mismanaged, it raised only temporary political issues. The removal of three established masters the following term created an open constitutional conflict that Boissier could not hide from the governors who, as often when faced with challenges to the Head Master's authority, displayed some sympathy with his opponents while formally lending him support. On 11 February 1942 the governors agreed to Boissier's proposals for the 'compulsory retirement' of Venables and the dismissal of Bostock and James.[197] Over the following weeks responsibility for choosing these victims was freely passed between the Head Master and the governing body, Boissier claiming he was merely doing his masters' bidding, while the governors made it clear that the policy was theirs but its implementation belonged to the Head. Venables recalled his experience with justified bitterness:

A master may be told that . . . his work is to be terminated, on the ground that the governors have found it necessary to make certain alterations in policy. He asks for an explanation from the Head Master, who tells him that the decision was not his, but that of the Governing Body. He then asks one of the Governors to see him, and is told that the decision was the Head Master's, and they cannot gainsay it . . . A great Head Master would never allow such things to happen, but personal power is a searching test of character.[198]

---

[194] HM/Boss/11 Dec. 1941.
[195] HM/Boss/Circular to Rendalls parents, Nov. 1941, 1 Dec. 1941, W. G. Mutter to Boissier.
[196] GBM, 17 Dec. 1941.   [197] GBM, 11 Feb. 1942.   [198] Venables, *Bases Attempted*, 173.

Protests came from all sides. On 7 March three masters, Henry, Gorse, and Plumptre, wrote to the Master's governor, Leo Amery, asking that the sacking of Venables be reconsidered. There had been no public explanation to the masters.

> There may be differences of opinion about the absolute merits of this decision, but the immediate reactions to it among boys and Parents and Old Harrovians seem to suggest that the method by which the matter has been handled here in Harrow is open to grave objection . . . Venables . . . with all his faults here has done, and is doing, so much for Harrow . . . his name carries considerable weight with Headmasters of many Preparatory Schools.[199]

Amery, then Secretary of State for India in the middle of a war, presented the letter to the governors at a meeting on 10 March. Meanwhile, it seems that Henry and Gorse had made private representations to Gerald Rivington, an increasingly influential new governor.[200] At the same time, governors had received letters of protest from prep. school heads, other masters, and even school monitors. Sir George Campbell, father of a monitor in The Park, demanded the governors receive a deputation representing 'a body of parents of boys at the Park and Rendalls', the addition of Bostock's house signalling that their attack was on Boissier's general conduct as much as the specific dismissals. Old boys were drawn in, Venables even receiving a letter of support from the octogenarian M. C. Kemp.[201] On 18 March the governors met Campbell's delegation which demanded an inquiry into Boissier's decisions. This the governors, after weeks of further consultations, refused. However, on 8 April their position over an inquiry still unresolved and with no successor chosen, they confirmed in an announcement to be given to the Press, that Boissier would be leaving at the same time as the dismissed masters, at the end of the Summer Term, as planned. They were keen to draw a line under the messy affair.[202]

Few of the participants emerge with much credit. Venables was only two years from retirement and would receive financial compensation; he had behaved outrageously for years and was not the only senior master to leave early during the war: Carrington did so in 1939, W. J. R. Calvert in 1940, and C. L. Bryant in 1941. Apparently, not all the boys in his house supported him, although this may have been a malicious rumour spread by Boissier.[203] James had proved increasingly difficult and irascible ever since Newlands closed. Bostock persisted in denying the precariousness of his position and, after his dismissal, displayed mulish obstinacy. Having moved into Flambards, a school house on the High Street between Moretons and The Park, he refused to leave after the end of the Summer Term,

---

[199] HM/Boss/8Mar. 1942; Gorse rather characteristically sent a copy of the letter to Amery to Boissier; he was keen to follow the proprieties and not be thought devious in any way.
[200] GBM, 10 Mar. 1942; HM/Boss/11 Mar. 1942, copy of Amery's subsequent reply to Henry.
[201] Venables, *Bases Attempted*, 15.   [202] GBM, 18 Mar., 8, 22 Apr. 1942.
[203] HM/Boss/7 Aug. 1942, Boissier to Moore.

clinging on for almost a year despite efforts to evict him.[204] Yet he may have had a genuine grievance. His teaching services were far from redundant. The school was not full of mathematicians: in 1943, to meet the shortage Bostock's dismissal had caused, the distinguished veteran A. W. Siddons, who had retired as senior master in 1936, was recalled to the staff for three years, finally retiring in 1946, aged 70, forty-seven years after he first began at Harrow, the last of the Victorian schoolmasters.[205] The governors scarcely covered themselves in glory, especially Amery who, in Venables' phrase, behaved as 'the Balaam of the Governing Body', in danger of appearing all things to all men.[206] But they were placed in an awkward position by Boissier and there was a war on.

Boissier's conduct was unfortunate. His failure to explain matters fuelled suspicion of his motives. These cannot be seen to have been entirely beyond reproach. However, faced with the need to reduce the teaching staff to save money, three senior figures had to go. Each of those chosen had proved difficult colleagues, arguably putting their own interests above those of the school. Easy alternatives did not exist, although Boissier admitted he had toyed with sacking Henry, who was to leave a couple of years later in any case.[207] Dismissing any of Leaf, Laborde, Browne of Elmfield, Housden of the Corps, or Baldwin of The Knoll would have proved just as unpopular. Vellacott might have dispensed with Bowlby's services, but Boissier seemed to admire his fellow Balliol man. As damaging as the choices made was Boissier's inability or refusal to discuss them. Whatever the justice of his case, his behaviour made a difficult situation worse. In his last year, July 1941 to July 1942, only seventy names had been registered for Harrow;[208] school numbers had settled below 300; almost half the school buildings were leased to Malvern College. The school's reputation was dangerously low. It was time for a fresh start.

Ralph Westwood Moore proved an inspired choice to succeed Boissier. Only 36, he had followed his Oxford Firsts in Mods and Greats with a meteoric teaching career. After seven years as Sixth Form Classics Master at Shrewsbury, he was appointed Head Master of Bristol Grammar School in 1938. The author of a *Greek and Latin Comparative Syntax*, he also wrote Christian devotional works and published poetry.[209] A deeply religious, scrupulously honest, and just man, Moore's character as much as his attainments suited Harrow's needs. In contrast to many Heads, Moore, educated at Wolverhampton Grammar School, affected no social airs. In the hard years of post-war austerity, he continued to throw the grand dinner parties expected of the Head Master of Harrow, even though he and his wife did not employ servants. When the grandees and acolytes had departed, they would

---

[204] GBM, 19 Aug., 4 Nov. 1942, 5 May 1943.
[205] *Harrow Register, 1971*, 701.   [206] Venables, *Bases Attempted*, 173.
[207] HM/Boss/7 Aug. 1942, Boissier to Moore.   [208] GBM, 4 Nov. 1942.
[209] In general, see his obituaries in HM/Moore, unsorted, Jan. 1953; *The Harrovian*, 28 Jan. 1953, pp. 47–52.

settle down to do the washing up themselves. When a friend expressed concern, Moore explained this was not simply a measure of perhaps excessive economy; he liked restoring order. In the school as in the kitchen, that is precisely what he did.

His appointment had been neither swift nor easy. The governors' search had begun before the end of 1941 when it was also decided that the new Head would continue to act as housemaster of the Head Master's. A strong academic selection committee was established in February 1942 comprising Pember, Butler, Pickard-Cambridge, and Rivington.[210] One difficulty they encountered was the restricted field available because of the war. Another was the perception of Harrow as a decayed snakepit. Walter Hamilton, master in college at Eton, future Head Master of Westminster and Rugby, and Master of Magdalene College, Cambridge, was told by one adviser, James Duff: 'I've always disliked Harrow so much that my opinion is prejudiced. But I think you would find Harrow parents, Harrow staff and Old Harrovians equally detestable; and what you as headmaster could do for the boys under those conditions I hardly see.'[211] The press announcement on 8 April followed an interim report by the committee and was in part designed to advertise their search. Further inconclusive reports followed over the next two months until, without formal interview, Moore was elected on 9 June. He had not applied, insisting that 'the appointment was none of my seeking'.[212] The governors had gone for an obviously rising star, a first-class classicist with experience of teaching and administration as a Head Master. Although Moore suffered from the social condescension of some of the older members of the Harrow staff, his lack of cradle nurturing in the public school ethos, as well as his acquaintance with two other HMC boarding schools (Rossall and Shrewsbury), afforded him an objectivity to assess the value of each part of the Harrow system without prejudice. His grammar school background suited the immediate post-war world where the talk was of integration and social cohesion, not segregation by snobbish elitism.

Figures alone chart Moore's achievement. He doubled the size of the school. Registrations in his first year, despite the war and continued bombing, rose from seventy to 192; in 1943–4 they leapt to 369.[213] From the low point of 292 at the beginning of 1943, numbers in the school rose steadily then rapidly: 350 in 1944; 400 in 1945; 500 in 1947–8; 550 in 1952. In Moore's first term as Head Master, the roll stood at 298; in his last, ten years later, it was 566, the highest since 1937, an increase of 90 per cent.[214] Harrow's rise mirrored increased demand across all public schools, yet Moore was adept at attracting new parents as much as Old Harrovians. Young, interested, persuasive, if a little prim, Moore worked hard to portray

[210] GBM, 12 Nov., 17 Dec. 1941; 11 Feb. 1942.
[211] Quoted during a later contest for the Head Mastership by N. R. Bomford, *The Harrovian*, 6 June 1998, p. 198.
[212] GBM, 8, 22 Apr., 9 June 1942; Masters' Files, P. H. M. Bryant, 18 June 1942, Moore to A. G. Elliott-Smith.   [213] GBM, 3 Nov. 1943, 1 Nov. 1944.
[214] Figures from the Head Master's termly report of numbers, GBM, *passim*, and *Harrow Register*.

Harrow as a school of diversity and excellence. While eager to maintain its sporting character, Moore's determination to revive the school's intellectual and cultural life was reflected in his immediate post-war appointments.

Moore was the Vaughan of the twentieth century. Presented with the requirement to restock the school with masters as well as boys, he had the opportunity to recreate Harrow in his own image. His task was aided by the availability of large numbers of recently demobilized members of the armed forces in search of work, men whom war had supplied with accelerated maturity and breadth of experience. Between 1944 and 1947 seventeen new appointments were made across the curriculum.[215] Although Dr James reaped the benefits, much of Harrow's success in the 1950s and 1960s relied on the men hired by Moore. To reassure the sporting lobby, he engaged cricketers such as J. Webster (1946–81) and M. Tindall (1946–76) and rugger players such as A. L. Warr (1946–75) and C. D. Laborde (1946–77), both Tindall and Laborde being usefully Old Harrovian. To replace Henry in 1944 to teach history, Moore attracted the experienced and worldly C. A. Lillingston from St Paul's (1944–68). First-class academic masters included the classicist M. S. Warman (1946–79), the mathematician J. B. Morgan (1946–71) and the modern linguist C. L. Walton (1947–82). The new Director of Music, H. J. McCurrach (1946–67) had been an assistant at Harrow 1938–41 and so knew the peculiar balance of refinement and philistinism demanded. M. M. Perceval, a talented minor artist himself, was poached from Malvern (1945–54) as Director of Art. Moore, believing that there remained a county constituency, fostered the school farm in peacetime as in war, appointing the Irishman, S. G. Patterson (1944–82) as its Director. He was later housemaster of The Grove and an excellent Bursar (1976–80). It says much for Moore's skill in recruitment that most of those he engaged spent the rest of their teaching careers at Harrow: seventeen or 70 per cent of his first twenty-four appointments made between 1944 and 1952 stayed until retirement. Moore saved the wartime school through his own efforts; in his choice of masters, he fashioned post-war Harrow for a generation.

Proof of Moore's success was provided by the Report of the School Inspectors in 1951. Not only was the education provided warmly praised, a number of individual masters such as Plumptre, Harris, and Morgan being especially commended, the staff as a whole drew the comment 'at least a quarter of them make outstanding contributions in the class-room'.[216] The Inspectors, showing an enthusiasm not matched by similar twentieth-century Reports, paid 'a very high tribute to the work done by the Head Master, the qualities that had enabled him to do it and the further benefits which they believed the school would get from him in the future'.[217] Moore played a full part in the school, to a degree unusual if not unique

---

[215] *Harrow Register, 1986*, pp. 808–12, 825.
[216] *Report by His Majesty's Inspectors on Harrow School, Middlesex, May 1951* (Ministry of Education, London, 1951), p. 8.   [217] GBM, 6 June 1951; *Report of Inspectors, 1951*, 8.

since the nineteenth century. Neither his nature nor the pressures of his job required he become a managerial administrator, although financial difficulties forced him to act briefly as his own secretary in 1948.[218] His energy was Butleresque. He taught divinity and English in the Sixth Form; acted as form master to the Classical Lower Sixth as well as sharing the teaching of Greek and Latin verse to the Classical Upper Sixth. Twice a week he read Homer in the evening with the Sixth Form. A poet himself, a volume of whose verse appeared while he was Head Master, *Trophy For an Unknown Soldier* (1952), he ran a Poetry Society. He used to attend and speak from the floor at school debates. He made himself available for routine consultations every day after lunch and after evening prayers. He customarily visited concert practices and rehearsals of the annual Shakespeare play.[219] Shakespeare had been performed regularly at Harrow since George Townsend Warner's pre-1914 productions on an unadorned Speech Room stage. Coade and Boissier continued the tradition with more lavish settings in the 1920s and 1930s. However, the custom of annually presenting a Shakespeare play in Speech Room on a stage and in costumes that recreated conditions recalling the playwright's own time, complete with constant light, thrust stage, and no scenery beyond a permanent backdrop of a tiring house, was a legacy from Boissier's time, one of the most unexpected but robust children of the wartime crisis. Begun in 1941, the plays were directed by the indefatigable bardolator A. R. D. Watkins in a style derived from the ideas of Dover Wilson on a stage imagined by the American Cranford Adams. Moore was an enthusiast for this tradition, prompting Watkins in 1944 to propose the school construct a replica of the original Globe Theatre in Harrow Park.[220]

There were few aspects of school life that Moore ignored. He unsuccessfully tried to persuade the governors to endow music entrance scholarships in 1947: it was one of the few criticisms voiced by the Inspectors in 1951 that the school's endowment of entrance scholarships was inadequate.[221] He oversaw the establishment of a Motor Driving Club to allow Harrovians to learn to drive.[222] He both played and watched games and, despite his concentration on cerebral matters, did not neglect sporting interests. To prevent the master in charge of cricket being seduced away by another school, additional money was found for him, even though his use as an academic beak was strictly limited.[223] More generally, there was encouragement for an exchange scheme with Princeton University.[224] Typically, Moore introduced the custom of Head Master's termly reports on every

---

[218] GBM, 8 May 1948; Vellacott had done the same.
[219] *The Harrovian*, 28 Jan. 1953, pp. 47–52; Minutes of Housemasters' Meetings 1949–67, 9 Dec. 1949.   [220] HM/Moore/8 Sept. 1944, Watkins to Moore.
[221] GBM, 15 Sept. 1947; *Report of Inspectors, 1951*, 29.
[222] GBM, 5 Mar. 1947: odd timing given the continuance of one of the worst winters of the century.
[223] GBM, 10 Nov. 1951.   [224] GBM, 12 Nov. 1949.

boy in the school, one that persisted until the 1980s when numbers rendered such termly reports prohibitively laborious. Not afraid to admit to shortcomings, Moore responded to the Inspector's recommendation of the need for a young specialist historian to teach in the Upper School by appointing R. W. Ellis (1952–67), a future Head Master of Rossall and Master of Marlborough.[225] Tradition was flouted by the experiment of voluntary Chapel. Obsessed with calligraphy, with an elegant, precise handwriting of his own, he imposed writing tests for new boys.[226]

Not everything Moore touched turned to gold. The Inspectors' criticisms of undue and premature specialization, the casual way A Level subjects were chosen by boys, and the lack of an effective English Sixth Form stayed largely unanswered. In 1952 it was admitted that there would be no science for most boys in the first year.[227] The renewed financial crisis of 1947–8 proved impervious to increasing numbers, a new round of austerity economies becoming necessary, with cuts of £10,000 a year sought in 1948–9, leading to a slight reduction in total academic staff. This was partly justified by a comparison with teaching ratios at other schools: Harrow's stood at one master to 11.95 boys; Winchester had 1:11.8 and Shrewsbury 1:11.25, but Repton's was 1:12.0, Rugby 1:12.6, Charterhouse 1:12.8, and Eton 1:12.87.[228] The behaviour of boys, judged by Moore's entries in his Punishment Book, appeared obstinately the same as their predecessors', his own approach to discipline similarly old-fashioned. Yet, as the 1950s began, Moore, backed by a staff of diversity, maturity, and some talent, still only in his mid-forties, must have viewed the immediate future with eager confidence. Like his nineteenth-century forerunners, Moore seemed at ease with the modern world.

One demonstration of this was his support for a visit by the Mass Radiography Unit in November 1951.[229] A caravan housing the X-ray equipment was parked in the High Street. To demonstrate his faith in the procedure, Moore led the way. When the plates were scrutinized, of all the hundreds taken, one showed a shadow on the lung. It was Moore's. He had cancer. An immediate operation was followed by convalescence and a return to the school for the Summer Term of 1952, the senior master Housden acting as Head in Moore's absence. The remission was brief. By the autumn, Moore was once again incapacitated, his duties devolving onto the new senior master, the stentorian and confident Baldwin. By the New Year, as it was obvious Moore would not recover, the governors decided, on 7 January, to place a notice in *The Times* and *Daily Telegraph*: 'The Governors of Harrow School regret to announce that owing to prolonged illness Dr R. W. Moore is unable to continue as Head Master of the School. Dr Moore is at Harrow and is seriously ill.'

---

[225] *Report of Inspectors, 1951*, 14.
[226] Minutes of Housemasters' Meetings 1949–67, 15 May 1950.
[227] *Report of Inspectors, 1951*, pp. 8, 13; Minutes of Housemasters' Meetings 1949–67, 7 July 1952.
[228] GBM, 6 Oct. 1948; 5 Feb. 1949.
[229] Minutes of Housemasters' Meetings 1949–67, 5 Nov. 1951.

A committee was established to find a successor. They needed to ensure any interregnum was as brief as possible.[230]

The last time the governors had felt compelled to retire a Head Master on his deathbed had been with the dying William Horne in 1685. Like Horne, Moore did not long survive the announcement of his retirement. He died suddenly on 10 January, two days after the governors' notice appeared. Astonishingly, but in keeping with the quite common practice of the day, Moore had not been told his illness was mortal; to the end he thought, or led others to believe he thought, that he would recover and return to work.[231]

R. L. James and 'a Confident Conservatism', 1953–1971[232]

The Head Mastership of Robert Leoline James, the longest of the twentieth century, was a triumph of accommodating conservatism. Fortunate to coincide with the economic revival of the 1950s and 1960s, by steadfast refusal to chase fashion or notoriety James 'guided Harrow from the old pattern towards the new without excessive travail or publicity'.[233] He gave the impression that the school he left in 1971 was much the same as it had been when he arrived eighteen years earlier. This was not true but he persuaded many that it was. If success is measured by the achievement of desired ends, James was the most successful Head Master of the century. Finding a school still establishing its direction and identity after the war, physically run down and nearly bankrupt, he left it full, solvent, well-furnished, and academically respected, its Oxbridge results better than Winchester's. Old Harrovians had been convinced into parting with their money as never before and in sending their sons to Harrow in unprecedented numbers. The range of prep. schools sending pupils to Harrow was greatly expanded, in type and region. The masters' habitual gossip and intrigue never spilt over into fratricide or rebellion. To a degree not matched since Welldon or Vaughan, James controlled Harrow without apparent effort. Unobtrusive, dapper in a seemingly never-ending supply of grey, sub-fusc three-piece suits, he quietly dominated the place. The internal success of his regime paid high dividends in refurbishing Harrow's image as one of the great public schools, an eminence recognized by the 861 diners at the Quarter-centenary dinner held during his last year at London's Guildhall, reputedly the largest ever served in the City.[234]

Not the least tribute to Ralph Moore was James' decision to swap the High Mastership of St Paul's for Harrow. James was Moore's exact Oxford contemporary,

---

[230] GBM, 9 Feb., 8 Nov., 10 Dec. 1952; 7 Jan. 1953; *The Times*, 9 Jan. 1953.
[231] *The Harrovian*, 28 Jan. 1953; cf. *The Times*, 12 Jan. 1953.
[232] The phrase is that of R. W. Ellis, *Harrow Association Record* (1982), p. 13.
[233] *The Harrovian*, 27 Nov. 1971, p. 38.   [234] GBM, 20 March 1971.

appearing with him only a few places apart in the list of Firsts in Mods. in 1926 and Greats in 1928. In some senses, he completed his predecessor's term, working with his masters and within his established system. It suited James' character not to be a reformer; it was his good fortune that he did not have to be. Only with the chapel did his policy demand change, but to a previous, uncontroversial state.[235] One of his closest associates observed that James 'gave little or no time to educational theory, and not a great deal to the curriculum'.[236] There was no need, especially as he desired to play no part in the modish debates over the future of public schools and the nature of secondary education. He disposed of Moore's legacy with skill. Surprisingly for such a long tenure, most of the dominant figures throughout had been appointed by his predecessors. Only from the mid-1960s did men he engaged rise to headships of departments in any numbers; none of his appointments became a full housemaster during his time. James was not a builder of institutions, parties, or bricks and mortar. He was a manager and a manipulator, a chairman rather than a chief executive, secure enough in his own convictions to delegate rather than interfere, to lead by precept not, like Moore, by example.

James was a Welshman, not the only schoolmaster in his family. Educated at Rossall, then Jesus College, Oxford, the Welshmen's college, James was sufficiently an outsider to understand the weaknesses and revere the strengths of the Establishment. Not that he was in any sense alienated from it. A freemason, he was comfortable in the world of insiders and deals struck behind the arras. Yet, when younger, he had displayed a certain effortful seriousness. A First Class classicist like all but two (Vellacott, with his History First, and Boissier) of his ten immediate predecessors, James was the first, and to date only, Head Master to have gained an academic doctorate by his own work. The doctorates borne by previous Head Masters since the eighteenth century, including Norwood's and Moore's D.Litt.s from Bristol, had come to them with the rations, as it were, bestowed for worldly success not intellectual achievement. Oddly, James's doctorate, awarded in 1938, attracted the disdain of some academic Harrow masters, including younger ones, possessed of neither his undergraduate Firsts nor higher degrees of their own, who sneered at the fact it came from the University of London. University snobbery, which, in a characteristic chameleon display of acculturation, James himself publicly affected,[237] was no less a bane of schools like Harrow than social snobbery, the two often marching arm in arm on the shady side of the street.

The election of Dr James in 1953 appeared to be without undue strain. The committee appointed in January, like that of 1942, including Butler and Rivington,

---

[235] Above pp. 459–60.
[236] Ellis, *Harrow Association Record* (1982), 12. Cf. Rae, *Public School Revolution*, 115 *et seq.*
[237] HM/James/4 Sept. 1968. James knew his audience. Only with the serious academic scholars among his appointees did he discuss his thesis: he understood the world in which he chose to succeed better than many of those more obviously born into it.

decided to approach James, who, in traditional Establishment style had not actually applied for the post, his acceptance being secured by 5 March.[238] It appeared an oustanding academic appointment. James had taught classics in the Sixth Form at St Paul's from 1928 to 1939 before becoming Head Master of Chigwell School, followed by his return to head St Paul's in 1946. It is testament to Harrow's governors' old-fashioned belief in Victorian principles that one of the basic criteria for appointment as Head remained until the 1980s a proven or prospective ability to teach, preferably classics. In the event, Dr James largely restricted himself to providing sporadic Latin verse classes for the talented, enthusiastic, or dragooned few. In contrast to his predecessor, he took surprisingly little active part in the ordinary business of the school. Yet he was always around and seemingly well-informed, paying visits to formrooms, attending school events, socializing, and padding around the playing fields accompanied by his small dog, Sappho. Beside him, his wife cut a dramatic contrast. He, small, neat, immaculate, understated, middle-aged; she, eternally youthful in striking, vividly imaginative, and often highly colourful clothes. It was a comparison that delighted observing Harrovians.

Known as 'Jimmy' to friends and colleagues, but 'Jankers' or 'Janks' to the boys, James's style mixed the Olympian with the Socratic.[239] Except to those in the Head Master's, he tended to be a remote figure, but his correspondence and letters reveal an acute understanding of adolescents and a realistic, unsentimental appraisal of human nature. In public, he possessed a remarkable ability to dominate almost any gathering without recourse to vanity, bombast, or intimidation: at parties there was no doubt who was Head Master. In Speech Room, his capacity to stand absolutely still—a very rare quality—concentrated attention on his slight frame. On one memorable occasion, he was confronted with a tittering school and a motorbike suspended far up in the roof. He simply ignored it and soon the school did the same. On Speech Days he delivered his long orations without notes, from memory, standing wrapped in his gown without lectern or table between him and his audience. For all his apparent unobtrusiveness, carefully calculated showmanship went into these public performances which, at least with parents and boys, proved highly effective. Without exhibitionism he conveyed authority, rather in the way Norwood had but without the pomposity.

Masters' photographs find James almost hunched, elfin-like, in the middle of the front row, crowded around by evidently larger egos. Yet, his quizzical smile and level stare exudes an absolute certainty as to who, despite the pretentions of others, was the boss. In contrast to his manner with boys, part of his hold over the staff was his accessibility. To them, his door was always open. He 'never seemed pressed for time', his discursive monologues which seemed to, and sometimes did, last for

---

[238] GBM, 7 Jan., 5 Mar. 1953; *Harrow Register, 1986*, 798.
[239] 'Jankers' was derived from British Army slang for punishment, convenient for a Head whose bark was professionally worse than his bite.

hours, becoming legendary, a humorous memory but a dreaded reality.[240] There was rarely such a thing as 'a quick word' with this Head Master. Such self-indulgence was possible because he delegated much, to masters or to his secretary, George Duvall, the most powerful occupant of the outer office since William Moss had served every Head from Butler to Norwood. James very rarely left the Hill during term, partly out of laziness, partly because he saw his work as centred on the school, partly because he disapproved of Head Masters parading themselves and their views in public. Explaining his refusal to enter the debate over the Royal Commission on Public Schools in 1966, he declared: 'I feel myself that the right attitude for a Head Master at least is to refrain from showing the cards in his hand . . . It is regrettable in fact that this is not the universal point of view.'[241]

One of James' most entrenched foibles was his dislike of any publicity and a pathological hostility to the press. He confided to Robert Birley, Head Master of Eton: 'I personally simply loathe being reported in the press before anything.' In 1966 he tried to dissuade the marquess of Aberdeen from mentioning Harrow in a House of Lords debate on the Royal Commission.[242] He was not always successful in keeping the school out of the news. In the autumn of 1967, a boy in the Knoll blew himself up with a home-made bomb he was making, another boy who happened to be in the room also receiving painful injuries. The headlines were suitably lurid. For such exigencies, James had installed a secret weapon. He reassured the father of the innocent victim of the Knoll explosion that he could prove any false reporting of his remarks, in the typically salacious *Daily Telegraph* for instance: 'I invariably record all telephone conversations with the press.'[243] Few of his colleagues knew that hidden in his desk was tape recording equipment. In this, and nothing else, James was keeping abreast with the latest transatlantic fashions.[244] A flavour of James' style and his relations with the press survives in a transcript of a telephone conversation with a *Daily Mail* journalist called Godwin on 21 January 1964. Godwin had rung to ask James about the merits of boxing as a school sport.

Godwin: Do you hold a personal opinion about the value of boxing?
James: Yes. I do, and I am not going to give it to you. Don't be stupid . . . This is a recorded conversation . . . I've got this on an Ultravox and you can't make anything up . . . I shall go straight off to the Press Council if you do because it is printed out by my secretary.[245]

---

[240] *The Harrovian*, 27 Nov. 1971, p. 38; in general, pp. 37–40.
[241] HM/J/16 Feb. 1966, James to marquess of Aberdeen.
[242] HM/J/16 June 1961, James to R. Birley, above, n. 241.   [243] HM/J/28 Nov. 1967.
[244] President L. B. Johnson also taped his telephone conversations; as yet there is no direct evidence whether Dr James anticipated President R. M. Nixon in taping personal conversations.
[245] HM/J/Transcript of telephone conversation with *Daily Mail*, 21 Jan. 1964.

James could be formidable if necessary. Not the least of his strengths as Head Master was that many of his staff and probably all of the boys were, to some degree, frightened of him.

James employed most of the black arts of rule to sustain the even tenor of his ordered life. His interminable monologues often acted as smokescreens for inaction or refusal. Some found him cold, vindictive, disloyal, and deceitful, a 'twister' according to one colleague. He perfected a curious, though undoubtedly useful, habit of disowning responsibility for his own or the school's failings or errors, as if he were merely an observer of the scene not its choreographer. An unpopular Head of Department wished to send a boy to James for severe punishment, perhaps even expulsion, for deliberately offensive behaviour directed at him. James insouciantly sent word that he would be delighted to see the boy and hear of his complaints. Yet the master concerned had only recently been appointed by James himself who subsequently did nothing to ease the tension caused by this appointee. This technique of disengagement operated most spectacularly with housemasters. At the end of the Summer Term of 1959, all the house monitors of Bradbys were asked to leave after an orgy of drinking, smoking, and breaking out at night. According to James, these habits 'had for some years been common in the leading members of that house' and he had been fully aware of them, as he admitted when writing to the former master, Leonard Henry: 'A week before Lord's the top blew off Bradbys. I had expected this to take place for years . . . I had told the House Master that it was only a matter of time before what he found impossible to believe would be proved to be true . . . there has been an exceedingly bad tradition in Bradbys ever since I have been here.'[246] Yet he had done nothing for six years, even though that housemaster's financial management was as inept as his discipline. Only after it was obvious to all that a new regime was required did James feel able to remove him a year early.[247]

This extreme caution and desire not to arouse opposition explained part of James' external popularity; he always set out to avoid trouble. Where he could act with relative impunity, such as when colleagues, parents, and old boys together murmured against a housemaster, he did so, engineering the departure of at least one housemaster five years before his term.[248] Others were allowed carte blanche despite financial incompetence or worse, brutal discipline, insensitive treatment of boys, and loud complaints from parents.[249] If a housemaster possessed powerful Old Harrovian or sporting credentials, he was unlikely to be publicly checked, however badly he behaved. Arguably, this was a prudent reaction to the trauma of Boissier's day. James' central concern was to protect Harrow's reputation. Messy sackings of men with strong social, masonic, or athletic contacts would make more

---

[246] HM/J/14 Jan. 1960, James to Henry. [247] GBM, 7 Nov. 1959, 13 Feb. 1960.
[248] GBM, 15 Feb. 1958. The Minutes are consistent: the only departures of housemasters recorded are of those who have been levered out. Cf. ibid., 13 Feb. 1960, etc.
[249] HM/J/14 Jan. 1960, 13 Jan. 1967, 12 and no date Dec. 1967 for relevant correspondence.

difficult the task of defending the school from political attack and maintaining its healthy numbers, especially as a major part of James' recruitment was aimed at old boys. Like Drury, Vaughan, Monty Butler, and Beer, James understood the importance of creating a positive atmosphere, of presenting the right image of confident unity whatever the reality. In his own aversion to publicity, James discovered a surprisingly effective form of public relations. However, James' selective laissez-faire hardly acted in the best interests of all his pupils. Yet the governors seemed content to share James' tolerance, as demonstrated when the Chairman freely admitted to a candidate to succeed James the problems with one violent, spendthrift drunken housemaster of almost a decade's standing who faced no prospect of removal.

The desire for a quiet life did not extend universally. Dr James had his prejudices and blind spots. He was a thorough-going philistine, if of the refined nineteenth-century type. He appeared suspicious of drama and the social evils of school plays, an opinion reinforced by a scandal involving the performers of *Antony and Cleopatra* in 1959. It was said of Harrow in the 1950s that it excelled at cricket and Shakespeare. More accurately, these two opposite poles provided representative symbols of the school's often irreconcilable diversity. The annual Shakespearian plays were tolerated because they had become traditional and attracted good publicity, not because James had any interest in them or understood their potential educational value. Similarly, he tolerated the continuation of the annual performances by the new Old Harrovian Players founded in 1952 by H. L. Harris and L. J. Verney, the only non-sporting old boys' society (the Harrow Lodge excepted).[250] Reflecting James' feelings, there were fewer plays and less depth of dramatic activity at Harrow in the 1950s and early 1960s than there had been in the days of Coade, Boissier, and Marjorie James in the 1920s and 1930s, or even in the time of George Townsend Warner and the Townsend Warner Players.[251] Apart from Watkins' Shakespeare, continued after 1964 by J. P. Lemmon, there were rare, sporadic house or masters' plays until an unstoppable revival of drama throughout the school from the mid-1960s. School music and musicians were regarded by James with similar detachment, his perennial inability to pronounce certain composers' names (e.g. Dvorak) providing a rich source of amusement to boys and masters alike. Both music and drama encouraged close, creative cooperation between masters and boys with which James appeared uneasy. He believed in maintaining an old-fashioned distance between teachers and taught.

However, this did not prevent him from appointing masters to whose cultural interests and activities he was either indifferent or hostile. His whole management style was relaxed, allowing individual masters and different sections of the school to operate as they saw fit provided nobody objected. His appointments reflected

---

[250] H. L. Harris, 'The Old Harrovian Players', *A Garland for the Harrow Globe 1941–91*, ed. H. L. Mallalieu and M. J. Levete (priv. pub., London, 1991), pp. 26–9.
[251] Above, n. 168.

his catholic approach.²⁵² In contrast to other Heads, he saw no need to impose uniformity, spurious or genuine. While continuing the tradition of games-players, he was alert to brains. Scholarship was sustained by the historians G. R. R. Treasure (1955–92) and D. J. Parry (1961–93), the mathematician S. L. Parsonson (1960–93), the physicist A. G. Bagnall (1962–97), the modern linguist J. Jeremy (1957–94), and the classicists A. T. Davis (1957–66) and J. H. W. Morwood (1966–96). Innovative techniques and courses were pioneered by the scientist A. A. Bishop (1955–95), who supervised the introduction of Nuffield Science, and M. W. Vallance (1961–72), the first Harrow English master to hold a degree in the subject, whose creation of a 'New Group' for less able O Level candidates, giving more time for English language and literature, proved one of Harrow's most successful educational developments, reflecting an imaginative understanding of the needs of the school's cherished broad intake. Harrow provided the springboard for the ambitious, such as the future Head Master of Westminster, J. M. Rae (1955–66). The composer R. J. Drakeford (1961–85) proved to be one of the most naturally gifted, if idiosyncratic, teachers of his generation. The talented Old Harrovian, J. P. Lemmon (1957–96), who taught English in the grand pedagogic manner, succeeded to Plumptre's mantle as the dominant intellectual force in the school, even though James rather disapproved of his wide cultural activities.

Just as the sporting life of the school developed, so did the intellectual. James was no enthusiast for new subjects, but with money largely provided by the Old Harrovian and future governor G. R. Simmonds he established Business Studies in 1967 under Dr J. S. Dugdale, whom he attracted with an inflated salary at the very top of the scale. However, James insisted he had 'no intention of making this a subject which can be examined. It is purely educative'.²⁵³ It was not a success and, when Dugdale was found dead one morning in July 1974, Business Studies was immediately closed down.²⁵⁴ More lasting were Political Studies (1967) and the reintroduction of Economics (1964).²⁵⁵ Otherwise, most curricular innovations occurred within existing disciplines or sprang directly from them, such as the influx of £10,000 from the Industrial Fund for the Advancement of Science in 1957.²⁵⁶ The traditional subjects held sway. The Oxford and Cambridge A Level examiners at the end of James' period believed Harrow's to be the largest history department in numbers of boys they encountered. English retained the peculiar status noted by the 1951 Inspectors by not having its own Sixth Forms. Notionally compulsory throughout the school, at A Level English was taken as a subsidiary subject, an anomaly that persisted into the mid-1970s. In classics, the witty, urbane, and erudite E. V. C. Plumptre had preserved something of the nineteenth-century depth

---

[252] *Harrow Register, 1986*, pp. 812–17.
[253] HM/J/28 July 1967, James to W. J. Nokes; HM/J/2, 10 May 1968, correspondence between James and Simmonds; GBM, 11 Feb., 11 Nov. 1967.
[254] HA Masters' Papers (unlisted), 'Economics at Harrow: A note by R.K. 6-3-81'.
[255] GBM, 9 June 1964.   [256] GBM, 13 June 1957.

of study and concentration on textual scholarship, producing a seemingly endless stream of outstanding classicists for the universities. He managed the trick of inspiring enthusiasm and belief in the subject as well as expertise; postcards to pupils could as easily be in elegant Greek as in his limpid English prose. After his early retirement in 1957 the tradition was maintained by his successors as Heads of Department, M. S. Warman and M. G. Balme (1952–85) but with a growing awareness of changes in learning techniques and teaching approaches which they helped promote through school textbooks, Balme being especially prominent in the 'new' classics. However, the classics department remained a model of certain traditional views on specialization that persisted in James' Harrow. Only *echt* classicists were allowed to study ancient history. Allegiance to other subjects was frowned upon. Much was the same in modern languages under the massive control of the cultured Roman Catholic C. L. Walton from whose pupils was expected almost monkish devotion to vocabulary learning and other basic skills. Although suffering the condescension of some and an unhelpful share of the timetable, the sciences and scientists were allowed freedom to experiment, often literally, before the tyranny of prescriptive national syllabuses placed a premium on non-exam-based learning. Even so, it was possible for intelligent boys to avoid any science at all throughout James' time, although it was agreed that a new physics block would be the prime objective for the Quartercentenary Appeal.[257] In mathematics, S. L. Parsonson continued the succession of elegant teaching, clear publications, and serious thought that stretched back through K. S. Snell (1930–61) to the indestructible A. W. Siddons.

The most distinctive feature of Harrow in mid-century as before was the extensive range of its pupils' academic ability, although Dr James was once moved to remark acidly on one new boy's appalling first term's reports 'we are not, after all, setting up to be a home for difficult children'.[258] The maintenance of a relatively low Common Entrance pass mark (50%) was deliberate. The exam was a qualification, not meant to be competitive. Even though the school was consistently overbooked for much of his time, James refused to raise the standard because he thought that would be betraying prep. schools which were accustomed to the Harrow entrance level and were advising parents accordingly.[259] It also allowed the Head and housemasters to perpetuate traditional dynastic as well as prep. school links. At one end of the spectrum were the scholars, by title or aptitude, rapidly matured by a system that allowed them to pass O Level within one or two years, leaving up to three, even four years in the Upper School. These precocious intellectuals were tested and extended to reach a level of interest and achievement often far beyond the requirements of A Level, as witnessed by some of the talks given to the Essay Club, a self-electing intellectual elite, originally founded by Dr Vaughan

---

[257] GBM, 15 Mar. 1969.   [258] HM/J/Reports, Mar. 1961.
[259] HM/J/23 Jan. 1967, James to Miss K. E. Higgins; *The Harrovian*, 27 Nov. 1971, p. 40.

for the sole purpose of hearing and discussing papers read by members.[260] At the other end of the spectrum were boys who entered in the Fourth Form, destined to spend three years before attempting a few O Levels. It was characteristic of Harrow of the 1950s and 1960s as before, that some Harrovians received a Rolls Royce intellectual education while others were allowed to wallow in an academic sump. Only a few masters managed to bridge this gulf, one of the most successful being the old-fashioned polymath H. L. Harris (Head of English 1948–66) equally at home teaching English to scholars in the Upper Sixth and, with a number of other subjects, to dullards in low Remove or Fifth Forms. Harris produced good results with both. While never flattering the clever, he never patronized the weak, famously given to appending to their work 'Much Better: 0'.

Increasingly, the academic structure of the school appeared fusty. The School Inspection of November 1965, the first since 1951 and the last for another thirty years, caught a whiff of this growing senescence. The Inspectors noted the growth in Upper School work from 35 per cent in 1951 to 47 per cent which had not been matched by adequate teaching resources, material or human.[261] As the Inspectors were conducting their investigation, the governors decided to invest in 'calculating machines' for maths A Level candidates.[262] It was agreed that the Vaughan Library, 'a somewhat comfortless and forbidding place' should cease to act as a gallery and concentrate on functioning as a library for school work.[263] Nothing came of discussions in 1968 on the introduction of a four-term year, a fashionable idea thirty years later.[264] James had remained wedded to the traditional system of form masters, especially in the pre-O Level years, generalists who taught a little Latin, English, history, Divinity, even French, much of it pretty badly. The Inspectors suggested more English and classics specialists. James rejected their proposal that the status of Heads of academic departments should be enhanced by greater remuneration to provided academic masters with an alternative to the customary trial of preferment towards housemastering. Teaching methods, while sound, were uninspiring. For example, the history department was criticized for giving verbatim notes, although the Inspectors failed to comment on the invariable habit of the Head of Department to dictate straight from Edward's *History Notes*. In general, the Inspectors observed 'a tendency . . . for the masters to do too much and not put quite enough responsibility on the boy for his own studies'.[265]

Responsibility for some problems lay with the unavoidable stagnation in staff. Harrow remained a comfortable berth. James himself encouraged a casual attitude where energy was the responsibility of the individual rather than part of the system.

---

[260] HA Essay Club Minute Books, 1914, *passim*.
[261] *Report by Her Majesty's Inspectors on Harrow School, Harrow, November 1965* (Dept. of Education and Science, London, 1966), esp. pp. 2, 6–7.
[262] GBM, 13 Nov. 1965.
[263] R. L. James, 'Comments on Inspectors' Report', Nov. 1966, p. 2.
[264] GBM, 26 Sept. 1968.   [265] *Report by Inspectors, 1965*, 5, 11, 13, 20.

Although Heads of Department had been appointed and paid additional sums since Ford's curriculum reforms, there was only rudimentary departmental organization or control once what was to be taught in any year had been established. The Head of History, the devious machiavel Charles Lillingston, combined his post with that of housemaster of Druries for a dozen years (1956–68). Only towards the end of that time did he hold informal departmental meetings, the first one being conducted from his bed. Most of the administrative work he delegated to Roger Ellis while retaining a close hold on the political dimensions of the job. The Inspectors tactfully pointed out this curious arrangement;[266] James studiously failed to take the hint and it continued until Ellis left for the Headship of James' old school, Rossall, in 1967.

Despite some glaring flaws, in structures and personnel, James' Harrow worked, saved by its variety, the relaxed reactionary nature of the regime responsible equally for its strengths and weaknesses. The experience of schoolboys could be conditioned by chance and by house. There were sensitive and cultured housemasters, such as the otherwise austere and meticulous Wykehamist Edward Malan at the Knoll (1948–63) or the liberal intellectual Salopian Mark Warman at Newlands (1961–72). There were housemasters of a very different stamp, such as Warman's predecessor at Newlands, J. W. Greenstock (housemaster 1946–61), C. D. Laborde at The Park (1960–74), M. Tindall at Bradbys (1960–74), and J. Webster at West Acre (1962–77). A few housemasters were intellectuals; some were effective. Unfortunate was the intellectual boy in a philistine house with an unsympathetic housemaster. A report supplied to the Head Master by one mid-1960s housemaster commented critically on one of his boys applying to Christ Church: 'As he grew up in the House, his influence was not particularly good. He was too clever by half for his contemporaries and could make a nonsense out of their arguments.'[267] James had little difficulty seeing through such weaknesses of his colleagues, even if he did nothing about them. The boy got in.

The standards of teaching, as had been noted by the 1951 Inspectors, varied enormously, from inspirational to unspeakable. James employed the system of two year's probation that had existed since Welldon's day, but that did not always weed out the hopeless. James was not above using the probation and subsequent formal confirmation of tenure as a crude expression of approval, a sort of teasing professional harassment of those whom he was not actually going to sack. One of the most distinguished and successful of his appointees, who stayed at Harrow for well over thirty years, claimed never to have been confirmed. James did not bother with the detail of teaching. In the information provided parents when they applied for their son's admission to Harrow, a single folded piece of paper, there were only two paragraphs, a total of some 130 words, on the academic programme.[268] In a

---

[266] *Report by Inspectors, 1965*, 19. [267] HM/J/11 Oct. 1966.
[268] Noted with surprise by Wakeford, *Cloistered Elite*, 35.

teaching system still run on horizontal lines, with masters allocated to years and abilities rather than by specialisms, clever boys could avoid some of the worst teaching which was the staple diet of their less able peers. As a result, James' Harrow lacked cohesion as well as uniformity.

A less adroit politician or one less alert to human nature could have failed badly. James succeeded not least because his aims were modest and conservative. He had no grand vision. He judged issues separately. In dealings with housemasters, he might publicly follow the majority while providing private succour and reassurance to the minority or isolated. In spite of a forbidding manner to most boys, he handled their problems with honesty and sensitivity. He understood that boys were interested in sex, drink, and smoking ('one cannot really expel boys for that');[269] this knowledge did not drive him to frenzies of self-righteous anger or puritanical absolutism when confronted with adolescent weakness. His empiricism did not mean he was sympathetic to modern youth. Homosexuals he advised to have psychological treatment. He regarded long hair as 'a dirty habit': his own was never out of place.[270] Yet despite the prejudices of a man old-fashioned even for his own generation, he steered Harrow through the 1960s with hardly a serious murmur. His conservatism was confident enough not to need to resort to repression. Ironically for one so fearful of publicity, he permitted satirical magazines, such as *Goulash*, to poke mild, heavily censored fun at the school and its inhabitants and allowed the semi-official school paper, the *Harrovian*, to change its nature. Founded in 1888 after a long line of transient failed predecessors, the *Harrovian* transformed itself from a monthly magazine of school events into a weekly newspaper in the 1930s under the editorship of A. R. D. Watkins, prominent English teacher as well Shakespearian producer. Until the 1960s the *Harrovian* remained weekly but retained a marmorial, literary tone of ponderous deference and unpointed wit. In the 1960s Geoffrey Treasure and a succession of talented and ebullient boy editors changed all that. While continuing as an organ of record, the *Harrovian* began to act as a forum for debate, commentary, and criticism as well as literary expression. It established a tradition of stubborn refusal to be incorporated into the school's propaganda machine which, if at times attentuated under pusillanimous or idle masters-in-charge, to the recurrent irritation of those uneasy with flexibility of discussion persisted for decades after Treasure handed on the paper in 1967. James censored the *Harrovian* himself, but understood that the lively exercise of schoolboy journalism could demonstrate even in criticism the strength of the institution not, as the paper's opponents asserted, its weakness. Unique among public school papers in continuing to appear weekly, the *Harrovian* of the later twentieth century was an unexpected legacy of James' Head Mastership, another tribute to his unwavering laissez-faire.

[269] HM/J/18 Jan. 1960, James to Leonard Henry.
[270] HM/J/14 Jan. 1960, James to Leonard Henry; HM/J/2 Feb. 1967.

James' conservative Harrow survived the 1960s without serious trouble, the seemingly unchanging sameness of the place, in organization, habits, people, and buildings acting as an anaesthetic. The Knoll bomb of 1967 was an almost isolated incident. On another occasion a similar device had been placed in the Old Schools' clock, timed to explode when the school was assembled below for Bill one Summer's afternoon at 6 p.m. In the event, only the detonator went off, enough to stop the clock. These were the work of one or two eccentric experimenters rather than signs of organized sedition of the sort portrayed in Lindsay Anderson's cult public school film *If*, in which the Head Master, played by an OH, sported a Harrow Association tie. In general, the boys were as conservative as their masters. While some indulged in vigorous sex or took increasingly available illegal drugs, many affected quite surprisingly traditional deference and respectability.[271] Tension was caused less by lack of institutional change or freedom than by restrictions of movement. James' pretence that Harrow was isolated from its surroundings, especially from the capital, became increasingly difficult to maintain, such as the rule that Sunday drives with parents must be 'in the direction away from London'. However, as James himself remarked to one correspondent, such difficulties hardly compared with 'the famous incidents in the twenties'.[272]

If James appeared supine it was in the Walpolean manner, *quieta non movere*, let sleeping dogs lie. When required, he acted. In 1956 he drew housemasters' attention to the 'fairly common' practice of cheating in GCE exams; increased space between desks was suggested. He reprimanded masters for failing to attend Speech Room or to set preps.[273] After 1966 he implemented the Inspectors' proposals regarding the Vaughan Library and the institution of paid house tutors.[274] Essential maintenance work in refurbishing houses was regularly conducted, much of it long overdue from wartime. The competition of the modern world intruded to the extent of his creation of a post of Universities' Liaison Master in 1969 and his nominal support for the Careers' Master.[275] Financially incompetent, profligate, or greedy housemasters were regularly brought to book, even if their domestic terrorism or feebleness went largely uncorrected. When one clerical master revealed smugly to an astounded Masters' Meeting in the 1950s that he believed private tuition was a splendid institution because its proceeds did not have to be declared to the Inland Revenue, James extracted from the governors an unequivocal statement that this was not the case.[276] The last thing Harrow could afford were headlines suggesting that masters were systematically defrauding the tax man. To avoid scandal of a different sort, in 1958 he insisted that masters entertaining boys to

---

[271] GBM, 7 Nov. 1970.
[272] Rae, *Public School Revolution*, 116; HM/J/18 Jan. 1960, James to Leonard Henry.
[273] Minutes of Housemasters' Meetings, 1949–67, 9 July, 1 Oct. 1956.
[274] GBM, 17 Feb., 9 Nov. 1968, 21 Mar. 1970, etc. for Vaughan changes under the Librarian, C. H. Shaw; 11 Nov. 1967 for House Tutors.
[275] GBM, 15 Mar. 1969.   [276] GBM, 12 Nov. 1955.

dinner offered them only two wines.[277] While homosexual problems within the school could be handled sympathetically, boys' liaisons with the opposite sex were strictly outlawed and policed. Boys were forbidden to be alone with girls. James circulated instructions to local shops that girls must not be allowed to serve alone and that care must be taken to hire shop assistants of good character. The local brothel, the Vienna Café at 17 High Street, was ruled out of bounds in James' first term.[278] Such regulations were probably inspired more by fear of bad publicity than by morality.

Yet such humdrum actions were in the nature of redecoration; the fabric of Harrow remained essentially unaltered. James' success lay in this being precisely what he intended. There were minor restorations: the full Harrow uniform after the end of rationing; morning coats at Lord's.[279] Yet James' Harrow was not a stagnant backwater, fetid with anachronism. Individual masters managed to inspire and excite their pupils far beyond the set curriculum, few more lastingly than Ronnie Watkins who surrounded himself with a coterie of acolytes devoted to the shrine of his vision of Shakespeare, an enthusiasm which for many lasted a lifetime. Cricketers retained their passion, as witnessed in the continuing power of the Field House Club and the popularity of the Harrow Wanderers. Scientists caught the excitement of empirical experimentation. Boys on Corps Camp could be diverted by eager masters to roaming the countryside in search of interesting parish churches. Musicians were encouraged to exploit the contrasting talents of Drakeford, G. L. Mendham (1941–59), and G. J. Higgins (1951–67). With the relaxed attitude towards public qualifications, even the formal curriculum provided ample scope for intellectual browsing and academic scholarship.

The statistics of James' success were impressive. When he arrived, the projected overdraft by the end of 1953 was nearly £90,000, almost 50 per cent of annual fee income. Most school property sat under mortgage. In April 1970 the last instalment of the repayable mortgage was paid off, in symbolic and fitting conclusion to James' Head Mastership, and money was beginning to flood in for the Quartercentenary Appeal.[280] In 1953 numbers hovered in the 570s. The 600 mark was reached and sustained after 1956–7; 650 in 1960; 700, for the first time in the school's history, in 1966. For James' last ten terms, 1968–71, the school roll recorded over 700 pupils in seven of them, that in his final term showing a new record of 727, 25 per cent higher than when he came. The pressures on space this increase provided needed careful management. Despite the fluctuations in size, the number of

---

[277] Minutes of Housemasters' Meetings, 1949–67, 3 Mar. 1958.
[278] Minutes of Masters' Meetings, 1949–67, 7 Oct. 1953, 5 Oct. 1954; Rae, *Public School Revolution*, 116; GBM, 14 Feb., 11 June 1959 for the school's purchase of 17 High Street.
[279] Minutes of Housemasters' Meetings, 1949–67, 10 May 1954. On uniform see Laborde, *Harrow School*, 209–14.
[280] GBM, 11 June 1953, 8 Nov. 1969. For numbers see GBM for termly reports and *Harrow Register, 1986*, 405–633.

Large Houses, eleven, remained an unaltered maximum since 1893. Each house simply took more boys. That such crowding did not lead to the sort of mayhem as it had in the 1920s was to the credit of James and some of his housemasters. However, it was entirely in character that in 1967 he rejected the idea of a new house.[281]

As with many successful and powerful leaders, Dr James stayed too long. Initially appointed to retirement age of 60, in 1965 his term was extended 'for at least two or three years'.[282] He stayed another six, determined to preside over the Quartercentenary celebrations, though this meant he had to insist on following the unhistorical precedent of George and Monty Butler in imagining 1571 as the year of foundation. In his last years the school ran on its own momentum along familiar grooves. James' interest waned with his energy. Although he obviously still much enjoyed being Head Master of Harrow, he cared less for the chores it entailed, apart from arranging for the Queen's Quartercentenary visit, her second in his time. Some appointments to the staff lacked distinction or foresight; others were the products of self-interested backstairs intrigue. There even appeared a limit to his cherished dictum; 'There is value in habit'.[283] Habit became routine. Changes to facilities, curriculum, and administration were postponed. There was a feeling of waiting for 'Jimmy' to go. When he did, in the Summer of 1971, many were surprised at how much he was missed. His small figure cast a long and deep shadow. His effective conservatism bred a culture of reaction that his successor found difficult to transform. A decade later, the writer of his successor's valediction in the *Harrovian* devoted an inordinate amount of space to a retrospective appraisal of Dr James.[284] His habit proved hard to shake off. The governors had no doubts about his 'outstanding Head Mastership', expressing grateful enthusiasm not seen since 1885.[285] Dr James had held aloof from the turbulent political fray of the 1960s; he had distanced the school even from public school propagandists. It was somehow appropriate that his tenure of office should end with the unexpected public victory of conservatism at the General Election of 1970. As his familiar vivid light-blue Armstrong Siddeley purred off the Hill for the last time, Dr James' refusal to be panicked into debate or change had seemingly paid off; Harrow's stability, popularity, and academic success provided their own vindication.

MODERNIZATION: PERCEPTION AND REALITY, 1971–1991

It was appropriate as well as symbolic that the governors' meeting in November 1970 at which the detailed terms for Dr James' successor were agreed also decided that the wearing of formal dress at Lord's should discontinue.[286] Change was

---

[281] HM/J/17, 18, 19 Jan. 1967, correspondence of James and N. P. Eadon.
[282] GBM, 6 Feb. 1965.   [283] HM/J/1 June 1962, James to Bishop Stopford of London.
[284] *The Harrovian*, 28 Nov. 1981.   [285] GBM, 6 Nov. 1971.   [286] GBM, 7 Nov. 1970.

inevitable because it was fashionable and therefore, for public schools, necessary. The later twentieth century witnessed the transmutation of public schools from introverted bastions of arcane customs and antediluvian practices into more or less successful educational businesses alert and sensitive to the requirements and aspirations of the newly expanded wealthy classes of the economic booms of the 1960s and 1980s. Increasingly schools were judged on the quantity of their facilities and examination successes. As never before, they became responsive to the demands of parents and the competitive pressures of national qualifications. Efficiency supplanted dignity, although at Harrow the useless retained a function. Bill, the laborious and inconvenient but traditional afternoon roll call of boys in the school yard on Summer half holidays designed to stop them going into London or worse, was reduced to a specially rehearsed ritual for family photographs on Speech Day. Older principles of character-building education were refashioned to promote public schools as gaining for their pupils a utilitarian advantage over their peers. In his report to the Harrow Association of 1985, wittingly or not, Ian Beer recalled the philosophy of John Dancy's 'total education' of the early sixties: 'the public schools of Great Britain will only survive if they cater for the whole man; his intellectual, cultural, technological, physical, emotional and spiritual growth and understanding'. However, he had been careful to preface this credo with a description of the new Sports Hall and Ducker, the annual improvement in public examination results and his excitement at government plans for 'changes at the 16+level and breadth in the Sixth Form'.[287] As public schools became less distinctive, Victorian ideals of *noblesse oblige* were replaced by an explicit imperative to equip pupils to help themselves. However, with boarding declining in relative popularity within the HMC, as important as results and equipment was the establishment of positive public perceptions.

Harrow responded to the new social, academic, and technological demands in ways similar to other schools. Extensive refurbishment of boarding accommodation was matched by new domestic and athletic facilities. Between the mid-1970s and mid-1990s, Harrow built itself to prosperity. Academically, the curriculum required constant tinkering and occasional overhauls to meet the demands of pupils and new examination syllabuses. The teaching staff was reorganized and expanded; the timetable cluttered. There were local variations. The Hill as well as the school was transformed almost out of recognition. Antique shops and estate agents replaced grocers, greengrocers, electricians, and butchers. For permanent residents, life could not be sustained on the Hill alone. Ironically, the school that had provided so much employment and wealth for local traders since the eighteenth century had now driven them off the Hill altogether, a suburban village being replaced by a plush middle-class dormitory.

---

[287] *Harrow Association Record* (1985), 9.

The twenty years between the departures of James and Beer present a paradox. Neatly divided into two equal Head Masterships (Hoban 1971–81; Beer 1981–91), anecdotal evidence would suggest a contrast between a troubled, ultimately unsuccessful decade followed by ten sunlit years of energetic progress towards modernity. The evidence draws a more complex picture. In only three of Hoban's thirty terms did numbers slip below 700 (and then no lower than 691). From 1977 to 1981 the lowest was 730; the 762 on the roll in the Summer Term of 1977, a school record, was not surpassed until the far more propitious circumstances of the autumn of 1986.[288] Of the major building developments of the period, the Central Feeding block, the new boarding house at the New Knoll, the new physics and maths schools and the Old Speech Room Gallery had been built, the refurbishment of houses, the Sports Hall, indoor swimming pool, Archives Room and theatre either planned or envisaged all before 1981, with only the CDT centre dating in conception as well as execution from the later decade.[289] The major assessment of long-term priorites occurred in 1978.[290] To the 1970s belonged the centralization of academic departments, both administratively and physically; the concentration of teaching within the central area of the school; the construction of a golf course; the promulgation of a stronger Central List to ensure a fuller school more evenly distributed across the houses; and the introduction of new tenure arrangements for housemasters and assistant masters.[291] The social structure of masters' lives was altered for ever by Michael Hoban's insistence on a masters' dining room in the new Central Feeding block where they could communally eat a free lunch, thus ending an enduring feature of traditional semi-detached Harrow.[292] In 1979–80 the school obtained its first 'micro-processor', an event presciently noted in print at the time by the Head Master as being 'of greater interest to future historians than anything else that has taken place at Harrow'; the information and computer revolution had arrived on the Hill.[293] By contrast, the widely recognized achievements of the 1980s appeared more managerial and presentational, in a skilful embrace and exploitation of that decade's *zeitgeist*.

There was nothing modern about the process of Hoban's election. A series of informal soundings, sometimes little more than casual encounters, spread over many months ended with the committee of Holt, R. A. Allan, and C. H. Stuart drawing up a shortlist of three by the autumn of 1970. One withdrew because he wanted to stay where he was and on 10 October 1970 it was agreed that B. M. S. Hoban, Head Master of Bradfield College was 'the more suitable of the two final contenders'.

---

[288] Statistics derived from Head Masters' termly then annual reports on numbers, GBM, *passim*.
[289] GBM, 21 Mar. 1971, 18 Mar., 25 May, 10 Nov. 1972, 17 Mar. 1973, 4 Jan., 30 May 1974, 8 Nov. 1975, 11 Nov. 1978, 3 Mar., 30 July, 10 Nov. 1979, 1 May, 8 Nov. 1980.
[290] GBM, 17 July 1978.
[291] GBM, 10 Nov. 1972, 17 Mar. 1973, 13 Mar., 23 May 1976, 10 Nov. 1979, 28 Feb. 1981.
[292] *The Harrovian*, 28 Nov. 1981.   [293] *Harrow Association Record* (1980), 6.

Unfortunately, the advertisement for the post had only just appeared and its stated closing date for applications was not until 21 October. This technical difficulty was brushed aside: 'the replies to the statutory advertisement has not altered [our] view', although the governors did agree to delay announcing the election until after the nominal closing date.[294] Charles Stuart, a Student of Christ Church, Oxford, appears to have played a particularly important role in choosing Hoban, believing him to have been 'the best teacher of classics in the country'. The Chairman, Lord McCorquodale, was less informed. In a scene that could have been written by P. G. Wodehouse, when he visited Hoban at Bradfield to offer him the job, the successful candidate ventured to enquire whether there was any remuneration attached to the post. There was, but the Chairman did not know how much, having to telephone the Chairman of the GPC, Holt, in London to find out. This was not the most auspicious start. In the event, Lord McCorquodale established a precedent, followed by his successors R. A. A. Holt and F. E. R. Butler after the next two Head Mastership elections, by retiring as Chairman after presiding over the appointment.

Brian Michael Stanislaus Hoban was 50. A Carthusian who read classics at Oxford, his university career was interrupted by the Second World War, in which he served with distinction, only the second Head Master of Harrow to have seen active military service. After teaching at Uppingham and Shrewsbury, he went as Head Master to St Edmund's School, Canterbury in 1960, proceeding to Bradfield in 1964, conforming to the pattern of Harrow being a third headship that lasted from 1953 to 1999.[295] A scholarly, thoughtful man, with a gentle wit, far shrewder than his mild appearance indicated, Hoban was confronted with the oppressive legacy of James, both in style and people. Harrow masters and Old Harrovians had grown accustomed to James. With a certain Celtic wizardry he had convinced or reassured many that change was never necessary but always evil. He did not think so, but it served his purposes to let some of his less reflective colleagues believe it. More damagingly, by his studious isolationism, James had led some to imagine that Harrow was immune to the outside world. Hoban was thus faced by confident and intransigent reactionary colleagues at a time when external political, economic, and journalistic forces turned against the school. All the while, there were insidious rumours of the views of the retired sage of Blenheim Drive, North Oxford as a few masters chose to spread mischief with their old chief.

To implement institutional changes after a long period of inertia requires both skill and luck. A poor politician, Hoban had none of the latter. Even nature conspired against him. The psychological effect of physical upheaval, the loss of the visually familar, on attitudes and behaviour is difficult to gauge. Yet it may not have aided Hoban's policy of innovation that he was forced to conduct it when surrounded by ravages to the landscape resulting from the building of the reservoir in

---

[294] GBM, 10 Oct. 1970.   [295] *Harrow Register, 1986*, 798.

Harrow Park, the consequent changes to the hydrology of the eastern slopes, and the sudden devastation caused by Dutch Elm disease that from 1972 rapidly destroyed over 300 mature trees on both sides of the Hill. The following year, the younger sycamores were attacked by 'Sooty Bark'.[296] Well-loved views vanished as hedges and tree screens were lost; ugly suburbia and the great pile of the Northwick Park Hospital appeared in sight for the first time, the sylvan cricket fields were revealed as barren municipal playing grounds. The Hill no longer looked the same; it looked worse, although the golfers (Hoban included) seized the opportunity to tame the fields below The Park by building a nine-hole golf course.[297]

Nationally, the public environment of the 1970s was the most unfavourable since the 1930s. Inflation, miners' strikes, the oil crisis followed by hyper-inflation, a collapse of the Stock Market, a hostile Labour government and marginal tax rates of 98 per cent caught Harrow in a vice; fees had to soar for the school to pay its bills while parents lacked the income or capital to afford them. In 1972, when planning to hold Churchill Songs in the Albert Hall in 1974, to mark the centenary of Sir Winston's birth, the governors felt they had to insure against its cancellation 'by reason of national emergency'.[298] Locally, misfortune shattered any pretence of Jamesian tranquillity. In 1974 an IRA bomb exploded at one of the masters' flats; the intended victim, a former Commanding Officer of the Harrow CCF, had in fact recently moved to become a housemaster. The main damage caused was to a fridge, but the sense that Harrow, with its clear imperial and military connections, was a soft target for terrorism was unsettling. The same year saw the scandal over The Grove fire. In November 1974 severe damage was caused to the boys' side of the house by arson. The perpetrator was a boy in the house, highly neurotic but of grand social connections. At his trial in May 1975 he revealed evidence of 'card and beer sessions' and claimed that he had been disturbed by repeated homosexual 'attack'; the police confirmed that his 'story about sexual advances was correct'.[299] The incident itself, the prolonged speculation and rumours, and the revelations at the trial were highly damaging, much of the burden of dealing with the concerns of parents, old boys, and press falling on the Head Master. Adding to his problems was an alleged vendetta conducted against him through criticism of Harrow by an education correspondent of a national broadsheet newspaper whose brother Hoban had removed from the school. To cap his troubles, an unfortunate appointment to the Bursarship led to mismanagement and suspicions of peculation and corruption that involved some familiar school suppliers.[300] Not only did this harm the school's attempts to combat financial difficulties, it created animosity to the Head from

---

[296] GBM, 11 Nov. 1967, *et seq.* for the Reservoir; 25 May for Dutch Elm Disease; M. Etheridge, 'Planting for the Future', *The Harrow Record* (1996), 100.
[297] GBM, 10 Nov. 1972, 8 Nov. 1975.   [298] GBM, 12 Sept. 1972.
[299] See the not untypical report, *Daily Mail*, 20 May 1975.
[300] GBM, 24 May 1973, 9 Mar. 1974, 27 May 1976.

those who, for reasons of friendship with those concerned, blamed him for his perfectly proper support of measures to restore bursarial probity.

Faced with such an array of problems not of his own making, Hoban never entirely overcame them. His style of leadership appeared ineffectual compared with his predecessor. Not a bully or a cheat, he lacked sufficient ruthlessness and adequate political support from senior masters and some governors to impose his will. Decisions did not come easily to him because he possessed a genuine desire to do the right thing. It is easy to be decisive if you are deciding to do nothing. Change is more difficult. Thoughtful hesitation appeared as congenital procrastination. Writing of Hoban's instant decision to close the Business Studies Department on hearing of Dr Dugdale's death, one less than loyal colleague recorded for posterity that 'this was possibly Mr Hoban's speadiest [sic] and most decisive move in his years at Harrow'.[301] Honesty had a habit of rebounding. Hoban's response to the trial of the Grove arsonist was to admit publicly that senior boys were allowed to drink beer in their houses even if under eighteen, adding 'I have not cracked down on this as a result of the Old Bailey case.'[302] In terms of public relations, this was Ford of 1925 *redivivus*. It was sadly ironic for a man eager for realistic adaptation to the modern world that he was inevitably pilloried as some out of touch reactionary. The boys scarcely helped when one Speech Day they daubed the Old Schools with an insulting whitewashed slogan against their Head.

No less undermining was his stand over academic standards. Entrance Scholarships served two functions for Harrow throughout the twentieth century: to attract very clever boys and to reward loyal prep. schools keen to fill their honours' boards. Most boys awarded scholarships had been destined for Harrow in any case, although successive academic Head Masters from Welldon onwards hoped that Harrow could catch more 'floaters'. Perennially, it was agreed that Harrow needed to offer greater numbers of more valuable awards. None the less, as part of the admissions ritual, a certain number of scholarships was expected to be given each year. In 1973 Hoban took a stand, reporting to the governors that all but three scholarship candidates had been of only 'moderate standard' and the number of awards had accordingly been tiny.[303] This produced negative reactions. It was portrayed as a sign of Harrow's falling academic standing; this was a self-fulfilling process as the intake of 1973, acknowledged to be academically weak, produced a particularly low percentage of leavers in 1977–8 proceeding to Oxbridge (between 12 per cent and 13 per cent depending on how the figures are calculated); this, in turn, prompted mutterings of a decline in academic standards which even found their way into Hoban's *Harrovian* exituary.[304] Another result of the 1973 decision was that prep. schools felt betrayed; numbers entered for Harrow scholarships in

---

[301] Master's Papers, unlisted, 'Economics at Harrow: A note by R.K. 6-3-81'.
[302] *Daily Mail*, 20 May 1975.   [303] GBM, 17 Mar. 1973.
[304] *The Harrovian*, 28 Nov. 1981.

subsequent years fell sharply. Honesty and principle had backfired. Hoban's naivety left indelible marks on his reputation and the perception of the school in the enclosed constituency for HMC schools.

For a most convivial man, as Head Master Hoban appeared strangely distant, aloof, isolated as troubles crowded in. He was well liked by those boys who knew him, especially those of intellectual or cultural bent. However, he failed to identify friendly groups or individuals on the staff, leaving him exposed and powerless when undermined by implacable traditionalists and reactionaries who, it must be said, sincerely believed that they held Harrow's interests most truly at heart. One of Hoban's difficulties lay in the chance of so many diehards combining at the top of the staff, men who had appropriated to themselves custody of what they regarded as the essence of Harrow's greatness. These self-appointed guardians of the Harrow myth dimly felt, rather than clearly thought, that Hoban posed a threat to their ordered world of discipline, compulsion, and inflexible adherence to the status quo, which they mistook, as had Harrow reactionaries for centuries, for immutable practice.

Despite such hostility and his own diffident management, Hoban implemented a wide range of overdue reforms which, inevitably, confirmed his critics in their opposition or contempt. Some innovations were uncontroversial, such as the building of a golf course after 1972; the introduction of Nuffield Physics in 1974; the establishment of a gallery in Old Speech room in 1976.[305] More unsettling for some were the reduction of housemasters' terms from fifteen to twelve years from 1976 and the revival of a strong central list of candidates for admission after 1976 which met concerted and sustained resistance from housemasters over the following years.[306] The ice-flow of habit was further eroded when the traditional date of Speech Day had to be altered to accommodate new timings of GCE exams in 1980.[307] In March 1973 he presented the governors with proposals that the Corps became voluntary; that Chapel remain obligatory but particular services a matter of choice; and that the value of Entrance Scholarships should be increased. At the same meeting, it was agreed that the masters' retirement age be raised from 60 to 62, a change that lasted until 1993, the Head Master retaining 'the overriding right' to ask a master to go at 60.[308] In 1979–80, after a debate that had surfaced sporadically over 140 years, the Head Master was relieved of his duties as a housemaster.[309] From 1980 the housemaster at the Head Master's became a full housemaster, the first incumbent, a forceful political figure in 1970s Harrow, the geographer E. J. H. Gould, later Head Master of Felsted and Master of Marlborough, inevitably being known as the 'Ed. Master'. Enemies regarded this as one more sign of Hoban's decline, unaware that governors had been suggesting it for decades. Ironically, its

---

[305] GBM, 10 Nov. 1972, 9 Mar. 1974, 8 Nov. 1975.
[306] GBM, 13 Mar., 23 May 1976.   [307] GBM, 10 Nov. 1979.
[308] GBM, 17 Mar. 1973.   [309] GBM, 30 July 1979.

implementation in 1980 was possible because the school could, for once, afford it, a sign of health not decay. In any case, the pressures placed not only on a Head Master but on his wife were becoming intolerable. Within two years, a new house had been specially built for Head Masters away from the hurly-burly of a boys' house and the High Street.

Hoban's reform of the academic organization of the school had profound consequences. While maths and science had been run as autonomous, centralized departments since the late nineteenth century, the Arts subjects had operated in a much less structured fashion. Even after Ford's introduction of a unified curriculum and greater specialization, departmental management consisted of agreeing to what was taught. Deciding who was to teach it to whom remained the prerogative of the Head Master until Norwood's time and, in some cases, long after. From the First World War, Heads of Department were recognized by additional payments.[310] The senior Sixth Form teacher was not necessarily the administrative head. J. W. Moir ran the Classics Department, although first N. K. Stephen, then E. V. C. Plumptre taught the Classical Sixth.[311] Until the 1960s the Middle and Lower Schools, i.e. up to School Certificate, later O Level, were arranged for many subjects in forms, considered by Norwood 'one of the best methods handed down from the old schools' (by which he meant pre-nineteenth-century reform).[312] Masters continued to be appointed as generalists, expected as form masters to teach many subjects or, if hired as specialists, attached to year blocks. As late as the 1960s one master could be appointed specifically to teach in the Upper School; another to act as a form master in the Lower School. Increasingly, the demands of examinations, the content of subjects, and teaching techniques rendered this system obsolete. Hoban, as well as physically centralizing teachers' formrooms in departmental buildings, altered the academic orientation of departments from a horizontal structure to a vertical one, from one centred on teachers allocated to years or ability groups to one based on specialist subject knowledge. Although in many cases not immediately marking a very extreme alteration in timetabling, the implications were considerable, for incumbents, future appointments, and the school's adaptibility to curriculum changes. Sixth Form teachers found themselves in the unfamiliar surroundings of 13-year-olds. Generalists were expected to teach A Level and academically to keep up to date. Inevitably not everybody was thrilled. However, these changes presaged the total divisionalization of all subjects which, with minor exceptions based on convenience, was completed by the late 1980s, providing the flexibility to grapple with rapid national curricular development after 1986.

---

[310] Masters' Files, L. W. Henry, 4 Apr. 1921, Ford to Henry offering him £50 a year as Head of History.
[311] Masters' Files, J. W. Moir, May 1925, Moir to Ford, 28 Sept. 1937, Moir to Vellacott.
[312] Norwood, *English Tradition of Education*, 42.

The most significant decision of Hoban's time was the introduction of central feeding and, with money from the sale of Shepherd's Market, the building of the Shepherd [*sic*] Churchill Hall and Room. The impact on the nature of the school constituted the most radical change since the 1820s and 1830s when Batten and Phelps began the modern system of boarding houses as homes instead of doss-houses. As the governors observed in November 1973, 'factors other than finance would also have to be taken into account' before any scheme could be agreed.[313] In fact they had no option. Eleven separate catering systems were inefficient and prohibitively expensive. In March 1973 it was calculated that central feeding could produce annual savings of £40,000, not counting the excess capacity released for boarders by the departure of chefs, staff, and kitchens.[314] For years house catering had presented almost insuperable problems of the cost and availability of staff and of matching price, quality, and quantity of food to budgets. Around 1960 some housemasters had hired professional catering firms who had found it impossible to provide food of adequate standard at the stipulated price.[315] The Inspectors' Report of 1965–6 had been highly critical of certain catering practices. Despite continued investment in new plant and even new house dining rooms, the situation had deteriorated.

When, early in 1973, the governors received a proposal to move to a system of central feeding, their reluctance was profound. A feasibility study recognized that 'Governors, Masters and boys would all prefer to keep the present system if there were any means of making it economically viable'.[316] There were not. After consultations with masters and investigation of schemes at St Paul's and Shrewsbury, in November 1973 the governors were presented with the 'only real solution', a central feeding block. Hoban 'regretfully' but consistently backed this plan, securing the governors' agreement in principle in January 1974. The public announcement was made on Speech Day 1974. Despite escalating costs and surrounding financial gloom, under the supervision of R. A. Allan, Deputy Chairman of the governors, the project proceeded, the building being finished in 1977.[317] Harrow was changed for ever.

The advent of central feeding not only saved money, crucial in the difficult years ahead, and spared housemasters and their wives much labour, inconvenience, and anxiety. It modified the relationship of houses to each other and the relationship of boys to their houses and the school. Eating together is one of the most socially affective of human activities. A significant element in the process of forging an individual's identification with his house and its inmates had been the experience of eating together, occasions that surface repeatedly in Harrovian memories. The shared communal activity strengthened bonds of familiarity, community, and exclusivity. Houses acted as homes; one definition of a home is a place in which

[313] GBM, 10 Nov. 1973.   [314] GBM, 17 Mar. 1973.
[315] GBM, 12 Nov. 1959, HM/J/10 Feb. 1961.
[316] GBM, 24 May 1973.   [317] GBM, 10 Nov. 1973, 4 Jan., 30 May 1974.

food is regularly provided. There were separate house areas in the Central Feeding Hall as a sop to those outraged at the prospect of dilution of house identity. This missed the point. Now the experience of meals was identical for the whole school. Before 1977 the only full corporate experiences occurred in Chapel or Speech Room, formal not social occasions. By eating together, Harrovians absorbed a greater sense of the unity of the school. Traditional rules restricting fraternization between houses were rendered irrelevant. Harrovians became easier to inform, easier to control. The riotous behaviour of many house mealtimes shaded into surprisingly ordered conduct in the central dining room. Food fights were now rare whole school experiences, assuming the status of collective ritual. More subtly, when led in the 1980s by a Head Master who valued direct leadership, corporate cohesion, and team spirit, there could be less structurally institutional resistance. Central feeding brought the school back together in a practical and symbolic acknowledgement of the reversal and defeat of the mid-nineteenth-century creation of the federal school. Housemasters who wished to perpetuate a keen sense of house separateness had to discover new techniques to make up the independence deficit and compensate for the blurring and merging of identities. The existence of a masters' dining room, on which Hoban had insisted, encouraged the solecism of the 1980s that Harrow, like many campus schools, possessed a Masters' Common Room. In fact, the masters' dining room was solely gastronomic, providing a canteen lunch, taken by most, and acting as a restaurant for dinner. The Masters' Room itself merely housed pigeon-holes and, except for mid-morning Break, remained deserted. More widely, the new hall provided the governors with greater long-term options. If they were to choose to increase numbers and revenue by admitting day pupils, a policy explicitly rejected in 1975, 1978, 1987, and 1989, central feeding had made it logistically possible.[318]

Harrow in the late 1970s began to resemble a building site, not necessarily a help to morale. After the Central Feeding Block was built, plans for redevelopment of the eastern side of Peterborough Road were revived. Plans to demolish houses on this site had first been aired in 1965.[319] Now, combined with a scheme to build a new boarding house, plans were devised from 1978–9 that resulted in the construction of the New Knoll, finished in 1981.[320] The whole project allowed the governors to raise money by selling Garlands for residential development and to begin a major refurbishment of all the boarding houses, some of which had degenerated into high-class slums. By moving the Knoll into the new house, the Old Knoll was available to accommodate houses whose buildings were being repaired. This hugely expensive process extended to the mid-1990s, constituting a vital part in Harrow's ability to attract pupils as well as customers for holiday lets.

[318] GBM, 14 July 1975, 17 July 1978, 6 June 1987; Long-Term Priorities Document 1989.
[319] GBM, 13 Nov. 1965; shelved, 8 June 1967.
[320] GBM, 11 Nov. 1978, 3 Mar., 30 July, 10 Nov. 1979, 1 Mar., 8 Nov. 1980.

Hoban received little credit for such preparation for the future. If anybody noticed, they ascribed it to the governors. A man of great affability, Hoban failed to communicate his ideas or personality to his colleagues, some of whom thought him too decent to cope with Harrow.[321] Not wishing to frighten, he became intimidated. To those accustomed to Dr James' rambling talk delivered from the fireplace in his study, Hoban, seeming to be trapped behind 'the Great Barrier desk', as the uncharitable *Harrovian* writer described it, appeared evasive and weak. Such reactions worsened the context for taking decisions, making them harder to reach which in turn increased irritation, forming a classic vicious circle. Few on the Hill emerged with much credit from the assassination of Hoban's Head Mastership. Constant sniping, not all of it behind his back, wore him down. Despite his effective actions behind the scenes, public and school perceptions were of disintegration, such opinions became self-fulfilling, as judgement on his policies was filtered through a web of hostility and criticism. Thus when he took the brave step of sacking an allegedly inept housemaster, his action was misconstrued as the behaviour of an impulsive and weak man.

In the Spring of 1979 it became clear that a senior, much-liked, and well-connected housemaster had apparently lost control of his house which had become the scene of extravagant bacchanalia. Hoban acted swiftly and decisively, removing the housemaster and installing a replacement. As Welldon had once remarked, 'if all my masters were to leave, I could fill their places in a week'.[322] Somebody was always available to benefit from another's misfortune. The repercussions of this, the most public dismissal of a housemaster since Venables, the most politically bold since Pope, reverberated for a year as an appeal was lodged with the governing body and proceedings for unfair dismissal instigated before an Industrial Tribunal. Individual governors appeared to sympathize with the ousted housemaster, whom many had known for decades. However, in subsequent negotiations with him and his solicitor, they collectively upheld the constitutional line, insisting that 'the Head Master had acted with [their] full support'. They rejected the suggestion that the removal had been unfair because that 'would be tantamount to saying that the Head Master's decision was wrong, which would not be true'. To the Head Master, in March 1980, they expressly 'wished to re-affirm their approval of the decision he had taken'. In the end the matter was settled without a Tribunal hearing by a payment of £4,000 with no admission of liability.[323]

The affair damaged Hoban. Nobody doubted the basis for the dismissal, but many wondered why this incidence of housemasterly ineptitude had drawn such ferocity while alleged failings elswhere had been ignored. Some assumed the Head Master had been more frightened of other malefactors. Others put it down

---

[321] This is implied in *The Harrovian*, 28 Nov. 1981.
[322] Quoted by Venables, *Bases Attempted*, 173.
[323] GBM, 31 May, 10 Nov. 1979, 1 Mar., 5 June (and GPC report) 1980.

to irrational behaviour born of fatigue and strain. Surprisingly few gave Hoban credit for sparing his successor an even messier inheritance than was likely. Despite his critics, Hoban had not acted unreasonably nor deviously. He showed the correspondence with the housemaster to his senior master. At most, he could be accused of sudden action which took many by surprise, especially those not appraised of the facts. Like Boissier, Hoban failed in explaining his actions. His difficulties were compounded by the master concerned remaining on the staff in receipt of sympathy from colleagues and governors.[324] The Harrow Establishment hated social embarrassment and did not lightly forgive whoever was deemed to have provoked it.

The whisperers alleged that the governors tired of Hoban and engineered his dismissal. The evidence suggests otherwise. Without telling his friends on the staff, Hoban had decided to retire just short of his sixtieth birthday in 1981. He announced his intention to the governors in November 1979.[325] Unfortunately, this coincided with the height of the row over the housemaster's sacking. The pressures of these difficult years exacted a toll. Illness forced Hoban to take the Summer Term of 1980 away from the Hill, the senior master, R. B. Venables substituting for him. It was ironic that one of Hoban's last acts in his final year was of the sort to gladden his most ardent enemies; he joined with the governors in rejecting the proposal by Eton that Lord's be abandoned after 1981.[326]

As a Head Master, as opposed to socially, Hoban had not been popular with staff and old boys. His constructive work largely escaped observers and he was not the man to blow his own trumpet. He was poor at manipulating people and opinion; supine instead of vulpine with the press. Decisions did not come easily to him, many were genuinely exasperated by what they took to be irresolute vacillation. Once entrenched, perceptions can be as concrete as reality. Hoban was freely traduced by masters, governors, OHs, and pupils; his failure to counter misperceptions providing a kind of self-destructive complicity. Yet his achievements were more positive and more lasting than many other Head Masters'. He tried to attune Harrow to a changing world. At the very least, when Michael Hoban retired in the Summer of 1981, he left the school a much less stuffy place than he had found ten years before.

Elected on 1 May from a shortlist of three 'all of whom impressed', Ian David Stafford Beer provided a most striking contrast to his predecessor.[327] Educated at Whitgift School in Croydon and Cambridge, he was the first Harrow Head to be a rugger blue and international. He was also the first to hold a degree in science, taking Zoology in Part II of the Natural Science Tripos after Part I.[328] One of the

---

[324] GBM, 8 Nov. 1980. Cf. Ibid., 14 Nov. 1981.   [325] GBM, 10 Nov. 1979.
[326] GBM, 5 June, 8 Nov. 1980, 28 Feb., 4 June 1981.   [327] GBM, 1 May 1980.
[328] *Harrow Association Record* (1980), 8–9; *Harrow Register, 1986*, 799.

memorable images of his years as Head Master was the sight of him striding along the High Street like a galleon in his billowing gown carrying a brightly coloured plastic brain under his arm, a scene inviting inevitable juvenile comment ('Getting it repaired, Sir?'; 'Old one run out, has it, Sir? etc.)

Like his predecessor, aged 50 on taking up office at Harrow, after teaching at Marlborough, Beer had become Head Master of Ellesmere College in 1961 before moving to the Head Mastership of Lancing in 1969. Where Hoban appeared quietly scholarly, Beer projected ebullient self-confidence. A tall, large man, he possessed the charisma of physical dominance. Not shy to press his views, he believed in his ability to direct affairs and lead men. Not equipped with a strong historical perspective, none the less Beer's metaphors drew on an almost Victorian well of community and team spirit. Unafraid to voice at times old-fashioned views on the centrality of spiritual and physical as well as intellectual training, he struck a chord with a school that seemed to yearn for control and direction.

Beer's term of office coincided with the heyday of Thatcherite conservatism. Ideologically and financially, these were easier days for public schools. Private enterprise and what were misleadingly described as Victorian values received fulsome praise; the rich enjoyed encouraging tax rates; the wealthy were re-branded as social benefactors. The context for independent education had not been so favourable since the 1950s. Mrs Thatcher had been a Harrow parent and was pleased to support the school. Beer took full advantage of these propitious circumstances. Immediately, he imposed his distinctive style. Having taken advice, he had insisted as a condition of accepting the post that the governors build a separate house for the Head Master, to avoid the awkwardness and inconvenience of the lodgings on the High Street. Originally to be called 'Shaftesbury House', the new house, finished in 1982, was named 'Peel House', a possibly deliberate statement of authority rather than philanthropy, either appropriate for a Head Master who believed in Christian mission and social responsibility and appreciated the realities of rule by an aristocracy of talent and wealth.[329]

For Beer meant to be presidential, a chief executive free from the chains that had tied down his predecessor, free to promulgate his message of Harrow's excellence. He harangued, charmed, cajoled, flattered, and browbeat until his enthusiastic mantra was received by parents, prospective parents, prep. schools, the press, and Old Harrovians alike. He enjoyed public speaking and being reported in the press. He became the school's chief and most effective publicity officer, unabashed in declaring his school one of the finest in the world. If nothing else, Harrow's recent past convinced him of the importance of perceptions. He wished Harrow to be regarded as a successful business, sensitive to the aspirations and needs of its clients to whose requirements the school would adapt. A key element in presenting this image was a clear set of principles concerning the all round training of boys that

---

[329] GBM, 5 June 1980, 14 Nov. 1981. There was also a suggestion of calling it Sheridan House.

would not have sounded entirely out of place a century earlier.[330] Yet no less important was an agressive embracing of modernity, whether in the field of computing, social education, or physical training. Assisted by new examination systems and syllabuses, the academic status of the school was conveniently refocused on A, O, then GCSE results. Beer successfully re-packaged and re-marketed Harrow.

He insisted on being positive. In Speech Room or elsewhere, his praise of individual or collective achievement regularly teetered on the edge of hyperbole. But what may have appeared as a generous, eccentric, or embarrassing quirk contained a serious purpose. He wanted members of the school to feel cherished and fulfilled, even at the cost of an orgy of mutual self-congratulation. For those with non-athletic interests, he created the Guild, a mock-Phil., a club for unclubbables. He understood the importance of creating receptive conditions for his policies by the repeated portrayal of them as innovative, popular, or successful. He was especially good at this in dealing with the governors. In November 1985 he proclaimed the term's roll of 752 boys a record, ignoring the 752 of 1978 or the 762 of 1977; it was only a record for an autumn term, a result of shifting entry patterns. In 1991 he declared 'broad interest' among masters in a link with a school in Osaka, Japan, when the majority had been either unaware or wholly indifferent to the idea. More boldly, he announced in 1989 the 'strongly favourable reaction' to the new 'Senior Masters' salary scale from the masters, by whom he actually meant the beneficiaries. Elsewhere there had been considerable unease at its substance and manner of devising.[331] Such economy with the truth was part of a management style that attempted, with remarkable success, to sweep people along into accepting Beer's analysis of events, actions, and projects on his terms. Criticism or undue discussion were equated with dissent which, he had learnt from Hoban's experience, could fatally undermine the smiling image being promoted and damage the school and the livelihood of those working in it. Masters' contracts, a new concept for Harrow, included clauses forbidding public utterances deemed prejudicial to the school's interests.

In establishing a mood of optimism within the school Beer was remarkably effective, although masters seemed more in awe of his relentless energy and frenetically busy administrative style than the boys, who called him 'Reggie'. Decisions flooded from the Head Master's study in profligate waves; his desk was always clear; his notes often abrupt, thoughts begun typically ending with a ubiquitous implication of continuance: '. . .'. Like Norwood, he painted with a broad brush, details often seeming irksome. He demanded written submissions to be brief, their main points highlighted. When not indulging in neo-Arnoldian rhetoric, his talk could slide into the language of management consultancy. The favourable contrast with the presentational skills of his predecessor was noted by veterans of the 1970s. Myth

---

[330] See e.g. Long-Term Priorities Document, 1989, *passim*.
[331] GBM, 10 Nov. 1985, 25 Feb. 1989, 23 Feb. 1991.

creation appeared as an almost unavoidable consequence of the project of renewal, under Beer as under Norwood, although some were repelled by the excessively negative picture of Hoban that was portrayed.

Beer's task, object, and achievement were to reinvigorate the school. A central element of his policy revolved around communication both within the school and with its various constituencies. Masters' views on general and specific future plans were formally canvassed when drawing up the Long-Term Priorities Document in 1989. Greater contact between the governors and the masters was encouraged. Summary minutes of Governing Body meetings were posted in the Masters' Room. More social contacts were arranged. Given the permanent Appeal, inherited from his predecessor, Beer recognized the importance of explaining policy and reassuring Old Harrovians. A sportsman and a conservative, alert to the new material opportunities offered the OH classes by Thatcher's Britain, Beer vigorously socialized with the old boys to some effect. An indefatigable visitor to prep. schools, he recognized the need to nurture links with the declining number of 'feeder' boarding schools. As early as 1965, it was noted that 35 per cent of Harrovians came from London, Middlesex, and Surrey;[332] the predominance of the South-East grew steadily, while the number of prep. schools sending significant numbers of boys to Harrow fell. Beer promoted visits of masters to prep. schools and open days, for sport or music, at Harrow. Parents were not ignored. Beer used to address parents of new boys on their first evening, to set the tone. In 1982 Beer instituted termly Newsletters and annual Parents' Evenings, this last a radical departure from tradition. Previously, almost all direct contact between school and parent had been conducted through housemasters, aided by termly reports. Parents enjoyed putting faces to the names their sons bandied about, and, in return, these encounters encouraged masters' diplomatic skills and a new style of oral opacity. If these meetings proved useful to parents, they enlightened masters even more to their pupils' backgrounds. Such contacts bound parents more closely to the school by information, involvement, and complicity. It also recognized that the old days when parents willingly ignored their children for the months of the school terms were over. Especially in a boarding school, access and a sense of shared responsibility were vital.

Within the school, given the sluggish turnover of staff and the resilience of pupils, Beer's energy was more dissipated. Individual masters pursued their own cultural, intellectual, technological, artistic, musical, dramatic, and sporting interests much as they always had, through societies and informally, although Beer was ever keen to publicize such activities. Boy culture remained robustly and predictably impervious and unmoved by much of the prevailing window-dressing. All Head Masters are the butt of teasing. Beer's habits provided a rich source of imitation and entertainment, his big personality creating commensurately large scope for schoolboy mockery.

---

[332] *Report of Inspectors, 1965,* 2.

Beer encouraged a new flavour to religious life, through bringing with him from Lancing a second chaplain, described by Beer as 'our priest on the Hill' to distinguish between the two, and the licensing of a Lay Reader. As passionately as any Arnoldian, he argued that 'much of the strength of the individual will come from... spiritual growth'.[333] Physical strength and growth were also a major enthusiasm, translated into practice by the appointment to the staff in 1982 of a rugger international and coach and the redesigning of the football fields. The new Sports Hall and indoor swimming pool, opened in 1985, constituted an appropriate memorial to a Head Master whose experience led him to elevate the educational role of sport as few had done so openly for decades.[334] In a modern context, Beer refashioned the ideals of Christian manliness. In Speech Room, when praising the First XV in defeat as in victory, Beer left his audience in no doubt of the value he placed on sport as a builder of character. Just as sport taught lessons available to all, so religion was seen as providing the essential, inescapable frame for social behaviour. The assigning of responsibility for the delivery of Personal and Social Education to the Religious Studies Department in 1989 spoke eloquently of Beer's world view, just as the trumpeted conception of the programme witnessed his enthusiasm for holistic education.

The academic curriculum presented more intractable problems. Beer supported the fashionable belief that secondary education was too narrow, encouraging too much specialization. Yet despite repeated official ululations about the resultant damage, government policy and educational practice failed materially to alter the status quo. If systems remained ossified, new subjects presented more superficially appealing scope for Beer's modernizing instincts. The building of the lavishly equipped CDT centre in 1988 seemed to open a new door of learning and skills.[335] In fact, many Harrovians still left school without being computer literate and few except the less academically able specialized in Design or Technology. Despite the rhetoric of newness, one of the more striking features of the 1980s was that traditional subjects served Harrow best. On the elitist scale of Oxbridge results, in many years the school depended heavily on the old staples of classics, chemistry, and history. At A Level, although the march of the sciences continued, the tenacity of arts subjects, including English and geography, reflected inescapable intellectual conservatism. Initiatives in Arabic and Japanese were only modestly successful.[336] The one unequivocal success was the introduction of Spanish in 1989.[337] For all the discussion and despite the introduction of AS Levels and the new GCSE exams in 1988, there was no radical strategic curriculum development, although they loomed as Beer left.[338] The extensive changes that did occur were in contents of

---

[333] *Harrow Association Record* (1985), 9.
[334] GBM, 12 Mar., 11 June 1983, 16 June 1984, 9 Feb. 1985.
[335] GBM, 9 Feb., 8 June, 16 Nov. 1985, 21 Feb. 1987, 27 Feb. 1988.
[336] GBM, 13 Nov. 1982, 12 Mar. 1983.   [337] GBM, 25 Feb. 1989.
[338] GBM, 2 June 1990.

courses and modes of examining, over neither of which school policy could have the slightest impact and the implementation of which was outside the Head Master's direct control.

The most important academic innovation of Beer's Head Mastership was imposed from outside. The abandonment by Cambridge and Oxford of the post-A Level Entrance examination presented all public schools with a problem, as it was almost exclusively they who had the resources and the wealthy parents to cater for pupils staying an extra term. Academically, the abolition of the post-A Level term constituted a major loss. Thereafter, A Level represented the summit of academic achievement causing a clear, unmistakable contraction of intellectual life. Standards of teaching and learning inevitably found their own pragmatic level. As serious were the financial implications of the loss of a term's fees from scores of pupils. Entry to Harrow had traditionally been every term, although from the late 1970s, fewer were joining in the Summer Term.[339] Boys had joined different year groups. In the 1960s scholars went straight into the Lower Fifth and sat O Levels in a year. In the Upper School it was not uncommon to find boys from three different years in the same division. The need to secure five years' fees without stealing boys early from prep. schools resulted in a fundamental change. From the mid-1980s, in a process complete by 1988, entry to Harrow was effectively restricted to the Autumn Term. Every boy, however clever or dull, joined the same year block (the Shells), thereafter progressing as a block through five years, ending together in the Sixth Form. This made for administrative convenience and academic neatness. The traditional acceleration for the bright with different paces for the average and the slow which in various guises had been a feature of Harrow's educational system since the seventeenth century gave way to a monolithic structure that creaked with strain at either intellectual extremity. The new system quickly assumed the status of immemorial custom: within a few years one master who had taught for twenty years under the old dispensation insisted it was impossible to organize a school or a house if boys of the same year were in different academic blocks. None the less, the experience of being a Harrovian had been significantly transformed. With central feeding in the 1970s, the unavoidable academic uniformity of the 1980s levelled the peaks and pits of the school's academic life, turning the variety of lush forests and parched deserts into even, flat, temperate grasslands. This was the experience of all public schools in the 1980s.

To compensate, greater emphasis was placed on extra-curricular activities, especially of the athletic variety, but importantly including music, art (both boosted by special Entrance Scholarships), and drama. This involved its own contradiction. In an age of informal and formal league tables, the school needed good examination results. As a result, the number of lessons taught and preps. set grew. To attract pupils, the school was required to provide excellent extra-curricular facilities and

---

[339] *Harrow Register, 1986, passim.*

opportunities which, as ever, could in practice compete for time with academic preparation: an old story in a new translation.

Harrow in the 1980s basked in a climate of public approval. However, it was inevitable that Beer's promotional efforts attracted greater cynicism within the school than outside. At times his laudable desire to portray the school in the best light stretched credulity. Both beating and fagging, especially the latter, persisted far longer than public statements indicated.[340] Administrative activity was not necessarily synonymous with effective decisions. Encouragement could sound like bombast; self-confidence appear vanity. When the band stopped playing and the stage cleared, many of the effects appeared transitory. There were fewer structural changes than may have been assumed. The Central List for admissions remained ineffectual. Traditional attitudes to class, and race, drink, and drugs persisted.[341] The increase in numbers, at less than 6 per cent over the ten years of his Head Mastership, was unspectacular. The great prosperity of the mid-1980s looked less secure with the bursting of the bubble of the Lawson boom after 1988. The early planning of the new theatre, an idea first conceived in the the late 1960s and completed under his successor in 1994, was, ironically, a presentational disaster with the local community, although this was not Beer's fault.[342] Not all felt easy with the creeping centralization of power in the hands of Bursars and Bursary; the exponential growth of the school bureaucracy; or the incorporation of business mentalities and practices in areas not apparently suited to them. Not all such features were integral to Beer's scheme of renewal. Some felt an appreciation of scholarship had been sacrificed to examination competence, although Beer insisted in 1983 that entry standards would not be lowered simply to maintain the annual surplus.[343]

When in 1989 the Chairman of the governors euphorically described Beer as 'one of the greatest Head Masters of the School', he was not necessarily thinking of such tangible matters.[344] Beer's achievement, like that of the school throughout its history, was of image as much as substance, the image that converts into pupils, fees, reputation, good publicity, and rich donations. This was one of Harrow's oldest and highest traditions, that of Bryan, Thackeray, Sumner, Drury, Vaughan, Monty Butler, Norwood, and James. Beer was immensely fortunate to lead Harrow at a time when it seemed that the school and others like it were striding once more to the heart of the British Establishment after years of faded grandeur and apologetic reticence. He seized the opportunity. At the Albert Hall in November 1990, at a special Songs concert to commemorate the fiftieth anniversary of Churchill's first visit in 1940, Harrow appeared in the heart of London *en fête* to celebrate this

---

[340] GBM, 21 Feb. 1987.   [341] GBM, 7 June 1986.
[342] GBM, 21 Nov. 1987, 24 Feb. 1990. Cf. ibid., 6 June 1987, 19 Nov. 1988.
[343] GBM, 11 June 1983.
[344] GBM, 25 Nov. 1989. Cf. ibid., June 1988 for praise of Beer's policy of opening communications between masters and governors.

modern school cult. The building was packed with the school, masters, OHs, and the great and good. If the occasion approached the apotheosis of Churchill, it also stood as a symbol of the confidence Beer had manufactured for Harrow. Yet, that same day Mrs Thatcher, who was to have been a guest, had announced her resignation. In a moment of symbolism no less telling than the event itself, when the Chairman of the governors, the Cabinet Secretary, F. E. R. Butler, in a remarkable address, ventured to send the assembly's best wishes to the fallen Prime Minister, there erupted an extraordinary roar of approval the like of which few present had ever experienced. It was the cry of a tribe that had lost its totem, the bellow of a herd in distress. Times would not be the same; but, then, they never are.

When Beer retired from the Head Mastership a few months later, at the end of the Summer Term 1991, his gilding of the modernization of Harrow appeared complete. Over twenty years, Harrow, yet again, had transformed itself without shedding the trappings of custom. If its certainty was more brittle than in the past; if its status was less genuinely august, the school was not showing it. In this confidence in its state of grace, modern Harrow found a bond with its history. On his final afternoon, as he passed through the ranks of cheering boys back for the last time to the front door of the old Head Master's house, in contrast to Montagu Butler who had trod the same path 106 years earlier, Ian Beer was smiling not weeping.

Conclusion

In the course of corresponding with the *Daily Sketch* over a series the paper was running on Harrow School in 1968, Dr James argued that 'one really must not destroy illusions because there isn't anything to be served by doing so', later adding that 'lots of people would be upset if what they have always been told was said to be no longer quite true'.[1] Historians must disagree with his first remark while recognizing the truth of the second. The Head Master's comments expose one central theme of the school's past. There are parallel histories of Harrow: what may actually have happened has been shadowed by what was said or believed to have happened. Since the eighteenth century the myth or myths of Harrow provided consistent support to the practical efforts of governors and masters to sustain the institution. The memories of former schoolboys are notoriously pliable, yet they provide the basis upon which their later support or disapproval is based. Those working within the institution rarely bother to question whatever interpretation is currently fashionable. Until the mid-nineteenth century, Harrow and Harrovians treasured an image of rowdy independence and found their poet in Byron. From Vaughan and Monty Butler, previous assumptions of power and rule became self-conscious and sought justification in the idea of duty, religion, and manliness. These found a voice with Edward Bowen. Both were some way removed from the daily routine of school life yet provided the intellectual and cultural framework in which members and observers of the school interpreted their experiences. The role of sentiment was and is fundamental not just to understanding the school's history but to how it actually operates. Harrow is bound to its past with hoops stronger than steel. In 1907, commemorating the fiftieth anniversary of the consecration of the school chapel, Joseph Wood described the essence of this intimacy: 'Every stone is eloquent with the memories of a personal past. The Chapel is not a monument, it is a Biography'.[2]

---

[1] HM/J/3 and 25 June 1968, James to Neville Randall.
[2] Laborde, *Harrow School*, 102.

One of the pitfalls of such institutional biography lies in the subject's persistent efforts to mislead, disguise, and manipulate opinion. Harrow's myths are legion and old. The eighteenth century displayed an interest only in an affective past, scenes of childhood. The Victorians demanded an ancient pedigree to bolster privilege. The twentieth century needed a smokescreen behind which the school could adapt and change. The original question persists. How was it that Harrow rose from modest obscurity to international fame? Well-connected governors, from the Gerrards onwards, were able to exploit the convenient site and the growing taste for public schools. By lacking the grand associations and rigid statutes of the collegiate schools, which some thought should be envied, Harrow retained flexibility and openness. It could adapt its entry to suit demand and its rhetoric to follow the times; seventeenth-century professionals, eighteenth-century aristocrats, nineteenth-century gentrified bourgeois, twentieth-century business; Calvinism; High Society; the British Empires; and the end of deference. If there is one conclusion to be taken from the 400 years of Harrow's history it is a paradox. From William Launce, the Suffolk-born first Lyonian Head Master, and Macharie Wildblood, the vicar's son and first recorded pupil, Harrow, like all other schools, could appear self-obsessed and introspective. Apparently hidebound by sentimentality, its social attitudes and educational policies frequently appearing atrophied, its survival and moments of eminence periodically demonstrated alert sensitivity to the requirements of the world outside, an awareness of the dangers of isolation vividly captured by Roger, Lord North, lord of the Rectory Manor of Harrow, writing from his house on the Hill, the old Rectory on the site of The Grove, to Sir Robert Cecil, Secretary of State, on 7 June 1596: 'At Harrow Steeple we see far and hear nothing.'[3]

---

[3] *Calendar of MSS preserved at Hatfield House, Royal Historical Manuscripts Commission*, vi (London, 1895), 211.

Select Bibliography

1. Manuscript Sources

Bodleian Library, Oxford, MS G. A. Middl. 65, 'Miscellaneous Papers' of Herbert Greene.
Bodleian Library, Oxford, MS Rawlinson D 1138.
British Library, Additional MSS 18,556, 29,254, 35,377, 35,384.
British Library, MS Harleian 2211.
Harrow School Archives.
Manuscripts of the late Rex Collings.

2. Printed Sources

ACKERMANN, R., *History of the Free School at Harrow* (London, 1816).

BALL, A. W., *Paintings, Prints and Drawings of Harrow on the Hill, 1562–1899* (London Borough of Harrow, 1978).
BENSON, A. C., *Diary*, ed. P. Lubbock (London, 1926).
BETJEMAN, J., *Letters*, ed. C. Lycett-Green, ii (London, 1995).
BOLTON, W., *A Poem upon a Laurel Leaf* (London, 1690).
BOWEN, W. E., *Edward Bowen: A Memoir* (London, 1902).
BUTLER G. (ed.), *Harrow School Speech Bills of Dr Drury and Dr Butler 1780–1829* (priv. pub., 1848).
BUTLER, H. M., *A Letter to the Governors of Harrow School on the Principal Recommendations of the Public Schools Commissioners* (priv. pub., 1864).
—— '*He Served his generation*': *A Sermon Preached in Llandaff Cathedral on 24 October 1897* (n.p., 1897).
BUTLER, S. (ed.), *The Life and Letters of Dr. Samuel Butler*, 2 vols. (London, 1896).
BYRON, GEORGE, LORD, *Letters and Journals*, ed. L. A. Marchand (London, 1973–82).
—— *Poetical Works*, i, ed. J. J. McGann (Oxford, 1980).

Calendar of Manuscripts preserved at Hatfield House, Historical Manuscripts Commission, vi (London, 1895).
Calendar of Patent Rolls, 1547–8.
Calendar of Patent Rolls, Elizabeth I.
Calendar of State Papers, Domestic. Addenda, 1566–79.
CANNON, G. (ed.), *The Letters of Sir William Jones*, 2 vols. (Oxford, 1970).
'C.L.H.', *Memorials of a Harrow Schoolboy* (London, 1873).
The Commemoration of the Tercentenary of Harrow School (Harrow, 1871).
COULTON, G. G., *Fourscore Years: An Autobiography* (Cambridge, 1943).

Daryl, S. ['An Old Harrovian'], *Harrow Recollections* (London, 1867).
Dibdin, T. F., *Reminiscences of a Literary Life*, 2 vols. (London, 1836).
Dictionary of National Biography.
Done Bushell, W., *Harrow Octocentenary Tracts*, ix, x, xi, xiii (Cambridge, 1897–1909).
—— et al., *William Done Bushell of Harrow* (Cambridge, 1919).
'D.P.H.', 'A Woman's Invasion of a Famous Public School', *Cornhill Magazine* (Oct. 1932).
Drury, C., *Memoir of the Rev. Joseph Drury DD, Annual Biography and Obituary*, i, (London, 1834), i. Part I.

Farmer, J. (ed.), *Harrow Songs and Glees* (London, 1885).
Farrar, F. W., *In the Days of Thy Youth* (London, 1889).
Field, W., *Memoirs of the Life, Writings and Opinions of the Rev. Samuel Parr LLD*, 2 vols. (London, 1828).
Fox, A., *Follow Up!* (London, 1908).
Frere, W. H., and W. M. Kennedy, *Visitation Articles and Injunctions*, 3 vols. (London, 1910).

Golland, J. S., *The Harrow Apprentices* (London Borough of Harrow, 1981).
—— *Eighteenth Century Harrow* (typescript, priv. circulated, 1986).
Greene, G. (ed.), *The Old School* (London, 1984).
Gregory, Lady (ed.), *Sir William Gregory: An Autobiography* (London, 1894).

Hare, A. J., *The Story of My Life*, i (London, 1896).
The Harrovian.
Harrow Association Record.
Harrow School Songs (Henley, 1993).
Hartley, L. P., 'The Conformer', in G. Greene (ed.), *The Old School* (London, 1984).
Historical Manuscripts Commission: Fifteenth Report. Appendix Pt. 1, *Manuscripts of the Earl of Dartmouth*, iii (London, 1896).
Historical Manuscripts Commission: National Register of Archives, Letters and Papers of C. T. Longley (Lambeth) Catalogue.
Holford, G., *The Cave of Neptune* (London, 1801).

Index of Wills Proved in the Prerogative Court of Canterbury, 1584–1604, ed. S. A. Smith and E. A. Fry, British Record Society (London, 1901).
Ingram, M. E., *Leaves from a Family Tree* (Hull, 1951).

Johnstone, J., *The Works of Samuel Parr LLD*, 8 vols. (London, 1828).
Jones, W., *Works* (London, 1799).

Leaf, C. M., *Walter Leaf, 1852–1927: Some Chapters of Autobiography* (London, 1932).
Lee, Nathaniel, *Sophonisba or Hannibal's Overthrow: A Tragedy* (London, 1697).
Lunn, A., *The Harrovians* (London, 1913).
—— *Memory to Memory* (London, 1956).

MACLURE, J. STUART, *Educational Documents: England and Wales 1816 to the Present Day* (5th edn., London, 1986).
'Martello Tower' [F. M. Norman], *At School and at Sea* (London, 1899).
MAURICE, T., *Memoirs of the Author of Indian Antiquities*, i (London, 1819).
MAYO, C. H. P., *Reminiscences of a Harrow Master* (London, 1928).
Medwin's Conversations of Lord Byron, ed. E. J. Lovell (Princeton, NJ, 1966).
MEINERTZHAGEN, R., *Diary of a Black Sheep* (London, 1964).
Memoir of Rev. F. Hodgson, ii (London, 1878).
MERIVALE, C., *Autobiography and Letters*, ed. J. A. Merivale (Oxford, 1898).

NEHRU, J., *An Autobiography* (Oxford, 1989).
NORDEN, J., *Speculum Britanniae* (London, 1593; repr. 1723).
NORWOOD, C., *The English Tradition of Education* (London, 1929).
—— *Religion and Education, The Teaching Church*, paper no. ix (London, 1932).
NOWELL, A., *A Catechisme or First Instruction and Learning of Christian Religion*, tr. T. Norton (London, 1570).

PART, A., *The Making of a Mandarin* (London, 1990).
PLAYFAIR, G., *My Father's Son* (London, 1937).
PREVOST, G., *The Autobiography of Isaac Williams BD* (London, 1892).
PRICE, C. (ed.), *The Letters of Richard Brinsley Sheridan* (Oxford, 1966).
PROTHERO, R. E., *Letters and Journals of Lord Byron* (London, 1898).
PRYME, J. T., and A. BAYNE, *Memorials of the Thackeray Family* (priv. pub., 1879).

RENDALL, E. D., and G. H. RENDALL, *Recollections and Impressions of the Rev. John Smith MA* (London, 1913).
RENDALL, F., *The Foundation of John Lyon: Remarks on the Present Distribution of its Funds* (Harrow, 1865).
Report by Her Majesty's Inspectors on Harrow School, Harrow, November 1965 (Dept. of Education and Science, London, 1966).
Report by His Majesty's Inspectors on Harrow School, Middlesex, May 1951 (Ministry of Education, London, 1951).
Report of the Royal Commission on Public Schools (The Clarendon Commission) (London, 1864).
Report on the Manuscripts of Lady de Cane, Historical Manuscripts Commission (London, 1906).
RUSSELL, G. W. E., *Fifteen Chapters of Autobiography* (London, n.d.).

Savillon's Elegies (London, 1795).
SCHOENBAUM, S., *William Shakespeare: A Compact Documentary Life* (Oxford, 1977).
SCOTT, E. J. L., *Records of the Grammar School Founded by John Lyon at Harrow-on-the-Hill AD 1572* (Harrow, 1886).
SENDALL, W. J., *The Literary Remains of C. S. Calverley* (London, 1885).
Shardloes Papers of the Seventeenth and Eighteenth Centuries, ed. G. Eland (London, 1947).
SOMERVELL, R., *Chapters of Autobiography* (London, 1935).

Statutes of the Realm.
STRETTON, C., *Memoirs of a Chequered Life*, 3 vols. (London, 1862).
SYMONDS, J. A., *Memoirs*, ed. P. Grosskurth (London, 1984).

TEIGNMOUTH, FIRST BARON, *Memoirs of the Life, Writings and Correspondence of Sir William Jones* (London, 1804).
TEIGNMOUTH, SECOND BARON, *Memoir of the Life and Correspondence of John, Lord Teignmouth*, 2 vols. (London, 1843).
TORRE, H. J., *Recollections of School Days at Harrow* (Manchester, 1890).
TOWNSEND WARNER, G., *On the Writing of English* (London, 1914).
TRENCH, F., *A Few Notes from Past Life, 1818–1832* (Oxford, 1862).
TRUEMAN, WOOD, SIR H., 'Harrow in the Fifties', *Cornhill Magazine* (Apr. 1921).

VACHELL, H. A., *The Hill* (9th edn., London, 1906).
—— *Fellow Travellers* (London, 1923).
VAUGHAN, C. J., *Harrow Sermons* (London, 1853).
—— *Memorials of Harrow Sundays* (London, 1863).
VENABLES, E. M., *Bases Attempted: Twenty-Five Years at Harrow* (typescript, priv. circulated, n.d.).
VINCENT, J. (ed.), *A Selection from the Diaries of Edward Henry Stanley, 15th earl of Derby, 1869–1878*, Camden Fifth Series, iv (London, 1994).

WELLDON, J. E. C., *Gerald Eversley's Friendship: A Study in Real Life* (London, 1895).
—— *Recollections and Reflections* (London, 1915).
—— *Forty Years On* (London, 1935).
WEST, SIR ALGERNON, *Recollections* (London, 1899).
WILKINS, C., *Concilia Magnae Britanniae et Hiberniae*, iii (London, 1737).
WILKINSON, T., *Memoirs*, 4 vols. (York, 1790).
WORDSWORTH, C., *Annals of My Early Life* (London, 1891).

Young Colt's Diary, 'ed.' C. Terrot (London, 1936).

3. Secondary Works

AKBAR, M. J., *Nehru: The Making of India* (London, 1989).
ALINGTON, C., *Lionel Ford* (London, 1934).
ALLEN, E. A., 'Public School Elites in Early-Victorian England', *Journal of British Studies*, 21 (1982).
ANNAN, N., 'The Intellectual Aristocracy', in *Studies in Social History: A Tribute to G. M. Trevelyan*, ed. J. H. Plumb (London, 1955).
ARNOLD, H. J. P., *William Henry Fox Talbot* (London, 1977).
ASHLEY, E., *The Life and Correspondence of Henry John Temple, Viscount Palmerston*, 2 vols. (London, 1879).

BAMFORD, T. W., 'Public Schools and Social Class, 1801–50', *British Journal of Sociology*, 12 (1961).

―― *The Rise of Public Schools* (London, 1967).
BARRETT-LENNARD, T., *An Account of the Families of Lennard and Barrett* (London, 1908).
BEST, G., 'Militarism', in B. Simon and I. Bradley (eds.), *The Victorian Public School* (London, 1975).
BOURNE, K., *Palmerston: The Early Years, 1784–1841* (London, 1982).
BOWEN, R., *Cricket: A History of its Growth and Development throughout the World* (London, 1970).
BRIGGS, A., *The Age of Improvement* (London, 1959).
BROWN, J. M., *Nehru* (London, 1999).
BURNETT, M., *History of the Harrow Mission and Club in Notting Dale* (London, 1983).
BRYANT, P. H. M., *Harrow* (London, 1936).

CANNON, G., *The Life and Mind of Oriental Jones* (Cambridge, 1990).
CANNON, J., *Aristocratic Century* (Cambridge, 1984).
CARLISLE, N., *A Concise Description of the Endowed Grammar Schools in England and Wales*, 2 vols. (London, 1818).
CHANDOS, J., *Boys Together* (London, 1984).
CHAPLIN, E. D. W., *The Book of Harrow* (London, n.d.).
CHARLTON, K., *Education in Renaissance England* (London, 1965).
CHURCHILL, R. S., *Winston S. Churchill*, i (London, 1966).
CHURCHILL, W. L. S., *My Early Life* (London, 1930).
CHURTON, R., *Life of Alexander Nowell* (Oxford, 1809).
CLARK, G. N., *The Later Stuarts* (Oxford, 1965).
CLARKE, M. L., *Greek Studies in England* (Cambridge, 1945).
―― *Classical Education in Britain, 1500–1900* (Cambridge, 1959).
CLAY, C. G. A., *Economic Expansion and Social Change in England, 1500–1700*, i (Cambridge, 1984).
COLLINSON, P., *Archbishop Grindal, 1519–83* (London, 1979).
Complete Peerage of England, Scotland, Ireland, Great Britain and the United Kingdom, ed. G. E. Cockayne; new edn., ed. V. Gibbs, G. H. White, H. A. Doubleday, *et al.*, 13 vols. (London, 1910–59).
CONNELL, B., *Portrait of a Whig Peer* (London, 1957).

DANCY, J. C., *The Public Schools and the Future* (London, 1963).
DARLOW, M., and G. HODSON, *Terence Rattigan: The Man and his Work* (London, 1979).
DAUGLISH, M. G., and P. K. STEPHENSON, *Harrow School Register, 1800–1911* (London, 1911).
DICKENS, A. G., *The English Reformation* (new edn., London, 1989).
DRAKE, W. R., *Heathiana* (priv. pub., 1881).
DRUETT, W. W., *Harrow through the Ages* (Uxbridge, 1935).

FARRAR, R., *The Life of Frederick William Farrar* (London, 1904).
FISCHER WILLIAMS, J., *Harrow* (London, 1901).
FOX, A., *Public School Life: Harrow* (London, 1911).
FROUDE, J. A., *Thomas Carlyle: A History of His Life in London*, 2 vols. (London, 1884).

GATHORNE-HARDY, J., *The Public School Phenomenon* (London, 1977).
GASH, N., *Mr Secretary Peel* (London, 1961).
GELDER, W. H., *Historic Barnet*, Barnet Historical Society (Barnet, n.d.).
GRAHAM, E., *The Harrow Life of H. M. Butler* (London, 1920).
GRAY, D., *Spencer Perceval* (Manchester, 1963).
GREIG, J. Y. T., *David Hume* (London, 1934).
GROGAN, LADY, *Reginald Bosworth Smith: A Memoir* (London, 1909).
GROSSKURTH, P., *John Addington Symonds* (London, 1964).
GUN, W. T. J., *The Harrow School Register, 1571–1800* (London, 1934).
GUY, J., *Tudor England* (Oxford, 1988).

HALLAM, G. H., F. E. MARSHALL, and G. W. E. RUSSELL, *Rev. H. M. Butler DD* (memorial vol., Harrow, 1918).
HARMAN, C., *Sylvia Townsend Warner* (London, 1989).
HAWKYARD, A., *William Henry Fox Talbot* (Harrow, 1989).
HOLE, C., *The Life of Archdeacon W. W. Phelps*, 2 vols. (London, 1871–3).
HONEY, J. R. DE S., *Tom Brown's Universe* (London, 1977).
HOWSON, E. W., and G. TOWNSEND WARNER (eds.), *Harrow School* (London, 1898).

JOHNSON, J., *Princely Chandos: John Brydges, 1674–1744* (London, 1984).

KALTON, G., *The Public Schools: A Factual Survey of Headmasters' Conference Schools in England and Wales* (London, 1966).
KREIDER, A., *English Chantries: The Road to Dissolution* (Cambridge, Mass., 1979).

LABORDE, E. D., *Harrow School: Yesterday and Today* (London, 1948).
LARPENT, F. DE H., *Reeves of Harrow School, 1745–1819* (London, 1911).
LAWSON, J., and H. SILVER, *A Social History of Education in England* (London, 1973).
LE MARCHANT, D., *Memoir of John Charles, Viscount Althorp, 3rd Earl Spencer* (London, 1876).

MACK, E. C., *Public Schools and British Opinion, 1780–1860* (London, 1938).
—— *Public Schools and British Opinion since 1860* (New York, 1941).
MANGAN, J. A., 'Philathletic Extraordinary: A Portrait of the Victorian Moralist Edward Bowen', *Journal of Sport History*, 9 (1982).
MARCHAND, L. A., *Byron. A Biography*, 3 vols. (London, 1957).
MARROT, H. V., *The Life and Letters of John Galsworthy* (London, 1935).
MAXWELL LYTE, SIR H. C., *A History of Eton College* (4th edn., Eton, 1911).
MAY, T., 'Relations between Harrow School and the Parishioners of Harrow', unpub. MA thesis, London, 1974.
MIDDLEMAS, K., and J. BARNES, *Baldwin. A Biography* (London, 1969).
MINCHIN, J. G. COTTON, *Old Harrow Days* (London, 1898).
MOIR, J. W., and L. J. VERNEY (eds.), *Harrow Register, 1885–1949* (London, 1951).
MOORE, R. W., *Charles John Vaughan Centenary Address* (Harrow, 1945).
MOORE, T., *Life of Lord Byron* (London, 1851).

MOORMAN, M., *George Macaulay Trevelyan* (London, 1980).
MORWOOD, J. H. W., *The Life and Works of Richard Brinsley Sheridan* (Edinburgh, 1985).

NEWSOME, D., *Godliness and Good Learning* (London, 1961).
—— *On the Edge of Paradise* (London, 1980).

O'DAY, R., *Education and Society, 1500–1800* (London, 1982).
OGILVIE, R. M., *Latin and Greek: A History of the Influence of the Classics on English Life from 1600 to 1918* (London, 1964).
OVERTON, J. E., and E. WORDSWORTH, *Christopher Wordsworth, Bishop of Lincoln* (London, 1890).

PARKER, C. S., *Sir Robert Peel*, i (London, 1899).
PATTENDEN, P., 'Peterhouse Honours May 1913', *Peterhouse Annual Record* (Cambridge, 1995–6).
PEACOCK, M. H., *History of the Free Grammar School of Queen Elizabeth at Wakefield* (Wakefield, 1892).
PORTER, R., *English Society in the Eighteenth Century* (London, 1982).
PURCELL, E. S., *The Life of Cardinal Manning*, 2 vols. (London, 1896).

QUIGLEY, I., *The Heirs of Tom Brown* (Oxford, 1982).

RAE, J., *The Public School Revolution, 1964–79* (London, 1981).

SANDERSON, M., *Educational Opportunity and Social Change in England* (London, 1987).
SHAW, R. A., 'Relations between Town and Gown in Nineteenth Century Harrow', unpub. London University MA thesis (1987).
SHROSBREE, C., *Public Schools and Private Education: The Clarendon Commission, 1861–64 and the Public Schools Act* (Manchester, 1988).
SIMON, B., *The Politics of Educational Reform, 1920–1940* (London, 1974).
—— *The Two Nations and the Educational Structure* (London, 1974).
—— and I. Bradley (eds.), *The Victorian Public School* (London, 1975).
SIMON, J., *Education and Society in Tudor England* (Cambridge, 1966).
STANLEY, A. P., *The Life of Thomas Arnold*, 2 vols. (London, 1858).
STOGDON, J. H. (ed.), *Harrow School Register, 1845–1937*, ii (London, 1937).
STRAY, C., *The Living Word. W. H. D. Rouse and the Crisis of Classics in Edwardian England* (Bristol, 1992).
—— *Classics Transformed* (Oxford, 1998).
STRUDWICK, V., *Christopher Wordsworth, bishop of Lincoln, 1869–85* (Lincoln, 1987).

THOMAS, K. V., *Rule and Misrule in the Schools of Early Modern England* (Reading, 1976).
THOMSON, A. A., *Hirst and Rhodes* (London, 1959).
THORNTON, P. M., *Harrow School and its Surroundings* (London, 1885).
TITTLER, R., *Nicholas Bacon. The Making of a Tudor Statesman* (London, 1976).
TOWNSEND WARNER, G. T., *Harrow in Prose and Verse* (London, 1913).

TRIPP, C. L., *A History of Queen Elizabeth's Grammar School, Barnet* (Cambridge, 1935).
TYERMAN, C. J., 'Byron's Harrow', *Journal of the Byron Society*, 17 (1989).

VANCE, N., 'The Ideal of Manliness', in B. Simon and I. Bradley (eds.), *The Victorian Public School* (London, 1975).
VERNEY, L. J. (ed.), *Harrow School Register, 1971* (London, 1971).
—— (ed.), *Harrow School Register, 1986* (London, 1987).
VICKERS, H., *Cecil Beaton* (London, 1993).
Victoria County History, Middlesex, iv (London, 1971).

WAKEFORD, J., *The Cloistered Elite* (London, 1969).
WALFORD, G., *Life in Public Schools* (London, 1986).
WANSELL, G., *Terence Rattigan* (London, 1995).
WARD, A., and A. WALLER, *Cambridge History of Literature*, vii, ix (Cambridge, 1911, 1912).
WATSON, F., *The English Grammar Schools to 1660* (Cambridge, 1908).
WATSON, J. STEVEN, *The Reign of George III* (Oxford, 1960).
WESTCOTT, A., *The Life and Letters of Brooke Foss Westcott*, 2 vols. (London, 1903).
WILKINSON, R., *The Prefects: British Leadership and the Public School Tradition* (London, 1964).
WRIGHTSON, K., *English Society, 1580–1680* (London, 1982).

YOUINGS, J., *Sixteenth Century England* (London, 1984).
YOUNG, G. M., *Victorian England: Portrait of an Age* (Oxford, 1936).

INDEX

Abbreviations: g = governor; HS = Harrow School; HM = Head Master; H = Harrow town; OH = Old Harrovian or Harrow boy; m = master at HS

Abercorn, James, 1st duke of, g 205, 219, 296, 311, 363, 427
Aberdeen, George, 4th earl of, g 163, 183, 204–5, 224, 234, 247, 251, 311
Aberdeen, Dudley, marquess of 536
Abbey, the, *see* Druries
Adair, A., g 424
Adair, Robert 202
Adkins, custos 61
aestheticism 340, 343–4
Akehurst, Sir John, g 424, 426
Aitken, P. A. 364
Alcock, C. W. 271
Alexander, Field Marshal Lord, g 424, 452
Alford School 24
All Souls College, Oxford 16, 60, 86
Allan, R. A., g 548, 554
Allegra, d. of Lord Byron 204
Allhusen, F. E., m 382
Althorp, George John, 2nd earl Spencer 98, 101, 106, 107, 110, 123, 26, 128, 137
Althorp, John Charles, 3rd earl Spencer 147, 163
Amery, John 511
Amery, L. S., g 344, 392, 400, 410, 416, 417, 422, 424, 426, 503, 511, 527, 528
Anderdon, John 193
Anderson, Henry 212
Anderson, Sir Hugh, g 409–10, 426
Anderson, Lindsay: *If* 544
Angelo, m 122
anti-semitism 321–2, 357, 396, 398–9, 463–6
Apcar, Gregory 421, 436–8

Apcar, J. A. 437
apprentices 46
Arabic 122
Archdall, Mervyn 90
archery 31, 62, 83
Armstrong, Mrs, house dame 153, 391
Army Class 256, 328, 333, 375, 379, 381, 383, 445, 446–7
Arnold, Matthew 298, 349
Arnold, Mrs, house dame 106, 110
Arnold, Thomas 171, 219, 203, 226, 228, 238, 248–9, 282
 and beating 195, 207
 and chapel 233
 and fagging 477–8
 influence of 221–2, 253, 256–9, 356, 461, 559
 and Vaughan 247–50
ARP wardens 444, 450–1
art 379, 562
Art Schools 379, 394
Ashford, C. E., m 332, 382
Ashwell, George 51
Assistant Masters' Association 386
assisted places scheme 407, 415, 416
Association Football 471
Asquith, H. H. 393
Athenaeum Club 184
athleticism, cult of 271, 334, 338–44, 354
 sex and 272
Attlee, Clement 445
Augmentations, court of 15

Bacon, Sir Nicholas 12, 24, 25
Baggs, boy at HS 83, 84

Index

Bagnall, A. G., m 539
Baldwin, R. M., m 385, 500, 528, 532
Baldwin, Stanley, g 241, 304, 309, 340–1, 345, 408, 409, 410, 411, 424, 430–1, 432, 448, 483, 503
Balfour, A. J. 359, 500
Balliol College, Oxford 91, 485, 528
Balme, M. G., m 540
Bamford, Gilbert, m 55–6
Bankes-Williams, I. W., m 450
Banks, Joseph 106–7
Baring, T. C. 264, 304
Barnard, Josias 50
Barnard, 'Mother' 160
Barnet 21, 24, 26, 36, 40
Barret-Lennard, Thomas, 17th Ld Dacre 89–90
Barrington, Daines 90
Barry, Alfred 310–11
Barrymore, earl of 115
Basil, I. (or T.) 83
Batt, Anne, school dame 153
Batten, George 187
Batten, S. E., m 188, 196, 201, 203, 206, 214, 215–17
Baxter, William 63
beating, *see* corporal punishment
Beaton, Cecil 408, 446, 481, 501, 520
Beaumont, T. W. 255
Beckwith, P. A., g 415, 436
Beddington, H. M. 321
beds, shared/single 110, 153
Beer, I.D.S., HM 405, 407, 416–17, 419, 432, 440, 441, 453, 455, 460–1, 465–6, 480, 490, 492, 548, 559
  election of 557
  and games 468, 470
  as HM 557–64
  and public relations 558–64
Bellamy, Thomas 19–20
Bennet, Philip: *The Beau's Adventures* 82
Bennet, William 107, 112, 120, 126, 130–1
Benson, A. C.: *The Schoolmaster* 398
Beresford-Hope, A. J. 233, 319–20
Bernard, Montagu, g 296
Besant, Annie 255
Bessborough, Lord 161

Betjeman, John 489, 490, 502
bill (i.e. call-over at HS) 125, 136–7
Billingsby, Capel 84, 85
Billingsby, Drope 85
biology 380
Bird, William 101
Birkett, J. P., m 226
Birley, Robert 536
Birmingham school 56–7
Biscoe, Elisha 110
Bishop, A. A., m 539
Blackwell, T. G. 418
Blake, Richard, m 144
Bland, Robert, m 153–4
Bliss, John, H publican 160, 180
Blithe, Mr, m 60, 86
Blount, Henry 82
Blundell, Peter 27
Board of Education 377–8, 411–13, 421, 432
Boas, P., m 514
Boer War 352, 356, 401–2, 445
Boissier, A. P., m and HM 134, 362, 374, 417, 418, 419, 420, 429, 445, 450, 463, 464, 479, 493, 500, 511, 516, 519–20, 522–3, 531, 534
  as HM 522–8
  feud with E. M. Venables 519, 522, 523
  reputation of 522
Bolton, William, HM 16, 45, 65, 67, 69–71, 229
  Poem on a Laurel Leaf 70–1
Bomford, N. R., HM 421
Bostock, J., m 419, 448, 514, 516, 523, 525–8
Bosworth-Smith, R., m 292, 320, 321, 329, 330, 331, 337, 338, 340, 360, 358, 366, 371, 379, 382, 388
botany 326, 331, 332, 380
Boucher, B. A., m 460
Bourchier, John 333
Bouverie, Jacob 98
Bowen, Dr, school doctor 192–3
Bowen, E. E., m 250, 261, 263, 264–5, 270, 297, 311, 314, 318, 319, 320, 321, 324–5, 342, 360, 365–6, 368, 371, 381, 385, 386, 388–9, 390, 394, 397, 419, 472, 475, 518

and athleticism 313, 339–40
benefactions of 392–3
candidate for HM 364, 366
influence of 334
legacy of 432, 436
obstructiveness of 379, 380, 382
and politics 359
and reform 291–2, 325–34
and Songs 344, 347–51
Bowlby, O. G., m 500, 513, 524, 528
boxing 159, 474
Boys' Own Paper 340–1
Bradby, E. H., m 255, 263, 386, 390, 391
Bradbys 255, 390, 431, 516, 517, 537
Bradley, Mr, schoolmaster 11, 40
Bradley, Mr, m 136
Bradshaw, T. E. J., m 500, 510–11
Bressy, Charles 84
Briod, M., m 154
Bromley, Rose (née Heath) 139, 147, 149
Bromley, Thomas, m 135–6, 143, 147, 149, 153, 154
Browning, O. 297, 343, 386
Brougham, Henry 168
Browne, C. R., m 445, 459, 467, 493, 500, 516, 528
Bruce, James 90
Brudenell, Lord, later earl of Cardigan 194
Brunel, Isambard Kingdom 252
Bryan, Samuel 79
Bryan, Thomas, HM 45, 66, 72–4, 78–87, 88, 362, 563
Bryan, Thomas, son of HM 79
Bryant, C. L., m 445, 527
Bryant, P. H. M., m 402, 458, 459, 461, 490, 514
Bryce Commission (1894–5) 330, 377, 385
Brydges, James, 1st duke of Chandos 74–8, 88, 91
Buchan, Agnes, countess of 294
Buck, Percy, m 352, 400, 456, 475–6
Bucknall, John, g 125, 126
Bucknall, William, g 85–6, 88, 89, 133
Buddhists 453
Bull, W. J. 263, 326, 388
bullying 151–2, 157, 159, 195, 272, 273, 317, 367, 396, 400, 446, 475, 480, 501

Burges, C. F. 319–20
bursars 302, 422
Bushell, W. D., m 312, 314, 323, 326, 367, 371, 373, 379, 381, 382, 388, 401
and sex 400
business studies 539, 551
Bute, earl of 115
Butler, E. M., m 307, 308–9, 342, 375, 418, 451, 499, 500
Butler, F. E. R., g 420, 426, 549, 563–4
Butler, George, HM 1, 144, 153, 164–6, 167, 168, 171, 172, 183–4, 186, 201–2, 204, 226, 228, 229, 230, 231, 234, 237, 253, 260, 306, 546
and beating 174, 194–5
and cult of HS 175–6
dismissal of 176
dynasticism of 203
failed discipline of 194–203
as HM 184–203
marriage of 184, 190–1
personality of 184, 194–5
and 'Pomposus' 155, 164–5, 166
resignation of 203
wealth of 184–6
Butler H. M., HM, g 41, 134, 201, 213, 250, 253, 263, 264, 265, 266, 273, 275, 276, 280, 316, 326, 353, 364, 369, 391, 394, 397, 401, 405, 417, 423, 428, 429, 437, 439, 456, 487, 489, 494, 536, 546, 563, 564
and curriculum 312–13
devotion to HS 306–10
and discipline 314, 365
election of 177–8, 202, 310–11
as HM 303–38, 342–4, 346, 353
influence of 354, 362
and fund-raising 307, 309
and masters 315–25
and music 346
personality of 304–6, 316
and politics 358, 359
and reform 286–302
resignation of 353
and sin 314
and Songs 344, 346
and sport 338, 342–4, 470

577

Butler H. M. (*cont.*):
  unpopularity of 354
  and Vaughan 245, 281–2, 283
  verses of 317
Butler, J. R. M., g 203, 373, 396, 426, 512, 529, 534–5
Butler, R. A. 412, 413
Butler, Samuel 110, 188, 204, 208–9, 220, 221, 228, 231–2, 331
Butterfield, Herbert 513
Butticaz, Jacques, m 154
Byrkhede, John 14, 16
Byron, George, Lord 107, 144, 146, 150, 151, 152, 157–66, 184, 186, 187, 197, 214, 307
  bully 153, 156
  disability of 157, 159–60
  influence of 169–70
  poetry of 140, 144–5, 154–4, 156–7, 158–9, 162, 164–6

Caius, John 9, 11
Calverley (né Blayds), C. S. 260, 264, 273
Calvert, W. J. R., m 527
Calvin, John 52
Catechism 30, 33
Calvinism 25
Cambridge University 210, 296
Cameron, Sir Donald, g 424
Campbell, Sir George 527
Canterbury, archbishops of 15, 16, 25, 29
Carlisle, K. R. M., g 424
Carlisle, I. M., 448
Caroline, Queen 198
Carrington, C. W., m 445, 464, 519, 527
Carroll, Lewis 221
Catholic Emancipation 123
Cecil, Sir Robert 566
Cecil, William, Lord Burghley 12, 24, 26
central feeding at HS 420, 422, 437, 441, 548, 554–5
central list for HS applications 493, 548, 552, 563
Champneys, Basil 354
Champneys, Thomas 106, 110, 111
chantries 14–15
Chantry of Blessed Virgin Mary, H 14–15
chapel 175, 186, 222, 233–5, 255, 256, 268, 276, 356, 361, 44, 459–60
  voluntary 532, 552
chaplains 371, 373, 458–61
Chapman, J. 247
Chapman, R. 267–8
Charity Commissioners 168, 284, 377, 393, 421
Charles I 52–3
Charles, William 89, 92
Charterhouse 69, 336, 363, 515
Chawner, William, g 427
Cheltenham College 172, 227, 288, 291, 313, 321, 357, 410
chemistry 380, 381–2, 561
Chester, Richard 105
Cholmley, John 85
Chotzner, J., housemaster 322
Christ Church, Oxford 15, 16, 205–6, 219
Christ's Hospital 26, 288
Church Hill House 255, 346
Church House, H 10, 13, 16
Churchill, A. Shepard 421, 436–7
Churchill, W. S. 157, 304, 328, 344–5, 357, 359, 367, 381, 383–4, 397, 401, 408, 410, 414, 416, 450, 451, 513, 523, 525
Churchill Memorial Appeal 414
Chute, Chaloner 137
City of London school 288
Clapham Sect, 215, 231
Clare, earl of 145
Clarendon, George, 4th earl of, g 285, 287, 292
Clarendon, Thomas, 2nd earl of, g 141, 142, 178
Clarendon Commission, the 251, 260, 271, 284–302
classical languages 31–3, 47, 56–8, 70, 99, 113, 118–19, 122–3, 161, 171, 181, 187, 191, 264–5, 285, 312–13, 326–9, 331, 379–85, 429, 495, 496–7, 506, 539–40, 553, 561
Claxton, Hammond 45
Clay, C. T. 363
Clifton College 321, 357, 387, 410
Clive, Robert 90
Coade, T. F., m 500, 522, 531
Cockerell, C. K. 186, 235, 237

Index

Coke, Edward 82
Coke-Norris, J. W., m 460, 500, 501, 511
Colbeck, C., M 329, 333, 381, 388, 391
Colenso, J. W., m 225–6, 228–30, 329
Common Entrance 378, 540
community service 452
comprehensive schools 486
Conington, John 278, 337
Connell, M. D., g 425, 426
Conservative Party 360, 407, 409, 413, 415, 415, 482, 546, 558
Contio, or Oration 46, 61–2, 83, 138, 141, 366, 429, 439, 498
Cooke, William 82
Cooke, Mr, m 136
Cookson, N. C. 271
Copse 389, 393, 394,
corporal punishment 30, 101, 102, 109, 116, 117–18, 135, 151, 174–5, 194–5, 197–8, 199, 207, 223, 257–9, 329, 336–7, 365, 367–8, 372, 475, 477, 478–80, 532
    failure of 195
    ritual of 195
Corpus Christi College, Oxford 136
Cory, W. S. 279, 340, 343, 345, 386
Cotton, G. E. C. 248, 253, 256, 339
Cottrell, G. C. 343
Coulton, G. G. 280
Coventry school 93
Cox, Elizabeth 100
Cox, James, m and HM 48, 64, 65, 73–4, 79, 80, 87–93, 134
    dismissal of 92–3
Cox, James, son of HM 91
Cox, Margaret 79
Cox, William, m 92, 117
Coxe, Richard 16–17
craft, design, technology 423, 432, 561
Crampton, Mrs, house dame 106, 110
cricket 108, 159, 174, 190, 192–3, 212, 270–1, 342–3, 469, 474, 538, 545
    and character forming 342
Crimean War 256
Crooke, John 132
Crosbie, James 105
Crosland, Anthony 406

Crown and Anchor public house 92, 160, 180
Cruikshank, J. A., m 367
Cuddesdon Theological College 456
Cunningham, J. W., g 175, 190–1, 204, 205, 247–8, 252, 276, 277, 311
    feud with H. Drury 321, 232–3
    feud with C. Wordsworth 230–41
    malignity of 171
    meddling of 201
    self-interest of 236
Curzon, G. N. 370
custodian of HS 61

Dahl, R. H. 470, 514
Dalrymple, Charles 245, 271, 279
dames:
    house 72, 105–6, 153, 172
    school 33, 46–7, 54, 59, 65, 73, 128, 268
dancing 99, 109, 122, 159
Danckwerts, Mr Justice 435
Dancy, John 485, 490–1, 547
Dartmouth, William, 2nd earl of 125, 127, 132
Dartmouth Naval College 445
Darwin, Charles 326, 331
Dauglish, M. G. 359
Davidson, H. O. D., m 333, 390
Davidson, Randall, g 262, 279, 304, 409, 424, 445, 457, 503
Davis, A. T., m 539
Davis, F. A. 321
debating society 256
declamations 121, 122, 107, 162–3, 191–2
    (1654, 1656) 56–8
Dedham school 31
Delawarre, 5th earl of 145, 156
Demainbray, Stephen 148
Denison, Michael 446, 521
Denne and Co., bankers 141
Dennis, John 61, 62
Derby, 15th earl of 258
Development Fund 433, 435
Development Trust 421
Devon, earl of 287
Dibdin, T. F. 1
Dickens, Charles 357

Digby, Kenelm 275
direct grant schools 416, 485–6
divinity 380
Dodington, Batholomew 57–8
Dodgson, Charles 219–21
Donaldson, S. 370
'Dons and Beaks' 386
Dorset, duke of 128, 145, 154, 156
Drakeford, R. J., m 539
drama 31, 83–6, 107, 116, 125, 520–1, 531, 538, 562
drawing 99, 109
drinking 152, 159, 172, 196, 211, 212
Drummond, Bulldog 409
Drummond, Edward 156
Drummond, Henry 148
Druries, formerly the Abbey 143, 147, 153, 174, 221, 226, 250, 260, 354, 391, 400, 526
Drury, Benjamin 149–50, 225, 226, 260, 263, 264, 266, 315, 386, 391
Drury, Charles 144, 149
Drury, Henry, m 149, 153, 154, 158, 168, 188, 189, 196, 198, 200–1, 210, 224, 228, 237, 319, 386
   candidate for HM 204–5
   decline of 208, 214–15, 218, 225
   feud with Cunningham 214, 231, 323–3
   income of 29
Drury, Joseph, HM 103, 105, 114, 121, 128, 129–31, 133, 138, 139, 176, 180, 197–8, 237, 251, 253, 563
   ambition of 147–8
   election of 134, 139
   as HM 140–66
   myth of 150
   personality of 148, 150
   profits of 141–4
   squeamishness of 118, 151
   succession to 176–8
Drury (née Heath), Louise 139, 149, 152, 157
Drury, Mark, m 64, 149, 153, 154, 155, 164, 197, 199–200
   candidate for HM 176–8
   profits 143–4
   resignation of 201
Drury, William, m 170, 199–200, 201

Dublin 104
'Ducker' 192, 255, 432
Dudley, Robert, earl of Leicester 24
Duff, James 529
Dugdale, J. S., m 539, 551
Duhamel, A. J., m 381, 383
Dundas, Henry 148
Dutch elm disease 550
Duvall, G. 536

Ealing Abbey 462
economics 539
Edgware Road 18, 21, 25, 28, 36, 37, 39, 101, 141–2
Edlyn, Richard, g 15
education:
   and class 46–7
   and government policy 23–6
   and segregation 46
Education Act (1870) 284
Education Act (1902) 378, 416
Education Act (1944) 413, 416, 486
Edward VI 12
Edward VII 337, 352, 374
Eiloart, R. 476
electricity 389, 400
Eleven-plus examination 413–14, 416
Elizabeth I 12, 26
Elizabeth II 546
Elkyn, Elizabeth 10
Elkyn, Nicholas 40
Elliot, C. 512
Elliott-Smith, A. G., m 521, 522
Ellis, R. W., 532, 542
Ellesmere, Lord Chancellor 36, 39
Elmfield 390, 391, 392, 424, 493, 497, 516
Emmanuel College, Cambridge 50, 100, 112
Enclosure Act (1803) 108, 142, 160, 343
Endowed Schools Act (1869) 284, 386
Endowment Fund 395, 418, 421, 423, 433, 435
Enfield, Lord 294–5
English 24, 120, 122, 163, 326, 327, 331, 333–4, 380–1, 532, 539
English Form 267–70
entrance examinations 300, 301, 313
entrance scholarships to HS 290–1, 301, 323, 365, 389, 436, 497, 531, 551, 552, 562

580

Essay Club 256, 306, 540–1
Eton College 28, 87, 92, 97, 100, 111, 154, 176, 208, 228, 290, 308, 356, 362, 387, 407, 410, 454, 462, 469, 473, 485
   compared with HS 145, 168, 274
   contacts with HS 386
   influence on HS 45, 65–6, 72–3, 81, 82, 89, 113–39
   and reform 284, 287
Euclid 332, 373, 384
evangelicalism 169, 171, 201, 206, 214, 215, 230–1
Evans, Benjamin, m 146, 153–4, 200, 201, 213–14
   candidate for HM 176–8
Evans, Mr, m 80, 81, 89, 109
examinations 188

Faisal, king of Iraq 465
Falklands War 452
fagging 151, 152, 174, 193, 196, 223, 227, 273, 336, 369, 440, 475, 477–8
Faning, E., m 351
Farmer, John, m 302, 319, 337, 345–51
Farrar, F. W., m 213, 261, 263, 264–5, 272, 278, 291, 311, 314, 317–18, 319, 326, 329–32, 340, 368, 386
   Eric: or Little by Little 261
fencing 99, 109, 122, 159
Fenn, William, g 9, 33, 55, 87
Ferguson, Adam 115
Fielding, Henry 121
Fifth Form Scholarship 392
fighting 107, 152, 159
Findlay, J. R., g 424
Finch, G. F. 425
fines (or finds) 210–11
First World War 341, 397, 402, 408, 409, 410, 442–9, 498, 504
Fisher, Geoffrey 497
Fitch, Alex 444, 453
fitness, cult of 474–5
FitzGerald, C. L. 273, 275
Fitzpatrick, T. C., g 428
Fladgate, Francis 425
Fladgate, Sir Francis 418, 444
Flambards, house at H 10, 52, 133

Fleming Report (1944) 412–13, 455
Fletcher, Frank 515
flogging, *see* corporal punishment
Folkestone, Jacob, Lord, 2nd earl of Radnor 98
football, HS variety of 159, 192–3, 213, 270, 339, 343, 471–2
Football Association 271
Football Field Trust 418, 421
Forbes, George, 4th earl of Granard 82, 106
Ford, L. G. B., HM 355, 361, 419, 429, 435–6, 441, 443–4, 447, 463, 467, 469, 470, 479, 488, 494, 495, 515
   candidate for HM 371
   dismissal of 503
   election of 375–6
   as HM 496–504
   and masters 499–500
   personality of 496–7, 502, 503–4
   and reform 128, 333, 376, 384–5
   religion and 454–5, 456–7, 458
   pigs and 504
   unpopularity of 497–8
Ford, May 496, 504
Ford, Richard 498
Forster, E. M. 408
Forty Years On 345, 348–9
Forwood, E. 373
Founder's Day 175, 251
Fourth Form Room 83, 164, 165, 195
Fox, A. 358, 398
   Follow Up! 396
   Harrow 401
Francis, Philip 109, 111
Franklyn, Sir Thomas, g 75
Frederick, prince of Wales 114
Free Scholars 32–3, 54, 70, 72, 88–9, 91, 100, 173, 178–84, 229, 233, 235–41, 267–70
Freeborn, E. W., m 445, 463, 465, 501
freemasonry 357, 362–4, 386, 424, 444, 462, 506, 534, 538
French 99, 109, 174, 208–10, 225, 262
Frere, George 239–40

Gaches, Lewis 299
Galba, Roman emperor 221

Index

Galsworthy, John 304, 329, 332, 356, 399, 440˙
Galton, Francis 307
Gambier, S. J. 231
games 31, 116, 108, 158–60, 192–3, 211, 270–1, 288, 338–44, 382
   claims for 466–7
   compulsory 174, 192–4, 213, 338, 475
   cost of 468
   cult of 192–4, 212–13, 249–50, 271, 317, 338–44, 396–400, 466–75
   and immaturity 340
   and intolerance 343–4
   and male beauty 343–4
   and morality 339–40
   and sex 272, 368
Gannon, E.D., m 514, 517
Garbett, James 219–20
Garlands 391, 516, 555
Genoa, duke of 298
geography 123, 331, 381
George II 114, 115
George III 115, 139, 160, 198
George IV 190, 198
George V 345, 355, 356, 361
George VI 525
General Purposes Committee 393, 422
General Strike, the (1926) 409
Gepp, G. E., m 218, 226
Gerrard, Sir Charles, Bt. 71, 75
Gerrard, Felix 9, 40
Gerrard, Sir Gilbert, Kt 8, 10, 21, 22–3, 25, 65
Gerrard, Sir Gilbert, Bt., g 48, 49, 52, 59
Gerrard, Philip 9, 10
Gerrard, Richard 8–9
Gerrard, Thomas, g 49
Gerrard, William 8, 10, 16, 21
Gilbart-Smith, J. B. 425
Gilbey, Geoffrey 447
Gilkes, A. D. 362
Gilliat, E., m 388
Gilson, R. C., m 381, 383
Girdler, Joseph 63, 69, 82
Girls' Public Day School Trust 345
Gladstone, W. E. 163, 251, 252, 286, 334, 337, 359
Glasse, Samuel 101, 105, 109, 125–8, 130

Glazebrook, M. G., m 312, 379, 401
Glover, Richard, m 136
Godmanchester school 24
Goffman, E. 489
Goderich, Viscount, Frederick Robinson, 1st earl of Ripon 158, 163, 204, 251
godliness 169–71, 221–2
Godley, A. D., g 428, 429
golf 474, 550, 552
Gomm, William 104
Gonville and Caius College, Cambridge 8, 9, 28, 50, 61, 63, 189, 263, 304
good form 397, 399
Goodden, C. P. 515
Goodhart, H. C. 364
Gordon, duke of 115
Gordon, General G. 334
Gore, Spencer 351, 391
Gorse, H. J. L., m 418–9, 460, 461, 473, 494, 519, 523, 527
Goulash 543
Gould, E. J. H., m 552
Governing Bodies Association 412, 413, 415
governors of HS 13, 15, 19, 21, 23, 25, 36–42, 48, 54, 58–9, 65, 66, 71, 74–8, 88, 91, 99, 116, 125–6, 140–2, 178–84, 224, 227, 234, 254, 267–70, 299, 301, 307, 321–2, 323–5, 335, 342, 358, 366–7, 386, 390–2, 393–5, 406–7, 411, 412, 413, 417–30, 502–3, 538
   amateurishness of 371–2
   clerks to 425
   conservatism of 429
   and cricket 468
   crisis of 1938–42 and 525–8
   dinners of 75–6
   and dismissals of HMs 239–41, 503, 532–3
   and dismissals of housemasters 556–7
   Eton policy of 131
   and freemasonry 363
   and HMs 125–7, 173, 201–2, 372, 417, 419, 429, 546, 556–7, 559
   and HM elections 203–6, 219–21 419; (1771) 131–4; (1805) 176–8; (1844) 247–9; (1859) 310–11; (1885) 364;

(1898) 370–2; (1910) 376; (1925) 504–5; (1934) 512–3; (1939) 522; (1942) 529; (1953) 534–5; (1970) 548–9; (1980) 557
improvidence of 229
interference of 136, 228, 233, 236–9, 497, 498, 501, 503
intolerance of 430
legalism of 236–9
and masters 387–8, 389, 419, 510
nepotism of 74–5, 76–7, 126
openness of 560
philistinism of 430
politics of 126, 358–9, 416
and reform 288, 289–90, 291, 292, 295–8
religion of 298, 426–7
and school 189, 417–20, 428–30
Graham, E., m 304, 315, 344, 457, 499, 500
Graham, William 90
Granard, earl of 115
Grant, Sir William 181–4
Gray, John, g 184
Gray, Charles 346
Greek 119, 122, 123, 312–13, 332, 380, 384, 439
Green, T. H. 246
Greene, Graham 406, 495
Greene, H. 363
Greenhill, William 9
Greenstock, J. W., m 542
Gregory, Isabella ('Jack the Sailor') 224
Gregory, Richard 224
Gregory, William 211, 213, 224
Grenfell, E. C., g 416, 418, 422, 426
Grey, Lord 359
Griffith, G., m 331–2, 382, 383, 400
Griffiths, Daniell 107
Grimston, Edward 205
Grimston, James, 3rd viscount 141, 142, 178
Grimston, Robert 255, 270, 343, 347
Grimston, Thomas 106, 110, 123
Grindall, Edmund 24
Grosskurth, Phyllis 277
Grove, The 13, 16, 133, 173, 174, 201, 213, 215–16, 218, 226, 240, 250, 255, 314, 321, 346, 390, 391, 392–3, 500
fire at: (1974) 482, 550–1

Grove Hill House 321, 324, 346
Guild 559
Guillemard, W. G., m 333, 381
Gyes, William 15
gymnastics 354, 394

Hadow, D. R. 339
Haggard, Rider 409
Haileybury College 387
Hale, Bernard 90
Halhed, Nathaniel 112
Hallam, G. H., m 356
Haly, Drope 85
Hamilton, Lord George, g 363, 424, 425, 427
Hamilton, John, 1st marquess of Abercorn 123–4
Hamilton, Walter 529
Hamilton, William 90
'hanging gardens', the at H 16
Hardy, M. Percival 425
Hare, Augustus 174, 265, 272, 273
Harris, G. F., m 226, 250, 260, 261, 263, 266, 314, 317, 346
Harris, H. L., m 450, 451, 541
  founder of OH Players 538
Harris, Dr Margaret 476 n.
Harrovian, The 543
Harrovians:
  academic distinction of 264
  age of 33, 83, 84–5, 106, 174
  careers of 174, 270, 303–4
  cheating by 544
  conservatism of 164
  and cross-dressing 223
  culture of 490–1, 520–1
  drunkenness of 207–8
  idleness of 172–3, 189–90, 312, 495, 501
  independence of 102, 132–3, 197–9, 314, 477–8, 481, 560
  indiscipline of 107, 172, 180, 195–6, 207–8, 211, 223–4, 250, 314, 367–8, 372–3, 400, 440, 495, 501–3, 532, 536, 543, 544, 550, 563
  ignorance of 314
  insularity of 164
  intelligence of 507–8, 540–1
  parents of 560

Index

Harrovians (cont.):
  pastimes of 106–8, 159–60, 191, 195–6, 211, 212–13, 268, 271–4, 440–2, 490–2, 520–1
  politics of 69, 124, 304, 359–60, 410
  snobbery of 183, 387
  under Vaughan 270–4
  underachievement of 270
  uniforms of 122, 175, 335, 439
  and war 442–5
Harrow Association 309, 418, 421, 425, 492, 547
Harrow Football Field Trust 391
Harrow Park Trust 391–2, 421
Harrow Road 18, 21, 22
Harrow Road Trust 28, 36–7, 39–40, 41, 53, 101, 141–2, 179, 302, 377, 393, 414–15, 421, 425
Harrow School:
  academic standards of 172, 208 264–5, 342, 383–4, 397, 540–1, 542, 551–2
  anti-Roman Catholicism of 456, 457, 462, 465, 506
  appeals for money for 186
  architecture of 441
  archives of 548
  and armed services 156, 357–8, 429
  boarders at 30, 31, 33, 34, 45–6, 54–5, 60–1, 66, 80
  centralization of 548, 553, 554–5
  change at 174, 440–2, 478, 480, 483–7, 495, 532, 544, 546–64
  charter of (1572) 20, 23–7
  closure of 519
  and commercialism 68, 142–4, 420, 435, 555, 563
  competition with 76–7, 127, 172
  composition of 32–3, 45–7, 48, 62–3, 72–3, 88–9, 90–1, 103–5, 168–9, 178–84, 253–4, 270, 376, 406, 414–16, 489–91, 529–30, 540, 560
  conformity at 335–6, 359–61, 395–402, 418, 486–7, 491, 562
  corruption at 548
  crisis of 1938–42 and 410–11, 418–9, 424, 428, 430–2, 515, 519, 521
  criticism of 168–71, 219, 356, 369, 399
  cult of 97–8, 175–6, 251, 306–10, 344–53, 354, 361, 439, 490
  culture at 337–8
  curriculum of 13, 30–3, 66, 81–2, 89–80, 99–100, 102, 107, 109, 118–20, 121–4, 137–8, 140, 157, 158, 160–2, 173, 174, 179–84, 187–8, 189–91, 208–9, 224–5, 264–5, 288–9, 313, 325–34, 360–1, 373, 378–85, 494–5, 539–40, 541, 542–3, 553, 561–3
  death at 110
  decadence of 501–3
  decline of 167–76, 227, 230, 250, 355
  discipline at 101–3, 111, 137, 174, 336, 397, 398, 440, 475–82, 488–9, 511, 543
  drinking at 152, 545
  elitism of 99–101, 122, 155–6, 269–70, 293, 329, 335, 563
  endowment of 26–7, 29, 37, 39
  estate of 374, 377–8
  expense of 109, 110–11, 142–4, 172, 211, 227, 288, 290–1, 324, 335, 372, 376–7, 423, 433
  family business and 79–80, 139, 147, 149–50
  favouritism at 211
  fees at 55, 66, 73, 109, 110–11 142–4, 185, 207, 211, 227, 254, 266, 300, 323, 324, 376–7, 394, 423, 433–4
  finances of 73, 141–4, 299, 254, 292, 300, 302, 391, 378, 392–5, 416–17, 430–9, 532, 545, 550
  foreigners at 358, 465–6, 492
  foundation of 7–42
  and freemasonry 363
  gifts to 438
  girls at 35
  and health 110, 145
  histories of 2, 88, 105
  holidays at 79, 116, 126, 137, 173, 190–1, 208
  ideals of 489
  independence of 378–9
  influence of 360, 386–7
  innovation at 380–1
  insanitary conditions at 250, 252
  introspection of 330, 335, 357, 487, 503–4, 533–46

Index

learning at 56–8, 161, 288, 333–4
legal problems of 19, 22, 53, 141, 173, 178–84, 236, 288
militarism at 446–9
myths of 7, 11–12, 26, 29, 34, 150, 164–5, 301–2, 329, 344–53, 441, 494, 552, 559–60
nature of 48, 53, 82, 106, 110, 127, 208–9, 334–8, 397, 399–400, 405, 428, 488–95, 501–2, 531–2, 543
non-Christians at 453–4, 462–66
numbers at 1–3, 91, 103, 114, 116, 120, 135, 139, 144, 145–6, 167, 187–8, 200, 202–3, 207, 226, 227, 239, 246, 250, 253, 303, 390, 410, 431, 443–4, 495, 497–8, 522, 524, 528, 529, 545–6, 548, 559
overcrowding at 128, 152, 185, 501–2, 508, 546
philistinism of 396, 397–8
politics of 76–7, 146, 163–4, 251–2, 358–60, 409–10
and progress 313
public subsidy for 432
publicity for 548
rats at 520
and reform 284–302
relations with Eton 11, 149, 386
reputation of 111, 120–1, 134, 137, 145, 154, 226, 251, 253, 272, 337, 357, 442, 444–5, 495, 529, 537–8, 547, 563
rituals at 61–2, 68, 69, 83, 115, 493, 547
rules of: (1591) 29–35
scandal at 173, 199, 502–3
and scholarship 111–12, 187, 373
schoolhouse of 29, 37–40, 42, 61, 70, 142, 160, 175, 186, 254
secularization of 361, 466
self-image of 78, 451–4, 475, 487, 564
slang of 335, 440
snobbery of 102, 335, 396, 397, 490, 508–9
and sport obsession 467–75
standardization of 494–5
status of 55, 60, 70, 72–3, 74, 82, 89–91, 93, 97–101, 115, 120–1, 134, 140, 177–8, 221, 251, 253, 303, 355, 360, 482–7, 557

statutes of (1591) 10, 13, 27–9, 33–4, 179–84, 267
structure of 256, 332–3, 380, 540–1
threats to 406–17
traditions of 439, 472, 482
and verse 107
violence of 151–2, 159, 195–7, 212, 257–9, 272, 273–4, 336–7, 481
and war 442–53
Harrow town 547
Harrow Trust 421, 423, 433, 436
Harrow Wanderers 545
Harrowby, Dudley Ryder, 1st earl of 102, 138, 148
Hartley, L. P. 396, 397, 398, 399, 400, 415
Hastings, Francis, 1st marquess of 149
Havergal, H., m 547, 514
Hawkins, F. V., g 264, 310
Hawkins, Mrs, house dame 106, 115
Haygarth, Arthur 167
Hayward, R. B., m 333, 388, 391
Hayward, Thomas 9
Head Masters of HS:
 academics as 535
 age of 371, 374
 authority of 101–2, 125–8, 136–7, 197, 200, 249, 284, 290, 300–1, 365–6, 389, 419
 and beating 479
 calibre of 499
 dismissals of 58–9, 65, 69, 92, 176, 239–41, 503, 532
 doctorates of 534
 duties of 29–30, 48
 education of 387, 484
 elections of 88, 114–15, 126, 139, 164, 203–5, 370–2, 504–5, (1805) 176–8; (1836) 219–21; (1844) 247–9; (1885) 364; (1910) 375–6; (1934) 512–3; (1939) 522; (1942) 529; (1953) 534–5; (1970) 548; (1980) 557
 and governors 419
 Holy Orders of 298, 454
 house of 55, 67, 70, 101, 106, 115, 152–3, 174, 84, 213, 225–6, 228–30, 250, 254, 257, 346, 354, 390, 391, 432, 481, 558, 564

585

Head Masters of HS (*cont.*):
  as housemasters 228, 230, 254–5, 372, 392–3, 524, 535, 552–3
  inadequacies of 172, 495–6
  incomes of 28, 55, 60, 66, 68, 80, 143–4, 207, 228–9, 239, 254, 265, 292, 300, 372, 374, 483
  laymen as 51–2
  marriages of 48, 67–8, 183
  power of 315, 317–20, 322–5
  qualifications of 178
  religion of 455
  status of 63, 64, 65, 66, 67–8, 70, 78–9, 148
  teaching of 530–1
  tenure of 374, 504–5, 520
  tutoring by 228
  undermining of 429, 498
  wives of 476
Headmasters' Conference 386–7, 407, 411, 412, 420
Heath, Baron 307
Heath, Benjamin, HM 62, 102, 106, 114, 122, 147, 150
  election of 132–4
  as HM 134–9
  profits of 110, 138–9
Heath, George 114
Hebrew 122
Henchman, Humphrey 88
Hendon District Council 393
Hendren, E. 473
Henry, L. W., m 418, 419, 445, 493, 500, 501, 523, 525, 527, 528, 537
Henty, G. A. 409
heraldry 422
Herbert, Lord 106
Herbert, Sydney 195
Herne, Francis, g 88, 125, 136
Hertford College, Oxford 304
Hewlett, Dr, HS doctor 258, 294
Hewlett, L. M. 438, 422
Hewlett, W. O. 13, 14
Hicks, F. C. N., g 363, 424, 512
Hide, William, HM 46, 60, 67, 68, 72, 87, 229, 251
  as HM 51–9

High Commission, court of 23, 24–5
Highgate school 24, 26, 34
Higgins, G. J., m 545
Hindus 453
Hine, W. E., m 379
Hirst, G. 473
history 323, 331, 333, 380, 381, 382, 495, 518, 539, 541, 561
Hoadly, Benjamin 114
Hoare, S. J. G., g 410, 424
Hoare, Samuel, custos 226
Hoban, B. M. S., HM 417, 441, 452, 483, 484, 548
  career of 549
  election of 548–9
  as HM 549–57
  reforms of 552–3
  resignation of 556–7
Hobbes, Thomas 71
Holford, George 145
Holland, Henry 223
Holland, Lancelot 151
Hollingsworth, J. H., m 445, 511
Holmes, C. F., m 262, 263, 314, 317, 319, 324, 325, 326, 391
Holmes, Mr, m 117, 119, 128
Holt, R. A. A., g 420, 424, 425, 548–9
Home Boarders 237, 293, 297, 298, 300, 334, 399, 443
Home Rule 251–2, 359
homosexuality 159, 174, 196, 271–3, 277–82, 328, 367–8, 448, 475, 477, 480–2, 502, 543, 550
Hooker, John, m 78, 79, 81, 85, 87
Hoord, Alan 21
Horne, General H. S. 424, 444
Horne, William, HM 45, 61, 63, 65–9, 533
Hort, Sir Arthur, m 500
Hope, Anthony 505
Housden, E. J., m 445, 456, 469, 496, 528, 532
house spirit 115, 193, 213, 174, 526
house system 105–6, 174, 216–17, 255, 274, 315–25, 389–92, 421–22, 431, 493, 509, 515–18, 555
  see HS: boarders at

housemasters 89, 128, 146, 153, 172, 201, 392, 413
  accounts of 516–7
  and beating 478–80
  commercialism of 217
  dismissal of 419, 429, 510, 537, 556–7
  diversity of 542
  fear of intellectuals of 542
  feebleness of 515
  inadequacies of 323, 537, 538, 542
  incomes of 143–4, 153, 323–4, 483–4, 516–17
  independence of 322–5, 509, 517–18
  power of 515–8
  religion and 461, 463
  status of 517–8
  tenure of 509, 510–11
  venality of 323–4, 517
Howley, William, archbishop of Canterbury 205, 241
Howson, E. W., m 307, 342, 351–2
Hubbard, Sir Henry 39
Hudson, George 252
Hughes, M. L., m 459–60
Hughes, R. T., m 465
Hughes, Thomas: *Tom Brown's Schooldays* 248, 338, 340, 357
Hume, David 115
Huntingdon, Francis Hastings, 12th earl of 111
Huntingdon, Henry Hastings, 3rd earl of 24, 27
Hussein, king of Jordan 452, 465
Hussey, Robert 219
Hutcheson, Francis 105
Hutton, H. E., m 226, 255, 264, 270, 388

Imhoff, Charles 104
imperialism 334–5, 355, 356–8, 359, 361
income tax 142
India 103
Indian Mutiny 256
Industrial Fund for the Advancement of Science 539
initiation rituals 196–7, 272, 481
Inspections of HS:
  (1906) 373, 384
  (1911) 378, 384
Intowne, John 13
Intowne, William 13
Ireland 103, 104–5, 115
Irish Republican Army 550

'Jack o'Lantern' 211
Jackson, Cyril 161
Jackson, F. Huth, g 393, 424
Jackson, F. S., g 382, 416, 424, 425, 474
Jackson, H. M. 280
Jacob, John 90
Jacobson, William 220
James, F. W. T., m 519, 523, 526
James, Marjorie 538
James, R. L., HM 363, 406, 413, 419, 432, 441–2, 454, 473–4, 469, 477, 479, 483, 485, 486, 492–3, 494, 530, 556, 563
  election of 534–5
  hatred of publicity of 536–8
  as HM 533–46
  laissez faire of 537, 538, 539, 541–2, 543, 544
  legacy of 549
  personality of 534–7
  and religion 459–60
  tapes of 536
Jameson Raid (1896) 356
Jenkins, J. W. 401, 402
Jenner, Robert 82
Jephson's sanitorium 241
Jeremy, J., m 539
Jews 298, 321–2, 357, 453, 463–6
  house at HS for 321–2
John Lyon School 286, 297, 299–300, 301–2, 415, 421
Johnson, Robert 24
Jones, N., g 424
Jones, William 97, 98, 101, 103, 106, 107, 108, 110, 111, 116, 118, 119, 120, 122, 123, 126, 129–30, 157
  and politics 118, 124
  and Sumner 130–1
Jonson, Ben 12
Jonson, Thomas, HM 59, 56, 60, 61, 64
Jowett, B. 326
Joyce, F. W. 293–5, 298

Kalton, G. 479
Kaye, Dean, of Lincoln 139
Kean, Edmund 148
Keary, H., m 255, 263
Keate, John 191, 195
Keble, John 169, 219
Keble College, Oxford 339
Kemmis, John 197, 198
Kemp, M. C., m 342, 400, 418, 469, 497, 498, 499, 500, 509, 527
Kempson, E. H., m 381
Kennedy, Benjamin, m 168, 175, 208, 212, 216, 217–18, 219, 221, 231
  Latin Primer 331
Kent, Claridge and Pearce, surveyors and accountants 141
Killick, E. T., m 457
King, Mrs, house dame 106
King, Rufus 155–6
King, W. G. 425
King Edward's School, Birmingham 263, 288
King's College, Cambridge 65, 66, 70, 72, 100, 113, 117, 121, 149, 362
King's College School, London 288
King's Head, at H 107, 142
Kingsley, Charles 338–9
Kirkby Stephen school 33
Kittermaster, D. B., m 445, 457, 458
Knoll, the new 420, 432, 548, 555
Knoll, the old 320, 368, 391, 536, 544
  foreigners at 321, 358
Knollys, Henry 24

Laborde, C. D., m 521, 530, 542
Laborde, E. D., m 314, 506–8, 514, 516
Labour Party 407, 409, 410, 413, 416, 550
Lake, Warwick, g 74–5
Lake, W. C. 248
Land Trust 418, 421
Lang, Robert 271
Lascelles, B. P., m 332, 381–2
Latham, Edward 280–1, 306
Launce, Thomas, m 41, 49–50
Launce, William, HM 11, 41–2, 49–50, 52, 565
Law, John 103

Layton, Robert 16
Leaf, F. A., m 411, 444, 525–6, 528
Leaf, Herbert 518
Leaf, Walter, g 330, 336, 337, 359, 393, 424, 428
Leaf Schools (formerly Sheridan Stables) 518
leaving scholarships 189, 436
Ledward, P. A. 515, 517
Lee, Nathaniel: *Sophonisba* 46, 83–6
Lee, Sir William 150
Leeson, Spencer 412, 512
Legh, W. L. 257, 272–3
Le Hunte, J., m 87
Leicester school 24, 27
Leigh, Thomas Pemberton 236
Leith, Mrs, house dame 153, 173, 189, 193, 213
Lemmon, J. P., m 538, 539
Lemon, Charles 199, 202
library, (later the Vaughan) 121, 313, 354, 541
Lillingston, C. A., m 530, 541, 542
local education authorities 412–14
Locke, John 98
  Thoughts Concerning Education 47
London, bishops of 25
London County Council 377
Long, Edward 156
Long, Walter, g 424, 425, 429, 498
Longley, Charles, HM 168, 171, 191, 228, 231, 234
  ambition of 218–19
  election of 203–5
  and Free Scholars 237
  as HM 206–19
  ineptitude of 172, 207–8
  nickname of ('Rose') 206
  profits of 207
Lonsdale, earl of 220
Lord's, Eton v Harrow at 114, 159–60, 192, 224, 270–1, 307, 337, 339, 343, 440, 465, 502, 557
  cult of 342, 396–7, 400
  dress at 546
  importance of 467, 468, 469, 520
  violence at 469
Lost, John 103

Lunn, Arnold 395–7, 399
  The Harrovians 395–7
Lupton, S., m 332
Lyon, Joan 7, 10, 21, 36, 37
Lyon, John, father of re-founder 15
Lyon, John, re-founder of HS 12, 13, 15, 16, 18–42, 47, 236, 395, 431
  Charity of 414–15, 421
  cult of 98
  death of 7
  estates of 20–2, 395
  memorial to (1813) 175
  motives of 7–8
  myth of 182
  piety of 17, 30
  religion of 9
  'will' of 27
Lyon, Sir John 22
Lyon Memorial Fund 307
Lyttleton, Edward 373
Lyttleton, Lord 287
Lytton, Richard 103

McConnell, G. R., m 473–4
McCorquodale, A., g 424
McCorquodale, M. M., g 424, 425, 538, 549
McCurrach, H. J., m 530
MacDonald, Audley 161
MacDonald, J. Ramsay 355–6
McFarlane, R. K. 442–3
MacLaren, A. C. 382, 474
Mack, E. C. 412
Maddox, John 63
Magdalene College, Cambridge 50
Maida Vale 393
Major, John 309
Malan, E. M., m 542
Malkyn, Richard 112
Maltby, C. J. 352
Malvern College 432, 451, 525, 528
Manchester Grammar School 154
manliness 328, 334, 561
Mann, M. A., g 424, 426
Manners-Sutton, Charles, archbishop of Canterbury 178
Manning, Henry 193
Manwood, Roger 24

Marillier, Jacob, m 201, 209, 218, 260, 264, 266, 315
Marillier, Jacques, m 209, 218, 225
Marlborough College 172, 227, 274, 288, 291, 320, 357, 387, 505
Marshall, F. E., g 389, 391
Martin, Richard 104–5
Martin, Thomas, HM 64–5, 520
Martineau, Arthur 192
Mary I 8, 12
Mason brothers 108
Masson, Gustav, m 262, 263, 264, 383
masters at HS 108–9, 135–6, 153–5, 175, 200–1, 225–6, 259–67, 388–9, 488–9
  and alcohol 515
  anxieties of 290
  and beating 101
  beliefs of 325–6
  boredom of 188
  and boys 330–1
  brutality of 117–18
  class of 117, 155
  conviviality of 109, 129
  cost of 388
  deference of 484
  deficiencies of 263–4, 382–3
  dishonesty of 286, 364–5
  disloyalty of 498, 552
  dismissal of 510–11, 522, 523
  distinction of 261, 263, 319, 330, 342, 530, 539, 545
  diversity of 538–40
  dullness of 208
  eccentricity of 400
  education of 387, 484
  elections of HMs and 364
  feuding of 519–20, 524
  and First World War 445, 451
  freedom of 538–40
  frustrations of 215, 317–18
  future HMs as 386–7
  and governors 324–5, 419
  and Holy Orders 263, 326, 362, 401, 457, 458
  homosexuality of 477
  hostility of 225–6
  idleness of 310, 362

masters at HS (*cont.*):
  incomes of 215–16, 227, 246, 254, 265–6, 292, 379, 390, 483–4
  incompetence of 209, 326, 327, 515
  independence of 315–25, 365–6, 389, 499–500, 508–11, 541–3, 555, 560
  indiscipline of 225, 499–500
  intellectual effort by 325–34
  irreligion of 362, 454, 459
  lack of specialization of 553
  marriage rituals of 476
  meetings of 499–500
  mercenary interests of 109, 260, 262
  mutiny of 318
  numbers of 117, 188, 261, 532
  obstructiveness of 213–18, 371
  politics of 251–2, 267, 359–60, 409–10
  professionalism of 362, 385–9
  prudery of 154
  quality of 383–4
  redundancy of 410–11
  secularization of 362
  sexuality of 475–7
  snobbery of 154–5
  and sport 338, 339, 340
  as sportsmen 213, 342, 469–70, 472–3, 530
  status of 387–9
  tax avoidance of 544
  and teaching 325–34, 381–2, 397
  tenure of 297, 342, 371, 388, 389, 419, 494, 500, 530, 542, 552
  unity of 389
  university snobbery of 534
  and war 451
  wives of 476–7
  as women 525
mathematics 81, 89, 99, 174, 208, 210, 224, 264, 326, 332, 333, 373, 380, 381, 384, 394, 432, 528, 540
Maulden, Beds. 21
Maurice, F. D. 329
Maurier, Gerald du 409
Mayo, C. H. P., m 358, 361, 383, 384, 408, 442–3, 450, 451, 465, 466, 477–8, 497, 500
Meaux, A. M. E. Begouën de 445, 499
Meek, W. A. 359

Meinertzhagen, R. 400
Melbourne, Lord 218
Mendham, G. L., m 545
Mercer, E. G., m 445, 449
Merchant Taylors' School 9, 26, 28, 288
Merivale, Charles 165, 183, 187, 188, 216
Merton College, Oxford 23, 88
Micklem, P. A., m 375
Middleditch, B., m 496
Middlemist, R., m 179, 255, 262–3, 264, 266, 267, 319, 346, 476
Middleton school 24, 26
Middlesex County Council 377, 393
Middlesex scholars at HS 413–4
Mildmay, Sir Walter 24, 26
Mill, J. S. 326, 335
Mill Hill school 387
Mills, Benjamin, m 199
Mills, William, m 201, 203–4, 215, 218
Milner, Alfred 359
Minchin, J. G. C. 343
Minsen, B. J., m 381, 383
Mitchell, Thomas 220
Mitford, Nancy 490
modern languages 265, 264, 380, 381, 382–3, 384, 540, 561
Modern Side, the 210, 292, 313, 318, 320, 325–34, 354, 360, 380, 382, 384
Moir, J. W., m 462, 470, 513, 515, 519, 553
Moira, John Rawdon, 1st earl of 111
Monckton, W. T., g 363, 407, 411, 418–19, 422, 424, 435
monitors 121, 222, 256–9, 289, 314, 335, 360–1, 389, 477–8
  authority of 196
  beating by 118, 151, 175, 199, 478–80
  rebellion of 197–8
Montagu, Matthew 107, 138
Montem, at Eton 62, 90, 136
Moore, R. W., HM 429, 451, 455, 458, 459, 470, 479, 493, 521, 523
  election of 529
  death of 69, 532–3
  as HM 528–33
  legacy of 533–4
  personality of 528–9, 529–30
  on Vaughan 245

590

Greek and Latin Comparative Syntax 528
Trophy For an Unknown Soldier 531
Moorsom, C. W. M., m 410, 445, 496, 498, 502
Moray, earl of 115
Morant, R. 360
Moreton, Matthew, 2nd Baron Ducie 82
Moretons 201, 215, 226, 250, 346, 383, 391, 392, 458, 511, 516, 519, 524
Morgan, J. B., m 530
Moriarty, L. M., m 381, 383, 500
Morris, John 268
Morwood, J. H. W., m 539
Moss, W. 312, 536
Motte, Edward de la 321
Mount Stuart, Lord 100, 103
Mulberry, William 22
muscular Christianity 249–50, 339–40
Museum Schools, the 354, 394
music 313, 319–20, 346-53, 394, 545, 562
Musical Society 256, 346
Muslims at HS 357, 453, 465
Mylne, J. E. 273

Napoleon I, emperor 163–4
National Curriculum, the 378
National School at H 268, 293
National Service 451–2
Nehru, J. 358, 380, 398–9, 463
Negus, Robin 449
Nettleship, Henry 337
'New Group' 539
New Schools 255, 268
Newcastle school 24
Newlands 368, 389, 391, 431, 516, 522, 524
Newman, J. H. 262
Newman, John 63
Newman, Nathaniel, school dame 63
Newsom Commission, the 405–6, 407, 413, 536
Newsome, David 340
Niblock, J. W. 203
Norden, John 11, 26
North, Lord, Prime Minister 125, 146
North, Dudley Lord, g 48, 49, 52
North, Sir Edward 17
North, Roger, Lord 566

North America 103, 104
Northcote, Sir Stafford 258, 287
Northwick, 2nd Baron, g 2, 177, 202, 205, 219, 220, 236, 247–8
Northwick, 3rd Baron, g 202, 296, 311
Northwick Park Hospital 550
Norwood, C., HM 363, 408, 411–12, 449, 455, 457, 458, 479, 488, 489, 494, 495, 497, 500, 509, 515, 521, 536, 553, 563
  election of 504–5
  and games 466–7, 469–70, 474
  as HM 504–11
  ideas of 505–6
  income of 483
  personality of 505–6, 511–12
  and Songs 352–3
  unpopularity of 508–11
  The English Tradition of Education 408, 467, 505–6
  The Higher Education of Boys in England 505
Nowell, Alexander 24, 26
  Catechism 30, 33

Oakham school 23
Old Harrovian Dramatic Society 511
Old Harrovian Lodge 444
Old Harrovian Players Society 538
Old Harrovians 146, 175–6
  and armed forces 256, 451, 447, 452
  benefactors among 309, 391–2, 395, 431, 433, 435–9
  and cricket 213–13
  distinction of 409
  early associations of 93, 98, 99
  and freemasonry 363
  ignorance of 327
  influence of 251, 418–19, 422, 424–5, 428, 491–4, 497, 510, 537, 558, 560
  loyalty of 439
  as masters 499, 518, 530
  as MPs 46, 63, 82, 359, 482
  morals of 327
  piety towards HS 251, 308
  and Songs 344–5
  sons of 491–3

Old Harrovians (*cont.*):
  and sports obsession 467, 468, 471–2, 473–4
  and university 485–6, 551
Old Harrovian Masonic Lodge 363
Old House, the at H 101
Orme, Robert 90
Orwell, George 345
Osborne Naval College 445
Oundle school 23, 24, 25, 34, 410
Outram, Edmund, m 154
Owen, E. C. E., m 367, 380, 383, 451, 500
Owen, N. A. S., g 420
Oxenham, H. 264
Oxenham, William, m 201, 203, 215, 218, 226, 229, 257, 259–61, 266, 307, 315, 386
Oxford and Cambridge Examination Board 313
Oxford Movement, the 169, 232, 456
Oxford university 210, 296
Ozanne, H., m 447–9, 511

Paddington 393
Page, John, g 19, 38
Page, Joseph 20
Page, Richard 49, 53, 117
Page, Thomas 38, 40
Page, T. E. 364
Pakeman, Thomas 52
Palmer, Sir Charles, g 125
Palmerston, 1st Viscount 147
Palmerston, Henry Temple, 2nd Viscount 144, 150, 152, 159, 163, 204, 251, 258, 278, 359
parish church, of St Mary, H 64
  HS attendance at 61, 236
parish of H 231
  foundation rights at HS 70, 100–1, 178–84, 235–9, 250, 267–70, 286–302, 399
  relations with HS 160, 170, 180–4, 234, 267–70
Park, The 173, 174, 201, 216–17, 227, 230, 250, 266, 314, 315, 337, 346, 391, 511, 516
Parker, Matthew, archbishop of Canterbury 24
Parnell, John 103

Parr, Samuel, m 79, 99, 107, 111, 116, 119, 120, 121, 122, 123, 128–31, 135, 146, 148, 157, 175, 197, 198, 217, 231, 386
  candidate for HM (1771) 126, 127, 131–4
  and cricket 108
  politics of 100, 124
Parry, D. J., m 539
Parsonson, S. L., m 539, 540
Part, Anthony 467, 507
Pater, Walter 326
Patrington church, Yorks. 398
Patterson, S. G., m 530
Peachey, William 100, 141, 197
Pears, S. A., m 246, 261, 386
Pearson, Hugh 278
Peel, G. F. 512
Peel, Sir Robert, 1st Bt. 147, 156
Peel, Sir Robert, 2nd Bt. 143, 146, 152, 156, 157, 159, 161, 163, 168, 204, 205, 208, 209, 217, 218, 226, 234, 241, 251, 442–3, 503
  benefactions of 189
peers at HS 72–3, 105, 145–7, 155–6
Peile, Thomas 220, 247
Pember F. W., g 418, 425, 428, 429, 512, 529
Pembroke College, Cambridge 154
Penrith school 24
Penrose, C. T. 247
pensions 388
People's Budget (1909) 352
Perceval, Spencer, Prime Minister 105, 146, 149, 163, 182, 309
Perceval, Spencer, grandson of PM 253
Percival, John 364
Percival, M. M., m 530
Perkins, E. 370
Personal and Social Education 461, 561
Peterhouse, Cambridge 520
Phelps, W. W., m 169, 174, 190, 201, 206, 214, 216–18, 225, 227, 229, 230, 232
Phillips, A. 247
Philathletic Club 256, 472–4
Philathletic Field Trust 421
physics 332, 380, 432, 495, 540, 552
Pickard-Cambridge, A. W., g 426, 512, 525, 529
Pinner 88, 117
  Sunday school at 141, 181

Pirie-Gordon, C. H. C. 363
Pitt, William, the Younger 145, 146, 181
Platt, H. E. 258
Platt-Stewart scandal (1853–4) 257–9, 289
Playfair, G. 410, 446, 449, 467, 481, 488, 501, 502, 511, 520
Plume, Thomas 49
Plumptre, E. V. C., m 385, 419, 456, 527, 539–40, 553
Pocock, N. 247
Political Studies 539
Pollard, Walter 132
Ponder, William, m 50
Ponsonby, Frederick 255, 270, 343, 347
Pontet, A. du, m 500, 510, 511
poor house at H 77, 91
Pope, C. G., m 342, 419, 457, 469, 471–2, 484, 500, 556
  dismissal of 509–11
pornography 273, 304, 367, 477
Port, Sir John 17
Pouchée, George 174, 213, 215
  dairy of 212
Powell, James 106, 111, 119
Powell, Thomas 132
Powys, Thomas, Lord Lilford 45, 149
Prentice, Reg 406
Preston Farm 18–19, 21, 28, 73, 75, 393, 395, 430, 431
Pretor, Alfred 278–82
Prior, William, m 92, 117–18, 124
  sadism of 122
prizes 186, 188–9
Proctor, Sir William Beauchamp 124
Profumo, J. D. 424, 521
public examinations 313, 378, 494–5, 506, 559, 561–2
public schools 386–7
  change at 547
  criticisms of 406–17
  divisiveness of 285, 405–6, 415–16
  HS as 45
  popularity of 98–100
  power of 409
  and religion 455
  and state aid 410–16
  tenacity of 251

Public Schools Act (1868) 41, 268, 269, 284–302, 406
Public Schools Shrewsbury and Harrow Act (1873) 296
public speaking 191–2
pupil-room system 188, 260–1, 373, 379, 384

Quartercentenary of HS 422, 466, 533, 546
Queens' College, Cambridge 154
Quick, Robert, m 317
quotas at HS 322, 464–6

Rae, J. M., m 441, 539
racism at HS 358, 465–6, 563
racquets 193
Radley school 387
Radnor, earls of 125, 425
railways 167, 186, 223–4, 377
Ramsay, James, marquis of Dalhousie 202
Rate, Anthony, schoolmaster 10, 11
Rattigan, T. M. 446, 447–8, 481, 501, 507, 520–1
  The Browning Version 460
Reade, E. 330
Reading school 34
rebellions 102–3
  (1771) 72, 132–5
  (1777) 137
  (1805) 164–5
  (1808) 165, 197–8
  (1820) 198–9
rectory, the, of H 13, 15, 16, 17
Red Nightcap Club 196
Redgrave school 24
Reeves, Henry, m 80, 105, 108, 115, 117, 153, 154, 200–1
regulations (1874) 300–1, 322–3, 324–5
religion 127, 137, 171, 206, 247–9, 252, 297–8, 300–1, 312, 320–2, 453–66, 561
  neglect of at HS 126–7, 162, 170, 171
  scepticism at 137
Rendall, F. 255, 263, 266, 297, 317–18, 319
Rendalls 174, 255, 326, 337, 368, 431, 493, 514, 516, 525–6
Rennie, J. K. 264
Repton school 17, 149, 220, 246, 288, 371, 375
reservoir at H 549–50

Index

Restoration, of Charles II 59, 69
Reuse, HS boy 84
Rewse, Francis 53
Rhodes, W. 473
Richardson, E. C. 367, 381–2, 397, 400
Richardson, John 137, 165
Richmond school 23
Ridley, Matthew, 1st Viscount, g 271, 272, 363
Rifle Corps (also known as Officer Training Corps, Junior Training Corps and Combined Cadet Force) 256, 313, 326, 357, 374, 394, 401–2, 408, 443, 446–9, 451–3, 545, 550
  mutinies in 447–9
rifle shooting 394, 402
Rivington, G. C., g 425, 426, 527, 534–5
Roberts, P. G. 448
Roberts, William, m 153–4
Robertson, J., m 297, 351
Robinson, Thomas, m 60, 64, 66, 68, 86–7
Roderick, Charles, provost of King's Cambridge 66
Roderick, Charles, m 121, 128, 129, 130, 131, 133, 135, 143
Rodney, George 76, 82
Rodney, Henry 76
Roman Catholics 137, 321, 357, 363, 453, 456, 461, 462, 463
Roper, George 8
Rosebery, earl of 345
Roseveare, W. N., m 375
Rothschild, Anthony de 427
Rothschild, E. A. R., g 424
Rothschild, Lionel de 427
Rothschild, N. C. 321
Rothwell school 23
Roundell, C. S. (*né* Currer), g 173, 358, 359, 364, 265, 296, 297, 310, 321, 426
Royal Society 296
Royal Society for the Protection of Animals 105
Ruault, A. J., m 260
Ruaul, P. M. G., m 260
Rugby Football 352–3, 429, 439, 471–2, 475, 508, 509, 510, 512

Rugby school 23, 24, 27, 167, 171, 175, 179, 182, 208–9, 221, 226, 228, 236, 238, 247, 260, 270, 290, 313, 332
  influence on HS 247, 257–9, 263
rules, ridicule of 318
Rushout, Sir John, g 75, 88, 91, 125
Rushout, Sir John, the younger, later 1st baron Northwick, g 114, 133, 134
Ruskin, John 331, 337
Russell, Bertrand 408
Russell, G. W. E. 359
Russell, Lord John 337

St Alban's school 24, 31, 34
St Bee's School 24, 33
St Catherine's College, Cambridge 280
St John, John, 2nd Viscount 82
St John's College, Cambridge 136, 154
St John's College, Oxford 508, 511
St Paul's School 46, 56, 288
St Vincent, earl of, admiral 143
Sadler, Sir Ralph 8, 10
Salisbury, marquess of 353
Sanatorium, the 313, 389, 394
Sanctuary, Thomas 238
Sanderson, Lancelot, m 317
Sandhurst, military college 452
Sandwich school 24, 26, 31, 34
sanitation 315, 324–5, 358, 388, 389, 390, 502
Sankey, Charles, m 322
Sappho, the dog 535
Sapte, Francis 104
Saunders, Francis, m and g 89, 92, 125, 126
Saunders, William, m 89, 92, 117
Savillon, pseudonomous OH poet 145
Sayer, John 123, 189
School Inspection (1931) 507–8, (1951) 423, 530, 532, 542, (1965) 541–2, 554
Schumann, Clara 337
science 264, 291, 307, 313, 331–2, 333, 337, 354, 379, 380, 381, 382, 497, 539, 540
Scotland 103, 104, 115
Scott, Edward 350
Scott, George Gilbert 255
Searle, F. C., m 383, 401
Second World War 414, 442, 444, 450–3, 521–2, 524–5

594

Index

Sedbergh school 387
Select Committee on Education (1920) 410
sex 271–3, 367–8, 396, 475–7, 480–2, 543, 545
sex education 477
sex panic 261, 318, 328
Seymour, Charles, 6th duke of Somerset 45, 63, 66
Seymour, Francis, 5th duke of Somerset 45, 63, 66
Shaftesbury, Anthony Ashley Cooper, 7th earl of 267, 308
Shakespeare, William 11–12, 333–4
    annual productions of plays by at HS 531, 538, 545
Sheafield, William 22
Sheldon, Gilbert, bishop of London 59
Sheldon, John 107–8
Shepherd's Market 437
Sheppard, Robert 169
Sherborne school 387, 396
Sheridan, R. B. 97, 104, 105, 121, 122, 130, 148
Sheridan, Thomas 104
Sheriff, R. C.: *Journey's End* 408
Sherington, William 21
Shilleto, Richard, m 173, 219, 240
Shore, Frederick 190
Shore, John, 1st Baron Teignmouth 103, 108, 118, 126–7
Shrewsbury school 23, 24, 33, 167, 179, 183, 226, 228, 260, 270, 379
Siddons, A. W., m 384, 501, 528, 540
Sidney Sussex College, Cambridge 177
Silver Arrow competition 62, 83, 90, 91, 102–3, 115, 122, 136, 352
Simmonds, G. R., g 420, 539
Simpkinson, J. N., m 255, 263, 264
Sixth Form, creation of 138
Sixth Form Ground 142, 192
Sixth Form Room 518
Sleeman, P. A., m 511
Sly, Mr or 'Old' 38, 40
Smith, Charles 39
Smith, Clifford 436
Smith, Drummond 174, 191
Smith, John, son of J. Wilkes 104
Smith, John, m 263, 266, 308, 316, 319, 327–8, 336
Smith, Sydney 168
Smith, Sir Thomas 24
Smith-Dorrien, General H. 444
smoking 58, 293
Smythe, Edmund 9
Sneezum, Thomas 294, 393
Snell, Elizabeth 9
Snell, K. S., m 540
Somervell, D. B., g 424, 425
Somervell, Robert, m 380, 381, 383, 391, 394
Somme, battle of 340
Songs of HS 307, 308, 319, 337, 344–53, 361, 401, 439, 440, 444–5, 472
    and W. S. Churchill 550, 563–4
    and games 347, 348–51
    and myths 301
    and philistinism 349
    and patriotism 349, 351
    purpose of 344, 345–7, 352–3
specialization 385
Speech Days 122, 136, 148, 165, 188, 191–2
'Speeches' 157–8, 163, 520–1
Speech Room 202, 307, 319–20, 354, 383, 450, 531
Speech Room, Old 191
    Gallery in 548, 552
Spencer, 5th earl, g 296, 358, 359, 425
Spencer, Herbert 397
Spencer, Matthew, scholmaster 10, 12
sports hall 423, 432, 548
Stanley, A. P. 248, 277, 278
Stanley, H. C. 273
Stanmore, Parr's secession to (1771) 133, 135, 136
statutes of HS (1874) 296–301, 322–3, 417
Stebbings, A. J. F. 425
Steel, T. H., m 173, 225, 226, 261, 263, 264, 314, 318, 319, 326
Stephen, Leslie 336
Stephen, N. K., m 383, 498, 500, 501, 505, 553
'Stet Fortuna Domus', HS motto 203
Stewart, Dr Alice 476
Stewart, L. D., m 476
Stewart, Rudolph 258
Stockdale, Leonard 53

Stocker, C. W. 203
Stogdon, E., m 401
Stogdon, J., m 324, 389, 390, 400
Stone, W. H., g 297, 298, 310, 393
stonethrowing 107, 273
Strangford, Percy Smythe, Viscount 223
Stretton, Charles 192, 194, 210
Stringe, John 9
Stuart, C. H., g 426, 548–9
Stuart, I. M. B., m 472
Stubbs, William: *Select Charters* 333
Studd, Sir Peter, g 424
suburbanization 377
Sumner, Humphrey 132
Sumner, Robert, HM 97, 99–111, 144, 251, 553
   decline of 130–1
   as HM 120–31
   politics of 123–5, 146
   popularity of 132
   teaching of 121–5, 128
   Concio ad Clerum 121
superannuation:
   of boys 300, 313, 380
   of masters 316, 365, 371, 388
Symonds, John Addington 174, 257, 271–2, 273, 278, 282, 337, 340, 343
   and Vaughan scandal 246, 277–82
Swift, Jonathan 104
swimming 174

Tacitus 221
Tait, A. C., archbishop of Canterbury 247
Talbot, Christopher 209
Talbot, Sir Gilbert 62
Talbot, Henry Fox 191, 196
Tassoni, m 107, 138
tariff reform 360
Tattershall, Cecil 151
Tawney, R. H. 409
taxation 47
Temple, William 502
Tercentenary of HS (1871) 301, 307, 350, 466
Terrot, C. H. 521
   Young Colt's Diary 521
Thackeray, Elias 114

Thackeray, Thomas, HM 45, 72, 74, 92, 97, 100, 102, 103, 106, 107, 108, 111, 371, 374, 563
   as HM 113–20
   wealth of 114–5
Thatcher, Margaret 416, 558, 564
Thatcher, R. S., m 353
theatre at HS 423, 430, 548
Thomas, Michael 424
Thompson, H. Yates 257, 259, 394
Thompson, W. H. 248, 287
Thornton, Percy 27, 29, 236, 350
Thring, Edward 246, 314, 330, 339
Tindall, M., m 530, 542
Titanic, the 355
Tomlin, J. W. S. 370
Tonbridge school 34, 46, 56, 57
Torre, Henry 207, 211
Tosswill, A. C., m 302, 312, 388
'total society', HS as a 489
Trade Union Congress 356, 378
Treasure, G. R. R. T., m 539, 543
Trench, Francis 170, 187, 189, 190
Trench, Richard 190, 193
Trevelyan, G. M. 333, 345, 360, 366, 381, 397, 409, 497
Trevelyan, G. O. 276
Trinity College, Cambridge 9, 49, 64, 220, 226, 263, 277, 304–5, 310, 353, 362, 467, 485
Trinity College, Dublin 105
Trollope, Anthony 179, 183, 194–5, 231, 232
Tunbridge school 26
Tunstall, Cuthbert 16
Turner, Sir John 82
tutors:
   as masters 109, 128, 156, 174, 260–1
   private 101, 105, 106, 109, 115, 125, 128, 126, 172, 237–8, 239
Twiss, E. F. 367
Twistleton, Edward 287
Tyndall, John, g 296, 323, 331, 337

Under Master (previously Usher) of HS 28, 48, 54, 55, 60, 61, 67, 68, 72, 73, 78–9, 80–1, 86–7, 89, 108, 115–16, 200, 289–90, 295, 300

unionism 360
United Ushers 300, 363, 386
University College, Oxford 91
Uppingham school 23, 24, 246
utilitarians 167–9

Vachell, H. A. 316, 335, 336, 344, 369, 396, 525
  The Hill 341, 440, 525
Vachell, Richard 341
Vallance, M. W., m 539
Vade, Vicesimus Knox 222–3
Valor Ecclesiasticus (1535) 15
Vassall, A., m 332, 356, 376, 381, 382, 383, 399, 494, 497, 500, 509, 511, 518
Vaughan, Catherine 262, 265, 267, 276, 278, 282
Vaughan, C. J., HM 72, 88, 150, 171, 173, 236, 245–7, 247, 290, 309, 307, 313, 368, 417, 454, 456, 481, 540–1, 563
  and discipline 195, 257–9, 273–4
  dislike of 266–7
  'doves' of 279
  election of 247–9
  and fagging 477
  funeral of 334
  and games 270–1
  as HM 249–83
  and local community 267–70
  personality of 245–6, 275–7
  philosophy of 249
  politics of 251–2, 358
  and Pretor scandal 246, 277–82
  reputation of 245
  resignation of 277–9
  sermons of 273, 276–7, 278–9, 282–3
  wealth of 265
Vaughan, Edwin, m 246, 263
Vaughan, H. H. 246, 287
Vaughan, W. W. 246
Vellacott, P. C., HM 311, 362, 363, 411, 422, 433–4, 442, 454, 457–8, 464, 469, 470, 477, 479, 494, 518–19, 525, 528, 534
  election of 512–13
  as HM 512–21
  honesty of 513–14
  personality of 512–15, 518
  resignation of 521
Velloni, Dominic, m 138
Venables, E. M., m 385, 417–18, 419, 443, 446, 454, 456, 457, 458, 467, 478, 497, 508, 511, 514, 516, 519, 556
  dismissal of 523, 526–8
  feud with A. P. Boissier 519, 522, 523
  'Jew-baiting' incident and 463–4
Venables, R. B., m 557
Verney, L. J., g 425, 538
Vernon, H. C. 238–9
Verulam, James, 2nd earl 205, 293, 296, 427
vicarage at H, as boys' house 255
vice 271–2
Victoria, Queen 190, 253
Villiers, F. H. 359
visitors of HS 182–3, 222

Wadeson, Richard, m 121, 128, 129, 131, 136, 149
Wadham College, Oxford 51
Wagner, Richard 346
Wakefield school 23, 26, 33–4
Waldo, Edmund 87
Waldo, Peter, g 76, 88
Wales 104
Waley, J. F. 321
Walker, D. F., m 469
Walkerne, Herts., parish of 114
Waller, Robert 103
Walton, C. L., m 530, 540
War Memorial of HS 408, 432, 441, 442, 444–5, 450
War Memorial Appeal 414, 418
War Memorial Trust 432
Warham, William 16
Warman, M. S., m 530, 540, 542
Warner, Billy 211, 223, 274
Warner, G. T., m 255, 263
Warner, G. Townsend, m 334, 336–7, 352, 361, 373, 375, 380, 381, 383, 397, 443, 469, 475–6, 499
  Warner G.T. Players 531, 538
Warner, Sylvia Townsend 352, 475–6
Warr, A. L., m 530
Warr, G. C. 305

Index

Watkins, A. R. D., m 519, 531, 538, 543, 545
Watkins, George 77
Watson, A. G., m 263, 379, 388, 390
Watson, H. W., m 263, 264
Waugh, Alec *Loom of Youth* 396
Webb, brothers 151–2
Webb, James, m 153, 154, 175
Webster, J., m 530, 542
Welldon, J. E. C., HM 241, 271, 280, 309, 326, 335, 342, 344, 356, 359, 389–90, 394, 409, 436, 454, 456, 470, 482, 488, 494, 499, 556
    election of 364
    and freemasonry 362–3
    as HM 361–70
    and imperialism 356–7, 367
    personality of 369–70
    and politics 360
    popularity of 366–7
    sermons of 367
    and reform 360–1, 379–84
    unpopularity of 366
    and Vaughan 245
    Gerald Eversley's Friendship 368–9
Wellingborough school 93
Wellington College 288, 290, 357
Welsford, J. W., m 367, 374–5, 381
Werner, C., m 443
West Acre 255, 287, 326, 390, 411, 431, 516, 517, 522, 525
West Indies 103
Westbee, John 50
Westcott, B. F., m and g 260–1, 263, 264, 265, 266, 289, 296, 297, 301, 316, 318, 346, 347
Westminster, marquess of 149
Westminster School 28, 31, 33, 34, 63, 97, 111, 113, 145, 147, 167, 226, 246, 290, 308, 432, 454
Weston, M. L. 109
Weston, Mr, m 80, 81, 89
whiggery 102–3, 124
White, Gilbert 90
White, Mrs P. H. F. 525
White-Thompson, Dean, g 424
Whittle, Robert, HM 50–1
Wickens, Sir John, g 296

Wickham, Edward 306
Wilbraham, G. F. 172
Wilcocks, Joseph 64, 65, 69
Wildblood (or Wildblud), Humphrey 40, 42
Wildblood (or Wildblud), Macharie 42, 566
Wilde, Oscar 368
Wildman, Thomas 146, 164–6
Wilkes, John, MP 100, 104, 124, 134
Wilkes, John, nephew of MP 104
Wilkinson, Ellen 413
Wilkinson, Tate 97, 115, 118, 125
Wilkinson, Thomas 16
William de Bosco 14, 16
Williams, B. 238–9
Williams, Charles 355
Williams, Dorian 521
Williams, Isaac 169–70, 187, 189
Wilson, L. C. 436
Winchester College 113, 119, 167, 168, 192, 197, 226, 288, 290, 308, 332, 336, 454, 486
Winckley, William 180, 294
Wingfield, John 156
Winlaw, R. de W. K., m 469
Winnington-Ingram, A. F., bishop of London 458
Winslow, Thomas 90–1
Withers, John 180
Withington, Peter 273, 369
Wood, J., HM 389, 390, 419, 456, 479, 494, 498, 565
    correspondence of 373, 374–5
    election of 370–2
    failure of 372–3
    as HM 370–5
    salary of 372, 394
    teaching of 384
    wealth of 374
Woodcock, orator 62
Woodstock school 23
Woolley, Geoffrey, m 446, 458, 522
Wordsworth, Charles 170, 187, 188–9, 192–4, 213, 219, 224
Wordsworth, Christopher, HM 88, 167, 168, 170, 171, 172, 173, 174, 190, 213, 248, 271, 297, 307, 432, 454, 456

achievements of 250–1
beliefs of 232
chapel of 175
and discipline 222–3, 257
dismissal of 240–1
election of 219–21
feud with Cunningham 230–41
and Free Scholars 184, 235–41
as HM 219–41
personality of 222
Wordsworth, William 326
Wrangham, William 104
writing master, the 51, 54, 108, 109
Wyatt-Smith, A., m 445, 446, 447, 457, 500, 510, 511

Wych, Jermyn 63, 69

Yarrow, C. D. 448
Yates, Dornford 409
Yerburgh, R. 320
Yorke, Philip, 3rd earl of Hardwicke 123, 137
Young, C. W. 298
Young, E. M., m 297, 317–18, 319, 330, 360, 387
Young, G. W. 425, 427
Young, H. 425
Young, W. G., m 500
youth, cult of 340–1, 348–51, 397

Zetland, 2nd marquess of, g 363, 424